Street by Street

MERSEYSIDE

Enlarged areas BIRKENHEAD, BOOTLE, ELLESMERE PORT, LIVERPOOL, RUNCORN, ST HELENS, SOUTHPORT, WARRINGTON, WIDNES

Plus Ashton-in-Makerfield, Bebington, Crosby, Formby, Heswall, Hoylake, Kirkby, Maghull, Neston, Ormskirk, Prescot, Skelmersdale, Wallasey, West Kirby

2nd edition November 2004

Original edition printed May 2001

Published by AA Publishing (a trading name of Automobile Association Developments Limited, whose registered office is Southwood East, Apollo Rise, Farnborough, Hampshire, GU14 0JW. Registered number 1878835).

Mapping produced by the Cartography Department of The Automobile Association. (A02238)

A CIP Catalogue record for this book is available from the British Library.

Printed by Oriental Press in Dubai.

Ref: ML049z

Key to map pages ii-iii

Key to map symbols iv–1

Enlarged map pages 2-19

Main map pages 20-203

Index – towns & villages 204

Index – streets 205-247

Index – featured places 247 -253

Acknowledgements 253

National Grid references are shown on the map frame of each page.
Red figures denote the 100 km square and blue figures the 1 km square.
Example, page 132: Brewery 335 389

The reference can also be written using the National Grid two-letter prefix shown on this page, where 3 and 3 are replaced by SJ to give SJ3589.

Scale of enlarged map pages 1:10,000 6.3 inches to 1 mile

0 1/4 miles 1/2

0 1/4 1/2 kilometres 3/4 1

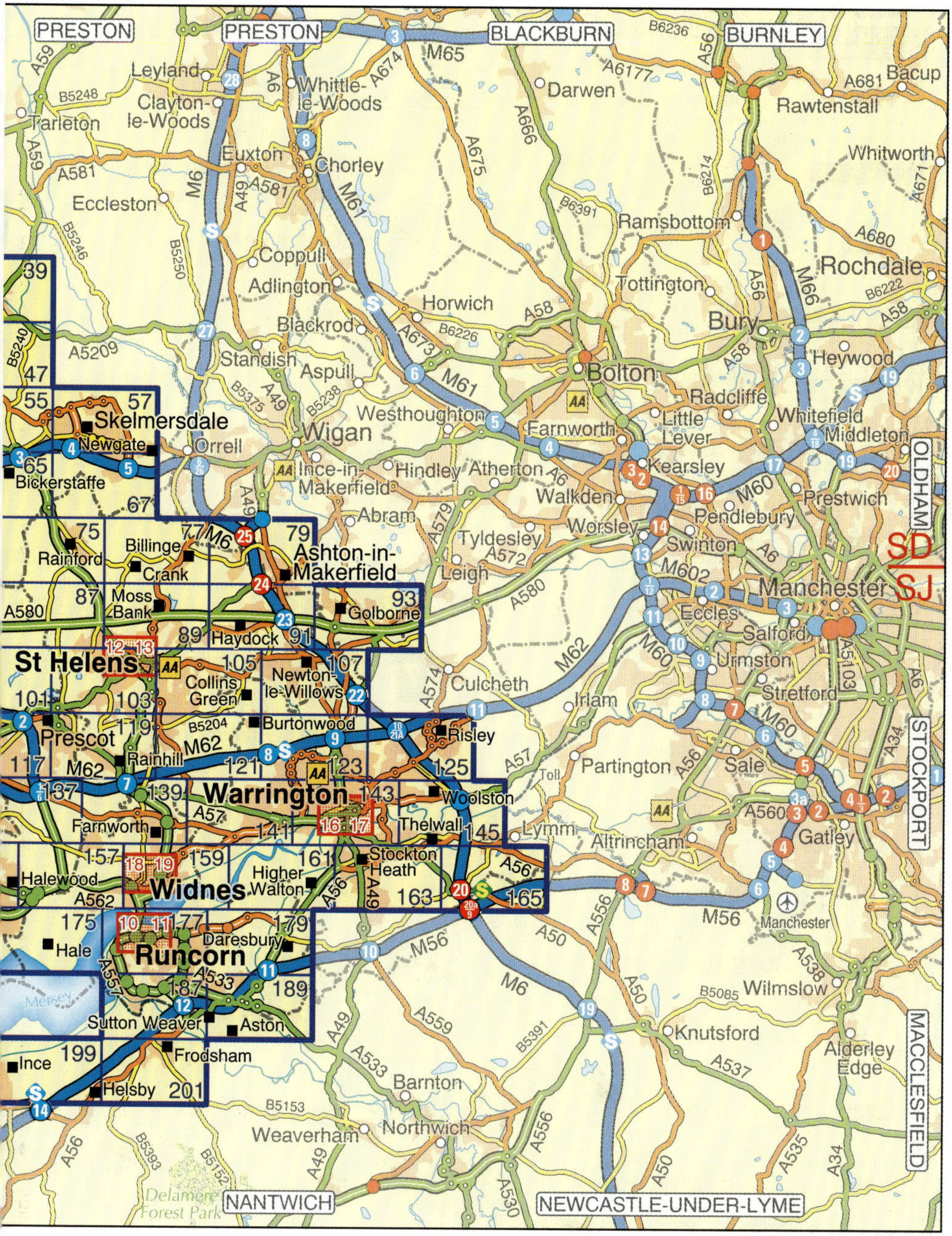

3.6 inches to 1 mile

Scale of main map pages **1:17,500**

0 — 1/2 — miles — 1

0 — 1/2 — 1 — kilometres — 1 1/2

Symbol	Meaning
Junction 9	Motorway & junction
Services	Motorway service area
	Primary road single/dual carriageway
Services	Primary road service area
	A road single/dual carriageway
	B road single/dual carriageway
	Other road single/dual carriageway
	Minor/private road, access may be restricted
	One-way street
	Pedestrian area
	Track or footpath
	Road under construction
	Road tunnel
AA	AA Service Centre
P	Parking
P+	Park & Ride
	Bus/coach station
	Railway & main railway station
	Railway & minor railway station
	Underground station
	Light railway & station
	Preserved private railway
LC	Level crossing
	Tramway
	Ferry route
	Airport runway
	County, administrative boundary
	Mounds
17	Page continuation 1:17,500
3	Page continuation to enlarged scale 1:10,000
	River/canal, lake
	Aqueduct, lock, weir
465 Winter Hill	Peak (with height in metres)
	Beach
	Woodland
	Park
	Cemetery
	Built-up area

Map Symbols

Symbol	Meaning
	Featured building
	City wall
A&E	Hospital with 24-hour A&E department
PO	Post Office
	Public library
	Tourist Information Centre
	Seasonal Tourist Information Centre
	Petrol station, 24-hour Major suppliers only
	Church/chapel
	Public toilets
	Toilet with disabled facilities
PH	Public house AA recommended
	Restaurant AA inspected
Madeira Hotel	Hotel AA inspected
	Theatre or performing arts centre
	Cinema
	Golf course
	Camping AA inspected
	Caravan site AA inspected
	Camping & caravan site AA inspected
	Theme park

Symbol	Meaning
	Abbey, cathedral or priory
	Castle
	Historic house or building
Wakehurst Place NT	National Trust property
	Museum or art gallery
	Roman antiquity
	Ancient site, battlefield or monument
	Industrial interest
	Garden
	Garden Centre Garden Centre Association Member
	Garden Centre Wyevale Garden Centre
	Farm or animal centre
	Zoological or wildlife collection
	Bird collection
	Nature reserve
	Aquarium
	Visitor or heritage centre
	Country park
	Cave
	Windmill
	Distillery, brewery or vineyard

2
CORPORATION ROAD
CORPORATION ROAD
LC
A5030
B5146
CORPORATION
ROAD
131
A
B
C
D
E
Price St
Merritt
Smith Av
Crutchley Av
Dawson Av
Street
Kilgarth School
Upr Beckwith St
Patten
Prim Sch
Cavendish
Price Road
CLEVELAND STREET
DUKE ST
Old Bidston Rd
Maddock St
Old Bidston Rd
Neston Gardens
Churchview Rd
St Edwards Cl
Beckwith St
Price Street Bus Centre
Arthur St
Marshall Street
Cleveland Business Park
Braid St
Massey St
Vardon St
Berner St
Brook St
A5030
Hilbre St
Lynas St
Neptune St
Works
Pool St
RENDEL STREET
Brassey Street
Prill St
Brett Street
Bray St
Cavendish Medical Centre
A5027
Birkenhead Park Stn
St Anne St
Annes Pl
St Annes Grove
St Annes Terrace
Fieldway
Street
Court
Parkview Cl
Parkview Close
Newhope Rd
Street
Works
Brook Street
Cottage St
Charles St
Street
Brook St
Brooklands
Watson St
Wood Close
Mortey Av
Churchill Av
Lloyd Av
Curzon Av
Hartington Av
Asquith Av
PO
PARK ROAD NORTH
DUKE
Beckwith Street
Harcourt St
Arthur Street
CH41
Livingstone
Livingstone Gardens
Anne St
Vittoria Medical Centre
Finch St
Price Street
Cathcart Street Primary School
St Anne Way
A5029
Park Drive
Cavendish Rd
PARK ROAD NORTH
Aspinall St
Newling St
Pr Edward St
The Priory CE Primary School
Aberdeen St
Trinity St
Vittoria
Vittoria Court
Banning Cl
Cathcart
WATSON STREET
Robert St
Park
PO
St Anne St
St Anne's Cl
Beckwith St E
Kinmel Cl
Birchwood Cl
A553
Ashville Rd
Park Drive
Park Drive
CONWAY
Newton Street
Kelghtley St
Hope St
Dover Cl
Dover Cl
Edgar Ct
St Laurences RC Primary School
Laurence
Park St
Europa Pool
3
Park Drive
STREET
Ashville Road
Knowles St
Craven Cl
Bentinck St
Exmouth Way
Conway Dr
A5029
A553
Hilton Close
Simpson St
Florence St
Parkfield Av
Council Building
130
Birkenhead Park
BIRKENHEAD
4
Birkenhead Park CC
Park Road East
Paterson Street
Craven Street
Park Cl
Fox St
Bright St
Gordon St
Gladstone Cl
Bentinck Cl
Street
Exmouth Gdns
Ambulance Station
Fire Stn
Craven Business Centre
EXMOUTH STREET
Sisters Wy
Park Field Pl
Sisters Wy
Cardigan Av
Hemingford St
Pine Ct
Elm Ct
Claughton
Superstore
Park Drive
Park Drive
Cannon Hill
St Helen's Cl
Park Dr
Cole Street Primary School
Bentinck St
Bright St
Cloughton Rd
Catherine St
Coventry St
St John St
Oliver St
Park High School Sports Centre
5
Park Road South
St Hugh's Cl
Francis Av
Hawarden Av
Radnor Pl
Merton Pl
Alvanley Pl
Cole St
South Cloughton Road
Oliver St
Road
Slatey Road
St Andrew's Road
Grange Road West
Bentinck Pl
Grange Pl
Eastbourne Rd
Menai St
Back Menai St
River St
Grange
Pyramids Shopping Centre
The Grange Shopping
Little Theatre
Charing Cross
Salisbury St
Grosvenor Road
Grosvenor Court
The Nook
Eaton Rd
Osborne Rd
Alexandra Rd
Ravenscroft Rd
Grange Mount
Hentmore St
Road
Barton St
Clayton St
Clayton Pl
WHETSTONE LANE
Cook St
BOROUGH ROAD A552
Fearnley Rd
Woodlands
Lowwood Gr
6
Place
Devonshire Road
Devonshire Cl
Claughton Gn
Palm
Caroline Pl
Grafton St
Alfred Rd
The Lindens
Westbourne Rd
Clarendon Cl
Warwick St
Carlisle Mews
Grange Vw
Oxton Rd
Quarrybank St
Wilkinson St
Whetstone Lane Health Cen
Hazel Rd
Lowwood Rd
Circular Rd
Lowwood Road
Brookland Rd
Slatey
Reedville Road
Balfour Road
Euston Grove
Road
Ridley Street
Town Vw
Belmont Grove
Oak Bank
Tetbury St
BOROUGH ROAD
Shaw St
Quarry Bank
B5148
The Hollybank
Cedar Street
Maple St
Park Gv
Council Building
Woodlands Primary School
Clifton
Charlesville
Grove
7
Williamson Art Gallery & Museum
Road
Belmont
Penrith St
Carnforth Cl
St Werburghs RC Primary School
Raffles
Whalley Rd
Rawcliffe Rd
Tatton Rd
Road
Mounsey Rd
Derby Rd
WHETSTONE LANE
Mather
Road
Enfield Ter
Barnard Rd
Road
Devaney Medical Centre
Ball's Road
Princess Terrace
Ball's Road E
Mount Grove Place
Mount Gv
Christchurch CE Primary Sch
Willmer
Larch Road
Wellington Ter
Elm Grove
Victoria Gardens
James St
Road
Ash Rd
Charlecombe St
Convent Cl
Rctr Cl
Chesnut
Grove
Kings M
Falcon Rd
Halcyon Road
Dingle Rd
Beech Rd
Beech Court
Laurel Rd
Milton Road
Milton Rd
Victoria
Marlborough Grove
Shrewsbury Road
CH42
1 grid square represents 250 metres

Twelve Quays Ferry Terminal
F
G
H
131
J
K
32
33
Works
Wharf
TOWER ROAD
Tower Wharf
Morpeth
QUEENSWAY (MERSEY TUNNEL)
A554
Egerton Dock
Wharf
Morpeth Dock
LC
Egerton
Wirral Metropolitan College
A554
FREEMAN STREET
Shore Road
TOWER ROAD
A554 CANNING STREET
Marcus St
Freeman St
Works
Bridge St
Park St
Works
Bridge St
Bridge Street
Taylor St
Works
Shore
Transport Museum
Pacific Road
Woodside Business Park
Road
Works
Queensway
Works
George St
CLEVELAND STREET
Wood St
Brook St
Russell St
Trinity La
Sandford St
Sidney St
A552
Bridge St
Pump House Museum
Woodside Ferry Landing Stage
Council Building
Elgin Wy
A5030
East
Price
Athol St
Lord St
Council Building
ARGYLE ST
Hamilton Square Stn
John St
Hamilton St
BR ST
A41
Woodside Ferry Approach
Brunswick Court
Conway Park Stn
Camden St
Boulevard
Boulevard
Street
Adelphi St
Brunswick Ms
Hamilton La
Hamilton Square
Hamilton Sq
ARGYLE ST
Town Hall & Registry Office
Albion St
Police Station
VUE Cinema
Wirral Metropolitan College
Market St
Adelphi St
Wirral Mus
Hamilton Sq
Mortimer St
Brandon St
CHESTER STREET
Wirral Borough Magistrates Court
89
Hornby St
Lorn St
Douglas Street
PO
Market St
DUNCAN ST
Church St
Castle St
Europa
Europa
Clwyd St
Marion St
A552
Henry Street
William Street
HAMILTON STREET
Albert St
Water Street
Wharf
Priory
Dacre Street
Marion St
ARGYLE ST
Market St
Council Building
Cross St
Pilgrim St
Gilbrook School
CONWAY STREET
HINSON ST
A552
Alma St
Henry St
County Court
Ivy Street
Alabama Wy
Road
Bank St
Argyle Hlth Cen
Hamilton St
Albion St
Priory Street
Church St
Works
Market Hall
Oliver St East
Oliver St E
Oliver La
Conway St
Market Place
Birkenhead Priory
Burgh's
Gra Rd
BOS
PO
Rd
ARGYLE ST
Grange
CHESTER STREET
Monks Ferry
St Werburgh's Sq
Grange Precinct
CLIFTON CRS
Borough Rd East
Jackson St
Tunnel Rd
St Mary's Ga
Knox St
Birkenhead Museum
A5227
BOROUGH RD
Abbey St
Hind St
Thomas St
Jackson St
A41
Abbey Close
ARGYLE STREET
Birkenhead Central Station
Blackpool St
Waterloo Place
TUNNEL RD
Road
Street
H St
B5147
Mollington St
Appin Road
Rock Retail Park
RD
NEW CHESTER
Works
ARGYLE STREET SOUTH
Mollington Link
Unicorn Wy
PEARSON RD
Hinderton Road
Works
388
Holt Hill
Hinderton
Hemingham
GREEN LANE
Green La
Marquis Street
Frodsham St
Green Lane Station
Valiant Way

BOOTLE
A565
Seaforth Rd
Riverside Cl
Bulwer Street
Deepdale Av
Collins Cl
PO
Surgery
81
KNOWSLEY ROAD
Moore St
Street
Eliot St
Hornby Blvd
Alpha
Mildmay Road
Works
STANLEY ROAD
Lathom Rd
Rufford Rd
Crx Rd
Markfield Rd
Ibstock Road
Malvern Rd
Thornton Rd
Byron Street
Burns St
Boswell St
Cowper Street
Dryden Street
Gray St
Hood Street
Keats St
Moore Street
Norton Street
Percy Street
Scott Street
Balfour Road
Chesnut Gv
North Park Health Centre
A566
Hornby Av
Parrs Corner Trading Estate
A567
Peel Road
Hemer Ter
Shore Rd
Shore Road
Works
Hemer Terrace
Rimrose Business Park
Baird Av
Anderson Av
Grimley Avenue
St Joan of Arc RC Primary School
Shakespeare St
Longfellow St
Hemans St
Goldsmith St
Bibby's Lane
Wordsworth Street
Tennyson Street
Shelley St
Southey St
Spencer St
Salisbury Rd
Peel Rd
Joseph Gardner Way
Thomas Gray Junior School
Thomas Gray Infant School
Bootle Leisure Centre
Hornby Road
STANLEY ROAD
Camelot Terrace
Avalon Terrace
Anvil Cl
Sandfield Pl
Chesnut Gv
Chestnut Court
Glover Pl
Glover Place
Hornby Road
Stanley Rd
Regent Road
Works
Grove Street
RIMROSE ROAD
MARSH
O'Neill St
Cleary St
Ronan Cl
Tullis Way
Halidon Ct
Browning St
Chaucer Street
Milton St
St James RC Prim School
LANE
A5098
The Strand Medical Cen
MARSH
Coleridge St
Sea View Road
Sea Vw Road
Pacific Road
Globe Road
Triam Road
St James
Bushley Cl
Dr
Capricorn Wy
Gemini Cl
Police Station
Delaware Rd
Washington Parade
Vermont Wa
Rimrose Business Park
Vulcan Street
Atlas Road
Irlam Place
Peter Mahon Way
Compton Walk
Newton Walk
Bootle New, Strand Station
Works
Strand Shopping Centre
The Tria
L20
Atlantic Rd
Baltic Rd
Pacific Road
Brook Road
Strand Road
Bank Road
Jersey St
Jersey Cl
Lyster Road
Rimrose Rd
Arctic Road
Liverpool Intermodal Freeport Terminal
Strand Rd
STRAND ROAD
IRLAM ROAD
St Marys Close
Waverley St
Kenilworth St
St Mary's Cl
St Marys CE Primary School
Carolina Street
Georgia St
St Winefrides Cath Primary Sch
Clairville Cl
Washington Parade
Merton
Summer Seat
Campbell St
CHURCH GDNS
Ashcroft St
A5057
MERTON ROAD
Church Street
Church Wk
Church View
Merton Rd
Ruskin Cl
Pembroke
St Catherine's Rd
Alexandra Dock
Chapel Ter
Pleasant Vw
Works
Grimshaw St
Pleasant St
Everton Vw
DERBY ROAD
Berry Street
Bootle Oriel Rd Station
B5090
ORIEL ROAD
St Edmond's Rd
Canal Street
South Sefton Business Cen
Trinity Road
Town Hall
Regent Road
Nelson Street
Benbow St
Byng St
Seymour St
William Henry St
Bridge St
A5058
BRIDGE
Marble Vw
College
Kings Terrace
Exeter
Hertford
Langton Dock
MILLER'S
Effingham St
Napier St
Douglas Pl
Lipton Close
St John's Ter
St John's Rd
Keble
Wadham
Bedford
Bedford Pl
Brocklebank Dock
Works
96
Howe Street
Keppel St
Drake St
Dundas St
REGENT R
Leeds & Liverpool Canal
BRASE
Princes
Works
Kin
1 grid square represents 250 metres

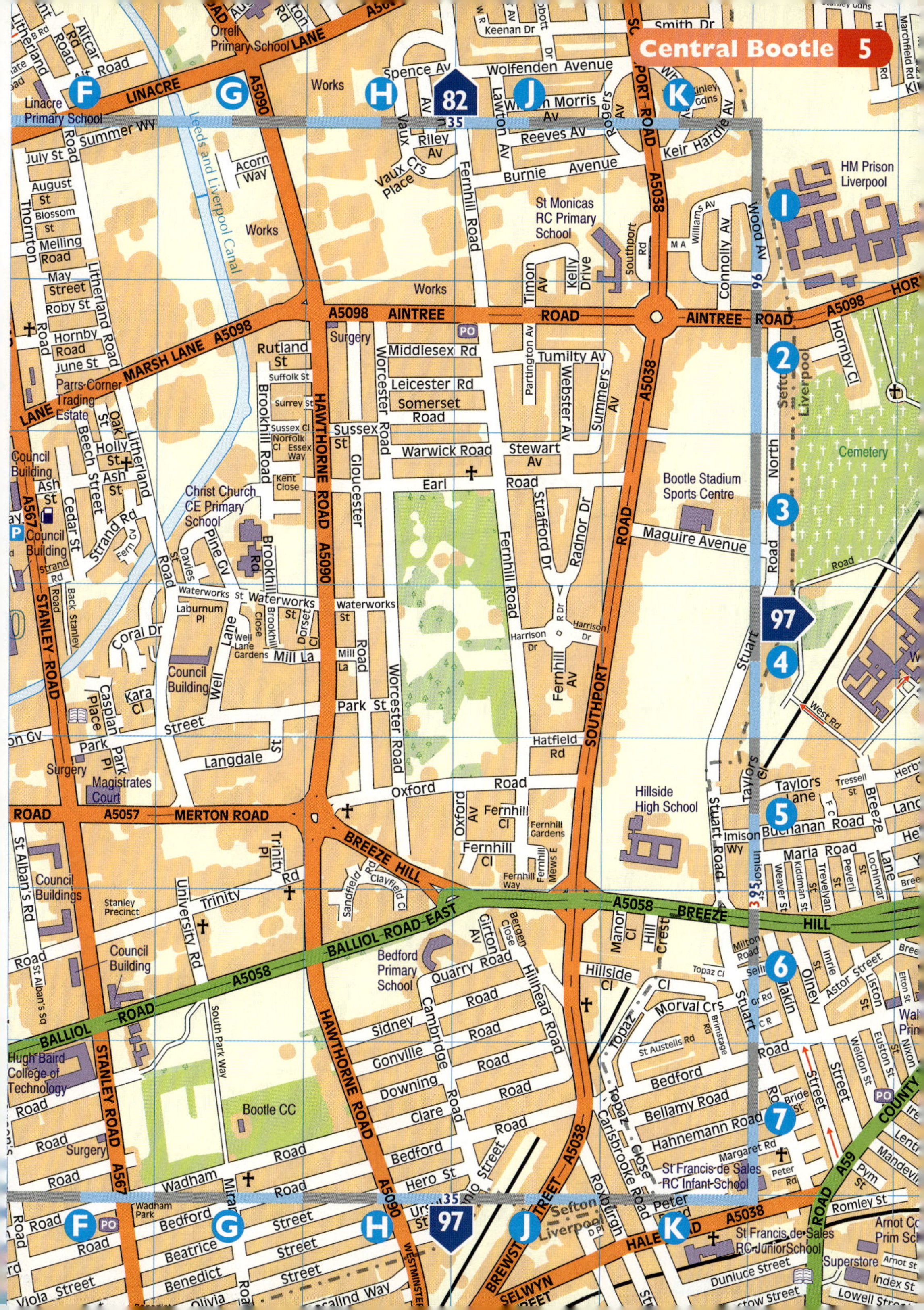

Linacre Primary School
Orrell Primary School
LINACRE
LANE
A5090
Works
Spence Av
Wolfenden Avenue
Keenan Dr
Smith Dr
William Morris Av
Reeves Av
Riley Av
Vaux Crs
Vaux Place
Burnie Avenue
Fernhill Road
Rogers Av
Keir Hardie Av
SOUTHPORT ROAD
A5038
HM Prison Liverpool
82
35
F
G
H
J
K
I
Summer Wy
July St
August St
Blossom St
Melling Road
May Street
Roby St
Hornby Road
June St
Thornton Road
Litherland Road
Leeds and Liverpool Canal
Acorn Way
Works
St Monicas RC Primary School
Timon Av
Kelly Drive
Southport Rd
Williams Av
Connolly Av
Wood Av
A5098
AINTREE
ROAD
AINTREE ROAD
HORNBY
MARSH LANE
A5098
Rutland St
Suffolk St
Surrey St
Sussex Cl
Norfolk Cl
Essex Way
Sussex St
Kent Close
Surgery
PO
Middlesex Rd
Leicester Rd
Somerset Road
Warwick Road
Stewart Av
Tumilty Av
Partington Av
Webster Av
Summers Av
Hornby Cl
Sefton Liverpool
Cemetery
2
3
4
5
6
7
Parrs Corner Trading Estate
Beech Street
Oak St
Holly St
Ash St
Cedar St
Council Building
Christ Church CE Primary School
Pine Gv
Brookhill Road
Gloucester
Worcester Road
Earl Road
Strafford Dr
Radnor Dr
Bootle Stadium Sports Centre
Maguire Avenue
North Road
Strand Rd
Fern Gv
Davies St
Waterworks St
Laburnum Pl
Coral Dr
Well Lane
Well Lane Gardens
Mill La
Dorset Cl
Brookhill Close
Harrison Dr
Fernhill Av
Stuart
97
West Rd
STANLEY ROAD
A567
Back Stanley
Casplan Place
Kara Cl
Council Building
Street
Park St
Worcester Road
Hatfield Rd
SOUTHPORT
Langdale St
Park Pl
Park
Surgery
Magistrates Court
Oxford Road
Oxford Av
Fernhill Cl
Fernhill Gardens
Fernhill Way
Fernhill Mews E
Hillside High School
Taylors Lane
Tressell St
Herbert
Breeze Lane
Stuart Road
Imison Wy
Buchanan Road
Maria Road
ROAD
A5057
MERTON ROAD
BREEZE HILL
Trinity Pl
Trinity Rd
Sandfield Rd
Clayfield Cl
St Alban's Rd
Council Buildings
Stanley Precinct
University Rd
A5058
BREEZE
HILL
BALLIOL ROAD EAST
Girton Av
Bergen Close
Manor Cl
Hill Crest
Milton Road
Council Building
Bedford Primary School
Quarry Road
Hillhead Road
Hillside Cl
Topaz Cl
Olney
Astor Street
Liston St
BALLIOL
ROAD
South Park Way
Sidney Road
Conville Road
Downing Road
Clare Road
Cambridge Road
Morval Crs
St Austells Rd
Brimstage Rd
Bedford
Bellamy Road
Hahnemann Road
Hugh Baird College of Technology
Bootle CC
HAWTHORNE ROAD
Bedford Road
Topaz Close
Carisbrooke Road
Roxburgh
Margaret Rd
St Francis de Sales RC Infant School
Peter Rd
Street
Surgery
Wadham Road
Hero St
Road
A5038
A59
ROAD
COUNTY
Pym St
Romley St
Wadham Park
Bedford
Beatrice Street
Benedict Street
Viola Street
Olivia
Selwyn Street
Brewster Street
HALE
St Francis de Sales RC Junior School
Superstore
Arnot St
Index St
Dunluce Street
Lowell Street
Arnot C Prim Sch
Westminster

1 grid square represents 250 metres

F
G
H
196
J
K
41
Boat Museum
Pier Road
Junction 9
Canalside
Canalside Industrial Estate
Oil Sites Road
Manchester Ship Canal
Yard Road
Dock
M53
CH65
Westminster Retail Park
Service Centre
Crescent Road
Meadow Lane
Meadow Lane Industrial Park
Works
Oil Sites Road
Bridges Road
Chapterhouse Cl
Cloister Way
Cromwell Road
Bridges Road
South Road
Lees Lane
Cambridge Road
Marchwiel Rd
Girton Cl
Girton Road
Lancing Road
Wolverham Primary School
Milton Road
Chesham Ct
Jubilee Green
Harrow Road
Eton Road
Telford Road
Burnell Rd
Repton Road
Winchester Av
Thornton Rd
Wolverham
PO
Avenue
St Andrew's Rd
Braemar Court
Dundee Court
Stokesay Court
Croft Court
Ellesmere Port Stadium
Edinburgh Court
Ruskin Rd
Ludlow
Deans Rd
New Bridge Road
Road
1
2
3
4
5
6
7
77
76

8
LIVERPOOL
KINGSWAY (TUNNEL)
QUEENSWAY (MERSEY TUNNEL)
A B C D E
1 2 3 4 5 6 7
112
132
Superstore
Retail Park
Chadwick Court Industrial Centre
Carruthers St
Blackstock Street
Pumpfields Road
Liverpool Community College
Business Centre
Eaton Street
Gascoyne Street
Paul St
Naylor St
Phillips Street
Freemasons Row
King Edward Industrial Estate
Calton St
Paisley St
Roberts St
King Edward Ind Est
LEEDS STREET
A5053
A5036
ROAD
GREAT HOWARD STREET
VAUXHALL ROAD
Works
Addison Street
Holy Cross Primary School
Midghall St
Marlborough St
Pickop St
Marybone
Lace St
GT CROSSHALL ST
A5046
LJMU Hatton Garden Ind Est
Council Building
Co Fire HQ
Mag Court
Police Stn
Primrose Hl
Trueman St
North St
LJMU
CHURCHILL WAY
Travelodge
Manchester St
Queensway
Cncl Bldg
Conservation Centre
WHITECHAPEL
Bus
Old Leeds St
Back Leeds St
Pall Mall
East Street
Rigby St
Paul's Sq
Edmund St
Bixteth Street
Brook St
Old Hall Street
Newspaper Office
Union St
Princes Dock
William Jessop Wy
BATH STREET
KING EDWARD ST
Princes Parade
Isle of Man Ferry Terminal
NEW QUAY
QUEENSWAY (MERSEY TUNNEL)
Council Building
Rumford Place
CHAPEL STREET
TITHEBARN ST
Cabinet War Rooms
Town Hall
Moorfields
Moorfields Station
Premier Lodge
DALE ST
A57
VICTORIA ST
Coll
Radio City
Council Building
Met Quarter (under development)
Dawson St
Williamson Square
George's Dock
St Nicholas Pl
Titanic Memorial
Royal Liver Building
WATER ST
Cncl Bldg
Castle St
COOK ST
Mathew St
Harrington Street
Cavern Club
Lord Street
Church St
Button Street
Whitechapel
Tarleton Street
Basnett Street
Police Station
Water St
Cunard Building
GEORGE'S DOCK GATES
THE STRAND
Brunswick St
Moor St
JAMES ST
Royal Coll of Nursing
Derby Square
James Street Stn
HM Coroners Court
Cable St
Paradise Street Bus Station
School La
College Lane
Mersey Ferries
St Nicholas Pl
Georges Pierhead
Georges Dockway
Pier Head
Mann Island
Red Cross St
Queen Elizabeth II Law Courts
National Discovery Park
S John St
BBC North & BBC Radio Merseyside
Hanover St
Peter's La
War Memorial
Port of Liverpool Building
Canning Dock
STRAND STREET
A562
Trans Pennine Trail
Fire Station
Campbell St
Cradwell Street
Museum of Liverpool Life
HM Customs & Excise National Museum
Merseyside Maritime Museum
Hartley Quay
Granada TV
Salthouse Dock
Salthouse Quay
CANNING PL
A5041
PRINCE STREET
Merseyside Police HQ
Paradise St
Seddon St
Argyle St
Fingerprints of Elvis
Albert Dock
Tate Gallery
Albert Dock Village
The Beatles Story
LIVER ST
Hotel Ibis
PARK LANE
Duke St
Maritime Way
Gower St
Premier Lodge
Wapping Basin
WAPPING
Express by Holiday Inn
Cornhill St
Tabley St
Sparling Street
Wapping Quay
YHA
Kings Dock St
Kings Dock
Blundell Street
1 grid square represents 250 metres

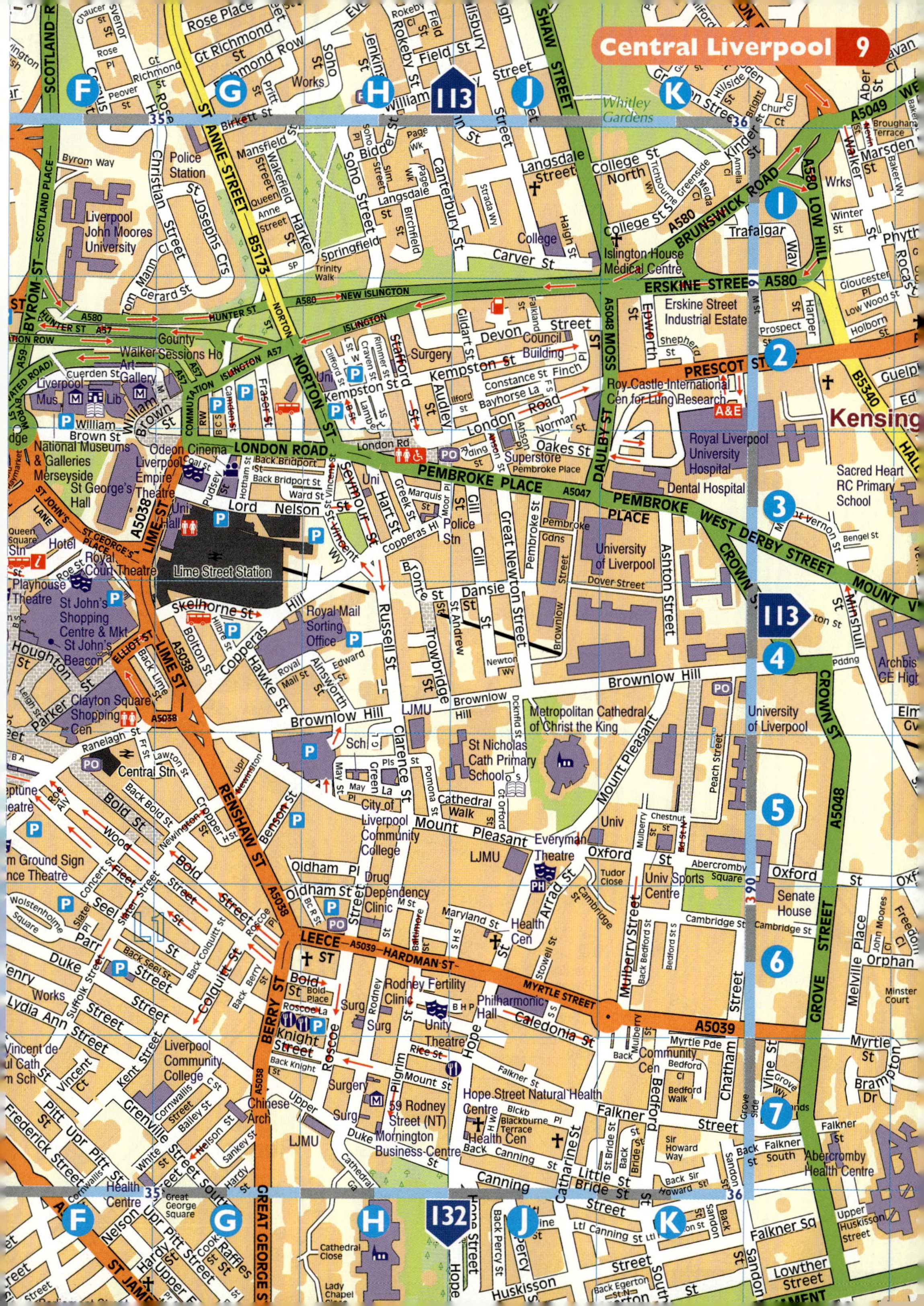

F
G
H
J
K
113
132
35
36
1
2
3
4
5
6
7
Scotland Rd
Rose Place
Gt Richmond St
Richmond Row
Soho St
Jenkinson St
Rokeby St
Field St
Shaw Street
Whitley Gardens
A5049
Brougham Terrace
Marsden St
Walker St
Byrom Way
Police Station
Christian Street
St Josephs Crs
St Anne Street
B5173
Mansfield St
Wakefield St
Queen Anne Street
Harker St
Soho Street
Bidder St
Canterbury St
Langsdale St
Springfield
Trinity Walk
Langsdale Street
College St North
Brunswick Road
Low Hill
A580
Trafalgar Way
College St S
Islington House Medical Centre
College
Carver St
Liverpool John Moores University
Gerard St
Scotland Place
Byrom St
Hunter St
A580
New Islington
Islington
A57
Norton St
Erskine Street
Erskine Street Industrial Estate
Prospect St
Harper St
Gloucester Pl
Low Wood St
Holborn St
County Sessions Ho
Walker Art Gallery
Devon Street
Council Building
Moss St
A5048
Epworth St
Shepherd St
Prescot St
B5340
Kempston St
Kempston Street
Surgery
Stafford St
Audley St
Constance St
Bayhorse La
Finch Pl
Roy Castle International Cen for Lung Research
A&E
Kensing
Liverpool Mus
Lib
William Brown St
Commutation Row
Islington
London Road
London Rd
Norman St
Oakes St
Daulby St
Royal Liverpool University Hospital
Dental Hospital
Superstore
Pembroke Place
Odeon Cinema
Liverpool Empire Theatre
National Museums & Galleries Merseyside
St George's Hall
Back Bridport St
Lord Nelson St
Ward St
Seymour St
Hart St
Greek St
Marquis St
Pembroke Place
A5047
West Derby Street
Mount Vernon St
Bengel St
Sacred Heart RC Primary School
Mount Vernon
Lime St
A5038
Hotel
Royal Court Theatre
Lime Street Station
St John's Lane
Queen Square
Copperas Hl
Police Stn
Gill St
Great Newton Street
Pembroke St
Pembroke Gdns
University of Liverpool
Dover Street
Ashton Street
Crown St
Playhouse Theatre
St John's Shopping Centre & Mkt
St John's Beacon
Skelhorne St
Royal Mail Sorting Office
Russell St
Bronte St
Dansie St
St Andrew St
Trowbridge St
Brownlow St
Minshull St
Archbis CE High
Houghton St
Elliot St
Bolton St
Copperas Hill
Hawke St
Ainsworth St
Edward St
Newton Wy
Brownlow Hill
Pddng
Parker St
Clayton Square Shopping Cen
Brownlow Hill
LJMU
Metropolitan Cathedral of Christ the King
University of Liverpool
Ranelagh St
Central Stn
Renshaw St
Sch
Clarence St
Pomona St
St Nicholas Cath Primary School
Mount Pleasant
Peach Street
A5048
Bold St
Back Bold St
Wood St
Newington
Benson St
City of Liverpool Community College
Cathedral Walk
Mount Pleasant
Everyman Theatre
Univ
Oxford St
Chestnut St
Abercromby Square
Oxford St
Senate House
Ground Sign Theatre
Concert St
Fleet St
Oldham Pl
Oldham St
Drug Dependency Clinic
LJMU
Tudor Close
Univ Sports Centre
Wolstenholme Square
Seel St
Slater St
Parr St
Colquitt St
Leece St
A5039
Hardman St
Maryland St
Health Cen
Mulberry Street
Cambridge St
Cambridge St
Grove Street
Melville Place
Orphan St
Minster Court
Duke St
Suffolk Street
Back Colquitt St
Berry St
Bold Place
Rodney Fertility Clinic
Philharmonic Hall
Myrtle Street
Caledonia St
A5039
Myrtle St
Brampton Dr
Henry St
Works
Lydia Ann Street
Kent Street
Liverpool Community College
Roscoe St
Knight Street
Surg
Unity Theatre
Rice St
Hope St
Community Cen
Bedford Walk
Chatham St
Vine St
Vincent de Paul Cath Sch
Vincent Ct
Grenville St
Cornwallis Street
Bailey St
Nelson St
Back Knight St
Surgery
Mount St
Falkner St
Hope Street Natural Health Centre
Blackburne Pl
Blackburne Terrace
Health Cen
Falkner Street
Sir Howard Way
Back Falkner St
Falkner St
Abercromby Health Centre
Chinese Arch
Upper Duke St
59 Rodney Street (NT)
Mornington Business Centre
Catharine St
Little St Bride St
Frederick Street
Pitt St
Upr Pitt St
Sankey St
LJMU
Canning Street
Back Canning St
Howard St
Sandon St
South Health Centre
Great George Square
Great George St
Cathedral Close
Lady Chapel Close
Hope Street
Back Percy St
Percy St
Huskisson St
Ltl Canning St
Egerton St
Falkner Sq
Lowther Street
Upper Huskisson Street
Nelson St
Upr Pitt Street
Cook St
Raffles St
Hardy St
St James

A
B
C
D
E
176
1
2
3
4
5
6
7
Runcorn Gap
Runcorn-Widnes Bridge
A533
QUEENSWAY
Manchester Ship
Mersey Road
Collier St
Blantyre St
Suffolk St
Cawdor St
Portland St
Bentinck Street
Trentham St
Leinster St
Algernon Street
Brackley Street
Leinster Gardens
Brindley St
Ashridge St
Edith St
Egerton St
Hankey St
Lord St
Grove St
Waterloo Road
Speakman St
All Saints CE Prim Sch
Canon St
Wellington St
Bridgewater St
Egerton St
Peel St
Station Rd
Cooper St
Church Street
Water St
King St
Public Hall St
Mkt
Loch St
B5155
HIGH STREET
High St
Back High Street
Works
Surgery
Brindley Arts Centre
Devonshire Pl
Bridgewater Canal
Duke Close
Percival Lane
Percival La
Works
DARESBURY EXPRESSWAY
Campanile Hotel
Lowlands Rd
CHAPEL ST
Okell St
Albert St
Oakmere St
Albany Ter
Cornwall Av
York Street
York Pl
Hill St
Walton St
Victoria Road
Victoria Road Primary School
Cemetery
Runcorn Station
Picow Farm Road
Shaw Street
Surrey St
New St
Vine St
Eaton St
Arthur St
Fox St
Salisbury St
Chaucer St
Byron St
Picow St
Roland Avenue
Adela Road
Cynthia Rd
Penn La
Roland Av
Burland Cl
Clayton Crs
Lane
Drayton Cl
Stapley Cl
Westfield Primary School
Westfield Mews
Holloway
Balfour Street
Havergal St
Queen's St
Curzon St
Queen's Cl
Lightburn St
Greenway Rd
Morley Rd
The Elms
Cormorant Dr
Works
Pimlico Rd
Pimlico Road
Docks Rd
Clifton Court
Runcorn
WESTON POINT EXPRESSWAY
Percival
A557
Works
Chandlers Court
Lane
Picow Farm Road
Works
Crofton Road
Westfield Road
Westfield Crescent
Cunningham Dr
Beaconsfield Road
Lingfield Rd
Cunningham Dr
War Memorial
Higher Runcorn
Southlands Ms
Johns Av
Whitley Cl
Tree Bank Close
St Clements RC Primary School
Ivy Street
Dale St
Hawthorn Av
Cawley St
Kingsley Road
Kingsley Crs
Norman Road
Oxford Rd
Hinton
Riley Drive
Royden
Hale View
WA7
West Bank Prim Sch
Parsonage Rd
Irwell
Oakland
Mersey
James Cl
Davies
Bridge Vw Cl
Beamont St
Alice Ct
St Mary's Rd
Hurst St
Works
Road
Macdermott
1 grid square represents 250 metres

F
G
H
177
J
K
52
I
2
3
4
5
6
7
Canal
Works
Fredric Place
Stanley St
Old Quay St
Dover St
Thomas St
Ann St
Fisher St
Irwell La
Grosvenor
Norfolk St
Pinellas
Pool Lane
John's St
Parker St
Bold St
Pool
St Edwards C Prim Sch
Runcorn AFC
Wivern Pl
Mason St
Astmoor Road
Astmoor Road
Lister Road
Works
Jensen Court
Hardwick Road
Hardwick Rd
Astmoor Industrial Estate
Astmoor Road
Faraday Rd
Edison Rd
Works
B5155
BRIDGE STREET
Penketh Court
Ellesmere St
Ellesmere St
Howarth Court
Sutherland Court
Works
Canal Street
Halton Rd
B5155
Windmill St
Victoria Rd
Wilding Av
ROAD
A533
DARESBURY EXPRESSWAY
A533
177
83
Cambridge St
Robert St
Cartwright St
Vahler Ter
G Rd N
Grange Rd
Easby Cl
Grange Pk Rd
Porter St
Halton Road
Taylors RW
Stonehills Lane
Sewell St
Perrey St
Ringway Road
Needham Cl
Needham Cl
Henley Ct
Fairfax Drive
Lane
Dudley Av
Renton Av
Works
Ashley Rd
Halton Road
Carlton Av
Manor Rd
Tenby Dr
Stanmore Rd
Halton Ct
Wicksten Drive
Saxon
Avenue
Grange Pk Av
Holmfield Av
Grange Road
Stenhills Crs
Malcolm St
Sewell St
Union St
Sutton St
HEATH
PO
Claremont Road
Marina Gv
Picton
Stenhills Crs
Stenhills Crescent
Stenhills Crs
The Grange Infant School
Castle Rise
Ivychurch Ms
LATHAM AV
B5155
Kent Gv
Duncan Av
Alexander Gv
Langdale Road
Poolside Rd
Ivy Street
RUNCORN SPUR ROAD
Latham
Quarry Cl
Boston Av
Halton Brook Av
The Grange Junior School
Harrop Rd
Coronation
Woodall Dr
Heath Road
Melford Dr
Adderley Close
Bickley Cl
Eccleston Dr
Eccleston Dr
Avenue
The Grange Comprehensive School
Lavender Cl
Halton Brook Av
The Winnows
Penfolds
Halton Brook
Fallowfield
Town Hall
B5155
Boston Av
Boston Avenue
Halton Brook Av
Halton Brook Av
Brook
Leaside
Leaside
Leaside
PO
Meadway
Road
Langdale Road
Road
RUNCORN
Latham Av
Morval Crs
Morval
Crescent
Halton
Fernhurst
382
Heath Rd Crs
Heath Road Medical Centre
Lyndon Gv
Boston
Avenue
Birch
Road
177
Festival
Elm Rd
Sycamore
RUNCORN SPUR ROAD
Cotterill
The Holy Spirit RC Aided Primary Sch
Castleview Prim Sch

88
102
103
A B C D E
1 2 3 4 5 6 7
Denton's Green
Eccleston
Newtown
West Park
Ravenhead
Hamblett School
Language College
Rivington Primary School
St Helens Cricket Club
Windle Vale
Juniper Close
Queens Park CE/URC Primary School
St Teresas Catholic Primary Sch
Leisure Centre
St Mary & Thomas CE Primary School
Superstore
Surgery
St Helens RLFC (Knowsley Road Stadium)
Swallow Ct
Sandfield Medical Centre
Council Building
Big Dam
Swallow Court
County Drive
A570
A58
RAINFORD RD
GREENFIELD ROAD
DENTONS GREEN LANE
LINGHOLME ROAD
KIRKLAND STREET
DUKE STREET
CROPPERS HL
WESTFIELD ST
BOROUGH ROAD
PRESCOT ROAD
Queens Drive
Rosebery Rd
Hartington Road
Kiln Lane
Moorfield
Fairfield Rd
Swinburne Road
Whitefield Rd
Beaconsfield Rd
St George's Avenue
St Andrew's Grove
Chaucer Rd
Kingsley Rd
Walton
Speakman Road
Windleshaw Road
Hammill Avenue
Carr St
Tennis St
Tennis St N
Bishop Road
Cowley Hill Lane
Moray Cl
Balker Dr
Rutland
Oxford St
Briars Gn
Canterbury St
Wynne Rd
Keswick
Wolseley Road
Harris Street
Atherton St
York St
Albion St
Spray St
Boundary Rd
Ruskin Drive
Ainsworth Rd
Arnold Av
Coleridge Avenue
Trafalgar St
Greenall St
Dilloway St
Cambridge Road
Horace St
Kitchener Street
Virgil St
Rodney St
Boundary St
Peter St
Grant Cl
Hope Close
Campbell St
Albion Street
Bruce St
Pigot St
Lewis St
Napier St
Havelock Cl
Abberley Cl
Dodd Ave
Percival Way
Marsden Avenue
Newfields
Fairclough
Ellison Drive
Beaumont Av
Melville
Morrissey Cl
Hopkins Cl
Stevenson Crs
Rivington Road
Drake St
Tamworth St
Sidney St
Bronte St
Devon Street
Exeter Street
Grafton Street
Douglas St
Windsor Road
Hewitt Avenue
Hewitt Av
Mulberry Avenue
Knowsley Road
Eccleston Street
Creswell St
Chisnall Av
McFarlane Av
Rennie Av
Hearne Rd
St Luke's Rd
St Teresa's Rd
Willow Road
Thorn Road
Hazel Gv
Poplar Gv
Maple Gv
Dunriding Lane
Balfour St
Gladstone Street
Chamberlain Street
Warwick St
Roscoe Street
Doulton Street
Silkstone St
Crowther St
Bridgeman St
Boundary Road
St Anns Road
Constance St
Moxon St
Laurel Road
Cedar St
St Georges Road
Haywood Gdns
West Pk Rd
Selby
Underhill Rd
Downs Rd
James Gv
Eldon St
Enfield St
Tullis St
Bank St
Carlton St
Sidgreave Street
Lawrenson St
Duncan St
Crispin St
Banner St
Manning St
Glover Street
Bold
Sandfield Crs
Greenbank Crs
The Shires
Cheshire Gdns
Shropshire Gdns
Flintshire Gdns
Worcester Cl
Cardigan Cl
Lanark Cl
Lancashire Gdns
Buckingham Cl
Berkshire Gdns
Hampshire Gdns
Ravenhead Road
Lyon Street
Wilson
Lyon Cl
1 grid square represents 250 metres

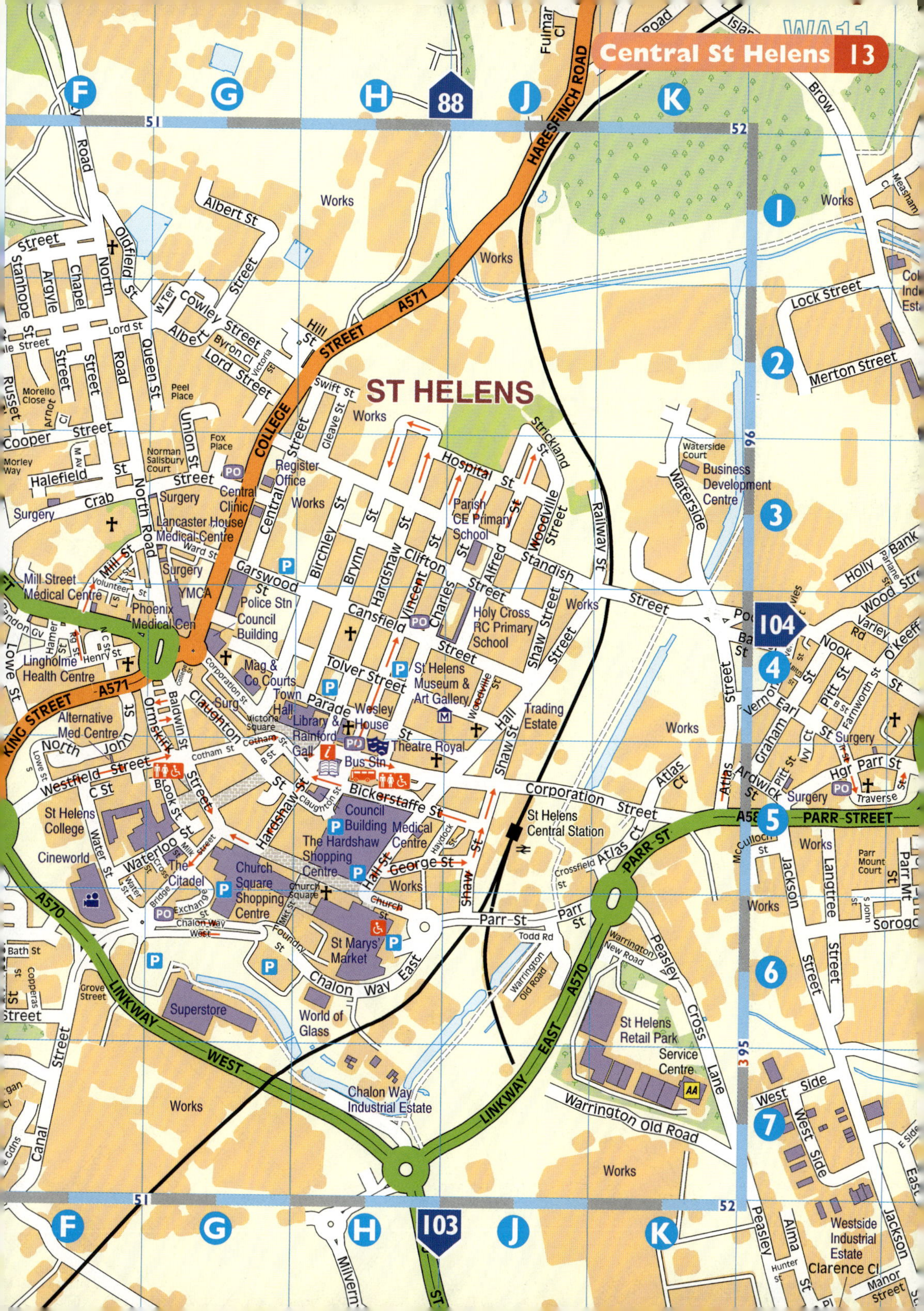
ST HELENS
F
G
H
J
K
88
103
104
51
52
96
395
1
2
3
4
5
6
7
HARESFINCH ROAD
COLLEGE STREET
A571
KING STREET
PARR STREET
A58
PARR ST
LINKWAY WEST
LINKWAY EAST
A570
Albert St
Works
Hill St
Swift St
Gleave St
Cowley Street
Albert
Lord Street
Byron Cl
Victoria St
Oldfield St
North Road
Stanhope St
Argyle Street
Chapel Street
Lord St
Queen St
Russet
Morello Close
Arnot Cl
Peel Place
Union St
Fox Place
Cooper Street
Morley Way
M Av
Halefield St
Norman Salisbury Court
Crab Street
Surgery
Central Clinic
Register Office
Central Street
Lancaster House Medical Centre
Ward St
Mill Street Medical Centre
Mill St
Volunteer St
Phoenix Medical Cen
YMCA
Lingholme Health Centre
Henry St
Hamer St
Lowe St
Garswood St
Police Stn
Council Building
Mag & Co Courts
Town Hall
Corporation St
Birchley St
Brynn St
Hardshaw St
Clifton St
Vincent St
Charles St
Alfred St
Woodville Street
Strickland St
Hospital St
Parish CE Primary School
Standish Street
Cansfield Street
Holy Cross RC Primary School
Shaw Street
Railway St
Tolver Street
St Helens Museum & Art Gallery
Parade St
Wesley House
Library & Rainford Gall
Theatre Royal
Bus Stn
Trading Estate
Hall St
Shaw St
Alternative Med Centre
North John St
Ormskirk St
Baldwin St
Claughton St
Victoria Square
Cotham St
Westfield Street
St Helens College
Water St
Cineworld
Waterloo St
The Citadel
Exchange St
Chalon Way West
Bickerstaffe St
Council Building
The Hardshaw Shopping Centre
Medical Centre
George St
Church Square Shopping Centre
Church St
St Marys' Market
Chalon Way East
Parr St
Todd Rd
St Helens Central Station
Corporation Street
Atlas Ct
Crossfield St
Superstore
World of Glass
Chalon Way Industrial Estate
Grove Street
Bath St
Canal Street
Warrington New Road
Warrington Old Road
Peasley Cross Lane
St Helens Retail Park
Service Centre
AA
Waterside Court
Business Development Centre
Waterside
Atlas Street
Lock Street
Merton Street
Brow
Measham Cl
Holly Bank
Wood Street
Varley Rd
Nook
Pitt St
Farnworth St
Graham
Ardwick St
Parr St
Traverse
Jackson Street
Langtree Street
Parr Mount Court
Parr Mt St
McCulloch St
West Side
Westside Industrial Estate
Clarence Cl
Manor Street
Alma St
Hunter St
Peasley
Milvern

SOUTHPORT
A
B
C
D
E
1
2
3
4
5
6
7
22
27
18
333
417
Southport Pier
Marine Drive
Southport Sailing Club
West Lancs Yacht Club
Marine Lake
Marine Parade
Lower Promenade
Theatre & Floral Hall
Bank Square
Bold St
Victoria St
Albert Place
Back Bath Street
Bath St
Funland
PROMENADE
Nevill Street
Cable St
Stanley St
London Sq
LORD STREET BOULEVARD
Pleasureland
Southport Zoo & Conservation Trust
Model Village
Promenade
Lower Promenade
B5245
Scarisbrick Avenue
Scarisbrick Hotel
Register Office
Royal Clifton Hotel
CORONATION WK
Hulme St
West St
Waverley Street
LORD ST
Cambridge Arcade
Cambridge Walks
Town Hall
Atkinson Art Gallery
Hodge St
ABC Cinema
Market Hall
Marble Shopping Centre
EASTBANK
Esplanade
Southport Swimming Baths
Victoria Way
Kingsway
Superstore
Garrick Pde
Southport Flower Show Site
Duke St
PO
LORD ST BOULEVARDS
A565
Metropole Hotel
Southport New Synagogue
Talbot St
Portland Street
Princes
King
Nelson St
Wellington St
Lord
Beach Priory Gdns
Priory Mews
Beechfield Gdns
Beechfield Gardens
Sunnymede School
Rotten Row
LORD ST WEST
Castle Walk
Works
St Paul's Sq
St Paul's Street
Duke Street
Trinity Gdns
Talbot Drive
Part Street
Cross St
PR8
Rimmer's Av
Beach Rd
Westcliffe Road
Southern Road
Belmont
Talbot Street
Kingswood
Rotten Row
Blandford Close
Palatine Road
Twistfield Close
AUGHTON ROAD
Hollybrook Road
Street
Duke St
Bentham St
The British Lawnmower Museum
1 grid square represents 250 metres

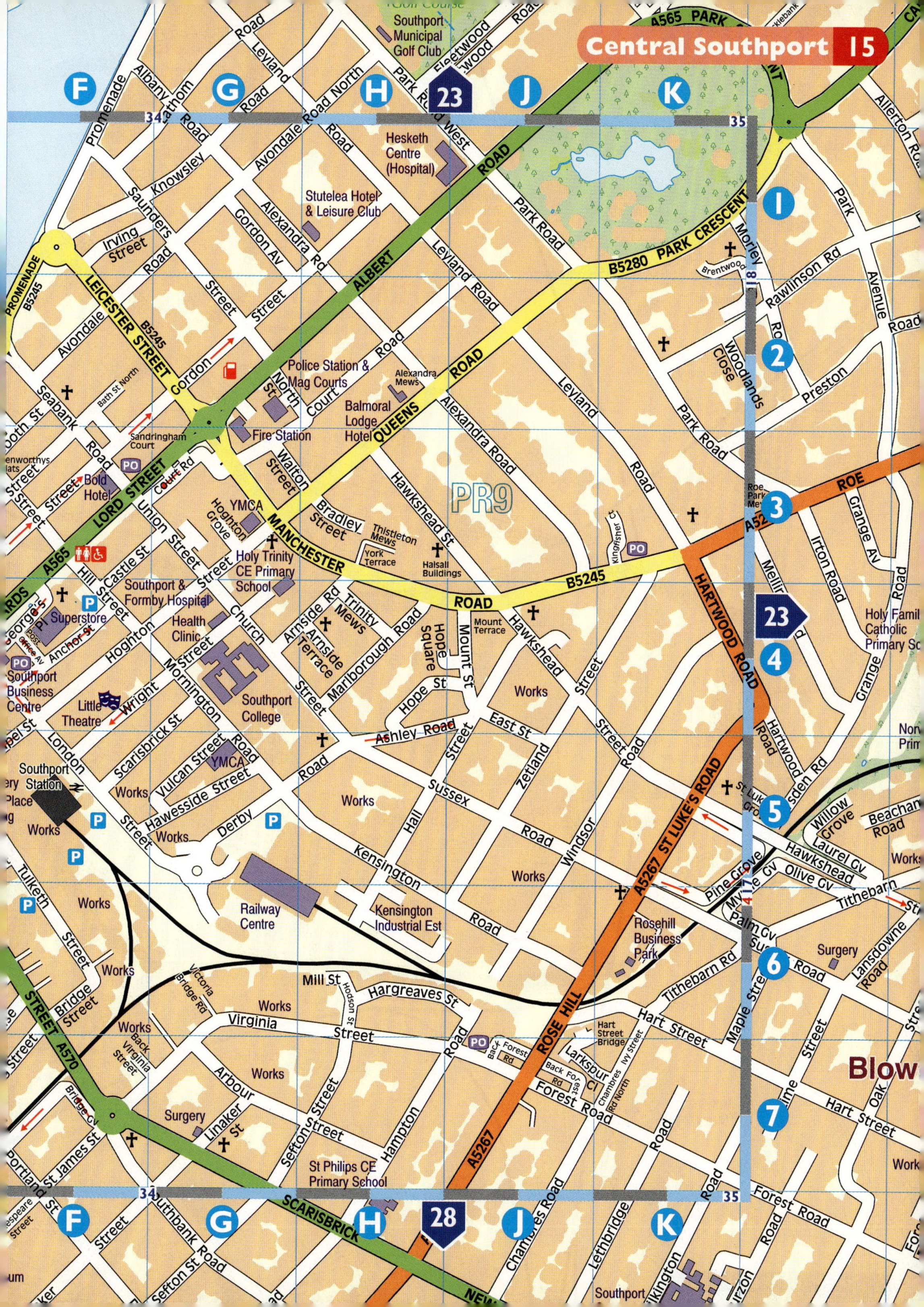
Southport Municipal Golf Club
Hesketh Centre (Hospital)
Stutelea Hotel & Leisure Club
Police Station & Mag Courts
Alexandra Mews
Balmoral Lodge Hotel
Fire Station
Sandringham Court
Bold Hotel
YMCA
Holy Trinity CE Primary School
Southport & Formby Hospital
Health Clinic
Superstore
Southport Business Centre
Little Theatre
Southport College
Southport Station
Railway Centre
Kensington Industrial Est
Rosehill Business Park
St Philips CE Primary School
Holy Family Catholic Primary Sc
Thistleton Mews
York Terrace
Halsall Buildings
Mount Terrace
Hart Street Bridge
Surgery
Works
PR9
A565 PARK CRESCENT
B5280 PARK CRESCENT
ALBERT ROAD
LORD STREET
LEICESTER STREET
PROMENADE
QUEENS ROAD
MANCHESTER ROAD
B5245
HARTWOOD ROAD
A5267 ST LUKE'S ROAD
ROSE HILL
A5267
ROE LANE
SCARISBRICK NEW ROAD
STREET A570
Leyland Road
Park Road
Park Road West
Alexandra Rd
Alexandra Road
Gordon Av
Hawkshead St
Hawkshead Street
Kensington Road
Sussex Road
Derby Road
Hawesside Street
Vulcan Street
Scarisbrick St
Mornington Road
Church Street
Hoghton Street
Wright Street
London Street
Tulketh Street
Bridge Street
Virginia Street
Hargreaves St
Mill St
Hodson St
Sefton Street
Arbour Street
Linaker St
Hampton Road
Chambres Road
Forest Road
Hart Street
Tithebarn Rd
Tithebarn Road
Windsor Road
Zetland Street
Hall Street
East St
Ashley Road
Hope St
Mount St
Hope Square
Marlborough Road
Arnside Rd
Arnside Terrace
Trinity Mews
Bradley Street
Walton Street
North St
Court Road
Union Street
Castle St
Hill Street
Anchor St
Seabank Road
Bath St North
Avondale Road
Irving Street
Knowsley Road
Saunders Street
Lathom Road
Albany Road
Avondale Road North
Morley Road
Rawlinson Rd
Woodlands Close
Preston Road
Park Avenue
Grange Road
Irton Road
Kingfisher Ct
Pine Grove
Myrtle Gv
Palm Gv
Olive Gv
Laurel Gv
Willow Grove
Beach Road
Lansdowne Road
Maple Street
Lime Street
Oak Street
Larkspur Cl
Ivy Street
Back Forest Rd
Victoria Bridge Rd
St James St
Portland St
Southbank Road
Lethbridge Road
Blow
23
28
34
35

16
WARRINGTON
Warrington Wolves RLFC (Halliwell Jones Stadium)
Warrington Central Trading Estate
Bewsey Industrial Estate
Bewsey Business Centre
St Albans RC Primary School
Bewsey Lodge Primary School
A&E
Warrington District General Hospital
Guardian Street Ind Estate
Medical Centre
Works
St Barnabas CE Primary School
Priestley Business Centre
Superstore
Council Building
Law Courts
Town Hall
Garven Place Clinic
Travel Lodge
Bus Station
Old Market Place
Golden Square Shopping Centre
Market Hall
Palace Theatre
Warrington Business Centre
Cockhedge Centre
Pinners Brow Retail Park
Warrington Central Station
Clinic for the Handicapped
Eric Moore Health Centre
YMCA
Queens Gdns
Surgery
Parr Hall
Pyramid
Museum & Library
Police Station
Medical Centre
Tanning Court Industrial Estate
Warrington Bank Quay Station
Bank Quay Trading Estate
Travel Inn
Latchford CE Primary School
MIDLAND WAY
FROGHALL LANE
TANNERS LANE
WINWICK ROAD
LYTHGOES LANE
ORFORD LANE
LONGFORD STREET
LIVERPOOL RD
PARKER STREET
WILSON PATTEN STREET
MERSEY STREET
WILDERSPOOL CAUSEWAY
BRIDGE ST
A49
A57
A5061
A574
B5210
A5060
1 grid square represents 250 metres

Howley
River Mersey
Victoria Park
Victoria Park Arena
St Elphins Park
Cemetery
WA1
Manchester Road
Marsh House Lane
Padgate Lane
King Edward St
Knutsford Road
Kingsway North
Farrell Street
Howley Lane
Church Street
School Brow
Howley Quay Industrial Estate
Church Street Industrial Estate
Riverside Retail Park
Parkdale Industrial Estate
Manor Industrial Estate
Fairfield Primary School
Beamont Infant School
Council Building
Superstore
Works
Surgery
Clinic
A57
A574
A50
A5061
A49
143

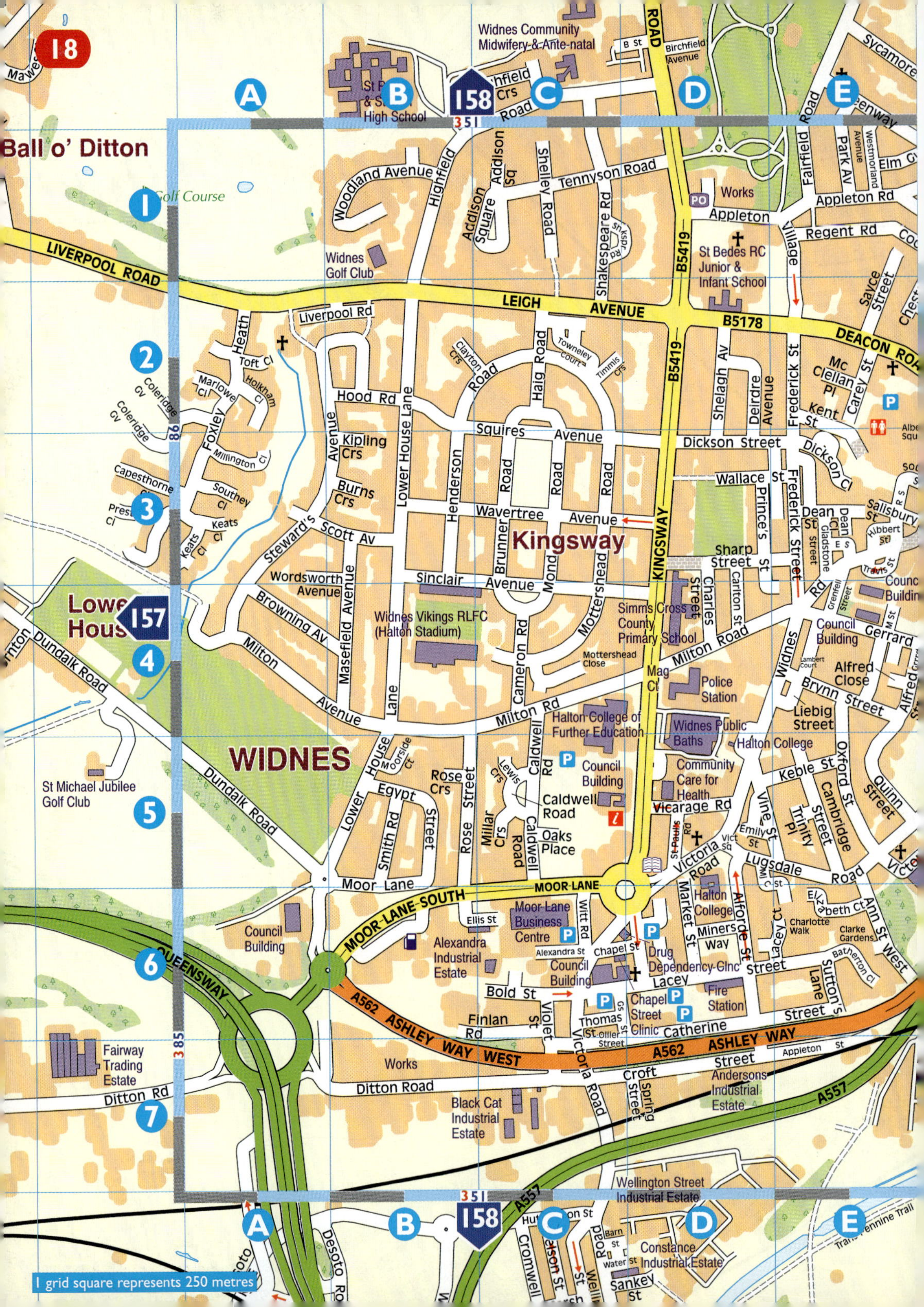
A
B
C
D
E
1
2
3
4
5
6
7
158
157
351
385
86
Ball o' Ditton
Golf Course
Widnes Golf Club
Widnes Community Midwifery & Ante-natal
St P & S High School
Highfield Crs
Highfield Road
Birchfield Avenue
B St
ROAD
Sycamore
Greenway
Fairfield Road
Park Av
Westmorland Avenue
Elm Gv
Woodland Avenue
Addison Sq
Addison Square
Shelley Road
Tennyson Road
Shakespeare Rd
Works
PO
Appleton Rd
Appleton
Village
Regent Rd
St Bedes RC Junior & Infant School
Sayce Street
B5419
LIVERPOOL ROAD
LEIGH AVENUE
B5178
DEACON ROAD
Liverpool Rd
Heath
Toft Cl
Holkham Cl
Marlowe Cl
Coleridge Gv
Foxley
Millington Cl
Capesthorne Cl
Southey Cl
Prestbury Cl
Keats Cl
Clayton Crs
Road
Haig Road
Towneley Court
Timmis Crs
Hood Rd
Kipling Crs
Burns Crs
Avenue
Lower House Lane
Squires Avenue
Shelagh Av
Deirdre Avenue
Frederick St
Mc Clellan Pl
Carey St
Kent St
Dickson Street
Dickson Cl
Wallace St
Prince's St
Frederick Street
Henderson
Brunner Road
Mond Road
Mottershead Road
Wavertree Avenue
Kingsway
KINGSWAY
Dean St
Dean Cl
Gladstone Street
Salisbury St
Hibbert St
Travis St
Sharp Street
Carlton St
Charles Street
Steward's Scott Av
Wordsworth Avenue
Masefield Avenue
Sinclair Avenue
Browning Av
Widnes Vikings RLFC (Halton Stadium)
Cameron Rd
Simms Cross County Primary School
Street
Grenfell Street
Council Building
Gerrard
Lambert Court
Alfred Close
Mottershead Close
Mag Ct
Milton Road
Police Station
Brynn Street
Liebig Street
Lowe House
Dundalk Road
Milton Avenue
Lane
Milton Rd
Halton College of Further Education
Widnes Public Baths
Halton College
WIDNES
Lower House
Moorside Ct
Rose Crs
Lewis Crs
Caldwell Rd
Council Building
Caldwell Road
Community Care for Health
Keble St
Oxford St
Quinn Street
Cambridge Street
Trinity Pl
St Michael Jubilee Golf Club
Egypt Street
Smith Rd
Rose Street
Millar Crs
Caldwell Road
Oaks Place
Vicarage Rd
St Paul's Rd
Victoria Road
Vict Sq
Emily St
Vine St
Lugsdale Road
Moor Lane
MOOR LANE
MOOR LANE SOUTH
Ellis St
Moor Lane Business Centre
Witt Rd
Market St
Halton College
Alforde St
Lacey Ct
Elizabeth Ct
Charlotte Walk
Clarke Gardens
Ann St West
Council Building
Alexandra Industrial Estate
Alexandra St
Chapel St
Drug Dependency Clinic
Miners Way
Street
Batherton Cl
Sutton's Lane
QUEENSWAY
Bold St
Council Building
Lacey
Chapel Street Clinic
Fire Station
Street
Finlan Rd
Violet St
Thomas St
Collier Street
Catherine
A562 ASHLEY WAY WEST
A562 ASHLEY WAY
Fairway Trading Estate
Works
Victoria Road
Croft Street
Spring Street
Street
Appleton St
Andersons Industrial Estate
Ditton Rd
Ditton Road
Black Cat Industrial Estate
A557
Wellington Street Industrial Estate
Desoto Road
Cromwell
Hutchinson St
Road
Barn St
Water St
Sankey St
Constance Industrial Estate
Trans Pennine Trail
1 grid square represents 250 metres

158
159
F
G
H
J
K
52
53
86
385
1
2
3
4
5
6
7
Fairfield County Junior & Infant School
Neil St
Reay St
Stanley Cl
Doward St
Kn St
Rd
Millfield
Susan St
William St
Peel House Lane
Pleasant St
Mount Street
Avenue
Eric St
Joseph St
Elaine Cl
Mill Brow
Houghton
Proctors Close
Ireland St
Smyth Road
Houghton St
Walter St
Drummond Ct
Raby Cl
Hadfield Close
Norbury Close
Halton Health
Close
Allerton Rd
Belvoir Road
Breck Rd
Taylor St
Edwin St
Cliffe St
Albert Rd
Halton Vw Rd
HALTON VIEW ROAD
B5178
WARRINGTON ROAD
Sandon Place
Sandon Pl
Ashford Way
Cheryl Drive
Wilson Close
Melville Close
Kingham Close
Edward St
Hargreaves Ct
Warrington Rd
East St
Castle St
Harris St
Christie St
Park Rd
Foster St
Midland Street
Ross St
Saxon Ter
Albert Road Medical Centre
Surgery
ALBERT ROAD
St Ambrose Road
St John Fisher Junior & Infant School
Gorsey Lane
Works
Denton Street
Bower St
Wood St
Sadler St
Page Lane
Frank Street
Naylor Road
Bell House Road
Denton's Pl
Black
Gregson Road
French St
Cross St
ROBERT ST
Bradley Way
Halton View
Mkt
Council Building
Green Oaks Shopping Centre
Green Oaks Way
WATKINSON WAY
A557
Page La
Green Oaks Path
FIDDLERS FERRY ROAD
A562
Winfield Way
Farrant St
Superstore
Windmill Shopping Centre
Greenoaks Farm Industrial Estate
Warrington Road
Tan House La
Walmsley Street
Simm's Cross
Lugsdale Rd
Street
Travelodge
A562 FIDDLERS FERRY RD
Moss Bank
Tan House Lane
Brown St
Moss Street
Mary St
Moss Bank Road
Ashley Retail Park
Bowers Business Park
Earle Road
Dennis Road
Tanhouse Industrial Estate
Cornubia Rd
Pool St
Lugsdale
Old Foundry Estate
ASHLEY WAY
Earle Rd
Trans Pennine Trail
St Helens Canal (disused)
River Mersey

Crossens Marsh
Works
Marshside RSPB Reserve
Marine Drive
Marshside Road
Stanley High School
Elswick Road
Garstang Rd
Freckleton Road
Hornby Rd
Inskip Road
Caton Close
Fylde Road
Ansdell Gv
Salwick Close
Pilling Close
Preesall Cl
Seaton Way
Coyford Dr
Fylde Road Industrial Estate
Fairhaven Road
Lane
Road
Totnes Drive
Salcombe Dr
Torcross Close
Northam Close
Seaton Close
Dawlish Dr
Slaidburn Crescent
Works
Truro Av
Millar's Pace
Menivale Close
Padstow Cl
Ottery Close
Talaton Cl
Glencoyne Drive
Treen Close
Bodmin Avenue
Crediton Av
Melrose Avenue
Eamont
Hartland Av
Seacroft Crescent
Fylde Road
Merepark Drive
Cros
23
1 grid square represents 500 metres

Banks Marsh
Old Hollow Farm
Marsh Rd
Marsh Road
Lancashire County
Sefton
Charnley's Lane
High Brow
George's Lane
Goose Dub Farm
Vicarage Lane
Glebe Lane
Bond's Lane
Chapel La
Long
Church Road
PO
Ralph's Wife's Lane
St Stephens School
Fleetwood Drive
Fleetwood Crescent
Hesketh Av
Todd's Lane
Schwartzman Drive
Hoole Lane
Fiddler's Ferry
Banks Road
Banks
Banks Health Centre
Caunce Av
Aveling Drive
Aveling
The Sluice
Crossens Way
Marine Drive
Harrogate Way
Skipton Avenue
Ilkley Av
Whitby Av
Fellview
Kingston Crs
Primrose Cl
Norbury Cl
Ferry Side Lane
Avenue
Meadow Brow
Bartons Cl
Station Road
The Avenue
Rufford Dr
Chorley Cl
Lancaster Gate
Abrams Green
Lancaster Drive
Abrams Fold
Guinea Hall Lane
Eversham Cl
Abington Drive
Levens Cl
Fareham Dr
WATER LANE
A565
Works
Primary School
Turnberry
Woodlea Close
Tarvin Cl
The Causeway
St Stephens Primary School
North Meols Community Leisure Centre
Greaves Hall Avenue
Westerdale
Gravel Lane
The Close
Pool Street
Ridge Cl
Brook Street
Land Lane
Works
Douglas Brade
Street
Road
Drewitt Crs
PO
Holmdale Av
Ribble Avenue
Roselea Drive
Hollywood Farm
Brooklyn Park
SOUTHP
24
37
38
39
23
22
21
20
F
G
H
J
K
1
2
3
4
5
6

A
B
C
D
E
1
2
3
4
5
6
Marshside Sands
SOUTHPORT
Southport Pier
14
15
Marine Drive
Marine Lake
Southport Sailing Club
West Lancs Yacht Club
Fairway
Golf Course
Southport Municipal Golf Club
Promenade
Leyland Road
Lathom Road
Albany Road
Knowsley Road
Avondale Road
Park Road West
Hesketh Centre (Hospital)
Gordon Avenue
Saunders St
Irving St
Leicester St
Stutelea Hotel & Leisure Club
Alexandra Road
Police Station & Mag Courts
Queens Road
Fire Station
Marine Parade
Theatre & Floral Hall
Funland
Pleasureland
Southport Zoo & Conservation Trust
Model Village
Royal Clifton Hotel
Promenade
Lord St
Boulevards
Bath Street
Seabank Road
Stanley St
Nevill St
Southport & Formby Hosp
Health Clnc
Southport College
Superstore
Little Thtr
Southport Business Cen
Atkinson Art Gal
Marble Place Shopping Cen
Southport Stn
ABC Cinema
Metropole Hotel
Esplanade
Southport Swimming Baths
Victoria Way
Southport Flower Show Site
Kingsway
Coronation Wk
Superstore
Kensington Industrial Estate
Works
Railway Cent
Mill St
Virginia St
Southport New Synagogue
King Street
Princes St
Portland St
Talbot St
Tulketh St
Strank St
Sunnymede School
Beechfield Gdns
Marine Drive
Esplanade
Row
West St
27
332
33
34
1 grid square represents 500 metres

Marshside RSPB Reserve
Marine Drive
Marshside Road
F
G
H
J
K
20
35
37
Elswick Rd
Garstang Rd
Freckleton Road
Hornby Rd
Inskip Road
Slaidburn Industrial Estate
Fylde Road Industrial Estate
Works
Slaidburn Crescent
Salcombe Dr
Crossens
Stanley High School
Caton Close
Fylde Road
Ansdell Gv
Manx Jane's La
Lytham Road
St Annes Road
Kirkham Road
Fairhaven Road
Glenpark Drive
Merepark Drive
Fylde Road
North
Poolside Walk
Holmdale Av
Asland Gardens
Drive
1
2
3
4
5
6
Rathmore Crescent
Shellfield Road
Cleveleys Road
Cleveleys Avenue
Larkfield Drive
Glamis Drive
Peterhouse School
Presfield Special Sch
Larkfield Primary Sch
Willowhey
St Michael's Cl
Granby Close
Paul's Lane
Knob Hall Lane
Cotty's Brow
Croston's Brow
Marshside
Golf Course
Fleetwood Road
Hesketh Road
Radnor
Denbigh Av
Links Avenue
Eden Av
Longacre
Baker's Lane
Marshside Rd
Mallee Avenue
Mallee Crs
The Ridings
A565 PRESTON NEW ROAD
Highfield Rd
Lexton
Balmoral
Merlewood Av
Verulam Road
BANKFIELD LANE
Hesketh Golf Club
Cockle Dick's La
Churchill Avenue
Threlfalls Lane
Emmanuel Rd
Cambridge Gdns
Cambridge Av
Drive
St Patricks RC Primary School
Churchtown Medical Centre
Churchtown Primary School
Sunny Road
St Cuthbert's Road
Sally's La
Botanic Gardens Museum
B5244
BOTANIC ROAD
Little Lane
24
The Lawns
A565 CAMBRIDGE ROAD
Tower Dene Preparatory School
Denmark Rd
CAMBRIDGE ROAD
MANOR ROAD
A5267
Cambridge Rd
Botanic Rd
Off Botanic Road
Hesketh Road
Argyle Lawn Tennis Club
Argyle Road
Brocklebank Rd
Cliff Rd
PARK CRESCENT
Beresford Gardens
Beresford Drive
Silverthorne Drive
Sandheys Dr
Chase Heys
Bibby Road
St Clair Drive
Churchgate
Peet's Lane
MILL LANE
Churchtown
Meol's Hall
North Meols Lawn Tennis Club
Southport Old Links Golf Club
Coudray Road
Allerton Rd
Hilbre Close
Montrose Drive
Kings Hey Dr
Carisbrooke Drive
Maybank Close
Rectory Rd
Bamber Gdns
Henley Drive
Rawlinson Road
Rookery Road
Grove Park
Derwent Avenue
Park Avenue
PARK CRESCENT
B5280
Brentwood Court
Morley Rd
Woodlands Close
Preston Road
Leyland Road
Parklands
High Park
High Park Pl
Chrc Cl
A5267 ROE LANE
Roe Lane
Farm Close
Tarleton Road
Warren Road
High Street
Old Links Cl
Moss Lane
Jane's Cl
Fosters Close
Fine Way
Pitts House Lane
Golf Course
Kingfisher Court
Ros Park Mews
Grange Avenue
Irton Road
Melling Road
NORWOOD AVENUE
Norwood Crescent
Chester Road
Chester Av
Bengarth Road
Gosforth Road
Vernon Rd
Park Road
Surgery
Griffiths Dr
Stretton Drive
Wennington Road
Sidney Road
Devonshire Road
Lawson Street
Fisher Drive
Heysham Road
Thornton Road
Old Road
Bishop David Sheppard CE Prim Sch
Holy Family Catholic Prim Sch
Norwood Primary School
HARTWOOD RD
A5267
Hartwood Road
Grange Road
Hawkshead Street
Hereford Road
Poulton Road
Bispham
Newton Street
Milton Street
Scott St
Russell Road
Teddar Av
Victory Av
Wavell Avenue
Brooke Cl
Wavell Cl
ST LUKE'S RD
Beech Gv
Blair Gv
Athole Gv
Meols Cop Stn
Bright Street
Byrom Street
Canning Road
Russell Avenue
Canning Road
Salisbury Street
Montgomery Avenue
Works
Zetland St
Windsor Road
East St
Mount St
CHESTER ROAD
Hawkshead St
Willow Gv
Beacham Road
Lesley Rd
Morven Grove
Tithebarn Road
Hazel Gv
Manning Road
NORWOOD RD
Hawthorne Rd
Clifton
28
Bus Station
Business Park
Old Hall Farm Business Park
Canning Road Industrial Estate
Cobden Rd
Palmerston Road
Crowland Street
Crowland
Rosehill Business Park
Tithebarn Rd
Maple St
Hart Street
ROSE HILL
Surgery
Sussex Road
Oak Street
Cypress Rd
Fir St
Blowick
Kts Ter
B5
Street

24
21
23
29
A
B
C
D
E
1
2
3
4
5
6
337
39
20
19
18
417
A565
Water Lane
Ferry Side La
Fylde Road
Merepark Drive
Works
Brd Wll La
Primary School
The Causeway
Tarvin Cl
Bartons Cl
Lancaster Drive
Abrams Fold
Gravel Lane
St Stephens Primary School
North Meols Community Leisure Centre
Hall Lane
The Close
Pool Street
Ridge Cl
Brook Street
Land Lane
Works
Douglas Brade Street
Drewitt Crs
PO
Crossens
Poolside Walk
Holmdale Av
Ribble Avenue
Roselea Drive
Asland Gardens
North Road
Rufford Road
Works
Crossens CC
New Lane
The Crescent
Three Pools
The Mallards
Lexton Drive
Merlewood Av
Bankfield Lane
Blundell Lane
PR9
Hollywood Farm
Brooklyn Park and Country Club
Gravel Lane
Bobbiners Lane
Mere Lane
Cabin Lane
New Lane
The Sluice
Three Pools Waterway
Dolly's Lane
Lane
Long Meanygate
Winacre Farm
Moss Lane
Dolly's Lane
Straight Up La
Moss Lane
Wyke Hey Farm
Wyke Wood Lane
Wyke Lane
Pitts House Lane
Lane
Wyke Farm
1 grid square represents 500 metres

Brightstone Close
Avenue
Westerdale Drive
Msbrk Cl
Oakford Cl
Boundary Lane
Moss Side Farm
Green Lane
Sugar Stubbs Lane
SOUTHPORT NEW ROAD
Boundary Farm
Gravel Lane
Dalweb Industrial Park
Gravel Lane
Moss Side
Mere Brow CE Primary School
A565
Mere
PO
THE GRAVEL
Mere Brow
Tabby Nook
B5246
Common Lane
THE MARSHES LANE
Leisure Lakes
Leisure Lakes
Sluice Farm
Long Meanygate
Meanygate Farm
Common Lane
The Sluice
Mere Farm
Mere
Nuck's Wood
F
G
H
J
K
40
41
42
20
19
18
17
2
3
4
5
6
30

A
B
C
D
E
330
31
17
1
2
16
3
4
15
5
6
14
Southport
Landing Area
Birkdale Sands
Westbourne
Granville Road
Selworthy
Road
Coastal Road
Sel
Hi
The Royal
Birkdale
Golf Club
Golf Course
Coastal Road
330
31
A
B
33
C
D
E
1 grid square represents 500 metres

Birkdale
Esplanade
Marine Drive
Victoria
Southport Swimming Baths
Southport Flower Show Site
Superstore
Lord St
Eastbank St
Scarisbrick New Rd
Ash Street
Southport Stn
Kensington Industrial Estate
Kensington Road
Railway Centre
Virginia St
Arbour Street
St Philips CE Primary School
PR8
Sunnymede School
West St
Aughton Road
Upr Aughton Rd
The British Lawnmower Museum
Chromolyte Ind Est
Linaker Prim Sch
Cemetery Road
Cemetery
Eastbourne Road
Lulworth Road
Waterloo Road
Birkdale Station
Atlanta Swimming
Infant School
Birkdale Primary School
Southport Business Park
Liverpool Road
Kew Rd
Claremont Road
Guildford Rd
Moss Road
Christ The King RC High School
Southport & Birkdale CC
Carlton Lawn Tennis Club
Birkdale Trading Estate
Our Lady of Lourdes RC Pri School
Lincoln Road Health Centre
Hillside
Hillside Station
Greenbank High Sch
Hillside Golf Club
Southport RFC
Arundel Road
Farnborough Road J&I School
Fine Jane's Farm
Sefton
Lancashire
22
28
34

28
23
15
27
35
A
B
C
D
E
1
2
3
4
5
6
Blowick
Pool Hey
Brown Edge
Catholic Prim Sch
Norwood Primary School
Rosehill Business Park
Kensington Ind Est
Surgery
Southport General Infirmary
Christina Hartley Maternity Hospital
Southport FC
King George V College
Meols Cop High School
Southport Girls FC
Service Centre
Meols Cop Retail Park
Sphynx Tennis Club
Southbank Tennis Club
A&E
Southport & Formby District General Hospital
Queenscourt Hospice
Kew Retail Park
Superstore
Primary School
Kew Medical Centre
Bus Station
Canning Road Industrial Estate
Crowland Street Industrial Est
Ak Business Park
Old Hall Farm Business Park
Blowick Business Centre
Old Hall Fm Business Park
Works
Southport Crematorium
Sefton Lancashire County
Moss Farm
SCARISBRICK NEW ROAD
A570
MEOLS COP ROAD
B5276
ROSE HILL
ASH STREET
ST LUKE'S RD
A5267
BIRKDALE COP
B5243
HEATHEY LANE
JACKSMERE
SOUTHPORT ROAD
Town Lane
Town Lane (Kew)
Wight Moss Way
Pool Hey Lane
Foul Lane
Crowland Street
Jane's Brook Road
Folkestone Rd
Ruddington Road
Winston Crescent
Fieldlands
Tinsley's Lane
Moss Gdns
1 grid square represents 500 metres

F
G
H
24
J
K
37
38
39
17
I
2
3
30
4
15
5
6
14
16
Wyke House Farm
Wyke Lane
Perch Pool Lane
The Avenue
Midge Hall Farms
Wyke Thorn Farm
Wyke Wood
Pool Hey Lane
LC
Shaw's Farm
Wyke Cop Road
Woodmoss Lane
Wyke Road Farm
Perch Pool Lane
PO
New Hall Drive
Pinewood Close
Greenfield Road
Hares Lane
Snape Green
Rimmer Green
Cat Tall Lane
Snape Gn
A570
SOUTHPORT ROAD
Carr Cross
36
Bescar Lane

1 grid square represents 500 metres

Holmeswood
Mere Side
Tarlscough
Holmeswood Methodist Primary School
Works
PO
Berry House
Windmill Farm
Wildfowl and Wetlands Trust Martin Mere
Mere Lane
Cabin Lane
Wiggins Lane
Chapel Lane
Smithy Lane
HOLMESWOOD ROAD
B5246
Sandy Lane
Cross Meanygate
Sandy Way
Berry House Road
Fish Lane
Curlew Lane
Tarlscough Lane
F
G
H
J
K
42
43
44
17
16
15
414
1
2
3
4
5
6

38

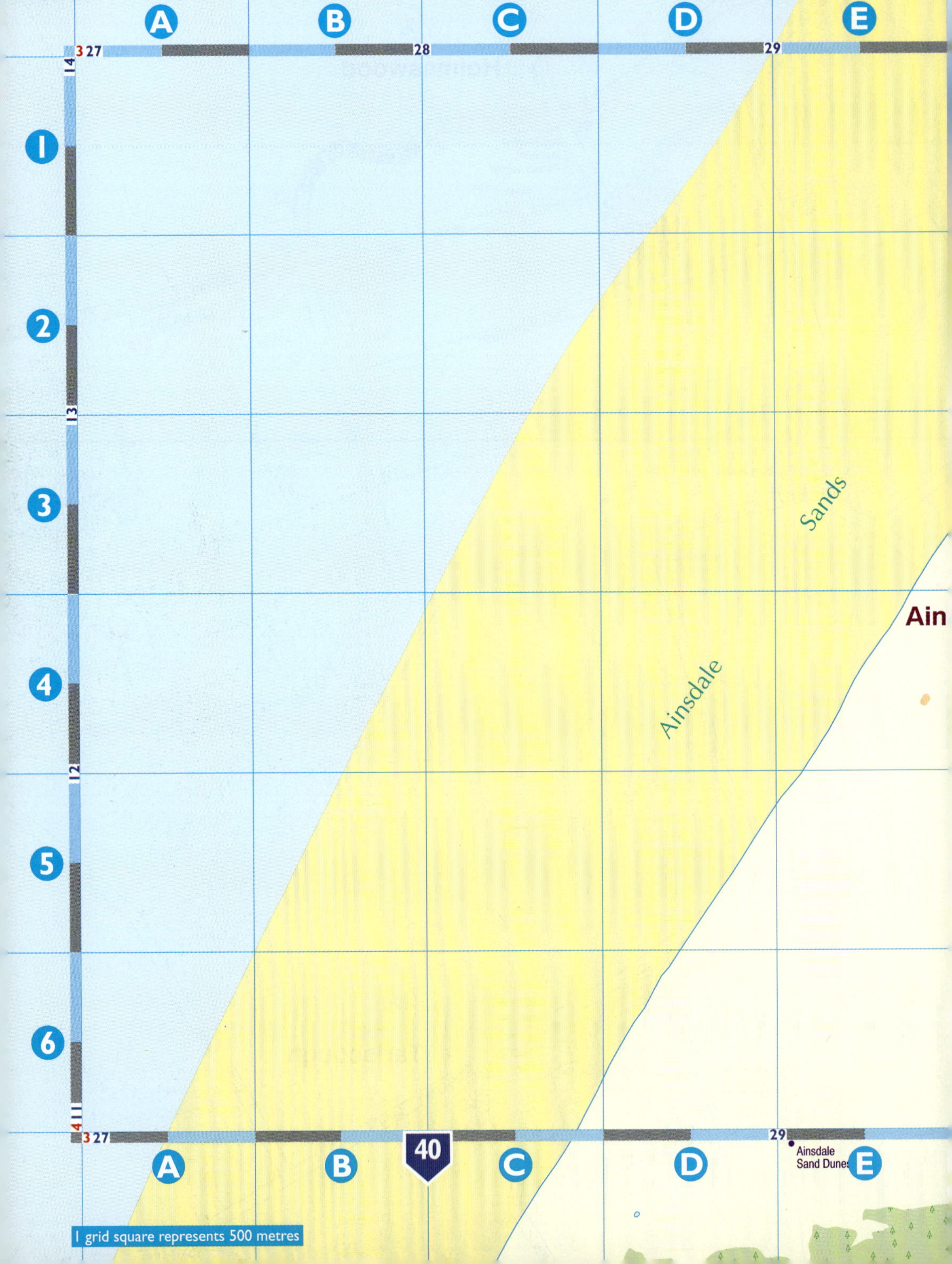
A
B
C
D
E
327
28
29
14
13
12
411
1
2
3
4
5
6
Sands
Ainsdale
Ain
40
Ainsdale
Sand Dunes
1 grid square represents 500 metres

Golf Club
Golf Course
Greenbank High Sch
Hillside Golf Club
F
G
H
J
K
26
30
32
14
13
12
11
1
2
3
4
5
6
34
41
Coastal Road
Lynton
Golf Course
Shore Rd
Promenade
Shore Rd
Shore
Road
Stratford Close
Barford Close
Arden Cl
Grafton Dr
Ettington Dr
Chipping Av
North Leach Dr
Alderdale Av
Rothwell Dr
Westminster Dr
Lighthorne Dr
Cantlow Fold
Pershore Gv
Shelton Dr
Quinton Cl
Harbury Av
Wigston Cl
Chiltern Road
Chatsworth Rd
Petworth Road
Chartwell Rd
Tavistock Dr
Blenheim Road
Tudor Rd
Daneway
Greyfriars Road
Mck Dr
Harvington Drive
Broadway Cl
Daresbury Avenue
Prestbury Av
Chandley Close
Barrington Dr
Arlington Close
Kettering Rd
Brinklow Close
Sevenoaks Avenue
Sambourn Fold
Meriden Cl
Rothley Av
Bosworth Dr
Wilmcote Gv
Kingsbury Cl
Drive
Avenue
Shoreside Primary School
Merefield Special School
Chatsworth Av
Upton Avenue
Harewood Av
Knowle Avenue
Road
Seafield Road
Carlton Road
Hatfield Road
Sandringham Road
Osborne Road
Belvedere Road
Shore Road
Delamere Road
Mandeville Road
Mossgiel Av
Chesterfield Rd
Ainsdale High School
Southport & Ainsdale Golf Club
Bradshaw's Lane
Berwick Av
Faulkner Cl
Burnley Road
Burnley Road
Fairfield Road
Ainsdale Station
Station Rd
Surgery
PO
Halifax Road
Leamington Road
Sanvino Avenue
Liverpool Rd
LIVERPOOL RD
LIVERPOOL
Mill Road
Segar's Lane
Limont Rd
Unit Road
Eldons Cft
Sandbrook Road
Ainsdale
Salford Road
Greenford Road
Hillsview Road
Chesterfield Cl
Frailey Close
Trevor Road
Stourton Rd
Stoneleigh Close
Kenilworth Road
Bridgend Dr
Longcliffe Drive
Midhurst Dr
The Paddock
Muirfield Drive
Sunbury Drive
Drive
Wentworth Close
Ainsdale CE Primary School
Staveley Rd
Briar Rd
Orchard Lane
Sandbrook
Orchard Lane
Hill House Farm
Shirdley Crescent
Mardale Close
Easedale Drive
Uldale Close
Gleneagles
Windermere Crs
Kendal Way
Woodside Av
Furness Cl
Thirlmere Drive
Penrith Av
Keswick Close
Bowness Av
Newby Cl
Coastal Road
Pinfold Lane
Woodvale
Pinfold Lane
Ainsdale Clinic
Kings Meadow Primary School
Kings Meadow
Sandbrook Road
PO
Meadow Lane
Meadow Lane
Cornwall Way
Dorset Avenue
Somerset Dr
Way
A565
LIVERPOOL ROAD
Rose Crs
Heather Cl
Cherry Road
Lilac Av
St John Stone Catholic Primary School
Willowbank Holiday Home & Touring Park
Woodvale Road
Woodvale
Birkdale Cemetery
Alston Ct
Welwyn Avenue
sdale-on-Sea

34
Greenbank High Sch
Hillside Golf Club
Lynton Drive
Sandon Road
Kirklees Road
Ashton
Langdale Gardens
Norfolk Gv
Works
Our Lady of Lourdes RC Pri School
Grantham Road
Shaw's Road
Grantham Ct
Lincoln Rd
Road Health Centre
PO
A
B
C
D
E
27
Southport RFC
332
34
Arundel Road
Dunbar Crescent
Woodstock Drive
LIVERPOOL
Shaftesbury Road
Suffolk Road
Essex Road
Shaftesbury Avenue
Halsall Road
Blythe Ms
Farnborough Road
Lynton
Clovelly Drive
14
1
Dunster Road
Ryder Crescent
Golf Course
Farnborough Road J&I School
Central Av
Guildford
New Cut Lane
PR8
Windy Harbour Road
St Mary's Gdns
Carr Lane
Birkdale High School
A565
2
Leybourne Av
Ranelagh Dr
East Crantum Farm
Birkdale Cemetery
Nixon's Lane
13
ROAD
Welwyn Avenue
Philip Drive
Charles Av
Elizabeth Av
Anne Av
3
Birkdale RC Cemetery
Alston Ct
Heathfield Road
Mary's Av
33
George Drive
Oakwood Drive
Mill Rd
Segar's Lane
Elm Park Dr
4
Unit Road
Sandbrook Road
12
White Otter Farm
Segar's Lane
Headbolt Lane
5
Hill House Farm
6
Spencer's La
Carr Moss Lane
Heather Farm
Meadow La
11
42
1 grid square represents 500 metres

28
F
G
H
J
K
35
37
Moss Farm
RKDALE
COP
HEATHEY LANE
Tinsley's
Lane
Turning
Lane
B5243
JACKSMERE
London Lane
Heathey
Lane
1
2
3
4
5
6
14
13
12
11
36
Shirdley Hill
Shaw Close
PO
Shaws Garth
Willow Brook
La Mancha
New Cut Lane
Cabin Lane
Renacres Lane
Manor House Farm
Barlow's Lane
Olverston House Farm
Renacres Hall Hospital
Renacres La
New Cut Lane
Halsall Moss
Green Kettle House
Gregory Lane
43
Carr Moss

36
29
35
44
Snape Green
Carr Cross
Scarisbrick
Bescar
Drummersdale
Pinfold
A570
SOUTHPORT ROAD
LANE
B5242
BESCAR BROW LANE
Woodland Avenue
Bescar Lane
Hillcrest Drive
Culshaw Wy
Everard Close
Bsc Brw La
Clyffes Farm Close
St Marys RC Primary School
HALL
Hall Road
Scarisbrick Hall
Kingswood College
St Marks CE Primary School
Sandy Brook
Hooton's Farm
Bullens Lane
Black
Moss Lane
Police Station
A5147
GORSUCH LANE
ROAD
Renacres Lane
Morris Hey
Morris Lane
Leeds & Liverpool Canal
Wharf
Pinfold Lane
Pinfold Primary School
Small Lane North
North Moor
Grange Farm
Hulmes Bridge Business Centre
1 grid square represents 500 metres
A
B
C
D
E
1
2
3
4
5
6
337
39
14
13
12
11

Drummersdale Lane
White House Lane
Copelands
30
38
45
40
42
LC
Martin Lane
Highfield Lane
Drummersdale Lane
Hall Road
ROAD
Merscar Lane
Gorst Lane
DAM WOOD LANE
Leeds & Liverpool Canal
Shaw Hall Caravan Park
Heatons Bridge
HEATONS BRIDGE ROAD
Smithy Lane
Rabbit Lane
Edge Farm
Hurlston Green
Moorfield La
Moorfield Lane
B5242
BARTON GREEN
PIPPIN
Stub Lane
Hurlston Hall Golf Club
F
G
H
J
K
1
2
3
4
5
6

Tarlscough
New Lane
Burscough Bridge
Burscough
Wildfowl and Wetlands Trust Martin Mere
Tarlscough Lane
Curlew Lane
Red Cat Lane
Marsh Moss Lane
Marsh Moss House
Crabtree Lane
New Lane Station
LC
New Lane
Lane
Works
Martin Hall
Burscough Industrial Estate
Langley Place
Langley Road
Plantation Road
Gilbert Place
Industrial Estate
L40
Ringtail Road
Ringtail Court
Ringtail Place
Higgin's Lane
Tollgate Road
Edge Farm
Rabbit Lane
Orrell Lane
Leeds & Liverpool Canal
Burscough Sports Centre
Burscough FC
Burscough Br Station
Mart Lane
Victoria St
Burscough Bridge Methodist Primary School
Burscough Priory High School
Vicarage Gardens
Trevor Road
Hesketh Road
Alexandra Road
Christines Crs
Liverpool Road North
A59
Junction Lane
Heather Close
Lordsgate Township Prim Sch
Lordsgate Drive
Liverpool Road South
Rivington Drive
Richmond Avenue
Elm Road
Square Lane
Moss Nook
Back Lane
Cherry Grove
Mere Avenue
Works
Ringtail Industrial Estate
Guys Industrial Estate
Springfield Close
Meadowbrook
Platts Lane Industrial Estate
Burscough RC Primary School
Manor Avenue
Stub Lane
PO
A B C D E
1 2 3 4 5 6
342 44
31 37 46
1 grid square represents 500 metres

F
G
H
J
K
45
46
47
14
13
12
11
I
2
3
4
5
6
Low Meadows
Burscough Moss
Prescott Bridge
Meadow Lane
Back Moss Lane
MOSS LANE
MOSS LANE A59
Leeds & Liverpool Canal (Rufford Branch)
Eller Brook
Meadow Lane
LC
Laburnum Grove
Rowan Cl
Avenue
Wil Crs
Warper's Moss Lane
Warper's Moss Lane
Trent Close
Weaver Avenue
New Sutch House Farm
St Johns CE Primary School
Surg
Burscough Primary Sch
School Lane
Colburne Close
Burscough Cricket Club
Sutch Lane
Bleak Lane
Wood Lane
Hoscar
Wanes
Daisy Lane
Meadow Lane
Moss Road
Hoscar Station
Hoscar Moss
Carr Lane
Wheat Lane
Frog Lane
Mill Lane
Green La
Boundary La
Willow End
Field Close
Gower Gardens
Rees Park
Abbey Dale
Carvel Way
Delph Dr
Croft Ave
Ellerbrook Dr
Council Building
BRIARS LANE
A5209
Brooklands Grove
Flaxfields
Briars Brook
Leeds & Liverpool Canal
Hollowford Lane
Ring O'B
47
Ring o' Bells
Flax Lane
Bridge Lane
Back Lane

A
B
32
C
D
E
327
29
11
10
09
408
1
2
3
4
5
6
Ainsdale Sand Dunes
Nature Reserve
LC
Golf Course
Clarence House School
Argarmeols Road
Fishermans Close
Argarmeols Road
Rimmer's Av
Stanlawe Road
Mersey Av
Gregson's Av
Queens Avenue
The Birches
Gores
Montagu Rd
Formby Golf Club
Formby Ladies Golf Club
Shireburn Road
Golf Road
Victoria Way
Badgers Rake
Tower End
Fairways Court
Freshfield
Freshfield Station
Grange Lane
Victoria Road
Victoria Road
College Path
Squirrel Green
Birch Green
Firs Crs
Firs Cl
Derby Road
48
Gorse Wy
Proctor Road
Harington
Larkhill
Dunes Drive
Oakfield Drive
St Peter's Way
Larch Way
St Peter's Close
College Close
Avenue
Holmwood Dr
Lenton Avenue
Vicarage Close
Vicarage Road
Vaughan Close
Lane
Barkfield
College Avenue
Freshfield Road
Town Green
Barkfield La
St George's R
FORM
PO
P
1 grid square represents 500 metres

Woodvale
Coastal Road
Newby Cl
Pinfold Lane
Pinfold Lane
Thirlmere Drive
Windermere
Keswick Close
Bowness
Penrith Av
Furness Cl
Kings Meadow Primary School
Sandbrook Road
Meadow Lane
Meadow
PO
33
Somerset Dr
Cornwall
Somerset
Dorset Avenue
Way
LIVERPOOL ROAD A565
Rose Crs
Heather Cl
Cherry Road
Lilac Av
St John Stone Catholic Primary School
Woodvale Road
Woodvale Road
Vale Crescent
Moor Close
Moor Lane
Willowbank Holiday Home & Touring Park
Dunlop Avenue
Liverpool Old Road
Plex Moss Lane
Tree Tops Country House Hotel
FORMBY BY-PASS A565
Southport Old Road
Southport Old Rd
Sixpenny Lane
Golf Course
Woodvale Airfield
Formby Hall Golf Club
42
FORMBY BY-PASS
North Moss Lane
Southport Old Road
A565
Hawksworth Dr
Hawksworth Drive
Hawksworth Close
Turnacre
Lingdales
Longton Dr
Deansgate Lane North
Gorsefield
Brackenway
Heather ways
The Rydinge
Brewery La
Brewery Lane
Old La
Kenton Cl
West Lane
St Anne's Cl
St Anne's Road
St Anne's Path
York Cl
Canterbury Cl
Spymers Croft
Heathfield Cl
Hthfld Cl
The Spinney
Wrigleys Lane
Wrigleys Cl
Paradise Lane
Green Lane
Timms Lane
Timms Close
Cricket Path
St Peters CE Primary School
SOUTHPORT ROAD B5424
Heather Close
Primrose Close
Longfield
Formby Junior Sports Club
Deansgate Lane
Mount House Road
Mount House Close
The Paddock
Formby CC
Formby Lawn Tennis Club
Deans Court
Piercefield Road
New Road
Clifton Rd
Surgery
Sefton
Lancashire
County
Downholland Brook
Freshfield Primary School
49
Side
Moss Lane
Cable Street
Old Mill Lane
Willow Grove
Dobbs Drive
Smithy Cl
Smt Gn
Lane
L37
30
32
F
G
H
J
K
1
2
3
4
5
6
10
11
09
408
BY

42
34
41
50
A
B
C
D
E
1
2
3
4
5
6
Meadow Lane
332
34
408
10
09
Spencer's La
Carr Moss Lane
Heather Farm
n Stone
ic Primary
vale Road
Plex Moss
Lancashire County
Sefton
Sixpenny Lane
Gettern Farm
Plex Moss Lane
Heathy Lane
Alder Lane
North Lane
Gorsey Lane
Gorsey
Cheshire Lines Path
Moss Lane
Old Moss Lane
Sefton
ncashire County
Downholland Moss
1 grid square represents 500 metres

F
G
H
J
K
35
Green Ketts House
Carr Moss Lane
Plumpton Lane
The Runnel
Cross Lane
A5147
PO
Chestnut Close
Halsall Hall Drive
Halsall Manor Court
NEW STREET
Halsall St Cuthberts CE Primary School
Carr Moss La
Linaker Drive
Park House Farm
Plex Moss Lane
44
Lane
SOUTHPORT ROAD A5147
Station Road
Shaw Lane
Well Lane
Barton
Smithy Lane
Plex Lane
WANISHAR LANE
Leeds & Liverpool Canal
Rosemary Lane
Haskayne
Jackson Close
Queens Green
Riding Lane
Park Crs
51
DELF
37
408
1
2
3
4
5
6

44
36
43
52
Halsall
Primrose Hill
Hulmes Bridge Business Centre
Grange Farm
North Moor
Diglake Farm
Works
PO
Halsall St Cuthberts CE Primary School
Bangor's Green
School
Leeds & Liverpool
Morris Hey
Morris Lane
Pinfold Lane
Gregory Lane
HALSALL ROAD
A5147
NEW STREET
Cross Lane
Runnel
Summerwood Lane
Chestnut Close
Small Lane North
North Moor Lane
Harridge Lane
Harridge
Jackson's
Asmall Lane
Cut Lane
Narrow Lane
(Clieves Hills)
Halsall Lane
Trundle Pie La
South Small Lane
Shepherd's Lane
Booth's Lane
A570 SOUTHPORT RD
1 grid square represents 500 metres

Green
Moorfield Lane
Barrison Green
B5242
Road
Pippin
37
46
53
40
42
F
G
H
J
K
1
2
3
4
5
6
Hurlston Hall Golf Club
Hurlston Hall Country Caravan Park
Hurlston Lane
Lane
Narrow Moss Lane
Blackacre Lane
Merrida Farm
Spout House Farm
A570
Southport Road
Heskin Hall
Heskin Lane
Renfrey Close
Marians Drive
Rutland Crs
Haslam Drive
Ludlow Drive
Douglas Drive
Courtfield
Fairfield Close
West End Primary School
Grimshaw Lane
Highfield Road
Hayfield Rd
Whittle Drive
Mawdsley Terrace
Carroll Crescent
Parker Crescent
Lea Crescent
Sturgess Close
Dawson Road
Tyrer Road
Sephton Drive
Scott Drive
A59
Blindman's Lane
Asmall House
Asmall Lane
Asmall Primary School
Tennyson Drive
Whiteralls Dr
Cotton Drive
Asmall Close
Halsall Lane
Church Hl Road
The Reeds
Cottage Lane
Rothwell Close
Kinloch Way
County Road
Ormskirk RUFC
Works
Green Lane
Hillcrest Rd
Farrington Drive
Yew Tree Road
Ashcroft Avenue
Clucas Gdns
Scarisbrick Street
Pennington Avenue
Burscough Street
B5319
Burscough Road
Ormskirk Business Park
Clinic
Hants Lane
Rosecroft Close
Civic Hall
Church Fields
Southport Rd
Derby St West
Church St
Pol-Mag Stn Ct
Ormskirk Station
Register Office
Surgery
Surg
Derby Street
Derby Hill Rd
Council Building
Moor St
Wigan Road
Ormskirk CE Primary School
Bath Springs
Pine Avenue
Pine Gv
Old Boundary Way
Brooklands
A&E
Vicarage Walk
Park Pool
Superstore
Kingsbury School
St Annes RC
Aughton St
Park Road
Mkt Hall
St Helens Road
Knowsley Road
A570
Windmill Av
Mill Street
School House
Ormskirk & District General Hospital
ORMSKIRK
Redgate
Ash Close
Beechwood Drive
Oak Ave
Cottage Ms
The Orch
Garnett Gdns
Cedar Crescent
Holborn Hill
A59
St Annes Road
St Bedes Catholic High School
Dyers Lane
Moorgate
Bridge Street
Chapel Mews
Brook Lane
Ravenscroft Avenue
Furness Av
Weldon Drive
Blairgowrie Gdns

38
45
54
A
B
C
D
E
1
2
3
4
5
6
342
44
11
10
09
408
Burscough
Westhead
SOUTH ROAD
A59
SQUARE LANE
Elm Road
Richmond Avenue
Rivington Drive
Springfield Close
Meadowbrook
Platts La
The Poplars
Chapel Lane
Burscough RC Primary School
Platts Lane Industrial Estate
Ringtail Industrial Estate
Guys Industrial Estate
Lordsgate Lane
Surgery
LIVERPOOL ROAD
Mill Dam Close
Manor Road
Manor Crs
Manor Avenue
Manor Gardens
Manor Dr
Mill Dam Lane
Stub Lane
PIPPIN STREET
B5242
Tollgate Road
Beaufort Hotel
Merridale Farm
Blackacre Lane
Abbey Lane
Abbey Lane Industrial Estate
Blythe Hall
Blythe Lane
Abbey Farm Caravan Park
Lady Alice's Drive
HIGH LANE
Tyrer Road
Sephton Drive
BURSCOUGH ROAD
Pine Gv
Avenue
Old Boundary Way
Brooklands
Works
Dark Lane
Sandy Lane
Lathom Lane
Cranes Lane
Ormskirk Golf Club
Golf Course
Lady's Walk
Castle Lane
Bath Farm
Waterworks Road
Nursery Avenue
Pendle Dr
Hill
Charlesbye Av
Ormskirk CE Primary School
Bath Springs
Register Office
Derby Street
Derby Hill Road
Greetby Hill
Thompson Avenue
Field Walk
Edgley Drive
Taylor Avenue
Tower Hill
Sunnyfields
Latham Avenue
WIGAN ROAD
A&E
PO
Ormskirk School
Ormskirk & District General Hospital
Hall Brow Close
A577
MOSSHALL BROW
Ormond Av
Halton Chase
Greenacre
Meadow Close
Weldon Drive
Milton Drive
Ruff
Mill Street
Windmill Av
School
Blairgowrie Gdns
Holly Close
Building
1 grid square represents 500 metres

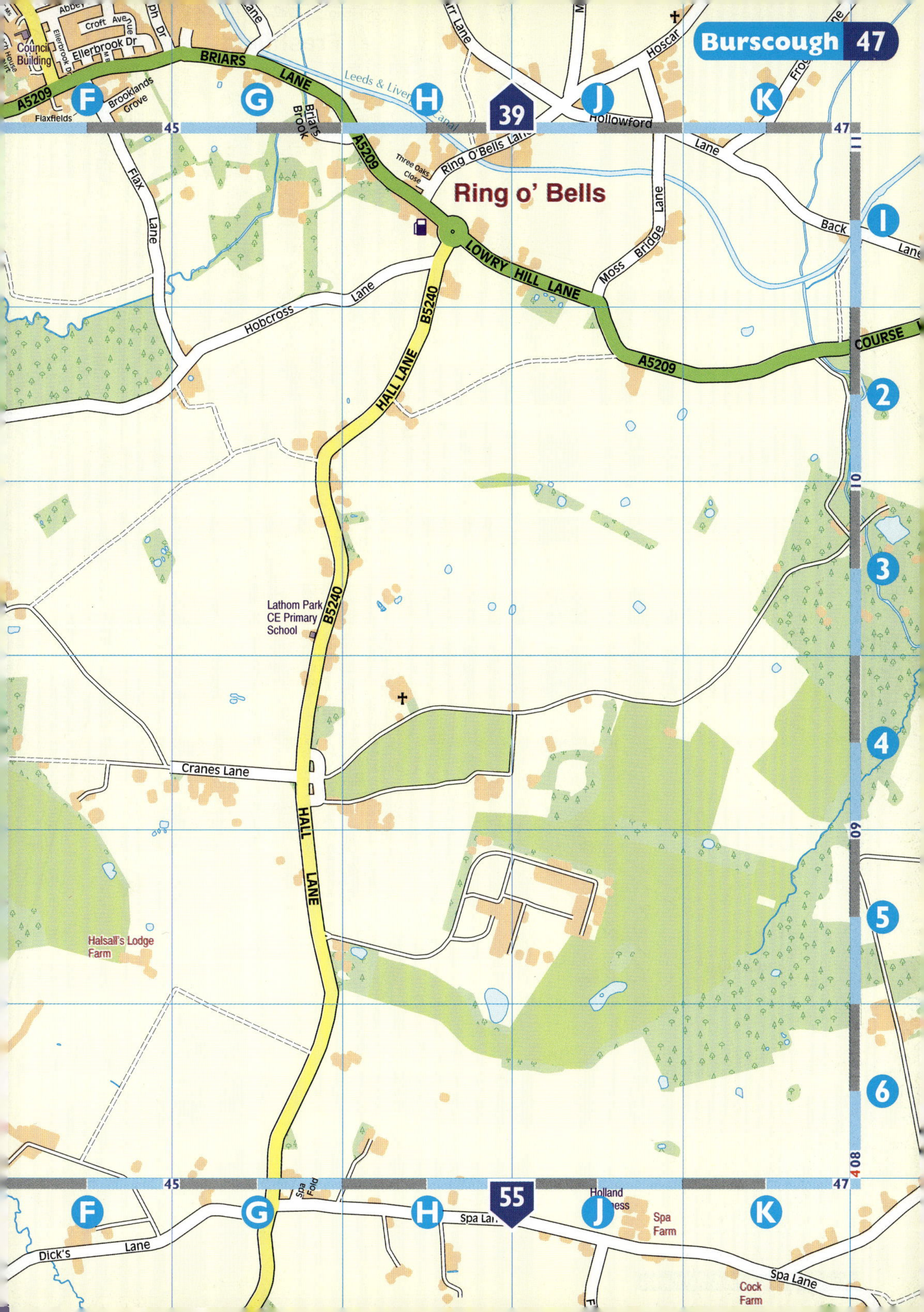
Council Building
Croft Ave
Ellerbrook Dr
A5209
BRIARS LANE
Brooklands Grove
Flaxfields
Briars Brook
Leeds & Liverpool Canal
39
Hollowford
Hoscar
Lane
Ring O'Bells Lane
Three Oaks Close
Ring o' Bells
Back Lane
Flax Lane
Moss Bridge Lane
LOWRY HILL LANE
Hobcross Lane
B5240
HALL LANE
COURSE
Lathom Park CE Primary School
Cranes Lane
Halsall's Lodge Farm
Spa Fold
55
Holland
Spa Farm
Spa Lane
Dick's Lane
Cock Farm
F
G
H
J
K
I
2
3
4
5
6
45
47
11
10
09
408

1 grid square represents 500 metres

F
G
H
41
J
K
30
32
L37
1
2
3
50
4
5
6
59
Southport Rd
Formby Junior Sports Club
Formby CC
Cricket Path
Timms Lane
The Paddock
Deansgate Lane
Mount House Road
Piercefield Road
New Road
Surgery
Byron Close
Graburn Road
Willow Grove
Freshfield Primary School
Moss Side
Moss Lane
Cable Street
Old Mill Lane
Dobbs Drive
Smithy Green
Alderson Crs
Halsall Lane
CHURCH ROAD
Hall
Davenham Road
Whitehouse Lane
Church Close
Watchyard Lane
Gardner Road
Shaw Crs
Norris Way
Police Stn
School Av
Holy Trinity CE Primary School
Shopping Centre
Chapel La
Three Tuns Lane
War Mem
Superstore
Kenyon's La
Ambulance Stn
Bull Cop
Our Lady of Compassion RC Prim Sch
Flaxfield Rd
Priesthouse Close
Glenmarsh Way
Burlington Av
Stephenson Way
Formby Business Park
Superstore
Formby's Farm
Sefton
Lancashire County
Downholland Brook
Formby AFC
Sumner Rd
Surg
Elbow La
Cropton Road
York Road
Chapelhouse Wk
ALTCAR ROAD
B5195
FORMBY BY-PASS
Works
Duke Street
Clinic
Whalley Drive
Hawthorne Crs
Ditchfield
Buckfast Dr
Cartmel Drive
Superstore
ALTCAR ROAD
LORD SEFTON WAY
Phillip's Lane
Walker Close
Glendale Way
Dickinson Road
Norburn Crs
Birkey La
LIVERPOOL ROAD
Crown Cl
Cheapside
Redgate
Redgate Primary School
Fountains Way
Friars Walk
Abbey Cl
Priory Close
Meols Lane
Nursery Drive
Park Av
Castle Drive
Park Road
Harebell Close
Ashcroft Rd
Kent Road
Royal Crs
Mayflower Industrial Estate
Abbots Close
Alt Road
River Close
Monks Drive
Savon Hook
Marina Road
Altcar Lane
Hill Road
Little Altcar
B5424
A565
Liverpool Rd
Alt Bridge
New Causeway
FORMBY-BY-PASS
Engine Lane
Lane
North End Farm
A565
LC
Road

50
42
49
60
A
B
C
D
E
1
2
3
4
5
6
332
34
405
08
07
06
Old Moss Lane
Downholland Moss
Sutton's Lane
Middle Moss Lane
Broad Lane
Broad
Lane
LORD SEFTON WAY
Doctor's Lane
Livesley's Lane
Aspinall Crs
BROAD LANE
Burgess' Lane
Middle Moss Lane
B5195
CAUSEWAY LANE
Hill House
Great Altcar
Broad Lane
Moss Lane
Rye
Acres La
New Meadow Lane
Middle Withins Lane
Linacre Lane
The Withins
Lower Carr Lane
Withins Lane
Engine Lane
Lancashire County
Sefton
Monks
1 grid square represents 500 metres

Haskayne
F
G
H
J
K
43
35
37
Rosemary Lane
Riding Lane
Sumner Avenue
Park Crs
Woods Close
Lane
08
I
DELF
LANE
School Lane
Old Lane
New Lane
Downholland Haskayne CE Primary School
2
B5195
BROAD
07
Downholland Cross
Works
Owen's Lane
Owen's
Lane
Black-A-Moor
Lane
BLACK-A-MOOR LANE
3
52
ALTCAR LANE
Worrall House Farm
A5147
WOOD
LANE
B5195
FLATMAN'S LANE
4
MAIRSCOUGH LANE
06
Acres Lane
Lancashire County
Sefton
5
Eager Lane
Church
Lane
Hollands Farm
Intake Lane
A5147
SOUTHPORT ROAD
6
Acres Lane
405
35
37
61
F
G
H
J
K
Station Road

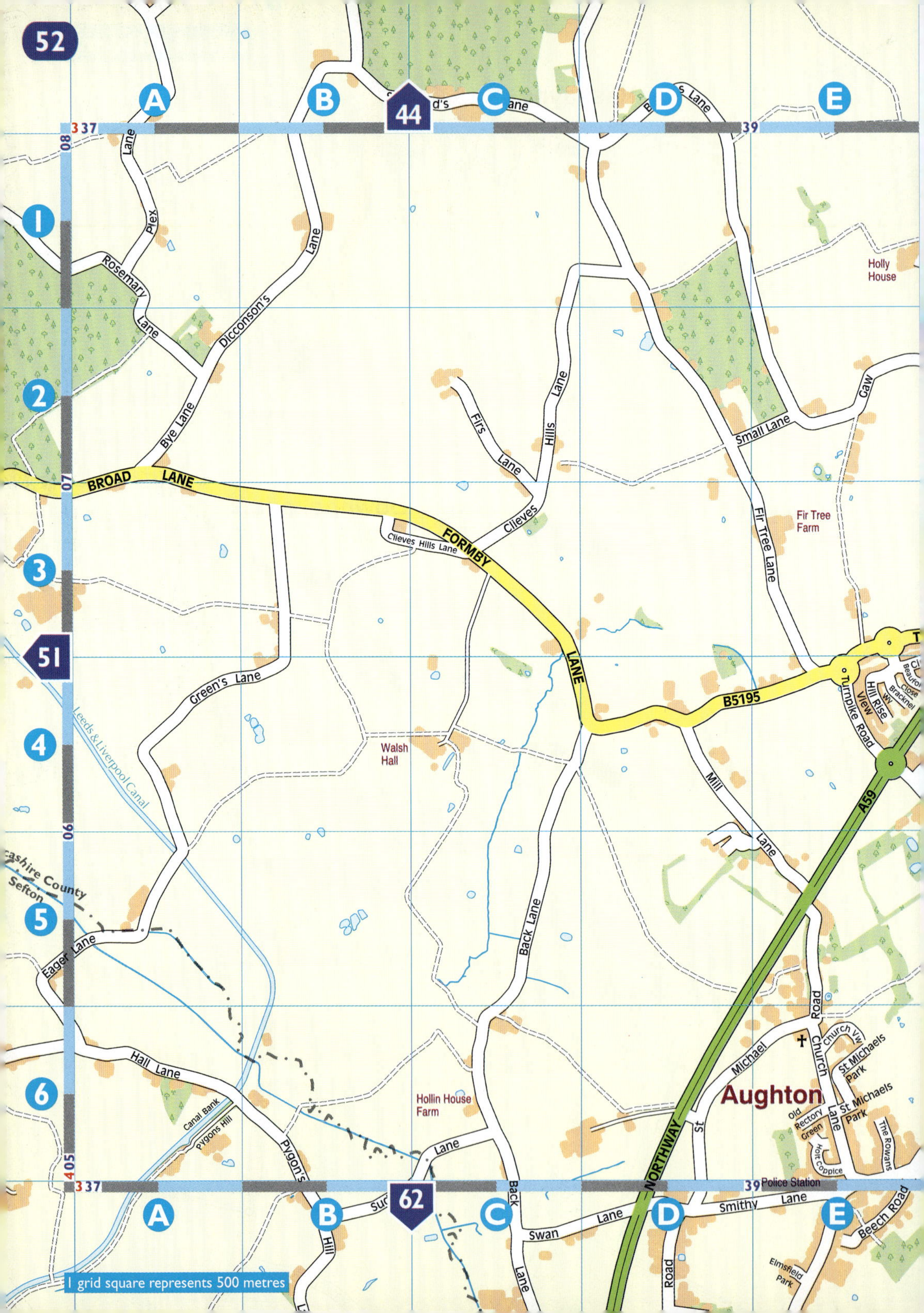

1 grid square represents 500 metres

ORMSKIRK
Aughton Park
Town Green
Holt Green
45
54
63
F
G
H
J
K
I
2
3
4
5
6
40
42
Redgate
Ash Close
Beechwood Drive
Oak Ave
Redgate
Cedar Crescent
Cottage Lane
Garnett Gdns
Holborn Hill
A59
HOLBORN HILL
LIVERPOOL ROAD
St Bedes Catholic High School
AUGHTON ST
St Annes RC Prim Sch
Park Pool
Vicarage Walk
A570
PARK ROAD
Mkt Hall
MOOR ST
WIGAN ROAD
ST HELENS ROAD
KNOWSLEY ROAD
Ormskirk & District General Hospital
A&E
Weldon Drive
Blairgowrie Gdns
Ormskirk Cricket Club
Edge Hill University Sector College
Derby Hill Rd
Bridge Street
Moorgate
Dyers Lane
Brook Farm
Chapel Mews
Chapel St
Surg
Brook Lane
Small Lane
Ravenscroft Avenue
Furness Av
Statham Way
Railway Path
Calder Avenue
Ryburn Road
Peet Av
B5197
PRESCOT ROAD
Black Moss
Chestnut Gra
Pontville School
Milman Close
Wimbrick Crescent
Hillside Av
Old Mill Hill
Parkfield
Bebles Road
Aughton Christ Church CE Primary School
PO
Holborn Drive
Holly Lane
Hill Lane
Lynwood Avenue
Victoria Road
Long Lane
The Paddock
Tarn Brow
Spinney Close
Woodfield Road
Claremont Drive
Red Sands
Red Fold
Rose Place
Aughton Park Station
High Moss Lane
Gore Drive
Barnes Road
Redcliffe Gdns
Convent Close
Moss Lane
Beaumont Crescent
Park Drive
Carmel Cl
Sch
Long Lane
Sandfield Park
Moss Bank
Black Moss
Halimoor Close
New Lane
Altys Lane
Scarth Hill Lane
Catharine's Lane
Cropper's
Long Lane
Greystokes
Rosehill
Cromwell Close
Cromfield
Drake Close
Meadow Drive
Greenbank
Swan Delph
Ryder Close
Ryder Crescent
Swanpool
Cygnet Cl
Teal Cl
Enderdale Dr
Eskdale Avenue
Sandhouse Lane
Liverpool Road
Rothwell Dr
Moss Delph Lane
Fernhurst Gate
Cherry Tree Lane
Avenue
East Mead
TURNPIKE ROAD
NORTHWAY
Narrow Lane
Croft Heys
Noel Gate
Park Link
St Michaels CE Primary School
Delph Common Road
Delph Lane
Quarry Drive
Greenwood Close
Westhaven Crescent
Dingle Close
Orchard View
Haven Brow
Delph Lane
Crescent Green
Delph Park
Granville Close
Granville Park West
Granville Park
Winifred Lane
Narrow Cft Road
Lane
Parr's Lane
Maltkiln Lane
Little Moor Hall Farm
Moss End
House Drive
Norris Cole Crescent
Town Green Primary Sch
Surgery
Granville Park
Capilano Park
Town Green Lane
Whalley Drive
Town Green Station
Molyneux Road
Middlewood Road
Middlewood Drive
Sunnyside
Belvedere Park
Ledson Gv
Bold Lane
Sandy Lane
PRESCOT ROAD
The Serpentine
Bleasdale Close
Sefton Gdns
Moor Hall
Moor Hall Farm
Grave-Yard
L39
405
406
407
408

54
46
53
64
A
B
C
D
E
1
2
3
4
5
6
Wigan Road
A&E
Ormskirk & District General Hospital
Ormskirk School
A577 Crosshall Brow
A577 Wigan Road
Hall Brow Close
Derby Hill Road
Edgley Drive
Taylor Avenue
Latham Avenue
Sunnyfields
Tower Hill
Thompson
Mill Street
School House
Ruff Lane
Milton Drive
Normanhurst
Beech Meadow
Blairgowrie Gdns
Woodlands Close
Edge Hill University Sector College
The Sporting Edge Track
Saint Helens Road
A570
Lady's Walk
Ruff Farm
Vicarage Close
St James Close
Varian Close
Bewcastle Dr
Wellfield Lane
Vicarage Lane
Westhead
Ormond Av
Halton Chase
Greenacre
Meadow Close
Holly Close
St James CE Primary School
School Lane
Works
Slack House Farm
Scarth Hill Lane
Whiteley's Lane
Scarth Hill
Cropper's Lane
Poppy Lane
Ormskirk Road
Clock House
High Lane
Long Lane
Grave-Yard Lane
Stanley Gate
Heyescroft
Stockley Crescent
1 grid square represents 500 metres

F
G
H
47
J
K
I
2
3
56
4
5
6
65
Spa Fold
Spa Lane
Holland Business Park
Spa Farm
Cock Farm
Dick's Lane
PLOUGH LANE
B5240
ROAD
Firswood Road
Stanley Place
Seaton
Seddon P
Works
Statham Road
Selby Place
Slate Lane
Chapel House
NEVERSTITCH ROAD
Old Engine Lane
Tintagel
Black Moss School
Brookfields Primary School
Turnberry
Sandy La
Bk Sl La
Clayton Street
Victoria Pk
School
Marchbank Road
Witham Road
Sherrat Street
Laburnum
Ash Grove
Olive Grove
Oxford Rd
DICKET'S LANE
A577
BLAGUEGATE LANE
ORMSKIRK ROAD
Holland's Lane
Blaguegate
Garden Centre
Bromilow Road
Orm Works
Taylor St
Sandy Lane
St Richards Catholic Primary Sch
Sandy Lane Health Cen
PO
Smith St
Westgate
Skelmersdale Park Primary School
Birch Street
Council Building
High
Pennylands
Liverpool Road
RAILWAY RD
Ashwall Street
Wallcroft Street
Wheatacre
LIVERPOOL RD
Kerfoot's Lane
Derby Rd
Old Town Cl
Old Town Wy
Village Cl
Skelmersdale United FC
B5312
RAIL
Gladden Pl
M58
LYELAKE LANE
Lyelake Farm
Road
White Moss Road
SKELMERSDALE ROAD
Stanley Farm
Ormskirk Rd
Old
RK ROAD
A570
RAINFORD ROAD
45
47
08
07
06
405

Dalton
Whalleys
Ashurst
Stanley
SKELMERSDALE
Birch Green
Digmoor
Whalleys Road
Beacon Lane
Cobb's Clough Road
Vale Lane
Glenburn Road
Our Lady Queen of Peace RC High School
Lathom County High School
Summer Street
Ashurst Road
St James RC Primary School
Ashurst Health Centre
Cobbs Brow Primary School
Manfield
Stanley Way
Seddon Place
Statham Road
Staveley Road
A577 HOUGHTONS ROAD
HOUGHTONS ROAD A577
Fairlie CP School
Birch Green Road
Irwell
Fawcett
Inskip
Tawd Valley Park
NEVERSTITCH ROAD
Crow Orchard Primary School
A5068 GLENBURN ROAD
Clough Fold Prim Sch
Superstore
Inchfield
Northway
Trinity Primary School
Skelmersdale Park Primary School
Skelmersdale & Ormskirk Colleges
Nye Bevan Swimming Pool
Market Hall Concourse Shop Cen
Police Station
St Johns RC Primary School
Hillside Health Centre
Yewdale
Glenburn High School
Southway
High Street
Council Building
Sandy Lane Health Cen
RAILWAY ROAD
B5312
HOPE ISLAND
GRIMSHAW ROAD
Delph Side Primary School
Glebe Road
Postal Delivery Office
Whiteledge Centre
Fire Station
Skelmersdale Sports Centre
West Gillbrands Industrial Estate
East Gillbrands Industrial Estate
Gillibrands Road
Junction 4
M58
White Moss Road South
Moss Lane
Little Digmoor Primary School
Works
1 grid square represents 500 metres

55
66

Dalton CE Primary School
Long Heys Lane
WN8
Beacon Park Public Golf Centre
Golf Course
Beacon CountryPark
Elmers Green
Stannanought Road
Crow Lane
Farley Lane
Beacon Lane
Roby Mill
Cemetery
Roby Mill CE Primary School
School Lane
Roby Mill
Stoney Brow
Elmers Green Lane
Elmers Wood Road
Beacon Park
Elmers Green Community Primary School
Evington
Tanhouse Road
Enstone
Earlswood
Eavesdale
Ennerdale
Tanhouse
Council Building
St Marks Catholic Primary School
Hart's Lane
Mill Lane
College Road
St Teresas County Primary School
Egerton
Beacon School
Hall Green
Hallbridge Gardens
Grove Road
Dingle Road
Parliament Street
B5312
Fir Tree Close
St Matthews RC Primary School
Parsonage Brow
Newgate Road
A577
Holland Moor Prim Sch
Collinton
Works
Ormskirk Road
Moorside Primary School
Back Lane
Tanhouse Road
Digmoor Road
Blakehall
Bishop Martin CE Primary School
Birleywood Health Cen
Clay Brow Road
Surgery
Newgate
Denholme
Dorchester Road
Carlton Avenue
St Thomas the Martyr CE Prim Sch
Stanley Road
Highgate Road
Mayfield Road
Windsor Road
Hall Green Clinic
Alma Hill
Ormskirk Road
Darfield
Ravenhead Drive
Highmeadow
Up Holland
Wellcross Road
Works
Belfield
Castlehey
Carfield
67
50
51
52
08
07
06
05
F
G
H
J
K
1
2
3
4
5
6

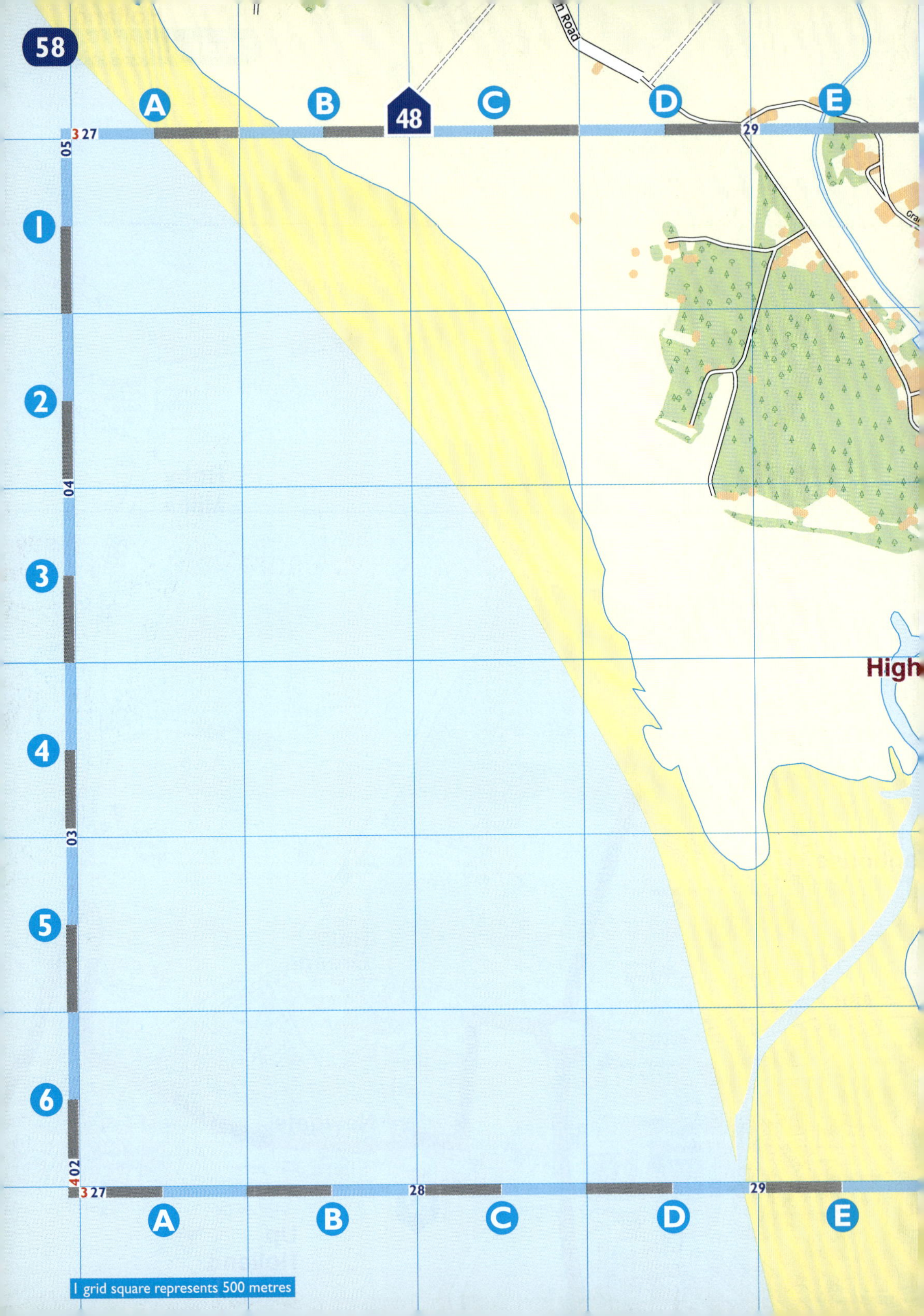
48
A
B
C
D
E
327
29
05
04
03
02
1
2
3
4
5
6
327
28
29
A
B
C
D
E
n Road
High
1 grid square represents 500 metres

F
G
H
J
K
49
30
32
North End Farm
A565
SCAFFOLD
LANE
Scaffold Lane
North End Lane
Alt Road
Whitedge Farm
Moss Lane
Marsh Lane
Lady Green
Garden Centre
Lady Green La
ORRELL HILL LANE
L38
60
Moor La
The Close
Moor Farm
B5193
Moss Farm
Gorsey Lane
MOSS LANE
Sandy Lane
Elmcroft Lane
Hightown Station
Emerson Cl
Surgery
Windermere Road
Thirlmere Road
Mark Road
Hester Cl
Kerslake Way
St George's Road
Lower Alt Road
Northdunes
Riverside
Westway
Village Way
School Road
Sndlnds Gv
Blundell Av
Bankside
The Roundway
Sandhills
Moorhouses
Thornbeck
Old Acre
Briary Cft
Blundell Grove
Thornbeck Av
Withins Fld
Avenue
Alton Close
Blundell Road
Elvington Road
Brentwood Close
Langley Cl
Oakfield Rd
Richmond Close
Marston Crs
Mayfair Cl
own
1
2
3
4
5
6
05
04
03
402
68
Delph Road
Ackers La
Little Crosby
St Marys

60
The Withins
Middle
Withins Lane
Lower Carr Lane
Lancashire County
Sefton
50
A
B
C
D
E
1
2
3
4
5
6
332
34
05
04
03
402
Monks Carr Lane
River Alt
Lady Green
Garden Centre
Lady Green Lane
59
Carr House Lane
Hall Lane
Carr Houses
Ince Blundell
Moor Lane
The Close
Victoria Rd
Back O The Town Lane
Cross Barn Lane
Park Wall Road
Blackcar Lane
Carr Side Lane
Carr Side Farm
A565
MOOR LANE
Moss Wood
East Lane
Lunt Road
Broad Lane
Home Green
Park Wall Road
Long Lane
Gates Lane
69
LANE
A565
Lunt
129
St Marys
1 grid square represents 500 metres

Lydiate
Acres Lane
Station Road
Punnell's Lane
Carr Lane
Lydiate Station Road
Gore House Farm
Pilling Lane
Altcar Lane
Cabin Lane
Crisp's Farm
Bell's Lane
Upper Gore Farm
River Alt
Lancashire County
Sefton
Green Lane
Moor Lane
Wingfield Close
Lane
SOUTHPORT ROAD
A5147 SOUTHPORT ROAD
Charlesworth Close
Sandhurst Way
Birchfield Way
Silver Birch Way
Manion Avenue
Manion Close
Avelon Cl
Woodleigh Close
Cadwell Rd
Silverstone Grove
Mallory Av
The Fieldings
The Moorings
Seafore Close
Bell's Close
High Banks
The Conifers
Rigby Road
Crawford Av
Turnbridge Road
Stonebarn
Green Park Primary School
Green Link
St John Bosco RC Primary School
North Meade
The Round
West Meade
Meade
Milton Way
Empress Close
South Meade
Glebe Cl
Green Park Drive
South Meade
Hinchley Green
B5422 GREEN LANE
Shop
Sefton Drive
Sefton Lane Industrial Estate
SEFTON LANE
B5422
Old Road
Claremont Medical Centre
Claremont Avenue
Rosslyn Avenue
Liverpool
Garden
Nursery
Roseland Cl
Clarendon Gv
Blackhurst Road
Upton Barn
Windle Ash
Dawson Gdns
Swalegate
35
37
05
04
03
02
51
62
70
F
G
H
J
K
I
2
3
4
5
6

62
52
61
71
Aughton
Moss Side
MAGHULL
Hall Lane
Canal Bank
Pygons Hill
Pygon's Hill Lane
Sudell Lane
Hollin House Farm
Rose Hill Farm
Back Lane
Swan Lane
Smithy Lane
Police Station
St Michaels Park
Old Rectory Green
Holt Coppice
The Rowans
Beech Road
Elmsfield Park
Brookfield House
Springfield Road
Aughton Chase
Nell's Lane
Butchers Lane
Brookfield Lane
Sandy Lane
Silver Birch Way
Moss Lane
Old Lane
NORTHWAY A59
LIVERPOOL ROAD B5407
Nursery Road
St Gregorys Catholic Primary School
Lambshear Lane
Lydiate Primary School
Liverpool Road
St Thomas CE Primary School
Coppull Road
Knutsford Weak
Kenyons Lane
A5147 SOUTHPORT ROAD
Marshall's Close
Barnes Drive
Nedens Lane
High Banks
The Conifers
Virginia Avenue
Sunnymede Dr
Ridgeway Dr
Coronation Road
Northway Primary School
Lathom Drive
Aragon Cl
Millbank Lane
Park Lane
Dodd's Lane
Moss Lane
Trent Avenue
Sudell Avenue
Mersey Avenue
Surgery
Ashworth Hospital
Parkbourn Drive
LIVERPOOL ROAD NORTH
Turnbridge Road
Greenbank Avenue
Hickson Avenue
Green Park Primary School
Upton Barn
North Meade
The Round
Westway
Eastway
Windermere Dr
Deyes Lane
School Lane
Police Station
Superstore
Maghull Health Cen
Red Lion Shopping Centre
Council Building
Deyes High School
St Andrews Maghull CE Prim Sch
B5422 GREEN LANE
LIVERPOOL ROAD SOUTH
A5147
DAMFIELD LA
South Meade
Westover Rd
Shop Lane
Parkfield Grove
Chilton Mews
Farmdale Drive
Waltho Avenue
Croft Field
Hillcrest
Foxhouse Lane
Newlyn Avenue
Aldykes
Damfield Lane
Claremont Medical Centre
Claremont Avenue
Avondale Av
Maricourt Catholic High School
Brookfield Lane
Poverty Lane
Town Hall
L31
1 grid square represents 500 metres

Moss Side 63
Town Green
Holt Green
Bowker's Green
Royal
53
64
72
F
G
H
J
K
1
2
3
4
5
6
40
42
05
04
03
402
Bold Lane
Sandy Lane
Belvedere Park
Sunnyside
Sefton Gdns
Moor Hall Farm
Hall
Mickering Farm
Mickering Lane
PRESCOT ROAD
B5197
Bowker's Green Lane
Billinges
Gerard Hall
Mossock Hall Golf Club
Golf Course
LIVERPOOL ROAD
Simonswood Lane
Butchers Lane
Works
Powderworks Lane
A506
CUNSCOUGH LANE
M58
Cunscough Hall
Old Prescot Close
Villas Road
Beechway
Outlet Lane
Outlet Farm
Sefton
Lancashire County
Junction 1
Maghull Lane
Land End
Lyon's Farm
Maghull-Lane
Whitegates Farm
Spurrier's Lane
Grave-Yard

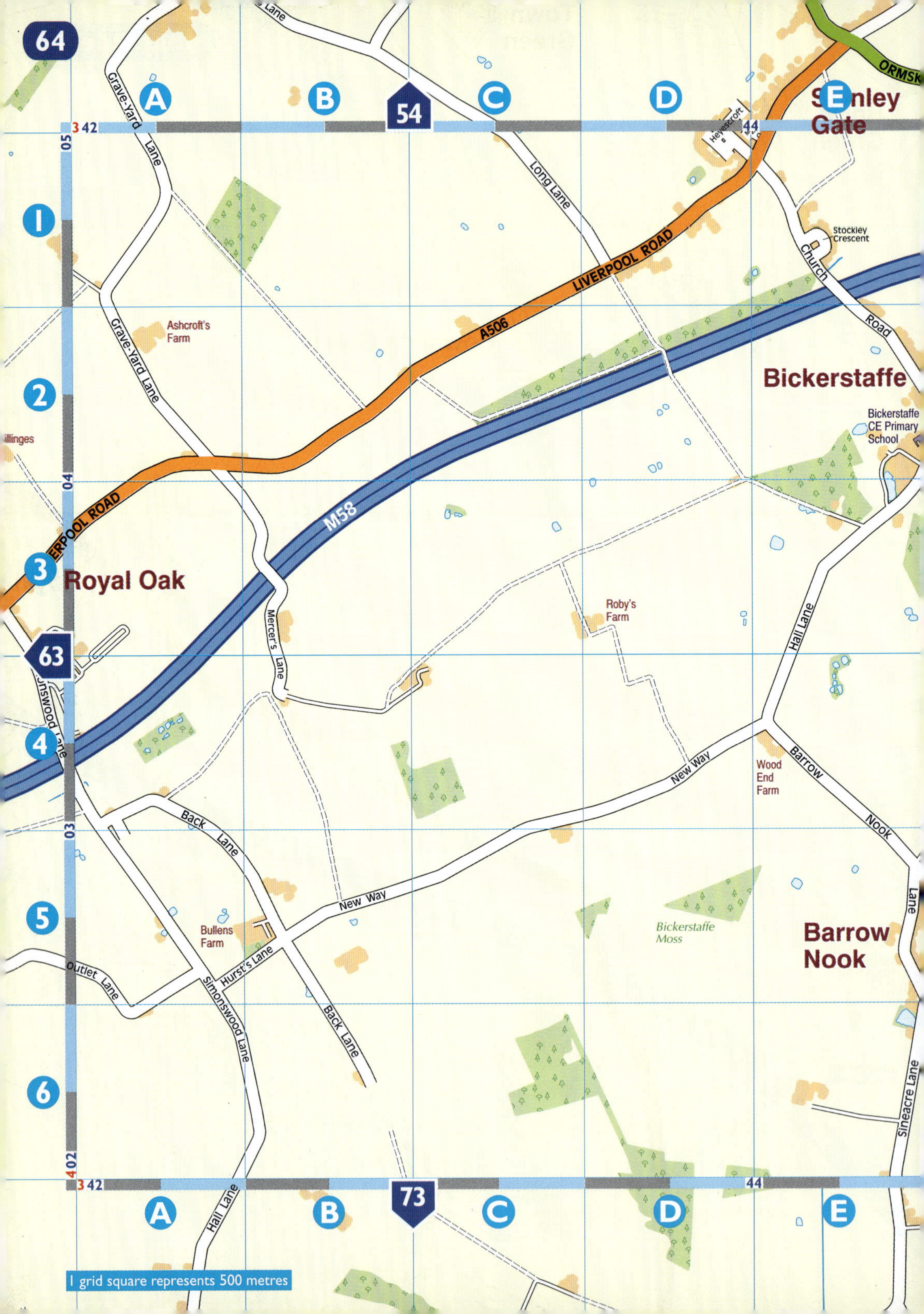
54
63
73
A
B
C
D
E
1
2
3
4
5
6
3 42
44
05
04
03
4 02
Stanley Gate
Heyescroft
Stockley Crescent
Church Road
Long Lane
LIVERPOOL ROAD
A506
ORMSK
Grave-Yard Lane
Ashcroft's Farm
Bickerstaffe
Bickerstaffe CE Primary School
M58
Royal Oak
Mercer's Lane
Roby's Farm
Hall Lane
New Way
Barrow Nook
Wood End Farm
Simonswood Lane
Back Lane
Bullens Farm
Hurst's Lane
Outlet Lane
Bickerstaffe Moss
Barrow Nook
Lane
Sineacre Lane
Hall Lane
1 grid square represents 500 metres

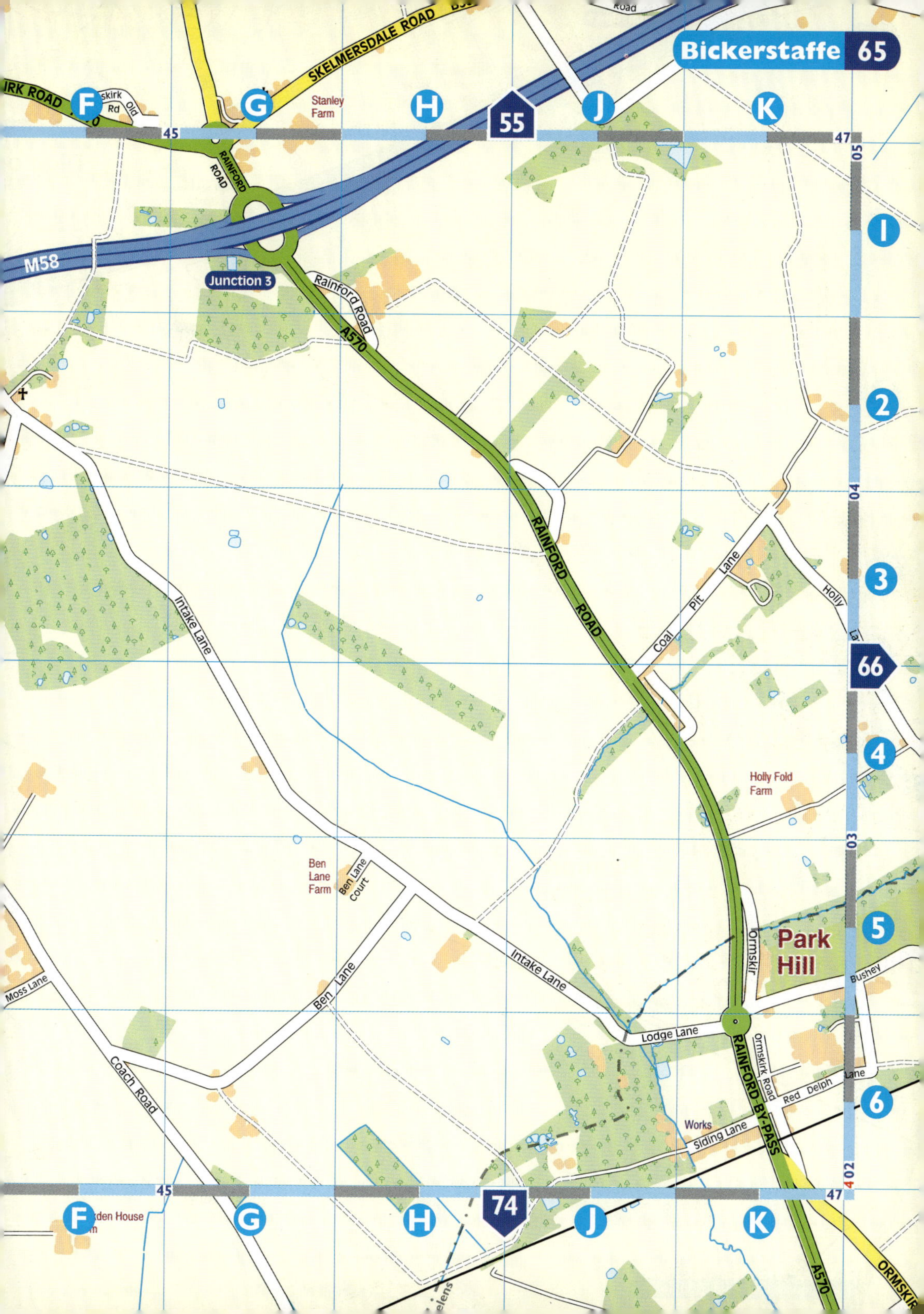
SKELMERSDALE ROAD
Stanley Farm
55
M58
Junction 3
RAINFORD ROAD
Rainford Road
A570
Intake Lane
Coal Pit Lane
Holly La
66
Holly Fold Farm
Ben Lane Farm
Ben Lane Court
Ben Lane
Moss Lane
Coach Road
Lodge Lane
Ormskirk
Park Hill
Bushey
Ormskirk Road
Red Delph Lane
Works
Siding Lane
RAINFORD BY-PASS
74
ORMSKIRK
F G H J K
1 2 3 4 5 6
45 47
05 04 03 402

Junction 4
A506
White Moss Road South
Gillibrands Road
Works
East Gillibrands Industrial Estate
Works
Grimrod
Daniels Lane
Amersham
Digmoor Drive
Sports Centre
Digmoor Road
Banksbarn
Gillibrands Road
Abbeystead
Abbeywood
Beecht
Acregate
Digmoor
Little Digmoor Primary School
Alderley
Digmoor
Whiteledge Road
M58
Moss Lane View
Moss Lane
White Moss Farm
Pennine Pl
Whiteledge Road
Works
Pikelaw Place
Pilling Place
Penketh Place
Holland Moss
Nipe Lane
Works
Works
Pimbo Road
Works
Pit Hey Place
Paddock Road
Works
Paxton Place
Ferny Knoll
Ferny Knoll Road
Holland Moss
Lancashire County
St. Helens
Holly Lane
Holly Fold Lane
Rainford Junction
Park Hill
Bushey Lane
News Lane
Windermere Drive
Buttermere Crs
Kendal Close
Kendal Drive
Rail Close
Spring Field
PO
Rainford Station
Nook Road
Works
News Lane
Maggots
Langwood
Henderson
Brow
Reeds
Hyde's Brow
Road
A570
Lane
1 grid square represents 500 metres
56
65
75

RC Primary School
Holland Moor Prim Sch
Brakehall
Whitstone Dr
Colinton
Works
Cornbrook
Ormskirk Road
Martins Lane
Nixons Lane
Digmoor Road
Meadow
A577
Denholme
Dorchester Road
Carlton Avenue
Dalton Rd
Millgreen Cl
Dayfield
Stanley Road
St Thomas the Martyr CE
Surgery
Newgate
ORMSKIRK R
Hall Green Clinic
Alma Hill
Alma Rd
F
G
H
J
K
57
Bishop Martin CE Primary School
50
Back Lane
Cherrycroft
Birleywood
Beavers La
Drive
Moor
Birleywood Health Cen
Surgery
PO
Back La
Clay Brow Road
Darfield
Danbers
Ravenhead Way
Brick Works
Ravenhead
Bardsley Cl
Fieldview
Meadowfield
Highmeadow
Vale Cft
Broadacre
Orchid Cl
Devon Av
Wellcross
Douglas Av
Up Holland
Works
52
05
Carfield
Castleheey
Belfield
Birkrig
Road
St Lukes RC Primary School
Brierfield
Chequer Lane
Tower Hill Road
Pimbo Road
M58
Works
Chequer Lane
Tower Nook
Junction 5
A577
STANNANOUGHT ROAD
Prospect Place
Chequer Cl
Potter Place
Peel Road
Industrial Estate
Industrial Estate
Quality Hotel
Priorswood Place
Works
04
Pinfold Place
Works
Pimbo Road
Prescott Road
Works
Up Holland Station
Penrose Pl
Works
Pimbo Lane
Place
Pendle
Higher Pimbo
LC
Duke's Wood Lane
Long Lane
Crawford Village Primary School
Manor House Dr
Millets
03
Bispham Ha Business Pa
Works
Crawford
Crawford Road
Oakleigh
Holland Court
Lancashire County
St. Helens
Maddocks
02
Lane
50
76
52
Brownlow
Lane
Pimbo Road
1
2
3
4
5
6

59
80
A
B
C
D
E
1
2
3
4
5
6
Little Crosby
Golf Course
Delph Road
Ackers Lane
Dibb Lane
Sefton Coastal Footpath
Hall Road Station
West Lancashire Golf Club
Hall Road West
Ward Road
Richard Road
Burbo Bank Road North
Warren Road
Spinney Crs
Paddock Close
Hall Road
St Andrew's Road
Saint Andrew's Drive
Sunningdale Drive
Prestwick Drive
Roehampton Drive
East Manor Road
Manor High School
St Michael's Road
Boundary Drive
Far Moss Road
Dowhills Road
Dowhills Dr
Waterloo FC
Crescent Road
Berwick Dr
College Road North
Cambridge Road
Ennismore Road
Sherwood Road
Bonnington Av
Manor Drive
Kaigh Avenue
Ilford Avenue
Manor Avenue
Miller Avenue
Primary School
Valewood Primary School
Cambridge Dr
Cambridge Av
Surgery
Fairways
Park Drive
The Serpentine
Holyrood
Merrilocks Road
Linville Avenue
Osbert Road
St Anthony's Road
Esthe Road North
Linden Avenue
Elton Av
Victoria Av
Victoria Road
Streatham House School
Kings Rd
Alexandra Road
York Av
Princes Av
Merchant Taylors School for Girls
Coronation Road
Coronation Drive
Atherton House School
Kingswood
Blundellsands
Bronte Cl
Nicholas Road
Burbo Bank
Devon Cl
Channel Rd
Warren Rd
The Mount St Marys Prep Sch
Ursuline RC Primary Sch
Blundellsands Road W
Byron Road
South Road
Blundellsands & Crosby Station
Ashbourne Av
Ivanhoe Rd
Kenilworth Rd
Abbotsford Rd
Agnes Road
Weld Rd
Mersey Road
Rossett Road
Marine FC
Abbotsford Gardens
St Nicholas CE Primary School
Surgery
Brighton le Sands
Harlech Rd
Cavendish
Bridge Rd
Jubilee Road
Sunnyside Road
Riversleа Rd
Warren House
Pinehurst Avenue
Rosebery Av
Mersey View
Holden Road
Leopold Road
Heathfield Rd
Endsleigh Road
Winchester
Brooke Road East
College Road
Park View
Waterloo
Crosby Baths
330
31
02
01
400
399
1 grid square represents 500 metres

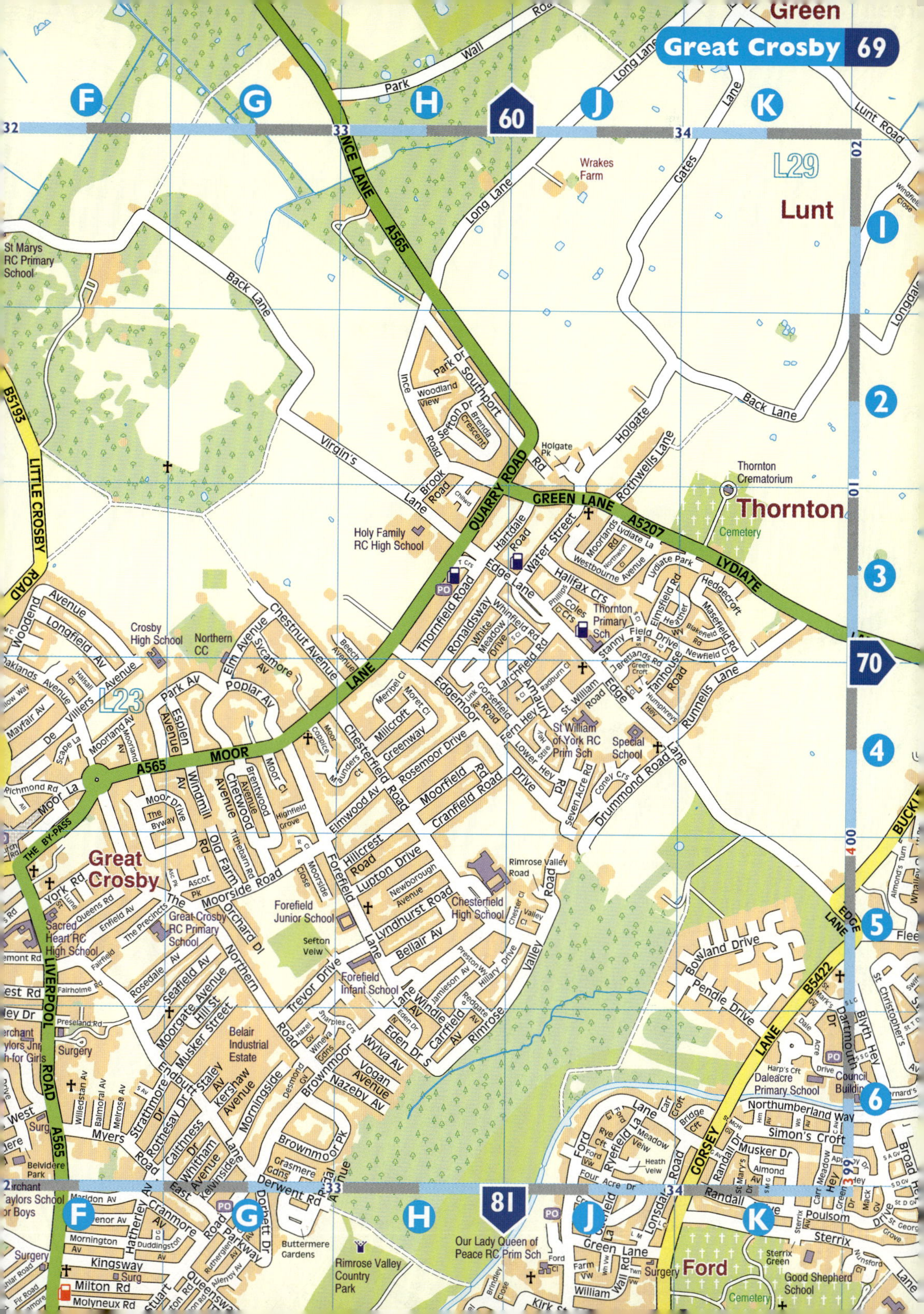

Green
Lunt
L29
Thornton
Thornton Crematorium
Cemetery
Great Crosby
L23
Ford
Wrakes Farm
Park Wall
Long Lane
Gates Lane
Lunt Road
Back Lane
Holgate
Holgate Pk
Rothwells Lane
GREEN LANE
A5207
LYDIATE
Lydiate Park
Hedgecroft
Masefield Rd
Newfield Cl
Runnells Lane
St Marys RC Primary School
INCE LANE
A565
Southport Road
QUARRY ROAD
Virgin's Lane
Brook Road
Woodland View
Sefton Dr
Brenda Crescent
Park Dr
Holy Family RC High School
Thornfield Road
Ronaldsway
Edge Lane
Water Street
Hartdale Road
Halifax Crs
Westbourne Avenue
Moorlands Rd
Thornton Primary Sch
Field Drive
Elmsfield Rd
Tanhouse Road
Edge Lane
St William Road
St William of York RC Prim Sch
Special School
Drummond Road
Seven Acre Rd
Coney Crs
Lower Hey
Fern Hey
Amaury Rd
Larchfield Rd
Whinfield Rd
White Meadow Drive
Corsefield Road
Edgemoor Drive
Rosemoor Drive
Moorfield Rd
Cranfield Road
Greenway
Millcroft
Chesterfield Road
Elmwood Av
Chestnut Avenue
Beech Avenue
Sycamore Av
Poplar Av
Elm Avenue
Park Av
Esplen Avenue
Crosby High School
Northern CC
Woodend Avenue
Longfield Av
Oaklands Avenue
Villiers Avenue
Mayfair Av
Moorland Av
MOOR LANE
A565
Windmill Av
Chetwood Avenue
Brentwood Avenue
Moor Cl
Moor Drive
The Byway
THE BY-PASS
Richmond Rd
Moor La
Old Farm Rd
Tithebarn Rd
Moorside Road
Orchard Dl
Forefield Lane
Hillcrest Road
Lupton Drive
Newborough Avenue
Lyndhurst Road
Chesterfield High School
Rimrose Valley Road
Valley Road
Forefield Junior School
Sefton Veiw
Forefield Infant School
Bellair Av
Trevor Drive
Hillary Drive
Rimrose
Redgate Av
Carrfield Av
Windle Av
Eden Dr S
Wyvia Av
Vogan Avenue
Nazeby Av
Brownmoor Pk
Brownmoor La
Grasmere Gdns
Derwent Rd
Great Crosby RC Primary School
The Precincts
Sacred Heart RC High School
York Rd
Queens Rd
Enfield Av
Rosedale Av
Seafield Av
Moorgate Avenue
Musker Street
Northern Road
Belair Industrial Estate
Morningside
Kershaw Avenue
Staley Av
Endbutt La
Strathmore Dr
Rothesay Dr
Caithness Dr
Whitham Avenue
Kelvinside
Myers Road
Melrose Av
Balmoral Av
Willedstan Av
Surgery
Preseland Rd
Fairholme Rd
LIVERPOOL ROAD
A565
LITTLE CROSBY ROAD
B5193
Belvidere Park
Merchant Taylors School for Boys
Marldon Av
Mornington Av
Kingsway
Milton Rd
Molyneux Rd
Hatherley Av
Cranmore Av
Duddingston Av
Parkway
Dorset Dr
Queensway
Buttermere Gardens
Rimrose Valley Country Park
Our Lady Queen of Peace RC Prim Sch
Green Lane
Farm Vw
William Wall Rd
Lonsdale Road
Four Acre Dr
Meadow Veiw
Heath Veiw
Bridge Cft
Croft
Northumberland Way
Simon's Croft
Musker Dr
Almond
Randall Dr
Randall Av
Poulsom Drive
Sterrix Lane
Sterrix Green
Good Shepherd School
Cemetery
CORSEY LANE
B5422
Dartmouth Dr
Blyth Hey
Daleacre Primary School
Council Building
Harp's Cft
Bowland Drive
Pendle Drive
EDGE LANE
St Christopher's Av
Almond's Turn
BUCKLEY
Fleet
Longdale
Windfield Close

70
61
69
82
Sefton
Netherton
Buckley Hill
Lunt
L30
Lunt Road
Longdale Lane
Wingfield Close
Sefton Mill Lane
Bridges Lane
Brickwall Lane
Glebe End
Old Rectory Green
Brickwall Green
BRIDGES LANE
BRICKWALL LANE
B5422
SEFTON LANE
Sefton Drive
Old Racecourse Road
Claremont Avenue
Rossiyn Avenue
Gainsborough
Lincoln Green
Meadway
Hathaway
Sefton Lane Industrial Estate
Sefton Lane Industrial Est
Garden Centre
Hinchley Green
South Meade
Fouracres
Trans Pennine Trail
Chapel Lane
Netherton Lane
A5207 NORTHERN PERIMETER ROAD
BUCKLEY HL LANE
EDGE LANE
Stanton Cl
Stonyfield
Grange Primary Sch
Waterside
Park Way
York Cl
St Benets RC Primary School
St Ambrose Barlow RC High School
Lunar Dr
Red Lomes
Granams Cft
St Raymonds RC Primary Sch
Harrops Croft
Fleetwood's Lane
Glover's La
Marian Way
Vale
Eden Vale
Westminster Av
Peterborough Drive
Canterbury Way
Apollo Way
Copy Lane
Witham Close
Fernbank Dr
Charlock Cl
Barberry Crs
Bootle High School
Albert Schweitzer Av
Council Building
Surgery
PO
Brown's Lane
Edward Jenner Av
Odeon Cinema
Megabowl
St Oswalds CE Primary School
St Oswald's Lane
Netherton Moss Primary School
Holy Spirit RC Primary School
Sefton Moss Lane
Swifts Lane
Bridge La
Elton Av
Regent Av
Travel Inn
DUNNINGS BR RD
Dooley Dr
Homestead Av
Orch Hey
Copy Lane
Manor Drive
Old Roan Station
Wakefield Industrial Estate
Wakefield Road
Grange Road
Leckwith Road
Bechers Business Centre
Heysham Road
Premier Lodge
Dunnings Br Rd
Our Lady of Walsingham RC Junior School
Our Lady of Walsingham RC Infant School
Golf Course
Good Shepherd School
Sterrix Green
Poulsom Drive
Broad Hey
Simon's Croft
Dartmouth Dr
Blyth Hey
St Christopher's Av
1 grid square represents 500 metres

MAGHULL
Melling
Waddicar
Aintree
62
72
83
F
G
H
J
K
I
2
3
4
5
6
37
38
39
02
01
400
399
Junction 7
M58
M57
A59
A5147
NORTHWAY
LIVERPOOL ROAD SOUTH
DAMFIELD LA
GREEN LANE
Deyes High School
St Andrews Maghull CE Prim Sch
Maricourt Catholic High School
Town Hall
Council Building
Maghull High School
St Georges RC Primary School
Glentworth Close
Summerhill Primary School
Maghull Station
Hudson Primary School
Surgery
Wood Hall Farm
Moorfield House
Superstore
Holy Rosary RC Junior School
Holy Rosary RC Primary School
Davenhill Primary School
Racecourse Retail Park
Works
Damfield Lane
Hall Lane
Station Road
Poverty Lane
Melling Lane
Leatherbarrows Lane
Weavers Lane
Rock Lane
Sandy Lane
Tithebarn Lane
School Lane
Brewery Lane
Spencer's Lane
Waddicar Lane
Chapel Lane
Woodland Road
Liddell Av
Station Rd
Moss Nook Lane
Foxhouse Lane
Bridge Road
Church Road
Old Hall Road
Sankey Road
Norfolk Road
York Road
Sussex Road
Grosvenor Road
Moorland Road
Dover Road
Cedar Grove
Moorhey Road
Eaton Rd
Derby Gv
Broadwood Av
Avondale Av
Brendale Av
Ormonde Drive
Buckingham Road
Deyes Lane
Eastway
Croft Field
Kebie Drive
Radley Drive
Oriel Drive
Altway
Sedbergh Avenue
Bradfield Avenue
Winchester Av
Lincoln Drive
Shrewsbury Av
Denstone Av
Harrow Drive
Wrekin Dr
Sandhurst Dr
Eton Drive
Dartmouth Dr
Aintree Lane
Bridge Lane
Summerhill Drive
Molyneux Road
Heathfield Road
Grange Park
Willow Hey
Bedford Av

72
Junction 1
Land End
Lyon's Farm
Maghull Lane
PRESCOT ROAD
63
Whitegates Farm
Spurrier's Lane
Outlet Lane
Lancashire
Moss Nook Lane
Moss Lane
Hall Lane
Moorfield House
Giddygate Lane
Melling Mount
Sefton
Knowlsey
Prescot Road
BANK LANE
A506
Lane
Angers Lane
71
Lane
Melling House
Waddicar Lane
Saxon Way
Tern Close
Deva Close
Swallow Close
Kingfisher Close
Turner Gv
Lowry Cl
Penda Dr
Elwood Cl
Hobart Dr
Weaver Avenue
Douglas
Severn Road
Dee Close
Whitebeam Close
Redwood Way
Shevington's Lane
Saxon Way
Yoxall Dr
Beattock Cl
Kelso Cl
Melrose Road
Moorfoot Way
Annandale Close
Washington Dr
Galston Cl
Lauder Cl
Jedburgh Drive
Bathgate Way
Perth Close
Salvia Way
Riesling Dr
Steeple View
Saints Peter & Paul Catholic Sch
Tower Hill Health Centre
Tower Hill
Ravenscroft Primary School
Eastcroft Park CP School
Riversdale Cl
Headbolt Lane
Knowsley Northern Prim Support Cen
Overdale Primary School
Windermere Drive
Rydal
Grasmere Close
Buttermere Close
Boyes Brow
Malvern Close
Pennine Way
Chiltern Drive
Cleveland Close
Mill Lane
Rainbow Drive
Surgery
Melling Primary School
Liddell Av
Station Rd
North Park Road
Sefton Drive
South Park Road
Kirkby Station
Elm Road
Willow Avenue
Poplar Drive
Millbrook Primary School
Church Way
Melling Drive
COUNTY ROAD
County Road
Kirkby CE Prim Sch
Hall Drive
Old Rough Lane
Roughwood Drive
Kennelwood Avenue
Wingate Road
Brook
Ruffwood Community School
Quarry Close
Quarry Green
Abbey Close
Scoter Road
Westhead
Kirkby Row
Delaware Crescent
Sidney Powell Avenue
William Roberts Avenue
84
Old Hall Lane
A506 HALL LANE
Westvale
Council Building
North Parade
Police Station
A5208
Westvale Primary
Health Cen
Satinwood Crs
Hickory Gv
Pickworth Way
1 grid square represents 500 metres

F
G
H
64
J
K
42
43
44
02
01
400
399
1
2
3
74
4
5
6
Hall Lane
Grayson's Farm
Stopgate Lane
Stopgate Lane
Simonswood Industrial Park
Pingwood Lane
Carl's Way
Freckleton Dr
Dorchester
Headbolt Lane
Dale Lane
Spencer's House
Urban Farm
North Perimeter Road
Works
Depot Road
North Mersey Business Centre
Woodward Road
Moss End Way
L33
Knowsley Industrial Park
Hammond Road
Bradman Road
Marl Road
Ashcroft Road
Woodlands Works
Courtyard Works
Perimeter Road
Boundary Lane
Lancashire County
Knowsley
Northwood
Lapford Crescent
Pentland Road
Shacklady Road
Trecastle Road
Roughwood Drive
Warrenhouse Road
Kenbury Road
Glisecroft Avenue
Jarrett Road
Watts Close
Changford Road
Wingate Medical Centre
Quernmore Road
St Marie RC Prim Sch
Bigdale Medical Cen
Birbeck Road
Simonswood Lane
Sanderling Road
Darmond Road
Moss Lane
Quarryside Drive
Colwall Road
Lees Road
Birchill Road
Stockpit Road
Draw Well Road
Knowsley Industrial Park
Kirkby Bank
Wyllin Road
Ormonde Crescent
Mintor Road
85

74
65
73
86
A
B
C
D
E
1
2
3
4
5
6
345
346
399
400
401
402
Coach Road
Walkden House Farm
Moss Farm
Lancashire County
St. Helens
Works
Siding Lane
Red Delph
A570
Dairy Farm Road
Simonswood Moss
Moor Game Farm
Brown Birch Farm
Mossborough Hall Lane
Boundary Lane
1 grid square represents 500 metres

RAINFORD
66
76
87
F
G
H
J
K
1
2
3
4
5
6
47
48
49
02
01
400
399
WA11
ORMSKIRK ROAD
B5203
CHURCH ROAD
MOSSBOROUGH ROAD
RAINFORD BY-PASS
A570
HIGHER LANE
B5205
CROSS PIT LANE
ROAD
News Lane
Nook
Langwood Lane
Henderson Drive
Brow
Reeds
Hyde's Brow
Brook Lodge Primary School
Rainford High School
Holiday Moss
Knowsley View
Junction Road
Tudor Close
Randle Brook Court
Randle Avenue
Graysons Road
Helen Bank Dr
Harrison Drive
Eden Avenue
Stanley Avenue
Old Lane
Works
Rufford Road
Witton Way
Scarisbrick
Lathom Drive
Duxbury Close
Standish Drive
Garswood Av
Higher Lane
Parklands
Corpus Christi Catholic Prim Sch
Beech Gardens
Pine Dale
Fern Bank
Ms Bw
Central Drive
Victoria St
Arnian Road
Arnian Wy
Brookside Avenue
Beech Gardens
Croxteth Drive
The Spinney
Muncaster Drive
Old Hall Gdns
Heyes Avenue
Heyes Grove
Sandon Grove
Rainford Health Centre
Rainford CE Prim Sch
Knwy
Ash Grove
Lime Gv
The Avenue
Whi Av
Leyland Road
Pilkington Street
Lakeside Gdns
Lakeside Court
Massam Cl
Parson's Brow
Moss Nook Lane
Inglenook Farm
Council Building
Medical Centre
PO
Southern's Lane
Eagle Crescent
Rookery Drive
Finch Av
Heron Gv
Derby Drive
Holly Crs
Festival Road
Walmesley Drive
Carter Avenue
Green Lane
Church Road
Thickwood Moss Lane
Rookery Lane
Rose Place
Rose Drive
Hopwood Crescent
Wellfield
Church Rd
Fire Clay Farm
Diamond Business Park
Hazel Business Park
Sandwash Close
Mill Lane
Pasture Lane
Rainford Industrial Estate
Millbrook Business Centre
Reed's Farm
Reed's Lane
Reed's Moss
Hill Top House
St Helens
Berrington's

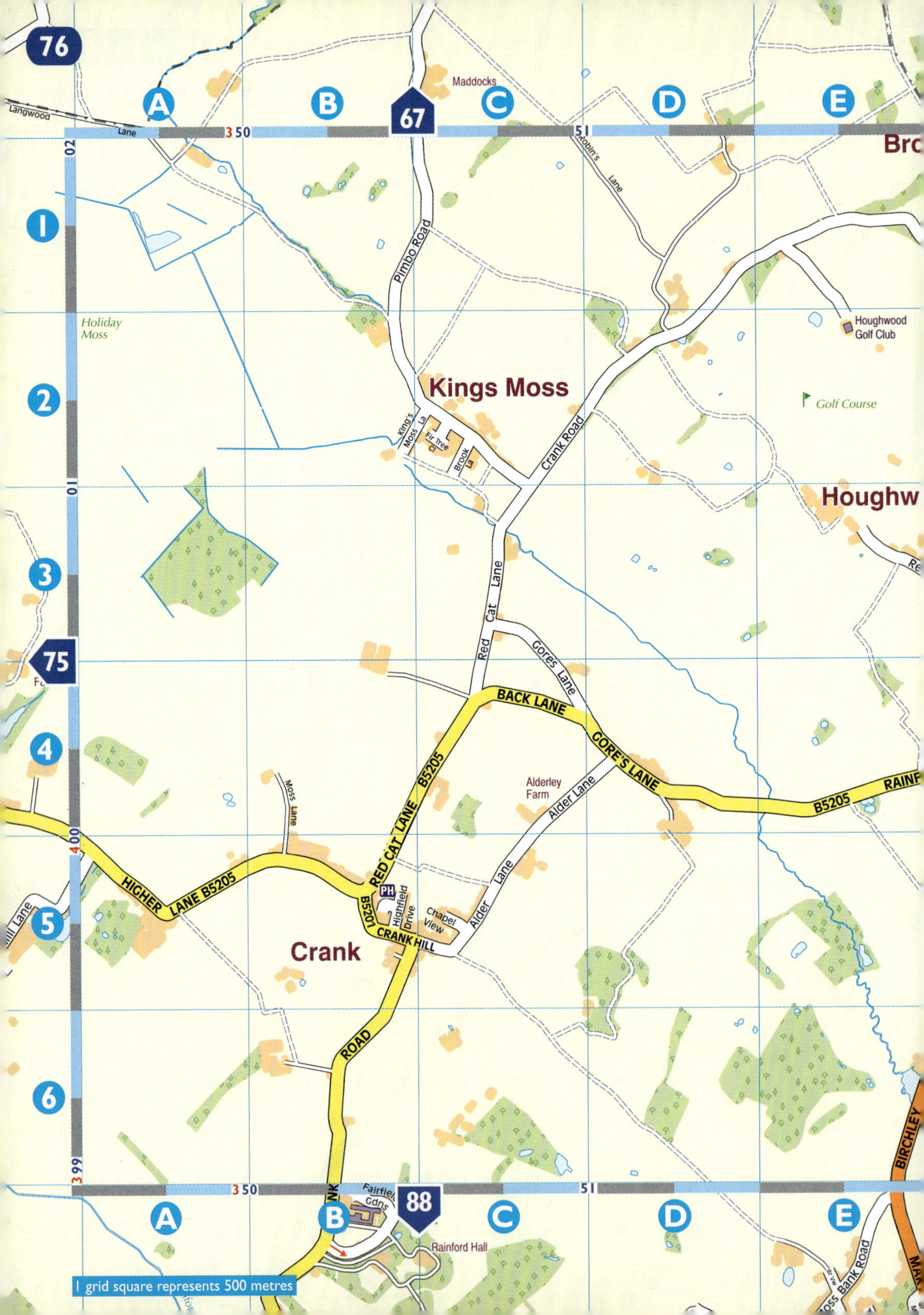

76
67
75
88
A
B
C
D
E
1
2
3
4
5
6
350
51
02
01
400
399
Langwood Lane
Maddocks
Robin's Lane
Pimbo Road
Holiday Moss
Kings Moss
King's Moss La
Fir Tree Cl
Brook La
Crank Road
Houghwood Golf Club
Golf Course
Houghw
Red Cat Lane
Gores Lane
BACK LANE
GORE'S LANE
B5205
RAINF
Alderley Farm
Alder Lane
Moss Lane
RED CAT LANE B5205
HIGHER LANE B5205
PH
B5201
Highfield Drive
Chapel View
CRANK HILL
Crank
ROAD
BIRCHLEY
Fairfield Gdns
Rainford Hall
Bank Road
1 grid square represents 500 metres

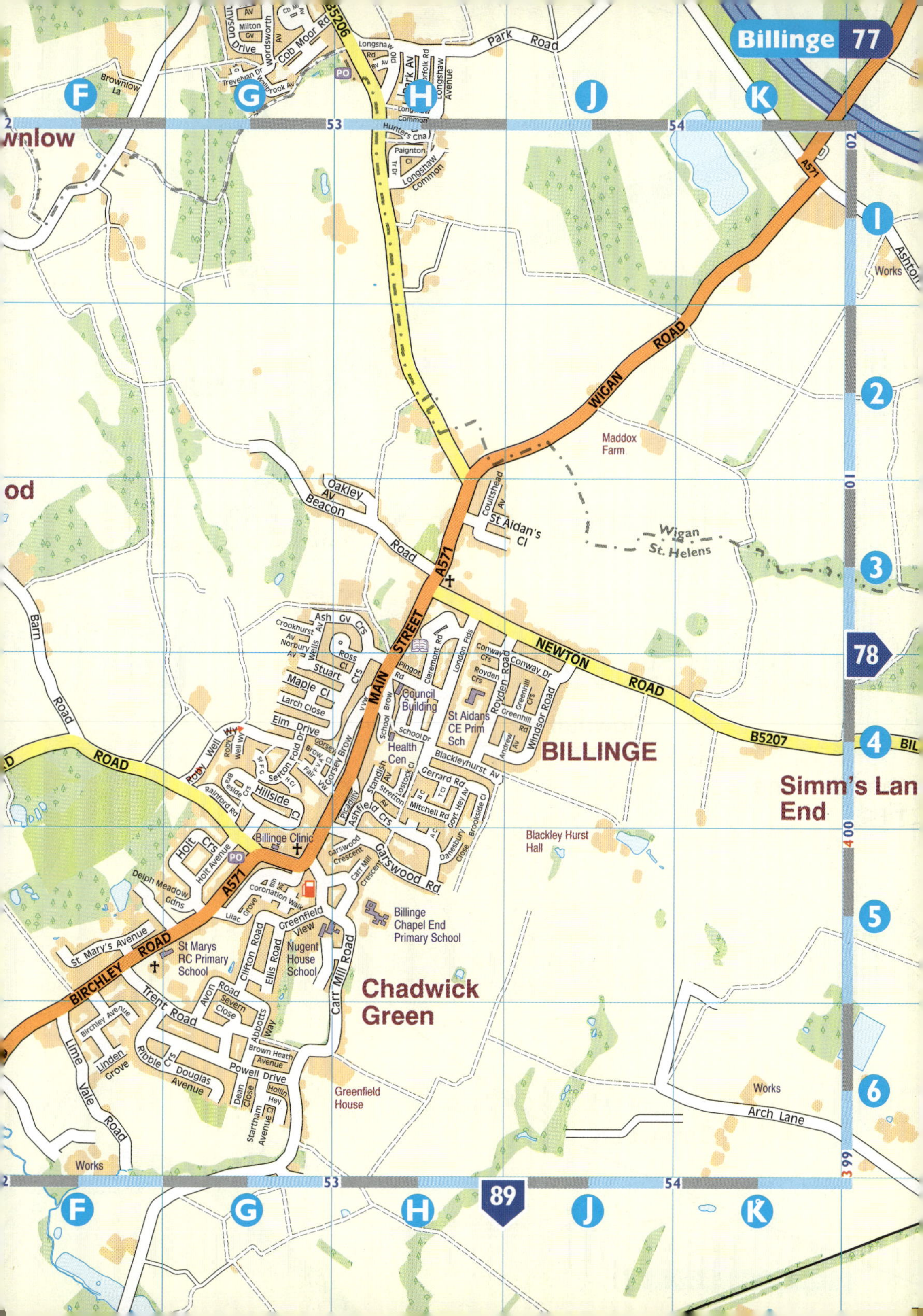

BILLINGE
Chadwick Green
Simm's Lan End
Maddox Farm
Blackley Hurst Hall
Greenfield House
Works
Wigan
St. Helens
WIGAN ROAD
NEWTON ROAD
MAIN STREET
BIRCHLEY ROAD
A571
B5207
B5206
Park Road
Arch Lane
Barn Road
Lime Vale Road
Beacon Road
Oakley Av
Coultshead Av
St Aidan's Cl
Council Building
Health Cen
Billinge Clinic
St Aidans CE Prim Sch
Billinge Chapel End Primary School
St Marys RC Primary School
Nugent House School
Carr Mill Road
Garswood Rd
Garswood Crescent
Ashfield Crs
Blackleyhurst Av
Windsor Road
Royden Road
Conway Dr
Elm Drive
Hillside Cl
Holt Crs
Holt Avenue
Delph Meadow Gdns
St Mary's Avenue
Trent Road
Clifton Road
Ellis Road
Powell Drive
Douglas Avenue
Ribble Crs
Linden Grove
Birchley Avenue
Brownlow La
Longshaw Common
Paignton Cl
Cob Moor Rd
Wordsworth Av
Milton Gv
F
G
H
J
K
53
54
78
89

78
77
90
A
B
C
D
E
1
2
3
4
5
6
355
56
02
01
400
399
M6
A571
A49
A58
B5207
Junction 25
Junction 24
WN4
Cranberry Ley Farm
Brocstedes Road
Brocstedes Farm
Ashton Road
Works
Winstanley Road
Drummer's Lane
Sougher's Lane
Dryden Avenue
Sunnyside Rd
Burns Cl
Chimes Rd
Eddleston St
Rosina Cl
Coralline Wy
Skelton St
Kielder Cl
Lyon St
Downall Green RC Primary School
DOWNALL GREEN ROAD
Brockstedes Av
Coronation St
Booth's Brow Rd
Pasture Cl
Meadowcroft
Leacroft
The Paddock
Sefton Road
Bryn
Clifton Rd
Chantry Wk
Clough Grove
Wootton Cl
Alder Av
Grange Road
Regent Av
Linden Av
Richmond
Hale Gv
Priory
Bevington St
Medway Wy
Harlech St
Bispham Dr
Lytham Rd
Ellesmere Rd
Clarence St
Tatton
Drive
Thornton Close
Road
Bank
Low
Wolfson Sq
Tenbury
Oriel Road
Balliol Way
Magdalen Drive
Greyfriars
Lazenby
Salkeld Av
Orton Way
Crs
Houghwood Gra
Rectory CE Primary School
Rectory Road
Delisle Cl
Leyland Green Road
Lilac Av
Hawthorn Av
Poplar Av
Palm Av
Elm Av
Birch Grove
Cedar Gv
Everton St
Bolton St
Fernlea Gv
The Brambles
Garswood United FC
Downall Green
BILLINGE ROAD
Simm's Lane End
Stirling Drive
Selkirk Avenue
Peebles Close
Thornhill Road
Smock Lane
Falkland Dr
Oban Drive
Argyll Close
Dunblane Close
Girvan Crs
Victoria Road
Elgin Avenue
Spindle Hillock
Gordon Avenue
Austin Avenue
The Clough
Elstead Grove
Abinger Road
Hillbeck Crescent
Camp Road
Langholm Road
Darvel Av
Kinross Avenue
Hamilton
Forres Gv
Garswood Prim Sch
Coldstone Drive
Hollins Close
Strange Road
Station Road
Manor Close
Old Colliery Yard
Surgery
PO
Garswood Road
School Lane
Garswood Station
Garswood
Gibbon's Road
Park Industrial Estate
Tithebarn Road
1 grid square represents 500 metres
Garswood Park

F
G
H
J
K
57
58
59
Park House Farm
Haslemere Industrial Estate
Landgate Industrial Estate
Bankside Av
Patterdale Road
Yewdale Road
Land Gate Lane
Bryn Gates Lane
Bamfurlong
Three Sisters Racing Circuit
Land Gate
Three Sisters Rd
South Lancashire Industrial Estate
Kingfisher Ct
Lockett Rd
Antler Ct
Redgate Rd
Lockett Road
Kestrel Dr
Beaver Ct
Ashton Grange Industrial Estate
Hall St
James St
Redland Ct
Beech Tree
A58
BRYN RD
ROAD
BRYN ROAD
Surg
Bryn Stn
Whitledge Rd
Highwoods Cl
Roman Rd
Drive
Benjamin Rd
Nicol Mere School
Lockett Road
South Lancashire Industrial Estate
Stubshaw Cross
BOLTON ROAD
Riding Lane
Bolton Rd
Severn Road
Avon Rd
Welland Road
Conway Rd
Willow Grove School
Luke St
Hope St
John St
School St
North St
Diane Road
Crossway
Linkway Av
Moorland Rd
Nicol Road
Ashton Medical Cen
Toothill Cl
Grasmere Dr
Hawes Crs
Ennerdale Av
Buttermere Av
Eskdale Rd
Welbeck Rd
Coniston Av
Rydal Close
Harold Av
Hardwick Rd
Surgery
Leisure Centre
Cansfield High Sch
Wolmer St
Alton Close
Fairholme Avenue
Laurel Grove
Bowland Avenue
Penrith Crs
Kendal Gv
Wood's La
East St
Recreation Avenue
Barrow St
Upland Drive
Heather Grove
Rushmoor Av
White Lodge Drive
Chestnut Grove
Cansfield Grove
Grove Street
Crescent Avenue
Alexandra Road
The Strand
Strand Avenue
Malvern Close
WIGAN ROAD
Sibley Av
Thompson St
Kilburn Avenue
Edge Gn St
Ashton Town AFC
Town Green
GOLBORNE ROAD
B5207
Jameson's Farm
Westfield Av
Osborne Rd
Grey Road
Briar Close
Pretoria Rd
Fairview Cl
Edward Dr
Bryn Road South
Cleveland Dr
Glendale Av
Belvedere Rd
Fleming Dr
Moxon Wy
Wotton Drive
Soane Cl
Wyatt Grove
Salvin Close
R L Hughes Primary School
Woodedge
Rigby Street
Morden Av
Adamson Street
Police Station
Queen's Avenue
A49
Hornbeam Crescent
BOLTON ROAD A58
Orchard St
Dunsdale Drive
St Thomas CE Prim Sch
Hilton Street
Walford Rd
Allscott Way
Bravsdale Dr
Mansart Cl
ASHTON-IN-MAKERFIELD
Berrington Grove
Alderton Drive
Liverpool Road
A58
Winchester Avenue
Townfields
St Oswalds RC J&I Sch
BRYN STREET
GERARD STREET
Princess Road
Duke St
Peter St
Tintern Avenue
Norwich Avenue
LIVERPOOL ROAD
York Road
Heath Road
Mill St
91
Lincoln Drive
Chester Drive
Blenheim Road
Ashton
Oakwood Av
Butcher Street
WARRINGTON ROAD
Vicarage Road
Violet Street
Flora Street
Glebe Av
Bransford Close
Premier Lodge
Townfield Avenue
Rookery Avenue
Old Hall Dr
Farefield Avenue
Edge
02
400
399
I
2
3
4
5
6
Bry

68
95
A
B
C
D
E
1
2
3
4
5
6
330
31
99
98
97
396
Blundellsands
St Nicholas CE Primary School
Surgery
Mersey Road
Abbotsford Gardens
Rossett Road
Marine FC
Woodville Av
Brookfield Av
Kingswood
Tudor Road
Myers Road
College Road
Harlech Rd
Crosender Rd
Jubilee Road
Sunnyside Road
Mariners Rd
Riverslea Rd
Crosby Baths
Warren House
Endsleigh Road
Holden Road
Bridge Rd
Devonshire Rd
Somerset Rd
Pinehurst Avenue
Rosebery Av
Mersey View
Leopold Road
Heathfield Rd
Brooke Road
Brooke Road West
Brooke Road East
Winchester Av
Park View
Waterloo
Sefton Coastal Footpath
River Beach
View Bank
Courtenay Av
Courtenay Road
Oxford Drive
Oxford Road
Sandheys Av
Manley Rd
Burdett Rd
Somerville Road
Lawton Road
St Johns CE Primary School
Works
St Edmunds & St Thomas CP Sch
St John's Rd
CROSBY
Harbord Rd
Beach Lawn
Blucher St
Picton Rd
Adelaide Terrace
Wellington St
Brighton Road
Mount St
King St
Marine Crs
East St
Mason St
Mt Pleasant
Albert Rd
Hyde Rd
Cross St
L22
Marine Terrace
Bath St
Dean St
Queen St
The Royal Hotel
Marine Lake
Works
DOUGLAS
DUBLIN
1 grid square represents 500 metres

Crosby 81
69
82
96
F
G
H
J
K
1
2
3
4
5
6
Ford
Litherland
Waterloo Park
Seaforth
L21
Rimrose Valley Country Park
Our Lady Queen of Peace RC Prim Sch
Hatton Hill Primary School
Good Shepherd School
Litherland High School
Cemetery
Moss Lane Sports Centre
Sefton Road Hlth Clinic
Industrial Estate
Town Hall
St Philips CE Primary School
St Robert Bellarmine RC Prim Sch
St Wilfrids RC High School
Kingfisher Business Park
Penpol Trading Estate
Penpol Industrial Estate
St Elizabeths Catholic Prim School
Orrell Primary School
Linacre Primary School
North Park Health Cen
Parrs Corner Trading Est
Bootle Leisure Centre
The Strand Medical Cen
Thomas Gray Infant School
St James RC Primary School
St Joan of Arc RC Prim School
Rimrose Business Park
Junior School
Our Lady Star of the Sea RC Prim Sch
Seaforth & Litherland Station
Hlth Clinic
Med Cen
Beach Road Primary School
William Gladstone CE Primary School
Rawson Road Primary School
Freight Terminal Buildings (Euro-Rail)
Port of Liverpool
Royal Seaforth Dock
Gladstone Dock
Waterloo Station
Waterloo Prim Sch
Plaza Cinema
Council Building
Abbey Sefton Hospitals
Merchant Taylors School for Boys
Buttermere Gardens
Leeds & Liverpool Canal
CROSBY ROAD NORTH
CROSBY ROAD SOUTH
A565
SANDY ROAD B5421 EWART ROAD
PRINCESS WAY
CHURCH ROAD
A5036
SEFTON ROAD
B5422
GORSEY LANE
A5090
HAWTHORNE ROAD
LINACRE ROAD
A567
STANLEY ROAD
KNOWSLEY ROAD
A566
LINACRE LANE
MARSH LANE
RIMROSE ROAD
A5098
Kirk Stone Road West
Sonning Avenue
Molyneux Rd
Milton Rd
Galloway Rd
Kingsway
Glenwyllin Rd
Cambridge Rd
Claremont Road
Church Road
Peel Road
Sea View Road

82
70
81
97
L30
A
B
C
D
E
1
2
3
4
5
6
335
36
396
98
97
Litherland
Orrell
Netherton Moss Primary School
St Oswalds CE Primary School
Odeon Cinema
Megabowl
Wakefield Industrial Estate
Old Roan Station
Trans Pennine Trail
Holy Spirit RC Primary School
Premier Lodge
Becher's Business Centre
Our Lady of Walsingham RC Junior School
Our Lady of Walsingham RC Infant School
Golf Course
Rowan Park Special Sch
Litherland High School
Litherland Moss Primary School
Moss Lane Sports Centre
Bootle Golf Club
Netherton Park Primary School
DUNNINGS BRIDGE ROAD
A5036
Savio Catholic High School
Netherton Industrial Estate
NETHERTON WAY
A5038
Senate Business Park
Sefton Business Park
Aintree Station
Sefton
Liverpool
ORMSKIRK ROAD
A59
WARBRECK MOOR
Melling
Captain's Lane
Galsworthy Avenue
St Robert Bellarmine RC Prim Sch
Roberts Primary School
BAILEY DRIVE
St George of England High School
Cemetery
Fernhill Sports Centre
Penpoll Trading Estate
Penpoll Industrial Estate
Orrell Primary School
LINACRE LA
A566
NORTHFIELD ROAD
MOSS LA
Orrell Park Stn
WALTON VALE
LONGMOOR LANE
B5187
Longmoor Community Prim Sch
Blessed Sacrament RC Infant School
Blessed Sacrament RC Junior School
Archbishop Beck Catholic Secondary School
Hartley Trading Estate
HM Prison Liverpool
St Monicas RC Primary School
SOUTHPORT ROAD
A5090
Rice Lane J&I Schools
Rice La Stn
RICE LANE
HORNBY ROAD
AINTREE ROAD
A5098
MARSH LANE
Walton Station
Sefton Avenue
Yew Tree Road
Rawcliffe Road
Aintree Estate
Bootle Stadium
Cemetery
Leeds & Liverpool Canal
1 grid square represents 500 metres

Orrell 83
71
84
98
M57
Aintree
Fazakerley
L10
L9
Holy Rosary RC Junior School
Holy Rosary RC Primary School
Davenhill Primary School
Aintree Racecourse Retail & Business Park
Aintree Racecourse
Racecourse Retail Park
Service Centre
Melling Road
Grand National
Leeds & Liverpool Canal
River Alt
Sefton
Knowsley
Redbridge High School
Watergate North Primary School
Meadow Bank Special School
Fazakerley Sports Centre
Fazakerley High School
Churchill Industrial Est
White Thorn Special School
Barlows Primary Sch
Cemetery
Aintree Osteopathic Clinic
Fazakerley Sth
Holy Name RC Primary School
Fazakerley Primary Sch
University Hospital Aintree
North Mersey Community Hospital
Edge Hill Enterprise Training Centre
A&E
HM Prison Altcourse
Council Building
Aintree Industrial Estate
Hanson Road Business Park
Liver Industrial Estate
Stonebridge Business Park (under development)
Police Station
Showcase Cinemas
Retail Park
Our Lady & St Philomenas Prim Sch
Copplehouse Medical Centre
Longmoor Lane
A506
B5187
Higher Lane
Lower Lane
Brookfield Drive
Seeds Lane
Signal Works Road
Sherwood's Lane
Aintree Lane
Wango Lane
School Lane
Spencer's Lane
Stonebridge Lane
Works

84
72
83
99
A
B
C
D
E
1
2
3
4
5
6
Westvale
KIRKBY
Southdene
Gillmoss
Croxteth
L32
L10
Kirkby Station
Holy Angels RC Prim Sch
Westvale Primary School
Family Health Cen
Westvale Health Cen
Trentham Road Medical Cen
Council Building
Knowsley Community College
Police Station
Ruffwood Community School
Kirkby CE Sch
All Saints Catholic School
St Laurence RC Prim School
St Josephs RC Inf Sch
Kirkby Sports Centre
Junction 6
Junction 5
Junction 4
Brookfield Comprehensive School
Parkfield Special School
Springfield Special School
Cherryfield Primary School
Peatwood Medical Cen
Surgery
Golf Course
Kirby-Liverpool Municipal Golf Club
Applehouse Medical Centre
Gillmoss Industrial Estate
Stonebridge Business Park (under development)
Centec Business Centre
Our Lady & St Swithins Catholic Prim Sch
Gillmoss Medical Cen
Croxteth Comprehensive School
Croxteth Family Health Centre
Croxteth Primary School
Showcase Cinemas
Howard Johnson Hotel
Knowsley
Liverpool
M57
A506
A580
A5208
HALL LANE
VALLEY ROAD
COUNTY ROAD
EAST LANCASHIRE ROAD
Ribbler's Lane
Bewley Drive
Stonebridge Lane
Moor Lane
Ingoe Lane
1 grid square represents 500 metres

Northwood
Quernmore Road
St Marie RC Prim Sch
Bigdale Medical Cen
Birbeck Road
Simonswood
Darmond Road
Moss
Quarryside Drive
Colwall Road
Wyllin Road
Minstead Avenue
Ormonde Crescent
Mintor Road
Madryn Avenue
Glegside Road
Simonswood Lane
Farrier Road
Arbour Lane
Marl Road
Hammond Road
Knowsley Industrial Park
Bradman Road
Woodlands Works
Courtyard Works
Newstet Road
Lodge Works
Lees Road
Birchill Road
Stockpit Road
Draw Well Road
Acornfield Road
Perimeter Road
Boundary Lane
Lancashire County
Knowsley
Kirkby Bank Road
Orchard Works
Cranston Road
Capitol Trading Estate
Acorn Business Centre
Gladeswood Road
Webber Road
Yardley Road
Venture Works
Arbour Works
Charley Wood Road
Kirkby Moss
Mosslawn Road
Surg
Crosland Road
Dulas Rd
Lees Rd
Cusson Road
Gores Road
Deltic Way
Dixon Road
Park Brow Primary School
New Lodge Industrial Estate
Beckett Cl
Gale Road
Admin Road
Business Resource Centre
Sandy Brow
A5208
SOUTH BOUNDARY ROAD
Lindby Road
Buxted Road
Lindby Cl
Southdene Medical Cen
Garth Road
Acornfield Close
Spinney Close
Spinney Road
Spinney Vw
Hornhouse Lane
Britonwood Trading Estate
Abercrombie Road
Owen Road
Faraday Road
Molly's Lane
Cut Lane
Sandy Brow Lane
Hewitt's Lane
Bainton Close
Sedburn Rd
COOPER'S LANE A5208
Moss Side
Knowsley Industrial Park
EAST LANCASHIRE ROAD A580
EAST LANC
Knowsley Business Park
Penrhyn Rd
Penrhyn Road
Villiers Road
Ormskirk Road
B5202
Ainsworth Lane
Unity Grove
Kitling Road
Canrow Lane
Lockton Road
SCHOOL LANE
B5194
Gellings Rd
Randles Road
Kitling Lane
Overbrook Lane
KNOWSLEY LANE
Gellings Lane
Caddick Road
Knowsley Business Park
Patten's Walk
Mill Lane
Dumbreeze
Old Mill Lane
Council Building
Whitegate Close
Longmeadow Road
Church
M57
KNOWSLEY
73
86
100
42
43
44
96
97
98
99
F
G
H
J
K
1
2
3
4
5
6

Brown Birch Farm
Coach Road
Mossborough Hall Lane
MOSSBOROUGH
Boundary Lane
New Cut Lane
Kirkby Moss
B5203
Blind Foot Farm
Sandy Brow
Red Cut Lane
Woodside Farm
BLIND FOOT ROAD
Cut Lane
EAST LANCASHIRE ROAD A580
Patten's Walk
A
B
C
D
E
1
2
3
4
5
6
74
85
101
345
46
399
398
397
396
1 grid square represents 500 metres

Reed's Farm
Reed's Lane
Millbrook
WA11
RAINFORD BY-PASS
75
Reed's Moss
Hill Top House
St Helens Road
Hilltop Road
Berrington's Lane
Inglemoss Drive
Longwood Close
Inglewood Road
RAINFORD BY-PASS
St Helens Road
RAINFORD ROAD A570
88
CRANK ROAD
Moss Lane
Liverpool St.Helens RUFC
Sadler's Lane
EAST LANCASHIRE ROAD
A580
St Helens Crematorium
Houghton's Lane
Windle Farm
Crantock Grove
The Nook
Portreath Way
Padstow Drive
BLEAK HILL ROAD
Windle Grove
Stuart Road
RAINFORD ROAD
Malt House Court
St Thomas of Canterbury Primary School
Lynton Way
Fistral Drive
Pentire Av
Calderhurst Drive
St. Mawes Way
Windlebrook Crescent
B5201
Rutherford Road
Lawrence Road
Sackville Road
Hamilton Road
Sidmouth Cl
Dartmouth Dr
B5203
Catchdale Moss
Green Lane
CATCHDALE MOSS LANE
Ecclesfield Road
Carmelite Crescent
Nicholl Road
Sandfield Road
Oaktree Road
Bleak Hill Primary School
Eccleston Medical Centre
Selkirk Drive
Melrose Av
Gunning Close
Queens Drive
Fair Way
The Grove
Coronation Road
St George's Avenue
A570
Hartington Road
Rosebery Road
Regal Drive
Kiln Lane
Sidmouth Close
Brookside Avenue
Beaconsfield Rd
Fairfield Rd
Moorfield
Walmesley Road
Osborne Road
Barrowfield Road
Pike House Road
Gunning Avenue
Ansdell Drive
Davy Close
Broadway
Green Lane
Villiers Crs
Springfield Lane
Lester Drive
The Close
Laresbury Road
Crockett's Wk
MILLBROOK LANE
Kiln Lane
Cranston Cl
Eccleston
Lynn Cl
Percival Way
102
Brookland Road
Pike Pl
Washbrook Cl
Clarke's Cl
WA10
Villiers Crs
Richmond Close
St Julie RC Primary School
Laurel Drive
Lane
Sp Cl
Fiveways
CHAPEL LANE
De La Salle School
Oleander Dr
Alpine Cl
Ellison
Fairclough Rd
Marsden
Kelsey
Morrissey
F
G
H
J
K
I
2
3
4
5
6
47
48
49
96
97
98
99

76
87
103
A
B
C
D
E
1
2
3
4
5
6
3 50
51
99
98
97
96
Fairfield Gdns
Fairfield Hospital
Rainford Hall
Rainford Brook
CRANK
ROAD
B5201
Berrington's Lane
Sandy La
Sandy Lane
Windle Hall
NFORD PASS
Cherry Tree Lane
Manor House Close
Moss Bank Road
Broad
Troutbeck Grove
Lane
Lingmell
Crossdale Way
Mosedale Av
Dalston Drive
Ingleton Drive
Crag Grove
Bampton Av
Ghyll Grove
Club Street
Moss Bank Road
Clinkham Wood
Moss Bank
Hillbrae Avenue
Devoke Av
Fell Grove
Lorton Avenue
Kingsway
Victoria Avenue
Bassenthwaite Av
Queensway
Africander Road
Woodside Avenue
Birch Tree Avenue
Ennerdale Avenue
Mardale Av
Avenue
Bowness Avenue
Grizedale Av
Windermere
Eskdale Av
Thirlmere Avenue
Tarn Grove
Ullswater Av
Carr Mill Infant Sch
Loughrigg Avenue
Yewdale Av
Wasdale
A580
EAST LANCASHIRE ROAD
LANCASHIRE ROAD
Scafell Road
Rydal Grove
Coniston Grove
Folds Lane
Grasmere Avenue
Clover Hey
Derwent Rd
Shirebourne Av
Dearham Avenue
Green Leach Avenue
The Brooks
A571 GREEN LEACH LANE
HARESFINCH VIEW
Washway Lane
Haresfinch
Buckingham Drive
Kingfisher Drive
Teal Close
Mallard Way
Fulmar Close
Lincoln Crs
Ewart Road
Furness Av
Windle Hall
Wyresdale Av
Cartmel Av
Drive
Whalley Av
Priory Gardens
City Road
Lane
Hard Lane
Birch Av
Birch Gdns
City Gardens
Seddon St
Friar St
PO
St Helens Crematorium
Borough Cemetery
St Thomas of Canterbury Catholic Primary School
Cowley Language College
Abbey Road
Gamble
Hurst School
Princess Avenue
Martin Av
Windlehurst Av
Rivington Av
Pine Av
City Road
Windle City
Works
Hamblett School
Eaton Road
Kingsley Road
Walton Road
Chaucer Road
Hard Lane
King Edward Rd
Speakman Road
Hammill Avenue
Huyton Av
Hillside Avenue
Windlehurst Primary School
Bishop Road
Rivington Prim Sch
RAINFORD ROAD
A570
Malt House Court
St George's Avenue
The Grove
Rosebery Road
Harrington Road
Kiln Lane
Moorfield Road
Swinburne Road
Fairfield Rd
DENTONS GREEN LANE
GREENFIELD ROAD
Windleshaw Road
Tennis St N
Carr St
Denton's Green
Moray Cl
St Helens Cricket Club
Balker Dr
Rutland St
Oldfield St
North Road
Queen St
Albert Street
Cowley St
Lord St
Hill Street
COLLEGE STREET
A571
13
12
Works
ST HELENS
Eccleston
Wynne Road
Briars Gn
Cowley Hill Lane
Windle Street
Morello Close
Peel Place
Fox Place
Swift St
Ruskin Drive
Queens Park CE/URC Prim Sch
Marsden Av
Rivington Rd
Horace St
DENTONS GREEN
Harris Street
ROAD
Cooper St
Surgery
Crab St
Central Clinic
Police Stn
Cncl
YMCA
DUKE STREET
Standish St
Birchley St
Hardshaw St
Hospital St
Woodville St
Parish CE Prim Sch
Waterside
Leisure Centre
Ellison
Fairclough Rd
Kelsey
BIRCHLEY
MARTIN
1 grid square represents 500 metres

Greenfield House
Arch Lane
Works
Carr Mill Dam
Carr Mill Junior Sch
Kentmere Avenue
Dunnail Avenue
CARR MILL ROAD
A571
Council Building
Honister Av
Kirkstone Av
Esthwaite Avenue
Hawes Avenue
Garswood Old Road
Old Garswood Hall Farm
Calday Grove
LIVERPOOL RD
A580
EAST LANCASHIRE ROAD
Premier Lodge
Newlands Rd
Carr Mill Road
Woodlands Rd
Laburnum Av
Laffak
Orchard Close
Chestnut Gv
Truro Close
Bodmin Gv
Newlyn Gv
Camborne Av
Helston Av
Penryn Av
Redruth Avenue
Litherland Crs
Roland Av
Chadwick Road
Finchley Dr
Irene Av
Allan Road
Paisley Avenue
Renfrew Avenue
Orkney Cl
Rothsay Cl
Peebles Av
Chain Lane
Desford Av
Old Nook Lane
Erskine Cl
Mallory Gv
Coalville Road
Shenton Av
Meriden Close
Enderby Av
Huncote Av
Ashurst Prim Sch
Hinckley Road
Syston Av
Bramcote Av
Arbury Av
Drayton Crs
Bosworth Road
Barwell Av
Mowbray Av
Wyken Gv
Ansty Cl
New Glade Hill
Ashurst Drive
Billinge Crs
Pendle Av
Parbold Av
Blackstone Av
Longridge Av
Caldy Grove
Bidston Way
Bidston Av
Frodsham Dr
Singleton Avenue
Markfield Crescent
Linford Gv
Birstall Av
Dalby Cl
Grantham Crs
St Helens Canal
Lock St
Collins Industrial Estate
Merton Street
Brow
Blackbrook St Marys Catholic Primary School
St Catherines Centre for Girls
Link Av
Council Building
BLACKBROOK ROAD
A58
Whiteside Av
Dearnley Av
O'Sullivan Crs
Callon Av
St Augustine of Canterbury RC High School
Richard Evans Community Primary School
Clipsley Brook View
Ebenezer St
WEST END ROAD
Lenfield Drive
W End Gv
W Side Av
Summer Street
Judd St
Tenfield St
Stanley Bank Road
VICARAGE RD
Vicarage Dr
Clipsley Crs
A599
CLIPSLEY
Cumberland Crs
Loweswater Road
Crescent
Winder Road
White Ho
Richard Evans Infant School
Cemetery
Park Av
Harrison Drive
Old Whint Road
Street
Hawkeswater Avenue
Arnside
Legh Vale Primary School
Edward St
Fairclough Crescent
Legh
Park Road
Fosters Road
Lloyd St
William Road
Holly Rd
Ledger Rd
Canniswood Rd
Caunce Av
Wagon
Sankey Road
Burrows Avenue
The Close
Redwood
Folds Road
Rowan Close
Laurel Road
Chestnut Avenue
Sycmr Av
Morris Close
Roberts Av
Whittle Avenue
Littler Road
Silver Av
Harty Road
Wedge Av
Troon Close
Gleneagles Dr
Carnoustie Grove
Tobermory Close
Blackbrook
Business Development Centre
Merton Bank Primary School
Bank Rd
Roper Street
Wood St
Varley Rd
O'Keeffe Rd
Cncl Bldg
PARK ROAD
A58
Cncl Bldg
Boardman
Lane
Murphy Grove
O'Brien Grove
Archer
Works
Broad Oak
Moorfoot Road
Delft
F
G
H
J
K
I
2
3
4
5
6
52
53
54
99
98
97
96
77
90
104

90
78
89
105
A
B
C
D
E
1
2
3
4
5
6
Garswood
Garswood Station
Garswood Road
School Lane
Surgery
PO
Gibbon's Road
Park Industrial Estate
Junction 24
M6
Lane
Tithebarn Road
A58
LIVERPOOL ROAD
Liverpool Road
Ashton-In-Makerfield Golf Club
Garswood Park
Golf Course
Millfield Lane
Hall Wood Avenue
Winchester Road
Andover Road
Salisbury Road
Haydock Lane
Haydock Lane Industrial Estate
Yew Tree Trading Estate
Bahama Close
Bahama Rd
North Florida Road
Florida Rd
Kilbuck
Fishwicks Industrial Estate
Withins Road
Millfield Lane
Kenyons Lane North
Calday Grove
A580
EAST
Travelodge
Primrose Grove
Bluebell Av
Piele Road
Wycliffe Road
Elizabeth Road
Manor Road
Beech Av
Jubilee Crs
Slag Lane
Avery Road
Avery Sq
Gt Delph
Chisledon Cl
Haydock Cricket Club
Willow Road
Birch Rd
Hall Rd
Pimblett Rd
Marian Rd
Alfred Road
James Road
Cook Avenue
Arrowsmith Rd
Harold Road
Sherlock Avenue
Oak Av
Woodside Rd
VICARAGE RD
Vicarage
Brookside Way
Brookside View
Clipsley Crs
Myrtle Av
Maple Av
Richmond Av
Regent Av
Grosvenor Rd
Darent Road
Avondale Road
Teesdale Road
Wyedale Road
Haydock Lane
Ashbury Drive
Albury Cl
Woolston Rd
Zara Ct
Woolston Road
Askett Cl
Mercer Road
Poplar Road
English Martyrs RC Prim Sch
HAYDOCK
CHURCH ROAD
Chapel St
Chapel Street
St James Primary School
Rose Avenue
Taylor
Moore Drive
Tulip Road
Lupin Drive
Hyacinth Cl
Aster Road
Close
Shaftway
Westminster Dr
New Boston
A599
CLIPSLEY LANE
Cumberland Crs
Loweswater Crescent
White House Cl
Windermere Road
Central Drive
Leyland Grove
O'Connell Close
Haydock Cricket Club
Haydock Medical Centre
Ireland Road
Greenwell Road
Branch Way
Haydock High Sch
Cooper Lane
Station Road
Oakthorn Grove
Works
Central Works
Lyme Street
Wrigley Road
Wharmby Road
Hunt Road
Shaw Street
Finney Grove
Nathan Dr
Legh Vale Primary School
Legh
Fairclough Crescent
Whiteside Road
Wagon Lane
Quayle Close
Caunce Av
Canniswood Rd
Ledger Rd
Wedge Av
Carnoustie Grove
Troon Close
Tobermory Close
Grange Valley
Gray Avenue
Canon Wilson Cl
Heyes Av
Grange Valley Prim School
Grange Road
Lancaster Close
Lyme Street
Lyme Community Primary School
Clarence
Brunswick Rd
Swan Road
Troutbeck Avenue
Birch Crs
Acacia St
Manor
3 55
56
3 96
97
98
99
1 grid square represents 500 metres

ASHTON-IN-MAKERFIELD
Old Boston
WA12
Haydock Park Racecourse
Haydock Park
Haydock Park Farm
Junction 23
M6
A580
EAST LANCASHIRE ROAD
LANCASHIRE ROAD
PENNY LANE
A599
A58
LIVERPOOL ROAD
WARRINGTON ROAD A49
LODGE LANE
A49 LODGE LANE
ASHTON ROAD
A49
VISTA ROAD
B5209
CROW LANE WEST
CROW LANE EAST
A572
HIGH STREET
York Road
Heath Road
Ashton Heath
Billington Avenue
Newton Lane
Wigan
St Helens
Old Boston Trading Estate
Holiday Inn
Woodlands Industrial Estate
St Oswalds RC J&I Sch
St Edmund Arrowsmith Catholic High Sch
Byrchall High School
Premier Lodge
Police Station
St Thomas CE Prim Sch
Newton-le-Willows Community High School
Borron Road Industrial Est
Newton-le-Willows Sports Club
Newton Health Clinic
Newton Bank Preparatory School
Surgery
St Aelreds RC
Works
Kilbuck Lane
Wilcock Road
Dixon Close
Pye Close
Coronation Drive
Princess Av
Norman Av
Queens Road
King George Road
Southward Road
Windsor Drive
Abby Av
Violet Street
Flora Street
Vicarage Road
Oakwood Av
Bransford Close
Glebe Av
Kiveton Dr
Farndale Grove
Chiltern Close
Newlyn Drive
Cheltenham Dr
Dixon Av
Martin Av
Elston Av
Speakman Av
Frawley Av
Johnson Avenue
Highmarsh Crs
Cole Avenue
Mercer St
Birley St
Castle Hill
Monmouth Crescent
Lincoln
Blenheim Road
Chester Drive
Ripon Drive
Norwich Avenue
Tintern Avenue
Harvey
Mansfield St
Helen Edge
Junction 23
79
92
106
57
58
59
F
G
H
J
K
1
2
3
4
5
6
96
97
98
99

92
91
107
A
B
C
D
E
1
2
3
4
5
6
Dam Lane
Edge
Ashton Road
B5207
Wigan Road
Ashton Road
Church Street
Manley Av
Millingford Av
Farefield Avenue
Linton Avenue
Justene Cl
Sandling Dr
Dove St
Rock St
Ash Street
May St
Edge Green Lane
Helen St
Park Avenue
Halewood Av
Dawlish Wy
Sycamore Av
Willow Gv
Elm Av
Beech Rd
Forster St
Duke Street
York St
Clarence St
Bank Street
Grimshaw St
Barton St
Charles St
Heath St
Talbot St
Turton St
Worsley St
Hell Nook
Mansfield St
Oakfield Av
Watson Avenue
Ringley Avenue
Gawsworth Road
Whitlow Avenue
Harvey Lane
Golborne CP School
John Street Medical Cen
High St
Surg
Cncl Bldg
Mill St
Legh Street
School St
Millingford Industrial Estate
Mitchell St
Brook St
Grundy St
Cross St
Dale Rd
Caunce Avenue
Dean Rd
Barn Lane
Wilmot Drive
Kings Rd
Park Road
Sandy Lane
Pierpoint St
Bridge Street
Golborne Clinic
Golborne High School
Rothwell Road
Heywood Av
Lowton Road
Elliott Av
Cottesmore Wy
St Thomas CE Prim School
Gloucester Av
Primary School
Hazel Rd
Barrowdale Rd
Briar Road
Oak Av
Naylor Av
Knowsley Avenue
West Av
Derby Road
East Av
Langley Cl
Windsor Rd
Twist Av
Manor Avenue
Holly Rd
Queens Dr
Holcombe Avenue
Tanner's Lane
Nook Lane
Yew Tree Way
GOLBORNE
Stone Cross Business Park
Travel Inn
Stone Cross Lane
Pennine La
Ullswater Rd
Rivington Av
Belmont Av
Pendle Rd
Rectory Av
Roadside Ct
Lowton West Prim Sch
Golborne Road
Lancaster Av
Manor Ct
Newlands Drive
North Lane
Rosedale Av
Welford Av
Longton Av
Upwood Rd
Garside Av
Haddon Road
Scott Road
Ivanhoe Av
Balmoral Av
Carlton Road
Hilary Avenue
Waverley Rd
Sawley Av
Crow Wd Rd
Lincoln Av
Surgery
The Cv
Braithwaite
Sarsfield Av
Laurel Gv
Cleveland Dr
Grampian Wy
Fieldfare Cl
Chester Av
Norwich Av
Mullein Cl
Primula Drive
Rostherne Av
Bourne Av
Upton Av
Meadway
Lapwing
Lowton
Church Lane
Rutland Av
Mirfield Cl
Bromley Avenue
Alderley Av
A580
East Lancashire Road
Heathmoor Av
Heath Lane
Cotswold
Stone Cross Lane South
Grange Cl
Lowton Heath
Golf Course
Haydock Park Golf Club
Warrington Road
A573
Town of Lowton
Lowton Gardens
Moss Lane
Highfield Lane
Highfield Farm
A572
Golborne Rd
Golborne Dale
Mere Road
360
61
99
98
97
396
1 grid square represents 500 metres

F
G
H
J
K
1
2
3
4
5
6
62
63
64
99
98
97
96
Pennington Flash Country Park
Aspull Common
Moss Industrial Estate
Gilded Hollins Primary School
Lowton Common
Council Building
Lowton St Marys CE Primary School
Lowton High Sch
Pocket Nook
Lowton St Mary's
Lowton J&I School
Lowton Business Park
Hesketh Meadow Lane
Brancaster Drive
Lane Head
Innkeeper's Lodge Warrington
St Catherines RC Primary School
St Lukes CE Prim Sch
Byrom Hall
Byrom Lane
Green Lane
Slag Lane
Sandy Lane
Woodvale Drive
Linbeck Grove
Brook-Lynn Avenue
The Pipers
Carton Drive
Beardsmore Dr
Garton
Edgerton Rd
Fir Tree Av
Elm Tree Rd
Laburnum Rd
Oaklands Road
Burnsall Av
Tarnway
Ridgeway
Bradwell Road
Wensley Road
Osborne Rd
Cranham Av
Kings Av
Beech Av
Cedar Av
Maple Av
Rowan Av
Mulberry Av
Spruce Cl
Larch Cl
The Elms
Pocket Nook Lane
Moorfield Crs
Stradbroke Cl
Carr La
Alfred Rd
Barford Dr
Milldale Road
Leighton Dr
The Poplars
Canaan
Abbey Road
Arlington Drive
Medway Cl
Fieldsend Dr
Dalesford Cl
Darlc Cl
Brook St
Bodden St
Pond St
Kane Ct
ST HELENS ROAD
A572
A579
A580
EAST LANCASHIRE ROAD
ATHERLEIGH
NEWTON ROAD
B5207
KENYON LANE
WILTON LANE
Diggle Green
BROSELEY LANE
Meadows Gn
Winton Rd
Delamere Avenue
Mather Av
Headland Cl
Lynwood Av
Wigan
Warrington
Leigh Golf Club
Golf Cou
Flash
PO

A
B
C
D
E
1
2
3
4
5
6
DUBLIN
A554
KING'S PARADE
King's Pde
Coastal Drive
Smugglers Way
Mockbeggar Dr
Burbo Way
Tide Wy
HARRISON DR
Bayview Drive
Sandcliffe Road
Harrison Park
Warren
Wallasey Golf Club
Wallasey Grove Road Stn
HARRISON DR
B5427
Parkway
Mere Lane
The Leas
The Willows
Coniston Av
Grove
Hotel
Wallasey Village
Golf Course
BAYSWATER
Bangor Rd
Barmouth Rd
Hillam Road
Stanley Av
Grosvenor Rd
Regent Rd
Leland Rd
Bidston Av
Lane
Wood La
WALLASEY
Farndon Av
PO
Gloucester Rd
Lynton
Taunton
Sand
Asbury Rd
110
1 grid square represents 500 metres

Royal Seaf
F
G
H
80
J
K
30
32
96
95
94
93
1
2
3
4
5
6
DUBLIN
BELFAST
DOUGLAS
Sefton
Wirral
96
Perch Rock
Marine Lake
King's Parade
A554 KING'S PARADE
Marine
Riverside Bowl
Floral Pavilion Theatre
Prom
Virginia Rd
Victoria Pde
Tollemache St
Tower Prom
Coastal Drive
Alexandra Road
Wellington Road
Portland St
Atherton
New Brighton Stn
Victoria Rd
Egerton Street
Faith House Yoga & Natural Hlth Cen
ROWSON STREET
Cressingham
Cavendish Road
Links View
Winton Cl
Montpellier Crs
Works
Albion Street
Prescot St
Dudley Road
Salisbury
Hamilton Road
New Brighton
St James Rd
Pickering Rd
St George's Mt
St George's Pk
Molyneux Drive
Rakersfield
Gregson Ct
Ross Tower Ct
New Tower Ct
Seymour St
Grosvenor Rd
Dalmorton Road
Vaughan Road
Kirkland
Ennerdale Rd
Warren Drive
Sea Road
Links Close
Linksway
Zetland Rd
Lansdowne
Sunningdale Rd
Langdale
Dovedale Rd
Mount Primary School
St Peter & Paul RC Primary School
Gorsehill Road
Sandymount Dr
Stoneby Drive
Sudworth Road
Bromley Rd
Dorset Rd
Field Rd
St Georges Medical Centre
Ormiston Rd
Manville
Onslow Rd
New Brighton Primary School
Vale Dr
Magazine Lane
Magazine Brow
Magazines Promenade
Aylesbury Rd
Nelson St
Fort St
Gordon Rd
ROWSON ST
A554
Coronation Road
Sutton Rd
Laburnum Road
Kirkway
Pleasant St
Clwyd St
The Coppice
The Orch
Elleray Park School
Glen Park Road
Elm Pk
Mount Pleasant
Warren Golf Club
Danehurst Road
Grove Rd
Hose Side Rd
Elleray Pk Rd
Sandrock Cl
Sandrock Rd
Sandfield Rd
Cambridge Road
Seabank Medical Cen
Birch Gv
Ash Gv
Cmbrin Rd
Wstmrl Rd
Orrell Rd
Dalton Rd
Holland Road
Osborne Av
SEABANK
LANE
RAKE
Beresford Road
Rollesston Dr
Lyndhurst Rd
Hamlet Road
Evesham
Lane
School
The Oval
Arundel Av
Queensway
Princesway
Kinnaird Rd
Castle Road
Turret Road
Earlston Road
Oarside Dr
Rose Mt
Derby
Apsley Avenue
Grange Avenue
Cemetery
Zig Zag Road
Penkett Road
Penkett Gv
Steel Av
Westbourne
Hale Road
Hertford Drive
Radnor Drive
Elgin Drive
Lincoln Drive
Caithness Drive
Haydock
Beach Cv
111
PO
CH45
Golf Course
Park

Royal Seaforth Dock
Works
Gladstone Dock
Alexandra Dock
Langton Dock
Brocklebank Dock
Canada Dock
Huskisson Dock
Sefton
Liverpool
BOOTLE
Sandhills
KNOWSLEY ROAD
Peel Road
Grove St
RIMROSE ROAD
A565
Sea View Road
Rimrose Business Park
Lyster Road
Strand Road
Church St
Regent Road
STRAND ROAD
CHURCH GDNS
MERTON ROAD
Oriel Rd
Bootle Oriel Rd Stn
South Sefton Business Centre
Town Hall
BALLIOL ROAD
Canal Street
DERBY ROAD
MILLER'S BRIDGE
REGENT ROAD
A5036
BRASENOSE ROAD
B5318
Bank Hall Station
BANKHALL STREET
A5056
BANKFIELD STREET
Juniper St
Belltower Rd
A5055
SANDHILLS LANE
Sandhills Station
Sandhills Business Park
Sandon Industrial Estate
Wellington Employment Park
A5038
A5098
A566
A567
L20
Bootle New Strand Stn
Strand Shopping Centre
Irlam Road
Bootle Leisure Centre
North Park Health Cen
Parrs Corner Trading Est
Linacre Primary School
Magistrates Court
Council Building
Surgery Park
Merton Gv
Stanley Road
Hornby Road
Washington Pde
Wadham
Bedford
Viola Street
Blanca St
Orlando St
Hertford
Keble
Exeter
Queen's Rd
Trinity Rd
Works
1 grid square represents 500 metres

81
95
112

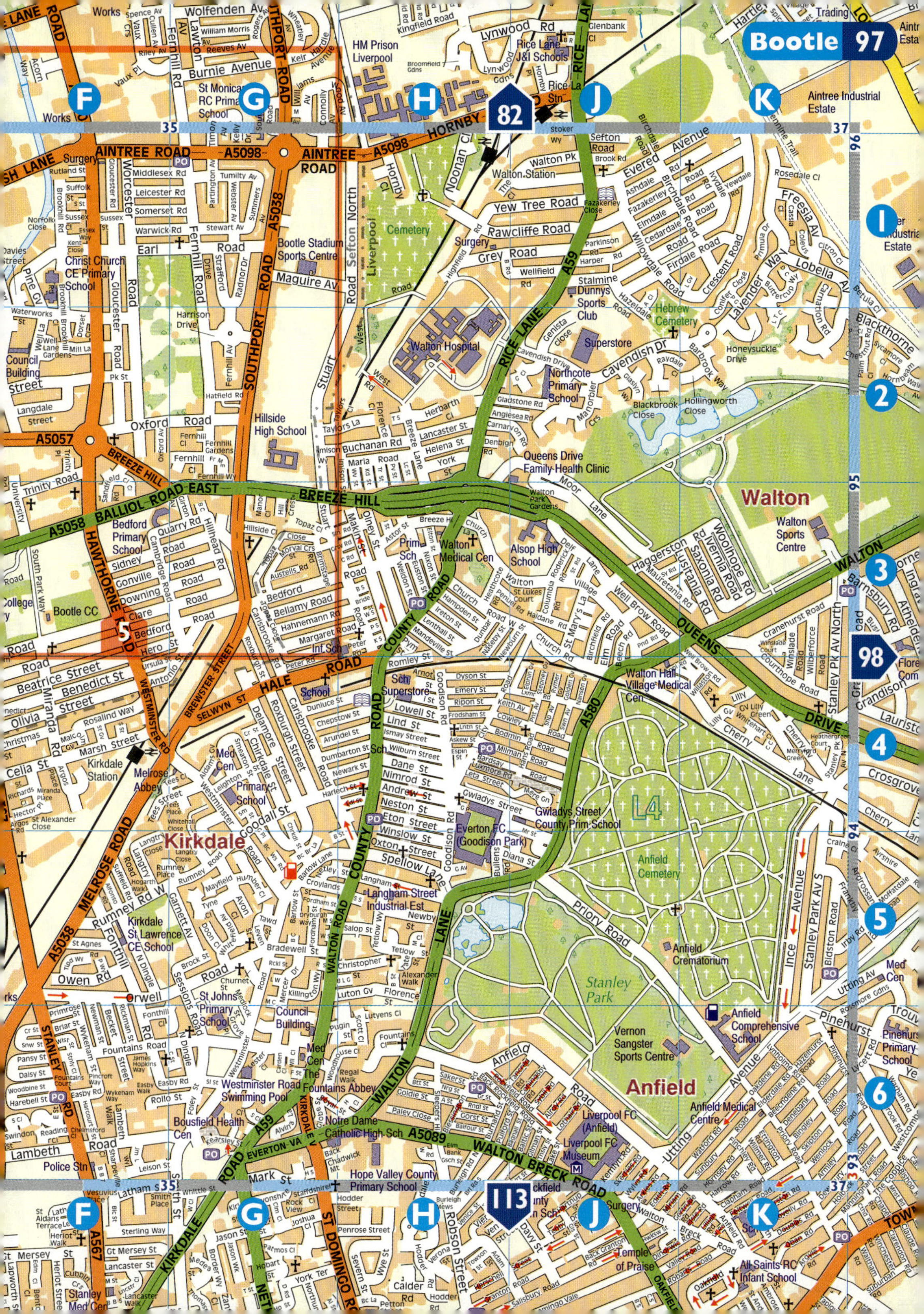

Bootle 97
82
98
113
F
G
H
J
K
I
2
3
4
5
6
35
37
96
95
94
93
Walton
Kirkdale
Anfield
L4
HM Prison Liverpool
Rice Lane J&I Schools
Aintree Industrial Estate
St Monica's RC Primary School
Works
AINTREE ROAD
A5098
HORNBY
Walton Station
Walton Pk
Yew Tree Road
Rawcliffe Road
Grey Road
Cemetery
Liverpool
Sefton North
Bootle Stadium Sports Centre
Maguire Av
Christ Church CE Primary School
Council Building
Harrison Drive
Walton Hospital
RICE LANE
A59
Superstore
Northcote Primary School
Hebrew Cemetery
Cavendish Dr
Honeysuckle Drive
Blackthorne
Hillside High School
A5057
Oxford Road
BREEZE HILL
Queens Drive Family Health Clinic
Moor Lane
Walton Sports Centre
A5058
BALLIOL ROAD EAST
Bedford Primary School
Walton Medical Cen
Alsop High School
Haggerston Rd
Well Brow Road
QUEENS
DRIVE
WALTON
Bootle CC
HAWTHORNE
WESTMINSTER RD
BREWSTER STREET
SELWYN ST
HALE ROAD
COUNTY ROAD
Superstore
Goodison Rd
Walton Hall Village Medical Cen
A580
Kirkdale Station
Melrose Abbey
MELROSE ROAD
A5038
Everton FC (Goodison Park)
Gwladys Street County Prim School
Anfield Cemetery
Langham Street Industrial Est
Priory Road
Anfield Crematorium
Stanley Park
Kirkdale St Lawrence CE School
St Johns Primary School
Council Building
WALTON ROAD
Anfield Comprehensive School
Vernon Sangster Sports Centre
Westminster Road Swimming Pool
Bousfield Health Cen
Notre Dame Catholic High Sch
A5089
WALTON BRECK ROAD
Liverpool FC (Anfield)
Liverpool FC Museum
Anfield Medical Centre
EVERTON VA
KIRKDALE
Hope Valley County Primary School
Police Stn
STANLEY RD
Lambeth
ST DOMINGO RD
Robson Street
Temple of Praise
All Saints RC Infant School
Stanley Med Cen
A567
Pinehurst Primary School

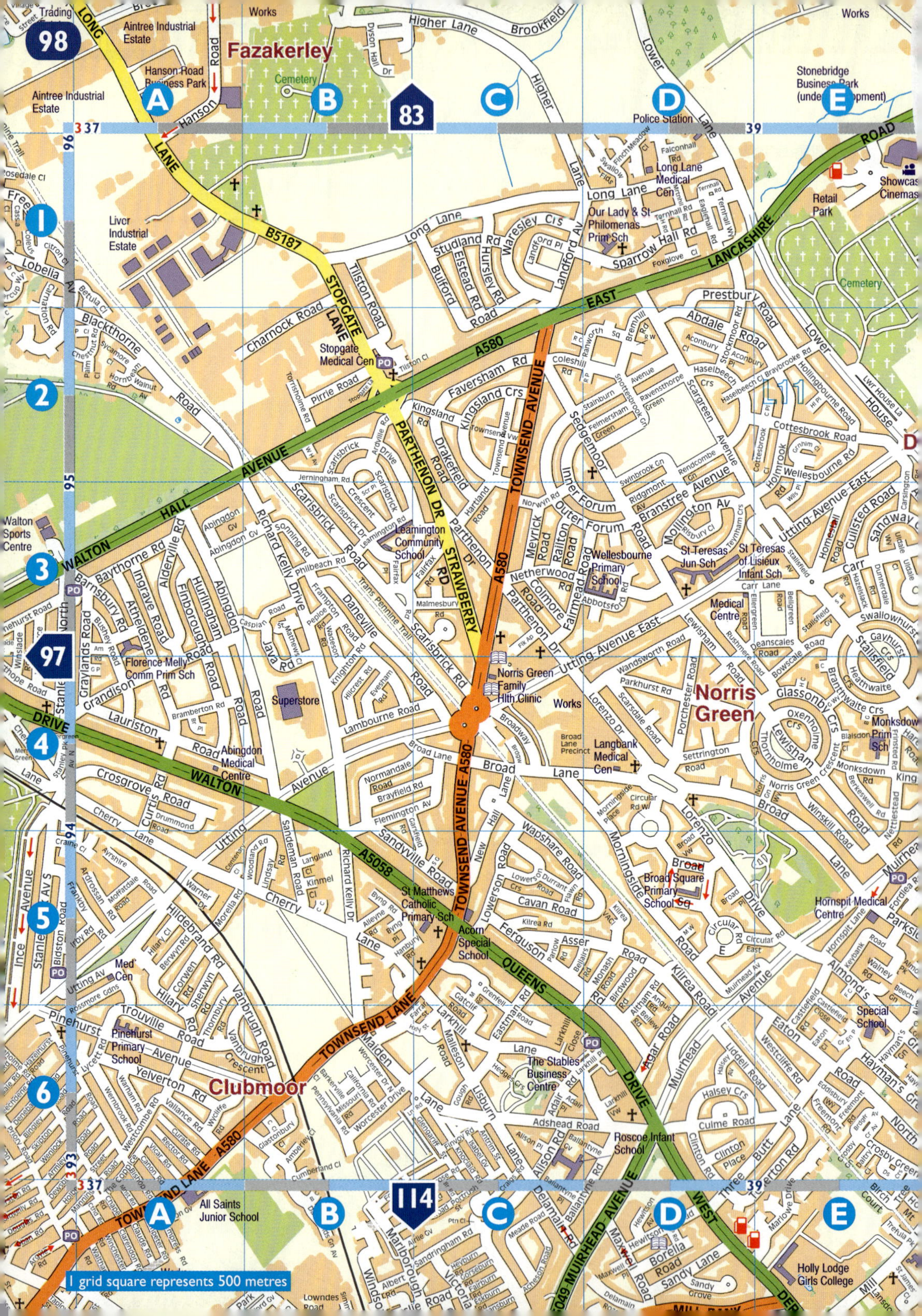

98
83
97
114
Fazakerley
Norris Green
Clubmoor
Aintree Industrial Estate
Hanson Road Business Park
Liver Industrial Estate
Stonebridge Business Park (under development)
Police Station
Long Lane Medical Cen
Our Lady & St Philomenas Prim Sch
Retail Park
Showcase Cinemas
Cemetery
Stopgate Medical Cen
Walton Sports Centre
Leamington Community School
Wellesbourne Primary School
St Teresas Jun Sch
St Teresas of Lisieux Infant Sch
Medical Centre
Florence Melly Comm Prim Sch
Superstore
Norris Green Family Hlth Clinic
Works
Broad Lane Precinct
Langbank Medical Cen
Abingdon Medical Centre
Broad Square Primary School
Hornspit Medical Centre
St Matthews Catholic Primary Sch
Acorn Special School
Med Cen
Pinehurst Primary School
The Stables Business Centre
Roscoe Infant School
Special School
All Saints Junior School
Holly Lodge Girls College
Long Lane
Stopgate Lane
B5187
East Lancashire Road
A580
Walton Hall Avenue
Townsend Avenue
Townsend Lane
Parthenon Dr
Strawberry Rd
Scarisbrick Road
Utting Avenue East
Broad Lane
Walton Drive
Queens Drive
A5058
West Derby
Muirhead Avenue
Lower Lane
Higher Lane
Brookfield
Trans Pennine Trail
L11
1 grid square represents 500 metres

Croxteth
West Derby
L12
84
100
115
F
G
H
J
K
1
2
3
4
5
6
40
42
96
95
94
93
Knowsley
Liverpool
A580
EAST
Centec Business Centre
Our Lady & St Swithins Catholic Prim Sch
Gillmoss Medical Cen
Croxteth Comprehensive School
Croxteth Sports Centre
Croxteth Family Health Centre
Croxteth Primary School
Oak Remedial Clnc
St John Bosco RC Secondary School
Jubilee Medical Centre
De La Salle RC High School
Croxteth Country Park
River Alt
Croxteth Hall
Fir Tree Drive South Medical Cen
Emmaus Primary School
St Marys West Derby Primary School
St Pauls & St Timothys RC J&I Sch
Deysbrook Med Cen
Blackmoor Park Infant School
West Derby Golf Club
Golf Cour
Baycliff Road Health Centre
Mab Lane Primary School
Ernest Cookson Special School
Cemetery
Surgery
St Alberts RC Prima
g & Gun
Stonebridge Lane
Hambleton Close
Stonedale Crescent
Storrington Avenue
Storrington Heys
Mansion Dr
Parkstile Lane
Altcross Road
Sceptre Road
Throne Rd
Sovereign Rd
Armill Rd
Dymoke Rd
Sword Wk
Coronet Rd
Ampulla Rd
Croxteth Hall Lane
Countess Pk
Oak Lane North
Abbeyfield Drive
Charnwood Cl
Moss Way
Petherick Rd
Redruth Road
Parkview Road
Tintagel Road
Newlyn Road
Middle Way
Trispen Rd
Cubert Road
Blackwater Rd
Fir Tree Drive North
Fir Tree Drive South
Pinewood Av
Mereview Crs
Crucian Wy
Trent Cl
Wood Lea
Craven Lea
Bracken Wood
Ashtree Grove
Burghill Road
Tupelo Close
Tiptree Close
Ledbury
Boxtree Close
The Oaks
Woodvale Road
Nightingale Road
Swallow Cl
Zander Gv
Lindisfarne Dr
Partridge Rd
Midhurst Road
Fir Tree Drive
Milford Dr
Ellerton Wy
Oakley Cl
Crompton Drive
Fulmar Gv
Turnstone
Chaucer Drive
Sandicroft Rd
Chiltern Cl
Albury Close
Inglewood
Hebden Rd
Oakgate Cl
Worrow Cl
Fieldton Road
Carr Lane East
Carr Cl
Dwerryhouse Lane
Beversbrook Road
Marshfield Road
Mentmore Crs
Eldersfield Rd
Hasfield Rd
Marshgate Rd
Cheldon Rd
Ashwater Rd
Stowford Cl
Oak Lane
Greenodd Av
Cumbria Way
Windermere Dr
Kents Bank
Cartmel Dr
Carnforth
Hawkshead
Oak Lane
Dalton Cl
East Avenue
Wingrave Wy
Dencourt
Fallbrook Drive
Meadow Way
Kerman
Templeton Crs
Pennant Av
Awelon Close
The Boulevard
Grove Park Av
Old Lodge Cl
Lingmell Road
Lydford Road
Marldon Road
Glentrees Rd
Norseman Cl
Meadow Lane
Castleview Rd
Castlesite Road
Town Row
The Croft
Barnfield Drive
Eaton Road
Melwood Drive
Crown Rd
Deysbrook La
Deysbrook Lane
Deysbrook Wy
Allerford Road
Halcombe Road
Minver Rd
Crawford Close
Crawford Cl
Lees La
Rockwell Rd
Sheldon Rd
Exford Rd
Berkley Av
Springfield Wy
Timway Dr
Claran Cl
Croxteth Hall Lane
The Meander
Riverside Dr
Coachmans Dr
Coachmans Dr
The Dell
Delta Dr
Oxbow Rd
Foxwood
Huntsman Wd
Lapwing Close
Manor View
Woodpecker Cl
Kingfisher Gv
Chaffinch Cl
Dalegarth Av
Peartree Av
Bridge Gdns
Brookside Cl
Old Kennel Cl
Deysbrook Lane
Chelsea Ct
Dumbrees Rd
Felwood Road
North Cantril Av
South Cantril Av
Baycliff
Princess Drive
Aspes Road
Mab Lane
Playfield Rd
Hare Cft
Waterpark Drive
Baron's Hey
Corner Brook
Steers Croft
Croxdale Rd W
Altfield Rd
Snowberry Rd
Gainford
Princess Drive
Rothbury
Lindridge Rd
Finch La
Yew Tree Cl
Lane
Tree St Andrews
Leyfield
Lislehome
Harbern Close
Thornhead La
Leyfield Close
South Parkside Dr
Town Row
Spring
Craven
Marlfield Rd
Barn Hey
Norris Gn Rd
Bonsall Rd
Hartington Rd
Rosthwaite Rd
Darley Drive
Marford Rd
Westerton
Langley
Chigwell Cl
Haddon Wk
Abbotsbury Wy
Measham Wy
Hanworth Cl
Grayling Dr
Hemlock
Lawson Wk
Ashwood
Mace Rd
Cartmel Cl
Elwick Drive
Meldon Cl
Knowle Cl
Hollocombe Rd
Riviera Dr
Unicorn Rd
Griffin Cl
Dragon Cl
Standard Road
Gillmoss Close
Preesall Way
Cockerham Wy
Altbridge Pk
Chalfont Rd
Marlborough Pk
Westfield Rd
Elm Dr
Cedars
Mullwood
Denham Cl
Hatfield Cl
Cardiff Dr
Carville Wy
Newbold Gv
Emmaus
Oaksmeade
Dumbrees
Kendal
Cunliffe Cl
Fallbrook
Woodside Cl
Marlcham

100
85
99
116
A
B
C
D
E
1
2
3
4
5
6
3 42
44
96
95
94
93
SCHOOL LANE
B5194
Overbrook Lane
Kipling Lane
Randles Road
Caddick
Mill Lane
Patten's Walk
Ormskirk Road
Old Mill Lane
Dumbreeze Gv
Teynham Avenue
Whitegate Close
Council Building
KNOWSLEY
Longmeadow Road
Middlehey Road
Guild Hey
Quakers Mdw
Tithebarn Road
Shop Road
St John Fisher RC Prim Sch
Singleton Dr
Homer Road
Frederick Lunt Av
Knowsley Medical Centre
The Coppice
Pinfold Lane
Maiden's Bower Farm
Sugar Lane
Parklands
Berry Hl Av
Riding Hill Road
Knowsley Village Prim Sch
Longborough Rd
Home Farm Road
Alder Lane
M57
KNOWSLEY LANE
Fir Tree Drive North
Fir Tree Drive South
Zander Gv
Nightingale Road
Lindisfarne Dr
Verwood Dr
Partridge Cl
Midhurst Road
Hebburn Wy
Carrville Way
Ingleword
Emmaus Primary School
Chiltern Cl
Albury Close
Liverpool
Knowsley
Brook Lane
Fluker's
Shannons La
Knowsley Cott
Jack's
Dark Entry
Nine Tree Primary School
St Alberts RC Primary School
Hollow Cft
Croxteth Lane
Boode Croft
Steers Croft
L28
Woodfarm Hey
Custley Hey
Blackmorne Crs
Milestone Hey
The Elms Special School
Stockbridge Village
Stockbridge Village Hlth Cen
Haswell Drive
Pool Hey
Junction 3
Waterpark Drive
Baron's Hey
Marled Hey
Corner Brook
Mab Lane Primary School
St Brigids RC Primary School
The Withens
Spruce Gv
Whitethorn Dr
Brandearth Hey
Lt Moss Hey
Cremorne Hey
Waterpark Dr
Boydell Cl
Brookside Primary School
St Christopher's Dr
STOCKBRIDGE LA
Pyes La
Knowsley La
Hillside Crs
Bruton Rd
Beechwood County Prim Sch
Hillside Avenue
George Hale Avenue
Newark Cl
KNOWSLEY LA
Croxdale Rd W
Altfield Rd
Princess Drive
Gainford Rd
Colwell Cl
Blueberry Park CP School
Callington
St Edmund Of Canterbury High School
St Dominics Sch
Melbury Road
Rothbury Rd
Linbridge Rd
Finch La
Surgery
A52
1 grid square represents 500 metres

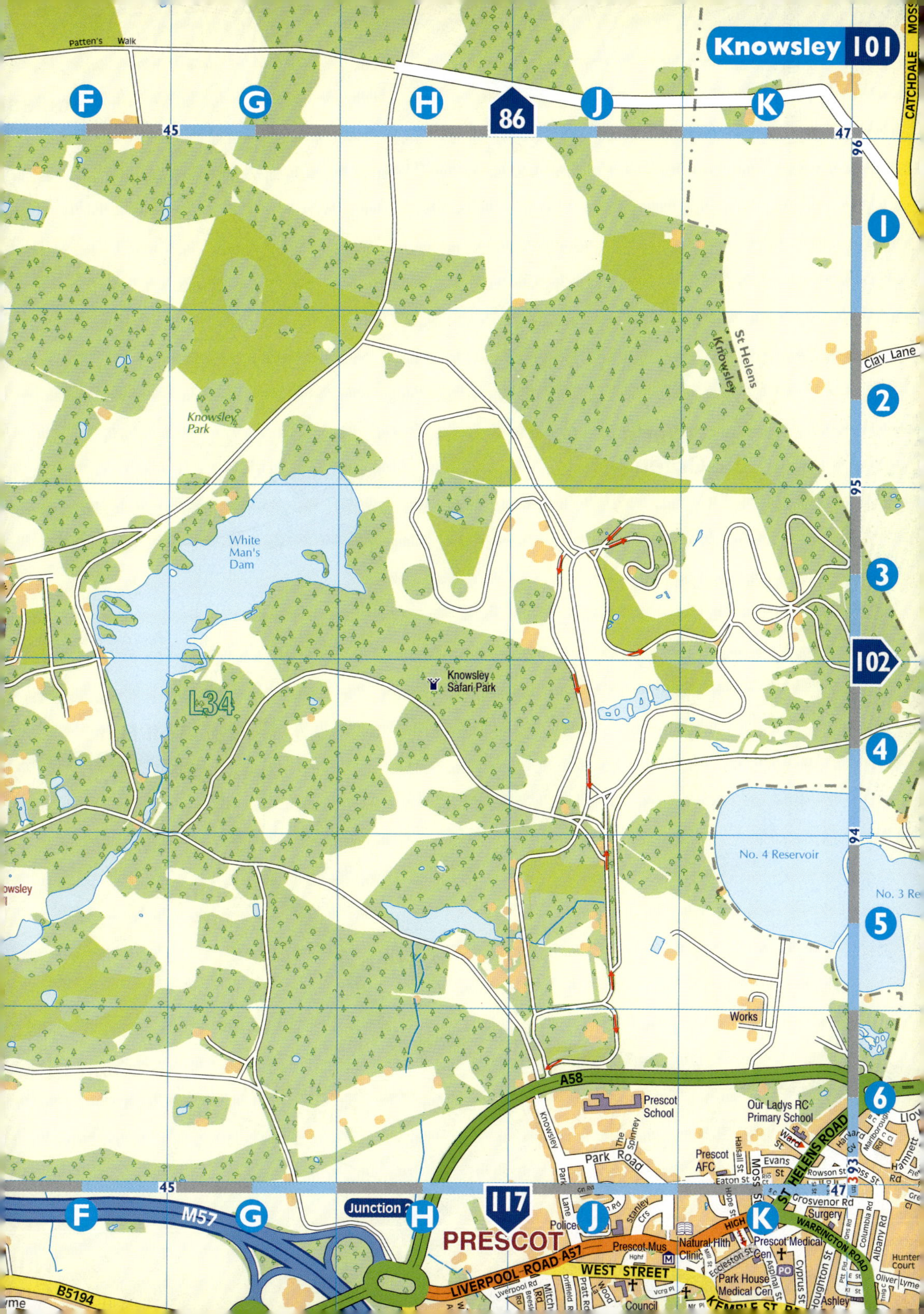
Knowsley 101
Patten's Walk
F
G
H
86
J
K
45
47
96
1
Clay Lane
St Helens
Knowsley
2
Knowsley Park
95
White Man's Dam
3
102
Knowsley Safari Park
L34
4
No. 4 Reservoir
94
No. 3 Re
5
Works
A58
6
Prescot School
Our Ladys RC Primary School
Knowsley
The Spinney
Park Road
Prescot AFC
Halsall St
Moss St
Evans St
Ward St
ST HELENS ROAD
Harvard Cv
Marlborough Rd
Hammett Rd
Rowson St
Moss St
Eaton St
Park Lane
Grosvenor Rd
Surgery
Columbia Rd
Albany Rd
Junction 2
117
PRESCOT
M57
B5194
Police
Stanley Crs
Hope St
HIGH
Prescot Mus
Natural Hlth Clinic
Prescot Medical Cen
WARRINGTON ROAD
LIVERPOOL ROAD A57
WEST STREET
Eccleston St
Aspinall St
Cyprus St
Houghton St
Park House Medical Cen
Hunter Court
Oliver Lyme
Liverpool Rd
Driffield Rd
Pratt Rd
Wood La
Vcrg Pl
Council
Mr Pl
KEMBLE ST
Ashley
CATCHDALE MOSS

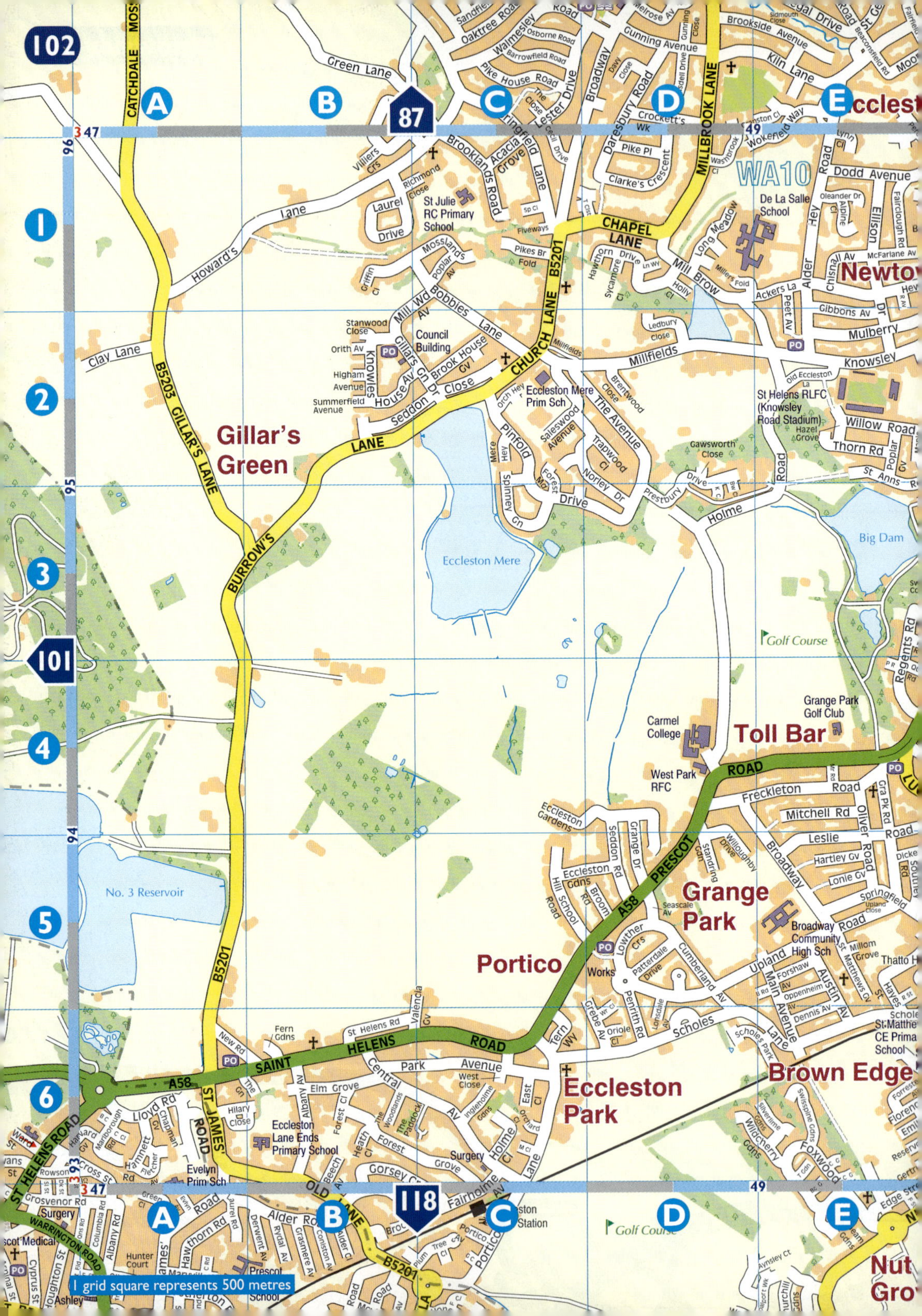

102
87
101
118
A
B
C
D
E
1
2
3
4
5
6
WA10
Gillar's Green
Toll Bar
Grange Park
Portico
Eccleston Park
Brown Edge
Newton
Eccleston
Eccleston Mere
Big Dam
No. 3 Reservoir
Golf Course
Grange Park Golf Club
Carmel College
West Park RFC
St Helens RLFC (Knowsley Road Stadium)
De La Salle School
St Julie RC Primary School
Eccleston Mere Prim Sch
Council Building
Broadway Community High Sch
Eccleston Lane Ends Primary School
Evelyn Prim Sch
St Matthew's CE Primary School
Eccleston Station
Works
Surgery
B5203 GILLAR'S LANE
BURROW'S LANE
CHURCH LANE B5201
CHAPEL LANE
MILLBROOK LANE
B5201
A58 PRESCOT ROAD
SAINT HELENS ROAD
ST HELENS ROAD
WARRINGTON ROAD
ST JAMES' ROAD
OLD LANE
CATCHDALE MOSS
Green Lane
Howard's Lane
Clay Lane
Holme Road
Knowsley Road
Broadway
Millfields
Bobbies Lane
Seddon Close
Brook House Gv
Kiln Lane
Brookside Avenue
Gunning Avenue
Dodd Avenue
Mulberry
Gibbons Av
Willow Road
Thorn Rd
St Anns
Freckleton Road
Mitchell Rd
Leslie Road
Oliver Road
Springfield
Upland Road
Main Avenue
Austin Av
Scholes Lane
Park Avenue
Elm Grove
Central Av
Forest Rd
Gorsey Grove
Fairholme Av
Alder Rd
Hawthorn Rd
Lloyd Rd
Cross St
Grosvenor Rd
Prescot School
Ashley
1 grid square represents 500 metres

Newtown 103
88
104
119
ST HELENS
Green
West Park
Ravenhead
Thatto Heath
Sutton Heath
St Helens Cricket Club
Queens Park CE/URC Prim Sch
St Teresas Catholic Prim Sch
Leisure Centre
LINGHOLME ROAD
KIRKLAND STREET
DENTONS GREEN LANE
DUKE STREET
COLLEGE STREET
WESTFIELD ST
CROPPERS HILL
BOROUGH RD
LINKWAY WEST
LINKWAY EAST
LINKWAY
PARR STREET
PRESCOT ROAD
THATTO HEATH ROAD
SAINT HELENS
SCORECROSS
MARSHALLS CROSS ROAD
Register Office
Central Clinic
Police Stn
Cncl Bldg
Mag & Co Cts
Town Hall
Thtr Royal
Hall St Med Cen
St Helens Museum & Art Gallery
Holy Cross RC Prim
Parish CE Prim Sch
St Helens College
Cineworld
Sandfield Medical Centre
St Helens Central Station
St Helens Retail Park
Service Centre
Chalon Way Industrial Estate
World of Glass
Market
Superstore
Trading Estate
Business Development Centre
Collins Industrial Est
Council Bldg
Works
Burtonhead Rd
Ravenhead Retail Park
Ravenhead Road
Ravenhead Nature Park
Sutton Heath Rd
Sherdley Road
Sherdley Business Park
Sherdley Park Golf Club
Sherdley Park
Golf Course
The Score
Council Building
Elmfield Close
Thatto Heath Community Prim Sch
Police Stn
The Bowry Health Cen
Nutgrove Methodist Prim Sch
Elephant Lane
Mayfield Avenue
Heathfield Av
Queensland Av
Adelaide Av
Canberra Avenue
Elm Road
Alexandra Drive
Stafford Road
Roby Street
Chamberlain St
Gladstone St
Doulton St
Eccleston St
Bold Street
Canal Street
Warrington Old Rd
Milverny Way
Roundwood Drive
Sherdley Rd
Eaves Lane
Eaves Prim Sch
Sutton Community Leisure Centre Track
Sutton High Sports College
Drake Gardens
Mallard Gardens
Swan Gardens
A58
A570
A571
A569
A57
12
13
50
52
F
G
H
I
J
K
1
2
3
4
5
6

104
89
103
120
A
B
C
D
E
1
2
3
4
5
6
352
354
393
395
394
396
Blackbrook
Broad Oak
Derbyshire Hill
Parr
Moss Nook
Peasley Cross
Sutton
WA9
St Helens Canal
Collins Industrial Estate
Business Development Centre
Merton Bank Primary School
St Augustine of Canterbury RC High School
Council Building
Moorfoot Road Industrial Estate
Cemetery
Works
Broad Oak Community Primary School
Holy Spirit Catholic Primary School
Maternity & Child Welfare Clinic
Parr Swimming Baths
St Helens Retail Park
Service Centre
Eastside Industrial Est
Westside Ind Est
Allanson Street CP School
Fleet Lane Industrial Estate
Parr Industrial Estate
St Cuthberts Catholic High Sch
St Helens Hospital
Fishwicks Industrial Est
Sherdley Business Park
Robins Lane Primary School
Sutton Oak CE Primary Sch
Irwin Road Health Centre
Rainbow Medical Cen
St Helens Junction Station
St Helens AFC
St Annes RC Primary School
Sutton Cricket Club
Eaves Prim Sch
Reginald Road Industrial Park
A58
PARK ROAD
PARR STREET
ASHCROFT
PARR STOCKS ROAD
CHANCERY LANE
BROAD OAK ROAD
A572
A569
MARSHALLS CROSS ROAD
BOLD ROAD
REGINALD ROAD
Peasley Cross
Fleet Lane
Nook Lane
Robins Lane
Station Road
1 grid square represents 500 metres

Collins Green
Earlestown
Newton Common
PENNINGTON LANE
COMMON ROAD
PENKFORD LANE
PENNY LANE
BOLD LANE
A572
B5204
Swan Road
Broad Lane
Collins Green Lane
Lumber Lane
Back Lane
Phipps' Lane
Forshaw's Lane
Green Lane
Fleet Lane
Wharf Road
Penkford School
Lyme Community Primary School
Grange Valley Prim School
Burtonwood Primary School
Burtonwood Industrial Centre
Bold Business Centre
Bold Industrial Park
Wheatacre Farm
Deacon Trading Estate
St Paul of the Cross Catholic Primary School
Chapel Lane
Cemetery
90
106
121
55
57

106
WA12
91
105
122
A
B
C
D
E
1
2
3
4
5
6
3 57
59
96
95
94
3 93
M6
VISTA ROAD
CROW LANE WEST
A572
CROW LANE EAST
HIGH STREET
A49 CHURCH ST
A49
ROAD
MILL LANE
WINWICK ROAD
NEWTON-LE- WILLOWS
Wargrave
Vulcan Village
Newton-le-Willows Community High School
Newton-le-Willows Sports Club
Borron Road Industrial Est
Newton Health Clinic
St Marys Catholic Junior School
St Marys Catholic Sch
St Aelreds RC Technology College
St Peters CE Prim Sch
Newton Bank Preparatory School
Kirkfield Hotel
Newton-le-Willows Station
Newton Le Willows Primary School
The District CE Prim Sch
Superstore
Council Building
Med Cen
Surgery
Earlestown Station
Deacon Trading Estate
Sankey Valley Industrial Estate
Wargrave Prim Sch
Newton Community Hospital
Wargrave House School
Vulcan Industrial Estate
Newton-le-Willows Cemetery
Sankey Valley Industrial Estate
Sankey Brook
Bradleigh Old Hall
Boarded Barn Farm
Red House Farm
Alder Root Golf Club
Golf Course
St Helens
Warrington
Hall Lane
Bradley Lane
Alder Lane
Alder Root Lane
Victoria Road
Wargrave Road
Bradleigh Road
Kingsway
Acorn Street
Oak Avenue
Alder Street
Laurel Avenue
Earle Street
Regent St
St John St
Market St
Haydock St
Bridge St
Cross Lane
Cole Avenue
Harrison Way
Hollins
1 grid square represents 500 metres

Town of Lowton
Lowton Gardens
Mos
Highfield Farm
A572
Colborne Dale Rd
Mere Road
SOUTHWORTH ROAD
Holford Way
Rosemary Dr
Green
Newton Park Drive
M6
A573
Parkside Farm
Kenyon Hall
WINWICK
Sandy
Newton Park
Barrow
Lane
Wigan
St. Helens
Warrington
St. Helens
Wood Head
PARKSIDE ROAD
Oven Back Farm
A49
Red Bank Avenue
Red Bank
Junction 22
Hermitage Green Lane
Gerosa Av
Colborne Rd
Hermitage Green
Cop Holt Farm
NEWTON ROAD
GOLBORNE ROAD
LINK ROAD
Highfield Lane
Lane
Old School House Lane
Green La Cl
Green Lane
Waterworks Lane
Southworth Lane
The Priory
Spires Cl
Winwick
Hornby La
Ilex Av
Myddle
Cem
Church Walk
PO
Hollins Lane
Winwick CE Primary School
Premier Lodge
Winwick Parish Leisure Centre
Ash
Maple Rd
Ballantyne Pl
Hollins Dr
Austen Dr
Marryat Cl
Rectory La
Linkside Av
Arbury Lane
Lane
F
G
H
J
K
92
123
60
62
96
95
94
93
1
2
3
4
5
6

A
B
C
D
E
322
23
24
93
92
91
390
1
2
3
4
5
6
Parkfield House
Lane
Park
Parkfields
Dove
Point
Great
Meols
Parade
Meols
Newlyn Road
Bennet's Lane
Cuffitts
Cl
Great Meols
Prim Sch
Road
Flowermead Cl
Dovepoint
Road
Roman Road
Firshaw
Rd
Garden Hey
Road
Beachcroft Rd
Mumfords
La
Rd
Forest
Close
The
Old
Forest
School Lane
Cuffitt's Rake
Drive
Centurion
Barnfield
Cl
Park
Celtic Rd
Cranborne
Rd
Lyndhurst
Ashley
Carr Lane
LC
Ashford
Rd
Shaws
Drive
Edgewood Rd
Egbert
Road
Meols Parade
Queen
Elizabeth II
Coronation Park
BIRKENHEAD ROAD
127
128
King's
Road
Foxfield
Road
Banks
Gorse
Avenue
Leighton Av
Manningtonn Cl
Derwent Rd
Meols
Station
PO
Hospital
Hoylake
1 grid square represents 500 metres

F
G
H
J
K
25
26
27
93
92
91
90
1
2
3
4
5
6
110
129
Leasowe Golf Club
Leasowe Castle Hotel
North Wirral Coastal Park
Lingham Lane
Lingham Farm
Lingham Lane
A551
PASTURE ROAD
Ditton Lane
Marshfield Court
The Sandhills
The Beeches
The Stakes
New Brighton RUFC
Wakefield Drive
Murrayfield Dr
Blackheath Dr
Reeds Lane
Farmside
Reeds Av
Birket Avenue
Cheltenham Crs
Epsom Rd
Surgery
Goodwood Dr
Dunstall Cl
Tarran Way N
Tarran Way West
Tarran Way E
Tarran Wy
Works
Moreton Station
Station Approch
Leasowe Station
Reedville Gv
Peninsula Business
The Birk
Pasture Avenue
Pasture Crescent
CH46
Sunfield Road
Kingsmead Road
Saxon Road
Yew Tree Lane
Danger Lane
East Way
West Way
Eastway Prim Sch
Blundells Dr
Oundle Rd
Ivy Lane
Witley Av
Daneswell Drive
Sacred Heart RC Primary Sch
Moreton
Fairmead Road
HOYLAKE ROAD
Stuart Av
Spencer Av
Pasture Road Health Centre
Knutsford Road
Orchard
Lyons Rd
Barnston Lane
Maryland Lane
Felicity Grove
Berrylands
Meadfoot Rd
Harvest Lane
Bramble Way
Lingham Lane
Heathmoor Road
Flaxhill
Lingham Primary School
Meadow Lane
Curlew Way
Curlew Court
Bradman Road
Glasier Rd
Eleanor Rd
PO
Wastdale Dr
Mallard Wy
Bermuda Road
Smillie Av
Hardie Av
Town Linear Park
Tern Way
Millhouse Lane
Millhouse Cl
Oakham Drive
Desford Cl
Belfry
Austell
Digg Lane
Works
Carr Lane
Kinnerton Cl
Rosewood Dr
Millhouse Dr
Alnwick
Rothbury Cl
Wooler Close
Kestrel Road
Macdonald Road
Edgehill Road
Bermuda
Joan Avenue
Fairfield Crs
Doreen Av
Neva Av
Drive
Douglas
Foxfield School
Surgery
Police Stn
Holt Av
Winston Gv
Dawpool Dr
Tintern Dr
Moreton Medical Centre
Sandbrook
Haig Avenue
Carnsdale Road
Lomond Grove
Pine Tree Grove
Burnley Road
Wimbrick Hey
Stuart Road
Stavordale Road
Orrets Meadow School
Sedgefield Rd
Castlewa
Castle Prima Schoo
Raven
Twick
Marram
Cornflow
P+

94
129
130
109
A
B
C
D
E
1
2
3
4
5
6
Wallasey Village
Leasowe
Bidston
Bidston Hill
Golf Course
Mockbeggar Wharf
Green Lane
Leasowe Golf Club
Wallasey Golf Club
Harrison Park
Bayview
Wallasey Grove Road Stn
Harrison Dr
Wallasey Village
Bayswater Rd
A554
A551
Leasowe Road
Greenleas School
Greenleas Road
Saltburn Rd
Malvern Rd
Northcote Rd
Kinross Rd
Keble Dr
Redcar Road
Asbury Rd
Bangor Rd
Barmouth Rd
Hillam Road
Stanley Av
Groveland Rd
Regent Rd
St Nicholas Rd
Moorcroft Rd
Southcroft Rd
Longacre Cl
Southbourne
Wallasey Village Station
Wallasey RFC
Burton Av
Lycett Road
Gainsborough Rd
Russell Rd
Radstock Rd
Mosslands Drive
Mosslands School
St Marys Catholic College
Surgery
Farndon Av
Dean Av
Sandiways Rd
Gloucester Rd
Lynton Rd
Taunton
Coniston Av
The Willows
The Leas
Grove
Hotel
Beechwood Av
Marlwood Av
Somerset Rd
Whitby Av
Beaufort Dr
Folly Lane
School Lane
Cross Lane
Works
Ashville FC
Wirral Hospital School
Heyes Dr
Our Lady of Lourdes RC Primary School
Meadowside
Gardenside
Shackleton Rd
Raleigh Rd
Cook Rd
Drake Road
Frobisher Rd
Leasowside
Castleway North
Castleway Primary School
Hudson Road
Franklin Rd
Baffin Cl
Livingstone Road
Leasowe Primary School
Leasowe Millennium Centre
Twickenham Dr
Grant Road
Ross Av
Scoresby Rd
Cameron Road
Boyd Cl
Wilkes Av
Mackenzie Road
Davis Rd
Oxley
Castleway South
Castle Close
Birket Close
Birket Avenue
Leasowe Recreation Centre
Wallasey School
The Birket
Peninsula Business Park
Murrayfield
Wakefield Drive
Fairhaven
Reeds La
Golf Course
Junction 1
A5139
Superstore
Junction 1 Retail Park
Bidston Moss
Bidston Industrial Estate
Bidston Golf Club
M53
Bidston Station
LC
Superstore
Wirral Tennis & Sports Centre
Superstore
Bidston Station Ap
Valley Road
Wildbrook Dr
Bluewood Dr
Treetops Dr
Hillburn Drive
Clover Drive
Fairbrook Drive
Valley Road
Works
Gautby
Holy Cross RC Prim School
Hoylake Road
A553
Challis St
Brow Rd
Vyner Primary School
Bidston Village Road
Lennox La
School Lane
St Oswald's CE Primary School
Keele Cl
Balliol Cl
Bidston Village Road
Fender Way
St Oswald's Av
Firbrook
Ashwood Ct
Lindwall Cl
Eleanor Rd
Fender Lane
A553
Claremount School
Marram Cl
Cornflower Way
Bullrush Dr
Willow Moss Cl
Hyacinth
Sunfield Road
Kingsmead Road
Saxon Road
Lombard Road
Poppy
Sacred Heart Primary School
Stuart Av
Spencer Av
Avondale Av
Burnley Road
Wimbrick Cl
Gabriel Close
Stavordale Road
Orrets School
Pine Tree Grove
Fender
Bidston Gn Dr
Parkland Court
Greenacres Close
Hillfoot Close
Fenderside Road
Statham Road
Lords Avenue
Truman
Lillie Close
Edgbaston Way
Boundary
Hoblyn Road
Flaybrick Road
Oakwood Dr
Maplewood Grove
Larch Grove
Lower
Mercer Rd
3 27
29
93
92
91
3 90
1 grid square represents 500 metres

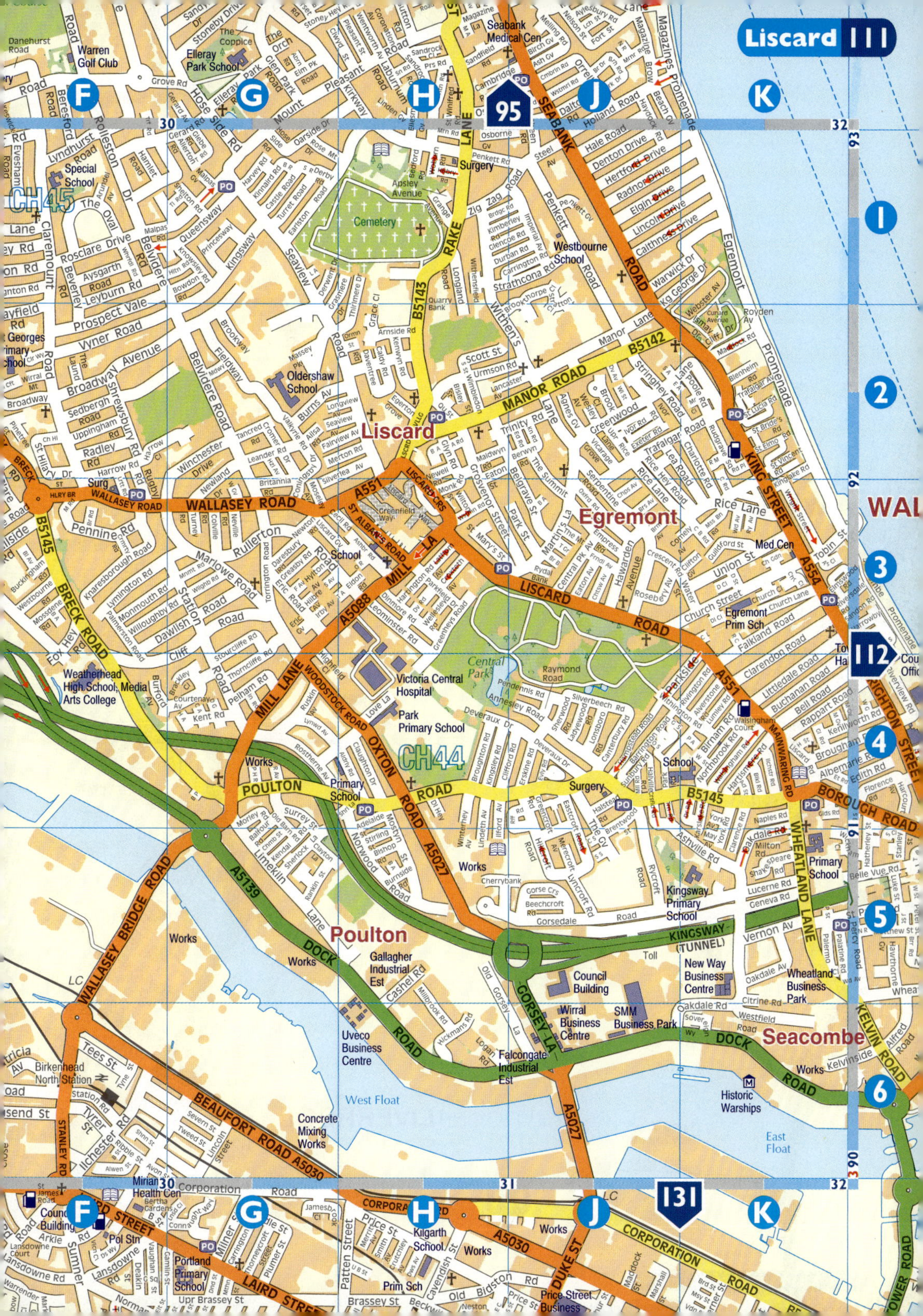
Liscard
Egremont
Poulton
Seacombe
CH45
CH44
95
112
131
WAL
Warren Golf Club
Elleray Park School
Special School
Cemetery
Seabank Medical Cen
Surgery
Westbourne School
Oldershaw School
Weatherhead High School Media Arts College
Victoria Central Hospital
Park Primary School
Central Park
Med Cen
Egremont Prim Sch
Primary School
Kingsway Primary School
Council Building
Wirral Business Centre
SMM Business Park
New Way Business Centre
Wheatland Business Park
Gallagher Industrial Est
Uveco Business Centre
Falcongate Industrial Est
Historic Warships
West Float
East Float
Concrete Mixing Works
Birkenhead North Station
Kilgarth School
Portland Primary School
Prim Sch
Price Street Business
Works
WALLASEY ROAD
BRECK ROAD
B5145
B5143
RAKE LANE
MANOR ROAD
B5142
SEABANK ROAD
KING STREET
A554
LISCARD ROAD
A551
MILL LANE
A5088
WOODSTOCK ROAD
OXTON ROAD
A5027
POULTON ROAD
BOROUGH ROAD
WHEATLAND LANE
KINGSWAY (TUNNEL)
DOCK ROAD
A5139
WALLASEY BRIDGE ROAD
GORSEY LA
BEAUFORT ROAD A5030
CORPORATION ROAD
A5030
DUKE ST
LAIRD STREET
KELVIN ROAD
TOWER ROAD
STANLEY RD
Promenade
F
G
H
J
K
1
2
3
4
5
6
30
31
32
90
91
92
93

A
B
96
C
D
E
I
2
3
111
4
5
6
131
132
8
WALLASEY
Seacombe
LIVERPOOL
Vauxhall
Huskisson Dock
Nelson Dock
Stanley Dock
Trafalgar Dock
Princes Dock
George's Dock
Albert Dock
Sandon Industrial Estate
Belltower Rd
Sandhills Station
Sandhills Business Park
Wellington Employment Park (under development)
A5055
SANDHILLS LANE
BOUNDARY STREET
A5054
A5036
A565
A5038
A5053
A554
REGENT ROAD
WATERLOO ROAD
GREAT HOWARD STREET
BLACKSTONE STREET
Walter St
Vauxhall Business Centre
Chadwick Court Industrial Cen
King Edward Industrial Estate
King Edward Industrial Est
Isle of Man Ferry Terminal
Princes Parade
BATH ST
NEW QUAY
THE STRAND
WATER ST
CHAPEL ST
DALE ST
LEEDS ST
Royal Liver Bldg
Cunard Building
Port of Liverpool Building
Mersey Ferries
Titanic Memorial
War Memorial
Newspaper Office
Town Hall
Museum of Liverpool Life
HM Customs & Excise Nat Mus
Merseyside Maritime Museum
Fingerprints of Elvis
Tate Gallery
Albert Dock Village
The Beatles Story
Granada TV
Merseyside Police HQ
National Discovery Park
Fire Stn
HM Coroners Court
Queen Elizabeth II Law Courts
BBC
James Street Stn
Liverpool
Wirral
KINGSWAY
(TUNNEL)
DOUGLAS
BELFAST
DUBLIN
DUBLIN
BRIGHTON STREET
BOROUGH ROAD
WHEATLAND LA
KELVIN ROAD
BIRKENHEAD ROAD
CHURCH RD
East Street
Council Offices
Guinea Gap Baths & Recreation Centre
Riverside Primary School
Primary School
Seacombe Promenade
Wheatland Business Park
Twelve Quays Ferry Terminal
Pump Road
Kings Wharf
Works
1 grid square represents 500 metres

Anfield
Liverpool FC (Anfield)
Westminster Road Swimming Pool
Bousfield Health Cen
Notre Dame Catholic High Sch
Hope Valley County Primary School
Breckfield County Prim Sch
Police Stn
97
BRECK ROAD
WALTON
KIRKDALE ROAD
NETHERFIELD ROAD NORTH
ST DOMINGO ROAD
BOUNDARY ST
SCOTLAND ROAD
A59
A580
A5089
A5050
BELMONT ROAD
Everton Park Sports Centre
Netherfield Family Hlth Clinic
The Beacon CE Primary School
Comprehensive School
Great Homer Street Medical Centre
St Anthony's Shopping Centre
Everton
HEYWORTH STREET
EVERTON ROAD
WEST DERBY ROAD
Whitefield JM&I Sch
Our Lady Catholic High School
Prince Edwin Adult Centre
Campion Catholic High School
Kingsway Industrial Park
Liverpool John Moores University
ST ANNE STREET
B5173
Boaler Street Industrial Est
New Park Primary Sch
Council Building
Kensington Medical Cen
KENSINGTON
A57
PRESCOT STREET
Royal Liverpool University Hospital
Sacred Heart RC Primary School
Kensington
Kensington CP J&I Schools
LONDON ROAD
Lime Street Station
PEMBROKE ROAD
University of Liverpool
Metropolitan Cathedral of Christ the King
Archbishop Blanch CE High School
EDGE LANE
A5047
WAVERTREE ROAD
Central Library
St George's Hall
Empire Thtr
Shopping Centre
MYRTLE ST
A5039
Philharmonic Hall
GROVE STREET
CROWN ST
133
Edge Hill
Edge Hill Station
Wavertree Retail Park
114
B5188
BROWNLOW HILL
MOUNT VERNON
IRVINE ST
NORTH VIEW
Police Stn
9
F
G
H
J
K
1
2
3
4
5
6
35
36
37
90
91
92
93

114
98
113
133
134
Clubmoor
Tuebrook
Fairfield
Old Swan
Newsham Park
Wavertree Park
TOWNSEND LANE
A580
ROCKY LANE
A5049
WEST DERBY ROAD
MILL BANK
WEST DERBY
A5058
A5049 MUIRHEAD AVENUE
B5189
GREEN LANE
PRESCOT ROAD
A57
EDGE LANE
A5047
A5080
B5188 SHEIL ROAD
HOLT ROAD
DURNING ROAD
A5089
B5178
PICTON ROAD
RATHBONE ROAD
B5179
ST OSWALD'S STREET
Newton Road
Dryden Road
Prospect Vale
Orphan Drive
Lister Drive
Gardner's Drive
Belmont Drive
Newsham Drive
Prescot Drive
Binns Road
Pighue Lane
Wavertree Boulevard
All Saints Junior School
Works
St Margarets Anfield CE Prim Sch
The Priory Medical Centre
Radnor Medical Cen
Police Station
Green Lane Medical Centre
Surgery
Cemetery
St Cecilias RC J&I School
Peter Lloyd Leisure Centre
Holly Lodge Girls College
Travel Inn
West Derby Comprehensive School
Roscoe Jn School
The Stables Business Centre
Lister Drive Infant School
Lister Drive Junior Sch
Council Building
Fairfield Medical Cen
Med Cen
St Cuthberts RC Primary School
St Annes CE Primary Sch
Derby Lane Medical Cen
Homoeopathic Medical Cen
Health Centre
St Oswalds Catholic Jr Sch
Hebrew Cem
University
Laurel Business Cen
Phoenix Primary School
St Sebastians Primary School
Edge Lane Retail Park
UGC Cinema
Virgin Cinemas
Hollywood Superbowl
Binns Road Industrial Estate
Wavertree Technology Park
Botanic Estate
Health Cen
Wavertree Retail Park
Edge Hill Station
Wavertree CC
Comm Prim Sch
Surgery
L13
1 grid square represents 500 metres

99
116
135
Fincham
Dovecot
Knotty Ash
Swanside
Broad Green
Court Hey
Eycroft
L14
M62
A57
A5058
A5080
Junction 4
EAST PRESCOT ROAD
PRESCOT ROAD
QUEENS DRIVE
STONEYCROFT
BROAD GREEN ROAD
EDGE LANE
BOWRING PK RD
BOWRING PARK ROAD
ROBY ROAD
St Marys West Derby Primary School
Deysbrook Med Cen
St Paschal Baylon RC Prim Sch
St Timothys RC J&I Sch
Golf Course
West Derby Golf Club
Cemetery
Surgery
Ernest Cookson Special School
Blackmoor Park Infant School
Leyfield Close
St Vincents School
St Edwards College (Secondary)
St Edwards Runnymede Junior School
Blackmoor Park Jnr Sch
Broughton Hall C High School Technology College
Cardinal Heenan Catholic High
Eaton Road Medical Centre
Sandfield Park Special School
Innkeeper's Lodge
Corinthian Primary Sch
Royal Liverpool Childrens Hospital (Alder Hey)
Police Station
Superstore
Knotty Ash Primary School
Dovecot Hlth Clinic
Works
Clifford Holroyde Centre of Expertise
Gresford Medical Centre
St Margaret Marys RC J&I School
Hebrew Cem
Broadgreen Community Comp School
Rocket Trading Cen
Broad Green Stn
Northway Primary School
National Wildflower Centre
Cricket Club
Valley Road Business Park
Trans Pennine Trail
Thomas Lane
Blackmoor Drive
Eaton Road
Alder Road
Honey's Green Lane
Pilch Lane
Thingwall Lane
Chelwood Avenue
Finch Lane
Princess Drive
Barnfield Drive
Melwood Drive
Whinmoor Road
Chatterton Rd
Warmington Road
Rennell Rd
Burnthwaite Rd
South Road
West Derby
Staplands Rd
Lingfield Gv
Seymour Rd
Malvern Av
Milton Avenue
Churchdown Road
Chedworth Road
Pilchbank Rd
Gordon Drive
Campbell Drive
Swanside Av
Coronation Dr
Kingsheath Av
Dunchurch Rd
Denford Rd
Ackers Rd
Woodford Rd
Prescot Road
Queens Dr (Wavertree)
Heywood Road
Orchard Av
Bentham Dr
Score Lane
Rocky Lane
Walsingham Rd
Thornton Road
Eastham Cl
Grangewood
40
41
42
90
91
92
93
F
G
H
J
K
1
2
3
4
5
6

116
100
115
135
136
A
B
C
D
E
1
2
3
4
5
6
342
93
92
91
390
44
Fincham
Woolfall Heath
Page Moss
HUYTON-WITH-ROBY
Roby
Huyton Park
Bowring Park
Junction 5
M62
M57
A57 LIVERPOOL ROAD
PRESCOT ROAD
A526 SETH POWELL WAY
STOCKBRIDGE LA
KNOWSLEY LANE
ROBY ROAD A5080
TARBOCK ROAD A5080
B5199 ARCHWAY ROAD
A5080
Brookside Primary School
St Edmund Of Canterbury High School
Blueberry Park CP School
St Dominics RC J&I Sch
St Brigids RC Primary School
Beechwood County Prim Sch
Longview J&I Sch
St Columbas RC Primary School
Cornerways Medical Centre
Council Building
Dinas Lane Medical Centre
Park View Primary School
St Aloysius RC Primary School
Twig Lane Clinc
Dovecot JMI Sch
Roby Park Prim Sch
Bowring Comprehensive School
Knowsley Community College
Huyton with Roby CE Prim Sch
Roby Medical Cen
Roby Station
Huyton Station
Premier Lodge
Bowring Park Golf Club
Golf Course
Blacklow Brow Prim Sch
St Annes RC Prim Sch
Oak Cottage Medical Cen
Lathom Road Health Cen
St Paschal Baylon RC Prim Sch
Princess Drive
Southdean Road
Wimborne Rd
St Davids Road
Melbury Road
Stockbridge Lane
Fairclough Road
Rosebank Road
Endmoor Road
Woolfall Heath Avenue
Huyton House Road
Stonefield Road
Winstone Rd
Aldwark Road
Dinas Lane
Western Avenue
Pagebank Rd
Moss Gate Rd
Beechburn Crs
Ashbourne Crs
Merton Crescent
Arnside Rd
Fairfield Avenue
Court Hey Avenue
Malvern Av
Crosswood Crs
Rupert Road
Larch Road
Church Road
Bridge Rd
Hawthorn Road
Kingsway
Alamein Road
Brookwood Road
Stanley Road
Lathom Road
Blacklow Brow
Bowring Park Avenue
Rimmer Av
Twickenham Drive
Acacia Avenue
Oak Road
Oulton Lane
Hillside Road
Wastle Bridge Rd
Primrose Drive
Nyland Road
Pennard Av
Altmoor Road
Bruton Rd
Hillside Crs
1 grid square represents 500 metres

101
Junction 2
M57
A58
PRESCOT
LIVERPOOL ROAD A57
WEST STREET
KEMBLE ST B5200
HIGH ST
ST HELENS ROAD
WARRINGTON ROAD
B5194
LIVERPOOL ROAD
B5199
HUYTON LANE
Longview
Huyton
Huyton Quarry
Whiston Cross
Whiston Lane Ends
Windy
Prescot AFC
Primary School
Police Station
Prescot Mus
Natural Hlth Clinic
Prescot Medical Cen
Park House Medical Cen
Council Building
Cemetery
Cables Retail Park
Prescot Station
Kings Bus Pk
Surgery
Alt Bridge Secondary Support Centre
Knowsley Central Primary Support Centre
Huyton & Prescot Golf Club
Golf Course
Works
St Mary & St Paul Prim Sch
Cedar Cross Medical Centre
Whiston Health Cen
Whiston Station
Halsnead Community Primary School
St Josephs RC Primary School
St Aidans RC Prim Sch
St Thomas Becket School
Mosscroft Prim Sch
Knowsley Hey School
St Gabriels CE Prim Sch
Wilson Bus Centre
St Agnes RC Primary School
Sylvester Primary School
Manor Farm Medical Cen
Interchange Motorway Industrial Est
Prince's House
Pottery Lane
Whiston Lane
Carr Lane
Manchester Rd
Central Avenue
South Avenue
Station Road
Hall La
Windy Arbor Road
Paradise Lane
Ashton Street
Link Rd
Stretton Wy
Fallows Wy
Seel Road
Wilson Road
Tarbock Road
118
137
F
G
H
J
K
1
2
3
4
5
6
45
46
47
390
391
392
393

118
102
117
137
138
A
B
C
D
E
1
2
3
4
5
6
Eccleston Park
Brown Edge
Nut Grov
Holt
Whiston
A58
Saint
St James' Road
St Helens Road
Warrington Road
A57 Warrington Road
B5200
B5201
B5204
B5413
Rainhill Road
Old Lane
Portico La
Delph Lane
Park Avenue
Central Av
Elm Grove
Albany Av
Hilary Close
Eccleston Lane Ends Primary Sch
Evelyn Prim Sch
West Close
Ingleholme Gdns
Orchard
East Cl
Surgery
Fairholme Av
Eccleston Park Station
Golf Course
Lloyd Rd
Haward
Marlborough
Hammett
Chapel Rd
Rowson St
Cross St
Grosvenor Rd
Columbia Rd
Albany Rd
Greenwood Cl
Hunter Court
Hawthorn Rd
Laurel Rd
Alder Road
Derwent Av
Rydal Av
Grasmere Av
Coniston Av
Alder Cl
Broom
Portico La
Prescot Primary School
Maryville Rd
Bretherton Rd
Oliver
Lyme Rd
St James' Rd
Sutherland Rd
Ashley Bus Cen
Scotchbarn Lane
Station Road
Sinclair
Grays Av
Vining Road
Mcvinnie Rd
Ford Road
Sundale Av
Chatel
Honeybourne Dr
Litchborough Grove
Watling Way
Two Butts Lane
Eccleston Park Golf Club
Wedgewood Gdns
Churchill Gdns
Aynsley Ct
Foxwood
Whitebeam Gdns
Silverlime Gdns
Wildcherry Gdns
Swisspine Gdns
Edge Street
Marlew Day Hospital
Nottingham Cl
Ellerslie Avenue
Brookfield Av
Field Wy
Gardeners Wy
Prescot Leisure Centre
BICC Athletic Club
St Edmund Arrowsmith RC Comprehensive Sch
Sinclair Av
Gilbert Road
Edward Rd
Time Pk
Fire Station Road
Sandstone
Gilleney Gv
Myers Av
Foster
Drive
Tarlton Cl
Croston Av
Amanda Road
Longton Lane
Sandhurst Road
St Winifred Rd
Longton Lane Community Primary School
Stapleton Road
Kg Edward Rd
Dorgan Cl
Francis
Stapleton Av
Elderswood Rd
Ellaby Rd
Ansdell Villas Rd
Roby Cl
Ritherup La
Vincent Rd
St Ann Pl
Warburton Hey
Park Av
Broadlands
Prescot Station
Bridge Road
Wy
Lovett Drive
Case Gv
Ogle Cl
Wyke Rd
Grove
Maple Gv
Poplar Gv
Willow
Beechwood
Rufford Ct
Windsor Rd
Cable Rd
Brook St
Cook St
Hayes Avenue
Lathum Cl
Ash
Kingsway
Gregson Rd
Fazakerley Rd
Mary & St Paul Prim
Bryer Rd
Shaw Lane
Brookside Cl
Youatt Av
St Lukes RC Primary School
Whiston Hospital
A&E
PO
Longview Road
Holt Lane
Council
Ruth Evans Court
Martin Av
Brancker Av
Norcliffe Rd
Batey Av
Millom Av
Chatsworth Road
Honiston Av
Horwood Av
Second Av
First Av
Ivy Farm Rd
Ratcliff Pl
Stoney Lane
Amb Stn
Works
Cartmel Dr
Kendal Drive
Warrington Rd
Higher Side Community Comprehensive Sch
Hulton Av
The Crs
Keats Av
Scott Av
Avenue
Walpole Av
Byron Av
Cumber Lane
Avenue
Saunders
Chestnut
Cedar
Birch Cl
Hazel Av
Dragon
Oak Road
Burns
Dryden
Milton
Weyman Av
Lunt
Willow Avenue
Harptree
Pinnington Rd
Whiston Station
Longton Medical Centre
Rainhill Station
Heskin Cl
Derwent
Weaver Av
Dee Road
Trent Cl
Severn Rd
Trent Road
Calder Drive
Stour
Ribble Av
Swale Av
St Anns CE Prim School
Commercial Business Cen
Victoria Terrace
Victoria Pl
Victoria T Estate
Station Rd
Surge
Priory The
Rainhill Clinic
Lowther Drive
Eden
Christophers
Marian Dr
Heyes Mt
Marian Cl
View Road
James
Owen Road
Saint
St James Mt
Ashton
Manor Av
The Mdw
Mill Lane
Hall Lane
Works
Blundells Hill Golf Club
Blundell's Lane
Lane
L35
Cronton Lane
Golf Course
Cemetery
Fox's Bank Lane
Driveway
Haslemere
Lyneham
Selborne
Kingsnorth
Dursley
Martock
Grovewood Gdns
Stanwood Gdns
Fellwood Gv
Copperwood Dr
Heywood Gdns
Manorwood Drive
Berrywood Dr
Parkwood Rd
St Leos RC Prim Sch
Southmead Prim Sch
Sherwood Dr
Lickers Lane
Halsnead Community Primary School
Dragon Lane
Langbar
Exeley
Skeffington
Domville
Rudgate
Pennywood Drive
Nelson Avenue
Raleigh Av
Beatty Cl
Windy Arbor Road
Prince's House
Main
Main Front
Orchard Cl
Old Orch
N Front
Lake Vw
East Front
S Front
Old Hall
Arbor
Whiston Lane
Tasker Ter
Hemmingsway
Kirkman
Kendricks Fold
Fairclough Rd
1 grid square represents 500 metres

Sutton Heath
Lea Green
Marshall's Cross
Rainhill
Rainhill Stoops
Sutton Manor
Elton Head Road
B5204
A570
Linkway
Saint Helens
Warrington Road
A57
Chester Lane
B5419
Marshalls Cross
A569
M62
Junction 7
Lea Green Station
Lea Green Business Park
Eurolink
Travel Inn
Micklehead Farm
Lowfield Industrial Estate
Lowfield Lane
Lea Green Road
Sherdley Park Golf Club
Sutton Community Leisure Centre Track
Sutton High Sports College
St John Vianney RC Primary School
Sutton Manor Community Primary School
Rainhill High Sch
St Bartholomews RC Primary School
Premier Lodge
Tower College
Nutgrove Methodist Prim Sch
St Theresas Prim Sch
Four Acre Lane Shop Cen
Chapel Lane
School Lane
Bell Lane
Mill Lane
Union Bank
Union Bank Farm
Works
103
120
139
50
51
52
90
91
92
93
F
G
H
J
K
1
2
3
4
5
6

120
104
119
139
140
Sutton
Sutton Leach
Clock Face
St Helens Junction Station
Station Road
Leonard St
Penlake Industrial Estate
Reginald Road Industrial Park
Reginald Road
Brindley Road
Bold Road
The Pastures
Marshalls Cross Road
Sutton Park Drive
Sandringham Dr
Sutton Cricket Club
Eaves Prim Sch
Eaves Lane
Sherdley Prim Sch
Mill Lane
Leach Lane
Belvedere Avenue
Hawthorne Rd
Wheatsheaf Avenue
Abbotsfield Road Industrial Park
Abbotsfield Road
Abbotsfield Farm
Woolacombe Avenue
Bideford Av
Porlock Av
Ilfracombe Rd
Taunton Avenue
Willow Tree Avenue
Willow Tree Primary School
Clock Face Road
A569
Lyon Industrial Estate
Crawford Cl
Gorsey Lane
Hall Lane
Home Farm
Clock Face Country Park
Four Acre Lane
Four Acre Lane Shop Cen
St Theresas Prim Sch
Gartons
Chester Lane
Farm Rd
Cranshaw Avenue
Abbots Hall Avenue
James Street
Lindsay St
Joy Lane
Bridge Road
M62
Finger House Lane
Bank Lane
Tibbs Cross Lane
Crow's Nest Farm
Union Bank Farm
A
B
C
D
E
1
2
3
4
5
6
1 grid square represents 500 metres

Clock Face 121
105
122
141
B5204
Bold Business Centre
Bold Industrial Park
Bold
Wheatacre Farm
Gorsey Lane
Nellis Road
Douglas Avenue
Rosehill Av
Celandine Wy
Columbine Wy
Orchid Wy
Peony Gdns
ERS' ENTRY
Lane
Phipps' Lane
Burtonwood Industrial Centre
St Paul of the Cross Catholic Primary School
Clay Lane
Chapel Lane
Jackson Street
Fairclough Street
Mercer St
Milnthorpe Road
Hawkshead Rd
Cemetery
Acton Rd
Haley Road North
Haley Road South
Mitchell Av
Kilshaw Road
Spurling Road
Perrins Road
Knight Rd
Almond Drive
Green Jones Brow
Weymouth Road
Sunning Drive
Aldridge Drive
Eastwood
Pinewood Rd
Cambourne Rd
Karen Close
Brookvale Cl
Fir Tree
Winsford Dr
Kinnock Pk
Burtonwood
St Helens
Warrington
Joy Lane Farm
Joy Lane
Limekiln Lane
Wright's Lane
Tan House
Junction 8
M62
Burtonwood
Orion Boulevard
Omega Bvd
Whittle Avenue
Matlo
Tunbridge Cl
Leamington Cl
Malvern Close
Lingley Green Av
Lonsda
Lingley Mere
F
G
H
J
K
I
2
3
4
5
6
55
56
57
90
91
92
93

122
106
121
141
142
A
B
C
D
E
1
2
3
4
5
6
Alder Lane
Hall Lane
Red House Farm
Alder Root Golf Club
Root Lane
Hollins
Watery Lane
Mill Lane
Eastwood Rd
Bakewell Road
Pinewood
Cambourne Rd
Karen Close
Brookvale
Fir Tree Lane
Farmer's Lane
Green Jones Brow
Knight Rd
Brook Head Farm
Tan House Lane
M62
Burtonwood Service Area
Welcome Lodge
Superstore
Gemini
Taurus Park
Europa Boulevard
Gemini Business Park
A574
Cromwell Avenue
Kingswood
Burtonwood Road
Falconers Green
Kingswood Road
Easter Court
Europa Bvd
Delta Crs
International Business Cen
Westbrook Crescent
Tourney Gn
Castle Green
Heralds Green
Kingswood Road
Coppice Green
Westbrook Way
St Philips Church Community School
Westbrook Medical Cen
Westbrook Crs
Westbrook Centre
Callands
Callands Road
Newbridge Cl
Penmark Close
Goldcliffe Cl
Welshpool Cl
Holyhead Cl
St Asaph Drive
Chepstow Cl
Ridgeborne Close
Newborough Cl
Cardigan Cl
Carmarthen Cl
Pendine Close
Barmouth Cl
St. Davids Drive
Kilford Cl
Wrexham Close
Gresford Close
Corwen Cl
Marcross Close
Candleston Close
Willoughby Cl
Raleigh Cl
Grant Close
Ladywood Rd
Purdy Cl
Beecroft Cl
Nares Close
Gulliver's World Theme Park
Sankey Valley Country Park
North Park Brook Road
Westbrook
Whittle Avenue
Ward Close
Blackshaw Dr
Barford Close
Garwood Close
Matlock
Harrogate Cl
Tunbridge Cl
Leamington Cl
Malvern Close
Burtonwood Road
Bristow Close
Bicknell Close
Skipton Close
Carter Cl
Twenty Acre
Morton Cl
Tasman Cl
A574 CROMWELL
Shackleton Close
Mawson Cl
Hudson Cl
Old Hall Primary School
Bewsey
Green Av
1 grid square represents 500 metres

Callands 123
107
124
143
F G H J K
1 2 3 4 5 6
60 61 62
93 92 91 90
Winwick
Green Lane
Old School House Lane
Hornby La
Myddleton Lane
Southworth
Hollins Lane
Lane
Winwick CE Primary School
Winwick Parish Leisure Centre
Premier Lodge
Maple Rd
Faringdon Road
Falcondale Road
Linkside Av
Arbury
Arbury Lane
WINWICK LINK
A49
A573
Austen Dr
Ballantyne Pl
Winwick Pk Av
Chesterton Dr
Warrington Community Health Care
Cemetery
Sheridan Pl
Beckett Dr
NEWTON RD
Junction 9
Delph Lane
M62
Peel Hall
Delph Lane
Midi Farm
Elm Road
Winwick Quay
WA2
Calver Road
Woburn Rd
Travel Inn
Birch Av
Cameron Ct
NEWTON ROAD
Mill Lane
Quay Business Cen
Poplars Av
Newhaven Road
Hastings Avenue
Poplars Avenue
Loweswater Close
Toll Bar Road
Cotswold Rd
Ulverston Av
Ennerdale Av
Cleveland Road
Petworth Avenue
Pentland Av
Cheviot Av
St Andrews CE Primary School
Windermere Av
Ullswater Av
Buttermere Av
Merewood Close
Linnet Cl
Grasmere
West Quay Road
Calver Rd
Fordton Leisure Centre
Hulme
Mendip Av
Sandy La W
St Stephen's Av
Sandy Lane
St Stephens Catholic Prim Sch
Borrowdale Av
Mardale Av
Bentham Av
Howson Road
Appleby Rd
Kirkstone Av
Keswick Av
Honister Av
Bowness Av
Poplars Avenue
Mallard Cl
Canberra Square
Meteor Crs
Greenwood Crs
Fairbrother Crs
WELL AVENUE
Alban Retail Park
A49 WINWICK ROAD
Winwick Road
Hunter Av
Crowe Avenue
Ajax Av
Mckee Av
Sinclair Av
Cooper Av
Locker Avenue
Patterdale Av
Statham Avenue
Sandy Lane
Northway
Small Crs
Small Av
Festival Av
Hughes Av
Festival Crs
Tenby Close
Rutter Av
Summerfield
Longshaw St
Dagnall Av
Conway Av
Marshall Avenue
Lewis Avenue
Council Building
Boulting Avenue
Dallam Community Prim Sch
Antrim Road
Service Centre
Gough Av
Marron Av
Densham Avenue
Council Building
Shakespeare Gv
Walpole Gv
Keats Gv
Burns Gv
Tennyson Dr
Dryden Pl
Infant School
Orford
Caldbeck Av
Poplars Av
Harding Av
Fisher Av
Long Lane County Primary School
Longford
Clive Avenue
Milvain Dr
Beatty Av
Marina Dr
School Rd
Capesthorne Road
Neville Av
Park Road
Warren Rd
Burton Rd
Brook Primary School
Martin Av
Boyle Avenue
Hawley's Lane
Eagle Pk Dr
Gale Avenue
Higham Av
Tavlin Av
Athlone Rd
Warrington Collegiate Institute
Winstanley Industrial Estate
LONG LANE A50
St Margarets CE Prim Sch
Longfield Road
Birtles Road
Bruce Av
Neville Av
Dallam
William Beamont Community School
Warrington Business Park
ORFORD GREEN
Malcolm Av
Works
Hallows
Tomlinson
Smith Crs
Drive
BIRCHWOOD WAY
A574
South Avenue
Molyneux Av
Longshaw St
Charter Av
Crosby Av
Hawthorne Business Park
Council Building
Kerfoot Business Park
Hawthorne
Grace Av
North Avenue
Lathom Av
Alder Lane
St Anns CE Primary School
Mortimer Av
Central Avenue
Alder Crs
Corbet
Ireland Street
Halfields
Ashbrook Crs
Smith
Withers Avenue
Brian Av
Stapleton Av
Venns Rd

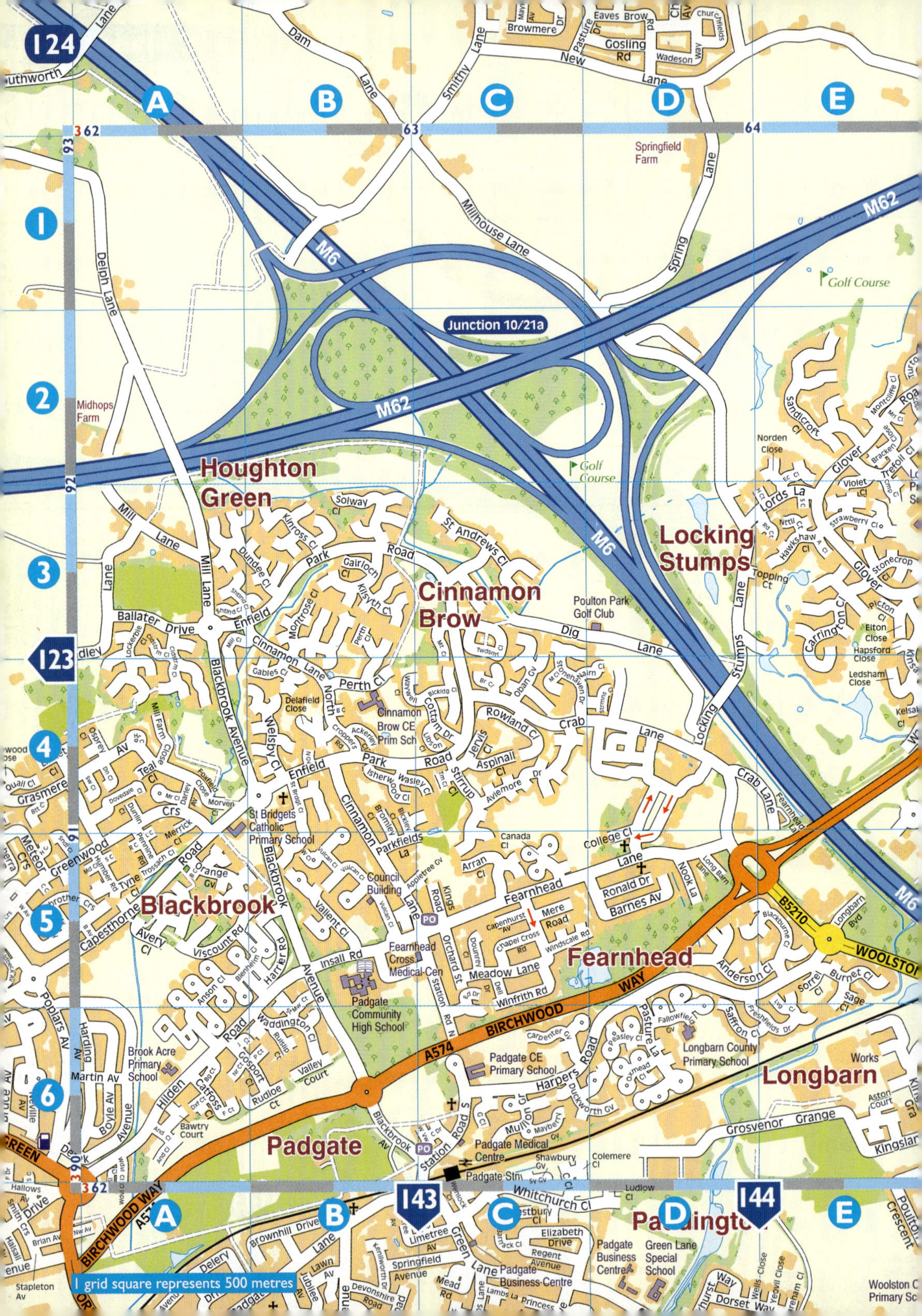
124
123
143
144
A
B
C
D
E
1
2
3
4
5
6
M6
M62
Junction 10/21a
Houghton Green
Cinnamon Brow
Locking Stumps
Blackbrook
Fearnhead
Padgate
Longbarn
Paddington
Midhops Farm
Springfield Farm
Golf Course
Poulton Park Golf Club
Cinnamon Brow CE Prim Sch
St Bridgets Catholic Primary School
Council Building
Fearnhead Cross Medical Cen
Padgate Community High School
Brook Acre Primary School
Padgate CE Primary School
Longbarn County Primary School
Padgate Medical Centre
Padgate Stn
Padgate Business Centre
Green Lane Special School
Padgate Business Centre
Works
A574
BIRCHWOOD WAY
B5210
Delph Lane
Mill Lane
Ballater Drive
Enfield Park Road
Cinnamon Lane
Blackbrook Avenue
Dig Lane
Crab Lane
Locking Stumps Lane
Fearnhead Lane
Insall Rd
Station Rd
Harpers Road
Grosvenor Grange
Whitchurch Cl
Millhouse Lane
Spring Lane
Smithy Lane
Dam Lane
New Lane
Glover Rd
Greenwood Crs
Poplars Av
Martin Av
Boyle Av
Harding Av
Hilden Rd
Blackbrook Av
Limetree Av
Springfield Avenue
Regent Avenue
Elizabeth Drive
Ludlow Cl
Colemere Cl
Woolston C Primary Sc
1 grid square represents 500 metres

Risley 125
Junction 11
M62
Silver Lane
Hey Farm
Cross Lane
Cross La S
WARRINGTON ROAD
Birchwood Golf Club
Kelvin
A574
Trident Industrial Est
Risley
Clayton Ct
Raglan
Melbury Ct
Road
Industrial Estate
Leacroft Road
Industrial Estate
Gorse Covert
Daten Av
Daten Avenue
Temple Ct
Heaton Court
Risley Rd
Daten Av
Kelburn Ct
Adlington Ct
Adlington Ct
Maxwell St
Reynolds Av
Kelvin Street
Griffith Av
Dewar St
Stokes St
Davy Av
Faraday St
Cavendish Avenue
Cavendish Pl
Joule Street
Ravenhurst Ct
Trinity Ct
BIRCHWOOD WAY A574
Warrington Rd
Dalton Rd
Chadwick Pl
Walton Rd
Wilson Lane
Thompson Street
Street
Newt Av
Astn Av
Dunscar
Havisham Av
BIRCHWOOD PARK
Heather Close
Garrett Fld
Nelson Rd
Barham Ct
Deleney Dr
Warrington Rd
Birchwood
Powell Av
Fern Cl
Armstrong Cl
Deanwater Close
Road
Ordnance Avenue
Moss Gate
Killingworth Lane
Dalby Close
Langwell Cl
Ashdown La
Gilderdale Cl
Ringwood Cl
Covert
Gorse Covert Rd
Fisherfield Drive
Bramshill Cl
Gorse Covert Prim Sch
PO
Aldewood Cl
Arden Cl
Hamsterley Cl
Falstone Cl
Darnaway Cl
Stanmore Cl
Woolmer Cl
Rd
Road
Rockingham Cl
Halelborough Close
Inglewood Cl
Risley Moss Nature Park
Keyes Cl
Admirals Road
Daniel Cl
Mansfield Cl
Redshank La
Pheasant Cl
Redshank La
Kingfisher Cl
Woodpecker Cl
Partridge Cl
Dunnock Gv
Dove Cl
Jay Cl
McCarthy Cl
Palliser Cl
Pennant Close
Ashmore Cl
Chaffinch Cl
Birchwood CE Prim Sch
PO
Whinchat Dr
Linnet Gv
Oakwood
Mallard La
Teal Gv
Admirals Rd
Halliday Cl
Oakwood Ga
Special School
Forbes Cl
Admirals Dr
Noble Cl
Chatfield Dr
Talbot Cl
Layton Cl
Curlew Gv
Pipit La
Road
Burrough Cl
Lyster Cl
Miles Cl
Rawlings Cl
Woodhouse Close
Dewhurst Road
Birchwood Community High School
Harcourt Cl
Leatham
Whitworth Cl
Ainscough Rd
Brock Rd
Benson Road
Birchwood Medical Cen
Birchwood One Business Park
PO
Birchwood Bvd
Dewhurst Road
Birchwood Station
Woolston Moss
Marshall's Farm
GRANGE AVENUE
Grange
Kingsland Gra
Hardwick Grange Works
M6
WOOLSTON GRANGE AVE
Nicol Av
Hollyhurst Lane
Long Barn Lane
Hardwick
Well Farm Cl
Brook
145
F G H J K
65 66 67
1 2 3 4 5 6
93 92 91 390

1 grid square represents 500 metres

HOYLAKE
Meols
CH47
Birkenhead Road
A553
Market Street
Meols Parade
Meols Drive
A540
Drummond Road
Carr Lane
Greenbank Road
Frankby Road
Hilbre View
Grange Rd
Manor Road Station
Hoylake Stn
Meols Station
Hoylake Cottage Hospital
Kingsmead School
Holy Trinity CE Primary School
Royal Liverpool Golf Club
Hoylake Golf Club
Golf Course
Great Meols Queen Elizabeth II Coronation Park
Police Station
Kings Gap Court Hotel
Lifeboat House
Carr Lane Industrial Estate
West Kirby Primary School
West Kirby Girls Grammar School
Black Horse Hill Junior School
Black Horse Hill Infant School
Hilbre High School
War Memorial
Cemetery
Fire Station
Health Cen & Swimming Pool
Brook House Business Centre
Corner House Clinic
Superstore
Hoylake Business Centre
Hoylake RFC
Industrial Estate
Works
108
128
146

128
108
127
147
Meols Station
Works
BIRKENHEAD ROAD
A553
HOYLAKE ROAD
Carr Farm
Saughall Massie
Heron Road
SAUGHALL MASSIE ROAD
WEST KIRBY RD
B5192
Oldfield Manor Farm
Three Lanes End
Oldfield Lane
Greasby
Greasby Brook
Pump Lane
FRANKBY ROAD
B5139
Larton
China Lane
Newton
Frankby
Lingham Primary School
Foxfield School
Surgery
Greasby Health Cen
Greasby Infant School
Our Lady of Pity
Barnacre Lane
Millhouse Lane
Carr Lane
Bermuda Road
Meadow Lane
Kingfisher Way
Birch Avenue
Elm Avenue
Beech Avenue
Oak Avenue
Lloyd Drive
Ferguson Avenue
The Nook
1 grid square represents 500 metres

Upton 129
109
110
130
148
Moreton
Upton
Noctorum
Arrowe Hill
Woodchurch
Junction 2
Junction 2a
M53
A553
A551
A5027
B5139
FENDER
Bidston Village
Fairmead Road
HOYLAKE ROAD
Sacred Heart RC Primary School
Pasture Road Health Centre
Police Stn
Moreton Medical Centre
Christ Church CE Primary School
Orrets Meadow School
UPTON ROAD
MORETON ROAD
UPTON BY-PASS
OLD GREASBY ROAD
GREASBY ROAD
ARROWE PK ROAD
ARROWE PARK ROAD
Hayfield School
Overchurch J&I School
Upton Hall FCJ School
St Josephs RC Primary School
Upton CC
Mount Haven Close
Surgery
Cemetery
Premier Lodge
Superstore
Police Station
Brookdale Primary School
Wirral Business Park
Arrowe Hill Primary School
Woodchurch CE Primary School
Fender Primary School
Woodchurch Leisure Centre
Woodchurch High School
St Pauls RC Primary School
Manor Primary School
Upton Station
St Peters RC Primary School
Hillside Primary School
Eleanor Road
Windermere Road
Beryl Road
Noctorum Av
Church Road
Ford Way
Big Meadow Road
Leeswood Road
Hey Road
Brook Road
Arrowe Road
Home Farm Road
New Hey Road
Grass Wood Road
Ganney's Meadow Road
Bridge Road
Hoole Road
Houghton Road
Woodland Road
Greenwood Road
Pemberton Road
Ferny Brow Rd
Westwood Road
Airdale Cl
Buttermere Avenue
Norwich Drive
Manor Drive
Upton Park Drive
Oakland Drive
Arborn Drive
Meadway
Ford Lane
Heath Drive
Shrewsbury Dr
Loretto Drive
Upland Road
Saughall Massie Lane
Royden Road
Gainsborough Road
Inman Road
Doncaster Drive
Caernarvon Close
Salacre Lane
Rake Lane
Greenacres Close
Chelford Close
Devisdale Grove
Beechwood Drive
Ravenstone Cl
Seaforth Dr
Cheshire Gv
Overchurch Road
Brookway
Greenway
Kirkway
Eastway
Cortsway
Dingwall Drive
Neale Drive
Appleton Dr
Brookdale Avenue South
F
G
H
J
K
I
2
3
4
5
6
26
27
28
87
88
89
90

130
110
129
149
Bidston
Bidston Hill
Claughton
Oxton
BIRKENHEAD
Birkenhead Park
Birkenhead North Station
West Float
Concrete Mixing Works
BEAUFORT ROAD A5030
CORPORATION RD
Corporation Road
HOYLAKE ROAD
A553
LAIRD STREET
PARK ROAD NORTH A5027
UPTON ROAD
A5027
BOUNDARY ROAD
B5151
BIDSTON ROAD
TALBOT ROAD
MILL HILL
INGESTRE ROAD
STORETON ROAD
WOODCHURCH ROAD
A552
M53
CH43
Holy Cross RC Prim School
Miriam Health Cen
Council Building
Pol Stn
Portland Primary School
Kilgarth School
Prim Sch
Cemetery
Bidston Avenue Primary School
Birkenhead Park RUFC
Cavendish Medical Centre
Park High Lower School
Claughton Medical Centre
North Clinic
Birkenhead Sixth Form College
Birkenhead Park CC
Park High Sports Col
Highfield School
Wirral Ladies Golf Club
Golf Course
St Anselms College
High School for Girls
Birkenhead High School
St Anselms Redcourt
Birkenhead Preparatory School
Birkenhead School
Hillside Primary School
Hanson Park
Ridgeway High School
Oxton CC
Bowler Hat Hotel
Riverhill Hotel
Prenton Preparatory School
Old Parkonians RFC
St Saviours CE Aided Primary School
Townfield Primary Sch
Woodchurch Leisure Centre
Woodchurch High School
Shopping Centre
Works
Surgery
1 grid square represents 500 metres

LIVERPOOL
111
112
132
150
Historic Warships
Twelve Quays Terminal
Pump Road
Corporation Road
Duke St
Cleveland Street
Price Street Business Centre
Cleveland Business Park
Tower Road
Tower Wharf
Morpeth Wharf
Morpeth Dock
Egerton Dock
Wirral Metropolitan College
Shore Road
Canning Street
Transport Museum
Woodside Business Park
Pacific Rd
Hamilton Square Stn
Queensway (Mersey Tunnel)
HM Customs Merseyside
Woodside Ferry Landing Stage
Woodside Ferry Approach
Conway Pk Stn
Conway Street
Conway St
Watson Street
Rendel Street
Exmouth Street
Argyle St
Hamilton St
Town Hall & Registry Office
Council Building
Wirral Mus
Wirral Borough Magistrates Court
Priory Wharf
Gilbrook School
Chester St
Birkenhead Co Ct
Pilgrim St
The Priory CE Primary School
Vittoria Medical Centre
Victoria St
Vue
Pyramids Shopping Ctr
The Grange Shopping Precinct
Grange Road West
Borough Road
Borough Rd
Tunnel Road
Birkenhead Museum
Birkenhead Priory
St Mary's
Birkenhead Central Station
Rock Retail Park
Mollington St
Unicorn Way
Works
Whetstone Lane
Whetstone Lane Health Cen
St Werburghs RC Primary Sch
Woodlands Primary School
Pearson Rd
Hinderton Road
Holt Hill
Green Lane Station
Campbeltown Road
Lairdside Technology Park
New Chester Road
Church Rd
Thompson St
Sidney Road
St Catherine's Hospital
Tranmere
Mersey Park
Mersey Park Prim Sch
Downham Rd
Borough Road
Singleton Avenue
Glenda Jackson Thtr
Fountain Street
Whitford Road
Elmswood Road
Harrowby Road
Maybank Rd
Victoria Fields
Expressway Business Park
Ferries Industrial Estate
Oil Terminal
Rock Ferry Primary Sch
Rock Ferry
Tranmere Rovers FC (Prenton Park)
Prenton Rd East
Devonshire Park Primary School
Bebington Road
Old Chester Road
Bedford Rd
Cole Street Primary School
Little Theatre
Park Road East
Cleveland
CH41

132
112
131
151
Titanic Memorial
Cunard Building
Mersey Ferries
War Memorial
Museum of Liverpool Life
HM Customs & Excise Nat Museum
Merseyside Maritime Museum
Fingerprints of Elvis
Tate Gallery
Albert Dock Village
The Beatles Story
Albert Dock
Express by Holiday Inn
Premier Lodge
Wapping Basin
Granada TV
Merseyside Police HQ
National Discovery Park
Fire Stn
Cavern Club
Police Station
Central Stn
Shopping Centre
BBC Radio
James Street Stn
Queen Elizabeth II Law Courts
Brownlow
Metropolitan Cathedral of Christ the King
Primary School
Philharmonic Hall
Community College
Natural Hlth Cen
Health Cen
Chinese Arch
Liverpool Anglican Cathedral
Kings Dock
Waterfront Business Area
Parliament St N'Waterfront Bus Area
Campanile Hotel
Queens Dock Business Centre
VAT House & HM Customs & Excise
Queens Dock
Liverpool Marina
Hill Street Business Centre
Navigation Wharf
Quebec Quay
Coburg Wharf
Small Business Centre
Brunswick Business Park
Brunswick Station
Travelodge
Toxteth
Primary School
Council Building
Ambulance Station
Hill Street Bus Cen
Toxteth Sports Centre
Park Rd Sports Cen
Beaufort Park County Prim Sch
Grain Industrial Estate
Our Lady Mount Ca RC Prim S
STRAND ST
WAPPING A562
PARK LANE
A561 ST JAMES ST
A5038 GT GEORGE ST
A5038 RENSHAW ST
BERRY ST
LEECE ST
MYRTLE ST
A5039
PARLIAMENT ST A562
UPPER PARLIAMENT
PRINCES RD
PARK PLACE A561
PARK RD
A5036
SEFTON STREET
CHALONER ST
CANNING PL
PRICE ST
Hill Street
Warwick Street
Northumberland Street
Park St
Caryl Street
Grafton St
Atlantic Way
Harrington Rd
Columbus Quay
Riverside Drive
Elleman Road
Cockburn Street
The Sloyne
Liverpool
Wirral
Works
Rock Ferry
A
B
C
D
E
1
2
3
4
5
6
90
89
88
3 87
3 34
35
1 grid square represents 500 metres

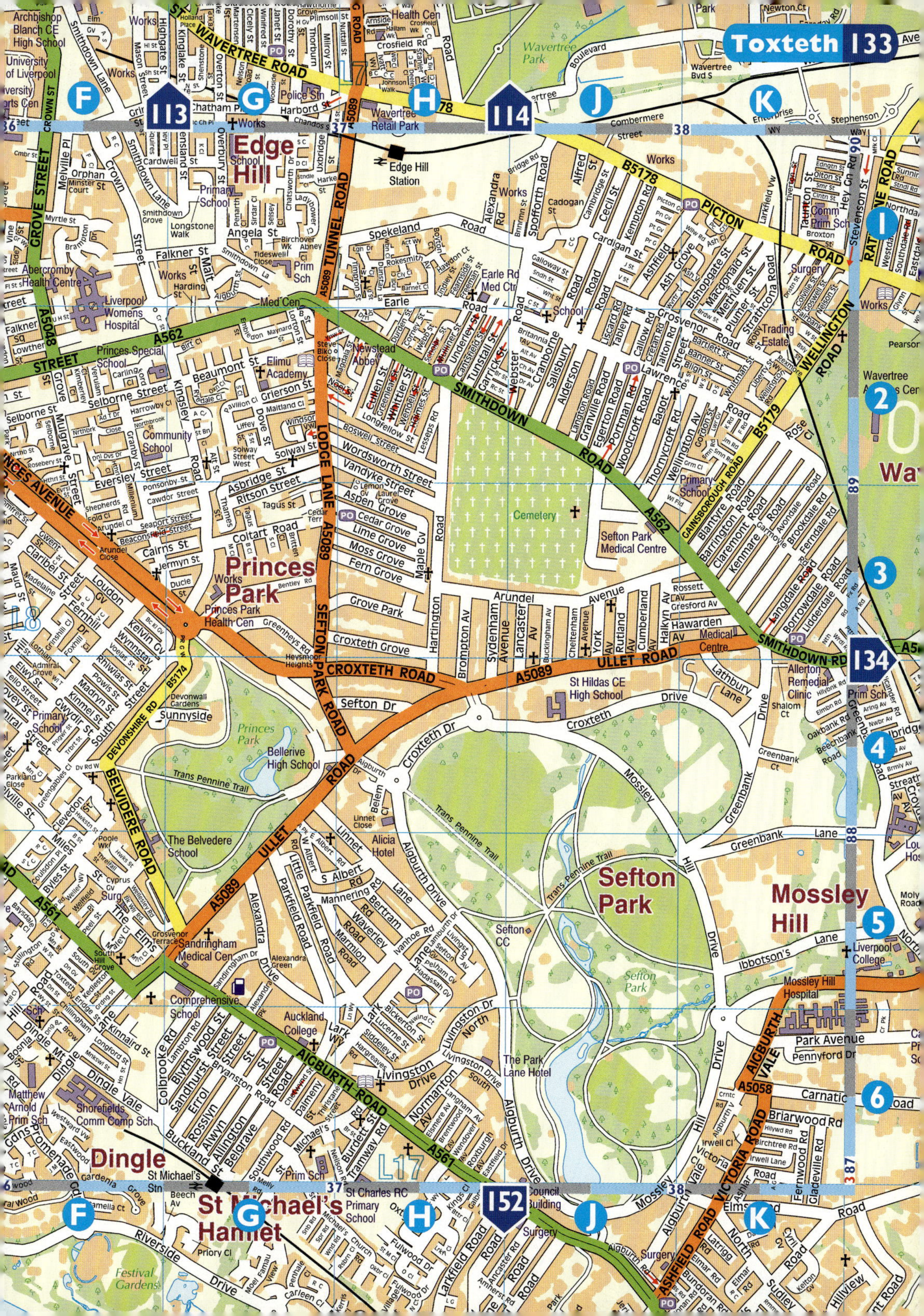

Toxteth 133
113
114
134
152
F
G
H
J
K
1
2
3
4
5
6
37
38
Edge Hill
Edge Hill Station
Wavertree Retail Park
Wavertree Park
Wavertree Road
Tunnel Road
Picton Road
Smithdown Road
Wellington Road
Lodge Lane A5089
Sefton Park Road
Princes Park
Princes Avenue
Croxteth Road
Ullet Road
Cemetery
Sefton Park Medical Centre
St Hildas CE High School
Belvidere Road
Devonshire Rd
Bellerive High School
The Belvedere School
Sefton Park
Mossley Hill
Mossley Hill Hospital
Aigburth Road
Aigburth Vale
Aigburth Drive
Aigburth Road
Victoria Road
Liverpool College
Greenbank Lane
Park Avenue
Carnatic Road
Dingle
Dingle Vale
St Michael's Hamlet
St Michael's Stn
Festival Gardens
Riverside Drive
Liverpool Womens Hospital
Abercromby Health Centre
Archbishop Blanch CE High School
University of Liverpool
Crown Street
Grove Street
Upper Parliament Street
Trans Pennine Trail
Sandringham Medical Cen
Comprehensive School
Auckland College
Shorefields Comm Comp Sch
The Park Lane Hotel
Alicia Hotel
Sefton CC
Council Building
St Charles RC Primary School
Livingston Drive
Mossley Hill Drive
Ibbotson's Lane
Newstead Abbey
Elmu Academy
Earle Rd Med Ctr
Allerton Remedial Clinic
Sunnyside
Smithdown Lane
Cemetery
L7
L8
L17

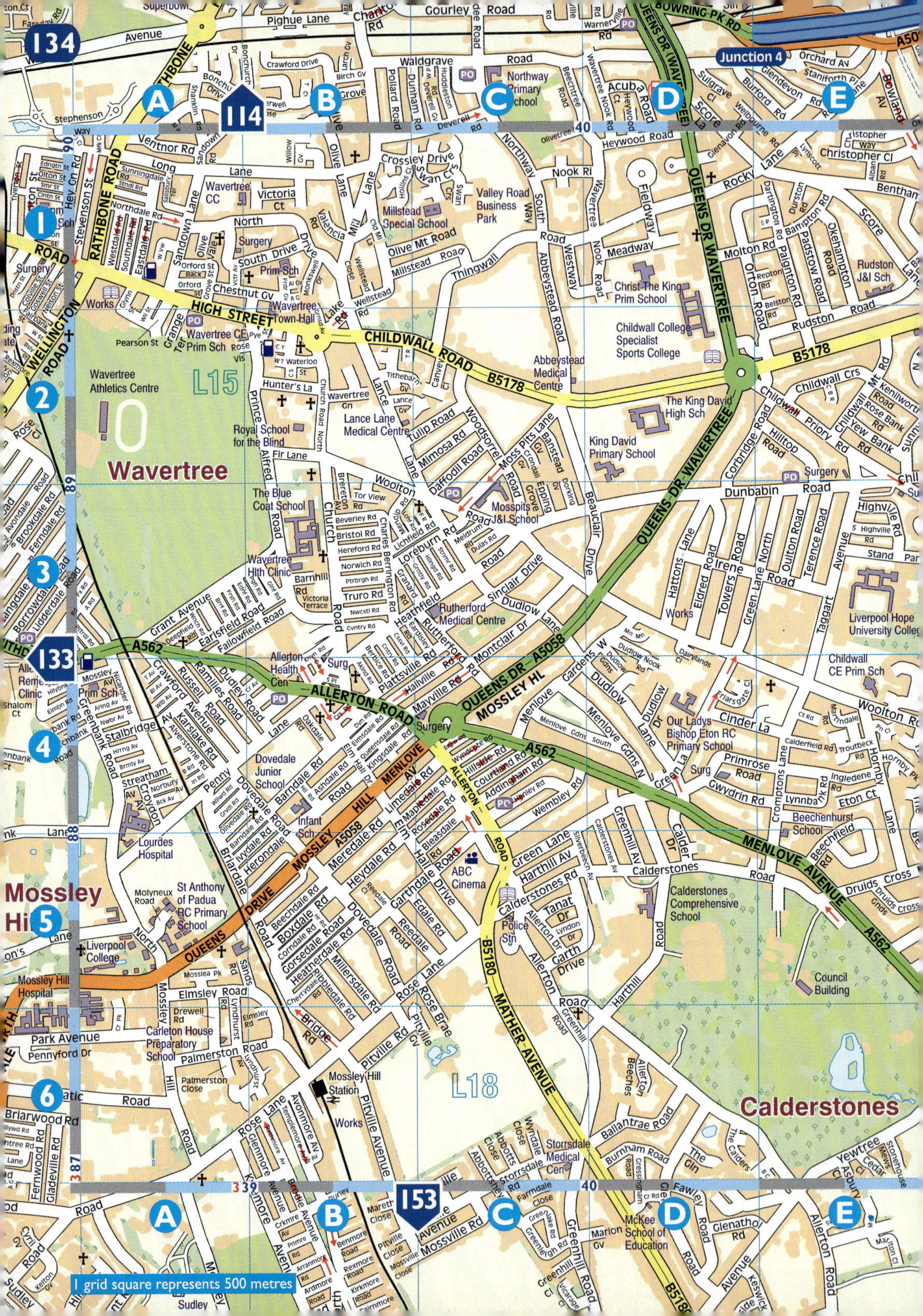

134
114
133
153
A
B
C
D
E
1
2
3
4
5
6
Junction 4
40
39
89
88
87
90
Wavertree
Mossley Hill
Calderstones
L15
L18
Pighue Lane
Gourley Road
Bowring Pk Rd
Waldgrave Road
Northway Primary School
Rathbone Road
Stephenson Way
Ventnor Rd
Long Lane
Heywood Road
Queens Dr Wavertree
Christopher Cl
Rocky Lane
Benthams
Wavertree CC
Victoria Ct
Crossley Drive
Swan Cr's
Valley Road Business Park
Millstead Special School
Olive Mt Road
Millstead Road
Nook Rd
Meadway
Wellington Road
High Street
Wavertree Town Hall
Childwall Road
B5178
Surgery
Prim Sch
Chestnut Gv
Thingwall
Christ The King Prim School
Childwall College Specialist Sports College
Rudston Road
Rudston J&I Sch
Molton Rd
Wavertree CE Prim Sch
Wavertree Athletics Centre
Abbeystead Medical Centre
Abbeystead Road
The King David High Sch
King David Primary School
Childwall Crs
Childwall Priory Rd
Hunter's La
Lance Lane Medical Centre
Royal School for the Blind
Fir Lane
Tulip Road
Mimosa Rd
Daffodil Road
Woodsorrel Road
Moss Pits Lane
Mosspits J&I School
Beauclair Drive
Dunbabin Road
The Blue Coat School
Church Road
Wavertree Hlth Clinic
Rutherford Medical Centre
Dudlow Lane
Sinclair Drive
Liverpool Hope University College
Childwall CE Prim Sch
Woolton Rd
Grant Avenue
Earlsfield Road
Fallowfield Road
A562
Allerton Health Cen
Allerton Road
Queens Dr
Mossley Hl
A5058
Menlove Gardens W
Our Ladys Bishop Eton RC Primary School
Cinder La
Primrose Road
Gwydrin Rd
Eton Ct
Beechenhurst School
Menlove Avenue
Mossley Prim Sch
Stalbridge
Crawford Avenue
Russell Road
Dovedale Junior School
Infant Sch
Menlove Av
Mossley Hill
Allerton Road
Surgery
Wembley Rd
Green Lane
Harthill Av
Calderstones Road
Calderstones Comprehensive School
Druids Cross
Lourdes Hospital
St Anthony of Padua RC Primary School
Liverpool College
Mossley Hill Hospital
Queens Drive
Dovedale Road
Heydale Rd
Garthdale Road
ABC Cinema
Police Stn
B5180
Mather Avenue
Council Building
Elmsley Road
Park Avenue
Pennyford Dr
Carleton House Preparatory School
Palmerston Road
Palmerston Close
Mossley Hill Station
Works
Pitville Avenue
Rose Lane
Booker Avenue
Storrsdale Medical Cen
Ballantrae Road
Burnham Road
Fawley Road
McKee School of Education
Briarwood Rd
Mossville Rd
Greenhill Road
Allerton Road
Sudley
1 grid square represents 500 metres

Court Hey
Bowring Park
Childwall
Belle Vale
Gateacre
Junction 5
Golf Course
BOWRING PARK ROAD
CHILDWALL VALLEY ROAD
B5178
B5171
GATEACRE BROW
ACREFIELD ROAD
BELLE VALE ROAD
MENLOVE AVENUE
A562
SPEKE RD
L16
115
116
136
154
F
G
H
J
K
1
2
3
4
5
6
42
43
National Wildflower Centre
St Paschal Baylon RC Prim Sch
Craighurst JM&I School
Our Lady of the Assumption Primary School
Belle Vale Health Centre
Belle Vale Swimming Pool
Belle Vale Shopping Centre
Police Station
Belle Vale JMI School
Gateacre Comprehensive School
Garden Centre
St Francis Xavier RC Coll
Abbots Lea Special School
Lower Lee Special Sch
Palmerston Special Sch
Harold Magnay Special Sch
Newborough School
Woolton J&I School
Bishop Martin CE Prim Sch
Picture House
Village Medical Cen
Watergate Special Sch
Lakeside School
Lee Park Golf Club
Mount Park Court
Trans Pennine Trail
Liverpool Loop Line
Woolton Road
Woolton Hill Road
Childwall Abbey Rd
Gateacre Park Drive
Hunts Cross Avenue
Halewood Road
Edenhurst Avenue
Walsingham Road
Chelwood Avenue
Barnham Drive
Score Lane
Quickswood Drive
Childwall Lane
Wallgate Road
Hartsbourne Avenue
Cranwell Road
Shrewton Road
Dorchester Park
Naylorsfield Drive
Lee Hall Drive
Kings Drive
Linkstor

136
116
135
155
A
B
C
D
E
1
2
3
4
5
6
Whitefield Lane End
Netherley
L27
M62
TARBOCK ROAD
A5080
CRONTON ROAD
NETHERLEY ROAD
B5178
CALDWAY DRIVE
Blacklow Brow Prim Sch
St Annes RC
Sylvester Primary School
Manor Farm Medical Cen
Oak Cottage Medical Cen
Interchange Motorway Industrial Est
Works
Lakeside School
Wheathill Farm
Hope School
The Childwall Golf Club
Golf Course
Wheathill Industrial Estate
St Gregorys RC JM&I Sch
Netherley Health Cen
Norman Pannell JM&I Sch
Netherley Sports Centre
Lee Park Golf Club
Cross Farm Primary School
Green's Bridge Farm
Liverpool
Knowsley
Naylor's Road
Wheat Hill Rd
Holt Lane
Coney Lane
Whitefield Lane
Knowsley Lane
Wood Lane
North End La
Foxhill Lane
Lydiate Lane
Greensbridge Lane
Acacia
Oak Rd
Laburnum Av
Rowan Gv
Lilac Gv
Cypress Rd
Yew Tree Rd
Willow Av
Oulton Lane
Twickenham Drive
Tennyson Rd
Logwood Rd
Manley Rd
Cringles Drive
Richmond Way
Mellor Cl
Smithford Wk
Winster Drive
Tothale Turn
Lee Hall Rd
Lulworth Rd
Cadnam Rd
Edenhall Drive
Banbury Av
Ribble Rd
Netherley Police Station
1 grid square represents 500 metres

Netherley 137
117
118
138
156
F
G
H
J
K
1
2
3
4
5
6
46
47
48
90
89
88
87
Mitre Cl
St Nicholas Rd
Windy Arbor
Foxs
Works
Windy Arbor Close
House
Main
Main Front
Orchard Cl
Old Orch
Lake Vw
Old Hall
S Front
Fox's Bank
Simons Cl
Windy Arbor Road
Windy Arbor
M57
M62
A5300
Junction 6/1
St Helens
Knowsley
Entry
Higher Shaw Farm
Shaw
Cronton
Dacre's Bridge Lane
A5080
CRONTON ROAD
Fox's Bank Lane
Penny Lane
Ox Lane
KNOWSLEY EXPRESSWAY
Works
Prescot Road
Lane
Tarbock Hall Farm
Water Lane Farm
Water Lane
Alder Lane
Tarbock Green
Works
NETHERLEY ROAD
B5178
Stockswell Road
Cross Hillocks Lane
Northern La
Brookdale
Cherry
Surgery
Bechers
St Basil RC Primary School
Brandon
Hough Green Rd
Avon
Aire
Alt
Arley
Arden
Lancaster Avenue
Cross Hillocks Farm
Lane

138
118
137
157
A
B
C
D
E
1
2
3
4
5
6
50
90
89
88
87
349
M62
Junction 7
A570
A557
WATKINS
WARRING
A5080
CRONTON RD
A5080 CRONTON LANE
Town End
Cronton
Upton Rocks
St Helens
Knowsley
Crontoc Lane
Hall Lane
Hall La
Mill Lane
Jackson Cl
Lincoln Way
Tower College
Premier Lodge
St Bartholomews RC Primary School
Caxton Road
Thorndyke Close
Norland's La
Loyola Hey
Norland's Lane
Norland Lane
Norland's Lane
Nicholford Hall Drive
Penny Lane
Tue Lane
The Ridgeway
Brook Cl
Cronton CE Primary School
Holy Family RC Primary School
The Rbt
Hall Lane
Mill Lane
Iver Cl
Hampton Dr
Woburn Dr
Lambourn Av
Kenley Av
Smithy Lane
Smithy Forge Cl
Wheatfield Road
Houghton Ct
PO
Chapel Lane
Hillcrest Hotel
Widnes & Runcorn 6th Form College
Stratton Park
Cowanway
Hill View
Tynwald Crs
Chetwood Dr
Upton Lane
Julian Way
Linden Wy
Tuson
Inghan Rd
Bembridge Cl
Upton Br
Lodge Lane
Sandy Lane
Upton Lane
Whitstable Pk
Rock La
Telford Cl
Chilwell Cl
Old Upton La
Kennington Park
Cleedon Wy
Upton Grange
Preece Cl
Upton Gra
Meadow
Rock Lane
Cornerhouse La
Bridgend Cl
Redbourne Dr
Chedworth Dr
Columbine Cl
Oxton
Cherrysutton
Darley Cl
Haddon Dr
Burnsall Dr
Lea Cross Gv
Aylsham Cl
Croston
Clanfield Av
Mortlake
Porthcawl Cl
Astley Cl
Blair Dr
Tiverton Cl
Ravenfield Dr
Parklands
Ash Priors
Prescot Road
All-Saints Upton Prim Sch
Surgery
Becher's
Danescroft
Downside
Dunsford
Deepdale
Simonside
Whernside
Blackbrook
Rainbow Cl
Great Ashfield
Heathfield Pk
Queensbury Wy
Northern La
Brookdale
Upton Medical Centre
Basil Primary School
Rushton Cl
Galloway
Campsey Ash
Lofthouse Ga
Higher Ashton
Lessingham Rd
Whickham
Marcien Wy
Belgravia Ct
Dinnington Ct
Holborn Ct
Wallsend Ct
Cornforth Wy
Hough Green Rd
Brandon
Avon
Aire
Alt
Edendale
Arley Dr
Foxcote
Fulbeck
Arley Dr
Atterbury Cl
Arkenstone Cl
Dunston Cl
Poleacre Dr
Rockfield Cl
Prescot
Crs
Lynton
Tabley Ave
St Peter & St Paul RC High School
WA8
1 grid square represents 500 metres

M62
Finger House Lane
Union Bank Lane
Union Bank Farm
Tibbs Cross Lane
A569
119
120
F
G
H
J
K
52
53
90
B5419
JUBITS LANE
Old Brook Hall
A57
Wilmere House
WARRINGTON ROAD
Bridge Farm
Halton
St Helens
CLOCK FACE RD
School La
Bold Heath
Ferndale Close
WILMERE LANE
A557
WATKINSON WAY
Twyford Lane
Mill Lane
89
Cranshaw Lane
140
LUNTS HEATH ROAD
Mill Green Farm
Mill Green Lane
Bold Industrial Est
Lunts Heath
Baileys Cl
Hartland Cl
Farndale
Gleneagles Dr
Churchfields
Birkdale Road
Minton Wy
Wenger Rd
Glebe Lane
Lunts Heath Primary School
Coroner's Lane
Twyford Cl
Tuscan Cl
Finsbury Pk
Eastbury Cl
Wilcote Cl
Garrigill Cl
South Lane
88
B5419
BIRCHFIELD ROAD
Buckingham Av
Holyrood Av
Clarence Avenue
Farnworth CE Primary School
Wedgwood Dr
Ryder Rd
Ganton Cl
Grosvenor Rd
Trent Cl
Mill La
DERBY ROAD A5080
Barrow's Green
St Luke's Crs
Marsh Hall Road
Claremont Dr
Derby Road
Moorfield Road
Camberwell Pk Rd
Cedardale Pk
Path
Pit Lane
Windsor Rd
Balmoral Road
Beaconsfield Crs
Beaconsfield Road
Mason Av
Widnes Cricket Club
Farnworth Street
Windermere St
Works
Greenwich Av
Kn Cl
Whalley Gv
Dykin Close
Lane
Daffodil Cl
Snowberry Cl
Weates Cl
Ribble Cl
Crossgates
Farnworth
Wellfield
Derby Road
Factory La
Moorfield Primary School
School Wy
Nursery Cl
Dykin Road
Green
Ramsey Cl
Close
Humber Cl
6
Borough Cemetery
Gloucester Rd
Lancaster Road
Alder Rd
Birch Rd
Acacia Av
Avenue
Peel House
Fairfield High School
Bishops Way
Hilary Cl
Chorley's La
Guernsey Rd
Orkney Cl
Skye Cl
Barneston Rd
Calder Cl
Severn Cl
Widnes Station
Victoria Av
Lockett Road
Cedar Av
Cypress Av
Lytham Rd
St Anne's Rd
Fairhaven Rd
Kirkham Rd
WAY
158
Bancroft Rd
Crow Wood La
Moorfield Road
Barrow's Lane
Romney
Kilsby Dr
Weates Cl
Shell Green
387
Wade Deacon County High Sch
Rose View Av
Elm Av
Chestnut Av
Lilac Av
Willow Av
Appleton
Ansdell Road
Neil St
Fairfield
Ireland St
Barnes
Crow Wood
Rossall Rd
Belmont Rd
Fieldway
Brookfield School
DANS ROAD A562
1
2
3
4
5

140
120
139
159
A
B
C
D
E
1
2
3
4
5
6
55
54
87
88
89
90
Bold Heath
Lingley Mere
Lingley Green
Penketh
Doe Green
Cuerdley Cross
Shell Green
Whittle Brook
A569
CLOCK FACE RD
A57
Dawson House
Sandy Lane
Laburnum Lane
Sandy Lane Farm
South Lane Farm
South Lane
St Helens
Warrington
SOUTH LANE
A5080
FARNWORTH ROAD
WIDNES ROAD
A562
Mowcroft Lane
Back Lane
Cuerdley Green
Wrights Lane
Tannery Lane
Cuerdley Road
Beech Av
Newlyn Gdns
Penrose Gdns
Rothay Dr
Roeburn Wy
The Park
Farnworth Rd
Haslemere Drive
Stocks Lane
Penketh Primary School
Liverpool Road
Edward Road
Henderson Cl
Friends Lane
Lingley Green Avenue
Lingley Green Av
Lingley Road
Fraser Road
Pyecroft Rd
Pyecroft Cl
Audre Cl
Muriel Cl
Hilary Cl
Paul Cl
Kintore
Mayfair Cl
Shanklin Cl
Bembridge Cl
Foreland Cl
Shorwell Cl
Park Road
Godshill Cl
Whitwell
Freshwater Cl
Snowberry Cl
Ribble Cl
Crossgates
Humber Cl
Close
Eltham Cl
Avebury Cl
Coulton Rd
Severn Cl
Calder Cl
Douglas Cl
Skye Cl
1 grid square represents 500 metres

Penketh 141
121
122
142
160
F
G
H
J
K
F
G
H
J
K
1
2
3
4
5
6
57
58
57
58
90
89
88
387
Westbrook
Great Sankey
Hood Manor
Sankey Bridges
WA5
RAF Burtonwood
Orion Boulevard
Westbrook Way
Omega Blvd
Lingley Green Av
Lingley Mere Business Park
Sankey Medical Centre
Great Sankey County High Sch
Barrow Hall County Prim Sch
Whittle Brook
Whittle Avenue
Burtonwood Road
Matlock Close
Malvern Close
Bicknell Close
Shipton Close
Garwood Close
Vincent Close
Twenty Acre Road
A574 CROMWELL AV
Old Hall Primary School
Boston Boulevard
Washington Drive
Gregory Cl
Kingsdale Road
Mossdale Cl
Swaledale Cl
Park Road
Vine Crescent
Halton Rd
Wilmot Av
Whittle Hall Lane
Alderbank Road
Belmont Crs
Cromdale Way Community Hall & Health Centre
Park Road Primary School
Thetford Road
Norfolk Drive
Yarmouth Rd
Campbell Crs
Sankey for Penketh Station
Station Road
LIVERPOOL ROAD
Elmsett Cl
Farmleigh Gdns
Hood Lane North
Sycamore Lane
Tankersley Grove
Mapplewell Crs
Sgt York Loop
Bradley Bvd
Molly Pitcher Way
Sankey Valley St James CE Primary School
Hood Manor Medical Centre
Dorchester Road
Winchester Av
Sycamore Lane Community Primary
Hood Lane
Warrington New Cricket Club
SANKEY WAY A57
SANKEY WAY
A574
Friars Avenue
St Josephs Catholic Primary
Windmill Lane
St Stephen Rd
St Mary's Road
Penketh County High School
Great Sankey Prim Sch
Ealing Rd
Liverpool Road
Heath Road
Penketh Swimming Baths
Penketh Health Clinic
Greystone Road
Birkdale Rd
Coronation Dr
PENKETH ROAD
A562
WARRINGTON ROAD
Eagle Sports Club
Rozel Crs
Marina Avenue
Buckingham Drive
Ridley Drive
Malpas Drive
Liverpool Road
Penketh Business Park
Sankey Bridge Industrial Est
Mersey Way
St Helens Canal (disused)
Trans Pennine Trail
Surgery
Ash Road
Maple Crs
Grange Drive
Clifford Road
Manston Road
Hamble Dr
Chapel Rd
Well Lane
St Austel Close
Penketh South Community Primary School
St Vincents Catholic Primary School
Ditchfield Rd
Falmouth Dr
Shaftesbury Av
LC

142
122
141
161
Gulliver's World Theme Park
Dallam
Bewsey
New Hall
Old Hall Primary School
Hawthorne Business Park
Council Building
Kerfoot Business Park
Record Business Park
Warrington Collegiate Institute
Winstanley Industrial Estate
Bewsey Lodge Primary School
Bewsey Business Centre
Bewsey Industrial Estate
Warrington Hospital
A&E
Guardian Street Industrial Estate
Guardian Medical Centre
Warrington Wolves RLFC (Halliwell Jones Stadium)
Warrington Central Trading Estate
Health Centre
Retail Park
Warrington Central Station
Cockhedge Centre
Warrington Bus Cen
Hood Manor
St Gregorys RC High School
Sankey Valley Park
Warrington New Town Cricket Club
Sacred Heart RC Primary Sch
St Barnabas CE Prim Sch
Priestley Business Cen
Postal Delivery Office
Cncl Bldg
Law Courts
Town Hall
Shopping Centre
Palace Theatre
YMCA
Sankey Bridges
Sankey Bridge Industrial Est
Evelyn Street Prim Sch
Gateworth Ind Estate
River Mersey
Warrington Bank Quay Station
Bank Quay Trading Estate
Superstore
Travel Inn
Latchford CE Primary School
Causeway Medical Centre
St Werburgh CE Primary School
A574 Cromwell Avenue
Sankey Way
A57
Liverpool Road A5061
Froghall Lane
Midland Way
Tanners Lane B5210
Wilson Patten Street
Winwick Road
Longford Street
Orford Lane
Lythgoes Lane
Folly Lane
Parker St
Crosfield Street
Chester Road
Knutsford
Wilderspool Causeway
A49
1 grid square represents 500 metres

LONG LANE
A50
ORFORD GREEN
Padgate
Padgate Stn
BIRCHWOOD WAY
A574
ORFORD ROAD
Bruche
Bruche Community Primary School
Padgate Business Centre
Paddington House Hotel
MANCHESTER ROAD
A57
NEW MANCHESTER ROAD
KING EDWARD ST
PADGATE LANE
MARSH HOUSE LANE
KINGSWAY NORTH
Cemetery
Surgery
Clinic
Council Building
St Elphins Park
SCHOOL BROW
Superstore
Church Street
Farrell Street
Howley Quay Industrial Estate
Howley Lane
River Mersey
Howley
WARRINGTON
Westy
Cardinal Newman RC High School
Victoria Park Arena
Victoria Park
Riverside Retail Park
Parkdale Industrial Estate
A5061
KNUTSFORD ROAD
THELWALL LANE
KINGSWAY SOUTH
Manor Industrial Estate
Alderman Bolton Com School
Latchford Medical Centre
Sir Thomas Boteler High School
Garden Centre
Our Lady RC Primary School
Palatine Industrial Estate
Priestley Sixth Form College
Latchford
WILDERSPOOL CAUSEWAY
Loushers Lane Special School
Warrington Town AFC
ACKERS ROAD
B5156
Station Road Industrial Estate
Fir Grove Hotel
A50
123
124
144
162
F
G
H
J
K
1
2
3
4
5
6
61
62
63
87
88
89
90

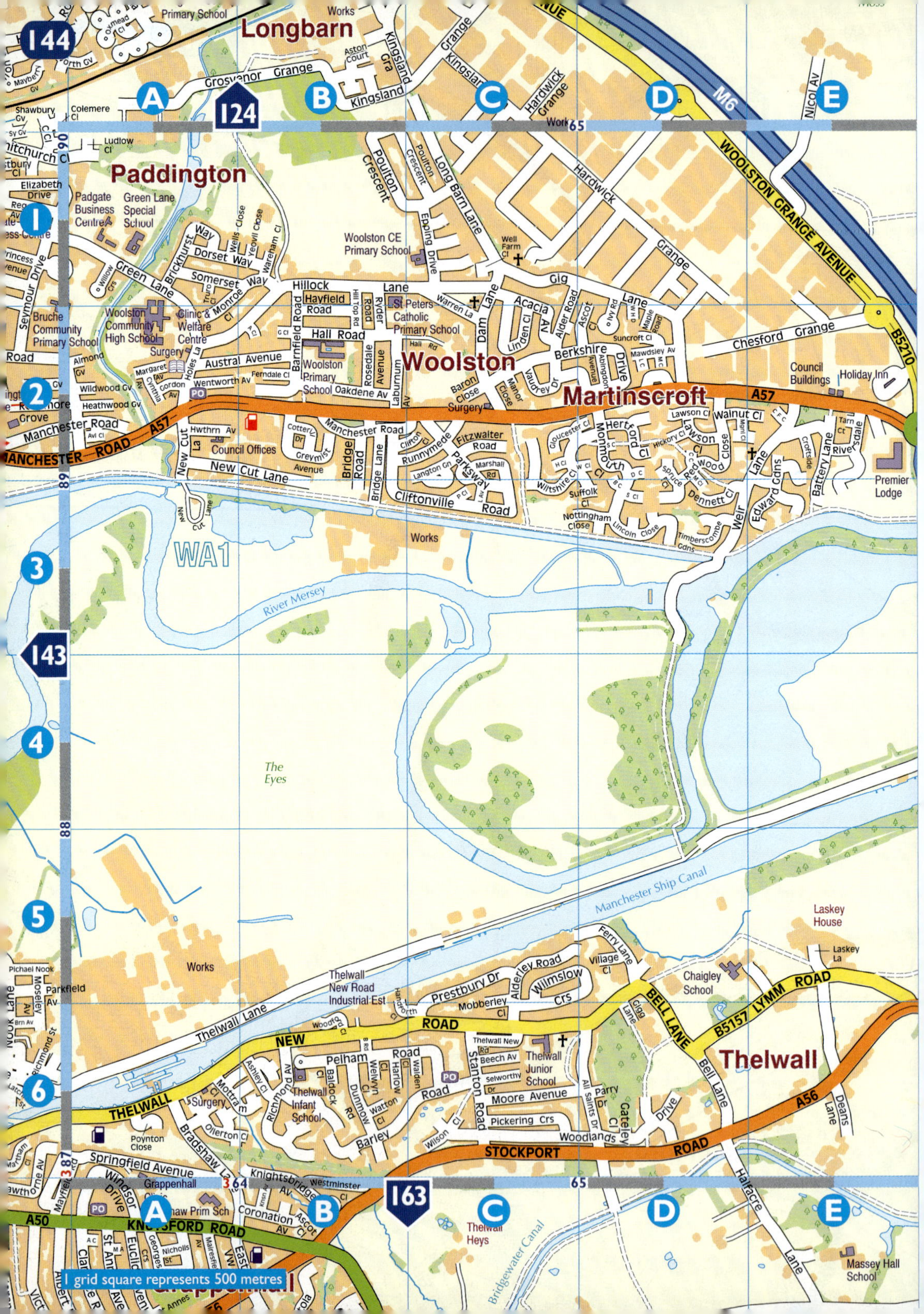
144
124
143
163
Longbarn
Paddington
Woolston
Martinscroft
Thelwall
Grappenhall
Primary School
Works
Grosvenor Grange
Kingsland Grange
Aston Court
Hardwick Grange
Nicol Av
M6
WOOLSTON GRANGE AVENUE
B5210
Shawbury Gv
Colemere Cl
Ludlow Cl
Whitchurch Cl
Elizabeth Drive
Padgate Business Centre
Green Lane Special School
Poulton Crescent
Long Barn Lane
Woolston CE Primary School
Epping Drive
Well Farm Cl
Hardwick Grange
Brickhurst Way
Dorset Way
Somerset Way
Wareham Cl
Green Lane
Seymour Drive
Bruche Community Primary School
Woolston Community High School
Clinic & Welfare Centre
Monroe Cl
Hillock Lane
Hayfield Road
Hall Road
St Peters Catholic Primary School
Warren La
Dam Lane
Acacia Av
Alder Road
Gig Lane
Chesford Grange
Council Buildings
Holiday Inn
Suncroft Cl
Berkshire Drive
Mawdsley Av
Austral Avenue
Woolston Primary School
Oakdene Av
Laburnum Av
Rosedale Avenue
Baron Close
Manor Close
Surgery
Wentworth Av
Ferndale Cl
Almond Gv
Wildwood Gv
Heathwood Gv
Manchester Road
A57
MANCHESTER ROAD
Council Offices
New Cut Lane
Greymist Avenue
Bridge Road
Bridge Lane
Runnymede
Fitzwalter Road
Parkway
Cliftonville Road
Gloucester Cl
Hertford Cl
Monmouth
Lawson Cl
Walnut Cl
Redwood Close
Dennett Cl
Suffolk Cl
Nottingham Close
Lincoln Close
Timberscombe Gdns
Weir Lane
Edward Gdns
Battery Lane
Riversdale
Premier Lodge
WA1
River Mersey
Works
The Eyes
Manchester Ship Canal
Laskey House
Laskey La
Works
Thelwall New Road Industrial Est
Thelwall Lane
Prestbury Dr
Alderley Road
Wilmslow Crs
Mobberley Cl
Village Cl
Ferry Lane
Chaigley School
BELL LANE
B5157 LYMM ROAD
NEW ROAD
THELWALL
Pelham Road
Thelwall Infant School
Thelwall Junior School
Stanton Road
Moore Avenue
Pickering Crs
Woodlands
Bell Lane
Deans Lane
A56
STOCKPORT ROAD
Halfacre Lane
Springfield Avenue
Knightsbridge Av
Westminster Cl
Grappenhall
KNUTSFORD ROAD
A50
Coronation Av
Thelwall Heys
Bridgewater Canal
Massey Hall School
Parkfield Av
Moseley Av
1 grid square represents 500 metres

Marshall's Farm
125
Holly Bush Lane
Green Alley Farm
Juniper Lane
Brook Lane
A57
MANCHESTER ROAD
Brookside Farm
Manchester Road
Junction 21
M6
River Mersey
Rixton Old Hall
Bollin Point
Golf Course
Lymm Golf Club
Thelwall Viaduct
Statham Lane
Pool Lane
Statham
Brookside Av
Whitbarrow Road
Oldfield Rd
Whitesands Rd
Star Lane
Warrington Road
Statham Primary School
Albany
Avenue
Statham Close
Lymm Hotel
Brook Rd
Lymmhay Lane
Yew Tree Close
Brooklyn Dr
Danebank Road
Reddish Lane
Millbank
Surgery
Maltmans Rd
Brookfield Cl
Statham
Lymmington Av
NEW ROAD
THE CROSS
Cross Clinic
Pepper Street
The Peppers
CAMSLEY LANE A56
BOOTH'S HILL ROAD
EAGLE BROW A6144
Thornley Rd
John Rd
David Rd
Booth's Hill La
Moston Gv
Grove
Rectory Lane
The Dingle
Dingle Bank Cl
Brookfield Rd
CHURCH RD
LYMM
164
Wychwood
Massey Brook Lane
Works
Weaste Lane
Heyes Dr
Hardy Road
Cherry Tree Primary School
ELM TREE RD
Parkwood Cl
Wayside Close
Lady Acre Cl
Surgery
Baycliffe
A56
Mayfield View
Greenwood Road
Manor Road
Hilton Rd

1 grid square represents 500 metres

Caldy 147
128
148
167
Frankby
Newton
Thurstaston
Larton
Dawpool
B5139
B5140
A540
TELEGRAPH ROAD
MONTGOMERY HILL
HILLBARK ROAD
Hillbark Road
Cemetery
Royden Park
Thurstaston Common
Irby Hill
Dawpool CE Primary School
Greasby Junior School
Greasby Infant School
Our Lady of Primary School
Caldy Golf Club
Golf Course
Wirral Way
Station Road
School Lane
Church Lane
Thurstaston Road
Sandy Lane
Sandy La North
Mill Lane
Mill Hill Road
Hillview Road
Heathbank
Thorstone Dr
Pikes Hey Road
Long Hey Rd
Links Hey Road
Grange Cross Lane
Gorse Lane
King's Drive
Birch Heys
Irbyside Road
Ferndale Avenue
The Nook
Bayfree Road
Newton Pk Rd
Springfield Avenue
Chantrell Rd
Hawthorn Dr
Bracken Drive
Sandstone Dr
Hinderton Dr
Frankby Cl
Greasby
Lombardy Avenue
Whitebeam Walk
Thorns Drive
Ashdown Dr
Juniper Cl
Danefield Rd
Allangate Close
Oakdale Dr
Sycamore Rise
Miles Lane
Barker Lane
Shaw Lane
Hall Dr
Ferguson Avenue
Harvey Av
Lloyd Dr
Loomsway
Far Meadow Lane
Martin Close
Lyndhurst Road
Greenheys Rd
South Drive
Dawlish Road
Thingwall Road
Manor Rd
Backford Rd
Townshend
F
G
H
J
K
1
2
3
4
5
6
23
24
25
84
85
86
87

148
129
147
167
168
CH49
CH61
Irby
Pensby
Wirral Business Park
Arrowe Country Park
Arrowe Park Hospital
A&E
Landican Cemetery
Greasby Infant School
Greasby Junior School
Our Lady of Pity Primary School
Irby CC
Irby Primary School
Arrowe Hill Primary School
Meadowside School
Woodchurch CE Primary School
Eltham Green Clnc
Surgery
Thingwall Primary School
Stanley School
Thingwall Recreation Centre
Pensby Recreation Centre
ARROWE PARK ROAD A551
A551
PARK ROAD
BARNSTON
PENSBY ROAD B5138
Arrowe Brook Lane
Arrowe Brook Road
Arrowe Road
Mill Lane
Mill Hill Road
Thingwall Road
Thingwall Rd E
Thingwall Drive
Irby Road
Coombe Road
Glenwood Drive
Seaview Av
Woodlands Road
Bridgenorth Road
Fishers Lane
Kenilworth Drive
Cornelius Drive
Bentley Rd
Heathbank Av
Far Meadow Lane
Hazel Grove
Laburnum Grove
Loomsway
Landican
Woodland Road
Greenwood Road
Home
Common
1 grid square represents 500 metres

Thingwall
149
130
150
169
Woodchurch
Woodchurch Leisure Centre
Fender Primary School
Woodchurch High School
Ganney's Meadow Road
Ackers Road
New Hey Road
SS Michael & All Angels RC Primary School
A552
Junction 3
M53
Landican
Landican Lane
Townfield Primary Sch
Noctorum Wy
Holmlands Drive
Prestbury Avenue
Aylesbury Avenue
Banbury Way
Woodchurch Road
Christleton Cl
Durley Drive
Kindale Road
Palmwood Close
Kenmore Rd
Ennerdale Road
Linden Drive
Prenton Way
Brookway
North Cheshire Trading Estate
Parkvale Avenue
Prenton Wy
Melford Drive
Prenton Dell Road
Prenton Hall Road
Boswell Road
Byron Close
Garrick Road
Holm Hey
Grainger Av
Layton Av
Northwood Road
Tilstock Crs
Waterpark Road
Queens Drive
Edinburgh Drive
Cornwall Drive
Glenavon Road
Prenton
Prenton Junior School
Bramwell Avenue
Wirral Stroke & Head Injury Clinic
Prenton Village Rd
Alastair Crs
Cumberland Avenue
Shopping Centre
Carlaw Road
Osmaston Road
Bryanston Road
Cambridge Road
Pulford Av
Gresford Av
Broxton Av
Reservoir Road N
Villa Medical Centre
Roman Road
Prenton Farm Road
Old Rockerrians RFC
Old RFC
Kelsall Close
Tarporley Close
Tabley Close
Marston Close
Overton Way
Overton Close
Davenham Av
Holm Lane
Holmside Lane
Dovedale Close
Welford Avenue
Storeton Road
Ltl Storeton Lane
Landican Lane
Station Road
Storeton
Murrayfield Hospital
Works
Holmwood Avenue
Holmwood Dr
Overdale Av
Private Drive
Lwr Thingwall La
A551
Woodlands Rd
Dale End Road
Low Wood Gro
Ley Farm
Keepers Lane
Red
F
G
H
J
K
I
2
3
4
5
6
28
29
30
84
85
86
87

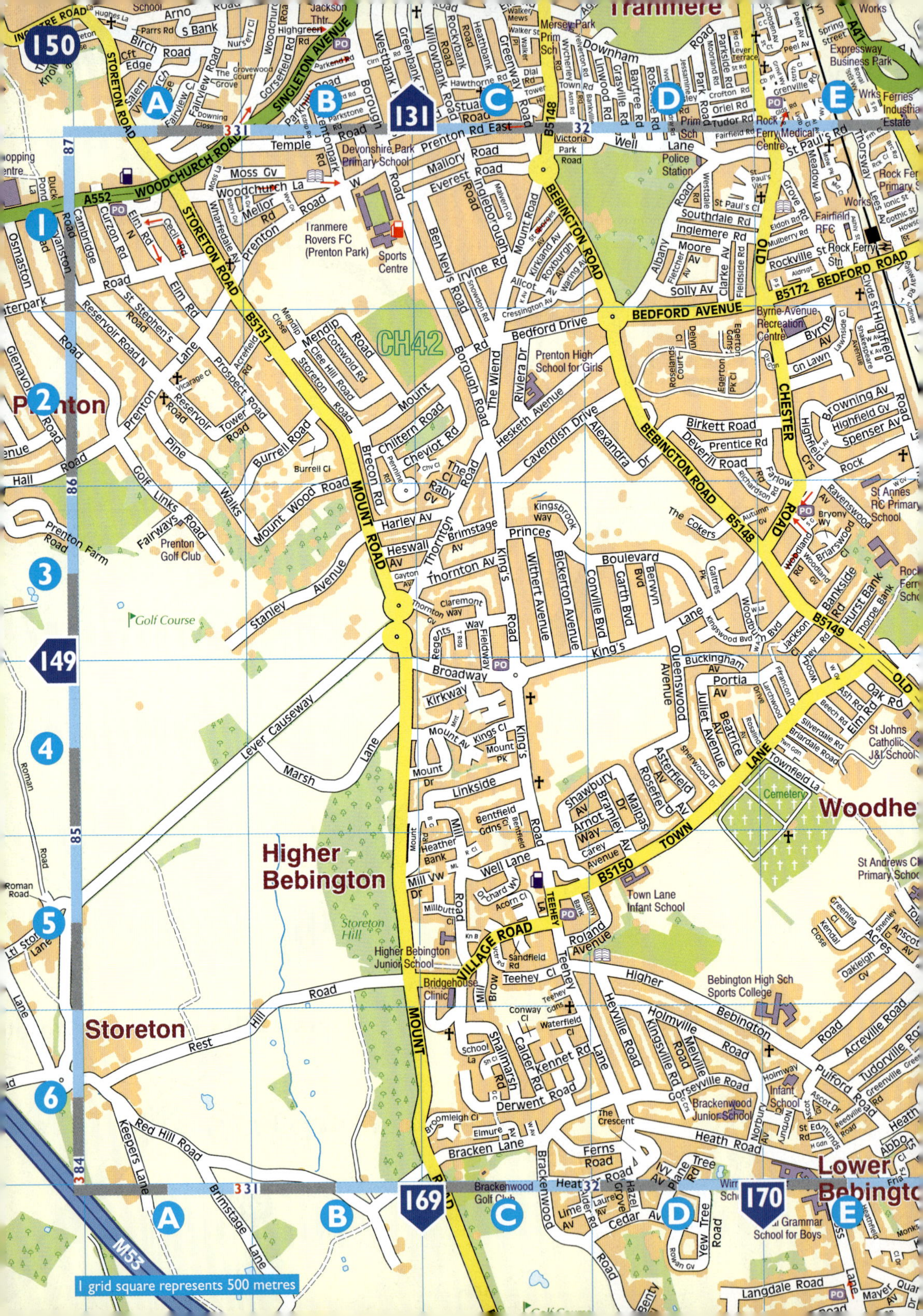
150
131
149
169
170
Tranmere
Prenton
Higher Bebington
Storeton
Woodhey
Lower Bebington
CH42
A B C D E
1 2 3 4 5 6
Storeton Road
Woodchurch Road
Singleton Avenue
Borough Road
Prenton Rd East
Bebington Road
Bedford Avenue
Bedford Drive
Mount Road
Chester Road
Town Lane
Village Road
Teehey La
Higher Bebington Road
Kings Road
Mount Wood Road
Golf Links Road
Prenton Farm Road
Lever Causeway
Marsh Lane
Rest Hill Road
Red Hill Road
Brimstage Lane
Keepers Lane
Heath Road
Heath Road
Pulford Road
Old Chester Road
Tranmere Rovers FC (Prenton Park)
Sports Centre
Devonshire Park Primary School
Prenton High School for Girls
Prenton Golf Club
Golf Course
Police Station
Byrne Avenue Recreation Centre
St Annes RC Primary School
St Johns Catholic J&I School
Cemetery
St Andrews CE Primary School
Town Lane Infant School
Bebington High Sch Sports College
Brackenwood Junior School
Higher Bebington Junior School
Bridgehouse Clinic
Brackenwood Golf Club
Grammar School for Boys
Storeton Hill
Rock Ferry Medical Centre
Ferries Industrial Estate
Expressway Business Park
Rock Ferry
M53
A552
B5151
B5148
B5150
B5149
B5172
1 grid square represents 500 metres

The Sloyne
Liverpool
Wirral
132
152
171
F
G
H
J
K
1
2
3
4
5
6
34
35
87
86
85
84
River Mersey
Rock Ferry
New Ferry
BEBINGTON
Bromborough Pool
Port Sunlight
Works
A41
ROCK FERRY BY-PASS
NEW CHESTER ROAD
NEW FERRY BY-PASS
CHESTER ROAD
B5136
BOUNDARY RD
BEBINGTON ROAD
THE VILLAGE
CHURCH ROAD
Bedford Rd East
Bedford Pl
Bedford Rd
Haddon Rd
Chatsworth Rd
Manor Rd
Mersey Rd
Mersey La S
Rock La East
Alpha Dr
Surgery
Morecroft Rd
Chatham Rd
Rochester Rd
Canterbury Rd
Nelson Rd
Grange
St Peter's Rd
Church Ms
King St
Acton
West
Melville Av
Victoria Drive
Knowsley Road
Rock Pk
Dell
The Dell Primary School
Cammell Laird's Sports Club
Procter Rd
The Dell
Thorburn Road
Onslow Rd
Tilstock Avenue
Boulton Av
Easton Rd
New Ferry Road
Seafield Road
Henthorne Road
Cecil Rd
Woodford Rd
Ingleby Rd
Napier Rd
Shore Bank
Shorefields
Merseybank Rd
Cornwall Cl
Starworth Dr
Oakworth Dr
Samaria Av
Alvega Close
Harrogate Road
Woodward Road
Power Rd
Hessal Road
Springwood Way
Stanley Road
Sefton Road
Parkfield Medical Centre
Grove Street Primary School
Longfellow Drive
Coleridge Dr
Larkin Cl
Eliot Cl
Bank Dene
The Oval Sports Cen
Rydal Bank
Grove Square
Grove St
Superstore
Windsor Cl
Beta Cl
Bebington Station
Lessington Catholic High Sch
Beresford Avenue
Stonehill Av
Stanbury Av
Barlow Av
Wellington Road
Lane
Brereton Av
Parkside Road
Greendale Road
Brook St
Primrose Hill
Circular Dr
Central Road
Osborne Ct
Pool Bank
Knox Cl
Lady Lever Art Gallery
Queen Mary's Drive
King George's Dr
Lodge Lane
Church Drive Primary School
Windy Bank
Church Drive
Corniche Rd
Kg Edward's Dr
Riverside
The Ginnel
Water St
Wharf St
Bolton Rd
Bolton Street
Bath Street
The Cswy
Park Road
Park Rd
Wood Street
Graylands Road
Ecclesahall Rd
Lewisham Rd
Corona Rd
Bolton Rd East
Dock Rd North
Woodhead Road
Shore Drive
Dock Rd South
York Street
The Gn
South
Manor Place
South View
Bromborough Pool Primary School
Lane
Old Ct House Road
Pool
Civic Wy
Police Station
The Grove
The Wiend
Ellen's La
Bromborough Road
Port Sunlight Stn
Highcroft Av
Birch Rd
Poplar
Erfurt Av
Trafalgar Dr
Carlton Rd
Road East
Church Road Medical Centre
Fellden Rd
Quarry Road
Avenue
Central Road
Main
Westgate
Dock
Port
Thermal
Riverside
Quay

152
133
151
171
A
B
C
D
E
1
2
3
4
5
6
Dingle
St Michael's Hamlet
Otterspool
AIGBURTH ROAD
A561
L17
Riverside Drive
Promenade Gdns
Festival Gardens
Works
Devil's Bank
River Mersey
Garston Channel
Liverpool
Wirral
Matthew Arnold Prim Sch
Shorefields Comm Comp Sch
St Charles RC Primary School
The Park Lane Hotel
Council Building
Surgery
Livingston Drive
Aigburth Drive
Otterspool Road
Jericho Lane
Fulwood Road
Ashbourne Road
Ampthill Road
Larkfield Road
Bempton Road
Priory Cl
Camelia Ct
Floral Wood
Glendale Cl
Dingle Vale
Dingle Rd
Southwood Rd
Tramway Rd
Normanton Av
Westbury Cl
Annesley Rd
Jericho Farm Cl
Osborne Wood
Silver Leigh
Acer Leigh
Fulwood Close
Carleen Cl
Moel Famau View
Park
Beech Av
Stn
Works
1 grid square represents 500 metres

L18
L19
134
154
172
F
G
H
J
K
1
2
3
4
5
6
39
40
Aigburth
Grassendale
Calderstones
Mossley Hill Station
West Allerton Station
Aigburth Station
Cressington Station
Hartington
Garston Station
Sudley House
Liverpool John Moores University
Sudley Infant School
Sudley Junior School
Mersey View Special Sch
Booker Avenue J&I School
Storrsdale Medical Cen
McKee School of Education
St Austins RC Prim School
Gilmour Infant School
Junior School
Greenways Special School
Liverpool CC
Innkeeper's Lodge
Garston Sports Centre
St Francis of Assisi RC Prim Sch
Sir Alfred Jones Memorial Hospital
Garston Leisure Cen
Garston Industrial Est
Holy Trinity Primary Sch
Banks Rd Prim Sch
Surgery
Works
PO
AIGBURTH ROAD
A561
ST MARY'S ROAD
GARSTON WAY
VICTORIA ROAD
A5058
MATHER AVENUE
B5180
HORROCKS AV
Carnatic Road
Briarwood Rd
Elmswood Road
Mossley Hill
Rose Lane
Pitville Avenue
Booker Avenue
Menlove
Mentmore Road
Rangemore Road
Tullimore Road
Martin Rd
Brockholme Rd
Holmefield Road
Aigburth Hall Avenue
Aigburth Hall Road
Mossley Hill Drive
Stairhaven Road
Brodie Avenue
Melbreck Road
Greenhill Road
Allerton Road
Heath Road
Woodlands Road
Dundonald Road
Riversdale Road
Mersey Road
Beechwood Road
Eastern Dr
Western Drive
North Road
South Road
Knowsley Road
Eaton Road
Salisbury Road
Grassendale Esp
Cressington Esp
Clarendon Road
Bowden Road
Garston Old Rd
Whitehedge Road
Long Lane
Church Rd
Dock Road
Window Lane
Chesterton Street
York Street
Canterbury Street

154
Calderstones
135
153
172
173
A
B
C
D
E
1
2
3
4
5
6
Allerton
Woolton
Garston
L25
Hun
Cro
Menlove Av
A562
B5171
B5180
A561
Allerton Road
Allerton High St
Woolton Road
Hillfoot Road
Speke Hall Road
Speke Road
Mather Avenue
Acrefield Rd
Horrocks Av
Allerton Park Golf Club
Golf Course
Springwood Crematorium
Allerton Cemetery
Springwood Avenue
Brunt Lane
Allerton Station
Garston Station
Woolton Golf Club
Camp Hill
Springwood Primary School
New Heys Comprehensive School
Hunts Cross Shop Park
Triumph Trading Park
Herald Avenue
Vitesse Road
Spitfire Road
Dolomite Av
Mayflower Av
Renown Way
Goodlass Road
North Av
Works
Edward's
Bridge Industrial Es
Barford
Leafield
Armscot Close
Garston Sports Centre
Garston CE Prim Sch
St John Almond RC Secondary Sch
Sir Alfred Jones Memorial Hospital
Garston Leisure Cen
Holy Trinity RC Primary School
Banks Prim Sch
New Mersey Retail Park
Liverpool Marriott Hotel
Estuary Business Park
Leeward Drive
Estuary Boulevard
Delf La
Woolton House Medical Cen
Picture House
Bishop Martin CE Prim Sch
Village Medical Cen
Woolton Swimming Pool
St Julies RC High School
Watergate Special Sch
Woolton J&I Sch
Newborough Sch
Surgery
Clarendon Road
Wheatcroft Road
Moorcroft Road
Cleveley Rd
Chalfont Road
Heath Road
Hardinge Road
Mostyn Av
Caldwell Road
Burman Rd
Woolton Rd
Holly Farm Rd
Northmead Rd
Southmead Rd
Drennan Road
Redington Rd
Ravenna Road
Clavell Rd
Darwall Rd
Longcroft Av
Perriam Rd
Lascelles Road
Blomfield Rd
Camphill Rd
School Lane
Speke Road
Charterhouse Rd
Stonyhurst Road
Haileybury
Jeudwine Close
Fairways
Manor Road
Kings Drive
Reservoir Road
Longworth Wy
Mount Park Court
Ridgetor Road
Linkstor Rd
Church Rd
Winchester Cl
Stowe Cl
Waylands
Salcombe Dr
Kingsmead
Hillfoot Rd
Farthing Cl
Vineyard St
Burnsall Street
Bank's Road
Byron Street
Canterbury St
Lincoln
Chesterton
York Street
Tonbridge Cl
Bexhill Cl
Sandgate Cl
Petworth Cl
1 grid square represents 500 metres

136
156
174
F
G
H
J
K
I
2
3
4
5
6
44
45
87
86
85
84
L26
Halewood
Foxhill Farm
Foxhill Lane
Lydiate Lane
Church Road
Carbridge Lane
Hever Dr
Court Av
Halewood CE Primary School
Lower Road
Baileys Lane
Mackets Primary School
Holy Family RC Primary School
Camberley Medical Cen
Southern Primary Support Centre
Liverpool Loop Line
Plantation Primary School
Halewood Station
Halewood St Marks Catholic Primary Sch
Halewood Comprehensive School
Roseheath Primary School
Council Bldg
Halewood Health Cen
Surgery
Halewood Sports Centre
Highfield Special School
Hunts Cross Station
St Andrews RC Prim Sch
Hunts Cross JM&I Sch
New Hutte County Prim Sch
Police Station
A562 HIGHER ROAD
Kingsthorne Park
Works
Edwards Lane Industrial Estate
Woodend Industrial Estate
Woodend Avenue
Shaw Road
Renaissance Way
North Road
Outer Central Road
Inner Central Rd
Middle Rd
East Road
South Road
SPEKE BOULEVARD
A561
Clough Road
Mackets Lane
Hollies Road
Okell Drive
Rainbow Drive
Wood Road
Woodland Road
Oakwood Rd
Beechwood Av
Boundary Farm Rd
Holland Road
Old Hutte Lane
Blakeacre
Roseheath Drive
Higher Rd

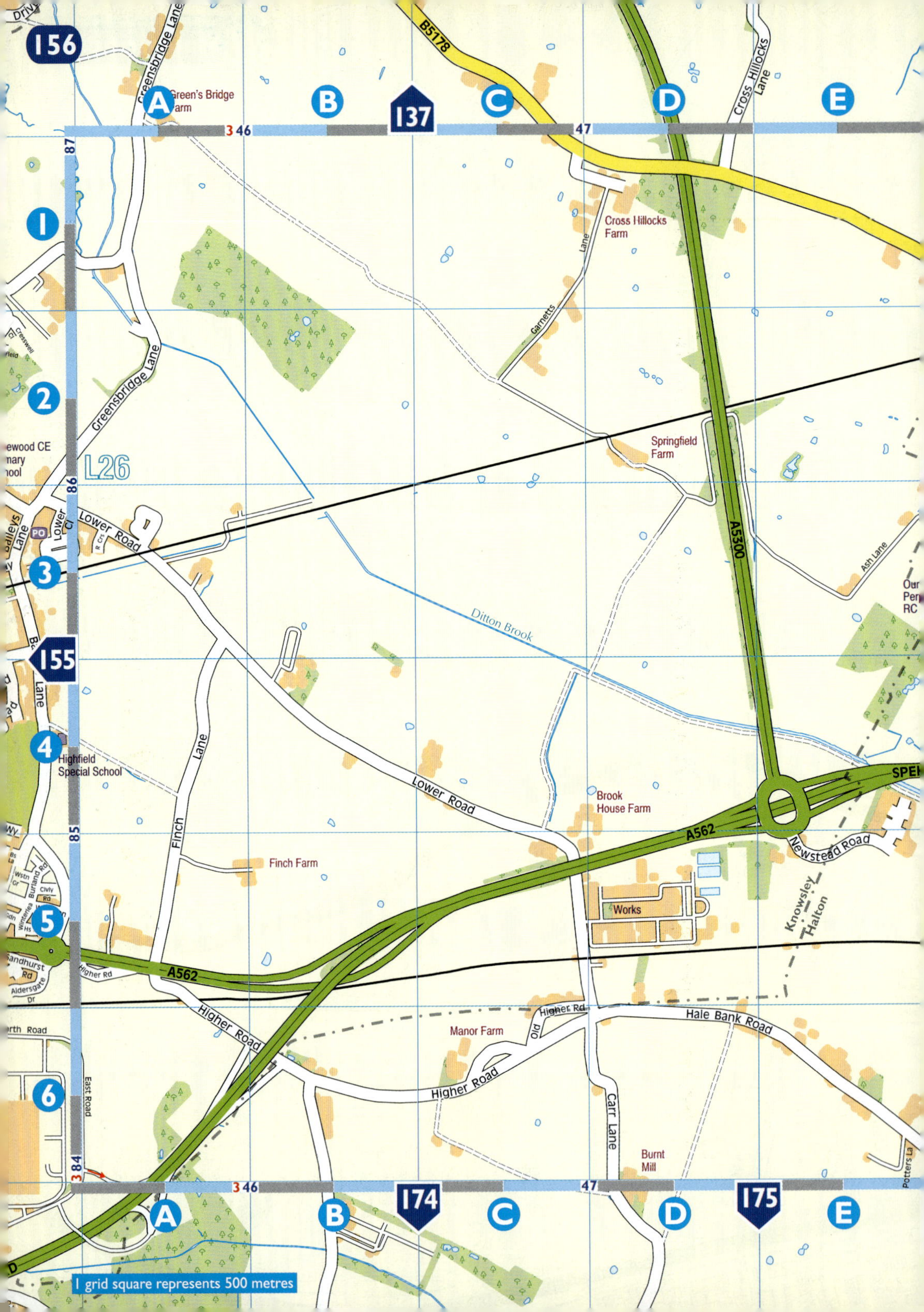

156
Greensbridge Lane
Green's Bridge Farm
B5178
Cross Hillocks Lane
A
B
137
C
D
E
3 46
47
87
1
2
3
4
5
6
Cross Hillocks Farm
Lane
Garnetts
Cresswell
Greensbridge Lane
ewood CE
nary
hool
L26
86
Lower Road
Lower Cl
Baileys Lane
PO
R Crs
Springfield Farm
A5300
Ash Lane
Our
Per
RC
Ditton Brook
155
Lane
Highfield Special School
Finch Lane
Lower Road
Brook House Farm
SPEKE
A562
Newstead Road
85
Finch Farm
Burland Rd
Works
Knowsley
Halton
Sandhurst Rd
Aldersgate Dr
Higher Rd
A562
Higher Road
Higher Rd
Old
Hale Bank Road
Manor Farm
erth Road
Higher Road
East Road
Carr Lane
Burnt Mill
Potters La
3 84
3 46
174
175
1 grid square represents 500 metres

Upton
Hough Green
Ditton
Ball o' Ditton
Lower House
Hale Bank
WIDNES
Runcorn Gap
LIVERPOOL ROAD
B5178
SPEKE RD A562 QUEENSWAY
A562
Speke Road
Ditton Road
Hale Rd
Hale Road
St Michael's Road
Prescot Road
Queensbury Wy
Dundalk Road
Ditchfield Road
Ditchfield Place
Hough Green Rd
Lancaster Avenue
Arley Drive
Grizedale
Bankfield Road
Delamere Av
Mayfield Avenue
New Bank Road
Manor Road
Royal Avenue
Coronation Drive
Abbey Road
Derwent Rd
Keswick Cl
Lonsdale Cl
Langdale Cl
Graham Rd
Crossway
Hanley Road
Borrowdale Road
Blundell Rd
Southway
Montgomery Road
Cunningham Road
Somerville Rd
Wavell Av
Canterbury Road
Wyncroft Road
Everite Road
Gavin Rd
Turnall Rd
Fieldgate
Marshgate
Oldgate
Foundry La
Clap Gate Crescent
Lovel Terrace
Baguley Avenue
Pickering Road
Mersey View Road
Mathieson Road
Ronan Road
Bush Road
Desoto
Vickers Road
Hough Green Station
Upton Medical Centre
St Basil RC Primary School
All-Saints Upton Prim Sch
Ditton CE Primary School
Chapelfield Clinic
Bankfield School
Oakfield Junior Sch
Council Building
Ditton Medical Centre
Ashley School
Chesnut Lodge School
St Michaels Catholic Prim Sch
Nazareth House
St Michael Jubilee Golf Club
Golf Course
Express Industrial Est
Everite Road Industrial Est
Pitville Terrace Industrial Estate
Golden Triangle Industrial Est
Superstore
Hale Road Industrial Estate
Fairway Trading Estate
West Bank Dock Estate
Ditton Works
Works
Trans Pennine Trail
138
158
176
F
G
H
J
K
I
2
3
4
5
6
48
49
50
84
85
86
87

158
139
176
177
157
A
B
C
D
E
1
2
3
4
5
6
WA8
WIDNES
Appleton
Crow Wood
Halton View
Kingsway
Simm's Cross
Moss Bank
Lugsdale
West Bank
Ball o' Ditton
BIRCHFIELD ROAD
LEIGH AVENUE
DEACON ROAD
ALBERT RD
HALTON VIEW RD
WARRINGTON RD
WATKINSON WAY
FIDDLERS FERRY ROAD
KINGSWAY
MOOR LANE SOUTH
ASHLEY WAY
ASHLEY WAY WEST
QUEENSWAY
Ditton Road
St Helens Canal (disused)
Trans Pennine Trail
Spike Island
Catalyst Science Discovery Centre
Widnes Vikings RLFC (Halton Stadium)
Halton College of Further Education
Greenoaks Farm Industrial Est
Black Cat Industrial Estate
Wellington Street Industrial Estate
Constance Industrial Estate
Widnes Golf Club
Wade Deacon County High Sch
St Peter & St Paul RC High School
Fairfield High Sch
Crematorium
Borough Cemetery
Widnes Station
Travelodge
Bowers Business Park
Old Foundry Estate
Ashley Retail Park
Green Oaks Shopping Centre
Windmill Shopping Centre
Queensway Business Cen
West Bank Medical Cen
West Bank Prim Sch
Fairway Trading Estate
Alexandria Industrial Estate
Andersons Ind Est
1 grid square represents 500 metres

Shell Green
Cuerdley Cross
Fiddler's
WIDNES ROAD
A562
DANS ROAD A562
WIDNES ROAD
Mowcroft Lane
Tannery Lane
Cuerdley Green
Back La
Wrights Lane
Weates Cl
Bennett's Lane
Works
Warrington
Halton
Johnson's Lane
Gorsey Lane
Marsh Lane
River Mersey
Hempstones Point
Wigg Island
Sewage Works
Warrington Road
Stuart
Christleton Ct
Manor Park Av
Manor
Chancellor Rd
Ramsey Cl
Rathlin
Skye Cl
Orkney
Barrow's
Kilsby Drive
Swinford Av
Severn Cl
Calder Cl
Douglas Cl
Barneston Rd
Coulton Rd
Avebury Cl
Hilary Cl
Trans Pennine
140
160
178

160
141
159
178
A
B
C
D
E
1
2
3
4
5
6
356
57
87
86
85
384
Tannery Lane
Penrose Gdns
Rothay Dr
Roeburn Wy
Radlett Close
Walkers Lane
Falmouth Dr
Ditchfield Rd
Brides Cl
Bramble Cl
Penketh South Community Primary School
St Vincents Cath
Manston Road
Hamble Dr
Trans Pennine Trail
Station
Shaftesbury Av
Road
LC
Fiddler's Ferry
PH
Riverside Trading Estate
St Helens Canal
River Mersey
Moss Side
Lapwing Lane
Norton Marsh
Moss Side Lane
Moore Lane
Moss Lane
Moore RUFC
Moore
Gigg Lane
Halton Moss
Manchester Ship Canal
Moore Prim Sch
Six Acre Lane
Six Acre Gdns
Eastgate Road
Lane
Blackheath
Runcorn Road
Hollybank
Beechmoore
Chancellor Rd
Rokeby Court
Warrington Road
Manor Park Av
Sunnyside Lane
Lane
Oakmoore
Calmington La
Keckwick Lane
1 grid square represents 500 metres

F
G
H
J
K
142
58
59
60
Forrest Way
River Mersey
Works
CHESTER ROAD
A5060
Eastford Road
Taylor St
Morley Rd
Works
B5156
Pool La
WALTON
Birch Wood
Grange Green Farm
A56 CHESTER ROAD
Lower Walton
Mill Lane
Walton Lea Crematorium
Warrington Sports Club
162
CHESTER NEW ROAD
Old Chester Road
Walton Lea Rd
Walton Lea Road
Higher Walton
Walton Hall Golf Club
Walton Hall
Bellhouse Lane
Runcorn Road
Hollyhedge Farm
Holly Hedge Lane
Cheshire Ring Canal Walk
Thomasons Br La
Underbridge La
Warrington Road
Golf Course
Hough's Lane
Runcorn Road
Canal Side
A56
Park Lane
Appleton Reservoir
ROAD
Hobb Lane
Lane
179
Norton House
CHESTER
Row's Wood
Halton
Warr
1
2
3
4
5
6
87
86
85
84
Rydal
Derwent
Avenue
Elgin Av
Silver
Copel
Gainsboro
Cranbo
Irwell
Manx
Greeba Av
Sulby Av
Worsley
Hill Cliffe Road
Brookwood Cl
Old H
Hillfoot Crs
Cranleigh
Slutchers
Meadow Av
St John Av
Wallis St
Hillberry Cresc

162
143
161
A
B
C
D
E
1
2
3
4
5
6
361
62
384
85
86
87
WA4
Wilderspool
Stockton Heath
Cobbs
Hillcliffe
Appleton Park
Dudlows Green
Latchford
Manchester Ship Canal
River Mersey
Palatine Industrial Estate
Priestley Sixth Form College
Works
Causeway Medical Centre
St Weburgh CE Primary School
Loushers Lane Special School
Warrington Town AFC
Our Lady RC Primary School
Sir Thomas Boteler High School
Latchford Medical Centre
Station Road Industrial Estate
Superstore
Medical Centre
Primary School
The Forge Shopping Centre
Police Station
St Thomas CE Prim Sch
Grappenhall Sports Club
Mountain Farm
Witherwin Farm
The Cobbs Infant School
Council Building
Broomfield County Junior School
St Monicas RC Primary School
Bridgewater Upper School
Bridgewater Community High School (Lower)
Warrington Sports Club
Hillfoot Farm
High Warren
Warrington Golf Club
Golf Course
Bellfield Farm
WILDERSPOOL CAUSEWAY
A49
LONDON ROAD
FAIRFIELD ROAD
B5156
ELLESMERE ROAD
GRAPPENHALL ROAD A56
WALTON NEW ROAD
A56
WALTON ROAD
KNUTSFORD ROAD
THELWALL LANE
STATION ROAD
ACKERS ROAD
CHESTER ROAD
A5060
Stockton Lane
Lumb Brook Road
Dale Lane
Bridge Lane
Broomfields Rd
Delphfields Road
Windmill Lane
Lyon's Lane
Cann Lane North
Dingle Lane
Green Lane
Longwood Road
Dudlow Green
Pineways
Fairways
Beechways
Highfield Avenue
Dipping Brook Av
1 grid square represents 500 metres

Thelwall
Stockton Heath 163
144
164
Grappenhall
Wright's Green
Appleton Thorn
Thelwall Lane
Dover Road
THELWALL
Fir Grove Hotel
Springfield Avenue
Grappenhall Clinic
Bradshaw Prim Sch
Bradshaw Lane
Surgery
Thelwall Infant School
Pelham Road
Barley
Knightsbridge Av
Westminster Cl
Coronation Av
Ascot Cl
Pickering Crs
Woodlands
Stanton Road
Moore
Selworthy Dr
Beech Av
A56
A50 KNUTSFORD ROAD
St Annes Avenue
Euclid Avenue
Clarence Road
Albert Road
Victoria Av
Kildonan Road
Middlehurst Road
Marifield Road
Tudor Close
York Drive
York Road
Harwood Gdns
Beechfield Rd
ROAD
Shadewood Crs
Lindi Av
St Wilfrid's Dr
Glebe
Portola Cl
Gilwell Cl
Barnswood Cl
Lane
Sharon Pk Cl
Cliff
Thelwall Heys
Bridgewater Canal
Weaste Lane
Cuerdon Dr
Marie Drive
Stoneleigh Gardens
St Wilfrids CE Aided Primary School
Church Lane
Stockton Lane
Bellhouse Lane
Laurel Bank
Canal Side
Australia Lane
Parrs Wd View
Grappenhall Hall School
Grappenhall Cricket Club
Gresham Dr
Bourchier Wy
Broad Lane
Hall Lane
Whitehouse Farm
KNUTSFORD ROAD
Grappenhall Heys
Chichester Cl
Dashwood Cl
Lichfield Av
Strickland Cl
Croft Gdns
Curzon Dr
Witherwin Avenue
Stansfield Dr
Keeper's Rd
Grappenhall Heys Primary School
Yew Tree Farm
Reddish Hall
Clifflane Farm
Cartridge Lane
GRAPPENHALL LANE
B5356
Bradley Hall
Appleton Thorn Trading Estate
Dodds Lane
New Lane
Lumb Brook Road
Ashberry Drive
Thorntree Green
GRAPPENHALL LANE
Yew Tree La
Booth's Farm
Barleycastle Lane
Villagate Lane
Lyncastle
Barleycastle Farm
Green Lane
Crofton Close
Parkland Cl
Greenlane Farm
Green Lane
HM Young Offenders Institute
Barleycastle Trading Estate
Blackcap Road
Langford Way
F
G
H
J
K
1
2
3
4
5
6
63
64
65
84
85
86
87

Thelwall
164
145
163
A56
Deans Lane
ROAD
CAMSLEY LANE A56
BOOTH'S HILL ROAD
Lymmington Av
Statham
Maltmans Rd
Brookfield Cl
Thornley Rd
John Rd
David Rd
Booth's Hill
Yeald Brow
Daisy Bank Rd
Newfield Rd
Moston Gv
Grove
Ash
Oak Rd
Ridgeway
Wychwood Av
Egerton Rd
Old Smithy La
Heyes Dr
Highfield Road
Hardy Road
Lyme Gv
ELM TREE RD
Surgery
Oaklands Dr
Parkwood Cl
Wayside Close
Lady Acre Cl
Hunts Field Cl
Cherry Tree Primary School
Hilltop Rd
Highfield Dr
Booth's Lane
Cherrylane Farm
Lakeside Road
Massey Brook Lane
Massey Av
Beech Gv
Works
Hyacre Lane
Massey Hall School
Weaste Lane
Massey Brook
Thelwall Grange
Cinder Lane
Higherhouse Farm
The Avenue
LANE
CHERRY
Cherry Hall Farm
M6
Oxheys Farm
Bradley Brook
A50 CLIFF LANE
Howshoots
B5158
Old Chrr La
Cherry Corner
A50 CLIFF LANE
Clifflane Farm
LANE
Junction 20
Travelodge
Lymm Service Area
Brook House Farm
Wither's Lane
Broadheys La
Primrose Hill
A50
Bradley Hall
Wither's La
Junction 9/20a
M56
Fanner's La
Fanner's Lane
Heath Lane
Barleycastle Farm
Wither's Lane
Crowsnest Farm
Swineyard Lane
Moss Brow La
Vineyard Lane
A B C D E
1 2 3 4 5 6
366 67
87 86 85 384
1 grid square represents 500 metres

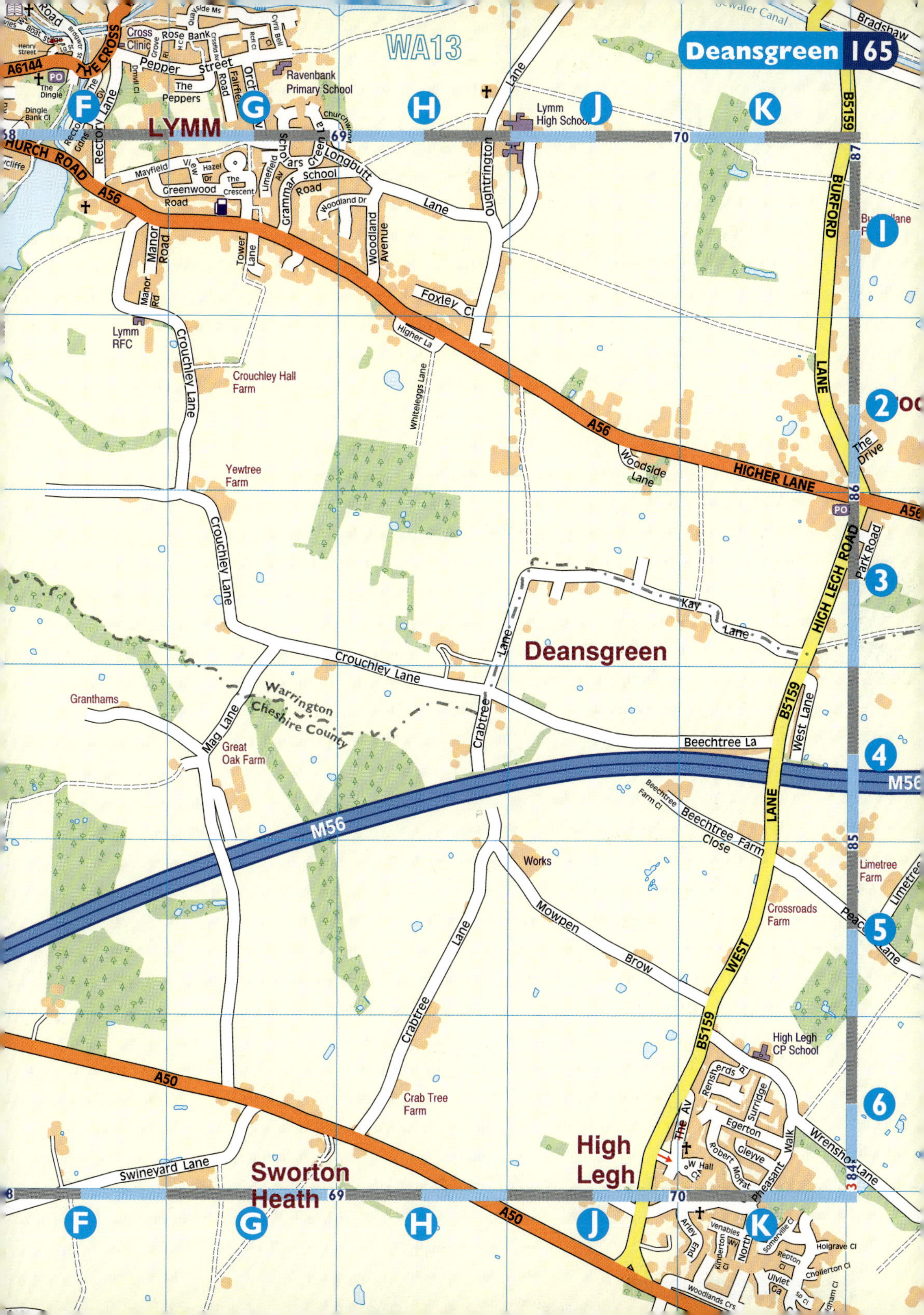
WA13
LYMM
Cross Clinic
Rose Bank
Pepper Street
The Peppers
THE CROSS
A6144
PO
The Dingle
Dingle Bank Cl
Rectory Lane
Fairfield Road
Ravenbank Primary School
Lymm High School
Lane
CHURCH ROAD
A56
Mayfield View
Hazel Dr
The Crescent
Greenwood Road
Limefield Av
Grammar School Road
Longbutt Lane
Woodland Dr
Woodland Avenue
Oughtrington Lane
Manor Road
Manor Rd
Tower Lane
Foxley Cl
Higher La
Lymm RFC
Crouchley Lane
Crouchley Hall Farm
Whiteleggs Lane
Yewtree Farm
Woodside Lane
HIGHER LANE
BURFORD LANE
B5159
The Drive
PO
Park Road
HIGH LEGH ROAD
Kay Lane
Deansgreen
Crouchley Lane
Granthams
Mag Lane
Great Oak Farm
Warrington
Cheshire County
Crabtree Lane
Beechtree La
West Lane
M56
Beechtree Farm Cl
Beechtree Farm Close
Works
Limetree Farm
Crossroads Farm
Mowpen Brow
WEST LANE
Peacock Lane
High Legh CP School
Wrenshot Lane
Crab Tree Farm
A50
Swineyard Lane
Sworton Heath
High Legh
Egerton
Surridge
Glebe
Robert Moffat
Pheasant Walk
The Av
Arley End
Venables Wy
Kinderton Cl
North
Somerville Cl
Holgrave Cl
Repton Cl
Chollerton Cl
Ulviet Ca
Woodlands Crs
F
G
H
J
K
I
2
3
4
5
6
68
69
70
84
85
86
87

1 grid square represents 500 metres

Heswall 167
147
148
168
180
F
G
H
J
K
1
2
3
4
5
6
25
27
84
83
82
81
CH60
HESWALL
Poll Hill
Pensby
Heswall
TELEGRAPH ROAD
A540
PENSBY ROAD
Wirral Way
The Dungeon
Oldfield
The Dales
Pensby High School for Girls
Pensby High School for Boys
Pensby Park Primary Sch
Ladymount RC Prim Sch
Pensby Infant School
Pensby Junior School
Pensby Clinic
Cemetery
Heswall Preparatory School
Heswall Health Centre
Silverdale Medical Cen
Surgery
St Peters CE Primary School
Church Farm Court
The Beacons
Gayton Primary School
Police Station
Telegraph Road
Mere Lane
Oldfield Drive
Oldfield Road
Piper's Lane
Broad Lane
Target Road
The Moorings
Banks Road
Wittering Lane
Davenport Road
Park West
Manners Lane
Station Road
Thurstaston Road
Delavor Road
Quarry Road East
Tower Road North
Farr Hall Drive
Rectory Lane
School Hill
Dawstone Road
Kylemore Drive
Bridgenorth Road
Fishers Lane
Rosemead Avenue
Ashlea Road
Greenbank Dr
Somerset Rd
Woodfield Road
Irby Road
Woodlands Road
Cornelius Drive
Ridgefield Rd
Woodend
Kenilworth Drive
Ridgewood Drive
Haddon Drive
Nelson Drive
Columbus Drive
Grenville Drive
Portal Road
Old Wd Rd
Nicholls Drive
Kentmere Drive
Hillfield Drive
Penmon Drive
Fairview Way
Richmond Way
Elmwood Drive
Berwyn Dr
Grange Rd
Quaker Lane
Circular Drive
Laurelbanks Way
Strathallan Close
Pine Way
Birchmere
The Ridge
Greenfield Lane
The Akbar
Broomfield Close
Redstone Drive
Ferns Close
Warren Way
Hatton Close
Sandfield Pk
Crossley Dr
Bush Way
Dalesway
Queens Dr
Phillips Way
Teals Way
Gulls Way
Rooks Wy
Linnets Wy
Hawks Way
Castle Dr
The Mt
Feather La
Dee View Rd
Church Meadow Lane
Wallrake
Village Road
Hinderton Drive
Westway
Riverbank Cl
Victoria Avenue
Gayton
Chantry Walk
Seabank Road
Hilbre Av
Seafield Av
Marine Dr
Mostyn Av
Broomlands
Rocky Lane
Beacon Lane
Dawstone Rise
Pye Rd
May Road
Daryl Road
Downham
Sandy Lane
Ravenswood Road
Florence Av
Holland Rd
Radnor Avenue
Poll Hill Road
Poll Avenue
Heath Dr
Dale Av
Tower Rd S
Highfields
Woodcot La
Quarry Rd West
Oldfield Gardens
Dale Gdns
Drayton Close
Backford Rd
Townshend Av
South Hey Road
Penrhyd Road
Sussex Cl
Dorset Dr
Devon Dr
Beeston Dr
Shearman Road
Langdale Av
Marksway
Rydal Cl
Derwent Dr
Rusland Avenue
Gleneagles Cl
Holmesway
Barleyfield
Copeland Close
Gibson Cl
Bader Cl
Portal Mews
Kylemore Way
Hannah Cl
Kylemore Close
Larchwood Close
Meadow Walk
Alexander Drive
Pensby Hall Lane
Pensall Drive
Woodcroft Drive
Ashcroft Drive
Belldene Grove
Quarry Close
Hillingdon Avenue
Erica Ct
Crossley Dr
Croftsway
Piper's End
Piper's Close
Dee Side
Raby Cl
The Lydiate
Brow Lane
St Peter's Cl
Hessle Dr
Strathearn
Chatsworth Road
Pensby Road
Lyndhurst Avenue
Birches Cl
Milton Cr
Greenway Rd
Chesnut Ct
Griffith Cl

168
148
167
181
Pensby
Barnston
Gayton
Thingwall
Pensby Road
B5138
A551
Barnston Road
A540
Telegraph Road
Chester Road
A5137
Brimstage Road
Station Road
Storeton Lane
Gills Lane
Whitehouse Lane
Whitfield Lane
Milner Road
Downham Road N
Rosemead Avenue
Ashlea Road
Greenbank Drive
Holmwood Avenue
Holmwood Dr
Private Drive
Overdale Av
Low Wood Grove
Woodlands Dr
Dale End Road
Thorncroft Drive
Marfield Lane
Fender Way
Laurelhurst Av
Marksway
Belmont Dr
Kentmere Drive
Hillfield Drive
Pine Vw Drive
Ravenswood Road
Napps Wy
Oaklands Dr
Shrewsbury Rd
Hesketh Drive
Gorsehill Rd
Milton Crs
Briary Close
Park Road
Pine Rd
Beech Rd
Buffs Lane
Topgate Cl
Andrew's Walk
Border Road
Moorway
Pinewood Drive
Acre Lane
Brunstath Close
Fieldway
Meadowcroft
Barcombe Rd
Brookfield Rd
Nigel Road
Lime Tree Gv
Speedwell Dr
Carol Dr
Lawford Drive
Barnston Towers Close
The Paddock
Pond Vw Cl
Redmere Dr
Heythrop Drive
Pullman Cl
Broadmead
Stevens Rd
Wheatland Road
Sandham Gv
Suncroft Rd
Kestrel Road
Fox Cover Rd
Ryecroft Road
Chalkwell Dr
Rhodesway
Larksway
Hill Top La
Tudorway
Mill Lane
Inglegreen
Briarfield Rd
Boundary Lane
Oban Dr
Milner Cop
Downham Dr
Fernlea Road
Forest Road
Birches Cl
Daryl Road
May Road
Pye Rd
Rocky Lane
Beacon Lane
Beacon La
West Drive
North Drive
South Drive
Hillside Road
Moorland Pk
The Ridgeway
Dawstone Rise
Dawstone
The Beacons
Wallrake
Beechfield Cl
Victoria Avenue
Chantry Walk
Gayton Road
Hinderton Drive
Lynton Crs
Beverley Dr
Gayton Lane
Manor House
Carnsdale Farm
Ley Farm
Works
Heswall Primary School
Heswall Station
Heswall FC
Barnston Primary School
Pensby Infant School
Pensby Clinic
Pensby Recreation
Police Station
Surgery
Health Centre
New Hall
PH
PO
CH60
1 grid square represents 500 metres

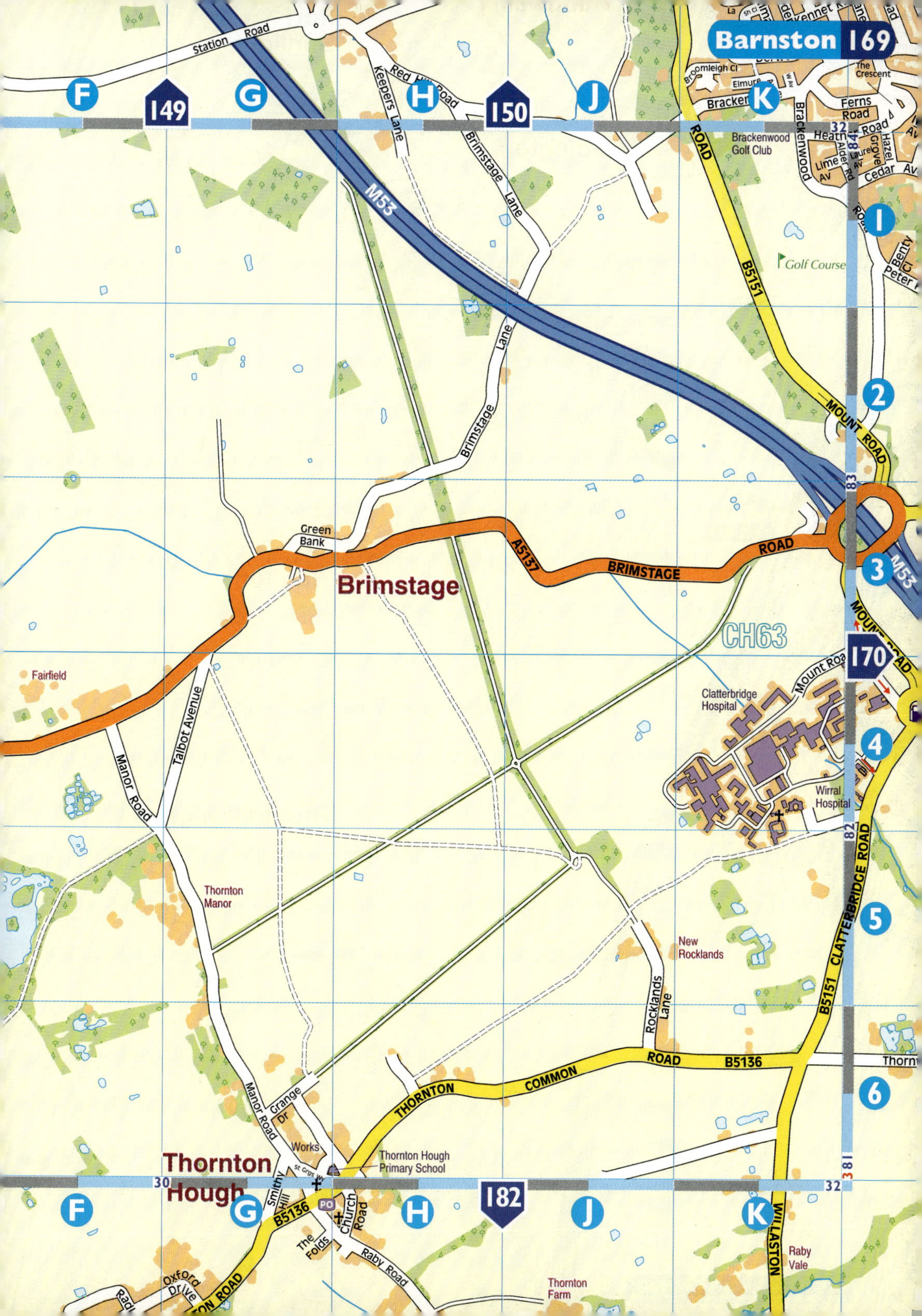
Barnston 169
Station Road
Red Hill Road
Keepers Lane
Brimstage Lane
Bromleigh Cl
Elmure
Bracken
Brackenwood
Ferns Road
Heath Road
Alder Rd
Laurel Av
Grove
Hazel
Lime Av
Cedar Av
The Crescent
Brackenwood Golf Club
Golf Course
Benty Cl
Peter
ROAD
B5151
M53
MOUNT ROAD
Green Bank
Brimstage
A5137
BRIMSTAGE ROAD
CH63
Fairfield
Talbot Avenue
Manor Road
Clatterbridge Hospital
Mount Road
Wirral Hospital
CLATTERBRIDGE ROAD
Thornton Manor
New Rocklands
Rocklands Lane
THORNTON COMMON ROAD
B5136
Thorn
Grange Dr
Works
Thornton Hough Primary School
Thornton Hough
Smithy Hill
St Grgs Wy
PO
Church Road
The Folds
Raby Road
Oxford Drive
THORNTON ROAD
WILLASTON
Raby Vale
Thornton Farm
149
150
170
182
F
G
H
J
K
I
2
3
4
5
6
30
32
81
82
83
84

170
150
167
183
Port Sunlight
Lower Bebington
Spital
Poulton
Bromborough
Junction 4
M53
B5137
B5136
B5151
BRIMSTAGE ROAD
SPITAL ROAD
MOUNT ROAD
CHURCH ROAD
CLATTERBRIDGE ROAD
WILLASTON
Wirral Grammar School for Girls
Wirral Grammar School for Boys
Brackenwood Junior School
Infant School
Police Sation
Church Road Medical Centre
Stanton Road Primary Sch
Poulton Lancelyn Primary School
Surgery
Wirral Hospital
Port Sunlight Stn
Spital Station
Bromborough Rake Station
Bromborough Station
Works
Golf Course
Poulton Hall
Nature Reserve
Blakeley Dene
Raby Hall
Raby Vale
Thornton Common Road
Poulton Road
Poulton Hall Road
Raby Mere Road
Dibbinsdale Road
Bromborough Road
Peter Price's Lane
Stanton Road
Langdale Road
Borrowdale Road
Heath Road
Bolton Street
Bath Street
Wood Street
Park Rd
A41
1 grid square represents 500 metres

F
G
H
J
K
151
152
184
37
35
84
83
82
81
1
2
3
4
5
6
York Street
Manor Place
South View
Old Ct House Road
Lane
Work
Dock
Port
Thermal Road
Causeway
Works
Fairway North
Crossways
Western Av
Eastern
Terminus Road
Magazine Lane
Georgia Av
Croft Business Park
Service Centre
Magazine Road
Multibowl
Odeon Cinema
Fairway South
Heather Dene
Welton Road
Welton Rd
Stadium Road
Commercial Road
Carrock Rd
Mosedale Road
Caldbeck Road
Bassendale Road
Skiddaw Rd
Wirral International Business Park
Plantation Business Park
Plantation Road
Power Road
Martindale Rd
Thursby Road
Spital Road
Croft Av E
Woodslee Primary School
Avenue
Stanhope Dr
Churchwood Close
Rake
Croft Lane
Hornby
A41
Bromborough
Travel Inn
The Cross
Mark
Athelstan Close
Ludlow Gv
Surgery
Allport La
Village
Old Hall Rd
Old Hall Road
Riverwood Road
Job's Ferry
Hardknott Road
CH62
Wrynose Rd
Tebay Road
Eastham Ferry
Ferry Road
Lock Rd
Eastham Country Park
Eastham Locks
Wirral Metropolitan College
Bradmoor Rd
Dale Avenue
Valley Rd
Mainwaring Rd
Forwood Rd
Gratrix Rd
Howard Av
June Av
Harrow Gv
Cambridge Rd
Heys Av
Otetey Avenue
Mossley Av
Hawthorn Lane
Meadowside Road
Mendell Primary School
Mendell Cl
Neville Road
Ambleside Close
Glyn Av
Gordon Av
Christ The King RC Primary School
Brancote Gdns
Allports
Allport Road
Woodyear Road
Caldicott Av
Westminster Dr
Bridle Park
Bridle Cl
Bridle Rd
Cemetery
New Chester Road
Morland Av
Raeburn Primary School
Manor Road
Princes Avenue
Kilburn Avenue
Dearnford Av
Dearnford Cl
Raeburn
Eastham Lodge Golf Club
Golf Course
Mayfield Dr
Seaview Av
Manchester Ship

153
Dock
Works
Railway St
Church Rd
Dale St
Byron Street
Bank's
Holy Trinity Primary School
Works
Vineyard St
Almond Ct
Cavalier Dr
Burnsall Street
SPEKE
ROAD
New Park
Hughes St
Sinclair St
King St
Campania St
Saunby St
Vulcan St
Window Lane
Canterbury Street
Lincoln
Chesterton Street
York Street
Stanley St
Hardy St
Durham St
Priory Road
PO
Banks Rd Prim Sch
Brunswick Street
Logfield Dr
Bank's Road
Liverpool Marriott Hotel
Estuary Boulevard
Garston Industrial Est
Windfield Road
Bank's La
Monkfield Wy
Blackburne Street
York Way
Works
Garston Rocks
Weaver Industrial Estate
Brunswick St
Mersey Way
Bank's Lane
Speke Hall (NT)
Liverpool
Cheshire County
A B C D E
1 2 3 4 5 6
84 83 82 381
340 41
1 grid square represents 500 metres

F
G
H
J
K
154
155
174
A561
A562
Delf La
Woodend Industrial Estate
Old Distillery Rd
Road
Evans
Physics Rd
Botany Rd
Speke Boulevard
Speke Bvd
Science Rd
Woodend
Shaw
Road
Gaskill Road
Renaissance Way
Inner West Road
Works
Rycot
Road
Bray
Road
Petworth Cl
Barnham Cl
Tonbridge Cl
Bexhill Cl
Sandgate Cl
Dymchurch
Appledore
Close
Lydd Cl
Gerneth Cl
PO
Speke Town La
Woodend La
Farm Road
Hall Road
Ramsbrook Rd
Blackrod Av
Goldfinch Farm Road
Western Avenue
SPEKE BOULEVARD
South Road
Clough Road
Tarbock Road
St Christophers RC Primary School
Speke
Parklands High School
Millwood
Clough Road
Leeward Drive
Banks
Speke Hall Av
Cartwright's Farm Rd
Speke Hall Avenue
Spindus Road
Speke Hall Industrial Estate
Stirling Rd
Blenheim Wy
Skypark Industrial Estate
Owen Dr
School Way
Gerneth Rd
Speke Church Rd
Greyhound
Blacklock
Stockton Wd Rd
Stockton Wood Community Prim Sch
All Saints Road
Hale Road
Sutton Wood Rd
Tewit Hall Rd
Tewit Hall Cl
Stapleton Avenue
Lovel Wy
Lovel Road
Linner Road
Central Avenue
Harefield Road
Conleach Road
Austin Rawlinson Sports Centre
Police Stn
North Parade
South Parade
Ganworth Road
Alder
Middlefield Primary School
Speke Family Health Clinic
Heath
Little
Oldbridge
Dunlop Road
Oglet Lane
Dam Wood Road
Dam Wood Rd
Hale Road
L24
Liverpool John Lennon International Airport
The Walk
Mersey Way
Oglet
Oglet Lane
Mersey Way
River Mersey
1
2
3
4
5
6

174
155
156
173
Hale
Speke Boulevard
Higher Road
East Road
South Road
Inner Central Rd
Works
Ramsbrook Lane
Hale Road
Hale Drive
Dungeon Lane
Bailey's Lane
Mersey Way
Liverpool
Halton
Brook Farm
Middlefield Primary School
St Ambrose RC Primary School
The Margaret Thompson Medical Cen
Police Station
Surgery
Clough Road
Millwood Road
Alder Wood Avenue
Central Way
Morcott Lane
High Street
1 grid square represents 500 metres

Carr Lane
Burn Mill
Potters La
Baguley
Aven
Heath View Rd
Kenview Cl
157
Blackburne Avenue
Foundry La
Pickering Road
Hale Road Industrial Estate
Mersey View Road
Hale Bank
Trans Pennine Trail
Pickerings Pasture
Garnetts Lane
Hale Gate Road
Trans Pennine Trail
Halegate Farm
River Mersey
Town Lane
Ellwood Cl
Curtender Wy
Hesketh Road
Hoghton Rd
As Wk
Hale CE Primary School
Ireland Road
Vicarage Close
Within Way
Church Road
176
Manchester Ship Canal
Salt Works Wharf
Works
Mersey View
Post Office
West Road
Weston Point Dock
Canal Side
Lighthouse Road
Mersey Way
Hale Head

157
158
175
186
West Bank
Runcorn Gap
Runcorn-Widnes Bridge
Vickers Road
Catalyst Science Discovery C
West Bank Medical Cen
West Bank Prim Sch
Manchester Ship Canal
All Saints CE Prim Sch
Mersey Road
Church Street
Old Quay
B5755 BRIDGE ST
HIGH ST
Arts Cen
Bridgewater Canal
DARESBURY EXPRESSWAY
QUEENSWAY
A533
A557
Campanile Hotel
Runcorn Station
Percival Lane
WESTON POINT EXPRESSWAY
Victoria Road Prim Sch
Cemetery
RUNCORN SPUR ROAD
HEATH RD
B5155
Westfield Prim Sch
Picow Farm Rd
Crofton Road
Higher Runcorn
War Mem
St.Clements RC Primary School
WA7
Runcorn Hill Nature Reserve
Heath Road Medical Cen
Weston Point
Weston Point Primary School
Highlands Road
Heath
Runcorn Golf Club
Pewithall Primary School
The Heath Comprehensive School
Weston
Clifton Road
Golf Course
Works
RUN
1 grid square represents 500 metres

Wigg Island
F
G
H
J
K
159
187
178
52
53
54
84
83
82
81
1
2
3
4
5
6
Sewage Works
Warrington Road
Astmoor
Astmoor Road
Astmoor Rd
Astmoor Industrial Estate
Brindley Road
Goddard
Davy Road
Dewar Ct
Dalton Ct
Lancer Ct
Chadwick
Arkwright Ct
Arkwright Road
Arkwright Rd
Hardwick Rd
Lister Road
Jensen Court
Edison Rd
Mason St
DARESBURY EXPRESSWAY
A533
A558
Astmoor Br La
North
Kingshead Cl
Astmoor Prim Sch
St Augustines RC Prim Sch
De Lacy Rw
Castlefields
Castlefields Avenue
Castlefields Health Centre
Castlefields Av East
Green
Bridge Cl
Plantation Cl
The Park Primary School
Halton Rd
Halton Road
Halton Brow
Robert St
Wicksten Dr
Porter St
Stonehills La
Taylors Rw
Stenhills Crs
Saxon Road
Works
Dudley Av
Renton Av
Brookfield Avenue
Richmond
Northwood
Carlton Av
Harrow Dr
Manor Rd
Castle Rise
Ivychurch Ms
The Grange Infant School
The Grange Junior School
The Grange Comprehensive Sch
Latham
Alexander
Duncan Av
Adderley Close
Avenue
Boston Av
Boston
RUNCORN SPUR ROAD
B5155
CORN
Morval Crs
Morval Crescent
Halton Brook
Halton Brook Avenue
The Glebe
Wheatlands
Fallowfield
Leaside
The Tithings
Meadway
Fernhurst
Cotterill
Hillcrest
Castleview Prim Sch
The Holy Spirit RC Aided Prim Sch
Brackendale
Littlegate
CENTRAL EXPRESSWAY
Roman Cl
Summer La
Spark Lane
St Mary's Road
Priory Cl
The Brow Primary School
The Clough
Halton House School
The Croft
Riversdale Rd
Hollybank Rd
Lodge Lane
Main Street
Castle Rd
The Underway
Mount Rd
School La
Pump La
Holt Lane
St Marys CE Primary School
Primrose Cl
Merlin Cl
Castlefields Av South
South
Norton View
Norton
Halton Link Rd
Council Building
Halton Magistrates Court
Runcorn Co Court
Police Stn
Northway
Second Av
Third Av
Fourth Av
Fifth Av
West Lane
Southway
East La
Halton
Cemetery
Stockham
Superstore
Trident Retail Park
Southgate
Cineworld
Crown Ga
Hospital Way
Surgery
The Uplands
Palace Fields Avenue
Rawdon Cl
Worthington Cl
Martin Cl
Cunliffe Cl
Sparrowhawk Cl
Charlton Cl
Badger Cl
Palacefields Prim Sch
Wren Cl
Our Lady Mother of the Saviour Catholic Prim
Fields Avenue
Lapwing
Cannell Ct
Stonebarn Lane
General Hospital
Roehampton Dr
Penshaw Ct
Plaistow Ct
Park Av
Earls Way
Parkers Ct
Falcons Wy
Hallwood
Roberts
Birch Road
Cherry Tree Av
Lilac Crs
Lime Gv
Festival Way
Elm Rd
Sycamore
Maple Avenue
Acacia Gv
Beech Rd
Ash Gv
Almond Av
Linkway
Grangeway
Grangeway Court
Halton Lodge Primary School
Grange
Thorn Road
Thorn Close
Oak Dr
Pear Tree
Poplar Av
Cedar Av
Larch Road
Cypress Gv
Grangemoor
Fieldhouse Row
Halton Lodge Av
YMCA
Woodside County Primary School
Shopping Centre
Whitchurch Way
St Chads Catholic High School
Birstall Ct
Bamford Cl
Rowan Close
Camrose Close
Tarvin Cl
Pickerings
Clifton Road
Trafford Crs
Whatcroft
Berchwood
CENTRAL EXPRESSWAY

1 grid square represents 500 metres

Gayton
Parkgate
The Beacons
Barnston Primary School
Gayton Primary School
Heswall Golf Club
Golf Course
New Hall
Leighton Hall Farm
Backwood Hall
Ashfield Hall
Parkgate Primary School
Westwood Court
Neston High School
Neston Station
Neston CC
Cemetery
A540 CHESTER ROAD
CHESTER ROAD A540
B5135
LANE
BOATHOUSE
THE PARADE
B5136 LIVERPOOL ROAD
PARKGATE RD
Parkgate Lane
The Runnell
Leighton Road
Wood Lane
Brook La
Wirral Way
North Parade
Gayton Lane
Gayton Road
Well Lane
Baskervyle Road
Baskervyle Close
Chantry Walk
Dee Park Road
Dee Park Close
Latchford Road
Oaksway
Kingsway
Queensway
Birchway
Parkway
St Stephens Close
The Spinney
Cedarway
Beverley Dr
Parklands Dr
Trent Way
Thornton Crs
Lynton Close
Porlock Close
Gayton Farm Rd
Moorland Pk
South Drive
The Ridgeway
Rhodesway
The Knap
Sandham
Suncroft Rd
Kestrel Road
Long Acres Road
Water Tower Rd
Ringway
Clayhill
Bulldwas Road
Coalbrookdale Rd
Westlands
Hawkins Road
Drake Road
Raleigh Rd
Shakespeare Rd
Jonson Rd
Raby Park
Breezehill
Breezehill Close
Blackeys Lane
Highfield Rd
Raby Gdns
Raby Pk Close
Frobisher Road
Pinehey
Leighton Chase
The Priory
Earle Crs
Albert Drive
Woodlands
The Leightons
Leighton Ct
Park St
Cross St
Mostyn Square
Holywell Close
Grenfell Cl
Grenfell Pk
Springcroft
Brooklands Road
Brooklands Gardens
Moorfield Drive
Hawthorn Road
Bowring Drive
Moorings Cl
School La
Coastguard La
Bevyl Road
The Looms
Looms
Brook Hey
Tithebarn Dr
Hamilton Cl
Greenway
Barnacre Drive
Carlton Cl
Paddock Dr
Marshall Rd
Hunters Way
The Parade
Manorial Rd
PO
P
F G H J K
I 2 3 4 5 6
27 28 29
78 79 80 81
168
182
191

Thornton Hough
Raby
Hinderton
A
B
C
D
E
1
2
3
4
5
6
169
181
192
330
31
81
80
79
378
THORNTON COMMON ROAD B5136
Manor Road
Grange Dr
Smithy Hill
B5136
PO
Church Road
The Folds
Raby Road
Thornton Hough Primary School
Oxford Drive
Radley Dr
Oxford Drive
Eton Drive
NESTON ROAD
Widgeons Covert
Parkgate Lane
B5136
Thornton Hall Hotel
NESTON ROAD
The Grange Country Club
Yew Tree Farm
LIVERPOOL ROAD B5136
CHESTER HIGH ROAD A540
Thornton Farm
Raby Vale
WILLASTON ROAD
Four Lanes End
Mere Road
Raby
The Crossway
The Green
Raby Road
Willowbrow Farm
Willow Lane
Willowbrow Road
Cherry Farm
Raby Road
Upper Raby Road
School Lane
Wirral
Cheshire County
WILLASTON
Liverpool Road
Buildwas Road
Coalbrookdale Rd
Clayhill
Windle Ct
Ringway
ROAD
Westwood Court
Tower
Ringway
Westlands Cl
Recreation Centre
Neston High School
Hawkins Rd
Sidney Rd
Raleigh Rd
Drake
Shakespeare Road
Jonson Rd
Spn Rd
Park Road
Quarry Road
Quarry Road
Hinderton La
CHESTER HIGH ROAD
Cemetery
LIVERPOOL
Raby
Mr Rd
Breezehill Close
Breezehill
Raby Pk
Close
Blackeys Lane
HINDERTON ROAD
HANNS HALL ROAD
Cherry Close
The Lydiat
Hanns Hall Farm
1 grid square represents 500 metres

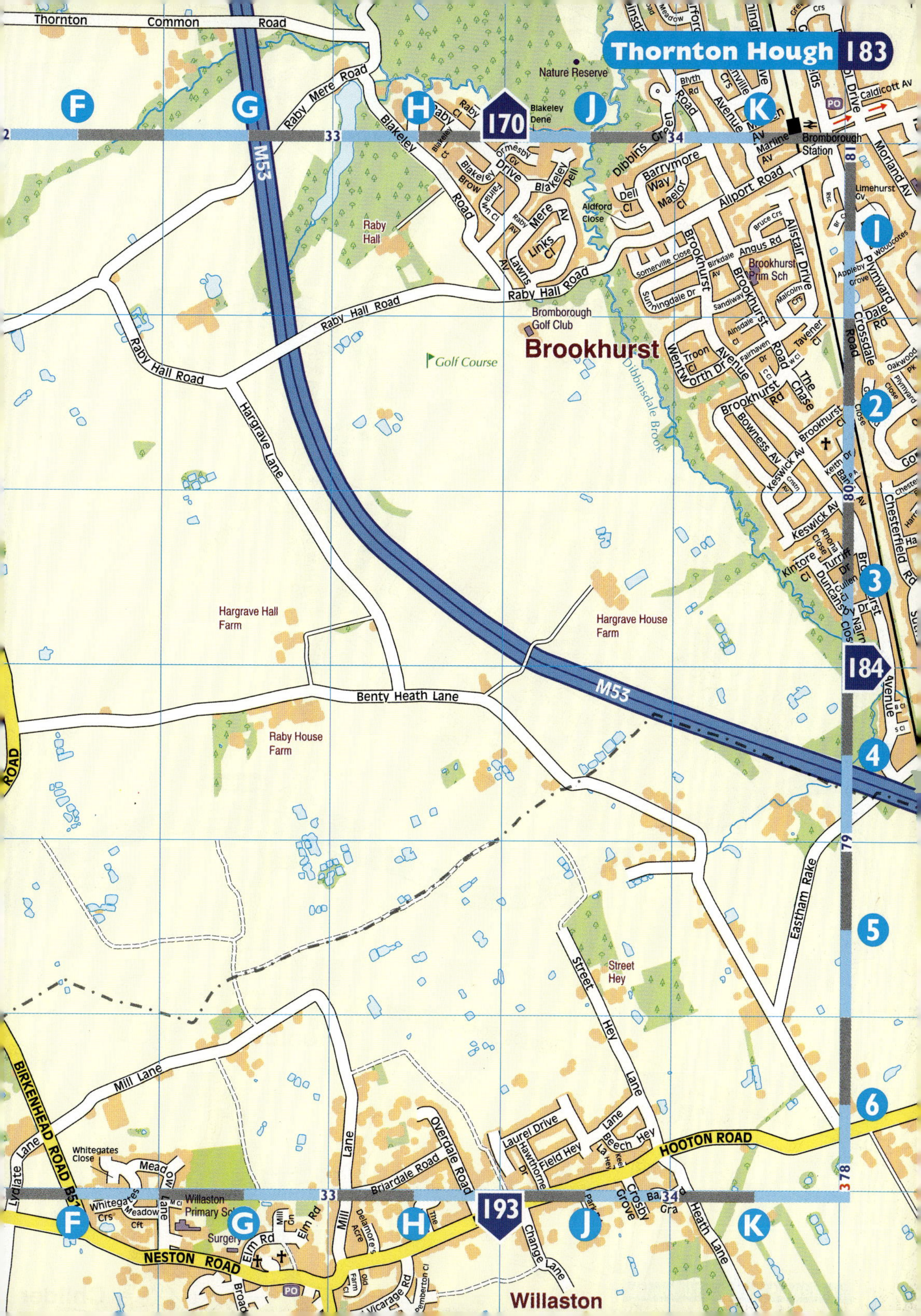
Thornton Common Road
Raby Mere Road
Nature Reserve
Blakeley Dene
170
Bromborough Station
Raby Hall
Raby Hall Road
Bromborough Golf Club
Brookhurst
Golf Course
Dibbinsdale Brook
Brookhurst Prim Sch
Allport Road
Hargrave Lane
Hargrave Hall Farm
Hargrave House Farm
Benty Heath Lane
M53
Raby House Farm
184
Eastham Rake
Street Hey
Street Hey Lane
Mill Lane
Birkenhead Road B5151
Hooton Road
Neston Road
Willaston Primary Sch
Surgery
193
Willaston
Heath Lane
Chester Road
Chesterfield Rd
Brookhurst Rd
Keswick Av
Overdale Road
Briardale Road
Change Lane

184
171
183
194
A
B
C
D
E
1
2
3
4
5
6
Eastham
Hooton
Childer
Eastham Locks
Wirral Metropolitan College
Eastham Lodge Golf Club
Golf Course
Christ The King RC Primary School
Raeburn Primary School
Heygarth Primary School
The Lyndale School
St Marys CE Primary School
South Wirral High School
Millfields Primary School
Childer Thornton Primary School
Eastham House
Travelodge
Woodcote Hotel
Works
Cemetery
Bromborough Station
Eastham Rake Station
Hooton Station
Junction 5
Junction 6
M53
A41
B5132
B5133
NEW CHESTER ROAD
EASTHAM VILLAGE ROAD
EASTHAM VILLAGE RD
RIVACRE ROAD
HOOTON ROAD
Westminster Dr
Allport Road
Woodyear Road
Bridle Road
Manor Road
Princes Avenue
Kilburn Avenue
Raeburn Avenue
Dearnford Avenue
Bettisfield Avenue
Plymyard Avenue
Heygarth Road
Elgar Avenue
Park Road
St David Road
St John's Road
Christopher Drive
Ferry Road
Mayfield Dr
Seaview Av
Eastham Rake
Grampian Way
Lyndale Av
Adaston Av
Brookhurst Avenue
Sutherland Avenue
Chesterfield Rd
Argyll Avenue
Rothesay Dr
Delamere Av
Tarvin Rd
Willington Avenue
Kelsall Avenue
Kingsley Avenue
Norley Av
Thornleigh Av
Crossdale Road
Gorsefield Av
Moorland Av
Caldicott Av
Vernon Av
Hooton Way
Hooton Green
Grange Crs
Woodclose
Welsh Road
School Lane
New School Lane
Waterworks Lane
Dale Hey
Oak Road
Hooton Road
Orchard La
New Road
Oaklands
1 grid square represents 500 metres

F
G
H
J
K
38
39
81
80
79
78
1
2
3
4
5
6
Wirral
Cheshire County
Manchester Ship Canal
Bankfields Drive
Eric Fountain Rd
North Road
River Mersey
Manchester Ship Canal
Booston Wood
Works
Rivacre Road
Lane
M53
Motor Vehicle Works
Junction 7
North Road
B5132
Poole Hall Industrial Estate
195
B5132
Rivacre Valley Country Park
Poole Hall Lane
Carlton Crs
Woodacre Grove
Plemston Court
Croughton Rd
Gowy Court
Stapleford Court
Huxley Court
Gateacre Court
Hillside Drive
ACRE ROAD
Poole Hall Rd
Poole Hall Industrial Estate

186
West Rd
Sandy
Road
Baker Road
South Parade
Canal Side
Leonard St
Sydney St
Roscoe Crescent
Castner Av
Primary School
Highlands Road
Weston
176
Heath Dr
Runcorn Golf Club
South
Beaufort Cl
Clifton Road
The Heath Comprehens School
A
B
C
D
E
Works
LC
Cheshyre's La
3 50
51
81
80
79
3 78
1
2
3
4
5
6
Works
Bankes' La
WESTON POINT EXPRESSWAY
Cheshyre's La
Weston Road
Works
South
Marion Dr
Weston Crs
Fieldsway
Montpelier Av
Lambsickle Lane
Heath Rd
Golf Course
Weston Primary School
Tildsley Crs
Weaver Rd
Bankes' La
Road
Cavendish Farm Rd
Works
A557
WESTON POINT EXPRESSWAY
Cow Hey Lane
Works
Works
Ashbourne Av
Springbank
Frodsham Marsh Farm
Alder Lane
Alder Lane
Brook Furlong
Frodsham Marsh
Weaver Lane
Lane
Moorditch Lane
Tadgers Lane
Brook Furlong
200
M56
Brookside Rd
Marsh Lane
Maori Dr
Chapelfields
MAIN STREET
PO
Greenfield Lane
Moor Lane
Frodsham Station
Surgery
Rodgers Close
Hawthorne Rd
Wayford Close
St Luke's Wy
Frodsham Science & Tech College
CHURCH ST
1 grid square represents 500 metres

Southgate
Palacefields
Beechwood
Clifton
Rocksavage
Newtown
Sutton Weaver
Woodside County Primary School
Trident Retail Park
Shopping Centre
Cineworld
Surgery
Hospital Way
St Chads Catholic High
Halton General Hospital
Hallwood Park Prim Sch
Palacefields Prim Sch
Our Lady Mother of the Saviour Catholic Prim
Beechwood Primary Sch
Hillview Primary School
Holiday Inn
Runcorn Rowing Club
Junction 12
Sutton Hall Golf Club
Golf Course
Marshgate Farm
Weaver Park Industrial Est
Weaver Vale Primary School
The Manor House Primary School
St Lukes RC Primary School
CENTRAL EXPRESSWAY
ROCKSAVAGE EXPRESSWAY
WHITEHOUSE EXPRESSWAY
A533
A557
M56
A56
CLIFTON ROAD A557
CHESTER ROAD
SUTTON CAUSEWAY
BRIDGE LANE
STREET
Halton
Cheshire County
Weaver Navigation
WA7
177
188
201
F
G
H
J
K
1
2
3
4
5
6
52
53
54
78
79
80
81

188
178
187
Murdishaw
Brookvale
Preston Brook
Sutton Weaver
Aston Heath
Aston
Runcorn Ski Slope
Folkstone Way
Fleetwood Walk
East Station
Murdishaw Health Centre
St Martins Catholic Prim Sch
Gorsewood Prim Sch
Palacefields Prim Sch
Our Lady Mother of the Saviour Catholic Prim
Brookvale Recreation Centre
Halton High School
Brookvale Primary School
Exmouth Crescent
Council Building
Travel Inn
Sutton Fields Farm
Aston Primary School
Aston Lodge
Beckett's Wood
Parkside Farm
Aston Grange
Weaver Navigation
M56
A533
CHESTER ROAD
NORTHWICH RD
Aston Fields Road
Rivington Road
Fairoak Lane
Fairoak Court
Aston Lane
Aston Lane South
Aston La North
Stockham Lane
Stockham La
Wood Lane
Palace Fields Avenue
Brookvale Av North
Brookvale Av S
Woodhatch Rd
Masseyfield Road
Ridding Lane
Northwich Road
Murdishaw Av
Barnfield Av
Ridgeway
Cedar Avenue
Beech Road
Station Road
Sycamore Drive
Sandy Lane
Bridgewater Grange
Canal Side
Waterfront
Wellfield
Heysham Cl
Hoylake
Tynemouth Rd
Waterford Wy
Cleethorpes Road
Warren Cft
Marina La
Gorsewood Rd
Mooring Cl
Sextant Cl
Chichester Cl
Compass Cl
Mariner Cl
Saltwood Dr
Pickmere Dr
Clovelly Cl
Helston Cl
Mevagissey Rd
Porthleven Rd
Newlyn Cl
Stratton Cl
Liskeard Cl
Saltash Cl
St Austell Cl
Wren Cl
Badger Cl
Martin Cl
Lockwood Vw
Coronation Rd
Dukes Wharf
Preston on the Hill
A
B
C
D
E
1
2
3
4
5
6
3 55
56
3 81
80
79
3 78
1 grid square represents 500 metres

Junction 11
Little Manor Farm
179
Hallamhall Farm
Lake Farm
Morphany Hall
Preston on the Hill
Windmill La
Barker's Hollow Road
New Manor Road
Morphany Lane
New Manor Farm
Higher Lane
Brook Farm
Turfland
Dutton
Tunnel Top North
Cheshire Ring Canal Walk
Redacre Cl
Vale Court
Marsh Lane
Higher Lane
Lightwood Farm
Union Farm
Bird's Wood
Delamere Way
Seven Acre Wood
Hill Farm
Hill Top Road
A533
NORTHWICH ROAD
Lodge Lane
Dutton Hollow Farm
Dutton Lodge Farm
Cheshire Ring Canal
F G H J K
1 2 3 4 5 6
58 59
378 79 80 81

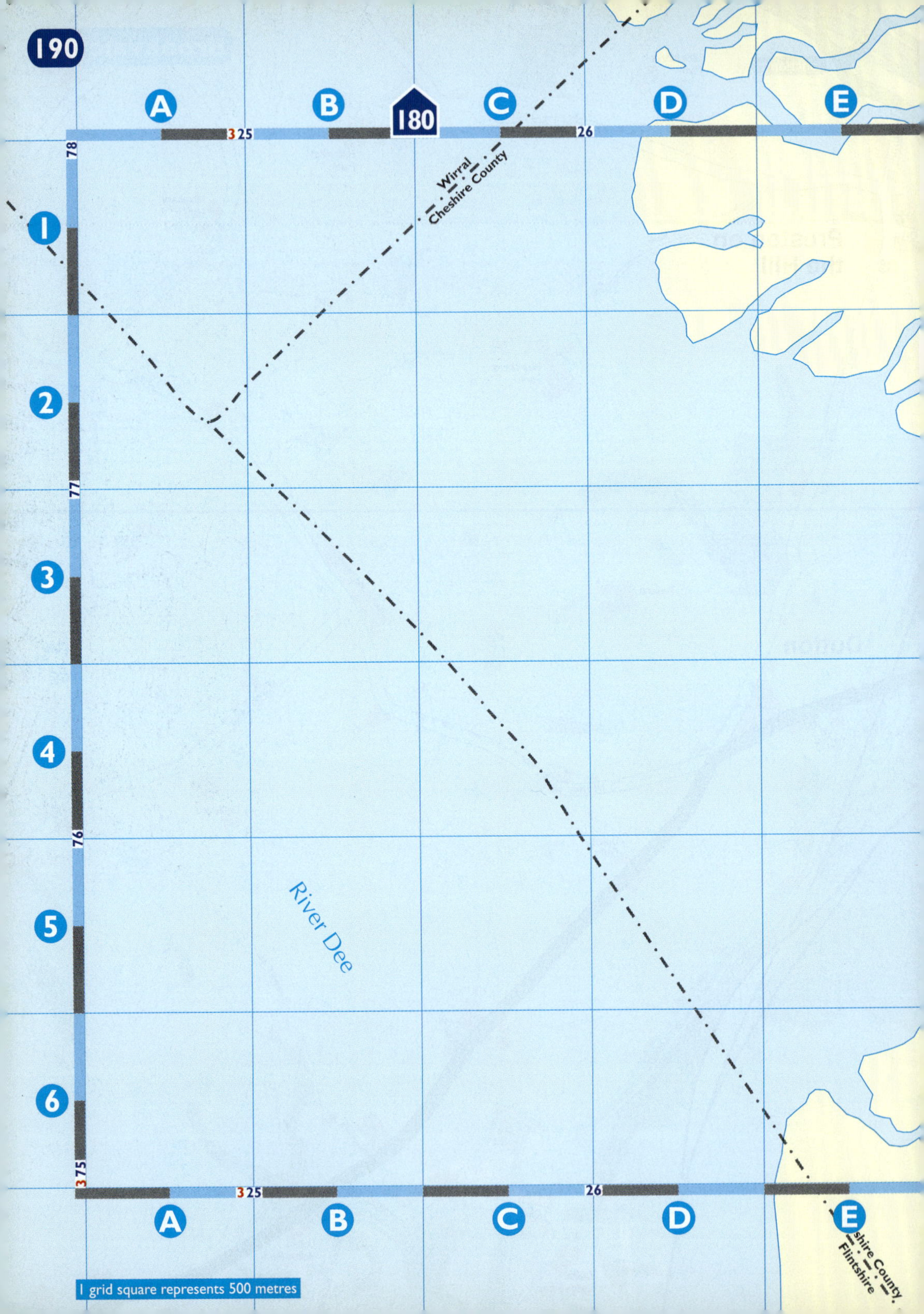
180
A
B
C
D
E
1
2
3
4
5
6
325
26
78
77
76
375
Wirral
Cheshire County
River Dee
shire County
Flintshire
1 grid square represents 500 metres

Neston 191
Parkgate
181
192
Moorside
NESTON
Little Neston
Nessho
F
G
H
J
K
F
G
H
J
K
I
2
3
4
5
6
28
29
78
77
76
375
STATION RD
PARKGATE RD
B5135
B5136
B5134
HIGH ST
CHESTER RD
THE PARADE
Brooklands Gardens
Mostyn Square
Wirral Way
Neston CC
Manorial Road
Hunters Way
Manorial Rd South
Moorside Avenue
Moorside
Boundary Pk
Old Quay Lane
Leighton Road
The Priory
Leighton Pk
Woodlands Rd
Albert Drive
Buggen Lane
Mill Street
Park St
Neston Station
Neston Medical Centre
Brook St
Church Lane
Bridge Street
Steeple Ct
Station Road
Neston Primary School
Romney Way
Cottage Cl
Meadow
Allans Meadow
Grasmere
West Vale
West Dr
Meadow Close
Sutton Av
Arden Dr
Henley Rd
Coniston
Hampton Crs
Kenilworth Rd
Stratford Rd
Riverside Walk
Warwick Cl
Leamington Cl
Merton Close
Holmcrofts
Somerville
Marshlands Road
New St
Colliery Green Dr
Orchard Dr
Grove
Foxglove Way
Tree Tops
Sunningdale Wy
Sea Vw
Quayside
Winstanley Rd
Darby Cl
Crofton
Snabwood Cl
Greenfields Drive
Brook Well
Wirral Crs
Turrocks Cft
Burton Road
Talbot Gdns
Breezehill
Blackeys Lane
Highfield
Olive Dr
Raby Rd
Sytch Croft
Frobisher Road
Drake Road
Shakespeare
Raleigh Rd
Cemetery

192
182
191
Hinderton
Neston High School
Windle Hill
Ness
Nessholt
Burton
CH64
B5134 HINDERTON ROAD
B5134 HINDERTON RD
CHESTER RD
CHESTER HIGH ROAD
B5133
HANNS HALL ROAD
Quarry Road
Hinderton La
Park Road
Cemetery
Raby Rd
Breezehill Rd
Gunn Grove
Cherry Close
Weatherstone Business Centre
Leahurst
Hanns Hall Farm
The Lydiate
Lees Lane
Wirral Way
Cuckoo Lane
Station Road
Bushell Road
The Quillet
Bendee Road
Bendee Av
Raymond Way
Dunraven Rd
Waterford Drive
Ashtree Dr
Mellock Lane
Surgery
St Winefrides RC Prim Sch
Yewtree Cl
Newtown
Romney Way
Raeburn Av
Cottage Cl
Sandy Lane
Stonebank Dr
Howards Way
Farm Dr
Talbot Av
Burton Road
Badger Bait
The Green
Town La
Ivy Farm Dr
Rocklee Gdns
Victoria Rd
Rock Farm Cl
Gorstons La
Woodfall Lane
Woodfall Junior School
Woodfall Infant School
Bull Hill
Glenton Pk
School Lane
Cliffe Rd
Riverview Rd
Furrocks La
Furrocks Wy
Coniston
Dawn Close
Cumbers Dr
Neston Road
Holt Hey
Well Lane
Cumbers La
Mill Lane
Hill Ct
Hill Cl
Flashes La
Hl Top Lane
Ml Bank
Palace Hey
Shones Cft
Snab La
Well Cl
Greenfields Drive
Brook Well
Wirral Crs
Snabwood Cl
Hyfield
Haddon Hall Farm
Haddon Lane
Liverpool University Botanic Gardens (Ness Gardens)
Denhall House Farm
Lane
Neston Road
Wood Lane
Haddon Road
A B C D E
1 2 3 4 5 6
330 31
378 377 376 375
1 grid square represents 500 metres

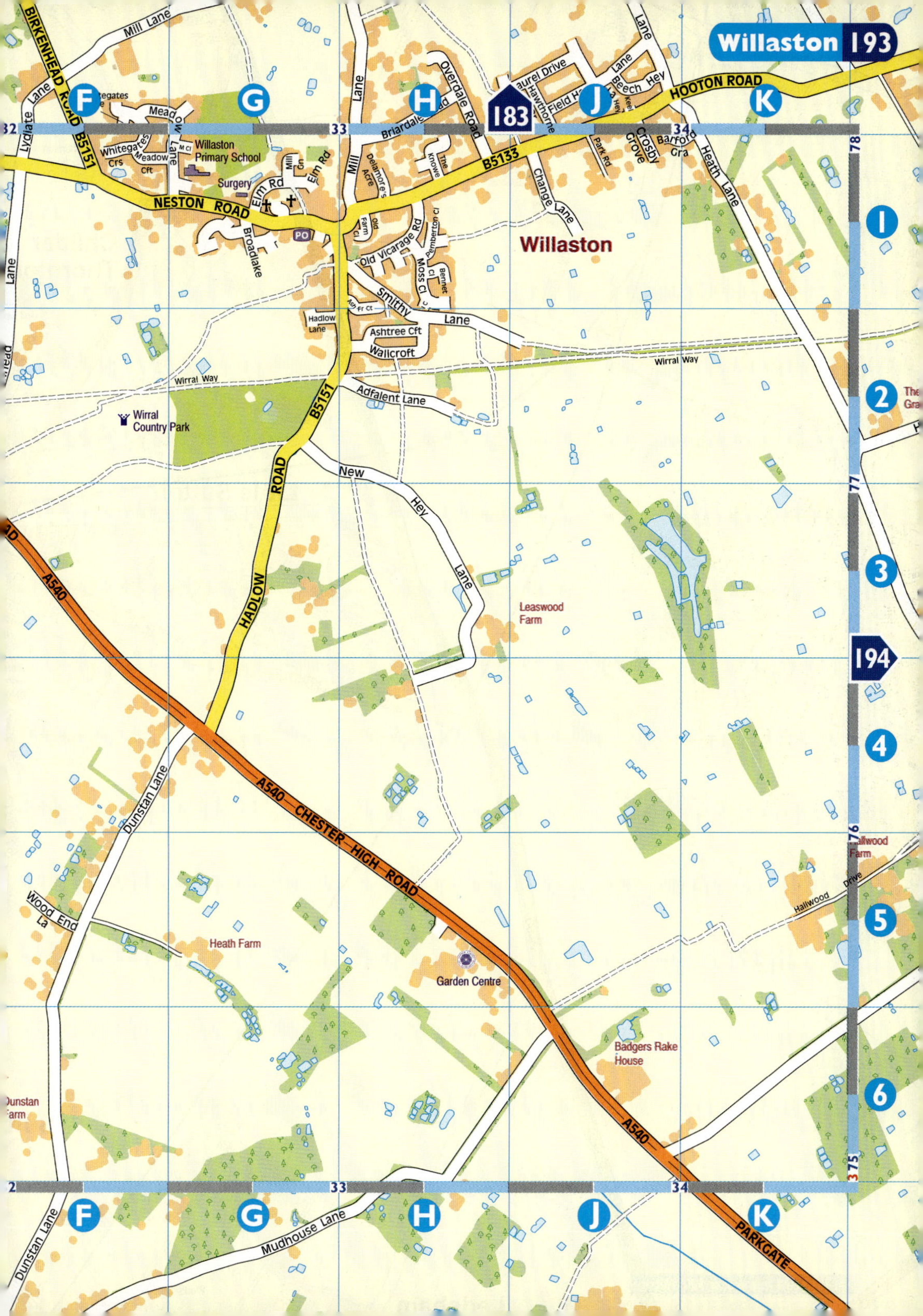

Willaston
Mill Lane
Birkenhead Road
B5151
Lydiate Lane
Whitegates
Meadow Lane
Meadow
Whitegates Crs
Meadow Cft
M Cl
Willaston Primary School
Surgery
Elm Rd
Mill Gn
Neston Road
Broadlake
PO
Mill Lane
Delamores Acre
Briardale Rd
Overdale Road
The Knowe
B5133
Laurel Drive
Hawthorne
Field Hey
Lane
Beech Hey
Hooton Road
Park Rd
Crosby Grove
Barford Gra
Heath Lane
Change Lane
Old Farm Cl
Old Vicarage Rd
Pemberton Cl
Moss Cl
Bennet Cl
Smithy Lane
Ash Fr Ct
Hadlow Lane
Ashtree Cft
Wallcroft
Wirral Way
Adfalent Lane
Wirral Country Park
Hadlow Road
New Hey Lane
Leaswood Farm
A540
A540 Chester High Road
Dunstan Lane
Wood End La
Heath Farm
Garden Centre
Badgers Rake House
Dunstan Farm
Hallwood Farm
Hallwood Drive
Mudhouse Lane
Parkgate
Lane
F
G
H
J
K
1
2
3
4
5
6
32
33
34
78
77
76
375
183
194

194
184
193
A
B
C
D
E
1
2
3
4
5
6
335
36
78
77
76
375
Hooton Station
Oak Road
Waterworks Lane
School Lane
Woodclose
Welsh Road
New School Lane
Childer Thornton Primary School
The Oaklands
Water Works Lane
Oakfield Road
A41
CHESTER ROAD
Orchard La
New Road
Childer Thornton
Cemetery
Ellesmere Golf Ce
Blackboards Lane
Heath Lane
St Pauls Gdns
Childer Crs
Childer Gdns
Meadway
Granville Dr
Fieldway
Beverley Way
Margaret's Lane
Heath Grove
Heathlands Road
The Grange
Heath Lane
A550
WELSH ROAD
Quality Hotel
Little Sutton
Berwick Road
Little Sutton CE Primary School
Snowdon Close
Stiperstones Cl
Weald Dr
Ben Nevis Dr
Ledsham Park Dr
Clwyd Way
Cambrian Close
Sidlaw Cl
Chevoit Close
Orchil Cl
Sutton Hall Gdns
Hillcrest Road
Hillcrest Drive
Wicklow Cl
Berwyn Cl
Cleveland Dr
Lochinvar Av
Ullapool Cl
Roxburgh Rd
Bredon Cl
Jedburgh Av
Coldstream Dr
Sutton Hall Dr
Stephens Ter
Berwick Gdns
Berwick Grove
B5463
Highfield Rd
Dudleston Road
Dunmore
Starbeck Dr
Askrigg Av
Sutton Green School
Scotton Av
Wetherby
Penistone Cl
Rudstone Cl
Collingham Gn
Oaks Farm
LEDSHAM ROAD
Sutton New Hall
CH66
Badgersrake Lane
Hallwood Farm
Hallwood Drive
Ledsham Lane
Sutt
Works
Ledsham
1 grid square represents 500 metres

Junction 7
F
G
H
185
J
K
North Road
B5132
RIVACRE ROAD
Rivacre Valley Country Park
Poole Hall Lane
Poole Hall Industrial Estate
Poole Hall Road
Poole Hall Industrial Estate
Junction 8
I
NETHERPOOL RD
Golf Course
Mossvale
Red Pike
Fairways
Hillfield Rd
Rossmore Primary School
Links Av
Trumans Lane
Pound Rd
Windways
Eagle La
Hillside Drive
Moorland Rd
Rivacre Brow
Rivacre Valley CP School
Rivacre Rd
Warren Dr
The Breck
Forest Rd
Naylor Crs
Rother Drive Business Park
Rother Dr
B5463
Overpool
Cemetery
ROSSMORE ROAD EAST
2
Rossbank Road
Rossmore Trading Estate
Rosscliffe Rd
Rossfield Road
Shallacres
STATION RD
ROSSMORE ROAD WEST
B5463
Little Sutton Station
Pius XII RC Primary School
Hawthorn Road
Parklands
Woodvale Rd
Ferguson Av
Crossley Av
Seymour Drive
OVERPOOL ROAD
Overpool Station
Bailey Avenue
Straker Av
Westenra Av
Westminster Industrial Park
Rossfield Road
Rosswood Road
3
Princes Road
CHESTER ROAD
Glenwood Road
Cedar Av
Maple Avenue
Fulwood Road
Parklands Primary School
Parklands
Heywood Road
Acre Road
Brook Rd
Valley Dr
Rivacre Business Cen
Sutton High School
B5132
Overpool Rd
Regent Street
Atherton Rd
Pooltown Rd
Festival Road
Atherton Infant School
Pooltown Junior School
Belgrave Dr
Dale Dr
Brooklyn Dr
Luton Road
196
6
Cannon St
Deansgate
Aldgate
Kensington Road
4
Ellesmere Port Business Cen
Great Sutton
Whetstone Hey
Valley View
A41
Great Sutton Health Cen
Mill Lane
Delamere Dr
Wilmslow Dr
Hargrave Dr
Waverton Rd
Gawsworth Road
Alvanley Rd
Sutton Way
SUTTON WAY
B5132
The Boulevard
Faraday Rd
Mallory Road
Tennyson Rd
Cavell Drive
WHITBY
A5032
5
Glen Road
Glenesk Road
Gleneagles Road
B5132 SUTTON WAY
Brookside Primary School
Singleton Road
Cholmondeley Road
Loxdale Drive
Green La
Old Chester Rd
Greystones
Bebington Road
Caldy Dr
Northern Rise
Ringway
Rostherne Avenue
Charter Crescent
Overpool Road
Hurford Av
Crappenhall Rd
Capenhurst Lane
Bradwell Close
Our Ladys RC Junior School
Gorsthills Primary School
Church Lane
Regal Cl
Seacombe Drive
St Saviour's RC J&I School
Mansfield Primary School
Ellesmere Port Catholic High School
Hinderton School
Our Ladys Catholic Infant School
CHESTER ROAD
Pennington Green
n Green
Holmfield Dr
The Paddock
Baker Drive
Brunswick Crs
Talbot Road
Nantwich Rd
Merton Road
202
Wenlock Lane
Overpool Road
Ellesmere Port Hospital
Fern Road
Fairfield Av
Orchard Rd
A5032
Kendal Drive
Dolphin Crescent
Capenhurst Grange
Meadow
Humber Rd
Council Building
38
39
37
78
77
76
75

196
A
B
C
D
E
340
41
78
77
76
375
1
2
3
4
5
6
Junction 8
Junction 9
ELLESMERE
PORT
Manchester Ship Canal
M53
MERSEYTON RD
DOCK ST
A5032
QUEEN ST
STATION ROAD
WHITBY ROAD
CHESTER ROAD
STANNEY LA
B5463
B5132
SUTTON WAY
EAST
Rother Drive
Business Park
Rossmore
Trading
Estate
Rossfield Road
Rosswood Road
Inward Way
Portside
North
Lower Mersey Street
South Pier Rd
Boat Museum
Canalside Industrial Estate
Oil Sites Road
Dock Yard Road
Works
Indigo Road
Westminster Retail Park
Crescent Rd
Service Centre
Meadow Lane
Meadow Lane Ind Park
Cedab Road
Cook St
Europa Wy
Station Rd
Ellesmere Port Station
Princes Road
William Stockton Primary School
Compton Place
Cromwell Road
Cloister Way
Chapterhouse Cl
Bridges Road
South Road
New Bridge Road
Deans Road
Newbridge Road
Mill Lane Industrial Estate
Shropshire Road
Stanney Mill Industrial Park
Stanney Mill Industrial Estate
Ellesmere Port Business Cen
Civic Hall
Council Building
Port Arcades
Market Hall
Surgery
Surg
Primary Sch
York Rd Clinic
Ellesmere Port Clinic
Epic Leisure Centre
Wolverham
Wolverham Primary School
Whitby
Whitby Heath Prim Sch
Tynesdale
Lees Lane
Thornton Road
Telford Road
Marchwiel Road
Girton Road
Cambridge Road
Milton Road
Eton Rd
Repton Rd
Winchester Av
St Andrew's Rd
Wolverham Road
Malvern Road
Marlborough Road
Sherbourne Rd
St Bernards RC Prim Sch
Rochester Drive
The Oaks Community Prim Sch
Ellesmere Port Stadium
Ellesmere Port Hospital
Christ Church CE Primary Sch
Stanney High School
The Oaks Community Prim Sch
Cheshire Oaks Retail Outlet
Bodiam Court
Alnwick Dr
Coliseum Wy
203
Works
Percival Road
Church Road
Westminster Rd
Wellington Road
McGarva Way
Grange Rd
Stoke Gdns
Newnham Dr
Somerville Crescent
Central Avenue
Park Road
Coronation Rd
Old Hall Dr
Thamesdale
Pembroke Drive
Wyedale
Clydesdale
Deesdale
Avondale
Buttermere Av
Underwood Drive
Crassmere Rd
Windermere Rd
Birkett Av
Fern Road
Silverne Dr
Beechcroft Drive
Fairfield Av
1 grid square represents 500 metres

F
G
H
J
K
42
43
44
78
77
76
375
1
2
3
4
5
6
198
Stanlow Point
Manchester Ship Canal
CH65
Corridor Road
Oil Sites Road
Stanlow
Stanlow & Thornton Station
Oil Refinery
Shellway Road
A5117
Poole Lane

Ince Banks
A
B
C
D
E
1
2
3
4
5
6
78
77
76
75
3 45
46
197
Holme Farm
Marsh Lane
Ince
Kinsey's Lane
Pool Lane
Station Road
Perimeter Road
Ince & Elton Stn
Ince Orchards
Cherry Tree Cl
Orchard Park Lane
Mt Pleasant
PO
Highfield
Hapsford Lane
Elton
Ince Lane
Anvil Cl
Coppice Green
Dove Cl
Redwood Dr
Elton Primary School
The Paddock
Farmdale Dr
Ryecroft
Whitefields
Marsh Lane
Holm Drive
Osier Cl
Holm Drive
Ash Road
Dlw Crs
Deansfield Way
Ferndale Av
Lane
Brackendale
Hallfield Dr
Greenfield Gdns
Pinewood Cl
Firbank
Mulberry Cl
Meadow View
School
Parkland
Lawnswood Grove
Hall Lane
Alvanley View
Drive
Manley View
Ince Lane
Lime Grove
Poplar Gv
Willow Grove
Old
A5117
Chester Service Area
Travel Inn
Cryers Lane
YERS LANE
Lane
Elton Green
Junction 14
1 grid square represents 500 metres

Manchester Ship Canal
Moorditch Lane
Cross Lane
Lordship Lane
Elton Lordship Lane
Ince Marshes
Rake Lane
Hill View Farm
Hornsmill Brook
Helsby Marsh
M56
Hoolpool Lane
Elton Lane
Lower Rake Lane
Helsby Station
Station Av
Lodge Hollow
Smithy Lane
Holly Ct
Plovers Lane
Hillside Primary School
Bank House La
Hallastone Rd
Vale Gdns
The Beeches
Vicarage Lane
Rake La
Red Stone Hl
High View
Hale View Road
Conery Cl
Cambridge Gdns
Old Chester Road
HELSBY
Longster Trail
Hill
Coppins Cl
Sandringham Av
Crescent Drive
Mountain View
Kings Dr
Queens Drive
Parkfield Dr
Sherwood Grove
Springfield Av
Lower Robin Hood Lane
Helsby Health Centre
Hill Road South
Freshmeadow Lane
Alvanley
The Orchard
CHESTER ROAD
Hood
Sandy Lane
The Paddock
Alvanley Dr
Road
Blue
Bridge
Lane
PO
200

200
186
199
A
B
C
D
E
1
2
3
4
5
6
M56
Lane
Tadgers Lane
Moorditch Lane
Brook Furlong
Hare's Lane
Straight Length
Hatley Lane
Godscroft Lane
Godscroft Hall
Bridge Lane
Blue Bridge
Marsh Lane
Brookside Rd
Chapelfields
Maori Dr
Millbank Court
MAIN STREET
PO
Greenfield Lane
Moor Lane
Rodgers Close
Hawthorne
Wayford
St Luke's Wy
Surgery
Frodsham Station
B5152 CHURCH STREET
Frodsham Science & Tech College
Fountain Lane
Princeway
Queensway
Martin Rd
Kingsway
Park Lane
St Lawrence Road
Council Building
Marsh Green
Castle Park
Netherton Drive
A56
Dig Lane
Matty's Lane
Howey Lane
Howey Ri
Howey Rise
Pinmill Brow
Hillfield
Mersey View
Middle Walk
War Memorial
Orchard Close
Carriage Drive
Erindale Crescent
CHESTER ROAD
Cemetery
Netherton
Dunsdale
Forest Hills Hotel & Leisure Complex
Bellemonte
Simons Lane
Sandstone Trail
Helsby High School
Hillside Primary School
Plovers Lane
Barn Cft
Hunters Ct
Cem
Landscape Dene
Foxhill Gv
Proffits Lane
High View
Cambridge Gdns
Hale View Road
Old Chester Road
Woodhouses
ROAD
TARVIN
Frodsham Golf Club
Golf Course
Mickledale
Covertside
Foxhill
Bates Lane
Shepherds Houses
HELSBY
North Road
B5393
WA6
Longster Trail
Willow Bank
350
51
375
76
77
78
1 grid square represents 500 metres

Newtown
FRODSHAM
Bradley
Fivecrosses
Newton
187
F
G
H
J
K
52
53
54
78
77
76
75
1
2
3
4
5
6
Bridge Lane
A56
Francis Rd
Ashton Drive
Ellis La
The Manor House Primary School
Langdale
Penrith Close
Thirlmere Close
Blue Hatch
Ennerdale Drive
Coniston Drive
Keswick Drive
Grasmere Road
The Willows
St Lukes RC Primary School
Fluin Lane
Lime Av
Beech Av
Ashlands
Churchfield Rd
Red Lane
Foxglove Court
Borrowdale Close
Silverdale Close
Matterdale Close
Townfield Lane
B5152
Vicarage Lane
Church Road
Frodsham CE Primary School
Doric Avenue
Hillsboro Avenue
Ranulph Court
Bickerton Av
Fairways
Greenside Av
Clover Av
Hillside Road
Arran Drive
Bradley Lane
Lansdowne
Oakdale Avenue
Royleen Drive
Manley Rd
Penkmans Lane
Newlands Cl
Eversley
Warren Ct
Hazlehurst Road
Kingsley Road
Top Road
Watery Lane
Eddisbury Way
Manley Road
Dobers Lane
Bradley Orchard
Weaver Navigation
Hatley Farm
Belleair
Newton Hall
Lady Heyes Farm
Pike Nook
Pike Lane
Hillfoot Lane
Hollow Lane
Middle Lane
Kingsley Community Primary School

Sutton Green
Pennington Green
195
Capenhurst
Capenhurst Learning Centre
Capenhurst Station
Capenhurst Lane
Dunkirk Lane
Whitbyheath
Dunkirk
Backford Cross
CHESTER ROAD
A41
A5117
A5032
LIVERPOOL ROAD
M56
Junction 16
Dunkirk Trading Estate
Coalpit Lane
Old Hall Farm
Heath Farm
Lea Manor Farm
Wood Farm
Strawberry Lane
Grove Road
Capenhurst Grange Special School
Meadow Primary School
Woodlands Infant School
Woodlands Junior School
The Whitby High School
Council Building
Garden Centre
Mansfield Primary School
Ellesmere Port Catholic High School
Hinderton School
Our Ladys Catholic Infant School
St Saviour's RC J&I School
Ellesmere Port Hospital
The Groves
Lea by
1 grid square represents 500 metres

196
Whitby Heath Prim Sch
Tynesdale
Park
Drive
Wyedale
Trentdale
Deeside
Avondale
Christ Church CE Primary Sch
Fern Road
Warrington
Woodland
Clare Drive
Woodsome Drive
Acorn Dr
Underwood Dr
Woodbank Rd
Greenlea
Buttermere Av
Underwood
Crasmere Rd
Windermere Rd
Ambleside Rd
Birkett
Thirlmere Rd
Rydal Cl
Ullswater Rd
Weaver Road
Stanney Lane
STANNEY LANE
Stanney High School
Wolverham
Rugby Road
Marlborough Rd
Sherbourne Rd
St Bernards RC Prim Sch
Harlech Way
Chirk Gardens
Denbigh Court
Rochester
The Oaks Community Prim Sch
Beaumaris Dr
Fotheringay Court
Rhuddlan Ct
Dover Court
Dover Dr
Alnwick
Bunbury
The Oaks Community Prim Sch
Edinburgh Court
Doune Court
Lancaster Gdns
Richmond Ct
Bamburgh Court
Pembridge Gardens
Langley Court
Arundel Court
Warwick Ct
Drive
Bodiam Court
Hylton Ct
Ellesmere Port Stadium
Thornton Road
Cheshire Oaks Retail Outlet
Cheshire Oaks Wy
Coliseum Wy
Coliseum Way
VUE Cinema
KINSEY RD
B5132
Longlooms Road
Blue Planet Aquarium
Stanney Lane
A5117
Little Stanney
Junction 10
Stanney Woods Country Park
Guernsey Drive
Arran Av
Jersey Av
Wight Cl
Avenue
St Kilda Cl
Kintyre Cl
Fair Isle Cl
Skye Cl
Hilbre Dr
Stanney Woods
Shetland Drive
Lloyd Dr
Rona Av
Stroma Av
Puffin Cl
Barry Cl
Lewis Cl
Islay Cl
Mill Close
Scilly Close
Handa Dr
Lundy Dr
M53
Stanney Mill Road
Mill Lane Industrial Estate
Stanney Ten Industrial Estate
Stanney Mill Lane
Stanney Mill Industrial Est
Stanney Mill Industrial Park
Industrial Estate
New Bridge Road
Dutton Gn
Shellway Road
Stoak Grange
Rake Lane
Rake Hall
Heath Farm
Little Stanney Lane
Heath Lane
Heath Lane
Poplarhall
M56
Stoak
Croughton Road
Junction 11/15
Mount Farm
The Grove
Croughton Road
Croughton Cottage
Wervin Road
Shropshire Union Canal
Gordon Lane
Rake Lane
Backford
Council Building
Church Lane
Church Lane
Chorlton Hall
LIVERPOOL
40
41
42
75
74
73
72
F
G
H
J
K
I
2
3
4
5
6
372

Aigburth 153 G2
Ainsdale 33 J4
Ainsdale-on-Sea 32 E4
Aintree 83 G1
Allerton 154 B2
Anfield 97 J6
Appleton 158 C1
Appleton Park 162 B6
Arrowe Hill 129 G6
Ashton-in-Makerfield 79 J6
Ashurst 56 D1
Aspull Common 93 J2
Astmoor 177 H2
Aston 188 C6
Aston Heath 188 C5
Aughton 52 D6
Aughton Park 53 J3
Backford Cross 202 D4
Ball o' Ditton 157 K2
Bamfurlong 79 K1
Banks 21 J5
Barnston 168 C2
Barrow Nook 64 E5
Barrow's Green 139 J5
Barton 43 H5
Bebington 151 H4
Beechwood 187 H2
Belle Vale 135 K4
Bescar 36 E2
Bewsey 142 B1
Bickerstaffe 64 E2
Bidston 110 D6
Bidston Hill 130 A1
Billinge 77 J4
Birch Green 56 E3
Birchwood 125 G3
Birkdale 27 G5
Birkenhead 2 A4
Blackbrook 89 K6
Blackbrook 124 A5
Blaguegate 55 H4
Blowick 28 B1
Blundellsands 68 B5
Bold Heath 139 K2
Bootle 4 A5
Bowker's Green 63 H2
Bowring Park 135 J1
Bradley 201 H2
Brighton le Sands 68 B6
Brimstage 169 H3
Broad Green 115 H5
Broad Oak 104 D1
Bromborough 170 D4
Bromborough Pool 151 J6
Brookhurst 183 J2
Brookvale 188 A2
Brown Edge 28 D5
Brown Edge 102 E6
Brownlow 76 E1
Bruche 143 J2
Bryn 78 E3
Buckley Hill 70 A5
Burscough 46 C1
Burscough Bridge 38 D3
Burtonwood 121 K1
Calderstones 134 D6
Caldy 146 E4
Callands 122 D5
Carr Cross 36 B1
Carr Houses 60 B3
Castlefields 177 J3
Chadwick Green 77 H5
Chapel House 55 K3
Childer Thornton 194 E1
Childwall 135 G3
Churchtown 23 K4
Cinnamon Brow 124 C3
Claughton 130 B4
Clifton 187 G3
Clinkham Wood 88 D2
Clock Face 120 B4
Clubmoor 98 A6
Cobbs 162 C3
Collins Green 105 H4
Court Hey 115 K6
Crank 76 B5
Crawford 66 E5
Cronton 138 A4
Crosby 80 C2
Crossens 23 K1
Crow Wood 158 E1
Croxteth 99 H1
Cuerdley Cross 140 B6
Dallam 123 F6
Daresbury 179 G4
Deansgreen 165 J3
Denton's Green 12 C1
Derbyshire Hill 104 D3
Digmoor 66 E1
Dingle 133 F6
Ditton 157 G4
Doe Green 140 D6
Dog & Gun 98 E2
Dovecot 115 K4
Downall Green 78 B4
Downholland Cross 51 J3
Drummersdale 36 D3
Dudlows Green 162 D6
Dunkirk 202 C4
Dutton 189 F3
Earlestown 105 K2
Eastham 184 B1
Eastham Ferry 171 J5
Eccleston 87 K6
Eccleston Park 102 C6
Edge Hill 133 G1
Egremont 111 J3
Ellesmere Port 6 B3
Elmers Green 57 F2
Elton 198 B5
Everton 113 H2
Fairfield 114 B4
Farnworth 139 F6
Fazakerley 83 F6
Fearnhead 124 C5
Fiddler's Ferry 21 G5
Fiddler's Ferry 159 K2
Fincham 115 K1
Fivecrosses 201 F4
Ford 81 K1
Formby 48 E1
Frankby 147 H1
Freshfield 40 C6
Frodsham 201 G2
Garston 154 A6
Garswood 78 A6
Gateacre 135 J5
Gayton 181 F1
Gemini 122 D4
Gillar's Green 102 A2
Gillmoss 84 B5
Golborne 92 C4
Gorse Covert 125 K1
Grange 146 E2
Grange 177 F6
Grange Park 102 D5
Grappenhall 163 G1
Grassendale 153 H4
Greasby 128 D5
Great Altcar 50 B4
Great Crosby 69 F5
Great Meols 108 D5
Great Sankey 141 J3
Great Sutton 195 G4
Hale 174 E3
Hale Bank 175 J1
Halewood 155 H3
Hall Green 57 J5
Halsall 44 A2
Halton 177 J5
Halton Brook 177 G4
Halton View 19 H2
Haresfinch 88 D4
Haskayne 43 G6
Haydock 90 C5
Heath 176 D6
Heaton's Bridge 37 H5
Helsby 199 K6
Hermitage Green 107 H5
Heswall 167 J5
High Legh 165 J6
High Park 23 H5
Higher Bebington 150 B5
Higher Runcorn 10 D7
Higher Walton 161 H4
Hightown 58 E4
Hillcliffe 162 B4
Hillside 26 E5
Hinderton 182 B6
Holmeswood 31 H1
Holt 118 C2
Holt Green 53 F6
Homer Green 60 E6
Hood Manor 141 K4
Hooton 184 C6
Hoscar 39 K5
Hough Green 157 F2
Houghton Green 124 A2
Houghwood 76 E3
Howley 17 J5
Hoylake 127 H2
Hulme 123 H4
Hunt's Cross 154 E5
Hurlston Green 37 F6
Huyton 117 F4
Huyton Park 116 C6
Huyton Quarry 117 H5
Huyton-With-Roby 116 C4
Ince 198 B3
Ince Blundell 60 A4
Irby 148 A5
Keckwick 178 E1
Kensington 113 J5
Kings Moss 76 C2
Kingsway 18 C3
Kingswood 122 A5
Kirkby 84 D2
Kirkdale 97 F5
Knotty Ash 115 H4
Knowsley 100 B1
Lady Green 60 A3
Laffak 89 H4
Land Gate 79 F2
Landican 149 F3
Lane Head 93 G5
Latchford 143 F6
Lea Green 119 H2
Leasowe 110 A3
Lingley Green 140 D2
Lingley Mere 140 E1
Liscard 111 H2
Litherland 81 K2
Little Altcar 49 G4
Little Crosby 68 D1
Little Neston 191 J3
Little Stanney 203 J2
Little Sutton 194 D3
Liverpool 112 C6
Locking Stumps 124 D3
Longbarn 124 E6
Longford 123 H6
Longview 117 F3
Lower Bebington 150 E6
Lower House 157 K3
Lower Walton 161 K3
Lowton 92 E3
Lowton Common 93 H3
Lowton Heath 92 D5
Lowton St Mary's 93 H4
Lugsdale 19 G5
Lunt 69 K1
Lunts Heath 139 F4
Lydiate 61 J2
Lymm 145 K6
Maghull 71 G1
Marsh Green 200 C1
Marshall's Cross 119 K2
Marshside 23 G2
Martinscroft 144 C2
Melling 71 J4
Melling Mount 72 C2
Meols 127 J1
Mere Brow 25 J3
Mere Side 31 G2
Moore 160 D5
Moorside 191 H2
Moreton 109 J6
Moss Bank 19 K4
Moss Bank 88 C2
Moss Nook 104 D4
Moss Side 62 E4
Moss Side 85 K4
Mossley Hill 133 K5
Murdishaw 178 D6
Ness 192 C4
Nessholt 191 K5
Neston 191 J2
Netherley 136 A5
Netherton 70 C4
Netherton 200 C3
New Boston 90 E5
New Brighton 95 G5
New Ferry 151 H3
New Lane 38 B2
Newgate 57 J6
Newton 147 G1
Newton Park 107 F3
Newton-le-Willows 106 D2
Newtown 102 E1
Newtown 187 G6
Noctorum 129 K4
Norris Green 98 D4
Northwood 73 G6
Norton 178 B4
Nut Grove 118 E1
Oakwood 125 G4
Oglet 173 J5
Old Boston 91 G4
Old Swan 114 D4
Orford 123 K6
Ormskirk 45 G6
Orrell 82 A5
Otterspool 152 E2
Overpool 195 J2
Overton 200 E2
Oxton 130 C6
Paddington 144 A1
Padgate 124 B6
Page Moss 116 B4
Palacefields 187 J2
Park Hill 65 K5
Parkgate 181 H6
Parr 104 C3
Peasley Cross 104 A4
Penketh 140 E5
Pennylands 55 J5
Pensby 167 K1
Pinfold 36 D5
Pocket Nook 93 K3
Poll Hill 167 K4
Pool Hey 28 E4
Port Sunlight 151 G6
Portico 102 C5
Poulton 111 G5
Poulton 170 D3
Prenton 149 K2
Prescot 117 H1
Preston Brook 188 E2
Preston on the Hill 189 F1
Primrose Hill 44 D3
Princes Park 133 G3
Raby 182 D3
Rainford 75 H2
Rainford Junction 66 B5
Rainhill 119 F4
Rainhill Stoops 119 G5
Ravenhead 103 G4
Ring o' Bells 47 H1
Risley 125 G1
Roby 116 B5
Roby Mill 57 K2
Rock Ferry 151 F1
Rocksavage 186 E2
Royal Oak 63 K3
Runcorn 11 G7
Sandhills 96 E5
Sankey Bridges 141 K5
Saughall Massie 128 C3
Scarisbrick 36 C2
Scarth Hill 54 C3
Seacombe 111 K6
Seaforth 81 F4
Sefton 70 C2
Sefton Park 133 J5
Shell Green 159 F1
Shirdley Hill 35 H3
Simm's Cross 19 F4
Simm's Lane End 77 K4
Skelmersdale 56 C3
Snape Green 29 H6
Southdene 84 D3
Southgate 177 H6
Southport 14 A2
Speke 173 K2
Spital 170 E2
St Helens 13 H2
St Michael's Hamlet 152 C1
Stanley 56 A2
Stanley Gate 54 E6
Stanlow 197 G4
Statham 145 J5
Stoak 203 K4
Stockbridge Village 100 A5
Stockton Heath 162 B2
Stoneycroft 114 E3
Storeton 150 A6
Stubshaw Cross 79 J4
Sutton 104 C6
Sutton Green 194 F6
Sutton Heath 119 G1
Sutton Leach 120 C2
Sutton Manor 119 J5
Sutton Weaver 188 A4
Swanside 115 K5
Sworton Heath 165 G6
Tanhouse 56 E5
Tarbock Green 137 F5
Tarlscough 31 J6
Thatto Heath 103 F5
Thelwall 144 D6
Thingwall 148 E6
Thornton 69 K3
Thornton Hough 169 G6
Thurstaston 147 H6
Toll Bar 102 D4
Tower Hill 72 E4
Town End 138 B3
Town Green 53 H6
Town Green 79 J5
Town of Lowton 92 B6
Town Park 178 A4
Toxteth 132 D4
Tranmere 131 H6
Tuebrook 114 D2
Up Holland 67 J1
Upton 129 G4
Upton 157 G1
Upton Rocks 138 D6
Vauxhall 112 D3
Vulcan Village 106 C5
Waddicar 71 K5
Wallasey 112 A3
Wallasey Village 110 C1
Walton 97 K3
Wargrave 106 C4
Warrington 16 B2
Waterloo 80 E1
Waterloo Park 81 G2
Wavertree 134 A2
West Bank 158 A6
West Derby 99 G6
West Kirby 146 A1
West Park 12 A7
Westbrook 122 A6
Westhead 54 D1
Weston 176 C6
Weston Point 176 A5
Westvale 84 C1
Westy 143 J4
Whiston 118 A4
Whiston Cross 117 K4
Whiston Lane Ends 117 J5
Whitby 6 C7
Whitbyheath 202 D2
Whitefield Lane End 136 E1
Widnes 18 A5
Wilderspool 162 B1
Willaston 193 J1
Windle Hill 192 D2
Windmill Hill 178 B3
Windy Arbor 137 G1
Winwick 107 H6
Winwick Quay 123 H3
Wolverham 6 E7
Woodchurch 129 K6
Woodhey 150 E4
Woodhouses 200 B5
Woodvale 33 H6
Woolfall Heath 116 C2
Woolston 144 B2
Woolton 154 D2
Wright's Green 163 F6

USING THE STREET INDEX

Street names are listed alphabetically. Each street name is followed by its postal town or area locality, the Postcode District, the page number, and the reference to the square in which the name is found.

Standard index entries are shown as follows:

Abacus Rd *CLB/OSW/ST* L13 .... **114** E3

Street names and selected addresses not shown on the map due to scale restrictions are shown in the index with an asterisk:

Abbeyway North *RNFD/HAY* WA11 * .. **90** A3

GENERAL ABBREVIATIONS

ACC ACCESS
ALY ALLEY
AP APPROACH
AR ARCADE
ASS ASSOCIATION
AV AVENUE
BCH BEACH
BLDS BUILDINGS
BND BEND
BNK BANK
BR BRIDGE
BRK BROOK
BTM BOTTOM
BUS BUSINESS
BVD BOULEVARD
BY BYPASS
CATH CATHEDRAL
CEM CEMETERY
CEN CENTRE
CFT CROFT
CH CHURCH
CHA CHASE
CHYD CHURCHYARD
CIR CIRCLE
CIRC CIRCUS
CL CLOSE
CLFS CLIFFS
CMP CAMP
CNR CORNER
CO COUNTY
COLL COLLEGE
COM COMMON
COMM COMMISSION
CON CONVENT
COT COTTAGE
COTS COTTAGES
CP CAPE
CPS COPSE
CR CREEK
CREM CREMATORIUM
CRS CRESCENT
CSWY CAUSEWAY
CT COURT
CTRL CENTRAL
CTS COURTS
CTYD COURTYARD
CUTT CUTTINGS
CV COVE
CYN CANYON
DEPT DEPARTMENT
DL DALE
DM DAM
DR DRIVE
DRO DROVE
DRY DRIVEWAY
DWGS DWELLINGS
E EAST
EMB EMBANKMENT
EMBY EMBASSY
ESP ESPLANADE
EST ESTATE
EX EXCHANGE
EXPY EXPRESSWAY
EXT EXTENSION
F/O FLYOVER

FC ... FOOTBALL CLUB
FK ... FORK
FLD ... FIELD
FLDS ... FIELDS
FLS ... FALLS
FLS ... FLATS
FM ... FARM
FT ... FORT
FWY ... FREEWAY
FY ... FERRY
GA ... GATE
GAL ... GALLERY
GDN ... GARDEN
GDNS ... GARDENS
GLD ... GLADE
GLN ... GLEN
GN ... GREEN
GND ... GROUND
GRA ... GRANGE
GRG ... GARAGE
GT ... GREAT
GTWY ... GATEWAY
GV ... GROVE
HGR ... HIGHER
HL ... HILL
HLS ... HILLS
HO ... HOUSE
HOL ... HOLLOW
HOSP ... HOSPITAL
HRB ... HARBOUR
HTH ... HEATH
HTS ... HEIGHTS
HVN ... HAVEN
HWY ... HIGHWAY
IMP ... IMPERIAL
IN ... INLET
IND EST ... INDUSTRIAL ESTATE
INF ... INFIRMARY
INFO ... INFORMATION
INT ... INTERCHANGE
IS ... ISLAND
JCT ... JUNCTION
JTY ... JETTY
KG ... KING
KNL ... KNOLL
L ... LAKE
LA ... LANE
LDG ... LODGE
LGT ... LIGHT
LK ... LOCK
LKS ... LAKES
LNDG ... LANDING
LTL ... LITTLE
LWR ... LOWER
MAG ... MAGISTRATE
MAN ... MANSIONS
MD ... MEAD
MDW ... MEADOWS
MEM ... MEMORIAL
MKT ... MARKET
MKTS ... MARKETS
ML ... MALL
ML ... MILL
MNR ... MANOR
MS ... MEWS
MSN ... MISSION
MT ... MOUNT
MTN ... MOUNTAIN
MTS ... MOUNTAINS
MUS ... MUSEUM
MWY ... MOTORWAY
N ... NORTH
NE ... NORTH EAST
NW ... NORTH WEST
O/P ... OVERPASS
OFF ... OFFICE
ORCH ... ORCHARD
OV ... OVAL
PAL ... PALACE
PAS ... PASSAGE
PAV ... PAVILION
PDE ... PARADE
PH ... PUBLIC HOUSE
PK ... PARK
PKWY ... PARKWAY
PL ... PLACE
PLN ... PLAIN
PLNS ... PLAINS
PLZ ... PLAZA
POL ... POLICE STATION
PR ... PRINCE
PREC ... PRECINCT
PREP ... PREPARATORY
PRIM ... PRIMARY
PROM ... PROMENADE
PRS ... PRINCESS
PRT ... PORT
PT ... POINT
PTH ... PATH
PZ ... PIAZZA
QD ... QUADRANT
QU ... QUEEN
QY ... QUAY
R ... RIVER
RBT ... ROUNDABOUT
RD ... ROAD
RDG ... RIDGE
REP ... REPUBLIC
RES ... RESERVOIR
RFC ... RUGBY FOOTBALL CLUB
RI ... RISE
RP ... RAMP
RW ... ROW
S ... SOUTH
SCH ... SCHOOL
SE ... SOUTH EAST
SER ... SERVICE AREA
SH ... SHORE
SHOP ... SHOPPING
SKWY ... SKYWAY
SMT ... SUMMIT
SOC ... SOCIETY
SP ... SPUR
SPR ... SPRING
SQ ... SQUARE
ST ... STREET
STN ... STATION
STR ... STREAM
STRD ... STRAND
SW ... SOUTH WEST
TDG ... TRADING
TER ... TERRACE
THWY ... THROUGHWAY
TNL ... TUNNEL
TOLL ... TOLLWAY
TPK ... TURNPIKE
TR ... TRACK
TRL ... TRAIL
TWR ... TOWER
U/P ... UNDERPASS
UNI ... UNIVERSITY
UPR ... UPPER
V ... VALE
VA ... VALLEY
VIAD ... VIADUCT
VIL ... VILLA
VIS ... VISTA
VLG ... VILLAGE
VLS ... VILLAS
VW ... VIEW
W ... WEST
WD ... WOOD
WHF ... WHARF
WK ... WALK
WKS ... WALKS
WLS ... WELLS
WY ... WAY
YD ... YARD
YHA ... YOUTH HOSTEL

POSTCODE TOWNS AND AREA ABBREVIATIONS

AIG/SPK ... Aigburth/Sefton Park
AIMK ... Ashton-in-Makerfield
AIN/FAZ ... Aintree/Fazakerley
ALL/GAR ... Allerton/Garston
ANF/KKDL ... Anfield/Kirkdale
BEB ... Bebington
BIRK ... Birkenhead
BTL ... Bootle
CALD/MH ... Calderstones/Mossley Hill
CHLDW ... Childwall
CL/PREN ... Claughton/Prenton
CLB/OSW/ST ... Clubmoor/Old Swan/Stoneycroft
CLVP ... Central Liverpool
CLVPS ... Central Liverpool south
CSBY/BLUN ... Crosby/Blundellsands
CSBY/WL ... Crosby/Waterloo
DV/KA/FCH ... Dovecot/Knotty Ash/Fincham
ECCL ... Eccleston
EHL/KEN ... Edge Hill/Kensington
EV ... Everton
FMBY ... Formby
FROD/HEL ... Frodsham/Helsby
GOL/RIS/CUL ... Golborne/Risley/Culcheth
GR/UP/WCH ... Greasby/Upton/Woodchurch
HES ... Heswall
HLWD ... Halewood
HOY ... Hoylake
HTWN ... Hightown
HUY ... Huyton
KKBY ... Kirkby
LITH ... Litherland
LYMM ... Lymm
MGHL ... Maghull
MOR/LEA ... Moreton/Leasowe
NEWLW ... Newton-le-Willows
NG/CROX ... Norris Green/Croxteth
NPK/KEN ... Newsham Park/Kensington
NSTN ... Neston
NTHLY ... Netherley
NTHTN ... Netherton
NWD/KWIPK ... Northwood/Knowsley Industrial Park
ORM ... Ormskirk
PEN/TH ... Pensby/Thingwall
PR/KW ... Prescot/Knowsley
PS/BROM ... Port Sunlight/Bromborough
RAIN/WH ... Rainhill/Whiston
RF/TRAN ... Rock Ferry/Tranmere
RNFD/HAY ... Rainford/Haydock
RUNC ... Runcorn
SFTN ... Sefton
SPK/HALE ... Speke/Hale
STBRV ... Stockbridge Village
STHEL ... St Helens
TOX ... Toxteth
VAUX/LVPD ... Vauxhall/Liverpool Docks
WAL/EG ... Wallasey/Egremont
WAL/NB ... Wallasey/New Brighton
WARR ... Warrington
WARRN/WOL ... Warrington north/Woolston
WARRS ... Warrington south
WARRW/BUR ... Warrington west/Burtonwood
WAV ... Wavertree
WD/CROXPK ... West Derby/Croxteth Park
WDN ... Widnes
WGNW/BIL/OR ... Wigan west/Billinge/Orrell
WKBY ... West Kirby
WLT/FAZ ... Walton/Fazakerley
WLTN ... Woolton

Index - streets

3rd St WGNE/HIN WN2 ... 79 K2

A

Abacus Rd CLB/OSW/ST L13 ... 114 E3
Abberley Cl ECCL WA10 ... 12 E5
Abberley Rd WLTN L25 ... 155 G4
Abberton Pk NTHTN L30 ... 70 D4
Abbey Cl BIRK CH41 ... 3 H6
FMBY L37 ... 49 H3
NWD/KWIPK L33 ... 84 E1
WDN WA8 ... 157 H3
Abbey Ct WLTN L25 ... 154 E1
Abbey Dl BRSC L40 ... 39 F6
Abbeyfield Dr WD/CROXPK L12 ... 99 H3
Abbey Fold BRSC L40 ... 38 D4
Abbey Gdns STHP PR8 ... 27 H3
Abbey Hey RUNC WA7 ... 178 B5
Abbey La BRSC L40 ... 46 C3
Abbey Rd ECCL WA10 ... 88 B4
GOL/RIS/CU WA3 ... 93 K3
RNFD/HAY WA11 ... 90 D4
WDN WA8 ... 157 G3
WKBY CH48 ... 146 C1
Abbeystead SKEL WN8 ... 56 D6
Abbeystead Av NTHTN L30 ... 82 D2
Abbeystead Rd WAV L15 ... 134 C1
Abbey St BIRK CH41 ... 3 H6
Abbeyvale Dr NTHLY L27 ... 135 K3
Abbey Vw CHLDW L16 ... 135 F2
Abbeyway North
RNFD/HAY WA11 * ... 90 A3
RNFD/HAY WA11 ... 91 F4
Abbeyway South
RNFD/HAY WA11 ... 91 F5
Abbeywood SKEL WN8 ... 56 E6
Abbeywood Gv RAIN/WH L35 ... 118 B5
Abbot Cl CL/PREN CH43 ... 129 K3
Abbotsbury Wy
WD/CROXPK L12 ... 99 J2
Abbots Cl FMBY L37 ... 49 G4
Abbots Dr BEB CH63 ... 150 E6
Abbotsfield Cl WARRS WA4 ... 162 D5
Abbotsfield Rd STHEL WA9 ... 120 C2
Abbotsford ORM L39 ... 45 K6
Abbotsford Cl GOL/RIS/CU WA3 ... 92 E2
Abbotsford Gdns
CSBY/BLUN L23 ... 68 D6
Abbotsford Rd CSBY/BLUN L23 ... 68 D6
NG/CROX L11 ... 98 C3
Abbotsford St WAL/EG CH44 ... 112 A5
Abbots Hall Av STHEL WA9 ... 120 B4
Abbots Ms EP CH65 ... 6 C2
Abbots Wy FMBY L37 ... 49 G3
NSTN CH64 ... 181 J6
Abbott Dr BTL L20 * ... 82 B6
Abbotts Cl CALD/MH L18 ... 134 C6
RUNC WA7 ... 176 D5
Abbottshey Av CALD/MH L18 ... 134 C6
Abbotts Wy WGNW/BIL/O WN5 ... 77 G6
Abdale Rd NG/CROX L11 ... 98 D2
Abercrombie Rd
NWD/KWIPK L33 ... 85 G4
Abercromby Sq EHL/KEN L7 ... 9 K5
Aberdale Rd CLB/OSW/ST L13 ... 115 F4
Aberdare Cl WARRW/BUR WA5 ... 122 E6
Aberdeen St BIRK CH41 ... 2 C3
Aberford Av WAL/NB CH45 ... 110 E2
Abergele Rd CLB/OSW/ST L13 ... 114 D5
Aber St NPK/KEN L6 ... 113 J4
Abingdon Av WARR WA1 ... 144 D2
Abingdon Gv ANF/KKDL L4 ... 98 A3
HLWD L26 ... 155 K2
Abingdon Rd ANF/KKDL L4 ... 98 A3
GR/UP/WCH CH49 ... 128 C6
Abinger Rd AIMK WN4 ... 78 C5
Abington Dr CHTN/BK PR9 ... 21 K6
Abney Cl EHL/KEN L7 ... 133 G1
Aboyne Cl WLT/FAZ L9 ... 97 J1
Abrams Fold CHTN/BK PR9 ... 21 J6
Abrams Gn CHTN/BK PR9 ... 21 J6
Abram St EV L5 ... 113 G3
Abratio St BIRK CH41 ... 2 D5
Abstone Cl WARR WA1 ... 144 B2
Abyssinia Cl WAV L15 * ... 133 K2
Acacia Av HUY L36 ... 116 D6
WARR WA1 ... 144 C1
WDN WA8 ... 139 G6
Acacia Cl CHNE CH2 ... 198 D6
GR/UP/WCH CH49 ... 147 K1
Acacia Dr GTS/LS CH66 ... 202 D2
Acacia Gv ECCL WA10 ... 102 C1
RUNC WA7 ... 177 F5
WAL/EG CH44 ... 112 A5
WKBY CH48 ... 146 B1
WLT/FAZ L9 ... 82 E5
Acacia St NEWLW WA12 ... 105 K1
Academy St WARR WA1 ... 16 E5
Academy Wy WARR WA1 ... 16 D5
Acanthus Rd CLB/OSW/ST L13 ... 114 E3
Access Rd WD/CROXPK L12 * ... 99 H6
Acer Leigh AIG/SPK L17 ... 152 E2
Acheson Rd CLB/OSW/ST L13 ... 114 C1
Achilles Av WARRN/WOL WA2 ... 123 H5
Ackerley Cl WARRN/WOL WA2 ... 124 B4
Ackers Hall Av DV/KA/FCH L14 ... 115 K3
Ackers Hall Cl DV/KA/FCH L14 ... 115 K2
Ackers La ECCL WA10 ... 102 E1
HTWN L38 ... 68 E1
WARRS WA4 ... 162 D2
Ackers Rd GR/UP/WCH CH49 ... 149 F1
WARRS WA4 ... 162 D2
Acland Rd WAL/EG CH44 * ... 111 H3
Aconbury Cl NG/CROX L11 ... 98 D2
Aconbury Pl NG/CROX L11 ... 98 D2
Acorn Cl BEB CH63 ... 150 C5
STHEL WA9 * ... 120 A3
Acorn Ct TOX L8 ... 132 E3
Acorn Dr EP CH65 ... 203 F2
Acornfield Cl NWD/KWIPK L33 ... 85 H3
Acornfield Rd NWD/KWIPK L33 ... 85 J2
Acorn St NEWLW WA12 ... 106 C2
Acorn Wy BTL L20 ... 5 G1
A Ct AIMK WN4 ... 91 G1
Acrefield Pk WLTN L25 ... 135 H6
Acrefield Rd RF/TRAN CH42 ... 150 A2
WDN WA8 ... 157 G2
WLTN L25 ... 135 H6
Acregate SKEL WN8 ... 66 E1
Acre Gn HLWD L26 ... 155 K5
Acre La HES CH60 ... 168 C4
PS/BROM CH62 ... 170 E6
Acre Rd GTS/LS CH66 ... 195 G4
Acresfield CLB/OSW/ST L13 * ... 115 F5
Acresgate Ct WLTN L25 ... 135 H4
Acres La FMBY L37 ... 50 A5
ORM L39 ... 51 G4
Acres Rd BEB CH63 ... 150 E5
HOY CH47 ... 127 K2
Acreville Rd BEB CH63 ... 150 E6
Acton Cl RNFD/HAY WA11 ... 90 B5
Acton Gv NPK/KEN L6 ... 114 A1
Acton La MOR/LEA CH46 ... 128 D2
Acton Rd KKBY L32 ... 84 B1
RF/TRAN CH42 ... 151 F2
WARRW/BUR WA5 ... 121 J1
Acton Wy EHL/KEN L7 ... 133 H1
Acuba Gv BIRK CH41 * ... 131 H5
Acuba Rd WAV L15 ... 115 G6
Adair Pl CLB/OSW/ST L13 ... 98 C6
Adair Rd CLB/OSW/ST L13 ... 98 C6
Adam Av GTS/LS CH66 ... 195 F6
Adam Cl ALL/GAR L19 ... 153 K6
GTS/LS CH66 ... 195 G5
Adams Cl NEWLW WA12 ... 106 D3
Adamson Ct WARRS WA4 ... 163 G1
Adamson St AIMK WN4 ... 79 F6
EHL/KEN L7 ... 114 B5
WARRS WA4 ... 142 E6
Adam St EV L5 ... 113 H1
WARRN/WOL WA2 ... 143 F2
Adaston Av PS/BROM CH62 ... 184 C3
Ada St STHEL WA9 ... 104 A4
Adcote Cl DV/KA/FCH L14 ... 115 K4
Adcote Rd DV/KA/FCH L14 ... 115 K4
Adderley Cl RUNC WA7 ... 11 H7
Adderley St EHL/KEN L7 ... 113 K5
Addingham Av WDN WA8 ... 157 H4
Addingham Rd CALD/MH L18 ... 134 C4
Addington St WAL/EG CH44 ... 111 K4
Addison Cl KKBY L32 ... 84 C3
Addison Sq WDN WA8 ... 18 C1
Addison St BTL L20 ... 81 H6
VAUX/LVPD L3 ... 8 E1
Addison Wy VAUX/LVPD L3 ... 8 E1
Adelaide Av STHEL WA9 ... 103 G6
Adelaide Pl EV L5 ... 113 G3
Adelaide Rd EHL/KEN L7 ... 113 K5
LITH L21 ... 81 G4
RF/TRAN CH42 ... 131 F5
Adelaide St WAL/EG CH44 ... 111 H5
Adelaide Ter CSBY/WL L22 ... 80 D2
Adela Rd RUNC WA7 ... 10 B5
Adele Thompson Dr TOX L8 ... 133 F2
Adelphi St BIRK CH41 ... 3 G3
Adfalent La NSTN CH64 ... 193 H2
Adkins St EV L5 * ... 113 J1
Adlam Crs WLT/FAZ L9 * ... 83 H4
Adlam Rd AIN/FAZ L10 ... 83 H4
Adlington Ct GOL/RIS/CU WA3 ... 125 H2
Adlington Rd RUNC WA7 ... 178 C3
Adlington St VAUX/LVPD L3 ... 8 E1
Admin Rd NWD/KWIPK L33 ... 85 H3
Admiral Gv TOX L8 ... 133 F4
Admirals Rd GOL/RIS/CU WA3 ... 125 H4
Admiral St TOX L8 ... 132 E4
Admiralty Cl BRSC L40 * ... 46 C1
Adrian's Wy KKBY L32 ... 84 D1
Adshead Rd CLB/OSW/ST L13 ... 98 C6
Adstone Rd WLTN L25 ... 135 K4
Adswood Rd HUY L36 ... 116 E4
Adwell Cl GOL/RIS/CU WA3 ... 93 H3
Africander Rd RNFD/HAY WA11 ... 88 D3
Afton WDN WA8 ... 157 F1
Agar Rd NG/CROX L11 ... 98 D6
Agate St NPK/KEN L6 ... 113 J2
Agincourt Rd WD/CROXPK L12 ... 115 G2
Agnes Gv WAL/EG CH44 ... 111 J2
Agnes Rd CSBY/BLUN L23 ... 68 D6
RF/TRAN CH42 ... 131 G6
Agnes St STHEL WA9 ... 120 A4
Agnes Wy EHL/KEN L7 ... 113 K6
Aiden Long Gv PR/KW L34 ... 116 E1
Aigburth Dr AIG/SPK L17 ... 133 H5
Aigburth Hall Av ALL/GAR L19 ... 153 H3
Aigburth Hall Rd ALL/GAR L19 ... 153 H3
Aigburth Rd AIG/SPK L17 ... 133 G6
Aigburth St TOX L8 ... 133 G1
Aigburth V AIG/SPK L17 ... 133 K6
Ailsa Rd WAL/NB CH45 ... 111 G2
Ainley Cl RUNC WA7 ... 187 K2
Ainscough Rd
GOL/RIS/CU WA3 ... 125 G4
Ainsdale Cl AIN/FAZ L10 ... 83 J3
BEB CH63 ... 183 K2
PEN/TH CH61 ... 148 D6
WARRW/BUR WA5 ... 141 G5
Ainsdale Rd BTL L20 ... 82 A6
Ainsworth Av MOR/LEA CH46 ... 128 D3
Ainsworth La PR/KW L34 ... 85 G5
Ainsworth Rd ECCL WA10 ... 12 B2
Ainsworth St VAUX/LVPD L3 ... 9 H4
Aintree Barracks WLT/FAZ L9 * ... 83 F6
Aintree Cl MOR/LEA CH46 ... 109 K4
Aintree Crs STHP PR8 ... 28 C4
Aintree Gv GTS/LS CH66 ... 195 G6
Aintree La AIN/FAZ L10 ... 83 F1
Aintree Rd BTL L20 ... 5 H2
WLT/FAZ L9 ... 83 G5
Aintree Wy WLT/FAZ L9 ... 83 F1
Airdale Cl CL/PREN CH43 ... 129 K3
Airdale Rd WAV L15 ... 134 A3
Airdrie Cl PS/BROM CH62 ... 184 A4
Aire WDN WA8 ... 157 G1
Aire Cl EP CH65 ... 195 K2
Airedale Cl WARRW/BUR WA5 ... 141 G2
Airegate MGHL L31 ... 61 K5
Airlie Gv CLB/OSW/ST L13 ... 114 B1
Airlie Rd HOY CH47 ... 127 G3
Aisthorpe Gv MGHL L31 ... 71 G2
Ajax Av WARRN/WOL WA2 ... 123 H5
The Akbar HES CH60 ... 167 G4
Akenside Ct LITH L21 * ... 81 H5
Akenside St BTL L20 ... 81 H5
Alabama Wy BIRK CH41 ... 3 J5
Alamein Crs
WARRN/WOL WA2 * ... 142 E2
Alamein Rd HUY L36 ... 116 D3
Alastair Crs CL/PREN CH43 ... 149 J2
Alban Rd CHLDW L16 ... 134 E1
Albany Av PR/KW L34 ... 102 B6
Albany Crs LYMM WA13 * ... 145 J5
Albany Gdns GTS/LS CH66 ... 195 F2
Albany Gv LYMM WA13 ... 145 H5
Albany Rd CLB/OSW/ST L13 ... 114 E3
EHL/KEN L7 ... 113 J5
LYMM WA13 ... 145 H6
PR/KW L34 ... 118 A1
RF/TRAN CH42 ... 150 D1
STHP PR8 ... 22 D4
WLT/FAZ L9 ... 82 E4
Albany Ter RUNC WA7 ... 10 D5
The Albany VAUX/LVPD L3 * ... 8 C3
Albemarle Rd WAL/EG CH44 ... 111 K4
Alberta Gv PR/KW L34 ... 117 F2
Albert Dr BTL L20 ... 82 C5
NSTN CH64 ... 191 J1
WARRW/BUR WA5 ... 140 E3
Albert Edward Rd EHL/KEN L7 ... 113 J5
Albert Gv CSBY/BLUN L23 * ... 68 E5
WAV L15 ... 134 B1
Albert Pk AIG/SPK L17 ... 133 G4
Albert Pl STHP PR8 ... 14 E3
Albert Rd CHTN/BK PR9 ... 15 H2
CLB/OSW/ST L13 ... 114 B1

CSBY/WL L22 80 E2
FMBY L37 48 B5
HOY CH47 127 G3
RF/TRAN CH42 131 F5
WARRS WA4 163 F1
WDN WA8 19 G1
WKBY CH48 146 B2
Albert Schweitzer Av
NTHTN L30 70 C6
Albert Sq WDN WA8 18 E3
Albert St AIMK WN4 79 G6
ECCL WA10 13 G2
EHL/KEN L7 113 J6
RUNC WA7 10 D5
Albert Ter STHP PR8 27 H2
Albion Pl WAL/NB CH45 95 H5
Albion St BIRK CH41 3 H5
ECCL WA10 12 E4
EV L5 113 G1
WAL/NB CH45 95 G5
Albourne Rd KKBY L32 85 F3
Albury Cl RNFD/HAY WA11 90 B4
WD/CROXPK L12 99 K3
Albury Rd KKBY L32 84 E4
Alcester Rd WD/CROXPK L12 115 G1
Alcock St RUNC WA7 10 E3
Alcott Pl WARRN/WOL WA2 123 G1
Aldams Gv ANF/KKDL L4 97 G4
Aldbourne Av CALD/MH L18 135 F4
Aldbourne Cl WLTN L25 135 F5
Aldcliffe GOL/RIS/CU WA3 93 G4
Alder Av AIMK WN4 78 E4
HUY L36 136 D1
WDN WA8 139 F6
WGNW/BIL/O WN5 * 77 G4
Alderbank Rd
WARRW/BUR WA5 141 H3
Alder Cl PR/KW L34 118 B1
Alder Crs KKBY L32 72 C6
WARRN/WOL WA2 143 F1
Alderdale Av STHP PR8 33 G4
Alder Dr GTS/LS CH66 202 D2
Alderfield Dr SPK/HALE L24 174 B3
Alder Gv CSBY/WL L22 80 E1
Alder Hey Rd ECCL WA10 102 E1
Alder La FROD/HEL WA6 186 B4
ORM L39 42 A3
PR/KW L34 100 B3
RNFD/HAY WA11 76 C5
WARRN/WOL WA2 142 E1
WARRW/BUR WA5 106 A6
WDN WA8 137 J5
Alderley SKEL WN8 66 E1
Alderley Av BIRK CH41 130 C2
GOL/RIS/CU WA3 92 E4
Alderley Rd HOY CH47 127 G2
WAL/EG CH44 111 H4
WARRS WA4 144 C5
Alderney Cl EP CH65 203 G2
Alderney Rd EV L5 113 F2
Alder Rd BEB CH63 169 K1
GOL/RIS/CU WA3 93 G3
PR/KW L34 118 B1
WARR WA1 144 C2
WD/CROXPK L12 115 F3
Alder Root La
WARRN/WOL WA2 106 D6
Aldersey Cl RUNC WA7 178 C4
Aldersey St VAUX/LVPD L3 113 F4
Aldersgate RF/TRAN CH42 150 E1
Aldersgate Av RUNC WA7 178 C6
Aldersgate Dr HLWD L26 155 K5
Alderson Crs FMBY L37 49 F1
Alderson Rd WAV L15 133 J2
Alder St NEWLW WA12 106 D2
Alderton Dr AIMK WN4 79 F6
Alderville Rd ANF/KKDL L4 98 A3
Alder Wood Av SPK/HALE L24 173 K2
Aldewood Cl GOL/RIS/CU WA3 125 J1
Aldford Cl BEB CH63 183 J1
CL/PREN CH43 149 H1
Aldford Rd KKBY L32 84 D4
Aldgate EP CH65 6 A5
Aldridge Cl WD/CROXPK L12 99 J2
Aldridge Dr WARRW/BUR WA5 105 K6
Aldrins La NTHTN L30 70 C5
Aldwark Rd DV/KA/FCH L14 116 A3
Aldwych Rd WD/CROXPK L12 115 G1
Aldykes MGHL L31 71 H1
Alexander Cl BRSC L40 39 F6
Alexander Dr MGHL L31 62 B4
PEN/TH CH61 167 J2
WDN WA8 157 J3
Alexander Fleming Av
NTHTN L30 70 C5
Alexander Gv RUNC WA7 11 H6
Alexander Wk ANF/KKDL L4 97 H5
Alexandra Cl NPK/KEN L6 113 K4
SKEL WN8 56 A5
Alexandra Dr AIG/SPK L17 133 G5
BTL L20 82 B5
ECCL WA10 12 C7
RF/TRAN CH42 150 D2
Alexandra Gn AIG/SPK L17 133 G5
Alexandra Ms CHTN/BK PR9 15 H2
ORM L39 45 J5
Alexandra Mt LITH L21 81 J3
Alexandra Pk AIG/SPK L17 133 G6
Alexandra Rd AIMK WN4 79 G5
BRSC L40 38 D5
CHTN/BK PR9 15 H2
CL/PREN CH43 2 B6
CLB/OSW/ST L13 114 E6
CSBY/BLUN L23 68 E5
CSBY/WL L22 81 F3
EHL/KEN L7 133 H1
FMBY L37 48 B5
WAL/NB CH45 95 G5
WARRS WA4 162 C2
WKBY CH48 146 B2
Alexandra St ECCL WA10 103 F4
EP CH65 * 6 D1
WARR WA1 17 K1
WDN WA8 18 C6
Alexandria Rd ALL/GAR L19 153 K4
Alex Cl TOX L8 132 E3
Alfonso Rd ANF/KKDL L4 97 F5
Alford Av STHEL WA9 119 K3
Alforde St WDN WA8 18 D6
Alford St EHL/KEN L7 114 C5
Alfred Cl WDN WA8 18 E4
Alfred Ms CLVPS L1 132 D2
Alfred Rd CL/PREN CH43 2 B6
GOL/RIS/CU WA3 93 H3
RNFD/HAY WA11 90 D4
WAL/EG CH44 112 A6
Alfred St ECCL WA10 13 J3
NEWLW WA12 106 E2
RNFD/HAY WA11 75 G2
WAV L15 133 J1
WDN WA8 18 E4
Alfriston Rd WD/CROXPK L12 115 G1
Algernon St RUNC WA7 10 B3
WARR WA1 17 H2
WARRS WA4 162 B2
Alice Ct WDN WA8 176 D1
Alice St STHEL WA9 104 C5
Alison Av RF/TRAN CH42 131 J6
Alison Pl CLB/OSW/ST L13 98 C6
Alison Rd CLB/OSW/ST L13 98 C6
Alistair Dr BEB CH63 183 K1
Allangate Cl GR/UP/WCH CH49 147 K1
Allangate Rd ALL/GAR L19 153 J3
Allan Rd RNFD/HAY WA11 89 F4
Allans Cl NSTN CH64 191 K3
Allans Meadow NSTN CH64 191 K3
Allanson St STHEL WA9 104 B3
Allcot Av RF/TRAN CH42 150 C1
Allenby Av CSBY/WL L22 81 G1
Allenby Sq CLB/OSW/ST L13 114 D5
Allendale RUNC WA7 188 A1
Allendale Av RAIN/WH L35 119 F4
WLT/FAZ L9 82 E4
Allengate CSBY/BLUN L23 69 F4
Allen Rd RUNC WA7 176 A6
Allen St WARRN/WOL WA2 16 C3
Allerby Wy GOL/RIS/CU WA3 93 F3
Allerford Rd WD/CROXPK L12 99 H5
Allerton Beeches
CALD/MH L18 134 D6
Allerton Dr CALD/MH L18 134 C5
Allerton Gv RF/TRAN CH42 131 G6
Allerton Rd CALD/MH L18 134 C5
CHTN/BK PR9 23 G4
RF/TRAN CH42 131 G6
WAL/NB CH45 111 G1
WDN WA8 19 F1
Allesley Rd DV/KA/FCH L14 115 K2
Alleyne Rd ANF/KKDL L4 98 B5
Allington St AIG/SPK L17 133 G6
Allonby Cl CL/PREN CH43 130 B5
Allport La PS/BROM CH62 171 F5
Allport Rd BEB CH63 183 K1
The Allports PS/BROM CH62 171 F6
All Saints Cl NTHTN L30 70 B6
All Saints Dr WARRS WA4 144 D6
All Saints Rd SPK/HALE L24 173 H2
Allscott Wy AIMK WN4 79 H6
Alma Cl AIN/FAZ L10 84 A4
Almacs Cl CSBY/BLUN L23 68 C6
Alma Hl SKEL WN8 57 K6
Alma Pl STHEL WA9 104 A3
Alma Rd AIG/SPK L17 153 F3
STHP PR8 27 H3
Alma St BIRK CH41 3 G5
NEWLW WA12 * 106 B2
PS/BROM CH62 * 151 F4
STHEL WA9 104 A3
Alma Vale Ter BTL L20 * 4 D5
Almeda Rd SPK/HALE L24 174 B3
Almer Dr WARRW/BUR WA5 141 K4
Almond Av BRSC L40 38 E3
NTHTN L30 69 K6
RUNC WA7 177 F5
Almond Cl HLWD L26 155 H4
RNFD/HAY WA11 89 J6
Almond Ct ALL/GAR L19 154 B6
Almond Dr WARRW/BUR WA5 121 K1
Almond Gv WARR WA1 144 A2
WDN WA8 157 J3
Almond Pl MOR/LEA CH46 129 G1
Almond's Gn WD/CROXPK L12 98 E5
Almond's Gv WD/CROXPK L12 98 E6
Almonds Pk WD/CROXPK L12 98 E5
Almond's Turn NTHTN L30 70 A5
Almond Wy
GR/UP/WCH CH49 * 147 K1
Alness Dr RAIN/WH L35 119 F5
Alnwick Dr EP CH65 203 H1
MOR/LEA CH46 128 D1
Aloeswood Cl NPK/KEN L6 113 K2
Alpass Rd AIG/SPK L17 * 133 G6
Alpha Dr RF/TRAN CH42 151 F2
Alpha St LITH L21 81 J6
Alpine Cl ECCL WA10 102 E1
Alpine St NEWLW WA12 106 A2
Alresford Rd ALL/GAR L19 153 G3
Alroy Rd ANF/KKDL L4 97 J6
Alscot Av AIN/FAZ L10 84 A4
Alscot Cl MGHL L31 71 G1
Alsop Ar VAUX/LVPD L3 * 9 K4
Alsop Ct VAUX/LVPD L3 * 9 K4
Alston Cl PS/BROM CH62 170 E4
Alston Ct STHP PR8 34 A3
Alstonfield Rd DV/KA/FCH L14 116 A3
Alston Rd AIG/SPK L17 153 F3
Alt WDN WA8 157 G1
Alt Av MGHL L31 71 F2
Altbridge Pk NG/CROX L11 84 A6
Alt Bridge Rd HUY L36 116 D3
Altcar Av WAV L15 133 J2
Altcar Dr MOR/LEA CH46 128 E2
Altcar La FMBY L37 49 F4
MGHL L31 61 J3
ORM L39 51 H4
Altcar Rd BTL L20 * 81 K6
FMBY L37 49 H3
Altcross Rd NG/CROX L11 99 G1
Altcross Wy NG/CROX L11 99 G1
Altfield Rd DV/KA/FCH L14 99 K6
Altfinch Cl DV/KA/FCH L14 100 A6
Altham Rd NG/CROX L11 98 D6
STHP PR8 28 B5
Althorpe Dr STHP PR8 28 B4
Althorp St TOX L8 132 E6
Altmoor Rd HUY L36 116 D2
Alton Av LITH L21 81 H2
Alton Cl AIMK WN4 79 F5
HTWN L38 59 F5
Alton Rd CL/PREN CH43 130 D4
NPK/KEN L6 114 B2
Alt Rd BTL L20 81 K6
FMBY L37 49 G4
HTWN L38 59 G3
HUY L36 116 E4
Alt Side Ct AIN/FAZ L10 84 A4
Alt St TOX L8 133 G2
Altway AIN/FAZ L10 71 F6
Altys La ORM L39 53 K2
Alundale Rd WD/CROXPK L12 115 J2
Alvanley Pl CL/PREN CH43 2 B5
Alvanley Rd GTS/LS CH66 195 H5
KKBY L32 84 B1
WD/CROXPK L12 115 G2
Alvanley Vw CHNE CH2 198 C6
Alvega Cl PS/BROM CH62 151 H4
Alverstone Av BIRK CH41 130 C2
Alverstone Cl
WARRW/BUR WA5 140 D2
Alverstone Rd CALD/MH L18 134 A4
WAL/EG CH44 111 K4
Alverton Cl WDN WA8 157 J3
Alvina La ANF/KKDL L4 97 G6
NWD/KWIPK L33 73 F4
Alwain Gn SPK/HALE L24 174 A3
Alwen St BIRK CH41 111 F6
Alwyn Av LITH L21 81 J2
Alwyn Gdns MOR/LEA CH46 129 G1
Alwyn St AIG/SPK L17 133 G6
Amanda Rd AIN/FAZ L10 84 A4
RAIN/WH L35 118 D2
Amanda Wy MGHL L31 * 72 A5
Amaury Cl CSBY/BLUN L23 69 J4
Amaury Rd CSBY/BLUN L23 69 J4
Ambassador Dr HLWD L26 155 K2
Ambergate SKEL WN8 56 D6
Ambergate Cl STHEL WA9 * 104 B6
Ambergate Rd ALL/GAR L19 153 J4
Amberley Av MOR/LEA CH46 128 D2
Amberley Cl MOR/LEA CH46 128 D2
NPK/KEN L6 98 B6
Amber Wy DV/KA/FCH L14 100 A6
Ambleside Av MOR/LEA CH46 128 E1
Ambleside Cl PEN/TH CH61 148 D5
PS/BROM CH62 171 G6
Ambleside Crs
WARRN/WOL WA2 123 J4
Ambleside Rd CALD/MH L18 154 A2
EP CH65 203 G1
MGHL L31 62 B5
Amelia Cl NPK/KEN L6 9 K1
WDN WA8 139 G5
Amelia St WARRN/WOL WA2 143 F2
Amersham SKEL WN8 56 D6
Amersham Rd ANF/KKDL L4 98 A3
Amery Gv RF/TRAN CH42 150 B1
Amethyst Cl NPK/KEN L6 113 K3
Amherst Rd AIG/SPK L17 152 D1
Amis Gv GOL/RIS/CU WA3 93 F3
Amity St TOX L8 132 E4
Amos Av LITH L21 81 K3
Ampleforth Cl KKBY L32 84 B2
Ampthill Rd AIG/SPK L17 152 D1
Ampulla Rd NG/CROX L11 99 G2
Ancaster Rd AIG/SPK L17 152 D1
Ancholme Cl RAIN/WH L35 118 C1
The Anchorage LYMM WA13 145 J6
NSTN CH64 191 H2
VAUX/LVPD L3 132 C3
Anchor Cl RUNC WA7 188 C1
Anchor Ctyd VAUX/LVPD L3 * 8 C7
Anchor St CHTN/BK PR9 15 F4
Ancient Mdw WLT/FAZ L9 82 E4
Ancroft Rd DV/KA/FCH L14 116 A4
Ancrum Rd NWD/KWIPK L33 72 C3
Anders Dr NWD/KWIPK L33 73 F4
Anderson Av BTL L20 4 A2
Anderson Cl PEN/TH CH61 148 D5
RAIN/WH L35 119 F6
WARRN/WOL WA2 124 D5
Anderson Rd LITH L21 82 A2
Anderson St EV L5 113 G1
Anderton Ter HUY L36 116 C5
Andover Cl WARRN/WOL WA2 124 A6
Andover Rd RNFD/HAY WA11 90 D3
Andover Wy WLTN L25 155 G3
Andreas Cl STHP PR8 27 J3
Andrew Av MGHL L31 71 K6
WGNW/BIL/O WN5 77 H4
Andrew Cl WDN WA8 157 H3
Andrews Cl FMBY L37 48 E4
Andrews La FMBY L37 48 E4
Andrew St ANF/KKDL L4 97 H4
Andrew's Wk HES CH60 168 B5
Andrews Yort FMBY L37 48 E4
Andromeda Wy STHEL WA9 104 E6
Anemone Wy STHEL WA9 104 E6
Anfield Rd ANF/KKDL L4 97 H6
Angela St EHL/KEN L7 133 G1
Angers La MGHL L31 72 A3
Anglesea Rd WLT/FAZ L9 97 H2
Anglesea Wy TOX L8 132 E5
Anglesey Cl EP CH65 203 G2
Anglesey Rd WAL/EG CH44 111 H2
WKBY CH48 127 F6
Anglezark Cl EHL/KEN L7 113 K5
Anglia Wy WLTN L25 155 F3
Anglican Ct TOX L8 * 132 D2
Anglo Cl WLT/FAZ L9 83 F3
Angus Rd BEB CH63 183 K1
NG/CROX L11 98 D5
Annandale Cl NWD/KWIPK L33 72 C3
Annandale Gdns SKEL WN8 57 J6
Annan Gv AIMK WN4 79 K4
Ann Cl GTS/LS CH66 195 G2
Anne Av STHP PR8 34 A3
Anne Gv STHEL WA9 104 A6
Annerley St EHL/KEN L7 * 133 H1
Annesley Rd AIG/SPK L17 152 D1
WAL/EG CH44 111 H4
Anne St STHEL WA9 120 B4
Annette Av NEWLW WA12 91 F6
Annie Rd BTL L20 82 A5
Annie St WARRN/WOL WA2 17 F2
Ann St RUNC WA7 11 F3
SKEL WN8 56 A4
Ann St West WDN WA8 18 E6
Anscot Av BEB CH63 150 E5
Ansdell Dr ECCL WA10 87 J6
Ansdell Gv CHTN/BK PR9 23 J1
Ansdell Rd WDN WA8 158 C1
Ansdell Villas' Rd RAIN/WH L35 118 E3
Anson Cl WARRN/WOL WA2 124 A5
Anson Pl VAUX/LVPD L3 9 J2
Anson St VAUX/LVPD L3 9 J3
Anstey Cl MOR/LEA CH46 109 F6
Anstey Rd CLB/OSW/ST L13 115 F4
Ansty Cl RNFD/HAY WA11 89 G6
Anthony's Wy HES CH60 168 A6
Anthorn Cl CL/PREN CH43 130 A5
Antler Ct AIMK WN4 79 G3
Antonio St BTL L20 97 F4
Antons Cl HLWD L26 155 J5
Antons Rd HLWD L26 155 J5
PEN/TH CH61 148 D6
Antony Rd WARRS WA4 162 A1
Antrim Cl RNFD/HAY WA11 90 B5
Antrim Dr GTS/LS CH66 202 D1
Antrim Rd WARRN/WOL WA2 123 G5
Antrim St CLB/OSW/ST L13 98 C6
Anvil Cl BTL L20 4 C2
CHNE CH2 198 C5
The Anzacs PS/BROM CH62 151 H5
Anzio Rd HUY L36 116 D3
Apex Ct PS/BROM CH62 * 171 G4
Apollo Crs NWD/KWIPK L33 72 D5
Apollo Wy NPK/KEN L6 * 113 K2
NTHTN L30 70 C5
Apostles Wy NWD/KWIPK L33 72 C4
Appin Rd BIRK CH41 3 F7
Appleby Cl WDN WA8 157 H3
Appleby Dr NTHTN L30 69 K6
Appleby Gn WD/CROXPK L12 115 H1
Appleby Gv PS/BROM CH62 183 K1
Appleby Lawn NTHLY L27 136 D5
Appleby Rd NWD/KWIPK L33 72 D5
WARRN/WOL WA2 123 J4
Appleby Wk WDN WA8 157 H3
Applecorn Cl STHEL WA9 120 B1
Apple Ct NPK/KEN L6 113 K4
Applecross Cl GOL/RIS/CU WA3 125 J1
Appledale Dr GTS/LS CH66 202 E3
Apple Dell Av GOL/RIS/CU WA3 92 D2
Appledore Cl SPK/HALE L24 173 G1
Appledore Gv STHEL WA9 120 A3
Appleford Cl WARRS WA4 162 D4
Applegarth MOR/LEA CH46 128 D3
Appleton Dr EP CH65 195 J6
GR/UP/WCH CH49 129 F6
Appleton Rd ANF/KKDL L4 97 J4
LITH L21 81 H2
SKEL WN8 56 B3
STHEL WA9 104 A3
WDN WA8 18 E1
Appleton St WDN WA8 18 E7
Appleton Village WDN WA8 18 D1
Appletree Cl CALD/MH L18 153 K2
Apple Tree Cl STBRV L28 100 B5
Apple Tree Gv GTS/LS CH66 202 D3
Appletree Gv
WARRN/WOL WA2 124 B5
April Gv NPK/KEN L6 114 B2
April Ri NTHTN L30 70 B6
Apsley Av WAL/NB CH45 111 H1
Apsley Brow MGHL L31 61 K6
Apsley Gv BEB CH63 151 F5
Apsley Rd PS/BROM CH62 151 G3
WD/CROXPK L12 115 G1
Aquarius Cl DV/KA/FCH L14 116 A3
Aragon Cl MGHL L31 62 C4
Aran Cl SPK/HALE L24 174 E3
Arborn Dr GR/UP/WCH CH49 129 H3
Arbour La NWD/KWIPK L33 85 F2
Arbour St STHP PR8 15 G7
Arbury Av RNFD/HAY WA11 89 G5
Arbury La WARRN/WOL WA2 123 J1
Arcadia Av MGHL L31 62 B4
Archbishop Worlock Ct
VAUX/LVPD L3 112 E3
Archer Av WARRS WA4 162 D1
Archer Cl ANF/KKDL L4 97 G6
Archerfield Rd CALD/MH L18 153 J2
Archer Gv STHEL WA9 104 C1
Archers Cft PS/BROM CH62 * 171 F4
Archers Fold MGHL L31 72 A5
Archers Gn PS/BROM CH62 184 B3
Archer St ANF/KKDL L4 * 97 G6
Archers Wy
GR/UP/WCH CH49 * 148 D1
GTS/LS CH66 202 C2
The Arches PR/KW L34 * 117 K1
Arch La AIMK WN4 77 K6
Archway Rd HUY L36 116 E5
Arctic Rd BTL L20 4 B4
Arden WDN WA8 157 F1
Arden Cl GOL/RIS/CU WA3 125 K1
STHP PR8 33 G3
Arden Dr NSTN CH64 191 K3
Ardennes Rd HUY L36 116 E4
Arderne Cl BEB CH63 170 D3
Ardleigh Av STHP PR8 28 B4
Ardleigh Cl CLB/OSW/ST L13 114 D5
Ardleigh Gv CLB/OSW/ST L13 114 D5
Ardleigh Pl CLB/OSW/ST L13 114 D5
Ardleigh Rd CLB/OSW/ST L13 114 C5
Ardmore Rd CALD/MH L18 153 H1
Ardrossan Rd ANF/KKDL L4 98 A5
Ardville Rd NG/CROX L11 98 B2
Ardwick Rd SPK/HALE L24 174 A2
Ardwick St STHEL WA9 13 K5
Argameols Cl STHP PR8 28 C2
Argarmeols Gv FMBY L37 40 E6
Argarmeols Rd FMBY L37 40 E5
Argo Rd CSBY/WL L22 80 E2
Argos Pl BTL L20 97 F4
Argos Rd BTL L20 97 F4
Argyle Rd ALL/GAR L19 153 K5
ANF/KKDL L4 113 K1
CHTN/BK PR9 23 F4
Argyle St BIRK CH41 3 G5
CLVPS L1 8 E6
ECCL WA10 13 F1
Argyle Street Hamilton Sq
BIRK CH41 3 G4
Argyle St South BIRK CH41 2 E7
Argyll Av PS/BROM CH62 184 A3
Argyll Cl AIMK WN4 78 B5
Aries Cl DV/KA/FCH L14 116 A2
Ariss Gv RAIN/WH L35 * 118 C2
Arkenstone Cl WDN WA8 157 H1
Arkle Rd CL/PREN CH43 130 C1
Arkles Rd ANF/KKDL L4 113 J1
Arklow Dr SPK/HALE L24 174 E3
Ark Royal Wy BIRK CH41 131 J5
Arkwood Cl PS/BROM CH62 170 E2
Arkwright Ct RUNC WA7 177 J2
Arkwright Rd RUNC WA7 177 J2
Arkwright St EV L5 113 G2
Arlescourt Rd WD/CROXPK L12 115 G2
Arley Av WARRS WA4 162 C2
Arley Cl CL/PREN CH43 129 K3
Arley Dr WDN WA8 157 G1
Arlington Av CALD/MH L18 134 A4
Arlington Cl STHP PR8 33 G4
Arlington Dr GOL/RIS/CU WA3 93 K3
WARRW/BUR WA5 141 F5
Arlington Rd WAL/NB CH45 110 E1
Armill Rd NG/CROX L11 99 G2
Armitage Gdns CALD/MH L18 153 J2
Armley Rd ANF/KKDL L4 97 K6
Armour Av WARRN/WOL WA2 123 H5
Armoury Bank AIMK WN4 79 G6
The Armoury WD/CROXPK L12 99 F6
Armscot Cl WLTN L25 154 E4
Armscot Pl WLTN L25 154 E4
Armstrong Cl GOL/RIS/CU WA3 125 F3
Armstrong Quay
VAUX/LVPD L3 132 E6
Armthorpe Dr GTS/LS CH66 194 E4
Arncliffe Dr WARRW/BUR WA5 121 K1
Arncliffe Rd WLTN L25 155 G2
Arndale RUNC WA7 187 H2
Arnhem Crs WARRN/WOL WA2 143 F2
Arnhem Rd HUY L36 116 D3
Arnian Rd RNFD/HAY WA11 75 G2
Arnian Wy RNFD/HAY WA11 75 G2
Arnold Av ECCL WA10 12 B2
Arnold Cl STHEL WA9 104 A4
TOX L8 133 F3
Arnold Crs TOX L8 132 E3
Arnold Gv WAV L15 134 B1
Arnold Pl WDN WA8 157 H4
Arnold St TOX L8 132 E3
WAL/NB CH45 * 111 H2
WARR WA1 17 J2
Arno Rd CL/PREN CH43 130 E6
Arnot Cl ECCL WA10 13 F2
Arnot St ANF/KKDL L4 97 H4
Arnot Wy BEB CH63 150 C5
Arnside LITH L21 82 A3
Arnside Av RAIN/WH L35 118 C3
RNFD/HAY WA11 89 K5
Arnside Gv WARRS WA4 162 A1
Arnside Rd CHTN/BK PR9 15 G4
CL/PREN CH43 130 D5
EHL/KEN L7 114 A6
HUY L36 116 B5
WAL/NB CH45 111 H2
Arnside Ter CHTN/BK PR9 15 H4
Arpley Rd WARR WA1 16 D7
Arpley St WARR WA1 16 B5
Arrad St EHL/KEN L7 9 J6
Arran Av EP CH65 203 G2
Arran Cl RNFD/HAY WA11 89 H5
WARRN/WOL WA2 124 C5
Arran Dr FROD/HEL WA6 201 F2
Arranmore Rd CALD/MH L18 153 H1
Arrowe Av MOR/LEA CH46 128 E2
Arrowe Brook La
GR/UP/WCH CH49 148 B2
Arrowe Brook Rd
GR/UP/WCH CH49 148 C1
Arrowe Park Rd
GR/UP/WCH CH49 129 G4
Arrowe Rd GR/UP/WCH CH49 128 E6
Arrowe Side GR/UP/WCH CH49 129 F5
Arrowe Vw
GR/UP/WCH CH49 * 129 H4
Arrowsmith Rd
RNFD/HAY WA11 90 E4
Arthur Av EP CH65 6 E5
Arthur St ALL/GAR L19 * 154 A6
BIRK CH41 2 B2
RUNC WA7 10 C5
WARRN/WOL WA2 16 B3
Arundel Av AIG/SPK L17 133 H3
WAL/NB CH45 111 F1
Arundel Cl PEN/TH CH61 148 B6
TOX L8 133 F3
Arundel Ct EP CH65 196 D6
Arundel Rd STHP PR8 34 B1
Arundel St ANF/KKDL L4 97 G4
Arvon St BTL L20 82 A5
Asbridge St TOX L8 133 G3
Asbury Cl CALD/MH L18 134 E6
Asbury Rd WAL/NB CH45 110 D1
Ascot Av LITH L21 81 H3
RUNC WA7 186 E1
Ascot Cl STHP PR8 27 F2
WARR WA1 144 D2

WARRS WA4 163 H1
Ascot Dr BEB CH63 150 E6
GTS/LS CH66 195 G6
NWD/KWIPK L33 72 D4
Ascot Gv BEB CH63 150 E6
Ascot Pk CSBY/BLUN L23 69 G5
Ascroft Rd WLT/FAZ L9 82 E3
Ash Av NEWLW WA12 106 C3
Ashbank Rd NG/CROX L11 98 E3
Ashberry Dr WARRS WA4 163 G6
Ashbourne Av CSBY/BLUN L23 68 D5
NTHTN L30 82 B1
RUNC WA7 186 E1
Ashbourne Cl GTS/LS CH66 202 C3
Ashbourne Crs HUY L36 116 B5
Ashbourne Rd AIG/SPK L17 152 D2
WARRW/BUR WA5 141 J4
Ashbrook Av RUNC WA7 187 J4
Ashbrook Crs
WARRN/WOL WA2 143 G1
Ashbrook Dr WLT/FAZ L9 83 F5
Ashburn Av NWD/KWIPK L33 72 D5
Ashburton Av CL/PREN CH43 130 C3
Ashburton Rd CL/PREN CH43 130 B3
WAL/EG CH44 111 H3
WKBY CH48 127 G6
Ashbury Cl RUNC WA7 178 C3
Ashbury Dr RNFD/HAY WA11 90 C4
Ashbury Rd DV/KA/FCH L14 116 B1
Ashby Cl MOR/LEA CH46 109 F6
Ash Cl GTS/LS CH66 202 D2
ORM L39 45 H6
WAV L15 133 K1
Ashcombe Rd DV/KA/FCH L14 115 G4
Ash Crs HUY L36 136 B1
Ashcroft Av ORM L39 45 K5
Ashcroft Dr PEN/TH CH61 167 K3
Ashcroft Rd FMBY L37 49 F4
NWD/KWIPK L33 73 H6
Ashcroft St BTL L20 4 D5
STHEL WA9 104 A2
Ashdale HUY L36 116 D5
Ashdale Cl FMBY L37 48 C3
Ashdale Pk GR/UP/WCH CH49 128 C6
Ashdale Rd CALD/MH L18 134 B4
CSBY/WL L22 80 E1
WLT/FAZ L9 97 J1
Ashdown Cl STHP PR8 28 A3
Ashdown Crs STHEL WA9 120 A3
Ashdown Dr
GR/UP/WCH CH49 147 K1
Ashdown Gv HLWD L26 155 K2
Ashdown La GOL/RIS/CU WA3 125 J2
Ashfarm Ct DV/KA/FCH L14 115 K4
Ashfield RAIN/WH L35 119 F4
WAV L15 133 J1
Ashfield Crs PS/BROM CH62 171 F5
WGNW/BIL/O WN5 77 H4
Ashfield Rd AIG/SPK L17 152 E1
PS/BROM CH62 170 E5
Ashfield Rd North EP CH65 6 D4
Ashford Cl HLWD L26 155 H4
Ashford Rd HOY CH47 127 H1
RF/TRAN CH42 131 F5
Ashford Wy WDN WA8 19 K1
Ash Gv FMBY L37 48 C4
GTS/LS CH66 195 F3
LITH L21 81 H5
RAIN/WH L35 118 A3
RNFD/HAY WA11 75 G3
RUNC WA7 177 F5
SKEL WN8 55 K4
STHEL WA9 120 A3
WAL/NB CH45 95 J6
WARRS WA4 143 G6
WAV L15 133 J1
WDN WA8 157 J3
Ash Grove Crs
WGNW/BIL/O WN5 77 G3
Ashland Av AIMK WN4 79 F5
Ashlands FROD/HEL WA6 201 F2
Ash La WARRS WA4 162 D3
WDN WA8 156 E3
Ashlar Gv AIG/SPK L17 153 F1
Ashlar Rd AIG/SPK L17 153 F1
CSBY/WL L22 81 F1
Ashlea Rd PEN/TH CH61 167 K2
Ashleigh Rd MGHL L31 71 J2
Ashley Av HOY CH47 108 D6
Ashley Cl NWD/KWIPK L33 72 D4
RAIN/WH L35 119 F5
WARRS WA4 144 B6
Ashley Rd CHTN/BK PR9 15 H5
RUNC WA7 11 K5
SKEL WN8 56 E1
Ashley St RF/TRAN CH42 150 E1
Ashley Wy WDN WA8 18 D7
Ashley Wy West WDN WA8 18 B6
Ashmead Rd SKEL WN8 56 C1
Ashmore Cl GOL/RIS/CU WA3 125 J4
Ashmuir Hey KKBY L32 84 E2
Ashover Av DV/KA/FCH L14 116 A3
Ash Priors WDN WA8 138 C6
Ashridge St RUNC WA7 10 C3
Ash Rd BEB CH63 150 E4
CHNE CH2 198 D6
LITH L21 81 H4
LYMM WA13 145 H6
RF/TRAN CH42 * 131 G5
RNFD/HAY WA11 90 D4
WARRN/WOL WA2 123 H1
WARRW/BUR WA5 141 G5
Ash St BTL L20 5 F3
GOL/RIS/CU WA3 92 C1
STHP PR8 15 J7
Ashton Av RAIN/WH L35 118 E5
Ashton Cl FROD/HEL WA6 187 F6
PS/BROM CH62 184 B4
RUNC WA7 186 C1
Ashton Dr FROD/HEL WA6 187 F6
WKBY CH48 146 B2
WLTN L25 154 E4
Ashton Heath AIMK WN4 91 H1
Ashton Rd GOL/RIS/CU WA3 92 A1
NEWLW WA12 91 H5
STHP PR8 27 G6
WGNW/BIL/O WN5 78 A1
Ashtons Green Dr STHEL WA9 104 D3
Ashton St CLB/OSW/ST L13 114 E4
VAUX/LVPD L3 9 K3
WARRN/WOL WA2 16 D3
Ashtree Cl NSTN CH64 192 B2
Ashtree Cft NSTN CH64 193 H2
Ashtree Dr NSTN CH64 192 B3
Ashtree Farm Ct NSTN CH64 193 H1
Ashtree Gv WD/CROXPK L12 99 J1
Ashurst Cl RNFD/HAY WA11 89 H5
SKEL WN8 56 C1
WLTN L25 135 J5
Ashurst Ct FMBY L37 48 E3
Ashurst Dr RNFD/HAY WA11 89 G5
Ashurst Gdns SKEL WN8 56 C1
Ashurst Rd SKEL WN8 56 D2
Ash V WAV L15 133 K1
Ash Vls WAL/EG CH44 * 111 K5
Ashville Rd BIRK CH41 2 A3
WAL/EG CH44 111 J5
Ashville Wy RUNC WA7 187 H4
Ashwall St SKEL WN8 55 K5
Ashwater Rd NG/CROX L11 99 G3
Ash Wy HES CH60 181 G2
Ashwell Av GOL/RIS/CU WA3 92 E2
Ashwell St TOX L8 132 D2
Ashwood SKEL WN8 56 C2
Ashwood Av AIMK WN4 91 F1
GOL/RIS/CU WA3 92 E3
WARR WA1 143 H2
Ashwood Cl GTS/LS CH66 * 202 B2
NWD/KWIPK L33 72 D4
Ashwood Ct CL/PREN CH43 110 C6
Ashwood Dr WD/CROXPK L12 99 H2
Askern Rd KKBY L32 84 E3
Askett Cl RNFD/HAY WA11 90 B4
Askew Cl WAL/EG CH44 111 K3
Askew St ANF/KKDL L4 97 H4
Askham Cl TOX L8 133 G2
Askrigg Av GTS/LS CH66 194 E4
Asland Gdns CHTN/BK PR9 24 A1
Asmall Cl ORM L39 45 H5
Asmall La ORM L39 44 C3
Aspen Cl GTS/LS CH66 202 C2
HES CH60 168 D5
NWD/KWIPK L33 72 E3
Aspendale Rd RF/TRAN CH42 131 G5
Aspen Gv FMBY L37 48 C4
TOX L8 133 H3
WARR WA1 143 K2
Aspenwood AIMK WN4 91 F1
Aspes Rd WD/CROXPK L12 99 J6
Aspinall Cl WARRN/WOL WA2 124 C4
Aspinall Crs FMBY L37 50 B4
Aspinall St BIRK CH41 2 B4
Aspinal St PR/KW L34 117 K1
Aspull Cl GOL/RIS/CU WA3 124 E3
Aspull Common LEIGH WN7 93 K2
Asquith Av BIRK CH41 2 A2
Asser Rd NG/CROX L11 98 C5
Assheton Wk SPK/HALE L24 175 F3
Assissian Crs NTHTN L30 70 B5
Astbury Cl GOL/RIS/CU WA3 93 J3
Aster Crs RUNC WA7 * 187 J3
Aster Dr NWD/KWIPK L33 72 C4
Asterfield Av BEB CH63 150 D4
Aster Rd RNFD/HAY WA11 90 E5
Astley Cl RNFD/HAY WA11 75 G2
WARRS WA4 142 E6
WDN WA8 138 B6
Astley Rd HUY L36 116 E1
Astmoor Bridge La RUNC WA7 177 J3
Astmoor Rd RUNC WA7 11 J3
Aston Av GOL/RIS/CU WA3 125 H3
Aston Cl CL/PREN CH43 130 C6
Aston Ct WARR WA1 124 E6
Aston Fields Rd RUNC WA7 188 C3
Aston Gn RUNC WA7 * 188 D1
Aston La RUNC WA7 188 A4
Aston La North RUNC WA7 188 D3
Aston La South RUNC WA7 188 D6
Aston St ALL/GAR L19 172 C1
Astonwood Rd RF/TRAN CH42 131 G6
Astor Dr WARRS WA4 162 E3
Astor St ANF/KKDL L4 98 A3
Atheldene Rd ANF/KKDL L4 98 A3
Athelstan Cl PS/BROM CH62 171 F4
Atherton Cl EV L5 113 H2
Atherton Dr GR/UP/WCH CH49 129 H6
Atherton Rd EP CH65 195 J3
WLT/FAZ L9 83 F5
Atherton St ECCL WA10 12 E2
PR/KW L34 * 117 K1
WAL/NB CH45 95 G4
Athlone Rd WARRN/WOL WA2 123 G6
Athol Cl NEWLW WA12 105 K1
PS/BROM CH62 184 B2
Athol Dr PS/BROM CH62 184 B2
Athole Gv CHTN/BK PR9 23 H6
Atholl Crs AIN/FAZ L10 83 G1
Athol St BIRK CH41 3 G3
EV L5 112 D2
Atkinson Gv HUY L36 117 F3
Atlanta Ct NWD/KWIPK L33 72 C3
Atlantic Point Village
VAUX/LVPD L3 113 F4
Atlantic Rd BTL L20 4 C1
Atlantic Wy NTHTN L30 82 B3
VAUX/LVPD L3 132 D5
Atlas Ct STHEL WA9 13 K5
Atlas Rd BTL L20 4 B4
Atlas St STHEL WA9 13 K5
Atterbury Cl WDN WA8 157 H1
Atterbury St TOX L8 132 D4
Attlee Rd HUY L36 117 G4
Attwood St ANF/KKDL L4 97 H6
Atwell St NPK/KEN L6 113 J3
Aubourn Cl WDN WA8 138 B6
Aubrey Ct NPK/KEN L6 113 J3
Auburn Rd CLB/OSW/ST L13 114 C2
WAL/NB CH45 95 G6
The Aubynes WAL/NB CH45 94 E6
Auckery Av GTS/LS CH66 195 G6
Audie Murphy Rd
WARRW/BUR WA5 141 J3
Audlem Av CL/PREN CH43 130 C6
Audlem Cl RUNC WA7 187 J3
Audley St VAUX/LVPD L3 9 H2
Audre Cl WARRW/BUR WA5 140 E3
Aughton Cl WGNW/BIL/O WN5 77 H5
Aughton Ms STHP PR8 27 H2
Aughton Park Dr ORM L39 53 H3
Aughton Rd BTL L20 82 A6
STHP PR8 27 H2
Aughton St ORM L39 53 J1
Augusta Cl CLB/OSW/ST L13 114 E5
August Rd NPK/KEN L6 114 A2
August St BTL L20 5 F1
Aukland Gv STHEL WA9 103 F6
Aukland Rd CALD/MH L18 134 B4
Aurorean Cl NTHLY L27 136 A3
Austell Cl RNFD/HAY WA11 89 G4
Austen Dr WARRN/WOL WA2 123 G1
Austin Av AIMK WN4 78 D5
ECCL WA10 102 E5
Austin Cl KKBY L32 84 C1
Austin St WAL/EG CH44 * 111 G5
Austral Av WARR WA1 144 A2
Australia La WARRS WA4 163 H2
Autumn Gv RF/TRAN CH42 150 D3
Avalon Ter BTL L20 4 B2
Avebury Cl GOL/RIS/CU WA3 93 F3
WDN WA8 139 K6
Aveley Cl WARR WA1 144 A2
Aveling Dr CHTN/BK PR9 21 K5
Avelon Cl CL/PREN CH43 130 A4
MGHL L31 61 K2
The Avenue ALL/GAR L19 154 B6
CHTN/BK PR9 21 J6
CHTN/BK PR9 29 J2
ECCL WA10 102 D2
HLWD L26 155 H4
HUY L36 116 E4
KNUT WA16 165 K6
LYMM WA13 164 D2
NEWLW WA12 106 C1
ORM L39 45 J5
PS/BROM CH62 170 E5
RNFD/HAY WA11 75 G3
Averham Cl AIMK WN4 91 G2
Avery Cl WARRN/WOL WA2 124 A5
Avery Crs RNFD/HAY WA11 90 B4
Avery Rd RNFD/HAY WA11 90 B4
Avery Sq RNFD/HAY WA11 90 B4
Aviary Ct WLT/FAZ L9 * 82 C5
Aviemore Cl AIMK WN4 78 C5
Aviemore Dr
WARRN/WOL WA2 124 C4
Aviemore Rd CLB/OSW/ST L13 114 D4
Avocet Cl NEWLW WA12 106 C1
WARRN/WOL WA2 123 K4
Avolon Rd WD/CROXPK L12 115 H2
Avon WDN WA8 157 F1
Avon Av WARRW/BUR WA5 141 G5
Avon Cl ANF/KKDL L4 97 G5
NWD/KWIPK L33 72 E3
Avondale EP CH65 196 A6
Avondale Av MGHL L31 71 F1
MOR/LEA CH46 109 K6
PS/BROM CH62 184 B2
Avondale Dr WDN WA8 157 G2
Avondale Rd CHTN/BK PR9 22 B5
HOY CH47 127 G2
RNFD/HAY WA11 90 B4
WAV L15 133 K3
Avondale Rd North
CHTN/BK PR9 15 G1
Avonmore Av CALD/MH L18 134 B6
Avon Rd AIMK WN4 79 K4
WGNW/BIL/O WN5 77 G6
Avon St BIRK CH41 111 F6
NPK/KEN L6 * 113 K2
Awelon Cl WD/CROXPK L12 99 G5
Axbridge Av STHEL WA9 120 B2
Axholme Cl PEN/TH CH61 148 E6
Axholme Rd PEN/TH CH61 148 D6
Ayala Cl BTL L20 82 C4
Aycliffe Rd STHEL WA9 * 119 F1
Aylesbury Av CL/PREN CH43 149 H1
Aylesbury Cl GTS/LS CH66 195 F6
Aylesbury Rd WAL/NB CH45 95 J6
Aylesford Rd CLB/OSW/ST L13 114 E4
Aylsham Cl WDN WA8 138 B6
Aylsham Dr GR/UP/WCH CH49 129 H2
Aylton Rd HUY L36 116 B3
Aylward Pl BTL L20 * 4 D2
Aynsley Ct STHEL WA9 118 E1
Ayr Cl STHP PR8 28 C3
Ayres Ct STHEL WA9 103 G4
Ayrshire Gdns ECCL WA10 12 D7
Ayrshire Rd ANF/KKDL L4 98 A5
Aysgarth Av WD/CROXPK L12 115 G1
Aysgarth Rd WAL/NB CH45 111 F1
Azalea Gv HLWD L26 155 G1
RUNC WA7 187 J3

B

Babbacombe Rd CHLDW L16 135 F3
WARRW/BUR WA5 141 F5
Back Barlow La ANF/KKDL L4 97 G5
Back Bath St STHP PR8 14 E3
Back Beau St EV L5 * 113 G3
Back Bedford St EHL/KEN L7 9 K6
Back Belmont Rd NPK/KEN L6 113 K2
Back Berry St CLVPS L1 9 G6
Back Blackfield Ter ANF/KKDL L4 97 F6
Back Bold St CLVPS L1 9 F5
Back Boundary St EV L5 113 F1
Back Bridge St NEWLW WA12 106 B2
Back Bridport St VAUX/LVPD L3 9 G3
Back Brook Pl WARRS WA4 143 H6
Back Canning St CLVPS L1 9 J7
Back Catharine St TOX L8 * 9 J7
Back Chadwick Mt EV L5 97 G6
Back Chatham Pl EHL/KEN L7 113 K6
Back Colquitt St CLVPS L1 9 G6
Back Commutation St
VAUX/LVPD L3 9 G3
Back Cross La NEWLW WA12 106 B1
Back Eastford Rd WARRS WA4 161 K2
Back Egerton St North
TOX L8 * 132 E2
Back Falkner St South TOX L8 9 K7
Backford Cl CL/PREN CH43 130 B6
RUNC WA7 188 B2
Backford Gdns GTS/LS CH66 202 D4
Backford Rd PEN/TH CH61 148 A6
Backford Wy CL/PREN CH43 130 B6
Back Forest Rd STHP PR8 15 J7
Back Forshaw St
WARRN/WOL WA2 17 F1
Back Gillmoss La NG/CROX L11 84 B5
Back Granton Rd EV L5 113 J1
Back Guilford St NPK/KEN L6 113 H3
Back High St RUNC WA7 10 D4
Back Holland Pl EHL/KEN L7 113 K6
Back Hope Pl CLVPS L1 9 J6
Back Huskisson St TOX L8 * 132 E2
Back Kelvin Gv TOX L8 133 F3
Back Knight St CLVPS L1 9 G7
Back La BRSC L40 38 E3
BRSC L40 47 K1
CSBY/BLUN L23 69 G1
ORM L39 52 C6
ORM L39 64 A4
RNFD/HAY WA11 76 C4
SKEL WN8 67 G1
WARRW/BUR WA5 105 H6
WARRW/BUR WA5 159 H1
Back Leeds St VAUX/LVPD L3 8 B1
Back Legh St NEWLW WA12 106 A2
Back Lime St CLVPS L1 9 F4
Back Little Canning St
TOX L8 * 132 E2
Back Luton Gv ANF/KKDL L4 97 G5
Back Market St NEWLW WA12 106 A1
Back Maryland St CLVPS L1 * 9 H6
Back Menai St CL/PREN CH43 2 C5
Back Mersey Vw CSBY/WL L22 80 D1
Back Moss La BRSC L40 39 F2
Back Mount St CSBY/WL L22 * 80 E2
Back Mount Vernon Gn
EHL/KEN L7 * 113 J6
Back Mulberry St EHL/KEN L7 9 K7
Back Oliver St BIRK CH41 3 G5
Back Orford St WAV L15 134 A1
Back o the Town La HTWN L38 60 B4
Back Percy St TOX L8 132 E1
Back Pickop St VAUX/LVPD L3 8 D2
Back Renshaw St CLVPS L1 9 H6
Back Rockfield Rd ANF/KKDL L4 97 H6
Back St Bride St EHL/KEN L7 9 K7
Back Sandon St TOX L8 132 E2
Back Sandstone Rd
CLB/OSW/ST L13 114 D3
Back School La SKEL WN8 55 K4
Back Seaview HOY CH47 127 G2
Back Seel St CLVPS L1 9 F6
Back Sir Howard St TOX L8 9 K7
Back South Rd CSBY/WL L22 81 F2
Back Stanley Rd BTL L20 5 F4
Back Towerlands St
EHL/KEN L7 113 K6
Back Virginia St STHP PR8 15 F7
Back Wellesley Rd TOX L8 133 F5
Back Westminster Rd
ANF/KKDL L4 97 G5
Back Windsor Vw TOX L8 * 133 G2
Back Winstanley Rd
CSBY/WL L22 81 F1
Back York Ter EV L5 * 113 G1
Badbury Cl RNFD/HAY WA11 90 C4
Badby Wd NWD/KWIPK L33 72 E5
Baden Rd CLB/OSW/ST L13 115 F4
Bader Cl PEN/TH CH61 167 J2
Badger Bait NSTN CH64 192 A3
Badger Cl RUNC WA7 187 K1
Badgers Cl GTS/LS CH66 202 D3
Badgers Pk NSTN CH64 192 A3
Badgers Rake FMBY L37 40 C6
Badgersrake La GTS/LS CH66 194 A5
Badger's Set WKBY CH48 146 E5
Badger Wy CL/PREN CH43 149 H3
Badminton St TOX L8 * 132 E6
Baffin Cl MOR/LEA CH46 110 A3
Bagnall Cl WARRW/BUR WA5 141 K4
Bagnall St ANF/KKDL L4 97 J6
Bagot Av WARRW/BUR WA5 142 C1
Bagot St WAV L15 133 J2
Baguley Av WDN WA8 157 F6
Bahama Cl RNFD/HAY WA11 90 C3
Bahama Rd RNFD/HAY WA11 90 C3
Bailey Av EP CH65 195 J3
Bailey Dr BTL L20 82 B5
Baileys Cl WDN WA8 139 F4
Baileys La HLWD L26 155 K3
SPK/HALE L24 174 B4
Bailey St CLVPS L1 9 G7
Bainbridge Av GOL/RIS/CU WA3 93 G3
Bainton Cl KKBY L32 85 F4
Bainton Rd KKBY L32 85 F4
Baird Av BTL L20 4 A2
Baker Dr GTS/LS CH66 195 H6
Baker Rd RUNC WA7 176 A6
Bakers Green Rd HUY L36 116 E3
Baker's La CHTN/BK PR9 23 J2
Bakers St HUY L36 117 G5
Baker St NPK/KEN L6 113 J4
STHEL WA9 104 A2
Baker Wy NPK/KEN L6 113 J4
Bakewell Cl GTS/LS CH66 202 C3
Bakewell Gv WLT/FAZ L9 82 E4
Bakewell Rd
WARRW/BUR WA5 106 A6
Bala Cl WARRW/BUR WA5 * 122 E5
Bala Gv WAL/EG CH44 * 111 G4
Bala St ANF/KKDL L4 113 K1
Balcarres Av CALD/MH L18 134 A4
Baldock Cl WARRS WA4 144 B6
Baldwin Av CHLDW L16 135 G1
Baldwin St ECCL WA10 13 G4
The Bales NTHTN L30 70 D5
Balfe St LITH L21 81 H5
Balfour Av BTL L20 * 4 D1
Balfour Rd BTL L20 4 C1
CL/PREN CH43 2 A7
STHP PR8 28 B2
WAL/EG CH44 111 G5
Balfour St ANF/KKDL L4 97 H6
ECCL WA10 12 A6
RUNC WA7 10 C6
Balham Cl WDN WA8 139 F5
Balharry Av RNFD/HAY WA11 90 E4
Balker Dr ECCL WA10 12 E1
Ballantrae Rd CALD/MH L18 134 D6
Ballantyne Dr CL/PREN CH43 110 C6
Ballantyne Gv BTL L20 82 B5
CLB/OSW/ST L13 98 C6
Ballantyne Pl CLB/OSW/ST L13 98 C6
WARRN/WOL WA2 123 G1
Ballantyne Rd
CLB/OSW/ST L13 114 C1
Ballantyne Wy GOL/RIS/CU WA3 93 F3
Ballard Rd WKBY CH48 127 K6
Ballater Dr WARRN/WOL WA2 124 A3
Ball Av WAL/NB CH45 95 G5
Balliol Cl CL/PREN CH43 110 C6
Balliol Gv CSBY/BLUN L23 80 C1
Balliol Rd BTL L20 5 F7
Balliol Rd East BTL L20 5 H6
Balliol Wy AIMK WN4 78 E5
Ball Pth WDN WA8 157 K2
Ball's Pl STHP PR8 14 E5
Ball's Rd CL/PREN CH43 2 B7
Ball's Rd East BIRK CH41 2 B7
Balmer St STHEL WA9 103 F6
Balmoral Av CSBY/BLUN L23 69 F6
GOL/RIS/CU WA3 92 E2
STHEL WA9 104 A6
Balmoral Cl CHTN/BK PR9 23 K2
NWD/KWIPK L33 72 D4
Balmoral Ct CLB/OSW/ST L13 114 C2
Balmoral Dr CHTN/BK PR9 23 K2
FMBY L37 48 E4
FROD/HEL WA6 199 J5
Balmoral Gdns
CL/PREN CH43 * 149 J2
EP CH65 203 H1
Balmoral Gv CL/PREN CH43 130 A6
Balmoral Rd AIMK WN4 79 F5
MGHL L31 62 A6
NPK/KEN L6 114 A4
WAL/NB CH45 95 H4
WARRS WA4 162 E1
WDN WA8 139 F5
WLT/FAZ L9 * 82 D5
Balmoral Wy HUY L36 117 F2
Balm St EHL/KEN L7 113 K5
Balniel St STHEL WA9 120 B4
Balsham Cl WLTN L25 155 F4
Baltic Rd BTL L20 4 C4
Baltic St ANF/KKDL L4 97 J6
Baltimore St CLVPS L1 9 H6
Bamber Gdns CHTN/BK PR9 23 J5
Bamboo Cl NTHLY L27 136 B3
Bamburgh Ct EP CH65 196 D6
Bamburgh Pl AIMK WN4 79 F4
Bamford Cl RUNC WA7 187 F1
Bampton Av RNFD/HAY WA11 88 E2
Bampton Rd CHLDW L16 134 E1
Banastre Dr NEWLW WA12 107 F2
Banastre Rd STHP PR8 27 H2
Banbury Av WLTN L25 155 F1
Banbury Dr WARRW/BUR WA5 141 K5
Banbury Wy CL/PREN CH43 149 H1
Bancroft Cl WLTN L25 155 F4
Bancroft Rd WDN WA8 158 E1
Bandon Cl SPK/HALE L24 174 E3
Banff Av BEB CH63 183 K2
Bangor Cl GTS/LS CH66 202 C3
Bangor Rd WAL/NB CH45 110 D1
Bangor St EV L5 112 E2
Bankburn Rd CLB/OSW/ST L13 114 C1
Bank Cl NSTN CH64 192 B3
Bank Dene RF/TRAN CH42 151 F3
Bankes' La RUNC WA7 186 C2
Bankfield SKEL WN8 56 E6
Bankfield Ct CLB/OSW/ST L13 114 D2
Bankfield La CHTN/BK PR9 23 K3
Bankfield Rd CLB/OSW/ST L13 114 D2
WDN WA8 157 G2
Bankfields Dr PS/BROM CH62 184 E2
Bankfield St BTL L20 96 D5
Bank Gdns WARRW/BUR WA5 141 F5
Bankhall La BTL L20 96 E6
Bankhall St BTL L20 96 E5
Bankhey NSTN CH64 192 A4
Bank House La FROD/HEL WA6 199 K5
Bankland Rd CLB/OSW/ST L13 114 D2
Bank La MGHL L31 72 B3
Bank Ms FROD/HEL WA6 * 199 K5
Bank Nook CHTN/BK PR9 * 23 H2
Bank Pas GOL/RIS/CU WA3 * 92 B2
Bank Rd BTL L20 4 D4
Banks Av HOY CH47 127 J1
Banksbarn SKEL WN8 56 E6
Banks Crs WARRS WA4 143 J5
Bankside HTWN L38 59 F4
RUNC WA7 178 D6
Bankside Av AIMK WN4 79 F1
Bankside Rd RF/TRAN CH42 150 E3
Bank's La ALL/GAR L19 172 C1
Bank Sq CHTN/BK PR9 14 E2
Bank's Rd ALL/GAR L19 153 K6
CHTN/BK PR9 21 G5
HES CH60 167 G5

WKBY CH48 146 B2
The Banks WAL/NB CH45 * 94 E6
Bank St BIRK CH41 3 G5
ECCL WA10 12 C6
GOL/RIS/CU WA3 92 B2
NEWLW WA12 105 K2
WARR WA1 16 E5
WDN WA8 176 D1
Bank's Wy ALL/GAR L19 172 C1
Bankville Rd RF/TRAN CH42 131 H6
Banner Hey RAIN/WH L35 117 K6
Bannerman St EHL/KEN L7 133 J1
Banner St ECCL WA10 12 F6
WAV L15 133 K2
Banner Wk ECCL WA10 12 D6
Banning Cl BIRK CH41 2 D3
Banstead Gv WAV L15 134 C2
Barbara Av AIN/FAZ L10 83 K4
Barbara St STHEL WA9 120 C4
Barbauld St WARR WA1 16 D6
Barberry Cl MOR/LEA CH46 128 C1
Barberry Crs NTHTN L30 70 D5
Barber St STHEL WA9 13 K4
Barbondale Cl
WARRW/BUR WA5 141 G2
Barbour Dr BTL L20 82 B5
Barbrook Wy WLT/FAZ L9 97 K2
Barchester Dr AIG/SPK L17 152 D2
Barclay St TOX L8 * 132 E5
Barcombe Rd HES CH60 168 D4
Bardale Gv AIMK WN4 79 F6
Bardley Crs HUY L36 136 D2
Bardney Av GOL/RIS/CU WA3 92 A1
Bardon Cl WLTN L25 135 K4
Bardsay Rd ANF/KKDL L4 97 H4
Bardsey Cl EP CH65 203 G2
Bardsley Av WARRW/BUR WA5 123 F5
Bardsley Cl SKEL WN8 57 J6
Barford Cl CL/PREN CH43 129 J3
SKEL WN8 57 J6
STHP PR8 33 G3
WARRW/BUR WA5 122 B6
Barford Dr GOL/RIS/CU WA3 93 H3
Barford Gra NSTN CH64 193 J1
Barford Rd HUY L36 117 F1
SPK/HALE L24 154 E5
Barham Ct GOL/RIS/CU WA3 125 F3
Barholm CL/PREN CH43 * 130 B5
Barington Dr RUNC WA7 178 D6
Barkbeth Rd HUY L36 116 C2
Barkeley Dr LITH L21 81 G5
Barker Cl HUY L36 136 C1
Barker La GR/UP/WCH CH49 147 K1
Barker Rd PEN/TH CH61 148 C5
Barker's Hollow Rd
WARRS WA4 189 F1
Barkerville Cl CLB/OSW/ST L13 98 B6
Barker Wy NPK/KEN L6 113 K2
Barkfield Av FMBY L37 48 E1
Barkfield La FMBY L37 48 E1
Barkhill Ct AIG/SPK L17 * 153 G2
Barkhill Rd AIG/SPK L17 153 G2
Barkiss Cl TOX L8 132 E4
Bark Rd LITH L21 81 K2
Barleycastle La WARRS WA4 163 J6
Barleyfield PEN/TH CH61 167 J1
Barley Mow Cl CH/BCN CH1 202 A1
Barley Rd WARRS WA4 144 B6
Barlow Av BEB CH63 151 F4
Barlow Gv STHEL WA9 104 E3
Barlow La ANF/KKDL L4 97 G5
Barlows Cl WLT/FAZ L9 83 G3
Barlow's La ORM L39 35 F4
WLT/FAZ L9 83 G3
Barlow St ANF/KKDL L4 97 G5
Barmouth Cl
WARRW/BUR WA5 122 E5
Barmouth Rd WAL/NB CH45 110 D1
Barmouth Wy EV L5 112 E2
Barnack Cl WARR WA1 143 K1
Barnacre Dr NSTN CH64 181 G5
Barnacre La WKBY CH48 128 C3
Barnard Rd CL/PREN CH43 2 A7
Barnard St WARRW/BUR WA5 142 A6
Barn Cl NTHTN L30 70 D5
Barn Cft FROD/HEL WA6 199 K5
Barncroft RUNC WA7 178 C6
Barn Croft Rd HLWD L26 155 K4
The Barncroft
GR/UP/WCH CH49 * 128 E5
Barndale Rd CALD/MH L18 134 B4
Barnes Av WARRN/WOL WA2 124 D5
Barnes Cl NWD/KWIPK L33 72 D3
WARRW/BUR WA5 141 H4
WDN WA8 * 158 E1
Barnes Dr MGHL L31 62 A3
Barnes Gn BEB CH63 170 C4
Barnes Rd ORM L39 53 J2
SKEL WN8 55 K4
WDN WA8 158 D1
Barnes St NPK/KEN L6 113 J2
Barneston Rd WDN WA8 139 K6
Barnet Cl EHL/KEN L7 133 H1
Barnett Av NEWLW WA12 105 J2
Barnfield Av RUNC WA7 188 C1
Barnfield Cl GTS/LS CH66 * 202 A1
HOY CH47 108 C6
NTHTN L30 82 B1
WD/CROXPK L12 115 F1
Barnfield Dr SKEL WN8 57 G6
WD/CROXPK L12 115 F1
Barnfield Rd WARR WA1 144 B2
Barnham Cl GOL/RIS/CU WA3 92 B3
SPK/HALE L24 173 G1
Barnham Dr CHLDW L16 135 F2
Barn Hey HOY CH47 127 F4
Barn Hey Crs HOY CH47 128 A2
Barn Hey Gn WD/CROXPK L12 115 F1
Barn Hey Rd NWD/KWIPK L33 85 F1
Barnhill Rd WAV L15 134 B3
Barnhurst Cl CHLDW L16 135 F2
Barnhurst Rd CHLDW L16 135 F2
Barn La GOL/RIS/CU WA3 92 A4
Barnmeadow Rd WLTN L25 135 H4
Barnsbury Rd ANF/KKDL L4 97 K3
Barnsdale Av PEN/TH CH61 148 E6
Barnside Ct CHLDW L16 135 F2
Barnstaple Wy
WARRW/BUR WA5 141 F5
Barnston Av EP CH65 195 J4
Barnston La MOR/LEA CH46 109 J6
Barnston Rd HES CH60 168 C5
PEN/TH CH61 148 E5
WLT/FAZ L9 82 D4
Barnston Towers Cl HES CH60 168 C5
Barnstream Cl NTHLY L27 135 K2
Barn St WDN WA8 158 B5
Barnswood Cl WARRS WA4 163 H2
Barnton Cl GOL/RIS/CU WA3 92 E4
Barn Wy NEWLW WA12 106 B2
Barnwell Av WAL/EG CH44 111 H2
Barnwood Rd HUY L36 116 B3
Baron Cl WARR WA1 144 C2
Baroncroft Rd WLTN L25 135 G5
Baron's Cl WDN WA8 157 H3
Baron's Hey STBRV L28 99 K5
Barren Gv CL/PREN CH43 130 E5
Barrett Av STHP PR8 27 H5
Barrett Rd STHP PR8 27 H5
Barrington Dr STHP PR8 33 H4
Barrington Rd WAL/EG CH44 111 J4
WAV L15 133 K3
Barrison Gn BRSC L40 45 J1
Barrow Av WARRN/WOL WA2 124 A5
Barrow Cl WD/CROXPK L12 99 G4
Barrowdale Rd
GOL/RIS/CU WA3 92 C3
Barrowfield Rd ECCL WA10 87 H6
Barrow Hall La
WARRW/BUR WA5 141 F2
Barrow La GOL/RIS/CU WA3 107 J3
Barrow Nook La ORM L39 64 E4
Barrow's Green La WDN WA8 159 F1
Barrow's Rw WDN WA8 139 G5
Barrow St AIMK WN4 79 J4
ECCL WA10 13 G5
Barrule Cl WARRS WA4 162 C4
Barry Cl EP CH65 203 G3
Barrymore Av WARRS WA4 143 J5
Barrymore Rd
CLB/OSW/ST L13 114 D4
RUNC WA7 176 E6
Barrymore Wy BEB CH63 183 J1
Barry St WARRS WA4 17 G7
Barsbank Cl LYMM WA13 145 H6
Barsbank La LYMM WA13 145 H6
Bartholomew Cl RAIN/WH L35 119 G6
Bartlegate RUNC WA7 188 A2
Bartlett St WAV L15 133 K2
Barton Av WARRS WA4 163 F1
Barton Cl ECCL WA10 12 E4
HOY CH47 126 E3
LITH L21 81 H1
RUNC WA7 178 C6
Barton Clough
WGNW/BIL/O WN5 77 H4
Barton Hey Dr WKBY CH48 146 D5
Barton Heys Rd FMBY L37 48 D4
Barton Rd HOY CH47 127 F3
WLT/FAZ L9 97 H1
Bartons Cl CHTN/BK PR9 21 G6
Barton St BIRK CH41 2 C6
GOL/RIS/CU WA3 92 B3
Barwell Av RNFD/HAY WA11 89 F5
Barwell Cl GOL/RIS/CU WA3 92 D2
Basil Cl CHLDW L16 135 F1
Basildon Cl STHEL WA9 119 G1
Basil Rd CHLDW L16 134 E1
Basing St ALL/GAR L19 153 K5
Baskervyle Cl HES CH60 181 F1
Baskervyle Rd HES CH60 181 F1
Basnett St CLVPS L1 8 E4
Bassendale Rd PS/BROM CH62 171 G3
Bassenthwaite Av
CL/PREN CH43 130 A4
NWD/KWIPK L33 72 C5
RNFD/HAY WA11 88 D3
Bates Crs ECCL WA10 103 F5
Bates La FROD/HEL WA6 200 A6
Batey Av RAIN/WH L35 118 D3
Batherton Cl WDN WA8 18 E6
Bathgate Wy NWD/KWIPK L33 72 C3
Bath Springs ORM L39 45 K6
Bath St CSBY/WL L22 80 E3
ECCL WA10 13 F6
PS/BROM CH62 151 G6
STHP PR8 14 E3
VAUX/LVPD L3 8 A2
WARR WA1 16 C4
Bath St North CHTN/BK PR9 15 F2
Bathurst Rd ALL/GAR L19 153 J4
Bathwood Dr NSTN CH64 191 K4
Batley St CLB/OSW/ST L13 114 E4
Battenberg St EHL/KEN L7 113 J5
Battersby La WARRN/WOL WA2 17 F2
Battersea Ct WDN WA8 * 138 E6
Battery Cl AIG/SPK L17 152 D1
Battery La WARR WA1 144 E3
Battle Wy FMBY L37 * 49 H3
Baucher Dr BTL L20 82 B4
Baumville Dr BEB CH63 170 B3
Bawtry Ct WARRN/WOL WA2 124 A6
Baxter Cl RUNC WA7 178 C6
Baxters La STHEL WA9 104 B5
Baxter St WARRW/BUR WA5 142 B4
Baycliffe LYMM WA13 164 E1
Baycliffe Cl RUNC WA7 187 G2
Baycliff Rd WD/CROXPK L12 99 J5
Bayfield Rd ALL/GAR L19 153 H4
Bayhorse La VAUX/LVPD L3 9 J2
Baysdale Cl TOX L8 133 F5
Bayswater Cl RUNC WA7 178 E1
Bayswater Gdns WAL/NB CH45 94 D6
Bayswater Rd WAL/NB CH45 110 D1
Baythorne Rd ANF/KKDL L4 98 A3
Baytree Cl CHTN/BK PR9 21 G6
GTS/LS CH66 202 D2
Baytree Gv MGHL L31 71 K6
Baytree Rd RF/TRAN CH42 131 H6
WKBY CH48 147 G1
Bayview Dr WAL/NB CH45 94 D6
Bayvil Cl RUNC WA7 178 D6
Beacham Rd STHP PR8 23 G6
Beach Bank CSBY/WL L22 80 D1
Beachcroft Rd HOY CH47 108 B6
Beach Gv WAL/NB CH45 95 J6
Beach Lawn CSBY/WL L22 80 D2
Beach Priory Gdns STHP PR8 14 C6
Beach Rd HOY CH47 126 E3
LITH L21 81 J4
STHP PR8 14 A7
Beach Wk WKBY CH48 146 C3
Beacon Dr WKBY CH48 146 D1
Beacon Gv RNFD/HAY WA11 89 G5
Beacon Hl WGNW/BIL/O WN5 * 77 G2
Beacon Hill Vw RUNC WA7 176 A6
Beacon La EV L5 113 H1
HES CH60 168 A6
SKEL WN8 57 H3
Beacon Rd WGNW/BIL/O WN5 77 G3
Beaconsfield Cl BIRK CH41 131 J6
Beaconsfield Crs WDN WA8 139 F5
Beaconsfield Gv WDN WA8 139 G5
Beaconsfield Rd CHTN/BK PR9 28 C1
ECCL WA10 87 K6
LITH L21 81 G4
PS/BROM CH62 151 G4
RUNC WA7 176 B5
WDN WA8 139 G6
WLTN L25 135 F6
Beaconsfield St TOX L8 133 F3
Beaconsfield Ter
ALL/GAR L19 * 153 J5
Beacon St EV L5 112 D1
Beacon View Dr SKEL WN8 57 K6
Beadnell Dr WARRW/BUR WA5 141 F6
Beames Cl EHL/KEN L7 114 A6
Beamont St WDN WA8 176 D1
Beardsmore Dr
GOL/RIS/CU WA3 93 F3
Bearncroft SKEL WN8 66 E1
Beasley Cl GTS/LS CH66 195 G6
Beatrice Av BEB CH63 150 D4
Beatrice St BTL L20 97 F4
WARRS WA4 143 G6
Beattock Cl NWD/KWIPK L33 72 C3
Beatty Av WARRN/WOL WA2 123 J6
Beatty Cl RAIN/WH L35 117 K5
WKBY CH48 * 146 D5
Beatty Rd CLB/OSW/ST L13 114 E5
STHP PR8 28 B2
Beauclair Dr WAV L15 134 C3
Beaufort FMBY L37 49 G3
Beaufort Cl ORM L39 52 E4
RUNC WA7 176 E6
WARRW/BUR WA5 141 H4
WDN WA8 157 F3
Beaufort Dr WAL/EG CH44 110 E3
Beaufort Rd BIRK CH41 111 G6
Beaufort St STHEL WA9 104 A4
TOX L8 132 D4
WARRW/BUR WA5 142 B5
Beaumaris Dr EP CH65 203 H1
PEN/TH CH61 148 E5
Beaumaris Rd WAL/NB CH45 110 D1
Beaumaris St BTL L20 96 D5
Beaumont Av ECCL WA10 12 A4
Beaumont Crs ORM L39 53 H3
Beaumont Dr AIN/FAZ L10 83 H2
Beaumont St TOX L8 133 G2
Beau St VAUX/LVPD L3 113 G4
Beauworth Av
GR/UP/WCH CH49 * 128 D6
Beaver Ct AIMK WN4 79 H3
Beaver Gv WLT/FAZ L9 82 D5
Beavers La SKEL WN8 67 F1
Bebington Rd GTS/LS CH66 195 G5
PS/BROM CH62 151 F5
RF/TRAN CH42 150 D2
Bebles Rd ORM L39 53 G2
Bechers WDN WA8 138 A6
Bechers Dr WLT/FAZ L9 83 F1
Bechers Rw WLT/FAZ L9 82 C4
Beck Cl AIN/FAZ L10 84 A4
Beckenham Av CALD/MH L18 134 A4
Beckenham Rd WAL/NB CH45 95 H4
Becket St ANF/KKDL L4 97 F6
Beckett Cl NWD/KWIPK L33 85 H3
Beckett Dr WARRN/WOL WA2 123 G2
Beckett Gv BEB CH63 150 C4
Beck Gv RNFD/HAY WA11 88 E3
Beck Rd BTL L20 81 K6
Beckwith St BIRK CH41 2 B2
CLVPS L1 8 E7
Beckwith St East BIRK CH41 2 E3
Becky St NPK/KEN L6 113 K2
Becontree Rd WD/CROXPK L12 115 H3
Bective St EHL/KEN L7 * 133 H1
Bedburn Dr HUY L36 116 A4
Bedford Av EP CH65 202 E1
MGHL L31 71 J3
RF/TRAN CH42 150 D2
Bedford Av East EP CH65 203 F1
Bedford Cl EHL/KEN L7 9 K7
HUY L36 117 G4
Bedford Dr RF/TRAN CH42 150 C2
Bedford Gdns RF/TRAN CH42 * 151 F1
Bedford Pl AIMK WN4 79 F4
BTL L20 96 E4
LITH L21 * 81 G4
RF/TRAN CH42 151 F1
Bedford Rd BTL L20 5 H7
RF/TRAN CH42 150 E1
STHP PR8 27 H5
WAL/NB CH45 111 H1
Bedford Rd East
RF/TRAN CH42 151 F1
Bedford St STHEL WA9 104 B3
WARRS WA4 162 B3
Bedford St North EHL/KEN L7 9 K5
Bedford St South EHL/KEN L7 9 K7
Bedford Wk EHL/KEN L7 9 K7
Beecham Cl HUY L36 116 D6
Beech Av AIG/SPK L17 152 C1
CSBY/BLUN L23 69 H3
FROD/HEL WA6 201 F1
GOL/RIS/CU WA3 93 G4
GR/UP/WCH CH49 128 E3
MGHL L31 72 A6
PEN/TH CH61 168 A1
PR/KW L34 118 B1
RNFD/HAY WA11 90 E4
STHEL WA9 120 A3
WARRS WA4 144 C6
WARRW/BUR WA5 140 D6
Beechbank Rd AIG/SPK L17 133 K4
Beechburn Crs HUY L36 116 B4
Beechburn Rd HUY L36 116 A4
Beech Cl KKBY L32 72 B6
NEWLW WA12 106 C3
SKEL WN8 56 A4
WD/CROXPK L12 99 H2
Beech Ct CALD/MH L18 134 E6
RF/TRAN CH42 131 G5
Beechcroft Dr EP CH65 196 A6
Beechcroft Rd WAL/EG CH44 111 J5
Beechdale Rd CALD/MH L18 134 B5
Beechdene Rd ANF/KKDL L4 97 K6
Beech Dr FMBY L37 48 D1
The Beeches CALD/MH L18 134 E4
FROD/HEL WA6 199 K5
GTS/LS CH66 195 G5
MOR/LEA CH46 109 J4
RF/TRAN CH42 * 151 F2
STHEL WA9 120 B2
Beechfield MGHL L31 62 C6
Beechfield Cl HES CH60 167 K6
HLWD L26 155 H5
Beechfield Gdns STHP PR8 14 B6
Beechfield Rd CALD/MH L18 134 E5
EP CH65 6 C4
WARRS WA4 163 F2
Beech Gdns RNFD/HAY WA11 75 F2
Beech Gn WD/CROXPK L12 98 E5
Beech Gv CHTN/BK PR9 23 G6
GTS/LS CH66 202 E3
LITH L21 81 G5
LYMM WA13 164 C1
NTHTN L30 82 D1
WARR WA1 143 K2
WLT/FAZ L9 * 82 E5
Beech Hey La NSTN CH64 183 J6
Beechill Cl WLTN L25 135 K5
Beech Lawn ALL/GAR L19 153 G4
Beech Meadow ORM L39 54 A1
Beech Mdw PR/KW L34 117 G2
Beechmoore WARRS WA4 160 E6
Beech Pk WD/CROXPK L12 114 E1
Beech Rd ANF/KKDL L4 97 J4
BEB CH63 150 E4
GOL/RIS/CU WA3 92 B2
HES CH60 168 C5
HUY L36 116 E6
ORM L39 62 E1
RF/TRAN CH42 131 F5
RUNC WA7 177 F5
RUNC WA7 188 A3
WARRS WA4 162 B3
Beech St BTL L20 5 F2
ECCL WA10 * 103 F5
EHL/KEN L7 114 A5
Beech Ter EHL/KEN L7 * 114 A5
Beechtree Farm Cl
KNUT WA16 165 K4
Beech Tree Houses
WGNE/HIN WN2 79 K3
Beechtree La KNUT WA16 165 K4
Beechtree Rd WAV L15 115 F6
Beechtrees SKEL WN8 56 E6
Beechurst Cl WLTN L25 135 J4
Beechurst Rd WLTN L25 135 J4
The Beechwalk
DV/KA/FCH L14 115 F3
Beechway BEB CH63 170 B2
MGHL L31 63 F6
Beechway Av MGHL L31 63 F5
Beechways WARRS WA4 162 C6
Beechways Dr NSTN CH64 191 J1
Beechwood SKEL WN8 56 E2
Beechwood Av AIMK WN4 91 F1
HLWD L26 155 H4
NEWLW WA12 106 D1
RUNC WA7 187 G2
WAL/NB CH45 110 E2
WARR WA1 143 H1
WARRW/BUR WA5 141 G4
Beechwood Cl ALL/GAR L19 153 H4
RAIN/WH L35 118 A3
Beechwood Dr CL/PREN CH43 129 J2
FMBY L37 48 C4
GTS/LS CH66 202 B2
ORM L39 53 H1
Beechwood Gdns ALL/GAR L19 153 G4
Beechwood Rd ALL/GAR L19 153 G4
LITH L21 81 J5
PS/BROM CH62 170 E5
Beechwood Rd South
ALL/GAR L19 153 G5
Beecroft Cl WARRW/BUR WA5 122 D6
Beesands Cl NTHLY L27 136 C5
Beesley Rd PR/KW L34 117 J1
Beeston Cl CL/PREN CH43 129 K3
GOL/RIS/CU WA3 125 F3
Beeston Ct RUNC WA7 * 178 B1
Beeston Dr NTHTN L30 70 E4
PEN/TH CH61 167 J1
Beeston Gn GTS/LS CH66 195 H4
Beeston Gv ALL/GAR L19 153 H4
Beeston St ANF/KKDL L4 97 G5
Begonia Gdns STHEL WA9 104 E6
Beilby Rd RNFD/HAY WA11 90 E4
Beldale Pk KKBY L32 72 B5
Beldon Crs HUY L36 116 B4
Belem Cl AIG/SPK L17 133 H4
Belfast Rd CLB/OSW/ST L13 115 F4
Belfield SKEL WN8 67 F1
Belfield Crs HUY L36 116 E6
Belfield Dr CL/PREN CH43 130 E6
Belford Dr MOR/LEA CH46 128 C1
Belfort Rd WLTN L25 135 J5
Belfry Cl MOR/LEA CH46 109 F6
WD/CROXPK L12 115 J1
Belgrave Av WAL/EG CH44 111 J3
WARR WA1 143 J2
Belgrave Cl LEIGH WN7 93 K3
WDN WA8 139 K6
Belgrave Dr EP CH65 195 J4
Belgrave Rd AIG/SPK L17 133 G6
LITH L21 81 G4
STHP PR8 27 G3
Belgrave St WAL/EG CH44 111 J2
Belgravia Ct WDN WA8 138 E6
Belhaven Rd CALD/MH L18 134 A4
Bellair Av CSBY/BLUN L23 69 H5
Bellairs Rd NG/CROX L11 98 C5
Bellamy Rd ANF/KKDL L4 5 K7
Bellcast Cl WARRS WA4 162 B5
Bell Cl HUY L36 136 C1
Belldene Gv HES CH60 167 K3
Bellefield Av WD/CROXPK L12 115 F1
Bellemonte Rd FROD/HEL WA6 200 E3
Belle Vale Rd WLTN L25 135 J5
Belle Vue Rd WAL/EG CH44 112 A5
WLTN L25 135 J4
Bellew Rd NG/CROX L11 98 D6
Bellfield Crs WAL/NB CH45 95 G5
Bellgreen Rd NG/CROX L11 98 E3
Bellhouse La WARRS WA4 161 G4
WARRS WA4 163 H2
Bell House Rd WDN WA8 19 H2
Bellingham Dr RUNC WA7 176 D5
Bellini Cl LITH L21 81 G6
Bellis Av CHTN/BK PR9 23 G3
Bellis Gv NWD/KWIPK L33 * 72 C4
Bell La RAIN/WH L35 119 J5
WARRS WA4 144 D6
Bellmore St ALL/GAR L19 153 K4
Bell Rd WAL/EG CH44 111 K4
Bell's Cl MGHL L31 61 K3
Bell's La MGHL L31 61 J4
Bell St CLB/OSW/ST L13 114 E4
Belltower Rd BTL L20 96 D6
Bellward Cl BEB CH63 170 B3
Belmont BIRK CH41 2 B7
Belmont Av GOL/RIS/CU WA3 92 D2
PS/BROM CH62 170 E4
WARRS WA4 143 J6
Belmont Cl BRSC L40 38 E6
Belmont Crs
WARRW/BUR WA5 141 H3
Belmont Dr NPK/KEN L6 114 A2
PEN/TH CH61 168 A2
Belmont Gv CL/PREN CH43 2 B7
NPK/KEN L6 114 A2
Belmont Rd NPK/KEN L6 113 K2
WAL/NB CH45 95 H4
WDN WA8 158 E1
WKBY CH48 127 G6
Belmont St ECCL WA10 12 A6
STHP PR8 14 C7
Beloe St TOX L8 132 E5
Belper St ALL/GAR L19 153 J5
Belston Rd CHLDW L16 134 E2
Belton Rd HUY L36 116 D1
Belvedere Av STHEL WA9 120 B1
Belvedere Cl FROD/HEL WA6 187 F6
PR/KW L34 102 A6
Belvedere Dr FMBY L37 49 F4
Belvedere Pk ORM L39 53 G6
Belvedere Rd AIMK WN4 79 H6
NEWLW WA12 106 B1
STHP PR8 33 J4
Belvidere Pk CSBY/BLUN L23 69 F6
Belvidere Rd CSBY/BLUN L23 68 E6
TOX L8 133 F4
WAL/NB CH45 111 G2
Belvoir Rd CALD/MH L18 153 K3
WARRS WA4 162 A3
WDN WA8 19 F1
Bembridge Cl
WARRW/BUR WA5 140 D2
WDN WA8 138 E5
Bempton Rd AIG/SPK L17 152 C1
Benbow Cl BIRK CH41 130 C1
Benbow St BTL L20 4 C7
Bendee Av NSTN CH64 192 B2
Bendee Rd NSTN CH64 192 A2
Benedict Ct BTL L20 96 E4
Benedict St BTL L20 97 F4
Bengarth Rd CHTN/BK PR9 23 H5
Bengel St EHL/KEN L7 113 J5
Benjamin Fold AIMK WN4 79 G4
Ben La RNFD/HAY WA11 65 H5
Ben Lane Ct ORM L39 65 H5
Benledi St EV L5 113 F2
Benmore Rd CALD/MH L18 153 H1
Bennet Cl NSTN CH64 193 H1
Bennet's La HOY CH47 108 C5
Bennett Av WARR WA1 143 J3
Bennetts Hl CL/PREN CH43 130 E5
Bennett's La WDN WA8 159 F2
Bennett St ALL/GAR L19 153 K5
WARR WA1 16 E5
Ben Nevis Dr GTS/LS CH66 194 C3
Ben Nevis Rd RF/TRAN CH42 150 C1
Bennison Dr ALL/GAR L19 * 153 H4
Ben's Ct PR/KW L34 85 G6
Benson Cl GR/UP/WCH CH49 129 G5
Benson Rd GOL/RIS/CU WA3 125 F5
Benson St CLVPS L1 9 G5
Bentfield AIG/SPK L17 153 G3
Bentfield Cl BEB CH63 150 C4
Bentfield Gdns BEB CH63 150 C4
Bentham Av WARRN/WOL WA2 123 J4
Bentham Cl CL/PREN CH43 130 B6
Bentham Dr CHLDW L16 134 E1
Bentham St STHP PR8 27 J2
Bentham's Wy STHP PR8 27 K5
Bentinck Cl BIRK CH41 2 C4
Bentinck Pl BIRK CH41 2 C5

Bentinck St BIRK CH41 ....2 D4
EV L5 ....112 D2
RUNC WA7 ....10 B3
STHEL WA9 ....104 B4
Bentley Rd CL/PREN CH43 ....130 E5
PEN/TH CH61 ....148 C6
TOX L8 ....133 G3
Bentley St STHEL WA9 ....120 A3
Benton Cl EV L5 ....113 F1
Benty Cl BEB CH63 ....170 A1
Benty Farm Gv PEN/TH CH61 ....148 D6
Benty Heath La NSTN CH64 ....183 H4
Benwick Rd KKBY L32 ....84 A2
Berbice Rd WAV L15 ....134 B3
Beresford Av BEB CH63 ....151 F5
Beresford Cl CL/PREN CH43 ....130 D4
Beresford Dr CHTN/BK PR9 ....23 H4
Beresford Gdns CHTN/BK PR9 ....23 H3
Beresford Rd CL/PREN CH43 ....130 D4
TOX L8 ....132 E5
WAL/NB CH45 ....95 F6
Beresford St BTL L20 ....96 D4
EV L5 ....113 G3
STHEL WA9 ....103 G6
WARR WA1 ....17 K1
Bergen Cl BTL L20 ....5 J6
Berkeley Av CL/PREN CH43 ....149 H2
Berkeley Cl LEIGH WN7 ....93 K3
Berkeley Dr WAL/NB CH45 ....95 J6
Berkeley Rd CSBY/BLUN L23 ....68 D4
Berkeswell Rd NG/CROX L11 ....98 E4
Berkley Av WD/CROXPK L12 ....99 H5
Berkley St TOX L8 ....132 E3
Berkshire Dr WARR WA1 ....144 C2
Berkshire Gdns ECCL WA10 ....103 H3
Bermuda Rd MOR/LEA CH46 ....109 G6
Bernard Av WAL/NB CH45 * 95 J6
WARRS WA4 ....162 C3
Berner's Rd ALL/GAR L19 ....153 J4
Berner St BIRK CH41 ....2 D1
Berrington Av WLTN L25 ....154 D1
Berrington Gv AIMK WN4 ....79 F6
Berrington's La
RNFD/HAY WA11 ....87 K1
Berry Cl GTS/LS CH66 ....195 F6
SKEL WN8 ....56 B3
Berry Dr GTS/LS CH66 ....195 F5
Berry Hill Av PR/KW L34 ....100 D2
Berry House Rd BRSC L40 ....31 F3
Berrylands Cl MOR/LEA CH46 ....109 H6
Berrylands Rd MOR/LEA CH46 ....109 H5
Berry Rd WDN WA8 ....157 J2
Berrys La STHEL WA9 ....104 D4
Berry St BTL L20 ....4 D5
CLVPS L1 ....9 G7
SKEL WN8 ....56 A3
Berrywood Dr RAIN/WH L35 ....118 B5
Bertha Gdns BIRK CH41 ....130 C1
Bertha St BIRK CH41 ....130 C1
Bertram Dr HOY CH47 ....127 H1
Bertram Dr North HOY CH47 ....127 J1
Bertram Rd AIG/SPK L17 ....133 H5
Bertram St NEWLW WA12 ....105 K2
Berwick Av PS/BROM CH62 ....184 B3
STHP PR8 ....33 J3
Berwick Cl CL/PREN CH43 * 129 K3
MOR/LEA CH46 ....128 C1
NPK/KEN L6 ....113 K3
WARR WA1 ....144 D3
Berwick Dr CSBY/BLUN L23 ....68 D4
Berwick Gdns GTS/LS CH66 ....194 E3
Berwick Gv GTS/LS CH66 ....194 E3
Berwick Rd GTS/LS CH66 ....194 D3
Berwick St NPK/KEN L6 ....113 K3
Berwyn Av HOY CH47 * 127 H2
PEN/TH CH61 * 148 D5
Berwyn Bvd BEB CH63 ....150 D3
Berwyn Cl GTS/LS CH66 ....194 D3
Berwyn Dr PEN/TH CH61 ....167 K3
Berwyn Gv STHEL WA9 ....104 D2
Berwyn Rd ANF/KKDL L4 ....98 A5
WAL/EG CH44 ....111 J2
Beryl Rd CL/PREN CH43 ....129 K4
Beryl St CLB/OSW/ST L13 ....114 E6
Bescar Brow La BRSC L40 ....36 D2
Bescar La BRSC L40 ....36 E1
CHTN/BK PR9 ....30 B5
Besford Rd WLTN L25 ....135 J4
Bessborough Rd
CL/PREN CH43 ....130 E5
Bessbrook Rd AIG/SPK L17 ....152 E1
Bessemer St TOX L8 ....132 E5
Beta Cl PS/BROM CH62 ....151 F4
Betchworth Crs RUNC WA7 ....187 G1
Bethany Cl RNFD/HAY WA11 ....89 K4
Betjeman Cl WARRS WA4 ....143 J5
Betjeman Gv CHLDW L16 ....135 F1
Betony Cl HLWD L26 ....155 H2
Bettisfield Av PS/BROM CH62 ....184 A2
Betula Cl WLT/FAZ L9 ....98 A1
Beulah Av WGNW/BIL/O WN5 ....77 G5
Bevan Cl STHEL WA9 ....119 F1
WARRW/BUR WA5 ....142 A3
Bevan's La WD/CROXPK L12 ....99 H6
Beverley Av WARRS WA4 ....162 C3
Beverley Cl CHTN/BK PR9 ....21 F6
Beverley Dr HES CH60 ....168 B6
Beverley Gdns PEN/TH CH61 ....148 E5
Beverley Rd PS/BROM CH62 ....151 G3
WAL/NB CH45 ....111 F1
WARRW/BUR WA5 ....141 K3
WAV L15 ....134 B3
Beverley Wy GTS/LS CH66 ....194 E2
Beversbrook Rd NG/CROX L11 ....99 F3
Bevington Bush
VAUX/LVPD L3 ....113 F4
Bevington St AIMK WN4 ....78 E4
VAUX/LVPD L3 ....113 F3
Bevyl Rd NSTN CH64 ....181 G5
Bewcastle Dr BRSC L40 ....54 B2
Bewey Cl TOX L8 ....132 D5
Bewley Dr KKBY L32 ....84 C2
Bewsey Farm Cl
WARRW/BUR WA5 ....142 B1
Bewsey Park Cl
WARRW/BUR WA5 ....142 C2
Bewsey Rd WARRW/BUR WA5 ....142 C2
Bewsey St ECCL WA10 ....103 F4
WARR WA1 ....16 D4
Bexhill Av WARRN/WOL WA2 ....123 H3
Bexhill Cl SPK/HALE L24 ....173 G1
Bianca St BTL L20 ....96 E4
Bibby Av WARR WA1 ....143 H3
Bibby Rd CHTN/BK PR9 ....23 J4
Bibby's La BTL L20 ....4 B1
Bibby St CLB/OSW/ST L13 ....114 D4
Bickerstaffe St ECCL WA10 ....13 H5
VAUX/LVPD L3 ....113 G4
Bickerton Av BEB CH63 ....150 C3
FROD/HEL WA6 ....201 G2
Bickerton Cl GOL/RIS/CU WA3 ....125 F3
Bickerton Rd STHP PR8 ....27 G3
Bickerton St AIG/SPK L17 ....133 H6
Bickley Cl RUNC WA7 ....11 H7
WARRN/WOL WA2 ....124 B4
Bicknell Cl WARRW/BUR WA5 ....141 J1
Bidder St VAUX/LVPD L3 ....9 H1
Bideford Av STHEL WA9 ....120 A2
Bideford Rd WARRW/BUR WA5 ....141 F5
Bidston Av BIRK CH41 ....130 C2
RNFD/HAY WA11 ....89 G6
WAL/NB CH45 ....110 E1
Bidston Gn GTS/LS CH66 ....195 G5
Bidston Green Ct
CL/PREN CH43 * 129 K1
Bidston Green Dr
CL/PREN CH43 ....129 K1
Bidston Moss WAL/EG CH44 ....110 D4
Bidston Rd ANF/KKDL L4 ....97 K5
CL/PREN CH43 ....130 C3
Bidston Station Ap
CL/PREN CH43 ....110 C5
Bidston Village Rd
CL/PREN CH43 ....110 B6
Bidston Wy RNFD/HAY WA11 ....89 G6
Bigdale Dr NWD/KWIPK L33 ....73 F6
Biggin Ct WARRN/WOL WA2 ....124 A6
Bigham Rd NPK/KEN L6 ....114 A4
Biglands Dr HUY L36 ....136 C1
Big Meadow Rd
GR/UP/WCH CH49 ....129 H5
Billinge Crs RNFD/HAY WA11 ....89 G5
Billinge Rd AIMK WN4 ....78 A4
Billingham Rd STHEL WA9 ....103 F6
Billings Cl EV L5 ....112 E1
Billington Av NEWLW WA12 ....91 H6
Billington Cl WARRW/BUR WA5 ....141 F1
Billington Rd WDN WA8 ....138 A5
Bilston Rd AIG/SPK L17 ....153 F3
Bilton Cl WDN WA8 ....159 F1
Bingley Rd ANF/KKDL L4 ....97 K6
Binns Rd CLB/OSW/ST L13 ....114 C5
Binns Wy CLB/OSW/ST L13 ....114 D6
Binsey Cl GR/UP/WCH CH49 ....128 E4
Birbeck Rd NWD/KWIPK L33 ....73 F6
Birchall St BTL L20 ....96 E6
Birch Av BRSC L40 ....38 E5
ECCL WA10 ....88 C5
GR/UP/WCH CH49 ....128 E3
WARRN/WOL WA2 ....123 G3
WLT/FAZ L9 ....82 E5
Birchcliffe Rd RF/TRAN CH42 ....150 E1
Birch Cl CL/PREN CH43 ....130 E6
MGHL L31 ....62 D6
RAIN/WH L35 ....118 A3
Birch Crs NEWLW WA12 ....105 K1
Birchdale Cl GR/UP/WCH CH49 ....128 E5
Birchdale Crs WARRS WA4 ....162 B3
Birchdale Rd CSBY/WL L22 ....80 E1
WARR WA1 ....143 K2
WARRS WA4 ....162 B4
WLT/FAZ L9 ....82 D6
Birchen Rd HLWD L26 ....155 K4
Birches Cl HES CH60 ....168 A4
The Birches FMBY L37 ....40 E6
STBRV L28 ....100 A6
WAL/EG CH44 ....112 A5
Birchfield MOR/LEA CH46 ....128 D2
Birchfield Av WDN WA8 ....158 B1
Birchfield Cl EHL/KEN L7 ....114 C5
MOR/LEA CH46 ....128 D3
Birchfield Rd ANF/KKDL L4 ....97 J4
EHL/KEN L7 ....114 C5
WARRW/BUR WA5 ....141 J4
WDN WA8 ....18 D1
Birchfield St STHEL WA9 ....103 F6
VAUX/LVPD L3 ....9 H1
Birchfield Wy MGHL L31 ....61 K2
Birch Gdns ECCL WA10 ....88 C5
Birch Gn FMBY L37 ....40 D6
Birch Green Rd SKEL WN8 ....56 E3
Birch Gv AIMK WN4 ....78 B4
GTS/LS CH66 ....202 E2
HUY L36 ....116 D5
RAIN/WH L35 ....118 A3
WAL/NB CH45 ....95 J6
WARR WA1 ....143 J2
WARRS WA4 ....143 G6
WAV L15 ....114 E6
Birch Heys WKBY CH48 ....147 H2
Birchill Rd NWD/KWIPK L33 ....85 H1
Birchley Av WGNW/BIL/O WN5 ....77 F6
Birchley Rd RNFD/HAY WA11 ....76 E6
WGNW/BIL/O WN5 ....77 F6
Birchley St ECCL WA10 ....13 H3
Birchley Vw RNFD/HAY WA11 ....88 E1
Birchmere HES CH60 ....167 J3
Birchmuir Hey KKBY L32 ....84 E2
Birchover Wk EHL/KEN L7 ....133 G1
Birchridge Cl PS/BROM CH62 ....170 E3
Birch Rd BEB CH63 ....170 C1
CL/PREN CH43 ....130 E6
HOY CH47 ....127 K1
HUY L36 ....116 E6
RNFD/HAY WA11 ....90 D4
RUNC WA7 ....177 F5
WDN WA8 ....139 F6
Birch St EV L5 ....112 D2
SKEL WN8 ....56 A4
STHP PR8 ....27 J3
Birch Tree Av RNFD/HAY WA11 ....88 C3
Birch Tree Ct WD/CROXPK L12 ....114 E1
Birchtree Rd AIG/SPK L17 ....133 K6
Birch Tree Rd GOL/RIS/CU WA3 ....93 G3
Birchview Wy CL/PREN CH43 ....130 A4
Birchway HES CH60 ....181 H1
Birchways WARRS WA4 ....162 D6
Birchwood Av BIRK CH41 ....2 E3
Birchwood Bvd
GOL/RIS/CU WA3 ....125 F5
Birchwood Cl BIRK CH41 ....2 E3
CHNE CH2 ....198 D5
GTS/LS CH66 ....202 B2
Birchwood Park Av
GOL/RIS/CU WA3 ....125 F2
Birchwood Wy
GOL/RIS/CU WA3 ....125 H3
NWD/KWIPK L33 ....73 F4
WARRN/WOL WA2 ....143 H1
Bird St EHL/KEN L7 ....133 H2
Birdwell Dr WARRW/BUR WA5 ....141 H4
Birdwood Rd NG/CROX L11 ....99 G3
Birkdale Av BEB CH63 ....183 K1
Birkdale Cl HUY L36 ....116 C6
NPK/KEN L6 ....114 B1
Birkdale Cop STHP PR8 ....28 B6
Birkdale Rd WARRW/BUR WA5 ....141 G5
WDN WA8 ....139 G4
Birkenhead Rd BIRK CH41 ....112 A6
HOY CH47 ....127 H1
NSTN CH64 ....183 F6
Birkenshaw Av CSBY/BLUN L23 ....68 C5
Birket Av MOR/LEA CH46 ....109 K4
Birket Cl MOR/LEA CH46 ....110 A4
Birket Sq MOR/LEA CH46 ....109 K4
Birkett Av EP CH65 ....203 G1
Birkett Rd RF/TRAN CH42 ....150 D2
WKBY CH48 ....127 G5
Birkett St VAUX/LVPD L3 ....9 G1
Birkey La FMBY L37 ....49 F3
Birkin Cl KKBY L32 ....85 F3
Birkin Rd KKBY L32 ....85 F3
Birkrig SKEL WN8 ....67 F1
Birley Ct TOX L8 ....132 E2
Birley St NEWLW WA12 ....106 D1
Birleywood SKEL WN8 ....67 F1
Birnam Dr RAIN/WH L35 ....119 F5
Birnam Rd WAL/EG CH44 ....111 K4
Birstall Av RNFD/HAY WA11 ....89 F6
Birstall Ct RUNC WA7 ....177 G6
Birstall Rd NPK/KEN L6 ....113 K4
Birt Cl TOX L8 ....133 G2
Birtles Rd WARRN/WOL WA2 ....123 J6
Bisham Pk RUNC WA7 ....178 C3
Bishopdale Cl
WARRW/BUR WA5 ....141 G2
Bishopdale Dr RAIN/WH L35 ....119 F5
Bishop Dr RAIN/WH L35 ....117 K6
Bishopgate St WAV L15 ....133 K2
Bishop Reeves Rd
RNFD/HAY WA11 ....90 D4
Bishop Rd ECCL WA10 ....12 D2
NPK/KEN L6 ....98 A6
WAL/EG CH44 ....111 H5
Bishops Ct WARRN/WOL WA2 ....123 F3
WLTN L25 ....154 E1
Bishops Gdns EP CH65 ....6 A4
Bishop Sheppard Ct
VAUX/LVPD L3 ....112 E3
Bishops Wy WDN WA8 ....139 J6
Bisley St WAL/NB CH45 ....111 H2
WAV L15 ....133 K2
Bispham Dr AIMK WN4 ....78 E4
HOY CH47 ....127 K2
Bispham Rd CHTN/BK PR9 ....23 H6
WARRW/BUR WA5 ....141 J5
Bittern Cl RUNC WA7 ....178 C5
WARRN/WOL WA2 ....123 G4
Bixteth St VAUX/LVPD L3 ....8 C2
Blackacre La BRSC L40 ....45 K2
Black-a-Moor La ORM L39 ....51 J3
Blackberry Gv HLWD L26 ....155 G1
Blackboards La GTS/LS CH66 ....194 D2
Blackbrook Av
WARRN/WOL WA2 ....124 A4
Blackbrook Cl WDN WA8 ....138 B6
WLT/FAZ L9 ....97 J2
Blackbrook Rd RNFD/HAY WA11 ....89 G4
Blackburn Cl GOL/RIS/CU WA3 ....93 G3
Blackburne Av WDN WA8 ....157 G6
Blackburne Cl
WARRN/WOL WA2 ....124 E5
Blackburne Dr WLTN L25 ....155 G4
Blackburne Pl TOX L8 ....9 J7
Blackburne St SPK/HALE L24 ....172 C2
Blackburne Ter TOX L8 ....9 J7
Blackcar La SFTN L29 ....60 C4
Black Denton's Pl WDN WA8 ....19 H2
Blackdown Cl GTS/LS CH66 ....194 D4
Blackdown Gv STHEL WA9 ....104 D3
Blackeys La NSTN CH64 ....191 K1
Blackfield St EV L5 ....113 F1
Blackheath Dr MOR/LEA CH46 ....109 K4
Blackheath La RUNC WA7 ....178 E1
Black Horse Cl WKBY CH48 ....127 H6
Black Horse Hl WKBY CH48 ....146 D1
Black Horse La
CLB/OSW/ST L13 ....115 F4
Black Horse Pl
CLB/OSW/ST L13 ....115 F4
Blackhorse St STHEL WA9 ....104 A1
Blackhurst Rd MGHL L31 ....62 A2
Blackhurst St WARR WA1 ....16 E5
Blackledge Cl
WARRN/WOL WA2 ....124 C4
Blackley Cl WARRS WA4 ....143 G6
Blackley Gv NWD/KWIPK L33 * 73 F3
Blackleyhurst Av
WGNW/BIL/O WN5 ....77 H4
Black Lion La GTS/LS CH66 ....194 E3
Blacklock Hall Rd
SPK/HALE L24 ....173 H2
Blacklow Brow HUY L36 ....116 D5
Blackmoor Dr WD/CROXPK L12 ....115 H2
Black Moss La BRSC L40 ....36 B2
ORM L39 ....53 H3
Blackpool St BIRK CH41 ....3 G6
Blackrod Av SPK/HALE L24 ....173 H2
Blackshaw Dr
WARRW/BUR WA5 ....122 B6
Blackstock St VAUX/LVPD L3 ....112 E4
Blackstone Av RNFD/HAY WA11 ....89 G6
Blackstone St EV L5 ....112 D2
Blackthorn Cl MOR/LEA CH46 ....129 G2
Blackthorne Av GTS/LS CH66 ....202 E3
Blackthorne Crs STBRV L28 ....100 B5
Blackthorne Rd WLT/FAZ L9 ....98 A2
Blackwater Rd NG/CROX L11 ....99 H1
Blackwood Av WLTN L25 ....135 G5
Blaguegate La SKEL WN8 ....55 H3
Blair Dr WDN WA8 ....138 A6
Blairgowrie Gdns ORM L39 ....54 A1
Blair Gv CHTN/BK PR9 ....23 H6
Blair Pk BEB CH63 ....170 D2
Blair St TOX L8 ....132 D2
Blaisdon Cl NG/CROX L11 ....98 E4
Blakeacre Cl HLWD L26 ....155 J5
Blakeacre Rd HLWD L26 ....155 J5
Blakefield Rd CSBY/BLUN L23 ....69 K3
Blakehall SKEL WN8 ....57 F6
Blakeley Brow BEB CH63 ....183 H1
Blakeley Ct BEB CH63 ....183 H1
Blakeley Dell BEB CH63 ....183 J1
Blakeley Dene BEB CH63 ....170 D6
Blakeley Rd BEB CH63 ....170 C6
Blakemere Ct EP CH65 ....6 D1
Blakeney Cl GR/UP/WCH CH49 ....129 H2
Blakenhall Wy
GR/UP/WCH CH49 ....128 E3
Blaking Dr PR/KW L34 ....100 D1
Blandford Cl STHP PR8 ....27 F2
Blandford Rd
WARRW/BUR WA5 ....141 J4
Blantyre Rd WAV L15 ....133 K3
Blantyre St RUNC WA7 ....10 B2
Blay Cl WLTN L25 ....155 G3
Blaydon Cl NTHTN L30 ....82 C2
Blaydon Gv STHEL WA9 ....103 F6
Blaydon Pk SKEL WN8 ....57 F6
Blaydon Wk CL/PREN CH43 ....130 B3
Bleak Hill Cl ECCL WA10 ....87 K4
Bleak Hill Rd ECCL WA10 ....87 K5
Bleak La BRSC L40 ....39 K4
Bleasdale Av AIN/FAZ L10 ....83 H1
Bleasdale Cl GR/UP/WCH CH49 ....129 F3
ORM L39 ....53 H6
Bleasdale Rd CALD/MH L18 ....134 C5
NEWLW WA12 ....106 B1
Blenheim Av LITH L21 ....81 K3
Blenheim Cl WARRN/WOL WA2 ....124 B5
Blenheim Dr HUY L36 ....117 F2
Blenheim Rd AIMK WN4 ....91 J1
CALD/MH L18 * 134 A4
STHP PR8 ....33 H3
WAL/EG CH44 ....111 K2
Blenheim St EV L5 ....112 E3
Blenheim Wy RNFD/HAY WA11 ....88 E5
SPK/HALE L24 ....173 G2
Blessington Rd ANF/KKDL L4 ....97 H6
Bletchley Av WAL/EG CH44 ....111 F3
Bligh St WAV L15 ....133 K2
Blind Foot Rd RNFD/HAY WA11 ....86 E4
Blindman's La ORM L39 ....45 G4
Blisworth St LITH L21 ....81 J5
Blomfield Rd ALL/GAR L19 ....154 A3
Bloomsbury Wy WDN WA8 ....138 C6
Blossom Gv KKBY L32 ....84 E4
Blossom St BTL L20 ....5 F1
Blucher St CSBY/WL L22 ....80 D2
Bluebell Av BIRK CH41 ....130 C1
RNFD/HAY WA11 ....90 D4
Bluebell Cl CSBY/WL L22 ....81 F2
Bluebell Ct RUNC WA7 ....187 J3
Blue Bell La HUY L36 ....116 E3
Blueberry Flds AIN/FAZ L10 ....83 J5
Blue Bridge La FROD/HEL WA6 ....199 K4
Bluecoat Chambers CLVPS L1 * 8 E5
Bluecoat St WARRN/WOL WA2 ....16 D1
Bluefields St TOX L8 ....132 E2
Blue Hatch FROD/HEL WA6 ....201 F1
Blue Jay Cl NTHLY L27 ....136 B4
Blue Ridge Cl
WARRW/BUR WA5 ....141 F2
Bluestone La MGHL L31 ....62 C6
Bluewood Dr BIRK CH41 ....110 D6
Blundell Av FMBY L37 ....48 B1
HTWN L38 ....59 F4
STHP PR8 ....27 G5
Blundell Crs STHP PR8 ....27 G5
Blundell Dr STHP PR8 ....27 G5
Blundell Gv HTWN L38 ....59 F4
Blundell La CHTN/BK PR9 ....24 A3
Blundell Rd HTWN L38 ....59 F5
WDN WA8 ....157 J3
Blundellsands Rd East
CSBY/BLUN L23 ....68 D5
Blundellsands Rd West
CSBY/BLUN L23 ....68 C6
Blundells Dr MOR/LEA CH46 ....109 J6
Blundell's La RAIN/WH L35 ....118 C6
Blundell St CLVPS L1 ....132 C2
Blyth Cl RUNC WA7 ....188 C2
Blythe Av WDN WA8 ....139 G5
Blythe La BRSC L40 ....46 E2
Blythe Ms STHP PR8 ....34 B1
Blythewood SKEL WN8 ....56 E6
Blyth Hey NTHTN L30 ....70 A6
Blyth Rd BEB CH63 ....170 E6
Blythswood St AIG/SPK L17 ....133 G6
Boaler St NPK/KEN L6 ....113 K4
Boardmans La STHEL WA9 ....104 C1
Boathouse La NSTN CH64 ....181 G5
Boat Stage LYMM WA13 ....145 K6
Bobbies La ECCL WA10 ....102 C1
Bobbiners La CHTN/BK PR9 ....24 E2
Bobby Langton Wy BRSC L40 ....38 E4
Bodden St GOL/RIS/CU WA3 ....93 H2
STHEL WA9 ....120 B3
Bodiam Ct EP CH65 ....203 J1
Bodley St ANF/KKDL L4 * 97 H6
Bodmin Av CHTN/BK PR9 ....20 E6
Bodmin Cl RUNC WA7 ....188 A1
Bodmin Gv RNFD/HAY WA11 ....89 G4
Bodmin Rd ANF/KKDL L4 ....97 H4
Bodmin Wy HLWD L26 ....155 H3
Bognor Cl SPK/HALE L24 ....173 G1
Bolan St CLB/OSW/ST L13 ....114 E4
Bolden Cl NTHTN L30 ....82 C2
Bolde Wy BEB CH63 ....170 C4
Bold La ORM L39 ....53 F6
WARRW/BUR WA5 ....105 G6
Bold Pl CLVPS L1 ....9 H6
Bold Rd STHEL WA9 ....104 D6
Bold St CHTN/BK PR9 ....14 E3
CLVPS L1 ....9 G6
ECCL WA10 ....12 E6
RUNC WA7 ....11 F3
WARR WA1 ....16 C6
WDN WA8 ....18 C6
Boleyn Ct RUNC WA7 ....178 B2
The Boleyn MGHL L31 ....62 C4
Bollington Cl CL/PREN CH43 ....130 C6
Bolton Av KKBY L32 ....84 B1
WARRS WA4 ....143 J5
Bolton Cl FMBY L37 ....49 G3
GOL/RIS/CU WA3 ....93 J3
Bolton Rd AIMK WN4 ....79 G6
PS/BROM CH62 ....151 H5
STHP PR8 ....27 H3
Bolton Rd East
PS/BROM CH62 ....151 H5
Bolton St AIMK WN4 ....78 C4
STHEL WA9 ....104 A1
VAUX/LVPD L3 ....9 G4
Bonchurch Dr
CLB/OSW/ST L13 ....114 D6
Bond Cl WARRW/BUR WA5 ....142 A5
Bond's La CHTN/BK PR9 ....21 K4
Bond St PR/KW L34 ....117 K1
VAUX/LVPD L3 ....113 F3
Bonnington Av CSBY/BLUN L23 ....68 D4
Bonsall Rd WD/CROXPK L12 ....115 F1
Boode Cft STBRV L28 ....100 B4
Booker Av CALD/MH L18 ....153 K2
Booth's Brow Rd AIMK WN4 ....78 C3
Booths Hill Cl LYMM WA13 ....164 E1
Booth's Hill La LYMM WA13 ....145 H6
Booth's Hill Rd LYMM WA13 ....145 H6
Booth's La LYMM WA13 ....164 C1
ORM L39 ....44 D6
Booth St CHTN/BK PR9 ....14 E3
CLB/OSW/ST L13 ....114 E4
STHEL WA9 ....103 F6
WARRW/BUR WA5 ....142 B5
Boothwood Cl EHL/KEN L7 ....113 K6
Borax St CLB/OSW/ST L13 ....114 E5
Border Rd HES CH60 ....168 B5
Border Wy EV L5 ....113 G1
Borella Rd CLB/OSW/ST L13 ....114 D1
Borough Pl BIRK CH41 * 3 G5
Borough Rd ECCL WA10 ....12 D7
RF/TRAN CH42 ....2 C7
WAL/EG CH44 ....111 K4
Borough Rd East BIRK CH41 ....3 G5
WAL/EG CH44 ....112 A5
Borough Wy WAL/EG CH44 ....112 A5
Borron Rd NEWLW WA12 ....91 G6
Borrowdale FMBY L37 ....41 F6
Borrowdale Av
WARRN/WOL WA2 ....123 H4
Borrowdale Cl FROD/HEL WA6 ....201 G1
Borrowdale Rd BEB CH63 ....170 A1
ECCL WA10 ....102 D5
MOR/LEA CH46 ....128 E1
WAV L15 ....133 K3
WDN WA8 ....157 H3
Boscow Crs STHEL WA9 ....104 B6
Bosnia St TOX L8 ....133 F6
Bostock Gn EP CH65 ....195 J4
Bostock St EV L5 ....113 F2
WARRW/BUR WA5 ....142 B3
Boston Av RUNC WA7 ....11 J7
Boston Bvd WARRW/BUR WA5 ....141 K2
Boswell Av WARRS WA4 ....162 A1
Boswell Rd CL/PREN CH43 ....149 J2
Boswell St BTL L20 ....4 B1
TOX L8 ....133 H2
Bosworth Cl BEB CH63 ....170 B3
Bosworth Dr STHP PR8 ....33 H5
Bosworth Rd RNFD/HAY WA11 ....89 F5
Botanic Gv EHL/KEN L7 ....114 A5
Botanic Pl EHL/KEN L7 ....114 A5
Botanic Rd CHTN/BK PR9 ....23 K3
EHL/KEN L7 ....114 A6
Botany Rd SPK/HALE L24 ....173 H1
Boteler Av WARRW/BUR WA5 ....142 C2
Botley Cl GR/UP/WCH CH49 * 128 E4
The Boulevard EP CH65 ....195 J5
WD/CROXPK L12 ....99 F5
Boulting Av WARRW/BUR WA5 ....123 F5
Boulton Av PS/BROM CH62 ....151 G3
WKBY CH48 ....127 G5
Boundary Dr CSBY/BLUN L23 ....68 D3
WLTN L25 ....155 G4
Boundary Farm Rd HLWD L26 ....155 G5
Boundary La BRSC L40 ....39 F6
HES CH60 ....168 A5
NPK/KEN L6 ....113 K3
NWD/KWIPK L33 ....85 J1
Boundary Pk NSTN CH64 ....191 J1
Boundary Rd CL/PREN CH43 ....130 A1
ECCL WA10 ....12 C6
HUY L36 ....136 C1
LITH L21 ....82 A2
PS/BROM CH62 ....151 G4
WKBY CH48 ....146 E3
Boundary St EV L5 ....112 E1
STHP PR8 ....27 J3
Boundary St East EV L5 ....113 F1
Bourchier Wy WARRS WA4 ....163 F3

Bourne Av GOL/RIS/CU WA3 92 E3
Bourne Gdns STHEL WA9 103 K4
Bournemouth Cl RUNC WA7 188 C1
Bourne St NPK/KEN L6 113 K4
Bourton Rd WLTN L25 154 E5
Bousfield St ANF/KKDL L4 * 97 G6
Bowden Cl ECCL WA10 102 D2
WD/CROXPK L12 99 J3
Bowden Rd ALL/GAR L19 153 J5
Bowden St LITH L21 81 J5
Bowdon Cl WARR WA1 * 143 J1
Bowdon Rd WAL/NB CH45 111 G1
Bowen Cl WDN WA8 138 C5
Bower Gv LITH L21 81 G4
Bower Rd HES CH60 168 C5
HUY L36 116 E3
WLTN L25 135 H5
Bower St WDN WA8 19 G1
Bowfell Cl BEB CH63 184 A4
Bowfield Rd ALL/GAR L19 153 J4
Bowgreen Cl CL/PREN CH43 129 K2
Bowker's Green La ORM L39 63 J2
Bowland Av AIMK WN4 79 G5
CHLDW L16 115 H6
GOL/RIS/CU WA3 92 D2
STHEL WA9 119 J4
Bowland Cl GOL/RIS/CU WA3 125 K2
PS/BROM CH62 171 F4
RUNC WA7 187 H2
Bowland Dr LITH L21 69 K5
Bowles St BTL L20 81 H6
Bowley Rd CLB/OSW/ST L13 114 D2
Bowling Green Cl STHP PR8 28 C2
Bowman Av WARRS WA4 143 K4
Bowness Av BEB CH63 183 K2
CL/PREN CH43 149 K1
RNFD/HAY WA11 88 E3
STHP PR8 33 J6
WARRN/WOL WA2 123 J5
Bowood Ct WARRN/WOL WA2 123 G3
Bowood St TOX L8 132 E6
Bowring Cl TOX L8 * 133 F5
Bowring Dr NSTN CH64 181 G6
Bowring Park Av CHLDW L16 116 A6
Bowring Park Rd
DV/KA/FCH L14 115 G6
Bowring St TOX L8 * 133 F5
Bowscale Cl
GR/UP/WCH CH49 * 129 F4
Bowscale Rd NG/CROX L11 98 E4
Boxdale Rd CALD/MH L18 134 B5
Boxgrove Cl WDN WA8 139 G6
Boxmoor Rd CALD/MH L18 153 H1
Boxtree Cl WD/CROXPK L12 99 K1
Boxwood Cl HUY L36 116 C5
Boycott St EV L5 113 J1
Boyd Cl MOR/LEA CH46 110 B4
Boydell Av WARRS WA4 143 J5
Boydell Cl STBRV L28 100 B6
Boyer Av MGHL L31 71 G2
Boyes Brow NWD/KWIPK L33 72 C5
Boyle Av WARRN/WOL WA2 124 A6
Boyton Ct EHL/KEN L7 133 H1
Brabant Rd AIG/SPK L17 153 F2
Braby Rd LITH L21 81 K5
Bracebridge Dr STHP PR8 28 C5
Bracewell Cl STHEL WA9 120 A1
Bracken Cl GOL/RIS/CU WA3 124 E2
Bracken Ct STHEL WA9 120 A3
Brackendale CHNE CH2 198 C6
GR/UP/WCH CH49 129 K6
RUNC WA7 177 G5
WLT/FAZ L9 * 82 E4
Brackendale Av WLT/FAZ L9 82 E4
Bracken Dr WKBY CH48 147 F1
Brackenhurst Dr WAL/NB CH45 95 J6
Brackenhurst Gn
NWD/KWIPK L33 84 D1
Bracken La BEB CH63 150 C6
Bracken Rd GTS/LS CH66 195 H5
Brackenside HES CH60 * 167 K3
Brackenway FMBY L37 41 G5
Bracken Wy FROD/HEL WA6 201 F3
Bracken Wd WD/CROXPK L12 99 J1
Brackenwood Dr WDN WA8 157 F4
Brackenwood Gv
RAIN/WH L35 118 B4
Brackenwood Rd BEB CH63 150 C6
Brackley Cl WAL/EG CH44 111 G4
Brackley St RUNC WA7 10 B3
WARRS WA4 162 B2
Bracknell Av KKBY L32 84 C3
Bracknell Cl KKBY L32 84 D2
Bracknel Wy ORM L39 52 E4
Bradbourne Cl WD/CROXPK L12 99 J2
Bradda Cl GR/UP/WCH CH49 129 G2
Braddan Av CLB/OSW/ST L13 * 114 C2
Bradden Cl BEB CH63 170 D3
Brade St CHTN/BK PR9 24 A1
Bradewell Cl ANF/KKDL L4 97 G5
Bradewell St ANF/KKDL L4 97 G5
Bradfield Av AIN/FAZ L10 71 F6
Bradfield St EHL/KEN L7 114 A5
Bradgate Cl MOR/LEA CH46 109 F6
Bradlegh Rd NEWLW WA12 106 C3
Bradley Bvd WARRW/BUR WA5 141 J3
Bradley Fold RAIN/WH L35 136 D1
Bradley La FROD/HEL WA6 201 G3
WARRW/BUR WA5 106 A4
Bradley Rd LITH L21 81 J2
Bradley St CHTN/BK PR9 15 H3
Bradley Wy WDN WA8 19 G2
Bradman Rd MOR/LEA CH46 109 G6
NWD/KWIPK L33 73 H6
Bradmoor Rd PS/BROM CH62 171 F5
Bradshaw Cl ECCL WA10 12 A3
Bradshaw La WARRS WA4 144 A6
Bradshaw's La STHP PR8 33 K3
Bradshaw St WDN WA8 158 B1
Bradstone Cl NG/CROX L11 84 A5
Bradville Rd WLT/FAZ L9 83 F4
Bradwall Cl EP CH65 195 K6
Bradwell Cl EP CH65 195 K5
WKBY CH48 146 E1
Bradwell Rd GOL/RIS/CU WA3 93 F4
Braehaven Rd WAL/NB CH45 95 J6
Braemar Av CHTN/BK PR9 23 H3
Braemar Cl RAIN/WH L35 118 B4
WARRN/WOL WA2 124 C4
Braemar Ct EP CH65 196 D6
Braemar St BTL L20 * 97 F4
Braemore Rd WAL/EG CH44 111 F3
Braeside Cl GTS/LS CH66 195 F4
Braeside Crs WGNW/BIL/O WN5 77 G4
Braeside Gdns
GR/UP/WCH CH49 129 G4
Brae St EHL/KEN L7 113 K5
Brahms Cl TOX L8 133 G3
Braid St BIRK CH41 2 D1
Brainerd St CLB/OSW/ST L13 114 C2
Braithwaite Cl RAIN/WH L35 118 E4
RUNC WA7 187 G2
Braithwaite Rd
GOL/RIS/CU WA3 92 E2
Brakenwood Ms WARRS WA4 * 163 H2
Bramberton Pl ANF/KKDL L4 98 A4
Bramberton Rd ANF/KKDL L4 98 A4
Bramble Av BIRK CH41 130 C1
Bramble Cl WARRW/BUR WA5 141 F6
The Brambles AIMK WN4 78 C4
NWD/KWIPK L33 * 85 G2
Bramble Wy MOR/LEA CH46 109 H5
RUNC WA7 187 H3
Bramblewood Cl
CL/PREN CH43 129 K5
NTHLY L27 136 B4
Brambling Cl RUNC WA7 187 H2
Brambling Pk HLWD L26 155 H2
Brambling Wy GOL/RIS/CU WA3 93 F4
Bramcote Av RNFD/HAY WA11 89 G5
Bramcote Cl NWD/KWIPK L33 73 F5
Bramcote Rd NWD/KWIPK L33 72 E5
Bramcote Wk NWD/KWIPK L33 72 E5
Bramerton Ct WKBY CH48 126 E6
Bramford Cl GR/UP/WCH CH49 129 F4
Bramhall Cl SPK/HALE L24 173 K3
WKBY CH48 146 E2
Bramhall Dr PS/BROM CH62 184 C4
Bramhall Rd CSBY/WL L22 81 F3
SKEL WN8 56 B3
Bramhall St WARRW/BUR WA5 142 B5
Bramley Av BEB CH63 150 D4
Bramley Cl GTS/LS CH66 202 D3
NTHLY L27 136 B4
Bramley Ms WARRS WA4 162 B3
The Bramleys MGHL L31 71 F2
Brampton Ct STHEL WA9 105 F2
Brampton Dr TOX L8 133 F1
Bramshill Cl GOL/RIS/CU WA3 125 J1
Bramwell Av CL/PREN CH43 149 K2
Bramwell St STHEL WA9 104 C1
Brancaster Dr GOL/RIS/CU WA3 93 H4
Brancepeth Ct EP CH65 196 C6
Branch Wy RNFD/HAY WA11 90 C5
Brancker Av RAIN/WH L35 118 D3
Brancote Gdns PS/BROM CH62 171 F6
Brancote Mt CL/PREN CH43 * 130 C3
Brancote Rd CL/PREN CH43 130 C3
Brandearth Hey STBRV L28 100 B6
Brandon WDN WA8 157 F1
Brandon Cl SKEL WN8 57 J6
Brandon St BIRK CH41 3 H4
Brandreth Cl RAIN/WH L35 118 E4
Brandwood Av
WARRN/WOL WA2 123 H5
Branfield Cl WD/CROXPK L12 99 J2
Bransdale Cl
WARRW/BUR WA5 141 F2
Bransdale Dr AIMK WN4 79 J6
Bransford Cl AIMK WN4 91 H1
Branson Cl GOL/RIS/CU WA3 92 B1
Branstree Av NG/CROX L11 98 D3
Brantfield Ct
WARRN/WOL WA2 124 A5
Branthwaite Cl NG/CROX L11 98 E4
Branthwaite Crs NG/CROX L11 98 E4
Branthwaite Gv NG/CROX L11 98 E4
Brasenose Rd BTL L20 96 D4
Brassey St BIRK CH41 130 E1
TOX L8 132 D3
Brathay Cl WARRN/WOL WA2 123 J4
Brattan Rd RF/TRAN CH42 131 F5
Braunton Rd AIG/SPK L17 153 F3
WAL/NB CH45 111 G1
Braybrooke Rd NG/CROX L11 98 E2
Bray Cl RUNC WA7 187 G1
Braydon Cl WLTN L25 * 155 F5
Brayfield Rd ANF/KKDL L4 98 B4
Bray Rd SPK/HALE L24 173 H1
Bray St BIRK CH41 130 E1
Brechin Rd NWD/KWIPK L33 84 E1
Breckfield Pl EV L5 * 113 H2
Breckfield Rd North EV L5 113 H1
Breckfield Rd South
NPK/KEN L6 113 J2
Breck Pl WAL/EG CH44 111 G4
Breck Rd NPK/KEN L6 113 J2
WAL/EG CH44 111 F3
WDN WA8 19 F1
Breckside Av WAL/EG CH44 110 E3
Breckside Pk NPK/KEN L6 114 A1
The Breck GTS/LS CH66 195 H2
Brecon Av NTHTN L30 82 C2
Brecon Dr GTS/LS CH66 202 C2
Brecon Rd RF/TRAN CH42 150 B2
Bredon Cl GTS/LS CH66 194 D3
Breeze Hl BTL L20 5 H5
Breezehill Cl NSTN CH64 191 K1
Breezehill Pk NSTN CH64 192 A1
Breezehill Rd NSTN CH64 192 A1
Breeze La WLT/FAZ L9 97 H2
Breeze Rd STHP PR8 27 F5
Brelade Rd CLB/OSW/ST L13 114 D3
Bremhill Rd NG/CROX L11 98 D2
Bremner Cl EHL/KEN L7 114 A6
Brenda Crs CSBY/BLUN L23 69 H2
Brendale Av MGHL L31 71 F1
Brendon Av LITH L21 81 H2
WARRN/WOL WA2 123 G4
Brendon Gv STHEL WA9 * 104 E1
Brendor Rd WLTN L25 154 E2
Brenig St BIRK CH41 111 F6
Brenka Av WLT/FAZ L9 82 E2
Brentfield WDN WA8 157 K1
Brentnall Cl
WARRW/BUR WA5 * 141 K4
Brent Wy HLWD L26 155 J5
Brentwood Av AIG/SPK L17 133 H6
CSBY/BLUN L23 69 G4
Brentwood Cl ECCL WA10 102 D2
HTWN L38 59 F5
Brentwood Ct CHTN/BK PR9 15 K1
Brentwood St WAL/EG CH44 111 J5
Brereton Av BEB CH63 151 F5
WAV L15 134 B2
Brereton Cl RUNC WA7 177 K5
Bretherton Pl RAIN/WH L35 118 E3
Bretherton Rd PR/KW L34 118 A1
Bretlands Rd CSBY/BLUN L23 69 J4
Bretton Fold STHP PR8 28 C2
Brett St BIRK CH41 130 E1
Brewery La FMBY L37 41 F5
MGHL L31 71 H6
Brewster St ANF/KKDL L4 97 G4
Brian Av PEN/TH CH61 148 C5
WARRN/WOL WA2 143 G1
WARRS WA4 162 D2
Briar Cl AIMK WN4 79 F5
Briardale Gdns GTS/LS CH66 195 F3
Briardale Rd BEB CH63 150 E4
CALD/MH L18 134 A5
GTS/LS CH66 195 F3
NSTN CH64 193 H1
RF/TRAN CH42 131 F5
WAL/EG CH44 112 A5
Briar Dr HES CH60 168 A5
HUY L36 116 D5
Briarfield Av WDN WA8 157 F2
Briarfield Rd EP CH65 6 C4
HES CH60 168 A5
Briar Rd GOL/RIS/CU WA3 92 C3
STHP PR8 33 K5
Briars Brook BRSC L40 39 G6
Briars Cl RAIN/WH L35 119 F6
Briars Gn ECCL WA10 12 E2
SKEL WN8 56 C1
Briars La BRSC L40 39 G6
MGHL L31 62 C6
The Briars STHP PR8 27 G6
Briar St ANF/KKDL L4 97 F6
Briarswood Cl RAIN/WH L35 118 B4
RF/TRAN CH42 150 E3
Briarwood RUNC WA7 178 A4
Briarwood Av WARR WA1 143 H2
Briarwood Rd AIG/SPK L17 133 K6
Briary Cl HES CH60 168 B4
Briary Cft HTWN L38 59 F4
Brickfields HUY L36 117 G6
Brickhurst Wy WARR WA1 144 A1
Brick St CLVPS L1 132 C2
NEWLW WA12 105 K2
WARR WA1 17 F4
Brickwall Gn SFTN L29 70 C2
Brickwall La SFTN L29 70 C2
Bride St ANF/KKDL L4 97 H3
Bridge Av ORM L39 53 J1
WARRS WA4 143 J5
Bridge Ct NSTN CH64 191 K2
STHEL WA9 * 120 B4
WKBY CH48 127 F6
Bridge Cft LITH L21 69 K6
Bridgecroft Rd WAL/NB CH45 111 H1
Bridge Farm Cl
GR/UP/WCH CH49 129 J5
Bridge Farm Dr MGHL L31 62 D5
Bridgefield Cl WLTN L25 135 J2
Bridgeford Av WD/CROXPK L12 98 E6
Bridge Gdns WD/CROXPK L12 99 K4
Bridge Gv STHP PR8 15 F7
Bridgehall Dr SKEL WN8 57 K6
Bridge La FROD/HEL WA6 187 F6
NTHTN L30 70 B6
WARR WA1 144 B3
WARRS WA4 162 D4
Bridgeman St ECCL WA10 12 B6
WARRW/BUR WA5 142 A5
Bridge Meadow GTS/LS CH66 202 D1
Bridgend Cl WDN WA8 138 C6
Bridgend Dr STHP PR8 33 H5
Bridgenorth Rd PEN/TH CH61 167 J1
Bridge Rd CALD/MH L18 134 B6
CSBY/BLUN L23 68 D6
EHL/KEN L7 133 J1
HUY L36 116 C5
LITH L21 81 J4
MGHL L31 71 G2
PR/KW L34 117 K2
STHEL WA9 120 B5
WARR WA1 144 B2
WKBY CH48 127 F6
Bridges La SFTN L29 70 C2
Bridges Rd EP CH65 7 K5
Bridge St BIRK CH41 3 F2
BTL L20 4 D7
ECCL WA10 13 G6
GOL/RIS/CU WA3 92 B4
NEWLW WA12 106 B2
NSTN CH64 191 K2
ORM L39 53 J1
RUNC WA7 11 F4
STHP PR8 15 F6
WARR WA1 16 E6
Bridge View Cl WDN WA8 176 D1
Bridgeview Dr NWD/KWIPK L33 72 E5
Bridge Wk RUNC WA7 * 177 J6
Bridgewater Av WARRS WA4 143 J5
Bridgewater Cl LITH L21 81 H1
Bridgewater Gra RUNC WA7 188 E1
Bridgewater Ms WARRS WA4 162 B3
Bridgewater St CLVPS L1 132 C2
LYMM WA13 145 K6
RUNC WA7 10 D3
Bridgewater Wy HUY L36 136 D1
Bridgeway NG/CROX L11 98 C4
Bridgeway East RUNC WA7 178 B3
Bridgeway West RUNC WA7 178 A3
Bridge Wills La CHTN/BK PR9 21 F6
Bridgewood Dr GTS/LS CH66 202 A1
Bridle Av WAL/EG CH44 112 A5
Bridle Cl CL/PREN CH43 129 J3
PS/BROM CH62 171 G6
Bridle Ct STHEL WA9 104 A5
Bridlemere Ct WARR WA1 143 H1
Bridle Pk PS/BROM CH62 171 F6
Bridle Rd NTHTN L30 82 D3
PS/BROM CH62 171 G6
WAL/EG CH44 112 A5
Bridle Wy GTS/LS CH66 195 G6
NTHTN L30 82 C3
Brierfield SKEL WN8 67 F2
Brierfield Rd WAV L15 134 A3
Brierley Cl NTHTN L30 70 E5
Brierley St WARRW/BUR WA5 16 A3
Briers Cl WARRN/WOL WA2 124 B4
Briery Hey Av NWD/KWIPK L33 84 E1
Brighouse Cl ORM L39 45 H5
Brightgate Cl EHL/KEN L7 * 133 G1
Brighton Rd CSBY/WL L22 80 E2
HUY L36 117 H4
STHP PR8 27 H4
Brighton St WAL/EG CH44 112 A4
WARRW/BUR WA5 142 B3
Brighton V CSBY/WL L22 80 D1
Bright St BIRK CH41 2 C5
CHTN/BK PR9 23 H6
NPK/KEN L6 113 J4
Brightwell Cl
GR/UP/WCH CH49 * 129 G5
WARRW/BUR WA5 141 F4
Brignall Gv GOL/RIS/CU WA3 92 E2
Brill St BIRK CH41 130 E1
Brimelow Crs
WARRW/BUR WA5 141 F6
Brimstage Av BEB CH63 150 C3
Brimstage Cl HES CH60 168 C5
Brimstage Gn HES CH60 * 168 D5
Brimstage La BEB CH63 169 H1
Brimstage Rd ANF/KKDL L4 5 K6
BEB CH63 169 J3
HES CH60 168 C5
Brimstage St BIRK CH41 131 F5
Brindley Av WARRS WA4 143 J5
Brindley Cl LITH L21 81 H1
Brindley Rd KKBY L32 84 B1
RUNC WA7 177 J2
STHEL WA9 120 C1
Brindley St RUNC WA7 10 C3
TOX L8 132 C3
Brinklow Cl STHP PR8 33 G4
Brinley Cl PS/BROM CH62 184 A2
Brinton Cl NTHLY L27 135 K3
WDN WA8 157 K3
Brisbane Av WAL/NB CH45 95 G5
Brisbane St STHEL WA9 103 F6
Briscoe Dr MOR/LEA CH46 129 F2
Bristol Av RUNC WA7 188 D1
WAL/EG CH44 111 J3
Bristol Dr GTS/LS CH66 202 C2
Bristol Rd WAV L15 134 B3
Bristow Cl WARRW/BUR WA5 141 J1
Britannia Av EHL/KEN L7 133 J2
Britannia Crs TOX L8 132 E6
Britannia Rd WAL/NB CH45 111 G3
Britannic Buildings
WAL/NB CH45 * 111 G3
Britonside Av KKBY L32 84 E3
Brittarge Brow NTHLY L27 136 B5
Britten Cl TOX L8 133 G3
Broadacre SKEL WN8 67 J1
Broadbelt St ANF/KKDL L4 97 H3
Broadbent Av WARRS WA4 143 J6
Broadfield Av CL/PREN CH43 129 K1
Broadfield Cl CL/PREN CH43 * 129 J2
Broadfields RUNC WA7 178 B5
Broadgate Av STHEL WA9 103 K4
Broad Green Rd
CLB/OSW/ST L13 115 F5
Broadheath Av CL/PREN CH43 129 K2
Broadheath Ter WDN WA8 157 J2
Broad Hey NTHTN L30 70 A6
Broad Hey Cl WLTN L25 135 J6
Broadheys La KNUT WA16 164 E5
Broadhurst Av
WARRW/BUR WA5 142 A5
Broadhurst St AIG/SPK L17 133 H6
Broadlake NSTN CH64 193 G1
Broadland Gdns GTS/LS CH66 202 D1
Broadland Rd GTS/LS CH66 202 D1
Broadlands RAIN/WH L35 118 A2
STHP PR8 27 F4
Broad La ANF/KKDL L4 98 B4
FMBY L37 49 K2
HES CH60 167 G4
KKBY L32 84 E3
ORM L39 52 A3
RNFD/HAY WA11 88 E1
SFTN L29 60 E6
WARRS WA4 163 G3
WARRW/BUR WA5 105 H5
Broad Lane Prec NG/CROX L11 98 C4
Broadley Av GOL/RIS/CU WA3 92 D4
Broadmead ALL/GAR L19 154 B4
HES CH60 168 C6
Broad Oak Av RNFD/HAY WA11 89 K5
WARRW/BUR WA5 141 F5
Broadoak Rd DV/KA/FCH L14 115 K4
MGHL L31 62 C6
Broad Oak Rd STHEL WA9 104 C2
Broadoaks GR/UP/WCH CH49 129 F3
Broad Pl NG/CROX L11 98 D5
Broad Sq NG/CROX L11 98 D5
Broadstone Dr BEB CH63 170 B3
Broad Vw NG/CROX L11 98 D5
Broadway BEB CH63 150 C4
ECCL WA10 87 J6
ECCL WA10 102 E5
GR/UP/WCH CH49 128 E4
NG/CROX L11 98 C4
WAL/NB CH45 111 F2
WDN WA8 157 F2
WLT/FAZ L9 83 H5
Broadway Av WAL/NB CH45 111 F2
Broadway Cl STHP PR8 33 H4
Broadwood Av MGHL L31 71 F2
Broadwood St WAV L15 133 K2
Brockenhurst Rd WLT/FAZ L9 82 D6
Brockhall Cl RAIN/WH L35 118 C1
Brock Hall Cl STHEL WA9 * 120 A3
Brockholme Rd CALD/MH L18 153 H2
Brocklebank La ALL/GAR L19 154 A3
Brocklebank Rd CHTN/BK PR9 23 G4
Brock Rd GOL/RIS/CU WA3 125 F4
Brockstedes Av AIMK WN4 78 D3
Brock St ANF/KKDL L4 97 G5
Brocstedes Rd AIMK WN4 78 C2
Brodie Av ALL/GAR L19 153 K3
CALD/MH L18 134 B6
Bromborough Rd BEB CH63 151 F6
Bromborough Village Rd
PS/BROM CH62 171 F4
Brome Wy BEB CH63 170 D3
Bromilow Rd SKEL WN8 55 J4
STHEL WA9 104 D3
Bromley Av CALD/MH L18 134 A4
GOL/RIS/CU WA3 92 E4
Bromley Cl HES CH60 167 J6
WARRN/WOL WA2 124 B4
Bromley Rd WAL/NB CH45 95 G6
Brompton Av AIG/SPK L17 133 H4
CSBY/BLUN L23 68 D6
WAL/EG CH44 111 J3
Brompton Gdns
WARRW/BUR WA5 142 B2
Brompton Rd STHP PR8 23 G6
Brompton Wy GTS/LS CH66 202 C2
Bromsgrove Rd
GR/UP/WCH CH49 128 D5
Bromyard Cl BTL L20 * 4 C3
Bronington Av PS/BROM CH62 184 A1
Bronte Cl CSBY/BLUN L23 68 C5
WARRN/WOL WA2 123 G1
Bronte St ECCL WA10 12 B4
VAUX/LVPD L3 9 H3
Brook Av MGHL L31 62 C5
WARRS WA4 143 J4
WARRS WA4 162 D2
Brookbank Ct AIN/FAZ L10 84 A4
Brookbridge Rd
CLB/OSW/ST L13 114 C1
Brook Cl WAL/EG CH44 111 J2
WDN WA8 138 B3
Brookdale RAIN/WH L35 137 K6
Brookdale Av North
GR/UP/WCH CH49 129 F5
Brookdale Av South
GR/UP/WCH CH49 129 F6
Brookdale Cl
GR/UP/WCH CH49 129 F5
Brookdale Rd WAV L15 133 K3
Brook Dr WARRW/BUR WA5 141 H4
Brooke Cl CHTN/BK PR9 23 K6
Brook End STHEL WA9 104 E4
Brooke Rd East CSBY/WL L22 80 E1
Brooke Rd West CSBY/WL L22 80 D1
Brook Farm ORM L39 53 J1
Brookfield Av CSBY/BLUN L23 68 E6
CSBY/WL L22 81 G3
RAIN/WH L35 118 E2
RUNC WA7 177 H3
Brookfield Cl LYMM WA13 145 J6
Brookfield Dr WLT/FAZ L9 83 F6
Brookfield Gdns WKBY CH48 146 C1
Brookfield La ORM L39 62 E2
Brookfield Pk WARRS WA4 163 F1
Brookfield Rd LYMM WA13 145 J6
WKBY CH48 146 C1
Brookfield St NEWLW WA12 106 B2
Brook Furlong FROD/HEL WA6 186 B5
Brook Hey NSTN CH64 181 G5
Brook Hey Dr NWD/KWIPK L33 72 E5
Brookhill Cl BTL L20 5 G4
Brookhill Rd BTL L20 5 G3
Brook House Ct LYMM WA13 * 145 K6
Brook House Gv ECCL WA10 102 C2
Brookhouse Rd ORM L39 45 H5
Brookhurst Av BEB CH63 183 K1
Brookhurst Cl BEB CH63 183 K2
Brookhurst Rd BEB CH63 183 K1
Brookland La STHEL WA9 104 E3
Brookland Rd BIRK CH41 2 E6
Brookland Rd East
CLB/OSW/ST L13 114 E4
Brookland Rd West
CLB/OSW/ST L13 114 E4
Brooklands BIRK CH41 2 E2
ORM L39 45 K5
Brooklands Av AIMK WN4 91 J1
CSBY/WL L22 81 F3
Brooklands Dr MGHL L31 71 G1
Brooklands Gdns NSTN CH64 181 H6
Brooklands Gv BRSC L40 39 F6
Brooklands Rd ECCL WA10 102 C1
NSTN CH64 181 H6
The Brooklands HUY L36 116 E6
Brookland St WARR WA1 143 H2
Brook La GOL/RIS/CU WA3 145 F1
NSTN CH64 181 H5
ORM L39 53 J1
RNFD/HAY WA11 76 C2
Brooklet Rd HES CH60 168 C5
Brooklyn Dr EP CH65 195 J4
LYMM WA13 145 K5
Brook Lynn Av
GOL/RIS/CU WA3 93 G2
Brook Meadow PEN/TH CH61 148 B4
Brook Pk MGHL L31 71 F2
Brook Pl WARRS WA4 * 143 H6
Brook Rd BTL L20 4 C4
CSBY/BLUN L23 69 H3
GTS/LS CH66 195 G4

LYMM WA13 145 J5
MGHL L31 71 H1
WLT/FAZ L9 97 J1
Brooks Aly CLVPS L1 9 F5
Brookside Av AIMK WN4 78 E1
CSBY/WL L22 81 G3
DV/KA/FCH L14 115 H4
ECCL WA10 87 J6
LYMM WA13 145 H5
RNFD/HAY WA11 75 F2
WARRS WA4 162 C2
WARRW/BUR WA5 141 H4
Brookside Cl RAIN/WH L35 118 A3
RNFD/HAY WA11 90 A4
WD/CROXPK L12 99 K4
WGNW/BIL/O WN5 77 H5
Brookside Crs
GR/UP/WCH CH49 128 E4
Brookside Dr
GR/UP/WCH CH49 * 129 F4
Brookside Rd FROD/HEL WA6 200 D1
RAIN/WH L35 118 A3
STHP PR8 27 K6
Brookside Vw RNFD/HAY WA11 90 A4
Brookside Wy RNFD/HAY WA11 90 A4
Brooks Rd FMBY L37 48 D3
The Brooks RNFD/HAY WA11 88 D4
Brook St AIMK WN4 91 H1
BIRK CH41 2 C1
CHTN/BK PR9 24 A1
ECCL WA10 13 G5
GOL/RIS/CU WA3 92 B4
GOL/RIS/CU WA3 93 H2
NSTN CH64 191 K1
PS/BROM CH62 151 F5
RAIN/WH L35 118 B2
RUNC WA7 10 D4
VAUX/LVPD L3 8 B2
Brook St East BIRK CH41 3 F3
Brooks Wy FMBY L37 48 D3
Brookthorpe Cl WAL/NB CH45 111 H2
Brook V CSBY/WL L22 81 G3
Brookvale Av North
RUNC WA7 188 A2
Brookvale Av South
RUNC WA7 188 A1
Brookvale Cl
WARRW/BUR WA5 121 K1
Brook Wk PEN/TH CH61 148 A4
Brookway CL/PREN CH43 149 H2
GR/UP/WCH CH49 129 F4
WAL/NB CH45 111 G2
Brook Wy WARRW/BUR WA5 141 H4
Brookway La STHEL WA9 104 D4
Brook Well NSTN CH64 191 K4
Brookwood Cl WARRS WA4 162 A3
Brookwood Rd HUY L36 116 E3
Broom Av WARRS WA4 162 D5
Broom Cl PR/KW L34 118 B1
Broome Cl STHP PR8 27 J4
Broome Ct RUNC WA7 188 A2
Broome Rd STHP PR8 27 J4
Broomfield Cl HES CH60 167 G4
Broomfield Gdns WLT/FAZ L9 82 C6
Broomfield Rd WLT/FAZ L9 82 C6
Broomfields Rd WARRS WA4 162 C4
Broom Hl CL/PREN CH43 130 C2
Broomhill Cl NTHLY L27 135 K3
Broomlands HES CH60 167 J5
Broomleigh Cl BEB CH63 150 C6
Broom Rd ECCL WA10 102 D5
Broomsgrove AIN/FAZ L10 83 H2
Broom Wy HLWD L26 155 G4
Broseley Av PS/BROM CH62 170 E4
Broster Av MOR/LEA CH46 128 D1
Broster Cl MOR/LEA CH46 128 D1
Brosters La HOY CH47 108 B6
Brotherhood Dr STHEL WA9 104 B6
Brotherton Cl PS/BROM CH62 170 E5
Brotherton Wy NEWLW WA12 106 B1
Brougham Av BIRK CH41 131 J6
Brougham Rd WAL/EG CH44 111 K4
Brougham Ter NPK/KEN L6 113 J4
Broughton Av GOL/RIS/CU WA3 92 A3
STHP PR8 28 A3
WKBY CH48 127 F6
Broughton Cl WARRS WA4 162 E3
Broughton Dr ALL/GAR L19 153 H4
Broughton Hall Rd
WD/CROXPK L12 115 J2
Broughton Rd WAL/EG CH44 111 H4
Brow La HES CH60 167 K6
Brownbill Bank NTHLY L27 136 B5
Brown Heath Av
WGNW/BIL/O WN5 77 G6
Brownhill Dr WARR WA1 143 J1
Browning Av RF/TRAN CH42 150 E2
WDN WA8 18 A4
Browning Cl HUY L36 117 F6
Browning Dr EP CH65 195 J5
WARRN/WOL WA2 123 F2
Browning Gn EP CH65 195 J5
Browning Rd CSBY/WL L22 80 E1
WAL/NB CH45 * 110 D2
Browning St BTL L20 4 B2
Brownlow Ar ECCL WA10 * 13 H6
Brownlow Hl VAUX/LVPD L3 9 G4
Brownlow Rd PS/BROM CH62 151 G4
Brownlow St VAUX/LVPD L3 9 J4
Brownmoor La CSBY/BLUN L23 69 H5
Brownmoor Pk CSBY/BLUN L23 69 G6
Brown's La NTHTN L30 70 D6
Brown St WDN WA8 19 J5
Brownville Rd
CLB/OSW/ST L13 * 114 B1
Brow Rd CL/PREN CH43 110 D6
Brows Cl FMBY L37 48 E2
Brow Side EV L5 113 H3
Brows La FMBY L37 48 E2
Broxholme Wy MGHL L31 71 G2
Broxton Av CL/PREN CH43 149 J1
WKBY CH48 127 G6
Broxton Cl WDN WA8 138 B6
Broxton Rd GTS/LS CH66 195 H4
Broxton St WAV L15 133 K1
Bruce Av WARRN/WOL WA2 123 K6
Bruce Crs BEB CH63 183 K1
Bruce Dr GTS/LS CH66 195 F5
Bruce St ECCL WA10 12 D5
TOX L8 133 F5
Bruche Av WARR WA1 143 J2
Bruche Dr WARR WA1 143 J1
Bruera Rd EP CH65 195 J5
Brunel Dr LITH L21 81 H1
Brunner Rd WDN WA8 18 C3
Brunsborough Cl
PS/BROM CH62 183 K1
Brunsfield Cl MOR/LEA CH46 128 D2
Brunstath Cl HES CH60 168 C4
Brunswick Cl ANF/KKDL L4 * 97 G5
Brunswick Ct BIRK CH41 3 F3
Brunswick Crs GTS/LS CH66 195 H6
Brunswick Ms BIRK CH41 3 G3
CSBY/WL L22 81 F3
Brunswick Pde CSBY/WL L22 80 E3
Brunswick Pl BTL L20 96 D5
Brunswick Rd NEWLW WA12 105 K1
NPK/KEN L6 9 K1
Brunswick St ALL/GAR L19 172 C1
CLVP L2 8 B5
STHEL WA9 104 E2
Brunswick Wy VAUX/LVPD L3 132 C4
Brunt La ALL/GAR L19 154 B4
Bruntleigh Av WARRS WA4 143 K6
Bruton Rd HUY L36 116 D1
Bryanston Rd AIG/SPK L17 133 G6
RF/TRAN CH42 149 K1
Bryant Av WARRS WA4 143 J5
Bryant Rd LITH L21 81 J5
The Bryceway
WD/CROXPK L12 115 H3
Brydges St EHL/KEN L7 * 113 J6
Bryer Rd RAIN/WH L35 117 K3
Bryn Bank WAL/EG CH44 111 J3
Bryn Gates La AIMK WN4 79 H1
Brynmor Rd CALD/MH L18 153 H2
Brynmoss Av WAL/EG CH44 111 F3
Brynn St ECCL WA10 13 H3
WDN WA8 18 E4
Bryn Rd AIMK WN4 79 F3
Bryn Rd South AIMK WN4 79 H5
Bryn St AIMK WN4 79 G6
Bryony Wy RF/TRAN CH42 150 E3
Brythen St CLVPS L1 9 F4
Buchanan Rd WAL/EG CH44 111 K4
WLT/FAZ L9 97 H2
Buchan Cl WARRW/BUR WA5 141 J1
Buckfast Av RNFD/HAY WA11 90 E4
Buckfast Cl NTHTN L30 70 C5
WARRW/BUR WA5 141 F6
Buckfast Ct RUNC WA7 178 D2
Buckfast Dr FMBY L37 49 H3
Buckingham Av AIG/SPK L17 133 J4
BEB CH63 150 D4
CL/PREN CH43 130 D6
WDN WA8 139 F5
Buckingham Cl ECCL WA10 103 G3
Buckingham Ct
NWD/KWIPK L33 72 E6
Buckingham Dr
RNFD/HAY WA11 88 D4
WARRW/BUR WA5 141 K5
Buckingham Gdns EP CH65 203 H1
Buckingham Gv FMBY L37 48 E3
Buckingham Rd
CLB/OSW/ST L13 114 B1
MGHL L31 71 H1
WAL/EG CH44 111 F3
WLT/FAZ L9 82 D5
Buckingham St EV L5 113 G2
Buckland Cl WDN WA8 157 J4
Buckland Dr BEB CH63 170 B3
Buckland St AIG/SPK L17 133 G6
Buckley Hill La NTHTN L30 70 A4
Buckley St WARRN/WOL WA2 16 C2
Buckthorn Cl STBRV L28 100 B6
Buckthorn Gdns STHEL WA9 118 E1
Buckton St WARR WA1 17 H1
Bude Cl CL/PREN CH43 129 K3
Bude Rd WDN WA8 157 K1
Budworth Av STHEL WA9 119 K4
WARRS WA4 143 J5
WDN WA8 157 J1
Budworth Cl CL/PREN CH43 130 B5
RUNC WA7 177 G6
Budworth Dr WLTN L25 155 F1
Budworth Rd CL/PREN CH43 130 B5
GTS/LS CH66 202 C1
Buerton Cl CL/PREN CH43 130 A5
Buffs La HES CH60 168 B5
Buggen La NSTN CH64 191 J1
Buildwas Rd NSTN CH64 181 K5
Bulford Rd WLT/FAZ L9 98 C1
Bulkeley Rd WAL/EG CH44 111 K4
Bull Bridge La AIN/FAZ L10 83 H1
Bull Cop FMBY L37 49 H2
Bullens La BRSC L40 36 B2
Bullens Rd ANF/KKDL L4 97 H5
KKBY L32 84 E2
Bullfinch Ct HLWD L26 155 H2
Bull Hl NSTN CH64 192 A3
Bull La WLT/FAZ L9 82 E4
Bullrush Dr MOR/LEA CH46 110 A5
The Bulrushes AIG/SPK L17 132 E6
Bulwer St BTL L20 81 H6
EV L5 * 113 J2
Bunbury Dr RUNC WA7 187 F1
Bunbury Gn EP CH65 203 H1
Bundoran Rd AIG/SPK L17 153 F1
Bungalow Rd NEWLW WA12 106 E4
The Bungalows Red Bank
NEWLW WA12 * 106 E4
Bunter Rd KKBY L32 84 E5
Bunting Cl GOL/RIS/CU WA3 93 F3
Bunting Ct HLWD L26 155 G1
Buntingford Rd WARRS WA4 144 B6
Burbo Bank Rd CSBY/BLUN L23 68 B5
Burbo Bank Rd North
CSBY/BLUN L23 68 A4
Burbo Bank Rd South
CSBY/BLUN L23 68 C6
Burbo Crs CSBY/BLUN L23 68 C6
Burbo Man CSBY/BLUN L23 * 68 C6
Burbo Wy WAL/NB CH45 94 E5
Burden Rd MOR/LEA CH46 128 D1
Burdett Av BEB CH63 170 B3
Burdett Cl BEB CH63 170 C3
Burdett Rd CSBY/WL L22 80 E2
GTS/LS CH66 202 C1
WAL/NB CH45 110 D2
Burdett St AIG/SPK L17 133 H6
Burfield Dr WARRS WA4 162 B5
Burford Av WAL/EG CH44 111 F4
Burford La LYMM WA13 165 K1
Burford Rd CHLDW L16 115 G6
Burgess Av WARRS WA4 142 E6
Burgess Gdns MGHL L31 62 A5
Burgess' La FMBY L37 50 C4
Burgess St VAUX/LVPD L3 9 H2
Burghill Rd WD/CROXPK L12 99 K1
Burgundy Cl AIG/SPK L17 152 D1
Burkhardt Dr NEWLW WA12 106 E2
Burland Cl RUNC WA7 10 C6
Burland Rd HLWD L26 155 K5
Burleigh Ms EV L5 113 H1
Burleigh Rd North EV L5 113 H1
Burleigh Rd South EV L5 113 H1
Burley Av GOL/RIS/CU WA3 92 E2
Burley Cl KKBY L32 84 E2
Burlingham Av WKBY CH48 146 D2
Burlington Av FMBY L37 49 H2
Burlington Rd STHP PR8 27 G4
WAL/NB CH45 95 H4
Burlington St BIRK CH41 3 F4
VAUX/LVPD L3 112 E3
Burman Crs ALL/GAR L19 153 K4
Burman Rd ALL/GAR L19 154 A4
Burnage Av STHEL WA9 120 A3
Burnage Cl SPK/HALE L24 174 A3
Burnand St ANF/KKDL L4 97 H6
Burnard Cl NWD/KWIPK L33 84 E1
Burnard Crs NWD/KWIPK L33 84 E1
Burnell Cl ECCL WA10 12 E4
Burnell Rd EP CH65 7 H7
Burnet Cl WARRN/WOL WA2 124 E5
Burnfell GOL/RIS/CU WA3 93 F4
Burnham Cl WARRW/BUR WA5 141 G4
WDN WA8 138 B6
Burnham Rd CALD/MH L18 134 D6
Burnie Av BTL L20 5 J1
Burnley Av MOR/LEA CH46 129 G1
Burnley Cl NPK/KEN L6 113 J3
Burnley Rd MOR/LEA CH46 129 G1
STHP PR8 33 J4
Burnsall Av GOL/RIS/CU WA3 93 G3
Burnsall Dr WDN WA8 138 B6
Burnsall St ALL/GAR L19 154 B6
Burns Av WAL/NB CH45 111 G2
Burns Cl AIMK WN4 78 E3
CHLDW L16 135 G1
GTS/LS CH66 195 H5
RAIN/WH L35 118 A4
Burns Crs WDN WA8 18 B3
Burns Gv HUY L36 117 G6
WARRN/WOL WA2 123 J5
WARRS WA4 162 C2
Burnside Av WAL/EG CH44 111 H5
Burnside Rd WAL/EG CH44 111 H5
Burns Rd STHEL WA9 119 J4
Burns St BTL L20 4 A1
Burnt Ash Cl ALL/GAR L19 153 G4
Burnthwaite Rd
DV/KA/FCH L14 115 G4
Burrell Cl RF/TRAN CH42 150 B2
Burrell Dr MOR/LEA CH46 128 E2
Burrell Rd RF/TRAN CH42 150 B2
Burrell St ANF/KKDL L4 97 H5
Burrough Cl GOL/RIS/CU WA3 125 H4
Burroughs Gdns
VAUX/LVPD L3 * 113 F3
Burrows Av RNFD/HAY WA11 89 J6
Burrows Ct VAUX/LVPD L3 112 E3
Burrow's La ECCL WA10 102 A3
Burrows St RNFD/HAY WA11 89 K5
Bursar Cl NEWLW WA12 106 D1
Burscough Rd ORM L39 45 K5
Burscough St ORM L39 45 K6
Burton Av RAIN/WH L35 118 C3
WAL/NB CH45 110 E2
Burton Cl CLVPS L1 8 E7
RAIN/WH L35 118 C3
WDN WA8 138 E6
Burton Gn GTS/LS CH66 195 G5
Burtonhead Rd STHEL WA9 103 H3
Burton Rd NSTN CH64 191 K3
WARRN/WOL WA2 123 K6
Burton St EV L5 112 E1
Burtons Wy NG/CROX L11 84 B4
Burtonwood Cottages
WARRW/BUR WA5 * 105 G2
Burtonwood Rd
WARRW/BUR WA5 121 K3
Burtree Rd DV/KA/FCH L14 116 A1
Burwell Av FMBY L37 48 D4
Burwen Dr WLT/FAZ L9 82 C5
Bury Rd STHP PR8 27 H4
Busby's Cottages WAL/NB CH45 95 H5
Bushby's La FMBY L37 48 C3
Bushby's Pk FMBY L37 48 C3
Bushell Cl NSTN CH64 192 A2
Bushell Rd NSTN CH64 192 A1
Bushel's Dr STHEL WA9 120 B5
Bushey La RNFD/HAY WA11 66 A5
Bushey Rd ANF/KKDL L4 98 A3
Bushley Cl BTL L20 4 D3
Bush Rd WDN WA8 158 A6
Bush Wy HES CH60 167 J5
Butchers La ORM L39 62 D2
Butcher St AIMK WN4 91 G1
Bute St EV L5 113 G4
Butleigh Rd HUY L36 116 D2
Butler Crs NPK/KEN L6 113 K4
Butler St NPK/KEN L6 113 K3
Buttercup Cl CSBY/WL L22 81 G2
MOR/LEA CH46 110 A5
Buttercup Wy WLT/FAZ L9 97 K1
Butterfield Gdns ORM L39 53 H2
Butterfield St ANF/KKDL L4 97 H6
Buttermarket St WARR WA1 16 E4
Buttermere Av AIMK WN4 79 G4
CL/PREN CH43 129 K3
EP CH65 196 B6
RNFD/HAY WA11 88 D3
WARRN/WOL WA2 123 J4
Buttermere Cl FMBY L37 48 D2
FROD/HEL WA6 201 G1
MGHL L31 62 B6
NWD/KWIPK L33 72 C5
Buttermere Crs
RNFD/HAY WA11 66 B5
Buttermere Gdns
CSBY/BLUN L23 81 G1
Buttermere Gv RUNC WA7 187 G1
Buttermere Rd CHLDW L16 135 H1
Buttermere St TOX L8 133 G2
Butterton Av
GR/UP/WCH CH49 128 E3
Butterwick Dr WD/CROXPK L12 99 J2
Button St CLVP L2 8 E4
Butts La STHP PR8 28 C2
Buxted Rd KKBY L32 85 F3
Buxton Cl WARRW/BUR WA5 141 H1
Buxton Rd RF/TRAN CH42 151 F1
Bxchange St West CLVP L2 * 8 C4
Bye La ORM L39 52 A2
Byerley St WAL/EG CH44 112 A4
Byland Cl FMBY L37 49 H3
WDN WA8 139 H4
Byles St TOX L8 133 F5
Byng Pl ANF/KKDL L4 98 B5
Byng Rd ANF/KKDL L4 98 B5
Byng St BTL L20 4 C7
The By-Pass CSBY/BLUN L23 69 F5
Byrne Av RF/TRAN CH42 150 E2
Byrom La GOL/RIS/CU WA3 93 G1
Byrom St CHTN/BK PR9 28 C1
VAUX/LVPD L3 9 F2
Byrom Wy VAUX/LVPD L3 9 F1
Byron Av RAIN/WH L35 118 B4
Byron Cl CL/PREN CH43 149 J3
ECCL WA10 13 G2
FMBY L37 49 F1
HUY L36 117 F6
Byron Ct WARRN/WOL WA2 123 J5
Byron Rd CSBY/BLUN L23 68 C5
MGHL L31 62 B4
Byron St ALL/GAR L19 153 K6
BTL L20 4 A1
RUNC WA7 10 C6
The Byway CSBY/BLUN L23 69 F4

C

Cabes Cl DV/KA/FCH L14 116 A1
Cabin La CHTN/BK PR9 24 C2
KIRK/FR/WA PR4 31 F1
MGHL L31 61 H3
ORM L39 35 F4
Cable Rd HOY CH47 127 G2
RAIN/WH L35 118 B2
Cable St CLVP L2 8 D5
FMBY L37 49 G1
STHP PR8 14 E4
Cabot Cl WARRW/BUR WA5 122 C6
Cabot Gn WLTN L25 135 F4
Cabul Cl WARRN/WOL WA2 143 F2
Caddick Rd PR/KW L34 85 G6
Cadnam Rd WLTN L25 136 A4
Cadogan St WAV L15 133 J1
Cadshaw Cl GOL/RIS/CU WA3 125 F2
Cadwell Rd MGHL L31 61 K2
Caernarvon Cl
GR/UP/WCH CH49 129 G3
Caernarvon Ct EP CH65 203 H1
Caerwys Gv RF/TRAN CH42 131 H5
Caird St NPK/KEN L6 113 J4
Cairn Ct STHEL WA9 103 F6
Cairnmore Rd CALD/MH L18 153 H1
Cairns St TOX L8 133 F3
Cairo St ANF/KKDL L4 97 G4
ECCL WA10 103 F4
WARR WA1 16 D5
Caister Cl SKEL WN8 57 F5
Caithness Ct RUNC WA7 10 E4
Caithness Dr CSBY/BLUN L23 69 G6
WAL/NB CH45 111 J1
Caithness Gdns
CL/PREN CH43 * 149 J2
Caithness Rd CALD/MH L18 153 J2
Calday Grange Cl WKBY CH48 146 E2
Calday Gv RNFD/HAY WA11 89 K3
Caldbeck Av WARRN/WOL WA2 123 K5
Caldbeck Cl AIMK WN4 79 G5
Caldbeck Gv RNFD/HAY WA11 89 F2
Caldbeck Rd PS/BROM CH62 171 G3
Calder Av CL/PREN CH43 149 K1
ORM L39 53 J1
Calder Cl NWD/KWIPK L33 72 E3
WDN WA8 140 A6
Calder Dr CALD/MH L18 134 D4
MGHL L31 62 D5
RAIN/WH L35 118 D4
Calderfield Cl WARRS WA4 162 A3
Calderfield Rd CALD/MH L18 134 E4
Calder Gra WLTN L25 135 F6
Calderhurst Dr ECCL WA10 87 J5
Calder Rd BEB CH63 150 C6
EV L5 113 H1
The Calders CALD/MH L18 134 D6
Calderstones Av CALD/MH L18 134 D4
Calderstones Rd CALD/MH L18 134 D5
Calder Wy GTS/LS CH66 195 F4
Calderwood Pk NTHLY L27 136 A3
Caldicott Av PS/BROM CH62 171 F6
Caldon Cl LITH L21 81 H2
Caldway Dr NTHLY L27 136 B4
Caldwell Av WARRW/BUR WA5 123 F5
Caldwell Cl NWD/KWIPK L33 72 E5
Caldwell Dr GR/UP/WCH CH49 148 E1
Caldwell Rd ALL/GAR L19 154 A3
WDN WA8 18 C5
Caldwell St STHEL WA9 104 B2
Caldy Chase Dr WKBY CH48 146 E4
Caldy Dr GTS/LS CH66 195 G5
Caldy Gv RNFD/HAY WA11 89 G6
Caldy Rd WAL/NB CH45 111 H2
WKBY CH48 146 E4
WLT/FAZ L9 82 D4
Caldy Wd WKBY CH48 146 E4
Caldywood Dr RAIN/WH L35 118 A4
Caledonia St EHL/KEN L7 9 J6
Calgarth Rd HUY L36 116 C2
California Cl WARRW/BUR WA5 141 K1
California Rd CLB/OSW/ST L13 98 B6
Callaghan Cl EV L5 113 F2
Callander Rd NPK/KEN L6 114 B4
Callands Rd WARRW/BUR WA5 122 D5
Callestock Cl NG/CROX L11 84 C6
Callington Cl DV/KA/FCH L14 116 A1
Callon Av RNFD/HAY WA11 89 H6
Callow Rd WAV L15 133 J2
Calmet Cl EV L5 113 G1
Calmington La RUNC WA7 178 E1
Calne Cl PEN/TH CH61 148 A4
Calstock Cl WARRW/BUR WA5 141 F6
Calthorpe St ALL/GAR L19 153 J5
Calthorpe Wy CL/PREN CH43 130 A3
Calton Av CALD/MH L18 * 134 B4
Calvados Cl AIG/SPK L17 152 D2
Calveley Av PS/BROM CH62 184 C3
Calveley Cl CL/PREN CH43 130 B6
Calveley Rd HLWD L26 155 K5
Calverhall Wy AIMK WN4 79 F6
Calverly Cl RUNC WA7 188 B2
Calver Rd WARRN/WOL WA2 123 G4
Camarthen Crs TOX L8 132 C3
Camberley Cl STHP PR8 27 F2
Camberley Dr WLTN L25 155 F3
Camberwell Park Rd
WDN WA8 139 J5
Camborne Av WLTN L25 155 F3
Camborne Cl RUNC WA7 188 B1
Cambourne Av
RNFD/HAY WA11 89 G4
Cambourne Rd
WARRW/BUR WA5 121 K1
Cambrai Av WARRS WA4 162 B1
Cambrian Cl GTS/LS CH66 194 D3
MOR/LEA CH46 * 128 C2
Cambrian Rd MOR/LEA CH46 128 D2
Cambrian Wy WLTN L25 135 J6
Cambria St NPK/KEN L6 113 K4
Cambridge Ar STHP PR8 14 E5
Cambridge Av CHTN/BK PR9 23 H3
CSBY/BLUN L23 68 E5
LITH L21 81 J3
Cambridge Cl WARRS WA4 162 A3
Cambridge Dr CSBY/BLUN L23 68 D4
HLWD L26 155 J3
Cambridge Gdns CHTN/BK PR9 23 H3
FROD/HEL WA6 200 A5
WARRS WA4 162 B5
Cambridge Rd BTL L20 5 H6
CHTN/BK PR9 23 G4
CSBY/BLUN L23 68 D4
ECCL WA10 12 C4
EP CH65 6 E5
FMBY L37 48 D4
LITH L21 81 F4
PS/BROM CH62 171 F5
RF/TRAN CH42 149 K1
SKEL WN8 56 A4
WAL/NB CH45 95 H6
WLT/FAZ L9 82 E3
Cambridge St EHL/KEN L7 9 J6
PR/KW L34 * 117 K1
RUNC WA7 11 H4
WAV L15 133 J1
WDN WA8 18 E5
Cambridge Wks STHP PR8 14 E5
Camdale Cl STBRV L28 100 B6
Camden Ct RUNC WA7 178 C4
Camden Pl BIRK CH41 3 F3
Camden Rd EP CH65 195 K4
Camden St BIRK CH41 3 F3
VAUX/LVPD L3 9 G2
Camelford Rd NG/CROX L11 84 B6
Camelia Ct AIG/SPK L17 152 B1
Camellia Gdns STHEL WA9 105 F6
Camelot Cl NEWLW WA12 105 K1
Camelot Ter BTL L20 4 C2
Cameo Cl NPK/KEN L6 113 K3
Cameron Av RUNC WA7 176 B5
Cameron Ct WARRN/WOL WA2 123 G3
Cameron Rd MOR/LEA CH46 110 B4
WDN WA8 18 C4
Cameron St EHL/KEN L7 114 A5
Campania St ALL/GAR L19 172 B1
Campbell Av RUNC WA7 176 D5
Campbell Crs
WARRW/BUR WA5 141 G3
Campbell Dr DV/KA/FCH L14 115 J4
Campbell St BTL L20 4 B5
CLVPS L1 8 E6
ECCL WA10 12 D4
Campbeltown Rd BIRK CH41 131 J5
Camperdown St BIRK CH41 3 H4
Camphill Rd WLTN L25 154 D4
Campion Cl GOL/RIS/CU WA3 124 E2
RNFD/HAY WA11 88 E4
Campion Gv AIMK WN4 78 E5
Campion Wy HUY L36 136 C2
Camp Rd AIMK WN4 78 D6
WLTN L25 154 E2
Campsey Ash WDN WA8 138 E6

Camrose Cl RUNC WA7 187 F1
Camsley La LYMM WA13 145 G6
Cam St WLTN L25 * 154 D2
Canaan GOL/RIS/CU WA3 93 K3
Canada Cl WARRN/WOL WA2 124 C5
Canal Bank BRSC L40 * 38 B3
Canal Bank Pygons Hl
MGHL L31 52 A6
Canal Reach RUNC WA7 178 B3
Canalside EP CH65 7 G2
Canal Side RUNC WA7 176 A6
WARRS WA4 161 F6
WARRS WA4 188 E1
Canalside Gv EV L5 112 E2
Canal St BTL L20 4 D6
ECCL WA10 13 F7
NEWLW WA12 105 K3
RUNC WA7 11 G4
Canal Vw LYMM WA13 * 145 H6
MGHL L31 83 K1
Canberra Av STHEL WA9 103 G6
Canberra La NG/CROX L11 84 B6
Canberra Sq WARRN/WOL WA2 123 K5
Candleston Cl
WARRW/BUR WA5 122 E6
Canford Cl WARRW/BUR WA5 141 K3
Cannell Ct RUNC WA7 187 K1
Cannell St WARRW/BUR WA5 142 A5
Canning Pl CLVPS L1 8 D6
Canning Rd CHTN/BK PR9 23 J6
Canning St BIRK CH41 3 G2
CSBY/WL L22 80 E2
TOX L8 9 J7
Canniswood Rd
RNFD/HAY WA11 89 K6
Cann La North WARRS WA4 162 D5
Cannock Cl GTS/LS CH66 202 C3
Cannock Gn MGHL L31 83 K3
Cannon Hl CL/PREN CH43 130 E3
Cannon St EP CH65 6 A4
STHEL WA9 120 A4
Canon Rd NPK/KEN L6 98 A6
Canons Rd WARRW/BUR WA5 142 A3
Canon St RUNC WA7 10 C3
Canon Wilson Cl
RNFD/HAY WA11 90 C5
Canrow La PR/KW L34 85 J6
Cansfield Gv AIMK WN4 79 F5
Cansfield St ECCL WA10 13 H4
Canterbury Av CSBY/WL L22 68 E6
GOL/RIS/CU WA3 92 E2
Canterbury Cl AIN/FAZ L10 83 H1
FMBY L37 41 F6
GTS/LS CH66 202 C3
PR/KW L34 102 A6
STHP PR8 27 G3
Canterbury Pk CALD/MH L18 153 K3
Canterbury Rd RF/TRAN CH42 151 F2
WAL/EG CH44 111 J4
WDN WA8 157 H4
Canterbury St ALL/GAR L19 172 B1
ECCL WA10 12 D2
VAUX/LVPD L3 9 H1
WARRS WA4 17 F7
Canterbury Wy NTHTN L30 70 C5
VAUX/LVPD L3 * 9 J1
Canter Cl WLT/FAZ L9 83 G3
Cantley Cl RUNC WA7 187 G1
Cantlow Fold STHP PR8 33 G5
Cantsfield St EHL/KEN L7 133 H2
Canvey Cl WAV L15 134 C2
Capenhurst Av
WARRN/WOL WA2 124 C5
Capenhurst La EP CH65 195 K6
Cape Rd WLT/FAZ L9 * 83 F5
Capesthorne Cl WDN WA8 157 K3
Capesthorne Rd
WARRN/WOL WA2 123 K6
Capilano Pk ORM L39 53 G5
Capper Gv HUY L36 116 E4
Capricorn Crs DV/KA/FCH L14 115 K2
Capricorn Wy BTL L20 4 D3
Captain's La AIMK WN4 79 H6
NTHTN L30 82 A3
Caradoc Rd LITH L21 81 G5
Caraway Cl CSBY/BLUN L23 69 J4
Caraway Gv ECCL WA10 12 A3
Carbis Cl AIN/FAZ L10 83 K5
Carden Cl ANF/KKDL L4 97 G6
GOL/RIS/CU WA3 124 E3
Cardeston Cl RUNC WA7 187 J4
Cardiff Cl GTS/LS CH66 202 C3
Cardiff St SKEL WN8 55 K4
Cardigan Av BIRK CH41 2 E4
Cardigan Cl ECCL WA10 12 E7
WARRW/BUR WA5 122 D5
Cardigan Rd STHP PR8 27 G6
WAL/NB CH45 95 H6
Cardigan St WAV L15 133 J1
Cardigan Wy NPK/KEN L6 113 K3
NTHTN L30 * 70 E5
Cardus Cl MOR/LEA CH46 128 C1
Cardwell St EHL/KEN L7 133 F1
Carey Av BEB CH63 150 C5
Carey St WDN WA8 18 E2
Carfax Rd NWD/KWIPK L33 73 F5
Carfield SKEL WN8 67 G1
Cargill Gv RF/TRAN CH42 151 G3
Carham Rd HOY CH47 127 H3
Carisbrooke Cl WKBY CH48 146 D3
Carisbrooke Dr CHTN/BK PR9 23 H4
Carisbrooke Pl ANF/KKDL L4 * 97 H4
Carisbrooke Rd ANF/KKDL L4 5 J7
Carkington Rd WLTN L25 155 F2
Carland Cl NG/CROX L11 84 A5
Carlaw Rd RF/TRAN CH42 149 K1
Carleen Cl AIG/SPK L17 152 C1
Carlett Bvd PS/BROM CH62 184 C2
Carlile Wy NWD/KWIPK L33 72 E3
Carlingford Cl TOX L8 133 F2
Carlingford Rd WARRS WA4 162 A3
Carlisle Cl ANF/KKDL L4 98 B5
Carlisle Ms CL/PREN CH43 2 C6
Carlisle Rd STHP PR8 27 H5
Carlisle St WARRS WA4 162 B3
Carlis Rd KKBY L32 84 E3
Carlow Cl SPK/HALE L24 174 D3
Carlow St ECCL WA10 103 F4
Carlsruhe Ct TOX L8 * 133 F4
Carl's Wy NWD/KWIPK L33 73 F3
Carlton Av RUNC WA7 177 G3
SKEL WN8 57 J6
Carlton Cl NSTN CH64 181 H5
Carlton Crs GTS/LS CH66 195 H1
Carlton La CLB/OSW/ST L13 114 E3
HOY CH47 127 H1
Carlton Mt RF/TRAN CH42 131 H6
Carlton Rd BEB CH63 170 D1
GOL/RIS/CU WA3 92 E2
RF/TRAN CH42 131 F5
STHP PR8 33 J3
WAL/NB CH45 95 H5
Carlton St ECCL WA10 12 D6
PR/KW L34 101 K6
VAUX/LVPD L3 112 D3
WARRS WA4 162 B3
WDN WA8 18 D3
Carlton Ter CSBY/BLUN L23 * 68 E5
HOY CH47 * 127 H1
Carlyle Crs GTS/LS CH66 195 H5
Carlyon Wy HLWD L26 * 155 H3
Carmarthen Cl
WARRW/BUR WA5 122 D5
Carmel Cl ORM L39 53 H3
Carmel Ct WDN WA8 139 G5
Carmelite Crs ECCL WA10 87 H6
Carmichael Av
GR/UP/WCH CH49 148 A1
Carnaby Cl HUY L36 136 D1
Carnarvon Rd STHP PR8 27 G6
WLT/FAZ L9 97 H2
Carnarvon St STHEL WA9 103 F6
Carnatic Rd AIG/SPK L17 133 K6
Carnation Rd WLT/FAZ L9 97 K1
Carnegie Av CSBY/BLUN L23 68 E6
Carnegie Crs STHEL WA9 104 C5
Carnegie Dr AIMK WN4 79 F4
Carnegie Rd CLB/OSW/ST L13 114 D3
Carnforth Av KKBY L32 84 E2
Carnforth Cl BIRK CH41 2 C7
WD/CROXPK L12 99 G4
Carnforth Rd CALD/MH L18 153 K1
Carno St WAV L15 * 133 K1
Carnoustie Cl MOR/LEA CH46 109 F6
STHP PR8 27 G3
WD/CROXPK L12 115 K1
Carnoustie Gv RNFD/HAY WA11 89 K6
Carnsdale Rd MOR/LEA CH46 129 G1
Carol Dr HES CH60 168 C5
Carole Cl STHEL WA9 120 C1
Carolina St BTL L20 4 E4
Caroline Pl CL/PREN CH43 130 E4
Caroline St WDN WA8 * 18 E6
Carol St WARRS WA4 143 G6
Caronia St ALL/GAR L19 * 172 B1
Carpathia St ALL/GAR L19 172 B1
Carpenter Gv
WARRN/WOL WA2 124 C6
Carpenter's La WKBY CH48 146 C1
Carpenters Rw CLVPS L1 8 D7
Carraway Rd NG/CROX L11 84 A5
Carr Bridge Rd
GR/UP/WCH CH49 129 J5
Carr Cl NG/CROX L11 99 F3
Carr Cft LITH L21 69 K6
Carrfield Av CSBY/BLUN L23 69 H6
Carr Ga MOR/LEA CH46 128 C2
Carr Hey MOR/LEA CH46 128 C1
Carr Hey Cl GR/UP/WCH CH49 149 F1
Carr House La HTWN L38 60 A3
MOR/LEA CH46 128 C1
Carriage Dr FROD/HEL WA6 200 D3
Carrick Dr EP CH65 203 F1
Carrickmore Av CALD/MH L18 153 H1
Carrington Cl GOL/RIS/CU WA3 124 E3
Carrington Rd WAL/NB CH45 111 H1
Carrington St BIRK CH41 130 D1
Carr La BRSC L40 39 H6
GOL/RIS/CU WA3 93 H4
HOY CH47 127 G3
HUY L36 116 C6
MGHL L31 61 H2
MOR/LEA CH46 128 C1
NG/CROX L11 98 E3
PR/KW L34 117 H2
SPK/HALE L24 174 E3
STHP PR8 34 B2
Carr La East NG/CROX L11 99 F3
Carr Meadow Hey NTHTN L30 81 K1
Carr Mill Crs WGNW/BIL/O WN5 77 H5
Carr Mill Rd RNFD/HAY WA11 89 F4
WGNW/BIL/O WN5 77 H6
Carr Moss La ORM L39 34 E6
Carrock Rd PS/BROM CH62 171 G3
Carroll Crs ORM L39 45 K4
Carrow Cl MOR/LEA CH46 128 C2
Carr Rd BTL L20 82 A4
Carr's Crs FMBY L37 48 D4
Carr's Crs West FMBY L37 48 D4
Carr Side La HTWN L38 60 C4
Carr St ECCL WA10 12 C1
Carruthers St VAUX/LVPD L3 112 E4
Carrville Wy WD/CROXPK L12 100 A3
Carrwood Cl RNFD/HAY WA11 89 K5
Carrwood Pk STHP PR8 23 J4
Carsdale Rd CALD/MH L18 134 B4
Carsgoe Rd HOY CH47 127 H3
Carsington Rd NG/CROX L11 98 E3
Carstairs Rd NPK/KEN L6 114 A3
Carsthorne Rd HOY CH47 127 H3
Cartbridge La HLWD L26 155 J2
Carter Av RNFD/HAY WA11 75 H4
The Carters GR/UP/WCH CH49 128 D5
NTHTN L30 70 D5
Carter St TOX L8 132 E3
Carterton Rd HOY CH47 127 H3
Cartier Cl WARRW/BUR WA5 141 K1
Cartmel Av ECCL WA10 88 B4
MGHL L31 62 C5
WARRN/WOL WA2 123 J4
Cartmel Cl BIRK CH41 * 2 C7
HUY L36 116 D3
STHP PR8 28 C4
WARRW/BUR WA5 122 E5
Cartmel Dr FMBY L37 49 H3
GTS/LS CH66 202 D1
MOR/LEA CH46 129 F2
RAIN/WH L35 118 C3
WD/CROXPK L12 99 G4
Cartmell Cl RUNC WA7 186 E1
Cartmel Rd HUY L36 116 D3
Cartmel Ter NG/CROX L11 99 G2
Cartmel Wy HUY L36 116 C3
Cartridge La WARRS WA4 163 J5
Cartwright's Farm Rd
SPK/HALE L24 173 F2
Cartwright St RUNC WA7 11 H5
WARRW/BUR WA5 142 B3
Carvel Wy BRSC L40 39 F6
Carver St VAUX/LVPD L3 9 J1
Caryl Gv TOX L8 132 D5
Caryl St TOX L8 132 D4
Cascades SKEL WN8 * 56 E6
Case Gv RAIN/WH L35 118 A2
Case Rd RNFD/HAY WA11 90 C5
Cashel Rd BIRK CH41 111 H5
Caspian Pl BTL L20 5 F4
Caspian Rd ANF/KKDL L4 98 A3
Cassia Cl WLT/FAZ L9 97 K1
Cassino Rd HUY L36 116 D4
Cassio St BTL L20 * 5 J7
Cassley Rd SPK/HALE L24 174 B2
Cassville Rd CALD/MH L18 134 B3
Castell Gv ECCL WA10 12 E5
Casterton St EHL/KEN L7 * 133 H1
Castle Av STHEL WA9 104 C2
Castle Cl MOR/LEA CH46 110 A4
Castle Dr EP CH65 195 K6
FMBY L37 49 F4
HES CH60 167 K5
Castlefield Cl WD/CROXPK L12 98 E5
Castlefield Rd WD/CROXPK L12 98 E6
Castlefields Av East
RUNC WA7 177 K4
Castlefields Av North
RUNC WA7 177 H3
Castlefields Av South
RUNC WA7 177 K5
Castle Fields Est
MOR/LEA CH46 109 K3
Castleford Ri MOR/LEA CH46 109 J4
Castleford St WAV L15 134 B2
Castlegate Gv WD/CROXPK L12 98 E6
Castlegrange Cl
MOR/LEA CH46 109 J3
Castle Gn WARRW/BUR WA5 122 B5
Castleheath Cl MOR/LEA CH46 109 J4
Castlehey SKEL WN8 67 G1
Castle Hl CLVP L2 * 8 C4
NEWLW WA12 106 E1
Castle La BRSC L40 46 D5
Castle Mt HES CH60 * 167 K5
Castle Ri RUNC WA7 11 K5
Castle Rd RUNC WA7 177 J5
WAL/NB CH45 111 G1
Castlesite Rd WD/CROXPK L12 99 F6
Castle St BIRK CH41 3 H4
CHTN/BK PR9 15 F4
CLVP L2 8 C4
WDN WA8 19 J2
WLTN L25 154 C1
Castleton Dr NTHTN L30 70 E5
Castletown Cl CHLDW L16 135 F1
Castleview Rd WD/CROXPK L12 99 F6
Castle Wk STHP PR8 14 C7
Castleway North
MOR/LEA CH46 110 A3
Castleway South
MOR/LEA CH46 110 A4
Castlewood Rd NPK/KEN L6 113 K2
Castner Av RUNC WA7 176 B6
Castor St NPK/KEN L6 113 K2
Catchdale Moss La ECCL WA10 87 F6
Catford Cl WDN WA8 157 H1
Catford Gn SPK/HALE L24 174 A2
Catfoss Cl WARRN/WOL WA2 124 A6
Catharine's La ORM L39 53 K3
Catharine St TOX L8 132 E2
Cathcart Quay BIRK CH41 * 2 E1
Cathcart St BIRK CH41 2 D3
Cathedral Cl CLVPS L1 132 D2
Cathedral Ga CLVPS L1 9 H7
Cathedral Rd NPK/KEN L6 114 A1
Cathedral Wk VAUX/LVPD L3 9 H5
Catherine St BIRK CH41 2 D5
LITH L21 81 J5
WARRW/BUR WA5 16 B1
WDN WA8 18 D7
Catherine Wy NEWLW WA12 106 B3
RNFD/HAY WA11 * 89 J5
Catkin Rd HLWD L26 155 G1
Caton Cl CHTN/BK PR9 23 H1
Catonfield Rd CALD/MH L18 134 E4
Cat Tail La STHP PR8 29 H6
Catterall Av STHEL WA9 120 B1
WARRN/WOL WA2 123 K5
Catterick Cl HLWD L26 155 J3
Catterick Fold STHP PR8 28 C4
Caulfield Dr GR/UP/WCH CH49 129 F6
Caunce Av CHTN/BK PR9 21 K5
GOL/RIS/CU WA3 92 B4
RNFD/HAY WA11 90 A5
Caunce's Rd CHTN/BK PR9 30 C1
Causeway Av WARRS WA4 143 F6
Causeway Cl PS/BROM CH62 151 G6
Causeway La FMBY L37 50 D4
The Causeway CHTN/BK PR9 21 F6
PS/BROM CH62 151 G6
WD/CROXPK L12 115 H3
Cavalier Dr ALL/GAR L19 154 B6
Cavan Rd NG/CROX L11 98 C5
Cavell Cl WLTN L25 154 D2
Cavell Dr EP CH65 6 A7
Cavendish Av GOL/RIS/CU WA3 125 G2
Cavendish Cl
WARRW/BUR WA5 142 A2
Cavendish Dr RF/TRAN CH42 150 C2
WLT/FAZ L9 97 J2
Cavendish Farm Rd
RUNC WA7 186 C2
Cavendish Gdns EP CH65 6 A7
TOX L8 * 133 F4
Cavendish Pl GOL/RIS/CU WA3 125 H2
Cavendish Rd BIRK CH41 130 E2
CSBY/BLUN L23 68 D6
STHP PR8 27 G4
WAL/NB CH45 95 H4
Cavendish St BIRK CH41 2 A1
RUNC WA7 10 C5
Cavendish Whf BIRK CH41 * 111 J6
Cavern Ct NPK/KEN L6 113 K4
Caversham Cl WARRS WA4 162 C4
Cawdor St RUNC WA7 10 B3
TOX L8 133 F3
WARRS WA4 162 B3
Cawfield Av WDN WA8 157 J2
Cawley St RUNC WA7 10 D7
Cawood Cl GTS/LS CH66 194 E4
Cawthorne Av KKBY L32 84 D4
WARRS WA4 163 F1
Cawthorne Cl KKBY L32 84 D3
Cawthorne Wk KKBY L32 * 84 D3
Caxton Cl CL/PREN CH43 129 K3
GTS/LS CH66 195 J5
WDN WA8 * 138 B6
Caxton Rd RAIN/WH L35 119 G6
Cazneau St VAUX/LVPD L3 113 F4
C' Ct AIMK WN4 91 G1
Cearns Rd CL/PREN CH43 130 D4
Cecil Dr ECCL WA10 87 H6
Cecil Rd LITH L21 81 G5
PS/BROM CH62 151 G3
RF/TRAN CH42 150 A1
WAL/EG CH44 111 G3
Cecil St STHEL WA9 104 D6
WAV L15 133 J1
Cedab Rd EP CH65 6 E3
Cedar Av BEB CH63 170 A1
GOL/RIS/CU WA3 93 G4
GTS/LS CH66 195 F3
RUNC WA7 177 F6
RUNC WA7 187 K3
WDN WA8 139 G6
Cedar Cl CALD/MH L18 134 E6
RAIN/WH L35 118 A3
Cedar Crs HUY L36 116 D6
NEWLW WA12 106 D3
ORM L39 53 G1
Cedardale Dr GTS/LS CH66 202 D2
Cedardale Pk WDN WA8 139 K5
Cedardale Rd WLT/FAZ L9 97 J1
Cedar Dr FMBY L37 48 C4
Cedar Gv AIMK WN4 78 C4
CSBY/WL L22 80 E1
MGHL L31 71 G3
NSTN CH64 192 A1
RNFD/HAY WA11 90 D4
SKEL WN8 56 A4
TOX L8 133 H3
WARR WA1 143 K2
WARRS WA4 143 G6
Cedar Rd RAIN/WH L35 117 K4
WARRW/BUR WA5 141 G3
WLT/FAZ L9 82 E5
The Cedars MOR/LEA CH46 128 D2
WD/CROXPK L12 99 K2
Cedar St BIRK CH41 2 D6
BTL L20 5 F3
ECCL WA10 12 A7
NEWLW WA12 * 106 C3
STHP PR8 27 K3
Cedar Ter TOX L8 133 G3
Cedarway HES CH60 181 G2
Cedarways WARRS WA4 162 C6
Cedarwood Cl
GR/UP/WCH CH49 128 C5
Cedarwood Ct HUY L36 136 B1
Celandine Wy STHEL WA9 105 F6
Celebration Dr NPK/KEN L6 114 A2
Celedine Cl WAV L15 * 114 C6
Celia St BTL L20 97 F4
Celtic Rd HOY CH47 108 C6
Celtic St TOX L8 133 F3
Celt St NPK/KEN L6 * 114 A3
Cemeas Cl EV L5 112 E2
Cemetery Rd STHP PR8 27 J3
Centenary Cl ANF/KKDL L4 98 A5
Central Av EP CH65 6 D6
PR/KW L34 117 J1
PS/BROM CH62 170 E4
SPK/HALE L24 173 J2
STHP PR8 34 B1
WARRN/WOL WA2 143 F1
WARRS WA4 142 E6
Central Buildings
CSBY/BLUN L23 * 69 F5
Central Dr RNFD/HAY WA11 75 G2
RNFD/HAY WA11 90 A5
WD/CROXPK L12 114 E2
Central Expy RUNC WA7 187 G1
Central Park Av WAL/EG CH44 111 J3
Central Rd PS/BROM CH62 151 G4
WARRS WA4 142 E6
Central Sq MGHL L31 62 B5
Central St ECCL WA10 13 G3
Central Wy NEWLW WA12 106 E3
SPK/HALE L24 173 K3
WARRN/WOL WA2 16 D3
Centre Ct LEIGH WN7 93 J2
Centre Pk WARR WA1 142 D6
Centre Park Sq WARR WA1 16 C7
Centreville Rd CALD/MH L18 134 B3
Centre Wy HUY L36 116 E5
Centurion Cl GOL/RIS/CU WA3 125 F3
HOY CH47 108 C6
Centurion Dr HOY CH47 108 C6
Ceres St BTL L20 96 E4
Cestrian Dr PEN/TH CH61 148 D6
Chadlow Rd KKBY L32 84 E4
Chadwell Rd NWD/KWIPK L33 72 E5
Chadwick Av WARRS WA4 162 D2
Chadwick Pl GOL/RIS/CU WA3 125 G2
Chadwick Rd RNFD/HAY WA11 89 F4
RUNC WA7 177 H2
Chadwick St MOR/LEA CH46 129 F1
VAUX/LVPD L3 112 D4
Chaffinch Cl GOL/RIS/CU WA3 125 H4
WD/CROXPK L12 99 K4
Chaffinch Gld HLWD L26 155 H2
Chainhurst Cl NTHLY L27 136 A3
Chain La RNFD/HAY WA11 89 G5
Chalfield Av GTS/LS CH66 195 F4
Chalfield Cl GTS/LS CH66 195 F4
Chalfont Cl WARRS WA4 162 D5
Chalfont Rd CALD/MH L18 154 A2
Chalfont Wy STBRV L28 100 B6
Chalgrave Cl WDN WA8 139 K6
Chalkwell Dr HES CH60 168 C6
Challis St BIRK CH41 110 E6
Challoner Cl HUY L36 136 C1
Chaloner Gv ALL/GAR L19 153 G4
Chaloner St VAUX/LVPD L3 132 C2
Chalon Wy East ECCL WA10 13 H6
Chalon Wy West ECCL WA10 13 G6
Chamberlain St BIRK CH41 * 131 H5
ECCL WA10 12 A6
WAL/EG CH44 111 G5
Chambres Rd STHP PR8 28 A2
Chambres Rd North STHP PR8 15 K7
Chancellor Rd RUNC WA7 160 A6
Chancel St ANF/KKDL L4 97 G6
Chancery La STHEL WA9 104 C2
Chandlers Ct RUNC WA7 10 A6
Chandler Wy GOL/RIS/CU WA3 93 F3
Chandley Cl STHP PR8 33 G4
Chandos St EHL/KEN L7 113 K6
Change La NSTN CH64 193 J1
Changford Rd NWD/KWIPK L33 73 F6
Channell Rd NPK/KEN L6 114 A4
Channel Rd CSBY/BLUN L23 68 C6
The Channel WAL/NB CH45 * 94 E5
Chantler Av WARRS WA4 143 H5
Chantrell Rd WKBY CH48 147 F1
Chantry Cl CL/PREN CH43 129 K3
Chantry Wk AIMK WN4 78 E4
HES CH60 181 F1
Chapel Av WLT/FAZ L9 82 D6
Chapel Cl EP CH65 6 D1
Chapel Cross Rd
WARRN/WOL WA2 124 C5
Chapelfields FROD/HEL WA6 200 D1
Chapel Gdns EV L5 113 F2
Chapelhill Rd MOR/LEA CH46 129 G1
Chapelhouse Wk FMBY L37 49 G2
Chapel La BRSC L40 46 E1
ECCL WA10 102 D1
FMBY L37 49 F2
KIRK/FR/WA PR4 31 G2
MGHL L31 71 K5
NTHTN L30 70 D4
RAIN/WH L35 119 H5
WARRS WA4 162 B3
WARRW/BUR WA5 121 K1
WDN WA8 138 B4
Chapel Ms EP CH65 6 B6
ORM L39 53 J1
Chapel Pl AIMK WN4 * 79 G6
ALL/GAR L19 153 K5
Chapel Rd ALL/GAR L19 153 K5
HOY CH47 127 G1
NPK/KEN L6 114 A1
WARRW/BUR WA5 141 F6
Chapel St AIMK WN4 79 G6
ECCL WA10 13 F1
NEWLW WA12 106 B2
ORM L39 45 K6
PR/KW L34 * 117 K1
RNFD/HAY WA11 90 D5
RUNC WA7 10 D4
STHP PR8 14 E5
VAUX/LVPD L3 8 B4
WDN WA8 18 C6
Chapel Ter BTL L20 4 C6
Chapel Vw RNFD/HAY WA11 76 C5
Chapel Yd WAV L15 134 B2
Chapman Cl TOX L8 * 132 D4
WDN WA8 138 C5
Chapman Gv PR/KW L34 102 A6
Chapterhouse Cl EP CH65 7 J4
Chardstock Dr WLTN L25 * 135 K5
Charing Cross BIRK CH41 2 D5
Charlecombe St
RF/TRAN CH42 131 G5
Charlecote St TOX L8 132 E6
Charles Av STHP PR8 34 A3
WARRW/BUR WA5 141 G3
Charles Berrington Rd
WAV L15 134 B3
Charlesbye Av ORM L39 46 A5
Charles Price Gdns EP CH65 6 D3
Charles Rd HOY CH47 127 G3
Charles St BIRK CH41 2 D2
ECCL WA10 13 H4
GOL/RIS/CU WA3 92 B2
WDN WA8 18 D3
Charleston Cl GTS/LS CH66 195 G6
Charleston Rd TOX L8 132 E5
Charlesville CL/PREN CH43 130 E4
Charles Wk DV/KA/FCH L14 115 K4
Charlesworth Cl MGHL L31 61 K2
Charley Wood Rd
NWD/KWIPK L33 85 G2
Charlock Cl NTHTN L30 70 D5
Charlotte Rd WAL/EG CH44 111 K2
Charlotte's Meadow BEB CH63 170 C1
Charlotte St CLVPS L1 * 8 E4
Charlotte Wk WDN WA8 18 E6
Charlotte Wy CLVPS L1 * 9 F4
Charlton Cl AIMK WN4 79 F4
RUNC WA7 177 K6

Charlton Ct CL/PREN CH43 130 C3
Charlton Pl CLB/OSW/ST L13 114 E6
Charlton Rd CLB/OSW/ST L13 114 E6
Charlton St WARRS WA4 143 J6
Charlwood Av HUY L36 116 E6
Charlwood Cl CL/PREN CH43 129 K3
Charminster Cl
WARRW/BUR WA5 141 J4
Charmouth Cl WD/CROXPK L12 99 J2
Charnley's La CHTN/BK PR9 21 H3
Charnock Av NEWLW WA12 105 K2
Charnock Rd WLT/FAZ L9 98 B2
Charnwood Cl
GOL/RIS/CU WA3 125 K2
WD/CROXPK L12 99 H2
Charnwood Rd HUY L36 116 B4
Charnwood St STHEL WA9 104 C1
Charter Av WARRW/BUR WA5 142 D1
Charter Crs GTS/LS CH66 195 H6
Charterhouse Dr AIN/FAZ L10 83 H1
Charterhouse Rd WLTN L25 154 E2
Chartmount Wy WLTN L25 135 J5
Chartwell Gv HLWD L26 155 K2
Chartwell Rd STHP PR8 33 H3
Chase Cl STHP PR8 27 G3
Chase Dr GTS/LS CH66 202 C1
Chase Heys CHTN/BK PR9 23 H4
Chaser Cl WLT/FAZ L9 83 F3
The Chase BEB CH63 183 K2
HUY L36 136 C1
Chase Wy EV L5 113 G3
GTS/LS CH66 202 B1
Chatburn Av GOL/RIS/CU WA3 92 D2
Chatburn Wk TOX L8 * 132 E5
Chater Cl RAIN/WH L35 118 C1
Chatfield Dr GOL/RIS/CU WA3 125 G4
Chatham Cl LITH L21 81 G4
Chatham Pl EHL/KEN L7 113 K6
Chatham Rd RF/TRAN CH42 151 F1
Chatham St EHL/KEN L7 9 K7
Chatsworth Av WAL/EG CH44 111 J3
WLT/FAZ L9 82 C6
Chatsworth Cl AIMK WN4 78 E5
GTS/LS CH66 195 F4
Chatsworth Dr EHL/KEN L7 133 G1
WDN WA8 * 138 B6
Chatsworth Rd PEN/TH CH61 148 C6
RAIN/WH L35 118 D3
RF/TRAN CH42 151 F1
STHP PR8 33 H3
Chatteris Pk RUNC WA7 178 D3
Chatterton Dr RUNC WA7 178 D5
Chatterton Rd DV/KA/FCH L14 115 G3
Chatwell Gdns WARRS WA4 162 E6
Chaucer Dr WD/CROXPK L12 99 K3
Chaucer Pl WARRS WA4 143 J5
Chaucer Rd ECCL WA10 88 A5
Chaucer St BTL L20 4 B2
RUNC WA7 10 D6
VAUX/LVPD L3 113 F4
Cheadle Av CLB/OSW/ST L13 114 D4
Cheapside CLVP L2 8 D2
FMBY L37 49 G3
Cheapside Aly CLVP L2 * 8 D3
Cheddar Cl WLTN L25 154 C1
Cheddar Gv KKBY L32 84 D4
WARRW/BUR WA5 105 K6
Cheddon Wy PEN/TH CH61 167 J1
Chedworth Dr WDN WA8 138 B5
Chedworth Rd DV/KA/FCH L14 115 J3
Cheldon Rd NG/CROX L11 99 G3
Chelford Av GOL/RIS/CU WA3 92 E4
Chelford Cl CL/PREN CH43 129 K2
WARRS WA4 162 B3
Chellowdene CSBY/BLUN L23 69 H3
Chelmarsh Av AIMK WN4 79 H6
Chelmsford Cl EV L5 97 F6
Chelsea Ct WD/CROXPK L12 99 J5
Chelsea Gdns
WARRW/BUR WA5 141 K5
Chelsea Rd LITH L21 81 J5
WLT/FAZ L9 82 D5
Cheltenham Av AIG/SPK L17 133 J4
Cheltenham Cl
WARRW/BUR WA5 141 H1
WLT/FAZ L9 83 H2
Cheltenham Crs HUY L36 116 D6
MOR/LEA CH46 109 J4
RUNC WA7 186 E1
Cheltenham Dr NEWLW WA12 91 H6
Cheltenham Rd EP CH65 196 C6
WAL/NB CH45 110 E1
Cheltenham Wy STHP PR8 28 C3
Chelwood Av CHLDW L16 115 J6
Chelwood Pk RNFD/HAY WA11 91 G2
Chemical St NEWLW WA12 106 B2
Chemistry Rd SPK/HALE L24 155 F6
Chenotrie Gdns CL/PREN CH43 130 A4
Chepstow Av WAL/EG CH44 111 J3
Chepstow Cl
WARRW/BUR WA5 122 E4
Chepstow St ANF/KKDL L4 97 G4
Chequer Cl SKEL WN8 67 H2
Chequer La SKEL WN8 67 H2
Chequers Gdns ALL/GAR L19 153 G3
Cheriton Av WKBY CH48 146 E1
Cheriton Cl HLWD L26 155 H3
Cheriton Pk STHP PR8 27 J2
STHP PR8 28 B4
Chermside Rd AIG/SPK L17 153 F2
Cherry Av ANF/KKDL L4 97 K4
Cherrybank WAL/EG CH44 111 H5
Cherry Blossom Rd RUNC WA7 187 J3
Cherry Cl ANF/KKDL L4 97 K4
NEWLW WA12 105 K1
NSTN CH64 192 D1
Cherry Cnr LYMM WA13 164 B5
Cherrycroft SKEL WN8 67 G1
Cherrydale Rd CALD/MH L18 134 B5
Cherryfield Crs KKBY L32 84 D1
Cherryfield Dr KKBY L32 84 D1
Cherry Gn ORM L39 53 F4
Cherry Gv BRSC L40 38 E3
GTS/LS CH66 202 E2

KKBY L32 84 E4
Cherry La ANF/KKDL L4 97 K4
LYMM WA13 164 C3
Cherry Rd STHP PR8 41 K1
Cherrysutton WDN WA8 138 A6
Cherrysutton Ms WDN WA8 * 138 A5
Cherry Tree Av LYMM WA13 164 E1
RUNC WA7 177 F5
WARRW/BUR WA5 141 G5
Cherry Tree Cl CHNE CH2 198 C5
RAIN/WH L35 117 K4
RNFD/HAY WA11 * 89 K6
Cherry Tree Dr STHEL WA9 104 E3
Cherry Tree La ORM L39 53 F4
RNFD/HAY WA11 88 D1
Cherry Tree Rd
GOL/RIS/CU WA3 93 G3
HUY L36 136 B1
MOR/LEA CH46 129 G2
Cherry V WLTN L25 135 J6
Cherry Vw NWD/KWIPK L33 72 E4
Cherwell Cl WARRN/WOL WA2 123 K5
Cheryl Dr WDN WA8 19 K1
Chesford Gra WARR WA1 144 D2
Chesham Ct EP CH65 7 F7
Cheshire Acre
GR/UP/WCH CH49 148 D1
Cheshire Av AIN/FAZ L10 84 A4
Cheshire Cl NEWLW WA12 106 E2
Cheshire Gdns ECCL WA10 12 D7
Cheshire Gv MOR/LEA CH46 129 F2
Cheshire Lines Pth FMBY L37 42 B5
Cheshire Oaks Wy EP CH65 203 J2
Cheshire Ring Canal Wk
WARRS WA4 161 F5
WARRS WA4 189 F3
Cheshyre Dr RUNC WA7 177 J4
Cheshyre's La RUNC WA7 176 B6
Chesnell Gv NWD/KWIPK L33 72 E4
Chesney Cl TOX L8 132 D3
Chesnut Gv BTL L20 4 D2
RF/TRAN CH42 131 G5
Chessington Cl WARRS WA4 162 E5
Chester Av CHTN/BK PR9 23 H5
GOL/RIS/CU WA3 92 E3
NTHTN L30 82 C2
Chester Cl CSBY/BLUN L23 69 J5
RUNC WA7 177 J3
Chester Dr AIMK WN4 91 J1
Chesterfield Cl STHP PR8 33 H5
Chesterfield Dr
NWD/KWIPK L33 72 D4
Chesterfield Rd CSBY/BLUN L23 69 H4
PS/BROM CH62 184 A3
STHP PR8 33 H5
Chesterfield St TOX L8 132 D2
Chester High Rd NSTN CH64 181 K3
Chester La STHEL WA9 119 K3
Chester New Rd WARRS WA4 161 J4
Chester Rd CHTN/BK PR9 23 H5
EP CH65 195 K6
FROD/HEL WA6 200 C3
GTS/LS CH66 194 E1
HES CH60 181 H1
HUY L36 117 G3
NPK/KEN L6 114 B1
NSTN CH64 191 K2
RUNC WA7 187 K4
WARRS WA4 161 K3
WARRS WA4 179 G4
Chester St BIRK CH41 3 H5
PR/KW L34 117 K1
TOX L8 132 D2
WAL/EG CH44 * 111 G4
WDN WA8 18 E2
Chesterton Dr
WARRN/WOL WA2 123 G2
Chesterton St ALL/GAR L19 172 B1
Chestnut Av CSBY/BLUN L23 69 G3
GTS/LS CH66 202 D2
HUY L36 136 A1
RNFD/HAY WA11 89 J6
WARRW/BUR WA5 141 G3
WDN WA8 158 C1
Chestnut Cl GR/UP/WCH CH49 147 K1
ORM L39 44 A2
RAIN/WH L35 118 A3
Chestnut Ct BTL L20 4 D2
ORM L39 45 K5
Chestnut Gra ORM L39 53 H2
Chestnut Gv AIMK WN4 79 J5
GOL/RIS/CU WA3 93 G3
PS/BROM CH62 170 E5
RNFD/HAY WA11 89 G4
WAV L15 134 A1
Chestnut Rd LITH L21 81 G4
WLT/FAZ L9 97 K2
Chestnut St EHL/KEN L7 9 K5
STHP PR8 27 K3
Chestnut Wk MGHL L31 71 K5
Chestnut Wy FMBY L37 48 C4
Cheswood Cl RAIN/WH L35 118 A5
Chetham Ct WARRN/WOL WA2 123 G4
Chetton Dr RUNC WA7 178 D6
Chetwode Av AIMK WN4 91 G1
Chetwood Av CSBY/BLUN L23 69 G4
Chetwood Dr WDN WA8 138 E5
Chetwynd Cl CL/PREN CH43 130 C5
Chetwynd Rd CL/PREN CH43 * 130 D4
Chetwynd St AIG/SPK L17 133 G6
Chevasse Wk WLTN L25 135 K6
Cheverton Cl
GR/UP/WCH CH49 129 J6
Cheviot Av STHEL WA9 104 D2
WARRN/WOL WA2 123 G4
Cheviot Cl RF/TRAN CH42 150 C2
Cheviot Rd EHL/KEN L7 114 C5
RF/TRAN CH42 150 B2
Cheviot Wy NWD/KWIPK L33 72 E3
Chevoit Cl GTS/LS CH66 194 D3
Cheyne Cl CSBY/BLUN L23 68 B6
Cheyne Gdns ALL/GAR L19 153 G3
Cheyne Wk STHEL WA9 119 H1
Chichester Cl RUNC WA7 188 C1

WARRS WA4 163 F4
WAV L15 133 J1
Chidden Cl GR/UP/WCH CH49 128 D6
Chidlow Cl WDN WA8 158 B6
Chigwell Cl WD/CROXPK L12 99 J2
Chilcott Rd CLB/OSW/ST L13 115 G4
Childer Crs GTS/LS CH66 194 E2
Childer Gdns GTS/LS CH66 194 E2
Childers St CLB/OSW/ST L13 114 E4
Childwall Abbey Rd
CHLDW L16 134 E3
Childwall Av MOR/LEA CH46 128 E2
WAV L15 133 J2
Childwall Bank Rd CHLDW L16 134 E2
Childwall Cl GR/UP/WCH CH49 128 E2
Childwall Crs CHLDW L16 134 E2
Childwall Gdns GTS/LS CH66 195 J1
Childwall Gn
GR/UP/WCH CH49 148 D1
Childwall Hts WLTN L25 135 G2
Childwall La DV/KA/FCH L14 116 A5
WLTN L25 135 G3
Childwall Mount Rd
CHLDW L16 134 E2
Childwall Park Av CHLDW L16 135 F3
Childwall Priory Rd
CHLDW L16 134 E2
Childwall Rd GTS/LS CH66 195 J1
WAV L15 134 B2
Childwall Valley Rd
CHLDW L16 134 E2
WLTN L25 135 G1
Chilhem Cl TOX L8 132 E5
Chilington Av WDN WA8 157 J3
Chillerton Rd WD/CROXPK L12 99 H5
Chillingham St TOX L8 133 F5
Chiltern Av WARRN/WOL WA2 123 G4
Chiltern Cl AIMK WN4 91 H1
WD/CROXPK L12 99 K3
Chiltern Crs WARRN/WOL WA2 123 G4
Chiltern Dr KKBY L32 72 B5
Chiltern Rd RF/TRAN CH42 150 B2
STHEL WA9 104 E2
STHP PR8 33 G3
WARRN/WOL WA2 123 G4
Chilton Cl MGHL L31 62 B6
Chilton Dr GTS/LS CH66 202 C1
Chilton Ms MGHL L31 62 B6
Chilwell Cl WDN WA8 138 C5
Chimes Rd AIMK WN4 78 E3
China Farm La WKBY CH48 127 K5
China La WARRS WA4 162 B1
Chindit Cl FMBY L37 48 E3
Chippenham Av
GR/UP/WCH CH49 128 D5
Chipping Av STHP PR8 33 G4
Chippingdall Cl
WARRW/BUR WA5 141 K4
Chirkdale St ANF/KKDL L4 97 G4
Chirk Gdns EP CH65 196 C6
Chirk Wy MOR/LEA CH46 129 G2
Chirton Cl RNFD/HAY WA11 90 C4
Chisenhale St VAUX/LVPD L3 112 E4
Chisledon Cl RNFD/HAY WA11 90 C4
Chislehurst Av WLTN L25 135 J3
Chislett Cl BRSC L40 * 38 D5
Chisnall Av ECCL WA10 102 E1
Chiswell St EHL/KEN L7 114 A5
Chiswick Cl RUNC WA7 * 178 C6
Chiswick Gdns WARRS WA4 162 E5
Cholmley Dr NEWLW WA12 106 E3
Cholmondeley Rd EP CH65 195 J5
RUNC WA7 187 G2
WKBY CH48 146 C1
Cholmondeley St WDN WA8 * 176 D1
Cholsey Cl GR/UP/WCH CH49 129 G5
Chorley Cl CHTN/BK PR9 21 H6
Chorley Rd PR/KW L34 117 H1
Chorley's La WDN WA8 139 J6
Chorley St ECCL WA10 12 E3
WARRN/WOL WA2 16 E2
Chorley Wy BEB CH63 170 C4
Chorlton Cl CHLDW L16 135 G1
RUNC WA7 178 C4
Chorlton Gv WAL/NB CH45 110 D2
Christchurch Rd
CL/PREN CH43 130 E5
Christian St VAUX/LVPD L3 9 F1
Christie Cl GTS/LS CH66 184 D5
Christie St WDN WA8 19 J1
Christines Crs BRSC L40 38 D5
Christleton Cl CL/PREN CH43 149 G1
Christleton Ct RUNC WA7 178 B1
Christleton Dr GTS/LS CH66 195 H3
Christmas St BTL L20 97 F4
Christopher Cl CHLDW L16 134 E1
RAIN/WH L35 118 D5
Christopher Dr PS/BROM CH62 184 D2
Christophers Cl
PEN/TH CH61 * 168 A1
Christopher St ANF/KKDL L4 97 H5
Christopher Wy CHLDW L16 134 E1
Chris Ward Cl EHL/KEN L7 114 A6
Chudleigh Cl HLWD L26 155 H2
Chudleigh Rd CLB/OSW/ST L13 114 D4
Church Av WLT/FAZ L9 82 E4
Church Cl CHTN/BK PR9 23 J5
FMBY L37 49 G2
WAL/EG CH44 111 K3
Church Close Ct FMBY L37 * 49 G2
Church Crs WAL/EG CH44 112 A5
Churchdown Gv
DV/KA/FCH L14 * 115 J3
Churchdown Rd
DV/KA/FCH L14 115 J3
Church Dr NEWLW WA12 106 C4
PS/BROM CH62 151 F6
WARRN/WOL WA2 124 C6
Church End SPK/HALE L24 174 E4
Church Farm Ct HES CH60 167 K6
Churchfield Rd FROD/HEL WA6 201 F2
WLTN L25 135 K4
Church Flds BRSC L40 36 D2
ORM L39 45 J6

Churchfields FROD/HEL WA6 199 K5
STHEL WA9 120 A3
STHP PR8 27 G4
WDN WA8 139 G4
Church Gdns BTL L20 4 C5
WAL/EG CH44 111 K3
Churchgate CHTN/BK PR9 23 J4
Churchgate Ms CHTN/BK PR9 23 J4
Church Gn CHLDW L16 135 G2
FMBY L37 48 C3
KKBY L32 72 D6
Church Gv LITH L21 81 G5
Church Hl WAL/EG CH44 111 F2
Churchhill Av BIRK CH41 2 A2
Church Hill Rd ORM L39 45 H5
Churchill Av CHTN/BK PR9 23 H3
Churchill Gdns STHEL WA9 118 E1
Churchill Gv WAL/EG CH44 * 111 J2
Churchill Wy NSTN CH64 191 K1
Churchill Wy (Elevated Rd)
CLVPS L1 8 E3
Church La AIG/SPK L17 153 F2
ANF/KKDL L4 97 H3
ECCL WA10 102 C2
GOL/RIS/CU WA3 92 E4
GR/UP/WCH CH49 148 E1
GTS/LS CH66 195 G5
NSTN CH64 191 K2
ORM L39 51 H5
ORM L39 52 E6
PEN/TH CH61 147 J6
PR/KW L34 100 C1
PS/BROM CH62 171 F4
PS/BROM CH62 184 D3
WAL/EG CH44 111 K3
WARRS WA4 163 G2
Churchmeadow Cl
WAL/EG CH44 111 K3
Church Meadow La HES CH60 167 J6
Church Meadow Wk
WDN WA8 157 G6
Church Ms RF/TRAN CH42 151 F2
Church Mt EHL/KEN L7 113 K6
Church Pde EP CH65 * 6 E2
Church Rd ALL/GAR L19 153 K6
ANF/KKDL L4 97 J3
BEB CH63 151 F6
BEB CH63 170 C1
BEB CH63 182 C1
BTL L20 82 A5
CHTN/BK PR9 21 K5
CLB/OSW/ST L13 114 D4
CSBY/BLUN L23 69 F5
CSBY/WL L22 81 F3
FMBY L37 49 G1
FROD/HEL WA6 201 F2
GR/UP/WCH CH49 129 H4
HLWD L26 155 J2
HUY L36 116 C5
LITH L21 81 K3
LYMM WA13 164 E1
MGHL L31 71 G2
ORM L39 64 E1
RF/TRAN CH42 131 G5
RNFD/HAY WA11 75 G3
RNFD/HAY WA11 90 D5
SKEL WN8 56 B4
SPK/HALE L24 175 F5
WAL/EG CH44 112 A5
WAV L15 134 B3
WKBY CH48 146 B2
WLTN L25 135 H6
Church Rd North WAV L15 134 B2
Church Rd South WLTN L25 154 D1
Church Rd West ANF/KKDL L4 97 H3
Church Sq ECCL WA10 13 G5
Church St BIRK CH41 3 J5
BTL L20 4 B5
CHTN/BK PR9 15 G4
CLVPS L1 8 E4
ECCL WA10 13 H6
EP CH65 6 E2
FROD/HEL WA6 200 E1
GOL/RIS/CU WA3 92 C2
NEWLW WA12 106 E2
ORM L39 45 J6
PR/KW L34 * 117 K1
RUNC WA7 10 D3
WAL/EG CH44 111 K3
WARR WA1 17 F4
WDN WA8 158 B6
Church Ter RF/TRAN CH42 131 G6
Church Vw BTL L20 4 D5
ORM L39 52 E6
Churchview Rd BIRK CH41 2 A1
Church Wk BTL L20 4 C5
EP CH65 6 E2
WARRN/WOL WA2 123 G1
Church Wy FMBY L37 48 C3
KKBY L32 72 D6
Churchway Rd SPK/HALE L24 174 B3
Churchwood Cl
PS/BROM CH62 171 F4
Churnet St ANF/KKDL L4 97 G5
Churn Wy GR/UP/WCH CH49 128 E5
Churston Rd CHLDW L16 135 F4
Churton Av CL/PREN CH43 130 C6
Churton Ct NPK/KEN L6 * 113 J4
Ciaran Cl WD/CROXPK L12 99 H5
Cicely St EHL/KEN L7 113 K6
Cinder La BTL L20 82 A4
CALD/MH L18 134 D4
KIRK/FR/WA PR4 25 K3
WARRS WA4 164 A3
Cinnamon La
WARRN/WOL WA2 124 B4
Cinnamon La North
WARRN/WOL WA2 124 B3
Cinnamon Pk
WARRN/WOL WA2 * 124 E5
Circular Dr GR/UP/WCH CH49 128 E6
HES CH60 167 J4
PS/BROM CH62 151 G4
Circular Rd BIRK CH41 2 E6

Circular Rd East NG/CROX L11 98 D5
Circular Rd West NG/CROX L11 98 D4
Cirencester Av
GR/UP/WCH CH49 128 D5
Cirrus Dr ORM L39 52 E4
Citrine Rd WAL/EG CH44 111 K5
Citron Cl WLT/FAZ L9 97 K1
City Gdns ECCL WA10 88 C5
City Rd ANF/KKDL L4 97 H4
ECCL WA10 88 C5
Civic Wy BEB CH63 151 F6
EP CH65 6 C4
HUY L36 116 E5
Clairville Cl BTL L20 4 E5
Clairville Wy CLB/OSW/ST L13 114 C2
Clandon Rd CALD/MH L18 154 A2
Clanfield Av WDN WA8 138 B6
Clanfield Rd NG/CROX L11 99 F4
Clap Gate Crs WDN WA8 157 G6
Clap Gates Rd
WARRW/BUR WA5 142 B2
Clapham Rd ANF/KKDL L4 113 K1
Clare Cl STHEL WA9 103 G6
Clare Crs WAL/EG CH44 110 E3
Clare Dr EP CH65 203 F2
Claremont Av MGHL L31 70 E1
STHP PR8 27 H3
WDN WA8 139 G5
Claremont Cl LITH L21 81 G4
Claremont Dr ORM L39 53 H2
WDN WA8 139 G5
Claremont Gdns STHP PR8 27 H3
Claremont Rd CSBY/BLUN L23 68 E5
LITH L21 81 G4
RUNC WA7 11 G5
STHP PR8 27 J4
WAV L15 133 K3
WGNW/BIL/O WN5 77 H4
WKBY CH48 127 G6
Claremont Ter CSBY/BLUN L23 * 68 E4
Claremont Wy BEB CH63 150 C3
Claremount Dr BEB CH63 170 B1
Claremount Rd WAL/NB CH45 111 F1
Clarence Av WARRW/BUR WA5 140 E3
WDN WA8 139 F5
Clarence Cl STHEL WA9 * 104 A3
Clarence Rd RF/TRAN CH42 131 F6
STHP PR8 27 H3
WAL/EG CH44 111 K5
WARRS WA4 163 G1
Clarence St AIMK WN4 78 E5
GOL/RIS/CU WA3 92 B2
NEWLW WA12 105 K1
RUNC WA7 10 C3
VAUX/LVPD L3 9 H4
WARR WA1 17 K1
Clarence Ter RUNC WA7 10 D3
Clarendon Cl CL/PREN CH43 2 B6
RUNC WA7 178 C6
Clarendon Ct
WARRN/WOL WA2 123 F3
Clarendon Gv MGHL L31 62 A2
Clarendon Rd ALL/GAR L19 153 K5
LITH L21 81 G5
NPK/KEN L6 114 A1
WAL/EG CH44 111 K4
Clare Rd BTL L20 5 H7
Clares Farm Cl WARR WA1 144 E2
Claret Cl AIG/SPK L17 152 D2
Clare Wy WAL/NB CH45 111 F2
Claribel St TOX L8 133 F3
Clarke Av RF/TRAN CH42 150 D1
WARRS WA4 162 C1
Clarke Gdns WDN WA8 18 E6
Clarke's Crs ECCL WA10 102 D1
Clarkes Ter RUNC WA7 176 A6
Clarkfield Cl BRSC L40 39 F6
Classic Rd CLB/OSW/ST L13 114 E3
Clatterbridge Rd BEB CH63 169 K5
Claude Rd NPK/KEN L6 114 A1
Claude St WARR WA1 17 G2
Claughton Cl EHL/KEN L7 114 A6
Claughton Dr WAL/EG CH44 111 H4
Claughton Firs CL/PREN CH43 130 E5
Claughton Gn CL/PREN CH43 130 E4
Claughton Pl BIRK CH41 2 C5
Claughton Rd BIRK CH41 2 E5
Claughton St ECCL WA10 13 H5
Clavell Rd ALL/GAR L19 154 A3
Claverton Cl RUNC WA7 186 E1
Clay Brow Rd SKEL WN8 67 G1
Clay Cross Rd WLTN L25 154 C1
Claydon Ct HLWD L26 155 K2
Clayfield Cl BTL L20 5 H5
Clayford Crs DV/KA/FCH L14 115 F3
Clayford Pl DV/KA/FCH L14 115 F3
Clayford Rd DV/KA/FCH L14 115 G3
Clayford Wy DV/KA/FCH L14 115 G3
Clayhill NSTN CH64 182 A5
Clayhill Gn GTS/LS CH66 195 F2
Clayhill Gv GOL/RIS/CU WA3 93 J3
Clay La ECCL WA10 102 A2
WARRW/BUR WA5 121 J1
Claypole Cl EHL/KEN L7 133 H1
Clay St VAUX/LVPD L3 112 D3
Clayton Av GOL/RIS/CU WA3 93 F3
Clayton Crs RUNC WA7 10 B6
WDN WA8 18 B2
Clayton Gdns BRSC L40 38 E5
Clayton La WAL/EG CH44 111 G5
Clayton Ms SKEL WN8 55 K4
Clayton Pl CL/PREN CH43 2 C6
Clayton Rd GOL/RIS/CU WA3 125 H1
Clayton St CL/PREN CH43 2 C6
SKEL WN8 55 K4
Cleadon Cl KKBY L32 85 F4
Cleadon Rd KKBY L32 84 E4
Cleadon Wy WDN WA8 138 D5
Clearwater Cl EHL/KEN L7 113 K5
Cleary St BTL L20 4 C2
Clee Hill Rd RF/TRAN CH42 150 B2
Cleethorpes Rd RUNC WA7 178 B6
Cleeves Cl WARR WA1 17 G5
Clegge St WARRN/WOL WA2 16 E1

Clegg St EV L5 113 G3
SKEL WN8 55 K4
Clelland St WARRS WA4 143 F6
Clematis Rd NTHLY L27 136 B3
Clement Gdns VAUX/LVPD L3 112 E3
Clementina Rd CSBY/BLUN L23 68 C5
Clemmey Dr BTL L20 82 B5
Clengers Brow CHTN/BK PR9 23 J2
Clent Av MGHL L31 62 A4
Clent Gdns MGHL L31 62 B4
Clent Rd MGHL L31 62 A5
Cleopas St TOX L8 132 E5
Clevedon St TOX L8 133 F5
Cleveland Buildings CLVPS L1 8 E6
Cleveland Cl KKBY L32 72 B5
Cleveland Dr AIMK WN4 79 H5
GOL/RIS/CU WA3 92 E3
GTS/LS CH66 194 D3
Cleveland Rd
WARRN/WOL WA2 123 H4
Cleveland Sq CLVPS L1 8 E6
Cleveland St STHEL WA9 104 A4
Cleveley Pk CALD/MH L18 154 A2
Cleveley Rd CALD/MH L18 154 A2
HOY CH47 127 K1
Cleveleys Av CHTN/BK PR9 23 J1
WDN WA8 139 J6
Cleveleys Rd CHTN/BK PR9 23 J2
WARRW/BUR WA5 141 J5
The Cleves MGHL L31 62 C4
Cleve Wy FMBY L37 49 H3
Clieves Hills La ORM L39 52 C3
Clieves Rd KKBY L32 84 E2
Cliff Dr WAL/EG CH44 111 K2
Cliffe Rd NSTN CH64 192 A4
WARRS WA4 162 B4
Cliffe St WARR WA1 16 A4
WDN WA8 19 G1
Cliff La WARRS WA4 163 J1
WARRS WA4 164 A4
Clifford Rd STHP PR8 27 H6
WAL/EG CH44 111 H4
WARRW/BUR WA5 141 H5
Clifford St BIRK CH41 130 D1
VAUX/LVPD L3 9 H2
Cliff Rd CHTN/BK PR9 23 F3
WAL/EG CH44 111 G4
Cliff St EHL/KEN L7 114 A5
Clifton Av HLWD L26 155 H2
PS/BROM CH62 184 B4
Clifton Cl WARR WA1 144 B2
Clifton Ct RUNC WA7 10 A6
RUNC WA7 186 E1
Clifton Crs BIRK CH41 3 F5
FROD/HEL WA6 187 F6
Clifton Dr AIN/FAZ L10 83 G1
Clifton Gdns EP CH65 196 B6
Clifton Gv EV L5 * 113 G3
WAL/EG CH44 111 K3
Clifton La RUNC WA7 187 H4
Cliftonmill Mdw
GOL/RIS/CU WA3 92 A3
Clifton Rd AIMK WN4 78 B4
BIRK CH41 2 E7
FMBY L37 41 G6
NPK/KEN L6 114 B2
RUNC WA7 176 E6
STHP PR8 28 C1
WGNW/BIL/O WN5 77 G5
Clifton Rd East NPK/KEN L6 114 B2
Clifton St ALL/GAR L19 153 K5
ECCL WA10 13 H3
WARRS WA4 17 G7
Clifton Vls EP CH65 * 202 E3
Cliftonville Rd PR/KW L34 118 A1
WARR WA1 144 B3
Clincton Cl WDN WA8 157 F3
Clincton Vw WDN WA8 157 F3
Clinning Rd STHP PR8 27 H5
Clinton Pl WD/CROXPK L12 98 D6
Clinton Rd WD/CROXPK L12 98 D6
Clint Rd EHL/KEN L7 114 A6
Clint Wy EHL/KEN L7 114 A6
Clipper Vw PS/BROM CH62 151 G3
Clipsley Brook Vw
RNFD/HAY WA11 89 J5
Clipsley Crs RNFD/HAY WA11 90 A4
Clipsley La RNFD/HAY WA11 90 A5
Clive Av WARRN/WOL WA2 123 J6
Clive Ldg STHP PR8 27 G5
Clive Rd CL/PREN CH43 131 F5
STHP PR8 27 G6
Clock Face Rd STHEL WA9 120 A3
Clocktower St ECCL WA10 13 F6
The Cloisters CSBY/BLUN L23 68 E6
ECCL WA10 102 D1
FMBY L37 * 49 F2
Cloister Wy EP CH65 7 J5
Clorain Rd NWD/KWIPK L33 73 F6
Closeburn Av HES CH60 * 180 D1
The Close, Red Bank School
NEWLW WA12 * 106 E4
Close St STHEL WA9 103 G6
The Close CHTN/BK PR9 21 K6
CSBY/BLUN L23 68 E6
ECCL WA10 87 H6
GR/UP/WCH CH49 148 A1
HTWN L38 60 A4
PEN/TH CH61 148 A5
RF/TRAN CH42 150 C2
RNFD/HAY WA11 89 J6
STBRV L28 100 C6
WLT/FAZ L9 97 H1
Cloudberry Cl NTHLY L27 136 C3
Clough Av WARRN/WOL WA2 123 H5
Clough Gv AIMK WN4 78 E4
Clough Rd SPK/HALE L24 173 J1
The Clough AIMK WN4 78 C5
RUNC WA7 177 J4
Cloughton Rd BIRK CH41 2 D5
Clovelly Av STHEL WA9 120 B1
WARRW/BUR WA5 141 F2
Clovelly Dr STHP PR8 34 A1
Clovelly Gv RUNC WA7 188 A2
Clovelly Rd ANF/KKDL L4 113 K1
Clover Av FROD/HEL WA6 201 G2
HLWD L26 155 G1
Clover Ct RUNC WA7 188 A2
Cloverdale Dr AIMK WN4 91 H1
Cloverdale Rd WLTN L25 135 J2
Clover Dr BIRK CH41 110 E6
Cloverfield RUNC WA7 * 178 B6
Cloverfield Gdns GTS/LS CH66 195 G2
Clover Hey RNFD/HAY WA11 88 E4
Club St RNFD/HAY WA11 88 D2
Clucas Gdns ORM L39 45 J5
Clwyd Gv WD/CROXPK L12 99 F5
Clwyd St BIRK CH41 2 E4
WAL/NB CH45 95 G6
Clwyd Wy GTS/LS CH66 194 D3
Clyde Rd CLB/OSW/ST L13 114 C5
Clydesdale EP CH65 196 A6
Clydesdale Rd HOY CH47 127 G1
WAL/EG CH44 111 K2
WARRS WA4 162 C3
Clyde St BTL L20 96 E5
RF/TRAN CH42 150 E1
Clyffes Farm Cl BRSC L40 36 E2
Coach House Ct BRSC L40 38 E6
Coachmans Dr WD/CROXPK L12 99 J4
Coach Rd ORM L39 65 F6
PR/KW L34 86 C4
Coalbrookdale Rd NSTN CH64 182 A5
Coalgate La RAIN/WH L35 117 K5
Coalpit La CH/BCN CH1 202 C6
Coal Pit La ORM L39 65 J3
Coalport Wk STHEL WA9 118 E1
Coal St CLVPS L1 9 G3
Coalville Rd RNFD/HAY WA11 89 G5
Coastal Dr WAL/NB CH45 94 D5
Coastal Rd STHP PR8 33 G3
Coastgaurd La NSTN CH64 181 G6
Coastline Ms CHTN/BK PR9 * 23 J1
Cobb Av LITH L21 81 J5
The Cobbles HLWD L26 155 G1
Cobblestone Cnr ALL/GAR L19 153 H4
Cobbs La WARRS WA4 162 D3
Cobden Av BIRK CH41 131 J6
Cobden Ct BIRK CH41 131 J6
Cobden Pl RF/TRAN CH42 131 J6
Cobden Rd CHTN/BK PR9 28 C1
Cobden St NEWLW WA12 106 D1
NPK/KEN L6 113 H4
WARRN/WOL WA2 16 E1
WLTN L25 154 C1
Cobden Vw WLTN L25 154 C1
Cobham Av WLT/FAZ L9 82 C5
Cobham Rd MOR/LEA CH46 128 E1
Coburg Whf VAUX/LVPD L3 132 B3
Cochrane St EV L5 113 H2
Cockburn St TOX L8 132 E5
Cockerell Cl ANF/KKDL L4 * 97 H6
Cockerham Wy NG/CROX L11 84 A6
Cockhedge La WARR WA1 16 E4
Cockhedge Wy WARR WA1 16 E4
Cocklade La SPK/HALE L24 174 E4
Cock Lane Ends WDN WA8 * 157 G6
Cockle Dick's La CHTN/BK PR9 23 G3
Cockshead Rd WLTN L25 135 J4
Cockshead Wy WLTN L25 135 J3
Cockspur St VAUX/LVPD L3 8 D2
Cockspur St West VAUX/LVPD L3 8 C2
Coerton Rd WLT/FAZ L9 82 E4
The Cokers BEB CH63 150 D3
Colbern Cl MGHL L31 71 H1
Colbrooke Rd AIG/SPK L17 133 G6
Colburne Cl BRSC L40 39 F4
Colby Cl CHLDW L16 135 F1
Colchester Rd STHP PR8 28 C5
Colden Cl WD/CROXPK L12 99 J6
Coldstone Dr AIMK WN4 78 C5
Coldstream Cl
WARRN/WOL WA2 124 A3
Coldstream Dr GTS/LS CH66 194 C4
Cole Av NEWLW WA12 106 C1
Colebrook Cl GOL/RIS/CU WA3 125 J3
Cole Crs ORM L39 53 G5
Coleman Dr GR/UP/WCH CH49 128 C6
Colemere Cl WARR WA1 124 D6
Colemere Ct EP CH65 6 C1
Colemere Dr PEN/TH CH61 148 E5
Coleridge Av ECCL WA10 12 B3
Coleridge Dr PS/BROM CH62 151 F4
Coleridge Gv WDN WA8 157 K2
Coleridge St BTL L20 4 B3
NPK/KEN L6 113 K4
Colesborne Rd NG/CROX L11 98 E3
Coles Crs CSBY/BLUN L23 69 J3
Coleshill Rd NG/CROX L11 98 C2
Cole St CL/PREN CH43 2 C5
Colette Rd AIN/FAZ L10 84 A4
Coleus Cl WLT/FAZ L9 97 K1
Colin Cl HUY L36 116 C6
Colindale Rd CHLDW L16 135 F2
Colin Dr VAUX/LVPD L3 112 E2
Colinmander Gdns ORM L39 53 G2
Colinton SKEL WN8 57 G6
Colinton St WAV L15 133 K1
Coliseum Wy EP CH65 203 H2
College Av CSBY/BLUN L23 68 E6
FMBY L37 48 E1
College Cl CL/PREN CH43 129 J3
FMBY L37 48 D1
STHP PR8 27 H4
WAL/NB CH45 110 E1
WARR WA1 17 H4
WARRN/WOL WA2 124 C5
College Ct WD/CROXPK L12 114 E2
College Dr BEB CH63 151 F4
College Flds HUY L36 116 E6
College La CLVPS L1 8 E5
College Pth FMBY L37 40 D6
College Rd CSBY/BLUN L23 68 E6
SKEL WN8 57 K4
College Rd North
CSBY/BLUN L23 68 D4
College St ECCL WA10 13 G4
College St North NPK/KEN L6 9 J1
College St South NPK/KEN L6 9 K1
College Vw BTL L20 4 E7
Collier's Rw RUNC WA7 176 B6
Collier St RUNC WA7 10 B2
Colliery Green Cl NSTN CH64 191 K4
Colliery Green Ct NSTN CH64 191 K4
Colliery Green Dr NSTN CH64 191 K4
Collingham Gn GTS/LS CH66 194 E4
Collingwood Rd BEB CH63 170 D1
NEWLW WA12 106 B2
Collin Rd CL/PREN CH43 130 B1
Collins Cl BTL L20 81 J6
Collins Green La
WARRW/BUR WA5 105 J4
Collin St WARRW/BUR WA5 142 B4
Colmore Av BEB CH63 170 B4
Colmore Rd NG/CROX L11 98 C3
Colne Dr STHEL WA9 104 B6
Colne Rd WARRW/BUR WA5 121 K1
The Colonnades VAUX/LVPD L3 * 8 C7
Colorado Cl WARRW/BUR WA5 141 K2
Colquitt St CLVPS L1 9 G6
Coltart Rd TOX L8 133 G3
Colton Rd WLTN L25 135 G2
Columban Cl NTHTN L30 70 B6
Columbia Rd ANF/KKDL L4 97 J3
PR/KW L34 118 A1
Columbine Cl WDN WA8 138 A5
Columbine Wy STHEL WA9 105 F6
Columbus Dr PEN/TH CH61 167 J2
Columbus Quay VAUX/LVPD L3 132 D6
Columbus Wy LITH L21 * 81 J4
Column Rd WKBY CH48 146 E2
Colville Ct WARRN/WOL WA2 123 G4
Colville Rd WAL/EG CH44 111 G3
Colville St WAV L15 133 K1
Colwall Cl NWD/KWIPK L33 85 F1
Colwall Rd NWD/KWIPK L33 85 F1
Colwell Cl DV/KA/FCH L14 100 A6
Colwell Rd DV/KA/FCH L14 116 A1
Colworth Rd SPK/HALE L24 173 G1
Colwyn Cl EP CH65 196 C6
WARRW/BUR WA5 122 E5
Colwyn Rd CLB/OSW/ST L13 114 D5
Colwyn St BIRK CH41 130 D1
Colyton Av STHEL WA9 120 B2
Combermere St TOX L8 * 132 E3
WAV L15 114 B6
Comely Av WAL/EG CH44 111 J3
Comely Bank Rd WAL/EG CH44 111 K3
Comer Gdns MGHL L31 62 A4
Comfrey Gv HLWD L26 155 H1
Commercial Rd EV L5 112 E1
PS/BROM CH62 171 G2
Common Field Rd
GR/UP/WCH CH49 148 E2
Common La CHTN/BK PR9 25 F3
WARRS WA4 162 D1
Common Rd NEWLW WA12 105 J2
Common St NEWLW WA12 105 J2
STHEL WA9 * 103 F6
Commutation Rw
VAUX/LVPD L3 8 E2
Company's Cl RUNC WA7 186 C1
Compass Cl RUNC WA7 188 C2
Compton Cl RNFD/HAY WA11 90 B4
Compton Pl EP CH65 6 C4
Compton Rd BIRK CH41 110 D6
NPK/KEN L6 113 J3
STHP PR8 27 J4
Compton Wk BTL L20 4 D3
Compton Wy HLWD L26 155 H5
Comus St VAUX/LVPD L3 113 F4
Concert St CLVPS L1 9 F6
Concorde Pl WARRN/WOL WA2 123 K5
Concordia Av
GR/UP/WCH CH49 129 H4
The Concourse WKBY CH48 * 127 F6
Concourse Wy STHEL WA9 104 D3
Condor Cl ALL/GAR L19 154 A5
Condron Rd North LITH L21 81 K2
Condron Rd South LITH L21 81 K2
Conery Cl FROD/HEL WA6 199 K5
Coney Crs CSBY/BLUN L23 69 J4
Coney Gv RUNC WA7 188 A2
Coney La HUY L36 136 C2
Coney Wk GR/UP/WCH CH49 128 E3
Conifer Cl GTS/LS CH66 202 E3
NWD/KWIPK L33 72 D4
WLT/FAZ L9 97 K2
Conifer Ct FMBY L37 49 F3
Conifer Gv WARRW/BUR WA5 141 G2
The Conifers MGHL L31 62 A4
Coningsby Dr WAL/NB CH45 111 G3
Coningsby Rd ANF/KKDL L4 97 J6
Coniston Av AIMK WN4 79 G5
BEB CH63 183 K2
CL/PREN CH43 129 K4
PR/KW L34 118 B1
WAL/NB CH45 94 E6
WARRW/BUR WA5 140 E5
Coniston Cl GTS/LS CH66 184 D6
NWD/KWIPK L33 72 C5
RUNC WA7 187 G1
WLT/FAZ L9 82 E4
Coniston Dr FROD/HEL WA6 201 G1
Coniston Gv RNFD/HAY WA11 88 D4
Coniston Rd FMBY L37 48 D3
MGHL L31 62 C5
NSTN CH64 191 K3
PEN/TH CH61 148 A5
Coniston St EV L5 113 J1
Coniston Wy RNFD/HAY WA11 66 B5
Conleach Rd SPK/HALE L24 173 K2
Connaught Av WARR WA1 143 H2
Connaught Dr NEWLW WA12 106 C3
Connaught Rd EHL/KEN L7 113 J5
Connaught Wy BIRK CH41 130 D1
Connolly Av BTL L20 5 K2
Conroy Wy NEWLW WA12 106 C4
Consett Rd STHEL WA9 119 F1
Constables Cl RUNC WA7 177 K4
Constance St ECCL WA10 12 A7
VAUX/LVPD L3 9 J2
Constance Wy WDN WA8 158 B6
Constantine Av HES CH60 168 A4
Convent Cl ALL/GAR L19 153 H4
ORM L39 53 H3
RF/TRAN CH42 131 G5
Conville Bvd BEB CH63 150 D3
Conway Av WARRW/BUR WA5 123 F5
Conway Cl BEB CH63 150 C6
NWD/KWIPK L33 72 C4
WARRW/BUR WA5 141 G3
Conway Crs WGNW/BIL/O WN5 77 H3
Conway Dr BIRK CH41 2 D4
NEWLW WA12 106 E2
WGNW/BIL/O WN5 77 J4
Conway Rd AIMK WN4 79 K4
Conway St BIRK CH41 2 C3
EV L5 113 G2
Conwy Dr NPK/KEN L6 113 K2
Conyers Av STHP PR8 27 G4
Coogee Av WARRW/BUR WA5 141 F2
Cook Av RNFD/HAY WA11 90 D4
Cooke St AIMK WN4 78 E3
Cook Rd MOR/LEA CH46 110 B3
Cooks Ct CSBY/BLUN L23 * 68 D4
Cookson Rd LITH L21 81 H5
Cookson St CLVPS L1 132 D2
Cook St BIRK CH41 2 D6
CLVP L2 8 D4
EP CH65 6 E3
RAIN/WH L35 118 B2
Coombe Dr RUNC WA7 176 C5
Coombe Pk GTS/LS CH66 195 F3
Coombe Rd PEN/TH CH61 148 B4
Cooperage Cl TOX L8 132 D5
Cooper Av NEWLW WA12 105 K2
WARRN/WOL WA2 123 H5
Cooper Av North
CALD/MH L18 153 H2
Cooper Av South
CALD/MH L18 153 H2
Cooper Cl ALL/GAR L19 153 H3
Cooper La RNFD/HAY WA11 90 B5
Cooper's La NWD/KWIPK L33 85 J5
Coopers Pl WARRS WA4 162 B2
Cooper St ECCL WA10 13 F5
RUNC WA7 10 D3
WDN WA8 18 E1
Copeland Cl PEN/TH CH61 167 J1
Copeland Gv RUNC WA7 187 H2
Copeland Rd WARRS WA4 162 A1
Copperas Hl VAUX/LVPD L3 9 H3
Copperas St ECCL WA10 13 F6
Copperfield Cl
GOL/RIS/CU WA3 124 E2
TOX L8 132 E4
Copperwood RUNC WA7 178 B4
Copperwood Dr RAIN/WH L35 118 A5
Coppice Cl CL/PREN CH43 129 J3
Coppice Crs HUY L36 117 F3
Coppice Gra MOR/LEA CH46 128 D2
Coppice Gn CHNE CH2 198 D5
WARRW/BUR WA5 122 A6
Coppice Gv
GR/UP/WCH CH49 * 147 K1
Coppice La RAIN/WH L35 136 E2
Coppice Leys FMBY L37 48 E2
The Coppice NPK/KEN L6 114 A1
PR/KW L34 100 D2
WAL/NB CH45 95 G6
Coppins Cl FROD/HEL WA6 199 J6
The Coppins WARRN/WOL WA2 123 J5
Copple House La AIN/FAZ L10 83 K4
Coppull Rd MGHL L31 62 A3
Copse Gv PEN/TH CH61 148 B4
The Copse CALD/MH L18 134 E4
NEWLW WA12 106 A1
RUNC WA7 187 K1
Copthorne Rd KKBY L32 84 A1
Copy La NTHTN L30 70 E6
Coral Av HUY L36 116 D4
STHEL WA9 103 H6
Coral Cl KKBY L32 84 B1
Coral Dr BTL L20 5 F4
Coralin Wy AIMK WN4 78 E2
Coral Rdg CL/PREN CH43 130 A3
Coral St CLB/OSW/ST L13 114 E6
Corbet Av WARRN/WOL WA2 142 E1
Corbet St WARRN/WOL WA2 * 142 E1
Corbridge Rd CHLDW L16 134 D3
Corbyn St WAL/EG CH44 112 A6
Corfu St BIRK CH41 * 2 C5
Corinthian Av CLB/OSW/ST L13 114 E3
Corinthian St LITH L21 81 G4
RF/TRAN CH42 * 150 E1
Corinto St TOX L8 132 E4
Cormorant Dr RUNC WA7 10 A5
Cornbrook SKEL WN8 57 G6
Corncroft Rd PR/KW L34 100 D2
Corndale Rd CALD/MH L18 134 B5
Cornelian Gv AIMK WN4 78 E4
Cornelius Dr PEN/TH CH61 148 C6
Cornel Wy HUY L36 136 C1
Corner Brook STBRV L28 99 K6
Cornerhouse La WDN WA8 138 C6
Cornett Rd WLT/FAZ L9 82 E4
Corney St EHL/KEN L7 133 H2
Cornfield Cl GTS/LS CH66 202 D2
Cornfields Cl ALL/GAR L19 153 K5
Cornflower Wy
MOR/LEA CH46 110 A5
Cornforth Wy WDN WA8 138 E6
Cornhill CLVPS L1 8 E7
Cornice Rd CLB/OSW/ST L13 114 E3
Corniche Rd PS/BROM CH62 151 G5
Corn St TOX L8 132 D4
Cornubia Rd WDN WA8 19 H5
Cornwall Av RUNC WA7 10 D5
Cornwall Cl PS/BROM CH62 151 G3
Cornwall Dr CL/PREN CH43 149 K2
Cornwallis St CLVPS L1 9 G7
Cornwall Rd WDN WA8 139 G6
Cornwall St STHEL WA9 104 B3
WARR WA1 17 K1
Cornwall Wy STHP PR8 41 H1
Cornwood Cl HUY L36 135 J2
Corona Av MGHL L31 62 A2
Corona Rd CLB/OSW/ST L13 114 E3
CSBY/WL L22 80 E2
PS/BROM CH62 151 H5
Coronation Av DV/KA/FCH L14 115 J4
FMBY L37 49 G3
WAL/NB CH45 95 H6
WARRS WA4 163 G1
Coronation Buildings
WAL/NB CH45 * 111 H2
Coronation Dr CSBY/BLUN L23 68 E6
DV/KA/FCH L14 115 J4
FROD/HEL WA6 187 G6
NEWLW WA12 106 E4
PS/BROM CH62 171 F2
RAIN/WH L35 117 J4
RNFD/HAY WA11 91 F4
WARRW/BUR WA5 141 G5
WDN WA8 157 G3
Coronation Rd CSBY/BLUN L23 68 E6
ECCL WA10 87 K5
EP CH65 6 D7
HOY CH47 126 E3
MGHL L31 62 B4
RUNC WA7 11 F6
RUNC WA7 188 E1
Coronation St AIMK WN4 78 C3
Coronation Vls
WD/CROXPK L12 * 99 H6
Coronation Wk STHP PR8 14 C5
WGNW/BIL/O WN5 77 G5
Coroner's La WDN WA8 139 F4
Coronet Rd NG/CROX L11 99 G2
Coronet Wy WDN WA8 157 G3
Corporation Rd BIRK CH41 130 E1
Corporation St ECCL WA10 13 G4
Corridor Rd EP CH65 197 G4
Corrie Dr BEB CH63 170 B1
Corsewall St EHL/KEN L7 133 J1
Corsican Gdns STHEL WA9 118 E1
Cortsway GR/UP/WCH CH49 129 F4
Cortsway West
GR/UP/WCH CH49 128 E4
Corwen Cl MOR/LEA CH46 129 G2
WARRW/BUR WA5 122 E6
Corwen Crs DV/KA/FCH L14 115 K5
Corwen Dr NTHTN L30 70 D5
Corwen Rd ANF/KKDL L4 98 A5
HOY CH47 127 H2
Cosgrove Cl NPK/KEN L6 98 B6
Cossack Av WARRN/WOL WA2 123 H6
Costain St BTL L20 96 E5
Cote Lea Ct RUNC WA7 * 187 J1
Cotham St ECCL WA10 13 G5
Cotsford Cl HUY L36 116 C3
Cotsford Pl HUY L36 116 C3
Cotsford Rd HUY L36 116 C3
Cotsford Wy HUY L36 116 C3
Cotswold Av GOL/RIS/CU WA3 92 E5
Cotswold Gv STHEL WA9 104 E2
Cotswold Rd RF/TRAN CH42 150 B2
WARRN/WOL WA2 123 H4
Cotswolds Crs HLWD L26 * 155 H4
Cotswold St EHL/KEN L7 113 K5
Cottage Cl BEB CH63 183 K2
KKBY L32 84 D4
NSTN CH64 191 K2
ORM L39 53 H1
Cottage Dr East HES CH60 180 E2
Cottage Dr West HES CH60 180 E2
Cottage La HES CH60 180 E2
ORM L39 45 H5
Cottage Ms ORM L39 45 H6
Cottage Pl STHEL WA9 * 120 A3
Cottage St BIRK CH41 2 D2
Cottam Dr WARRN/WOL WA2 124 C4
Cottenham St NPK/KEN L6 113 K4
Cotterdale Cl STHEL WA9 120 A1
WARRW/BUR WA5 141 G2
Cotterill RUNC WA7 177 G5
Cotterill Dr WARR WA1 144 B2
Cottesbrook Cl NG/CROX L11 98 E2
Cottesbrook Pl NG/CROX L11 98 E2
Cottesbrook Rd NG/CROX L11 98 E2
Cottesmore Dr HES CH60 * 168 D5
Cottesmore Wy
GOL/RIS/CU WA3 92 C2
Cotton Dr ORM L39 45 H5
Cotton La RUNC WA7 177 G5
Cotton St VAUX/LVPD L3 112 D3
Cottonwood AIG/SPK L17 132 E6
Cottrell Cl ALL/GAR L19 172 B1
Cotty's Brow CHTN/BK PR9 23 H2
Coudray Rd CHTN/BK PR9 23 G4
Coulport Cl DV/KA/FCH L14 116 A3
Coulsdon Pl TOX L8 133 F5
Coulthard Rd RF/TRAN CH42 151 F3
Coulton Rd WDN WA8 139 K6
Coultshead Av WGNW/BIL/O WN5 77 H3
Council Av AIMK WN4 79 G6
Council St RAIN/WH L35 118 C2
Countess Pk NG/CROX L11 99 G3
Countisbury Dr CHLDW L16 135 F3
County Dr ECCL WA10 12 D7
County Rd ANF/KKDL L4 97 H5
KKBY L32 72 D6
ORM L39 45 H6
Court Av HLWD L26 155 K2
Courtenay Av CSBY/WL L22 80 D1
WAL/EG CH44 111 G4
Courtenay Rd CSBY/WL L22 80 D1
HOY CH47 127 F2
WLTN L25 135 G5
Courtfield ORM L39 45 H4
Courtfields Cl WD/CROXPK L12 115 F2
Courtgreen ORM L39 45 H4
Court Hey Av DV/KA/FCH L14 116 A5
Court Hey Dr CHLDW L16 115 K6
Court Hey Rd CHLDW L16 115 K6
Courthope Rd ANF/KKDL L4 97 K4
Courtland Rd CALD/MH L18 134 C4
Court Ms CHTN/BK PR9 * 23 J4
Courtney Av WAL/EG CH44 111 G4

Courtney Rd RF/TRAN CH42 151 F3
Court Rd CHTN/BK PR9 15 H2
The Court BEB CH63 * 170 C1
NSTN CH64 192 A3
STBRV L28 * 100 C6
Covent Gdn CLVP L2 8 C4
Coventry Av GTS/LS CH66 202 C3
Coventry Rd WAV L15 134 B3
Coventry St BIRK CH41 2 E5
Coverdale Av RAIN/WH L35 119 F5
Coverdale Cl
WARRW/BUR WA5 141 G2
Covertside WKBY CH48 146 E1
Cowan Dr NPK/KEN L6 113 J3
Cowanway WDN WA8 138 E5
Cowdell St WARRN/WOL WA2 142 E2
Cowdrey Av CL/PREN CH43 110 C6
Cow Hey La RUNC WA7 186 D2
Cowley Cl GR/UP/WCH CH49 * 128 E4
Cowley Ct ECCL WA10 * 12 E3
Cowley Hill La ECCL WA10 12 D1
Cowley Rd ANF/KKDL L4 97 H4
Cowley St ECCL WA10 13 G2
Cowper Rd CLB/OSW/ST L13 115 F5
Cowper St BTL L20 4 B1
STHEL WA9 * 104 A4
Cowper Wy HUY L36 117 G6
Coyford Dr CHTN/BK PR9 23 J1
Coylton Av RAIN/WH L35 119 F5
Crab La WARRN/WOL WA2 124 D4
Crab St ECCL WA10 13 F3
Crabtree Cl BRSC L40 38 D5
NEWLW WA12 106 E2
NTHLY L27 136 A4
Crabtree Fold RUNC WA7 178 B5
Crabtree La BRSC L40 38 C4
KNUT WA16 165 H4
Cradley WDN WA8 157 H1
Crag Gv RNFD/HAY WA11 88 E2
Craigburn Rd CLB/OSW/ST L13 114 C1
Craig Gdns GTS/LS CH66 195 H2
Craighurst Rd WLTN L25 135 H2
Craigleigh Gv PS/BROM CH62 184 C3
Craigmore Rd CALD/MH L18 153 H2
Craigside Av WD/CROXPK L12 98 E6
Craigs Rd CLB/OSW/ST L13 114 C1
Craigwood Wy HUY L36 116 B4
Craine Cl ANF/KKDL L4 97 K5
Cramond Av CALD/MH L18 134 B4
Cranage Cl RUNC WA7 177 G6
Cranberry Cl ECCL WA10 12 E2
Cranborne Av HOY CH47 108 C6
WARRS WA4 162 A2
Cranborne Rd WAV L15 133 J2
Cranbourne Av BIRK CH41 130 C2
MOR/LEA CH46 128 E2
Cranbrook Av AIMK WN4 79 F5
Crane Av STHEL WA9 120 B1
Cranehurst Rd ANF/KKDL L4 97 K3
Cranes La BRSC L40 46 D4
Cranfield Rd CSBY/BLUN L23 69 H4
Cranford Cl PS/BROM CH62 184 C3
Cranford Ct WARR WA1 * 144 D1
Cranford Rd ALL/GAR L19 153 J3
Cranford St WAL/EG CH44 111 J5
Cranham Av GOL/RIS/CU WA3 93 F4
Crank Hl RNFD/HAY WA11 76 B5
Crank Rd RNFD/HAY WA11 76 C2
RNFD/HAY WA11 87 K4
Cranleigh Cl WARRS WA4 162 A4
Cranleigh Pl WLTN L25 135 H3
Cranleigh Rd WLTN L25 135 H4
Cranmer St EV L5 112 E2
Cranmore Av CSBY/BLUN L23 81 F1
Cranshaw Av STHEL WA9 120 B4
Cranshaw La WDN WA8 139 G4
Cranston Cl ECCL WA10 87 J6
Cranston Rd NWD/KWIPK L33 85 H1
Cranswick Gn GTS/LS CH66 195 F4
Crantock Cl HLWD L26 155 J3
NG/CROX L11 * 99 G1
Crantock Gv ECCL WA10 87 K5
Cranwell Cl AIN/FAZ L10 83 F1
Cranwell Rd GR/UP/WCH CH49 128 C6
WLTN L25 135 H2
Craven Av GOL/RIS/CU WA3 93 F4
Craven Cl BIRK CH41 2 D4
Craven Ct WARRN/WOL WA2 123 F3
Craven Lea WD/CROXPK L12 99 J2
Craven Rd RAIN/WH L35 118 E4
WD/CROXPK L12 115 G1
Craven St BIRK CH41 2 C5
VAUX/LVPD L3 9 H2
Cravenwood Rd HLWD L26 155 J4
Crawford Av CALD/MH L18 134 A4
MGHL L31 61 K4
WDN WA8 157 G2
Crawford Cl STHEL WA9 120 B3
WD/CROXPK L12 99 H6
Crawford Dr WAV L15 114 E6
Crawford Pk CALD/MH L18 134 A6
Crawford Pl RUNC WA7 186 E1
Crawford Rd SKEL WN8 67 F5
Crawford St STHEL WA9 120 C3
Crawford Wy CLB/OSW/ST L13 114 C5
Crawley Av
WARRN/WOL WA2 * 123 G4
Crawley Cl WLTN L25 155 G3
Crediton Av CHTN/BK PR9 20 E6
Crediton Cl NG/CROX L11 84 B6
The Creek WAL/NB CH45 94 E5
Cremorne Hey STBRV L28 100 B6
Crescent Av AIMK WN4 79 F5
FMBY L37 48 E4
Crescent Ct LITH L21 81 H5
Crescent Dr FROD/HEL WA6 199 J6
Crescent Gn ORM L39 53 F4
Crescent Rd CSBY/BLUN L23 68 C4
EP CH65 7 F3
LITH L21 81 H5
STHP PR8 27 G4
WAL/EG CH44 111 J3
WLT/FAZ L9 97 K1
The Crescent BEB CH63 150 D6
CHTN/BK PR9 24 A2
CSBY/BLUN L23 69 H3
CSBY/WL L22 81 F2
EP CH65 195 J4
GR/UP/WCH CH49 128 E6
HUY L36 117 G5
LYMM WA13 165 G1
MGHL L31 71 F2
PEN/TH CH61 148 C5
RAIN/WH L35 118 B3
WKBY CH48 146 B1
The Cresents RAIN/WH L35 118 C3
Cressbrook Rd WARRS WA4 162 B3
Cressingham Rd WAL/NB CH45 95 H5
Cressington Av RF/TRAN CH42 150 C2
Cressington Esp ALL/GAR L19 153 G5
Cressington Gdns EP CH65 6 D2
Cresswell Cl HLWD L26 155 K2
WARRW/BUR WA5 122 D5
Cresswell St NPK/KEN L6 113 J3
Cresta Dr RUNC WA7 186 C1
Cresttor Rd WLTN L25 135 G6
Creswell St ECCL WA10 12 C5
Cretan Rd WAV L15 133 J2
Crewe Gn GR/UP/WCH CH49 148 D1
Criccieth Ct EP CH65 203 H1
Cricket Pth FMBY L37 41 F6
STHP PR8 27 G4
Cricklade Cl BTL L20 4 C3
Criftin Cl GTS/LS CH66 202 A1
Cringles Dr RAIN/WH L35 136 D2
Crispin Rd NTHLY L27 136 A4
Crispin St ECCL WA10 12 D6
Critchley Rd SPK/HALE L24 174 B3
Critchley Wy NWD/KWIPK L33 72 E4
Croasdale Dr RUNC WA7 187 H2
Crockett's Wk ECCL WA10 87 J6
Crockleford Av STHP PR8 28 B4
Crocus Av BIRK CH41 130 C1
Crocus Gdns STHEL WA9 104 E6
Crocus St EV L5 97 F6
Croesmere Dr GTS/LS CH66 202 B1
Croft Av BRSC L40 39 F6
GOL/RIS/CU WA3 92 A1
PS/BROM CH62 170 E4
Croft Av East PS/BROM CH62 171 F3
Croft Cl CL/PREN CH43 130 B5
Croft Ct EP CH65 196 D6
Croft Dr GR/UP/WCH CH49 129 F2
WKBY CH48 146 D5
Croft Dr East WKBY CH48 146 E5
Croft Dr West WKBY CH48 146 D4
Croft Edge CL/PREN CH43 130 E6
Croft End STHEL WA9 104 D4
Croften Dr NSTN CH64 191 K4
Crofters Cl GTS/LS CH66 202 C2
Crofters Heath GTS/LS CH66 202 C2
The Crofters
GR/UP/WCH CH49 128 E5
Croft Fld MGHL L31 62 C6
Croft Gdns WARRS WA4 163 F4
Croft Gn PS/BROM CH62 171 F2
Croft Heys ORM L39 53 F4
Croft La PS/BROM CH62 171 F4
WLT/FAZ L9 83 G4
Crofton Cl WARRS WA4 163 H6
Crofton Crs CLB/OSW/ST L13 115 F4
Crofton Rd CLB/OSW/ST L13 115 F4
RF/TRAN CH42 131 H6
RUNC WA7 176 B4
Croftside WARR WA1 144 E2
Croftson Av ORM L39 45 K4
Croft St GOL/RIS/CU WA3 * 92 B3
WDN WA8 18 C7
Croftsway HES CH60 167 H5
The Croft GR/UP/WCH CH49 148 A1
MGHL L31 61 K2
RUNC WA7 177 J4
STBRV L28 * 100 A5
WD/CROXPK L12 99 F6
Croftwood Gv RAIN/WH L35 118 A5
Cromarty Rd CLB/OSW/ST L13 114 D5
WAL/EG CH44 111 F3
Cromdale Gv STHEL WA9 104 C3
Cromdale Wy
WARRW/BUR WA5 141 F3
Cromer Dr WAL/NB CH45 111 G2
Cromer Rd AIG/SPK L17 153 F2
HOY CH47 127 F3
STHP PR8 27 F5
Cromer Wy HLWD L26 155 J5
Cromfield ORM L39 53 G3
Cromford Rd HUY L36 116 E2
Crompton Dr
WARRN/WOL WA2 123 G1
WD/CROXPK L12 99 J2
Cromptons La CALD/MH L18 134 E4
Crompton St EV L5 113 F2
Cromwell Av
WARRW/BUR WA5 122 C5
Cromwell Av South
WARRW/BUR WA5 141 K5
Cromwell Cl NEWLW WA12 106 A1
ORM L39 53 G3
Cromwell Ct WARR WA1 16 B5
Cromwell Rd ANF/KKDL L4 97 H3
EP CH65 6 E4
Cromwell St WDN WA8 158 B5
Crondall Gv WAV L15 134 C2
Cronton Av MOR/LEA CH46 109 J4
Cronton La RAIN/WH L35 118 D6
WDN WA8 138 E4
Cronton Park Cl WDN WA8 138 B3
Cronton Rd RAIN/WH L35 136 E2
WAV L15 134 B4
Cronulla Dr WARRW/BUR WA5 140 E2
Crookall St AIMK WN4 79 H5
Crookhurst Av
WGNW/BIL/O WN5 77 G3
Croome Dr WKBY CH48 146 D1
Croppers Hl ECCL WA10 12 D6
Cropper's La ORM L39 54 A4
Croppers Rd WARRN/WOL WA2 124 B4
Cropper St CLVPS L1 9 G5
Cropton Rd FMBY L37 49 F2
Crosby Av WARRW/BUR WA5 142 D1
Crosby Cl GR/UP/WCH CH49 129 G3
Crosby Gn WD/CROXPK L12 98 E6
Crosby Gv ECCL WA10 103 F4
NSTN CH64 183 J6
Crosby Rd STHP PR8 27 G4
Crosby Rd North CSBY/WL L22 81 F2
Crosby Rd South CSBY/WL L22 81 F3
Crosender Rd CSBY/BLUN L23 68 D6
Crosfield Cl EHL/KEN L7 114 A6
Crosfield Rd EHL/KEN L7 114 A6
RAIN/WH L35 118 B3
WAL/EG CH44 111 J4
Crosfield St WARR WA1 16 B4
Crosfield Wk EHL/KEN L7 114 A6
Crosgrove Rd ANF/KKDL L4 98 A4
Crosland Rd KKBY L32 85 F2
Crossacre Rd WLTN L25 135 J2
Cross Barn La HTWN L38 60 A5
Crossdale Rd CSBY/BLUN L23 68 D6
PS/BROM CH62 184 A1
Crossdale Wy RNFD/HAY WA11 88 E2
Crossens Wy CHTN/BK PR9 21 F5
Cross Farm Rd STHEL WA9 104 A4
Crossfield Rd SKEL WN8 56 E5
Crossfield St STHEL WA9 13 J5
Crossford Rd DV/KA/FCH L14 116 A1
Crossgates WDN WA8 140 A6
Cross Green Cl FMBY L37 49 G3
Crosshall Brow BRSC L40 54 C1
Crosshall St CLVPS L1 8 E3
Cross Hey LITH L21 81 J1
MGHL L31 * 71 H2
Cross Hey Av CL/PREN CH43 130 A4
Cross Hillocks La RAIN/WH L35 137 H6
The Crossings NEWLW WA12 106 C2
Cross La BEB CH63 170 B1
FROD/HEL WA6 199 J1
NEWLW WA12 106 B2
NSTN CH64 191 K4
ORM L39 43 K2
RAIN/WH L35 117 K3
WAL/NB CH45 110 D2
WARRS WA4 163 F1
Cross La South
GOL/RIS/CU WA3 125 F1
Crossley Av GTS/LS CH66 195 H3
Crossley Dr HES CH60 167 H5
WAV L15 134 B1
Crossley Rd ECCL WA10 103 F5
Crossley St WARR WA1 17 F3
Cross Meanygate
KIRK/FR/WA PR4 31 H2
Cross Pit La RNFD/HAY WA11 75 G3
Cross St BIRK CH41 3 H4
CSBY/WL L22 80 E3
ECCL WA10 13 G5
GOL/RIS/CU WA3 92 B4
NSTN CH64 191 K1
PR/KW L34 101 K6
PS/BROM CH62 * 151 G6
RUNC WA7 * 10 D3
STHP PR8 14 E7
WARRN/WOL WA2 142 E2
WDN WA8 19 F2
The Cross HTWN L38 59 K4
LYMM WA13 145 K6
MOR/LEA CH46 * 129 F1
PS/BROM CH62 151 G5
Crossvale Rd HUY L36 116 E6
Crossway CL/PREN CH43 130 B1
WDN WA8 157 J3
Crossway Cl AIMK WN4 79 K4
Crossways PS/BROM CH62 171 F2
The Crossway BEB CH63 182 C3
Crosswood Crs HUY L36 116 C4
Crosthwaite Av
PS/BROM CH62 184 C3
Croston Av RAIN/WH L35 118 D2
Croston Cl WDN WA8 138 B5
Croston's Brow CHTN/BK PR9 23 H2
Crouchley Hall Ms
LYMM WA13 * 165 G2
Crouchley La LYMM WA13 165 G2
Crouch St EV L5 113 J1
STHEL WA9 * 104 B5
Croughton Rd CHNE CH2 203 K5
GTS/LS CH66 195 J1
Crowe Av WARRN/WOL WA2 123 H4
Crowland Cl CHTN/BK PR9 28 D1
Crowland St CHTN/BK PR9 28 D1
Crowland Wy FMBY L37 49 H3
Crow La SKEL WN8 57 H2
Crow La East NEWLW WA12 106 C1
Crow La West NEWLW WA12 106 B1
Crowmarsh Cl
GR/UP/WCH CH49 * 129 G5
Crown Acres Rd WLTN L25 155 F2
Crown Av WDN WA8 157 G3
Crown Cl FMBY L37 49 G3
Crown Fields Cl NEWLW WA12 91 G6
Crown Gdns NEWLW WA12 106 B1
Crown Ga RUNC WA7 177 J6
Crown Park Dr NEWLW WA12 106 B1
Crown Rd WD/CROXPK L12 99 G6
Crown St EHL/KEN L7 9 K3
NEWLW WA12 106 A2
STHEL WA9 * 103 F6
TOX L8 133 F2
WARR WA1 16 D4
Crownway HUY L36 116 D3
Crow St TOX L8 132 C3
Crowther St ECCL WA10 12 C6
Crow Wood La WDN WA8 158 E1
Crow Wood Pl WDN WA8 * 139 J6
Crow Wood Rd
GOL/RIS/CU WA3 92 E2
Croxdale Rd DV/KA/FCH L14 100 A6
Croxdale Rd West
DV/KA/FCH L14 99 K6
Croxteth Av LITH L21 81 H4
WAL/EG CH44 111 H3
Croxteth Cl MGHL L31 62 C4
Croxteth Dr AIG/SPK L17 133 J4
RNFD/HAY WA11 75 G2
Croxteth Gv TOX L8 133 G3
Croxteth Hall La NG/CROX L11 99 G2
Croxteth La STBRV L28 100 B4
Croxteth Rd BTL L20 81 J6
TOX L8 133 G4
Croxteth Vw KKBY L32 84 E5
Croyde Cl CHTN/BK PR9 20 E6
Croyde Pl STHEL WA9 120 A3
Croyde Rd SPK/HALE L24 174 B2
Croydon Av CALD/MH L18 134 A4
Croylands St ANF/KKDL L4 97 G5
Crucian Wy WD/CROXPK L12 99 H2
Crump St CLVPS L1 132 D2
Crutchley Av BIRK CH41 130 E1
Cubbin Crs EV L5 113 F1
Cubert Rd NG/CROX L11 99 G1
Cuckoo Cl CHTN/BK PR9 135 H5
Cuckoo La NSTN CH64 192 C2
WLTN L25 135 H4
Cuerden St VAUX/LVPD L3 9 F2
Cuerdley Gn WDN WA8 159 H1
Cuerdley Rd WARRW/BUR WA5 140 D6
Cuerdon Dr WARRS WA4 163 J2
Culbin Cl GOL/RIS/CU WA3 125 J1
Culford Cl RUNC WA7 178 C4
Cullen Av BTL L20 82 A6
Cullen Cl BEB CH63 183 K3
Cullen Rd RUNC WA7 176 A6
Cullen St TOX L8 133 H2
Culme Rd WD/CROXPK L12 98 D6
Culshaw Wy BRSC L40 36 D2
Culzean Cl WD/CROXPK L12 99 J2
Cumberland Av AIG/SPK L17 133 J3
CL/PREN CH43 149 K1
ECCL WA10 102 D5
NTHTN L30 69 K6
Cumberland Cl NPK/KEN L6 114 B1
Cumberland Crs
RNFD/HAY WA11 89 K5
Cumberland Ga NTHTN L30 70 D5
Cumberland Gv GTS/LS CH66 195 F6
Cumberland Rd STHP PR8 28 A2
WAL/NB CH45 95 J6
Cumberland St CLVPS L1 * 8 D3
WARRS WA4 143 G6
Cumber La RAIN/WH L35 118 B4
Cumbers Dr NSTN CH64 192 B4
Cumbers La NSTN CH64 192 B4
Cumbrae Dr EP CH65 203 G2
Cumbria Wy WD/CROXPK L12 99 G4
Cummings St CLVPS L1 9 G7
Cumpsty Rd LITH L21 81 K2
Cunard Av WAL/EG CH44 111 K2
Cunard Cl CL/PREN CH43 129 K3
Cunard Rd LITH L21 81 J4
Cunliffe Av NEWLW WA12 91 G6
Cunliffe Cl RUNC WA7 177 K6
Cunliffe St CLVP L2 8 D2
Cunningham Cl
WARRW/BUR WA5 141 G4
WKBY CH48 * 146 D5
Cunningham Dr BEB CH63 170 E6
RUNC WA7 10 A7
Cunningham Rd
CLB/OSW/ST L13 114 E5
WDN WA8 157 J3
Cunscough La MGHL L31 63 H5
Cuper Crs HUY L36 116 D3
Curate Rd NPK/KEN L6 98 A6
Curlender Cl BIRK CH41 110 E6
Curlender Wy SPK/HALE L24 175 F3
Curlew Av GR/UP/WCH CH49 128 E3
Curlew Cl GOL/RIS/CU WA3 92 E3
GR/UP/WCH CH49 128 E3
Curlew Ct MOR/LEA CH46 109 G6
Curlew Gv GOL/RIS/CU WA3 125 G4
Curlew La BRSC L40 31 K6
Curlew Wy MOR/LEA CH46 109 G6
Currans Rd WARRN/WOL WA2 123 G5
Curtana Crs NG/CROX L11 99 G2
Curtis Rd ANF/KKDL L4 98 A4
Curwell Cl BEB CH63 170 D2
Curzon Av BIRK CH41 2 A2
WAL/NB CH45 95 H5
Curzon Dr WARRS WA4 163 F4
Curzon Rd CSBY/WL L22 81 F2
HOY CH47 127 F2
RF/TRAN CH42 150 A1
STHP PR8 28 B2
Curzon St RUNC WA7 10 C6
Cusson Rd NWD/KWIPK L33 85 G2
Custley Hey STBRV L28 100 B5
Custom House La CLVPS L1 * 8 D5
Cut La BRSC L40 44 D3
NWD/KWIPK L33 85 K4
Cygnet Cl GTS/LS CH66 195 G5
ORM L39 53 G3
Cygnet Ct NWD/KWIPK L33 85 F1
WARR WA1 142 D6
Cynthia Av WARR WA1 144 A2
Cynthia Rd RUNC WA7 10 B6
Cypress Av GTS/LS CH66 202 D2
WDN WA8 139 G6
Cypress Cl MGHL L31 71 K6
WARR WA1 144 D2
Cypress Cft BEB CH63 170 D2
Cypress Gdns STHEL WA9 102 E6
Cypress Gv RUNC WA7 177 F6
Cypress Rd HUY L36 136 A1
STHP PR8 28 B1
Cyprus Gv TOX L8 133 F5
Cyprus St PR/KW L34 117 K1
Cyprus Ter WAL/NB CH45 * 95 H6
Cyril Gv AIG/SPK L17 153 F1
Cyril St WARRN/WOL WA2 16 E1

D

Dacre's Bridge La RAIN/WH L35 137 G2
Dacre St BIRK CH41 3 F4
BTL L20 96 D4
Dacy Rd EV L5 113 J2
Daffodil Cl WDN WA8 139 K5
Daffodil Rd BIRK CH41 130 C2
WAV L15 134 C3
Dagnall Av WARRW/BUR WA5 123 F5
Dagnall Rd KKBY L32 84 B2
Dahlia Cl WLT/FAZ L9 97 K1
Dailton Rd SKEL WN8 57 J6
Dairy Farm Rd RNFD/HAY WA11 74 E2
Dairylands Cl CALD/MH L18 134 D3
Daisy Av NEWLW WA12 106 C3
Daisy Bank Rd LYMM WA13 145 H6
WARRW/BUR WA5 * 141 G5
Daisy La BRSC L40 39 H5
Daisy Ms LITH L21 81 J5
Daisy Mt MGHL L31 71 H1
Daisy St EV L5 97 F6
Daisy Wy STHP PR8 27 J5
Dalby Cl GOL/RIS/CU WA3 125 K2
RNFD/HAY WA11 89 F6
Dale Acre Dr NTHTN L30 69 K6
Dale Av GTS/LS CH66 195 F3
HES CH60 167 K4
PS/BROM CH62 171 F5
Dalebrook Cl WLTN L25 135 J2
Dale Cl MGHL L31 62 A5
WARRW/BUR WA5 142 A5
WDN WA8 157 F3
Dale Crs STHEL WA9 120 B1
Dale Dr EP CH65 195 J4
Dale End Rd PEN/TH CH61 168 C1
Dale Farm RAIN/WH L35 * 136 E5
Dale Gdns HES CH60 167 H4
Dalegarth Av WD/CROXPK L12 99 K6
Dalehead Pl RNFD/HAY WA11 88 E2
Dale Hey GTS/LS CH66 184 B5
WAL/EG CH44 111 H4
Dalehurst Cl WAL/EG CH44 111 K3
Dale La NWD/KWIPK L33 73 F5
WARRS WA4 162 D4
Dalemeadow Rd
DV/KA/FCH L14 115 H4
Dale Ms WLTN L25 135 J5
Dale Rd GOL/RIS/CU WA3 92 B4
PS/BROM CH62 184 A2
Dalesford Cl LEIGH WN7 93 K3
Daleside Av AIMK WN4 79 F1
Daleside Cl PEN/TH CH61 148 C5
Daleside Rd NWD/KWIPK L33 72 E6
Dales Rw HUY L36 117 H5
Dale St ALL/GAR L19 153 K6
CLVP L2 8 D3
RUNC WA7 10 D7
Dalesway HES CH60 167 J5
The Dale NSTN CH64 191 J3
WARRW/BUR WA5 141 G4
Dale Vw NEWLW WA12 106 E1
Dale View Cl PEN/TH CH61 148 D6
Dalewood WD/CROXPK L12 99 J2
Dalewood Cl WARRN/WOL WA2 16 B3
Dalewood Crs CHNE CH2 198 B6
Dalewood Gdns RAIN/WH L35 118 B5
Daley Pl BTL L20 82 B4
Daley Rd LITH L21 81 K2
Dallam Ct WARRN/WOL WA2 * 16 C1
Dallam La WARRN/WOL WA2 16 C3
Dallas Gv WLT/FAZ L9 82 D5
Dalmeny St AIG/SPK L17 133 G6
Dalmorton Rd WAL/NB CH45 95 J5
Dalry Crs KKBY L32 84 E4
Dalrymple St EV L5 113 F2
Dalston Dr RNFD/HAY WA11 88 E2
Dalton Av WARRW/BUR WA5 142 C2
Dalton Bank WARR WA1 17 G3
Dalton Cl WD/CROXPK L12 99 G3
Dalton Ct RUNC WA7 177 H2
Dalton Gv AIMK WN4 79 F5
Dalton Rd WAL/NB CH45 95 J6
Dalton St GOL/RIS/CU WA3 125 G2
RUNC WA7 177 G3
Daltry Cl WD/CROXPK L12 98 E6
Dalwood Cl RUNC WA7 178 D6
Damerham Ms WLTN L25 135 H2
Damfield La MGHL L31 62 A6
Damhead La NSTN CH64 193 F2
Damian Dr NEWLW WA12 91 F6
Dam La WARR WA1 144 C2
Damson Rd NTHLY L27 136 B4
Dam Wood La BRSC L40 37 G4
Dam Wood Rd SPK/HALE L24 173 J3
Danbers SKEL WN8 67 H1
Danby Cl EV L5 113 H2
RUNC WA7 187 G1
WARRW/BUR WA5 142 B2
Danby Fold RAIN/WH L35 118 D4
Danebank Rd LYMM WA13 145 K5
Danebank Rd East
LYMM WA13 145 K5
Dane Cl GR/UP/WCH CH49 148 C5
Danefield Pl ALL/GAR L19 154 A3
Danefield Rd ALL/GAR L19 154 B3
GR/UP/WCH CH49 147 K1
Danehurst Rd WAL/NB CH45 95 F6
WLT/FAZ L9 82 E4
Danesbury Cl
WGNW/BIL/O WN5 77 H5
Danescourt Rd BIRK CH41 130 D1
WD/CROXPK L12 115 G2
Danescroft WDN WA8 138 A6
Dane St ANF/KKDL L4 97 H4
Daneswell Dr MOR/LEA CH46 109 K6
Daneswell Rd SPK/HALE L24 174 B3
Daneville Rd ANF/KKDL L4 98 B3
Daneway STHP PR8 33 H3
Danger La MOR/LEA CH46 109 K5
Daniel Cl GOL/RIS/CU WA3 125 J3
LITH L21 81 H5

Daniel Davies Dr TOX L8 133 F2
Daniels La SKEL WN8 56 E6
Dannette Hey STBRV L28 116 C1
Dansie St VAUX/LVPD L3 9 J4
Dans Rd WDN WA8 159 F1
Dante Cl WLT/FAZ L9 83 F3
Danube St TOX L8 * 133 H2
Darby Cl NSTN CH64 191 K5
Darby Gv ALL/GAR L19 153 J5
Darby Rd ALL/GAR L19 153 H3
Darent Rd RNFD/HAY WA11 90 A5
Daresbury Av STHP PR8 33 G4
Daresbury Cl KKBY L32 84 B1
Daresbury Expy RUNC WA7 10 C4
WARRS WA4 179 F2
Daresbury La WARRS WA4 179 J3
Daresbury Rd ECCL WA10 102 D1
WAL/EG CH44 111 G3
Darfield SKEL WN8 57 H6
Daric Cl LEIGH WN7 93 K2
Dark Entry PR/KW L34 100 E4
Dark La BRSC L40 46 B5
MGHL L31 62 B6
Darley Av WARRN/WOL WA2 124 A4
Darley Cl WDN WA8 138 A6
Darleydale Dr PS/BROM CH62 184 C2
Darley Dr WD/CROXPK L12 115 G1
Darlington Cl WAL/EG CH44 111 K3
Darlington St WAL/EG CH44 111 K3
Darmond Rd NWD/KWIPK L33 73 F6
Darmond's Gn WKBY CH48 127 G6
Darmonds Green Av
NPK/KEN L6 114 B1
Darnaway Cl GOL/RIS/CU WA3 125 K1
Darnley St TOX L8 132 D4
Darrel Dr EHL/KEN L7 133 H2
Darsefield Rd CHLDW L16 135 F2
Dartington Rd CHLDW L16 134 E1
Dartmouth Av AIN/FAZ L10 83 F1
Dartmouth Dr ECCL WA10 87 K5
NTHTN L30 69 K5
Darvel Av AIMK WN4 78 B5
Darwall Rd ALL/GAR L19 154 A3
Darwen St EV L5 * 112 E2
Darwick Dr HUY L36 136 D1
Darwin Gv STHEL WA9 103 G6
Daryl Rd HES CH60 168 A4
Dashwood Cl WARRS WA4 163 F4
Daten Av GOL/RIS/CU WA3 125 H1
Dauiby St VAUX/LVPD L3 9 K3
Dauntsey Brow WLTN L25 135 J2
Dauntsey Ms WLTN L25 135 J2
Davenham Av CL/PREN CH43 130 C6
WARR WA1 143 H1
Davenham Cl CL/PREN CH43 149 J1
Davenham Rd FMBY L37 49 F1
Davenhill Pk WLT/FAZ L9 83 F1
Davenport Av WARRS WA4 143 J4
Davenport Cl WKBY CH48 146 D5
Davenport Gv NWD/KWIPK L33 72 D5
Davenport Rd HES CH60 167 J6
Davenport Rw RUNC WA7 177 G5
Daventree Rd WAL/NB CH45 111 H2
Daventry Rd AIG/SPK L17 153 F1
David Rd LYMM WA13 145 H6
David's Av WARRW/BUR WA5 141 J4
Davidson Rd CLB/OSW/ST L13 114 D4
David St TOX L8 132 E5
Davids Wk WLTN L25 135 K6
Davies Av NEWLW WA12 106 C1
WARRS WA4 143 J5
Davies Cl WDN WA8 176 D1
Davies St BTL L20 5 G3
CLVPS L1 * 8 D3
STHEL WA9 104 A1
Davies Wy LYMM WA13 145 J6
Davis Rd MOR/LEA CH46 110 B4
Davy Av GOL/RIS/CU WA3 125 G2
Davy Cl ECCL WA10 87 J6
Davy Rd RUNC WA7 177 H2
Davy St EV L5 113 J1
Dawber Cl NPK/KEN L6 113 J3
Dawber St AIMK WN4 79 J5
Dawley Cl AIMK WN4 79 F6
Dawlish Cl WLTN L25 155 F3
Dawlish Dr CHTN/BK PR9 20 D6
Dawlish Rd PEN/TH CH61 147 K6
WAL/EG CH44 111 F3
Dawlish Wy GOL/RIS/CU WA3 92 A2
Dawn Cl NSTN CH64 192 A4
STHEL WA9 103 G6
Dawn Gdns EP CH65 6 B7
Dawpool Dr MOR/LEA CH46 129 F1
PS/BROM CH62 170 E6
Dawpool Farm PEN/TH CH61 * 147 J6
Dawson Av BIRK CH41 130 E1
CHTN/BK PR9 21 F6
STHEL WA9 104 B6
Dawson Gdns MGHL L31 62 A5
Dawson Rd ORM L39 45 K4
Dawson St CLVPS L1 8 E4
Dawson Wy CLVPS L1 * 9 F4
Dawstone Ri HES CH60 167 K6
Dawstone Rd HES CH60 167 K6
Daybrook SKEL WN8 67 H1
Dayfield SKEL WN8 57 J6
Days Meadow
GR/UP/WCH CH49 128 D6
Day St CLB/OSW/ST L13 114 E4
Deacon Cl CSBY/WL L22 80 E3
Deacon Ct CSBY/WL L22 80 E3
WLTN L25 154 E1
Deacon Rd WDN WA8 18 E2
Deakin St BIRK CH41 130 C1
Dean Av WAL/NB CH45 110 E1
Dean Cl WDN WA8 18 E3
WGNW/BIL/O WN5 77 G6
Dean Ct GOL/RIS/CU WA3 92 B4
Dean Crs WARRN/WOL WA2 123 H5
Deane Rd EHL/KEN L7 114 A5
Dean Meadow NEWLW WA12 106 C1
Dean Rd GOL/RIS/CU WA3 92 B4
Deansburn Rd
CLB/OSW/ST L13 114 C1
Deanscales Rd NG/CROX L11 98 D3
Deans Ct FMBY L37 41 F6
Deansfield Wy CHNE CH2 198 B6
Deansgate EP CH65 6 A4
Deansgate La FMBY L37 41 H6
Deansgate La North FMBY L37 41 G5
Deans La WARRS WA4 144 E6
Deans Rd EP CH65 196 E6
Dean St CSBY/WL L22 80 E3
WDN WA8 18 E3
Deans Wy CL/PREN CH43 130 C1
Deansway WDN WA8 157 H3
Deanwater Cl
GOL/RIS/CU WA3 125 F5
Dean Wy STHEL WA9 119 K4
Dean Wood Cl RAIN/WH L35 118 B5
Dearham Av RNFD/HAY WA11 88 D4
Dearne Cl WD/CROXPK L12 115 J2
Dearnford Av PS/BROM CH62 184 A1
Dearnford Cl PS/BROM CH62 184 A1
Dearnley Av RNFD/HAY WA11 89 K6
Deauville Rd WLT/FAZ L9 83 F4
Debra Cl GTS/LS CH66 195 F5
MGHL L31 72 A5
Debra Rd GTS/LS CH66 195 F6
Dee Cl NWD/KWIPK L33 72 E3
Dee La WKBY CH48 146 B1
Deeley Cl EHL/KEN L7 114 A6
Dee Park Cl HES CH60 181 G1
Dee Park Rd HES CH60 181 G1
Deep Dl WARRW/BUR WA5 141 G3
Deepdale WDN WA8 138 B6
Deepdale Av BTL L20 81 H6
RNFD/HAY WA11 * 89 F2
Deepdale Cl CL/PREN CH43 129 K3
Deepdale Dr RAIN/WH L35 119 F4
Deepdale Rd WLTN L25 135 H2
Deepfield Dr HUY L36 136 C1
Deepfield Rd WAV L15 134 A3
Deepwood Gv RAIN/WH L35 118 A5
Deerbarn Dr NTHTN L30 70 E6
Deerbolt Cl KKBY L32 72 B6
Deerbolt Crs KKBY L32 72 B6
Deerbolt Wy KKBY L32 72 B6
Dee Rd RAIN/WH L35 118 D4
Deer Park Ct RUNC WA7 187 J1
Deerwood Cl GTS/LS CH66 195 G2
Deerwood Crs GTS/LS CH66 195 G2
Deeside EP CH65 196 A6
Dee Side HES CH60 167 G5
Deeside Cl CL/PREN CH43 129 J3
EP CH65 203 F1
Dee View Rd HES CH60 167 K5
De Grouchy St WKBY CH48 * 127 G6
Deirdre Av WDN WA8 18 D2
Delabole Rd NG/CROX L11 84 C6
De Lacy Rw RUNC WA7 177 K3
Delafield Cl WARRN/WOL WA2 124 B4
Delagoa Rd AIN/FAZ L10 83 J5
Delamain Rd CLB/OSW/ST L13 114 D1
Delamere Av GOL/RIS/CU WA3 93 F5
GTS/LS CH66 195 H4
PS/BROM CH62 184 B3
STHEL WA9 119 J4
WDN WA8 157 H2
Delamere Cl CL/PREN CH43 129 J3
PS/BROM CH62 184 B3
WD/CROXPK L12 99 H2
Delamere Dr GTS/LS CH66 195 H5
Delamere Gv WAL/EG CH44 * 112 A5
Delamere Rd SKEL WN8 56 B3
STHP PR8 33 H4
Delamere St
WARRW/BUR WA5 142 B4
Delamere Wy FROD/HEL WA6 201 F4
SKEL WN8 57 J6
Delamore Pl ANF/KKDL L4 * 97 G4
Delamore's Acre NSTN CH64 193 H1
Delamore St ANF/KKDL L4 97 G4
Delavor Cl HES CH60 167 J5
Delavor Rd HES CH60 167 J5
Delaware Crs KKBY L32 72 B6
Delaware Rd BTL L20 4 E3
Delenty Dr GOL/RIS/CU WA3 125 F3
Delery Dr WARR WA1 143 H1
Delfby Crs KKBY L32 85 F2
Delf La ANF/KKDL L4 97 J3
ORM L39 43 J6
SPK/HALE L24 154 E6
Dell Cl BEB CH63 183 J1
Dell Dr WARRN/WOL WA2 124 C5
Dellfield La MGHL L31 62 C6
Dell Gv RF/TRAN CH42 151 F3
Dell La HES CH60 168 B6
Dellside Cl AIMK WN4 78 C3
Dellside Gv STHEL WA9 104 A5
Dell St EHL/KEN L7 114 A5
The Dell RF/TRAN CH42 151 G2
SKEL WN8 57 K6
WD/CROXPK L12 99 J4
Delph Common Rd ORM L39 53 F4
Delph Dr BRSC L40 39 F6
Delphfields Rd WARRS WA4 162 B4
Delphfield RUNC WA7 178 C5
Delph La FMBY L37 48 C2
ORM L39 53 G4
RAIN/WH L35 118 B3
WARRN/WOL WA2 123 F3
WARRN/WOL WA2 124 A1
WARRS WA4 179 F2
Delph Meadow Gdns
WGNW/BIL/O WN5 77 F5
Delph Park Av ORM L39 53 F4
Delph Rd HTWN L38 68 E1
Delphwood Dr STHEL WA9 103 K4
Delta Crs WARRW/BUR WA5 122 C5
Delta Dr WD/CROXPK L12 99 J5
Delta Rd LITH L21 81 J4
STHEL WA9 104 D1
Delta Rd East RF/TRAN CH42 151 G2
Delta Rd West RF/TRAN CH42 * 151 G2
Deltic Wy NTHTN L30 82 D3
NWD/KWIPK L33 85 G3
Delves Av BEB CH63 170 B2
WARRW/BUR WA5 142 C2
Delyn Cl RF/TRAN CH42 150 D2
Demage Dr GTS/LS CH66 195 G6
Demesne St WAL/EG CH44 112 A4
Denbigh Av CHTN/BK PR9 23 H2
STHEL WA9 104 A6
Denbigh Ct EP CH65 196 C6
Denbigh Gdns EP CH65 196 B6
Denbigh Rd WLT/FAZ L9 97 H2
Denbigh St EV L5 112 D2
Denbury Av WARRS WA4 162 E1
Dencourt Rd NG/CROX L11 99 F4
Dene Av NEWLW WA12 105 K1
Denebank Rd ANF/KKDL L4 97 K6
Denehurst Cl
WARRW/BUR WA5 141 G5
Deneshey Rd HOY CH47 127 H1
Denes Wy STBRV L28 100 A6
Denford Rd DV/KA/FCH L14 115 K2
Denham Av WARRW/BUR WA5 141 J4
Denham Cl WD/CROXPK L12 99 K2
Denholme SKEL WN8 57 H6
Denise Av WARRW/BUR WA5 141 F4
Denise Rd AIN/FAZ L10 84 A4
Denison Gv STHEL WA9 * 103 G6
Denman Dr NPK/KEN L6 114 A3
Denman Gv WAL/EG CH44 * 112 A4
Denman St NPK/KEN L6 113 K4
Denman Wy NPK/KEN L6 114 A3
Denmark Rd CHTN/BK PR9 23 J3
Denmark St CSBY/WL L22 80 E2
Dennett Cl MGHL L31 71 G2
WARR WA1 144 D3
Dennett Rd RAIN/WH L35 117 J3
Denning Dr PEN/TH CH61 148 A4
Dennis Av ECCL WA10 102 E6
Dennis Rd WDN WA8 19 G5
Denny Cl GR/UP/WCH CH49 129 G5
Densham Av
WARRN/WOL WA2 123 H5
Denston Cl CL/PREN CH43 129 J2
Denstone Av AIN/FAZ L10 83 G1
Denstone Cl WLTN L25 154 E3
Dentdale Dr EV L5 113 G3
Denton Dr WAL/NB CH45 111 J1
Denton Gv NPK/KEN L6 114 A2
Dentons Green La ECCL WA10 12 B2
Denton St TOX L8 132 E5
WDN WA8 19 G2
Dentwood St TOX L8 133 F5
Denver Rd KKBY L32 84 B2
WARRS WA4 143 K6
Depot Rd NWD/KWIPK L33 73 H5
Derby Cl NEWLW WA12 106 B2
Derby Dr RNFD/HAY WA11 75 H4
WARR WA1 143 J2
Derby Gv MGHL L31 71 G3
Derby Hill Crs ORM L39 46 A6
Derby Hill Rd ORM L39 46 A6
Derby La CLB/OSW/ST L13 114 E4
Derby Rd BTL L20 4 C6
CHTN/BK PR9 15 G5
FMBY L37 48 E1
GOL/RIS/CU WA3 92 D2
HUY L36 116 E5
RF/TRAN CH42 131 G5
SKEL WN8 55 J5
WAL/NB CH45 111 G1
WARRS WA4 162 B3
WDN WA8 139 G6
Derby Rw NEWLW WA12 106 C5
Derbyshire Hill Rd STHEL WA9 104 E2
Derby Sq CLVP L2 8 D5
PR/KW L34 118 A1
Derby St CLB/OSW/ST L13 * 114 D4
HUY L36 117 G5
NEWLW WA12 106 B2
ORM L39 45 K6
Derby St West ORM L39 45 J6
Dereham Av
GR/UP/WCH CH49 129 H2
Dereham Crs AIN/FAZ L10 83 J4
Dereham Wy RUNC WA7 178 C2
Derek Av WARRN/WOL WA2 123 K6
Derna Rd HUY L36 116 D4
Derringstone Cl ECCL WA10 103 F4
Derwent Av CHTN/BK PR9 23 H4
FMBY L37 48 D3
GOL/RIS/CU WA3 92 D2
PR/KW L34 118 B1
Derwent Cl BEB CH63 * 150 C6
MGHL L31 62 D5
NWD/KWIPK L33 72 C5
RAIN/WH L35 118 D4
Derwent Dr GTS/LS CH66 184 E5
LITH L21 82 A3
PEN/TH CH61 167 K1
WAL/NB CH45 111 G1
Derwent Rd AIMK WN4 79 K4
BEB CH63 150 C6
CL/PREN CH43 130 E5
CSBY/BLUN L23 81 G1
HOY CH47 127 K1
RNFD/HAY WA11 88 E4
WARRS WA4 161 K1
WDN WA8 157 H2
Derwent Rd East
CLB/OSW/ST L13 114 E3
Derwent Rd West
CLB/OSW/ST L13 114 D3
Derwent Sq CLB/OSW/ST L13 114 E3
Derwent Wy NSTN CH64 192 A3
Desborough Crs
WD/CROXPK L12 98 E6
Desford Av RNFD/HAY WA11 89 G5
Desford Cl MOR/LEA CH46 109 F6
Desford Rd ALL/GAR L19 153 F3
Desilva St HUY L36 117 G5
Desmond Cl CL/PREN CH43 129 K2
Desmond Gv CSBY/BLUN L23 69 G6
Desoto Rd WDN WA8 157 K6
Desoto Rd East WDN WA8 158 A5
Desoto Rd West WDN WA8 158 A5
Deva Cl NWD/KWIPK L33 72 D2
Deva Rd WKBY CH48 146 B1
Deveraux Dr WAL/EG CH44 111 J4
Deverell Gv WAV L15 115 F6
Deverell Rd WAV L15 115 F6
Deverill Rd RF/TRAN CH42 150 D2
Devilla Cl DV/KA/FCH L14 116 A2
De Villiers Av CSBY/BLUN L23 69 F4
Devisdale Gv CL/PREN CH43 129 K2
Devizes Dr PEN/TH CH61 148 A4
Devizes Ms WLTN L25 135 J2
Devoke Av RNFD/HAY WA11 88 D2
Devon Av SKEL WN8 67 K1
WAL/EG CH44 111 J2
Devon Cl CSBY/BLUN L23 68 B5
Devon Ct EV L5 113 J2
Devondale Rd CALD/MH L18 134 B4
Devon Dr PEN/TH CH61 167 J1
Devon Farm Wy FMBY L37 49 H2
Devonfield Rd WLT/FAZ L9 82 C6
Devon Gdns CHLDW L16 135 F4
RF/TRAN CH42 150 E2
Devon Pl WDN WA8 139 F6
Devonport St TOX L8 132 E4
Devonshire Cl CL/PREN CH43 2 A6
NWD/KWIPK L33 72 D5
Devonshire Gdns
NEWLW WA12 106 C3
Devonshire Pl CL/PREN CH43 130 D4
EV L5 113 G1
RUNC WA7 10 D4
Devonshire Rd CHTN/BK PR9 23 J6
CL/PREN CH43 130 E4
CSBY/WL L22 80 D1
ECCL WA10 12 A1
GR/UP/WCH CH49 129 F4
PEN/TH CH61 167 J1
TOX L8 133 F4
WAL/EG CH44 111 H3
WARR WA1 143 J1
WKBY CH48 146 D2
Devonshire Rd West TOX L8 133 F4
Devon St ECCL WA10 12 B4
VAUX/LVPD L3 9 J2
Devonwall Gdns TOX L8 133 G4
Devon Wy CHLDW L16 135 F3
HUY L36 117 G3
Dewar Ct RUNC WA7 177 H2
Dewar St GOL/RIS/CU WA3 125 G2
Dewberry Cl RF/TRAN CH42 131 G5
Dewberry Flds SKEL WN8 57 K6
Dewey Av WLT/FAZ L9 82 E3
Dewhurst Rd GOL/RIS/CU WA3 125 F5
Dewlands Rd LITH L21 81 G3
Dewsbury Rd ANF/KKDL L4 113 K1
Dexter St TOX L8 132 D3
Deycroft Av NWD/KWIPK L33 73 F5
Deyes End MGHL L31 62 C6
Deyes La MGHL L31 62 B6
Deysbrook La WD/CROXPK L12 115 G1
Deysbrook Side
WD/CROXPK L12 115 G1
Deysbrook Wy WD/CROXPK L12 99 H5
Dial Rd RF/TRAN CH42 131 G6
Dial St EHL/KEN L7 114 A5
WARR WA1 16 E4
Diamond St EV L5 113 F3
Diana Rd BTL L20 82 A4
Diana St ANF/KKDL L4 97 H5
Diane Rd AIMK WN4 79 K5
Dibbinsdale Rd BEB CH63 170 D6
Dibbins Gn BEB CH63 183 J1
Dibbins Hey BEB CH63 170 C3
Dibbinview Gv BEB CH63 170 D3
Dibb La CSBY/BLUN L23 68 D2
Dicconson's La ORM L39 52 A2
Dicconson St ECCL WA10 * 13 G3
Dicconson Wy ORM L39 * 54 A1
Dickens Av CL/PREN CH43 149 J2
Dickens Cl CL/PREN CH43 149 J2
Dickenson St CLVPS L1 * 8 E7
WARRN/WOL WA2 17 F1
Dickens Rd ECCL WA10 102 E5
Dickens St TOX L8 * 132 E3
Dicket's La SKEL WN8 55 G3
Dickinson Cl FMBY L37 49 F3
RNFD/HAY WA11 89 K5
Dickinson Rd FMBY L37 49 F3
Dick's La BRSC L40 55 F1
Dickson Cl WDN WA8 18 E3
Dickson St VAUX/LVPD L3 112 D3
WDN WA8 18 D3
Didcot Cl WLTN L25 155 G3
Didsbury Cl NWD/KWIPK L33 84 E1
Digg La MOR/LEA CH46 109 H6
Dig La FROD/HEL WA6 200 D2
WARRN/WOL WA2 124 C3
Digmoor Dr SKEL WN8 56 D6
Digmoor Rd KKBY L32 84 E4
SKEL WN8 66 E1
Dignum Md NTHLY L27 136 B3
Dilloway St ECCL WA10 12 C3
Dinas La DV/KA/FCH L14 116 A3
Dinesen Rd ALL/GAR L19 153 K4
Dingle Av NEWLW WA12 105 K3
SKEL WN8 57 K5
Dingle Bank Cl LYMM WA13 145 K6
Dingle Brow TOX L8 133 F6
Dingle Cl ORM L39 53 G4
Dingle Gv TOX L8 133 F5
Dingle La TOX L8 133 F6
WARRS WA4 162 E5
Dingle Mt TOX L8 133 F6
Dingle Rd RF/TRAN CH42 131 F5
SKEL WN8 57 K6
TOX L8 132 E6
The Dingle LYMM WA13 145 K6
Dingle V TOX L8 133 F6
Dingleway WARRS WA4 162 C3
Dingley Av WLT/FAZ L9 82 C5
Dingwall Dr GR/UP/WCH CH49 129 F6
Dinmore Rd WAL/EG CH44 111 H3
Dinnington Ct WDN WA8 138 E6
Dinorwic Rd ANF/KKDL L4 113 J1
STHP PR8 27 H4
Ditchfield FMBY L37 49 G3
Ditchfield Pl WDN WA8 157 G3
Ditchfield Rd
WARRW/BUR WA5 141 F6
WDN WA8 157 G3
Ditton La MOR/LEA CH46 109 J4
Ditton Rd WDN WA8 18 B7
Dixon Av NEWLW WA12 91 H6
Dixon Cl RNFD/HAY WA11 91 F3
Dixon Rd NWD/KWIPK L33 85 G3
Dixon St WARR WA1 16 B5
Dobbs Dr FMBY L37 49 G1
Dobers La FROD/HEL WA6 201 G5
Dobson St NPK/KEN L6 113 J3
Dock Rd ALL/GAR L19 153 J6
BIRK CH41 111 G5
WDN WA8 158 B6
Dock Rd North PS/BROM CH62 151 H5
Dock Rd South
PS/BROM CH62 171 F1
Dock St EP CH65 6 E1
WDN WA8 158 B6
Dock Yard Rd EP CH65 7 G3
Doctor's La FMBY L37 50 A4
Dodd Av ECCL WA10 102 E1
GR/UP/WCH CH49 128 E6
Doddridge Rd TOX L8 132 D4
Dodd's La MGHL L31 62 B5
WARRS WA4 163 F6
Dodleston Cl CL/PREN CH43 130 A5
Dodman Rd NG/CROX L11 84 C6
Dodworth Av STHP PR8 28 B2
Doe Park Ctyd WLTN L25 * 154 E3
Doe's Meadow Rd BEB CH63 170 D6
Dolly's La CHTN/BK PR9 24 C4
Dolomite Av ALL/GAR L19 154 C5
Dolphin Crs GTS/LS CH66 202 C1
Domar Cl KKBY L32 84 D3
Dombey St TOX L8 132 E3
Domingo Dr NWD/KWIPK L33 72 C4
Dominic Cl CHLDW L16 135 F1
Dominic Rd CHLDW L16 135 F1
Dominion St NPK/KEN L6 * 114 A2
Domville RAIN/WH L35 118 A5
Domville Cl LYMM WA13 145 K6
Domville Rd CLB/OSW/ST L13 114 E6
Donaldson St EV L5 113 J1
Donalds Wy AIG/SPK L17 153 F2
Doncaster Dr
GR/UP/WCH CH49 129 G3
Donegal Rd CLB/OSW/ST L13 115 F4
Donne Av BEB CH63 170 B2
Donne Cl BEB CH63 170 C2
Donnington Cl HUY L36 136 A1
Donsby Rd WLT/FAZ L9 82 E5
Don Wk EP CH65 195 K2
Dooley Dr NTHTN L30 70 E5
Doon Cl ANF/KKDL L4 97 G5
Dorbett Dr CSBY/BLUN L23 81 G1
Dorchester Cl
GR/UP/WCH CH49 129 G5
Dorchester Dr NWD/KWIPK L33 73 F4
Dorchester Pk CL/PREN CH43 130 A6
RUNC WA7 178 C2
WLTN L25 135 J3
Dorchester Rd SKEL WN8 57 J6
WARRW/BUR WA5 141 J4
Dorchester Wy
WARRW/BUR WA5 121 K1
Doreen Av MOR/LEA CH46 128 E1
Dorgan Cl RAIN/WH L35 118 D3
Doric Av FROD/HEL WA6 201 F2
Doric Rd CLB/OSW/ST L13 114 E3
Doric St LITH L21 81 G4
RF/TRAN CH42 * 150 E1
Dorien Rd CLB/OSW/ST L13 114 D5
Dorking Gv WAV L15 134 C2
Dorney Cl WARRS WA4 162 D5
Dorothea St WARRN/WOL WA2 143 F2
Dorothy St EHL/KEN L7 113 K6
STHEL WA9 103 G6
Dorrington Cl RUNC WA7 178 C5
Dorrit St TOX L8 132 E3
Dorset Av STHP PR8 41 J1
WAV L15 133 J2
Dorset Cl BTL L20 5 H4
Dorset Dr PEN/TH CH61 167 J1
Dorset Rd ECCL WA10 103 F4
HUY L36 117 G4
NPK/KEN L6 114 B1
WAL/NB CH45 95 G6
WKBY CH48 127 H6
Dorset Wy WARR WA1 144 A1
Douglas Av SKEL WN8 57 K6
STHEL WA9 121 F1
WGNW/BIL/O WN5 77 G6
Douglas Cl CLB/OSW/ST L13 114 D3
WDN WA8 140 A6
Douglas Dr MGHL L31 62 D5
MOR/LEA CH46 128 D1
ORM L39 45 H4
Douglas Pl BTL L20 4 D7
Douglas Rd ANF/KKDL L4 113 K1
CHTN/BK PR9 24 A1
WKBY CH48 127 J6
Douglas St BIRK CH41 3 G4
ECCL WA10 12 B5
Douglas Wy NWD/KWIPK L33 72 E3
Doulton Cl CL/PREN CH43 129 J2
Doulton St ECCL WA10 12 A6
Doune Ct EP CH65 196 C6
Dounrey Cl WARRN/WOL WA2 124 C5
Douro Pl CLB/OSW/ST L13 114 D5
Douro St EV L5 113 G3
Dove Cl CHNE CH2 198 D5
EP CH65 195 J2
FROD/HEL WA6 199 K4
GOL/RIS/CU WA3 125 H3
Dovecot Av DV/KA/FCH L14 115 K3
Dovecote Dr RNFD/HAY WA11 90 B4
Dovecote Gn
WARRW/BUR WA5 122 A6
Dove Ct WLTN L25 154 E1
Dovedale Av MGHL L31 62 A5

PS/BROM CH62 184 B2
Dovedale Cl CL/PREN CH43 149 J1
WARRN/WOL WA2 124 A4
Dovedale Crs AIMK WN4 79 F1
Dovedale Rd AIMK WN4 79 F1
CALD/MH L18 134 B5
HOY CH47 127 G1
WAL/NB CH45 95 G6
Dovepoint Rd HOY CH47 108 C6
Dovercliffe Rd
CLB/OSW/ST L13 115 F4
Dover Cl BIRK CH41 2 D3
RUNC WA7 188 D1
Dover Ct EP CH65 203 H1
Dover Dr EP CH65 203 H1
Dover Gv CHLDW L16 135 G1
Dove Rd WLT/FAZ L9 82 C5
Dover Rd MGHL L31 71 F3
STHP PR8 27 G5
WARRS WA4 143 K6
WLT/FAZ L9 82 C5
Dover St RUNC WA7 11 F3
VAUX/LVPD L3 9 J4
Dovesmead Rd HES CH60 * 168 C6
Dovestone Cl EHL/KEN L7 133 G1
Dove St GOL/RIS/CU WA3 92 B1
TOX L8 133 G2
Dovey St TOX L8 132 E4
Doward St WDN WA8 158 D1
Dowhills Dr CSBY/BLUN L23 68 C4
Dowhills Pk CSBY/BLUN L23 68 C3
Dowhills Rd CSBY/BLUN L23 68 C4
Downall Green Rd AIMK WN4 78 D3
Downes Gn BEB CH63 170 C4
Downham Cl WLTN L25 135 G4
Downham Dr HES CH60 168 A5
Downham Gn WLTN L25 135 G4
Downham Rd RF/TRAN CH42 131 H6
Downham Rd North
PEN/TH CH61 168 A3
Downham Rd South HES CH60 168 A5
Downham Wy WLTN L25 135 G4
Downing Cl CL/PREN CH43 130 E6
Downing Rd BTL L20 5 H7
Downing St EV L5 113 J2
Downland Wy STHEL WA9 104 D4
Downside WDN WA8 138 A6
Downside Cl NTHTN L30 70 B5
Downside Dr AIN/FAZ L10 83 J2
Downs Rd ECCL WA10 12 B7
RUNC WA7 10 E7
Downway La STHEL WA9 104 E4
Dowsefield La CALD/MH L18 135 F6
Dragon Cl NG/CROX L11 99 G1
Dragon Crs RAIN/WH L35 118 B3
Dragon La RAIN/WH L35 117 K5
Dragon Yd WDN WA8 139 G5
Drake Cl AIN/FAZ L10 83 K4
ORM L39 53 G3
RAIN/WH L35 118 A5
WARRW/BUR WA5 122 D6
Drake Crs AIN/FAZ L10 83 K4
Drakefield Rd NG/CROX L11 98 C2
Drake Gdns STHEL WA9 119 G1
Drake Pl AIN/FAZ L10 * 83 J4
Drake Rd AIN/FAZ L10 83 J4
MOR/LEA CH46 110 B3
NSTN CH64 181 K6
Drake St BTL L20 96 D4
ECCL WA10 12 B4
Drake Wy AIN/FAZ L10 83 K4
Draw Well Rd NWD/KWIPK L33 85 J1
Draycott St TOX L8 132 E6
Drayton Cl PEN/TH CH61 148 A6
RUNC WA7 10 B6
Drayton Crs RNFD/HAY WA11 89 G5
Drayton Rd ANF/KKDL L4 * 97 J3
WAL/EG CH44 111 K4
Drennan Rd ALL/GAR L19 154 B3
Drewell Rd CALD/MH L18 134 A6
Drewitt Crs CHTN/BK PR9 24 A1
Driffield Rd PR/KW L34 117 J1
Drinkwater Gdns
VAUX/LVPD L3 113 G4
The Drive WD/CROXPK L12 115 F2
Driveway RAIN/WH L35 118 B5
Droitwich Av
GR/UP/WCH CH49 128 D5
Dromore Av CALD/MH L18 134 B6
Dronfield Wy WLTN L25 135 G2
Druids Cross Gdns
CALD/MH L18 134 E5
Druids Cross Rd CALD/MH L18 134 E5
Druids Pk CALD/MH L18 135 F5
Druid St AIMK WN4 91 H1
Druidsville Rd CALD/MH L18 135 F5
Druids Wy GR/UP/WCH CH49 148 D1
Drum Cl DV/KA/FCH L14 116 A2
Drummersdale La BRSC L40 30 A6
Drummer's La AIMK WN4 78 D2
Drummond Av GTS/LS CH66 195 F5
Drummond Ct WDN WA8 158 E1
Drummond Rd ANF/KKDL L4 98 A4
CSBY/BLUN L23 69 J4
HOY CH47 127 F4
Druridge Dr WARRW/BUR WA5 141 G5
Drury La CLVP L2 8 C4
Dryburgh Wy ANF/KKDL L4 97 G5
Dryden Av AIMK WN4 78 E2
Dryden Cl CL/PREN CH43 129 K2
RAIN/WH L35 118 A4
Dryden Gv HUY L36 117 F6
Dryden Pl WARRN/WOL WA2 123 J5
Dryden Rd EHL/KEN L7 114 C6
Dryden St BTL L20 4 B1
EV L5 113 F3
Dryebeck Gv STHEL WA9 120 B1
Dryfield Cl GR/UP/WCH CH49 * 128 E5
Drysdale St TOX L8 133 F5
Drysdale Wk TOX L8 133 F5
Dublin Cft GTS/LS CH66 202 C2
Dublin St VAUX/LVPD L3 112 D3
Ducie St TOX L8 133 G3
Duckinfield St VAUX/LVPD L3 9 J4
Duck Pond La RF/TRAN CH42 149 K1
Duckworth Gv
WARRN/WOL WA2 124 C6
Duddingston Av
CALD/MH L18 * 134 B4
CSBY/BLUN L23 81 F1
Duddon Av MGHL L31 62 D5
Duddon Cl CL/PREN CH43 130 C5
Dudleston Rd GTS/LS CH66 194 E3
Dudley Av RUNC WA7 177 G3
Dudley Cl CL/PREN CH43 130 E5
Dudley Crs PS/BROM CH62 184 E4
Dudley Gv CSBY/BLUN L23 81 F1
Dudley Pl STHEL WA9 104 B2
Dudley Rd CALD/MH L18 134 A4
EP CH65 6 C5
WAL/NB CH45 95 G5
Dudley St AIMK WN4 79 F4
WARRN/WOL WA2 142 E2
Dudlow Dr CALD/MH L18 134 D4
Dudlow Gdns CALD/MH L18 134 D3
Dudlow Green Rd WARRS WA4 162 C6
Dudlow La CALD/MH L18 134 D4
Dudlow Nook Rd
CALD/MH L18 134 D3
Dugdale Cl ALL/GAR L19 153 H4
Duke Av STHP PR8 27 K3
Duke Cl RUNC WA7 10 B4
Dukes Rd EV L5 113 G1
Duke St AIMK WN4 79 H6
ALL/GAR L19 153 K5
BIRK CH41 2 B1
CLVPS L1 9 F6
CSBY/WL L22 80 E3
ECCL WA10 12 E3
FMBY L37 48 E3
GOL/RIS/CU WA3 92 B2
NEWLW WA12 106 B2
PR/KW L34 101 K6
STHP PR8 14 C6
WAL/NB CH45 95 H5
Duke Street La CLVPS L1 * 8 E6
Dukes Wy FMBY L37 49 F3
Dukes Whf RUNC WA7 188 E1
Duke's Wood La SKEL WN8 67 F4
Dulas Gn KKBY L32 85 F2
Dulas Rd KKBY L32 85 F2
WAV L15 134 C3
Dulverton Rd AIG/SPK L17 153 F3
Dumbarton St ANF/KKDL L4 97 G4
Dumbrees Rd WD/CROXPK L12 99 J5
Dumbreeze Gv PR/KW L34 100 D1
Dumfries Wy NWD/KWIPK L33 72 C3
Dunacre Wy HLWD L26 155 J4
Dunbabin Rd CHLDW L16 134 D3
Dunbar Cl GTS/LS CH66 195 F4
Dunbar Crs STHP PR8 34 B1
Dunbar Rd STHP PR8 27 F6
Dunbar St ANF/KKDL L4 97 H3
Dunbeath Av RAIN/WH L35 119 F6
Dunbeath Cl RAIN/WH L35 119 F6
Dunblane Cl AIMK WN4 78 B5
Duncan Av NEWLW WA12 91 H6
RUNC WA7 11 H6
Duncan Cl ECCL WA10 12 E7
Duncan Dr GR/UP/WCH CH49 128 E5
Duncansby Crs
WARRW/BUR WA5 141 F3
Duncansby Dr BEB CH63 183 K3
Duncan St BIRK CH41 3 H4
CLVPS L1 132 D2
ECCL WA10 12 D6
WARRN/WOL WA2 143 F2
Dunchurch Rd DV/KA/FCH L14 115 K2
Duncombe Rd North
ALL/GAR L19 153 J4
Duncombe Rd South
ALL/GAR L19 153 J4
Duncote Cl CL/PREN CH43 130 D5
RAIN/WH L35 118 C2
Dundale Rd CLB/OSW/ST L13 115 F4
Dundalk Rd WDN WA8 157 K3
Dundas St BTL L20 96 D4
Dundee Cl WARRN/WOL WA2 124 A3
Dundee Ct EP CH65 196 D6
Dundee Gv WAL/EG CH44 111 G4
Dundonald Av WARRS WA4 162 B2
Dundonald Rd AIG/SPK L17 153 F2
Dundonald St BIRK CH41 130 D1
Dunedin St STHEL WA9 103 G6
Dunes Dr FMBY L37 48 C1
Dunes Wy EV L5 112 E1
Dunfold Cl KKBY L32 84 E2
Dungeon La SPK/HALE L24 174 A4
Dunham Av GOL/RIS/CU WA3 92 A2
Dunham Cl PS/BROM CH62 184 C3
Dunham Rd WAV L15 114 E6
Dunkeld Cl NPK/KEN L6 113 J4
Dunkeld St NPK/KEN L6 * 113 J4
Dunkirk Dr EP CH65 202 E2
Dunkirk La CH/BCN CH1 202 A3
Dunkirk Rd STHP PR8 27 G5
Dunley Cl GOL/RIS/CU WA3 125 J1
Dunlin Av NEWLW WA12 106 C1
Dunlin Cl NTHLY L27 136 B5
RUNC WA7 187 J2
WARRN/WOL WA2 124 A4
Dunlop Av STHP PR8 41 J1
Dunlop Dr MGHL L31 72 A5
Dunlop Rd SPK/HALE L24 173 G3
Dunlop St WARRS WA4 142 E6
Dunluce St ANF/KKDL L4 97 G4
Dunmail Av RNFD/HAY WA11 89 F2
Dunmail Gv RUNC WA7 187 H3
Dunmore Crs GTS/LS CH66 194 E3
Dunmore Rd CLB/OSW/ST L13 114 C4
GTS/LS CH66 194 E3
Dunmow Rd WARRS WA4 144 B6
Dunmow Wy WLTN L25 155 F3
Dunnerdale Rd NG/CROX L11 98 E3
Dunnett St BTL L20 96 D4
Dunning Cl GR/UP/WCH CH49 129 F4
Dunnings Bridge Rd NTHTN L30 70 E5
Dunnock Cl WARRN/WOL WA2 124 A4
WLTN L25 135 H4
Dunnock Gv GOL/RIS/CU WA3 125 G3
Dunraven Rd NSTN CH64 192 B2
WKBY CH48 146 B1
Dunriding La ECCL WA10 12 A6
Dunscar Cl GOL/RIS/CU WA3 125 F2
Dunscroft STHEL WA9 104 B6
Dunsdale Dr AIMK WN4 79 H6
Dunsdon Cl CALD/MH L18 135 F5
Dunsdon Rd CALD/MH L18 135 F4
Dunsford WDN WA8 138 B6
Dunsmore Cl RNFD/HAY WA11 90 B4
Dunsop Av STHEL WA9 120 B3
Dunstall Cl MOR/LEA CH46 109 J4
Dunstan La EHL/KEN L7 133 H1
Dunstan St WAV L15 133 K1
Dunster Gv HES CH60 168 B6
STHEL WA9 120 B3
Dunster Rd STHP PR8 34 A1
Durban Rd CLB/OSW/ST L13 115 F5
WAL/NB CH45 111 H1
Durden St EHL/KEN L7 133 H2
Durham Av NTHTN L30 82 D2
Durham Cl WARR WA1 144 D2
Durham Ms East NTHTN L30 * 82 D2
Durham Ms West NTHTN L30 * 82 D2
Durham Rd LITH L21 81 F4
WDN WA8 * 139 G6
Durham St ALL/GAR L19 172 C1
Durham Wy NTHTN L30 82 D2
Durley Dr CL/PREN CH43 149 H2
Durley Rd WLT/FAZ L9 82 E5
Durliston Cl WDN WA8 157 H1
Durning Rd EHL/KEN L7 114 A6
Durrant Rd NG/CROX L11 98 C5
Durrell Wy GOL/RIS/CU WA3 93 F3
Dursley RAIN/WH L35 118 B5
Dursley Dr AIMK WN4 79 J5
Durston Rd CHLDW L16 134 E1
Durweston Wk NTHLY L27 135 K3
Dutton Dr BEB CH63 170 B3
Dutton Gn EP CH65 196 E6
Dutton St WARR WA1 17 F5
Duxbury Cl MGHL L31 62 C4
RNFD/HAY WA11 75 G2
Duxford Ct WARRN/WOL WA2 124 A6
Dwerryhouse La NG/CROX L11 99 F3
Dwerryhouse St TOX L8 132 C3
Dyers La ORM L39 53 J1
Dyer St GOL/RIS/CU WA3 92 A3
Dyke St NPK/KEN L6 113 J3
Dykin Cl WDN WA8 139 K6
Dykin Rd WDN WA8 139 J6
Dymchurch Rd SPK/HALE L24 173 G1
Dymoke Rd NG/CROX L11 99 G2
Dyson Hall Dr WLT/FAZ L9 83 G6
Dyson St ANF/KKDL L4 97 H4

E

Eager La MGHL L31 51 K5
Eagle Brow LYMM WA13 145 J6
Eagle Crs RNFD/HAY WA11 75 H3
Eaglehall Rd WLT/FAZ L9 98 D1
Eaglehurst Rd WLTN L25 135 J5
Eagle La GTS/LS CH66 195 G2
Eagle Park Dr
WARRN/WOL WA2 123 G6
Eagles Ct KKBY L32 84 D1
Eaglesfield Cl STHEL WA9 * 104 A6
Eagles Wy RUNC WA7 187 H1
Ealing Rd WARRW/BUR WA5 141 H4
WLT/FAZ L9 82 E4
Eamont Av CHTN/BK PR9 20 E6
Eanleywood La RUNC WA7 178 B6
Eardisley Rd WAV L15 134 B3
Earle Cl NEWLW WA12 105 K2
Earle Crs NSTN CH64 181 J6
Earle Dr NSTN CH64 191 J1
Earle Rd EHL/KEN L7 133 H1
WDN WA8 19 G5
Earle St NEWLW WA12 105 K3
VAUX/LVPD L3 8 C2
Earl Rd BTL L20 5 H3
Earl's Cl CSBY/BLUN L23 68 E6
Earlsfield Rd WAV L15 134 A3
Earls Gdns EP CH65 6 B4
Earlston Rd WAL/NB CH45 111 G1
Earl St PS/BROM CH62 151 G4
STHEL WA9 104 A1
WARRN/WOL WA2 142 E2
Earls Wy RUNC WA7 187 H1
Earlswood SKEL WN8 57 G4
Earlswood Cl MOR/LEA CH46 128 C1
Earlwood Gdns RAIN/WH L35 118 A5
Earp St ALL/GAR L19 153 K5
Easby Cl FMBY L37 49 G3
RUNC WA7 11 H5
Easby Rd ANF/KKDL L4 97 F6
Easby Wk ANF/KKDL L4 97 F6
Easedale Dr STHP PR8 33 H5
Easedale Wk NWD/KWIPK L33 72 C4
Easenhall Cl WDN WA8 139 G5
Easington Rd STHEL WA9 119 F1
East Albert Rd AIG/SPK L17 133 G5
East Av GOL/RIS/CU WA3 92 D2
WARRN/WOL WA2 143 F1
WARRS WA4 162 C2
WARRW/BUR WA5 141 H5
Eastbank St STHP PR8 14 E5
Eastbourne Rd CL/PREN CH43 2 C5
CSBY/WL L22 80 C1
STHP PR8 27 H4
WLT/FAZ L9 82 E4
Eastbourne Wy NPK/KEN L6 113 H4
Eastbury Cl WDN WA8 139 H4
Eastcliffe Rd CLB/OSW/ST L13 115 F4
East Cl PR/KW L34 102 C6
Eastcote Rd ALL/GAR L19 153 K3
Eastcott Cl GR/UP/WCH CH49 128 D6
Eastcroft NWD/KWIPK L33 72 E4
Eastcroft Rd WAL/EG CH44 111 J4
Eastdale Rd WARR WA1 143 K2
WAV L15 134 A1
East Dam Wood Rd
SPK/HALE L24 174 A3
Easter Ct WARRW/BUR WA5 122 B5
Eastern Av PS/BROM CH62 171 F1
SPK/HALE L24 174 A3
Eastern Dr ALL/GAR L19 153 H4
Eastfield Dr AIG/SPK L17 133 H6
Eastfield Wk KKBY L32 84 B2
East Float BIRK CH41 * 111 K6
Eastford Rd WARRS WA4 161 K2
East Front RAIN/WH L35 118 A6
Eastgate Rd RUNC WA7 160 B6
Eastham Cl CHLDW L16 115 K6
Eastham Crs STHEL WA9 120 A3
Eastham Gn SPK/HALE L24 173 K1
Eastham Ms PS/BROM CH62 184 D3
Eastham Rake GTS/LS CH66 183 K5
Eastham Village Rd
PS/BROM CH62 184 D3
Eastlake Av EV L5 113 H2
East Lancashire Rd ECCL WA10 88 C4
GOL/RIS/CU WA3 92 C5
NG/CROX L11 98 D2
NWD/KWIPK L33 85 F5
RNFD/HAY WA11 89 G3
East La RUNC WA7 177 J6
SFTN L29 60 D5
East Leigh SKEL WN8 57 F4
Eastleigh Dr PEN/TH CH61 148 A4
East Mains SPK/HALE L24 174 B2
Eastman Rd CLB/OSW/ST L13 98 C6
East Md ORM L39 53 F4
East Meade MGHL L31 62 A5
East Millwood Rd
SPK/HALE L24 174 B1
Easton Rd HUY L36 116 B4
PS/BROM CH62 151 G3
East Orchard La WLT/FAZ L9 83 G4
East Park Ct WAL/EG CH44 112 A4
East Prescot Rd
DV/KA/FCH L14 115 K3
East Rd DV/KA/FCH L14 115 G5
SPK/HALE L24 156 A6
East Side STHEL WA9 104 A3
East St AIMK WN4 79 J5
BIRK CH41 112 A5
CHTN/BK PR9 15 J4
CSBY/WL L22 80 E2
PR/KW L34 118 A1
VAUX/LVPD L3 8 C2
WDN WA8 19 J1
East Vw WARRS WA4 163 G1
Eastview Cl CL/PREN CH43 130 A5
East Wy MOR/LEA CH46 109 J6
Eastway GR/UP/WCH CH49 129 F5
GTS/LS CH66 195 G2
MGHL L31 62 B5
WDN WA8 157 J2
Eastwell Rd AIMK WN4 79 F6
Eastwood AIG/SPK L17 133 F6
RUNC WA7 178 B4
Eastwood Av NEWLW WA12 107 F2
Eastwood Rd
WARRW/BUR WA5 105 K6
Eaton Av BTL L20 82 A5
LITH L21 81 J4
WAL/EG CH44 111 J3
Eaton Cl HUY L36 116 C5
WD/CROXPK L12 98 E6
Eaton Gdns WD/CROXPK L12 115 H2
Eaton Rd ALL/GAR L19 153 H5
CL/PREN CH43 2 A6
ECCL WA10 88 A5
MGHL L31 71 G3
WD/CROXPK L12 99 F6
WKBY CH48 146 B2
Eaton Rd North
WD/CROXPK L12 98 E6
Eaton St PR/KW L34 117 K1
RUNC WA7 10 D5
VAUX/LVPD L3 8 C1
WAL/EG CH44 111 H3
Eavesdale SKEL WN8 57 G5
Eaves La STHEL WA9 119 K1
Ebenezer Howard Rd LITH L21 81 K1
Ebenezer Rd EHL/KEN L7 114 A5
Ebenezer St RF/TRAN CH42 151 F1
RNFD/HAY WA11 89 J5
Eberle St CLVP L2 8 D3
Ebony Cl MOR/LEA CH46 * 128 C1
Ebony Wy NWD/KWIPK L33 72 D4
Ebor La EV L5 113 G3
Ebrington St ALL/GAR L19 153 K5
Ecclesall Av LITH L21 81 K3
Eccles Dr WLTN L25 * 135 J2
Ecclesfield Rd ECCL WA10 87 H6
Eccles Gv STHEL WA9 120 C4
Eccleshall Rd PS/BROM CH62 151 H5
Eccleshill Rd CLB/OSW/ST L13 114 E2
Eccles Rd FMBY L37 48 D4
Eccleston Av GTS/LS CH66 195 H4
PS/BROM CH62 170 E4
Eccleston Cl CL/PREN CH43 130 C6
GOL/RIS/CU WA3 124 E3
Eccleston Dr RUNC WA7 11 J7
Eccleston Gdns ECCL WA10 102 C5
Eccleston Rd WLT/FAZ L9 82 C5
Eccleston St ECCL WA10 12 C5
PR/KW L34 117 K1
Edale Cl PS/BROM CH62 184 B2
Edale Rd CALD/MH L18 134 B5
Eddisbury Rd GTS/LS CH66 202 D1
WAL/EG CH44 111 J2
WKBY CH48 127 F5
Eddisbury Wy WD/CROXPK L12 98 E6
Eddleston St AIMK WN4 78 E3
Edelsten St WARRW/BUR WA5 142 C4
Eden Av CHTN/BK PR9 23 H2
RNFD/HAY WA11 75 F2
Eden Cl GTS/LS CH66 195 F4
NWD/KWIPK L33 72 E3
RAIN/WH L35 118 D5
Edendale WDN WA8 157 G1
Eden Dr North CSBY/BLUN L23 69 H6
Eden Dr South CSBY/BLUN L23 69 H6
Edenfield Cl STHP PR8 28 B4
Edenfield Crs HUY L36 117 F3
Edenfield Rd WAV L15 134 A3
Edenhall Dr WLTN L25 135 K6
Edenhurst Av CHLDW L16 135 H1
WAL/EG CH44 111 J2
Edenhurst Cl FMBY L37 48 C3
Edenhurst Ct HUY L36 * 116 B3
Edenhurst Dr FMBY L37 48 C3
Edenpark Rd RF/TRAN CH42 131 F6
Eden V NTHTN L30 70 C5
Edgar Ct BIRK CH41 2 D3
LITH L21 81 J2
Edgars Dr WARRN/WOL WA2 124 C5
Edgar St VAUX/LVPD L3 113 F4
Edgbaston Cl HUY L36 116 C6
Edgbaston Wy CL/PREN CH43 129 K1
Edgefield Cl CL/PREN CH43 130 A5
Edgefold Rd KKBY L32 84 E2
Edge Green La GOL/RIS/CU WA3 92 A4
Edge Green St AIMK WN4 79 J5
Edge Gv EHL/KEN L7 114 C5
Edgehill Rd MOR/LEA CH46 128 D1
Edge La CLB/OSW/ST L13 114 C5
CSBY/BLUN L23 69 H3
EHL/KEN L7 113 K6
Edge Lane Dr CLB/OSW/ST L13 115 F6
Edgeley Gdns WLT/FAZ L9 82 C5
Edgemoor Cl CL/PREN CH43 129 J2
WD/CROXPK L12 115 H2
Edgemoor Dr AIN/FAZ L10 83 K4
CSBY/BLUN L23 69 H4
PEN/TH CH61 147 K4
Edgemoor Rd WD/CROXPK L12 115 H2
Edgerley Pl AIMK WN4 79 F6
Edgerton Rd CL/PREN CH43 130 D3
GOL/RIS/CU WA3 93 F3
Edge St STHEL WA9 118 E1
Edgewood Dr PS/BROM CH62 184 A2
Edgewood Rd
GR/UP/WCH CH49 129 F3
HOY CH47 108 B6
Edgeworth Cl STHEL WA9 104 C5
Edgeworth Rd GOL/RIS/CU WA3 92 A2
Edgeworth St STHEL WA9 104 C6
Edgley Dr ORM L39 46 A6
Edgworth Rd ANF/KKDL L4 113 K1
Edgworth St WARR WA1 16 C4
Edinburgh Cl NTHTN L30 82 C3
Edinburgh Ct EP CH65 196 C6
Edinburgh Dr CL/PREN CH43 149 K2
HUY L36 136 D1
Edinburgh Rd EHL/KEN L7 113 K5
FMBY L37 48 E4
WAL/NB CH45 * 111 H2
WDN WA8 157 F3
Edington St WAV L15 133 K1
Edison Rd RUNC WA7 177 G2
Edith Rd ANF/KKDL L4 113 J1
BTL L20 82 A5
WAL/EG CH44 112 A4
Edith St RUNC WA7 10 C3
STHEL WA9 * 104 D6
Edith Vls BTL L20 * 5 J2
Edmondson St STHEL WA9 * 104 D2
Edmonton Cl EV L5 113 F1
Edmund St VAUX/LVPD L3 8 C3
Edna Av AIN/FAZ L10 83 K4
Edrich Av CL/PREN CH43 * 129 K1
Edward Dr AIMK WN4 79 G5
Edward Gdns WARR WA1 144 E3
Edward Jenner Av NTHTN L30 70 C6
Edward Rd HOY CH47 127 H3
RAIN/WH L35 118 B2
WARRW/BUR WA5 140 E3
Edward's La SPK/HALE L24 154 E5
Edward St EP CH65 * 6 D1
RNFD/HAY WA11 89 K5
STHEL WA9 104 B4
VAUX/LVPD L3 9 H4
WDN WA8 19 J1
Edwards Wy WDN WA8 157 H3
Edwin St WDN WA8 19 G1
Effingham St BTL L20 96 D4
Egan Rd CL/PREN CH43 130 B1
Egbert Rd HOY CH47 127 H1
Egdon Cl WDN WA8 159 F1
Egerton KNUT WA16 165 K6
SKEL WN8 57 F5
Egerton Av WARR WA1 143 H2
Egerton Dr WKBY CH48 146 C1
Egerton Gdns RF/TRAN CH42 150 D2
Egerton Gv WAL/NB CH45 111 H2
Egerton Park Cl
RF/TRAN CH42 150 D2
Egerton Rd LYMM WA13 164 D1
PR/KW L34 117 J1
PS/BROM CH62 151 G4
WAV L15 133 J2
Egerton St EP CH65 6 D2
RUNC WA7 10 C3
STHEL WA9 104 B4
TOX L8 132 E2
WAL/NB CH45 95 H5
WARR WA1 17 G4
WARRS WA4 162 B2
Egerton Whf BIRK CH41 3 G2
Eglington Av RAIN/WH L35 117 K5
Egremont Cl NTHLY L27 136 D5
Egremont Lawn NTHLY L27 136 D5
Egremont Prom WAL/EG CH44 111 K1
Egypt St WARR WA1 16 C5
WDN WA8 18 B5
Eighth Av WLT/FAZ L9 83 G4
Eilian Gv DV/KA/FCH L14 115 H5
Eisenhower Cl
WARRW/BUR WA5 141 J4
Elaine Cl AIMK WN4 79 J4

GTS/LS CH66 195 F5
WDN WA8 19 G1
Elaine St TOX L8 132 E3
WARR WA1 17 J1
Elbow La FMBY L37 49 F2
Elcombe Av GOL/RIS/CU WA3 93 F4
Elderdale Rd ANF/KKDL L4 97 K6
Elder Gdns ALL/GAR L19 153 J3
Elder Gv WKBY CH48 146 C1
Eldersfield Rd NG/CROX L11 99 F3
Elderswood Rd RAIN/WH L35 118 E3
Elderwood Rd RF/TRAN CH42 131 H6
Eldon Cl ECCL WA10 12 C7
Eldon Gdns AIMK WN4 79 F3
Eldonian Wy VAUX/LVPD L3 112 E3
Eldon Pl VAUX/LVPD L3 112 E3
Eldon Rd RF/TRAN CH42 150 E1
WAL/EG CH44 111 H3
Eldons Cft STHP PR8 33 K4
Eldon St ECCL WA10 12 C7
VAUX/LVPD L3 112 E3
WARR WA1 17 G4
Eldon Ter NSTN CH64 191 K2
Eldred Rd CHLDW L16 134 D3
Eleanor Pk CL/PREN CH43 129 K1
Eleanor Rd BTL L20 82 A5
CL/PREN CH43 110 D6
MOR/LEA CH46 109 G6
Eleanor St BTL L20 96 D4
EP CH65 6 E2
WDN WA8 * 18 D6
Elephant La STHEL WA9 103 G6
Elfet St BIRK CH41 130 C1
Elgar Av PS/BROM CH62 184 B2
Elgar Cl EP CH65 195 J6
Elgar Rd DV/KA/FCH L14 115 K2
Elgin Av AIMK WN4 78 C5
WARRS WA4 161 K1
Elgin Ct RAIN/WH L35 * 119 F5
Elgin Dr WAL/NB CH45 111 J1
Elgin Wy BIRK CH41 3 G3
Eliot Cl PS/BROM CH62 151 F4
Eliot St BTL L20 81 J6
Elizabeth Av STHP PR8 34 A3
Elizabeth Ct WDN WA8 18 E6
Elizabeth Dr WARR WA1 143 K1
Elizabeth Rd AIN/FAZ L10 84 A4
BTL L20 82 A5
HUY L36 136 D1
RNFD/HAY WA11 90 D4
Elizabeth St STHEL WA9 104 C5
STHEL WA9 120 B4
VAUX/LVPD L3 * 9 K3
Elizabeth Ter WDN WA8 157 J2
Eliza St STHEL WA9 104 D6
Elkan Cl WDN WA8 139 K6
Elkan Rd WDN WA8 139 J6
Elkstone Rd NG/CROX L11 99 F4
Ellaby Rd RAIN/WH L35 118 E3
Ellamsbridge Rd STHEL WA9 104 C6
Elland Dr GTS/LS CH66 195 F4
Ellel Gv NPK/KEN L6 114 A2
Ellen Gdn STHEL WA9 104 C6
Ellen's La BEB CH63 151 F6
Ellen St STHEL WA9 104 C6
WARRW/BUR WA5 16 A1
Elleray Dr TOX L8 132 E5
Elleray Park Rd WAL/NB CH45 95 G6
Ellerbrook Dr BRSC L40 39 F6
Ellerbrook Wy ORM L39 45 J5
Ellerby Cl RUNC WA7 178 D6
Ellergreen Rd NG/CROX L11 98 D3
Ellerman Rd VAUX/LVPD L3 132 E6
Ellerslie Av RAIN/WH L35 118 E2
Ellerslie Rd CLB/OSW/ST L13 114 B1
Ellerton Av GTS/LS CH66 195 F4
Ellerton Cl WDN WA8 138 C6
Ellerton Wy WD/CROXPK L12 99 J2
Ellesmere Dr AIN/FAZ L10 83 F1
Ellesmere Gv WAL/NB CH45 111 H1
Ellesmere Rd AIMK WN4 78 E4
WARRS WA4 162 A2
Ellesmere St RUNC WA7 11 F4
WARR WA1 17 G5
Ellesworth Cl
WARRW/BUR WA5 141 K1
Elliot St CLVPS L1 9 F4
ECCL WA10 12 C5
WDN WA8 18 E3
Elliott Av GOL/RIS/CU WA3 92 C2
WARR WA1 17 K1
Ellis Ashton St HUY L36 117 G5
Ellis La FROD/HEL WA6 187 G6
Ellison Dr ECCL WA10 102 E1
Ellison Gv HUY L36 116 D5
Ellison St CLB/OSW/ST L13 114 D3
WARRS WA4 162 C2
Ellis Pl TOX L8 132 E4
Ellis Rd WGNW/BIL/O WN5 77 G5
Ellis St WDN WA8 18 B6
Ellon Av RAIN/WH L35 119 F5
Elloway Rd SPK/HALE L24 174 B2
Ellwood Cl SPK/HALE L24 175 F3
Elmar Rd AIG/SPK L17 153 F1
Elm Av AIMK WN4 78 C4
CSBY/BLUN L23 69 G4
GOL/RIS/CU WA3 92 B2
GR/UP/WCH CH49 128 E3
WDN WA8 158 C1
Elm Bank EV L5 97 H6
Elmbank Rd CALD/MH L18 133 K4
PS/BROM CH62 151 G5
Elmbank St WAL/EG CH44 * 111 J4
Elm Cl PEN/TH CH61 167 K1
WD/CROXPK L12 99 K2
Elmcroft Cl WLT/FAZ L9 83 G4
Elmcroft La HTWN L38 59 G4
Elmdale Cl FMBY L37 48 D3
Elmdale Rd WLT/FAZ L9 97 J1
Elmdene Ct
GR/UP/WCH CH49 * 147 K1
Elm Dr FMBY L37 48 D4
GR/UP/WCH CH49 128 D6
LITH L21 81 G5
WGNW/BIL/O WN5 77 G4
Elmers Gn SKEL WN8 57 F4
Elmer's Green La SKEL WN8 56 E1
Elmers Wood Rd SKEL WN8 57 G2
Elmfield Cl STHEL WA9 103 G5
Elmfield Rd WLT/FAZ L9 82 D6
Elm Gdns LITH L21 * 81 H5
RNFD/HAY WA11 75 G3
Elm Gv EHL/KEN L7 113 J6
GTS/LS CH66 202 E2
HOY CH47 127 G2
PR/KW L34 102 B6
RF/TRAN CH42 131 G5
SKEL WN8 * 56 A4
WARR WA1 143 J2
WDN WA8 18 E1
Elm Hall Dr CALD/MH L18 134 B4
Elmham Crs AIN/FAZ L10 83 J4
Elm House Ms WLTN L25 135 J5
Elmhurst Rd WLTN L25 135 H2
Elmore Cl EV L5 113 H2
RUNC WA7 178 C4
Elm Park Dr STHP PR8 34 A4
Elm Park Rd WAL/NB CH45 95 G6
Elm Pl ORM L39 53 J1
Elmridge SKEL WN8 57 F5
Elm Ri FROD/HEL WA6 201 F2
Elm Rd ANF/KKDL L4 97 J4
BEB CH63 150 E4
BRSC L40 38 E6
ECCL WA10 103 F5
KKBY L32 72 C6
LITH L21 81 G5
NSTN CH64 193 G1
PEN/TH CH61 148 C5
RF/TRAN CH42 131 G6
RNFD/HAY WA11 * 90 D4
RUNC WA7 177 F5
STHP PR8 27 J3
WARRN/WOL WA2 123 H3
WARRW/BUR WA5 141 G6
Elm Rd North RF/TRAN CH42 150 A1
Elmsbury St AIMK WN4 78 E4
Elmsdale Rd CALD/MH L18 134 B4
Elmsett Cl WARRW/BUR WA5 141 F4
Elmsfield Cl WLTN L25 135 H4
Elmsfield Pk ORM L39 62 E1
Elmsfield Rd CSBY/BLUN L23 69 J3
Elms House Rd
CLB/OSW/ST L13 114 D4
Elmsley Rd CALD/MH L18 134 A6
Elms Rd MGHL L31 71 F3
Elm St EP CH65 196 B2
Elmstead SKEL WN8 57 F5
The Elms GOL/RIS/CU WA3 93 G4
MGHL L31 62 B4
RUNC WA7 10 C7
TOX L8 133 F5
Elm St BIRK CH41 2 E4
HUY L36 117 G5
Elmswood Av RAIN/WH L35 119 F5
Elmswood Ct CALD/MH L18 * 134 A6
Elmswood Gv HUY L36 116 B4
Elmswood Rd AIG/SPK L17 153 F1
RF/TRAN CH42 131 F5
WAL/EG CH44 111 K3
Elm Ter EHL/KEN L7 * 114 A5
HOY CH47 127 H2
Elm Tree Av LYMM WA13 164 E1
WARR WA1 143 J1
Elmtree Cl WD/CROXPK L12 99 G6
Elmtree Gv CL/PREN CH43 130 B1
Elm Tree Rd GOL/RIS/CU WA3 93 G4
LYMM WA13 164 E1
Elmure Av BEB CH63 150 C6
Elm V NPK/KEN L6 114 B4
Elmway Cl CLB/OSW/ST L13 114 D5
Elmwood RUNC WA7 178 B4
SKEL WN8 56 E2
Elmwood Av AIMK WN4 91 F1
CSBY/BLUN L23 69 G5
WARR WA1 17 K1
Elmwood Dr PEN/TH CH61 167 K3
Elphin Gv ANF/KKDL L4 97 J4
Elsbeck Gv STHEL WA9 120 B1
Elsie Rd ANF/KKDL L4 113 K1
Elsmere Av AIG/SPK L17 133 H6
Elson Rd FMBY L37 48 D4
Elstead Gv AIMK WN4 78 C5
Elstead Rd KKBY L32 84 B2
WLT/FAZ L9 98 C1
Elston Av NEWLW WA12 91 G6
Elstow St EV L5 97 F6
Elstree Rd NPK/KEN L6 114 B4
Elswick SKEL WN8 56 E5
Elswick Rd CHTN/BK PR9 23 H1
Elswick St TOX L8 132 E6
Elsworth Cl FMBY L37 48 C5
Eltham Av LITH L21 81 J2
Eltham Cl AIMK WN4 79 J6
GR/UP/WCH CH49 148 E1
WDN WA8 139 K6
Eltham Gn GR/UP/WCH CH49 148 D1
Eltham St EHL/KEN L7 114 B5
Elton Av CSBY/BLUN L23 68 D5
NTHTN L30 70 B6
Elton Cl GOL/RIS/CU WA3 93 F4
GOL/RIS/CU WA3 124 E3
PS/BROM CH62 184 B4
Elton Dr BEB CH63 170 C3
Elton Head Rd STHEL WA9 119 F2
Elton La FROD/HEL WA6 199 F5
Elton Lordship La
FROD/HEL WA6 199 H2
Elton St ANF/KKDL L4 97 H3
Elvington Cl RUNC WA7 187 J4
Elvington Rd HTWN L38 59 G5
Elway Rd AIMK WN4 79 H6
Elwick Dr NG/CROX L11 99 G3
Elwood Cl NWD/KWIPK L33 72 D3
Elworth Av WDN WA8 139 F4
Elworthy Av HLWD L26 155 J2
Elwyn Dr HLWD L26 155 K3
Elwyn Rd HOY CH47 108 C6
Elwy St TOX L8 133 F4
Ely Av MOR/LEA CH46 128 D1
Ely Cl GTS/LS CH66 202 C3
NTHTN L30 82 C2
Ely Ms CHTN/BK PR9 23 J3
Ely Pk RUNC WA7 178 D3
Ember Crs NPK/KEN L6 113 H3
Embledon St TOX L8 133 G2
Embleton Ct RUNC WA7 187 G2
Emerald Cl NTHTN L30 70 E6
Emerald St TOX L8 132 E6
Emerson Cl HTWN L38 59 G3
Emerson St TOX L8 132 E2
Emery St ANF/KKDL L4 97 H4
Emily St STHEL WA9 102 E6
WDN WA8 18 D5
Emlyn St STHEL WA9 104 B4
Emmanuel Rd CHTN/BK PR9 23 H3
Emmett St STHEL WA9 104 A4
Empire Rd LITH L21 81 J5
Empress Cl MGHL L31 61 K6
Empress Rd EHL/KEN L7 113 K5
NPK/KEN L6 114 A1
WAL/EG CH44 111 J3
Emslie Ct NSTN CH64 191 H1
Endborne Rd WLT/FAZ L9 82 D5
Endbutt La CSBY/BLUN L23 69 F6
Enderby Av RNFD/HAY WA11 89 F5
Endfield Pk ALL/GAR L19 153 J3
Endmoor Rd HUY L36 116 C2
Endsleigh Rd CLB/OSW/ST L13 114 C4
CSBY/WL L22 80 C1
Enerby Cl CL/PREN CH43 129 K2
Enfield Av CSBY/BLUN L23 69 F5
Enfield Park Rd
WARRN/WOL WA2 124 A3
Enfield Rd CLB/OSW/ST L13 115 F5
EP CH65 6 C4
Enfield St ECCL WA10 12 C7
Enfield Ter CL/PREN CH43 2 A7
Enford Dr STHEL WA9 104 B6
Engine La FMBY L37 49 K6
Enid St TOX L8 132 E3
Ennerdale SKEL WN8 57 F5
Ennerdale Av AIMK WN4 79 G5
MGHL L31 62 C5
PS/BROM CH62 184 C3
RNFD/HAY WA11 88 E3
WARRN/WOL WA2 123 H4
Ennerdale Cl FMBY L37 48 D2
NWD/KWIPK L33 72 C4
SPK/HALE L24 155 F6
Ennerdale Dr FROD/HEL WA6 201 F1
NTHTN L30 82 A3
ORM L39 53 F3
Ennerdale Rd CL/PREN CH43 149 H2
FMBY L37 48 D2
WAL/NB CH45 95 F5
WLT/FAZ L9 83 G5
Ennerdale St VAUX/LVPD L3 113 F3
Ennis Cl SPK/HALE L24 174 E3
Ennisdale Dr WKBY CH48 146 E1
Ennismore Rd
CLB/OSW/ST L13 114 D4
CSBY/BLUN L23 68 D4
Ennis Rd WD/CROXPK L12 115 J1
Ensor St BTL L20 96 D4
Enstone SKEL WN8 57 F4
Enstone Av LITH L21 81 H2
Enstone Rd WLTN L25 154 E5
Ensworth Rd CALD/MH L18 134 C4
Enterprise Wy WAV L15 114 C6
Enville St WARRS WA4 17 F7
Epping Av STHEL WA9 119 K4
Epping Cl RAIN/WH L35 119 F5
Epping Ct HES CH60 168 A4
Epping Dr WARR WA1 144 C1
Epping Gv WAV L15 134 C3
Epsom Cl WLT/FAZ L9 83 H2
Epsom Gdns WARRS WA4 162 D4
Epsom Gv NWD/KWIPK L33 73 F3
Epsom Rd MOR/LEA CH46 109 K4
Epsom St STHEL WA9 104 D1
Epsom Wy EV L5 113 F2
Epstein Ct NPK/KEN L6 113 K4
Epworth Cl CL/PREN CH43 130 D3
Epworth Gra CL/PREN CH43 * 130 D3
Epworth St NPK/KEN L6 9 K2
Eremon Cl WLT/FAZ L9 83 G3
Erfurt Av BEB CH63 170 C1
Erica Ct HES CH60 167 J3
Eric Av WARR WA1 143 H1
Eric Fountain Rd EP CH65 185 G4
Eric Gv WAL/EG CH44 111 G3
Eric Rd WAL/EG CH44 111 G3
Eric St WDN WA8 19 G1
Eridge St TOX L8 133 F5
Erin Cl TOX L8 132 D4
Erindale Crs FROD/HEL WA6 200 D3
Erl St WLT/FAZ L9 82 D5
Ermine Crs EV L5 113 H2
Errington Av EP CH65 6 D2
Errington Ct AIG/SPK L17 153 F3
Errington St EV L5 112 D1
Errol St AIG/SPK L17 133 G6
Erskine Cl RNFD/HAY WA11 89 H5
Erskine Rd WAL/EG CH44 111 J4
Erskine St NPK/KEN L6 9 K2
Erwood St WARRN/WOL WA2 16 C2
Erylmore Rd CALD/MH L18 153 H2
Escolme Dr GR/UP/WCH CH49 129 F6
Escor Rd WLTN L25 135 G3
Escort Cl WLTN L25 155 F3
Eshelby Cl CSBY/WL L22 81 F2
Esher Cl CL/PREN CH43 129 K2
Eshe Rd CSBY/BLUN L23 68 D5
Eshe Rd North CSBY/BLUN L23 68 D5
Esher Rd NPK/KEN L6 114 A4
PS/BROM CH62 151 G3
Eskbank SKEL WN8 56 E5
Eskbrook SKEL WN8 56 E4
Eskburn Rd CLB/OSW/ST L13 114 C1
Eskdale EP CH65 196 A6
SKEL WN8 56 D5
Eskdale Av ORM L39 53 G3
PS/BROM CH62 184 B2
RNFD/HAY WA11 88 E3
Eskdale Cl FMBY L37 48 D3
RUNC WA7 187 G2
Eskdale Dr FMBY L37 48 D3
MGHL L31 62 B5
Eskdale Rd AIMK WN4 79 G4
WLT/FAZ L9 82 D5
Esk St BTL L20 96 D5
Eslington St ALL/GAR L19 153 H4
Esmond St NPK/KEN L6 113 K2
Esonwood Rd RAIN/WH L35 117 K4
Espin St ANF/KKDL L4 97 H4
Esplanade STHP PR8 14 B5
Esplen Av CSBY/BLUN L23 69 G4
Essex Rd HUY L36 117 G3
STHP PR8 34 C1
WKBY CH48 127 H6
Essex St TOX L8 132 E4
Essex Wy BTL L20 5 G3
Esther St WDN WA8 19 F2
Esthwaite Av RNFD/HAY WA11 89 F3
Estuary Banks SPK/HALE L24 172 E1
Estuary Bvd SPK/HALE L24 172 E1
Etal Cl NG/CROX L11 99 F4
Ethelbert Rd HOY CH47 127 H1
Ethel Rd WAL/EG CH44 111 K4
Etna St CLB/OSW/ST L13 114 D4
Eton Ct CALD/MH L18 134 E4
Eton Dr AIN/FAZ L10 83 F1
BEB CH63 182 A1
Eton Hall Dr STHEL WA9 104 A6
Eton Rd EP CH65 7 F7
Eton St ANF/KKDL L4 97 H4
Etruria St ALL/GAR L19 172 B1
Etruscan Rd CLB/OSW/ST L13 114 E3
Ettington Dr STHP PR8 33 G4
Ettington Rd ANF/KKDL L4 97 K6
Ettrick Cl NWD/KWIPK L33 72 C3
Euclid Av WARRS WA4 163 G1
Eurolink STHEL WA9 119 H3
Europa Bvd BIRK CH41 3 F4
WARRW/BUR WA5 122 D4
Europa Wy EP CH65 6 E3
Eustace St WARRN/WOL WA2 16 B3
Euston Gv CL/PREN CH43 2 B7
Euston St ANF/KKDL L4 97 H3
Evans Cl RNFD/HAY WA11 90 E4
Evans Pl WARRS WA4 143 G6
Evans Rd HOY CH47 127 G2
SPK/HALE L24 155 F6
Evans St PR/KW L34 101 K6
Evellynne Cl KKBY L32 84 B1
Evelyn Av PR/KW L34 118 A1
STHEL WA9 104 C2
Evelyn Rd WAL/EG CH44 111 J4
Evelyn St WARRW/BUR WA5 142 A5
Evenwood SKEL WN8 57 F4
STHEL WA9 120 A1
Evenwood Ct SKEL WN8 * 56 E4
Everard Cl BRSC L40 36 D2
Everard Rd STHP PR8 28 A3
Everdon Wd NWD/KWIPK L33 72 D6
Evered Av WLT/FAZ L9 97 J1
Everest Cl GTS/LS CH66 195 J6
Everest Rd CSBY/BLUN L23 68 E5
RF/TRAN CH42 150 C1
Evergreen Cl
GR/UP/WCH CH49 128 E3
NTHLY L27 136 B3
The Evergreens FMBY L37 48 D1
Evergreen Wy STHEL WA9 104 E6
Everite Rd WDN WA8 157 G4
Everleigh Cl CL/PREN CH43 129 J2
Eversham Cl CHTN/BK PR9 21 K6
Eversleigh Dr BEB CH63 170 C1
Eversley SKEL WN8 57 F4
WDN WA8 157 G1
Eversley Cl FROD/HEL WA6 201 F3
WARRS WA4 162 E6
Eversley Pk CL/PREN CH43 * 130 E6
Eversley St TOX L8 133 F3
Everton Brow VAUX/LVPD L3 113 G4
Everton Gv RNFD/HAY WA11 89 G6
Everton Rd NPK/KEN L6 113 H3
STHP PR8 27 H3
Everton St AIMK WN4 78 C4
Everton Ter EV L5 113 H3
Everton Va ANF/KKDL L4 97 G6
Everton Vw BTL L20 4 C6
Every St NPK/KEN L6 113 K3
Evesham Cl WARRS WA4 162 B3
WLTN L25 154 C1
Evesham Rd ANF/KKDL L4 98 B4
WAL/NB CH45 111 F1
Evington SKEL WN8 57 F4
Ewanville HUY L36 116 E6
Ewart Rd CHLDW L16 135 H1
LITH L21 81 G4
RNFD/HAY WA11 88 E5
Ewden Cl CHLDW L16 135 F2
Ewloe Ct EP CH65 203 H1
Exchange Pas West CLVP L2 * 8 C3
Exchange Pl RAIN/WH L35 118 E4
Exchange St ECCL WA10 13 G6
Exchange St East CLVP L2 8 C3
Exeley RAIN/WH L35 118 A5
Exeter Cl WLT/FAZ L9 83 H2
Exeter Rd BTL L20 4 E7
EP CH65 6 D4
WAL/EG CH44 111 J2
Exeter St ECCL WA10 12 B5
Exford Rd WD/CROXPK L12 99 H5
Exmoor Cl CHTN/BK PR9 20 E5
PEN/TH CH61 148 C6
Exmouth Cl BIRK CH41 2 D4
Exmouth Crs RUNC WA7 188 D1
Exmouth Gdns BIRK CH41 2 D4
Exmouth St BIRK CH41 2 D5
Exmouth Wy BIRK CH41 2 D4
WARRW/BUR WA5 121 K1
Extension Vw STHEL WA9 104 B5

F

Factory La WARR WA1 16 B6
WDN WA8 139 G6
Factory Rw ECCL WA10 103 G4
Fairacre Rd ALL/GAR L19 153 H4
Fairacres Rd BEB CH63 170 B1
Fairbairn Rd CSBY/WL L22 81 F2
Fairbank St WAV L15 133 K2
Fairbeech Ct CL/PREN CH43 129 K2
Fairbeech Ms CL/PREN CH43 * 129 K2
Fairbourne Cl
WARRW/BUR WA5 122 E4
Fairbrook Dr BIRK CH41 110 D6
Fairbrother Crs
WARRN/WOL WA2 123 K5
Fairburn SKEL WN8 56 D2
Fairburn Cl WDN WA8 139 K6
Fairburn Rd CLB/OSW/ST L13 114 C1
Fairclough Av WARR WA1 17 F6
Fairclough Crs RNFD/HAY WA11 89 K5
Fairclough La CL/PREN CH43 130 E5
Fairclough Rd ECCL WA10 102 E1
HUY L36 116 C3
RAIN/WH L35 118 D4
Fairclough St CLVPS L1 9 F5
NEWLW WA12 106 B2
WARRW/BUR WA5 121 J1
Fairfax Dr RUNC WA7 177 G3
Fairfax Pl NG/CROX L11 98 B3
Fairfax Rd NG/CROX L11 98 C3
RF/TRAN CH42 131 H5
Fairfield CSBY/BLUN L23 69 F5
Fairfield Av DV/KA/FCH L14 116 A5
EP CH65 202 E1
Fairfield Cl HUY L36 116 A5
ORM L39 45 J4
Fairfield Crs HUY L36 116 A5
MOR/LEA CH46 128 E1
NPK/KEN L6 114 B4
Fairfield Dr ORM L39 45 J4
WKBY CH48 127 K6
Fairfield Gdns RNFD/HAY WA11 88 B1
WARRS WA4 162 D1
Fairfield Rd ECCL WA10 87 K6
RF/TRAN CH42 150 D1
STHP PR8 33 J3
WARRS WA4 162 C1
WDN WA8 18 E1
Fairfield St EHL/KEN L7 114 C4
WARR WA1 17 G2
Fairford Crs DV/KA/FCH L14 115 F3
Fairford Rd DV/KA/FCH L14 115 F3
Fairhaven NWD/KWIPK L33 72 D4
SKEL WN8 56 D2
Fairhaven Cl RF/TRAN CH42 150 E1
WARRW/BUR WA5 141 J5
Fairhaven Dr BEB CH63 183 K2
Fairhaven Rd CHTN/BK PR9 23 K1
WDN WA8 158 D1
Fairholme Av AIMK WN4 79 G5
NSTN CH64 181 J6
PR/KW L34 118 C1
Fairholme Cl WD/CROXPK L12 98 E5
Fairholme Rd CSBY/BLUN L23 69 F5
Fairhurst Ter PR/KW L34 * 118 A1
Fair Isle Cl EP CH65 203 G2
Fairlawn Cl BEB CH63 183 H1
Fairlawne Cl NWD/KWIPK L33 72 D5
Fairlie SKEL WN8 56 E2
Fairlie Crs BTL L20 82 A4
Fairlie Dr RAIN/WH L35 119 F5
Fairmead Rd MOR/LEA CH46 109 J6
NG/CROX L11 98 C3
Fairoak Cl CL/PREN CH43 129 K2
Fairoak Ct RUNC WA7 188 E4
Fairoak La RUNC WA7 188 E4
Fairoak Ms CL/PREN CH43 * 129 K2
Fairstead SKEL WN8 56 E2
Fairview BIRK CH41 131 H5
Fair Vw WGNW/BIL/O WN5 77 G4
Fairview Av WAL/NB CH45 111 G2
Fair View Av WGNW/BIL/O WN5 77 G4
Fairview Cl AIMK WN4 79 G5
CL/PREN CH43 130 E6
Fair View Pl TOX L8 * 133 F5
Fairview Rd CL/PREN CH43 130 E6
GTS/LS CH66 202 E1
Fairview Wy PEN/TH CH61 167 K2
Fairway CHTN/BK PR9 22 E3
Fair Wy ECCL WA10 87 K6
Fairway HUY L36 117 G3
Fairway Crs PS/BROM CH62 171 F1
Fairway North PS/BROM CH62 171 F1
Fairways CL/PREN CH43 150 A3
CSBY/BLUN L23 68 E4
FROD/HEL WA6 201 G2
WARRS WA4 162 C6
Fairways Cl WLTN L25 154 E3
Fairways Ct FMBY L37 40 C6
Fairways Dr GTS/LS CH66 195 G2
Fairways South PS/BROM CH62 171 F2
The Fairways AIMK WN4 90 C1
SKEL WN8 57 F2
The Fairway WD/CROXPK L12 115 H3
Falcondale Rd
WARRN/WOL WA2 123 H1
Falconers Gn
WARRW/BUR WA5 122 B5
Falconer St BTL L20 81 H5
Falconhall Rd WLT/FAZ L9 98 D1
Falcon Hey AIN/FAZ L10 83 K5
Falcon Rd GTS/LS CH66 195 J6
RF/TRAN CH42 131 F5
Falcons Wy RUNC WA7 187 H1
Falkland SKEL WN8 56 E2
Falkland Dr AIMK WN4 78 B5
Falkland Rd STHP PR8 28 A2
WAL/EG CH44 111 K3
Falklands Ap NG/CROX L11 98 C3
Falkland St BIRK CH41 130 D1
VAUX/LVPD L3 9 J2

Falkner Sq TOX L8 133 F2
Falkner St TOX L8 9 J7
Fallbrook Dr WD/CROXPK L12 99 F5
Fallow Cl STHEL WA9 120 A3
Fallowfield NWD/KWIPK L33 72 D5
RUNC WA7 177 G4
Fallowfield Gv
WARRN/WOL WA2 124 D6
Fallowfield Rd WAV L15 134 A3
Fallows Wy RAIN/WH L35 117 J6
Falmouth Dr
WARRW/BUR WA5 141 F6
Falmouth Pl RUNC WA7 188 D1
Falmouth Rd NG/CROX L11 84 B6
Falstaff St BTL L20 96 E5
Falstone Cl GOL/RIS/CU WA3 125 K1
Falstone Dr RUNC WA7 178 D5
Fanner's La KNUT WA16 164 D6
Faraday Rd CLB/OSW/ST L13 114 C6
EP CH65 195 K5
NWD/KWIPK L33 85 G4
Faraday St EV L5 113 J2
GOL/RIS/CU WA3 125 G2
Farefield Av GOL/RIS/CU WA3 92 A1
Fareham Cl GR/UP/WCH CH49 128 E3
Fareham Dr CHTN/BK PR9 21 K6
Fareham Rd EHL/KEN L7 114 B5
Faringdon Cl WLTN L25 * 154 E5
Faringdon Rd
WARRN/WOL WA2 123 H1
Farley Av PS/BROM CH62 170 E4
Farley La SKEL WN8 57 J2
Farlow Rd RF/TRAN CH42 150 E2
Farmbrook Rd WLTN L25 135 J2
Farm Cl CHTN/BK PR9 23 J5
GR/UP/WCH CH49 128 D5
Farmdale Cl CALD/MH L18 153 J1
Farmdale Dr CHNE CH2 198 B6
MGHL L31 62 C6
Far Meadow La PEN/TH CH61 147 K5
Farmer Pl BTL L20 82 B4
Farmers Heath GTS/LS CH66 202 B1
Farmer's La WARRW/BUR WA5 122 A1
Farmfield Dr CL/PREN CH43 129 K2
Farm La WARRS WA4 162 D3
Farmleigh Gdns
WARRW/BUR WA5 141 K3
Far Moss Rd CSBY/BLUN L23 68 C3
Farm Rd STHEL WA9 120 B4
Farmside MOR/LEA CH46 109 K4
Farmside Cl WARRW/BUR WA5 142 B2
Farmstead Wy GTS/LS CH66 202 C2
Farm Vw LITH L21 81 J1
Farmview Cl NTHLY L27 135 K2
Farm Wy NEWLW WA12 106 E4
Farnworth St NPK/KEN L6 113 K4
Farnborough Gv HLWD L26 155 J2
Farnborough Rd STHP PR8 34 B1
Farndale WDN WA8 139 F4
Farndale Cl WARRW/BUR WA5 141 G2
Farndale Gv AIMK WN4 91 H1
Farndon Av STHEL WA9 119 K3
WAL/NB CH45 110 E1
Farndon Dr WKBY CH48 127 K6
Farndon Rd GTS/LS CH66 195 H3
Farndon Wy CL/PREN CH43 130 C5
Farne Cl EP CH65 203 G3
Farnham Cl KKBY L32 84 E2
WARRS WA4 162 D4
Farnhill Cl RUNC WA7 178 C5
Farnley Cl RUNC WA7 178 C4
Farnworth Av MOR/LEA CH46 109 J4
Farnworth Cl WDN WA8 139 G5
Farnworth Gv NWD/KWIPK L33 72 D4
Farnworth Rd
WARRW/BUR WA5 140 E5
Farnworth St STHEL WA9 104 A1
WDN WA8 139 G5
Farrant St WDN WA8 19 F3
Farrar St CLB/OSW/ST L13 98 B6
Farrell Cl MGHL L31 72 A5
Farrell Rd WARRS WA4 162 B3
Farrell St WARR WA1 17 H4
Farr Hall Dr HES CH60 167 J6
Farr Hall Rd HES CH60 167 J5
Farrier Rd NWD/KWIPK L33 85 F1
Farriers Wy NTHTN L30 82 C3
WKBY CH48 147 J1
Farrier Wk STHEL WA9 120 A3
Farringdon Cl STHEL WA9 119 H2
Farrington Dr ORM L39 45 J5
Farthing Cl WLTN L25 154 D4
Farthingstone Cl RAIN/WH L35 118 C1
Fatherside Dr NTHTN L30 * 69 K6
Faulkner Cl STHP PR8 33 J4
Faulkner Gdns STHP PR8 33 J3
Faversham Rd NG/CROX L11 98 C2
Fawcett SKEL WN8 56 D2
Fawcett Rd MGHL L31 62 B4
Fawley Rd CALD/MH L18 153 K1
RAIN/WH L35 119 G6
Fazakerley Cl WLT/FAZ L9 97 J1
Fazakerley Rd RAIN/WH L35 118 A3
WLT/FAZ L9 97 J1
Fazakerley St VAUX/LVPD L3 8 C3
Fearnhead Cross
WARRN/WOL WA2 * 124 A6
Fearnhead La
WARRN/WOL WA2 124 C5
Fearnley Rd BIRK CH41 2 E6
Fearnside St EHL/KEN L7 133 H1
Feather La HES CH60 167 K5
Feeny St STHEL WA9 * 119 K5
Feilden Rd BEB CH63 170 C1
Felicity Gv MOR/LEA CH46 109 H6
Fell Gv RNFD/HAY WA11 88 D3
Fell St EHL/KEN L7 113 K5
WAL/EG CH44 112 A5
Fellitor Cl WLTN L25 135 G6
Fellview CHTN/BK PR9 21 G5
Fellwood Gv RAIN/WH L35 118 A5
Felmersham Gn NG/CROX L11 98 D2
Felspar Rd KKBY L32 84 D4
Felstead SKEL WN8 56 D3
Felsted Av WLTN L25 155 F1
Felsted Dr AIN/FAZ L10 83 H2
Felthorpe Cl GR/UP/WCH CH49 129 J2
Felton Gv CLB/OSW/ST L13 114 D3
Feltons SKEL WN8 56 D3
Feltwell Rd ANF/KKDL L4 113 K1
Feltwood Cl WD/CROXPK L12 99 K6
Feltwood Rd WD/CROXPK L12 99 K5
Fender La MOR/LEA CH46 110 A6
Fenderside Rd CL/PREN CH43 129 K1
Fender View Rd
MOR/LEA CH46 129 H1
Fender Wy CL/PREN CH43 129 J2
PEN/TH CH61 168 A1
Fenham Dr WARRW/BUR WA5 141 F5
Fennel St WARR WA1 17 F4
Fenney Ct SKEL WN8 56 E4
Fenton Cl ECCL WA10 12 E3
NTHTN L30 82 E3
SPK/HALE L24 173 J2
WDN WA8 138 B6
Fenton Gn SPK/HALE L24 173 J3
Fenwick La RUNC WA7 187 G1
Fenwick Rd GTS/LS CH66 202 C1
Fenwick St CLVP L2 8 C4
Ferguson Av
GR/UP/WCH CH49 128 D6
GTS/LS CH66 195 H3
Ferguson Dr
WARRN/WOL WA2 123 K6
Ferguson Rd LITH L21 81 K2
NG/CROX L11 98 C5
Fern Av NEWLW WA12 106 D3
Fern Bank RNFD/HAY WA11 75 F2
Fernbank Av HUY L36 116 D5
Fernbank Cl GOL/RIS/CU WA3 125 G3
Fernbank Dr NTHTN L30 70 D5
Fern Cl GOL/RIS/CU WA3 125 F3
NTHLY L27 136 B5
SKEL WN8 56 A4
Ferndale SKEL WN8 56 D3
Ferndale Av CHNE CH2 198 B6
WAL/EG CH44 111 J3
WKBY CH48 147 J2
Ferndale Cl WARR WA1 144 B2
WDN WA8 139 K2
WLT/FAZ L9 82 D4
Ferndale Rd CSBY/WL L22 80 E1
HOY CH47 127 G2
WAV L15 133 K3
Fern Gdns PR/KW L34 102 B6
Fern Gv BTL L20 5 F3
CL/PREN CH43 130 A4
TOX L8 133 H3
Fern Hey CSBY/BLUN L23 69 H4
Fern Hl WAL/NB CH45 95 H5
Fernhill Av BTL L20 5 J4
Fernhill Cl BTL L20 5 J5
Fernhill Dr TOX L8 133 F3
Fernhill Gdns BTL L20 5 J5
Fernhill Ms East BTL L20 5 J5
Fernhill Ms West BTL L20 * 5 J5
Fernhill Rd BTL L20 82 A6
Fernhill Wy BTL L20 5 J5
Fernhurst RUNC WA7 177 G5
Fernhurst Ga ORM L39 53 F3
Fernhurst Rd KKBY L32 84 B2
Fernlea Av STHEL WA9 103 F6
Fernlea Gv AIMK WN4 78 C4
Fernlea Ms CL/PREN CH43 129 K1
Fernlea Rd HES CH60 168 A5
Fernleigh Rd
CLB/OSW/ST L13 * 115 F4
Fernley Rd STHP PR8 27 H2
Fern Rd EP CH65 202 E1
Ferns Cl HES CH60 167 G4
Ferns Rd BEB CH63 150 C6
Fern Vls WAL/EG CH44 * 112 A5
Fernwood RUNC WA7 178 A4
Fernwood Dr HLWD L26 155 H3
Fernwood Rd AIG/SPK L17 153 F1
Ferny Brow Rd
GR/UP/WCH CH49 129 J6
Ferny Knoll Rd
RNFD/HAY WA11 66 B3
Ferrer St AIMK WN4 78 E3
Ferrey Rd AIN/FAZ L10 83 K4
Ferries Cl RF/TRAN CH42 * 151 F3
Ferry La WARRS WA4 144 D5
Ferry Rd PS/BROM CH62 171 J5
Ferryside WAL/EG CH44 112 A5
Ferry Side La CHTN/BK PR9 21 F6
Ferry View Rd WAL/EG CH44 112 A5
Festival Av WARRN/WOL WA2 123 K5
Festival Ct NG/CROX L11 * 99 F2
Festival Crs WARRN/WOL WA2 123 K5
Festival Rd EP CH65 195 J4
RNFD/HAY WA11 75 H4
Festival Wy RUNC WA7 177 F5
Ffrancon Dr BEB CH63 150 E4
Fiddlers Ferry Rd WDN WA8 19 J3
Fidler St ECCL WA10 103 F4
Field Av LITH L21 81 H3
Field Cl BRSC L40 39 F6
PS/BROM CH62 151 G3
Fieldfare Cl GOL/RIS/CU WA3 92 E3
GOL/RIS/CU WA3 125 H3
WLTN L25 135 H4
Fieldgate WDN WA8 157 G5
Field Hey La NSTN CH64 183 J6
Fieldhouse Rw RUNC WA7 177 G6
The Fieldings MGHL L31 61 K3
Fielding St NPK/KEN L6 * 113 J4
Fieldlands STHP PR8 28 D5
Field La AIN/FAZ L10 84 A4
LITH L21 81 H2
WARRS WA4 162 B5
Field Rd STHEL WA9 120 B4
WAL/NB CH45 95 H6
Field's End HUY L36 136 B1
Fieldsend Cl NTHLY L27 136 B5
Fieldsend Dr LEIGH WN7 93 K3
Fieldside Rd RF/TRAN CH42 150 D1
Field St VAUX/LVPD L3 113 G4
Fieldsway RUNC WA7 186 D1
Fieldton Rd NG/CROX L11 99 G2
Field Vw LITH L21 81 H2
Fieldview SKEL WN8 57 J6
Fieldview Dr
WARRN/WOL WA2 123 J6
Field Wk ORM L39 46 B6
Field Wy RAIN/WH L35 118 E2
Fieldway BEB CH63 150 C3
FROD/HEL WA6 201 F2
GTS/LS CH66 194 E2
HES CH60 168 C4
HOY CH47 128 A2
HUY L36 136 C1
MGHL L31 71 H2
WAL/NB CH45 111 G2
WAV L15 134 D1
WDN WA8 159 F1
Fieldway Ct BIRK CH41 2 B1
Fife Rd WARR WA1 17 K1
Fifth Av CL/PREN CH43 129 J2
RUNC WA7 177 J6
WLT/FAZ L9 83 H4
Filbert Cl NWD/KWIPK L33 72 E3
Fildes Cl WARRW/BUR WA5 141 K4
Filton Rd DV/KA/FCH L14 116 B2
Finborough Rd ANF/KKDL L4 98 A3
Fincham Cl DV/KA/FCH L14 116 B2
Fincham Gn DV/KA/FCH L14 116 B2
Fincham Rd DV/KA/FCH L14 116 A2
Fincham Sq DV/KA/FCH L14 116 A2
Finch Av RNFD/HAY WA11 75 H4
Finch Cl DV/KA/FCH L14 * 115 K1
STHEL WA9 120 B4
Finch Ct BIRK CH41 2 D2
Finchdale Gdns
GOL/RIS/CU WA3 93 J3
Finchdean Cl
GR/UP/WCH CH49 128 D5
Finch Dene DV/KA/FCH L14 115 K1
Finch La DV/KA/FCH L14 115 K1
HLWD L26 156 A5
Finch Lea Dr DV/KA/FCH L14 116 A2
Finchley Dr RNFD/HAY WA11 89 F4
Finchley Rd ANF/KKDL L4 97 K6
Finch Meadow Cl WLT/FAZ L9 98 D1
Finch Pl VAUX/LVPD L3 9 J2
Finch Rd DV/KA/FCH L14 116 A1
Finch Wy DV/KA/FCH L14 115 K2
Findlay Cl NEWLW WA12 106 C3
Findley Dr MOR/LEA CH46 109 K4
Findon SKEL WN8 56 D4
Findon Rd KKBY L32 84 E3
Fine Jane's Wy CHTN/BK PR9 23 K5
Fingall Rd WAV L15 134 C3
Finger House La WDN WA8 120 B6
Fingland Rd WAV L15 133 K2
Finlan Rd WDN WA8 18 B6
Finlay Av WARRW/BUR WA5 141 F6
Finlay St NPK/KEN L6 114 A4
Finney Gv RNFD/HAY WA11 90 D5
The Finney WKBY CH48 * 146 E5
Finningley Ct
WARRN/WOL WA2 124 A6
Finsbury Cl WARRW/BUR WA5 141 K5
Finsbury Pk WDN WA8 139 H4
Finstall Rd BEB CH63 170 B3
Finvoy Rd CLB/OSW/ST L13 98 C6
Fir Av HLWD L26 155 K3
Firbank CHNE CH2 198 D6
Firbank Cl RUNC WA7 178 C4
Firbeck SKEL WN8 56 E4
Firbrook Ct CL/PREN CH43 110 C6
Fir Cl HLWD L26 155 K3
Firdale Rd WLT/FAZ L9 97 J1
Firdene Crs CL/PREN CH43 130 B5
Fire Station Rd RAIN/WH L35 118 B2
Firethorne Rd HLWD L26 155 G1
Fir Gv WARR WA1 143 J2
WLT/FAZ L9 83 F3
Fir La WAV L15 134 B2
Firman Cl WARRW/BUR WA5 141 J1
Fir Rd CSBY/WL L22 81 F1
Firs Av BEB CH63 170 B2
Firs Cl FMBY L37 40 D6
Firs Crs FMBY L37 40 D6
Firshaw Rd HOY CH47 108 A6
Firs La ORM L39 52 C2
WARRS WA4 162 A5
Firs Link FMBY L37 48 D1
First Av CL/PREN CH43 129 K3
CSBY/BLUN L23 * 68 E5
RAIN/WH L35 118 D3
WLT/FAZ L9 83 F4
Firstone Gv KKBY L32 84 D3
Fir St ECCL WA10 102 E5
STHP PR8 28 C1
WDN WA8 158 D1
Firswood Rd BRSC L40 55 J1
Firthland Wy STHEL WA9 104 D3
Fir Tree Av GOL/RIS/CU WA3 93 G3
Firtree Av WARR WA1 143 K1
Fir Tree Cl RNFD/HAY WA11 76 C2
SKEL WN8 57 F6
Fir Tree Dr North
WD/CROXPK L12 99 H2
Fir Tree Dr South
WD/CROXPK L12 99 H2
Firtree Gv GTS/LS CH66 202 E3
Fir Tree La ORM L39 52 E3
WARRW/BUR WA5 122 A1
Fir Wy HES CH60 181 G2
Firwood SKEL WN8 57 F2
Firwood Gv AIMK WN4 90 E1
Fisher Av RAIN/WH L35 117 K5
WARRN/WOL WA2 123 H6
Fisher Dr CHTN/BK PR9 23 H6
Fisherfield Dr
GOL/RIS/CU WA3 125 J1
Fishermans Cl FMBY L37 40 E5
Fisher Pl RAIN/WH L35 117 K5
Fishers La PEN/TH CH61 167 J1
Fisher St RUNC WA7 11 G3
STHEL WA9 104 C6
TOX L8 132 C3
Fishguard Cl NPK/KEN L6 113 H3
Fish La BRSC L40 31 G4
Fistral Cl AIN/FAZ L10 84 A5
Fistral Dr ECCL WA10 87 J5
Fitzclarence Wy NPK/KEN L6 113 H3
Fitzgerald Rd CLB/OSW/ST L13 114 E4
Fitzherbert St
WARRN/WOL WA2 143 F2
Fitzpatrick Ct VAUX/LVPD L3 112 E3
Fitzroy Wy NPK/KEN L6 113 J4
Fitzwalter Rd WARR WA1 144 C2
Fiveways ECCL WA10 102 C1
Flag La NSTN CH64 192 A2
Flail Cl GR/UP/WCH CH49 128 D5
Flambards GR/UP/WCH CH49 129 J6
Flamstead SKEL WN8 56 E4
Flander Cl WDN WA8 157 H1
Flashes La NSTN CH64 192 C4
Flatfield Wy MGHL L31 62 C6
Flatman's La ORM L39 51 G4
Flatt La CL/PREN CH43 130 C6
EP CH65 6 B4
Flawn Rd NG/CROX L11 98 C5
Flaxfield Rd FMBY L37 49 G2
Flaxfields BRSC L40 39 F6
Flaxhill MOR/LEA CH46 109 H6
Flax La BRSC L40 47 F1
Flaxley Cl GOL/RIS/CU WA3 125 J2
Flaxman St EHL/KEN L7 * 114 A5
Flaxton SKEL WN8 56 E4
Flaybrick Cl CL/PREN CH43 130 B1
Fleck La WKBY CH48 146 E2
Fleet Croft Rd
GR/UP/WCH CH49 148 D1
Fleet La STHEL WA9 104 C3
Fleet St CLVPS L1 9 F5
EP CH65 6 A4
Fleetwood Cl CHTN/BK PR9 23 H2
WARRW/BUR WA5 141 J5
Fleetwood Crs CHTN/BK PR9 21 K5
Fleetwood Dr CHTN/BK PR9 21 K5
NEWLW WA12 106 B1
Fleetwood Gdns
NWD/KWIPK L33 72 E4
Fleetwood Rd CHTN/BK PR9 22 E4
Fleetwood's La NTHTN L30 70 A5
Fleetwood Wk RUNC WA7 178 B6
Fleming Ct VAUX/LVPD L3 112 E3
Fleming Dr AIMK WN4 79 J5
WARRN/WOL WA2 123 G1
Fleming Rd SPK/HALE L24 155 F5
Fleming St EP CH65 6 E2
Flemington Av ANF/KKDL L4 98 B4
Flers Av WARRS WA4 143 F6
Fletcher Av PR/KW L34 102 A6
RF/TRAN CH42 150 D1
Fletcher Cl GR/UP/WCH CH49 148 D1
Fletcher Dr ALL/GAR L19 153 H4
Fletcher's Dr BRSC L40 38 D6
Fletcher St WARRS WA4 142 E6
Flimby SKEL WN8 57 F4
Flint Cl NSTN CH64 191 J3
Flint Ct EP CH65 203 H1
Flint Dr NSTN CH64 191 K2
Flint Meadow NSTN CH64 191 K2
Flintshire Gdns ECCL WA10 12 E7
Flint St CLVPS L1 132 C2
Floral Wd AIG/SPK L17 152 A1
Flora St AIMK WN4 91 G1
Flordon SKEL WN8 57 F4
Florence Av HES CH60 167 K4
Florence Cl WLT/FAZ L9 97 H2
Florence Nightingale Cl
NTHTN L30 70 C5
Florence Rd WAL/EG CH44 112 A4
Florence St ANF/KKDL L4 97 H5
BIRK CH41 2 E4
STHEL WA9 102 E6
WARRS WA4 143 G6
Florentine Rd CLB/OSW/ST L13 114 E3
Florida Cl WARRW/BUR WA5 141 K2
Florida Ct ALL/GAR L19 153 J3
Flowermead Cl HOY CH47 108 D6
Fluin La FROD/HEL WA6 201 F1
Fluker's Brook La PR/KW L34 100 B4
Foinavon Cl BTL L20 82 C4
Folds La RNFD/HAY WA11 88 D4
Folds Rd RNFD/HAY WA11 89 J5
The Folds BEB CH63 182 B1
Fold St GOL/RIS/CU WA3 92 B2
Foley St ANF/KKDL L4 97 G6
Folkestone Rd STHP PR8 28 B4
Folkstone Wy RUNC WA7 178 B6
Folly La WAL/EG CH44 110 E2
WARRW/BUR WA5 142 D2
Fontenoy St CLVP L2 8 E2
Fonthill Cl ANF/KKDL L4 97 F6
Fonthill Rd ANF/KKDL L4 97 F5
Forbes Cl GOL/RIS/CU WA3 125 G3
Ford Av NWD/KWIPK L33 72 D3
Ford Cl BTL L20 82 B4
GR/UP/WCH CH49 129 J5
LITH L21 81 J1
Fordcombe Rd WLTN L25 135 K5
Ford Dr GR/UP/WCH CH49 129 J4
Fordham Cl STHP PR8 28 B4
Fordham St ANF/KKDL L4 97 G5
Fordhill Vw MOR/LEA CH46 129 H1
Fordington Rd
WARRW/BUR WA5 141 J4
Fordland Cl GOL/RIS/CU WA3 93 F2
Ford La GR/UP/WCH CH49 129 J4
LITH L21 69 J6
Fordlea Rd WD/CROXPK L12 98 E5
Fordlea Wy WD/CROXPK L12 99 F5
Ford Rd GR/UP/WCH CH49 129 H4
RAIN/WH L35 118 B1
Ford St VAUX/LVPD L3 112 E4
WARR WA1 17 H2
Ford Vw LITH L21 69 J6
Ford Wy GR/UP/WCH CH49 129 H5
Forefield La CSBY/BLUN L23 69 G5
Foreland Cl WARRW/BUR WA5 140 D2
Forest Cl HOY CH47 108 B6
PR/KW L34 102 B6
Forest Ct CL/PREN CH43 130 C3
Forest Dr HUY L36 116 C4
SKEL WN8 56 E2
Forest Gn WD/CROXPK L12 99 F5
Forest Gv PR/KW L34 102 B6
Forest Lawn WD/CROXPK L12 99 F5
Forest Md ECCL WA10 102 C2
Forest Rd CL/PREN CH43 130 D3
GTS/LS CH66 195 H2
HES CH60 168 A5
HOY CH47 108 B6
STHEL WA9 119 J4
STHP PR8 15 J7
Forest Wk RUNC WA7 * 177 J6
Forfar Rd CLB/OSW/ST L13 114 B1
Forge Cl BRSC L40 54 E1
WDN WA8 138 B4
Forge Rd GTS/LS CH66 195 F3
WARRW/BUR WA5 141 G4
Forge St BTL L20 96 E5
Formby Br FMBY L37 48 E3
Formby By-Pass FMBY L37 41 H2
Formby Cl WARRW/BUR WA5 141 G5
Formby Flds FMBY L37 49 G3
Formby Gdns FMBY L37 49 F1
Formby La ORM L39 52 C3
Formby Rd ECCL WA10 103 F4
Formby St FMBY L37 48 E3
Formosa Dr AIN/FAZ L10 83 J4
Formosa Rd AIN/FAZ L10 83 J4
Formosa Wy AIN/FAZ L10 83 J4
Fornalls Green La HOY CH47 127 K2
Forres Gv AIMK WN4 78 B5
Forrester Av STHEL WA9 102 E6
Forrest St CLVPS L1 8 E6
Forrest Wy WARRW/BUR WA5 142 A6
Forshaw Av ECCL WA10 102 E5
Forshaw's La
WARRW/BUR WA5 105 J5
Forshaw St WARRN/WOL WA2 17 F1
Forster St GOL/RIS/CU WA3 92 B2
WARRN/WOL WA2 16 E1
Forsythia Cl WLT/FAZ L9 * 98 A2
Forthlin Rd CALD/MH L18 153 K2
Forth St BTL L20 96 E4
Forton Lodge Flats
CSBY/BLUN L23 * 68 D5
Fort St WAL/NB CH45 95 J6
Forwood Rd PS/BROM CH62 171 F5
Foscote Rd NWD/KWIPK L33 73 F5
Foster Cl RAIN/WH L35 118 C2
Foster Rd FMBY L37 48 D3
Fosters Cl CHTN/BK PR9 23 K5
Fosters Green Rd SKEL WN8 56 E3
Fosters Gv RNFD/HAY WA11 89 J5
Fosters Rd RNFD/HAY WA11 89 J5
Foster St BTL L20 96 E6
WDN WA8 19 F1
Fothergill St WARR WA1 17 J1
Fotheringay Ct EP CH65 203 H1
Foul La STHP PR8 28 D3
Foundry La WDN WA8 157 H6
Foundry St ECCL WA10 13 G6
NEWLW WA12 106 B2
WARRN/WOL WA2 16 D3
Fountain Ct CSBY/BLUN L23 68 B4
Fountain La FROD/HEL WA6 200 D1
Fountain Rd PR/KW L34 100 D2
WAL/NB CH45 95 H6
Fountains Av RNFD/HAY WA11 90 E4
Fountains Cl ANF/KKDL L4 97 H6
RUNC WA7 188 B2
Fountains Ct EV L5 97 F6
Fountains Rd ANF/KKDL L4 97 G6
Fountain St RF/TRAN CH42 131 F6
STHEL WA9 118 E1
Fountains Wk GOL/RIS/CU WA3 93 J3
Fountains Wy FMBY L37 49 G3
Four Acre Dr LITH L21 69 J6
Four Acre La STHEL WA9 120 A3
Fouracres MGHL L31 70 E2
Fourth Av CL/PREN CH43 129 J3
RUNC WA7 177 J6
WLT/FAZ L9 83 H4
Fourways Cl NTHLY L27 136 A2
Fowell Rd WAL/NB CH45 95 H5
Fowler Cl EHL/KEN L7 114 A6
Foxall Wy GTS/LS CH66 202 B1
Foxcote WDN WA8 157 G1
Fox Cover Rd HES CH60 168 C6
Foxcovers Rd BEB CH63 170 C2
Fox Covert RUNC WA7 178 B6
Foxdale Cl CL/PREN CH43 130 D4
STHP PR8 28 B4
Foxdale Rd WAV L15 134 A3
Foxdell Cl CLB/OSW/ST L13 114 E5
The Foxes PEN/TH CH61 148 D5
Foxfield Cl WARRN/WOL WA2 124 A4
Foxfield Rd HOY CH47 127 J1
Foxfold SKEL WN8 57 F2
Fox Gdns LYMM WA13 145 H5
Foxglove Av HLWD L26 155 H2
Foxglove Cl WLT/FAZ L9 98 D1
Foxglove Ct FROD/HEL WA6 201 F1
Foxglove Rd BIRK CH41 * 130 C2
Foxglove Wy NSTN CH64 191 K4
Fox Hey Rd WAL/EG CH44 111 F4
Foxhill Cl FMBY L37 48 C2
TOX L8 133 F4
Foxhill Gv FROD/HEL WA6 200 A5
Foxhill La HLWD L26 155 J1
Foxhouse La MGHL L31 71 H1
Foxhunter Dr WLT/FAZ L9 83 F3
Foxleigh HLWD L26 155 G2
Foxley Cl LYMM WA13 165 H1
Foxley Hall Ms LYMM WA13 * 165 H2
Foxley Heath WDN WA8 18 A3
Fox Pl ECCL WA10 13 G3
Fox's Bank La RAIN/WH L35 137 J2
WDN WA8 118 B6
Foxshaw Cl RAIN/WH L35 117 K6
Fox St BIRK CH41 2 C4

RUNC WA7 10 D6
VAUX/LVPD L3 113 G3
WARRW/BUR WA5 142 B4
Foxton Cl MOR/LEA CH46 109 F6
RNFD/HAY WA11 * 89 G6
Foxwood STHEL WA9 102 E6
WD/CROXPK L12 99 J5
Foxwood Cl WKBY CH48 127 K6
Foy St AIMK WN4 * 79 G6
Frailey Cl STHP PR8 33 J5
Frampton Rd ANF/KKDL L4 98 B3
Franceys St VAUX/LVPD L3 * 9 H4
Francine Cl EV L5 112 E2
Francis Av CL/PREN CH43 2 A5
MOR/LEA CH46 128 E1
Francis Cl RAIN/WH L35 118 E3
WDN WA8 157 H3
Francis Rd FROD/HEL WA6 187 F6
WARRS WA4 162 A2
Francis St STHEL WA9 104 D6
Francis Wy CHLDW L16 135 F1
Frankby Av WAL/EG CH44 111 G3
Frankby Cl GR/UP/WCH CH49 128 C6
Frankby Gv GR/UP/WCH CH49 129 G4
Frankby Rd ANF/KKDL L4 97 K5
GR/UP/WCH CH49 128 D6
HOY CH47 127 J1
WKBY CH48 127 J6
Franklin Cl WARRW/BUR WA5 141 K1
Franklin Pl NPK/KEN L6 * 113 K2
Franklin Rd MOR/LEA CH46 110 A3
Frank St TOX L8 132 D4
WDN WA8 19 H2
Fraser Rd WARRW/BUR WA5 140 E3
Fraser St VAUX/LVPD L3 9 G2
Frawley Av NEWLW WA12 91 G6
Freckleton Cl
WARRW/BUR WA5 141 J5
Freckleton Dr NWD/KWIPK L33 73 F4
Freckleton Rd CHTN/BK PR9 23 H1
ECCL WA10 102 D4
Freda Av STHEL WA9 * 120 A1
Frederick Banting Cl
NTHTN L30 70 C5
Frederick Gv WAV L15 134 B1
Frederick Lunt Av PR/KW L34 100 C2
Frederick St AIMK WN4 79 F4
CLVPS L1 8 D6
STHEL WA9 104 D6
WARRS WA4 143 G6
WDN WA8 18 E3
Fredric Pl RUNC WA7 11 F3
Freedom Cl EHL/KEN L7 133 F1
Freehold St EHL/KEN L7 114 B4
Freeland St ANF/KKDL L4 * 97 G6
Freeman St BIRK CH41 3 F2
EHL/KEN L7 133 H1
Freemantle Av STHEL WA9 103 H6
Freemasons Rw VAUX/LVPD L3 8 E1
Freemont Rd WD/CROXPK L12 98 E6
Freeport Gv WLT/FAZ L9 82 E4
Freesia Av WLT/FAZ L9 97 K1
Freme Cl NG/CROX L11 99 F2
French St ECCL WA10 103 F4
WDN WA8 19 J2
Frensham Cl BEB CH63 170 B3
Frensham Wy WLTN L25 155 G3
Freshfield Cl HUY L36 116 C4
Freshfield Rd FMBY L37 40 E6
WAV L15 134 A3
Freshfields Dr
WARRN/WOL WA2 124 D6
Freshford STHEL WA9 120 B1
Freshwater WARRW/BUR WA5 140 E2
Freshwater Cl
WARRW/BUR WA5 140 E2
Friars Av WARRW/BUR WA5 141 F4
Friars Cl BEB CH63 170 B1
Friars Ga WARR WA1 16 D6
Friarsgate Cl CALD/MH L18 134 D4
Friars La WARR WA1 16 D6
Friar St ECCL WA10 88 C4
EV L5 * 113 J2
Friars Wk FMBY L37 49 H3
Friends La WARRW/BUR WA5 140 E3
Frinsted Rd NG/CROX L11 98 E4
Frobisher Ct
WARRW/BUR WA5 142 A1
Frobisher Rd MOR/LEA CH46 110 A3
NSTN CH64 191 K1
Froda Av FROD/HEL WA6 200 E2
Frodsham Dr RNFD/HAY WA11 89 G6
Frodsham St ANF/KKDL L4 97 H4
BIRK CH41 131 H5
Froghall La WARR WA1 16 A3
WARRW/BUR WA5 142 C4
Frog La BRSC L40 39 K6
Frogmore Rd CLB/OSW/ST L13 114 C4
Frome Cl PEN/TH CH61 148 A4
Frome Ct EP CH65 196 A2
Frome Wy WLTN L25 155 G2
Frost Dr PEN/TH CH61 147 K4
Frosts Ms EP CH65 6 C2
Frost St EHL/KEN L7 114 A5
Fry St STHEL WA9 104 C2
Fuchsia Cl GTS/LS CH66 202 D2
Fuchsia Wk GR/UP/WCH CH49 147 K1
Fulbeck WDN WA8 157 H1
Fulbrook Cl BEB CH63 170 B3
Fulbrook Rd BEB CH63 170 B3
Fulford Cl DV/KA/FCH L14 115 K1
Fulford Pk MOR/LEA CH46 129 F2
Fullerton Gv HUY L36 116 E3
Fulmar Cl NTHLY L27 136 B5
RNFD/HAY WA11 88 E5
Fulmar Gv WD/CROXPK L12 99 J2
Fulshaw Cl NTHLY L27 136 A3
Fulton Av WKBY CH48 127 J6
Fulton St EV L5 112 D1
Fulwood Av STHP PR8 28 A3
Fulwood Cl AIG/SPK L17 152 E1
Fulwood Dr AIG/SPK L17 152 D1
Fulwood Gdns GTS/LS CH66 195 F3
Fulwood Ms GTS/LS CH66 195 F3
Fulwood Pk AIG/SPK L17 152 D2
Fulwood Rd AIG/SPK L17 152 D1
GOL/RIS/CU WA3 93 F5
GTS/LS CH66 195 F3
Funchal Av FMBY L37 48 D4
Furlong Cl WLT/FAZ L9 83 G3
Furness Av ECCL WA10 88 B4
FMBY L37 49 F2
ORM L39 53 J1
WD/CROXPK L12 99 G4
Furness Cl STHP PR8 33 H6
Furness St ANF/KKDL L4 97 G6
Furnival Dr BRSC L40 38 D5
Furrocks Cl NSTN CH64 192 A4
Furrocks La NSTN CH64 192 A4
Furrocks Wy NSTN CH64 192 A4
The Furrows GTS/LS CH66 202 C3
Fylde Rd CHTN/BK PR9 20 E6

G

Gable Ct NG/CROX L11 * 98 C2
Gables Cl WARRN/WOL WA2 124 B4
The Gables MGHL L31 * 71 H2
Gable St NEWLW WA12 106 A2
Gable Vw NG/CROX L11 * 98 C2
Gabriel Cl MOR/LEA CH46 129 G1
Gainford Cl WDN WA8 138 B6
Gainford Rd DV/KA/FCH L14 116 A1
Gainsborough Av MGHL L31 70 E1
Gainsborough Cl
WD/CROXPK L12 115 J2
Gainsborough Ct WDN WA8 157 G2
Gainsborough Rd
GR/UP/WCH CH49 129 F3
STHP PR8 27 F4
WAL/NB CH45 110 E2
WARRS WA4 162 A1
WAV L15 133 K3
Gairloch Cl WARRN/WOL WA2 124 B3
Gaisgill Ct WDN WA8 157 H2
Galbraith Cl AIG/SPK L17 152 D1
Gale Av WARRW/BUR WA5 123 F6
Galemeade NG/CROX L11 * 99 F2
Gale Rd LITH L21 81 K2
NWD/KWIPK L33 85 H3
Galion Wy WDN WA8 138 E5
Galloway Rd CSBY/WL L22 81 F1
Galloway St EHL/KEN L7 133 J1
Galston Av RAIN/WH L35 119 F5
Galston Cl NWD/KWIPK L33 72 C3
Galsworthy Av NTHTN L30 82 A4
Galsworthy Pl NTHTN L30 82 B3
Galton St VAUX/LVPD L3 8 A1
Galtres Pk BEB CH63 150 D3
Gambier Ter CLVPS L1 132 D2
Gamble Av ECCL WA10 88 B5
Gamlin St BIRK CH41 130 C1
Gamston Wd KKBY L32 84 B2
Ganney's Meadow Rd
GR/UP/WCH CH49 129 K6
Gannock St EHL/KEN L7 114 A5
Ganton Cl STHP PR8 28 B3
WDN WA8 139 G5
Ganworth Cl SPK/HALE L24 173 K3
Ganworth Rd SPK/HALE L24 173 K3
Garage Rd SPK/HALE L24 155 J6
Gardeners Vw NWD/KWIPK L33 72 E3
Gardeners Wy RAIN/WH L35 118 E2
Garden Hey Rd HOY CH47 127 H1
MOR/LEA CH46 128 C2
Gardenia Gv AIG/SPK L17 152 B1
Garden La MOR/LEA CH46 109 J6
VAUX/LVPD L3 * 113 H3
WLT/FAZ L9 83 G4
Garden Lodge Gv NTHLY L27 136 A4
Garden Pl BTL L20 * 5 F4
Gardenside MOR/LEA CH46 110 B3
Gardenside St NPK/KEN L6 113 H4
Gardens Rd BEB CH63 151 G6
Garden St WLTN L25 154 D1
Garden Wk PR/KW L34 117 K2
Gardiner Av RNFD/HAY WA11 90 B5
Gardiners Pl SKEL WN8 56 A5
Gardner Av BTL L20 82 A4
Gardner Rd CLB/OSW/ST L13 114 C2
FMBY L37 49 G2
Gardner's Dr NPK/KEN L6 114 A3
Gareth Av RNFD/HAY WA11 88 E5
Garfield Ter
GR/UP/WCH CH49 * 129 H4
Garfourth Cl ALL/GAR L19 154 A4
Garfourth Rd ALL/GAR L19 154 A4
Garmoyle Cl WAV L15 133 K2
Garmoyle Rd WAV L15 133 K3
Garner St WARRN/WOL WA2 143 F2
Garnet St CLB/OSW/ST L13 114 D6
STHEL WA9 104 B6
Garnett Av ANF/KKDL L4 97 G5
WARRS WA4 143 J5
Garnett Gdns ORM L39 53 H1
Garnett Pl SKEL WN8 56 C6
Garnetts La RAIN/WH L35 156 C2
WDN WA8 175 H2
Garrett Fld GOL/RIS/CU WA3 125 F2
Garrick Av MOR/LEA CH46 128 D1
Garrick Pde STHP PR8 14 C6
Garrick Rd CL/PREN CH43 149 J3
Garrick St EHL/KEN L7 133 H2
Garrigill Cl WDN WA8 139 G4
Garrowby Dr HUY L36 116 C4
Garsdale Av RAIN/WH L35 119 F5
Garsdale Cl WARRW/BUR WA5 141 G2
Garsfield Rd ANF/KKDL L4 98 B4
Garside Av GOL/RIS/CU WA3 92 E4
Garstang Rd CHTN/BK PR9 23 H1
Garston Old Rd ALL/GAR L19 153 K4
Garston Wy ALL/GAR L19 153 K6
Garswood Av RNFD/HAY WA11 75 H2
Garswood Cl MGHL L31 62 C4
MOR/LEA CH46 109 J3
Garswood Crs
WGNW/BIL/O WN5 77 G5
Garswood Old Rd AIMK WN4 89 J2
Garswood Rd AIMK WN4 78 B6
WGNW/BIL/O WN5 77 H5
Garswood St AIMK WN4 79 G6
ECCL WA10 13 G3
TOX L8 132 E6
Garter Cl NG/CROX L11 99 G2
Garth Bvd BEB CH63 150 D3
Garthdale Rd CALD/MH L18 134 B5
Garth Dr CALD/MH L18 134 C5
Garthowen Rd EHL/KEN L7 114 B5
Garth Rd KKBY L32 85 F3
The Garth HUY L36 116 E4
Garton Dr GOL/RIS/CU WA3 93 F2
Gartons La STHEL WA9 120 A4
Garven Pl WARR WA1 16 C5
Garway WLTN L25 135 K6
Garwood Cl WARRW/BUR WA5 122 B6
Gascoyne St VAUX/LVPD L3 8 C1
Gaskell Av WARRS WA4 143 K6
Gaskell St STHEL WA9 104 B4
WARRS WA4 162 B2
Gaskill Rd SPK/HALE L24 173 J1
Gatclif Rd CLB/OSW/ST L13 98 C5
Gateacre Brow WLTN L25 135 H5
Gateacre Ct GTS/LS CH66 195 J1
Gateacre Park Dr WLTN L25 135 G3
Gateacre Ri WLTN L25 135 J5
Gateacre Vale Rd WLTN L25 135 J6
Gateley Cl WARRS WA4 144 D6
Gateside Cl NTHLY L27 136 B4
Gates La SFTN L29 69 J1
Gate Warth St
WARRW/BUR WA5 * 142 A6
Gathurst Ct WDN WA8 157 J3
Gatley Dr MGHL L31 71 H1
Gaunts Wy RUNC WA7 187 H1
Gautby Rd BIRK CH41 110 E6
Gavin Rd WDN WA8 157 G4
Gaw Hill La ORM L39 52 E2
Gaw Hill Vw ORM L39 53 F2
Gawsworth Cl CL/PREN CH43 130 C6
ECCL WA10 102 D2
Gawsworth Ct
GOL/RIS/CU WA3 * 125 H1
Gawsworth Rd
GOL/RIS/CU WA3 92 A2
GTS/LS CH66 195 H5
Gaybeech Cl CL/PREN CH43 129 K1
Gayhurst Av
WARRN/WOL WA2 * 124 B5
Gayhurst Crs NG/CROX L11 98 E3
Gaynor Av RNFD/HAY WA11 90 E4
Gayton Av BEB CH63 150 B3
WAL/NB CH45 95 H5
Gayton Farm Rd HES CH60 181 F2
Gayton La HES CH60 181 G1
Gayton Mill Cl HES CH60 * 168 B6
Gayton Pkwy HES CH60 181 G2
Gayton Rd HES CH60 180 E1
Gaywood Av KKBY L32 84 E3
Gaywood Cl CL/PREN CH43 * 129 K2
KKBY L32 84 E3
Gellings La PR/KW L34 85 F6
Gellings Rd PR/KW L34 85 F6
Gelling St TOX L8 132 E4
Gemini Cl BTL L20 4 D3
Gemini Dr DV/KA/FCH L14 115 K3
General St WARR WA1 17 F4
Geneva Rd NPK/KEN L6 114 A4
WAL/EG CH44 111 K5
Genista Cl WLT/FAZ L9 97 J2
Genoa Cl WLTN L25 135 K2
Gentwood Rd HUY L36 116 C3
George Dr STHP PR8 34 A4
George Hale Av PR/KW L34 116 E1
George Harrison Cl
NPK/KEN L6 113 K4
George Moore Ct
CSBY/BLUN L23 * 69 K3
George Rd HOY CH47 127 H3
WARRW/BUR WA5 141 K5
Georges Crs WARRS WA4 163 G1
George's Dock Gates
VAUX/LVPD L3 8 B3
Georges Dockway
VAUX/LVPD L3 8 B5
George's La CHTN/BK PR9 21 J3
Georges Pierhead
VAUX/LVPD L3 8 B5
George St AIMK WN4 79 H5
BIRK CH41 3 G2
ECCL WA10 13 H5
EP CH65 6 D1
NEWLW WA12 * 106 A1
VAUX/LVPD L3 8 C3
Georgia Av NWD/KWIPK L33 72 C3
PS/BROM CH62 171 G2
Georgian Cl HLWD L26 155 J5
RAIN/WH L35 118 C1
Georgian Pl FMBY L37 48 E4
Georgia St BTL L20 4 E4
Geraint St TOX L8 132 E3
Gerald Rd CL/PREN CH43 130 D5
Gerard Av WAL/NB CH45 95 G6
Gerard Rd WAL/NB CH45 111 G1
WKBY CH48 127 G6
Gerards Ct RNFD/HAY WA11 * 89 F3
Gerards La STHEL WA9 104 B6
Gerard St AIMK WN4 79 G6
VAUX/LVPD L3 9 F2
Germander Cl HLWD L26 155 H2
Gerneth Cl SPK/HALE L24 173 H1
Gerneth Rd SPK/HALE L24 173 G2
Gerosa Av WARRN/WOL WA2 107 H5
Gerrard Av GTS/LS CH66 195 F5
WARRW/BUR WA5 142 C2
Gerrard Pl SKEL WN8 56 B6
Gerrard Rd WGNW/BIL/O WN5 77 H4
Gerrard's La HLWD L26 155 H1
Gerrard St WDN WA8 18 E4
Gertrude Rd ANF/KKDL L4 113 J1
Gertrude St BIRK CH41 3 H4
STHEL WA9 118 E1
Geves Gdns CSBY/WL L22 81 F2
Ghyll Gv RNFD/HAY WA11 88 E2
Gibbons Av ECCL WA10 102 E2
Gibbon's Rd AIMK WN4 90 C1
Gibraltar Rw VAUX/LVPD L3 8 B2
Gibson Cl PEN/TH CH61 167 K2
Gibson Ct EP CH65 * 196 A1
Gibson Rd TOX L8 132 E2
Gibson St TOX L8 132 E2
WARR WA1 17 G5
WARRS WA4 162 C2
Giddygate La MGHL L31 72 A3
Gidlow Rd CLB/OSW/ST L13 114 D4
Gidlow Rd South
CLB/OSW/ST L13 114 D4
Gigg La WARRS WA4 144 D5
WARRS WA4 160 E6
Gig La WARR WA1 144 C1
Gilbert Cl BEB CH63 170 B3
Gilbert Pl BRSC L40 38 B5
Gilbert Rd RAIN/WH L35 118 B2
Gilbert St CLVPS L1 8 E6
Gilbrook Sq BIRK CH41 130 C1
Gildarts Gdns VAUX/LVPD L3 * 113 F3
Gildart St VAUX/LVPD L3 9 J2
Gilderdale Cl GOL/RIS/CU WA3 125 K2
Gilead St EHL/KEN L7 113 K5
Gillan Cl RUNC WA7 188 B2
Gillars Green Dr ECCL WA10 102 B2
Gillar's La ECCL WA10 102 A2
Gilleney Gv RAIN/WH L35 118 C2
Gillibrands Rd SKEL WN8 56 D6
Gillmoss Cl NG/CROX L11 99 G1
Gillmoss La NG/CROX L11 84 B6
Gills La PEN/TH CH61 168 A1
Gill St VAUX/LVPD L3 9 J3
Gilman St ANF/KKDL L4 97 J6
Gilmour Mt CL/PREN CH43 130 E5
Gilpin Av MGHL L31 62 C5
Gilroy Rd NPK/KEN L6 113 K4
WKBY CH48 127 J6
Gilsecroft Av NWD/KWIPK L33 73 F6
Giltbrook Cl WDN WA8 138 E6
Gilwell Av MOR/LEA CH46 129 F2
Gilwell Cl MOR/LEA CH46 129 F2
WARRS WA4 163 H1
The Ginnel PS/BROM CH62 151 G6
Gipsy Gv CALD/MH L18 135 F4
Gipsy La CALD/MH L18 135 F4
Girton Av AIMK WN4 78 E5
BTL L20 5 J6
Girton Cl EP CH65 7 F6
Girton Rd EP CH65 7 F6
Girtrell Cl GR/UP/WCH CH49 128 E4
Girtrell Rd GR/UP/WCH CH49 128 E4
Girvan Crs AIMK WN4 78 B5
Girvin Dr NSTN CH64 191 K3
Gisburn Av GOL/RIS/CU WA3 92 A1
Givenchy Cl CHLDW L16 135 F2
Gladden Pl SKEL WN8 56 A5
Glade Rd HUY L36 116 E3
Gladeswood Rd
NWD/KWIPK L33 85 G2
The Glade HOY CH47 108 B6
Gladeville Rd AIG/SPK L17 153 F1
Gladstone Av CHLDW L16 135 H1
LITH L21 81 G4
Gladstone Cl BIRK CH41 2 C4
Gladstone Hall Rd
PS/BROM CH62 * 170 D1
Gladstone Rd ALL/GAR L19 153 K5
CHTN/BK PR9 28 C1
EHL/KEN L7 113 K6
LITH L21 81 G5
NSTN CH64 191 K1
RF/TRAN CH42 131 J6
WAL/EG CH44 111 K4
WLT/FAZ L9 97 H2
Gladstone St BIRK CH41 * 2 C4
ECCL WA10 12 A6
VAUX/LVPD L3 8 D1
WARRN/WOL WA2 16 B3
WDN WA8 18 E3
WLTN L25 154 C1
Gladstone Wy NEWLW WA12 106 B1
Glaisdale Cl AIMK WN4 79 H6
Glaisdale Dr STHP PR8 28 C4
Glaisher St EV L5 113 J1
Glamis Dr CHTN/BK PR9 23 K2
Glamis Gv STHEL WA9 104 A6
Glamis Rd CLB/OSW/ST L13 114 B1
Glamorgan Cl ECCL WA10 12 E7
Glan Aber Pk WD/CROXPK L12 99 J5
Glasier Rd MOR/LEA CH46 109 G6
Glaslyn Wy WLT/FAZ L9 97 J2
Glassonby Crs NG/CROX L11 98 E4
Glassonby Wy NG/CROX L11 98 E4
Glastonbury Av
GOL/RIS/CU WA3 93 J3
Glastonbury Cl NPK/KEN L6 98 B6
RUNC WA7 178 D2
Glasven Rd NWD/KWIPK L33 72 E6
Glazebrook St WARR WA1 17 H3
Gleadmere WDN WA8 157 H1
Gleaston Cl PS/BROM CH62 170 E4
Gleave Crs NPK/KEN L6 113 H3
Gleave Rd WARRW/BUR WA5 121 K1
Gleave St ECCL WA10 13 H3
Glebe Av AIMK WN4 91 G1
WARRS WA4 163 H2
Glebe Cl MGHL L31 61 K6
Glebecroft Av CHNE CH2 198 B6
Glebe End SFTN L29 70 B2
Glebe Hey NTHLY L27 136 B4
Glebe Hey Rd
GR/UP/WCH CH49 129 H6
Glebelands Rd MOR/LEA CH46 129 F1
Glebe La CHTN/BK PR9 21 K4
WDN WA8 139 F4
Glebe Pl STHP PR8 14 E4
Glebe Rd SKEL WN8 56 C6
WAL/NB CH45 111 G1
The Glebe RUNC WA7 177 H4
Gleggside WKBY CH48 146 D1
Glegg St VAUX/LVPD L3 112 D3
Glegside Rd NWD/KWIPK L33 85 F1
Glenacres WLTN L25 * 135 H6
Glenalmond Rd
WAL/EG CH44 * 111 K3
Glenathol Rd CALD/MH L18 153 K1
GTS/LS CH66 195 F5
Glenavon Rd CHLDW L16 134 D1
CL/PREN CH43 149 K2
Glenbank CSBY/WL L22 80 D1
Glenbank Cl WLT/FAZ L9 82 D6
Glenburn Av PS/BROM CH62 184 B3
Glenburn Rd SKEL WN8 56 A1
SKEL WN8 56 B6
WAL/EG CH44 111 K4
Glenby Av CSBY/BLUN L23 81 G1
Glencairn Rd CLB/OSW/ST L13 114 D5
Glencoe Rd GTS/LS CH66 195 F5
WAL/NB CH45 111 H1
Glenconner Rd CHLDW L16 115 J6
Glencourse Rd WDN WA8 139 F4
Glencoyne Dr CHTN/BK PR9 20 E5
Glencroft Cl HUY L36 116 C2
Glendale Av AIMK WN4 79 H5
CHNE CH2 198 B6
Glendale Cl TOX L8 132 E6
Glendale Gv BEB CH63 170 D3
Glendale Wy FMBY L37 49 F3
Glendevon Rd CHLDW L16 115 H6
HUY L36 116 E6
Glendower Rd CSBY/WL L22 81 F2
Glendower St BTL L20 96 E5
Glendyke Rd CALD/MH L18 153 K1
GTS/LS CH66 195 F5
Gleneagles Cl NWD/KWIPK L33 72 C3
PEN/TH CH61 167 K2
Gleneagles Dr RNFD/HAY WA11 89 K6
STHP PR8 33 H6
WDN WA8 139 F4
Gleneagles Rd CHLDW L16 115 H6
GTS/LS CH66 195 F5
Glenesk Rd GTS/LS CH66 195 F5
Glenfield Cl CL/PREN CH43 129 K1
MOR/LEA CH46 109 F6
Glenfield Rd WAV L15 134 B3
Glengariff St CLB/OSW/ST L13 98 C6
Glenham Cl HOY CH47 127 K1
Glenhead Rd ALL/GAR L19 153 J3
Glenholm Rd MGHL L31 * 71 F2
Glenluce Rd ALL/GAR L19 153 J3
Glenmarsh Cl BEB CH63 150 C6
WD/CROXPK L12 115 G1
Glenmarsh Wy FMBY L37 49 H2
Glenmaye Cl WD/CROXPK L12 99 J3
Glenmaye Rd GTS/LS CH66 195 F5
Glenmore Av CALD/MH L18 134 A6
Glenmore Rd CL/PREN CH43 130 D5
Glenn Pl WDN WA8 157 J2
Glenpark Dr CHTN/BK PR9 23 K1
Glen Park Rd WAL/NB CH45 95 G6
Glen Rd CLB/OSW/ST L13 115 F5
GTS/LS CH66 195 F5
Glen Ronald Dr
GR/UP/WCH CH49 128 E4
Glenrose Ter STHP PR8 27 H2
Glenroyd Dr BRSC L40 38 E5
Glenside CALD/MH L18 153 K1
The Glen CALD/MH L18 134 D6
PS/BROM CH62 170 E2
RUNC WA7 187 J2
Glenton Pk NSTN CH64 192 A3
Glentrees Cl GR/UP/WCH CH49 128 E4
Glentrees Rd WD/CROXPK L12 99 F5
Glentworth Cl MGHL L31 71 G1
Glenville Cl RUNC WA7 186 E1
WLTN L25 135 J6
Glen Vine Cl CHLDW L16 * 135 G1
Glenway NWD/KWIPK L33 72 E3
Glenwood Cl GTS/LS CH66 195 F3
Glenwood Dr PEN/TH CH61 148 B4
Glenwood Gdns GTS/LS CH66 195 F3
Glenwood Rd GTS/LS CH66 195 F3
Glenwyllin Rd CSBY/WL L22 81 F1
Gleyve KNUT WA16 165 K6
Globe Rd BTL L20 4 C3
Globe St ANF/KKDL L4 97 G6
Gloucester Av GOL/RIS/CU WA3 92 C2
Gloucester Cl GTS/LS CH66 202 C3
WARR WA1 144 C2
Gloucester Ct NPK/KEN L6 113 J4
Gloucester Pl NPK/KEN L6 113 J5
Gloucester Rd BTL L20 5 H3
HUY L36 117 G4
NPK/KEN L6 114 B2
STHP PR8 27 G2
WAL/NB CH45 110 E1
WDN WA8 139 G6
Gloucester Rd North
NPK/KEN L6 114 B1
Gloucester St STHEL WA9 104 B3
Gloucestor Ct NPK/KEN L6 113 J4
Glover Pl BTL L20 4 D2
Glover Rd GOL/RIS/CU WA3 124 E2
Glover's Brow KKBY L32 72 B5
Glover's La NTHTN L30 70 B5
Glover St ECCL WA10 12 E7
NEWLW WA12 106 C2
RF/TRAN CH42 131 F5
Glyn Av PS/BROM CH62 171 G6
Glynne Gv CHLDW L16 135 H1
Glynne St BTL L20 82 A5
Glynn St WAV L15 134 A2
Glyn Rd WAL/EG CH44 111 H2
Goddard Rd RUNC WA7 177 H2
Godetia Cl WLT/FAZ L9 * 98 D1
Godfrey St WARRN/WOL WA2 17 H1
Godscroft La FROD/HEL WA6 200 B3
Godshill Cl WARRW/BUR WA5 140 E2
Godstow RUNC WA7 178 D1

Golborne Dale Rd
NEWLW WA12 92 B6
Golborne Rd AIMK WN4 79 J5
GOL/RIS/CU WA3 92 D3
WARRN/WOL WA2 107 H5
Golborne St NEWLW WA12 106 E1
WARR WA1 16 C4
Goldcliffe Cl WARRW/BUR WA5 122 D5
Goldcrest Cl RUNC WA7 187 J2
WD/CROXPK L12 99 K1
Goldcrest Ms HLWD L26 155 H2
Golden Gv ANF/KKDL L4 97 J4
Goldfinch Cl HLWD L26 155 H2
Goldfinch Farm Rd
SPK/HALE L24 173 H2
Goldfinch La GOL/RIS/CU WA3 125 G3
Goldie St ANF/KKDL L4 97 H6
Goldsmith Rd CL/PREN CH43 149 J2
Goldsmith St BTL L20 4 B2
NPK/KEN L6 * 113 K4
Goldsmith Wy CL/PREN CH43 * 149 J2
Goldsworth Fold RAIN/WH L35 118 D4
Golf Links Rd RF/TRAN CH42 150 A2
Golf Rd FMBY L37 40 D6
Gondover Av WLT/FAZ L9 82 C5
Gonville Rd BTL L20 5 H7
Gooch Dr NEWLW WA12 106 D3
Goodacre Rd WLT/FAZ L9 82 E4
Goodaker's Meadow
GR/UP/WCH CH49 * 148 D1
Goodall Pl ANF/KKDL L4 97 G4
Goodall St ANF/KKDL L4 97 G5
Goodban St STHEL WA9 104 C5
Goodison Av ANF/KKDL L4 97 H5
Goodison Pl ANF/KKDL L4 97 H4
Goodison Rd ANF/KKDL L4 97 H5
Goodlass Rd SPK/HALE L24 154 D6
Goodleigh Pl STHEL WA9 120 A2
Good Shepherd Cl
NG/CROX L11 99 F3
Goodwood Cl HUY L36 116 D6
Goodwood Ct STHEL WA9 119 F1
Goodwood Dr MOR/LEA CH46 109 J4
Goodwood Gv GTS/LS CH66 195 G6
Goodwood St EV L5 113 F2
Gooseberry La RUNC WA7 178 C4
Goostrey Cl BEB CH63 170 D4
Gordale Cl WARRW/BUR WA5 141 G2
Gordon Av AIMK WN4 78 D5
CHTN/BK PR9 15 G1
CSBY/WL L22 80 D1
GR/UP/WCH CH49 129 F6
MGHL L31 62 A4
PS/BROM CH62 171 G6
RNFD/HAY WA11 90 E4
WARR WA1 144 A2
Gordon Ct GR/UP/WCH CH49 129 F6
Gordon Dr ALL/GAR L19 153 H4
DV/KA/FCH L14 115 J4
Gordon La CHNE CH2 203 F6
Gordon Rd LITH L21 81 G5
WAL/NB CH45 95 H6
Gordon St BIRK CH41 2 C5
CHTN/BK PR9 15 G2
WAV L15 133 K2
Gore Dr ORM L39 53 J2
Goree Piazza CLVP L2 * 8 C4
Gores La FMBY L37 40 E6
RNFD/HAY WA11 76 D4
Gores Rd NWD/KWIPK L33 85 G2
Gore St TOX L8 132 D3
Gorleston Wy KKBY L32 84 E2
Gorse Av WD/CROXPK L12 99 G4
Gorsebank Rd CALD/MH L18 * 133 K4
Gorsebank St WAL/EG CH44 111 J4
Gorseburn Rd
CLB/OSW/ST L13 114 C1
Gorse Covert Rd
GOL/RIS/CU WA3 125 K1
Gorse Crs WAL/EG CH44 111 J5
Gorsedale Pk WAL/EG CH44 * 111 K5
Gorsedale Rd CALD/MH L18 134 B5
WAL/EG CH44 111 J5
Gorsefield FMBY L37 41 G5
STHEL WA9 103 F6
Gorsefield Av PS/BROM CH62 184 A2
Gorsefield Cl PS/BROM CH62 184 A2
Gorsefield Rd CSBY/BLUN L23 69 H4
RF/TRAN CH42 131 F6
Gorse Hey Ct WD/CROXPK L12 114 E2
Gorsehill Rd HES CH60 168 A4
WAL/NB CH45 95 G6
Gorse La WKBY CH48 147 F2
Gorse Rd HOY CH47 127 J1
Gorse Wy FMBY L37 48 C1
Gorsewood Gv WLTN L25 135 J4
Gorsewood Rd RUNC WA7 188 C1
WLTN L25 135 J4
Gorsey Av NTHTN L30 69 K6
Gorsey Brow
WGNW/BIL/O WN5 77 G4
Gorsey Brow Cl
WGNW/BIL/O WN5 77 G4
Gorsey Cop Wy WLTN L25 135 H3
Gorsey Cft PR/KW L34 102 B6
Gorsey La HTWN L38 59 G6
LITH L21 81 K2
NTHTN L30 69 K6
ORM L39 42 C4
STHEL WA9 120 D3
WAL/EG CH44 111 J5
WARRN/WOL WA2 143 G2
WDN WA8 159 F3
Gorsey Pl SKEL WN8 56 D6
Gorseyville Crs BEB CH63 150 D6
Gorseyville Rd BEB CH63 150 D6
Gorseywell La RUNC WA7 188 E1
Gorst La CHTN/BK PR9 37 K3
Gorstons La NSTN CH64 192 B3
Gorst St ANF/KKDL L4 97 H6
Gorsuch La BRSC L40 36 B5
Gorton Rd CLB/OSW/ST L13 115 F5
Gort Rd HUY L36 116 E4
Goschen St CLB/OSW/ST L13 114 D4
EV L5 97 H6
Gosford St TOX L8 132 E5
Gosforth Rd CHTN/BK PR9 23 H5
Gosport Cl WARRN/WOL WA2 124 A6
Goswell St WAV L15 133 K2
Gotham Rd BEB CH63 170 C3
Gothic St RF/TRAN CH42 150 E1
Gough Av WARRN/WOL WA2 123 H5
Gough Rd CLB/OSW/ST L13 98 C6
Goulden St WARRW/BUR WA5 142 B3
Goulders Ct RUNC WA7 188 A2
Gourley Rd CLB/OSW/ST L13 115 F6
Gourley's La WKBY CH48 146 E2
Government Rd HOY CH47 127 G2
Govett Rd STHEL WA9 102 E6
Gower Gdns BRSC L40 39 F6
Gower St BTL L20 81 H6
STHEL WA9 104 B4
VAUX/LVPD L3 8 C7
Gowrie Gv LITH L21 81 H4
Gowy Ct GTS/LS CH66 195 H1
Goyt Hey Av WGNW/BIL/O WN5 77 H5
Graburn Rd FMBY L37 49 F1
Grace Av AIN/FAZ L10 83 K4
WARRN/WOL WA2 142 E1
Grace Cl WAL/NB CH45 111 H2
Grace Rd EP CH65 6 D2
WLT/FAZ L9 82 D5
Grace St STHEL WA9 104 A5
TOX L8 132 E5
Gradwell St CLVPS L1 8 E5
Grafton Crs TOX L8 132 D3
Grafton Dr GR/UP/WCH CH49 129 H5
STHP PR8 33 G4
Grafton Gv TOX L8 132 D5
Grafton Rd EP CH65 6 D1
WAL/NB CH45 95 H6
Grafton St CL/PREN CH43 2 A6
ECCL WA10 12 B5
NEWLW WA12 106 B2
WARRW/BUR WA5 142 B3
Grafton Wk WKBY CH48 146 D1
Graham Av GTS/LS CH66 195 G4
Graham Cl WDN WA8 157 H3
Graham Dr HLWD L26 155 K3
Graham Rd WDN WA8 157 H3
WKBY CH48 127 F6
Graham's Rd HUY L36 117 F5
Graham St STHEL WA9 104 A1
Grainger Av BTL L20 82 B5
CL/PREN CH43 149 J1
WKBY CH48 127 G5
Graley Cl HLWD L26 155 J5
Grammar School Ct
WARRS WA4 * 143 J6
Grammar School La
WKBY CH48 146 E2
Grammar School Rd
LYMM WA13 165 G1
WARRS WA4 143 J6
Grampian Av MOR/LEA CH46 129 F1
Grampian Rd EHL/KEN L7 114 C5
Grampian Wy GOL/RIS/CU WA3 92 E2
MOR/LEA CH46 129 F1
NSTN CH64 191 K4
PS/BROM CH62 184 B3
Granams Cft NTHTN L30 70 A5
Granard Rd WAV L15 134 B3
Granary Wy VAUX/LVPD L3 132 C3
Granborne Cha KKBY L32 72 A6
Granby Cl CHTN/BK PR9 23 H2
RUNC WA7 * 188 B2
Granby Crs BEB CH63 170 C3
Granby Rd WARRS WA4 162 A3
Granby St TOX L8 133 F2
Grandison Rd ANF/KKDL L4 98 A4
Grand National Av WLT/FAZ L9 82 E2
Grange Av CHTN/BK PR9 23 G5
WAL/NB CH45 111 H1
WARRS WA4 143 H5
WD/CROXPK L12 115 J2
WLTN L25 155 G4
Grange Av North
WD/CROXPK L12 115 K2
Grange Cl GOL/RIS/CU WA3 92 D5
Grange Crs GTS/LS CH66 184 D6
Grange Cross Cl WKBY CH48 147 F2
Grange Cross Hey WKBY CH48 147 F2
Grange Cross La WKBY CH48 147 F2
Grange Dr BEB CH63 169 G6
ECCL WA10 102 D4
HES CH60 167 K4
WARRW/BUR WA5 141 H5
WDN WA8 157 J2
Grange Farm Cl
WARRW/BUR WA5 142 A3
Grange Farm Crs WKBY CH48 127 K6
Grange Green Mnr
WARRS WA4 * 161 H4
Grangehurst Ct WLTN L25 135 J5
Grange La FMBY L37 40 E6
WLTN L25 135 H4
Grangemeadow Rd WLTN L25 135 H4
Grange Ms WLTN L25 * 135 J5
Grangemoor RUNC WA7 177 G6
Grange Mt CL/PREN CH43 2 B6
HES CH60 167 K4
WKBY CH48 146 E1
Grange Old Rd WKBY CH48 146 D1
Grange Pk MGHL L31 71 H2
Grange Park Av RUNC WA7 11 H5
Grange Park Rd ECCL WA10 102 E4
RUNC WA7 11 H5
Grange Pl CL/PREN CH43 2 C5
Grange Rd AIMK WN4 78 E3
BIRK CH41 2 D5
CHTN/BK PR9 23 G6
EP CH65 6 D5
HES CH60 167 K3
HTWN L38 58 E1
NTHTN L30 82 E1
RNFD/HAY WA11 90 C6
RUNC WA7 11 H5
WKBY CH48 146 C1
Grange Rd North RUNC WA7 11 H4
Grange Rd West CL/PREN CH43 2 B5
Grangeside WLTN L25 135 H4
Grange St NPK/KEN L6 114 B2
Grange Ter WAV L15 134 A2
The Grange WAL/EG CH44 111 J3
Grange V RF/TRAN CH42 151 F2
Grange Va RNFD/HAY WA11 90 C5
Grange Vw CL/PREN CH43 2 B6
Grangeway RUNC WA7 177 F6
Grange Wy WLTN L25 135 H4
Grangeway Ct RUNC WA7 177 F6
Grange Weint WLTN L25 135 H5
Grangewood CHLDW L16 115 K6
Granston Cl WARRW/BUR WA5 122 E5
Grant Av WAV L15 134 A3
Grant Cl DV/KA/FCH L14 116 A4
ECCL WA10 12 D4
WARRW/BUR WA5 122 D6
Grantham Av WARR WA1 143 H2
WARRS WA4 162 A3
Grantham Cl PEN/TH CH61 167 J1
STHP PR8 27 H6
Grantham Crs RNFD/HAY WA11 89 F6
Grantham Rd NWD/KWIPK L33 72 D4
STHP PR8 27 H6
Grantham St NPK/KEN L6 113 K4
Grantham Wy NTHTN L30 70 D5
Grantley Rd WAV L15 134 B3
Grantley St AIMK WN4 79 F4
Granton Cl FMBY L37 48 E2
Granton Rd EV L5 113 H1
Grant Rd DV/KA/FCH L14 115 K4
MOR/LEA CH46 110 B3
WARRW/BUR WA5 141 J3
Grantwood AIMK WN4 79 F4
Granville Av MGHL L31 62 A5
Granville Cl ORM L39 53 F4
WAL/NB CH45 110 E1
Granville Dr GTS/LS CH66 194 E2
Granville Pk ORM L39 53 G5
Granville Pk West ORM L39 53 F5
Granville Rd ALL/GAR L19 * 153 K5
STHP PR8 26 E4
WAV L15 133 J2
Granville St RUNC WA7 10 E3
STHEL WA9 104 B2
WARR WA1 17 H2
Grappenhall La WARRS WA4 163 J6
Grappenhall Rd EP CH65 195 J6
WARRS WA4 162 C2
Grappenhall Wy
CL/PREN CH43 129 K2
Grasmere Av CL/PREN CH43 129 K4
PR/KW L34 118 B1
RNFD/HAY WA11 88 E4
SKEL WN8 57 K5
WARRN/WOL WA2 123 K4
Grasmere Cl NWD/KWIPK L33 72 C5
RNFD/HAY WA11 * 88 E4
Grasmere Ct RNFD/HAY WA11 88 D4
Grasmere Dr AIMK WN4 79 G4
LITH L21 82 B2
RUNC WA7 187 G2
WAL/NB CH45 111 G2
Grasmere Fold RNFD/HAY WA11 88 E4
Grasmere Gdns CSBY/BLUN L23 69 G6
Grasmere Rd EP CH65 203 G1
FMBY L37 48 D2
FROD/HEL WA6 201 F1
MGHL L31 62 B5
NSTN CH64 191 K3
Grasmere St EV L5 113 J1
Grassendale Esp ALL/GAR L19 153 G5
Grassendale La ALL/GAR L19 153 H4
Grassendale Rd ALL/GAR L19 153 H4
Grassington Crs WLTN L25 155 G1
Grassmoor Cl PS/BROM CH62 171 G5
Grass Wood Rd
GR/UP/WCH CH49 148 E1
Grasville Rd RF/TRAN CH42 131 H6
Gratrix Rd PS/BROM CH62 171 F5
Gratton Pl SKEL WN8 56 C5
Gravel La CHTN/BK PR9 21 J6
The Gravel KIRK/FR/WA PR4 25 K3
Grave-Yard La ORM L39 54 A6
Gray Av RNFD/HAY WA11 90 C5
Gray Gv HUY L36 136 C1
Graylag Cl RUNC WA7 187 J2
Graylands Pl ANF/KKDL L4 98 A4
Graylands Rd ANF/KKDL L4 98 A4
PS/BROM CH62 151 H5
Grayling Dr WD/CROXPK L12 99 H2
Grays Av RAIN/WH L35 118 B1
Graysons Rd RNFD/HAY WA11 75 G1
Grayson St CLVPS L1 8 D7
Grayston Av STHEL WA9 120 B1
Gray St BTL L20 81 H6
Greasby Dr GTS/LS CH66 195 H5
Greasby Rd GR/UP/WCH CH49 128 E6
WAL/EG CH44 111 G3
Great Ashfield WDN WA8 138 C6
Great Charlotte St CLVPS L1 9 F4
Great Crosshall St
VAUX/LVPD L3 8 E2
Great Delph RNFD/HAY WA11 90 C4
Great George Pl CLVPS L1 132 D2
Great George Sq CLVPS L1 132 D2
Great George's Rd CSBY/WL L22 80 E3
Great George St CLVPS L1 9 G7
Great Hey NTHTN L30 70 A4
Great Homer St EV L5 113 G2
Great Howard St EV L5 112 D2
VAUX/LVPD L3 8 B1
Great Mersey St EV L5 113 F1
Great Nelson St VAUX/LVPD L3 113 F3
Great Newton St VAUX/LVPD L3 9 J3
Great Orford St VAUX/LVPD L3 9 J5
Great Richmond St
VAUX/LVPD L3 113 G4
Great Riding RUNC WA7 178 B6
Greaves Cl CHTN/BK PR9 21 K6
Greaves Hall Av CHTN/BK PR9 21 K6
Greaves St TOX L8 * 132 E4
Grebe Av ECCL WA10 102 C5
Grecian St LITH L21 81 G3
Grecian Ter EV L5 113 H1
Gredington St TOX L8 133 F6
Greeba Av WARRS WA4 142 E6
Greek St RUNC WA7 10 C3
VAUX/LVPD L3 9 H3
Greenacre BRSC L40 54 E1
Greenacre Cl WLTN L25 155 F3
Greenacre Dr BEB CH63 170 D6
Greenacre Rd WLTN L25 155 F3
Greenacres FROD/HEL WA6 201 F3
Greenacres Cl CL/PREN CH43 129 K1
GOL/RIS/CU WA3 93 J3
Greenall Av WARRW/BUR WA5 140 E5
Greenall's Av WARRS WA4 162 B2
Greenall St AIMK WN4 79 G4
ECCL WA10 12 B3
Green Bank BEB CH63 169 G3
Greenbank CSBY/WL L22 81 F3
ORM L39 53 G3
Greenbank Av GTS/LS CH66 195 F2
MGHL L31 62 A4
WAL/NB CH45 95 H6
Greenbank Cl AIG/SPK L17 133 K4
Greenbank Crs ECCL WA10 12 E6
Greenbank Dr AIG/SPK L17 133 K4
AIN/FAZ L10 84 A4
PEN/TH CH61 167 K2
STHP PR8 27 F5
Greenbank Gdns WARRS WA4 162 E1
Greenbank La AIG/SPK L17 133 K5
Greenbank Rd CALD/MH L18 134 A4
RF/TRAN CH42 131 F6
WARRS WA4 162 E1
WKBY CH48 127 G5
Greenbank St WARRS WA4 162 B1
Green Bridge Cl RUNC WA7 177 K4
Greenbridge Rd RUNC WA7 178 A3
Greenburn Av RNFD/HAY WA11 89 F2
Green Coppice RUNC WA7 178 B5
Green Ct GOL/RIS/CU WA3 93 J2
Green Cft CSBY/BLUN L23 69 J4
Greencroft Rd WAL/EG CH44 111 J4
Greendale Rd PS/BROM CH62 151 F5
WLTN L25 135 G5
Green End La STHEL WA9 103 K5
Green End Pk WD/CROXPK L12 98 E6
Greene's Rd RAIN/WH L35 117 K5
Greenfield Dr HUY L36 136 C1
Greenfield Gdns CHNE CH2 198 C6
Greenfield Gv HUY L36 136 C1
Greenfield La FROD/HEL WA6 186 E6
HES CH60 167 G3
LITH L21 81 H2
Greenfield Rd CLB/OSW/ST L13 114 E4
ECCL WA10 12 B1
GTS/LS CH66 194 E2
STHP PR8 29 F6
Greenfields Av PS/BROM CH62 170 E6
WARRS WA4 162 C3
Greenfields Cl NEWLW WA12 106 C1
NSTN CH64 192 A4
WARR WA1 144 B2
Greenfields Crs AIMK WN4 79 G5
PS/BROM CH62 170 E6
Greenfields Cft NSTN CH64 191 K4
Greenfields Dr NSTN CH64 191 K5
Greenfield Vw
WGNW/BIL/O WN5 77 G5
Greenfield Wy CALD/MH L18 153 K2
WAL/EG CH44 111 H3
Greenfinch Cl HLWD L26 155 H2
WD/CROXPK L12 99 K2
Greenford Rd STHP PR8 33 J5
Greengables Cl TOX L8 133 F4
Green Gates HUY L36 116 E1
Greengates Crs NSTN CH64 191 H4
Greenham Av NWD/KWIPK L33 72 E3
Greenhaven Cl AIN/FAZ L10 83 K4
Greenheath Wy
MOR/LEA CH46 109 K4
Green Hey Dr NTHTN L30 81 K1
Greenhey Pl SKEL WN8 56 B5
Green Heys Dr MGHL L31 62 D5
Greenheys Gdns TOX L8 * 133 G3
Greenheys Rd PEN/TH CH61 147 K6
TOX L8 133 G3
WAL/EG CH44 111 H3
Greenhill Av CALD/MH L18 134 D4
Greenhill Cl CALD/MH L18 153 J1
Greenhill Crs
WGNW/BIL/O WN5 77 J4
Greenhill Pl HUY L36 116 E6
Greenhill Rd CALD/MH L18 134 C6
WGNW/BIL/O WN5 77 H4
Greenholme Cl NG/CROX L11 98 E2
Greenhouse Farm Rd
RUNC WA7 188 A1
Greenhow Av WKBY CH48 127 G6
Greenings La CHTN/BK PR9 30 B4
Green Jones Brow
WARRW/BUR WA5 121 K1
Greenlake Rd CALD/MH L18 153 J1
Greenlands HUY L36 116 E6
Greenland St CLVPS L1 132 C2
Green La BEB CH63 150 E6
BIRK CH41 131 H5
BRSC L40 39 F5
CALD/MH L18 134 D4
CHTN/BK PR9 25 G1
CLB/OSW/ST L13 114 D3
CSBY/BLUN L23 69 J3
CSBY/WL L22 80 D1
ECCL WA10 87 F5
EP CH65 6 D7
FMBY L37 41 F5
GOL/RIS/CU WA3 93 H1
GTS/LS CH66 195 G5
LITH L21 81 H4
MGHL L31 61 J5
ORM L39 45 J5
RNFD/HAY WA11 75 H4
VAUX/LVPD L3 9 H5
WAL/NB CH45 110 B2
WARR WA1 143 K1
WARRN/WOL WA2 107 G6
WARRS WA4 162 E6
WARRW/BUR WA5 105 J6
WDN WA8 157 K2
Green Lane Av ORM L39 * 45 J5
Green Lane Cl
WARRN/WOL WA2 107 G6
Green La North CHLDW L16 134 D3
Green Lawn HUY L36 117 G3
RF/TRAN CH42 150 E2
Green Lawn Gv
RF/TRAN CH42 * 150 E2
Green Lawns Dr GTS/LS CH66 202 D3
Green Leach Av
RNFD/HAY WA11 88 E4
Green Leach Ct
RNFD/HAY WA11 88 E4
Green Leach La
RNFD/HAY WA11 88 E4
Greenlea Cl BEB CH63 150 E5
EP CH65 203 F1
Greenleaf St TOX L8 133 H2
Greenleas Cl WAL/NB CH45 110 D1
Greenleas Rd WAL/NB CH45 110 D1
Greenleigh Rd CALD/MH L18 153 J1
Green Link MGHL L31 61 K5
Greenloon's Dr FMBY L37 48 C3
Greenloon's Wk FMBY L37 48 C3
Green Mt GR/UP/WCH CH49 129 H4
Green Oaks Pth WDN WA8 19 H3
Green Oaks Wy WDN WA8 19 G3
Greenock St VAUX/LVPD L3 8 A1
Greenodd Av WD/CROXPK L12 99 G4
Greenore Dr SPK/HALE L24 174 E3
Greenough Av RAIN/WH L35 118 E2
Greenough St WLTN L25 154 C1
Green Pk NTHTN L30 70 C4
Green Park Dr MGHL L31 61 K6
Green Rd PR/KW L34 117 J1
Greensbridge La HLWD L26 156 A2
Greenshank Cl NEWLW WA12 106 C1
Greenside NPK/KEN L6 9 K1
Greenside Av AIN/FAZ L10 83 G1
FROD/HEL WA6 201 G2
WAV L15 134 B2
Greenside Cl NWD/KWIPK L33 73 F3
Green's La MGHL L31 52 A4
Green Strawberry EP CH65 202 E3
Green St EV L5 112 E3
WARRW/BUR WA5 142 C4
The Green BEB CH63 182 D3
CLB/OSW/ST L13 115 G5
EP CH65 203 F1
NSTN CH64 191 J1
NSTN CH64 192 A3
PR/KW L34 102 A6
PS/BROM CH62 151 K6
RUNC WA7 177 J4
WKBY CH48 146 E4
Greenville Cl BEB CH63 150 E6
Greenville Dr MGHL L31 62 A6
Greenville Rd BEB CH63 150 E6
NSTN CH64 182 A6
Green Wk STHP PR8 33 K4
Green Wy HUY L36 116 B3
Greenway AIMK WN4 79 F5
CSBY/BLUN L23 69 H4
GR/UP/WCH CH49 129 F5
NSTN CH64 181 G5
PEN/TH CH61 167 J1
PS/BROM CH62 171 F2
WARR WA1 143 J2
WARRS WA4 162 C4
WARRW/BUR WA5 141 F2
Greenway Av SKEL WN8 56 D6
Greenway Cl FROD/HEL WA6 199 J6
Green Way Cl HUY L36 116 B3
Greenway Cl SKEL WN8 56 A3
Greenway Rd RF/TRAN CH42 131 G6
RUNC WA7 10 C7
SPK/HALE L24 174 B2
WDN WA8 158 C1
The Greenway
WD/CROXPK L12 115 J3
Greenwell Rd RNFD/HAY WA11 90 B5
Greenwich Av WDN WA8 139 J5
Greenwich Ct WLT/FAZ L9 82 E3
Greenwich Rd WLT/FAZ L9 82 E3
Greenwood Cl ORM L39 53 G4
PR/KW L34 118 A1
Greenwood Ct STHEL WA9 120 A3
Greenwood Crs
WARRN/WOL WA2 123 K5
Greenwood Dr NEWLW WA12 106 D3
Greenwood La WAL/EG CH44 111 J2
Greenwood Rd CALD/MH L18 153 J2
GR/UP/WCH CH49 129 H6
HOY CH47 127 K1
LYMM WA13 165 F1
Greetby Hl ORM L39 46 A6
Greetby Pl SKEL WN8 56 C5
Greetham St CLVPS L1 * 8 E7
Gregory Cl CHLDW L16 135 F1
WARRW/BUR WA5 141 K2
Gregory La ORM L39 35 K6
Gregory Wy CHLDW L16 135 F1
Gregson Ct WAL/NB CH45 95 J5
Gregson Rd DV/KA/FCH L14 115 G4
RAIN/WH L35 117 K2
WDN WA8 19 H2
Gregson's Av FMBY L37 40 E6
Gregson St NPK/KEN L6 113 H4
Grenfell Cl NSTN CH64 181 H6
Grenfell Pk NSTN CH64 181 H6
Grenfell Rd CLB/OSW/ST L13 98 C5
Grenfell St WDN WA8 18 E4
Grennan Ct WAL/NB CH45 * 95 H5
The Grennan WAL/NB CH45 * 95 H5
Grenville Crs BEB CH63 170 E6
Grenville Dr PEN/TH CH61 167 J2
Grenville Rd RF/TRAN CH42 131 J6
Grenville St South CLVPS L1 9 F7

Grenville Wy RF/TRAN CH42 131 J6
Gresford Av AIG/SPK L17 133 J3
CL/PREN CH43 149 K1
WKBY CH48 127 H6
Gresford Cl RAIN/WH L35 118 B4
WARRW/BUR WA5 122 E6
Gresham St EHL/KEN L7 114 B5
Gresley Cl EHL/KEN L7 * 114 A6
Gressingham Rd CALD/MH L18 134 D6
Gretton Rd DV/KA/FCH L14 116 B2
Greyfriars AIMK WN4 78 E6
Greyfriars Rd STHP PR8 33 H3
Greyhound Farm Rd
SPK/HALE L24 173 H2
Greymist Av WARR WA1 144 B2
Grey Rd AIMK WN4 79 F5
WLT/FAZ L9 97 H1
Greys Ct WARR WA1 * 124 E6
Greystoke Cl
GR/UP/WCH CH49 129 G5
Greystokes ORM L39 53 H3
Greystone Crs DV/KA/FCH L14 115 J4
Greystone Pl AIN/FAZ L10 83 J4
Greystone Rd AIN/FAZ L10 83 H4
DV/KA/FCH L14 115 J5
WARRW/BUR WA5 141 G5
Greystones GTS/LS CH66 195 G5
Grey St TOX L8 132 E3
WARR WA1 17 F3
Gribble Rd AIN/FAZ L10 83 K4
Grice St WARRS WA4 162 B2
Grierson St TOX L8 133 G2
Grieve Rd AIN/FAZ L10 83 K4
Griffin Av MOR/LEA CH46 129 F1
Griffin Cl ECCL WA10 102 B1
NG/CROX L11 99 G1
WARRW/BUR WA5 121 J1
Griffin Ms WDN WA8 139 G6
Griffin St STHEL WA9 104 C6
Griffith Av GOL/RIS/CU WA3 125 J4
Griffiths Cl GR/UP/WCH CH49 128 D6
Griffiths Dr CHTN/BK PR9 23 H5
Griffith's Rd HUY L36 116 E5
Griffiths St CLVPS L1 * 9 G7
WARRS WA4 143 J5
Grimley Av BTL L20 4 A2
Grimrod Pl SKEL WN8 56 C6
Grimshaw La ORM L39 45 J5
Grimshaw Rd SKEL WN8 56 D5
Grimshaw St BTL L20 4 C6
GOL/RIS/CU WA3 92 B2
STHEL WA9 120 A1
Grindley Gdns EP CH65 203 G1
Grinfield St EHL/KEN L7 113 J6
Grinshill Cl TOX L8 133 F3
Grinstead Cl STHP PR8 27 G6
Grinton Crs HUY L36 116 D5
Grisedale Av WARRN/WOL WA2 123 H4
Grisedale Cl FMBY L37 48 E2
RUNC WA7 187 H2
Grisedale Rd PS/BROM CH62 171 G5
Grizedale WDN WA8 157 G1
Grizedale Av RNFD/HAY WA11 88 E3
Grizedale Rd EV L5 113 H1
Groarke Dr WARRW/BUR WA5 140 E4
Groes Rd ALL/GAR L19 153 J4
Grogan Sq BTL L20 82 A5
Gronow Pl BTL L20 * 82 B5
Grosmont Rd KKBY L32 84 E3
Grosvenor Av CSBY/BLUN L23 81 F1
GOL/RIS/CU WA3 92 E3
WARR WA1 143 H2
WKBY CH48 146 C1
Grosvenor Cl STHP PR8 27 F4
WARRW/BUR WA5 141 K4
Grosvenor Ct CL/PREN CH43 130 E4
WAV L15 * 134 D2
Grosvenor Dr WAL/NB CH45 95 H5
Grosvenor Gdns NEWLW WA12 106 B3
STHP PR8 27 G4
Grosvenor Gra WARR WA1 124 D6
Grosvenor Pl CL/PREN CH43 130 D4
STHP PR8 27 G4
Grosvenor Rd ALL/GAR L19 153 H5
ANF/KKDL L4 5 K6
CL/PREN CH43 130 D3
ECCL WA10 102 E3
HOY CH47 127 G3
MGHL L31 71 F3
PR/KW L34 117 K1
RNFD/HAY WA11 90 A5
STHP PR8 27 F3
WAL/NB CH45 95 H5
WAV L15 133 J2
WDN WA8 139 G5
Grosvenor St RUNC WA7 11 G3
WAL/EG CH44 111 H2
Grosvenor Ter TOX L8 133 F5
Grounds St WARRN/WOL WA2 16 E1
The Grove BEB CH63 151 F6
CL/PREN CH43 130 E6
CLB/OSW/ST L13 * 114 D2
ECCL WA10 87 K6
GOL/RIS/CU WA3 92 E2
LYMM WA13 145 K6
ORM L39 53 G6
STBRV L28 116 C1
WAL/EG CH44 111 J4
WARRW/BUR WA5 141 G5
Grove Av HES CH60 167 K4
LYMM WA13 145 H6
Grovedale Rd CALD/MH L18 134 A4
Grovehurst Av DV/KA/FCH L14 115 K3
Groveland Av HOY CH47 127 G2
WAL/NB CH45 110 D1
Groveland Rd WAL/NB CH45 110 D1
Grovelands EHL/KEN L7 * 133 F1
Grove Md MGHL L31 62 D6
Grovenor Cl NTHTN L30 70 C6
Grove Pk CHTN/BK PR9 23 H4
ORM L39 45 K4
TOX L8 133 H3
Grove Park Av WD/CROXPK L12 99 F5
Grove Pl ANF/KKDL L4 97 G6
HOY CH47 127 G2
Grove Ri LYMM WA13 145 K6
Grove Rd CH/BCN CH1 202 C6
HOY CH47 127 G2
NPK/KEN L6 114 B4
RF/TRAN CH42 150 E1
SKEL WN8 57 K5
WAL/NB CH45 110 E1
Grove Side EHL/KEN L7 133 F1
Groveside WKBY CH48 146 B1
Grove Sq PS/BROM CH62 151 F4
The Groves EHL/KEN L7 * 133 F1
EP CH65 202 E3
KKBY L32 84 D4
Grove St AIMK WN4 79 F5
BTL L20 4 A2
ECCL WA10 13 F6
PS/BROM CH62 151 G4
RUNC WA7 10 C3
STHP PR8 27 H2
TOX L8 133 F2
WARRS WA4 17 G7
WAV L15 134 A1
Grove Ter HOY CH47 127 G2
STHP PR8 27 H2
Grove Wy EHL/KEN L7 133 F1
Grovewood STHP PR8 27 F3
Grovewood Ct CL/PREN CH43 130 E6
Grovewood Gdns
RAIN/WH L35 118 A4
Grundy Cl STHP PR8 28 B2
WDN WA8 138 E6
Grundy St EV L5 112 D1
GOL/RIS/CU WA3 92 B4
Guardian St WARRW/BUR WA5 16 A3
Guelph St EHL/KEN L7 113 J5
Guernsey Cl WARRS WA4 162 C3
Guernsey Dr EP CH65 203 G2
Guernsey Rd CLB/OSW/ST L13 114 D3
WDN WA8 139 K6
Guest St WDN WA8 18 C6
Guffitts Cl HOY CH47 108 C6
Guffitt's Rake HOY CH47 108 C6
Guildford Cl WARRN/WOL WA2 124 C6
Guildford Rd STHP PR8 27 J5
Guildford St WAL/EG CH44 111 K3
Guildhall Rd WLT/FAZ L9 82 D5
Guild Hey PR/KW L34 100 D1
Guillemot Wy HLWD L26 155 H2
Guilsted Rd NG/CROX L11 98 E3
Guinea Hall La CHTN/BK PR9 21 K6
Guion Rd LITH L21 81 J4
Guion St NPK/KEN L6 113 K3
Gulls Wy HES CH60 167 H5
Gunn Gv NSTN CH64 192 A1
Gunning Av ECCL WA10 87 J6
Gunning Cl ECCL WA10 87 J6
Gurnall St ANF/KKDL L4 97 H6
Gutticar Rd WDN WA8 157 G3
Gwendoline Cl PEN/TH CH61 148 D6
Gwendoline St TOX L8 132 E3
Gwenfron Rd NPK/KEN L6 113 K4
Gwent Cl NPK/KEN L6 113 K2
Gwent St TOX L8 133 F3
Gwladys St ANF/KKDL L4 97 H4
Gwydir St TOX L8 133 F4
Gwydrin Rd CALD/MH L18 134 D4

H

Hackett Av BTL L20 82 A5
Hackins Hey CLVP L2 8 C3
Hackthorpe St EV L5 97 G6
Hadassah Gv AIG/SPK L17 133 H5
Hadden Cl RAIN/WH L35 * 118 C3
Haddock St BTL L20 96 D4
Haddon Av WLT/FAZ L9 82 C5
Haddon Dr PEN/TH CH61 167 K1
WDN WA8 138 B6
Haddon La NSTN CH64 192 C5
Haddon Rd GOL/RIS/CU WA3 92 E2
RF/TRAN CH42 151 F1
Haddon Wk WD/CROXPK L12 99 J2
Hadfield Av HOY CH47 127 G2
Hadfield Cl WDN WA8 159 F1
Hadfield Gv WLTN L25 135 K6
Hadleigh Cl WARRW/BUR WA5 140 E4
Hadleigh Rd KKBY L32 84 E4
Hadley Av PS/BROM CH62 170 E4
Hadlow Gdns RF/TRAN CH42 131 H6
Hadlow La NSTN CH64 193 G2
Hadlow Rd NSTN CH64 193 G3
Hadstock Av FMBY L37 48 D4
Haggerston Rd ANF/KKDL L4 97 J3
Hague Bush Cl
GOL/RIS/CU WA3 * 93 F2
Hahnemann Rd ANF/KKDL L4 5 K7
Haig Av MOR/LEA CH46 129 F1
STHP PR8 28 C2
WARRW/BUR WA5 141 H5
Haigh Crs MGHL L31 62 A3
Haigh Rd CSBY/WL L22 81 F2
Haigh St VAUX/LVPD L3 9 J1
Haig Rd WDN WA8 18 C2
Haileybury Av AIN/FAZ L10 83 G1
Haileybury Rd WLTN L25 154 E3
Hailsham Rd ALL/GAR L19 153 F3
Halby Rd WLT/FAZ L9 82 E5
Halcombe Rd WD/CROXPK L12 99 H5
Halcyon Rd RF/TRAN CH42 131 F5
Haldane Av BIRK CH41 130 C2
Haldane Rd ANF/KKDL L4 97 J3
Hale Bank Rd WDN WA8 156 D6
Hale Dr SPK/HALE L24 174 A3
Halefield St ECCL WA10 12 E3
Hale Gate Rd WDN WA8 175 G2
Hale Gv AIMK WN4 78 E4
WARRW/BUR WA5 141 H3
Hale Rd ANF/KKDL L4 97 G4
SPK/HALE L24 173 H2
WAL/NB CH45 111 J1
WDN WA8 157 G5
Hale St CLVP L2 8 D3
WARRN/WOL WA2 16 D1
Hale Vw RUNC WA7 176 B5
Hale View Rd FROD/HEL WA6 199 K5
HUY L36 117 G5
Halewood Av GOL/RIS/CU WA3 92 A2
Halewood Cl WLTN L25 135 J5
Halewood Dr WLTN L25 154 E1
Halewood Pl WLTN L25 135 K6
Halewood Rd WLTN L25 135 J6
Halewood Wy WLTN L25 155 F1
Haley Rd North
WARRW/BUR WA5 121 J1
Haley Rd South
WARRW/BUR WA5 121 J1
Halfacre La WARRS WA4 144 D6
Half Crown St EV L5 112 E1
Halfpenny Cl ALL/GAR L19 153 J4
Halidon Ct BTL L20 4 B2
Halifax Cl WARRN/WOL WA2 123 K5
Halifax Crs CSBY/BLUN L23 69 J3
Halifax Rd STHP PR8 33 J4
Halkirk Rd CALD/MH L18 153 K3
Halkyn Av AIG/SPK L17 133 J3
Halkyn Dr EV L5 113 J2
Hallam Wk EHL/KEN L7 114 A6
Hallastone Rd FROD/HEL WA6 199 J5
Hall Av WDN WA8 157 F2
Halla-way WARRS WA4 143 H6
Hallbridge Gdns SKEL WN8 57 K5
Hall Brow Cl BRSC L40 54 B1
Hallcroft SKEL WN8 56 E3
Hallcroft Pl WARRS WA4 163 F1
Hall Dr GR/UP/WCH CH49 128 D6
KKBY L32 84 D1
WARRS WA4 162 C5
Hallfield Dr CHNE CH2 198 C6
Hallfield Pk GTS/LS CH66 195 G5
Hallfields Rd
WARRN/WOL WA2 143 G1
Hall Gn SKEL WN8 57 K6
Hall Green Cl SKEL WN8 57 K6
Halliday Cl GOL/RIS/CU WA3 125 H4
Hall La BRSC L40 47 G4
EHL/KEN L7 113 J5
HTWN L38 60 B3
HUY L36 117 G5
KKBY L32 84 D1
MGHL L31 52 A6
MGHL L31 71 G1
NWD/KWIPK L33 72 E3
ORM L39 64 E3
PR/KW L34 117 K2
RAIN/WH L35 118 E6
STHEL WA9 120 E3
WARRS WA4 163 G3
WARRS WA4 179 J3
WARRW/BUR WA5 106 B5
WLT/FAZ L9 82 E4
Hallmoor Cl ORM L39 53 H3
Hall Nook WARRW/BUR WA5 141 G5
Hallows Av WARRN/WOL WA2 143 G1
Hall Rd BRSC L40 36 E3
RNFD/HAY WA11 90 D4
WARR WA1 144 C2
Hall Rd East CSBY/BLUN L23 68 C3
Hall Rd West CSBY/BLUN L23 68 B3
Hallsands Rd KKBY L32 84 D3
Hallside Cl ALL/GAR L19 153 H3
Hall St CHTN/BK PR9 15 H5
ECCL WA10 13 J4
STHEL WA9 120 C4
WARR WA1 17 F5
WGNE/HIN WN2 79 K2
Hall Ter WARRW/BUR WA5 141 F2
Halltine Cl CSBY/BLUN L23 68 B4
Hallville Rd CALD/MH L18 134 B4
Hall Wood Av RNFD/HAY WA11 90 E3
Hallwood Cl RUNC WA7 186 E1
Hallwood Dr GTS/LS CH66 193 K5
Hallwood Link Rd RUNC WA7 187 H1
Hallwood Park Av RUNC WA7 187 H1
Hallworthy Cl LEIGH WN7 93 J2
Halsall Av WARRN/WOL WA2 143 G1
Halsall Buildings CHTN/BK PR9 15 H3
Halsall Cl CSBY/BLUN L23 69 F4
RUNC WA7 188 B2
Halsall Gn BEB CH63 170 D4
Halsall Hall Dr ORM L39 43 K2
Halsall La FMBY L37 49 F1
ORM L39 44 B5
ORM L39 45 H5
Halsall Manor Ct ORM L39 43 K2
Halsall Rd BTL L20 82 B4
ORM L39 44 A1
STHP PR8 34 C1
Halsalls Cottages WDN WA8 * 156 D6
Halsall St PR/KW L34 101 K6
Halsbury Rd NPK/KEN L6 114 A4
WAL/NB CH45 111 H1
Halsey Av WD/CROXPK L12 98 D6
Halsey Crs WD/CROXPK L12 98 D6
Halsnead Av RAIN/WH L35 117 J6
Halstead Rd WAL/EG CH44 111 J4
WLT/FAZ L9 82 C5
Halton Brook Av RUNC WA7 11 K7
Halton Brow RUNC WA7 177 H4
Halton Cha BRSC L40 54 E1
Halton Ct RUNC WA7 11 K5
Halton Crs GR/UP/WCH CH49 128 C6
GTS/LS CH66 202 D1
Halton Hey RAIN/WH L35 117 K6
Halton Link Rd RUNC WA7 177 H5
Halton Lodge Av RUNC WA7 177 G6
Halton Rd GTS/LS CH66 202 C2
MGHL L31 62 B4
RUNC WA7 11 J5
WAL/NB CH45 111 G1
WARRW/BUR WA5 141 G3
Halton Station Rd RUNC WA7 187 J4
Halton St RNFD/HAY WA11 * 90 D5
Halton View Rd WDN WA8 19 H1
Halton Wy GTS/LS CH66 202 C2
Halton Wd KKBY L32 72 A6
Halville Rd WAL/EG CH44 111 J4
Hambledon Cl GTS/LS CH66 194 D3
Hambledon Dr
GR/UP/WCH CH49 128 D5
Hamble Dr WARRW/BUR WA5 141 G6
Hambleton Cl NG/CROX L11 99 F1
WDN WA8 * 138 B6
Hamblett Crs RNFD/HAY WA11 88 E5
Hamer St ECCL WA10 13 F4
Hamil Cl HOY CH47 108 C6
Hamilton Cl NSTN CH64 181 G5
Hamilton La BIRK CH41 3 G3
Hamilton Rd AIMK WN4 78 B5
ECCL WA10 87 J5
EV L5 113 H2
WAL/NB CH45 95 G5
Hamilton Sq BIRK CH41 3 H3
Hamilton St BIRK CH41 3 G5
Hamlet Rd WAL/NB CH45 111 F1
Hammersley Av STHEL WA9 120 A4
Hammersley St STHEL WA9 * 120 A4
Hammill Av ECCL WA10 88 B5
Hammill St ECCL WA10 12 B1
Hammond Rd NWD/KWIPK L33 73 H6
Hammond St STHEL WA9 104 B3
Hamnett Ct GOL/RIS/CU WA3 125 G4
Hamnett Rd PR/KW L34 102 A6
Hampden Gv RF/TRAN CH42 131 H5
Hampden Rd RF/TRAN CH42 131 G5
Hampden St ANF/KKDL L4 97 H3
Hampshire Av NTHTN L30 69 K6
Hampshire Gdns ECCL WA10 103 H3
Hampson Cl AIMK WN4 91 G1
Hampson St NPK/KEN L6 114 A2
Hampstead Rd NPK/KEN L6 114 B3
WAL/EG CH44 111 J4
Hampton Cl NSTN CH64 191 K3
WDN WA8 139 K6
Hampton Court Rd
WD/CROXPK L12 115 G2
Hampton Crs NSTN CH64 191 K4
Hampton Dr
WARRW/BUR WA5 141 K5
WDN WA8 138 B4
Hampton Gdns EP CH65 195 K4
Hampton Pl RNFD/HAY WA11 88 E5
Hampton Rd FMBY L37 48 E4
STHP PR8 15 H7
Hampton St TOX L8 132 E2
Hamsterley Cl
GOL/RIS/CU WA3 125 K1
Hanbury Rd ANF/KKDL L4 98 B5
Handa Dr EP CH65 203 G3
Handel Ct TOX L8 * 133 G3
Handel Rd NTHLY L27 135 K3
Handfield Pl EV L5 113 J2
Handfield Rd CSBY/WL L22 80 E2
Handfield St EV L5 113 J2
Handford Av PS/BROM CH62 184 C2
Handforth Cl WARRS WA4 144 B5
Handforth La RUNC WA7 187 G1
Handley Ct ALL/GAR L19 153 G3
Hands St LITH L21 81 J5
Hanford Av WLT/FAZ L9 82 C5
Hankey Dr BTL L20 82 B6
Hankey St RUNC WA7 10 C4
Hankin St EV L5 113 F2
Hanley Cl WDN WA8 157 H2
Hanley Rd WDN WA8 157 H2
Hanlon Av BTL L20 82 A5
Hanmer Rd KKBY L32 84 A1
Hannah Cl PEN/TH CH61 167 J2
Hannan Rd NPK/KEN L6 114 A4
Hanns Hall Rd NSTN CH64 192 D1
Hanover Cl CL/PREN CH43 130 C3
Hanover St CLVPS L1 8 E5
WARR WA1 16 B6
Hanson Pk CL/PREN CH43 130 B4
Hanson Rd WLT/FAZ L9 83 F6
Hans Rd ANF/KKDL L4 97 J4
Hants La ORM L39 45 J5
Hanwell St NPK/KEN L6 113 K1
Hanworth Cl WD/CROXPK L12 99 H2
Hapsford Cl GOL/RIS/CU WA3 124 E3
Hapsford La CHNE CH2 198 E5
Hapsford Rd LITH L21 81 J5
Hapton St EV L5 113 G1
Harbern Cl WD/CROXPK L12 115 H1
Harbord Rd CSBY/WL L22 80 D2
Harbord St EHL/KEN L7 113 K6
WARR WA1 17 G6
Harborne Dr BEB CH63 170 B3
Harbury Av STHP PR8 33 G5
Harcourt Av WAL/EG CH44 112 A4
Harcourt Cl GOL/RIS/CU WA3 125 G4
Harcourt St ANF/KKDL L4 97 F6
BIRK CH41 2 B2
Hardacre St ORM L39 45 K5
Hardie Av MOR/LEA CH46 109 G6
Hardie Cl STHEL WA9 119 J4
Hardie Rd HUY L36 117 G4
Harding Av BEB CH63 170 B1
WARRN/WOL WA2 123 K6
Harding Cl EV L5 113 J2
Hardinge Rd ALL/GAR L19 153 K3
Harding Rd BRSC L40 38 D5
Harding St TOX L8 133 G1
Hardknott Rd PS/BROM CH62 171 G4
Hard La ECCL WA10 88 B5
Hardman St CLVPS L1 9 H6
Hardshaw St ECCL WA10 13 H4
Hardwick Gra WARR WA1 125 F6
Hardwick Rd AIMK WN4 79 F4
RUNC WA7 11 K3
Hardy Cl GTS/LS CH66 195 J6
Hardy Rd LYMM WA13 164 D1
Hardy St ALL/GAR L19 172 C1
CLVPS L1 132 D2
WARRN/WOL WA2 16 E2
Harebell Cl FMBY L37 49 F4
Harebell St EV L5 97 F6
Hare Cft STBRV L28 99 K5
Harefield Gn SPK/HALE L24 173 J2
Harefield Rd SPK/HALE L24 173 J2
Haresfinch Rd RNFD/HAY WA11 13 J1
Haresfinch Vw RNFD/HAY WA11 88 E5
Hare's La FROD/HEL WA6 200 B1
STHP PR8 29 G6
Harewell Rd NG/CROX L11 98 E4
Harewood Av GTS/LS CH66 195 F5
STHP PR8 33 J3
Harewood Cl HUY L36 116 E4
Harewood Rd WAL/NB CH45 95 G6
Harewood St NPK/KEN L6 * 113 J3
Harfield Gdns GTS/LS CH66 195 F4
Harford Cl WARRW/BUR WA5 141 G5
Hargate Rd NWD/KWIPK L33 84 E1
Hargrave Av CL/PREN CH43 130 B6
Hargrave Cl CL/PREN CH43 130 B6
Hargrave Dr GTS/LS CH66 195 H4
Hargrave La BEB CH63 183 G2
Hargreaves Ct WDN WA8 19 J1
Hargreaves Rd AIG/SPK L17 133 H6
Hargreaves St STHEL WA9 104 C1
STHP PR8 15 H6
Harington Cl FMBY L37 48 D2
Harington Gn FMBY L37 48 D2
Harington Rd FMBY L37 48 C1
Harker St VAUX/LVPD L3 9 G1
Harke St EHL/KEN L7 133 G1
Harland Dr AIMK WN4 79 H6
Harland Gn SPK/HALE L24 174 A2
Harland Rd RF/TRAN CH42 131 G5
Harlech Cl WARRW/BUR WA5 122 E5
Harlech Rd CSBY/BLUN L23 68 D6
Harlech St AIMK WN4 78 E4
ANF/KKDL L4 97 G4
WAL/EG CH44 112 A6
Harlech Wy EP CH65 196 C6
Harleston Rd NWD/KWIPK L33 73 F6
Harley Av BEB CH63 150 B3
Harley St WLT/FAZ L9 82 D5
Harlian Av MOR/LEA CH46 128 E2
Harlow Cl STHEL WA9 103 H6
WARRS WA4 144 B6
Harlow St TOX L8 132 D5
Harlyn Cl HLWD L26 155 H5
Harlyn Gdns WARRW/BUR WA5 140 E6
Harmony Wy CLB/OSW/ST L13 114 E6
The Harn GTS/LS CH66 195 F6
Harold Av AIMK WN4 79 F4
Haroldene Gv HUY L36 117 F2
Harold Rd RNFD/HAY WA11 90 E4
Harper Cl GTS/LS CH66 195 G5
Harper Rd WLT/FAZ L9 97 J1
Harpers Rd WARRN/WOL WA2 124 C6
Harp's Cft NTHTN L30 69 K6
Harptree Cl RAIN/WH L35 118 A4
Harradon Rd WLT/FAZ L9 82 E4
Harridge La BRSC L40 44 E2
Harrier Dr HLWD L26 155 H2
Harrier Rd WARRN/WOL WA2 124 B5
Harringay Av CALD/MH L18 134 A4
Harrington Av HOY CH47 127 H2
Harrington Rd CSBY/BLUN L23 68 E5
LITH L21 82 A2
VAUX/LVPD L3 132 D5
Harrington St CLVP L2 8 D4
Harris Cl BEB CH63 170 B3
Harris Dr BTL L20 82 A4
Harris Gdns STHEL WA9 103 K4
Harrismith Rd AIN/FAZ L10 83 J4
Harrison Dr BTL L20 5 J4
RNFD/HAY WA11 75 G2
RNFD/HAY WA11 89 K5
WAL/NB CH45 94 E6
Harrison Hey HUY L36 116 D6
Harrison St WDN WA8 157 G5
Harrisons Yd PS/BROM CH62 * 184 C1
Harrison Wy NEWLW WA12 106 C1
VAUX/LVPD L3 132 D5
Harris St ECCL WA10 12 D3
WDN WA8 19 H1
Harrocks Cl NTHTN L30 70 A4
Harrock Wood Cl
PEN/TH CH61 148 B5
Harrod Dr STHP PR8 27 F4
Harrogate Cl PS/BROM CH62 184 A3
WARRW/BUR WA5 141 H1
Harrogate Dr EV L5 113 H2
Harrogate Rd PS/BROM CH62 184 A3
RF/TRAN CH42 151 F3
Harrogate Wy CHTN/BK PR9 21 F5
Harrop Rd RUNC WA7 11 F7
Harrops Cft NTHTN L30 70 B5
Harrowby Cl TOX L8 133 F2
Harrowby Rd LITH L21 81 G4
RF/TRAN CH42 131 F5
WAL/EG CH44 112 A3
Harrowby Rd South
RF/TRAN CH42 131 F5
Harrowby St TOX L8 * 133 F2
Harrow Cl NTHTN L30 70 C6
WAL/EG CH44 111 F2
WARRS WA4 162 D5
Harrow Dr AIN/FAZ L10 83 G1
RUNC WA7 177 H3
Harrow Gv PS/BROM CH62 171 G5
Harrow Rd ANF/KKDL L4 113 K1
EP CH65 7 F7
WAL/EG CH44 111 F2
Harsnips SKEL WN8 56 E3
Hartdale Rd CALD/MH L18 134 B5
CSBY/BLUN L23 69 H3
Hartford Cl CL/PREN CH43 130 C6
Hartford Dr EP CH65 195 J5
Harthill Av CALD/MH L18 134 C5
Harthill Rd CALD/MH L18 134 D6
Hartington Av BIRK CH41 2 A2
Hartington Rd ALL/GAR L19 153 K5
ECCL WA10 87 K6
TOX L8 133 H3
WAL/EG CH44 111 H3
WD/CROXPK L12 115 G1
Hartismere Rd WAL/EG CH44 111 K4

Hartland Av CHTN/BK PR9 ....20 E6
Hartland Cl WDN WA8 ....139 F4
Hartland Gdns STHEL WA9 ....119 F1
Hartland Rd NG/CROX L11 ....98 C3
Hartley Av WLT/FAZ L9 ....82 E6
Hartley Cl ANF/KKDL L4 ....97 H6
Hartley Crs STHP PR8 ....27 G5
Hartley Gv ECCL WA10 ....102 E5
Hartley Quay VAUX/LVPD L3 ....8 B6
Hartley Rd STHP PR8 ....27 G5
Hartleys Village WLT/FAZ L9 ....82 E6
Hartnup St EV L5 ....113 J1
Hartopp Rd WLTN L25 ....135 H3
Hartsbourne Av WLTN L25 ....135 G2
Hartsbourne Cl WLTN L25 ....135 G2
Hartsbourne Wk WLTN L25 ....135 H2
Hartshead SKEL WN8 ....56 E3
Hart's La SKEL WN8 ....57 H5
Hart St STHP PR8 ....15 K6
VAUX/LVPD L3 ....9 H3
Hart Street Br STHP PR8 ....15 K6
Hartswell Cl GOL/RIS/CU WA3 ....92 B2
Hartwell St LITH L21 ....81 J5
Hartwood Cl KKBY L32 ....84 E4
Hartwood Rd CHTN/BK PR9 ....15 K3
KKBY L32 ....84 E4
Hartwood Sq KKBY L32 * 84 E4
Harty Rd RNFD/HAY WA11 ....89 K6
Harvard Cl RUNC WA7 ....178 C3
Harvard Ct WARRN/WOL WA2 ....123 G4
Harvard Gv PR/KW L34 ....101 K6
Harvester Wy
GR/UP/WCH CH49 * 128 D5
NTHTN L30 ....70 D5
Harvest La MOR/LEA CH46 ....109 H6
Harvest Wy STHEL WA9 ....120 A3
Harvey Av GR/UP/WCH CH49 ....128 E6
NEWLW WA12 ....105 K2
Harvey Ct GOL/RIS/CU WA3 ....93 J2
WARRN/WOL WA2 ....123 H4
Harvey La GOL/RIS/CU WA3 ....92 A2
Harvey Rd WAL/NB CH45 ....111 G1
Harvington Dr STHP PR8 ....33 G4
Harwich Gv CHLDW L16 ....135 G1
Harwood Gdns WARRS WA4 ....163 F1
Harwood Rd ALL/GAR L19 ....154 A5
Haryngton Av
WARRW/BUR WA5 ....142 C2
Haselbeech Cl NG/CROX L11 ....98 D2
Haselbeech Crs NG/CROX L11 ....98 D2
Haseldine St AIMK WN4 ....78 E3
Hasfield Rd NG/CROX L11 ....99 F3
Haslam Dr ORM L39 ....45 H4
Haslemere RAIN/WH L35 ....118 B4
Haslemere Dr
WARRW/BUR WA5 ....140 E5
Haslemere Rd WLTN L25 ....135 H3
Haslemere Wy WLTN L25 ....135 J3
Haslingden Cl CLB/OSW/ST L13 ....115 F5
Haslington Gv HLWD L26 ....155 K5
Hassal Rd RF/TRAN CH42 ....151 F3
Hastings Av WARRN/WOL WA2 ....123 H3
Hastings Dr HUY L36 ....136 D1
Hastings Rd CSBY/WL L22 ....80 C1
STHP PR8 ....27 F6
Haswell Dr STBRV L28 ....100 B5
Hatchmere Cl CL/PREN CH43 ....130 C6
WARRW/BUR WA5 ....142 B4
Hatfield Cl STHEL WA9 ....103 H6
WD/CROXPK L12 ....99 K2
Hatfield Gdns HUY L36 ....117 F6
Hatfield Rd BTL L20 ....5 J5
STHP PR8 ....33 J3
Hathaway MGHL L31 ....70 E2
Hathaway Cl WLTN L25 ....135 H3
Hathaway Rd WLTN L25 ....135 H3
Hatherley Av CSBY/WL L22 ....81 F1
Hatherley Cl TOX L8 ....133 F2
Hatherley St TOX L8 ....133 F3
WAL/EG CH44 ....112 A5
Hathersage Rd HUY L36 ....116 E2
Hatley La FROD/HEL WA6 ....200 C2
Hatters Rw WARR WA1 * 16 D4
Hatton Av PS/BROM CH62 ....184 B4
Hatton Cl HES CH60 ....167 H4
Hatton Gdn VAUX/LVPD L3 ....8 D2
Hatton Hill Rd LITH L21 ....81 H3
Hattons La CHLDW L16 ....134 D3
Hauxwell Gv RNFD/HAY WA11 ....89 F5
Havannah La STHEL WA9 ....105 F2
Havelock Cl ECCL WA10 ....12 D5
Haven Brow ORM L39 ....53 G5
Haven Rd AIN/FAZ L10 ....83 J3
Havergal St RUNC WA7 ....10 C6
Haverstock Rd NPK/KEN L6 ....114 B4
Haverton Wk WD/CROXPK L12 ....99 J2
Havisham Cl GOL/RIS/CU WA3 ....125 F2
Hawarde Cl NEWLW WA12 ....106 A1
Hawarden Av AIG/SPK L17 ....133 J3
CL/PREN CH43 ....2 B5
WAL/EG CH44 ....111 J3
Hawarden Gdns EP CH65 ....196 C6
Hawarden Gv LITH L21 ....81 H5
Hawdon Ct EHL/KEN L7 ....133 H1
Hawes Av RNFD/HAY WA11 ....89 F3
Hawes Crs AIMK WN4 ....79 G4
Hawesside St CHTN/BK PR9 ....15 F5
Haweswater Av
RNFD/HAY WA11 ....89 K5
Haweswater Cl
NWD/KWIPK L33 ....72 C4
RUNC WA7 ....187 K2
Haweswater Gv MGHL L31 ....62 D5
Hawgreen Rd KKBY L32 ....84 A2
Hawick Cl GTS/LS CH66 ....194 D4
NWD/KWIPK L33 ....72 C3
Hawke Gn HUY L36 ....136 D2
Hawke St VAUX/LVPD L3 ....9 G4
Hawkesworth St ANF/KKDL L4 ....113 J1
Hawkhurst Cl TOX L8 ....132 E5
Hawkins Rd NSTN CH64 ....182 A6
Hawkins St NPK/KEN L6 ....113 K4
Hawksclough SKEL WN8 ....56 E3
Hawks Ct RUNC WA7 ....187 H1
Hawkshaw Cl
GOL/RIS/CU WA3 ....124 E3
Hawkshead Av
WD/CROXPK L12 ....99 G4
Hawkshead Cl MGHL L31 ....62 C5
RUNC WA7 * 187 K2
Hawkshead Dr LITH L21 ....82 A3
Hawkshead Rd
PS/BROM CH62 ....171 G4
WARRW/BUR WA5 ....121 J1
Hawkshead St CHTN/BK PR9 ....15 J4
Hawksmoor Cl AIN/FAZ L10 ....83 K4
Hawksmoor Rd AIN/FAZ L10 ....83 K5
Hawksmore Cl
GR/UP/WCH CH49 ....128 E3
Hawkstone Gv FROD/HEL WA6 ....199 K5
Hawkstone St TOX L8 ....133 F5
Hawkstone Wk TOX L8 * 133 F5
Hawks Wy HES CH60 ....167 J5
Hawksworth Cl FMBY L37 ....41 G5
Hawksworth Dr FMBY L37 ....41 G5
Hawley's La WARRN/WOL WA2 ....123 G6
Haworth Dr BTL L20 ....82 A4
Hawthorn Av AIMK WN4 ....78 B4
NEWLW WA12 ....106 C2
RUNC WA7 ....10 E6
WDN WA8 * 158 C1
Hawthorn Cl WGNW/BIL/O WN5 ....77 G4
Hawthorn Crs SKEL WN8 ....56 A4
Hawthorn Dr ECCL WA10 ....102 D1
PEN/TH CH61 ....167 K3
WKBY CH48 ....147 F1
Hawthorne Av HLWD L26 ....155 H5
WARR WA1 ....144 A2
WARRW/BUR WA5 ....141 G3
Hawthorne Cl RNFD/HAY WA11 ....89 K6
Hawthorne Crs FMBY L37 ....49 G3
Hawthorne Dr NSTN CH64 ....183 J6
Hawthorne Gv CHTN/BK PR9 ....23 H6
EHL/KEN L7 ....113 K6
WAL/EG CH44 ....112 A5
WARR WA1 ....143 J2
Hawthorne Rd BTL L20 ....5 H6
FROD/HEL WA6 ....186 E6
LITH L21 ....81 J4
RF/TRAN CH42 ....131 G6
STHEL WA9 ....120 B1
WARRS WA4 ....162 B3
The Hawthornes NTHLY L27 * 135 K3
Hawthorne St
WARRW/BUR WA5 ....142 D1
Hawthorn Gv EHL/KEN L7 ....113 K6
WARRS WA4 ....143 G6
WARRS WA4 ....162 C2
Hawthorn La PS/BROM CH62 ....171 F5
Hawthorn Rd GTS/LS CH66 ....195 F3
HUY L36 ....116 C5
LYMM WA13 ....145 J6
NSTN CH64 ....181 G5
PR/KW L34 ....118 A1
Hawthorns Gv
WD/CROXPK L12 ....115 F1
Haxted Gdns ALL/GAR L19 ....154 A5
Haycroft Cl GTS/LS CH66 ....202 B1
Haydn Rd DV/KA/FCH L14 ....115 K2
Haydock La RNFD/HAY WA11 ....90 B5
Haydock Park Gdns
NEWLW WA12 ....91 G2
Haydock Park Rd AIN/FAZ L10 ....71 H6
Haydock Rd WAL/NB CH45 ....95 J6
Haydock St AIMK WN4 ....91 G1
ECCL WA10 ....13 J5
NEWLW WA12 ....106 A1
WARRN/WOL WA2 ....16 D3
Hayes Av RAIN/WH L35 ....118 A2
Hayes Crs FROD/HEL WA6 ....186 E6
Hayes Dr MGHL L31 ....72 A6
Hayes St ECCL WA10 ....102 E5
Hayfield Rd ORM L39 ....45 J4
WARR WA1 ....144 B1
Hayfield St ANF/KKDL L4 * 97 H6
Hayfield Cl HLWD L26 ....155 K2
Hayles Cl WLTN L25 ....135 H3
Hayles Gn WLTN L25 ....135 H3
Hayles Gv WLTN L25 ....135 H3
Haylock Cl TOX L8 ....132 E5
Hayman's Cl WD/CROXPK L12 * 98 E6
Haymans Gn MGHL L31 ....62 C6
WD/CROXPK L12 ....98 E6
Hayman's Gv WD/CROXPK L12 ....98 E6
Hayscastle Cl
WARRW/BUR WA5 ....122 E6
Haywood Cl GOL/RIS/CU WA3 ....93 F2
Haywood Crs RUNC WA7 ....178 C3
Haywood Gdns ECCL WA10 ....12 A7
Hazel Av KKBY L32 ....72 B6
RAIN/WH L35 ....118 A3
RUNC WA7 ....176 B5
Hazelbank Gdns FMBY L37 * 40 E6
Hazelborough Cl
GOL/RIS/CU WA3 ....125 K1
Hazel Cl GTS/LS CH66 ....202 D2
Hazeldale Rd WLT/FAZ L9 ....97 J1
Hazeldene Av PEN/TH CH61 ....148 D5
WAL/NB CH45 ....111 G2
Hazeldene Wy PEN/TH CH61 ....148 E5
Hazel Dr LYMM WA13 ....165 G1
Hazelfield Ct STHEL WA9 * 120 A3
Hazel Gv BEB CH63 ....170 A1
CSBY/BLUN L23 ....69 G6
ECCL WA10 ....102 E2
GOL/RIS/CU WA3 ....92 C3
PEN/TH CH61 ....148 A4
STHP PR8 ....23 G6
WARR WA1 ....143 K1
WLT/FAZ L9 ....82 E5
Hazelhurst Rd ANF/KKDL L4 ....97 K6
Hazel La SKEL WN8 ....56 D1
Hazel Ms MGHL L31 * 72 A6
Hazel Rd BIRK CH41 ....2 D6
HOY CH47 ....127 G2
HUY L36 ....117 F2
Hazelslack Rd NG/CROX L11 ....98 E3
Hazel St WARR WA1 ....17 J1
Hazelwood GR/UP/WCH CH49 ....128 E5
Hazelwood Av BRSC L40 ....38 E5
Hazelwood Cl STHEL WA9 ....119 K4
WDN WA8 ....157 F3
Hazelwood Gv HLWD L26 ....155 G1
Hazelwood Ms WARRS WA4 ....163 H2
Hazlehurst Cl FMBY L37 ....48 C3
Hazlehurst Gv AIMK WN4 ....79 H6
Hazlehurst Rd FROD/HEL WA6 ....201 F4
Hazleton Rd DV/KA/FCH L14 ....115 G4
Headbolt La NWD/KWIPK L33 ....72 D5
STHP PR8 ....34 C5
Headbourne Cl WLTN L25 ....135 G2
Headingley Cl HUY L36 ....135 K1
STHEL WA9 ....120 A1
Headington Rd
GR/UP/WCH CH49 ....128 E4
Headland Cl
GOL/RIS/CU WA3 ....93 F5
WKBY CH48 ....146 C3
Headley Cl ECCL WA10 ....12 D5
Head St TOX L8 ....132 D3
Heald St ALL/GAR L19 ....153 K5
NEWLW WA12 ....105 K2
Heanor Dr STHP PR8 ....28 C4
Hearne Rd ECCL WA10 ....102 E1
Heartwood Cl WLT/FAZ L9 ....82 D4
Heath Av GTS/LS CH66 ....202 E2
Heathbank Av PEN/TH CH61 ....147 K4
WAL/EG CH44 ....111 G4
Heathbank Rd RF/TRAN CH42 ....131 G6
Heath Cl PR/KW L34 ....102 B6
WKBY CH48 ....146 C3
WLTN L25 ....135 G4
Heathcote Cl EHL/KEN L7 * 133 H1
Heathcote Gdns BEB CH63 ....150 E6
Heathcote Rd ANF/KKDL L4 ....97 H3
Heath Dl BEB CH63 ....170 B2
Heath Dr GR/UP/WCH CH49 ....129 H4
HES CH60 ....167 K4
RUNC WA7 ....176 D6
Heather Bank BEB CH63 ....150 C5
Heather Brae NEWLW WA12 ....106 A1
Heather Brow CL/PREN CH43 ....130 C3
Heather Cl ANF/KKDL L4 * 97 H5
BRSC L40 ....38 E5
FMBY L37 ....41 H6
GOL/RIS/CU WA3 ....125 F2
GTS/LS CH66 ....195 H6
RUNC WA7 ....187 H3
STHP PR8 ....41 K1
Heatherdale Cl CL/PREN CH43 ....130 E6
Heatherdale Rd CALD/MH L18 ....134 B5
Heather Dene PS/BROM CH62 ....171 F2
Heatherdene Rd WKBY CH48 ....127 G6
Heathergreen Ct ANF/KKDL L4 ....97 K4
Heather Gv AIMK WN4 ....79 K5
Heatherleigh STHEL WA9 ....119 F1
WKBY CH48 ....146 E5
Heatherleigh Cl WLT/FAZ L9 ....82 D4
Heather Rd BEB CH63 ....169 K1
HES CH60 ....168 A4
Heathers Cft NTHTN L30 ....70 B6
Heather Wy CSBY/BLUN L23 ....69 J3
Heatherways FMBY L37 ....41 G5
Heathey La STHP PR8 ....35 J1
Heathfield Av STHEL WA9 ....103 G5
Heathfield Cl FMBY L37 ....41 G5
LITH L21 ....81 K5
Heathfield Dr NWD/KWIPK L33 ....72 D5
Heathfield Pk WARRS WA4 ....163 F1
WDN WA8 ....138 C6
Heathfield Rd BEB CH63 ....170 B1
CL/PREN CH43 ....131 F5
CSBY/WL L22 ....80 D1
EP CH65 ....6 C4
MGHL L31 ....71 J2
STHP PR8 ....34 A4
WAV L15 ....134 B3
Heathfield St CLVPS L1 ....9 G5
Heathgate SKEL WN8 ....56 E3
Heathgate Av SPK/HALE L24 ....174 B3
Heath Gv GTS/LS CH66 ....194 E2
Heath Hey WLTN L25 ....135 G4
Heathland Rd STHEL WA9 ....120 A3
Heathlands Rd GTS/LS CH66 ....194 E2
The Heathlands
MOR/LEA CH46 ....109 J3
Heath La CHNE CH2 ....203 J4
GOL/RIS/CU WA3 ....92 E5
GTS/LS CH66 ....194 D2
NSTN CH64 ....193 K1
Heathmoor Av
GOL/RIS/CU WA3 ....92 E5
Heathmoor Rd MOR/LEA CH46 ....109 H6
Heath Park Gv RUNC WA7 ....176 C6
Heath Rd AIMK WN4 ....91 G1
ALL/GAR L19 ....153 K3
BEB CH63 ....150 D6
HUY L36 ....116 B2
RUNC WA7 ....11 G5
WARRW/BUR WA5 ....141 G4
WDN WA8 ....157 K2
Heath Road Crs RUNC WA7 ....11 F7
Heathside HES CH60 ....167 G4
Heath St AIMK WN4 ....91 H1
GOL/RIS/CU WA3 ....92 B3
STHEL WA9 ....103 F6
WARRS WA4 ....162 B3
The Heath RUNC WA7 * 176 D6
Heath Vw LITH L21 ....69 J6
Heathview Rd WDN WA8 ....175 H1
Heathwaite Crs NG/CROX L11 ....98 E4
Heathway HES CH60 ....168 B6
Heathwood WD/CROXPK L12 ....115 F2
Heathwood Gv WARR WA1 ....144 A2
Heathy La ORM L39 ....42 C3
Heatley Cl CL/PREN CH43 ....129 K2
Heaton Cl BRSC L40 ....38 D5
SKEL WN8 ....57 J6
SPK/HALE L24 ....174 A2
Heaton Ct GOL/RIS/CU WA3 ....125 H1
Heatons Bridge Rd BRSC L40 ....37 H5
Hebburn Wy WD/CROXPK L12 ....100 A2
Hebden Rd NG/CROX L11 ....99 G2
Hebdon Cl AIMK WN4 ....79 F4
Hector Pl BTL L20 ....97 F4
Hedgebank Cl WLT/FAZ L9 ....83 G3
Hedgecroft CSBY/BLUN L23 ....69 K3
Hedgefield Rd WLTN L25 ....135 J4
Hedge Hey RUNC WA7 ....177 K4
The Hedgerows
RNFD/HAY WA11 ....90 E4
Hedges Crs CLB/OSW/ST L13 ....98 C6
Hedingham Cl HLWD L26 ....155 K5
Hedworth Gdns STHEL WA9 ....119 F1
The Heights FROD/HEL WA6 ....199 K5
Helena Rd STHEL WA9 ....104 D6
Helena St BIRK CH41 ....3 F6
EHL/KEN L7 ....113 K6
WLT/FAZ L9 ....97 H2
Helen Bank Dr RNFD/HAY WA11 ....75 G1
Helen St AIMK WN4 ....79 F5
GOL/RIS/CU WA3 ....92 A1
Helford Cl RAIN/WH L35 ....118 C1
Helford Rd NG/CROX L11 ....84 C6
Heliers Rd CLB/OSW/ST L13 ....115 F5
Hell Nook GOL/RIS/CU WA3 ....91 K2
Helmdon Cl NG/CROX L11 ....98 E4
Helmingham Gv BIRK CH41 ....131 H5
Helmsdale SKEL WN8 ....56 E3
Helmsdale La
WARRW/BUR WA5 ....141 K3
Helmsley Cl WARRW/BUR WA5 ....142 B2
Helmsley Rd HLWD L26 ....155 J4
Helsby Av PS/BROM CH62 ....184 C4
Helsby Rd WLT/FAZ L9 ....82 E4
Helsby St EHL/KEN L7 ....113 J6
STHEL WA9 ....104 B4
WARR WA1 ....17 J2
Helston Av HLWD L26 ....155 J2
RNFD/HAY WA11 ....89 G4
Helston Cl CHTN/BK PR9 ....20 E6
RUNC WA7 ....188 A2
WARRW/BUR WA5 ....141 F4
Helston Rd NG/CROX L11 ....84 C6
Helton Cl CL/PREN CH43 ....130 B6
Hemans St BTL L20 ....4 B2
Hemer Ter BTL L20 ....4 A1
Hemingford Cl GTS/LS CH66 ....202 B1
Hemingford St BIRK CH41 ....2 E4
Hemlock Cl WD/CROXPK L12 ....99 H2
Hemmingsway RAIN/WH L35 ....118 C4
Hempstead Cl STHEL WA9 ....103 H6
Hemsworth Av GTS/LS CH66 ....195 F4
Henbury Pl RUNC WA7 ....186 E1
Henderson Cl
GR/UP/WCH CH49 ....128 E3
WARRW/BUR WA5 ....140 E3
Henderson Dr RNFD/HAY WA11 ....75 H1
Henderson Rd HUY L36 ....117 G4
WDN WA8 ....18 B3
Hendon Rd NPK/KEN L6 ....114 B3
Hendon Wk GR/UP/WCH CH49 ....128 D6
Henglers Cl NPK/KEN L6 * 113 J4
Henley Av LITH L21 ....81 H3
Henley Cl BEB CH63 ....170 C3
NSTN CH64 ....191 K3
WARRS WA4 ....162 D5
Henley Ct ECCL WA10 ....103 F4
RUNC WA7 ....177 G3
Henley Dr CHTN/BK PR9 ....23 G4
Henley Rd CALD/MH L18 ....134 C4
NSTN CH64 ....191 K3
Henllan Gdns STHEL WA9 ....104 D6
Henlow Av KKBY L32 ....84 E3
Hennawood Cl NPK/KEN L6 ....113 K2
Henry Edward St
VAUX/LVPD L3 * 8 E1
Henry St BIRK CH41 ....3 G5
CLB/OSW/ST L13 ....114 D5
CLVPS L1 ....8 E6
ECCL WA10 ....13 F4
LYMM WA13 ....145 K6
WARR WA1 ....16 B5
WDN WA8 * 19 H1
Henshall Av WARRS WA4 ....143 J5
Henthorne Rd PS/BROM CH62 ....151 G3
Henthorne St CL/PREN CH43 ....2 B5
Hepherd St WARRW/BUR WA5 ....142 A5
Hepworth Cl GOL/RIS/CU WA3 ....92 A1
Herald Av ALL/GAR L19 ....154 B5
Herald Cl NG/CROX L11 ....99 G2
Heralds Cl WDN WA8 ....157 G3
Heralds Gn WARRW/BUR WA5 ....122 A5
Herbarth Cl WLT/FAZ L9 ....97 H2
Herbert St STHEL WA9 ....104 D6
WARRW/BUR WA5 * 121 J1
Herbert Taylor Cl NPK/KEN L6 ....114 A1
Herculaneum Ct TOX L8 ....132 E6
Herculaneum Rd TOX L8 ....132 D5
Herdman Cl WLTN L25 ....135 J4
Hereford Av GOL/RIS/CU WA3 * 92 C3
GR/UP/WCH CH49 ....129 F3
GTS/LS CH66 ....202 C3
Hereford Cl AIMK WN4 ....91 H1
WARR WA1 ....144 C2
Hereford Dr NTHTN L30 ....82 C2
Hereford Rd CHTN/BK PR9 ....23 H6
LITH L21 ....81 F4
WAV L15 ....134 B3
Heriot St EV L5 ....113 F1
Heriot Wk EV L5 ....113 F1
Hermes Cl NTHTN L30 ....82 B3
Hermes Rd NG/CROX L11 ....84 B5
Hermitage Green La
WARRN/WOL WA2 ....107 G5
Hermitage Gv BTL L20 ....82 A4
Hern Rd EV L5 ....112 E2
Heron Cl RUNC WA7 * 178 C5
Heron Ct HLWD L26 ....155 H2
NSTN CH64 ....191 H2
Herondale Rd CALD/MH L18 ....134 A5
Heron Gv RNFD/HAY WA11 ....75 J4
Heronhall Rd WLT/FAZ L9 ....98 D1
Heronpark Wy BEB CH63 ....170 D2
Heron Rd WKBY CH48 ....128 B3
Herons Wy RUNC WA7 ....178 E1
Hero St BTL L20 ....5 H7
Herrick St CLB/OSW/ST L13 ....114 D4
Herschell St EV L5 ....113 H1
Hertford Cl HLWD L26 ....155 J4
WARR WA1 ....144 D2
Hertford Dr WAL/NB CH45 ....111 J1
Hertford Rd BTL L20 ....4 E7
Hertford St STHEL WA9 ....104 B3
Hesketh Av CHTN/BK PR9 ....21 K5
RF/TRAN CH42 ....150 C2
Hesketh Cl WARRW/BUR WA5 ....141 G5
Hesketh Dr CHTN/BK PR9 ....23 G3
HES CH60 ....168 A4
MGHL L31 ....62 D5
Hesketh Meadow La
GOL/RIS/CU WA3 ....93 H4
Hesketh Rd BRSC L40 ....38 D5
CHTN/BK PR9 ....23 G3
SPK/HALE L24 ....175 F3
Hesketh St North
WARRW/BUR WA5 ....142 A5
Hesketh St AIG/SPK L17 * 133 H5
WARRW/BUR WA5 ....142 A5
Heskin Cl KKBY L32 ....84 D4
MGHL L31 ....62 B3
RAIN/WH L35 ....118 D4
Heskin La ORM L39 ....45 H3
Heskin Rd KKBY L32 ....84 D4
Heskin Wk KKBY L32 ....84 D4
Hessle Dr HES CH60 ....167 K6
Hester Cl HTWN L38 ....59 F3
Heswall Av BEB CH63 ....150 B3
STHEL WA9 ....119 K3
Heswall Mt PEN/TH CH61 ....148 D6
Heswall Rd GTS/LS CH66 ....195 G5
WLT/FAZ L9 ....82 E4
Hever Dr HLWD L26 ....155 K2
Heversham SKEL WN8 ....56 E3
Heward Av STHEL WA9 * 120 A1
Hewitson Av CLB/OSW/ST L13 ....114 D1
Hewitson Rd CLB/OSW/ST L13 ....114 D1
Hewitt Av ECCL WA10 ....102 E1
Hewitt's La PR/KW L34 ....85 K4
Hewitts Pl CLVP L2 * 8 D3
Hewitt St WARRS WA4 ....143 F6
Hexham Cl STHEL WA9 ....103 F6
Heyburn Rd CLB/OSW/ST L13 ....114 C1
Heydale Rd CALD/MH L18 ....134 B5
Heydean Rd CALD/MH L18 ....153 K2
Heydon Cl FMBY L37 ....48 D4
Heyes Av RNFD/HAY WA11 ....75 H3
RNFD/HAY WA11 ....90 C6
Heyescroft ORM L39 ....64 D1
Heyes Dr LYMM WA13 ....164 D1
WAL/NB CH45 ....110 C3
Heyes Gv RNFD/HAY WA11 ....75 H3
Heyes La WARRS WA4 ....162 D3
Heyes Mt RAIN/WH L35 ....118 E5
Heyes Rd WDN WA8 ....157 H3
Heyes St EV L5 ....113 J2
The Heyes WLTN L25 ....154 E1
Heyfield Park Rd GTS/LS CH66 ....194 E2
Heygarth Dr
GR/UP/WCH CH49 ....128 E5
Heygarth Rd PS/BROM CH62 ....184 B2
Hey Green Rd WAV L15 ....133 K1
Hey Lock Cl NEWLW WA12 * 106 C5
Hey Rd HUY L36 ....117 F5
Heys Av PS/BROM CH62 ....171 F5
Heyscroft Rd WLTN L25 ....154 E1
Heysham Cl RUNC WA7 ....188 C1
Heysham Lawn NTHLY L27 ....136 D5
Heysham Rd CHTN/BK PR9 ....23 H6
NTHTN L30 ....82 D1
Heysmoor Hts TOX L8 ....133 G4
The Heys RUNC WA7 ....177 H4
The Hey STBRV L28 ....100 C6
Heythrop Dr HES CH60 ....168 C5
Heyville Rd BEB CH63 ....150 D5
Heywood Av GOL/RIS/CU WA3 ....92 C2
Heywood Bvd PEN/TH CH61 ....148 D5
Hey Wood Cl NEWLW WA12 * 106 C5
Heywood Cl FMBY L37 ....48 E2
PEN/TH CH61 ....148 D5
Heywood Ct WAV L15 ....115 G6
Heywood Gdns RAIN/WH L35 ....118 A5
Heywood Rd GTS/LS CH66 ....195 G4
WAV L15 ....134 D1
Heyworth St EV L5 ....113 H2
Hibbert St WDN WA8 ....18 E3
Hickmans Rd BIRK CH41 ....111 H6
Hickory Cl WARR WA1 ....144 D2
Hickory Gv MGHL L31 ....83 K1
Hickson Av MGHL L31 ....62 A4
Hicks Rd CSBY/WL L22 ....81 F2
Higgin's La BRSC L40 ....38 C5
Highacre Rd WAL/NB CH45 * 95 G6
Higham Av ECCL WA10 ....102 B2
WARRW/BUR WA5 ....123 F6
Higham Sq EV L5 ....113 G3
High Bank Cl CL/PREN CH43 * 130 A4
Highbank Dr ALL/GAR L19 ....154 A5
High Banks MGHL L31 ....62 A4
High Beeches CHLDW L16 ....115 K6
High Beeches Crs AIMK WN4 ....79 F3
High Carrs HUY L36 ....116 B5
High Clere Crs HUY L36 ....116 E2
Highcroft Av BEB CH63 ....151 F6
Highcroft Gn BEB CH63 ....151 F6
The Highcroft BEB CH63 ....150 E6
Higher Ashton WDN WA8 ....138 E6
Higher Bebington Rd
BEB CH63 ....150 D5
Higher End Pk NTHTN L30 ....70 B4
Higher La LYMM WA13 ....165 H2
RNFD/HAY WA11 ....75 H3
WARRS WA4 ....189 G4
WLT/FAZ L9 ....83 F4
Higher Parr St STHEL WA9 ....104 A2
Higher Rd HLWD L26 ....155 H4
SPK/HALE L24 ....156 A6
Highfield CHNE CH2 ....198 C5
NWD/KWIPK L33 ....72 E3
Highfield Av GOL/RIS/CU WA3 ....92 A3

WARRW/BUR WA5 141 H4
Highfield Cl NSTN CH64 191 K1
WAL/EG CH44 111 G4
Highfield Crs RF/TRAN CH42 150 E2
WDN WA8 158 B1
Highfield Dr GR/UP/WCH CH49 128 E5
LYMM WA13 164 D1
RNFD/HAY WA11 76 B5
Highfield Gv CSBY/BLUN L23 69 G4
RF/TRAN CH42 150 E2
Highfield La BRSC L40 37 G2
GOL/RIS/CU WA3 92 D6
WARRN/WOL WA2 107 J5
Highfield Pk MGHL L31 62 D6
Highfield Pl PR/KW L34 * 117 K1
Highfield Rd CHTN/BK PR9 23 K2
CLB/OSW/ST L13 114 E3
GTS/LS CH66 194 E3
LITH L21 81 H3
LYMM WA13 164 D1
NSTN CH64 191 K1
ORM L39 45 J5
RF/TRAN CH42 150 E2
WDN WA8 18 B1
WLT/FAZ L9 97 H1
Highfield Rd North EP CH65 6 D4
Highfields HES CH60 167 K4
PR/KW L34 117 J1
Highfield South RF/TRAN CH42 150 E2
Highfield St STHEL WA9 104 B5
VAUX/LVPD L3 8 D2
Highfield Vw CLB/OSW/ST L13 114 D3
Highgate Cl HES CH60 167 K4
RUNC WA7 178 C4
Highgate Ct EHL/KEN L7 113 J6
Highgate Rd MGHL L31 62 B4
SKEL WN8 57 K6
High Gates Cl
WARRW/BUR WA5 142 B2
Highgate St EHL/KEN L7 113 J6
Highgreen Rd RF/TRAN CH42 131 F6
Highgrove Pk ALL/GAR L19 153 H3
Highlands Rd RUNC WA7 176 C5
High La BRSC L40 46 A3
ORM L39 54 C5
High Legh Rd LYMM WA13 165 K3
Highmarsh Crs NEWLW WA12 91 G6
Highmeadow SKEL WN8 67 J1
High Moss ORM L39 53 J2
Highoaks Rd WLTN L25 154 E2
High Park Pl CHTN/BK PR9 23 J5
High Park Rd CHTN/BK PR9 23 J5
Highpark Rd RF/TRAN CH42 * 131 F6
High Park St TOX L8 132 E4
Highsted Gv NWD/KWIPK L33 72 D4
High St CLVP L2 8 C3
FROD/HEL WA6 186 E6
GOL/RIS/CU WA3 92 B3
NEWLW WA12 106 D1
NSTN CH64 191 K2
PR/KW L34 117 K1
PS/BROM CH62 * 171 G4
RUNC WA7 10 D4
SKEL WN8 55 K5
SPK/HALE L24 174 E4
WARR WA1 17 F3
WAV L15 134 A2
WLTN L25 154 D1
Hightor Rd WLTN L25 135 G6
High Vw FROD/HEL WA6 199 K5
Highville Rd CHLDW L16 134 E3
High Warren Cl WARRS WA4 162 B6
Highwood Ct NWD/KWIPK L33 72 D5
Highwood Rd WARRS WA4 162 B4
Highwoods Cl AIMK WN4 79 F4
Hignett Av STHEL WA9 104 E3
Hilary Av DV/KA/FCH L14 115 J5
GOL/RIS/CU WA3 92 E2
Hilary Cl ANF/KKDL L4 98 A5
PR/KW L34 102 A6
WARRW/BUR WA5 140 E3
WDN WA8 139 K6
Hilary Dr GR/UP/WCH CH49 129 H3
Hilary Rd ANF/KKDL L4 98 A5
Hilberry Av CLB/OSW/ST L13 114 C2
Hilbre Av HES CH60 180 D1
WAL/EG CH44 111 G3
Hilbre Cl CHTN/BK PR9 23 G4
Hilbre Ct WKBY CH48 146 B2
Hilbre Dr EP CH65 203 G2
Hilbre Rd WKBY CH48 146 C2
Hilbre St BIRK CH41 2 D1
VAUX/LVPD L3 9 G4
Hilbre Vw WKBY CH48 146 C1
Hilcrest Rd ANF/KKDL L4 98 B4
Hilda Rd WD/CROXPK L12 115 J2
Hildebrand Rd ANF/KKDL L4 98 A5
Hilden Rd WARRN/WOL WA2 124 A6
Hillaby Cl TOX L8 * 133 F3
Hillam Rd WAL/NB CH45 110 D1
Hillary Crs MGHL L31 62 B6
Hillary Dr CSBY/BLUN L23 69 H5
Hillary Rd PS/BROM CH62 184 B2
Hillary Wk CSBY/BLUN L23 * 69 H5
Hillbark Rd WKBY CH48 147 J2
Hillbeck Crs AIMK WN4 78 C5
Hillberry Crs WARRS WA4 142 E6
Hillbrae Av RNFD/HAY WA11 88 D3
Hillburn Dr BIRK CH41 110 E6
Hill Cliffe Rd WARRS WA4 161 K2
Hill Cl NSTN CH64 192 B4
Hill Ct NSTN CH64 192 C4
Hill Crest ANF/KKDL L4 5 K6
Hillcrest MGHL L31 71 J1
RUNC WA7 177 G4
SKEL WN8 56 D6
Hillcrest Av HUY L36 117 G5
Hillcrest Dr BRSC L40 36 D1
GR/UP/WCH CH49 128 D6
GTS/LS CH66 194 D3
Hillcrest Rd CSBY/BLUN L23 69 H5
GTS/LS CH66 194 E3
ORM L39 45 J5
Hillcroft Rd WAL/EG CH44 111 J5
WLTN L25 135 G5
Hillerton Cl NG/CROX L11 * 99 G3
Hillfield FROD/HEL WA6 200 E2
RUNC WA7 178 C5
Hillfield Dr PEN/TH CH61 167 K2
Hillfield Rd GTS/LS CH66 195 G2
Hillfoot Av WLTN L25 154 E5
Hillfoot Cl CL/PREN CH43 129 K1
Hillfoot Crs WARRS WA4 162 A4
Hillfoot Gn WLTN L25 154 D4
Hillfoot La FROD/HEL WA6 201 H6
Hillfoot Rd WLTN L25 154 D2
Hill Gv MOR/LEA CH46 129 F2
Hillhead Rd BTL L20 5 J6
Hillingden Av HLWD L26 155 J4
Hillingdon Av PEN/TH CH61 167 K3
Hillingdon Rd WAV L15 134 C3
Hillock Cl BRSC L40 36 E2
Hillock La BRSC L40 36 E2
WARR WA1 144 B1
Hill Rdg CL/PREN CH43 130 A4
Hill Rise Vw ORM L39 52 E4
Hill Rd CL/PREN CH43 130 B2
Hill Rd North FROD/HEL WA6 199 K6
Hill Rd South FROD/HEL WA6 199 K6
Hillsboro Av FROD/HEL WA6 201 F2
Hill School Rd ECCL WA10 102 C5
Hillsdown Wy GTS/LS CH66 202 A1
Hillside Av AIMK WN4 78 E1
ECCL WA10 88 B5
HUY L36 116 D1
NEWLW WA12 105 K3
ORM L39 53 H1
RUNC WA7 176 B5
Hillside Cl BIRK CH41 131 H5
BTL L20 5 J6
FROD/HEL WA6 200 A5
WGNW/BIL/O WN5 77 G5
Hillside Ct BIRK CH41 131 H5
Hillside Crs HUY L36 116 C1
Hillside Dr GTS/LS CH66 195 H2
WLTN L25 135 J6
Hillside Gv WARRW/BUR WA5 141 G4
Hillside Rd BIRK CH41 131 H5
CALD/MH L18 134 C4
CL/PREN CH43 130 A1
FROD/HEL WA6 201 F2
HES CH60 168 A6
HUY L36 116 E2
STHP PR8 27 F6
WAL/EG CH44 110 E3
WKBY CH48 146 E1
Hillside St NPK/KEN L6 113 H4
Hillside Vw CL/PREN CH43 130 D6
Hills Moss Rd STHEL WA9 104 D6
Hills Pl WAV L15 * 134 B2
Hill St CHTN/BK PR9 15 F3
CSBY/BLUN L23 69 G6
ECCL WA10 13 H2
RUNC WA7 10 E5
TOX L8 132 D3
WARR WA1 16 D4
Hillsview Rd STHP PR8 33 J5
Hill Top La HES CH60 168 B5
NSTN CH64 192 C4
Hilltop Rd CHLDW L16 134 E2
LYMM WA13 164 D1
RNFD/HAY WA11 87 J1
Hill Top Rd WARR WA1 144 B1
WARRS WA4 162 E1
WARRS WA4 189 H6
Hilltop Wk ORM L39 53 G2
Hillview AIG/SPK L17 153 F1
Hill Vw WDN WA8 138 E4
Hillview Av WKBY CH48 127 G6
Hillview Cl FROD/HEL WA6 201 F2
Hill View Dr GR/UP/WCH CH49 129 H3
Hillview Gdns WLTN L25 135 F6
Hillview Rd PEN/TH CH61 147 K5
Hillwood Cl BEB CH63 170 C4
Hilton Av WARRW/BUR WA5 141 J4
Hilton Cl BIRK CH41 2 C4
Hilton Gv WKBY CH48 127 F6
Hilton St AIMK WN4 79 G6
Hinchley Gn MGHL L31 61 K6
Hinckley Rd RNFD/HAY WA11 89 F5
Hindburn Av MGHL L31 62 D5
Hinderton Cl BIRK CH41 131 H5
Hinderton Dr HES CH60 180 E1
WKBY CH48 147 F2
Hinderton Gn NSTN CH64 192 A1
Hinderton La NSTN CH64 182 B6
Hinderton Rd BIRK CH41 3 F7
NSTN CH64 192 B1
Hindle Av WARRW/BUR WA5 123 F6
Hindley Beech MGHL L31 62 A5
Hindlip St TOX L8 133 F6
Hind St BIRK CH41 3 G6
Hinson St BIRK CH41 3 G4
Hinton Crs WARRS WA4 162 D3
Hinton Rd RUNC WA7 10 E7
Hinton St LITH L21 81 J5
NPK/KEN L6 114 A4
Hitchen's Cl RUNC WA7 178 C6
Hobart Dr NWD/KWIPK L33 72 D3
Hobart St EV L5 113 G1
STHEL WA9 103 F5
Hobb La WARRS WA4 161 F6
Hobby Ct RUNC WA7 187 H1
Hobcross La BRSC L40 47 G2
Hobhouse Ct CL/PREN CH43 * 2 A5
Hoblyn Rd CL/PREN CH43 130 B1
Hockenhall Aly CLVP L2 8 D3
Hockenhull Cl BEB CH63 * 170 C3
Hodder Av MGHL L31 62 D5
Hodder Cl RNFD/HAY WA11 88 E4
Hodder Rd EV L5 113 H1
Hodder St EV L5 113 H1
Hodge St STHP PR8 14 E5
Hodgkinson Av
WARRW/BUR WA5 123 F6
Hodnet Dr AIMK WN4 79 H6
Hodson Pl NPK/KEN L6 113 H3
Hodson St STHP PR8 15 H6
Hogarth Dr CL/PREN CH43 130 A6
Hogarth St LITH L21 81 H5
Hogarth Wk ANF/KKDL L4 97 F5
Hoggs Hill La FMBY L37 48 E5
Hoghton Cl STHEL WA9 104 D5
Hoghton Gv CHTN/BK PR9 15 G3
Hoghton Rd SPK/HALE L24 175 F4
STHEL WA9 104 D6
Hoghton St CHTN/BK PR9 15 F4
Holbeck RUNC WA7 178 B6
Holbeck St ANF/KKDL L4 113 K1
Holborn Ct WDN WA8 138 E6
Holborn Dr ORM L39 53 G2
Holborn Hl BIRK CH41 131 H5
ORM L39 53 H1
Holborn Sq BIRK CH41 131 H5
Holbrook Cl STHEL WA9 120 A1
WARRW/BUR WA5 140 E3
Holcombe Av GOL/RIS/CU WA3 92 D3
Holcombe Cl
GR/UP/WCH CH49 * 128 E5
Holden Gv CSBY/WL L22 80 D1
Holden Rd CSBY/WL L22 80 C1
RAIN/WH L35 117 J3
Holden Rd East CSBY/WL L22 * 80 D1
Holden Ter CSBY/WL L22 80 D1
Holdsworth St EHL/KEN L7 113 K5
Holes La WARR WA1 144 A2
Holford Av WARRW/BUR WA5 142 C1
Holford Wy NEWLW WA12 107 F2
Holgate CSBY/BLUN L23 69 J2
Holgate Pk CSBY/BLUN L23 69 J2
Holkham Cl WDN WA8 18 A2
Holland Ct SKEL WN8 67 F5
Holland Gv HES CH60 167 K4
Holland Moss SKEL WN8 66 C2
Holland Pl EHL/KEN L7 113 K6
Holland Rd HLWD L26 155 H5
SPK/HALE L24 173 K3
WAL/NB CH45 95 J6
Holland's La SKEL WN8 55 G3
Holland St EHL/KEN L7 114 B4
Holland Wy HLWD L26 155 H5
Hollies Rd HLWD L26 155 J4
The Hollies RUNC WA7 * 177 G5
WLTN L25 135 F6
Hollingbourne Pl NG/CROX L11 98 E2
Hollingbourne Rd NG/CROX L11 98 E2
Hollinghurst Rd
NWD/KWIPK L33 72 E4
Hollingwood Cl AIMK WN4 79 F6
Hollingworth Cl WLT/FAZ L9 97 K2
Hollinhey Cl NTHTN L30 70 D4
Hollin Hey Cl WGNW/BIL/O WN5 77 G6
Hollins Cl AIMK WN4 78 C5
WAV L15 134 B1
Hollins Dr WARRN/WOL WA2 123 G1
Hollins La WARRN/WOL WA2 122 E1
Hollocombe Rd NG/CROX L11 99 G3
Holloway RUNC WA7 10 C6
Hollow Cft STBRV L28 100 A4
Hollow Dr WARRS WA4 162 D2
Hollowford La BRSC L40 39 J6
Hollow La FROD/HEL WA6 201 K6
Holly Av BEB CH63 170 B2
NEWLW WA12 106 D2
Holly Bank LYMM WA13 * 164 E1
Hollybank WARRS WA4 160 D6
Hollybank Ct WDN WA8 * 18 B1
Holly Bank Gv STHEL WA9 104 A1
Hollybank Rd BIRK CH41 2 D6
CALD/MH L18 133 K4
RUNC WA7 177 J5
Hollybrook Rd STHP PR8 27 H2
Hollybush Sq GOL/RIS/CU WA3 93 F2
Holly Cl BRSC L40 54 E1
ECCL WA10 102 D1
SKEL WN8 56 A4
SPK/HALE L24 174 E4
Holly Ct FROD/HEL WA6 199 K4
Holly Crs RNFD/HAY WA11 75 H4
Hollydale Rd CALD/MH L18 134 B4
Holly Farm Rd ALL/GAR L19 154 A5
Hollyfield Rd EP CH65 6 C4
WLT/FAZ L9 82 C6
Holly Fold La RNFD/HAY WA11 66 A4
Holly Gv BIRK CH41 131 H5
HUY L36 116 B5
LITH L21 81 G5
WARR WA1 143 K2
Holly Hedge La WARRS WA4 161 G5
Holly Hey RAIN/WH L35 117 K6
Holly La ORM L39 53 F1
SKEL WN8 65 K3
Holly Mt WD/CROXPK L12 114 E1
Holly Pl MOR/LEA CH46 129 G2
Holly Rd EHL/KEN L7 114 B5
EP CH65 6 E4
GOL/RIS/CU WA3 92 D3
RNFD/HAY WA11 89 J6
WARRW/BUR WA5 141 F4
Hollyrood PR/KW L34 117 F2
Holly St BTL L20 5 F3
Holly Ter WARRW/BUR WA5 141 G4
Hollytree Rd WLTN L25 135 J6
Hollywood Rd AIG/SPK L17 133 K6
Holman Rd ALL/GAR L19 154 A5
Holm Cottages CL/PREN CH43 149 J1
Holmcrofts NSTN CH64 191 K4
Holmdale Av CHTN/BK PR9 24 A1
Holm Dr CHNE CH2 198 D6
Holme Cl PR/KW L34 102 C6
Holmefield Av ALL/GAR L19 153 H3
Holmefield Gv MGHL L31 62 A6
Holmefield Rd ALL/GAR L19 153 G2
Holme Rd ECCL WA10 102 D3
Holmes Ct GOL/RIS/CU WA3 124 E3
Holmes La LITH L21 * 81 H4
Holmes St TOX L8 133 H2
Holme St EV L5 112 E1
Holmesway PEN/TH CH61 167 K1
Holmeswood Rd
KIRK/FR/WA PR4 31 J1
Holmfield CL/PREN CH43 149 K1
Holmfield Av RUNC WA7 11 H5
Holmfield Dr GTS/LS CH66 195 G6
Holmfield Gv HUY L36 136 C1
Holmfield Pk FMBY L37 48 D1
Holm Hey Rd CL/PREN CH43 149 J1
Holm Hl WKBY CH48 146 D2
Holmlands Crs
CL/PREN CH43 * 149 H1
Holmlands Dr CL/PREN CH43 149 H1
Holmlands Wy CL/PREN CH43 149 H1
Holm La CL/PREN CH43 149 J1
Holmleigh Rd WLTN L25 135 H3
Holm Oak Wy GTS/LS CH66 202 C3
Holmrook Rd NG/CROX L11 98 E3
Holmsfield Rd WARR WA1 17 J4
Holmside Cl MOR/LEA CH46 129 G1
Holmside La CL/PREN CH43 149 J1
Holm View Cl CL/PREN CH43 130 D6
Holmville Rd BEB CH63 150 D6
Holmway BEB CH63 150 E6
Holmwood Av PEN/TH CH61 149 F6
Holmwood Cl AIMK WN4 79 F4
FMBY L37 48 D2
Holmwood Dr EP CH65 203 F1
FMBY L37 48 D1
PEN/TH CH61 149 F6
Holmwood Gdns FMBY L37 48 D1
Holt Av MOR/LEA CH46 129 F1
WGNW/BIL/O WN5 77 G5
Holt Coppice ORM L39 52 E6
Holt Crs WGNW/BIL/O WN5 77 G5
Holt Hey NSTN CH64 192 B4
Holt Hl BIRK CH41 131 H5
Holt Hill Ter BIRK CH41 2 E7
Holt La NTHLY L27 136 B2
RAIN/WH L35 118 C3
RUNC WA7 177 J6
Holt Rd BIRK CH41 131 H5
EHL/KEN L7 114 A5
Holtswell Cl GOL/RIS/CU WA3 93 F2
Holyhead Cl WARRW/BUR WA5 122 D4
Holyrood CSBY/BLUN L23 68 B5
Holyrood Av WDN WA8 139 F5
Holywell Cl NSTN CH64 181 G6
STHEL WA9 120 B1
Home Farm Cl
GR/UP/WCH CH49 149 F1
Home Farm Rd
GR/UP/WCH CH49 148 E1
PR/KW L34 100 C3
Homer Rd PR/KW L34 100 C2
Homerton Rd NPK/KEN L6 114 B4
Homestall Rd NG/CROX L11 98 E3
Homestead Av NTHTN L30 70 E6
RNFD/HAY WA11 * 90 D4
Homestead Cl HUY L36 117 G4
Homestead Ms WKBY CH48 * 146 C1
Honeybourne Dr RAIN/WH L35 118 C1
Honey Hall Rd HLWD L26 155 H5
Honeys Green Cl
WD/CROXPK L12 115 H2
Honey's Green La
WD/CROXPK L12 115 H2
Honey St STHEL WA9 * 102 E6
Honeysuckle Cl GTS/LS CH66 202 D3
HLWD L26 155 G1
WDN WA8 139 G5
Honeysuckle Dr WLT/FAZ L9 97 K2
Honister Av RNFD/HAY WA11 89 F3
WARRN/WOL WA2 123 J5
Honister Gv RUNC WA7 187 H2
Honister Wk NTHLY L27 136 D6
Honiston Av RAIN/WH L35 118 D3
Honiton Rd AIG/SPK L17 153 F3
Honiton Wy WARRW/BUR WA5 141 F5
Hood La WARRW/BUR WA5 141 K4
Hood La North
WARRW/BUR WA5 141 K3
Hood Rd WDN WA8 18 B2
Hood St BTL L20 4 B1
CLVPS L1 8 E3
WAL/EG CH44 111 K4
Hookstone Dr GTS/LS CH66 195 F3
Hoole La CHTN/BK PR9 21 K5
Hoole Rd GR/UP/WCH CH49 129 J6
Hoolpool La FROD/HEL WA6 199 G4
Hooton Gn GTS/LS CH66 184 D5
Hooton La GTS/LS CH66 184 E6
Hooton Rd NSTN CH64 183 J6
WLT/FAZ L9 82 E4
Hooton Wy GTS/LS CH66 184 C5
Hope Cl ECCL WA10 12 D4
Hope Cft GTS/LS CH66 202 D1
Hope Farm Rd GTS/LS CH66 202 C2
Hope Island SKEL WN8 56 B5
Hope Pl CLVPS L1 * 9 H6
Hope Sq CHTN/BK PR9 15 H4
Hope St AIMK WN4 79 J4
BIRK CH41 2 D3
CHTN/BK PR9 15 H4
CLVPS L1 9 J7
NEWLW WA12 106 B2
PR/KW L34 117 K1
WAL/NB CH45 95 H5
Hope Wy TOX L8 9 J7
Hopfield Rd MOR/LEA CH46 129 G1
Hopkins Cl ECCL WA10 12 A4
Hopwood Cl GOL/RIS/CU WA3 93 G3
Hopwood Crs RNFD/HAY WA11 75 H4
Hopwood St EV L5 112 E2
WARR WA1 17 F3
Horace Black Gdns EP CH65 6 D3
Horace St ECCL WA10 12 C4
Horbury Gdns GTS/LS CH66 195 F4
Hornbeam Av GTS/LS CH66 202 D2
Hornbeam Cl MOR/LEA CH46 * 128 C1
RNFD/HAY WA11 89 J6
RUNC WA7 178 B5
Hornbeam Crs AIMK WN4 79 G6
Hornbeam Rd HLWD L26 155 K4
WLT/FAZ L9 98 A2
Hornby Av BTL L20 4 D1
PS/BROM CH62 171 F4
Hornby Bvd LITH L21 81 J5
Hornby Cha MGHL L31 71 G2
Hornby Cl WLT/FAZ L9 97 H1
Hornby Crs STHEL WA9 120 B3
Hornby Flats LITH L21 * 81 J5
Hornby La CALD/MH L18 134 E4
WARRN/WOL WA2 123 G1
Hornby Pk CALD/MH L18 134 E4
Hornby Pl WLT/FAZ L9 82 D6
Hornby Rd BTL L20 4 E2
CHTN/BK PR9 23 J1
PS/BROM CH62 170 E4
WLT/FAZ L9 97 H1
Hornby St BIRK CH41 3 H4
CSBY/BLUN L23 * 69 F5
LITH L21 81 H5
Hornby Wk EV L5 112 E3
Horncastle Cl GOL/RIS/CU WA3 93 G3
Horne St NPK/KEN L6 113 K3
Hornet Cl NPK/KEN L6 113 J3
Hornhouse La NWD/KWIPK L33 85 G3
Hornsey Rd ANF/KKDL L4 113 K1
Hornspit La WD/CROXPK L12 98 E5
Horridge Av NEWLW WA12 91 H6
Horringford Rd ALL/GAR L19 153 G3
Horrocks Av ALL/GAR L19 154 A5
Horrocks Cl HUY L36 116 D3
Horrocks La WARR WA1 16 D5
Horrocks Rd HUY L36 116 D4
Horseman Pl WAL/EG CH44 112 A5
Horseshoe Crs
WARRN/WOL WA2 124 A4
Horseshoe Dr AIN/FAZ L10 84 A4
Horsfall Gv TOX L8 132 D5
Horsfall St TOX L8 132 D5
Horstone Crs GTS/LS CH66 202 D1
Horstone Gdns GTS/LS CH66 202 D1
Horstone Rd GTS/LS CH66 202 D1
Horwood Av RAIN/WH L35 118 D3
Horwood Cl NG/CROX L11 * 99 G3
Hoscar Ct WDN WA8 157 J4
Hoscar Moss Rd BRSC L40 39 J6
Hoscote Pk WKBY CH48 146 B1
Hose Side Rd WAL/NB CH45 95 G6
Hospital St ECCL WA10 13 H3
Hospital Wy RUNC WA7 177 J6
Hosta Cl NWD/KWIPK L33 72 C4
Hostock Cl RAIN/WH L35 117 K5
Hotel St NEWLW WA12 106 B2
Hotham St VAUX/LVPD L3 9 G3
Hothfield Rd WAL/EG CH44 * 111 K4
Hotspur St BTL L20 96 E5
Hough Green Rd WDN WA8 157 F1
Hough's La WARRS WA4 161 K5
Houghton Cl NEWLW WA12 * 106 B2
WDN WA8 158 D1
Houghton Cft WDN WA8 138 B4
Houghton La CLVPS L1 * 9 F4
Houghton Rd
GR/UP/WCH CH49 129 J6
Houghton's La ECCL WA10 87 G4
SKEL WN8 56 E4
Houghtons Rd SKEL WN8 56 C2
Houghton St CLVPS L1 9 F4
NEWLW WA12 106 B2
PR/KW L34 117 K1
RAIN/WH L35 * 118 E4
WARRN/WOL WA2 16 D2
WDN WA8 158 E1
Houghton Wy CLVPS L1 * 9 F4
Houghwood Gra AIMK WN4 78 E6
Hougoumont Av CSBY/WL L22 81 F2
Hougoumont Gv CSBY/WL L22 81 F2
Houlding St ANF/KKDL L4 * 113 J1
Houlgrave Rd EV L5 112 E2
Houlston Rd KKBY L32 84 A1
Houlton St EHL/KEN L7 114 A5
The Hove RUNC WA7 188 C1
Howard Av PS/BROM CH62 171 F5
Howard Cl LITH L21 81 K1
MGHL L31 62 D6
Howard Dr ALL/GAR L19 153 H4
Howard Florey Av NTHTN L30 70 C5
Howard's La ECCL WA10 102 A1
Howards Rd PEN/TH CH61 148 E5
Howard St ECCL WA10 * 102 E5
Howards Wy NSTN CH64 192 B3
Howarth Ct RUNC WA7 11 F4
Howbeck Cl CL/PREN CH43 130 C3
Howbeck Dr CL/PREN CH43 130 C3
Howbeck Rd CL/PREN CH43 130 C4
Howden Dr HUY L36 116 A5
Howell Dr GR/UP/WCH CH49 148 A1
Howell Rd PS/BROM CH62 151 F4
Howells Av GTS/LS CH66 195 F6
Howells Cl MGHL L31 62 B5
Howe St BTL L20 96 D4
Howey La FROD/HEL WA6 200 E2
Howey Ri FROD/HEL WA6 200 D2
Howley La WARR WA1 17 H5
Howley Quay WARR WA1 * 17 H5
Howson Rd WARRN/WOL WA2 123 J5
Howson St RF/TRAN CH42 150 E1
Hoylake Cl RUNC WA7 188 B1
Hoylake Gv STHEL WA9 120 A3
Hoylake Rd BIRK CH41 110 E6
MOR/LEA CH46 109 K6
Hoyle Rd HOY CH47 127 G1
Hoyle St WARRW/BUR WA5 16 A1
Huddleston Cl
GR/UP/WCH CH49 129 J6
Huddleston Rd WAV L15 115 F6
Hudson Cl WARRW/BUR WA5 142 A1
Hudson Rd MGHL L31 71 G2
MOR/LEA CH46 110 A3
Hudswell Cl NTHTN L30 82 E2
Hughenden Rd
CLB/OSW/ST L13 114 D2
Hughes Av RAIN/WH L35 117 K3
WARRN/WOL WA2 123 K5
Hughes Cl EHL/KEN L7 114 A6
Hughes Dr BTL L20 82 B5
Hughes La CL/PREN CH43 130 E6
Hughes Pl WARRN/WOL WA2 123 K5
Hughes St ALL/GAR L19 153 K6

NPK/KEN L6 113 J4
STHEL WA9 104 B5
WARRS WA4 143 F6
Hughestead Gv ALL/GAR L19 153 J5
Hughson St TOX L8 132 E4
Hulme St STHP PR8 14 D5
Hulmewood BEB CH63 151 F4
Hulton Av RAIN/WH L35 118 B3
Humber Cl ANF/KKDL L4 97 G5
WDN WA8 140 A6
Humber Crs STHEL WA9 120 A2
Humber Rd GTS/LS CH66 202 D1
WARRN/WOL WA2 124 A5
Hume Ct HOY CH47 127 H1
Hume St WARR WA1 17 H2
Humphrey's Cl RUNC WA7 * 178 C6
Humphreys Hey
CSBY/BLUN L23 69 J4
Humphrey St BTL L20 81 K5
Huncote Av RNFD/HAY WA11 89 G5
Hunslett Rd WLT/FAZ L9 82 E5
Hunstanton Cl
GR/UP/WCH CH49 129 H2
Hunt Cl WARRW/BUR WA5 * 141 J1
Hunter Av WARRN/WOL WA2 123 H5
Hunter Ct PR/KW L34 118 A1
Hunters Ct FROD/HEL WA6 200 A5
RUNC WA7 187 H1
Hunter's La WAV L15 134 B2
Hunter St STHEL WA9 * 104 A3
VAUX/LVPD L3 9 G2
Hunters Wy NSTN CH64 191 H1
Huntingdon Cl MOR/LEA CH46 128 C1
Huntingdon Ct CHTN/BK PR9 * 23 J3
Huntingdon Gv MGHL L31 62 A3
Huntley Gv STHEL WA9 104 A6
Huntley St WARRW/BUR WA5 141 K5
Huntly Rd NPK/KEN L6 114 A4
Hunt Rd MGHL L31 62 B6
RNFD/HAY WA11 90 D5
Hunts Cross Av WLTN L25 135 J6
Hunts Field Cl LYMM WA13 164 E1
Hunts La WARRS WA4 162 E1
Huntsman Wd WD/CROXPK L12 99 J5
Hurford Av EP CH65 195 J5
Hurley Cl WARRW/BUR WA5 141 K4
Hurlingham Rd ANF/KKDL L4 98 A3
Hurlston Av SKEL WN8 * 56 E5
Hurlston Dr ORM L39 45 J4
Hurlston La BRSC L40 45 G2
Hurrell Rd BIRK CH41 110 D6
Hursley Rd WLT/FAZ L9 98 C1
Hurst Bank RF/TRAN CH42 150 E3
Hurstlyn Rd CALD/MH L18 153 K2
Hurst Park Cl HUY L36 * 117 G3
Hurst Park Dr HUY L36 117 G4
Hurst Rd MGHL L31 71 H2
Hurst's La ORM L39 64 A5
Hurst St CLVPS L1 8 D7
WDN WA8 10 D1
Huskisson St TOX L8 132 E2
Huskisson Wy NEWLW WA12 106 B1
Hutchinson St NPK/KEN L6 113 J4
WDN WA8 158 B5
Hutchinson Wk NPK/KEN L6 113 J4
Huttfield Rd SPK/HALE L24 174 B1
Hutton Ct SKEL WN8 55 K4
Hutton Rd SKEL WN8 55 K4
Hutton Wy ORM L39 45 J6
Huxley Cl MOR/LEA CH46 128 C1
Huxley Ct GTS/LS CH66 195 J1
Huxley St CLB/OSW/ST L13 98 B6
Huyton Av ECCL WA10 88 B5
Huyton Brook HUY L36 136 C1
Huyton Church Rd HUY L36 116 E5
Huyton Hall Crs HUY L36 * 116 E5
Huyton Hey Rd HUY L36 117 F5
Huyton House Cl HUY L36 116 B3
Huyton House Rd HUY L36 116 B3
Huyton La HUY L36 117 F4
Hyacinth Cl RNFD/HAY WA11 90 E5
Hyacinth Gv MOR/LEA CH46 110 A5
Hyde Cl EP CH65 195 J5
RUNC WA7 * 187 G1
Hyde Rd CSBY/WL L22 80 E2
Hyde's Brow RNFD/HAY WA11 75 H1
Hydro Av WKBY CH48 146 C2
Hygeia St NPK/KEN L6 113 J3
Hylton Av WAL/EG CH44 111 G3
Hylton Ct EP CH65 203 J1
Hylton Rd ALL/GAR L19 154 A3
Hyslop St TOX L8 132 D3
Hythe Av LITH L21 81 K3
Hythe Cl STHP PR8 28 B4
Hythedale Cl AIG/SPK L17 152 D1

I

Ibbotson's La AIG/SPK L17 133 K5
Ibis Ct WARR WA1 142 D6
Ibstock Rd BTL L20 81 J6
Iffley Cl GR/UP/WCH CH49 128 E4
Ikin Cl CL/PREN CH43 110 C6
Ilchester Rd BIRK CH41 111 F6
CHLDW L16 115 J6
WAL/EG CH44 111 K4
Ilex Av WARRN/WOL WA2 123 H1
Ilford Av CSBY/BLUN L23 68 E4
WAL/EG CH44 111 H5
Ilford St VAUX/LVPD L3 9 H2
Ilfracombe Rd STHEL WA9 120 A2
Iliad St EV L5 113 G3
Ilkley Av CHTN/BK PR9 21 F5
Ilsley Cl GR/UP/WCH CH49 129 G5
Imber Rd KKBY L32 84 E3
Imison St WLT/FAZ L9 97 H2
Imison Wy WLT/FAZ L9 5 K5
Imperial Av WAL/NB CH45 111 J1
Imperial Ms EP CH65 6 C2
Imrie St ANF/KKDL L4 97 H3
Ince Av ANF/KKDL L4 97 K5
CSBY/BLUN L23 68 D4
LITH L21 81 J4
PS/BROM CH62 184 B4
Ince Cl CL/PREN CH43 * 130 C5
Ince Crs FMBY L37 48 D2
Ince Gv CL/PREN CH43 130 C6
Ince La CHNE CH2 198 C5
CSBY/BLUN L23 60 B6
Incemore Rd CALD/MH L18 153 J2
Ince Orchards CHNE CH2 198 C5
Ince Rd CSBY/BLUN L23 69 H2
Inchcape Rd CHLDW L16 115 J6
WAL/NB CH45 * 110 D2
Inchfield SKEL WN8 56 D3
Index St ANF/KKDL L4 97 H4
Indigo Rd EP CH65 196 E4
Ingestre Rd CL/PREN CH43 130 D6
Ingham Rd WDN WA8 138 E5
Ingleborough Rd
RF/TRAN CH42 150 C1
Ingleby Rd PS/BROM CH62 151 G3
WAL/EG CH44 111 G4
Ingledene Rd CALD/MH L18 134 E4
Ingle Gn CSBY/BLUN L23 68 B4
Inglegreen HES CH60 168 A5
Ingleholme Gdns PR/KW L34 102 C6
Ingleholme Rd CALD/MH L18 153 H2
Inglemere Rd RF/TRAN CH42 150 D1
Inglemoss Dr RNFD/HAY WA11 87 J2
Inglenook Rd
WARRW/BUR WA5 141 G5
Ingleton Cl
GR/UP/WCH CH49 * 128 E5
NEWLW WA12 * 106 B1
Ingleton Dr RNFD/HAY WA11 88 E2
Ingleton Gn KKBY L32 84 E3
Ingleton Gv RUNC WA7 187 G2
Ingleton Rd CALD/MH L18 134 A4
KKBY L32 84 E3
STHP PR8 28 B4
Inglewhite SKEL WN8 56 C3
Inglewood WD/CROXPK L12 100 A3
Inglewood Av MOR/LEA CH46 128 E2
Inglewood Cl GOL/RIS/CU WA3 125 K1
Inglewood Rd RNFD/HAY WA11 87 J2
Inglis Rd WLT/FAZ L9 82 E4
Ingoe Cl KKBY L32 84 A3
Ingoe La KKBY L32 84 A3
Ingram SKEL WN8 56 D4
Ingrave Rd ANF/KKDL L4 98 A3
Ingrow Rd NPK/KEN L6 113 K4
Inigo Rd CLB/OSW/ST L13 115 F3
Inley Cl BEB CH63 170 C3
Inley Rd BEB CH63 170 B3
Inman Av STHEL WA9 105 F3
Inman Rd GR/UP/WCH CH49 129 F3
LITH L21 81 J4
Inner Central Rd
SPK/HALE L24 155 J6
Inner Forum NG/CROX L11 98 C2
Inner South Rd SPK/HALE L24 174 A1
Inner West Rd SPK/HALE L24 175 F1
Innisfree Cl GTS/LS CH66 195 F4
Insall Rd CLB/OSW/ST L13 115 F6
WARRN/WOL WA2 124 B5
Inskip SKEL WN8 56 C3
Inskip Rd CHTN/BK PR9 23 J1
Intake Cl NSTN CH64 193 H2
Intake La ORM L39 65 F2
ORM L39 65 G3
Inveresk Ct CL/PREN CH43 130 B3
Invincible Cl NTHTN L30 82 B3
Invincible Wy NG/CROX L11 84 B5
Inward Wy EP CH65 196 A2
Inwood Rd ALL/GAR L19 153 K4
Iona Cl WD/CROXPK L12 100 A2
Ionic Rd CLB/OSW/ST L13 114 E3
Ionic St LITH L21 * 81 G4
RF/TRAN CH42 150 E1
Irby Av WAL/EG CH44 111 G3
Irby Cl GTS/LS CH66 195 H5
Irby Rd ANF/KKDL L4 97 K5
PEN/TH CH61 148 A6
Irbyside Rd WKBY CH48 147 J2
Ireland Rd RNFD/HAY WA11 90 B5
SPK/HALE L24 175 F4
Ireland St WARRN/WOL WA2 142 E1
WDN WA8 158 E1
Irene Av RNFD/HAY WA11 89 F4
Irene Rd CHLDW L16 134 D3
Ireton St ANF/KKDL L4 97 H3
Iris Av BIRK CH41 130 C1
Iris Cl WDN WA8 157 H1
Irlam Dr KKBY L32 84 D1
Irlam Pl BTL L20 4 C3
Irlam Rd BTL L20 4 C4
Ironbridge Vw TOX L8 132 D5
Ironside Rd HUY L36 116 D3
Irton Rd CHTN/BK PR9 23 G5
Irvin Av CHTN/BK PR9 21 F6
Irvine Rd RF/TRAN CH42 150 C1
Irvine St EHL/KEN L7 113 J6
Irving St CHTN/BK PR9 15 F1
Irwell SKEL WN8 56 C2
Irwell Cl AIG/SPK L17 133 K6
Irwell La AIG/SPK L17 133 K6
RUNC WA7 11 G3
Irwell Rd WARRS WA4 162 A1
Irwell St WDN WA8 176 D1
Irwin Rd STHEL WA9 104 A6
Isaac St TOX L8 132 E5
Isabel Gv CLB/OSW/ST L13 98 C6
Isherwood Cl
WARRN/WOL WA2 124 B4
Island Pl ALL/GAR L19 * 153 K5
Island Rd ALL/GAR L19 153 K5
Island Rd South ALL/GAR L19 153 K5
Islands Brow RNFD/HAY WA11 88 E5
Islay Cl EP CH65 203 G3
Isleham Cl CALD/MH L18 153 K3
Islington CSBY/BLUN L23 68 E5
VAUX/LVPD L3 9 H2
Islip Cl PEN/TH CH61 148 A4
Ismay Dr WAL/EG CH44 111 K2
Ismay Rd LITH L21 81 J4
Ismay St ANF/KKDL L4 97 H4
Ivanhoe Av GOL/RIS/CU WA3 92 E2
Ivanhoe Rd AIG/SPK L17 133 H5
CSBY/BLUN L23 68 D6
Ivatt Wy EHL/KEN L7 114 A6
Iveagh Cl RUNC WA7 177 K6
Iver Cl WDN WA8 138 B3
Ivernia Rd ANF/KKDL L4 97 K3
Ivor Rd WAL/EG CH44 111 J2
Ivory Dr NWD/KWIPK L33 72 D4
Ivy Av ALL/GAR L19 153 H4
BEB CH63 150 D6
NEWLW WA12 106 C3
Ivybridge SKEL WN8 56 D3
Ivychurch Ms RUNC WA7 11 K5
Ivy Ct STHEL WA9 * 104 A2
Ivydale SKEL WN8 56 D3
Ivydale Rd CALD/MH L18 134 A5
RF/TRAN CH42 131 H6
WLT/FAZ L9 97 K1
Ivy Farm Dr NSTN CH64 192 A3
Ivy Farm Rd RAIN/WH L35 118 D3
Ivy House Rd GOL/RIS/CU WA3 92 E2
Ivyhurst Cl ALL/GAR L19 153 G3
Ivy La MOR/LEA CH46 109 J6
Ivy Leigh CLB/OSW/ST L13 114 C2
Ivy Rd GOL/RIS/CU WA3 92 C3
WARR WA1 144 D2
Ivy St BIRK CH41 3 H5
RUNC WA7 10 E6
STHP PR8 15 K7

J

Jack McBain Ct
VAUX/LVPD L3 * 112 E3
Jack's Brow PR/KW L34 100 E3
Jacksfield Wy ALL/GAR L19 153 G4
Jacksmere La BRSC L40 35 K1
Jackson Av WARR WA1 143 J2
Jackson Cl BEB CH63 150 E3
ORM L39 43 H6
RAIN/WH L35 119 F6
Jackson's Common La
BRSC L40 44 E2
Jacksons Pond Dr WLTN L25 135 G2
Jackson St ALL/GAR L19 153 K5
BIRK CH41 3 G6
RNFD/HAY WA11 * 89 K4
STHEL WA9 104 A2
WARRW/BUR WA5 121 J1
Jacobs Cl LITH L21 81 J5
Jacob St TOX L8 132 E5
Jacqueline Dr HUY L36 117 G3
Jade Cl NWD/KWIPK L33 72 E6
Jade Rd NPK/KEN L6 113 H1
Jamaica St CLVPS L1 132 C2
James Av GTS/LS CH66 195 F6
Jamesbrook Cl BIRK CH41 130 D1
James Clarke St EV L5 112 E3
James Cl WDN WA8 176 D1
James Ct WLTN L25 154 E1
James Gv ECCL WA10 12 C7
James Holt Av KKBY L32 84 C2
James Hopkins Wy
ANF/KKDL L4 97 F6
James Larkin Wy ANF/KKDL L4 97 G6
James Rd RNFD/HAY WA11 90 E4
WLTN L25 154 E1
James St ALL/GAR L19 153 K6
CL/PREN CH43 2 B7
CLVPS L1 8 C5
STHEL WA9 120 B4
WAL/EG CH44 112 A5
WARR WA1 16 E4
WGNE/HIN WN2 79 K2
Jamieson Av CSBY/BLUN L23 69 H5
Jamieson Rd WAV L15 133 K2
Jane's Brook Rd STHP PR8 28 A3
Jane St STHEL WA9 104 D6
Janet St EHL/KEN L7 113 K6
Jarrett Rd NWD/KWIPK L33 73 F5
Jarrow Cl CL/PREN CH43 130 E5
Jasmine Cl EV L5 113 H3
MOR/LEA CH46 128 E2
Jasmine Ct HUY L36 117 F2
Jasmine Gdns STHEL WA9 104 E6
Jasmine Gv WDN WA8 157 J3
Jasmine Ms AIG/SPK L17 133 F6
Jason St EV L5 113 G1
Jason Wk EV L5 113 G1
Java Rd ANF/KKDL L4 98 B3
Jay Cl GOL/RIS/CU WA3 125 J3
Jays Cl RUNC WA7 178 D6
Jedburgh Av GTS/LS CH66 194 D3
Jedburgh Dr NWD/KWIPK L33 72 C3
Jeffereys Crs HUY L36 116 B5
Jeffereys Dr HUY L36 116 A4
Jeffreys Dr GR/UP/WCH CH49 128 E2
Jellicoe Cl WKBY CH48 * 146 E5
Jenkinson St VAUX/LVPD L3 113 G4
Jennet Hey AIMK WN4 78 E3
Jensen Ct RUNC WA7 11 K3
Jericho Cl AIG/SPK L17 152 E1
Jericho Ct AIG/SPK L17 * 152 E1
Jericho Farm Cl AIG/SPK L17 152 E2
Jericho La AIG/SPK L17 152 E2
Jermyn St TOX L8 133 F3
Jerningham Rd NG/CROX L11 98 B2
Jersey Av EP CH65 203 G2
LITH L21 81 J2
Jersey Cl BTL L20 4 E4
Jersey St BTL L20 4 E4
STHEL WA9 120 A4
Jervis Cl WARRN/WOL WA2 124 C4
Jesmond St WAV L15 133 J1
Jessamine Rd RF/TRAN CH42 131 H6
Jet Cl NPK/KEN L6 113 K3
Jeudwine Cl WLTN L25 154 E3
Joan Av GR/UP/WCH CH49 129 F5
MOR/LEA CH46 128 E1
Jocelyn Cl BEB CH63 170 C2
Jockey St WARRN/WOL WA2 142 E2
John Bagot Cl EV L5 113 G2
John F Kennedy Hts
VAUX/LVPD L3 113 G3
John Hunter Wy NTHTN L30 70 C6
John Lennon Dr NPK/KEN L6 113 K4
John Moores Cl EHL/KEN L7 * 133 F1
John Nicholas Crs EP CH65 6 E3
John Rd LYMM WA13 145 H6
Johns Av RUNC WA7 10 C7
Johnson Av NEWLW WA12 91 G6
RAIN/WH L35 117 J3
Johnson Gv WD/CROXPK L12 115 J2
Johnson Rd CL/PREN CH43 149 J2
Johnson's La WDN WA8 159 F3
Johnson St STHEL WA9 104 A1
VAUX/LVPD L3 8 E2
Johnson Wk EHL/KEN L7 114 A6
Johnston Av BTL L20 82 B5
John St AIMK WN4 79 J4
BIRK CH41 3 H3
ECCL WA10 * 13 G4
EP CH65 6 C2
GOL/RIS/CU WA3 92 B3
VAUX/LVPD L3 113 G4
WARRN/WOL WA2 16 E3
Jones Farm Rd WLTN L25 135 K5
Jonson Rd NSTN CH64 181 K6
Jonville Rd WLT/FAZ L9 83 F4
Jordan St CLVPS L1 132 C2
Joseph Gardner Wy BTL L20 4 D2
Joseph Groome Towers
EP CH65 6 D3
Joseph Lister Cl NTHTN L30 70 C6
Joseph St STHEL WA9 104 C6
WDN WA8 158 D1
Joshua Cl EV L5 113 G1
Joule St GOL/RIS/CU WA3 125 H2
Joy La STHEL WA9 120 C5
WARRW/BUR WA5 121 J3
Jubilee Av DV/KA/FCH L14 115 H6
ORM L39 45 K5
WARR WA1 143 J1
WARRW/BUR WA5 141 F5
Jubilee Crs PS/BROM CH62 151 G6
RNFD/HAY WA11 90 E4
Jubilee Dr EHL/KEN L7 113 K5
NTHTN L30 82 D2
RAIN/WH L35 117 K5
SKEL WN8 56 A5
WKBY CH48 127 F5
Jubilee Gn EP CH65 7 F7
Jubilee Gv LYMM WA13 145 H5
Jubilee Rd CSBY/BLUN L23 68 D6
FMBY L37 48 D4
LITH L21 81 J4
Jubilee Wy WDN WA8 157 K2
Jubits La WDN WA8 139 F1
Juddfield St RNFD/HAY WA11 89 K5
Judges Dr NPK/KEN L6 114 A3
Judges Wy NPK/KEN L6 114 A3
Julian Wy WDN WA8 138 E5
Julie Gv WD/CROXPK L12 115 J2
Juliet Av BEB CH63 150 D4
Juliet Gdns BEB CH63 * 150 D4
July Rd NPK/KEN L6 114 B2
July St BTL L20 5 F1
Junction La BRSC L40 38 E5
NEWLW WA12 106 B3
STHEL WA9 104 C6
Junction Rd RNFD/HAY WA11 75 F1
June Av PS/BROM CH62 171 G5
June Rd NPK/KEN L6 114 B2
June St BTL L20 5 F2
Juniper Cl ECCL WA10 12 A3
GR/UP/WCH CH49 147 K1
STBRV L28 100 B6
Juniper Dr GTS/LS CH66 202 C2
Juniper Gdns CSBY/BLUN L23 69 J3
Juniper Gv GTS/LS CH66 202 D2
Juniper La GOL/RIS/CU WA3 145 F1
Juniper St BTL L20 96 E6
Jurby Ct WARRN/WOL WA2 124 B6
Justene Cl GOL/RIS/CU WA3 92 B1
Justin Wy RAIN/WH L35 118 D2
Juvenal Pl VAUX/LVPD L3 113 G3
Juvenal St VAUX/LVPD L3 113 F4

K

Kaigh Av CSBY/BLUN L23 68 E4
Kale Cl WKBY CH48 146 C2
Kale Gv NWD/KWIPK L33 73 F4
Kane Ct GOL/RIS/CU WA3 93 H2
Kara Cl BTL L20 5 F4
Karan Wy MGHL L31 71 K6
Karen Cl WARRW/BUR WA5 121 K1
Karen Wy GTS/LS CH66 195 G6
Karonga Rd AIN/FAZ L10 83 H4
Karonga Wy AIN/FAZ L10 83 J4
Karslake Rd CALD/MH L18 134 A4
WAL/EG CH44 111 K5
Kay La LYMM WA13 165 K3
Kearsley Cl ANF/KKDL L4 * 97 G6
Kearsley St ANF/KKDL L4 97 G6
Keates St STHEL WA9 104 D5
Keats Av RAIN/WH L35 118 B4
Keats Cl GTS/LS CH66 * 202 C3
WDN WA8 18 A3
Keats Gn HUY L36 117 F6
Keats Gv WARRN/WOL WA2 123 J5
Keats St BTL L20 4 C1
Keats Ter STHP PR8 28 C1
Keble Dr AIN/FAZ L10 71 F6
WAL/NB CH45 110 D1
Keble Rd BTL L20 96 E4
Keble St NPK/KEN L6 113 J4
WDN WA8 18 E5
Keckwick La RUNC WA7 178 E1
WARRS WA4 179 G3
Kedleston St TOX L8 133 F5
Keegan Dr WAL/EG CH44 112 A5
Keele Cl CL/PREN CH43 110 C6
Keel Hey NSTN CH64 183 J6
Keenan Dr BTL L20 82 B6
Keepers La BEB CH63 150 A6
Keeper's Rd WARRS WA4 163 F4
Keighley Av WAL/NB CH45 110 E2
Keightley St BIRK CH41 2 D3
Keir Hardie Av BTL L20 5 K1
Keith Av ANF/KKDL L4 97 H4
WARRW/BUR WA5 141 F3
Keith Dr BEB CH63 183 K2
Kelbrook Cl STHEL WA9 120 B1
Kelburn Ct GOL/RIS/CU WA3 125 H1
Kelby Cl TOX L8 * 133 F5
Kelday Cl NWD/KWIPK L33 84 D1
Kelkbeck Cl MGHL L31 62 D5
Kellett Rd MOR/LEA CH46 110 B4
Kellitt Rd WAV L15 133 K2
Kelly Dr BTL L20 5 J2
Kelly St PR/KW L34 117 K1
Kelmscott Cl GTS/LS CH66 202 B1
Kelmscott Dr WAL/EG CH44 110 E3
Kelsall Av PS/BROM CH62 184 B4
STHEL WA9 119 K3
Kelsall Cl CL/PREN CH43 130 D6
GOL/RIS/CU WA3 124 E4
PS/BROM CH62 184 B4
WDN WA8 157 J1
Kelsey Cl ECCL WA10 12 A3
Kelso Cl NWD/KWIPK L33 72 C3
Kelso Rd NPK/KEN L6 114 A4
Kelton Gv AIG/SPK L17 153 F1
Kelvin Cl AIMK WN4 * 78 C5
GOL/RIS/CU WA3 125 F1
Kelvin Gv TOX L8 133 F3
Kelvin Pk BIRK CH41 * 112 A6
Kelvin Rd BIRK CH41 131 H5
WAL/EG CH44 112 A6
Kelvinside CSBY/BLUN L23 81 G1
WAL/EG CH44 111 K6
Kelvin St GOL/RIS/CU WA3 125 G1
Kemberton Dr WDN WA8 139 F4
Kemble St EHL/KEN L7 * 113 K5
PR/KW L34 117 K1
Kemlyn Rd ANF/KKDL L4 113 J1
Kemmel Av WARRS WA4 162 B1
Kempsell Wy HLWD L26 155 K4
Kempsey Gv STHEL WA9 103 G6
Kempson Ter BEB CH63 170 B1
Kempston St VAUX/LVPD L3 9 H2
Kempton Cl HUY L36 116 C6
NEWLW WA12 91 J6
RUNC WA7 187 F1
Kempton Park Fold STHP PR8 28 C4
Kempton Park Rd AIN/FAZ L10 83 H1
Kempton Rd PS/BROM CH62 151 G3
WAV L15 133 J1
Kemsley Rd DV/KA/FCH L14 115 K4
Kenbury Cl NWD/KWIPK L33 73 F5
Kenbury Rd NWD/KWIPK L33 73 F5
Kendal Av WARRN/WOL WA2 123 J5
Kendal Cl BEB CH63 150 E5
GTS/LS CH66 202 B1
RNFD/HAY WA11 66 B5
Kendal Dr GTS/LS CH66 202 B1
MGHL L31 62 B5
RAIN/WH L35 118 C4
RNFD/HAY WA11 66 B6
RNFD/HAY WA11 89 F3
Kendal Gv AIMK WN4 79 G5
Kendal Pk WD/CROXPK L12 115 H1
Kendal Ri RUNC WA7 187 G2
Kendal Rd CHLDW L16 135 F2
WAL/EG CH44 111 G5
WDN WA8 * 157 H2
Kendal St BIRK CH41 * 3 F5
Kendal Wy STHP PR8 33 H6
Kendricks Fold RAIN/WH L35 118 D4
Kendrick St WARR WA1 16 B4
Kenilworth Av RUNC WA7 176 E5
Kenilworth Cl WLTN L25 135 F6
Kenilworth Ct EP CH65 203 J1
Kenilworth Dr PEN/TH CH61 148 B6
WARR WA1 143 J1
Kenilworth Gdns
GR/UP/WCH CH49 129 F3
NEWLW WA12 106 C3
Kenilworth Rd CHLDW L16 134 E2
CSBY/BLUN L23 68 D6
GOL/RIS/CU WA3 93 F4
NSTN CH64 191 K3
STHP PR8 33 J5
WAL/EG CH44 111 K4
Kenilworth St BTL L20 4 D4
Kenilworth Wy WLTN L25 135 F6
Kenley Av WDN WA8 138 C4
Kenley Cl NPK/KEN L6 114 A3
Kenley Pde NPK/KEN L6 114 A3
Kenmare Rd WAV L15 133 K3
Kenmore Cottages LITH L21 * 69 K6
Kenmore Gv AIMK WN4 78 C6
Kenmore Rd CL/PREN CH43 149 H2
Kennelwood Av
NWD/KWIPK L33 72 E6
Kennessee Cl MGHL L31 71 H1
Kenneth Cl NTHTN L30 70 B6
Kenneth Rd WDN WA8 157 H4
Kennet Rd BEB CH63 150 C6
RNFD/HAY WA11 90 B5
Kennford Rd NG/CROX L11 84 B6
Kennington Pk WDN WA8 138 D6
Kensington EHL/KEN L7 113 K5
Kensington Av STHEL WA9 104 A6
WARRS WA4 163 H1
Kensington Cl WDN WA8 139 J5

Kensington Dr HUY L36 .....117 G2
Kensington Gdns
MOR/LEA CH46 .....129 F1
Kensington Rd CHTN/BK PR9 .....15 H5
EP CH65 .....6 A5
FMBY L37 .....48 E4
Kensington St NPK/KEN L6 .....113 J4
Kent Av FMBY L37 .....49 G4
LITH L21 .....81 K3
Kent Cl BEB CH63 .....170 D5
BTL L20 .....5 G3
Kent Gv RUNC WA7 .....11 G6
Kentmere Av RNFD/HAY WA11 .....89 F2
Kentmere Dr PEN/TH CH61 .....167 K2
Kentmere Pl
WARRN/WOL WA2 .....123 G4
Kenton Cl FMBY L37 .....41 F5
Kenton Rd HLWD L26 .....155 J4
Kentridge Dr GTS/LS CH66 .....195 G6
Kent Rd FMBY L37 .....49 G4
STHEL WA9 .....104 A5
STHP PR8 .....27 H3
WAL/EG CH44 .....111 G4
WARRW/BUR WA5 .....141 K5
Kents Bank WD/CROXPK L12 .....99 G4
Kent St CLVPS L1 .....9 F7
WARRS WA4 .....17 F7
WDN WA8 .....18 E2
Kenview Cl WDN WA8 .....175 H1
Kenway RNFD/HAY WA11 .....75 H3
Kenwick Cl GTS/LS CH66 .....195 F6
Kenworthys Flats
CHTN/BK PR9 .....14 E3
Kenwright Crs STHEL WA9 .....104 A5
Kenwyn Rd WAL/NB CH45 .....111 H2
Kenyon Av WARRW/BUR WA5 .....141 F4
Kenyon Cl NWD/KWIPK L33 .....72 E3
Kenyon La GOL/RIS/CU WA3 .....93 G5
Kenyon Rd WAV L15 .....134 B4
Kenyon's La FMBY L37 .....49 G2
MGHL L31 .....62 B3
Kenyons La North
RNFD/HAY WA11 .....90 E3
Kenyon's La South
RNFD/HAY WA11 .....90 E3
Kepler St LITH L21 .....81 H5
Keppel St BTL L20 .....96 D4
Kerfoot's La SKEL WN8 .....55 J5
Kerfoot St WARRN/WOL WA2 .....142 D2
Kerman Cl WD/CROXPK L12 .....99 F4
Kerr Gv STHEL WA9 .....104 C2
Kerris Cl AIG/SPK L17 .....152 D1
Kerry Cft GTS/LS CH66 .....202 C2
Kerrysdale Cl STHEL WA9 .....104 B6
Kersey Rd KKBY L32 .....84 E3
Kershaw Av CSBY/BLUN L23 .....69 G6
Kershaw St WDN WA8 .....157 J2
Kershaw Wy NEWLW WA12 .....91 H6
Kerslake Wy HTWN L38 .....59 F3
Kerswell Cl STHEL WA9 .....120 B1
Kerton Rw STHP PR8 * 27 G3
Kestral Gv HLWD L26 .....155 G2
Kestral Pk SKEL WN8 .....56 E1
Kestrel Av GR/UP/WCH CH49 .....128 E3
Kestrel Cl GR/UP/WCH CH49 .....128 E3
RNFD/HAY WA11 .....88 E5
Kestrel Dr AIMK WN4 .....79 H3
Kestrel La GOL/RIS/CU WA3 .....125 G3
Kestrel Ms SKEL WN8 .....56 E1
Kestrel Rd HES CH60 .....168 C6
MOR/LEA CH46 .....128 D1
Kestrels Wy RUNC WA7 .....187 J1
Keswick Av BEB CH63 .....183 K3
WARRN/WOL WA2 .....123 J5
Keswick Cl MGHL L31 .....62 C5
STHP PR8 .....33 J6
WDN WA8 .....157 H2
Keswick Crs WARRN/WOL WA2 .....123 J5
Keswick Dr FROD/HEL WA6 .....201 G1
LITH L21 .....82 B3
Keswick Pl CL/PREN CH43 .....110 D6
Keswick Rd CALD/MH L18 .....153 K1
ECCL WA10 .....12 D2
WAL/NB CH45 .....95 F6
Keswick Vls CHLDW L16 * 135 H1
Keswick Wy CHLDW L16 .....135 H1
RNFD/HAY WA11 .....66 B5
Kettering Rd STHP PR8 .....33 H4
Kevelioc Cl BEB CH63 .....170 B2
Kew Rd FMBY L37 .....48 D4
STHP PR8 .....27 J5
Keybank Rd WD/CROXPK L12 .....98 E5
Keyes Cl GOL/RIS/CU WA3 .....125 H3
Keyes Gdns GOL/RIS/CU WA3 .....125 H3
Kiddman St WLT/FAZ L9 .....97 H2
Kidstone Cl STHEL WA9 .....104 B6
Kielder Cl AIMK WN4 .....78 E2
Kilbuck La RNFD/HAY WA11 .....90 E3
Kilburn Av AIMK WN4 .....79 J5
PS/BROM CH62 .....184 B1
Kilburn Gv STHEL WA9 .....103 G6
Kilburn St LITH L21 .....81 J5
Kildale Cl MGHL L31 .....62 A5
Kildare Cl SPK/HALE L24 .....174 E3
Kildonan Rd AIG/SPK L17 .....152 E1
WARRS WA4 .....163 F1
Kilford Cl WARRW/BUR WA5 .....122 E5
Kilgraston Gdns AIG/SPK L17 .....153 G2
Killarney Gv WAL/EG CH44 * 111 G4
Killarney Rd CLB/OSW/ST L13 .....114 E4
Killester Rd WLTN L25 .....135 J5
Killingbeck Cl BRSC L40 .....38 D5
Killington Wy ANF/KKDL L4 .....97 G5
Killingworth La
GOL/RIS/CU WA3 .....125 K2
Kilmalcolm Cl CL/PREN CH43 .....130 C5
Kilmore Cl WLT/FAZ L9 .....83 F3
Kilmory Av WLTN L25 .....155 F1
Kilncroft RUNC WA7 * 188 A2
Kiln Hey WD/CROXPK L12 .....115 G2
Kiln La ECCL WA10 .....87 K6
SKEL WN8 .....56 A3
Kiln Rd GR/UP/WCH CH49 .....129 H6
Kilnyard Rd CSBY/BLUN L23 .....68 E5
Kilrea Cl NG/CROX L11 .....98 D5
Kilrea Rd NG/CROX L11 .....98 D5
Kilsail Rd KKBY L32 .....85 F4
Kilsby Dr WDN WA8 .....159 F1
Kilshaw Rd WARRW/BUR WA5 .....121 K1
Kilshaw St NPK/KEN L6 .....113 J3
Kilsyth Cl WARRN/WOL WA2 .....124 B3
Kimberley Av CSBY/BLUN L23 * 68 E6
STHEL WA9 .....103 H6
Kimberley Cl TOX L8 .....133 F2
Kimberley Dr CSBY/BLUN L23 .....68 E6
WARRS WA4 .....162 B2
Kimberley Pl AIMK WN4 .....79 H6
Kimberley Rd WAL/NB CH45 .....111 H1
Kimberley St
WARRW/BUR WA5 .....142 B4
Kindale Rd CL/PREN CH43 .....149 H2
Kinder Gv AIMK WN4 .....78 E3
Kinder St NPK/KEN L6 .....9 K1
King Av BTL L20 .....82 B5
King Edward Rd ECCL WA10 .....88 A5
RAIN/WH L35 .....118 D3
King Edward's Dr
PS/BROM CH62 .....151 G5
King Edward St VAUX/LVPD L3 .....8 B2
WARR WA1 .....143 H2
Kingfield Rd WLT/FAZ L9 .....82 C6
Kingfisher Cl GOL/RIS/CU WA3 .....125 H3
NTHLY L27 .....136 C4
NWD/KWIPK L33 .....72 D3
RUNC WA7 .....187 J2
Kingfisher Ct AIMK WN4 .....79 G3
CHTN/BK PR9 .....15 K3
Kingfisher Dr RNFD/HAY WA11 .....88 E5
Kingfisher Gv WD/CROXPK L12 .....99 K4
Kingfisher Pk SKEL WN8 .....56 E1
Kingfisher Wy
GR/UP/WCH CH49 .....128 E3
King George Cl AIMK WN4 .....79 G6
King George Crs WARR WA1 .....17 K1
King George Dr WAL/NB CH45 .....111 J2
King George Rd
RNFD/HAY WA11 .....91 F4
King George's Dr
PS/BROM CH62 .....151 G5
Kingham Cl WDN WA8 .....19 K1
WLTN L25 .....155 F1
King James Ct RUNC WA7 .....187 H1
Kinglake Rd WAL/EG CH44 .....111 K3
Kinglake St EHL/KEN L7 .....113 K6
Kinglass Rd PS/BROM CH62 .....170 D2
King's Av GOL/RIS/CU WA3 .....93 G4
HOY CH47 .....127 J1
Kingsbrook Wy BEB CH63 .....150 C3
King's Brow BEB CH63 .....150 C5
Kingsbury WKBY CH48 .....127 J6
Kingsbury Cl STHP PR8 .....33 G5
Kingsbury Ct SKEL WN8 .....56 E1
Kings Cl AIG/SPK L17 .....152 D1
BEB CH63 .....150 C4
FMBY L37 .....48 E3
Kings Ct HOY CH47 .....127 F2
LITH L21 .....81 G4
RUNC WA7 * 178 C1
Kingscourt Rd
WD/CROXPK L12 .....115 G2
Kingsdale Av RAIN/WH L35 .....119 F4
RF/TRAN CH42 .....150 C1
Kingsdale Rd CALD/MH L18 .....134 B4
WARRW/BUR WA5 .....141 G2
Kings Dock St CLVPS L1 .....132 C2
Kingsdown Rd NG/CROX L11 .....98 E4
Kingsdown St BIRK CH41 .....131 H5
Kings Dr FROD/HEL WA6 .....199 J6
PEN/TH CH61 .....148 C5
WKBY CH48 .....146 E3
WLTN L25 .....154 E1
Kingsfield Rd MGHL L31 .....71 F2
The King's Gap HOY CH47 .....127 F2
Kingshead Cl RUNC WA7 .....177 K3
Kingsheath Av DV/KA/FCH L14 .....115 K2
Kings Hey Dr CHTN/BK PR9 .....23 H4
Kingsland Crs NG/CROX L11 .....98 C2
Kingsland Gra WARR WA1 .....125 F6
Kingsland Rd NG/CROX L11 .....98 B2
RF/TRAN CH42 .....131 F5
King's La BEB CH63 .....150 D4
Kingsley Av PS/BROM CH62 .....184 B4
Kingsley Cl MGHL L31 .....62 A2
PEN/TH CH61 .....168 A2
Kingsley Crs RUNC WA7 .....10 E7
Kingsley Dr WARRS WA4 .....162 B4
Kingsley Rd ECCL WA10 .....88 A5
EP CH65 .....6 E4
FROD/HEL WA6 .....201 H4
RUNC WA7 .....10 E6
TOX L8 .....133 G2
WAL/EG CH44 .....111 H4
Kingsley St BIRK CH41 .....130 D1
Kingsmead Dr WLTN L25 .....154 E4
Kingsmead Gv CL/PREN CH43 .....130 C4
Kings Meadow RUNC WA7 .....178 B5
STHP PR8 .....33 K6
Kingsmead Rd CL/PREN CH43 .....130 C4
MOR/LEA CH46 .....109 K5
Kingsmead Rd North
CL/PREN CH43 .....130 C4
Kingsmead Rd South
CL/PREN CH43 .....130 C4
Kings Ms WARRS WA4 * 162 B3
King's Moss La
RNFD/HAY WA11 .....76 B2
Kings Mt CL/PREN CH43 .....130 E5
Kingsnorth RAIN/WH L35 .....118 B5
Kings Pde VAUX/LVPD L3 * 132 B3
Kings Pk LITH L21 .....81 G4
King's Rd AIMK WN4 .....79 F4
BEB CH63 .....150 C4
BTL L20 .....96 E3
CSBY/BLUN L23 .....68 E5
ECCL WA10 .....102 E3
FMBY L37 .....48 E3
GOL/RIS/CU WA3 .....92 B4
GTS/LS CH66 .....195 F2
WARRN/WOL WA2 .....124 C5
Kings Ter BTL L20 .....4 E7
Kingsthorne Pk SPK/HALE L24 .....155 F5
Kingsthorne Rd WLTN L25 .....155 F5
Kingston Av
WARRW/BUR WA5 .....141 F3
Kingston Cl MOR/LEA CH46 .....129 F1
RUNC WA7 .....177 H3
WD/CROXPK L12 .....115 J2
Kingston Crs CHTN/BK PR9 .....21 F6
King St ALL/GAR L19 .....172 B1
CSBY/WL L22 .....80 E2
ECCL WA10 .....13 F5
EP CH65 .....6 E2
NEWLW WA12 .....106 B2
RF/TRAN CH42 .....151 F2
RUNC WA7 .....10 E3
STHP PR8 .....14 D6
WAL/EG CH44 .....111 K2
Kings Vw HOY CH47 * 126 E3
Kingsville Rd BEB CH63 .....150 D6
Kingswalk WKBY CH48 .....146 D1
Kingsway CSBY/WL L22 .....81 F1
FROD/HEL WA6 .....200 E2
HES CH60 .....181 H1
HUY L36 .....116 D3
NEWLW WA12 .....106 C3
RAIN/WH L35 .....117 K2
RNFD/HAY WA11 .....88 D3
STHP PR8 .....14 C5
WAL/NB CH45 .....111 G1
WDN WA8 .....18 D3
Kingsway Ct VAUX/LVPD L3 .....113 F3
Kingsway North WARR WA1 .....143 H4
Kingsway Pk VAUX/LVPD L3 * 113 F3
Kingsway South WARRS WA4 .....143 J5
Kingsway (Tunnel)
WAL/EG CH44 .....111 J5
Kingswell Cl EHL/KEN L7 .....133 G1
Kings Whf BIRK CH41 .....112 A6
Kingswood Av CSBY/WL L22 .....81 G2
WLT/FAZ L9 .....82 E4
Kingswood Bvd BEB CH63 .....150 D3
Kingswood Ct NWD/KWIPK L33 .....72 E5
Kingswood Dr CSBY/BLUN L23 .....68 E6
Kingswood Pk STHP PR8 .....14 A7
Kingswood Rd WAL/EG CH44 .....111 J2
WARRW/BUR WA5 .....122 B5
Kington Rd WKBY CH48 .....127 F6
Kinley Gdns BTL L20 * 82 B6
Kinloch Cl HLWD L26 .....155 K4
Kinloch Wy ORM L39 .....45 H6
Kinloss Rd GR/UP/WCH CH49 .....128 D6
Kinmel Cl ANF/KKDL L4 .....98 B5
BIRK CH41 .....2 E3
Kinmel St STHEL WA9 .....104 A5
TOX L8 .....133 F4
Kinnaird Rd WAL/NB CH45 .....111 G1
Kinnaird St TOX L8 .....133 F6
Kinnerley Rd EP CH65 .....195 K6
Kinnerton Cl MOR/LEA CH46 .....128 C1
Kinnington Wy GTS/LS CH66 * 202 D4
Kinnock Pk WARRW/BUR WA5 .....121 J1
Kinross Av AIMK WN4 .....78 B5
Kinross Cl WARRN/WOL WA2 .....124 B3
Kinross Rd AIN/FAZ L10 .....83 H4
CSBY/WL L22 .....81 F3
WAL/NB CH45 .....110 D1
Kinsale Dr GOL/RIS/CU WA3 .....124 E3
Kinsey Rd EP CH65 .....203 J2
Kinsey's La EP CH65 .....198 A3
Kintore Cl BEB CH63 .....183 K3
Kintore Dr WARRW/BUR WA5 .....140 E3
Kintore Rd ALL/GAR L19 .....153 J4
Kintyre Cl EP CH65 .....203 G2
Kipling Av HUY L36 .....117 G6
RF/TRAN CH42 .....150 E2
WARRN/WOL WA2 .....123 J6
Kipling Crs WDN WA8 .....18 B3
Kipling Gv STHEL WA9 .....119 J4
Kipling St BTL L20 .....81 H6
Kirby Cl WKBY CH48 .....146 C2
Kirby Mt WKBY CH48 .....146 D3
Kirby Pk WKBY CH48 .....146 C2
Kirby Park Man WKBY CH48 * 146 C2
Kirby Rd BTL L20 .....82 A5
Kirkacre Av NEWLW WA12 .....106 C5
Kirkbride Cl NTHLY L27 .....136 D5
Kirkburn Cl TOX L8 * 132 E5
Kirkby Bank Rd
NWD/KWIPK L33 .....85 G1
Kirkby Rw KKBY L32 .....72 B6
Kirkcaldy Av
WARRW/BUR WA5 .....140 E3
Kirkdale Gdns SKEL WN8 * 57 H6
Kirkdale Rd EV L5 .....113 F1
Kirkdale V ANF/KKDL L4 .....97 G6
Kirket Cl BEB CH63 .....170 C1
Kirket La BEB CH63 .....170 B1
Kirkfield Gv RF/TRAN CH42 .....151 F2
Kirkham Av GOL/RIS/CU WA3 * 93 F5
Kirkham Cl WARRW/BUR WA5 .....141 J5
Kirkham Rd CHTN/BK PR9 .....23 J1
WDN WA8 .....158 D1
Kirklake Bank FMBY L37 .....48 C3
Kirklake Rd FMBY L37 .....48 C3
Kirkland Av RF/TRAN CH42 .....150 C1
Kirkland Cl WLT/FAZ L9 * 82 C4
Kirkland Rd WAL/NB CH45 .....95 J5
The Kirklands WKBY CH48 .....146 D1
Kirkland St ECCL WA10 .....12 E4
Kirklees Rd STHP PR8 .....27 G6
Kirkmaiden Rd ALL/GAR L19 .....153 J3
Kirkman Fold RAIN/WH L35 .....118 D4
Kirkmore Rd CALD/MH L18 .....153 H1
Kirkmount GR/UP/WCH CH49 .....129 H4
Kirk Rd BTL L20 .....81 K5
Kirkside Cl WD/CROXPK L12 .....99 H2
Kirkstall Dr FMBY L37 .....49 H3
Kirkstall Rd STHP PR8 .....27 G5
Kirkstead Rd KKBY L32 .....72 A6
Kirkstead Wk GOL/RIS/CU WA3 .....92 B3
Kirkstone Av RNFD/HAY WA11 .....89 F3
WARRN/WOL WA2 .....123 J4
Kirkstone Crs RUNC WA7 .....187 K3
Kirkstone Rd North LITH L21 .....81 K2
Kirkstone Rd South LITH L21 .....82 A3
Kirk Stone Rd West LITH L21 .....81 J1
Kirk St EV L5 .....113 G1
Kirkwall Dr WARRW/BUR WA5 .....141 H6
Kirkway BEB CH63 .....150 C4
GR/UP/WCH CH49 .....129 G4
WAL/NB CH45 .....95 H6
Kitchener Dr WLT/FAZ L9 .....82 C5
Kitchener St ECCL WA10 .....12 C4
Kitchen St CLVPS L1 .....132 C2
Kitling La PR/KW L34 .....85 H6
Kitling Rd PR/KW L34 .....85 H6
Kiverley Cl WLTN L25 .....135 F6
Kiveton Dr AIMK WN4 .....91 H1
The Knap HES CH60 .....181 F1
Knaresborough Rd WAL/EG CH44 .....111 F3
Knighton Rd ANF/KKDL L4 .....98 B4
Knight Rd WARRW/BUR WA5 .....121 K1
Knightsbridge Av WARRS WA4 .....144 B6
Knightsbridge Cl WDN WA8 .....139 J5
Knightsbridge Ct
CL/PREN CH43 .....130 A5
WARR WA1 * 16 C5
Knightsbridge Wk
NWD/KWIPK L33 .....72 C3
Knights Gra STHEL WA9 .....104 A1
Knight St CLVPS L1 .....9 G7
Knightsway CSBY/WL L22 .....81 G1
Knob Hall Gdns CHTN/BK PR9 .....23 H2
Knob Hall La CHTN/BK PR9 .....23 H2
Knoclaid Rd CLB/OSW/ST L13 .....98 C6
The Knoll CL/PREN CH43 .....130 D6
Knottingley Dr GTS/LS CH66 .....195 F4
Knotty Ms WLTN L25 .....135 K6
The Knowe NSTN CH64 .....193 H1
Knowle Av STHP PR8 .....33 J3
Knowle Cl GTS/LS CH66 .....195 H6
NG/CROX L11 .....99 G3
Knowles House Av ECCL WA10 .....102 B2
Knowles St BIRK CH41 .....2 C3
WDN WA8 .....158 D1
Knowl Hey Rd HLWD L26 .....155 K5
Knowsley Av GOL/RIS/CU WA3 .....92 C2
Knowsley Cl RF/TRAN CH42 .....151 F2
Knowsley Expy RAIN/WH L35 .....137 G3
WDN WA8 .....156 D3
Knowsley La PR/KW L34 .....85 H6
Knowsley Park La PR/KW L34 .....101 J6
Knowsley Rd ALL/GAR L19 .....153 H5
BTL L20 .....81 J6
CHTN/BK PR9 .....15 G1
ECCL WA10 .....102 E2
ORM L39 .....53 K1
RAIN/WH L35 .....119 F5
RF/TRAN CH42 .....151 F2
WAL/NB CH45 .....111 G1
Knowsley St ANF/KKDL L4 .....97 H3
Knowsley Vw RNFD/HAY WA11 .....75 F1
Knox Cl PS/BROM CH62 .....151 G5
Knox St BIRK CH41 .....3 H5
Knutsford Cl ECCL WA10 .....102 D3
Knutsford Gn MOR/LEA CH46 .....109 J6
Knutsford Old Rd WARRS WA4 .....163 F1
Knutsford Rd MOR/LEA CH46 .....109 J6
WARRS WA4 .....17 F7
Knutsford Wk MGHL L31 .....62 B3
Kremlin Dr CLB/OSW/ST L13 .....114 D2
Kronsbec Av GTS/LS CH66 .....195 G3
Kylemore Av CALD/MH L18 .....134 A6
Kylemore Cl PEN/TH CH61 .....167 J2
Kylemore Dr PEN/TH CH61 .....167 J2
Kylemore Rd CL/PREN CH43 .....130 D5
Kylemore Wy HLWD L26 .....155 G4
PEN/TH CH61 .....167 J2
Kynance Rd NG/CROX L11 .....84 C6

L

Laburnum Av HUY L36 .....136 B1
RNFD/HAY WA11 .....89 G4
WARR WA1 .....144 B2
Laburnum Crs KKBY L32 .....72 C6
Laburnum Dr SKEL WN8 .....55 K4
Laburnum Farm Cl NSTN CH64 .....192 B4
Laburnum Gv BRSC L40 .....39 F3
GTS/LS CH66 .....202 E3
MGHL L31 .....62 D6
PEN/TH CH61 .....148 A5
RUNC WA7 .....176 E5
STHP PR8 .....23 H6
Laburnum La
WARRW/BUR WA5 .....140 D3
Laburnum Pl BTL L20 .....5 G4
Laburnum Rd CL/PREN CH43 .....131 F5
EHL/KEN L7 .....114 B4
GOL/RIS/CU WA3 .....93 G3
WAL/NB CH45 .....95 H6
Laburnum St AIMK WN4 .....91 G1
Laburnum Ter ALL/GAR L19 * 153 K5
Lace St VAUX/LVPD L3 .....8 E2
Lacey Ct WDN WA8 .....18 E6
Lacey Rd PR/KW L34 .....118 A2
Lacey St ECCL WA10 .....103 F5
WDN WA8 .....18 D6
Lad La VAUX/LVPD L3 * 8 B2
Lady Acre Cl LYMM WA13 .....164 E1
Lady Alice's Dr BRSC L40 .....46 E3
Ladybarn Av GOL/RIS/CU WA3 .....92 A4
Ladybower Cl EHL/KEN L7 .....133 G1
Lady Chapel Cl CLVPS L1 .....132 D2
Ladycroft Cl WARR WA1 .....144 D2
Ladyewood Rd WAL/EG CH44 .....111 J4
Ladyfield CL/PREN CH43 .....129 K2
Ladyfields WD/CROXPK L12 .....115 F2
Lady Green Cl HTWN L38 * 60 A4
Lady Green La HTWN L38 .....59 K3
Ladypool SPK/HALE L24 .....174 D4
Lady Richeld Cl RUNC WA7 .....178 C2
Ladysmith Av AIMK WN4 .....79 H6
Ladysmith Rd AIN/FAZ L10 .....83 J4
Lady's Wk BRSC L40 .....46 C5
Ladywood Rd
WARRW/BUR WA5 .....122 C6
Laffak Rd RNFD/HAY WA11 .....89 G3
Laggan St EHL/KEN L7 * 113 K5
Lagrange Ar ECCL WA10 * 13 G5
Laira Ct WARRN/WOL WA2 * 17 F1
Laira St WARRN/WOL WA2 .....17 F1
Laird Cl CL/PREN CH43 .....130 C1
Lairds Pl VAUX/LVPD L3 .....113 F3
Laird St BIRK CH41 .....130 D1
Laithwaite Cl STHEL WA9 .....119 K4
Lakeland Av AIMK WN4 .....79 H5
Lakeland Cl CLVPS L1 .....8 E6
Lakemoor Cl STHEL WA9 .....104 B6
Lakenheath Rd HLWD L26 .....155 H5
Lake Pl HOY CH47 .....127 G2
Lake Rd HOY CH47 .....127 G2
WAV L15 .....134 B2
Lakeside Cl WDN WA8 .....157 F4
Lakeside Ct RNFD/HAY WA11 .....75 H3
STHP PR8 * 14 E3
WAL/NB CH45 .....95 J5
Lakeside Dr WARR WA1 .....142 D6
Lakeside Gdns RNFD/HAY WA11 .....75 H3
Lakeside Rd LYMM WA13 .....164 E2
Lakeside Vw CSBY/WL L22 * 80 E3
Lakes Rd WLT/FAZ L9 .....83 G4
Lake St ANF/KKDL L4 .....97 J6
Lake Vw RAIN/WH L35 .....118 A6
Laleston Cl WDN WA8 .....157 K3
Lambert Ct WDN WA8 .....18 E4
Lambert St VAUX/LVPD L3 .....9 H2
Lambert Wy VAUX/LVPD L3 .....9 H2
Lambeth Rd EV L5 .....97 F6
Lambeth Wk ANF/KKDL L4 .....97 F6
Lambourn Av WDN WA8 .....138 B4
Lambourne SKEL WN8 .....56 D1
Lambourne Cl GTS/LS CH66 .....202 D3
Lambourne Gv STHEL WA9 .....104 E2
Lambourne Rd ANF/KKDL L4 .....98 B4
Lambshear La MGHL L31 .....62 A3
Lambsickle Cl RUNC WA7 .....186 C1
Lambsickle La RUNC WA7 .....186 C1
Lambs La WARR WA1 .....143 K2
Lambton Rd AIG/SPK L17 .....133 G6
Lamburth Dr AIG/SPK L17 .....133 H5
Lamerton Cl WARRW/BUR WA5 .....140 E5
Lammermoor Rd
CALD/MH L18 .....153 H1
Lampeter Cl
WARRW/BUR WA5 * 122 E5
Lampeter Rd NPK/KEN L6 .....114 A1
Lamport Cl WDN WA8 .....139 K6
Lamport St TOX L8 .....132 D3
Lanark Cl ECCL WA10 .....12 E7
Lancashire Gdns ECCL WA10 .....12 E7
Lancaster Av AIG/SPK L17 .....133 J4
CSBY/BLUN L23 .....68 E6
GOL/RIS/CU WA3 .....92 D3
RAIN/WH L35 .....117 K4
RAIN/WH L35 .....157 F1
RUNC WA7 .....176 B5
WAL/NB CH45 .....111 H2
Lancaster Cl EV L5 .....113 F1
MGHL L31 .....62 D6
NEWLW WA12 .....90 E6
PS/BROM CH62 .....151 G5
STHP PR8 .....27 F3
WARRN/WOL WA2 * 124 B5
Lancaster Ct WARRS WA4 * 162 D2
Lancaster Crs SKEL WN8 .....56 A4
Lancaster Dr CHTN/BK PR9 .....21 H6
Lancaster Gdns EP CH65 .....196 C6
Lancaster Ga CHTN/BK PR9 .....21 J6
Lancaster Rd FMBY L37 .....48 E4
HUY L36 .....117 G3
STHP PR8 .....27 F3
WDN WA8 .....139 F6
Lancaster St EV L5 .....113 F1
WARRW/BUR WA5 .....142 B4
WLT/FAZ L9 .....97 H2
Lancaster Ter PR/KW L34 * 118 A1
Lancaster Wk EV L5 .....113 F1
Lance Cl EV L5 .....113 H3
Lancefield Rd WLT/FAZ L9 * 82 C6
Lance Gv WAV L15 .....134 B2
Lance La WAV L15 .....134 B2
Lancelyn Prec BEB CH63 * 170 C2
Lancelyn Ter BEB CH63 .....170 B1
Lancer Ct RUNC WA7 .....177 H2
Lancers Cft GTS/LS CH66 .....202 C2
Lancing Av WARRN/WOL WA2 .....123 G3
Lancing Cl WLTN L25 .....155 G2
Lancing Dr AIN/FAZ L10 .....83 G1
Lancing Rd EP CH65 .....7 E6
WLTN L25 .....155 G3
Lancing Wy WLTN L25 .....155 G2
Lancots La STHEL WA9 .....104 B5
Land Cut La GOL/RIS/CU WA3 .....125 F4
Land End MGHL L31 .....63 G6
Lander Cl WARRW/BUR WA5 .....142 A2
Lander Rd LITH L21 .....81 J5
Landford Av WLT/FAZ L9 .....98 C1
Landford Pl WLT/FAZ L9 .....98 C1
Land Gate La AIMK WN4 .....79 F2
Landican La BEB CH63 .....149 K5
GR/UP/WCH CH49 .....149 F2
Landican Rd GR/UP/WCH CH49 .....148 E4
Land La CHTN/BK PR9 .....24 A1
Landor Cl EV L5 .....112 E2
GOL/RIS/CU WA3 .....93 F3
Landscape Dene
FROD/HEL WA6 .....200 A5
Landseer Av NSTN CH64 .....192 A2
WARRS WA4 .....162 A2
Landseer Rd EV L5 .....113 H2
Lane Head Av GOL/RIS/CU WA3 .....93 F3
Lanfranc Cl CHLDW L16 .....135 F1
Lanfranc Wy CHLDW L16 .....135 F1
Langbar RAIN/WH L35 .....118 A5

Langdale Av FMBY L37 48 D2
GOL/RIS/CU WA3 92 D2
PEN/TH CH61 167 K1
Langdale Cl FMBY L37 48 D3
KKBY L32 84 E2
WARRN/WOL WA2 124 A5
WDN WA8 157 H3
Langdale Dr BRSC L40 38 E5
MGHL L31 62 C5
Langdale Gdns STHP PR8 27 G6
Langdale Gv RNFD/HAY WA11 88 E4
Langdale Rd BEB CH63 170 A1
RUNC WA7 11 F6
WAL/NB CH45 95 G6
WAV L15 133 K3
Langdale St BTL L20 5 G5
Langdale Wy FROD/HEL WA6 187 F6
Langfield GOL/RIS/CU WA3 93 F4
Langfield Gv PS/BROM CH62 184 A2
Langford SPK/HALE L24 174 D4
Langford Rd ALL/GAR L19 153 G3
Langham Av AIG/SPK L17 133 H6
Langham St ANF/KKDL L4 97 H5
Langholm Rd AIMK WN4 78 B5
Langland Cl ANF/KKDL L4 98 B5
WARRW/BUR WA5 122 E5
Lang La WKBY CH48 127 G6
Lang La South WKBY CH48 127 H6
Langley Cl BEB CH63 170 C4
GOL/RIS/CU WA3 92 D2
HTWN L38 59 F5
WD/CROXPK L12 99 K2
Langley Ct EP CH65 196 D6
Langley Pl BRSC L40 38 B5
Langley Rd BEB CH63 170 C3
BRSC L40 38 B5
Langley St TOX L8 * 132 D3
Langrove St EV L5 113 G2
Langsdale St VAUX/LVPD L3 9 J1
Langshaw Lea NTHLY L27 136 C5
Langstone Av
GR/UP/WCH CH49 147 J1
Langton Cl NEWLW WA12 106 A1
WDN WA8 138 A6
Langton Gn WARR WA1 144 C2
Langton Rd NWD/KWIPK L33 72 E5
WAV L15 133 J2
Langtree SKEL WN8 56 D2
Langtree St STHEL WA9 104 A2
Langtry Cl ANF/KKDL L4 97 G5
Langtry Rd ANF/KKDL L4 97 F5
Langwell Cl GOL/RIS/CU WA3 125 J2
Langwood La RNFD/HAY WA11 66 E6
Lansbrook Ct RUNC WA7 * 11 H5
Lansbury Av STHEL WA9 104 C3
Lansbury Rd HUY L36 117 G5
Lansdown WD/CROXPK L12 114 E1
Lansdowne FROD/HEL WA6 201 G3
Lansdowne Cl BIRK CH41 130 D1
Lansdowne Ct CL/PREN CH43 130 C1
Lansdowne Pl EV L5 113 H1
Lansdowne Rd BIRK CH41 130 C1
STHP PR8 28 B1
WAL/NB CH45 95 F5
Lanville Rd ALL/GAR L19 153 J2
Lanyork Rd VAUX/LVPD L3 8 B1
Lapford Crs NWD/KWIPK L33 73 F5
Lapwing Cl GOL/RIS/CU WA3 92 E3
WD/CROXPK L12 99 J4
Lapwing Ct HLWD L26 155 H2
Lapwing Gv RUNC WA7 187 K1
Lapwing La WARRS WA4 160 C4
Lapworth Cl MOR/LEA CH46 128 C1
Lapworth St EV L5 113 F1
Larch Av NEWLW WA12 106 C3
WARRW/BUR WA5 141 F4
WDN WA8 158 C1
Larch Cl ALL/GAR L19 153 G4
GOL/RIS/CU WA3 93 G5
RUNC WA7 177 G6
SKEL WN8 56 A4
WGNW/BIL/O WN5 77 G4
Larchdale Cl GTS/LS CH66 202 D3
Larchdale Gv WLT/FAZ L9 97 K1
Larchfield Rd CSBY/BLUN L23 69 H4
Larch Gv CL/PREN CH43 130 B1
WAV L15 114 E6
Larch Lea NPK/KEN L6 113 K2
Larch Rd HUY L36 116 C5
RF/TRAN CH42 2 C7
RNFD/HAY WA11 * 90 D4
RUNC WA7 177 F6
Larch St STHP PR8 28 B2
Larch Wy FMBY L37 48 D1
Larchways WARRS WA4 162 C6
Larchwood Av MGHL L31 71 F2
Larchwood Cl PEN/TH CH61 167 K2
WLTN L25 135 J4
Larchwood Dr BEB CH63 150 E4
Larcombe Av
GR/UP/WCH CH49 129 G4
Larkfield Av WARR WA1 143 J2
Larkfield Cl AIG/SPK L17 152 D1
Larkfield Gv AIG/SPK L17 152 D1
Larkfield La CHTN/BK PR9 23 J2
Larkfield Rd AIG/SPK L17 152 D1
Larkfield Vw WAV L15 133 K1
Larkhill SKEL WN8 56 D1
Larkhill Av GR/UP/WCH CH49 129 H3
Larkhill Cl CLB/OSW/ST L13 98 C6
Larkhill Gv HTWN L38 59 F4
Larkhill La CLB/OSW/ST L13 98 C6
FMBY L37 48 C1
Larkhill Pl CLB/OSW/ST L13 98 C6
Larkhill Vw CLB/OSW/ST L13 98 D6
Larkhill Wy GR/UP/WCH CH49 129 H2
Larkin Cl PS/BROM CH62 151 F4
Lark La AIG/SPK L17 133 H6
Larkspur Cl RUNC WA7 187 J3
STHP PR8 15 J7
Larkstoke Cl WARRS WA4 162 D5
Larksway HES CH60 168 B5
Lark Wy AIG/SPK L17 133 G6
Larton Farm Cl WKBY CH48 127 K6
Larton Rd WKBY CH48 127 J6
Lartonwood WKBY CH48 147 F1
Lascelles Rd ALL/GAR L19 154 A4
Lascelles St STHEL WA9 104 A2
Laskey La WARRS WA4 144 E5
Latchford Rd HES CH60 181 G1
Latchford St WARRS WA4 143 K6
Late Moffatt Rd West
WLT/FAZ L9 * 82 E4
Latham Av NEWLW WA12 106 C1
ORM L39 46 A6
RUNC WA7 11 G6
Latham St EV L5 113 F1
Latham Wy BEB CH63 170 D3
Lathbury La AIG/SPK L17 133 K4
Lathom Av LITH L21 81 G5
WAL/EG CH44 111 H3
WARRN/WOL WA2 142 E1
Lathom Cl BRSC L40 38 E5
Lathom Dr MGHL L31 62 C4
RNFD/HAY WA11 75 G2
Lathom La BRSC L40 46 C4
Lathom Rd BTL L20 81 K6
CHTN/BK PR9 15 G1
HUY L36 116 E5
ORM L39 55 F6
Lathum Cl RAIN/WH L35 118 A2
Latimer St EV L5 113 F2
Latrigg Rd AIG/SPK L17 153 F1
Lauder Cl NWD/KWIPK L33 72 C3
Launceston Cl RUNC WA7 188 B1
Launceston Dr
WARRW/BUR WA5 141 F6
The Laund WAL/NB CH45 111 F2
Laurel Av BEB CH63 170 A1
BRSC L40 38 E3
HES CH60 167 K4
NEWLW WA12 106 D3
WARR WA1 * 144 C2
Laurel Bank WARRS WA4 163 H2
WDN WA8 139 F6
Laurelbanks HES CH60 167 J4
Laurel Ct RNFD/HAY WA11 88 E4
Laurel Dr ECCL WA10 102 B1
EP CH65 203 F1
NSTN CH64 183 J6
SKEL WN8 56 A3
Laurel Gv AIMK WN4 79 G5
CHTN/BK PR9 23 G6
CSBY/WL L22 80 E1
GOL/RIS/CU WA3 92 E3
HUY L36 136 B1
TOX L8 133 H3
Laurelhurst Av PEN/TH CH61 168 A1
Laurel Rd ECCL WA10 12 A7
EHL/KEN L7 114 B5
PR/KW L34 118 A1
RF/TRAN CH42 131 G5
RNFD/HAY WA11 89 J6
Laurels Farm Ct CHNE CH2 * 198 C6
Laurel Wy ECCL WA10 * 103 F3
Laurelwood Dr GTS/LS CH66 202 C3
Laurence Deacon Ct
BIRK CH41 * 2 D2
Lauren Cl HUY L36 117 H5
Lauriston Rd ANF/KKDL L4 98 A4
Laurus Cl NTHLY L27 136 C4
Lavan Cl NPK/KEN L6 113 J4
Lavan St NPK/KEN L6 113 J4
Lavender Cl RUNC WA7 11 J7
Lavender Crs PR/KW L34 118 A1
Lavender Wy WLT/FAZ L9 97 K2
Lavrock Bank TOX L8 132 D5
Lawford Dr HES CH60 168 C5
Lawler St LITH L21 81 J5
Lawn Av WARR WA1 143 J1
Lawns Av BEB CH63 183 J1
Lawnside Cl RF/TRAN CH42 150 E2
The Lawns CHTN/BK PR9 23 H3
CL/PREN CH43 130 A2
Lawnswood Gv CHNE CH2 198 C6
Lawrence Cl ALL/GAR L19 153 H4
Lawrence Gv WAV L15 133 K2
Lawrence Rd ECCL WA10 87 K5
WAV L15 133 J2
Lawrenson St ECCL WA10 12 D6
Lawson Cl WARR WA1 144 D2
Lawson St CHTN/BK PR9 23 J6
Lawson Wk WD/CROXPK L12 99 H2
Lawton Av BTL L20 82 B6
Lawton Rd CSBY/WL L22 80 E1
HUY L36 116 C5
RAIN/WH L35 119 F5
Lawton St CLVPS L1 9 G5
Laxey Av WARR WA1 144 C3
Laxey St TOX L8 132 D3
Laxton Cl GTS/LS CH66 202 D3
Laxton Rd WLTN L25 155 F5
Layford Cl HUY L36 116 D1
Layford Rd HUY L36 116 D2
Layton Av CL/PREN CH43 149 J1
Layton Cl GOL/RIS/CU WA3 125 G4
WLTN L25 155 F1
Layton Rd WLTN L25 155 F1
Lazenby Crs AIMK WN4 78 E6
Leach Cft STBRV L28 100 A6
Leach La STHEL WA9 120 B2
Leach St ECCL WA10 13 F4
Leach Vw RNFD/HAY WA11 * 88 E4
Leach Wy PEN/TH CH61 147 K5
Lea Cl CL/PREN CH43 130 B5
Lea Crs ORM L39 45 J4
Leacroft AIMK WN4 78 D3
Leacroft Rd GOL/RIS/CU WA3 125 J1
Lea Cross Gv WDN WA8 138 B6
Leadenhall Cl EV L5 113 H1
Leafield Cl PEN/TH CH61 148 C5
Leafield Rd WLTN L25 154 E5
Leagate AIN/FAZ L10 83 J3
Lea Green Rd STHEL WA9 119 J3
Leamington Av NEWLW WA12 106 C4
Leamington Cl NSTN CH64 191 K3
WARRW/BUR WA5 141 H1
Leamington Rd NG/CROX L11 98 B3
STHP PR8 33 J4
Leander Rd WAL/NB CH45 111 G2
Lea Rd WAL/EG CH44 111 J2
Leas Cl GTS/LS CH66 195 F4
Leaside RUNC WA7 11 K7
Leasowe Av WAL/NB CH45 110 E1
Leasowe Gdns MOR/LEA CH46 109 J4
Leasowe Rd MOR/LEA CH46 110 A3
WLT/FAZ L9 82 E4
Leasoweside MOR/LEA CH46 110 A3
Leas Pk HOY CH47 127 F5
The Leas PEN/TH CH61 148 E5
WAL/NB CH45 94 E6
Leatham Cl GOL/RIS/CU WA3 125 G4
Leatherbarrows La MGHL L31 71 K2
Leather La CLVP L2 8 D3
Leather's La HLWD L26 155 J4
Leathwood MGHL L31 * 71 H1
Leaway GR/UP/WCH CH49 128 E5
Leawood Gv MOR/LEA CH46 129 G1
Leckwith Rd NTHTN L30 70 E6
Ledburn SKEL WN8 56 D2
Ledbury Cl CL/PREN CH43 149 H1
ECCL WA10 102 D2
WD/CROXPK L12 99 K1
Ledger Rd RNFD/HAY WA11 89 K6
Ledmore Gv AIMK WN4 78 C6
Ledsham Cl CL/PREN CH43 130 B5
GOL/RIS/CU WA3 124 E4
Ledsham La GTS/LS CH66 194 C6
Ledsham Park Dr GTS/LS CH66 194 D3
Ledsham Rd GTS/LS CH66 194 D4
KKBY L32 84 B1
Ledson Gv ORM L39 53 F6
Ledston Cl RUNC WA7 178 C4
Ledyard Cl WARRW/BUR WA5 142 A2
Leece St CLVPS L1 9 G6
Lee Cl RAIN/WH L35 119 F6
Lee Ct WARRN/WOL WA2 123 J5
Leecourt Cl WD/CROXPK L12 115 H2
Leeds St VAUX/LVPD L3 8 C1
Lee Hall Rd WLTN L25 135 K4
Leeming Cl ALL/GAR L19 153 K6
Lee Park Av WLTN L25 135 K5
Lee Rd HOY CH47 127 H2
WARRW/BUR WA5 * 141 J3
Lees Av RF/TRAN CH42 150 E1
Leeside Av KKBY L32 84 E3
Leeside Cl KKBY L32 84 E2
Lees La EP CH65 7 G7
NSTN CH64 192 C1
WD/CROXPK L12 99 H6
Lees Rd NWD/KWIPK L33 85 G2
Lee St STHEL WA9 104 C5
Leeswood SKEL WN8 56 D2
Leeswood Rd
GR/UP/WCH CH49 129 H6
Lee Vale Rd WLTN L25 135 K5
Leeward Dr SPK/HALE L24 173 F1
Legh Rd PS/BROM CH62 151 G4
RNFD/HAY WA11 89 K5
Legh St AIMK WN4 91 G1
GOL/RIS/CU WA3 92 B3
LYMM WA13 145 K6
NEWLW WA12 106 A2
WARR WA1 16 C4
Legion La PS/BROM CH62 171 F4
Legion Rd ECCL WA10 103 F5
Leicester Av CSBY/WL L22 80 E1
Leicester Rd BTL L20 5 H2
Leicester St CHTN/BK PR9 15 F2
STHEL WA9 103 F5
WARRW/BUR WA5 142 B4
Leigh Av WDN WA8 18 C2
Leigh Pl CLVPS L1 * 9 F4
Leigh Rd WKBY CH48 127 G6
Leighs Hey Crs KKBY L32 84 E2
Leigh St CLVPS L1 9 F4
Leighton Av HOY CH47 127 K1
MGHL L31 62 B5
Leighton Cha NSTN CH64 181 J6
Leighton Ct NSTN CH64 191 J1
Leighton Dr LEIGH WN7 93 J2
Leighton Pk NSTN CH64 191 J1
Leighton Rd BIRK CH41 131 H5
NSTN CH64 181 H4
The Leightons NSTN CH64 191 J1
Leighton St ANF/KKDL L4 97 G4
Leinster Gdns RUNC WA7 10 B3
Leinster Rd CLB/OSW/ST L13 115 F4
Leinster St RUNC WA7 10 B3
Leison St ANF/KKDL L4 97 F6
Leiston Cl PEN/TH CH61 148 B4
Lemon Cl EHL/KEN L7 114 A6
Lemon Gv TOX L8 133 H3
Lemon St EV L5 113 F1
Lemon Tree Wk ECCL WA10 103 F4
Lendel Cl FMBY L37 48 E2
Lenfield Dr RNFD/HAY WA11 89 J5
Lenham Wy SPK/HALE L24 173 G1
Lennox Av WAL/NB CH45 * 95 H6
Lennox La CL/PREN CH43 110 C6
Lenthall St ANF/KKDL L4 97 H3
Lenton Av FMBY L37 48 D1
Lenton Rd WLTN L25 135 K4
Leo Cl DV/KA/FCH L14 115 K3
Leominster Rd WAL/EG CH44 111 H3
Leonard Cheshire Dr
NTHTN L30 70 C6
Leonards Cl HUY L36 116 D1
Leonard St RUNC WA7 176 A6
STHEL WA9 104 D6
WARRN/WOL WA2 17 F1
WARRS WA4 162 B2
Leon Cl WARRW/BUR WA5 * 140 E2
Leonora St TOX L8 * 133 F5
Leopold Gv STHEL WA9 120 A2
Leopold Rd CSBY/WL L22 80 D1
EHL/KEN L7 113 K5
Leopold St WAL/EG CH44 * 112 A4
Lesley Rd STHP PR8 23 G6
Leslie Av GR/UP/WCH CH49 128 E6
Leslie Rd ECCL WA10 102 E5
Lesseps Rd TOX L8 133 H2
Lessingham Rd WDN WA8 138 E6
Lester Cl ANF/KKDL L4 97 G6
Lester Dr ECCL WA10 87 H6
PEN/TH CH61 147 K4
Lester Gv HUY L36 * 117 F3
Lestock St TOX L8 132 D2
Leta St ANF/KKDL L4 97 H4
Letchworth St NPK/KEN L6 114 A2
Lethbridge Cl EV L5 112 E1
Lethbridge Rd STHP PR8 28 A2
Letitia St TOX L8 132 E4
Levens Cl CHTN/BK PR9 21 K6
Levens Hey MOR/LEA CH46 128 E1
Leven St ANF/KKDL L4 97 G5
Levens Wy WDN WA8 157 H3
Leven Wk EP CH65 195 K1
Lever Av WAL/EG CH44 112 A5
Lever Cswy BEB CH63 150 A4
Leveret Rd SPK/HALE L24 174 B2
Lever St STHEL WA9 120 B3
Lever Ter RF/TRAN CH42 131 H6
Leveson Rd CLB/OSW/ST L13 115 F6
Levisham Gdns
WARRW/BUR WA5 142 B2
Lewis Av WARRW/BUR WA5 123 F5
Lewis Cl CHNE CH2 203 G3
Lewis Crs WDN WA8 18 C5
Lewis Gv WDN WA8 157 J2
Lewisham Rd NG/CROX L11 98 E4
PS/BROM CH62 151 H5
Lewis St ECCL WA10 12 D5
Lexden St WARRW/BUR WA5 142 B3
Lexham Rd DV/KA/FCH L14 115 G4
Lexington Wy NWD/KWIPK L33 72 C3
Lexton Dr CHTN/BK PR9 23 K2
Leybourne Av STHP PR8 34 B2
Leybourne Cl WLTN L25 135 H3
Leybourne Gn WLTN L25 135 H4
Leybourne Gv WLTN L25 135 H4
Leybourne Rd WLTN L25 135 H3
Leyburn Cl KKBY L32 84 D4
Leyburn Rd WAL/NB CH45 111 F2
Ley Cl STHEL WA9 120 A3
Leyfield Cl WD/CROXPK L12 115 H1
Leyfield Rd WD/CROXPK L12 115 G1
Leyland Cl CHTN/BK PR9 21 H6
Leyland Green Rd AIMK WN4 78 B4
Leyland Gv RNFD/HAY WA11 90 A5
Leyland Rd CHTN/BK PR9 15 J2
RNFD/HAY WA11 75 G3
STHP PR8 22 E4
Leyland St PR/KW L34 117 K1
Leyland Wy ORM L39 45 K6
Leyton Cl RUNC WA7 186 E1
Liberton Ct EV L5 113 H1
Liberty St WAV L15 133 K2
Libra Cl DV/KA/FCH L14 116 A2
Libson Cl WARRN/WOL WA2 124 C4
Lichfield Av CSBY/WL L22 68 E6
GOL/RIS/CU WA3 92 E3
WARRS WA4 163 F4
Lichfield Cl NTHTN L30 82 D2
Lichfield Dr GTS/LS CH66 202 C3
Lichfield Gv AIMK WN4 91 H1
Lichfield Rd HLWD L26 155 H5
WAV L15 134 B3
Lichfield St WAL/NB CH45 95 J6
Lickers La RAIN/WH L35 118 A5
Liddell Av MGHL L31 71 K5
Liddell Rd WD/CROXPK L12 98 D6
Lidderdale Rd WAV L15 133 K3
Lidgate Cl NWD/KWIPK L33 72 D4
Liebig St WDN WA8 18 E4
Lifeboat Rd FMBY L37 48 A4
Liffey St TOX L8 133 G2
Lifton Rd NWD/KWIPK L33 84 E1
Lightbody St EV L5 112 D2
Lightburn St RUNC WA7 10 C7
Lightfoot Cl HES CH60 * 168 B6
Lightfoot La HES CH60 168 B6
Lighthorne Dr STHP PR8 33 G5
Lighthouse Rd HOY CH47 127 F3
SPK/HALE L24 175 F6
Lightwood Dr EHL/KEN L7 133 H1
Lightwood St EHL/KEN L7 133 H1
Lilac Av AIMK WN4 78 C4
STHP PR8 41 K1
WARRW/BUR WA5 141 H4
WDN WA8 158 C1
Lilac Crs RUNC WA7 177 F5
Lilac Gv GTS/LS CH66 202 E3
HUY L36 136 A1
RNFD/HAY WA11 89 J6
SKEL WN8 56 A4
WARRS WA4 162 D2
WGNW/BIL/O WN5 77 G5
Lilac Rd GOL/RIS/CU WA3 92 B2
Lilford Av WARRW/BUR WA5 142 C1
WLT/FAZ L9 82 C5
Lilford Dr WARRW/BUR WA5 141 G3
Lilford St WARRW/BUR WA5 16 A1
Lilley Rd EHL/KEN L7 114 B4
Lillian Rd ANF/KKDL L4 113 K1
Lillie Cl CL/PREN CH43 129 K1
Lillyfield HES CH60 180 E1
Lilly Gn ANF/KKDL L4 97 K4
Lilly Gv ANF/KKDL L4 97 K4
Lilly V EHL/KEN L7 114 B4
Lily Av NEWLW WA12 106 C3
Lily Pl AIMK WN4 91 H1
Lily Rd LITH L21 81 J5
Lily St AIMK WN4 79 K4
Lime Av BEB CH63 169 K1
FROD/HEL WA6 201 F1
WDN WA8 * 158 C1
Lime Cl CLB/OSW/ST L13 114 E4
Limedale Rd CALD/MH L18 134 B4
Limefield Av LYMM WA13 165 G1
Limefield Dr SKEL WN8 57 G6
Lime Gv CHNE CH2 198 B6
GOL/RIS/CU WA3 92 E5
LITH L21 81 H5
RNFD/HAY WA11 75 G3
RUNC WA7 177 F5
SKEL WN8 56 A4
TOX L8 133 H3
Limehurst Gv PS/BROM CH62 184 A1
Limekiln Ct EV L5 113 F3
Limekiln La EV L5 113 F2
WAL/EG CH44 111 G5
WARRW/BUR WA5 121 J4
The Limes GOL/RIS/CU WA3 92 E5
GR/UP/WCH CH49 129 G4
Lime St CLVPS L1 9 F4
EP CH65 6 D1
STHP PR8 28 B1
Limetree Av WARR WA1 143 J1
WARRS WA4 162 D2
Lime Tree Cl GTS/LS CH66 202 E3
WLT/FAZ L9 97 K2
Lime Tree Gv HES CH60 168 C5
Lime Tree Wy FMBY L37 48 C3
Lime Vale Rd WGNW/BIL/O WN5 77 F6
Limeways WARRS WA4 162 D6
Limont Rd STHP PR8 33 K4
Linacre La BTL L20 81 K6
HTWN L38 50 C5
Linacre Rd LITH L21 81 J5
Linaker Dr ORM L39 43 K3
Linaker St STHP PR8 15 G7
Linbeck Gv GOL/RIS/CU WA3 93 F2
Linbridge Rd DV/KA/FCH L14 115 K1
Lincoln Av GOL/RIS/CU WA3 92 E2
Lincoln Cl GOL/RIS/CU WA3 93 K3
HUY L36 117 H4
RUNC WA7 187 F1
WARR WA1 144 D3
Lincoln Crs RNFD/HAY WA11 88 E5
Lincoln Dr AIMK WN4 91 H1
AIN/FAZ L10 71 G6
WAL/NB CH45 111 J1
Lincoln Gdns BIRK CH41 * 130 D1
Lincoln Gn MGHL L31 70 E1
Lincoln Rd ECCL WA10 103 F3
GTS/LS CH66 195 G6
STHP PR8 27 H6
Lincoln Sq WDN WA8 158 C1
Lincoln St ALL/GAR L19 172 B1
BIRK CH41 111 G6
Lincoln Wy RAIN/WH L35 119 F6
Lincombe Rd HUY L36 116 B3
Lindale Dr STHEL WA9 120 A3
Lindale Rd EHL/KEN L7 114 C4
Lindby Cl KKBY L32 85 F3
Lindby Rd KKBY L32 85 F3
Linden Av AIMK WN4 78 E4
CSBY/BLUN L23 68 D5
NTHTN L30 82 C1
Linden Cl GTS/LS CH66 202 D3
WARR WA1 144 C2
Linden Ct WDN WA8 * 138 E5
Linden Dr CL/PREN CH43 149 H2
HUY L36 136 B1
Linden Gv RNFD/HAY WA11 77 F6
WAL/NB CH45 95 H6
Linden Rd NTHLY L27 136 B4
Lindens SKEL WN8 56 D1
The Lindens CL/PREN CH43 2 B6
MGHL L31 71 F2
Linden Wy ECCL WA10 102 D1
WDN WA8 138 E5
Lindenwood KKBY L32 84 E3
Lindeth Av WAL/EG CH44 111 H5
Lindfield Cl TOX L8 132 D5
WARRS WA4 160 D6
Lindholme SKEL WN8 56 E2
Lindi Av WARRS WA4 163 G2
Lindisfarne Av EP CH65 203 G2
GOL/RIS/CU WA3 93 K3
Lindisfarne Dr
WD/CROXPK L12 100 A2
Lindley Av WARRS WA4 143 J5
Lindley Cl EHL/KEN L7 133 H1
Lindley St EHL/KEN L7 133 H1
Lindrick Cl RAIN/WH L35 118 C3
Lindsay Rd ANF/KKDL L4 98 B5
Lindsay St STHEL WA9 120 C4
Lind St ANF/KKDL L4 97 H4
Lindsworth Cl
WARRW/BUR WA5 * 141 K3
Lindwall Cl CL/PREN CH43 110 C6
Linear Pk MOR/LEA CH46 109 G6
Linear Vw NEWLW WA12 106 C5
Lineside Cl WLTN L25 135 J4
Linford Gv RNFD/HAY WA11 89 F6
Lingdale Av CL/PREN CH43 130 C3
Lingdale Rd CL/PREN CH43 130 C2
WKBY CH48 127 F6
Lingdale Rd North BIRK CH41 130 C2
Lingdales FMBY L37 41 H5
Lingfield Cl HUY L36 116 C6
Lingfield Gv DV/KA/FCH L14 115 H5
Lingfield Rd DV/KA/FCH L14 115 G5
RUNC WA7 176 B5
Lingford Cl NTHLY L27 136 C5
Lingham Cl MOR/LEA CH46 109 H6
Lingham La MOR/LEA CH46 109 G5
Lingholme Rd ECCL WA10 12 D3
Lingley Green Av
WARRW/BUR WA5 141 G1
Lingley Rd WARRW/BUR WA5 140 E3
Lingmell Av RNFD/HAY WA11 88 E2
Lingmell Rd WD/CROXPK L12 99 F5
Ling St EHL/KEN L7 113 K5
Lingtree Rd KKBY L32 84 A1
Lingwell Av WDN WA8 157 J1
Lingwood Rd
WARRW/BUR WA5 141 F3
Linhope Wy AIG/SPK L17 133 H6
Link Av CSBY/BLUN L23 69 H4
RNFD/HAY WA11 89 H6
Link Rd HUY L36 117 H6
Links Av CHTN/BK PR9 23 G3
GTS/LS CH66 195 F2
Links Cl BEB CH63 183 J1
WAL/NB CH45 95 F5
Links Hey Rd WKBY CH48 147 F5
Linkside BEB CH63 150 C4

Linkside Av WARRN/WOL WA2 123 H1
Linkside Wy GTS/LS CH66 202 D3
Links Rd KKBY L32 85 F3
The Links COL/RIS/CU WA3 * 125 F1
Linkstor Rd WLTN L25 154 C1
Links Vw CL/PREN CH43 130 B4
WAL/NB CH45 95 F5
Links View Cl WLTN L25 135 G6
Linksway WAL/NB CH45 95 F6
Linkway ECCL WA10 87 J5
RUNC WA7 177 F5
Linkway Av AIMK WN4 79 K4
Linkway East STHEL WA9 13 J7
Linkway West ECCL WA10 13 F6
Linner Rd SPK/HALE L24 173 J2
Linnet Cl AIG/SPK L17 133 H4
NEWLW WA12 106 C2
WARRN/WOL WA2 123 K4
Linnet Gv GOL/RIS/CU WA3 125 G4
Linnet La AIG/SPK L17 133 G4
Linnets Wy HES CH60 167 J5
Linnet Wy NWD/KWIPK L33 72 D2
Linosa Cl NPK/KEN L6 114 A3
Linslade Cl NWD/KWIPK L33 72 E5
Linslade Crs NWD/KWIPK L33 72 E5
Linton Av GOL/RIS/CU WA3 92 A1
Linton St ANF/KKDL L4 97 H4
Linum Gdns STHEL WA9 105 F6
Linville Av CSBY/BLUN L23 68 C5
Linwood Cl RUNC WA7 188 B2
Linwood Gv RAIN/WH L35 118 A5
Linwood Rd RF/TRAN CH42 131 H6
Lionel St STHEL WA9 104 D6
Lion Hotel Yd WARR WA1 * 16 D5
Lipton Cl BTL L20 4 D7
Lisburn La CLB/OSW/ST L13 98 C6
Lisburn Rd AIG/SPK L17 153 F1
Liscard Crs WAL/EG CH44 111 H2
Liscard Gv WAL/EG CH44 111 G3
Liscard Rd WAL/EG CH44 111 K4
WAV L15 133 J2
Liscard Village WAL/NB CH45 111 H2
Liscard Wy WAL/EG CH44 111 H3
Liskeard Cl RUNC WA7 188 A1
Lisleholme Crs
WD/CROXPK L12 115 G1
Lisleholme Rd
WD/CROXPK L12 115 G1
Lismore Rd CALD/MH L18 153 H2
Lister Crs EHL/KEN L7 114 A5
Lister Dr CLB/OSW/ST L13 114 C3
Lister Rd EHL/KEN L7 114 A5
RUNC WA7 11 H3
Liston St ANF/KKDL L4 * 97 H3
Litcham Cl GR/UP/WCH CH49 129 H2
Litchborough Gv RAIN/WH L35 118 C1
Litherland Av MOR/LEA CH46 109 H6
Litherland Crs
RNFD/HAY WA11 89 F4
Litherland Pk LITH L21 81 J3
Litherland Rd BTL L20 5 F1
Lithou Cl EV L5 113 F2
Little Acre MGHL L31 71 H1
Little Barn Hey NTHTN L30 70 A5
Little Brook La KKBY L32 84 C3
Little Canning St TOX L8 132 E2
Little Catharine St TOX L8 132 E2
Littlecote Cl STHEL WA9 120 A3
Littlecourt VAUX/LVPD L3 112 E3
Little Crosby Rd
CSBY/BLUN L23 69 F2
Little Dl DV/KA/FCH L14 * 115 H4
Littledale Rd DV/KA/FCH L14 115 H4
WAL/EG CH44 111 K4
WARRW/BUR WA5 141 G2
Little Delph RNFD/HAY WA11 90 B4
Littlegate RUNC WA7 177 H5
Little Gn GTS/LS CH66 195 G6
Little Hardman St CLVPS L1 * 9 H6
Little Heath Rd SPK/HALE L24 173 K3
Little Heyes St EV L5 113 J1
Little Hey La FMBY L37 49 H1
Little Howard St
VAUX/LVPD L3 112 D3
Little Huskisson St TOX L8 132 E2
Little La CHTN/BK PR9 23 K4
NSTN CH64 181 G6
Littlemore Cl
GR/UP/WCH CH49 128 E4
Little Moss Hey STBRV L28 100 B6
Little Parkfield Rd AIG/SPK L17 133 G5
Littler Rd RNFD/HAY WA11 89 K6
Little St Bride St TOX L8 9 J7
Little Stanney La CHNE CH2 203 J3
Littlestone Cl WDN WA8 139 F5
Little Storeton La BEB CH63 149 K5
Little St STHEL WA9 104 C4
Littleton Cl CL/PREN CH43 * 130 B5
WARRW/BUR WA5 142 A5
Little Wissage GTS/LS CH66 202 D1
Little Woolton St EHL/KEN L7 113 J6
Littondale Av RAIN/WH L35 * 119 F5
Liverpool Loop Line WLTN L25 135 G2
Liverpool Old Rd STHP PR8 41 J2
Liverpool Pl WDN WA8 157 H2
Liverpool Rd AIMK WN4 78 E6
CH/BCN CH1 202 D4
CSBY/BLUN L23 69 F5
FMBY L37 49 G3
MGHL L31 62 B3
NSTN CH64 181 K6
ORM L39 53 G2
ORM L39 63 K3
PR/KW L34 117 H1
RNFD/HAY WA11 90 B2
SKEL WN8 55 K5
STHP PR8 41 J1
WARRW/BUR WA5 16 A5
WARRW/BUR WA5 140 E3
WDN WA8 18 A2
Liverpool Rd North BRSC L40 38 E5
MGHL L31 62 A5
Liverpool Rd South BRSC L40 38 D6
MGHL L31 62 A6
Liverpool Rw NEWLW WA12 106 D5
Liverpool St ECCL WA10 13 F6
Liverside Rd RF/TRAN CH42 131 G5
Liver St CLVPS L1 8 D7
Livesley's La FMBY L37 50 B3
Livingston Av AIG/SPK L17 133 H5
Livingston Dr AIG/SPK L17 133 H6
Livingston Dr North
AIG/SPK L17 133 H6
Livingston Dr South
AIG/SPK L17 133 H6
Livingstone Cl
WARRW/BUR WA5 142 A2
Livingstone Gdns BIRK CH41 2 C2
Livingstone Rd EP CH65 6 D1
MOR/LEA CH46 110 A3
RF/TRAN CH42 131 J6
Livingstone St BIRK CH41 2 C2
Llandaff Cl GTS/LS CH66 202 C2
Llanrwst Cl TOX L8 132 D4
Lloyd Av BIRK CH41 2 A2
Lloyd Cl NPK/KEN L6 113 H3
Lloyd Crs NEWLW WA12 105 K2
Lloyd Dr EP CH65 203 G2
GR/UP/WCH CH49 128 E6
Lloyd Rd PR/KW L34 102 A6
Lloyd St RNFD/HAY WA11 89 J5
Lobelia Av WLT/FAZ L9 97 K1
Lobelia Gv RUNC WA7 187 J3
Lochinvar Av GTS/LS CH66 194 C3
Lochinvar St WLT/FAZ L9 97 H2
Lochmore Rd CALD/MH L18 153 H2
Lochryan Rd ALL/GAR L19 153 J3
Loch St RUNC WA7 10 D4
Locker Av WARRN/WOL WA2 123 H5
Lockerbie Cl WARRN/WOL WA2 124 A3
Lockerby Rd EHL/KEN L7 114 B4
Locker Pk GR/UP/WCH CH49 128 D5
Locke St ALL/GAR L19 172 B1
Lockett Rd AIMK WN4 79 H4
WDN WA8 158 B1
Lockett St WARRS WA4 143 J6
Lockfields Vw VAUX/LVPD L3 112 E2
Lockgate East RUNC WA7 178 B3
Lockgate West RUNC WA7 178 B3
Locking Stumps La
WARRN/WOL WA2 124 D4
Lockington Cl TOX L8 133 F5
Lock Rd PS/BROM CH62 171 K6
WARR WA1 143 J2
Lock St STHEL WA9 89 F6
Lockton La WARRW/BUR WA5 142 B2
Lockton Rd PR/KW L34 85 G6
Lock Vls WARRS WA4 * 144 A6
Lockwood Vw RUNC WA7 188 E2
Loddon Cl GR/UP/WCH CH49 129 H2
Lodge Hollow FROD/HEL WA6 199 J6
Lodge La NEWLW WA12 91 G2
PS/BROM CH62 151 G5
RNFD/HAY WA11 65 J6
RUNC WA7 177 H5
TOX L8 133 G2
WARRW/BUR WA5 142 B2
WDN WA8 138 A5
Lodge Rd WDN WA8 157 G3
Lodwick St BTL L20 96 D4
Lofthouse Ga WDN WA8 138 E6
Logan Rd BIRK CH41 111 H6
Logfield Dr ALL/GAR L19 154 A6
Lognor Rd KKBY L32 84 B1
Logwood Rd HUY L36 136 D1
Lombard Rd MOR/LEA CH46 109 K5
Lombardy Av
GR/UP/WCH CH49 147 J1
Lomond Gv EP CH65 195 J6
MOR/LEA CH46 129 G1
Lomond Rd EHL/KEN L7 114 C5
Londonderry Rd
CLB/OSW/ST L13 98 B6
London Flds WGNW/BIL/O WN5 77 H4
London La STHP PR8 35 F1
London Rd FROD/HEL WA6 200 E1
VAUX/LVPD L3 9 G3
WARRS WA4 162 C3
London Rw NEWLW WA12 106 D5
London Sq STHP PR8 14 E4
London St CHTN/BK PR9 15 F5
Longacre CHTN/BK PR9 23 H2
Longacre Cl WAL/NB CH45 110 D2
Long Acres GR/UP/WCH CH49 128 E4
Long Acres Rd NSTN CH64 181 K5
Long Av WLT/FAZ L9 82 E5
Longbarn Bvd
WARRN/WOL WA2 124 E5
Long Barn La
WARRN/WOL WA2 124 D5
Longborough Rd PR/KW L34 100 C2
Longbutt La LYMM WA13 165 G1
Longcliffe Dr STHP PR8 33 H5
Longcroft Av ALL/GAR L19 154 A4
Longcroft Sq ALL/GAR L19 154 A4
Longdale La SFTN L29 70 A2
Longdin St WARRS WA4 143 J6
Longdown Rd NG/CROX L11 84 A5
Longfellow Dr RF/TRAN CH42 151 F3
Longfellow St BTL L20 4 B1
TOX L8 133 H2
Longfield FMBY L37 41 H6
Longfield Av CSBY/BLUN L23 69 F3
Longfield Cl GR/UP/WCH CH49 128 E5
Longfield Rd LITH L21 81 J5
WARRN/WOL WA2 123 J6
Longfold MGHL L31 62 C6
Longford Rd STHP PR8 27 H5
Longford St TOX L8 133 F6
WARRN/WOL WA2 142 E2
Long Hey RAIN/WH L35 117 K5
Longhey SKEL WN8 56 E1
Long Hey Rd WKBY CH48 147 F4
Longland Rd WAL/NB CH45 111 H1
Long La ALL/GAR L19 153 K4
ORM L39 53 G2
SFTN L29 69 H1
SKEL WN8 67 G4
WARRN/WOL WA2 123 J6
WAV L15 134 A1
WLT/FAZ L9 83 F6
Longlooms Rd EP CH65 203 H2
Longmead Av AIMK WN4 79 H5
Long Meadow ECCL WA10 102 D1
HES CH60 180 E1
Longmeadow Rd PR/KW L34 100 D1
Long Meanygate CHTN/BK PR9 24 D5
Longmoor Cl AIN/FAZ L10 83 H4
Longmoor Gv WLT/FAZ L9 82 E4
Longmoor La WLT/FAZ L9 82 E5
Longreach Rd DV/KA/FCH L14 115 K4
Longridge Av
GR/UP/WCH CH49 129 F3
RNFD/HAY WA11 89 G6
Longridge Wk ANF/KKDL L4 97 G5
Longshaw Common
WGNW/BIL/O WN5 77 H1
Longshaw St
WARRW/BUR WA5 123 F5
Long Spinney RUNC WA7 178 B5
Longster Trail FROD/HEL WA6 199 K6
Longstone Wk EHL/KEN L7 133 G1
Longton Av GOL/RIS/CU WA3 92 D3
Longton Dr FMBY L37 41 G5
Longton La RAIN/WH L35 118 D2
Longview Av RAIN/WH L35 118 C3
WAL/NB CH45 111 G2
Longview Crs HUY L36 117 F4
Longview Dr HUY L36 117 G4
Longview La HUY L36 117 F2
Longview Rd HUY L36 117 F3
RAIN/WH L35 118 C3
Longville St TOX L8 132 D4
Longwood Cl RNFD/HAY WA11 87 J2
Longwood Rd WARRS WA4 162 D6
Longworth Wy WLTN L25 135 H6
Lonie Gv ECCL WA10 102 E5
Lonsboro Rd WAL/EG CH44 111 J4
Lonsdale Av ECCL WA10 102 D6
ORM L39 45 K4
WAL/NB CH45 111 G1
Lonsdale Cl LITH L21 81 J1
WARRW/BUR WA5 141 F1
WDN WA8 157 H3
Lonsdale Ms LITH L21 81 J1
Lonsdale Rd FMBY L37 48 E2
HLWD L26 155 H5
LITH L21 81 J1
STHP PR8 28 A3
Lonsdale Vls WAL/NB CH45 * 111 G1
Looe Cl WDN WA8 157 K1
Looe Rd NG/CROX L11 84 C6
The Looms NSTN CH64 181 G5
Loomsway PEN/TH CH61 147 K5
Loraine St EV L5 113 H2
Lordens Cl DV/KA/FCH L14 116 A2
Lordens Rd DV/KA/FCH L14 116 B1
Lord Nelson St CLVPS L1 9 G3
WARR WA1 17 F5
Lords Av CL/PREN CH43 129 K1
Lord Sefton Wy FMBY L37 49 K3
Lordsgate Dr BRSC L40 38 E6
Lordsgate La BRSC L40 46 B1
Lordship La FROD/HEL WA6 199 G3
Lords La GOL/RIS/CU WA3 124 E3
Lord St AIMK WN4 * 79 J5
ALL/GAR L19 172 B1
BIRK CH41 3 G3
BRSC L40 38 E4
CHTN/BK PR9 15 F3
CLVP L2 8 D4
ECCL WA10 13 G2
NEWLW WA12 106 A2
RUNC WA7 10 C3
STHP PR8 14 C6
WARRS WA4 16 E7
Lord St Boulevards STHP PR8 14 C6
Lord St West STHP PR8 14 C7
Loreburn Rd WAV L15 134 B3
Lorenzo Dr NG/CROX L11 98 D4
Loretto Dr GR/UP/WCH CH49 129 H3
Loretto Rd WAL/EG CH44 111 F2
Lorn Ct BIRK CH41 * 3 G4
Lorne Ct CL/PREN CH43 * 130 E4
Lorne Rd CL/PREN CH43 130 D5
CSBY/WL L22 80 E2
Lorne St EHL/KEN L7 114 C4
Lorn St BIRK CH41 3 G4
Lorton Av RNFD/HAY WA11 88 D3
Lorton St TOX L8 133 G2
Lostock Av WARRW/BUR WA5 * 142 C1
Lostock Cl WGNW/BIL/O WN5 77 H4
Lothair Rd ANF/KKDL L4 97 J6
Lothian St TOX L8 133 F3
Lotus Gdns STHEL WA9 104 E6
Loudon Gv TOX L8 133 F3
Lough Gn BEB CH63 170 C3
Loughlin Dr NWD/KWIPK L33 72 E4
Loughrigg Av RNFD/HAY WA11 88 E2
Louis Braille Cl NTHTN L30 70 C5
Louis Pasteur Av NTHTN L30 70 C5
Loushers La WARRS WA4 162 C1
Lovage Cl WARRN/WOL WA2 124 E5
Lovelace Rd ALL/GAR L19 153 J4
Love La VAUX/LVPD L3 112 E3
WAL/EG CH44 111 H4
Lovel Rd SPK/HALE L24 173 J3
Lovel Ter WDN WA8 157 G6
Lovel Wy SPK/HALE L24 173 J2
Lovely La WARRW/BUR WA5 142 C2
Lovett Dr RAIN/WH L35 118 A2
Low Bank Rd AIMK WN4 78 D5
Lowcroft SKEL WN8 56 E2
Lowden Av LITH L21 81 J1
Lowe Av WARRS WA4 143 J5
Lowell St ANF/KKDL L4 97 H4
Lower Alt Rd HTWN L38 59 F3
Lower Appleton Rd WDN WA8 19 F1
Lower Bank Vw BTL L20 96 D4
Lower Breck Rd NPK/KEN L6 114 A1
Lower Carr La HTWN L38 50 D6
Lower Castle St CLVP L2 8 C4
Lower Church St WDN WA8 158 B6
Lower Cl HLWD L26 155 K3
Lower Farm Rd WLTN L25 135 G2
Lower Flaybrick Rd
CL/PREN CH43 130 B1
Lower Gn GR/UP/WCH CH49 129 H6
Lower Hey CSBY/BLUN L23 69 J4
Lower House La NG/CROX L11 98 E2
WDN WA8 18 B5
Lower La WLT/FAZ L9 83 H4
Lower Mersey St EP CH65 196 B2
Lower Mersey Vw BTL L20 96 D4
Lower Milk St VAUX/LVPD L3 8 D2
Lower Prom STHP PR8 14 C4
Lower Rake La FROD/HEL WA6 199 J5
Lower Rd HLWD L26 156 A3
PS/BROM CH62 151 G5
Lower Robin Hood La
FROD/HEL WA6 199 J6
Lowerson Crs NG/CROX L11 98 C5
Lowerson Rd NG/CROX L11 98 C5
Lower Thingwall La
PEN/TH CH61 149 F5
Lower Wash La WARRS WA4 143 H6
Lowes Gn FMBY L37 49 H2
Lowe St ECCL WA10 13 F4
GOL/RIS/CU WA3 92 B3
Lowe St South ECCL WA10 13 F5
Loweswater Cl
WARRN/WOL WA2 123 H4
Loweswater Crs
RNFD/HAY WA11 89 K5
Loweswater Wy
NWD/KWIPK L33 72 C5
Lowfield La STHEL WA9 119 H2
Lowfield Rd DV/KA/FCH L14 115 G4
Lowfields Av PS/BROM CH62 184 A4
Lowfields Cl PS/BROM CH62 184 B4
Lowlands Rd RUNC WA7 10 C5
Lowndes Rd NPK/KEN L6 114 B1
Lowry Bank WAL/EG CH44 112 A4
Lowry Cl NWD/KWIPK L33 72 D3
WARRW/BUR WA5 142 A3
Lowry Hill La BRSC L40 47 H1
Lowther Av AIN/FAZ L10 83 G1
MGHL L31 62 C5
Lowther Crs ECCL WA10 102 D5
Lowther Dr RAIN/WH L35 118 D4
Lowther St TOX L8 133 F2
Lowton Gdns GOL/RIS/CU WA3 92 C6
Lowton Rd GOL/RIS/CU WA3 92 C2
Lowwood Gv BIRK CH41 2 E6
Low Wood Gv PEN/TH CH61 168 C1
Lowwood Rd BIRK CH41 2 E6
Low Wood St NPK/KEN L6 113 J5
Loxdale Cl TOX L8 133 F6
Loxdale Dr EP CH65 195 J5
Loxley Cl WARRW/BUR WA5 141 H1
Loxley Rd STHP PR8 28 A3
Loyola Hey RAIN/WH L35 138 D1
Lucania St ALL/GAR L19 172 B1
Lucan Rd AIG/SPK L17 153 F1
Lucerne Rd WAL/EG CH44 111 K5
Lucerne St AIG/SPK L17 133 H6
Lucius Cl WLT/FAZ L9 82 C4
Lucknow St AIG/SPK L17 * 133 H5
Ludlow SKEL WN8 56 E1
Ludlow Cl WARR WA1 144 A1
Ludlow Crs RUNC WA7 176 E5
Ludlow Dr EP CH65 196 D6
ORM L39 45 H4
WKBY CH48 146 C2
Ludlow Gv PS/BROM CH62 171 F4
Ludlow St ANF/KKDL L4 97 H4
Ludwig Rd ANF/KKDL L4 113 K2
Lugard Rd AIG/SPK L17 153 F1
Lugsdale Rd WDN WA8 18 D5
Lugsmore La ECCL WA10 102 E4
Luke St AIMK WN4 79 J4
TOX L8 132 E3
WAL/EG CH44 112 A5
Lulworth SKEL WN8 56 E1
Lulworth Av CSBY/WL L22 80 D2
Lulworth Rd STHP PR8 27 G3
WLTN L25 135 K4
Lumb Brook Rd WARRS WA4 162 D3
Lumber La WARRW/BUR WA5 105 J5
Lumby Av HUY L36 116 E4
Lumley Rd WAL/EG CH44 111 K4
Lumley St ALL/GAR L19 153 J5
Lunar Dr NTHTN L30 70 C5
Lunar Rd WLT/FAZ L9 82 E5
Lundy Dr EP CH65 203 G3
Lune Av MGHL L31 62 C5
Lunehurst GOL/RIS/CU WA3 93 F3
Lunesdale Av WLT/FAZ L9 82 E4
Lune St CSBY/BLUN L23 69 F5
Lune Wy WDN WA8 157 H2
Lunsford Rd DV/KA/FCH L14 115 K3
Lunt Av NTHTN L30 82 D1
RAIN/WH L35 118 A4
Lunt Rd BTL L20 81 K6
SFTN L29 60 E5
Lunt's Heath Rd WDN WA8 139 G4
Lupin Dr RNFD/HAY WA11 90 E5
Lupton Dr CSBY/BLUN L23 69 H5
Lupus Wy GTS/LS CH66 195 J6
Luscombe Cl HLWD L26 155 K3
Lusitania Rd ANF/KKDL L4 97 J4
Luther Gv STHEL WA9 105 F3
Luton Gv ANF/KKDL L4 97 H5
Luton Rd EP CH65 195 K4
Luton St EV L5 112 E1
WDN WA8 * 18 D6
Lutyens Cl ANF/KKDL L4 97 H6
Luxmore Rd ANF/KKDL L4 97 J4
Lycett Rd ANF/KKDL L4 98 A6
WAL/EG CH44 110 E2
Lychgate WARRS WA4 161 J4
Lycroft Cl RUNC WA7 186 E1
Lydbrook Cl RF/TRAN CH42 131 J6
Lydbury Cl WARRW/BUR WA5 122 D5
Lydbury Crs KKBY L32 84 E3
Lydd Cl SPK/HALE L24 173 G1
Lydden Rd EP CH65 6 C1
Lydford Rd WD/CROXPK L12 99 F5
Lydia Ann St CLVPS L1 9 F6
Lydiate La CSBY/BLUN L23 69 K3
NSTN CH64 193 F1
RUNC WA7 176 B6
WLTN L25 155 G1
Lydiate Pk CSBY/BLUN L23 69 J3
Lydiate Rd BTL L20 81 K6
Lydiate Station Rd MGHL L31 61 G2
The Lydiate HES CH60 167 K6
Lydieth Lea NTHLY L27 136 B3
Lydney Rd HUY L36 116 D3
Lydstep Ct WARRW/BUR WA5 * 122 E5
Lyelake Cl KKBY L32 84 E2
Lyelake La BRSC L40 55 F4
Lyelake Rd KKBY L32 84 E2
Lyle St EV L5 113 F2
Lyme Cl HUY L36 117 G1
Lyme Cross Rd HUY L36 117 F1
Lyme Gv HUY L36 117 F2
LYMM WA13 164 D1
Lyme St NEWLW WA12 105 J1
RNFD/HAY WA11 90 D5
Lymington Gv NTHTN L30 70 C6
Lymington Rd WAL/EG CH44 111 F3
Lymmhay La LYMM WA13 145 K5
Lymmington Av LYMM WA13 145 H6
Lymm Rd CL/PREN CH43 129 K2
WARRS WA4 144 E6
Lynas Gdns ALL/GAR L19 153 J3
Lynas St BIRK CH41 2 D1
Lyncot Rd WLT/FAZ L9 82 E3
Lyncroft Rd WAL/EG CH44 111 J5
Lyndale SKEL WN8 56 D1
Lyndale Av PS/BROM CH62 184 B3
WARRN/WOL WA2 143 G1
Lyndene Rd WLTN L25 135 H3
Lyndhurst SKEL WN8 56 D1
Lyndhurst Av CALD/MH L18 134 A6
PEN/TH CH61 168 A2
Lyndhurst Cl PEN/TH CH61 148 D6
Lyndhurst Rd CALD/MH L18 134 A5
CSBY/BLUN L23 69 H5
HOY CH47 108 C6
PEN/TH CH61 147 K6
STHP PR8 27 H5
WAL/NB CH45 111 F1
Lyndhurst Wy HUY L36 116 E5
Lyndon Dr CALD/MH L18 134 C5
Lyndon Gv RUNC WA7 176 E5
Lyndor Cl WLTN L25 154 E2
Lyndor Rd WLTN L25 154 E2
Lyneal Av GTS/LS CH66 202 A1
Lyneham RAIN/WH L35 118 B5
Lynham Av
WARRW/BUR WA5 * 141 J4
Lynholme Rd ANF/KKDL L4 97 K6
Lynmouth Rd AIG/SPK L17 153 F3
Lynnbank CL/PREN CH43 130 E5
Lynnbank Rd CALD/MH L18 134 E4
Lynn Cl ECCL WA10 102 E1
RUNC WA7 177 F6
Lynndene GTS/LS CH66 195 G2
Lynscott Pl CHLDW L16 134 E1
Lynsted Rd DV/KA/FCH L14 115 K4
Lynton Cl ALL/GAR L19 153 J3
HES CH60 181 G1
WARRW/BUR WA5 141 F5
Lynton Crs WDN WA8 157 K1
Lynton Dr BEB CH63 170 C2
STHP PR8 27 F6
Lynton Gn WLTN L25 135 G5
Lynton Gv STHEL WA9 120 A2
Lynton Rd HUY L36 117 H4
STHP PR8 34 A1
WAL/NB CH45 110 E1
Lynton Wy ECCL WA10 87 J5
Lynwood Av GOL/RIS/CU WA3 93 F5
ORM L39 53 G2
WAL/EG CH44 111 G4
WARRS WA4 162 B4
Lynwood Cl SKEL WN8 57 F6
Lynwood Dr PEN/TH CH61 148 B5
Lynwood End ORM L39 * 53 G2
Lynwood Gdns WLT/FAZ L9 82 C6
Lynwood Rd WLT/FAZ L9 82 C6
The Lynxway WD/CROXPK L12 115 H2
Lyon Cl ECCL WA10 12 E5
Lyon Rd ANF/KKDL L4 113 K1
Lyons Cl MOR/LEA CH46 109 J6
Lyon's La WARRS WA4 162 C5
Lyons Pl WLTN L25 155 G3
Lyons Rd MOR/LEA CH46 109 J6
STHP PR8 27 H2
WARRW/BUR WA5 141 G5
Lyon St AIMK WN4 78 E2
ALL/GAR L19 172 B1
ECCL WA10 12 D5
WARRS WA4 143 J6
Lyra Rd CSBY/WL L22 80 E2
Lyster Cl GOL/RIS/CU WA3 125 H4
Lyster Rd BTL L20 4 B4
Lytham Cl WLT/FAZ L9 83 J2
Lytham Ct KKBY L32 72 B5
Lytham Rd AIMK WN4 78 E4
CHTN/BK PR9 23 J1
WDN WA8 158 C1
Lytham Wy WD/CROXPK L12 115 J1
Lythgoes La WARRN/WOL WA2 16 E3
Lytles Cl FMBY L37 49 G3
Lyttelton Rd AIG/SPK L17 153 F1
Lytton Av RF/TRAN CH42 150 E2
Lytton Gv LITH L21 81 H5
Lytton St NPK/KEN L6 113 H4

M

Mab La WD/CROXPK L12 99 K5

Macalpine Cl GR/UP/WCH CH49 129 H3
Macarthur Rd WARRW/BUR WA5 * 141 J3
Macbeth St BTL L20 96 E4
Macdermott Rd WDN WA8 158 A6
Macdona Dr WKBY CH48 146 C3
Macdonald Av RNFD/HAY WA11 * 89 H6
Macdonald Dr GR/UP/WCH CH49 128 E6
Macdonald Rd MOR/LEA CH46 128 D1
Macdonald St WAV L15 133 K1
Mace Rd NG/CROX L11 99 G2
Macfarren St CLB/OSW/ST L13 114 E4
Mackenzie Rd MOR/LEA CH46 110 B4
Mackenzie St NPK/KEN L6 113 J2
Mackets Cl WLTN L25 155 F2
Macket's La WLTN L25 155 F2
Mack Gv NTHTN L30 82 A1
Macqueen St CLB/OSW/ST L13 114 E5
Maddock Rd WAL/EG CH44 111 K2
Maddocks St CLB/OSW/ST L13 114 E5
Maddock St BIRK CH41 2 C1
Maddrell St VAUX/LVPD L3 112 D3
Madelaine St TOX L8 133 F3
Madeley Cl WKBY CH48 146 C2
Madeley Dr WKBY CH48 146 C2
Madeley St NPK/KEN L6 114 A3
Madeline McKenna Ct WDN WA8 * 138 B6
Madiera Dr WLTN L25 135 J3
Madingley Ct CHTN/BK PR9 * 23 H3
Madryn Av NWD/KWIPK L33 85 F1
Madryn St TOX L8 133 F4
Maelor Cl BEB CH63 183 J1
Mafeking Cl WAV L15 * 114 D6
Mafeking Pl AIMK WN4 79 H6
Magazine Av WAL/NB CH45 95 H6
Magazine Brow WAL/NB CH45 95 J6
Magazine La PS/BROM CH62 171 G2
WAL/NB CH45 95 J6
Magazine Rd PS/BROM CH62 171 F2
Magazines Prom WAL/NB CH45 95 J6
Magazine Wk PS/BROM CH62 * 171 F2
Magdala St TOX L8 133 H2
Magdalen Dr AIMK WN4 78 E5
Magdalene Sq NTHTN L30 * 70 C5
Maggots Nook Rd RNFD/HAY WA11 66 C6
Maghull La MGHL L31 63 G6
Maghull St CLVPS L1 8 D7
Mag La LYMM WA13 165 G4
Magnolia Cl GTS/LS CH66 202 D2
HLWD L26 155 G1
RNFD/HAY WA11 89 J6
WARR WA1 144 D2
Magnolia Dr RUNC WA7 187 J3
Magnolia Wk GR/UP/WCH CH49 147 K1
Magnum St EV L5 113 G2
Maguire Av BTL L20 5 K3
Mahon Av BTL L20 82 A5
Mahon Ct TOX L8 * 132 E2
Maiden Gdns EP CH65 196 C6
Maiden La CLB/OSW/ST L13 98 B6
Maidford Rd DV/KA/FCH L14 115 K2
Maidstone Dr DV/KA/FCH L14 115 K2
Main Av ECCL WA10 102 E5
Main Cl RNFD/HAY WA11 89 K5
Main Dr RAIN/WH L35 118 A6
Main Front RAIN/WH L35 118 A6
Main Rd PS/BROM CH62 170 D1
Mainside Rd KKBY L32 84 E2
Main St FROD/HEL WA6 200 D1
RUNC WA7 177 J5
WGNW/BIL/O WN5 77 H4
Maintree Crs SPK/HALE L24 174 B1
Mainwaring Rd PS/BROM CH62 171 F5
WAL/EG CH44 111 K4
Mairesfield Av WARRS WA4 163 G1
Mairscough La ORM L39 51 J5
Maitland Cl TOX L8 133 G2
Maitland Rd WAL/NB CH45 95 J5
Maitland St TOX L8 * 133 G2
Major Cross St WDN WA8 18 D5
Major St EV L5 113 F1
Makerfield Dr NEWLW WA12 106 A1
Makin St ANF/KKDL L4 97 H3
Malcolm Av WARRN/WOL WA2 123 K6
Malcolm Crs BEB CH63 183 K1
Malcolm Gv BTL L20 97 F4
Malcolm Pl WAV L15 114 D6
Malcolm St RUNC WA7 11 G5
Malden Rd NPK/KEN L6 114 A4
Maldon Cl HLWD L26 155 J5
Maldwyn Rd WAL/EG CH44 111 H2
Maley Cl TOX L8 133 F5
Malham Cl STHP PR8 28 B4
Malhamdale Av RAIN/WH L35 119 F5
Malika Pl AIMK WN4 * 78 D3
Malin Cl SPK/HALE L24 174 E3
Maliston Rd WARRW/BUR WA5 141 J4
Mallaby St BIRK CH41 130 D1
Mallard Cl HLWD L26 155 H2
ORM L39 53 G3
RUNC WA7 187 J2
WARRN/WOL WA2 123 K4
WD/CROXPK L12 99 K2
Mallard Gdns STHEL WA9 119 G1
Mallard La GOL/RIS/CU WA3 125 H4
The Mallards CHTN/BK PR9 24 A2
Mallard Wy MOR/LEA CH46 109 G6
RNFD/HAY WA11 88 E5
Mallee Av CHTN/BK PR9 23 J2
Mallee Crs CHTN/BK PR9 23 J2
Malleson Rd CLB/OSW/ST L13 98 C6
Mallins Cl TOX L8 133 F5
Mallory Av MGHL L31 61 K3
Mallory Gv RNFD/HAY WA11 89 G5
Mallory Rd EP CH65 6 A6
RF/TRAN CH42 150 C1
Mallowdale Cl PS/BROM CH62 184 B2
Mallow Rd NPK/KEN L6 114 A4
Mallow Wy HUY L36 136 C1
The Mall NPK/KEN L6 * 113 J2
Malmesbury Cl GR/UP/WCH CH49 128 D5
Malmesbury Pk RUNC WA7 178 C2
Malmesbury Rd NG/CROX L11 98 C3
Malpas Av CL/PREN CH43 149 K1
Malpas Dr BEB CH63 150 D4
WARRW/BUR WA5 141 K5
Malpas Gv WAL/NB CH45 111 G1
Malpas Rd EP CH65 195 J5
NG/CROX L11 84 C6
RUNC WA7 176 E6
WAL/NB CH45 111 F1
Malpas Wy WARRW/BUR WA5 * 141 K5
Malta Cl HUY L36 116 D4
Malta St TOX L8 132 E4
Malta Wk TOX L8 132 E4
Malt House Ct ECCL WA10 87 K5
Maltkiln La ORM L39 53 J5
Maltmans Rd LYMM WA13 145 J6
Malton Av GOL/RIS/CU WA3 93 F4
Malton Cl WDN WA8 138 B4
Malton Rd WLTN L25 155 F2
Malt St TOX L8 133 G1
Malvern Av DV/KA/FCH L14 115 K5
EP CH65 196 B6
Malvern Cl AIMK WN4 79 G5
KKBY L32 72 B5
WARRW/BUR WA5 141 H1
Malvern Crs DV/KA/FCH L14 115 K5
Malvern Gv RF/TRAN CH42 150 C1
WLT/FAZ L9 83 F1
Malvern Rd BTL L20 81 K6
NPK/KEN L6 114 A4
STHEL WA9 104 D2
WAL/NB CH45 110 D2
The Malverns CL/PREN CH43 * 130 D6
Malwood St TOX L8 132 E6
Manchester Rd CHTN/BK PR9 15 G3
PR/KW L34 117 K2
WARR WA1 144 E2
Manchester Rw NEWLW WA12 106 D5
Manchester St (Queensway) CLVPS L1 8 E3
Mancroft Cl WARR WA1 144 D2
Mandeville Rd STHP PR8 33 H4
Mandeville St ANF/KKDL L4 97 H3
Manesty's La CLVPS L1 8 E5
Manfield SKEL WN8 56 C2
Manica Crs AIN/FAZ L10 83 J5
Manion Av MGHL L31 61 K2
Manion Cl MGHL L31 61 K2
Manley Av GOL/RIS/CU WA3 92 A1
Manley Cl CL/PREN CH43 130 C6
Manley Gdns WARRW/BUR WA5 142 C4
Manley Pl STHEL WA9 103 G6
Manley Rd CSBY/WL L22 80 D1
HUY L36 136 D1
Manley Vw CHNE CH2 198 D6
Manna Dr CHNE CH2 198 D6
Mannering Rd AIG/SPK L17 133 G5
Manners La HES CH60 180 D1
Manningham Rd NPK/KEN L6 113 K1
Manning Rd STHP PR8 28 B1
Manning St ECCL WA10 12 E6
Mannington Cl HOY CH47 127 K1
Mann Island VAUX/LVPD L3 8 B5
Mann St TOX L8 132 D3
Manor Av BRSC L40 46 D1
CSBY/BLUN L23 68 E4
GOL/RIS/CU WA3 92 D3
NEWLW WA12 105 K1
RAIN/WH L35 118 E5
Manorbier Crs WLT/FAZ L9 97 J2
Manor Cl AIMK WN4 78 B6
BTL L20 5 K6
NSTN CH64 191 H2
WARR WA1 144 C2
Manor Ct GOL/RIS/CU WA3 92 D3
Manor Crs BRSC L40 46 D1
WLTN L25 154 E2
Manor Dr BRSC L40 46 D1
CSBY/BLUN L23 68 E4
GR/UP/WCH CH49 129 G2
NTHTN L30 70 E6
Manor Farm Rd HUY L36 117 F6
RUNC WA7 178 C1
Manor Fell RUNC WA7 178 A6
Manor Gdns BRSC L40 46 D1
Manor Gv KKBY L32 84 A1
SKEL WN8 56 B4
Manor Hl CL/PREN CH43 130 D3
Manor House Cl MGHL L31 62 A6
RNFD/HAY WA11 88 D1
Manor House Dr SKEL WN8 67 G4
Manorial Rd NSTN CH64 191 H1
Manorial Rd South NSTN CH64 191 H1
Manor La GTS/LS CH66 195 G6
RF/TRAN CH42 151 F1
WAL/NB CH45 111 J2
Manor Ldg FMBY L37 48 E1
Manor Ms WAL/NB CH45 * 111 J2
Manor Park Av RUNC WA7 178 B1
Manor Park Dr GTS/LS CH66 202 B1
Manor Pl PS/BROM CH62 151 J6
Manor Rd BEB CH63 169 F4
BRSC L40 46 D1
CHTN/BK PR9 23 J3
CSBY/BLUN L23 68 D4
FROD/HEL WA6 187 F6
HOY CH47 127 H1
LYMM WA13 165 F1
PEN/TH CH61 148 A5
PS/BROM CH62 184 B1
RNFD/HAY WA11 90 E4
RUNC WA7 177 G3
WAL/EG CH44 111 H2
WDN WA8 157 G2
WLTN L25 154 E2
Manorside Cl GR/UP/WCH CH49 129 G3
Manor St GOL/RIS/CU WA3 92 C2
STHEL WA9 104 A3
Manor Vw WD/CROXPK L12 99 K4
Manor Wy WLTN L25 154 E2
Manorwood Dr RAIN/WH L35 118 A5
Mansart Cl AIMK WN4 79 J6
Manse Gdns NEWLW WA12 106 D1
Mansell Cl WDN WA8 139 H4
Mansell Dr HLWD L26 155 H5
Mansell Rd NPK/KEN L6 113 K4
Mansfield Cl GOL/RIS/CU WA3 125 J3
Mansfield Rd EP CH65 202 E1
Mansfield St GOL/RIS/CU WA3 91 K2
VAUX/LVPD L3 9 G1
Mansion Dr NG/CROX L11 99 F1
Manston Rd WARRW/BUR WA5 141 G6
Manton Rd NPK/KEN L6 114 A4
Manuel Perez Rd WARRW/BUR WA5 141 J3
Manvers Rd CHLDW L16 115 J6
Manville Rd WAL/NB CH45 95 H6
Manville St STHEL WA9 104 A4
Manx Jane's La CHTN/BK PR9 23 J1
Manx Rd WARRS WA4 142 E6
Maori Dr FROD/HEL WA6 200 D1
Maple Av BRSC L40 38 E5
GOL/RIS/CU WA3 93 G4
GTS/LS CH66 195 F3
NEWLW WA12 106 D3
RNFD/HAY WA11 90 A4
RUNC WA7 177 F5
RUNC WA7 187 K3
WDN WA8 * 19 F1
Maple Cl FMBY L37 48 C4
LITH L21 81 H5
RAIN/WH L35 118 A4
WD/CROXPK L12 99 H2
WGNW/BIL/O WN5 77 G4
Maple Crs HUY L36 116 D5
WARRW/BUR WA5 141 G5
Mapledale Rd CALD/MH L18 134 B4
Maple Gv ECCL WA10 102 E2
GTS/LS CH66 202 E2
PS/BROM CH62 170 E5
RAIN/WH L35 118 A2
TOX L8 133 H3
WARRS WA4 143 G6
Maple Rd WARR WA1 144 D2
WARRN/WOL WA2 123 H1
Maple St AIMK WN4 79 F3
BIRK CH41 2 D7
STHP PR8 15 K7
Mapleton Cl CL/PREN CH43 149 H2
Mapleton Dr RUNC WA7 187 J4
Maple Tree Gv HES CH60 168 C4
Maplewood KKBY L32 84 E3
SKEL WN8 56 C1
Maplewood Cl NTHLY L27 136 B4
Maplewood Gv CL/PREN CH43 130 B1
Mapplewell Crs WARRW/BUR WA5 141 H3
Marathon Cl NPK/KEN L6 113 H3
Marble Cl BTL L20 4 E7
Marbury Gdns EP CH65 195 J3
Marbury Rd KKBY L32 84 B1
Marbury St WARRS WA4 17 F7
Marc Av MGHL L31 72 A5
Marcham Wy NG/CROX L11 99 F4
Marchant Cl NTHTN L30 82 D3
Marchbank Rd SKEL WN8 55 K4
Marchfield Rd WLT/FAZ L9 82 C6
March Rd NPK/KEN L6 114 B2
Marchwiel Rd EP CH65 7 G6
Marchwood Wy WLTN L25 135 H2
Marcien Wy WDN WA8 138 E6
Marcot Rd NPK/KEN L6 114 B3
Marcross Cl WARRW/BUR WA5 122 E6
Marcus St BIRK CH41 3 F2
Mardale Av RNFD/HAY WA11 88 E3
WARRN/WOL WA2 123 J4
Mardale Cl NTHLY L27 136 D6
STHP PR8 33 H5
Mardale Lawn NTHLY L27 136 D6
Mardale Rd HUY L36 116 C2
Mareth Cl CALD/MH L18 153 H1
Marford Rd WD/CROXPK L12 99 F6
Marfords Av BEB CH63 170 E6
Margaret Av BTL L20 81 K4
STHEL WA9 104 A6
WARR WA1 144 A2
Margaret Ct WDN WA8 * 18 E6
Margaret Rd ANF/KKDL L4 5 K7
CSBY/BLUN L23 68 B4
Margaret's La GTS/LS CH66 194 D2
Margaret St NPK/KEN L6 113 J3
STHEL WA9 * 120 C4
Margery Rd ECCL WA10 102 E4
Marian Av NEWLW WA12 105 J2
Marian Cl RAIN/WH L35 118 E5
The Marian Cl NTHTN L30 70 B5
Marian Dr MOR/LEA CH46 129 F1
RAIN/WH L35 118 D5
Marian Rd RNFD/HAY WA11 90 D4
Marians Dr ORM L39 45 J3
The Marian Sq NTHTN L30 70 B6
The Marian Wy NTHTN L30 70 B6
Maria Rd WLT/FAZ L9 97 H2
Marie Curie Av NTHTN L30 70 C5
Marie Dr WARRS WA4 163 J1
Marigold Wy STHEL WA9 104 E6
Marina Av LITH L21 81 J4
STHEL WA9 104 A6
WARRW/BUR WA5 141 J5
Marina Crs HUY L36 116 D6
NTHTN L30 82 D2
Marina Dr EP CH65 6 D5
WARRN/WOL WA2 123 J6
Marina Gv RUNC WA7 11 G5
Marina La RUNC WA7 178 D6
Marina Rd FMBY L37 49 F4
The Marina CSBY/WL L22 * 80 D1
Marina Village RUNC WA7 178 D6
Marine Crs CSBY/WL L22 80 E2
Marine Dr CHTN/BK PR9 20 B6
CHTN/BK PR9 21 F5
HES CH60 167 H6
STHP PR8 14 A4
STHP PR8 14 D1
STHP PR8 22 D3
STHP PR8 27 F1
Marine Gate Man CHTN/BK PR9 * 15 F2
Marine House VAUX/LVPD L3 * 132 C3
Marine Pde STHP PR8 14 C2
Marine Pk WKBY CH48 127 G5
Marine Prom WAL/NB CH45 95 H4
Mariner Cl RUNC WA7 188 C1
Marine Rd HOY CH47 127 F2
Mariners Rd CSBY/BLUN L23 80 C1
WAL/NB CH45 95 J6
Mariners Whf VAUX/LVPD L3 132 B3
Marine Ter CSBY/WL L22 80 E3
Marion Dr RUNC WA7 186 C1
Marion Gv CALD/MH L18 153 K1
Marion Rd BTL L20 82 A5
Marion St BIRK CH41 3 G4
Maritime Cl NEWLW WA12 91 H6
Maritime Ct NTHTN L30 70 C4
Maritime Pk BIRK CH41 * 2 C6
Maritime Pl VAUX/LVPD L3 * 9 H1
Maritime Vw RF/TRAN CH42 131 G6
Maritime Wy CLVPS L1 8 E6
Mariton Cl CALD/MH L18 154 A1
Marius Cl ANF/KKDL L4 97 H5
Mark Av GTS/LS CH66 195 F5
Market Ap AIMK WN4 * 79 G6
Market Ga WARR WA1 16 D5
Market Pl BIRK CH41 3 G5
PR/KW L34 117 K1
Market Sq CLVPS L1 * 9 F4
Market St BIRK CH41 3 H4
ECCL WA10 13 G6
EP CH65 6 C6
HOY CH47 127 G2
NEWLW WA12 106 A1
STHP PR8 14 D5
WDN WA8 18 D5
Market Wy CLVPS L1 * 9 F4
Markfield Crs RNFD/HAY WA11 89 F6
WLTN L25 155 G2
Markfield Rd BTL L20 81 J6
Markham Dr STHP PR8 28 B5
Markham Gv BIRK CH41 130 C1
Mark Rake PS/BROM CH62 171 F4
Mark Rd HTWN L38 59 F3
Mark St EV L5 113 G1
Marksway PEN/TH CH61 168 A1
Marland SKEL WN8 56 C1
Marlborough SKEL WN8 56 C1
Marlborough Av MGHL L31 62 B4
NTHTN L30 82 D1
Marlborough Crs WARRS WA4 162 E1
WDN WA8 139 F4
Marlborough Gv CL/PREN CH43 130 E5
Marlborough Pl VAUX/LVPD L3 * 8 D1
Marlborough Rd CHTN/BK PR9 15 H4
CLB/OSW/ST L13 114 B1
CSBY/WL L22 81 F3
EP CH65 196 C6
PR/KW L34 102 A6
Marlborough St VAUX/LVPD L3 8 D1
Marlborough Wk EP CH65 196 B6
Marlbrook Rd WLTN L25 135 J3
Marldon Av CSBY/BLUN L23 81 F1
Marldon Rd WD/CROXPK L12 99 F5
Marled Hey STBRV L28 100 A5
Marley Cl RAIN/WH L35 119 G6
Marlfield La PEN/TH CH61 168 A1
Marlfield Rd WARRS WA4 163 F1
WD/CROXPK L12 115 F1
Marline Av BEB CH63 183 K1
Marling Cl FROD/HEL WA6 201 G3
Marling Pk WDN WA8 157 G2
Marlow Cl GOL/RIS/CU WA3 124 E2
Marlowe Cl ALL/GAR L19 153 K6
WDN WA8 18 A2
Marlowe Dr WD/CROXPK L12 114 E1
Marlowe Rd NSTN CH64 191 K1
WAL/EG CH44 111 G3
Marl Rd NTHTN L30 70 E6
NWD/KWIPK L33 73 H6
Marlsford St NPK/KEN L6 114 A4
Marlston Av PEN/TH CH61 148 C5
Marlston Pl RUNC WA7 186 E1
Marlwood Av WAL/EG CH44 110 E2
Marmaduke St EHL/KEN L7 113 K6
Marmion Av BTL L20 82 B4
Marmion Cl GOL/RIS/CU WA3 93 F2
Marmion Rd AIG/SPK L17 133 G5
HOY CH47 127 G2
Marmonde St ANF/KKDL L4 97 G5
Marnwood Rd KKBY L32 84 C2
Marple Cl CL/PREN CH43 130 B6
Marquis St BIRK CH41 131 H5
PS/BROM CH62 151 G4
VAUX/LVPD L3 9 H3
Marram Cl MOR/LEA CH46 110 A6
Marron Av WARRN/WOL WA2 123 H5
Marryat Cl WARRN/WOL WA2 123 G1
Marsden Av ECCL WA10 12 A3
WARRS WA4 143 K5
Marsden Cl WAL/EG CH44 111 K2
Marsden Ct WDN WA8 138 D5
Marsden Rd CHTN/BK PR9 23 G6
HLWD L26 155 J5
Marsden St NPK/KEN L6 113 J4
Marsden Wy NPK/KEN L6 * 113 J4
Marshall Av STHEL WA9 * 104 A5
WARRW/BUR WA5 123 F5
Marshall Pl VAUX/LVPD L3 * 112 E3
Marshall Rd WARR WA1 144 C2
Marshallsay FMBY L37 49 G3
Marshall's Cl MGHL L31 62 A3
Marshalls Cross Rd STHEL WA9 119 K1
Marshall St BIRK CH41 2 C1
Marsham Cl GR/UP/WCH CH49 * 129 H2
Marsham Rd WLTN L25 135 K4
Marsh Av BTL L20 82 B5
Marsh Brows FMBY L37 48 E3
Marshfield Cl HUY L36 117 F4
Marshfield Ct MOR/LEA CH46 109 J4
Marshfield Rd NG/CROX L11 99 F4
Marshgate WDN WA8 157 G5
Marshgate Pl FROD/HEL WA6 187 F5
Marshgate Rd NG/CROX L11 99 F3
Marsh Hall Rd WDN WA8 139 G5
Marsh House Ln WARRN/WOL WA2 17 G1
Marshlands Rd NSTN CH64 191 K4
WAL/NB CH45 110 E1
Marsh La BEB CH63 150 B4
BTL L20 4 C2
CHNE CH2 198 B3
FROD/HEL WA6 200 D1
HTWN L38 59 K3
RUNC WA7 177 J2
WARRS WA4 189 J4
WARRW/BUR WA5 159 K1
Marsh Moss La BRSC L40 38 C2
Marsh Rd CHTN/BK PR9 21 K2
Marshside Cl TOX L8 132 E4
Marshside Rd CHTN/BK PR9 20 B6
Marsh St BTL L20 97 F4
WARR WA1 17 J1
WDN WA8 158 B5
Marshway Dr NEWLW WA12 106 B1
Marsland Gv STHEL WA9 104 C5
Marson St WARRN/WOL WA2 16 C3
Marston Cl CL/PREN CH43 149 J1
PS/BROM CH62 184 B4
Marston Crs HTWN L38 59 G5
Marston Gdns EP CH65 195 J3
Marten Av BEB CH63 170 E6
Martensen St EHL/KEN L7 113 K6
Martham Cl WARRS WA4 143 K6
Martin Av ECCL WA10 88 C5
NEWLW WA12 91 G6
WARRN/WOL WA2 123 K6
Martin Cl CALD/MH L18 153 H2
PEN/TH CH61 147 K5
RAIN/WH L35 118 C3
RUNC WA7 177 K6
Martindale Gv RUNC WA7 187 G2
Martindale Rd CALD/MH L18 134 E4
PS/BROM CH62 171 G4
RNFD/HAY WA11 88 E1
WGNW/BIL/O WN5 77 G5
Martine Cl MGHL L31 72 A5
Martin Gv RAIN/WH L35 118 A2
Martinhall Rd WLT/FAZ L9 98 D1
Martin La BRSC L40 37 J1
Martin Rd CALD/MH L18 153 H2
FROD/HEL WA6 200 E1
Martins La SKEL WN8 57 F6
WAL/EG CH44 111 J3
Martland Av AIN/FAZ L10 71 H6
GOL/RIS/CU WA3 92 E4
Martland Rd WLTN L25 135 K5
Mart La BRSC L40 38 E4
Martlesham Crs GR/UP/WCH CH49 128 C6
Martlett Rd WD/CROXPK L12 115 H2
Martock RAIN/WH L35 118 B5
Marton Cl SPK/HALE L24 173 J3
Marton Gn SPK/HALE L24 * 173 J3
Marton Rd HUY L36 116 E1
Marvin St NPK/KEN L6 113 J4
Mary Av STHP PR8 34 A3
Marybone VAUX/LVPD L3 8 D2
Maryfield Cl GOL/RIS/CU WA3 92 B4
Maryhill Rd RUNC WA7 176 D5
Maryland La MOR/LEA CH46 109 H6
Maryland St CLVPS L1 9 H6
Marylebone Av STHEL WA9 119 H1
Mary Rd BTL L20 82 A5
Mary Stockton Ct LITH L21 * 81 H5
Mary St STHEL WA9 120 C4
WDN WA8 19 K5
Maryton Gra CALD/MH L18 154 A1
Maryville Cl EP CH65 6 E1
Maryville Rd PR/KW L34 118 A1
Marywell Cl STHEL WA9 104 B6
Masefield Av WDN WA8 18 B4
Masefield Cl PS/BROM CH62 151 F4
Masefield Crs NTHTN L30 82 A3
Masefield Gv CHLDW L16 135 G1
ECCL WA10 12 A1
Masefield Pl NTHTN L30 82 B3
Masefield Rd CSBY/BLUN L23 69 K3
Maskell Rd CLB/OSW/ST L13 114 D4
Mason Av WARR WA1 143 H1
WDN WA8 139 F5
Mason Cl AIMK WN4 79 J5
GTS/LS CH66 202 B1
Mason St CSBY/WL L22 80 E2
EHL/KEN L7 113 J6
RUNC WA7 11 H3
WAL/NB CH45 95 H5
WARR WA1 17 G5
WLTN L25 154 D1
Massam Cl RNFD/HAY WA11 75 H3
Massam's La FMBY L37 40 E5
Massey Av LYMM WA13 164 B1
WARRW/BUR WA5 123 F5
Massey Brook La LYMM WA13 164 C1
Masseyfield Rd RUNC WA7 187 K2
Massey Pk WAL/NB CH45 111 G2
Massey St BIRK CH41 2 D1
STHEL WA9 104 A5
Masters Wy ALL/GAR L19 172 C1
Mather Av CALD/MH L18 134 C5
GOL/RIS/CU WA3 93 F5
STHEL WA9 104 C2
Mather Rd CL/PREN CH43 130 E4
Mathers Cl WARRN/WOL WA2 124 C3
Mathew St CLVP L2 8 D4

Mathieson Rd WDN WA8 157 K6
Matlock Av WLT/FAZ L9 82 D5
Matlock Cl WARRW/BUR WA5 141 H1
Matlock Crs STHP PR8 27 J3
Matlock Rd STHP PR8 27 J4
Matterdale Cl FROD/HEL WA6 201 G2
Matthew Cl WAL/EG CH44 112 A5
Matthews St WARR WA1 17 H1
Matthew St WAL/EG CH44 112 A5
Matty's La FROD/HEL WA6 200 D2
Maud St TOX L8 133 F3
Maunders Ct CSBY/BLUN L23 69 G4
Mauretania Rd ANF/KKDL L4 97 J3
Mavis Dr GR/UP/WCH CH49 129 H6
Mawdsley Av WARR WA1 144 D2
Mawdsley Cl FMBY L37 49 H2
Mawdsley Ter ORM L39 45 K3
Mawson Cl WARRW/BUR WA5 142 A1
Max Rd DV/KA/FCH L14 115 K2
Maxton Rd NPK/KEN L6 114 A4
Maxwell Cl EP CH65 202 E1
GR/UP/WCH CH49 129 H3
Maxwell Pl CLB/OSW/ST L13 114 D1
Maxwell Rd CLB/OSW/ST L13 114 D1
Maxwell St ECCL WA10 12 D6
GOL/RIS/CU WA3 125 G1
May Av WAL/EG CH44 111 K5
Maybank Cl CHTN/BK PR9 23 J4
Maybank Gv AIG/SPK L17 153 G2
Maybank Rd RF/TRAN CH42 131 G5
Mayberry Gv
WARRN/WOL WA2 124 C6
Maybury Wy AIG/SPK L17 152 D1
May Cl LITH L21 81 J5
Mayer Av BEB CH63 170 B1
Mayew Rd PEN/TH CH61 148 C5
Mayfair Av CSBY/BLUN L23 69 F4
DV/KA/FCH L14 115 K4
Mayfair Cl HTWN L38 59 F5
NPK/KEN L6 113 K3
WARRW/BUR WA5 140 E2
Mayfair Gv WDN WA8 157 J2
Mayfayre Av MGHL L31 61 K2
Mayfield ANF/KKDL L4 97 G5
Mayfield Av FMBY L37 48 C4
STHEL WA9 103 G5
WDN WA8 157 G2
Mayfield Cl WD/CROXPK L12 115 G1
Mayfield Ct FMBY L37 40 E6
Mayfield Dr GOL/RIS/CU WA3 93 K3
PS/BROM CH62 184 E1
Mayfield Gdns ALL/GAR L19 153 H4
Mayfield Rd ALL/GAR L19 153 H4
BEB CH63 170 C2
SKEL WN8 57 J6
WAL/NB CH45 110 E2
WARRS WA4 163 F1
Mayfields North
PS/BROM CH62 151 G4
Mayfields South
PS/BROM CH62 151 G4
Mayfield St AIMK WN4 * 79 F6
Mayfield Vw LYMM WA13 165 F1
Mayflower Av SPK/HALE L24 154 D5
Maynard St TOX L8 133 G2
May Pl VAUX/LVPD L3 9 H5
Maypole Ct NTHTN L30 70 A4
May Rd HES CH60 168 A5
May St BTL L20 5 F2
GOL/RIS/CU WA3 92 C1
VAUX/LVPD L3 9 H5
Maytree Cl NTHLY L27 135 K3
Maytree Wk SKEL WN8 56 D1
Mayville Rd CALD/MH L18 134 C4
Mazenod Ct VAUX/LVPD L3 8 E1
Mazzini Cl EV L5 113 G2
McBride St ALL/GAR L19 153 K5
McCarthy Cl GOL/RIS/CU WA3 125 J4
Mc Clellan Pl WDN WA8 18 E2
McCormack Av STHEL WA9 104 C1
McCulloch St STHEL WA9 13 K5
McFarlane Av ECCL WA10 102 E1
McGarva Wy EP CH65 6 E6
McGough Cl STHEL WA9 119 J4
McGregor St EV L5 113 G2
McKee Av WARRN/WOL WA2 123 H5
McKeown Cl EV L5 113 F2
McMinnis Av STHEL WA9 104 E3
McVinnie Rd RAIN/WH L35 118 B1
Mead Av LITH L21 81 K3
Meade Cl RAIN/WH L35 119 F6
Meade Rd CLB/OSW/ST L13 114 C1
Meadfoot Rd MOR/LEA CH46 109 H6
Meadow Av STHEL WA9 120 B4
STHP PR8 27 K3
WARRS WA4 161 K1
Meadow Bank MGHL L31 61 K5
ORM L39 * 45 K6
Meadowbank Cl
WD/CROXPK L12 115 J2
Meadowbridge Cl BRSC L40 54 E1
Meadowbrook BRSC L40 46 D1
Meadow Brook Cl AIN/FAZ L10 84 A4
Meadowbrook Rd
MOR/LEA CH46 128 E2
Meadow Brow CHTN/BK PR9 21 G6
Meadow Cl BRSC L40 54 E1
NSTN CH64 191 K3
NSTN CH64 193 G1
SKEL WN8 57 F6
WDN WA8 138 C6
Meadow Clough SKEL WN8 56 D1
Meadow Crs
GR/UP/WCH CH49 148 E1
Meadow Cft NSTN CH64 193 F1
Meadowcroft AIMK WN4 78 E3
FMBY L37 49 F3
HES CH60 168 C4
SKEL WN8 56 D1
STHEL WA9 120 A1
Meadowcroft Pk
WD/CROXPK L12 115 H3
Meadowcroft Rd HOY CH47 108 C6
Meadow Dr HUY L36 136 C1
ORM L39 53 G3
Meadowfield SKEL WN8 57 J6
Meadowfield Cl RF/TRAN CH42 150 E1
WLT/FAZ L9 82 D4
Meadow Hey BTL L20 81 H6
Meadow Hey Cl WLTN L25 135 J6
Meadow La BRSC L40 39 J1
BRSC L40 39 J6
EP CH65 7 F3
MGHL L31 62 C6
NSTN CH64 183 F6
RF/TRAN CH42 150 E1
STHEL WA9 104 D4
STHP PR8 33 K6
WARRN/WOL WA2 124 C5
WD/CROXPK L12 99 F6
Meadow Oak Dr WLTN L25 135 H5
Meadow Pk RF/TRAN CH42 150 E1
Meadow Rd WKBY CH48 128 A6
Meadows Gn GOL/RIS/CU WA3 93 F6
Meadowside MOR/LEA CH46 110 B3
Meadowside Av AIMK WN4 79 F1
Meadowside Dr
NWD/KWIPK L33 72 E3
Meadowside Rd
PS/BROM CH62 171 F6
The Meadows NSTN CH64 192 A3
RAIN/WH L35 118 E5
STHP PR8 * 33 K5
Meadow St WAL/NB CH45 95 G5
The Meadow
GR/UP/WCH CH49 129 J6
Meadow Vw CHNE CH2 198 B6
LITH L21 69 J6
STHP PR8 28 A3
Meadow View Dr
FROD/HEL WA6 200 D2
Meadow Wk PEN/TH CH61 167 J2
RUNC WA7 * 177 J6
Meadow Wy WD/CROXPK L12 99 F4
Mead Rd WARR WA1 143 K1
Meadway GOL/RIS/CU WA3 92 E3
GR/UP/WCH CH49 129 J3
GTS/LS CH66 194 E2
HES CH60 180 E1
MGHL L31 70 E2
NTHTN L30 82 C1
PS/BROM CH62 170 E3
RAIN/WH L35 118 B3
RUNC WA7 177 G4
SKEL WN8 56 C1
WAL/NB CH45 111 G2
WAV L15 134 D1
WDN WA8 157 F2
The Meander WD/CROXPK L12 99 J4
Measham Cl RNFD/HAY WA11 * 89 F6
Measham Wy WD/CROXPK L12 99 J2
Medbourne Crs KKBY L32 84 E3
Medea St EV L5 113 G1
Medlar Wy AIMK WN4 78 E4
Medlock St ANF/KKDL L4 97 G5
Medway Cl AIMK WN4 * 78 E3
LEIGH WN7 93 K3
WARRN/WOL WA2 124 A5
Medway Rd RF/TRAN CH42 151 F2
Meeting La WARRW/BUR WA5 140 E4
Melbreck SKEL WN8 56 C1
Melbreck Rd CALD/MH L18 153 J2
Melbury Ct GOL/RIS/CU WA3 125 H1
Melbury Rd DV/KA/FCH L14 116 B1
Melda Cl NPK/KEN L6 9 K1
Meldon Cl NG/CROX L11 99 G3
Meldreth Cl FMBY L37 48 C4
Meldrum Rd WAV L15 134 C3
Melford Ct WARR WA1 * 144 C1
Melford Dr AIMK WN4 79 F5
CL/PREN CH43 149 H2
RUNC WA7 11 H7
Melford Gv NPK/KEN L6 114 B1
Meliden Gdns STHEL WA9 104 D6
Melksham Dr PEN/TH CH61 148 A4
Melling Av WLT/FAZ L9 82 E4
Melling Dr KKBY L32 72 D6
Melling La MGHL L31 71 H2
Melling Rd BTL L20 5 F1
CHTN/BK PR9 23 G5
WAL/NB CH45 95 J6
WLT/FAZ L9 82 E3
Melling Wy KKBY L32 72 D6
Mellock Cl NSTN CH64 192 A3
Mellock La NSTN CH64 192 A2
Melloncroft Dr WKBY CH48 146 C3
Melloncroft Dr West
WKBY CH48 146 D4
Mellor Cl RAIN/WH L35 136 D2
RUNC WA7 178 C5
Mellor Rd RF/TRAN CH42 150 B1
Melly Rd AIG/SPK L17 133 G6
Melmerby Cl AIMK WN4 78 E6
Melrose Av CHTN/BK PR9 20 E6
CSBY/BLUN L23 69 F6
ECCL WA10 87 J6
HOY CH47 127 G2
WARRS WA4 162 C3
WARRW/BUR WA5 105 K6
Melrose Crs AIMK WN4 78 B6
Melrose Dr GTS/LS CH66 202 D3
Melrose Gdns CL/PREN CH43 * 149 J2
Melrose Rd ANF/KKDL L4 97 F5
CSBY/WL L22 81 F3
NWD/KWIPK L33 72 C3
Melton Av WARRS WA4 162 A3
Melton Cl GR/UP/WCH CH49 129 F4
Melton Rd RUNC WA7 186 E1
Melverley Rd KKBY L32 84 A1
Melville Av RF/TRAN CH42 151 F2
Melville Cl ECCL WA10 12 A4
WARRN/WOL WA2 16 D1
WDN WA8 19 K1
Melville Pl EHL/KEN L7 133 F1
Melville Rd BEB CH63 150 D6
BTL L20 81 K4
Melville St TOX L8 132 E4
Melwood Dr WD/CROXPK L12 99 G6
Menai Ms PR/KW L34 * 118 A1
Menai Rd BTL L20 82 A5
Menai St BIRK CH41 2 C5
Mendell Cl PS/BROM CH62 171 G5
Mendip Av WARRN/WOL WA2 123 H4
Mendip Cl GTS/LS CH66 195 H6
HLWD L26 155 H4
RF/TRAN CH42 150 B2
Mendip Gv STHEL WA9 104 D2
Mendip Rd RF/TRAN CH42 150 B2
WAV L15 134 B3
Menin Av WARRS WA4 143 F6
Menivale Cl CHTN/BK PR9 20 D5
Menlo Av PEN/TH CH61 148 C5
Menlo Cl CL/PREN CH43 130 B5
Menlove Av CALD/MH L18 134 B4
Menlove Gdns North
CALD/MH L18 134 C4
Menlove Gdns South
CALD/MH L18 134 C4
Menlove Gdns West
CALD/MH L18 134 C4
Menlove Man CALD/MH L18 134 D3
Menlow Cl WARRS WA4 163 H2
Menstone Rd CLB/OSW/ST L13 114 D3
Mentmore Crs NG/CROX L11 99 F4
Mentmore Gdns WARRS WA4 162 E6
Mentmore Rd CALD/MH L18 153 G2
Menzies St TOX L8 133 F5
Meols Cl FMBY L37 48 E3
GTS/LS CH66 195 H5
Meols Cop Rd STHP PR8 28 C2
Meols Dr HOY CH47 127 F5
Meols Pde HOY CH47 127 G1
Mercer Av KKBY L32 84 B2
Mercer Ct WD/CROXPK L12 115 J2
Mercer Dr ANF/KKDL L4 97 G5
Mercer Rd CL/PREN CH43 130 B1
RNFD/HAY WA11 90 B5
Mercer's La ORM L39 64 B3
Mercer St ALL/GAR L19 * 153 K6
NEWLW WA12 106 D1
WARRW/BUR WA5 121 J1
Mercer Wk EP CH65 6 D5
Merchants Crs
GOL/RIS/CU WA3 93 F2
Mere Av BEB CH63 183 J1
BRSC L40 38 E3
Merebank CL/PREN CH43 130 B5
Merebrook Gv
NWD/KWIPK L33 72 E4
Mere Cl GTS/LS CH66 202 B1
SKEL WN8 56 B3
Merecroft Av WAL/EG CH44 111 J5
Meredale Rd CALD/MH L18 134 B5
Meredith Av WARRS WA4 163 G1
Meredith St ALL/GAR L19 154 B6
Mere Farm Gv CL/PREN CH43 130 C5
Mere Farm Rd CL/PREN CH43 130 B5
Mere Fld CL/PREN CH43 * 130 C5
Mere Gn ANF/KKDL L4 97 J4
Mere Gv RNFD/HAY WA11 88 E2
Mereheath MOR/LEA CH46 109 J4
Mere Hey ECCL WA10 102 C2
Mereland Wy STHEL WA9 104 D3
Mere La BRSC L40 31 J4
CHTN/BK PR9 24 E2
EV L5 113 H2
HES CH60 167 J3
WAL/NB CH45 94 E6
Merepark Dr CHTN/BK PR9 23 K1
Mere Park Rd
GR/UP/WCH CH49 128 D6
Mere Rd AIMK WN4 79 H5
FMBY L37 48 D3
NEWLW WA12 107 F1
WARRN/WOL WA2 124 C5
Meres Rd WLT/FAZ L9 83 H4
Meres Wy STHP PR8 27 J5
Merevale Cl RUNC WA7 187 H1
Mereview Crs WD/CROXPK L12 99 H2
Merewood KKBY L32 84 E3
SKEL WN8 56 C1
Merewood Cl
WARRN/WOL WA2 123 K4
Mereworth WKBY CH48 146 E5
Meribel Cl CSBY/BLUN L23 69 H4
Meriden Av BEB CH63 170 C4
Meriden Cl RNFD/HAY WA11 89 G5
STHP PR8 33 H4
Meriden Rd WLTN L25 135 J3
Merlewood Av CHTN/BK PR9 23 K2
Merlin Av GR/UP/WCH CH49 128 E3
Merlin Cl GR/UP/WCH CH49 128 D3
RNFD/HAY WA11 88 E5
RUNC WA7 177 K5
Merlin Ct HLWD L26 155 G2
Merlin St TOX L8 132 E3
Merrick Cl WARRN/WOL WA2 124 A5
Merrills La GR/UP/WCH CH49 129 H4
Merrilocks Rd CSBY/BLUN L23 68 C5
Merrilox Av MGHL L31 62 B5
Merrion Cl WLTN L25 135 G6
Merritt Av BIRK CH41 130 E1
Merrivale Rd WLTN L25 155 F1
Merrydale Dr NG/CROX L11 99 G2
Merryford Gn ANF/KKDL L4 97 K4
Merscar La BRSC L40 37 H3
Mersey Av ALL/GAR L19 153 G3
FMBY L37 40 E5
MGHL L31 62 D5
Merseybank Rd
PS/BROM CH62 151 G3
Mersey La South
RF/TRAN CH42 151 F1
Mersey Mt RF/TRAN CH42 131 H6
Mersey Rd AIG/SPK L17 153 F3
CSBY/BLUN L23 68 D6
RF/TRAN CH42 131 K6
RUNC WA7 10 D3
WDN WA8 176 D1
Mersey St STHEL WA9 104 E2
WAL/EG CH44 112 A5
WARR WA1 16 E6
Merseyton Rd EP CH65 196 B2
Mersey Vw ALL/GAR L19 153 K5
CSBY/WL L22 80 D1
RUNC WA7 176 A6
Mersey View Rd WDN WA8 175 J1
Mersey View South Rd
RUNC WA7 176 A5
Mersey Wk WARRS WA4 143 J4
Mersey Wy SPK/HALE L24 172 C3
WARRW/BUR WA5 141 K5
Mersham Ct WDN WA8 138 E5
Merstone Cl HLWD L26 155 J4
Merthyr Gv CHLDW L16 115 J6
Merton Bank Rd STHEL WA9 89 F6
Merton Cl NSTN CH64 191 K4
Merton Crs HUY L36 116 B5
Merton Dr GR/UP/WCH CH49 129 H6
HUY L36 116 A5
Merton Gv BTL L20 4 E5
CSBY/BLUN L23 68 D6
Merton Pl CL/PREN CH43 2 B5
Merton Rd BTL L20 4 E5
GTS/LS CH66 195 H6
PS/BROM CH62 184 E4
WAL/NB CH45 111 G2
Merton St STHEL WA9 89 F6
Mertoun Rd WARRS WA4 162 A2
Mesham Cl GR/UP/WCH CH49 129 F4
Meteor Crs WARRN/WOL WA2 123 K5
Methuen St BIRK CH41 130 D1
WAV L15 133 K2
Mevagissey Rd RUNC WA7 188 B2
The Mews AIG/SPK L17 153 G2
STBRV L28 100 C6
STHP PR8 27 H2
WARRW/BUR WA5 * 121 J1
Meyrick Rd NG/CROX L11 98 C3
Micawber Cl TOX L8 132 E4
Michael Dragonette Ct
VAUX/LVPD L3 112 E3
Michaels Cl FMBY L37 48 E2
Mickering La ORM L39 63 G1
Micklefield Rd WAV L15 * 134 A3
Micklegate RUNC WA7 178 C6
Mickleton Dr STHP PR8 33 G4
Middlefield Rd CALD/MH L18 135 F6
Middleham Cl KKBY L32 84 B2
Middlehey Rd PR/KW L34 100 D1
Middlehurst Av ECCL WA10 13 F3
Middlehurst Cl PR/KW L34 102 C6
Middlehurst Rd WARRS WA4 163 F1
Middlemass Hey NTHLY L27 136 B4
Middle Moss La FMBY L37 50 B2
Middle Rd SPK/HALE L24 155 J6
Middlesex Rd BTL L20 5 H2
Middleton Rd CSBY/WL L22 81 G1
EHL/KEN L7 114 C5
Middle Wk FROD/HEL WA6 200 E2
Middle Wy NG/CROX L11 84 C6
Middle Withins La HTWN L38 50 B6
Middlewood GOL/RIS/CU WA3 93 F3
KKBY L32 84 E3
SKEL WN8 56 C1
Middlewood Cl ORM L39 53 G6
Middlewood Dr ORM L39 53 G6
Middlewood Rd ORM L39 53 G6
Midge Hall La CHTN/BK PR9 30 B5
Midghall St VAUX/LVPD L3 8 D1
Midhurst Dr STHP PR8 33 H5
Midhurst Rd WD/CROXPK L12 99 K2
Midland St BIRK CH41 * 2 C6
WDN WA8 19 F2
Midland Ter CSBY/WL L22 80 E2
Midland Wy WARR WA1 16 B3
Midlothian Dr CSBY/BLUN L23 68 D6
Midway Rd HUY L36 116 E3
Midwood St WDN WA8 18 E4
Milbrook Crs KKBY L32 72 D6
Milbrook Dr KKBY L32 72 D6
Mildenhall Rd WLTN L25 135 H3
Mildmay Rd BTL L20 81 J6
NG/CROX L11 * 98 C3
Mile End EV L5 113 F3
Miles Cl GOL/RIS/CU WA3 125 H4
GR/UP/WCH CH49 147 K1
Miles La GR/UP/WCH CH49 147 K1
Miles St TOX L8 133 F5
Milestone Hey STBRV L28 100 B5
Milford Cl FMBY L37 48 C4
Milford Dr WD/CROXPK L12 99 J2
Milford St EV L5 112 D1
Milk St ECCL WA10 13 G5
Milland Cl NG/CROX L11 99 G2
Millar Crs WDN WA8 18 C5
Millar's Pace CHTN/BK PR9 20 E6
Mill Av WARRW/BUR WA5 141 F2
Mill Bank CLB/OSW/ST L13 114 D1
Millbank LYMM WA13 145 K6
Mill Bank NSTN CH64 192 B4
Millbank Brow BRSC L40 39 F6
Millbank Ct FROD/HEL WA6 200 D1
Millbank La MGHL L31 62 D4
Millbank Rd WAL/EG CH44 * 111 G4
Millbeck Gv RNFD/HAY WA11 88 E2
Millbrook Cl SKEL WN8 56 A3
Millbrook La ECCL WA10 102 D1
Millbrook Rd BIRK CH41 111 H5
Mill Brow BEB CH63 150 C5
ECCL WA10 102 D1
STHEL WA9 120 B2
WDN WA8 19 H1
Mill Brow Cl STHEL WA9 120 B2
Millbutt Cl BEB CH63 150 C5
Mill Cl CSBY/BLUN L23 69 F3
EP CH65 203 G2
WARRN/WOL WA2 124 A3
Mill Ct NTHTN L30 70 A4
Millcroft CSBY/BLUN L23 69 H4
Millcroft Pk GR/UP/WCH CH49 128 C6
Millcroft Rd WLTN L25 155 F2
Milldale Rd LEIGH WN7 93 J2
Mill Dam Cl BRSC L40 46 C1
Mill Dam La BRSC L40 46 D2
Millenium Rd TOX L8 133 F3
Miller Av CSBY/BLUN L23 68 E4
Miller Cl TOX L8 132 E5
Miller's Br BTL L20 4 D7
Millers Cl MOR/LEA CH46 128 C2
Millers Ct ORM L39 45 K6
Millerscroft KKBY L32 72 B6
Millersdale STHEL WA9 120 A3
Millersdale Av WLT/FAZ L9 82 E4
Millersdale Cl PS/BROM CH62 184 C2
Millersdale Gv RUNC WA7 187 G2
Millersdale Rd CALD/MH L18 134 B5
Millers Fold ECCL WA10 102 D1
Miller St WARRS WA4 17 G7
Millers Wy MOR/LEA CH46 * 128 D1
Mill Farm Cl WARRN/WOL WA2 124 A4
Millfield Cl CLB/OSW/ST L13 114 E1
Millfield La RNFD/HAY WA11 90 E3
Millfield Rd WDN WA8 158 D1
Millfields ECCL WA10 102 D2
Mill Gn NSTN CH64 193 G1
Millgreen Cl SKEL WN8 57 J6
WD/CROXPK L12 99 J2
Mill Green La WDN WA8 139 J4
Mill Hey RAIN/WH L35 119 G6
Mill Hey Rd WKBY CH48 146 E5
Mill Hl CL/PREN CH43 130 D6
Mill Hill Rd PEN/TH CH61 147 K4
Millhouse Av WARRS WA4 162 C2
Millhouse Cl MOR/LEA CH46 109 F6
Millhouse La GOL/RIS/CU WA3 124 C1
MOR/LEA CH46 109 F6
Millingford Av GOL/RIS/CU WA3 92 A1
Millingford Gv AIMK WN4 79 G6
Millington Cl CL/PREN CH43 149 H2
RUNC WA7 187 J3
WDN WA8 18 A3
Mill La BRSC L40 38 E4
BTL L20 5 G4
CHTN/BK PR9 23 J4
FROD/HEL WA6 187 H5
GR/UP/WCH CH49 147 K2
GTS/LS CH66 195 G5
HES CH60 168 B5
KKBY L32 72 B5
NEWLW WA12 106 E2
NSTN CH64 183 F6
NSTN CH64 192 D4
NSTN CH64 193 H1
ORM L39 52 D4
PR/KW L34 85 J6
RAIN/WH L35 118 E6
RNFD/HAY WA11 75 K5
SKEL WN8 56 B3
SKEL WN8 57 J5
STHEL WA9 120 A2
VAUX/LVPD L3 9 F2
WAL/EG CH44 111 H3
WARRN/WOL WA2 122 E2
WARRN/WOL WA2 124 A3
WARRS WA4 161 H4
WARRS WA4 162 D1
WAV L15 134 B1
WD/CROXPK L12 114 E1
WDN WA8 138 C4
WDN WA8 139 J4
Mill Meadow NEWLW WA12 106 E2
Millom Av RAIN/WH L35 118 D3
Millom Gv ECCL WA10 102 E5
WD/CROXPK L12 99 G4
Mill Park Dr PS/BROM CH62 184 B4
Mill Rd BEB CH63 150 C4
NPK/KEN L6 113 J4
PEN/TH CH61 148 D5
PS/BROM CH62 171 F2
STHP PR8 33 K4
Mill Sq AIN/FAZ L10 83 H1
Millstead Rd WAV L15 134 B1
Mill St AIMK WN4 91 H1
ECCL WA10 13 F3
GOL/RIS/CU WA3 92 B3
NSTN CH64 191 K1
ORM L39 53 K1
PR/KW L34 117 K1
RF/TRAN CH42 131 G5
STHP PR8 15 H6
TOX L8 132 D4
WLTN L25 154 D1
Mill Ter BEB CH63 * 150 C6
Millthwaite Rd WAL/EG CH44 111 F3
Millvale St NPK/KEN L6 114 A4
Mill Vw TOX L8 132 D4
Mill View Ct ORM L39 64 D1
Mill View Dr BEB CH63 150 B5
Millway Rd SPK/HALE L24 174 B1
Millwood BEB CH63 150 C5
RUNC WA7 178 B4
Mill Wood Av ECCL WA10 102 B2
Millwood Cl AIMK WN4 79 F4
Millwood Ct SPK/HALE L24 * 174 B1
Millwood Gdns RAIN/WH L35 118 B5
Millwood Rd SPK/HALE L24 173 K2
Milman Cl GR/UP/WCH CH49 129 G5
ORM L39 53 H2
Milman Rd ANF/KKDL L4 97 H4
Milner Cop HES CH60 168 A5
Milne Rd CLB/OSW/ST L13 98 C5
Milner Rd AIG/SPK L17 153 F2
HES CH60 168 A5
Milner St BIRK CH41 130 D1
WARRW/BUR WA5 16 A5
Milnthorpe Cl ANF/KKDL L4 97 G5
Milnthorpe Rd
WARRW/BUR WA5 121 J1
Milnthorpe St ALL/GAR L19 153 K5
Milroy St EHL/KEN L7 113 K6
Milton Av DV/KA/FCH L14 115 K5
NEWLW WA12 106 B2
RAIN/WH L35 118 A4
WDN WA8 18 A4
Milton Cl RAIN/WH L35 118 A4
Milton Crs HES CH60 168 A4
Milton Dr ORM L39 54 A1
Milton Gn PEN/TH CH61 148 E5
Milton Gv WARRS WA4 143 G6

Milton Rd ANF/KKDL L4 5 K6
CSBY/WL L22 81 F1
EHL/KEN L7 114 C5
EP CH65 7 G7
GOL/RIS/CU WA3 92 E4
RF/TRAN CH42 131 F5
WAL/EG CH44 111 K5
WDN WA8 18 C4
WKBY CH48 127 F6
Milton Rd East RF/TRAN CH42 131 G5
Milton St BTL L20 4 C2
CHTN/BK PR9 23 J6
STHEL WA9 119 J5
WDN WA8 158 B6
Milton Wy MGHL L31 61 K6
Milvain Dr WARRN/WOL WA2 123 J6
Milverny Wy STHEL WA9 103 J3
Milverton St NPK/KEN L6 114 A3
Mimosa Rd WAV L15 134 C2
Minehead Gv STHEL WA9 120 B2
Minehead Rd AIG/SPK L17 153 F2
Miners Wy SPK/HALE L24 174 B2
WDN WA8 18 D6
Minerva Cl WARRS WA4 162 C1
Mines Av AIG/SPK L17 153 G4
PR/KW L34 118 A1
Mine Wy RNFD/HAY WA11 * 90 E4
Minshull St EHL/KEN L7 113 J6
Minstead Av NWD/KWIPK L33 85 F1
Minster Ct EHL/KEN L7 133 F1
RUNC WA7 176 B5
Minto Cl EHL/KEN L7 114 A5
Minton Cl WD/CROXPK L12 99 K2
Minton Wy WDN WA8 139 G4
Mintor Rd NWD/KWIPK L33 85 F1
Minto St EHL/KEN L7 113 K5
Minver Rd WD/CROXPK L12 99 H6
Miranda Pl BTL L20 97 F4
Miranda Rd BTL L20 5 G7
Mirfield Cl GOL/RIS/CU WA3 92 E4
HLWD L26 155 J5
Mirfield St NPK/KEN L6 113 K4
Miriam Rd ANF/KKDL L4 113 J1
Miskelly St BTL L20 96 E5
Mission Wk NPK/KEN L6 113 K4
Missouri Rd CLB/OSW/ST L13 98 B6
Mistlethrush Wy
WD/CROXPK L12 99 K2
Misty Cl WDN WA8 157 H1
Mitchell Av WARRW/BUR WA5 121 J2
Mitchell Crs LITH L21 81 J3
Mitchell Rd ECCL WA10 102 E4
PR/KW L34 117 J1
WGNW/BIL/O WN5 77 H4
Mitchell St AIMK WN4 91 H1
GOL/RIS/CU WA3 92 B4
WARRS WA4 162 B3
Mithril Cl WDN WA8 139 K6
Mitre Cl RAIN/WH L35 117 K6
Mitylene St EV L5 * 113 G1
Mobberley Cl WARRS WA4 144 C6
Mobberley Wy BEB CH63 170 C2
Mockbeggar Dr WAL/NB CH45 94 D6
Mockbeggar Whf WAL/NB CH45 94 D6
Modred St TOX L8 132 E4
Moel Famau Vw AIG/SPK L17 152 C1
Moffatdale Rd ANF/KKDL L4 98 A5
Moffat Rd WLT/FAZ L9 * 83 F4
Moffatt Rd WLT/FAZ L9 82 E4
Molesworth Gv CHLDW L16 115 K6
Molineux Av DV/KA/FCH L14 115 H6
Molland Cl WD/CROXPK L12 99 H5
Mollington Av NG/CROX L11 98 D3
Mollington Link BIRK CH41 3 G7
Mollington Rd KKBY L32 84 B1
WAL/EG CH44 111 J4
Mollington St BIRK CH41 3 F6
Molly Pitcher Wy
WARRW/BUR WA5 141 J4
Molly's La NWD/KWIPK L33 85 J4
Molton Rd CHLDW L16 134 D1
Molyneux Av
WARRW/BUR WA5 142 C1
Molyneux Cl
GR/UP/WCH CH49 129 G4
HUY L36 117 F5
RAIN/WH L35 117 K3
Molyneux Ct NG/CROX L11 * 99 F2
Molyneux Dr RAIN/WH L35 117 K3
WAL/NB CH45 95 H5
Molyneux Rd CALD/MH L18 134 A5
CSBY/WL L22 81 F1
MGHL L31 71 J2
NPK/KEN L6 113 K4
ORM L39 53 G6
Molyneux Wy AIN/FAZ L10 71 F6
Monaghan Cl WLT/FAZ L9 82 C4
Monash Rd NG/CROX L11 98 D5
Monastery La STHEL WA9 104 B6
Monastery Rd NPK/KEN L6 114 A1
STHEL WA9 104 C6
Mona St BIRK CH41 130 C2
BTL L20 82 A5
ECCL WA10 12 A6
Mond Rd AIN/FAZ L10 83 J4
WDN WA8 18 C4
Monfa Rd BTL L20 81 K5
Monica Dr WDN WA8 139 F4
Monica Rd WLTN L25 154 E2
Monica Ter AIMK WN4 91 G1
Monkfield Wy ALL/GAR L19 172 C1
Monk Rd WAL/EG CH44 111 H3
Monks Carr La HTWN L38 60 C1
Monks Cl FMBY L37 49 G4
Monksdown Rd NG/CROX L11 98 E4
Monks Dr FMBY L37 49 G4
Monks Ferry BIRK CH41 3 J5
Monksferry Wk ALL/GAR L19 153 G4
Monks Gv EP CH65 6 C3
Monks St WARRW/BUR WA5 * 142 B3
Monk St EV L5 * 113 H1
Monks Wy BEB CH63 170 B1
WKBY CH48 146 C1
WLTN L25 154 E1
Monkswell Dr WAV L15 134 B1
Monkswell St TOX L8 133 F6
Monkswood Cl
WARRW/BUR WA5 122 E5
Monmouth Cl WARR WA1 144 D2
Monmouth Crs AIMK WN4 91 H1
Monmouth Dr AIN/FAZ L10 83 J2
Monmouth Gv STHEL WA9 104 B3
Monmouth Rd WAL/EG CH44 111 G3
Monro Cl TOX L8 * 132 E5
Monroe Cl WARR WA1 144 A2
Monro St TOX L8 132 E5
Montague Rd CLB/OSW/ST L13 114 E5
Montagu Rd FMBY L37 40 E6
Montclair Dr CALD/MH L18 134 C4
Montclare Crs WARRS WA4 162 D2
Montcliffe Cl GOL/RIS/CU WA3 124 E2
Monterey Rd CLB/OSW/ST L13 115 F5
Montfort Dr ALL/GAR L19 153 H4
Montgomery Av CHTN/BK PR9 28 D1
Montgomery Cl RAIN/WH L35 117 K5
Montgomery Hl WKBY CH48 147 H3
Montgomery Rd HUY L36 116 D3
WDN WA8 157 J3
WLT/FAZ L9 82 D5
Montgomery Wy NPK/KEN L6 113 K3
Montpelier Av RUNC WA7 186 C1
Montpelier Dr TOX L8 132 E5
Montpellier Crs WAL/NB CH45 95 G5
Montreal Rd NTHLY L27 136 B4
Montrey Crs AIMK WN4 78 B6
Montrose Av WAL/EG CH44 112 A6
Montrose Cl WARRN/WOL WA2 124 B3
Montrose Dr CHTN/BK PR9 23 H4
Montrose Rd CLB/OSW/ST L13 114 C1
Montrose Wy CLB/OSW/ST L13 114 D5
Montrovia Crs AIN/FAZ L10 83 J4
Monville Rd WLT/FAZ L9 83 F4
Moorbridge Cl NTHTN L30 70 D5
Moor Cl CSBY/BLUN L23 69 G4
STHP PR8 41 J1
Moor Coppice CSBY/BLUN L23 69 G4
Moorcroft Rd CALD/MH L18 153 K2
HUY L36 116 E2
WAL/NB CH45 110 D2
Moorditch La FROD/HEL WA6 186 C6
Moor Dr CSBY/BLUN L23 69 F4
SKEL WN8 57 F6
Moore Av RF/TRAN CH42 150 D1
STHEL WA9 104 E2
WARRS WA4 144 C6
Moore Cl WDN WA8 158 E1
Moore Dr RNFD/HAY WA11 90 E5
Moore La WARRS WA4 160 E4
Moore St BTL L20 4 C1
Mooreway RAIN/WH L35 119 G6
Moorfield NWD/KWIPK L33 72 E4
Moorfield Crs GOL/RIS/CU WA3 93 H4
Moorfield Dr NSTN CH64 181 H5
Moorfield La BRSC L40 37 F6
Moorfield Rd CSBY/BLUN L23 69 H4
ECCL WA10 87 K6
WDN WA8 139 J5
Moorfields CLVP L2 8 D3
Moorfields Av CL/PREN CH43 130 A5
Moorfoot Rd STHEL WA9 104 D2
Moorfoot Wy NWD/KWIPK L33 72 C3
Moorgate ORM L39 53 J1
Moorgate Av CSBY/BLUN L23 69 F6
Moorgate Rd NWD/KWIPK L33 84 E5
Moorgate St EHL/KEN L7 113 K6
Moorhey Rd MGHL L31 71 G3
Moorhouses HTWN L38 59 F4
Mooring Cl RUNC WA7 188 C1
Moorings Cl NSTN CH64 181 G6
The Moorings BIRK CH41 * 2 E6
HES CH60 167 G5
MGHL L31 61 K3
Moorland Av CSBY/BLUN L23 69 F4
Moorland Cl HES CH60 168 A6
Moorland Dr RUNC WA7 178 D6
Moorland Pk HES CH60 168 A6
Moorland Rd AIMK WN4 79 K4
GTS/LS CH66 195 H1
MGHL L31 71 F3
RF/TRAN CH42 131 H6
Moorlands Rd CSBY/BLUN L23 69 J3
Moor La AIN/FAZ L10 83 K4
ANF/KKDL L4 97 J2
CSBY/BLUN L23 69 G4
FROD/HEL WA6 200 E1
HES CH60 167 K5
HTWN L38 59 K4
SFTN L29 61 F6
STHP PR8 41 J1
WDN WA8 18 C6
Moor La South WDN WA8 18 B6
Moor Pl VAUX/LVPD L3 9 H3
Moorside Av NSTN CH64 191 H1
Moorside Cl CSBY/BLUN L23 69 G5
Moorside Ct WDN WA8 18 B5
Moorside La NSTN CH64 191 H2
Moorside Rd CSBY/BLUN L23 69 G5
Moor St CLVP L2 8 C5
ORM L39 45 K6
Moorway HES CH60 168 B5
Moorwood Crs STHEL WA9 120 A3
Moray Cl ECCL WA10 12 D1
Morcott La SPK/HALE L24 174 E3
Morden Av AIMK WN4 79 G6
Morden St NPK/KEN L6 114 A4
Morecambe St NPK/KEN L6 * 114 A2
Morecroft Rd RF/TRAN CH42 151 F1
Morella Rd ANF/KKDL L4 98 A5
Morello Cl ECCL WA10 13 F2
Morello Dr BEB CH63 170 D3
Moresby Cl RUNC WA7 178 D6
Moret Cl CSBY/BLUN L23 69 H4
Moreton Av STHEL WA9 120 A3
Moreton Cl GOL/RIS/CU WA3 92 A2
Moreton Gv WAL/NB CH45 110 E1
Moreton Rd GR/UP/WCH CH49 129 G3
Morgan Av WARRN/WOL WA2 123 J5
Morgan Ms NTHTN L30 70 A6
Morgan St STHEL WA9 104 B3
Morland Av NSTN CH64 192 A2
PS/BROM CH62 171 F6
Morley Av BIRK CH41 130 E2
Morley Rd CHTN/BK PR9 15 K1
RUNC WA7 10 D7
WAL/EG CH44 111 G4
WARRS WA4 161 K2
Morley St ANF/KKDL L4 * 97 G6
ECCL WA10 12 E1
WARR WA1 17 G3
Morley Wy ECCL WA10 13 F3
Morningside CSBY/BLUN L23 69 G6
Morningside Pl NG/CROX L11 98 D4
Morningside Rd NG/CROX L11 98 D5
Morningside Wy NG/CROX L11 98 D5
Mornington Av CSBY/BLUN L23 81 F1
EP CH65 6 E5
Mornington Rd CHTN/BK PR9 15 G4
WAL/NB CH45 111 H1
Mornington St TOX L8 132 D4
Morpeth Cl MOR/LEA CH46 128 C1
Morpeth Rd HOY CH47 127 F4
Morpeth St TOX L8 132 E2
Morpeth Whf BIRK CH41 3 G1
Morphany La WARRS WA4 189 K1
Morris Av WARRS WA4 143 J5
Morris Cl RNFD/HAY WA11 89 K6
Morris Hey ORM L39 36 B6
Morris La ORM L39 36 B6
Morrison Cl WARRW/BUR WA5 141 H4
Morris Rd SKEL WN8 57 J6
Morrissey Cl ECCL WA10 12 A3
Morris St STHEL WA9 104 C4
Morston Av KKBY L32 84 D3
Morston Crs KKBY L32 84 D3
Mort Av WARRS WA4 143 K5
Mortimer Av
WARRN/WOL WA2 142 E1
Mortimer St BIRK CH41 3 H4
Mortlake Cl WDN WA8 138 B6
Morton Cl WARRW/BUR WA5 141 K1
Morton Rd RUNC WA7 178 C5
Morton St TOX L8 132 E4
Morvah Cl NG/CROX L11 99 G3
Morval Crs ANF/KKDL L4 5 K6
RUNC WA7 11 K7
Morven Cl WARRN/WOL WA2 124 A4
Morven Gv STHP PR8 23 G6
Moscow Dr CLB/OSW/ST L13 114 D2
Mosedale Av RNFD/HAY WA11 88 E2
Mosedale Gv RUNC WA7 * 187 H2
Mosedale Rd PS/BROM CH62 171 G3
WLT/FAZ L9 82 D6
Moseley Av WAL/NB CH45 111 G3
WARRS WA4 143 K5
Moseley Rd BEB CH63 170 C4
Moses St TOX L8 132 E5
Mosley St STHP PR8 27 J3
Moss Bank ORM L39 53 H3
Moss Bank Pk LITH L21 81 H3
Moss Bank Rd RNFD/HAY WA11 88 D2
WDN WA8 19 J5
Mossborough Hall La
RNFD/HAY WA11 74 D6
Mossborough Rd
RNFD/HAY WA11 75 G4
Moss Bridge La BRSC L40 47 J1
Moss Brow RNFD/HAY WA11 75 F2
Mossbrow Rd HUY L36 116 E3
Moss Cl NSTN CH64 193 H1
WARRS WA4 162 D1
Mosscroft Cl HUY L36 117 G3
Mossdale Cl WARRW/BUR WA5 141 H2
Mossdale Dr RAIN/WH L35 119 F4
Mossdale Rd AIMK WN4 79 F1
NWD/KWIPK L33 72 E4
Moss Delph La ORM L39 53 G4
Mossdene Rd WAL/EG CH44 111 F3
Moss End Wy NWD/KWIPK L33 73 J6
Mossfield Rd WLT/FAZ L9 82 C5
Moss Gdns STHP PR8 27 K5
Moss Ga GOL/RIS/CU WA3 125 J2
Moss Gate Gv DV/KA/FCH L14 116 A4
Moss Gate Rd DV/KA/FCH L14 116 A4
Mossgiel Av STHP PR8 33 H4
Moss Green Wy STHEL WA9 104 E4
Moss Gv RF/TRAN CH42 150 A1
TOX L8 133 H3
Mosshill Cl MGHL L31 62 A4
Mosslands ECCL WA10 102 C1
Mosslands Cl GTS/LS CH66 202 C1
Mosslands Dr WAL/EG CH44 110 E3
Moss La BRSC L40 39 G2
BTL L20 82 B5
CHTN/BK PR9 23 K5
FMBY L37 49 J1
GOL/RIS/CU WA3 92 C6
HTWN L38 59 H2
LITH L21 81 K3
MGHL L31 62 B2
NWD/KWIPK L33 72 E1
NWD/KWIPK L33 73 G6
ORM L39 65 F5
RF/TRAN CH42 150 A1
RNFD/HAY WA11 76 B4
RNFD/HAY WA11 87 H4
SKEL WN8 66 B1
STHEL WA9 104 E4
WARRS WA4 160 D5
Moss Lane Vw SKEL WN8 66 B1
Mosslawn Rd KKBY L32 85 F2
Mosslea Pk CALD/MH L18 134 A5
Mossley Av CALD/MH L18 134 A4
PS/BROM CH62 171 F5
Mossley Hill Dr AIG/SPK L17 133 J4
Mossley Hill Rd CALD/MH L18 153 G1
Mossley Rd RF/TRAN CH42 131 H6
Moss Nook BRSC L40 38 E3
ORM L39 * 53 G3
Moss Nook La MGHL L31 72 A1
RNFD/HAY WA11 75 F3
Moss Pits Cl AIN/FAZ L10 83 H4
Moss Pits La AIN/FAZ L10 83 H4
WAV L15 134 C2
Moss Rd STHP PR8 27 K5
WARRS WA4 143 K6
Moss Side DV/KA/FCH L14 116 A4
FMBY L37 49 H1
Moss Side La KIRK/FR/WA PR4 25 K2
WARRS WA4 160 B4
Moss St ALL/GAR L19 153 K5
NPK/KEN L6 9 K2
PR/KW L34 101 K6
WDN WA8 19 K5
Mossvale GTS/LS CH66 195 G1
Moss Vw LITH L21 81 K3
MGHL L31 62 D6
Mossville Cl CALD/MH L18 153 H1
Mossville Rd CALD/MH L18 153 J1
Moss Wy NG/CROX L11 99 G1
Mossy Bank Rd WAL/EG CH44 111 K3
Moston Gv LYMM WA13 145 J6
Moston Wy GTS/LS CH66 195 J6
Mostyn Av AIN/FAZ L10 83 F1
ALL/GAR L19 154 A3
HES CH60 167 G5
WKBY CH48 146 C2
Mostyn Cl ANF/KKDL L4 * 97 G6
Mostyn Sq NSTN CH64 181 G6
Mostyn St WAL/EG CH44 111 H4
Motherwell Crs STHP PR8 28 C4
Mottershead Cl WDN WA8 18 C4
Mottershead Rd WDN WA8 18 C4
Mottram Cl NWD/KWIPK L33 84 E1
WARRS WA4 144 A6
Moughland La RUNC WA7 176 D5
Moulders La WARR WA1 16 E6
Mould St EV L5 113 F2
Moulton Cl RUNC WA7 187 J3
Mounsey Rd RF/TRAN CH42 2 D7
Mountain Vw FROD/HEL WA6 199 J6
Mount Av BEB CH63 150 C4
BTL L20 82 A5
HES CH60 * 167 K5
Mount Cl KKBY L32 72 B5
Mount Ct HES CH60 * 167 K5
Mount Crs KKBY L32 72 B5
Mount Dr BEB CH63 150 B4
Mount Farm Wy GTS/LS CH66 202 A1
Mount Gv BIRK CH41 2 C7
Mount Grove Pl BIRK CH41 2 B7
Mount Haven Cl
GR/UP/WCH CH49 129 H4
Mount House Cl FMBY L37 41 H6
Mount House Rd FMBY L37 41 H6
Mount Ms HES CH60 * 167 K5
Mount Olive CL/PREN CH43 130 D6
Mount Pk BEB CH63 150 C4
WLTN L25 135 H6
Mount Park Ct WLTN L25 135 H6
Mount Pleasant CHNE CH2 198 B5
CL/PREN CH43 130 E6
CSBY/WL L22 80 E2
VAUX/LVPD L3 9 H5
WDN WA8 158 C1
Mount Pleasant Av
STHEL WA9 104 E2
Mount Pleasant Rd
WAL/NB CH45 95 G6
Mount Rd BEB CH63 150 B5
BEB CH63 169 K2
GR/UP/WCH CH49 129 H4
KKBY L32 72 A6
RF/TRAN CH42 150 C1
RUNC WA7 177 J5
WAL/NB CH45 95 G5
WKBY CH48 146 D2
Mount St CHTN/BK PR9 15 J4
CLVPS L1 9 H7
CSBY/WL L22 80 E2
WDN WA8 19 F1
WLTN L25 154 D1
Mount Ter CHTN/BK PR9 15 J4
The Mount HES CH60 167 K5
SKEL WN8 * 56 D5
WAL/EG CH44 111 J3
Mount Vernon EHL/KEN L7 113 J5
Mount Vernon St EHL/KEN L7 113 J5
Mount Vernon Vw EHL/KEN L7 113 J5
Mountview Cl TOX L8 133 F4
Mountway BEB CH63 150 C4
Mountwood SKEL WN8 56 C1
Mount Wood Rd
RF/TRAN CH42 150 B3
Mourne Cl GTS/LS CH66 194 D3
Mowbray Av RNFD/HAY WA11 89 F6
Mowbray Gv CLB/OSW/ST L13 114 E6
Mowcroft La
WARRW/BUR WA5 140 C6
Mowpen Brow KNUT WA16 165 J5
Moxon Av WARRS WA4 143 J4
Moxon St ECCL WA10 102 E3
Moxon Wy AIMK WN4 79 J5
Moyles Cl WDN WA8 157 J1
Mozart Cl TOX L8 133 G3
Muirfield Cl WARRN/WOL WA2 124 C4
WD/CROXPK L12 115 J1
Muirfield Dr STHP PR8 33 J5
Muirfield Rd HUY L36 116 C6
Muirhead Av CLB/OSW/ST L13 114 C1
Muirhead Av East
WD/CROXPK L12 98 E5
Mulberry Av ECCL WA10 102 E2
GOL/RIS/CU WA3 93 G4
Mulberry Cl CHNE CH2 198 D6
NWD/KWIPK L33 72 E3
WARR WA1 144 D2
Mulberry Ct WARRS WA4 * 162 C2
Mulberry Gv WAL/EG CH44 111 K4
Mulberry Pl EHL/KEN L7 * 9 K6
Mulberry Rd RF/TRAN CH42 150 E1
Mulberry St EHL/KEN L7 9 K6
Mulcrow Cl STHEL WA9 104 B1
Mulgrave St TOX L8 133 F2
Mullein Cl GOL/RIS/CU WA3 92 E3
Mullen Cl WARRW/BUR WA5 * 142 C3
Mulliner St EHL/KEN L7 133 H2
Mullins Av NEWLW WA12 91 H6
Mullion Cl CHTN/BK PR9 20 E6
HLWD L26 155 H3
RUNC WA7 188 A1
Mullion Gv WARRN/WOL WA2 124 C6
Mullion Rd NG/CROX L11 99 G1
Mullion Wk NG/CROX L11 * 84 B6
Mullwood Cl WD/CROXPK L12 99 K2
Mulveton Rd BEB CH63 170 B2
Mumfords La HOY CH47 108 C6
Muncaster Cl PS/BROM CH62 171 F4
Muncaster Dr RNFD/HAY WA11 75 H2
Munster Rd CLB/OSW/ST L13 115 F4
Murat Gv CSBY/WL L22 80 D2
Murat St CSBY/WL L22 80 D2
Murcote Rd DV/KA/FCH L14 115 K2
Murdishaw Av RUNC WA7 188 B2
Muriel Cl WARRW/BUR WA5 140 E3
Muriel St ANF/KKDL L4 97 J5
Murphy Gv STHEL WA9 104 C1
Murrayfield Dr MOR/LEA CH46 109 K3
Murrayfield Rd WLTN L25 135 H3
Murray Gv WKBY CH48 127 F6
Museum St WARR WA1 16 B6
Musker Dr NTHTN L30 69 K6
Musker St CSBY/BLUN L23 69 G6
Muspratt Rd LITH L21 81 H6
Myddleton La
WARRN/WOL WA2 123 H1
Myers Av RAIN/WH L35 118 C2
Myerscough Av BTL L20 5 K1
Myers Rd East CSBY/BLUN L23 69 F6
Myers Rd West CSBY/BLUN L23 68 E6
Mynsule Rd BEB CH63 170 B2
Myrtle Av AIMK WN4 78 E3
NEWLW WA12 106 C3
RNFD/HAY WA11 90 A4
Myrtle Gv CHTN/BK PR9 15 K6
CSBY/WL L22 80 E1
STHP PR8 28 B1
WAL/EG CH44 111 K4
WARRS WA4 143 G6
WDN WA8 157 J3
WGNW/BIL/O WN5 * 77 G5
Myrtle Pde EHL/KEN L7 9 K7
Myrtle St EHL/KEN L7 9 J6
EP CH65 196 B2

N

Nairn Cl BEB CH63 184 A3
WARRN/WOL WA2 124 C4
Nansen Cl WARRW/BUR WA5 142 A2
Nansen Gv ANF/KKDL L4 97 J4
Nant Park Ct WAL/NB CH45 95 J5
Nantwich Cl GR/UP/WCH CH49 148 D1
Nantwich Rd GTS/LS CH66 195 J6
Napier Cl ECCL WA10 12 D5
Napier Dr MOR/LEA CH46 129 G1
Napier Rd PS/BROM CH62 151 G3
Napier St BTL L20 96 D4
ECCL WA10 12 D5
WARR WA1 17 F5
Napier Ter STHP PR8 27 H2
Naples Rd WAL/EG CH44 111 K4
Napps Cl WLTN L25 135 G2
Napps Wy PEN/TH CH61 168 A3
WLTN L25 135 G1
Nares Cl WARRW/BUR WA5 122 C6
Narrow Croft Rd ORM L39 53 F4
Narrow La ORM L39 53 F4
Narrow La (Clieves Hills)
ORM L39 44 B4
Narrow Moss La BRSC L40 45 H1
Naseby Cl CL/PREN CH43 129 K5
Naseby St ANF/KKDL L4 97 H3
Natal Rd WLT/FAZ L9 82 E5
Nathan Dr RNFD/HAY WA11 90 D5
Nathan Gv NWD/KWIPK L33 72 E5
Navigation Cl NTHTN L30 70 D5
RUNC WA7 188 C1
Navigation St WARR WA1 17 H5
Navigation Whf VAUX/LVPD L3 132 C3
Naylor Av GOL/RIS/CU WA3 92 C3
Naylor Crs GTS/LS CH66 195 J1
Naylor Rd CL/PREN CH43 130 B1
WDN WA8 19 J2
Naylorsfield Dr NTHLY L27 135 K3
Naylor's Rd NTHLY L27 136 A3
Naylor St VAUX/LVPD L3 8 D1
WARR WA1 16 E4
Nazeby Av CSBY/BLUN L23 69 G6
Neale Dr GR/UP/WCH CH49 129 F6
Neales Fold CHTN/BK PR9 21 G6
Neasham Cl HLWD L26 155 J4
Nedens Gv MGHL L31 62 A4
Nedens La MGHL L31 62 A4
Needham Cl RUNC WA7 11 K4
Needham Rd EHL/KEN L7 114 A5
Needwood Dr BEB CH63 170 B2
Neills Rd STHEL WA9 121 F1
Neilson Rd AIG/SPK L17 133 G6
Neil St WDN WA8 158 C1
Nell's La ORM L39 62 D2
Nelson Av RAIN/WH L35 118 A5
Nelson Ct STHP PR8 27 G3
Nelson Dr PEN/TH CH61 167 J2
Nelson Pl RAIN/WH L35 118 A5
Nelson Rd EHL/KEN L7 113 K6
EP CH65 6 D1
GOL/RIS/CU WA3 125 F3
LITH L21 * 81 J4
RF/TRAN CH42 151 F2
Nelson's Cft BEB CH63 170 C2
Nelson St BTL L20 4 C7
CLVPS L1 9 G7
NEWLW WA12 106 A2
STHP PR8 14 D6
WAL/NB CH45 95 J6

WAV L15 133 K2
WDN WA8 158 B5
Nelville Rd *WLT/FAZ* L9 83 F4
Neptune Cl *RUNC* WA7 178 C6
Neptune St *BIRK* CH41 2 E2
Ness Gv *KKBY* L32 84 B1
Neston Av *STHEL* WA9 119 K3
Neston Gdns *BIRK* CH41 2 A1
Neston Gn *GTS/LS* CH66 195 G5
Neston Rd *BEB* CH63 182 B1
NSTN CH64 192 A4
NSTN CH64 193 F1
Neston St *ANF/KKDL* L4 97 H4
Netherby St *TOX* L8 132 E6
Netherfield *WDN* WA8 157 J3
Netherfield Cl *CL/PREN* CH43 129 K5
Netherfield Rd North *EV* L5 113 G2
Netherfield Rd South *EV* L5 113 G3
Netherley Rd *RAIN/WH* L35 136 C4
Netherpool Rd *GTS/LS* CH66 195 J1
Netherton Dr *FROD/HEL* WA6 200 D2
Netherton Gra *NTHTN* L30 70 E6
Netherton Gn *NTHTN* L30 70 C4
Netherton La *NTHTN* L30 70 B4
Netherton Park Rd *LITH* L21 82 A3
Netherton Rd *BTL* L20 82 A5
CALD/MH L18 153 H2
MOR/LEA CH46 129 F1
Netherton Wy *NTHTN* L30 82 B3
Netherwood Rd *NG/CROX* L11 98 C3
Netley St *ANF/KKDL* L4 97 G5
Nettlestead Rd *NG/CROX* L11 98 E5
Neva Av *MOR/LEA* CH46 128 E1
Nevada Cl *WARRW/BUR* WA5 141 J2
Neverstitch Cl *SKEL* WN8 * 56 B3
Neverstitch Rd *SKEL* WN8 55 K3
Neville Av *STHEL* WA9 105 F3
WARRN/WOL WA2 123 K6
Neville Cl *CL/PREN* CH43 129 K5
Neville Crs *WARRW/BUR* WA5 141 H6
Neville Rd *CSBY/WL* L22 81 F2
PS/BROM CH62 171 G6
WAL/EG CH44 111 G3
Neville St *NEWLW* WA12 106 A2
Nevill St *STHP* PR8 14 E3
Nevin St *NPK/KEN* L6 113 J4
Nevison St *EHL/KEN* L7 113 K6
Nevitte Cl *STBRV* L28 100 A5
New Acres Cl *CL/PREN* CH43 129 K1
Newark Cl *CL/PREN* CH43 129 K5
HUY L36 116 D1
NTHTN L30 70 E4
Newark St *ANF/KKDL* L4 97 G4
New Bank Rd *WDN* WA8 157 G2
New Barn Av *AIMK* WN4 79 H6
New Barnet *WDN* WA8 138 E5
New Bird St *CLVPS* L1 132 C2
Newbold Crs *WKBY* CH48 127 K6
Newbold Gv *WD/CROXPK* L12 99 K3
Newborough Av
CALD/MH L18 134 A4
CSBY/BLUN L23 69 H5
Newborough Cl
WARRW/BUR WA5 122 D5
Newbridge Cl *AIMK* WN4 78 C6
GR/UP/WCH CH49 129 J5
RUNC WA7 188 B1
WARRW/BUR WA5 122 C5
New Bridge Rd *EP* CH65 7 K7
Newbridge Rd *EP* CH65 196 E6
Newburgh Cl *RUNC* WA7 178 C4
Newburns La *CL/PREN* CH43 130 E6
Newburn St *ANF/KKDL* L4 97 H4
Newbury Cl *HUY* L36 116 D6
WDN WA8 138 E6
Newbury Wy *MOR/LEA* CH46 109 J4
WD/CROXPK L12 115 J2
Newby Av *RAIN/WH* L35 118 C3
Newby Cl *STHP* PR8 33 H6
Newby Dr *HUY* L36 116 C4
Newby Gv *WD/CROXPK* L12 99 G3
Newby St *ANF/KKDL* L4 97 H5
Newcastle Rd *WAV* L15 134 B3
New Cswy *HTWN* L38 49 H5
New Chester Rd *BIRK* CH41 3 H6
PS/BROM CH62 184 D4
RF/TRAN CH42 151 F2
Newcombe Av
WARRN/WOL WA2 143 G1
Newcombe St *NPK/KEN* L6 113 K2
New Court Wy *ORM* L39 45 K6
Newcroft Rd *WLTN* L25 135 G5
New Cross St *ECCL* WA10 13 F5
PR/KW L34 * 101 K6
New Cut La *NWD/KWIPK* L33 86 B3
STHP PR8 34 C1
WARR WA1 144 A3
Newdales Cl *CL/PREN* CH43 129 K2
Newdown Rd *NG/CROX* L11 84 C6
Newell Rd *WAL/EG* CH44 111 H3
Newenham Crs
DV/KA/FCH L14 115 J4
New Ferry By-Pass
PS/BROM CH62 151 G4
New Ferry Rd *PS/BROM* CH62 151 G4
Newfield Cl *CSBY/BLUN* L23 69 K3
Newfield Rd *LYMM* WA13 145 J6
Newfields *ECCL* WA10 102 E1
New Fort Wy *BTL* L20 81 H5
New Foul La *STHP* PR8 28 C3
Newgate Rd *SKEL* WN8 57 H6
New Glade Hl *RNFD/HAY* WA11 89 G5
New Grey Rock Cl *NPK/KEN* L6 113 K3
New Grosvenor Rd *EP* CH65 6 C1
New Hall Dr *STHP* PR8 29 F6
Newhall La *HOY* CH47 127 G3
New Hall La *NG/CROX* L11 98 C5
Newhall St *CLVPS* L1 * 132 D2
Newhaven Rd *WAL/NB* CH45 95 J6
WARRN/WOL WA2 123 H3
New Hedley Gv *EV* L5 112 E2
New Henderson St *TOX* L8 132 D3
New Hey *WD/CROXPK* L12 114 E2
New Hey La *NSTN* CH64 193 H2
New Hey Rd *GR/UP/WCH* CH49 129 J6
Newholme Cl *WD/CROXPK* L12 99 J2
Newhope Rd *BIRK* CH41 2 B2
Newhouse Rd *WAV* L15 * 133 J2
New Hutte La *HLWD* L26 155 J5
Newick Rd *KKBY* L32 84 B2
Newington *CLVPS* L1 9 G5
New Islington *VAUX/LVPD* L3 9 H2
Newland Cl *WDN* WA8 138 B6
Newland Ct *AIG/SPK* L17 133 H6
Newland Dr *WAL/EG* CH44 111 G3
Newlands Av *BRSC* L40 39 F5
Newlands Cl *FROD/HEL* WA6 201 F3
Newlands Dr *GOL/RIS/CU* WA3 92 D3
Newlands Rd *BEB* CH63 * 170 C1
RNFD/HAY WA11 89 F4
WARRS WA4 162 E1
New La *BRSC* L40 38 B3
CHTN/BK PR9 24 B1
ORM L39 51 F2
ORM L39 53 J3
WARRS WA4 163 G6
Newling St *BIRK* CH41 2 B3
Newlyn Av *LITH* L21 81 H2
MGHL L31 62 C6
Newlyn Cl *HOY* CH47 108 C5
RUNC WA7 188 A1
Newlyn Dr *AIMK* WN4 91 G1
SKEL WN8 57 F6
Newlyn Gdns
WARRW/BUR WA5 140 E6
Newlyn Gv *RNFD/HAY* WA11 89 G4
Newlyn Rd *HOY* CH47 108 C6
NG/CROX L11 84 C6
Newlyn Wk *NG/CROX* L11 * 84 C6
New Manchester Rd
WARR WA1 143 K2
New Manor Rd *WARRS* WA4 189 G1
Newman St *ANF/KKDL* L4 97 F5
WARRS WA4 143 J6
New Market Rd *LITH* L21 81 J3
New Meadow La *FMBY* L37 50 A5
New Mill Stile *WLTN* L25 135 H6
Newmoore La *RUNC* WA7 178 E1
Newmorn Ct *AIG/SPK* L17 152 D1
Newnham Dr *EP* CH65 6 E7
Newport Av *WAL/NB* CH45 94 D6
Newport Cl *CL/PREN* CH43 129 K5
Newport Ct *EV* L5 112 E2
New Quay *VAUX/LVPD* L3 8 B3
Newquay Cl *RUNC* WA7 188 A1
New Rd *CLB/OSW/ST* L13 114 C2
FMBY L37 41 G6
GTS/LS CH66 194 D1
LYMM WA13 145 K6
PR/KW L34 102 A6
WARRS WA4 16 E7
New School La *GTS/LS* CH66 194 E1
Newsham Cl *WDN* WA8 138 A5
Newsham Dr *NPK/KEN* L6 114 A2
Newsham Rd *HUY* L36 136 D1
Newsham St *EV* L5 113 F2
News La *RNFD/HAY* WA11 66 B5
Newstead Av *CSBY/BLUN* L23 68 C6
Newstead Rd *TOX* L8 * 133 H2
WDN WA8 156 E5
Newstet Rd *NWD/KWIPK* L33 85 G1
New St *NSTN* CH64 191 K4
ORM L39 43 K2
RUNC WA7 10 D5
STHEL WA9 120 A1
WAL/EG CH44 112 A5
Newton Av *GOL/RIS/CU* WA3 125 G2
Newton Cl *WD/CROXPK* L12 99 F5
Newton Ct *CLB/OSW/ST* L13 114 C6
Newton Cross La *WKBY* CH48 147 F1
Newton Dr *WKBY* CH48 147 F1
Newton Gv *WARRN/WOL* WA2 124 B4
Newton La *NEWLW* WA12 91 K5
WARRS WA4 166 B5
Newton Park Dr *NEWLW* WA12 107 F3
Newton Park Rd *WKBY* CH48 147 F1
Newton Rd *CLB/OSW/ST* L13 114 C3
EP CH65 6 E4
GOL/RIS/CU WA3 92 C6
HOY CH47 127 H2
STHEL WA9 104 E2
WAL/EG CH44 111 G3
WARRN/WOL WA2 107 F5
WGNW/BIL/O WN5 77 J3
Newton St *BIRK* CH41 2 C3
CHTN/BK PR9 23 J6
Newton Wk *BTL* L20 4 D3
Newton Wy *GR/UP/WCH* CH49 129 G4
VAUX/LVPD L3 9 J4
New Tower Ct *WAL/NB* CH45 95 J5
Newtown *NSTN* CH64 192 A3
Newway *DV/KA/FCH* L14 116 A2
New Wy *ORM* L39 64 B5
Nicander Rd *CALD/MH* L18 134 A4
Nicholas Rd *CSBY/BLUN* L23 68 C5
WDN WA8 157 H3
Nicholas St *VAUX/LVPD* L3 * 113 F4
Nicholford Hall Dr *WDN* WA8 138 E3
Nicholl Rd *ECCL* WA10 87 H5
Nicholls Dr *PEN/TH* CH61 167 K1
Nicholls St *WARRS* WA4 163 G1
Nicholson St *STHEL* WA9 104 C1
WARR WA1 16 A4
Nickleby Cl *TOX* L8 132 E4
Nicol Av *GOL/RIS/CU* WA3 125 H6
Nicol Mere Dr *AIMK* WN4 79 G4
Nicol Rd *AIMK* WN4 79 F4
Nidderdale Av *RAIN/WH* L35 119 F4
Nigel Rd *HES* CH60 168 C5
Nightingale Cl
GOL/RIS/CU WA3 125 H3
KKBY L32 72 A6
NTHLY L27 136 C4
RUNC WA7 187 H2
Nightingale Rd *WD/CROXPK* L12 99 K2
Nimrod St *ANF/KKDL* L4 97 H4
Ninth Av *WLT/FAZ* L9 83 G4
Nipe La *SKEL* WN8 66 D2
Nithsdale Rd *WAV* L15 133 K3
Nixons La *SKEL* WN8 57 F6
STHP PR8 34 A2
Nixon St *ANF/KKDL* L4 97 H3
Noble Cl *GOL/RIS/CU* WA3 125 G4
Noctorum Av
GR/UP/WCH CH49 129 K4
Noctorum Dell *CL/PREN* CH43 130 A5
Noctorum La *CL/PREN* CH43 130 B3
Noctorum Rd *CL/PREN* CH43 130 A4
Noctorum Wy *CL/PREN* CH43 130 B6
Noel Ga *ORM* L39 53 F4
Noel St *TOX* L8 133 G2
Nolan St *STHP* PR8 27 K2
Nook La *GOL/RIS/CU* WA3 92 C3
STHEL WA9 104 D4
WARRN/WOL WA2 124 D5
WARRS WA4 143 K6
Nook Ri *WAV* L15 134 C1
The Nook *CL/PREN* CH43 2 A6
ECCL WA10 87 J5
WKBY CH48 147 J1
WLTN L25 135 J6
Noonan Cl *WLT/FAZ* L9 97 H1
Nora St *WARR* WA1 17 G5
Norbreck Av *DV/KA/FCH* L14 115 J5
Norbreck Cl *WARRW/BUR* WA5 141 H5
Norbreck Crs
WARRW/BUR WA5 141 H5
Norburn Crs *FMBY* L37 49 F3
Norbury Av *BEB* CH63 150 D6
CALD/MH L18 134 A4
WARRN/WOL WA2 143 G1
WGNW/BIL/O WN5 77 G3
Norbury Cl *BEB* CH63 150 E6
CHTN/BK PR9 21 F6
WDN WA8 19 K1
Norbury Fold *RAIN/WH* L35 119 G6
Norbury Rd *KKBY* L32 84 C1
Norcliffe Rd *RAIN/WH* L35 118 D3
Norcott Av *WARRS* WA4 162 C1
Norcott Dr *WARRW/BUR* WA5 121 K1
Norden Cl *GOL/RIS/CU* WA3 124 E2
Norfolk Cl *BTL* L20 5 G3
CL/PREN CH43 129 K4
Norfolk Dr *WARRW/BUR* WA5 141 F3
WKBY CH48 146 D2
Norfolk Gv *STHP* PR8 27 G6
Norfolk Pl *LITH* L21 * 81 H4
WDN WA8 157 H3
Norfolk Rd *ECCL* WA10 103 F4
EP CH65 6 D5
MGHL L31 71 F2
STHP PR8 27 G6
Norfolk St *CLVPS* L1 132 C2
RUNC WA7 11 G3
Norgate St *ANF/KKDL* L4 97 H6
Norgrove Cl *RUNC* WA7 178 C5
Norland's La *RAIN/WH* L35 138 D1
Norland St *WDN* WA8 19 J1
Norleane Crs *RUNC* WA7 176 E5
Norley Av *EP* CH65 195 J3
PS/BROM CH62 184 B4
Norley Dr *ECCL* WA10 102 C2
Norley Pl *HLWD* L26 155 H5
Norman Av *NEWLW* WA12 106 E2
RNFD/HAY WA11 91 F4
Normanby Cl
WARRW/BUR WA5 142 B2
Norman Cl *GTS/LS* CH66 202 D3
Normandale Rd *ANF/KKDL* L4 98 B4
Normandy Rd *HUY* L36 116 D4
Normanhurst *ORM* L39 54 A1
Norman Rd *BTL* L20 81 K4
CSBY/BLUN L23 68 E6
RUNC WA7 10 D7
WAL/EG CH44 112 A5
Norman Salisbury Ct
ECCL WA10 13 F3
Normans Rd *STHEL* WA9 104 D6
Normanston Rd
CL/PREN CH43 130 E5
Norman St *BIRK* CH41 130 C1
VAUX/LVPD L3 9 J3
WARRN/WOL WA2 16 E2
Normanton Av *AIG/SPK* L17 133 H6
Normanton Cl *CL/PREN* CH43 130 D5
Norma Rd *CSBY/WL* L22 81 F2
Norreys Av *WARRW/BUR* WA5 142 C1
Norric Ct *SPK/HALE* L24 * 154 E6
Norris Cl *CL/PREN* CH43 129 K5
Norris Green Crs *NG/CROX* L11 98 E4
Norris Green Rd
WD/CROXPK L12 115 F1
Norris Green Wy *NG/CROX* L11 98 E4
Norris House Dr *ORM* L39 53 G5
Norris Rd *PR/KW* L34 117 J1
Norris St *WARRN/WOL* WA2 143 F1
Norris Wy *FMBY* L37 49 H2
Norseman Cl *WD/CROXPK* L12 99 F5
Northam Cl *CHTN/BK* PR9 20 D6
North Av *AIN/FAZ* L10 83 H1
SPK/HALE L24 154 D5
WARRN/WOL WA2 142 E1
North Barcombe Rd
CHLDW L16 134 E2
Northbrook Cl *TOX* L8 133 F2
Northbrook Rd *WAL/EG* CH44 111 K4
Northbrook St *TOX* L8 133 F2
Northbury Rd *GTS/LS* CH66 202 C2
North Cantril Av
WD/CROXPK L12 99 J5
North Cl *PS/BROM* CH62 170 E3
Northcote Cl *EV* L5 113 H3
Northcote Rd *WAL/NB* CH45 110 D2
WLT/FAZ L9 * 97 H2
Northdale Rd *WARR* WA1 143 K1
WAV L15 134 A1
North Dingle *ANF/KKDL* L4 97 G6
North Dr *HES* CH60 168 A6
WAV L15 134 A1
WD/CROXPK L12 115 F2
Northdunes *HTWN* L38 59 F3
North End La *HLWD* L26 136 B6
HTWN L38 59 G2
Northern La *RAIN/WH* L35 137 K6
Northern Perimeter Rd
NTHTN L30 70 B4
Northern Ri *GTS/LS* CH66 195 H5
Northern Rd *SPK/HALE* L24 173 K1
The Northern Rd
CSBY/BLUN L23 69 F5
Northfield *SKEL* WN8 56 D1
Northfield Cl *NWD/KWIPK* L33 73 F5
STHEL WA9 120 B4
Northfield Rd *BTL* L20 82 B5
North Florida Rd
RNFD/HAY WA11 90 C3
North Front *RAIN/WH* L35 118 A6
Northgate Rd *CLB/OSW/ST* L13 114 D2
North Gv *CALD/MH* L18 153 K2
North Hill St *TOX* L8 132 E4
North John St *CLVP* L2 8 D4
ECCL WA10 13 F5
North Leach Dr *STHP* PR8 33 G4
North Linkside Rd *WLTN* L25 155 F2
North Manor Wy *WLTN* L25 155 F2
North Meade *MGHL* L31 61 K5
Northmead Rd *ALL/GAR* L19 154 B4
North Moor La *ORM* L39 44 D3
North Moss La *FMBY* L37 41 K4
North Mossley Hill Rd
CALD/MH L18 134 A5
North Mount Rd *KKBY* L32 72 B5
Northolt Ct *WARRN/WOL* WA2 124 A6
North Pde *HOY* CH47 127 F2
KKBY L32 84 D1
NSTN CH64 181 F5
SPK/HALE L24 173 K2
North Park Brook Rd
WARRW/BUR WA5 122 E6
North Park Ct *WAL/EG* CH44 112 A4
North Park Rd *KKBY* L32 72 B5
North Perimeter Rd
NWD/KWIPK L33 73 J5
Northridge Rd *PEN/TH* CH61 148 D6
North Rd *ALL/GAR* L19 153 G5
CHTN/BK PR9 23 K1
DV/KA/FCH L14 115 G5
ECCL WA10 13 F1
EP CH65 185 G4
RF/TRAN CH42 131 F6
SPK/HALE L24 155 K6
WKBY CH48 146 B1
North St *AIMK* WN4 79 J4
CHTN/BK PR9 15 G2
NEWLW WA12 105 K1
RNFD/HAY WA11 90 D5
VAUX/LVPD L3 8 E2
North Sudley Rd *AIG/SPK* L17 153 F1
Northumberland Gv *TOX* L8 132 C4
Northumberland St *TOX* L8 132 E4
Northumberland Ter *EV* L5 113 G1
Northumberland Wy
NTHTN L30 69 K6
North Vw *EHL/KEN* L7 113 K6
HUY L36 117 G5
WARRW/BUR WA5 141 F2
Northway *HES* CH60 * 168 D4
LYMM WA13 145 J5
MGHL L31 71 F2
RUNC WA7 177 J5
SKEL WN8 56 D4
WARRN/WOL WA2 123 H5
WAV L15 134 C1
WDN WA8 157 J2
Northways *PS/BROM* CH62 171 F2
Northwich Cl *CSBY/BLUN* L23 69 J3
Northwich Rd *RUNC* WA7 188 C3
North William St
WAL/EG CH44 * 112 A5
Northwood Av *NEWLW* WA12 107 F1
Northwood Rd *CL/PREN* CH43 149 J1
HUY L36 117 F3
RUNC WA7 177 H3
Norton Av *WARRW/BUR* WA5 141 F4
Norton Dr *PEN/TH* CH61 147 K4
Norton Ga *RUNC* WA7 178 B5
Norton Gv *MGHL* L31 71 G3
STHEL WA9 103 F6
Norton Hl *RUNC* WA7 178 B4
Norton La *RUNC* WA7 178 A5
Norton Rd *WKBY* CH48 127 F6
Norton Station Rd *RUNC* WA7 178 C5
Norton St *BTL* L20 4 C1
VAUX/LVPD L3 9 G2
Norton Vw *RUNC* WA7 177 K5
Norton Village *RUNC* WA7 178 C5
Nortonwood La *RUNC* WA7 178 B4
Norville *GTS/LS* CH66 195 G2
Norville Rd *DV/KA/FCH* L14 115 G5
Norwich Av *AIMK* WN4 91 J1
GOL/RIS/CU WA3 92 E3
Norwich Dr *GR/UP/WCH* CH49 129 H2
GTS/LS CH66 202 C3
Norwich Rd *WAV* L15 134 B3
Norwich Wy *KKBY* L32 84 D1
Norwood Av *AIMK* WN4 78 E3
CHTN/BK PR9 23 G5
GOL/RIS/CU WA3 93 F4
LITH L21 81 J2
Norwood Ct *GR/UP/WCH* CH49 128 E6
Norwood Crs *CHTN/BK* PR9 23 G5
Norwood Gv *NPK/KEN* L6 113 K3
RNFD/HAY WA11 75 H3
Norwood Rd
GR/UP/WCH CH49 128 E5
STHP PR8 23 H6
WAL/EG CH44 111 H5
Norwyn Rd *NG/CROX* L11 98 C3
Nostell Rd *AIMK* WN4 79 F4
Nottingham Cl *RAIN/WH* L35 118 E2
WARR WA1 144 C3
Nottingham Rd *HUY* L36 116 C6
Nowshera Av *PEN/TH* CH61 148 C6
Nuffield Cl *GR/UP/WCH* CH49 129 G5
Nun Cl *CL/PREN* CH43 130 E5
Nunn St *STHEL* WA9 104 B2
Nunsford Cl *LITH* L21 82 A1
Nunthorpe Rd *PR/KW* L34 85 G6
The Nurseries *FMBY* L37 49 G3
Nurse Rd *PEN/TH* CH61 148 E5
Nursery Av *ORM* L39 46 A5
Nursery Cl *CL/PREN* CH43 130 E6
WDN WA8 139 J6
WLTN L25 155 F3
Nursery Dr *FMBY* L37 49 F3
Nursery La *ALL/GAR* L19 153 K4
Nursery Rd *MGHL* L31 62 A3
STHEL WA9 103 F6
Nutgrove Av *STHEL* WA9 * 103 F6
Nutgrove Hall Dr *STHEL* WA9 103 F6
Nutgrove Rd *STHEL* WA9 118 E1
Nuthall Rd *STHP* PR8 28 B4
Nut St *STHEL* WA9 103 F6
Nuttall Ct *GOL/RIS/CU* WA3 124 E3
Nuttall St *EHL/KEN* L7 114 A6
Nyland Rd *HUY* L36 116 D2

O

Oak Av *GOL/RIS/CU* WA3 92 C3
GR/UP/WCH CH49 128 E3
NEWLW WA12 106 C2
ORM L39 53 H1
RNFD/HAY WA11 90 D4
WLT/FAZ L9 82 E5
Oak Bank *BIRK* CH41 2 C6
Oakbank Rd *AIG/SPK* L17 133 K4
Oakbank St *WAL/EG* CH44 111 J4
Oakbourne Cl *AIG/SPK* L17 152 D1
Oak Cl *MOR/LEA* CH46 128 E2
RAIN/WH L35 118 A4
WD/CROXPK L12 99 K4
Oak Crs *SKEL* WN8 55 K4
Oakdale Av *FROD/HEL* WA6 201 G3
WAL/EG CH44 111 K5
WARRS WA4 162 C2
Oakdale Dr *GR/UP/WCH* CH49 147 K1
Oakdale Rd *CALD/MH* L18 134 B4
CSBY/WL L22 80 E1
WAL/EG CH44 111 K6
Oakdene Av *GTS/LS* CH66 195 F4
WARR WA1 144 B2
Oakdene Cl *PS/BROM* CH62 184 A2
Oakdene Rd *ANF/KKDL* L4 97 K6
RF/TRAN CH42 131 F6
Oak Dr *RUNC* WA7 177 F6
Oakenden Cl *AIMK* WN4 79 F3
Oakenholt Rd *MOR/LEA* CH46 109 J6
Oakes St *VAUX/LVPD* L3 9 J3
Oakfield *ANF/KKDL* L4 113 K1
Oakfield Av *GOL/RIS/CU* WA3 92 A2
WLTN L25 135 H5
Oakfield Cl *STHEL* WA9 103 F6
Oakfield Dr *FMBY* L37 48 D1
HUY L36 136 C1
WDN WA8 157 F3
Oakfield Gv *HUY* L36 136 C1
Oakfield Rd *ANF/KKDL* L4 113 J1
GTS/LS CH66 194 B1
HTWN L38 59 F5
PS/BROM CH62 170 E5
Oakgate Cl *NG/CROX* L11 99 F2
Oak Gn *ORM* L39 45 K6
Oak Gv *EP* CH65 195 K6
Oakham Ct *CHTN/BK* PR9 * 15 H3
Oakham Dr *AIN/FAZ* L10 83 J2
MOR/LEA CH46 109 F6
Oakham St *TOX* L8 132 C3
Oakhill Cl *MGHL* L31 62 B5
WD/CROXPK L12 99 H2
Oakhill Cottage La *MGHL* L31 62 B3
Oakhill Dr *MGHL* L31 62 A3
Oakhill Pk *CLB/OSW/ST* L13 115 F5
Oakhill Rd *CLB/OSW/ST* L13 115 F5
MGHL L31 62 B5
Oakhurst Cl *WLTN* L25 135 J5
Oakland Cl *LITH* L21 81 K5
Oakland Dr *GR/UP/WCH* CH49 129 H3
Oakland Rd *ALL/GAR* L19 153 G3
Oaklands *RAIN/WH* L35 118 E4
Oaklands Av *CSBY/BLUN* L23 69 F4
Oaklands Ct *STHEL* WA9 120 A3
Oaklands Dr *BEB* CH63 151 F5
HES CH60 168 A4
LYMM WA13 164 E1
Oaklands Rd *GOL/RIS/CU* WA3 93 G4
Oaklands Ter *PEN/TH* CH61 * 168 A3
Oakland St *WARR* WA1 143 H2
WDN WA8 176 D1
Oak La *WD/CROXPK* L12 99 G3
Oak La North *WD/CROXPK* L12 99 G3
Oakleaf Ms *CL/PREN* CH43 130 A4
Oaklea Rd *PEN/TH* CH61 148 C5
Oaklee Gv *NWD/KWIPK* L33 73 F5
Oak Leigh *CLB/OSW/ST* L13 114 C2
Oakleigh *SKEL* WN8 67 F5
Oakleigh Gv *BEB* CH63 150 E5
Oakley Av *WGNW/BIL/O* WN5 77 G3
Oakley Cl *WD/CROXPK* L12 99 J2
Oakley Ct *EP* CH65 6 E7
Oak Meadows Ct *RAIN/WH* L35 119 G6
Oakmere Cl *MOR/LEA* CH46 109 J3
WLT/FAZ L9 82 D4
Oakmere Dr *GR/UP/WCH* CH49 128 D5
GTS/LS CH66 202 D3
WARRW/BUR WA5 141 G6
Oakmere St *RUNC* WA7 10 D5
Oakmoore *RUNC* WA7 178 E1
Oakridge Cl *PS/BROM* CH62 170 E3
Oakridge Rd *PS/BROM* CH62 170 E3
Oak Rd *BEB* CH63 150 E4
GTS/LS CH66 184 B6
HUY L36 136 A1
LYMM WA13 145 H6
RAIN/WH L35 118 A4

WARRW/BUR WA5 141 G6
Oaks Cl STHEL WA9 120 B4
Oaks La PEN/TH CH61 168 A1
Oaksmeade Cl WD/CROXPK L12 99 K2
Oaks Pl WDN WA8 18 C5
The Oaks PS/BROM CH62 170 E5
WD/CROXPK L12 99 K2
WKBY CH48 * 146 D2
Oakston Av RAIN/WH L35 119 F5
Oak St BTL L20 5 F2
EP CH65 196 B2
STHEL WA9 104 C5
STHP PR8 28 B1
Oaksway HES CH60 181 G1
Oak Ter EHL/KEN L7 * 114 A5
Oakthorn Gv RNFD/HAY WA11 90 B5
Oak Tree Ct SKEL WN8 57 F2
Oaktree Pl RF/TRAN CH42 131 J6
Oaktree Rd ECCL WA10 87 H6
Oak V CLB/OSW/ST L13 115 F5
Oak Vw SPK/HALE L24 174 B2
Oakways WARRS WA4 162 C6
Oak Wharf Ms WARRS WA4 * 162 B3
Oakwood SKEL WN8 * 57 F2
Oakwood Av AIMK WN4 91 F1
STHP PR8 33 K3
WARR WA1 17 J1
Oakwood Cl WLTN L25 135 J4
Oakwood Dr CL/PREN CH43 130 B1
HUY L36 117 F6
STHP PR8 34 A4
Oakwood Ga GOL/RIS/CU WA3 125 F3
Oakwood Pk PS/BROM CH62 184 A2
Oakwood Rd HLWD L26 155 H4
Oakworth Cl NWD/KWIPK L33 72 D5
Oakworth Dr HUY L36 136 D2
PS/BROM CH62 151 H4
Oarside Dr WAL/NB CH45 111 G1
Oatfield La LITH L21 81 J1
Oatlands Rd KKBY L32 * 84 B1
The Oatlands WKBY CH48 146 D2
Oban Dr AIMK WN4 78 B5
HES CH60 168 A5
Oban Gv WARRN/WOL WA2 124 C4
Oban Rd ANF/KKDL L4 113 K1
Oberon St BTL L20 96 E4
O'Brien Gv STHEL WA9 104 C1
Observatory Rd
CL/PREN CH43 130 A1
Oceanic Rd CLB/OSW/ST L13 114 D5
Ocean Rd LITH L21 81 J4
O'Connell Cl RNFD/HAY WA11 90 B5
O'Connell Rd VAUX/LVPD L3 113 F3
Octavia Ct HUY L36 117 G6
Octavia Hill Rd LITH L21 81 K2
Odsey St EHL/KEN L7 114 A5
Off Botanic Rd CHTN/BK PR9 23 J4
Ogle Cl RAIN/WH L35 118 A2
Oglet La SPK/HALE L24 173 H3
Oil Sites Rd EP CH65 7 F2
Oil St VAUX/LVPD L3 112 D3
O'Keeffe Rd STHEL WA9 104 A1
Okehampton Rd CHLDW L16 134 E1
Okell Dr HLWD L26 155 H1
Okell St RUNC WA7 10 D5
Old Acre HTWN L38 59 F4
Old Barn Rd ANF/KKDL L4 113 K1
WAL/EG CH44 111 G4
Old Bidston Rd BIRK CH41 2 B1
Old Boston RNFD/HAY WA11 91 F4
Old Boundary Wy ORM L39 45 K5
Oldbridge Rd SPK/HALE L24 174 A2
Old Cherry La LYMM WA13 164 B5
Old Chester Rd
FROD/HEL WA6 199 J6
GTS/LS CH66 195 G5
RF/TRAN CH42 150 E1
WARRS WA4 161 J4
Old Church Cl EP CH65 * 6 E1
Old Church Yd CLVP L2 8 C4
Old Colliery Rd RAIN/WH L35 117 K4
Old Colliery Yd AIMK WN4 78 B6
Old Court House Rd
PS/BROM CH62 151 J6
Old Distillery Rd SPK/HALE L24 154 E6
Old Dover Rd HUY L36 135 K1
Old Eccleston La ECCL WA10 102 E2
Old Engine La SKEL WN8 55 J3
Old Farm Cl NSTN CH64 193 H1
Old Farm Rd CSBY/BLUN L23 69 G5
KKBY L32 84 E5
Oldfield Cl HES CH60 167 J3
Oldfield Dr HES CH60 167 G4
Oldfield Gdns HES CH60 167 H4
Oldfield La WKBY CH48 128 B4
Oldfield Rd ALL/GAR L19 153 H2
EP CH65 6 C5
HES CH60 167 H3
LYMM WA13 145 H5
Oldfield St ECCL WA10 13 F1
Oldfield Wy HES CH60 167 H3
Oldgate WDN WA8 157 H5
Old Gorsey La WAL/EG CH44 111 H5
Old Greasby Rd
GR/UP/WCH CH49 129 G4
Old Hall RAIN/WH L35 137 H1
Old Hall Cl MGHL L31 71 G2
WARRS WA4 161 K3
Old Hall Dr AIMK WN4 91 F1
EP CH65 6 C7
Old Hall Gdns RNFD/HAY WA11 75 H3
Old Hall La CHNE CH2 198 C6
KKBY L32 84 C1
Old Hall Rd MGHL L31 71 G2
PS/BROM CH62 171 H4
WARRW/BUR WA5 142 A1
Old Hall St VAUX/LVPD L3 8 B2
Oldham Pl CLVPS L1 9 G5
Oldham St CLVPS L1 9 G6
WARRS WA4 143 G6
Old Haymarket CLVPS L1 9 F3
Old Higher Rd WDN WA8 156 C6
Old Hutte La SPK/HALE L24 155 K6
Old Kennel Cl STBRV L28 99 K5
Old La FMBY L37 41 F5
MGHL L31 62 C3
ORM L39 51 G2
PR/KW L34 118 B1
RAIN/WH L35 118 D5
RNFD/HAY WA11 75 G2
Old Leeds St VAUX/LVPD L3 8 B2
Old Links Cl CHTN/BK PR9 23 K5
Old Liverpool Rd
WARRW/BUR WA5 142 B5
Old Lodge Cl WD/CROXPK L12 99 F5
Old Market Pl WARR WA1 16 C4
Old Maryland La
MOR/LEA CH46 109 J6
Old Meadow PR/KW L34 85 J6
Old Meadow Rd PEN/TH CH61 167 J2
Old Mill Av STHEL WA9 120 B2
Old Mill Cl HES CH60 168 B6
Old Mill Hl ORM L39 53 H2
Old Mill La FMBY L37 49 F1
PR/KW L34 100 E1
WAV L15 134 B1
Old Moss La ORM L39 42 E6
Old Nook La RNFD/HAY WA11 89 H5
Old Orch RAIN/WH L35 118 A6
Old Park La CHTN/BK PR9 23 J6
Old Post Office Pl CLVPS L1 * 8 E5
Old Prescot Cl MGHL L31 63 G5
Old Pump La
GR/UP/WCH CH49 128 D6
The Old Quarry WLTN L25 154 D1
Old Quay Cl NSTN CH64 191 H2
Old Quay La NSTN CH64 191 J2
Old Quay St RUNC WA7 11 G3
Old Racecourse Rd MGHL L31 70 E1
Old Rectory Gn ORM L39 52 E6
SFTN L29 70 B2
Old Riding DV/KA/FCH L14 115 K2
Old Rd AIMK WN4 79 F4
WARRS WA4 16 E7
Old Ropery CLVP L2 * 8 D4
Old Rough La NWD/KWIPK L33 84 D1
Old School Cl NSTN CH64 192 A4
Old School House La
WARRN/WOL WA2 107 G6
Old School Pl AIMK WN4 79 F6
Old School Wy
CL/PREN CH43 * 130 B2
Old Smithy La LYMM WA13 164 D1
Old Thomas La DV/KA/FCH L14 115 H6
Old Town Cl SKEL WN8 55 K5
Old Town La FMBY L37 48 E1
Old Town Wy SKEL WN8 55 K5
Old Upton La WDN WA8 138 D5
Old Vicarage Rd NSTN CH64 193 H1
Old Wargrave Rd
NEWLW WA12 106 B2
Old Whint Rd RNFD/HAY WA11 89 K5
Old Wood Rd PEN/TH CH61 167 K1
Oleander Dr ECCL WA10 102 E1
O'Leary St WARRN/WOL WA2 143 F2
Olga Rd STHEL WA9 104 A6
Olinda St PS/BROM CH62 151 G4
Olive Cl MGHL L31 * 83 K1
Olive Crs BIRK CH41 131 H5
Olivedale Rd CALD/MH L18 134 A5
Olive Dr NSTN CH64 191 K1
Olive Gv HUY L36 116 D5
NTHTN L30 82 D2
SKEL WN8 56 A4
STHP PR8 23 G6
WAV L15 114 E6
Olive La WAV L15 114 E6
Olive Mt BIRK CH41 131 H5
Olive Mount Rd WAV L15 134 B1
Oliver La BIRK CH41 3 F5
GTS/LS CH66 195 G5
Oliver Lyme Rd PR/KW L34 118 A1
Olive Rd CSBY/WL L22 81 F3
NSTN CH64 191 K1
Oliver Rd ECCL WA10 102 E4
Oliver St BIRK CH41 2 E5
WARRN/WOL WA2 16 D2
Oliver St East BIRK CH41 3 F5
Olivetree Rd WAV L15 134 C1
Olive V WAV L15 134 A1
Olivia Cl CL/PREN CH43 129 K5
Olivia St BTL L20 97 F4
Ollerton Cl CL/PREN CH43 129 K5
WARRS WA4 144 A6
Ollery Gn NTHTN L30 70 E5
Ollier St WDN WA8 18 C6
Olney St ANF/KKDL L4 97 H3
Olton St WAV L15 133 K1
Olympia St NPK/KEN L6 113 J4
Olympic Wy WLT/FAZ L9 82 D3
Omega Bvd WARRW/BUR WA5 121 H6
O'Neill St BTL L20 4 C2
Onslow Crs STHP PR8 27 H5
Onslow Rd NPK/KEN L6 114 A4
PS/BROM CH62 151 G3
WAL/NB CH45 95 H5
Opal Cl LITH L21 81 K3
NPK/KEN L6 113 K3
Openfields Cl HLWD L26 155 H1
Oppenheim Av ECCL WA10 102 E5
Orange Gv TOX L8 133 H3
WARRN/WOL WA2 124 A5
Orange Tree Cl STBRV L28 * 100 B5
Oran Wy HUY L36 116 D4
Orb Cl NG/CROX L11 99 G2
Orchard Av CHLDW L16 115 H6
Orchard Cl FROD/HEL WA6 200 D3
GTS/LS CH66 202 D2
PR/KW L34 102 C6
RAIN/WH L35 118 A6
RNFD/HAY WA11 89 G4
Orchard Ct BIRK CH41 131 J6
Orchard Dl CSBY/BLUN L23 69 G5
Orchard Dr NSTN CH64 191 K4
Orchard Gra MOR/LEA CH46 128 D2
Orchard Hvn GTS/LS CH66 202 C2
Orchard Hey ECCL WA10 102 C2
MGHL L31 71 H1
NTHTN L30 70 E6
Orchard La GTS/LS CH66 194 D1
STHP PR8 33 K5
Orchard Park La CHNE CH2 198 C5
Orchard Pl FROD/HEL WA6 199 K5
Orchard Rd EP CH65 202 E1
MOR/LEA CH46 109 J6
Orchard St AIMK WN4 79 H6
WARR WA1 17 F4
WARRN/WOL WA2 124 C5
WARRS WA4 162 B3
The Orchard AIG/SPK L17 153 G2
HUY L36 116 E6
ORM L39 45 H6
WAL/NB CH45 95 G6
Orchard Vw ORM L39 53 H4
Orchard Wk RUNC WA7 * 177 J6
Orchard Wy BEB CH63 150 C5
WDN WA8 137 K6
Orchid Cl SKEL WN8 67 K1
Orchid Gv AIG/SPK L17 132 E6
Orchid Wy STHEL WA9 105 F6
Orchil Cl GTS/LS CH66 194 D3
Ordnance Av GOL/RIS/CU WA3 125 H3
O'Reilly Ct VAUX/LVPD L3 112 E3
Orford Av WARRN/WOL WA2 143 F2
Orford Gn WARRN/WOL WA2 123 K6
Orford La WARRN/WOL WA2 16 E1
Orford Rd WARRN/WOL WA2 143 G1
Orford St WARR WA1 16 E4
WAV L15 134 A1
Oriel Cl AIN/FAZ L10 71 G6
Oriel Crs BTL L20 96 E4
Oriel Dr AIN/FAZ L10 71 G6
Oriel Rd AIMK WN4 78 E5
BTL L20 4 D6
RF/TRAN CH42 131 H6
Oriel St VAUX/LVPD L3 112 E4
Orient Dr WLTN L25 135 J6
Origen Rd CHLDW L16 115 H6
Oriole Cl ECCL WA10 102 D6
Orion Bvd WARRW/BUR WA5 121 J6
Orith Av ECCL WA10 102 B2
Orkney Cl EP CH65 203 G2
RNFD/HAY WA11 89 G4
WDN WA8 139 K6
Orlando Cl CL/PREN CH43 129 K5
Orlando St BTL L20 96 E4
Orleans Rd CLB/OSW/ST L13 114 E4
Ormande St STHEL WA9 103 K4
Ormesby Gv BEB CH63 183 H1
Ormiston Rd WAL/NB CH45 95 H6
Ormond Av BRSC L40 54 D1
Ormonde Av MGHL L31 71 F2
Ormonde Crs NWD/KWIPK L33 85 F1
Ormonde Dr MGHL L31 71 F1
Ormond St VAUX/LVPD L3 8 C3
WAL/NB CH45 111 H2
Ormond Wy CL/PREN CH43 129 K5
Ormsby St WAV L15 133 K2
Ormside Gv STHEL WA9 104 B6
Ormskirk Old Rd ORM L39 55 F6
Ormskirk Rd ORM L39 54 C4
PR/KW L34 85 J6
RNFD/HAY WA11 65 K6
SKEL WN8 55 J4
WLT/FAZ L9 82 E1
Ormskirk St ECCL WA10 13 F4
Orms Wy FMBY L37 48 E2
Orphan Dr NPK/KEN L6 114 B2
Orphan St EHL/KEN L7 133 F1
Orrell Cl WARRW/BUR WA5 141 H3
Orrell Hey BTL L20 82 A4
Orrell Hill La HTWN L38 59 J3
Orrell La BRSC L40 38 D4
BTL L20 82 C4
Orrell Ms BRSC L40 * 38 E4
Orrell Mt BTL L20 81 K4
Orrell Rd BTL L20 81 K4
WAL/NB CH45 95 J6
Orrell St STHEL WA9 104 A2
Orret's Meadow Rd
GR/UP/WCH CH49 129 J6
Orrysdale Rd WKBY CH48 127 F6
Orry St EV L5 113 F2
Orsett Rd KKBY L32 84 E3
Orston Crs BEB CH63 170 C3
Ortega Cl PS/BROM CH62 151 H4
Orthes St VAUX/LVPD L3 9 J5
Orton Rd CHLDW L16 134 D1
Orton Wy AIMK WN4 78 E6
Orville St STHEL WA9 104 D6
Orwell Cl FMBY L37 48 D4
STHEL WA9 119 J4
Orwell Rd ANF/KKDL L4 97 F5
Osbert Rd CSBY/BLUN L23 68 C5
Osborne Av WAL/NB CH45 95 H6
WARRN/WOL WA2 123 K6
Osborne Ct PS/BROM CH62 151 G4
Osborne Gv PR/KW L34 117 G2
WAL/NB CH45 111 H1
Osborne Rd AIMK WN4 79 F5
CL/PREN CH43 2 A6
CLB/OSW/ST L13 114 C1
ECCL WA10 87 H6
FMBY L37 48 E4
GOL/RIS/CU WA3 93 F4
LITH L21 81 K2
STHP PR8 33 H3
WAL/NB CH45 95 J6
WARRS WA4 162 A2
Osborne Wd AIG/SPK L17 152 E2
Osbourne Cl PS/BROM CH62 171 G6
Osier Cl CHNE CH2 198 D6
Osmaston Rd RF/TRAN CH42 149 K1
Osprey Cl NTHLY L27 136 C4
RUNC WA7 187 J2
WARRN/WOL WA2 124 A4
Ossett Cl CL/PREN CH43 129 K5
RUNC WA7 178 C5
Osterley Gdns WLT/FAZ L9 82 C5
O'Sullivan Crs RNFD/HAY WA11 89 H6
Oteley Av PS/BROM CH62 171 F5
Othello Cl BTL L20 96 E4
Otterburn Cl MOR/LEA CH46 128 C1
Otterspool Dr AIG/SPK L17 152 E3
Otterspool Rd AIG/SPK L17 152 E2
Otterton Rd NG/CROX L11 84 B6
Ottery Cl CHTN/BK PR9 20 D6
Ottley St NPK/KEN L6 114 A4
Otway St ALL/GAR L19 172 B1
Queenswood Av BEB CH63 150 D3
Oughtrington La LYMM WA13 165 H1
Oulton Cl CL/PREN CH43 130 B6
MGHL L31 61 K3
Oulton La HUY L36 135 K1
Oulton Rd CHLDW L16 134 E3
Oulton Wy CL/PREN CH43 149 H1
Oundle Dr AIN/FAZ L10 71 F6
Oundle Pl WLTN L25 154 E4
Oundle Rd MOR/LEA CH46 109 J6
Outer Central Rd
SPK/HALE L24 155 H6
Outer Forum NG/CROX L11 98 C3
Out La WLTN L25 154 E1
Outlet La MGHL L31 63 J6
The Oval EP CH65 196 B6
WAL/NB CH45 111 F1
Overbrook La PR/KW L34 85 H6
Overbury St EHL/KEN L7 113 K6
Overchurch Rd
GR/UP/WCH CH49 129 F3
Overdale Av PEN/TH CH61 149 G6
Overdale Rd NSTN CH64 183 H6
Overdene Wk KKBY L32 84 E2
Overgreen Gv MOR/LEA CH46 109 H6
Overpool Gdns GTS/LS CH66 195 J6
Overpool Rd EP CH65 195 J4
Overton Av LITH L21 81 J2
Overton Cl CL/PREN CH43 130 C6
KKBY L32 84 C2
Overton Dr FROD/HEL WA6 201 F3
Overton Rd WAL/EG CH44 111 H3
Overton St EHL/KEN L7 113 K6
Overton Wy CL/PREN CH43 130 C6
Ovington Cl RUNC WA7 187 J3
Ovington Dr STHP PR8 28 B4
Ovolo Rd CLB/OSW/ST L13 114 E3
Owen Av ORM L39 45 K5
Owen Cl ECCL WA10 102 E4
Owen Dr SPK/HALE L24 173 G3
Owen Rd ANF/KKDL L4 97 F5
NWD/KWIPK L33 85 H4
RAIN/WH L35 118 E5
Owen's La ORM L39 51 G3
Owen St ECCL WA10 102 E4
WARRN/WOL WA2 16 C1
Owlsfield NEWLW WA12 106 E2
Oxborough Cl WDN WA8 138 E6
Oxbow Rd WD/CROXPK L12 99 J5
Oxendale Cl TOX L8 133 G2
Oxenham Rd
WARRN/WOL WA2 123 G4
Oxenholme Crs NG/CROX L11 98 E4
Oxford Av BTL L20 5 J5
LITH L21 81 J3
Oxford Cl AIG/SPK L17 152 D1
GTS/LS CH66 202 C1
Oxford Ct STHP PR8 27 G3
Oxford Dr BEB CH63 182 B1
CSBY/WL L22 80 D2
HLWD L26 155 J3
Oxford Gdns STHP PR8 27 F3
Oxford Rd BTL L20 5 H5
CSBY/WL L22 80 D1
HUY L36 117 G3
RUNC WA7 10 D7
SKEL WN8 56 A4
STHP PR8 27 F3
WAL/EG CH44 111 J3
WLT/FAZ L9 82 E3
Oxford St ECCL WA10 12 E3
EHL/KEN L7 9 J5
NEWLW WA12 106 A2
WARRS WA4 17 G7
WDN WA8 18 E5
Oxheys RUNC WA7 178 B5
Ox La RAIN/WH L35 137 F3
Oxley Av MOR/LEA CH46 110 B4
Oxley St STHEL WA9 104 B6
Oxmead Cl WARRN/WOL WA2 124 D6
Oxmoor Cl RUNC WA7 187 K2
Oxton Cl AIG/SPK L17 152 D1
KKBY L32 84 A3
WDN WA8 138 B5
Oxton Gn GTS/LS CH66 195 G5
Oxton Rd BIRK CH41 2 C7
WAL/EG CH44 111 H4
Oxton St ANF/KKDL L4 97 H5

P

Pacific Rd BIRK CH41 3 H2
BTL L20 4 C4
Packenham Rd
CLB/OSW/ST L13 114 D1
Paddington EHL/KEN L7 113 J6
Paddington Bank WARR WA1 143 J3
Paddock Cl CSBY/BLUN L23 68 C3
Paddock Dr NSTN CH64 181 J5
Paddock Gv STHEL WA9 120 B4
Paddock Hey NTHLY L27 136 A3
Paddock Ri RUNC WA7 187 H3
Paddock Rd SKEL WN8 66 E2
The Paddock AIMK WN4 78 E3
CHNE CH2 198 B6
FMBY L37 41 G6
GR/UP/WCH CH49 129 J4
GTS/LS CH66 195 G6
HES CH60 168 C5
KKBY L32 84 C4
MOR/LEA CH46 128 D2
ORM L39 53 G2
PR/KW L34 102 B6
STHP PR8 33 H5
WLTN L25 135 J5
Padeswood Cl STHEL WA9 120 A1
Padgate La WARR WA1 17 K1
Padstow Cl CHTN/BK PR9 20 D6
HLWD L26 155 H3
WARRW/BUR WA5 141 F6
Padstow Dr ECCL WA10 87 J5
Padstow Rd CHLDW L16 134 E1
GR/UP/WCH CH49 147 K1
Pagebank Rd DV/KA/FCH L14 116 A4
Page Ct FMBY L37 49 F2
Pagefield Rd WAV L15 134 B3
Page La WDN WA8 19 H2
Page Moss Av HUY L36 116 B3
Page Moss La HUY L36 116 B3
Page Wk VAUX/LVPD L3 9 H1
Pagewood Cl CL/PREN CH43 130 A5
Paignton Cl HUY L36 117 H5
WARRW/BUR WA5 141 F5
WGNW/BIL/O WN5 77 H1
Paignton Rd CHLDW L16 134 E1
WAL/NB CH45 110 E1
Painswick Rd GTS/LS CH66 202 C1
Paisley Av PS/BROM CH62 184 B3
RNFD/HAY WA11 89 G4
Paisley St VAUX/LVPD L3 8 B1
Palace Ar AIMK WN4 79 G6
Palace Fields Av RUNC WA7 177 K6
Palace Hey NSTN CH64 192 B4
Palace Rd STHP PR8 27 F2
WLT/FAZ L9 82 D5
Palatine Ar ECCL WA10 * 13 G5
Palatine Rd PS/BROM CH62 170 E4
STHP PR8 27 G2
WAL/EG CH44 111 K5
Palermo Cl WAL/EG CH44 111 K5
Paley Cl ANF/KKDL L4 97 H6
Palin Dr WARRW/BUR WA5 141 G3
Palladio Rd CLB/OSW/ST L13 115 F3
Palliser Cl GOL/RIS/CU WA3 125 J4
Pall Ml VAUX/LVPD L3 8 C2
Palm Av AIMK WN4 78 C4
Palm Cl WLT/FAZ L9 98 A2
Palm Ct SKEL WN8 56 A3
Palmer Cl CL/PREN CH43 130 A6
ECCL WA10 12 E4
Palmer Crs WARRW/BUR WA5 142 A1
Palmerston Av LITH L21 81 H4
Palmerston Cl CALD/MH L18 134 A6
Palmerston Crs ALL/GAR L19 153 K5
Palmerston Dr LITH L21 81 J5
Palmerston Rd ALL/GAR L19 153 K5
CALD/MH L18 134 A6
CHTN/BK PR9 28 C1
WAL/EG CH44 111 F3
Palmerston St RF/TRAN CH42 150 E1
Palm Gv CHTN/BK PR9 15 K6
CL/PREN CH43 130 E4
GTS/LS CH66 202 E2
STHP PR8 28 B1
WLTN L25 154 E2
Palm Hl CL/PREN CH43 130 E5
Palmwood Av RAIN/WH L35 119 F5
Palmwood Cl CL/PREN CH43 149 H2
Palmyra Sq North WARR WA1 16 C5
Palmyra Sq South WARR WA1 16 C5
Paltridge Wy PEN/TH CH61 167 K1
Pamela Cl AIN/FAZ L10 84 A4
Pampas Gv WLT/FAZ L9 97 K1
Pangbourne Cl WARRS WA4 162 D5
Pankhurst Rd LITH L21 81 K2
Pansy St EV L5 97 F6
Parade Crs SPK/HALE L24 173 K3
Parade St ECCL WA10 13 H4
The Parade NSTN CH64 181 G6
Paradise La FMBY L37 41 G6
RAIN/WH L35 117 K5
Paradise Rw WLTN L25 * 135 J5
Paradise St CLVPS L1 8 E4
Paragon Cl WDN WA8 139 G4
Parbold Av RNFD/HAY WA11 89 G6
Parbold Cl BRSC L40 38 E6
Parbold Ct WDN WA8 157 J4
Parbrook Cl HUY L36 116 D1
Parbrook Rd HUY L36 116 D2
The Parchments
NEWLW WA12 106 D1
Park Av CALD/MH L18 133 K6
CHTN/BK PR9 23 G4
CSBY/BLUN L23 69 F4
FMBY L37 49 F4
GOL/RIS/CU WA3 92 A1
MGHL L31 62 B4
ORM L39 45 J6
PR/KW L34 102 B6
RAIN/WH L35 118 E3
RNFD/HAY WA11 89 K5
WAL/EG CH44 111 K4
WARRS WA4 143 G6
WDN WA8 18 E1
WLT/FAZ L9 83 G4
Park Av North NEWLW WA12 106 C3
Park Av South NEWLW WA12 106 C3
Park Bvd WARR WA1 16 D7
Parkbourn MGHL L31 62 E5
Parkbourn Dr MGHL L31 62 E5
Parkbourn North MGHL L31 62 E5
Parkbourn Sq MGHL L31 62 E5
Parkbridge Rd RF/TRAN CH42 131 F6
Park Brow Dr KKBY L32 84 E3
Parkbury Ct CL/PREN CH43 130 D6
Park Cl BIRK CH41 2 C4
FMBY L37 48 E5
KKBY L32 72 A6
Park Ct CSBY/WL L22 81 F2
RUNC WA7 176 D5
Park Crs CHTN/BK PR9 15 K1
ORM L39 51 H1
WARRS WA4 162 C5
Parkdale WKBY CH48 146 E5
Parkdale Av WLT/FAZ L9 82 D4
Parkdale Rd WARR WA1 143 K2

Park Dr BIRK CH41 2 B5
CSBY/BLUN L23 68 B5
CSBY/BLUN L23 69 H2
EP CH65 196 B6
Parkend Rd RF/TRAN CH42 131 F6
Parker Av LITH L21 81 G4
Parker Cl NTHTN L30 82 E2
Parker Crs ORM L39 45 K4
Parkers Ct RUNC WA7 187 H1
Parker St CLVPS L1 9 F5
RUNC WA7 11 F3
WARR WA1 16 B6
Parkfield Av BIRK CH41 2 E4
NTHTN L30 82 D2
WARRS WA4 143 K5
Parkfield Cl ORM L39 53 G2
Parkfield Dr EP CH65 202 E1
FROD/HEL WA6 199 J6
WAL/EG CH44 111 H3
Parkfield Gv MGHL L31 62 A6
Parkfield Pl BIRK CH41 2 D4
Parkfield Rd AIG/SPK L17 133 G5
BEB CH63 170 C2
CSBY/WL L22 81 F1
Parkfields La
WARRN/WOL WA2 124 B5
Parkgate Cl AIG/SPK L17 153 F2
Parkgate La NSTN CH64 181 K2
Parkgate Rd NSTN CH64 191 H1
WARRS WA4 162 C2
Parkgate Wy RUNC WA7 178 B6
Park Gv BIRK CH41 2 D7
Parkhill Ct TOX L8 132 E5
Parkhill Rd RF/TRAN CH42 131 F6
Park Hill Rd TOX L8 132 E5
Parkhurst Rd NG/CROX L11 98 D4
RF/TRAN CH42 * 150 B1
Parkinson Rd WLT/FAZ L9 97 J1
Parkland Cl TOX L8 133 F4
Parkland Ct CL/PREN CH43 129 K1
Parkland Dr CHNE CH2 198 C6
Parklands CHTN/BK PR9 23 G5
GTS/LS CH66 195 G4
PR/KW L34 100 D2
RNFD/HAY WA11 75 G2
SKEL WN8 57 F3
WDN WA8 138 B6
Parklands Dr HES CH60 181 G1
Parklands Gdns GTS/LS CH66 195 G3
Parklands Vw GTS/LS CH66 195 G3
Parklands Wy CSBY/WL L22 81 G2
Park La BTL L20 82 B4
CLVPS L1 8 E6
FROD/HEL WA6 200 E1
HOY CH47 108 E5
MGHL L31 62 C4
NTHTN L30 82 C1
WARRS WA4 161 J6
Park Lane Dr MGHL L31 63 F5
Park La West NTHTN L30 70 C6
Parklea GTS/LS CH66 195 G3
Park Link ORM L39 53 F4
Park Pl BTL L20 5 F5
TOX L8 132 E3
Park Rd CHTN/BK PR9 15 J1
CSBY/WL L22 81 F2
EP CH65 6 D7
FMBY L37 48 E4
HES CH60 168 B4
HOY CH47 108 C6
KKBY L32 72 B6
NEWLW WA12 92 A4
NSTN CH64 193 J1
ORM L39 45 J6
PR/KW L34 101 J6
PS/BROM CH62 151 G6
PS/BROM CH62 184 C1
RF/TRAN CH42 131 H6
RUNC WA7 176 C5
STHEL WA9 104 B1
TOX L8 132 E4
WAL/EG CH44 111 J4
WARRN/WOL WA2 123 K6
WARRW/BUR WA5 140 D2
WDN WA8 19 F1
WKBY CH48 146 B1
Park Rd East BIRK CH41 2 C5
Park Rd North BIRK CH41 2 A2
NEWLW WA12 106 E2
Park Rd South CL/PREN CH43 2 B5
NEWLW WA12 106 D3
Park Rd West CHTN/BK PR9 22 E4
CL/PREN CH43 130 D3
Parkside WAL/EG CH44 111 J4
Parkside Av AIMK WN4 78 E1
STHEL WA9 119 K4
Parkside Cl BEB CH63 151 F5
NSTN CH64 191 J1
NTHLY L27 136 B5
Parkside Dr WD/CROXPK L12 98 E5
Parkside Rd BEB CH63 151 F5
NEWLW WA12 107 H4
RF/TRAN CH42 131 H6
Parkside St NPK/KEN L6 113 H4
The Parks RNFD/HAY WA11 91 G2
Parkstile La NG/CROX L11 99 G1
Parkstone Rd RF/TRAN CH42 131 F6
Park St BIRK CH41 2 E4
BTL L20 5 F5
NSTN CH64 191 K1
RNFD/HAY WA11 89 J5
STHEL WA9 104 A1
TOX L8 132 D4
WAL/EG CH44 111 J3
Parksway WARR WA1 144 C2
Park Ter CSBY/WL L22 81 F3
The Park HUY L36 116 E6
WARRW/BUR WA5 140 E6
Parkvale Av CL/PREN CH43 149 H3
Park Vale Rd WLT/FAZ L9 82 D5
Park Vw AIMK WN4 91 G1
CSBY/WL L22 80 E1
HUY L36 116 C3
NPK/KEN L6 114 B2
PS/BROM CH62 170 E5
WARRN/WOL WA2 * 124 A4
Parkview Cl BIRK CH41 2 C2
Parkview Dr NTHLY L27 136 B5
Park View Flats LITH L21 * 81 H3
Parkview Rd NG/CROX L11 99 H1
Park Wall Rd HTWN L38 60 B4
Park Wy FMBY L37 49 F4
HOY CH47 127 K1
HUY L36 100 D6
TOX L8 132 E2
Parkway CSBY/BLUN L23 81 G1
NTHTN L30 70 B4
WAL/NB CH45 94 E6
Parkway Cl GR/UP/WCH CH49 148 C4
Park Wy West KKBY L32 * 72 A6
Park West HES CH60 167 H6
Parkwood Cl LYMM WA13 164 E1
PS/BROM CH62 171 G4
Parkwood Rd RAIN/WH L35 118 A5
WLTN L25 135 H5
Park Works SPK/HALE L24 * 154 E5
Parlane St STHEL WA9 104 A1
Parliament Cl CLVPS L1 132 D2
Parliament Pl TOX L8 132 E2
Parliament St STHEL WA9 103 F6
Parliament Wy GTS/LS CH66 202 D3
Parlington Cl WDN WA8 157 H4
Parlow Rd NG/CROX L11 98 G5
Parnell Rd BEB CH63 170 C3
Parren Av RAIN/WH L35 117 J6
Parr Gv GR/UP/WCH CH49 128 D5
RNFD/HAY WA11 89 K5
Parr Mount Ct STHEL WA9 104 A2
Parr Mount St STHEL WA9 104 A2
Parr's La ORM L39 53 H5
Parrs Rd CL/PREN CH43 130 E6
Parr Stocks Rd STHEL WA9 104 B2
Parr St CLVPS L1 9 F6
LITH L21 81 J2
STHEL WA9 13 K5
WARR WA1 16 E6
WDN WA8 * 19 G1
Parrs Wood View WARRS WA4 163 F2
Parry Dr WARRS WA4 144 D6
Parry St WAL/EG CH44 111 K5
Parsonage Brow SKEL WN8 57 H5
Parsonage Cl SKEL WN8 57 J6
Parsonage Rd SKEL WN8 57 J6
WDN WA8 176 D1
Parsonage Wy
WARRW/BUR WA5 141 H4
Parson's Brow
RNFD/HAY WA11 75 F3
Parthenon Dr NG/CROX L11 98 C3
Partington Av BTL L20 5 J2
Parton St NPK/KEN L6 114 A4
Partridge Cl GOL/RIS/CU WA3 125 G4
WD/CROXPK L12 99 K2
Partridge Rd CSBY/BLUN L23 68 C5
KKBY L32 72 A6
Part St STHP PR8 27 H2
Pasture Av MOR/LEA CH46 109 J5
Pasture Cl AIMK WN4 78 D3
STHEL WA9 120 A3
WLTN L25 154 E2
Pasture Crs MOR/LEA CH46 109 J6
Pasture La RNFD/HAY WA11 75 H5
WARRN/WOL WA2 124 D6
Pasture Rd MOR/LEA CH46 109 H4
The Pastures CHTN/BK PR9 21 G6
STHEL WA9 104 E6
WKBY CH48 147 G1
Pateley Cl KKBY L32 84 B6
Paterson St BIRK CH41 2 C5
Patmos Cl EV L5 113 G1
Paton Cl WKBY CH48 127 H6
Patricia Av BIRK CH41 110 E6
Patricia Gv BTL L20 82 A5
Patrick Av BTL L20 82 A4
Patrivale Cl WARR WA1 143 J2
Patten La WARR WA1 * 16 D5
Patten's Cl NTHTN L30 70 A5
Patten St BIRK CH41 130 E1
Patten's Wk PR/KW L34 85 K6
Patterdale Av
WARRN/WOL WA2 123 J5
Patterdale Cl STHP PR8 33 H6
Patterdale Crs MGHL L31 62 C5
Patterdale Dr ECCL WA10 102 D5
Patterdale Rd AIMK WN4 79 F1
BEB CH63 170 B2
WAV L15 133 K3
Patterson Cl GOL/RIS/CU WA3 125 G4
Patterson St NEWLW WA12 106 B1
Paul Cl WARRW/BUR WA5 140 E3
Paul McCartney Wy
NPK/KEN L6 113 K4
Paul Orr Ct VAUX/LVPD L3 112 E3
Paulsfield Dr MOR/LEA CH46 129 F2
Paul's La CHTN/BK PR9 23 H2
Paul St VAUX/LVPD L3 112 E4
WARRN/WOL WA2 16 B3
Paulton Cl TOX L8 132 E5
Paveley Bank NTHLY L27 136 A4
Pavilion Cl TOX L8 133 G2
Paxton Pl SKEL WN8 66 E3
Paxton Rd HUY L36 116 E3
Payne Cl WARRW/BUR WA5 142 A3
Peace Dr WARRW/BUR WA5 142 A4
Peacehaven Cl CHLDW L16 135 G1
Peach Gv MGHL L31 72 A5
RNFD/HAY WA11 * 90 D4
Peach St EHL/KEN L7 9 K5
Peacock Av WARR WA1 143 H3
Peacock La KNUT WA16 165 K5
Pearce Cl WLTN L25 135 G3
Pear Gv NPK/KEN L6 113 K4
Pearl Wy NPK/KEN L6 113 K3
Pearson Av WARRS WA4 162 C1
Pearson Ct WAV L15 * 134 B3
Pearson Dr BTL L20 82 B4
Pearson Rd BIRK CH41 3 F7
Pearson St WAV L15 134 A2
Pear Tree Av RUNC WA7 177 F6
Peartree Av WD/CROXPK L12 99 K4
Peartree Cl FROD/HEL WA6 187 G6
Pear Tree Cl HES CH60 168 C4
Peartree Pl WARR WA1 142 D6
WARRS WA4 17 F7
Pear Tree Rd HUY L36 136 B1
Pear Tree Wy GTS/LS CH66 * 202 C2
Peasefield Rd DV/KA/FCH L14 116 A3
Peasley Cl WARRN/WOL WA2 124 D6
Peasley Cross La STHEL WA9 13 K6
Peatwood Av KKBY L32 84 E4
Peckers Hill Rd STHEL WA9 104 C6
Peckfield Cl RUNC WA7 187 K2
Peckforton Cl
CLB/OSW/ST L13 114 C1
Peckforton Dr GTS/LS CH66 195 H6
RUNC WA7 187 J3
Peckmill Gn NTHLY L27 136 C5
Pecksniff Cl TOX L8 132 E4
Peebles Av RNFD/HAY WA11 89 G5
Peebles Cl AIMK WN4 78 B5
GTS/LS CH66 * 194 C3
NWD/KWIPK L33 72 C3
Peel Av BIRK CH41 131 J6
Peel Cl RAIN/WH L35 118 A4
WARR WA1 144 C3
Peel House La WDN WA8 139 G6
Peel Pl ECCL WA10 13 G2
TOX L8 132 E2
Peel Rd BTL L20 4 A1
SKEL WN8 67 G2
Peel St NEWLW WA12 106 A2
RUNC WA7 10 C3
STHP PR8 28 C1
TOX L8 133 F5
Peerswood Ct NSTN CH64 191 K4
Peet Av ECCL WA10 102 E1
ORM L39 53 H1
Peet's La CHTN/BK PR9 23 J4
Peet St EHL/KEN L7 113 K6
Pelham Gv AIG/SPK L17 133 H5
Pelham Rd WAL/EG CH44 111 G4
WARRS WA4 144 B6
Pemberton Cl NSTN CH64 193 H1
Pemberton Rd
CLB/OSW/ST L13 114 E4
GR/UP/WCH CH49 129 J6
Pembertons Ct PR/KW L34 118 A1
Pemberton St ECCL WA10 * 12 D6
Pembrey Wy WLTN L25 155 G3
Pembridge Gdns EP CH65 196 D6
Pembroke Av MOR/LEA CH46 129 F2
Pembroke Ct BIRK CH41 131 H5
Pembroke Dr EP CH65 195 K6
Pembroke Gdns VAUX/LVPD L3 9 J3
Pembroke Pl VAUX/LVPD L3 9 H3
Pembroke Rd BTL L20 4 E5
VAUX/LVPD L3 9 K3
Pembroke St VAUX/LVPD L3 9 J3
Pembury Cl WD/CROXPK L12 99 J2
Penare Gorran Hvn RUNC WA7 188 B1
Penarth Cl EHL/KEN L7 133 G1
Pencombe Rd HUY L36 116 B3
Penda Dr NWD/KWIPK L33 72 D3
Pendennis Rd WAL/EG CH44 111 H4
Pendennis St NPK/KEN L6 113 K2
Pendine Cl NPK/KEN L6 114 A3
WARRW/BUR WA5 122 C5
Pendle Av RNFD/HAY WA11 89 G6
Pendlebury St STHEL WA9 120 A3
WARRS WA4 143 J6
Pendle Cl GR/UP/WCH CH49 * 129 F3
Pendle Dr LITH L21 69 K5
ORM L39 46 A5
Pendle Pl SKEL WN8 67 F3
Pendle Rd GOL/RIS/CU WA3 92 D2
Pendleton Gn HLWD L26 155 H4
Pendleton Rd ANF/KKDL L4 97 J3
Penfold MGHL L31 62 C6
Penfold Cl CALD/MH L18 134 E4
Penfolds RUNC WA7 177 G4
Pengallo Hey NTHLY L27 136 C4
Pengwern Gv WAV L15 133 J1
Pengwern St TOX L8 133 F4
Penhale Cl AIG/SPK L17 152 C1
Peninsula Cl WAL/NB CH45 94 E5
Penistone Dr GTS/LS CH66 194 E4
Penketh Av WARRW/BUR WA5 142 C1
Penketh Ct RUNC WA7 10 E4
Penketh Gn SPK/HALE L24 173 K1
Penketh Pl SKEL WN8 66 E2
Penketh Rd WARRW/BUR WA5 141 H5
Penketh's La RUNC WA7 10 E3
Penkett Gv WAL/NB CH45 111 J1
Penkett Rd WAL/NB CH45 111 J1
Penkford La
WARRW/BUR WA5 105 H4
Penkmans La FROD/HEL WA6 201 F3
Penlake La STHEL WA9 104 C6
Penley Crs KKBY L32 84 A1
Penlinken Dr NPK/KEN L6 113 K3
Penmann Cl HLWD L26 * 155 J4
Penmann Crs HLWD L26 155 J4
Penmark Cl WARRW/BUR WA5 122 C5
Penmon Dr PEN/TH CH61 167 K2
Pennant Av WD/CROXPK L12 99 G4
Pennant Cl GOL/RIS/CU WA3 125 J4
Pennard Av HUY L36 116 D2
Penn Gdns EP CH65 6 C4
Pennine Cl STHEL WA9 104 C2
Pennine Dr STHEL WA9 104 D2
Pennine La GOL/RIS/CU WA3 92 D2
Pennine Pl SKEL WN8 66 D1
Pennine Rd RF/TRAN CH42 150 B2
WAL/EG CH44 111 F3
WARRN/WOL WA2 124 A5
Pennine Wy KKBY L32 72 B5
Pennington Av BTL L20 82 B4
ORM L39 45 J5
Pennington Cl FROD/HEL WA6 187 F6
Pennington Dr NEWLW WA12 106 E2
Pennington Gn GTS/LS CH66 195 F6
Pennington La
WARRW/BUR WA5 105 G2
Pennington Rd BTL L20 81 K5
Pennington St ANF/KKDL L4 97 H3
Penn La RUNC WA7 10 B6
Pennsylvania Rd
CLB/OSW/ST L13 98 B6
Pennyford Dr CALD/MH L18 133 K6
Penny La CALD/MH L18 134 A4
RAIN/WH L35 137 K2
RNFD/HAY WA11 91 F4
WARRW/BUR WA5 105 H5
Pennystone Cl
GR/UP/WCH CH49 128 E3
Pennywood Dr RAIN/WH L35 118 A5
Penrhos Rd HOY CH47 126 E3
Penrhyd Rd PEN/TH CH61 148 A6
Penrhyn Av LITH L21 81 J4
PEN/TH CH61 148 D5
Penrhyn Crs RUNC WA7 176 D6
Penrhyn Rd PR/KW L34 85 H5
Penrhyn St EV L5 113 F2
Penrith Av STHP PR8 33 H6
WARRN/WOL WA2 123 J4
Penrith Cl FROD/HEL WA6 201 G1
Penrith Crs AIMK WN4 79 G5
MGHL L31 62 C5
Penrith Rd ECCL WA10 102 D5
Penrith St BIRK CH41 2 C7
Penrose Av East
DV/KA/FCH L14 115 J5
Penrose Av West
DV/KA/FCH L14 115 J5
Penrose Gdns
WARRW/BUR WA5 140 E6
Penrose Pl SKEL WN8 67 G3
Penrose St EV L5 113 H1
Penryn Av RNFD/HAY WA11 89 G4
Penryn Cl WARRW/BUR WA5 141 F5
Pensall Dr PEN/TH CH61 167 K3
Pensarn Gdns
WARRW/BUR WA5 * 122 D5
Pensarn Rd CLB/OSW/ST L13 114 D5
Pensby Cl PEN/TH CH61 148 D6
Pensby Dr GTS/LS CH66 195 G5
Pensby Hall La PEN/TH CH61 167 K3
Pensby Rd HES CH60 168 A4
PEN/TH CH61 148 D5
Penshaw Ct RUNC WA7 177 H6
Pentire Av ECCL WA10 87 J5
Pentire Cl NG/CROX L11 84 A5
Pentland Av ANF/KKDL L4 97 J4
STHEL WA9 104 D2
WARRN/WOL WA2 123 H4
Pentland Pl WARRN/WOL WA2 123 H4
Pentland Rd NWD/KWIPK L33 73 F5
Penuel Rd ANF/KKDL L4 97 H3
Penvalley Crs NPK/KEN L6 114 A3
Peony Gdns STHEL WA9 105 F6
Peover St VAUX/LVPD L3 113 F4
Peploe Rd ANF/KKDL L4 98 B3
Peplow Rd KKBY L32 84 A1
Pepper St LYMM WA13 145 K6
SPK/HALE L24 174 E4
Pera Cl NPK/KEN L6 113 J4
Perch Pool La CHTN/BK PR9 29 J2
Percival La RUNC WA7 10 B4
Percival Rd EP CH65 6 C3
Percival St WARR WA1 17 F5
Percival Wy ECCL WA10 87 K6
Percy Rd WAL/EG CH44 112 A5
Percy St BTL L20 4 C1
STHEL WA9 104 D6
TOX L8 132 E2
WARRW/BUR WA5 * 142 B4
Percy Vls WLT/FAZ L9 * 97 J1
Perimeter Rd CHNE CH2 198 D4
NWD/KWIPK L33 85 J3
Perrey St RUNC WA7 11 G4
Perriam Rd ALL/GAR L19 154 A3
Perrin Av RUNC WA7 176 B5
Perrin Rd WAL/NB CH45 110 E2
Perrins Rd WARRW/BUR WA5 121 K1
Perrygate Cl EHL/KEN L7 133 G1
Perry St TOX L8 132 G3
Pershore Gv STHP PR8 33 G5
Pershore Rd KKBY L32 84 D3
Perth Av STHEL WA9 103 G6
Perth Cl NWD/KWIPK L33 72 C3
WARRN/WOL WA2 124 B3
Perth St NPK/KEN L6 113 J4
Peterborough Cl GTS/LS CH66 202 D4
Peterborough Dr NTHTN L30 70 B5
Peterborough Rd WAV L15 134 B3
Peterlee Cl STHEL WA9 103 H6
Peter Mahon Wy BTL L20 4 C3
Peter Price's La BEB CH63 170 A1
Peter Rd ANF/KKDL L4 97 H3
Peter Salem Dr
WARRW/BUR WA5 141 J3
Peters Av BRSC L40 38 E5
Petersfield Cl NTHTN L30 82 C2
Petersgate RUNC WA7 178 C6
Petersham Dr WARRS WA4 162 D6
Peter's La CLVPS L1 8 E5
Peterstone Cl
WARRW/BUR WA5 122 D5
Peter St AIMK WN4 79 H6
CLVPS L1 8 E4
ECCL WA10 12 D4
GOL/RIS/CU WA3 92 B3
WAL/EG CH44 112 A5
Peterwood RF/TRAN CH42 151 F2
Petherick Rd NG/CROX L11 84 B6
Petton St EV L5 113 H1
Petunia Cl DV/KA/FCH L14 * 116 A3
STHEL WA9 104 E6
Petworth Av
WARRN/WOL WA2 123 H4
Petworth Cl SPK/HALE L24 173 G1
Petworth Rd STHP PR8 33 H3
Peveril Cl WARRS WA4 162 C4
Peveril St WLT/FAZ L9 97 H2
Pheasant Cl GOL/RIS/CU WA3 125 H3
Pheasant Fld SPK/HALE L24 174 D3
Pheasant Gv HLWD L26 155 H2
Philbeach Rd ANF/KKDL L4 98 B3
Philip Dr STHP PR8 34 A3
Philip Gv STHEL WA9 104 A6
Philip Rd WDN WA8 157 G3
Philips Dr WARRW/BUR WA5 141 F3
Philips La GTS/LS CH66 195 F5
Phillimore Rd NPK/KEN L6 * 114 A4
Phillip Gv WD/CROXPK L12 115 K2
Phillips Cl CSBY/BLUN L23 69 J3
FMBY L37 49 F3
Phillip's La FMBY L37 49 F3
Phillips St VAUX/LVPD L3 8 D1
Phillips Wy HES CH60 167 J5
Phipps' La WARRW/BUR WA5 105 J6
Phoenix Av WARRW/BUR WA5 123 F5
Phoenix Dr DV/KA/FCH L14 116 A3
Physics Rd SPK/HALE L24 155 F6
Phythian Cl NPK/KEN L6 113 K4
Phythian Crs
WARRW/BUR WA5 141 G5
Phythian St NPK/KEN L6 113 J4
RNFD/HAY WA11 89 J5
Picadilly WGNW/BIL/O WN5 77 H4
Pichael Nook WARRS WA4 143 K5
Pickerill Rd GR/UP/WCH CH49 128 E6
Pickering Crs WARRS WA4 144 C6
Pickering Rd WAL/NB CH45 95 H5
WDN WA8 157 G6
Pickerings Cl RUNC WA7 187 F1
Pickering St NPK/KEN L6 113 J2
Pickles Dr BRSC L40 38 D5
Pickmere Dr PS/BROM CH62 184 C4
RUNC WA7 188 B2
Pickmere St WARRW/BUR WA5 142 B4
Pickop St VAUX/LVPD L3 8 D2
Pickwick St TOX L8 132 E3
Pickworth Wy KKBY L32 84 A1
Picow Farm Rd RUNC WA7 176 B4
Picow St RUNC WA7 10 C6
Picton Av EP CH65 6 E5
RUNC WA7 11 G6
Picton Cl CL/PREN CH43 130 C5
GOL/RIS/CU WA3 124 E3
PS/BROM CH62 184 A4
Picton Crs WAV L15 133 K1
Picton Gv WAV L15 133 J1
Picton Rd CSBY/WL L22 80 E2
WAV L15 133 K1
Piele Rd RNFD/HAY WA11 90 D4
Piercefield Rd FMBY L37 49 F1
Pier Head VAUX/LVPD L3 8 B5
Pierpoint St NEWLW WA12 92 B4
WARRW/BUR WA5 16 A1
Pighue La CLB/OSW/ST L13 114 C6
Pigot Pl WARRS WA4 143 J4
Pigot St ECCL WA10 12 D5
Pike House Rd ECCL WA10 87 H6
Pike La FROD/HEL WA6 201 K6
Pikelaw Pl SKEL WN8 66 E2
Pike Pl ECCL WA10 102 D1
Pikes Bridge Fold ECCL WA10 102 C1
Pikes Hey Rd WKBY CH48 147 G4
Pike St WARRS WA4 162 B2
Pilchbank Rd DV/KA/FCH L14 115 J3
Pilch La DV/KA/FCH L14 115 J4
Pilch La East HUY L36 116 A5
Pilgrim Cl WARRN/WOL WA2 123 G1
Pilgrim St BIRK CH41 3 H4
CLVPS L1 9 H7
Pilkington Rd STHP PR8 28 A2
Pilkington St RNFD/HAY WA11 75 G3
Pilling Cl CHTN/BK PR9 20 C6
Pilling La MGHL L31 61 J2
Pilling Pl SKEL WN8 66 E2
Pilot Gv WAV L15 133 J1
Pimblett Rd RNFD/HAY WA11 90 D4
Pimblett St GOL/RIS/CU WA3 * 92 B4
Pimbley Gv East MGHL L31 71 F3
Pimbley Gv West MGHL L31 71 F3
Pimbo La SKEL WN8 67 H4
Pimbo Rd RNFD/HAY WA11 76 B1
SKEL WN8 66 E2
Pimhill Cl TOX L8 133 F3
Pimlico Rd RUNC WA7 10 A6
Pincroft Wy ANF/KKDL L4 97 F6
Pine Av BEB CH63 170 B2
ECCL WA10 88 C5
NEWLW WA12 106 C3
ORM L39 45 K4
WDN WA8 158 C1
Pine Cl HUY L36 116 D3
KKBY L32 72 B6
RAIN/WH L35 118 A4
RNFD/HAY WA11 90 B5
SKEL WN8 56 B4
Pine Ct BIRK CH41 2 E4
Pine Crest ORM L39 53 F3
Pine Dl RNFD/HAY WA11 75 F2
Pinedale Cl CL/PREN CH43 130 A5
GTS/LS CH66 202 D3
Pine Dr ORM L39 45 K5
Pine Gv BTL L20 5 G3
CHTN/BK PR9 15 K6
CSBY/WL L22 80 E1
GOL/RIS/CU WA3 92 D3
GTS/LS CH66 202 E2
ORM L39 46 A4
WARR WA1 143 K2
Pinehey NSTN CH64 181 J6
Pinehurst Av ANF/KKDL L4 97 K6
CSBY/WL L22 68 D6
Pinehurst Rd ANF/KKDL L4 97 K6
Pinellas RUNC WA7 11 G3
Pine Ms CLVPS L1 132 D2
Pinemore Rd CALD/MH L18 153 H1
Pineridge Cl PS/BROM CH62 170 E2
Pine Rd HES CH60 168 C4
RUNC WA7 177 F6
The Pines BEB CH63 170 D2
WD/CROXPK L12 99 K1
Pinetop Cl NPK/KEN L6 113 K3
Pine Tree Av CL/PREN CH43 129 K5

Pine Tree Cl MOR/LEA CH46 129 G1
Pinetree Cl NTHTN L30 70 C6
Pinetree Ct WAL/EG CH44 111 F2
Pinetree Dr WKBY CH48 146 E2
Pine Tree Gv MOR/LEA CH46 129 G1
Pine Tree Rd HUY L36 136 A1
Pine View Dr PEN/TH CH61 167 K3
Pine Wks RF/TRAN CH42 150 A2
Pine Wy HES CH60 167 J3
Pineways WARRS WA4 162 C6
Pinewood AIMK WN4 91 F1
SKEL WN8 57 F2
Pinewood Av FMBY L37 48 D4
WARR WA1 143 H2
WD/CROXPK L12 99 H2
Pinewood Cl CHNE CH2 198 D6
FMBY L37 48 D3
NTHLY L27 136 B3
STHP PR8 29 F6
Pinewood Dr HES CH60 168 B5
Pinewood Gdns
NWD/KWIPK L33 72 D4
Pinewood Rd
WARRW/BUR WA5 105 K6
Pinfold Cl NTHTN L30 70 A4
Pinfold Crs KKBY L32 85 F3
Pinfold Dr ECCL WA10 102 C2
Pinfold La BRSC L40 36 D6
PR/KW L34 100 B2
STHP PR8 33 H6
WKBY CH48 127 F5
Pinfold Pl SKEL WN8 67 F3
Pinfold Rd WLTN L25 155 F4
Pingot Rd WGNW/BIL/O WN5 77 H4
Pingwood La NWD/KWIPK L33 73 F3
Pinmill Brow FROD/HEL WA6 200 E2
Pinmill Cl FROD/HEL WA6 200 E2
Pinners Brow
WARRN/WOL WA2 16 D2
Pinners Fold RUNC WA7 178 A4
Pinnington Pl HUY L36 116 D5
Pinnington Rd RAIN/WH L35 118 A4
Pintail Cl RNFD/HAY WA11 88 E5
Piper's Cl HES CH60 167 H5
Piper's End HES CH60 167 H5
Piper's La HES CH60 167 G3
The Pipers GOL/RIS/CU WA3 93 G3
Pipit Av NEWLW WA12 106 C2
Pipit Cl HLWD L26 155 H1
Pipit La GOL/RIS/CU WA3 125 G4
Pippin St BRSC L40 46 A1
Pippits Rw RUNC WA7 187 H3
Pirrie Rd WLT/FAZ L9 98 B2
Pitch Cl GR/UP/WCH CH49 * 128 E5
Pit Hey Pl SKEL WN8 66 E2
Pit La WDN WA8 139 F5
Pit Pl WLTN L25 154 D1
Pitsmead Rd KKBY L32 84 D2
Pitts Heath La RUNC WA7 178 D2
Pitts House La CHTN/BK PR9 23 K5
Pitt St CHTN/BK PR9 28 C1
CLVPS L1 9 F7
STHEL WA9 104 A1
WARRW/BUR WA5 16 A2
WDN WA8 158 B6
Pitville Av CALD/MH L18 134 B6
Pitville Cl CALD/MH L18 153 H1
Pitville Gv CALD/MH L18 134 B6
Pitville Rd CALD/MH L18 134 B6
Pitville Ter WDN WA8 157 H4
Plaistow Ct RUNC WA7 177 H6
Plane Cl WLT/FAZ L9 98 A2
Plane Tree Gv
RNFD/HAY WA11 * 91 F4
Plane Tree Rd BEB CH63 170 A1
Planetree Rd WD/CROXPK L12 99 K6
Plantation Cl RUNC WA7 177 K4
Plantation Dr GTS/LS CH66 195 H2
Plantation Rd BRSC L40 38 B5
PS/BROM CH62 171 H4
The Planters
GR/UP/WCH CH49 128 D5
NTHTN L30 70 D5
Platt Gv RF/TRAN CH42 151 F3
Platts La BRSC L40 46 D1
Platts St RNFD/HAY WA11 89 K5
Plattsville Rd CALD/MH L18 134 B4
Playfield Rd WD/CROXPK L12 99 K6
Pleasance Wy NEWLW WA12 106 C1
Pleasant Hill St TOX L8 132 C3
Pleasant St BTL L20 4 C6
VAUX/LVPD L3 9 H5
WAL/NB CH45 95 H6
Pleasant Vw BTL L20 4 C6
Pleasington Cl CL/PREN CH43 130 B5
Pleasington Dr CL/PREN CH43 130 B5
Pleck Rd EP CH65 202 E1
Plemont Rd CLB/OSW/ST L13 114 E2
Plemston Ct GTS/LS CH66 195 J1
Plex La ORM L39 43 K5
Plex Moss La ORM L39 42 C3
STHP PR8 41 K2
Plimsoll St EHL/KEN L7 113 K6
Plinston Av WARRS WA4 143 J5
Plough La BRSC L40 55 G2
Ploughmans Wy GTS/LS CH66 202 C3
Plover Cl NEWLW WA12 106 C2
Plover Dr RUNC WA7 178 C5
Plovers La FROD/HEL WA6 199 K4
Plover Wy GOL/RIS/CU WA3 93 F3
Pluckington Rd HUY L36 117 H5
Plumbers Wy HUY L36 117 F5
Plumer St BIRK CH41 130 D1
WAV L15 133 K2
Plumley Gdns RAIN/WH L35 157 F2
Plumpstons La FROD/HEL WA6 186 E6
Plumpton La ORM L39 43 G1
Plumpton St NPK/KEN L6 113 H3
Plumtree Av WARRW/BUR WA5 142 C1
Plum Tree Cl RAIN/WH L35 118 B1
STBRV L28 100 B6
Plymouth Cl RUNC WA7 188 D1
Plymyard Av PS/BROM CH62 184 A1
Plymyard Cl PS/BROM CH62 184 A2
Poachers' La WARRS WA4 143 J6
Pochard Ri RUNC WA7 178 C5
Pocket Nook La
GOL/RIS/CU WA3 93 H3
Pocket Nook St STHEL WA9 13 K4
Pocklington Ct
WARRN/WOL WA2 124 B6
Podium Rd CLB/OSW/ST L13 114 E3
Poets Cnr PS/BROM CH62 * 151 G6
Poleacre Dr WDN WA8 157 J1
Pollard Rd WAV L15 114 E6
Poll Hill Rd HES CH60 167 K4
Pollitt Crs STHEL WA9 120 A4
Pollitt Sq PS/BROM CH62 151 H3
Polperro Cl WARRW/BUR WA5 141 F6
Pomfret St TOX L8 132 E3
Pomona St VAUX/LVPD L3 9 H5
Pond Green Wy STHEL WA9 104 D4
Pond St GOL/RIS/CU WA3 93 H3
Pond View Cl HES CH60 168 C5
Pond Wk STHEL WA9 104 E4
Ponsonby Rd WAL/NB CH45 110 E2
Ponsonby St TOX L8 133 F3
Pool Bank PS/BROM CH62 151 G4
Poolbank Rd PS/BROM CH62 151 G4
Poole Av WARRN/WOL WA2 123 H5
Poole Crs WARRN/WOL WA2 123 H5
Poole Hall La GTS/LS CH66 195 H1
Poole Hall Rd EP CH65 195 J1
Pool End STHEL WA9 104 D3
Poole Rd WAL/EG CH44 111 K2
Poole Wk TOX L8 133 F5
Pool Hey STBRV L28 100 B5
Pool Hey La STHP PR8 28 E4
Pool La CHNE CH2 198 A4
GR/UP/WCH CH49 148 D1
LYMM WA13 145 H5
PS/BROM CH62 170 E1
RUNC WA7 11 F3
WARRS WA4 161 K2
Poolside Rd RUNC WA7 11 F6
Poolside Wk CHTN/BK PR9 23 K1
Pool St BIRK CH41 2 E2
CHTN/BK PR9 24 A1
WDN WA8 19 F5
Pooltown Rd EP CH65 195 J3
Poolwood Rd
GR/UP/WCH CH49 129 J5
Pope St BTL L20 81 J6
Poplar Av AIMK WN4 78 C4
CSBY/BLUN L23 69 G4
ECCL WA10 102 C1
GR/UP/WCH CH49 129 G4
NEWLW WA12 106 D2
RUNC WA7 177 F6
WARRW/BUR WA5 141 F5
Poplar Bank HUY L36 116 E5
Poplar Cl EP CH65 6 B7
RUNC WA7 177 F6
Poplar Dr BEB CH63 170 C1
EV L5 113 J2
KKBY L32 72 C6
SKEL WN8 56 B4
Poplar Farm Cl MOR/LEA CH46 128 D3
Poplar Gv CHNE CH2 198 B6
ECCL WA10 102 E2
LITH L21 81 G1
RAIN/WH L35 118 A2
RNFD/HAY WA11 90 B5
Poplar Rd CL/PREN CH43 130 E5
RNFD/HAY WA11 90 B5
WLTN L25 135 G6
Poplars Av WARRN/WOL WA2 123 H3
The Poplars BRSC L40 46 E1
LEIGH WN7 93 K3
LYMM WA13 145 J5
Poplar St GOL/RIS/CU WA3 92 C2
STHP PR8 28 C1
Poplar Vw WARRS WA4 * 160 D4
Poplar Wy ANF/KKDL L4 97 F5
Poppleford Cl WLTN L25 135 K5
Poppy Cl MOR/LEA CH46 110 A5
Poppy La ORM L39 54 B5
Porchester Rd NG/CROX L11 98 D4
Porchfield Cl NG/CROX L11 99 F2
Porlock Av CHLDW L16 135 F4
STHEL WA9 120 A2
Porlock Cl HES CH60 181 G1
WARRW/BUR WA5 141 F5
Portal Ms PEN/TH CH61 167 K2
Portal Rd PEN/TH CH61 167 K2
Portbury Cl PS/BROM CH62 151 H5
Port Cswy PS/BROM CH62 171 F1
Portelet Rd CLB/OSW/ST L13 114 E3
Porter Av NEWLW WA12 91 H6
Porter Cl RAIN/WH L35 119 F6
Porter St RUNC WA7 11 J4
VAUX/LVPD L3 112 D3
Portgate Cl NG/CROX L11 99 G3
Porthcawl Cl WDN WA8 138 B6
Porthleven Rd RUNC WA7 188 A2
Portia Av BEB CH63 150 D4
Portia Gdns BEB CH63 * 150 D4
Portia St BTL L20 96 E5
Portico Av RAIN/WH L35 118 C1
Portico La RAIN/WH L35 118 C1
Portland Av CSBY/WL L22 80 D1
Portland Gdns EV L5 112 E3
Portland Pl EV L5 113 G3
FROD/HEL WA6 199 K5
Portland St BIRK CH41 130 D1
EV L5 112 E3
NEWLW WA12 105 K1
RUNC WA7 10 B3
STHP PR8 14 D6
WAL/NB CH45 95 G4
Portland Wy STHEL WA9 104 D4
Portlemouth Rd NG/CROX L11 84 B6
Portloe Av HLWD L26 155 J2
Portman Rd WAV L15 133 J2
Porto Hey Rd PEN/TH CH61 148 A6
Portola Cl WARRS WA4 163 H1
Porton Rd KKBY L32 84 B2
Portreath Wy ECCL WA10 87 J5
Portree Av BEB CH63 184 A2
Portree Cl WLT/FAZ L9 82 D6
Portrush St CLB/OSW/ST L13 114 C1
Portside North EP CH65 196 A1
Portsmouth Pl RUNC WA7 188 D1
Portwood Cl TOX L8 * 133 G1
Post Office Av CHTN/BK PR9 15 F4
Post Office La RUNC WA7 176 A6
Potter Pl SKEL WN8 67 F2
Potters La WDN WA8 175 G1
Pottery Flds PR/KW L34 117 K1
Pottery La RAIN/WH L35 117 J4
Poulsom Dr NTHTN L30 81 K1
Poulter Rd WLT/FAZ L9 82 E4
Poulton Cl HLWD L26 155 G5
Poulton Crs WARR WA1 144 C1
Poulton Dr AIMK WN4 * 78 E5
WDN WA8 157 J4
Poulton Green Cl BEB CH63 170 B4
Poulton Hall Rd BEB CH63 170 C6
WAL/EG CH44 111 G4
Poulton Rd BEB CH63 170 C4
CHTN/BK PR9 23 H6
WAL/EG CH44 111 G4
Poulton Royd Dr BEB CH63 170 B3
Pound Rd GTS/LS CH66 195 F2
Poverty La MGHL L31 71 J1
Povey Rd WARRN/WOL WA2 123 J6
Powderworks La MGHL L31 63 G4
Powell Av GOL/RIS/CU WA3 125 G3
Powell Dr WGNW/BIL/O WN5 77 G6
Powell St STHEL WA9 104 C6
WARRS WA4 143 J6
Power Rd PS/BROM CH62 171 H4
RF/TRAN CH42 151 F3
Powis St TOX L8 133 F4
Pownall St CLVPS L1 8 E7
Powys St WARRW/BUR WA5 142 C4
Poynter St STHEL WA9 103 G6
Poynton Cl WARRS WA4 144 A6
Pratt Rd PR/KW L34 117 J1
The Precincts CSBY/BLUN L23 69 F5
Preece Cl WDN WA8 138 C6
Preesall Cl CHTN/BK PR9 20 C6
Preesall Wy NG/CROX L11 84 B6
Premier St EV L5 113 H2
Prentice Rd RF/TRAN CH42 150 D2
Prenton Av STHEL WA9 119 K3
Prenton Dell Av
CL/PREN CH43 149 K3
Prenton Dell Rd
CL/PREN CH43 149 H2
Prenton Farm Rd
CL/PREN CH43 149 K3
Prenton Gn SPK/HALE L24 173 K2
Prenton Hall Rd
CL/PREN CH43 149 K3
Prenton La RF/TRAN CH42 150 A2
Prentonpark Rd
RF/TRAN CH42 131 F6
Prenton Rd East
RF/TRAN CH42 150 C1
Prenton Rd West
RF/TRAN CH42 150 B1
Prenton Village Rd
CL/PREN CH43 149 K3
Prenton Wy CL/PREN CH43 149 H3
Prescot Dr NPK/KEN L6 114 B4
Prescot Gn ORM L39 53 H2
Prescot Rd CLB/OSW/ST L13 114 C4
ECCL WA10 102 D5
MGHL L31 72 B3
WDN WA8 137 J4
WDN WA8 138 C6
Prescot St EHL/KEN L7 9 K2
WAL/NB CH45 95 G5
Prescott Av GOL/RIS/CU WA3 92 A1
Prescott Br BRSC L40 39 J1
Prescott Rd SKEL WN8 67 G3
Prescott St GOL/RIS/CU WA3 92 B2
WARRS WA4 143 H6
Preseland Rd CSBY/BLUN L23 69 F6
Prestbury Av CL/PREN CH43 149 H1
STHP PR8 33 H4
Prestbury Cl CL/PREN CH43 149 H1
WDN WA8 157 K3
Prestbury Dr ECCL WA10 102 D3
WARRS WA4 144 C6
Prestbury Rd NG/CROX L11 98 D1
Preston Av PR/KW L34 117 J2
Preston Gv NPK/KEN L6 114 A2
Preston New Rd CHTN/BK PR9 23 J2
Preston on the Hl WARRS WA4 188 E1
Preston Rd CHTN/BK PR9 23 G5
Preston St CLVPS L1 8 E3
STHEL WA9 119 K5
Preston Wy CSBY/BLUN L23 69 H5
Prestwick Dr CSBY/BLUN L23 68 D3
Prestwood Rd DV/KA/FCH L14 115 K3
Pretoria Rd AIMK WN4 79 F5
WLT/FAZ L9 82 E5
Price Gv STHEL WA9 104 E3
Price's La CL/PREN CH43 130 E5
Price St BIRK CH41 2 B1
BIRK CH41 3 F3
CLVPS L1 * 8 E6
Pride Cl NEWLW WA12 106 E3
Priestfield Rd EP CH65 6 C4
Priesthouse Cl FMBY L37 49 G2
Priesthouse La FMBY L37 49 G2
Primrose Cl CHTN/BK PR9 21 F5
FMBY L37 41 H6
RUNC WA7 177 K5
WARRN/WOL WA2 123 J6
WDN WA8 157 K2
Primrose Dr HUY L36 116 E2
Primrose Gv RNFD/HAY WA11 90 D4
WAL/EG CH44 * 112 A5
Primrose Hl PS/BROM CH62 151 G5
VAUX/LVPD L3 8 E2
Primrose Rd BIRK CH41 130 C2
CALD/MH L18 134 D4
Primrose St ANF/KKDL L4 97 F6
Primrose Vw AIMK WN4 91 G1
Primula Dr GOL/RIS/CU WA3 92 E3
WLT/FAZ L9 97 K1
Prince Albert Ms CLVPS L1 132 D2
Prince Alfred Rd WAV L15 134 B2
Prince Andrew's Gv ECCL WA10 87 K5
Prince Charles Gdns STHP PR8 27 G2
Prince Edward St BIRK CH41 2 C3
Prince Edwin St EV L5 113 G3
Princes Av CSBY/BLUN L23 68 E5
PS/BROM CH62 184 B1
TOX L8 132 E2
WKBY CH48 146 C1
Princes Bvd BEB CH63 150 C3
Princes Gdns VAUX/LVPD L3 8 D2
Princes Ga West TOX L8 133 G3
Princes Pde VAUX/LVPD L3 8 A2
Princes Pl WDN WA8 157 K2
Princes Rd ECCL WA10 102 E4
EP CH65 195 J3
TOX L8 132 E2
Princess Av AIMK WN4 79 H6
ECCL WA10 88 B5
RNFD/HAY WA11 91 F4
WARR WA1 143 J3
WARRW/BUR WA5 141 F3
Princess Crs WARR WA1 143 J3
Princess Dr DV/KA/FCH L14 115 K1
WD/CROXPK L12 99 J6
Princess Rd AIMK WN4 79 G6
LYMM WA13 145 H6
WAL/NB CH45 95 H6
Princess St CLVP L2 8 D4
RUNC WA7 10 D3
WARRW/BUR WA5 142 A5
Princess Ter CL/PREN CH43 2 B7
Princes St BTL L20 96 D4
CLVP L2 8 D3
NEWLW WA12 106 B2
STHP PR8 14 D6
WDN WA8 18 D3
Princess Wy LITH L21 81 H4
Prince St AIMK WN4 79 F4
CLVPS L1 8 D6
CSBY/WL L22 80 E3
Princes Wy RNFD/HAY WA11 88 D3
Princesway WAL/NB CH45 111 G1
Princeway FROD/HEL WA6 200 E1
Prince William St TOX L8 132 D3
Prior Farm Cl ALL/GAR L19 153 H4
Priors Cl WLTN L25 154 E1
Priorsfield MOR/LEA CH46 129 F1
Priorsfield Rd WLTN L25 154 E1
Prior St BTL L20 81 H5
Priorswood Pl SKEL WN8 67 H3
Priory Cl AIG/SPK L17 152 C1
BEB CH63 170 C2
BRSC L40 38 D4
FMBY L37 49 H3
RAIN/WH L35 117 J6
RUNC WA7 177 K4
Priory Ct HUY L36 * 116 E5
RUNC WA7 * 188 D2
Priory Gdns ECCL WA10 88 C4
STHP PR8 27 G3
Priory Gra STHP PR8 27 H3
Priory Gv ORM L39 53 H1
Priory Ms BIRK CH41 * 3 J5
STHP PR8 14 B6
Priory Rd AIMK WN4 78 E4
ANF/KKDL L4 97 J5
RUNC WA7 * 178 B3
WAL/EG CH44 112 A4
WKBY CH48 146 C1
Priory St ALL/GAR L19 172 C1
BIRK CH41 3 J5
WARRS WA4 142 E6
The Priory NSTN CH64 181 J6
RAIN/WH L35 118 E4
WARRN/WOL WA2 107 G6
Priory Wy WLTN L25 154 E1
Priory Whf BIRK CH41 3 J4
Pritchard Av LITH L21 81 G4
Pritt St VAUX/LVPD L3 113 G4
Private Dr PEN/TH CH61 149 G6
Prizett Rd ALL/GAR L19 153 J4
Probyn Rd WAL/NB CH45 110 E2
Procter Rd RF/TRAN CH42 151 F2
Proctor Rd FMBY L37 48 C1
HOY CH47 127 H3
Proctors Cl WDN WA8 158 D1
Proffits La FROD/HEL WA6 200 B5
Promenade STHP PR8 14 E3
STHP PR8 22 D4
STHP PR8 33 F3
Promenade Gdns AIG/SPK L17 133 F6
The Promenade WARRS WA4 * 160 D4
Prospect Ct NPK/KEN L6 * 114 B4
Prospect Pl SKEL WN8 67 H2
Prospect Rd RF/TRAN CH42 150 A2
STHEL WA9 104 B1
Prospect Rw RUNC WA7 176 C6
Prospect V NPK/KEN L6 114 B3
WAL/NB CH45 111 F2
Prospect Wy NTHTN L30 70 E6
Providence Crs TOX L8 132 D3
Provident St STHEL WA9 104 E2
Province Rd BTL L20 82 A5
Prussia St VAUX/LVPD L3 * 8 C2
Public Hall St RUNC WA7 10 E3
Pudsey St CLVPS L1 9 G3
Puffin Cl EP CH65 203 G3
Pugin St ANF/KKDL L4 97 G6
Pulford Av CL/PREN CH43 149 K1
Pulford Cl RUNC WA7 187 G1
Pulford Rd BEB CH63 150 E6
EP CH65 195 J5
Pulford St ANF/KKDL L4 97 H6
Pullman Cl HES CH60 168 D5
Pumpfields Rd VAUX/LVPD L3 112 E4
Pump La RUNC WA7 177 J5
WKBY CH48 128 C5
Pump Rd BIRK CH41 131 H1
Punnell's La MGHL L31 61 H2
Purbeck Dr PEN/TH CH61 148 A4
Purdy Cl WARRW/BUR WA5 122 D6
Purley Gv CALD/MH L18 153 H1
Purley Rd CSBY/WL L22 * 80 D1
Purser Gv WAV L15 133 J1
Putney Ct RUNC WA7 * 177 H6
Pye Cl RNFD/HAY WA11 91 G3
Pyecroft Cl WARRW/BUR WA5 140 E3
Pyecroft Rd WARRW/BUR WA5 140 E3
Pye Rd HES CH60 168 A5
Pyes Gdns RNFD/HAY WA11 88 E4
Pyes La HUY L36 100 C6
Pye St WAV L15 134 B2
Pygon's Hill La MGHL L31 52 B6
Pym St ANF/KKDL L4 97 H3
The Pyramids BIRK CH41 * 2 E5
Pyrus Gv FROD/HEL WA6 * 199 K5

Q

Quadrangle VAUX/LVPD L3 * 9 K4
The Quadrangle
CALD/MH L18 * 134 C5
Quadrant Cl RUNC WA7 188 C1
Quail Cl WARRN/WOL WA2 123 K4
Quaker La HES CH60 167 J4
Quakers Meadow PR/KW L34 100 D1
Quantock Cl GTS/LS CH66 194 D3
Quarry Av BEB CH63 170 B1
Quarry Bank BIRK CH41 2 D6
NWD/KWIPK L33 72 E6
WAL/NB CH45 111 H1
Quarrybank St BIRK CH41 2 C6
Quarry Cl CLB/OSW/ST L13 114 D2
HES CH60 167 K3
NWD/KWIPK L33 72 E6
RUNC WA7 11 K6
Quarry Ct HES CH60 * 167 J4
WDN WA8 157 H2
Quarry Dl NWD/KWIPK L33 72 E6
Quarry Dr ORM L39 53 G4
Quarry Gn NWD/KWIPK L33 72 E6
Quarry Hey NWD/KWIPK L33 72 E6
Quarry La PEN/TH CH61 148 D5
WARRS WA4 162 C5
Quarry Mt ORM L39 46 A5
Quarry Rd BTL L20 5 H6
CLB/OSW/ST L13 114 E2
CSBY/BLUN L23 69 H3
NSTN CH64 182 D6
Quarry Rd East BEB CH63 170 C1
HES CH60 167 J4
Quarry Rd West HES CH60 167 J4
Quarryside Dr NWD/KWIPK L33 85 F1
Quarry St WLTN L25 135 G6
Quarry St South WLTN L25 154 D1
Quartz Wy LITH L21 81 K3
Quay Fold WARRS WA4 142 B5
Quayle Cl RNFD/HAY WA11 90 A5
Quay Pl RUNC WA7 178 D6
Quay Side FROD/HEL WA6 187 G6
Quayside NSTN CH64 191 J4
The Quay FROD/HEL WA6 187 G5
Quebec Quay VAUX/LVPD L3 132 B3
Quebec Rd WARRN/WOL WA2 143 G2
Queen Anne St STHP PR8 14 E5
VAUX/LVPD L3 9 G1
Queen Av CLVP L2 * 8 D4
Queen Mary's Dr
PS/BROM CH62 151 G5
Queen's Av AIMK WN4 79 G5
EP CH65 195 K6
FMBY L37 40 E6
HOY CH47 127 J1
WARR WA1 143 H2
WDN WA8 157 G3
Queensberry St TOX L8 132 E4
Queensbury WKBY CH48 127 J6
Queensbury Av
PS/BROM CH62 171 G4
Queensbury Wy WDN WA8 138 C6
Queen's Cl RUNC WA7 10 C7
Queens Ct NPK/KEN L6 113 J2
Queenscourt Rd
WD/CROXPK L12 115 G2
Queens Crs WARR WA1 * 143 K1
Queens Cft FMBY L37 48 D3
Queensdale Rd CALD/MH L18 134 B4
Queens Dr CL/PREN CH43 149 K2
ECCL WA10 87 K5
FROD/HEL WA6 199 J6
GOL/RIS/CU WA3 92 D3
HES CH60 167 J5
NEWLW WA12 91 H6
WARRS WA4 162 E1
Queens Drive Mossley Hl
CALD/MH L18 134 A5
Queens Drive Stoneycroft
CLB/OSW/ST L13 115 F3
Queens Drive (Stoneycroft)
CLB/OSW/ST L13 115 G5
Queens Drive Walton
ANF/KKDL L4 97 J3
Queens Drive (Wavertree)
DV/KA/FCH L14 115 G6
Queens Drive Wavertree
WAV L15 134 D3
Queens Drive West Derby
CLB/OSW/ST L13 98 C5
Queens Gdns EP CH65 6 B4
Queens Gn ORM L39 43 H6
Queensland Av STHEL WA9 103 G6
Queensland Pl STHEL WA9 103 G6
Queensland St EHL/KEN L7 113 K6
Queens Ms NPK/KEN L6 113 J2
Queen Sq CLVPS L1 9 F3
Queen's Rd AIMK WN4 79 G6
BTL L20 4 E7
CHTN/BK PR9 15 H3
CSBY/BLUN L23 69 F5

ECCL WA10 102 E4
FMBY L37 48 D3
GTS/LS CH66 195 F2
HOY CH47 127 F2
NPK/KEN L6 113 J3
PR/KW L34 118 A1
RF/TRAN CH42 151 F2
RNFD/HAY WA11 91 F4
RUNC WA7 10 C6
WAL/EG CH44 112 A4
Queen St ALL/GAR L19 153 K6
BIRK CH41 131 H5
CSBY/WL L22 80 E3
ECCL WA10 13 F2
EP CH65 6 E1
GOL/RIS/CU WA3 * 92 C3
NEWLW WA12 106 B2
ORM L39 53 J1
RUNC WA7 10 D3
WAL/NB CH45 111 H2
Queensway CSBY/WL L22 81 G1
FROD/HEL WA6 200 E2
HES CH60 181 H1
RNFD/HAY WA11 75 H4
RNFD/HAY WA11 88 D3
RUNC WA7 10 C3
WAL/NB CH45 111 G1
WDN WA8 157 K4
Queensway (Mersey Tunnel)
BIRK CH41 3 F2
VAUX/LVPD L3 8 B3
Queens Whf VAUX/LVPD L3 132 B2
Quernmore Rd
NWD/KWIPK L33 73 F6
Quernmore Wk
NWD/KWIPK L33 73 F6
Quickswood Cl WLTN L25 135 G4
Quickswood Dr WLTN L25 135 G4
Quickswood Gn WLTN L25 135 G4
Quickthorn Crs STBRV L28 100 B6
Quigley Av NTHTN L30 82 D2
Quigley St BIRK CH41 131 H5
The Quillet NSTN CH64 192 A2
Quinesway GR/UP/WCH CH49 129 H4
Quinn St WDN WA8 18 E5
Quintbridge Cl HLWD L26 155 H4
Quinton Cl STHP PR8 33 G5
Quorn St EHL/KEN L7 113 K5

R

Rabbit La BRSC L40 37 K6
Raby Av BEB CH63 183 J1
Raby Cl BEB CH63 170 C6
HES CH60 167 K6
WDN WA8 158 E1
Raby Dr BEB CH63 170 C6
MOR/LEA CH46 128 E2
Raby Gdns NSTN CH64 191 K1
Raby Gv RF/TRAN CH42 150 C3
Raby Hall Rd BEB CH63 183 F2
Raby Mere Rd BEB CH63 182 D2
Raby Park Cl NSTN CH64 191 K1
Raby Park Rd NSTN CH64 191 K1
Raby Rd BEB CH63 182 C1
NSTN CH64 191 K1
Rachel St EV L5 113 F3
Radburn Cl CSBY/BLUN L23 69 J4
Raddon Pl WARRS WA4 * 143 H6
Radford Av BEB CH63 170 D3
Radford Cl WDN WA8 157 H4
Radlett Cl WARRW/BUR WA5 141 F6
Radley Dr AIN/FAZ L10 71 F6
BEB CH63 182 A1
Radley La WARRN/WOL WA2 123 K4
Radley Rd WAL/EG CH44 111 F2
Radleys Ct TOX L8 * 132 E3
Radley St STHEL WA9 103 G6
Radmore Rd DV/KA/FCH L14 115 H4
Radnor Av HES CH60 167 K4
Radnor Cl HLWD L26 155 G5
Radnor Dr BTL L20 5 J4
CHTN/BK PR9 23 H2
WAL/NB CH45 111 J1
WDN WA8 157 J1
Radnor Pl CL/PREN CH43 2 B5
NPK/KEN L6 114 B2
Radnor St WARRW/BUR WA5 142 B3
Radstock Gv STHEL WA9 120 B2
Radstock Rd NPK/KEN L6 114 A4
WAL/EG CH44 110 E2
Radway Gn GTS/LS CH66 195 H4
Radway Rd HUY L36 117 F2
Raeburn Av NSTN CH64 192 A2
PS/BROM CH62 184 A1
WKBY CH48 127 H6
Raffles Rd RF/TRAN CH42 2 D7
Raffles St CLVPS L1 132 D2
Rafter Av BTL L20 82 B5
Raglan Ct GOL/RIS/CU WA3 125 H1
Rail Cl RNFD/HAY WA11 66 B5
Railside Ct EV L5 * 112 E2
Railton Av RAIN/WH L35 119 F5
Railton Cl RAIN/WH L35 119 F6
Railton Rd NG/CROX L11 98 C3
Railway Ap ORM L39 45 K6
Railway Pth ORM L39 53 J1
Railway Rd GOL/RIS/CU WA3 * 92 C3
RF/TRAN CH42 150 E1
SKEL WN8 55 K5
Railway St ALL/GAR L19 153 K6
NEWLW WA12 106 B2
STHEL WA9 13 J3
STHP PR8 27 J2
Railway Ter STHP PR8 27 H2
Rainbow Cl WDN WA8 138 B6
Rainbow Dr HLWD L26 155 H3
MGHL L31 72 A5
Raines Cl GR/UP/WCH CH49 129 F5
Rainford Av BTL L20 82 B6
Rainford By-Pass
RNFD/HAY WA11 74 E2
Rainford Rd ORM L39 65 G1
RNFD/HAY WA11 87 K4
WGNW/BIL/O WN5 76 E4
Rainham Cl ALL/GAR L19 153 K3
Rainhill Rd RAIN/WH L35 118 E2
Rake Hey MOR/LEA CH46 128 C1
Rake Hey Cl MOR/LEA CH46 128 D1
Rake La CHNE CH2 203 H6
FROD/HEL WA6 199 H3
GR/UP/WCH CH49 129 H5
WAL/NB CH45 111 H1
Rakersfield Ct WAL/NB CH45 95 J5
Rakersfield Rd WAL/NB CH45 95 J5
The Rake PS/BROM CH62 171 G4
Raleigh Av RAIN/WH L35 117 K5
Raleigh Cl WARRW/BUR WA5 122 D6
Raleigh Rd MOR/LEA CH46 110 B3
NSTN CH64 181 K6
Raleigh St BTL L20 96 D4
Ralph's Wife's La
CHTN/BK PR9 21 J5
Rame Cl NG/CROX L11 84 A5
Ramford St STHEL WA9 104 B3
Ramilies Rd CALD/MH L18 134 A4
Ramleh Cl CSBY/BLUN L23 68 C6
Rampit Cl RNFD/HAY WA11 90 E4
Ramsay Cl GOL/RIS/CU WA3 125 G4
Ramsbrook Cl SPK/HALE L24 173 H1
Ramsbrook La SPK/HALE L24 174 D2
Ramsbrook Rd SPK/HALE L24 173 H1
Ramsey Cl AIMK WN4 91 G1
ALL/GAR L19 154 A3
RAIN/WH L35 118 A4
WDN WA8 139 K6
Ramsey Ct WKBY CH48 146 C2
Ramsey Rd ALL/GAR L19 154 A3
EP CH65 203 G2
Ramsfield Rd SPK/HALE L24 174 B1
Ramsons Cl HLWD L26 155 H2
Randall Dr NTHTN L30 69 K6
Randle Av RNFD/HAY WA11 75 F1
Randle Brook Ct
RNFD/HAY WA11 75 F1
Randle Cl BEB CH63 170 C3
Randle Meadow GTS/LS CH66 202 D1
Randles Rd PR/KW L34 85 F6
Randolph St ANF/KKDL L4 97 H6
Randon Gv ECCL WA10 12 E4
Ranelagh Av LITH L21 81 H3
Ranelagh Dr STHP PR8 34 B2
Ranelagh Dr North
ALL/GAR L19 153 H3
Ranelagh Dr South
ALL/GAR L19 153 H4
Ranelagh St CLVPS L1 9 F5
Ranfurly Rd ALL/GAR L19 153 J4
Rangemoor Cl
GOL/RIS/CU WA3 125 J1
Rangemore Rd CALD/MH L18 153 H2
Rankin St WAL/EG CH44 111 G5
Ranmore Av AIMK WN4 78 C5
Rannoch Cl GTS/LS CH66 195 J6
Ranulph Ct FROD/HEL WA6 201 F2
Ranworth Cl NG/CROX L11 98 C2
Ranworth Dr GOL/RIS/CU WA3 93 F4
Ranworth Pl NG/CROX L11 98 D2
Ranworth Rd
WARRW/BUR WA5 141 F3
Ranworth Sq NG/CROX L11 98 D2
Ranworth Wy NG/CROX L11 98 D2
Rappart Rd WAL/EG CH44 111 K4
Ratcliff Pl RAIN/WH L35 118 D3
Rathbone Rd HTWN L38 59 F3
WAV L15 134 A1
Rathlin Cl WDN WA8 139 K6
Rathmore Av CALD/MH L18 134 B6
Rathmore Cl CL/PREN CH43 130 D6
Rathmore Crs CHTN/BK PR9 23 K2
Rathmore Dr CL/PREN CH43 130 D5
Rathmore Rd CL/PREN CH43 130 D5
Raven Cl NPK/KEN L6 * 113 J4
Ravendale Cl CL/PREN CH43 130 A5
Ravenfield Cl HLWD L26 155 H3
Ravenfield Dr WDN WA8 138 B6
Ravenglass Av MGHL L31 62 B5
Ravenhead Av KKBY L32 84 D4
Ravenhead Colliery Yd
STHEL WA9 * 103 J4
Ravenhead Dr SKEL WN8 57 J6
Ravenhead Rd ECCL WA10 103 G4
Ravenhead Rw ECCL WA10 * 103 G4
Ravenhead Wy SKEL WN8 67 H1
Ravenhill Crs MOR/LEA CH46 109 K4
Ravenhurst Ct
GOL/RIS/CU WA3 125 H2
Ravenhurst Wy RAIN/WH L35 117 J6
Raven Meols La FMBY L37 48 E3
Ravenna Rd ALL/GAR L19 154 A3
Ravenscourt HLWD L26 * 155 J4
Ravenscroft FMBY L37 49 F3
Ravenscroft Av ORM L39 53 J1
Ravenscroft Rd CL/PREN CH43 2 B6
Ravensdale Cl
WARRN/WOL WA2 123 K4
The Ravens FMBY L37 49 F4
Ravensthorpe Gn NG/CROX L11 98 D2
Ravenstone Cl
GR/UP/WCH CH49 129 F2
Ravenstone Dr STHEL WA9 104 B6
Ravenstone Rd ALL/GAR L19 153 J3
Ravenswood Av
RF/TRAN CH42 150 E3
Ravenswood Rd
CLB/OSW/ST L13 114 E4
PEN/TH CH61 168 A3
Rawcliffe Cl WDN WA8 138 E5
Rawcliffe Rd RF/TRAN CH42 2 D7
WLT/FAZ L9 97 H1
Rawdon Cl RUNC WA7 177 K6
Rawlings Cl GOL/RIS/CU WA3 125 H4
Rawlinson Ct CHTN/BK PR9 * 15 K2
Rawlinson Crs HLWD L26 156 A3
Rawlinson Gv CHTN/BK PR9 23 G4
Rawlinson Rd CHTN/BK PR9 23 G4
CLB/OSW/ST L13 114 D4
Rawlins St EHL/KEN L7 114 B4
Rawson Cl LITH L21 81 G4
Rawson Rd LITH L21 81 G5
Raydale Cl GOL/RIS/CU WA3 93 F2
WLT/FAZ L9 97 J2
Raymond Av NTHTN L30 82 D2
WARRS WA4 162 C1
Raymond Pl EV L5 113 F3
Raymond Rd WAL/EG CH44 111 J4
Raymond Wy NSTN CH64 192 B2
Raynham Rd CLB/OSW/ST L13 114 D5
Reade Cl BEB CH63 170 C4
Reading Cl EV L5 97 F6
Reads Ct WLT/FAZ L9 82 C5
Reaper Cl WARRW/BUR WA5 142 A3
Reapers Wy NTHTN L30 70 D5
Reay St WDN WA8 158 D1
Rebecca Gdns STHEL WA9 104 A6
Recreation Av AIMK WN4 79 J5
Recreation Dr
WGNW/BIL/O WN5 * 77 H4
Recreation St STHEL WA9 104 A2
Rector Rd NPK/KEN L6 98 A6
Rectory Av GOL/RIS/CU WA3 92 D3
Rectory Cl HES CH60 167 K6
RF/TRAN CH42 131 G5
WARRN/WOL WA2 123 G1
Rectory Dr HLWD L26 155 J2
Rectory Gdns LYMM WA13 165 F1
STHEL WA9 120 A1
Rectory La HES CH60 167 J6
LYMM WA13 165 F1
WARRN/WOL WA2 123 G1
Rectory Rd AIMK WN4 78 C4
CHTN/BK PR9 23 H4
WKBY CH48 146 C2
Redacre Cl RUNC WA7 188 E4
Red Bank Av NEWLW WA12 107 F4
Red Barnes FMBY L37 41 F5
Red Barn Rd WGNW/BIL/O WN5 76 E3
Redbourne Av HLWD L26 155 J5
Redbourne Dr WDN WA8 138 A5
Redbourn St NPK/KEN L6 114 A1
Redbrook Cl PS/BROM CH62 184 A1
Redbrook St NPK/KEN L6 114 A1
Red Brow La RUNC WA7 178 D5
Redbrow Wy NWD/KWIPK L33 72 D5
Redburn Cl TOX L8 133 F5
Redcap Cl WAL/NB CH45 94 E5
Redcar Cl STHP PR8 28 C4
Redcar Dr PS/BROM CH62 184 A2
Redcar Ms NPK/KEN L6 113 K1
Redcar Rd WAL/NB CH45 110 D1
Redcar St NPK/KEN L6 114 A1
Red Cat La BRSC L40 38 E1
RNFD/HAY WA11 76 C4
Redcliffe Gdns ORM L39 53 J2
Redcroft GR/UP/WCH CH49 * 128 D6
Red Cross St CLVPS L1 8 C5
Red Cut La NWD/KWIPK L33 86 A3
Red Delph La RNFD/HAY WA11 65 K6
Reddish La LYMM WA13 145 K5
Redditch Cl GR/UP/WCH CH49 128 D5
Redesdale Cl
WARRN/WOL WA2 124 A5
Redfern St BTL L20 96 E5
Redfield Cl WAL/EG CH44 111 K3
Red Fold ORM L39 53 G3
Redford Cl GR/UP/WCH CH49 128 D5
Redford St NPK/KEN L6 114 A2
Redgate FMBY L37 49 G3
ORM L39 53 H1
Redgate Av CSBY/BLUN L23 69 H5
Redgate Dr FMBY L37 49 H3
STHEL WA9 104 B2
Redgate Rd AIMK WN4 79 G3
Redgrave St EHL/KEN L7 114 A5
Redhill Av KKBY L32 84 E3
Redhill Ms EP CH65 6 C2
Red Hill Rd BEB CH63 150 A6
Redhills Dr STHP PR8 28 C4
Redhouse Bank WKBY CH48 127 F6
Redhouse La WKBY CH48 127 F6
Redington Rd ALL/GAR L19 154 A3
Redland Ct WGNE/HIN WN2 79 K2
Redland Rd WLT/FAZ L9 82 E3
Red La FROD/HEL WA6 201 F1
WARRS WA4 162 B4
Red Lion Cl MGHL L31 62 A6
Red Lion La GTS/LS CH66 195 F2
Red Lomes NTHTN L30 70 A4
Redmain Gv GOL/RIS/CU WA3 93 F3
Redmain Wy WD/CROXPK L12 99 K4
Redmayne Cl NEWLW WA12 106 B1
Redmere Dr HES CH60 168 C5
Redmires Cl EHL/KEN L7 * 133 G1
Redmond St BIRK CH41 131 H5
Redmoor Crs NWD/KWIPK L33 72 D5
Red Pike GTS/LS CH66 195 G2
Redpoll Gv HLWD L26 155 H1
Redpoll La GOL/RIS/CU WA3 125 G3
Red Rock St NPK/KEN L6 113 K3
Red Rum Cl WLT/FAZ L9 83 G3
Redruth Av RNFD/HAY WA11 89 G4
Redruth Cl RUNC WA7 188 B1
Redruth Rd NG/CROX L11 84 C6
Red Sands ORM L39 53 H2
Redshank Cl NEWLW WA12 106 C1
Redshank La GOL/RIS/CU WA3 125 H3
Redstart Cl GOL/RIS/CU WA3 93 F3
Redstone Cl HOY CH47 127 J1
Redstone Dr HES CH60 167 G4
Red Stone Hl FROD/HEL WA6 199 J5
Redstone Pk WAL/NB CH45 * 95 G5
Redstone Ri CL/PREN CH43 130 A3
Redvales Ct GOL/RIS/CU WA3 124 E3
Redvers Av GTS/LS CH66 184 D5
Redvers Dr WLT/FAZ L9 82 C5
Redwald Cl NWD/KWIPK L33 72 E3
Redwing La WLTN L25 135 H5
Redwing Wy HLWD L26 155 G1
Redwood Av MGHL L31 62 A4
Redwood Cl CL/PREN CH43 * 149 J1
WARR WA1 144 D3
Redwood Dr CHNE CH2 198 D5
GTS/LS CH66 202 D2
ORM L39 53 H1
RNFD/HAY WA11 89 J6
Redwood Gv BTL L20 * 5 F3
Redwood Rd WLTN L25 135 J4
Redwood Wy NWD/KWIPK L33 72 D3
Reedale Cl CALD/MH L18 134 B5
Reedale Rd CALD/MH L18 134 B5
Reeds Av East MOR/LEA CH46 109 K4
Reeds Av West MOR/LEA CH46 109 K4
Reeds Brow RNFD/HAY WA11 75 J1
Reeds La MOR/LEA CH46 109 K4
RNFD/HAY WA11 75 G6
Reedsmere Cl WARRS WA4 162 D1
Reeds Rd HUY L36 116 E3
The Reeds ORM L39 45 H5
Reedville CL/PREN CH43 2 A7
Reedville Gv MOR/LEA CH46 109 K5
Reedville Rd BEB CH63 150 E6
Rees Pk BRSC L40 39 F6
Reeves Av BTL L20 5 J1
Reeves St STHEL WA9 104 C2
Reeve St GOL/RIS/CU WA3 93 J3
Regal Cl GTS/LS CH66 195 H6
Regal Crs WDN WA8 157 G3
Regal Dr ECCL WA10 87 K6
Regal Rd NG/CROX L11 99 G2
Regal Wk ANF/KKDL L4 97 H6
Regency Gdns STHP PR8 27 F3
Regent Av AIMK WN4 78 E4
DV/KA/FCH L14 115 J5
NTHTN L30 70 C6
RNFD/HAY WA11 90 A4
WARR WA1 143 K1
Regent Cl STHP PR8 27 G3
Regent Ms STHP PR8 27 G3
Regent Rd BTL L20 4 A4
CSBY/BLUN L23 68 E5
EV L5 112 D1
STHP PR8 27 F3
WAL/NB CH45 110 D1
WDN WA8 18 E1
Regents Cl PEN/TH CH61 148 E5
Regents Fld FMBY L37 * 40 D6
Regents Rd ECCL WA10 102 E4
Regent St EP CH65 195 K4
NEWLW WA12 106 A2
RUNC WA7 10 D3
VAUX/LVPD L3 112 D3
WARR WA1 16 C5
Regents Wy BEB CH63 150 C4
Regina Av CSBY/WL L22 80 D1
Reginald Rd STHEL WA9 120 C1
Regina Rd WLT/FAZ L9 82 D5
Reid Av WARRW/BUR WA5 142 C1
Reid Ct GTS/LS CH66 195 F2
Reigate Cl WLTN L25 155 F1
Rembury Pl RUNC WA7 188 E4
Renacres La ORM L39 35 G4
Renaissance Wy SPK/HALE L24 173 J1
Rendal Cl EV L5 113 J2
Rendcombe Gn NG/CROX L11 98 D2
Rendel Cl NEWLW WA12 106 D3
Rendelsham Cl
GR/UP/WCH CH49 129 F4
Rendel St BIRK CH41 2 E2
Rendlesham Cl
GOL/RIS/CU WA3 125 K1
Renfrew Av PS/BROM CH62 184 B2
RNFD/HAY WA11 89 H4
Renfrew St EHL/KEN L7 113 J5
Renfrey Cl ORM L39 45 J3
Rennell Rd DV/KA/FCH L14 115 G4
Rennie Av ECCL WA10 102 E1
Renown Cl GOL/RIS/CU WA3 125 F3
Renown Wy SPK/HALE L24 154 D5
Renshaw St CLVPS L1 9 G5
Rensherds Pl KNUT WA16 165 K6
Renton Av RUNC WA7 177 G3
Renville Rd DV/KA/FCH L14 115 G6
Renwick Av RAIN/WH L35 118 C3
Renwick Sq AIMK WN4 78 E6
Repton Gv WLT/FAZ L9 83 F1
Repton Rd CHLDW L16 134 E1
EP CH65 7 G7
Reservoir Rd RF/TRAN CH42 150 A2
WLTN L25 135 G6
Reservoir Rd North
RF/TRAN CH42 150 A1
Reservoir St NPK/KEN L6 113 J3
STHEL WA9 102 E6
Rest Hill Rd BEB CH63 150 A6
Retford Rd NWD/KWIPK L33 84 E1
Reva Rd DV/KA/FCH L14 115 K5
Revesby Cl WDN WA8 157 J1
Rexmore Rd CALD/MH L18 153 H1
Rexmore Wy WAV L15 133 K2
Reynolds Av GOL/RIS/CU WA3 125 G2
STHEL WA9 105 F3
Reynolds Cl NPK/KEN L6 113 J3
Reynolds St WARRS WA4 143 H6
Reynolds Wy WLTN L25 154 D1
Rhiwlas St TOX L8 133 F4
Rhodesia Rd WLT/FAZ L9 82 E5
Rhodes St WARRN/WOL WA2 143 F2
Rhodesway HES CH60 168 B6
Rhona Cl BEB CH63 183 K3
Rhona Dr WARRW/BUR WA5 141 F3
Rhosesmor Cl KKBY L32 84 E5
Rhosesmor Rd KKBY L32 84 E5
Rhuddlan Ct EP CH65 203 H1
Rhum Cl EP CH65 203 G2
Rhyl St TOX L8 132 E4
WDN WA8 * 18 B6
Rialto Cl TOX L8 132 E2
Ribble Av CHTN/BK PR9 24 A1
MGHL L31 62 C5
RAIN/WH L35 118 E4
Ribble Cl WDN WA8 140 A6
Ribble Crs WGNW/BIL/O WN5 77 F6
Ribbledale Rd CALD/MH L18 134 B5
Ribble Rd WLTN L25 135 K6
Ribbler's La KKBY L32 84 C4
Ribblesdale EP CH65 195 K6
Ribblesdale Av WLT/FAZ L9 82 E4
Ribblesdale Cl PS/BROM CH62 184 C2
Ribble St BIRK CH41 111 F6
Ribchester Wy RAIN/WH L35 136 D2
Rice Hey Rd WAL/EG CH44 111 J2
Rice La WAL/EG CH44 111 K3
WLT/FAZ L9 97 J1
Rice St CLVPS L1 9 H7
Richard Allen Wy EV L5 113 G3
Richard Gv WD/CROXPK L12 115 J2
Richard Hesketh Dr KKBY L32 84 B1
Richard Kelly Cl ANF/KKDL L4 * 98 B5
Richard Kelly Dr ANF/KKDL L4 98 B3
Richard Kelly Pl ANF/KKDL L4 * 98 B5
Richard Martin Rd LITH L21 * 81 K2
Richard Rd CSBY/BLUN L23 68 B3
Richards Gv STHEL WA9 104 C1
Richardson Rd RF/TRAN CH42 150 D2
Richardson St EHL/KEN L7 133 H2
WARRN/WOL WA2 143 F1
Richland Rd CLB/OSW/ST L13 114 D2
Richmond Av BRSC L40 38 E6
LITH L21 81 H3
RNFD/HAY WA11 90 A4
RUNC WA7 177 H3
WARRS WA4 143 J5
Richmond Cl BEB CH63 150 E5
ECCL WA10 102 B1
HTWN L38 59 F5
Richmond Ct EP CH65 196 C6
LITH L21 * 81 J4
Richmond Cresent NTHTN L30 70 C6
Richmond Gdns NEWLW WA12 106 C3
Richmond Gv MGHL L31 62 C4
Richmond Ms BRSC L40 38 E6
Richmond Pk NPK/KEN L6 113 K1
Richmond Rd AIMK WN4 78 E4
BEB CH63 150 E5
CSBY/BLUN L23 69 F4
STHP PR8 27 G5
Richmond Rw VAUX/LVPD L3 113 G4
Richmond St CLVPS L1 * 8 E4
WAL/NB CH45 95 H4
WARRS WA4 143 K6
WDN WA8 19 G1
Richmond Ter NPK/KEN L6 113 J2
Richmond Wy HUY L36 136 D2
PEN/TH CH61 * 148 D5
PEN/TH CH61 167 K3
Rickaby Cl BEB CH63 170 E5
Rickman St ANF/KKDL L4 97 F5
Rickman Wy HUY L36 136 C1
Ridding La RUNC WA7 188 A2
The Riddings EP CH65 6 B7
Riddock Rd LITH L21 81 J6
Ridgeborne Cl
WARRW/BUR WA5 122 D5
Ridge Cl CHTN/BK PR9 24 A1
Ridgefield Rd PEN/TH CH61 148 C6
Ridgemere Rd PEN/TH CH61 148 C6
The Ridge HES CH60 167 H3
Ridgetor Rd WLTN L25 135 H6
Ridgeview Rd CL/PREN CH43 130 A4
Ridgeway GOL/RIS/CU WA3 93 F4
Ridgeway Cl GTS/LS CH66 202 A1
Ridgeway Dr MGHL L31 62 B4
Ridgeway Gdns LYMM WA13 145 J6
The Ridgeway BEB CH63 150 C3
HES CH60 168 B6
HOY CH47 127 K2
RUNC WA7 188 C1
WDN WA8 138 B3
WLTN L25 135 H6
Ridgewell Av GOL/RIS/CU WA3 92 E3
Ridgewood Dr PEN/TH CH61 167 K1
STHEL WA9 120 B1
Ridgewood Wy WLT/FAZ L9 82 D4
Ridgmont Av NG/CROX L11 98 D3
Ridgway St WARRN/WOL WA2 143 G2
Riding Cl STHEL WA9 * 120 A3
Riding Fold HLWD L26 155 G1
Riding Hill Rd PR/KW L34 100 D3
Riding La AIMK WN4 79 K4
ORM L39 51 G1
Ridings Hey CL/PREN CH43 130 A5
The Ridings CHTN/BK PR9 23 J2
CL/PREN CH43 130 A4
Riding St STHP PR8 14 E7
VAUX/LVPD L3 9 J3
Ridley Dr WARRW/BUR WA5 141 K5
Ridley Gv WKBY CH48 127 F6
Ridley La MGHL L31 62 B6
Ridley Rd NPK/KEN L6 114 A4
Ridley St CL/PREN CH43 2 B6
Ridsdale WDN WA8 157 H3
Riesling Dr NWD/KWIPK L33 72 D4
Rigby Dr GR/UP/WCH CH49 148 A1
Rigby Rd MGHL L31 61 K4
Rigbys La AIMK WN4 79 J6
Rigby St AIMK WN4 79 F6
ECCL WA10 13 F4
GOL/RIS/CU WA3 92 B3
VAUX/LVPD L3 8 B2
Riley Av BTL L20 5 H1
Riley Dr RUNC WA7 176 D5
Rimington Av GOL/RIS/CU WA3 92 D2
Rimmer Av CHLDW L16 116 A6
Rimmer Cl LITH L21 81 J4
Rimmer Gn STHP PR8 29 G6
Rimmer Gv STHEL WA9 104 C2
Rimmer's Av FMBY L37 40 E5
STHP PR8 14 E7
Rimmers Ct BIRK CH41 * 130 C2
Rimmer St VAUX/LVPD L3 9 H2
Rimmington Rd AIG/SPK L17 153 F1
Rimrose Rd BTL L20 4 B2
Rimrose Valley Rd
CSBY/BLUN L23 69 J5
Ringcroft Rd CLB/OSW/ST L13 115 F4

Ringley Av GOL/RIS/CU WA3 ....92 A2
Ring O'bells La BRSC L40 ....47 H1
Ringo Starr Dr NPK/KEN L6 * 113 K4
Ringsfield Rd SPK/HALE L24 ......174 B2
Ringtail Ct BRSC L40 ....38 B5
Ringtail Pl BRSC L40 ....38 B6
Ringtail Rd BRSC L40......................38 B5
Ringway GTS/LS CH66 ....195 H5
NSTN CH64 ....182 A5
Ringway Rd RUNC WA7 ....11 K5
WLTN L25 ....135 K5
Ringways PS/BROM CH62 ....171 F2
Ringwood CL/PREN CH43 ....130 D6
Ringwood Av DV/KA/FCH L14 ......115 K5
Ringwood Cl GOL/RIS/CU WA3 ..125 K2
Ringwood Ct CL/PREN CH43 * 130 D6
Rio Ct PR/KW L34.........................101 K6
Ripley Av LITH L21 ....81 J2
Ripley Cl MGHL L31 ....62 C6
Ripley St WARRW/BUR WA5........142 B2
Ripon Av GOL/RIS/CU WA3...........92 E3
Ripon Cl HUY L36 ....117 G4
NEWLW WA12 ....106 C1
NTHTN L30 ....82 C2
STHP PR8 ....28 C4
Ripon Dr AIMK WN4.........................91 J1
Ripon Rd WAL/NB CH45 ....110 E1
Ripon St ANF/KKDL L4 ....97 H4
BIRK CH41 * 131 H5
Rippon Av GTS/LS CH66 ....195 F4
Risbury Cl NG/CROX L11 ....98 D3
Rishton Cl EV L5............................113 J2
Risley Rd GOL/RIS/CU WA3.........125 H1
Ritchie Av WLT/FAZ L9 ....83 F4
Ritherup La RAIN/WH L35 ....118 E3
Ritson St TOX L8 ....133 G3
Rivacre Brow GTS/LS CH66 ....195 H2
Rivacre Rd EP CH65 ....185 F5
GTS/LS CH66 ....195 H2
PS/BROM CH62 ....184 D3
River Avon St TOX L8 * 133 H2
Riverbank Cl HES CH60................180 E1
Riverbank Rd ALL/GAR L19 ....153 H4
HES CH60 ....180 D1
River Cl FMBY L37 ....49 H4
River Gv PS/BROM CH62 ....151 G3
Rivermeade STHP PR8 ....28 A3
River Rd WARRS WA4 ....142 E6
Riversdale FROD/HEL WA6..........187 F6
WARR WA1 ....144 E2
Riversdale Cl NWD/KWIPK L33.....72 D5
Riversdale Ct AIG/SPK L17 ....153 G3
Riversdale Ms ALL/GAR L19 ....153 G3
Riversdale Rd ALL/GAR L19 ....153 G4
LITH L21 ....81 G4
RUNC WA7 ....177 H4
WAL/EG CH44...............................111 K3
WKBY CH48 ....146 B1
Riverside HTWN L38 ....59 F3
PS/BROM CH62 ....151 G6
WD/CROXPK L12 ....99 J4
WKBY CH48 ....146 C3
Riverside Cl BTL L20 ....81 H6
WARR WA1 ....17 G5
Riverside Dr AIG/SPK L17 ....152 B1
VAUX/LVPD L3 ....132 E6
Riverside Gv STHEL WA9.............104 B6
Riverside Wk NSTN CH64 ....191 J4
Riverslea Rd CSBY/WL L22 ....80 C1
River St BIRK CH41 ....2 D5
River Vw CSBY/WL L22 ....80 C1
Riverview Rd NSTN CH64 ....192 A4
WAL/EG CH44...............................112 A4
Riverview Wk TOX L8 ....132 E5
River Wk RUNC WA7 * 177 J6
Riverwood Rd PS/BROM CH62 ..171 H4
Riviera Dr RF/TRAN CH42............150 C2
WD/CROXPK L12 ....99 G1
Rivington Av CL/PREN CH43 ....130 B5
ECCL WA10 ....88 B5
GOL/RIS/CU WA3.............................92 D2
Rivington Cl STHP PR8 ....27 H4
Rivington Ct WARR WA1 * 144 D1
Rivington Dr BRSC L40 ....38 E6
Rivington Rd ECCL WA10 ....12 B4
EP CH65 ....6 C5
RUNC WA7 ....188 E4
WAL/EG CH44................................111 K4
Rivington St ECCL WA10..................12 A7
Rixton Av WARRW/BUR WA5.......142 C1
Roadside Ct GOL/RIS/CU WA3 ......92 D3
Roadwater Cl WLTN L25...............135 J2
Robarts Rd ANF/KKDL L4 ....113 J1
Robeck Rd CLB/OSW/ST L13 ....115 F6
Robert Dr GR/UP/WCH CH49 ......129 F6
Robert Gv WD/CROXPK L12 ....115 J2
Robert Moffat KNUT WA16 ....165 K6
Roberts Av RNFD/HAY WA11 ....89 K6
Roberts Ct RUNC WA7..................187 H1
Roberts Dr BTL L20 ....82 B5
Robertson St TOX L8....................132 D4
Roberts St VAUX/LVPD L3 ....8 A1
Robert St BIRK CH41 ....2 E3
RUNC WA7 ....11 H4
WARRW/BUR WA5.........................142 C3
WDN WA8..19 F2
Robina Rd STHEL WA9 ....104 B5
Robin Cl RUNC WA7......................178 C6
Robins Cft GTS/LS CH66 ....202 D1
Robin's La RNFD/HAY WA11.........76 C1
STHEL WA9 ....104 A5
Robinson Ms BIRK CH41 * 3 H4
Robinson Pl STHEL WA9 ....104 B2
Robinson Rd LITH L21 ....81 K2
Robin Wy GR/UP/WCH CH49 ......148 E1
Rob La NEWLW WA12 ....106 E1
Robsart St EV L5 ....113 G2
Robson St CLB/OSW/ST L13.........114 D6
EV L5...113 H1
WARR WA1 ....17 H2
Robson Wy GOL/RIS/CU WA3 ....93 G3
Roby Cl RAIN/WH L35 ....118 E3
Roby Gv WARRW/BUR WA5 ....141 H3
Roby Ml SKEL WN8 ....57 K2
Roby Mount Av HUY L36 ....116 D5
Roby Rd HUY L36...........................116 A5
Roby St BTL L20 ....5 F2
ECCL WA10 ....103 F4
WAV L15 ....133 K2
Roby Well Wy
WGNW/BIL/O WN5 ....77 G4
Rocastle Cl NPK/KEN L6 ....113 J4
Rochester Av NTHTN L30 ....82 C2
Rochester Cl GOL/RIS/CU WA3 ....92 B3
WARRW/BUR WA5........................141 K4
Rochester Dr EP CH65 ....196 C6
Rochester Gdns ECCL WA10........103 F4
Rochester Rd RF/TRAN CH42......151 F1
Rock Av HES CH60........................167 K4
Rockbank Rd CLB/OSW/ST L13 ..114 D2
Rockbourne Av WLTN L25 ....135 G4
Rockbourne Gn WLTN L25 ....135 G4
Rockbourne Wy WLTN L25 ....135 G4
Rock Cl RF/TRAN CH42 ....150 E1
Rock Ct CLB/OSW/ST L13 ....114 E4
Rock Dr FROD/HEL WA6 ....187 F6
Rock Farm Cl NSTN CH64 ....192 B3
Rock Farm Dr NSTN CH64 ....192 B3
Rock Farm Gv NSTN CH64 * 192 B3
Rock Ferry By-pass
RF/TRAN CH42..............................151 F1
Rockfield Cl WDN WA8 ....157 J1
Rockfield Rd ANF/KKDL L4.............97 H6
Rockford Av KKBY L32 ....84 D4
Rockford Cl KKBY L32.....................84 D4
Rockford Wk KKBY L32....................84 D4
Rock Gv CLB/OSW/ST L13.............114 E4
Rockhill Rd WLTN L25 ....154 E2
Rockhouse St NPK/KEN L6...........114 A2
Rockingham Cl
GOL/RIS/CU WA3 ....125 K1
Rockingham Ct
NWD/KWIPK L33 * 72 E5
Rockland Rd CSBY/WL L22.............80 E1
Rocklands Av BEB CH63..............151 F4
Rocklands La BEB CH63 ....169 J6
Rock La MGHL L31 ....71 J4
WDN WA8.......................................138 E5
Rock La East RF/TRAN CH42 ......151 F2
Rock La West RF/TRAN CH42......150 E2
Rocklee Gdns NSTN CH64............192 B3
Rockley St ANF/KKDL L4.................97 G5
Rock Mount Cl WLTN L25 ....135 G6
Rockmount Rd AIG/SPK L17 ....153 G2
Rock Park Rd RF/TRAN CH42......151 G2
Rockpoint Av WAL/NB CH45 ....95 J6
Rocksavage Expy RUNC WA7 ....187 F2
Rockside Rd CALD/MH L18..........153 H1
Rock St CLB/OSW/ST L13 ....114 E4
GOL/RIS/CU WA3............................92 C3
STHEL WA9 ....102 E5
Rock Vw EV L5 ....113 G1
MGHL L31 ....71 K5
Rockville Rd DV/KA/FCH L14 ......115 G6
Rockville St RF/TRAN CH42 ....150 E1
Rockwell Rd WD/CROXPK L12 ......99 H5
Rockybank Rd RF/TRAN CH42....131 G6
Rocky La CHLDW L16...................115 H6
HES CH60 ....167 K5
NPK/KEN L6 ....114 A2
Rocky La South HES CH60 ....168 A5
Roderick Rd ANF/KKDL L4 ....97 J3
Roderick St VAUX/LVPD L3 * 9 H1
Rodgers Cl FROD/HEL WA6 ....186 E6
Rodick St WLTN L25.....................154 C1
Rodmell Rd WLT/FAZ L9 ....82 E5
Rodney St BIRK CH41 ....2 E7
CLVPS L1 ....9 H6
ECCL WA10 ....12 C5
WARRN/WOL WA2...........................16 D2
Roe Aly CLVPS L1 ....9 F5
Roeburn Wy
WARRW/BUR WA5.........................140 E6
Roedean Cl MGHL L31 ....62 B5
WLTN L25 ....154 E3
Roehampton Dr
CSBY/BLUN L23 ....68 D3
RUNC WA7 ....177 H6
Roe La CHTN/BK PR9.....................23 G5
Roemarsh Ct RUNC WA7 ....187 H1
Roe Park Ms CHTN/BK PR9 ....15 K3
Roe St CLVPS L1 ....9 F4
Rogers Av BTL L20...........................5 K1
Rogerson's Gn HLWD L26 ....155 H1
Rokeby Av GOL/RIS/CU WA3 ....92 E2
Rokeby Cl VAUX/LVPD L3 ....113 G4
Rokeby Ct RUNC WA7 ....160 A6
Rokeby St VAUX/LVPD L3 ....113 G4
Rokeden NEWLW WA12 ....106 D1
Roker Av WAL/EG CH44 ....111 G4
Rokesmith Av EHL/KEN L7...........133 H1
Roland Av BEB CH63.....................150 C5
RNFD/HAY WA11 ....89 F4
RUNC WA7 ....10 C5
Roleton Cl NTHTN L30....................70 E5
Rolleston Dr BEB CH63................170 C1
WAL/NB CH45 ....95 F6
Rolleston St WARRN/WOL WA2 .....16 B3
Rolling Mill La STHEL WA9 ....104 D5
Rollo St ANF/KKDL L4 ....97 F6
Roman Cl NEWLW WA12...............106 C3
RUNC WA7 ....177 H4
Roman Ct NSTN CH64 ....192 A2
Roman Rd AIMK WN4 ....79 F4
CL/PREN CH43..............................149 K3
HOY CH47......................................108 B6
WARRS WA4 ....162 B2
Rome Cl HUY L36 ....116 D4
Romer Rd NPK/KEN L6 ....114 A4
Romford Wy HLWD L26 ....155 J5
Romiley Dr SKEL WN8....................56 B3
Romiley Rd GTS/LS CH66 ....195 H3
Romilly St NPK/KEN L6 ....113 J4
Romley St ANF/KKDL L4 ....97 H4
Romney Cl WDN WA8 ....158 E1
Romney Wy NSTN CH64 ....192 A2
Romsey Av FMBY L37 ....49 H3
Romulus St EHL/KEN L7 ....114 B5
Rona Av EP CH65 ....203 G2
Ronald Cl CSBY/WL L22..................81 G2
Ronald Dr WARRN/WOL WA2 ......124 D5
Ronald Rd CSBY/WL L22................81 G2
Ronald Ross Av NTHTN L30 ....70 C6
Ronaldshay WDN WA8 ....159 F1
Ronald St CLB/OSW/ST L13 ....114 D4
Ronaldsway AIN/FAZ L10...............83 K4
CSBY/BLUN L23 ....69 H3
GR/UP/WCH CH49.........................129 G3
HES CH60 ....180 E1
HLWD L26 ....155 K3
Ronan Cl BTL L20 ....4 B2
Ronan Rd WDN WA8 ....157 K6
Rone Cl MOR/LEA CH46 ....128 E1
Rookery Av AIMK WN4 ....91 G1
Rookery Dr ALL/GAR L19 ....153 G3
RNFD/HAY WA11 ....75 H4
Rookery La RNFD/HAY WA11.........75 H4
Rookery Rd CHTN/BK PR9 ....23 G4
The Rookery NEWLW WA12 ....106 D1
Rook Rd WARRS WA4 ....143 H5
Rooks Wy HES CH60 ....167 J5
The Rooley HUY L36 ....116 D6
Roome St WARRN/WOL WA2 ......143 F2
Roosevelt Dr WLT/FAZ L9..............82 E6
Ropers Bridge Cl RAIN/WH L35 ..117 K5
Roper St STHEL WA9 ....104 A1
TOX L8..132 E4
The Ropewalk NSTN CH64 ....191 H1
Rosalind Av BEB CH63 ....150 D4
Rosalind Wy BTL L20......................97 F4
Rosam Ct RUNC WA7....................187 H1
Rosclare Dr WAL/NB CH45 ....111 F1
Roscoe Av NEWLW WA12 ....106 E2
WARRN/WOL WA2 ....143 G1
Roscoe Cl RAIN/WH L35 ....136 D2
Roscoe Crs RUNC WA7 ....176 B6
Roscoe La CLVPS L1 ....9 G6
Roscoe Pl CLVPS L1 ....9 G6
Roscoe St CLVPS L1 ....9 H7
ECCL WA10 ....12 B6
Roscommon St EV L5 ....113 G3
Roscote Cl HES CH60 * 167 K6
The Roscote HES CH60................167 K6
Roseacre WKBY CH48 ....127 F6
Rose Av BTL L20.............................81 K4
RNFD/HAY WA11 ....90 D5
STHEL WA9 ....104 A6
Rose Bank LYMM WA13 ....145 K6
Rose Bank Rd CHLDW L16 ....134 E2
Rosebank Rd HUY L36 ....116 C1
Rosebank Wy HUY L36.................116 C2
Rosebay Cl FMBY L37 ....49 G2
Roseberry Rd AIMK WN4 ....79 F4
Rosebery Av CSBY/WL L22............80 D1
WAL/EG CH44................................111 J3
Rosebery Gv RF/TRAN CH42 ......150 A1
Rosebery Rd ECCL WA10 ....88 A5
Rosebery St CHTN/BK PR9............28 D1
TOX L8...133 F2
Rosebourne Cl AIG/SPK L17 ....152 D1
Rose Brae CALD/MH L18..............134 C5
Rose Brow WLTN L25 ....135 H5
Rose Cl RUNC WA7.......................188 C2
WAV L15 ....133 K2
Rose Crs SKEL WN8 ....56 A4
STHP PR8 ....41 J1
WDN WA8...18 B5
Rosecroft PS/BROM CH62 ....183 K1
Rosecroft Cl ORM L39....................45 J5
Rosecroft Ct HOY CH47 * 127 F3
Rosedale Av CSBY/BLUN L23 ....69 F5
GOL/RIS/CU WA3.............................92 D4
WARR WA1 ....144 B2
Rosedale Cl WLT/FAZ L9 ....97 K1
Rosedale Rd CALD/MH L18 ....134 B5
RF/TRAN CH42..............................131 H6
Rose Dr RNFD/HAY WA11..............75 H4
Rosefield Av BEB CH63................150 D4
Rosefield Rd WLTN L25................155 F2
Roseheath Dr HLWD L26 ....155 J5
Rose Hl STHP PR8 ....15 J7
VAUX/LVPD L3 ....113 F4
Rosehill Av STHEL WA9 ....121 F2
Rosehill Ct WLTN L25...................135 H5
Rosehill Dr ORM L39 ....53 G3
Rose Hill Vw AIMK WN4 ....78 E2
Roseland Cl MGHL L31 ....61 K3
Roselands Ct RF/TRAN CH42 ......150 D2
Rose La CALD/MH L18..................134 A6
Rose Lea Cl WDN WA8..................139 F5
Roselea Dr CHTN/BK PR9 ....24 A1
Rosemary Av RUNC WA7 ....187 J3
WARRS WA4 ....162 D1
Rosemary Cl CL/PREN CH43 ....130 B1
EHL/KEN L7 ....133 F1
WARRW/BUR WA5 * 141 K3
Rosemary Dr NEWLW WA12.........107 F2
Rosemary La FMBY L37 ....48 E2
ORM L39 ....43 J6
Rosemead Av PEN/TH CH61 ....167 K1
Rosemere Dr GTS/LS CH66.........202 D4
Rosemont Rd AIG/SPK L17..........153 G1
Rosemoor Dr CSBY/BLUN L23 ......69 H4
Rosemoor Gdns WARRS WA4 ......162 E6
Rose Mt CL/PREN CH43 ....130 E6
CSBY/WL L22 * 80 D2
RUNC WA7 * 188 E1
Rose Mount Cl CL/PREN CH43....130 D6
Rose Mount Dr WAL/NB CH45....111 G1
Rose Pl ORM L39 ....53 H3
RF/TRAN CH42..............................131 G5
RNFD/HAY WA11 ....75 H4
VAUX/LVPD L3 ....113 G4
Rose St CLVPS L1 * 9 F3
WDN WA8...18 B5
WLTN L25 ....154 C1
Rose V EV L5 ....113 G3
Rose View Av WDN WA8 ....158 B1
Rose Vls WAV L15.........................134 A2
Rosewarne Cl AIG/SPK L17.........152 C1
Rosewell Ct STBRV L28 ....116 B1
Rosewood Av FROD/HEL WA6....201 G2
WARR WA1 ....143 H2
Rosewood Cl NTHLY L27..............136 B4
STBRV L28 ....100 B6
Rosewood Dr MOR/LEA CH46 ....128 C1
Rosewood Gdns NG/CROX L11 ....99 F4
Roseworth Av WLT/FAZ L9 ....82 D4
Rosina Cl AIMK WN4 ....78 E3
Roskell Rd WLTN L25....................155 F4
Roslin Rd CL/PREN CH43 ....130 E5
PEN/TH CH61.................................148 A5
Roslyn St BIRK CH41 ....131 J6
Rossall Av AIN/FAZ L10 ....71 G6
Rossall Gv GTS/LS CH66 ....195 G3
Rossall Rd CLB/OSW/ST L13........115 F5
MOR/LEA CH46 ....109 K6
WARRW/BUR WA5..........................141 J5
WDN WA8.......................................158 E1
Ross Av MOR/LEA CH46 ....110 C3
Rossbank Rd EP CH65 ....195 K2
Rosscliffe Rd EP CH65 ....195 K3
Ross Cl PR/KW L34.......................100 D2
WARRW/BUR WA5.........................142 A1
WGNW/BIL/O WN5 ....77 H4
Ross Dr GTS/LS CH66 ....195 F4
Rossendale Cl CL/PREN CH43 ....130 A5
Rossendale Dr
GOL/RIS/CU WA3 ....125 J1
Rossett Av AIG/SPK L17 ....133 J3
Rossett Cl WARRW/BUR WA5.......122 E5
Rossett Rd CSBY/BLUN L23 ....68 D6
Rossett St NPK/KEN L6................114 A2
Rossfield Rd EP CH65 ....195 K3
Rossini St LITH L21 ....81 H5
Rosslyn Av MGHL L31 ....70 E1
Rosslyn Crs MOR/LEA CH46 ....129 F1
Rosslyn Dr MOR/LEA CH46..........129 F1
Rosslyn Pk MOR/LEA CH46 ....129 F2
Rosslyn St AIG/SPK L17...............133 G6
Rossmore Gdns ANF/KKDL L4 ......97 K6
GTS/LS CH66 ....195 G3
Rossmore Rd East EP CH65........195 J2
Rossmore Rd West
GTS/LS CH66 ....195 G2
Rossmount Rd EP CH65 ....195 K3
Ross Rd EP CH65 ....6 A3
Ross St STHEL WA9 ....104 A1
WDN WA8...19 F2
Ross Tower Ct WAL/NB CH45 ......95 J5
Rosswood Rd EP CH65....................6 A2
Rostherne Av GOL/RIS/CU WA3 ..92 E3
GTS/LS CH66 ....195 H5
WAL/EG CH44...............................111 G4
Rostherne Cl
WARRW/BUR WA5.........................142 A5
Rostherne Crs WDN WA8 ....157 J1
Rosthwaite Gv
RNFD/HAY WA11 ....88 E2
Rosthwaite Rd
WD/CROXPK L12 ....115 G1
Rostron Crs FMBY L37 ....48 E4
Rothay Dr WARRW/BUR WA5 .....140 E6
Rothbury Cl MOR/LEA CH46 ....128 D1
RUNC WA7 ....187 G1
Rothbury Ct STHEL WA9..............119 K5
Rothbury Rd DV/KA/FCH L14.......115 K1
Rother Dr EP CH65 ....195 K2
Rotherham Cl HUY L36................116 E3
Rotherwood Cl BEB CH63 ....150 C5
Rothesay Dr CSBY/BLUN L23........69 F6
PS/BROM CH62 ....184 A3
Rothesay Gdns
CL/PREN CH43 * 149 J2
Rothley Av STHP PR8 ....33 G5
Rothsay Cl RNFD/HAY WA11 ....89 H4
Rothwell Cl ORM L39 ....45 H6
Rothwell Dr ORM L39 ....53 F3
STHP PR8 ....33 G4
Rothwell Rd GOL/RIS/CU WA3......92 D2
Rothwells La CSBY/BLUN L23 ....69 J3
Rothwell St NPK/KEN L6 ....113 J3
Rotten Rw STHP PR8 ....27 F2
Rotunda St EV L5..........................113 F2
Roughdale Av KKBY L32................84 E4
STHEL WA9 * 119 K3
Roughdale Cl KKBY L32 ....84 E4
Roughley Av
WARRW/BUR WA5.........................142 A5
Roughwood Dr
NWD/KWIPK L33 ....72 E6
The Roundabout WDN WA8 ....138 C3
Round Hey STBRV L28 ....100 A5
The Round Meade MGHL L31 ......61 K5
The Roundway HTWN L38 ....59 F4
Roundwood Dr STHEL WA9 ....103 K4
Routledge St WDN WA8 ....19 F1
Rowan Av GOL/RIS/CU WA3...........93 G4
WD/CROXPK L12 ....99 K4
Rowan Cl BRSC L40 ....39 F3
RNFD/HAY WA11 ....89 G4
RUNC WA7 ....177 F6
WARRW/BUR WA5.........................141 G3
Rowan Ct AIG/SPK L17 ....153 F1
GR/UP/WCH CH49.........................147 J1
Rowan Dr KKBY L32 ....72 C6
Rowan Gv BEB CH63....................170 A1
HUY L36 ....136 A1
Rowan La SKEL WN8.......................56 D1
The Rowans ORM L39....................52 E6
Rowan Tree Cl
GR/UP/WCH CH49.........................128 C6
Rowena Cl CSBY/BLUN L23 ....69 G5
Rowland Cl WARRN/WOL WA2.....124 C4
Rowsley Gv WLT/FAZ L9 ....82 E4
Rowson St PR/KW L34 ....101 K6
WAL/NB CH45 ....95 H5
Rowthorn Cl WDN WA8 ....157 K3
Rowton Cl CL/PREN CH43 ....130 C6
Roxborough Cl
WARRW/BUR WA5.........................122 A1
Roxborough Wk WLTN L25 ....135 K6
Roxburgh Av AIG/SPK L17 ....133 H6
RF/TRAN CH42..............................150 C1
Roxburgh Rd GTS/LS CH66 ....194 C3
Roxburgh St ANF/KKDL L4 ....5 J7
Royal Av WDN WA8 ....157 G3
Royal Cl FMBY L37 ....49 G4
Royal Crs FMBY L37........................49 G4
Royal Cft WD/CROXPK L12 ....115 F3
Royal Gv ECCL WA10 ....103 F4
Royal Mail St VAUX/LVPD L3 ....9 G4
Royal Standard Wy
RF/TRAN CH42..............................131 J6
Royal St ANF/KKDL L4 ....97 G6
Royal Ter STHP PR8........................14 D5
The Royal HOY CH47 ....126 E3
Royden Av RUNC WA7 ....176 C5
WAL/EG CH44................................111 K2
Royden Crs WGNW/BIL/O WN5 ....77 H4
Royden Rd GR/UP/WCH CH49 ....129 F3
WGNW/BIL/O WN5 ....77 H4
Royden Wy VAUX/LVPD L3..........132 D6
Royhsay Cl EV L5 ....113 G3
Royleen Dr FROD/HEL WA6 ....201 G3
Roysten Gdns STHEL WA9 ....104 B3
Royston Av WAL/EG CH44 ....111 K3
WARR WA1 ....143 J2
Royston Cl GOL/RIS/CU WA3 ....93 F3
GTS/LS CH66 ....202 D1
Royston St EHL/KEN L7 ....113 K6
Royton Rd CSBY/WL L22 ....81 G1
Rozel Crs WARRW/BUR WA5 ....141 J5
Rubbing Stone WKBY CH48 * 146 E5
Ruby Cl LITH L21 ....81 K3
Ruby St TOX L8..............................132 E6
Rudd Av STHEL WA9 ....104 E3
Ruddington Rd STHP PR8 ....28 B5
Rudd St HOY CH47........................127 G2
Rudgate RAIN/WH L35 ....118 A5
Rudgrave Ms WAL/EG CH44.........111 K2
Rudgrave Pl WAL/EG CH44 ....111 K2
Rudgrave Sq WAL/EG CH44 ....111 K2
Rudloe Ct WARRN/WOL WA2 ....124 B6
Rudstone Cl GTS/LS CH66............194 E4
Rudston Rd CHLDW L16 ....134 E2
Rudyard Cl DV/KA/FCH L14 ....115 G4
Rudyard Rd DV/KA/FCH L14 ....115 G4
Ruff La ORM L39 ....54 A1
Rufford Av MGHL L31 ....62 C4
Rufford Cl AIN/FAZ L10..................83 J2
RAIN/WH L35 ....118 B2
WDN WA8.......................................157 H1
Rufford Dr CHTN/BK PR9 ....21 J6
Rufford Rd BTL L20........................81 K6
CHTN/BK PR9..................................24 A2
NPK/KEN L6 ....114 A4
RNFD/HAY WA11 ....75 G1
WAL/EG CH44................................111 J4
Rugby Dr AIN/FAZ L10...................83 H2
Rugby Rd EP CH65 ....196 C6
WAL/EG CH44................................111 F2
WLT/FAZ L9 ....82 E3
Rugby Wk EP CH65 ....196 C6
Ruislip Cl WLTN L25 ....155 F1
Ruislip Ct WARRN/WOL WA2 ....124 B6
Rullerton Rd WAL/EG CH44 ....111 G3
Rumford Pl VAUX/LVPD L3..............8 B3
Rumford St CLVP L2 ....8 C3
Rumney Pl ANF/KKDL L4 ....97 F5
Rumney Rd ANF/KKDL L4...............97 G5
Rumney Rd West ANF/KKDL L4....97 F5
Runcorn Docks Rd RUNC WA7 ....10 A5
Runcorn Rd WARRS WA4 ....161 F6
Runcorn Spur Rd RUNC WA7........11 G6
Runcorn-widnes Br WDN WA8 ....10 D1
Rundle Rd AIG/SPK L17...............153 F1
Rundle St BIRK CH41....................130 D1
Runic St CLB/OSW/ST L13............114 D5
Runnells La CSBY/BLUN L23..........69 K4
The Runnell NSTN CH64 ....181 J3
The Runnel ORM L39.......................43 K1
Runnymede WARR WA1 ....144 B2
Runnymede Cl WLTN L25 ....135 H5
Runnymede Dr
RNFD/HAY WA11 * 89 K5
Runnymede Wk WDN WA8 * 158 D1
Runton Rd WLTN L25 ....135 K4
Rupert Dr NPK/KEN L6 ....113 J4
Rupert Rd HUY L36 ....116 C4
Ruscar Cl HLWD L26 ....155 H1
Ruscolm Cl WARRW/BUR WA5....140 E2
Ruscombe Rd DV/KA/FCH L14.....115 K1
Rushden Rd KKBY L32....................85 F2
Rushey Hey Rd KKBY L32 ....84 D2
Rushfield Crs RUNC WA7 ....188 A2
Rushgreen Cl CL/PREN CH43.......129 K2
Rushlake Dr NTHLY L27 ....136 A4
Rushmere Rd NG/CROX L11 ....98 D3
Rushmoor Av AIMK WN4 ....79 K5
Rushmore Gv WARR WA1 ....143 K2
Rusholme Cl HLWD L26................155 K5
Rushton Av NEWLW WA12 ....106 B1
Rushton Cl WDN WA8 ....138 E6
Rushton Pl WLTN L25 ....154 D1
Rushy Vw NEWLW WA12 ....106 A1
Ruskin Av NEWLW WA12 ....106 C1
RF/TRAN CH42 * 150 E2
WAL/EG CH44................................111 G4
WARRN/WOL WA2 ....123 J5
Ruskin Cl BTL L20............................4 E5
Ruskin Dr ECCL WA10 ....12 B3
EP CH65 ....196 C6
Ruskin Wy CL/PREN CH43 ....130 A6
HUY L36 ....116 D6
Rusland Av PEN/TH CH61.............167 K1
Rusland Rd KKBY L32 ....84 E3
Russell Av CHTN/BK PR9...............23 J6
Russell Rd ALL/GAR L19 ....153 K5
CALD/MH L18 ....134 A4
CHTN/BK PR9..................................23 J6
HUY L36 ....117 H5
RF/TRAN CH42..............................131 J6
RUNC WA7 ....176 B5
WAL/EG CH44................................110 E2
Russell St BIRK CH41 ....3 F3
VAUX/LVPD L3 ....9 H4
Russet Cl ECCL WA10.....................13 F2
NTHLY L27 ....136 B4
Russian Dr CLB/OSW/ST L13 ......114 D2

Rutherford Cl *CLB/OSW/ST* L13..114 C6
Rutherford Rd *CALD/MH* L18 ....134 C3
ECCL WA10 ....87 K5
MGHL L31 ....71 H2
Rutherglen Av *CSBY/BLUN* L23...81 G1
Ruth Evans Ct *RAIN/WH* L35 ......118 C3
Ruthin Cl *WARRW/BUR* WA5 * 122 E4
Ruthin Ct *EP* CH65 ....196 C6
Ruthven Rd *CLB/OSW/ST* L13 ....115 F6
LITH L21 ....81 H4
Rutland Av *AIG/SPK* L17 ....133 J3
GOL/RIS/CU WA3 ....92 E4
HLWD L26 ....155 J3
WARRS WA4 ....162 A3
Rutland Cl *EV* L5 ....113 J2
Rutland Crs *ORM* L39 ....45 H4
Rutland Dr *AIMK* WN4 ....79 H5
Rutland Rd *STHP* PR8 ....28 A2
Rutland St *BTL* L20 ....5 G2
ECCL WA10 ....12 E2
RUNC WA7 ....10 C4
Rutter Av *WARRW/BUR* WA5 ......123 F5
Rutter St *TOX* L8 ....132 D4
Ryburn Rd *ORM* L39 ....53 H1
Rycot Rd *SPK/HALE* L24 ....173 H1
Rycroft Rd *AIN/FAZ* L10 ....83 H3
HOY CH47 ....127 K1
WAL/EG CH44 ....111 J5
Rydal Av *CL/PREN* CH43 ....129 K4
CSBY/BLUN L23 ....81 G1
FMBY L37 ....48 D3
PR/KW L34 ....118 B1
WARRS WA4 ....161 K1
Rydal Bank *BEB* CH63 ....151 F4
WAL/EG CH44 ....111 J3
Rydal Cl *AIMK* WN4 ....79 H5
AIN/FAZ L10 ....83 J1
EP CH65 ....203 G1
NSTN CH64 ....192 A3
NWD/KWIPK L33 ....72 C5
PEN/TH CH61 ....167 K1
Rydal Gv *RNFD/HAY* WA11 ....88 D4
RUNC WA7 ....176 E5
Rydal Rd *HUY* L36 ....116 E6
Rydal St *EV* L5 ....113 J2
NEWLW WA12 ....106 C2
Rydal Wy *WDN* WA8 ....157 H3
Ryder Cl *ORM* L39 ....53 G3
RAIN/WH L35 ....118 C3
Ryder Crs *ORM* L39 ....53 G4
STHP PR8 ....34 A1
Ryder Rd *WARR* WA1 ....144 B1
WDN WA8 ....139 G5
The Rydinge *FMBY* L37 ....41 G5
Rye Cl *STHEL* WA9 ....120 A3
Ryecote *KKBY* L32 ....84 D4
Ryecroft *CHNE* CH2 ....198 C6
Rye Cft *LITH* L21 ....69 J6
Ryecroft Av *GOL/RIS/CU* WA3 ......93 F2
Ryecroft Rd *HES* CH60 ....188 C6
Ryedale Cl *TOX* L8 ....133 G2
Ryefield La *LITH* L21 ....69 J6
Ryegate Rd *ALL/GAR* L19 ....153 J4
Rye Gv *WD/CROXPK* L12 ....115 J1
Rye Hey Rd *KKBY* L32 ....84 D1
Rye Moss La *FMBY* L37 ....50 C5
Ryland Pk *PEN/TH* CH61 ....148 D6
Rylands Hey
GR/UP/WCH CH49 ....128 E5
Rylands St *WARR* WA1 ....16 D5
WDN WA8 ....18 E3
Ryleys Gdns *CLVP* L2 ....8 D3
Rymer Gv *ANF/KKDL* L4 ....97 J4
Rymers Gn *FMBY* L37 ....48 E1

S

Sabre Cl *RUNC* WA7 * 178 C6
Sackville Rd *ECCL* WA10 ....87 K5
Saddle Cl *WLT/FAZ* L9 ....83 G3
Saddlers Ri *RUNC* WA7 ....178 B5
Sadler's La *RNFD/HAY* WA11 ....87 F4
Sadler St *WDN* WA8 ....19 G1
Saffron Cl *GOL/RIS/CU* WA3 ....93 F3
WARRN/WOL WA2 ....124 D6
Saffron Gdns *STHEL* WA9 ....104 B3
Saffron Ms *CSBY/BLUN* L23 ....69 J3
Sagar Fold *ORM* L39 ....53 H5
Sage Cl *WARRN/WOL* WA2 ....124 E5
St Agnes Rd *ANF/KKDL* L4 ....97 F5
HUY L36 ....117 F5
St Aidan's Cl *WGNW/BIL/O* WN5 ..77 H3
St Aidans Ct *CL/PREN* CH43 ....130 C3
St Aidan's Ter *CL/PREN* CH43 ....130 C3
EV L5 ....113 F1
St Aidan's Wy *NTHTN* L30 ....70 A6
St Aiden's Gv *PR/KW* L34 ....100 C6
St Alban Rd *WARRW/BUR* WA5 ..141 F4
St Albans *NPK/KEN* L6 ....113 K2
St Albans Cl *RNFD/HAY* WA11 ....90 E4
St Albans Ct *EV* L5 ....112 E2
St Alban's Rd *BTL* L20 ....5 F5
CL/PREN CH43 ....130 D2
WAL/EG CH44 ....111 H3
St Alban's Sq *BTL* L20 ....5 F6
St Alexander Cl *BTL* L20 ....97 F4
St Ambrose Cft *NTHTN* L30 ....70 B5
St Ambrose Gv *ANF/KKDL* L4 ....113 K1
St Ambrose Rd *WDN* WA8 ....19 H1
St Ambrose Wy *EV* L5 ....113 G3
St Andrew Rd *ANF/KKDL* L4 ....113 K1
St Andrews Av
WD/CROXPK L12 ....115 J1
St Andrews Cl
WARRN/WOL WA2 ....124 C3
St Andrew's Dr *CSBY/BLUN* L23 ..68 C3
PR/KW L34 ....100 C6
St Andrew's Gv *NTHTN* L30 * 69 K6
RNFD/HAY WA11 ....88 E5
St Andrew's Pl *STHP* PR8 ....14 E6
St Andrews Rd *BEB* CH63 ....170 C2
BTL L20 ....81 K6
CL/PREN CH43 ....130 E3
CSBY/BLUN L23 ....68 C2
EP CH65 ....196 C6
St Andrew St *VAUX/LVPD* L3 ....9 H4
St Andrew's Vw
NWD/KWIPK L33 ....72 D4
St Annes Av *WARRS* WA4 ....163 G1
St Annes Av East *WARRS* WA4 ...163 G1
St Anne's Cl *BIRK* CH41 ....2 E3
FMBY L37 ....41 F5
St Annes Ct *VAUX/LVPD* L3 * 113 G4
St Annes Gdns *AIG/SPK* L17 ....153 G2
St Anne's Gv *AIG/SPK* L17 ....153 F2
BIRK CH41 ....2 B1
St Anne's Pth *FMBY* L37 ....41 F5
St Anne's Pl *BIRK* CH41 ....2 B1
St Anne's Rd *AIG/SPK* L17 ....153 F2
CHTN/BK PR9 ....23 H1
FMBY L37 ....41 F5
HUY L36 ....116 E6
ORM L39 ....53 H1
WDN WA8 ....158 C1
St Annes Ter *BIRK* CH41 ....2 B2
St Anne St *BIRK* CH41 ....2 C2
VAUX/LVPD L3 ....113 G4
St Anne Wy *BIRK* CH41 ....2 E3
St Ann Pl *RAIN/WH* L35 ....118 E3
St Anns Rd *ECCL* WA10 ....102 E2
St Anthony Pl
WARRN/WOL WA2 ....123 H1
St Anthony's Cl *PR/KW* L34 ....100 C6
St Anthony's Gv *NTHTN* L30 ....70 A6
St Anthony's Rd
CSBY/BLUN L23 ....68 C5
St Asaph Dr *WARRW/BUR* WA5 ..122 D5
St Asaph Gv *NTHTN* L30 ....82 C2
St Asaph Rd *GTS/LS* CH66 ....202 C3
St Augustine's Av *WARRS* WA4 ..143 J5
St Augustine St *EV* L5 * 113 F2
St Augustine's Wy *NTHTN* L30 ....70 A5
St Austel Cl *WARRW/BUR* WA5 ..141 F6
St Austell Cl *MOR/LEA* CH46 ....109 F6
RUNC WA7 ....188 A1
St Austells Rd *ANF/KKDL* L4 ....5 K7
St Austins La *WARR* WA1 ....16 C6
St Barnabas Pl
WARRW/BUR WA5 ....142 B3
St Bedes Cl *ORM* L39 ....53 H2
St Benard's Cl *TOX* L8 ....133 G2
St Benedicts Cl
WARRN/WOL WA2 ....16 E1
St Benedict's Gv *PR/KW* L34 ....100 C6
St Benet's Wy *NTHTN* L30 ....70 B6
St Bernard's Cl *NTHTN* L30 ....70 A6
St Bernard's Dr *NTHTN* L30 ....70 A6
St Brendan's Cl *HUY* L36 ....100 C6
St Brides Cl *WARRW/BUR* WA5 ..141 F6
St Bride's Rd *WAL/EG* CH44 ....111 K2
St Bride St *EHL/KEN* L7 ....9 K7
St Bridget's Cl
WARRN/WOL WA2 ....124 B4
St Bridget's Gv *NTHTN* L30 * 70 A6
St Bridget's La *WKBY* CH48 * 146 C2
St Brigids Crs *EV* L5 ....112 E2
St Catherine's *RF/TRAN* CH42 ....131 G5
St Catherines Cl *HUY* L36 ....116 E6
St Catherines Gdns
RF/TRAN CH42 ....131 G5
St Catherine's Rd *BTL* L20 ....4 E5
St Chad's Dr *KKBY* L32 ....84 D1
St Christopher's Av *NTHTN* L30....70 A5
St Christopher's Dr *PR/KW* L34..100 C6
St Clair Dr *CHTN/BK* PR9 ....23 J4
St Columba's Cl
WAL/EG CH44 * 111 K2
St Cuthbert's Cl
WD/CROXPK L12 * 99 J2
St Cuthbert's Rd *CHTN/BK* PR9 ....23 K3
St Cyrils Cl *NTHLY* L27 ....135 K2
St Damian's Cft *NTHTN* L30 ....70 B6
St David Rd *CL/PREN* CH43 ....130 D3
PS/BROM CH62 ....184 D1
St Davids Cl *RAIN/WH* L35 ....118 E3
St Davids Dr *GTS/LS* CH66 ....202 D3
WARRW/BUR WA5 ....122 E5
St Davids Gv *NTHTN* L30 ....82 A1
St Davids La *CL/PREN* CH43 ....130 A4
St David's Rd *ANF/KKDL* L4 ....113 K1
DV/KA/FCH L14 ....115 K4
St Domingo Gv *EV* L5 ....113 J1
St Domingo Rd *EV* L5 ....113 G1
St Domingo V *EV* L5 ....113 J1
St Dunstan's Gv *NTHTN* L30 ....82 A1
St Edmond's Rd *BTL* L20 ....4 E6
St Edmunds Rd *BEB* CH63 ....150 E6
St Edwards Cl *BIRK* CH41 ....2 A1
St Edwards Ms *BIRK* CH41 * 2 A1
St Elmo Rd *WAL/EG* CH44 ....111 K2
St Elphins Cl *WARR* WA1 ....17 G4
St Gabriel's Av *HUY* L36 ....117 G5
St George's Av *ECCL* WA10 ....87 K6
GTS/LS CH66 ....202 D3
RF/TRAN CH42 ....150 C1
St Georges Ct *WDN* WA8 ....157 J3
St Georges Gv *NTHTN* L30 ....82 A1
St George's Hl *EV* L5 ....113 H2
St George's Mt *WAL/NB* CH45 ....95 H5
St George's Pk *WAL/NB* CH45 ....95 H5
St George's Pl *CHTN/BK* PR9 ....14 E4
CLVPS L1 ....9 F3
St Georges Rd *ECCL* WA10 ....12 A7
FMBY L37 ....48 E1
HTWN L38 ....59 F2
HUY L36 ....116 E2
WAL/NB CH45 ....110 E1
St George's Wy *BEB* CH63 ....169 G6
CLVPS L1 * 9 F4
St Gregory's Cft *NTHTN* L30 ....70 B5
St Helen's Cl *BIRK* CH41 ....2 A5
St Helens Linkway *STHEL* WA9 ..103 H6
St Helens Rd *LEIGH* WN7 ....93 K2
ORM L39 ....45 K6
ORM L39 ....53 K1
PR/KW L34 ....102 B6
PR/KW L34 ....117 K1
RNFD/HAY WA11 ....87 J1
St Hilary Brow *WAL/EG* CH44 ....111 F3
St Hilary Dr *WAL/EG* CH44 ....111 F2
St Hilda's Dr *FROD/HEL* WA6 ....187 F6
St Hilda St *ANF/KKDL* L4 * 97 G5
St Hugh's Cl *CL/PREN* CH43 ....2 A5
St Ives Gv *CLB/OSW/ST* L13 ....114 D4
St Ives Rd *CL/PREN* CH43 ....130 D3
St Ives Wy *HLWD* L26 ....155 J3
St James Cl *BRSC* L40 ....54 C2
GR/UP/WCH CH49 ....128 E5
WD/CROXPK L12 ....114 E1
St James Dr *BTL* L20 ....4 C3
St James Mt *RAIN/WH* L35 ....118 E5
St James Pl *TOX* L8 ....132 D2
St James Rd *CL/PREN* CH43 ....130 C1
CLVPS L1 ....132 D2
HUY L36 ....116 E6
PR/KW L34 ....102 A6
RAIN/WH L35 ....118 E5
WAL/NB CH45 ....95 H5
St James St *CLVPS* L1 ....132 C2
STHP PR8 ....27 J2
St Jerome's Wy *NTHTN* L30 ....70 B5
St John Av *WARRS* WA4 ....162 A1
St John's Av *WLT/FAZ* L9 ....82 D6
St John's Brow *RUNC* WA7 * 11 F3
St John's Cl *HOY* CH47 ....127 J1
St Johns Ct *STHP* PR8 * 33 K5
St John's La *CLVPS* L1 ....9 F3
St John's Pl *CSBY/WL* L22 ....80 E2
St John's Rd *BTL* L20 ....96 D4
CSBY/WL L22 ....80 E2
HUY L36 ....117 F6
PS/BROM CH62 ....184 D2
STHP PR8 ....27 G6
WAL/NB CH45 ....110 E2
St Johns Sq *CLVPS* L1 * 9 F4
St John's St *RUNC* WA7 ....11 F3
St John's Ter *BTL* L20 * 96 D4
St John St *BIRK* CH41 ....2 E5
ECCL WA10 ....103 F5
NEWLW WA12 ....106 A2
St Johns Wy *CLVPS* L1 * 9 F4
St Josephs Cl *PR/KW* L34 ....100 C6
WARRW/BUR WA5 ....141 F4
St Josephs Crs *VAUX/LVPD* L3 ....9 G1
St Jude's Cl *HUY* L36 * 100 C6
St Katherines Wy *WARR* WA1 ....17 H4
St Kilda Cl *EP* CH65 ....203 G2
St Kilda's Rd *MOR/LEA* CH46 ....128 E2
St Laurence Cl *BIRK* CH41 ....2 E3
St Laurence Dr *BIRK* CH41 ....2 E4
St Laurence Gv *KKBY* L32 * 84 E3
St Lawrence Cl *TOX* L8 ....133 F5
St Lawrence Rd
FROD/HEL WA6 ....200 E2
St Leonard's Cl *NTHTN* L30 ....70 A5
St Lucia Rd *WAL/EG* CH44 ....111 K2
St Luke's Av *GOL/RIS/CU* WA3 ....92 E3
St Luke's Church Rd *FMBY* L37 ....48 C3
St Lukes Cl *DV/KA/FCH* L14 ....115 K1
St Lukes Ct *ANF/KKDL* L4 ....97 J3
St Luke's Crs *WDN* WA8 ....139 G5
St Luke's Dr *FMBY* L37 ....48 C3
St Luke's Gv *CHTN/BK* PR9 ....15 K5
NTHTN L30 ....70 A5
St Luke's Rd *CHTN/BK* PR9 ....15 K6
CSBY/BLUN L23 ....68 E5
ECCL WA10 ....12 A5
St Luke's Wy *FROD/HEL* WA6 ....186 E6
HUY L36 ....100 C6
St Margaret's Av
WARRN/WOL WA2 ....123 K6
St Margaret's Gv *NTHTN* L30 ....81 K1
St Margaret's Rd *HOY* CH47 ....127 F2
St Marks Crs *GTS/LS* CH66 ....202 D4
St Mark's Gv *NTHTN* L30 ....69 K5
St Mark's Rd *HUY* L36 ....117 F6
St Mark's St *RNFD/HAY* WA11 ....89 K5
St Martins Dr *GTS/LS* CH66 ....202 B1
St Martins Gv *KKBY* L32 ....84 E3
St Martins La *RUNC* WA7 ....178 C6
St Martin's Ms *EV* L5 ....113 G3
St Marys Ar *ECCL* WA10 * 13 H6
St Mary's Av *ANF/KKDL* L4 * 97 J3
WGNW/BIL/O WN5 ....77 F5
St Mary's Cl *BTL* L20 ....4 D4
WARRS WA4 ....162 B5
St Marys Ct *WLTN* L25 ....154 D1
St Mary's Dr *NTHTN* L30 ....81 K1
St Mary's Gdns *STHP* PR8 ....34 B2
St Mary's Ga *BIRK* CH41 ....3 H5
St Mary's Gv *ANF/KKDL* L4 * 97 J3
St Mary's La *ANF/KKDL* L4 ....97 J3
St Marys Market *ECCL* WA10 * 13 H6
St Mary's Pl *ANF/KKDL* L4 * 97 J3
WLTN L25 ....154 D1
St Mary's Rd *ALL/GAR* L19 ....153 K5
CSBY/WL L22 ....81 G3
HUY L36 ....116 E5
RUNC WA7 ....177 J4
WARRW/BUR WA5 ....141 G4
WDN WA8 ....10 D1
St Mary's St *WAL/EG* CH44 ....111 H3
St Mathews Cl *ANF/KKDL* L4 ....98 B3
St Matthews Av *LITH* L21 ....81 K3
St Matthew's Cl *HUY* L36 * 117 F4
WARRS WA4 ....162 C4
St Matthews Gv *ECCL* WA10 ....102 E5
St Mawes Cl *WDN* WA8 ....157 K1
St Mawes Wy *ECCL* WA10 ....87 J5
St Mawgan Ct
WARRN/WOL WA2 ....124 B6
St Michael Rd *ORM* L39 ....52 D6
St Michael's Church Rd
AIG/SPK L17 ....152 C1
St Michael's Cl *AIG/SPK* L17 ....152 D1
CHTN/BK PR9 ....23 H2
WDN WA8 ....157 H4
St Michaels Ct *HUY* L36 ....116 E4
St Michael's Gv *NPK/KEN* L6 ....113 K3
NTHTN L30 ....69 K6
St Michaels Pk *ORM* L39 ....52 E6
St Michael's Rd *AIG/SPK* L17 ....133 G6
CSBY/BLUN L23 ....68 D3
STHEL WA9 ....119 J4
WDN WA8 ....157 H4
St Monicas Cl *WARRS* WA4 ....162 C4
St Monica's Dr *NTHTN* L30 ....70 A5
St Nicholas' Dr *NTHTN* L30 ....70 A6
St Nicholas Gv *STHEL* WA9 * 104 B6
St Nicholas Pl *VAUX/LVPD* L3 ....8 B4
St Nicholas Rd
GOL/RIS/CU WA3 ....93 H2
RAIN/WH L35 ....117 J6
WAL/NB CH45 ....110 D2
St Oswald's Av *CL/PREN* CH43 ..110 C6
St Oswalds Cl
WARRN/WOL WA2 * 123 H1
St Oswalds Ct *NTHTN* L30 * 70 C6
St Oswald's La *NTHTN* L30 ....70 C5
St Oswald's Ms *CL/PREN* CH43 ..110 C6
St Oswalds Rd *AIMK* WN4 ....91 F1
St Oswald's St *CLB/OSW/ST* L13 114 E5
St Paschal Baylon Bvd
CHLDW L16 ....135 G1
St Patrick's Cl
NWD/KWIPK L33 * 72 D4
St Patrick's Dr *NTHTN* L30 * 70 A5
St Pauls Av *WAL/EG* CH44 ....112 A5
St Pauls Cl *NWD/KWIPK* L33 ....72 C4
RF/TRAN CH42 ....150 D1
St Pauls Gdns *GTS/LS* CH66 ....194 E2
St Pauls Ms *RUNC* WA7 * 10 E4
St Paul's Pas *STHP* PR8 ....14 D7
St Paul's Rd *RF/TRAN* CH42 ....150 E1
WAL/EG CH44 ....111 K5
WDN WA8 ....18 D5
St Paul's Sq *STHP* PR8 ....14 C7
VAUX/LVPD L3 ....8 C2
St Paul's St *STHP* PR8 ....14 C7
St Paul St *ECCL* WA10 ....12 D5
St Paul's Vls *RF/TRAN* CH42 ....150 D1
St Peter's Av *FMBY* L37 ....48 D1
St Peter's Cl *FMBY* L37 ....48 D1
HES CH60 ....167 K6
NWD/KWIPK L33 ....72 C4
St Peters Ct *AIG/SPK* L17 * 133 G5
St Peter's Ms *RF/TRAN* CH42 ....151 G2
St Peter's Rd *RF/TRAN* CH42 ....151 F2
STHP PR8 ....27 H4
WLT/FAZ L9 ....83 F4
St Peter's Wy *CL/PREN* CH43 ....129 K5
WARRN/WOL WA2 ....16 E3
St Philip's Av *LITH* L21 ....81 K3
St Richards Cl *BTL* L20 ....97 F4
St Seiriol Gv *CL/PREN* CH43 ....130 D3
St Stephen Rd
WARRW/BUR WA5 ....141 G4
St Stephen's Av
WARRN/WOL WA2 ....123 H4
St Stephens Cl *HES* CH60 ....181 H1
WLTN L25 ....135 K4
St Stephen's Gv *NTHTN* L30 ....70 A6
St Stephen's Rd *HTWN* L38 ....59 F3
RF/TRAN CH42 ....150 A1
St Teresa's Rd *ECCL* WA10 ....12 A4
St Thomas Ct *WDN* WA8 * 157 K2
St Thomas's Dr *NTHTN* L30 ....70 A6
St Thomas' Vw *EP* CH65 ....6 B7
St Vincent Rd *CL/PREN* CH43 ....130 D3
WAL/EG CH44 ....111 K2
WARRW/BUR WA5 ....141 G4
St Vincent's Cl
WD/CROXPK L12 ....115 J1
St Vincent St *VAUX/LVPD* L3 ....9 H3
St Vincent's Wy *STHP* PR8 ....27 G3
St Vincent Wy *VAUX/LVPD* L3 ....9 H3
St Werburgh's Sq *BIRK* CH41 ....3 F5
St Wilfrid's Dr *WARRS* WA4 ....163 H2
St William Rd *CSBY/BLUN* L23 ....69 J4
St Winifred Rd *RAIN/WH* L35 ....118 D2
WAL/NB CH45 ....95 H6
Saker St *ANF/KKDL* L4 ....97 H6
Salacre Cl *GR/UP/WCH* CH49 ....129 H5
Salacre Crs *GR/UP/WCH* CH49 ....129 H5
Salacre La *GR/UP/WCH* CH49 ....129 H4
Salacre Ter *GR/UP/WCH* CH49 * 129 H4
Salcombe Dr *CHTN/BK* PR9 ....20 D6
WLTN L25 ....154 E4
Salem Vw *CL/PREN* CH43 ....130 E6
Salerno Dr *HUY* L36 ....116 D4
Saleswood Av *ECCL* WA10 ....102 C2
Salford Rd *STHP* PR8 ....33 J4
Saline Cl *DV/KA/FCH* L14 ....116 A1
Salisbury Av *NTHTN* L30 ....82 D2
WKBY CH48 ....146 B1
Salisbury Cl *GTS/LS* CH66 ....202 D3
Salisbury Dr *PS/BROM* CH62 ....151 G4
Salisbury Pk *CHLDW* L16 ....135 F4
Salisbury Rd *AIMK* WN4 * 79 F4
ALL/GAR L19 ....153 H5
BTL L20 ....4 C2
EV L5 ....113 J1
RNFD/HAY WA11 ....90 D2
WAL/NB CH45 ....95 G5
WAV L15 ....133 J2
Salisbury St *BIRK* CH41 ....2 D6
CHTN/BK PR9 ....28 D1
GOL/RIS/CU WA3 ....92 B3
PR/KW L34 ....101 K6
RUNC WA7 ....10 D6
VAUX/LVPD L3 ....113 H4
WARR WA1 ....17 H3
WDN WA8 ....18 E3
Salisbury Ter *WAV* L15 ....134 A1
Salkeld Av *AIMK* WN4 ....78 E6
Sally's La *CHTN/BK* PR9 ....23 J3
Salop St *ANF/KKDL* L4 ....97 H5
Saltash Cl *HLWD* L26 ....155 H3
RUNC WA7 ....188 A1
Saltburn Rd *WAL/NB* CH45 ....110 D2
Saltersgate *GTS/LS* CH66 ....202 D1
Salthouse Quay *VAUX/LVPD* L3 ....8 C6
Saltney St *VAUX/LVPD* L3 ....112 D3
Salton Gdns
WARRW/BUR WA5 ....142 B2
Saltpit La *MGHL* L31 ....62 C6
Saltwood Dr *RUNC* WA7 ....188 B2
Saltworks Cl *FROD/HEL* WA6 ....187 G5
Salvin Cl *AIMK* WN4 ....79 J6
Salvia Wy *NWD/KWIPK* L33 ....72 C4
Salwick Cl *CHTN/BK* PR9 ....20 C6
Samaria Av *PS/BROM* CH62 ....151 H4
Sambourn Fold *STHP* PR8 ....33 G4
Samphire Gdns *STHEL* WA9 ....105 F6
Samuel St *STHEL* WA9 ....103 F6
WARRW/BUR WA5 ....142 B5
Sanbec Gdns *WDN* WA8 ....138 C4
Sandalwood *RUNC* WA7 ....178 A4
Sandalwood Cl *NPK/KEN* L6 ....113 K2
WARRN/WOL WA2 ....123 K5
Sandalwood Dr *CL/PREN* CH43..130 A5
Sandalwood Gdns *STHEL* WA9 ..104 A6
Sandbeck St *TOX* L8 ....132 E6
Sandbrook La *MOR/LEA* CH46....129 F1
Sandbrook Rd *STHP* PR8 ....33 J6
WLTN L25 ....135 H1
Sandcliffe Rd *WAL/NB* CH45 ....94 E5
Sandeman Rd *ANF/KKDL* L4 ....98 B4
Sanderling Rd *NWD/KWIPK* L33 ..73 F6
Sanders Hey Cl *RUNC* WA7 ....187 K2
Sanderson Cl
WARRW/BUR WA5 * 140 E3
Sandfield *HUY* L36 ....116 D5
Sandfield Av *HOY* CH47 ....108 B6
Sandfield Cl *BEB* CH63 * 150 C5
GOL/RIS/CU WA3 ....93 F3
WD/CROXPK L12 ....115 G2
Sandfield Ct *FROD/HEL* WA6 ....200 E1
Sandfield Crs *ECCL* WA10 ....12 E6
Sandfield Pk *HES* CH60 ....167 H5
ORM L39 ....53 H3
Sandfield Pk East
WD/CROXPK L12 ....115 G1
Sandfield Pl *BTL* L20 ....4 C2
Sandfield Rd *BEB* CH63 ....150 C5
BTL L20 ....5 H6
ECCL WA10 ....87 H6
GR/UP/WCH CH49 ....148 E2
WAL/NB CH45 ....95 H6
WLTN L25 ....135 J5
Sandfields *FROD/HEL* WA6 ....200 E1
Sandfield Wk *CLB/OSW/ST* L13 ..115 F3
Sandford Dr *MGHL* L31 ....62 B5
Sandford St *BIRK* CH41 ....3 G3
Sandforth Cl *WD/CROXPK* L12....114 E2
Sandforth Ct
WD/CROXPK L12 * 114 E2
Sandforth Rd *WD/CROXPK* L12..114 E2
Sandgate Cl *SPK/HALE* L24 ....173 G1
Sandham Gv *HES* CH60 ....168 C6
Sandham Rd *SPK/HALE* L24 ....174 B2
Sandhead St *EHL/KEN* L7 ....133 J1
Sandhey Rd *HOY* CH47 ....127 H1
Sandheys *NSTN* CH64 ....181 H6
Sandheys Av *CSBY/WL* L22 ....80 D2
Sandheys Cl *ANF/KKDL* L4 ....97 G6
Sandheys Dr *CHTN/BK* PR9 ....23 H4
Sandheys Gv *CSBY/WL* L22 ....80 D1
Sandheys Rd *WAL/NB* CH45 ....95 H6
Sandheys Ter *CSBY/WL* L22 ....80 D2
Sandhills *HTWN* L38 ....59 F4
Sandhills La *EV* L5 ....96 E6
The Sandhills *MOR/LEA* CH46 ....109 J4
Sandhills Vw *WAL/NB* CH45 ....110 D2
Sandhurst Cl *FMBY* L37 ....48 C4
LITH L21 ....81 G4
Sandhurst Dr *AIN/FAZ* L10 ....83 H1
Sandhurst Rd *HLWD* L26 ....155 K5
RAIN/WH L35 ....118 C2
Sandhurst St *AIG/SPK* L17 ....133 G6
WARRS WA4 ....143 J6
Sandhurst Wy *MGHL* L31 ....61 K2
Sandicroft Cl *GOL/RIS/CU* WA3 ..124 E2
Sandicroft Rd *WD/CROXPK* L12....99 K3
Sandilands Gv *HTWN* L38 ....59 F4
Sandino St *TOX* L8 ....132 D3
Sandringham Dr *AIG/SPK* L17 ....133 G5
Sandiway *BEB* CH63 ....183 K1
HOY CH47 ....108 B6
HUY L36 ....117 F6
RAIN/WH L35 ....117 K5
Sandiway Av *WDN* WA8 ....157 F2
Sandiways Av *NTHTN* L30 ....82 C1
Sandiways Rd *WAL/NB* CH45....110 E1
Sandlea Pk *WKBY* CH48 ....146 B1
Sandlewood Gv
NWD/KWIPK L33 ....72 E5
Sandling Dr *GOL/RIS/CU* WA3 ....92 B1
Sandon Cl *RAIN/WH* L35 ....118 D3
Sandon Crs *NSTN* CH64 ....191 K4
Sandon Gv *RNFD/HAY* WA11 ....75 H3
Sandon Pl *WDN* WA8 ....19 K1
Sandon Rd *STHP* PR8 ....27 G6
WAL/EG CH44 ....111 K3
Sandon St *CSBY/WL* L22 ....80 E2
TOX L8 ....9 K7
Sandon Wy *EV* L5 ....112 D1
Sandown Cl *RUNC* WA7 ....187 F1
Sandown La *WAV* L15 ....134 A1
Sandown Park Rd *AIN/FAZ* L10....71 H6
Sandown Rd *WAV* L15 ....134 A1
Sandpiper Cl
GR/UP/WCH CH49 ....128 E3
NEWLW WA12 ....106 C1
Sandpiper Gv *HLWD* L26 * 155 H2
Sandra Dr *NEWLW* WA12 ....106 D2
Sandridge Rd *PEN/TH* CH61 ....148 C6
WAL/NB CH45 * 95 H6
Sandringham Av *CSBY/WL* L22 ....81 F3
FROD/HEL WA6 ....199 J6
HOY CH47 ....127 H2
Sandringham Cl *HOY* CH47 * 127 H2
NWD/KWIPK L33 ....72 D4
PS/BROM CH62 ....151 F4
Sandringham Ct *CHTN/BK* PR9 ....15 F3

Sandringham Dr STHEL WA9......120 A1
WAL/NB CH45......95 G5
WARRW/BUR WA5......141 K5
Sandringham Gdns EP CH65......203 H1
Sandringham Ms HOY CH47 *......127 H1
Sandringham Rd
CLB/OSW/ST L13......114 C1
CSBY/WL L22......81 F3
FMBY L37......48 E4
MGHL L31 *......71 F1
STHP PR8......27 F4
STHP PR8......33 J4
WDN WA8......138 E5
Sandrock Cl WAL/NB CH45......95 H6
Sandrock Rd WAL/NB CH45......95 H6
Sands Rd CALD/MH L18......134 A5
Sandstone Cl RAIN/WH L35......118 E6
Sandstone Dr RAIN/WH L35......118 B2
WKBY CH48......147 F1
Sandstone Rd East
CLB/OSW/ST L13......114 E3
Sandstone Rd West
CLB/OSW/ST L13......114 D3
Sandstone Wk HES CH60......168 A6
Sandwash Cl RNFD/HAY WA11......75 J5
Sandway Crs NG/CROX L11......98 E3
Sandy Brow La NWD/KWIPK L33..85 K4
Sandy Gn WLT/FAZ L9......83 F5
Sandy Gv CLB/OSW/ST L13......114 D1
Sandy Knowe WAV L15 *......134 B1
Sandy La BRSC L40......46 D4
CLB/OSW/ST L13......114 D1
GOL/RIS/CU WA3......93 H1
HES CH60......168 A4
HTWN L38......59 G4
KIRK/FR/WA PR4......31 H1
LITH L21......81 G4
MGHL L31......62 A2
MGHL L31......71 K4
NEWLW WA12......92 A3
NSTN CH64......192 B3
ORM L39......63 F1
PEN/TH CH61......147 K4
RNFD/HAY WA11......88 A3
RUNC WA7......176 A6
RUNC WA7......188 D1
SKEL WN8......55 K4
WAL/NB CH45......110 E1
WARRN/WOL WA2......123 J5
WARRS WA4......162 C3
WARRW/BUR WA5......141 H5
WDN WA8......138 D5
WDN WA8......140 C3
WKBY CH48......146 C3
WLT/FAZ L9......82 E5
Sandy La North PEN/TH CH61......147 K3
Sandy La West
WARRN/WOL WA2......123 G4
Sandy Moor La RUNC WA7......178 C2
Sandymoor La RUNC WA7......178 C2
Sandymount Dr BEB CH63 *......170 B1
WAL/NB CH45......95 G6
Sandy Rd LITH L21......81 H4
Sandyville Gv ANF/KKDL L4......98 C5
Sandyville Rd ANF/KKDL L4......98 B5
Sandy Wy BRSC L40......31 J3
CL/PREN CH43......130 D4
Sanfield Cl ORM L39......45 H5
Sangness Dr STHP PR8......28 B4
Sankey Mnr
WARRW/BUR WA5 *......141 F3
Sankey Rd MGHL L31......71 G2
RNFD/HAY WA11......89 J6
Sankey St CLVPS L1......9 G7
GOL/RIS/CU WA3......92 B3
NEWLW WA12......106 A2
STHEL WA9......104 B3
WARR WA1......16 C5
WDN WA8......158 B5
Sankey Wy WARRW/BUR WA5......141 K4
Santon Av CLB/OSW/ST L13......114 C2
Santon Dr GOL/RIS/CU WA3......93 F3
Sanvino Av STHP PR8......33 K4
Sapphire Dr NWD/KWIPK L33......72 D4
Sapphire St CLB/OSW/ST L13......114 D6
Sarah's Cft NTHTN L30......70 B6
Sark Av EP CH65......203 F2
Sark Rd CLB/OSW/ST L13......114 D3
Sarsfield Av GOL/RIS/CU WA3......92 E3
Sartfield Cl CHLDW L16......135 F1
Sarum Rd WLTN L25......135 H2
Satinwood Cl AIMK WN4......78 E6
Satinwood Crs MGHL L31......71 K6
Saughall Massie La
GR/UP/WCH CH49......129 F4
Saughall Massie Rd
WKBY CH48......128 B5
Saughall Rd MOR/LEA CH46......128 D2
Saunby St ALL/GAR L19......172 B1
Saunders Av RAIN/WH L35......117 K3
Saundersfoot Cl
WARRW/BUR WA5......122 E5
Saunders St CHTN/BK PR9......15 F1
Saunderton Cl RNFD/HAY WA11..90 B4
Saville Av WARRW/BUR WA5......142 C2
Saville Rd CLB/OSW/ST L13......115 F5
MGHL L31......62 A4
Savon Hook FMBY L37......49 H4
Savoylands Cl AIG/SPK L17......152 D1
Sawdon Av STHP PR8......28 B3
Sawley Av GOL/RIS/CU WA3......92 E2
Sawley Cl RUNC WA7......178 D6
Sawpit La HUY L36......117 F5
Sawyer Dr AIMK WN4......79 J6
Saxby Rd DV/KA/FCH L14......116 A1
Saxon Cl NPK/KEN L6......113 K2
WARRS WA4......162 A6
Saxonia Rd ANF/KKDL L4......97 K3
Saxon Rd CSBY/BLUN L23......68 E6
HOY CH47......127 H1
MOR/LEA CH46......109 K6
RUNC WA7......11 H5
STHP PR8......27 G2
Saxon Ter WDN WA8......19 F2
Saxon Wy GTS/LS CH66......202 D3
NWD/KWIPK L33......72 D3
Saxony Rd EHL/KEN L7......113 J5
Sayce St WDN WA8......18 E2
Scafell Av WARRN/WOL WA2......123 J4
Scafell Cl BEB CH63......184 A4
Scafell Lawn NTHLY L27......136 D6
Scafell Rd ECCL WA10......88 D4
Scaffold La HTWN L38......59 J2
Scape La CSBY/BLUN L23......69 F4
Scargreen Av NG/CROX L11......98 D2
Scarisbrick Av LITH L21......81 J4
STHP PR8......14 D4
Scarisbrick Cl MGHL L31......62 C4
Scarisbrick Crs NG/CROX L11......98 B2
Scarisbrick Dr NG/CROX L11......98 B2
Scarisbrick New Rd STHP PR8......27 K2
Scarisbrick Pl NG/CROX L11......98 B3
Scarisbrick Rd NG/CROX L11......98 B3
RNFD/HAY WA11......75 G2
Scarisbrick St CHTN/BK PR9......15 F5
ORM L39......45 J5
Scarsdale Rd NG/CROX L11......98 D4
Scarth Hill La BRSC L40......54 B3
ORM L39......53 J3
Scarth Pk SKEL WN8......56 E6
Sceptre Cl NEWLW WA12......106 A2
Sceptre Rd NG/CROX L11......99 G2
Sceptre Wk NG/CROX L11 *......99 G2
Scholar St EHL/KEN L7......133 H2
Scholes La ECCL WA10......102 D6
Scholes Pk ECCL WA10......102 D6
Schomberg St NPK/KEN L6......113 J4
School Av FMBY L37......49 F2
NSTN CH64......192 A3
School Brow WARR WA1......17 F4
WGNW/BIL/O WN5......77 H4
School Cl MOR/LEA CH46......109 K5
NTHLY L27......135 K2
ORM L39 *......53 G4
STHP PR8......27 J5
School Dr WGNW/BIL/O WN5......77 H4
Schoolfield Cl
GR/UP/WCH CH49......148 E1
Schoolfield Rd
GR/UP/WCH CH49......148 E1
School Hl HES CH60......167 K6
School House Gn ORM L39......45 K6
School House Gv BRSC L40......38 D4
School Houses SKEL WN8 *......56 D5
School La AIMK WN4......78 B6
AIN/FAZ L10......83 G2
BEB CH63......150 C6
BRSC L40......39 F4
BRSC L40......54 E2
CHNE CH2......198 B6
CL/PREN CH43......110 C6
CLVPS L1......8 E5
FMBY L37......49 F2
FROD/HEL WA6......201 F2
GTS/LS CH66......184 C6
HOY CH47......108 B6
HOY CH47......127 G2
HUY L36......117 G5
LITH L21......81 J3
MGHL L31......62 E6
MGHL L31......71 K4
NSTN CH64......181 G6
NSTN CH64......182 C5
NSTN CH64......192 A3
ORM L39......51 H2
PEN/TH CH61......147 J5
PR/KW L34......85 F6
PS/BROM CH62......151 G4
RAIN/WH L35......119 H6
RUNC WA7......177 J5
SKEL WN8......55 K4
SKEL WN8......57 K2
WAL/EG CH44......110 E3
WDN WA8......139 K2
WLTN L25......154 D2
School Rd EP CH65......6 B4
HTWN L38......59 F3
WARRN/WOL WA2......123 J6
School St AIMK WN4......79 J4
GOL/RIS/CU WA3......92 B3
NEWLW WA12......106 B2
RNFD/HAY WA11......89 J5
WARRS WA4......16 E7
School Ter GOL/RIS/CU WA3 *......92 B3
School Wy SPK/HALE L24......173 G2
WDN WA8......139 J6
Schooner Cl RUNC WA7......188 C1
Schwartzman Dr
CHTN/BK PR9......21 K5
Science Rd SPK/HALE L24......173 H1
Scilly Cl EP CH65......203 G2
Scone Cl NG/CROX L11......99 G2
Scorecross STHEL WA9......103 K5
Score La CHLDW L16......115 G6
Scoresby Rd MOR/LEA CH46......110 B4
The Score STHEL WA9......119 J1
Scorpio Cl DV/KA/FCH L14......116 A2
Scorton St NPK/KEN L6......114 A2
Scotchbarn La PR/KW L34......118 A1
Scoter Rd NWD/KWIPK L33......84 E1
Scotia Av PS/BROM CH62......151 H4
Scotia Rd CLB/OSW/ST L13......114 E3
Scotland Pl VAUX/LVPD L3......9 F1
Scotland Rd EV L5......113 F2
WARR WA1......16 D4
Scott Av HUY L36......136 D1
RAIN/WH L35......118 B4
WDN WA8......18 A3
Scott Cl ANF/KKDL L4......97 H6
MGHL L31......62 B6
Scott Dr ORM L39......45 K4
Scotton Av GTS/LS CH66......194 E4
Scott Rd GOL/RIS/CU WA3......92 E2
Scotts Av STHEL WA9......119 J4
Scotts Pl BIRK CH41......130 C2
Scotts Quays BIRK CH41......112 A6
Scott St BTL L20......4 C1
CHTN/BK PR9......23 J6
WAL/NB CH45......111 H2
WARRN/WOL WA2......16 E2
The Scythes GR/UP/WCH CH49..128 D5
NTHTN L30......70 E5
Scythia Cl PS/BROM CH62......151 H3
Seabank Av WAL/EG CH44......111 J2
Seabank Rd CHTN/BK PR9......15 F2
HES CH60......180 D1
WAL/NB CH45......95 J6
Seabury St WARRS WA4......143 K6
Seacombe Dr GTS/LS CH66......195 H6
Seacombe Prom
WAL/EG CH44......112 A4
Seacombe Vw WAL/EG CH44......112 A5
Seacroft Cl DV/KA/FCH L14......116 A1
Seacroft Crs CHTN/BK PR9......20 E6
Seacroft Rd DV/KA/FCH L14......116 A1
Seafield FMBY L37......49 G3
Seafield Av CSBY/BLUN L23......69 G5
HES CH60......180 D1
Seafield Cottages
ALL/GAR L19 *......153 K5
Seafield Rd BTL L20 *......4 C2
PS/BROM CH62......151 G3
STHP PR8......33 J3
Seaford Cl RUNC WA7......178 C4
Seaford Pl WARRN/WOL WA2......123 G3
Seafore Cl MGHL L31......61 K3
Seaforth Dr MOR/LEA CH46......129 F2
Seaforth Rd LITH L21......81 H5
Seaforth V North LITH L21......81 H4
Seaforth V West LITH L21......81 H5
Seagram Cl WLT/FAZ L9......83 F3
Sealand Av FMBY L37......48 D3
Sealand Cl FMBY L37......48 D3
WARRN/WOL WA2......143 H1
Sea La RUNC WA7......177 G3
Sealy Cl BEB CH63......170 C4
Seaman Rd WAV L15......133 K2
Seaport St TOX L8......133 F3
Sea Rd WAL/NB CH45......95 F5
Seascale Av ECCL WA10......102 D5
Seath Av STHEL WA9......104 C1
Seathwaite Cl CSBY/BLUN L23....68 C6
Seathwaite Crs
NWD/KWIPK L33......72 C5
Seathwaite Grove Cl
RUNC WA7......187 H2
Seaton Cl WD/CROXPK L12......100 A2
Seaton Gv STHEL WA9......119 F1
Seaton Pk RUNC WA7......178 D2
Seaton Pl SKEL WN8......56 A2
Seaton Rd RF/TRAN CH42......131 F5
WAL/NB CH45......111 G1
Seaton Wy CHTN/BK PR9......20 D6
Sea Vw HOY CH47......127 G2
NSTN CH64......191 K5
Seaview Av PEN/TH CH61......148 A5
PS/BROM CH62......184 E1
WAL/NB CH45......111 G2
Sea View La PEN/TH CH61......148 A5
Sea View Rd BTL L20......4 B3
Seaview Rd WAL/NB CH45......111 G1
Seawood Gv MOR/LEA CH46......128 E2
Secker Av WARRS WA4......162 C1
Secker Cl WARRS WA4......162 C1
Second Av CL/PREN CH43......129 J3
CSBY/BLUN L23 *......68 E5
RAIN/WH L35......118 D3
RUNC WA7......177 J5
WLT/FAZ L9......83 F4
Sedbergh Av AIN/FAZ L10......71 F6
Sedbergh Gv RUNC WA7......187 H2
Sedbergh Rd WAL/EG CH44......111 F2
Sedburgh Gv HUY L36......116 B4
Sedburn Rd KKBY L32......85 F4
Seddon Cl ECCL WA10......102 B2
Seddon Pl SKEL WN8......56 A2
Seddon Rd ALL/GAR L19......153 K5
ECCL WA10......102 D4
Seddons Ct PR/KW L34......117 K1
Seddon St CLVPS L1......8 E6
ECCL WA10......88 C4
Sedgefield Rd MOR/LEA CH46....129 H1
Sedgemoor Rd NG/CROX L11......98 C2
Sedgewick Crs
WARRW/BUR WA5......121 J1
Sedley St NPK/KEN L6......113 K1
Sedum Gv NWD/KWIPK L33......72 C4
Seeds La WLT/FAZ L9......83 F4
Seeley Av BIRK CH41......130 D2
Seel Rd HUY L36......117 F5
Seel St CLVPS L1......9 F6
Sefton Av LITH L21......81 J4
WDN WA8......139 F6
Sefton Cl KKBY L32......72 B6
Sefton Coastal Footpath
CSBY/WL L22......80 C1
HTWN L38......68 A3
Sefton Dr AIN/FAZ L10......83 H1
CSBY/BLUN L23......69 H2
KKBY L32......72 B6
MGHL L31......70 E1
TOX L8......133 H4
Sefton Fold Dr
WGNW/BIL/O WN5......77 G4
Sefton Fold Gdns
WGNW/BIL/O WN5......77 G4
Sefton Gdns ORM L39......53 H6
Sefton Gv AIG/SPK L17......133 H5
Sefton La MGHL L31......70 E1
Sefton Mill Ct SFTN L29 *......70 C2
Sefton Mill La SFTN L29......70 C2
Sefton Moss La NTHTN L30......70 A6
Sefton Moss Vls LITH L21......81 J3
Sefton Park Rd TOX L8......133 G3
Sefton Rd AIMK WN4......79 G4
BTL L20......82 A6
FMBY L37......48 E3
LITH L21......81 J3
RF/TRAN CH42......151 F3
WAL/NB CH45......95 H6
WLT/FAZ L9......97 J1
Sefton St LITH L21......81 J4
NEWLW WA12......105 K2
STHP PR8......15 G7
VAUX/LVPD L3......132 C3
Sefton Vw CSBY/BLUN L23......69 G5
Sefton Vls BTL L20 *......5 J2
Segar's La STHP PR8......33 K4
Selborne RAIN/WH L35......118 B5
Selborne Cl TOX L8......133 F2
Selborne St TOX L8......133 F2
Selbourne Cl
GR/UP/WCH CH49......129 J6
Selby Cl ECCL WA10......12 B7
RUNC WA7......178 D1
Selby Dr FMBY L37......49 H3
Selby Gn GTS/LS CH66......194 E4
Selby Gv HUY L36......117 H3
Selby Pl SKEL WN8......55 K2
Selby Rd WLT/FAZ L9......82 D5
Selby St WAL/NB CH45......111 H2
WARRW/BUR WA5......142 B4
Seldon St EHL/KEN L7 *......113 K5
Selina Rd ANF/KKDL L4......5 K6
Selkirk Av AIMK WN4......78 C5
PS/BROM CH62......184 B3
WARRS WA4......143 K6
Selkirk Cl GTS/LS CH66 *......194 C4
Selkirk Dr ECCL WA10......87 J6
Selkirk Rd CLB/OSW/ST L13......114 D5
Sellar St ANF/KKDL L4......97 G6
Selsdon Rd CSBY/WL L22......80 D1
Selsey Cl EHL/KEN L7......133 G1
Selside Wk NTHLY L27......136 D6
Selston Cl BEB CH63......170 C3
Selworthy Dr WARRS WA4......144 C6
Selworthy Gn CHLDW L16 *......134 E3
Selworthy Rd STHP PR8......26 E4
Selwyn Cl NEWLW WA12......91 G6
WDN WA8......139 J6
Selwyn St ANF/KKDL L4......97 G4
Senator Point
NWD/KWIPK L33 *......85 G3
Seneschal Ct RUNC WA7......187 H1
Sennen Cl RUNC WA7......188 A2
Sennen Rd KKBY L32......84 E3
Sentinel Wy NTHTN L30......82 E3
Sephton Dr ORM L39......45 K4
September Rd NPK/KEN L6......114 A2
Serenade Rd NWD/KWIPK L33......72 E3
Sergeant York Loop
WARRW/BUR WA5......141 J4
Sergrim Rd HUY L36......116 D4
Serin Cl NEWLW WA12......106 C2
Serpentine Rd WAL/EG CH44......111 J2
The Serpentine South
CSBY/BLUN L23......68 B5
The Serpentine ALL/GAR L19......153 H3
CSBY/BLUN L23......68 B5
ORM L39......53 H5
Servia Rd LITH L21......81 J4
Servite Cl CSBY/WL L22......80 D1
EP CH65......195 J3
Sessions Rd ANF/KKDL L4......97 G5
Seth Powell Wy HUY L36......116 C1
Settrington Rd NG/CROX L11......98 D4
Seven Acre Rd CSBY/BLUN L23....69 J4
Seven Acres La PEN/TH CH61......148 D5
Sevenoaks Av STHP PR8......33 H4
Sevenoaks Cl EV L5......113 G2
Seventh Av WLT/FAZ L9 *......83 G4
Severn Cl STHEL WA9......120 A2
WARRN/WOL WA2......124 A5
WDN WA8......140 A6
WGNW/BIL/O WN5......77 G5
Severn Rd AIMK WN4......79 K4
NWD/KWIPK L33......72 E3
RAIN/WH L35......118 D4
Severn St BIRK CH41......111 G6
EV L5......113 H1
Severnvale EP CH65......195 K6
Severs St NPK/KEN L6......113 J3
Sewell St PR/KW L34......117 K1
RUNC WA7......11 G5
Sextant Cl RUNC WA7......188 C1
Sexton Av STHEL WA9......105 F3
Sexton Wy DV/KA/FCH L14......115 J5
Seymour Dr GTS/LS CH66......195 H3
MGHL L31......62 C4
WARR WA1......143 K2
Seymour Pl West
WAL/NB CH45......95 H5
Seymour Rd DV/KA/FCH L14......115 H6
LITH L21......81 J4
Seymour St BTL L20......4 C7
RF/TRAN CH42......131 G5
VAUX/LVPD L3......9 H3
WAL/NB CH45......95 H5
Sgt York Loop
WARRW/BUR WA5......141 J3
Shacklady Rd NWD/KWIPK L33....73 F5
Shackleton Cl
WARRW/BUR WA5......142 A1
Shackleton Rd MOR/LEA CH46..110 B3
Shadewood Crs WARRS WA4......163 G1
Shadwell Cl EV L5......112 D2
Shadwell St EV L5......112 D2
Shaftesbury Av STHP PR8......34 C1
WARRW/BUR WA5......160 B1
Shaftesbury Gv STHP PR8......27 H6
Shaftesbury Rd CSBY/BLUN L23..68 E5
STHP PR8......34 C1
Shaftesbury St TOX L8......132 D3
Shaftesbury Ter
CLB/OSW/ST L13 *......114 E4
Shaftesbury Wy
WARRW/BUR WA5......105 K6
Shaftsbury Av NWD/KWIPK L33..72 C4
Shaftway Cl RNFD/HAY WA11......90 E4
Shakespeare Av KKBY L32......84 C2
RF/TRAN CH42......150 E2
Shakespeare Cl NPK/KEN L6......113 J3
Shakespeare Gv
WARRN/WOL WA2......123 J5
Shakespeare Rd NSTN CH64......181 K6
STHEL WA9......119 J5
WAL/EG CH44......111 K5
WDN WA8......18 C2
Shakespeare St ALL/GAR L19......153 K6
BTL L20......4 B1
STHP PR8......27 J2
Shakspeare Cl NPK/KEN L6......113 J3
Shalcombe Cl HLWD L26......155 K4
Shaldon Cl KKBY L32......85 F3
Shaldon Gv KKBY L32......85 F3
Shaldon Rd KKBY L32......85 F4
Shalford Gv WKBY CH48......146 E1
Shallacres EP CH65......195 J2
Shallcross Ct NPK/KEN L6......113 J3
Shallcross Pl NPK/KEN L6......113 J3
Shallmarsh Cl BEB CH63......150 C6
Shallmarsh Rd BEB CH63......150 C6
Shalom Ct AIG/SPK L17......133 K4
Shamrock Rd BIRK CH41......130 C2
Shanklin Cl WARRW/BUR WA5......140 D3
Shanklin Rd WAV L15......114 D6
Shannons La PR/KW L34......100 C4
Shannon St BIRK CH41......111 F6
Shard Cl NG/CROX L11......84 A6
Shard St STHEL WA9......104 C6
Sharon Park Cl WARRS WA4......163 H2
Sharpeville Cl ANF/KKDL L4......97 F6
Sharples Crs CSBY/BLUN L23......69 G6
Sharp St WARRN/WOL WA2......16 E1
WDN WA8......18 D3
Sharwood Rd NTHLY L27......136 C5
Shavington Av CL/PREN CH43..130 C6
Shawbury Av BEB CH63......150 C4
Shawbury Gv WARR WA1......124 C6
Shaw Cl GTS/LS CH66......195 H5
ORM L39......35 H3
Shaw Crs FMBY L37......49 H1
Shawell Ct WDN WA8......159 F1
Shaw Entry WDN WA8......137 K2
Shaw Hill St CLVPS L1 *......8 E3
Shaw La GR/UP/WCH CH49......147 K1
ORM L39......43 F5
RAIN/WH L35......118 A3
Shaw Rd SPK/HALE L24......155 G6
Shaws Aly CLVPS L1......8 E7
Shaw's Av STHP PR8......27 H6
WARRN/WOL WA2......142 E1
Shaws Dr HOY CH47......127 J1
Shaws Garth ORM L39......35 H3
Shaw's Rd STHP PR8......27 H6
Shaw St AIMK WN4......79 G4
BIRK CH41......2 D7
ECCL WA10......13 J4
HOY CH47......127 G2
NPK/KEN L6......113 H4
RNFD/HAY WA11......90 D5
RUNC WA7......10 C5
Shawton Rd CHLDW L16......134 E1
Shearman Cl PEN/TH CH61......168 A1
Shearman Rd PEN/TH CH61......167 K1
Sheen Rd WAL/NB CH45......95 J6
Sheepfield Cl GTS/LS CH66......195 F2
Sheerwater Cl WARR WA1......143 J2
Sheffield Cl WARRW/BUR WA5..141 K4
The Sheilings GOL/RIS/CU WA3....93 G3
Sheil Rd NPK/KEN L6......114 A4
Shelagh Av WDN WA8......18 D2
Sheldon Cl BEB CH63......170 C4
Sheldon Rd WD/CROXPK L12......99 H5
Sheldrake Gv NSTN CH64......191 K4
Shelley Cl HUY L36......117 F6
Shelley Ct KKBY L32......84 C3
Shelley Dr ORM L39......45 H5
Shelley Gv ALL/GAR L19......153 K6
STHP PR8......23 H6
WARRS WA4......143 J5
Shelley Pl RAIN/WH L35......118 B4
Shelley Rd WDN WA8......18 C1
Shelley St BTL L20......4 C2
STHEL WA9......119 K5
Shelley Wy WKBY CH48......146 C3
Shellfield Rd CHTN/BK PR9......23 J2
Shellingford Rd
DV/KA/FCH L14......116 A3
Shellway Rd EP CH65......197 F6
Shelmore Dr TOX L8......132 D5
Shelton Cl CLB/OSW/ST L13......114 E5
WDN WA8......140 A6
Shelton Dr STHP PR8......33 G5
Shelton Rd WAL/NB CH45......111 G1
Shenley Cl BEB CH63......150 E5
Shenley Rd WAV L15 *......134 D1
Shenley Wy CHTN/BK PR9 *......21 G6
Shenstone St EHL/KEN L7......113 K6
Shenton Av RNFD/HAY WA11......89 G5
Shepherd Cl GR/UP/WCH CH49..128 D5
Shepherds Fold Cl TOX L8......133 F3
Shepherd's La ORM L39......44 B6
Shepherd St NPK/KEN L6......9 K2
Sheppard Av CHLDW L16......135 H1
Shepperton Cl WARRS WA4......162 C5
Shepsides Cl GTS/LS CH66......195 F6
Shepston Av ANF/KKDL L4......97 J4
Shepton Rd GTS/LS CH66......202 C1
HUY L36......116 D1
Sherborne Av WLTN L25......155 G3
Sherborne Cl RUNC WA7......178 E2
Sherbourne Rd EP CH65......196 C6
Sherbourne Wy
WARRW/BUR WA5......121 K1
Sherbrooke Cl
WD/CROXPK L12......115 J2
Sherburn Cl WLT/FAZ L9......83 G3
Sherdley Park Dr STHEL WA9....119 K1
Sherdley Rd STHEL WA9......103 H6
Sheridan Av GOL/RIS/CU WA3......92 E4
Sheridan Pl WARRN/WOL WA2..123 G2
Sheri Dr NEWLW WA12......106 D3
Sheriff Cl EV L5 *......113 G3
Sheringham Cl
GR/UP/WCH CH49......129 H2
STHEL WA9......104 B2
Sheringham Rd
WARRW/BUR WA5......141 F3
Sherlock Av RNFD/HAY WA11......90 D4

Sherlock La WAL/EG CH44 111 H4
Sherman Dr RAIN/WH L35 119 F6
Sherrat St SKEL WN8 55 K4
Sherringham Rd STHP PR8 27 F5
Sherry Ct AIG/SPK L17 * 133 K4
Sherry La GR/UP/WCH CH49 148 D1
Sherwell Cl WAV L15 114 E6
Sherwood Av AIMK WN4 * 79 H5
CSBY/BLUN L23 68 E4
ORM L39 53 G3
PEN/TH CH61 147 K4
Sherwood Cl RAIN/WH L35 118 D2
WDN WA8 157 H2
Sherwood Ct HUY L36 117 F5
WD/CROXPK L12 99 K2
Sherwood Crs
WARRW/BUR WA5 121 J1
Sherwood Dr BEB CH63 150 D4
RAIN/WH L35 118 B5
SKEL WN8 57 F2
Sherwood Gv FROD/HEL WA6 199 H6
HOY CH47 128 A2
Sherwood Rd CSBY/BLUN L23 68 D4
HOY CH47 128 A1
WAL/EG CH44 111 J4
Sherwood's La AIN/FAZ L10 83 J3
Sherwood St VAUX/LVPD L3 112 D3
Sherwyn Rd ANF/KKDL L4 98 A6
Shetland Cl WARRN/WOL WA2 124 A3
WDN WA8 139 K6
Shetland Dr EP CH65 203 G2
PS/BROM CH62 171 G5
Shevington Cl STHEL WA9 104 A6
WDN WA8 139 K6
Shevington's La
NWD/KWIPK L33 72 D4
Shewell Cl RF/TRAN CH42 131 G5
Shiel Rd WAL/NB CH45 95 G6
Shiggins Cl WARRW/BUR WA5 142 A3
Shillingford Cl WARRS WA4 162 D6
Shimmin St EHL/KEN L7 113 J6
Ship St FROD/HEL WA6 186 E6
Shipton Cl ALL/GAR L19 153 J3
CL/PREN CH43 149 H2
WARRW/BUR WA5 141 J1
WDN WA8 138 C6
Shirdley Av KKBY L32 84 E4
Shirdley Crs STHP PR8 33 J6
Shirdley Wk KKBY L32 84 E4
Shirebourne Av
RNFD/HAY WA11 88 E4
Shireburn Rd FMBY L37 40 C6
Shire Gn STHEL WA9 120 A1
The Shires ECCL WA10 12 D7
Shirley Dr WARRS WA4 163 F1
Shirley Rd ALL/GAR L19 153 K3
Shirley St WAL/EG CH44 112 A4
Shirwell Gv STHEL WA9 120 A3
Shobdon Cl WD/CROXPK L12 99 K1
Shones Cft NSTN CH64 192 B4
Shop La MGHL L31 62 A6
Shop Rd PR/KW L34 100 C1
Shore Bank PS/BROM CH62 151 H3
Shore Dr PS/BROM CH62 151 H5
Shorefields PS/BROM CH62 151 H4
Shorefields Village TOX L8 132 E6
Shoreham Dr
WARRW/BUR WA5 141 H6
Shore Rd BIRK CH41 3 H2
LITH L21 81 G6
STHP PR8 33 F3
WKBY CH48 146 D4
Short Cl NEWLW WA12 105 J2
Shortfield Rd
GR/UP/WCH CH49 129 H5
Shortfield Wy
GR/UP/WCH CH49 * 129 H5
Short St GOL/RIS/CU WA3 * 92 C2
NEWLW WA12 105 J2
RNFD/HAY WA11 90 D5
WDN WA8 158 B6
Shortwood Rd DV/KA/FCH L14 115 K4
Shorwell Cl WARRW/BUR WA5 140 D2
Shrewsbury Av AIN/FAZ L10 71 F6
CSBY/WL L22 68 E6
Shrewsbury Cl CL/PREN CH43 130 C3
Shrewsbury Dr
GR/UP/WCH CH49 129 H3
Shrewsbury Rd ALL/GAR L19 153 K5
CL/PREN CH43 130 C2
HES CH60 168 A4
WAL/NB CH45 111 F2
WKBY CH48 146 B2
Shrewsbury St WARRS WA4 143 G6
Shrewton Rd WLTN L25 135 H2
Shropshire Cl NTHTN L30 70 D5
WARR WA1 144 D3
Shropshire Gdns ECCL WA10 12 F7
Shropshire Rd EP CH65 196 E6
Sibford Rd WD/CROXPK L12 115 H2
Sibley Av AIMK WN4 79 J5
Siddall St ECCL WA10 88 C4
Siddeley Dr NEWLW WA12 105 K2
Siddeley St AIG/SPK L17 133 H6
Sidgreave St ECCL WA10 12 D6
Siding La RNFD/HAY WA11 65 K6
The Sidings RF/TRAN CH42 150 E1
Sidlaw Av STHEL WA9 104 D2
Sidlaw Cl GTS/LS CH66 194 D3
Sidmouth Cl ECCL WA10 87 K6
WARRW/BUR WA5 141 F5
Sidney Av WAL/NB CH45 95 G5
Sidney Gdns RF/TRAN CH42 131 H5
Sidney Pl EHL/KEN L7 113 J6
Sidney Powell Av KKBY L32 84 B1
Sidney Rd BIRK CH41 131 H5
BTL L20 5 H6
CHTN/BK PR9 23 H5
NSTN CH64 182 A6
Sidney St BIRK CH41 3 G3
ECCL WA10 12 B4
Sidney Ter RF/TRAN CH42 131 H6
Sidwell St ALL/GAR L19 153 K6
Signal Works Rd WLT/FAZ L9 83 H3
Silcock St GOL/RIS/CU WA3 92 B3
Silcroft Rd KKBY L32 84 D3
Silkstone Cl ECCL WA10 12 B6
EHL/KEN L7 133 G1
Silkstone Crs RUNC WA7 178 A6
Silkstone St ECCL WA10 12 C6
Silsden Av GOL/RIS/CU WA3 93 J3
Silver Av RNFD/HAY WA11 89 K6
Silverbeech Av CALD/MH L18 134 C5
Silverbeech Rd WAL/EG CH44 111 J4
Silver Birch Gv AIMK WN4 79 F4
Silverbirch Wy GTS/LS CH66 202 D3
Silver Birch Wy MGHL L31 61 K2
Silverbrook Rd NTHLY L27 135 K2
Silverburn Av MOR/LEA CH46 109 J6
Silverdale Av CLB/OSW/ST L13 114 C2
Silverdale Cl FROD/HEL WA6 201 F2
HUY L36 136 B1
Silverdale Dr LITH L21 82 A3
Silverdale Gv RNFD/HAY WA11 88 D3
Silverdale Rd BEB CH63 150 E4
CL/PREN CH43 130 D5
NEWLW WA12 106 B1
WARRS WA4 162 A1
Silverlea Av WAL/NB CH45 111 G3
Silver Leigh AIG/SPK L17 152 E2
Silverlime Gdns STHEL WA9 102 E6
Silverne Dr EP CH65 202 E1
Silverstone Dr HUY L36 136 A1
Silverstone Gv MGHL L31 61 K2
Silver St WARRN/WOL WA2 16 D2
Silverthorne Dr CHTN/BK PR9 23 H4
Silverton Rd AIG/SPK L17 153 F3
Silverwell Rd NG/CROX L11 84 C6
Silvester St EV L5 112 E2
Simkin Av WARRS WA4 143 J5
Simms Av STHEL WA9 104 C2
Simm's Rd NPK/KEN L6 114 B1
Simnel Cl WLTN L25 135 J3
Simonsbridge WKBY CH48 * 146 E5
Simons Cl RAIN/WH L35 137 F1
Simon's Cft NTHTN L30 69 K6
Simonside WDN WA8 157 H1
Simons La FROD/HEL WA6 200 E3
Simonstone Gv STHEL WA9 104 B6
Simonswood La
NWD/KWIPK L33 85 F1
ORM L39 63 K4
Simpson St BIRK CH41 2 E4
CLVPS L1 * 132 C2
Sim St VAUX/LVPD L3 9 H1
Sinclair Av RAIN/WH L35 118 B2
WARRN/WOL WA2 123 H5
WDN WA8 18 B3
Sinclair Cl RAIN/WH L35 118 B1
Sinclair Dr CALD/MH L18 134 C3
Sinclair St ALL/GAR L19 153 K6
Sineacre La ORM L39 64 E6
Singleton Av RF/TRAN CH42 131 F6
RNFD/HAY WA11 89 G6
Singleton Ct FROD/HEL WA6 201 F1
Singleton Dr PR/KW L34 100 D2
Singleton Rd EP CH65 195 J5
Sirdar Cl EHL/KEN L7 133 G1
Sir Howard St EHL/KEN L7 * 9 K7
Sir Howard Wy EHL/KEN L7 9 K7
Sir Thomas St CLVPS L1 8 E3
Siskin Cl NEWLW WA12 106 C2
Siskin Gn WLTN L25 135 H5
Sisters Wy BIRK CH41 2 D4
Six Acre Gdns WARRS WA4 160 D6
Six Acre La RUNC WA7 160 D6
Sixpenny La STHP PR8 41 K2
Sixth Av WLT/FAZ L9 83 H4
Skeffington RAIN/WH L35 118 A5
Skelhorne St VAUX/LVPD L3 9 G4
Skelmersdale Rd ORM L39 55 G6
Skelton Cl RNFD/HAY WA11 88 D4
Skelton St AIMK WN4 78 E3
Skerries Rd ANF/KKDL L4 113 J1
Skiddaw Cl RUNC WA7 187 K3
Skiddaw Rd PS/BROM CH62 171 G3
Skipton Av CHTN/BK PR9 21 F5
Skipton Dr GTS/LS CH66 195 F5
Skipton Rd ANF/KKDL L4 97 K6
HUY L36 117 H4
Skirving Pl EV L5 113 F1
Skirving St EV L5 113 F1
Skye Cl EP CH65 203 G2
WDN WA8 139 K6
Slackey La CHTN/BK PR9 24 A1
Slag La GOL/RIS/CU WA3 93 G1
RNFD/HAY WA11 90 A4
Slaidburn Crs CHTN/BK PR9 20 D6
GOL/RIS/CU WA3 92 A1
Slate La SKEL WN8 55 J3
Slater Pl CLVPS L1 9 F6
Slater St CLVPS L1 9 F6
WARRS WA4 17 G7
Slatey Rd CL/PREN CH43 2 A7
Sleaford Rd DV/KA/FCH L14 116 B2
Sleepers Hl ANF/KKDL L4 97 H6
Slenna Cl NTHLY L27 135 K3
Slessor Av WKBY CH48 127 J6
Slim Rd HUY L36 116 E3
Slingsby Dr GR/UP/WCH CH49 129 H5
Slutchers La WARR WA1 16 C7
Small Av WARRN/WOL WA2 123 J5
Small Crs WARRN/WOL WA2 123 J5
The Smallholdings MGHL L31 * 62 E4
Small La BRSC L40 37 J1
ORM L39 52 D2
ORM L39 53 K1
Small La North ORM L39 44 B1
Small La South ORM L39 44 A6
Smallridge Cl PEN/TH CH61 * 167 J1
Smallshaw Cl AIMK WN4 91 F1
Smallwoods Ms HES CH60 * 167 J4
Smeaton St ANF/KKDL L4 97 G4
Smilie Av MOR/LEA CH46 109 G6
Smith Av BIRK CH41 130 E1
Smith Crs WARRN/WOL WA2 143 G1
Smithdown Gv EHL/KEN L7 133 F1
Smithdown La EHL/KEN L7 113 J6
Smithdown Pl WAV L15 134 B4
Smithdown Rd EHL/KEN L7 133 H2
Smith Dr BTL L20 82 B6
WARRN/WOL WA2 143 G1
Smithfield St CLVP L2 8 D2
STHEL WA9 104 A3
Smithford Wk RAIN/WH L35 136 E2
Smithills Cl GOL/RIS/CU WA3 125 F2
Smith Pl EV L5 113 F1
Smith Rd WDN WA8 18 B5
Smith St EV L5 97 G6
PR/KW L34 * 118 A1
SKEL WN8 55 K4
STHEL WA9 104 C6
WARR WA1 16 E4
Smithy Cl FMBY L37 49 H1
NSTN CH64 192 B5
WDN WA8 138 B3
Smithy Gn FMBY L37 49 H1
Smithy Hey WKBY CH48 146 D1
Smithy Hl BEB CH63 182 B1
Smithy La BRSC L40 37 G5
FROD/HEL WA6 199 K4
GTS/LS CH66 195 F3
KIRK/FR/WA PR4 31 H1
NSTN CH64 193 H1
ORM L39 43 J5
ORM L39 62 D1
WDN WA8 138 B4
Smock La AIMK WN4 78 B5
Smollett St BTL L20 81 H5
EHL/KEN L7 * 113 K5
Smugglers Wy WAL/NB CH45 94 E5
Smyth Rd WDN WA8 158 E1
Snab La NSTN CH64 192 A5
Snabwood Cl NSTN CH64 191 K4
Snaefell Av CLB/OSW/ST L13 114 C2
Snaefell Gv CLB/OSW/ST L13 114 C2
Snaefell Ri WARRS WA4 162 B4
Snape Gn STHP PR8 36 B1
Snave Cl LITH L21 81 J6
Snottesbrook Gn NG/CROX L11 98 D2
Snowberry Cl WDN WA8 139 K5
Snowberry Rd DV/KA/FCH L14 115 K1
Snowden Rd MOR/LEA CH46 128 D1
Snowdon Cl GTS/LS CH66 194 D3
WARRW/BUR WA5 141 F3
Snowdon Gv STHEL WA9 104 A6
Snowdon La EV L5 112 E2
Snowdon Rd RF/TRAN CH42 150 C1
Snowdrop Av BIRK CH41 130 C1
Snowdrop Cl RUNC WA7 187 J3
Snowdrop Ms LITH L21 81 J5
Snowdrop St EV L5 97 F6
Soane Cl AIMK WN4 79 J6
Soho Pl VAUX/LVPD L3 9 H1
Soho St VAUX/LVPD L3 9 H1
Solar Rd WLT/FAZ L9 82 E5
Solly Av RF/TRAN CH42 150 D1
Solomon St EHL/KEN L7 113 K5
Solway Cl AIMK WN4 79 F5
WARRN/WOL WA2 124 B3
Solway Gv RUNC WA7 187 G2
Solway St TOX L8 133 G2
Solway St West TOX L8 133 G2
Soma Av LITH L21 81 K3
Somerford Rd DV/KA/FCH L14 116 A3
Somerset Dr STHP PR8 41 J1
Somerset Pl NPK/KEN L6 114 B2
Somerset Rd BTL L20 5 H2
CSBY/WL L22 80 D1
PEN/TH CH61 167 J1
WAL/NB CH45 110 E2
WKBY CH48 127 H6
Somerset St STHEL WA9 104 B3
Somerset Wy WARR WA1 144 A1
Somerton St WAV L15 133 K1
Somerville Cl BEB CH63 183 J1
NSTN CH64 191 K4
Somerville Crs EP CH65 6 E7
Somerville Gv CSBY/WL L22 80 E1
Somerville Rd CSBY/WL L22 80 E1
WDN WA8 157 J3
Sommer Av WD/CROXPK L12 * 98 E6
Sonning Av LITH L21 81 J2
Sonning Rd ANF/KKDL L4 98 B3
Sorany Cl CSBY/BLUN L23 69 J3
Sorbus Cl CHNE CH2 198 D6
Sorogold St STHEL WA9 104 A2
Sorrel Cl CL/PREN CH43 130 A4
WARRN/WOL WA2 124 E5
Sougher's La AIMK WN4 78 E3
South Albert Rd AIG/SPK L17 133 G5
Southampton Wy RUNC WA7 188 D1
South Av PR/KW L34 117 J2
WARRN/WOL WA2 142 E1
WARRS WA4 162 B2
South Bank CL/PREN CH43 130 E6
South Bank Rd ALL/GAR L19 153 J4
EHL/KEN L7 114 B5
Southbank Rd STHP PR8 27 J1
South Bank Ter RUNC WA7 10 C3
South Barcombe Rd
CHLDW L16 135 F2
South Boundary Rd
NWD/KWIPK L33 85 G3
Southbourne Rd
WAL/NB CH45 110 D2
Southbrook Rd NTHLY L27 135 K3
South Cantril Av
WD/CROXPK L12 99 K6
South Chester St TOX L8 132 D3
South Cloughton Rd BIRK CH41 2 D5
Southcroft Rd WAL/NB CH45 110 D2
South Dl WARRW/BUR WA5 141 G4
Southdale Rd RF/TRAN CH42 150 D1
WARR WA1 143 K2
WAV L15 134 A1
Southdean Rd DV/KA/FCH L14 116 B1
South Dr GR/UP/WCH CH49 129 H4
HES CH60 168 A6
PEN/TH CH61 147 K6
WAV L15 134 A1
WD/CROXPK L12 115 G2
Southern Crs TOX L8 132 D4
Southern Rd SPK/HALE L24 173 K3
STHP PR8 14 C7
Southern's La RNFD/HAY WA11 75 H3
Southern St WARRS WA4 162 B2
Southey Cl WDN WA8 18 A3
Southey Gv MGHL L31 71 G3
Southey Rd ECCL WA10 102 E5
Southey St BTL L20 4 C2
WAV L15 133 K2
South Ferry Quay
VAUX/LVPD L3 132 C3
Southfield Rd GTS/LS CH66 195 F3
WLT/FAZ L9 82 C5
Southfields Av
WARRW/BUR WA5 141 G3
South Front RAIN/WH L35 137 H1
Southgate Cl WD/CROXPK L12 99 J2
Southgate Rd
CLB/OSW/ST L13 115 F4
South Gv CALD/MH L18 153 K2
TOX L8 133 F5
South Heath Rd RUNC WA7 176 D6
South Hey Rd PEN/TH CH61 167 H1
South Highville Rd CHLDW L16 134 E3
South Hill Gv CL/PREN CH43 130 E6
TOX L8 133 F5
South Hill Rd CL/PREN CH43 130 E5
TOX L8 132 E6
South Hunter St CLVPS L1 9 J6
South John St CLVPS L1 8 D4
STHEL WA9 * 104 A2
Southlands Av
WARRW/BUR WA5 141 G6
Southlands Ct RUNC WA7 * 10 C7
South La WDN WA8 139 K4
South Manor Wy WLTN L25 155 F2
South Meade MGHL L31 61 K6
Southmead Gdns ALL/GAR L19 154 B4
Southmead Rd ALL/GAR L19 154 B4
South Mossley Hill Rd
ALL/GAR L19 153 H2
Southney Cl KKBY L32 84 A1
South Pde KKBY L32 84 D1
RUNC WA7 176 A6
SPK/HALE L24 173 K3
WKBY CH48 146 B1
South Park Ct WAL/EG CH44 112 A4
South Park Rd KKBY L32 72 B6
South Parkside Dr
WD/CROXPK L12 99 G6
South Park Wy BTL L20 5 G6
South Pier Rd EP CH65 196 C2
Southport New Rd
CHTN/BK PR9 25 F1
Southport Old Rd FMBY L37 41 H4
Southport Rd BTL L20 5 J5
CSBY/BLUN L23 69 H2
FMBY L37 41 G6
MGHL L31 51 J6
ORM L39 43 J5
ORM L39 45 H3
STHP PR8 28 D5
Southport St STHEL WA9 104 E2
Southridge Rd PEN/TH CH61 148 D6
South Rd ALL/GAR L19 153 G5
CSBY/WL L22 80 E3
DV/KA/FCH L14 115 H4
EP CH65 7 K5
RF/TRAN CH42 150 B1
SPK/HALE L24 173 K1
WKBY CH48 146 B2
WLT/FAZ L9 83 G5
South Station Rd WLTN L25 135 J4
South St STHEL WA9 103 F6
TOX L8 133 F4
WDN WA8 18 E3
South Sudley Rd ALL/GAR L19 153 H2
South Ter ORM L39 53 J1
South Vw CSBY/WL L22 * 81 F3
HUY L36 117 H5
PS/BROM CH62 151 J6
TOX L8 * 133 F5
South Vls WAL/NB CH45 95 H6
Southward Rd RNFD/HAY WA11 91 F4
South Wy WAV L15 134 C1
Southway RUNC WA7 177 H6
SKEL WN8 56 E4
WDN WA8 157 J3
Southway Av WARRS WA4 162 C4
Southwell Cl GOL/RIS/CU WA3 92 D3
Southwell Pl TOX L8 132 D4
Southwick Rd RF/TRAN CH42 131 H6
Southwood Av RUNC WA7 178 B3
Southwood Cl KKBY L32 85 F4
Southwood Rd AIG/SPK L17 152 C1
Southworth Av
WARRW/BUR WA5 142 C1
Southworth La
WARRN/WOL WA2 107 K6
Southworth Rd NEWLW WA12 107 F1
Sovereign Cl GOL/RIS/CU WA3 93 F4
RUNC WA7 178 C5
Sovereign Ct GOL/RIS/CU WA3 124 E3
Sovereign Rd NG/CROX L11 99 G2
Sovereign Wy BIRK CH41 111 K6
NG/CROX L11 99 G2
Spa Fold BRSC L40 55 G1
Spa La BRSC L40 55 H1
Spark La RUNC WA7 177 J4
Sparks La PEN/TH CH61 148 E5
Sparling St CLVPS L1 132 C2
Sparrow Hall Cl WLT/FAZ L9 * 98 D1
Sparrow Hall Rd WLT/FAZ L9 98 D1
Sparrowhawk Cl HLWD L26 155 H2
RUNC WA7 177 K6
Spawell Cl GOL/RIS/CU WA3 93 F2
Speakman Av NEWLW WA12 91 G6
Speakman Rd ECCL WA10 88 A5
Speakman St RUNC WA7 10 C3
Speedwell Cl GOL/RIS/CU WA3 93 F3
HES CH60 * 168 C5
Speedwell Dr HES CH60 168 C5
Speedwell Rd BIRK CH41 130 C2
Speke Bvd SPK/HALE L24 173 G1
Speke Church Rd
SPK/HALE L24 173 G2
Speke Hall Av SPK/HALE L24 173 F2
Speke Hall Rd WLTN L25 154 D4
Spekeland Rd EHL/KEN L7 133 H1
Speke Rd HLWD L26 156 A5
WDN WA8 156 E4
WLTN L25 154 E2
Speke Town La SPK/HALE L24 173 G1
Spellow La ANF/KKDL L4 97 H5
Spence Av BTL L20 82 A6
Spencer Av MOR/LEA CH46 110 A6
Spencer Cl HUY L36 * 136 C1
WDN WA8 150 A2
Spencer Gdns STHEL WA9 104 B5
Spencer Pl BTL L20 82 A4
CHTN/BK PR9 * 15 H5
Spencer's La MGHL L31 71 J6
ORM L39 34 D6
SKEL WN8 56 D5
Spencer St BTL L20 4 C2
NPK/KEN L6 113 H3
Spennymoor Ct RUNC WA7 177 H6
Spenser Av RF/TRAN CH42 150 E2
Spenser Rd NSTN CH64 191 K1
Spicer Gv KKBY L32 84 D1
Spice St WLT/FAZ L9 82 E6
Spindle Cl NPK/KEN L6 113 H3
Spindle Hillock AIMK WN4 78 C5
Spindus Rd SPK/HALE L24 173 F2
Spinnaker Cl RUNC WA7 188 C1
Spinney Av WDN WA8 157 F2
Spinney Cl NWD/KWIPK L33 85 H3
ORM L39 53 H2
STHEL WA9 120 A3
Spinney Crs CSBY/BLUN L23 68 C3
Spinney Dr GTS/LS CH66 202 B1
Spinney Gn ECCL WA10 102 C2
Spinney Houses CLVPS L1 * 8 E5
Spinney Rd NWD/KWIPK L33 85 H3
The Spinney BEB CH63 170 D2
FMBY L37 41 G6
HES CH60 181 H2
NSTN CH64 191 J1
PR/KW L34 101 J6
RNFD/HAY WA11 75 G2
STBRV L28 100 A6
WKBY CH48 146 E1
Spinney Vw NWD/KWIPK L33 85 J3
Spion Kop AIMK WN4 79 F6
Spires Cl WARRN/WOL WA2 107 G6
Spital Heyes BEB CH63 170 D2
Spital Rd BEB CH63 170 D2
Spitfire Rd ALL/GAR L19 154 C5
Spofforth Rd WAV L15 133 J1
Spooner Av LITH L21 81 K4
Sprainger St VAUX/LVPD L3 112 D3
Sprakeling Pl BTL L20 82 B4
Spray St ECCL WA10 12 D3
Spreyton Cl NG/CROX L11 99 G3
Sprig Cl WLT/FAZ L9 83 G3
Spring Av GTS/LS CH66 195 F3
Springbank Cl RUNC WA7 186 E1
Spring Bank Rd ANF/KKDL L4 113 K2
Springbourne FROD/HEL WA6 201 G3
Springbourne Rd AIG/SPK L17 152 C1
Springbrook Cl ECCL WA10 102 C1
Spring Cl NWD/KWIPK L33 * 73 F4
STHP PR8 27 H2
Spring Ct RUNC WA7 10 E4
Springcroft NSTN CH64 181 H6
Springdale Cl WD/CROXPK L12 99 G6
Spring Fld RNFD/HAY WA11 66 A5
Springfield VAUX/LVPD L3 9 H1
Springfield Av FROD/HEL WA6 199 J6
GOL/RIS/CU WA3 92 A3
LITH L21 81 K3
WARR WA1 143 J1
WARRS WA4 144 A6
WKBY CH48 127 K6
Springfield Cl BRSC L40 46 D1
FMBY L37 48 C3
GR/UP/WCH CH49 149 F1
Springfield La ECCL WA10 87 H6
Springfield Pk RNFD/HAY WA11 90 B4
Springfield Rd ECCL WA10 102 E5
ORM L39 62 D2
WDN WA8 157 F3
Springfield Sq ANF/KKDL L4 97 H5
Springfield St WARR WA1 16 C5
Springfield Wy WD/CROXPK L12 99 J5
Spring Gdns GTS/LS CH66 195 F3
MGHL L31 71 H1
Spring Gv WD/CROXPK L12 115 G1
Springhill Av PS/BROM CH62 184 A1
Spring La GOL/RIS/CU WA3 124 D1
Springmeadow Rd WLTN L25 135 H4
Springmount GOL/RIS/CU WA3 93 F4
Springpool STHEL WA9 104 B6
Springs Cl BTL L20 * 5 G3
Spring St RF/TRAN CH42 131 J6
WDN WA8 18 D7
Spring V WAL/NB CH45 94 E6
Spring Vls CL/PREN CH43 * 130 E5
Springville Rd WLT/FAZ L9 * 83 F4
Springwell Rd BTL L20 81 K4
Springwood Av ALL/GAR L19 154 A3
Springwood Gv KKBY L32 84 E4
Springwood Wy
RF/TRAN CH42 151 F3
Spruce Cl GOL/RIS/CU WA3 93 G4
RF/TRAN CH42 131 G5
WARR WA1 144 D2
Spruce Gv STBRV L28 100 B6
Spruce Wy FMBY L37 48 C2
Sprucewood Cl NPK/KEN L6 113 K2
Spunhill Av GTS/LS CH66 195 F6
Spur Cl NG/CROX L11 99 G2
Spurgeon Cl EV L5 113 H2
Spurling Rd WARRW/BUR WA5 121 K1
Spurrier's La MGHL L31 72 C1
Spurstow Cl CL/PREN CH43 130 C6
The Spur CSBY/BLUN L23 68 E6

Spymers Cft FMBY L37 41 G5
Square La BRSC L40 38 E6
BRSC L40 39 F6
Squires Av WDN WA8 18 C3
Squires Cl RNFD/HAY WA11 90 A5
Squires St EHL/KEN L7 113 J6
Squirrel Gn FMBY L37 40 C6
Stable Cl GR/UP/WCH CH49 128 D5
The Stables CSBY/BLUN L23 * 69 H4
The Stackfield WKBY CH48 127 K6
Stadium Rd PS/BROM CH62 171 G2
Staffin Av EP CH65 203 F3
Stafford Cl HUY L36 117 G3
Stafford Gdns EP CH65 6 C4
Stafford Moreton Wy
MGHL L31 * 62 A6
Stafford Rd ECCL WA10 103 F4
STHP PR8 27 H6
WARRS WA4 162 B1
Staffordshire Cl EV L5 113 G1
Stafford St SKEL WN8 55 K3
VAUX/LVPD L3 9 H2
Stainburn Av NG/CROX L11 98 D2
Stainer Cl DV/KA/FCH L14 115 K2
NEWLW WA12 91 G6
Staines Cl WARRS WA4 162 D6
Stainmore Cl GOL/RIS/CU WA3 125 K1
Stainton Cl HLWD L26 155 H3
RNFD/HAY WA11 88 E3
Stairhaven Rd ALL/GAR L19 153 J3
The Stakes MOR/LEA CH46 109 J4
Stalbridge Av CALD/MH L18 134 A4
Staley Av CSBY/BLUN L23 69 G6
Staley St BTL L20 81 K5
Stalisfield Av NG/CROX L11 98 E3
Stalisfield Gv NG/CROX L11 98 E3
Stalisfield Pl NG/CROX L11 98 E3
Stalmine Rd WLT/FAZ L9 97 J1
Stamford Ct LYMM WA13 145 K6
Stamfordham Dr ALL/GAR L19 153 K3
Stamfordham Gv ALL/GAR L19 154 A4
Stamfordham Pl ALL/GAR L19 154 A4
Stamford Rd STHP PR8 27 J4
Stamford St EHL/KEN L7 114 A5
EP CH65 195 K4
Stanbury Av BEB CH63 151 F5
Standale Rd WAV L15 134 A1
Standard Pl RF/TRAN CH42 131 J6
Standard Rd NG/CROX L11 99 G1
Standen Cl ECCL WA10 12 D4
Stand Farm Rd
WD/CROXPK L12 99 K2
Standhouse La ORM L39 53 G3
Standish Av WGNW/BIL/O WN5 77 H4
Standish Ct WDN WA8 157 J3
Standish Dr RNFD/HAY WA11 75 H2
Standish St ECCL WA10 13 J3
VAUX/LVPD L3 8 E2
Stand Park Av NTHTN L30 82 C1
Stand Park Cl NTHTN L30 * 82 C1
Stand Park Rd CHLDW L16 134 E3
Stand Pkwy NTHTN L30 82 B1
Standring Gdn ECCL WA10 102 D5
Stanfield Av EV L5 113 H2
Stanfield Dr BEB CH63 170 B2
Stanford Av WAL/NB CH45 95 H6
Stanford Crs WLTN L25 155 G3
Stangate MGHL L31 61 K5
Stanhope Dr HUY L36 116 C4
PS/BROM CH62 171 F4
Stanhope St ECCL WA10 13 F1
TOX L8 132 C3
Stanier Wy EHL/KEN L7 114 A6
Staniforth Pl CHLDW L16 115 H6
Stanlawe Rd FMBY L37 40 E5
Stanlaw Rd EP CH65 6 E6
Stanley Av BEB CH63 150 B3
RNFD/HAY WA11 75 F2
STHP PR8 27 G5
WAL/NB CH45 110 D1
WARRS WA4 162 E1
WARRW/BUR WA5 140 E2
Stanley Bank Rd
RNFD/HAY WA11 89 K4
Stanley Bungalows
PR/KW L34 * 100 C1
Stanley Cl ANF/KKDL L4 97 F6
WAL/EG CH44 112 A5
WDN WA8 158 D1
Stanley Ct BIRK CH41 131 J6
BRSC L40 38 E4
Stanley Crs PR/KW L34 117 J1
Stanley Gdns WLT/FAZ L9 82 C6
Stanley La PS/BROM CH62 184 C2
Stanley Pk LITH L21 81 J2
Stanley Park Av North
ANF/KKDL L4 97 K4
Stanley Park Av South
ANF/KKDL L4 97 K5
Stanley Pl WARRS WA4 * 162 E1
Stanley Prec BTL L20 5 F6
Stanley Rd BIRK CH41 111 F6
BTL L20 4 E2
CSBY/WL L22 81 F3
EP CH65 196 B2
FMBY L37 40 E5
HOY CH47 127 F3
HUY L36 116 E5
MGHL L31 71 F3
RF/TRAN CH42 151 F3
SKEL WN8 57 J6
Stanley St ALL/GAR L19 172 B1
CHTN/BK PR9 14 E4
CLVP L2 8 D4
EHL/KEN L7 114 C4
NEWLW WA12 * 106 A2
RUNC WA7 11 F3
WAL/EG CH44 112 A5
WARR WA1 16 D6
Stanley Vls RUNC WA7 * 10 C7
Stanley Wy SKEL WN8 56 A2
Stanlowe Vw ALL/GAR L19 153 G5
Stanmore Pk
GR/UP/WCH CH49 128 C6
Stanmore Rd WAV L15 134 C3
Stannanought Rd SKEL WN8 57 F2
SKEL WN8 67 G2
Stanner Cl WARRW/BUR WA5 122 D5
Stanney Cl PS/BROM CH62 184 B4
Stanney La EP CH65 6 C7
Stanney Mill La CHNE CH2 203 K2
Stanney Mill Rd EP CH65 203 K1
Stanney Woods Av EP CH65 203 G2
Stannyfield Cl CSBY/BLUN L23 69 J3
Stanny Field Dr CSBY/BLUN L23 69 J3
Stansfield Av MGHL L31 62 D6
WARR WA1 143 J3
Stansfield Dr WARRS WA4 163 F4
Stanstead Av
WARRW/BUR WA5 141 G6
Stanton Av LITH L21 81 H2
Stanton Cl NTHTN L30 70 A4
RNFD/HAY WA11 90 B5
Stanton Ct NSTN CH64 191 K1
Stanton Crs KKBY L32 84 B1
Stanton Rd BEB CH63 170 A2
CALD/MH L18 * 134 A4
WARRS WA4 144 C6
Stanwood Cl ECCL WA10 102 B2
Stanwood Gdns RAIN/WH L35 118 A4
Stapehill Cl CLB/OSW/ST L13 115 F5
Stapeley Gdns HLWD L26 155 K5
Staplands Rd DV/KA/FCH L14 115 H5
Stapleford Ct GTS/LS CH66 195 J1
Stapleford Rd WLTN L25 135 K3
Staplehurst Cl WD/CROXPK L12 99 J2
Stapleton Av
GR/UP/WCH CH49 128 E5
RAIN/WH L35 118 E3
SPK/HALE L24 173 J2
WARRN/WOL WA2 143 G1
Stapleton Cl RAIN/WH L35 118 E3
WLTN L25 135 J2
Stapleton Rd FMBY L37 48 D5
RAIN/WH L35 118 D2
Stapley Cl RUNC WA7 10 B6
Starbeck Dr GTS/LS CH66 194 E3
Starkey Gv WARRS WA4 * 143 J5
Star La LYMM WA13 145 H5
Starling Cl RUNC WA7 178 C6
Starling Gv WD/CROXPK L12 99 K4
Star St TOX L8 132 D3
Startham Av WGNW/BIL/O WN5 77 G6
Starworth Dr PS/BROM CH62 151 H4
Statham Av LYMM WA13 145 H6
WARRN/WOL WA2 123 J5
Statham Cl LYMM WA13 145 J6
Statham Dr LYMM WA13 145 J6
Statham La LYMM WA13 145 G4
Statham Rd CL/PREN CH43 129 K1
SKEL WN8 55 K2
Statham Wy ORM L39 53 J1
Station Ap BRSC L40 38 E4
HOY CH47 127 K1
MOR/LEA CH46 109 J5
ORM L39 * 45 K6
Station Av FROD/HEL WA6 199 J5
GTS/LS CH66 195 F2
Station Cl NSTN CH64 192 A2
Station Gn GTS/LS CH66 195 F2
Station Ms AIMK WN4 78 C6
KKBY L32 * 72 B6
Station Rd AIMK WN4 78 B6
BEB CH63 149 K6
BIRK CH41 111 F6
CHNE CH2 198 B4
CHTN/BK PR9 21 J6
EP CH65 6 E3
GTS/LS CH66 195 F3
HES CH60 180 E1
HOY CH47 127 G3
HUY L36 116 C5
MGHL L31 61 J1
MGHL L31 71 H1
MGHL L31 72 A6
NSTN CH64 191 H1
ORM L39 43 H5
ORM L39 45 K5
PEN/TH CH61 149 H6
PR/KW L34 117 K1
RAIN/WH L35 118 E4
RNFD/HAY WA11 90 B5
RUNC WA7 10 C4
RUNC WA7 188 A3
STHEL WA9 104 C6
STHP PR8 33 J4
WAL/EG CH44 111 G3
WARRS WA4 162 D1
WARRW/BUR WA5 140 E6
WLTN L25 135 J4
Station Rd North
WARRN/WOL WA2 124 C5
Station Rd South
WARRN/WOL WA2 124 C6
Station St RAIN/WH L35 * 118 E4
Station Yd WARRN/WOL WA2 * 143 K1
Statton Rd CLB/OSW/ST L13 115 F6
Staveley Av BRSC L40 38 E5
Staveley Rd ALL/GAR L19 153 J3
SKEL WN8 56 A2
STHP PR8 33 K5
Stavert Cl NG/CROX L11 99 F2
Staverton Rd KKBY L32 84 B2
Stavordale Rd MOR/LEA CH46 129 H1
Steble St TOX L8 132 E4
Steel Av WAL/NB CH45 111 J1
Steel Ct EV L5 112 E2
Steel St WARR WA1 143 H2
Steeplechase Cl WLT/FAZ L9 83 F3
Steeple Ct NSTN CH64 191 K2
The Steeple WKBY CH48 146 E5
Steeple Vw NWD/KWIPK L33 72 D4
Steers Cft STBRV L28 99 K5
Stein Av GOL/RIS/CU WA3 93 F3
Steinberg Ct VAUX/LVPD L3 112 E3
Steley Wy PR/KW L34 117 K2
Stella Prec LITH L21 * 81 H5
Stenhills Crs RUNC WA7 11 H6
Stephens La CLVP L2 * 8 D3
Stephenson Ct EHL/KEN L7 * 114 A6
Stephenson Rd
CLB/OSW/ST L13 * 114 E5
NEWLW WA12 106 C3
Stephenson Wy FMBY L37 49 J2
WAV L15 114 C6
Stephens Ter GTS/LS CH66 194 E3
Stephen St WARR WA1 17 J2
Stephen Wy RAIN/WH L35 * 118 D2
Stepney Gv ANF/KKDL L4 97 J4
Sterling Wy EV L5 113 F1
Sterndale Cl EHL/KEN L7 133 G1
Sterrix Av LITH L21 81 K1
Sterrix Gn LITH L21 81 K1
Sterrix La LITH L21 81 K1
Stetchworth Rd WARRS WA4 162 A2
Steve Biko Cl TOX L8 133 G2
Stevenage Cl STHEL WA9 103 H6
Steven Dr BEB CH63 170 B2
Stevenson Crs ECCL WA10 12 B4
Stevenson Dr BEB CH63 170 B2
Stevenson St WAV L15 134 A1
Stevens Rd HES CH60 168 C6
Stevens St STHEL WA9 103 F5
Steventon RUNC WA7 178 D1
Steward Ct RAIN/WH L35 118 B2
Steward's Av WDN WA8 18 A3
Stewart Av BTL L20 5 J3
Stewart Cl PEN/TH CH61 167 K2
Stewerton Cl GOL/RIS/CU WA3 92 A1
Stile Hey CSBY/BLUN L23 69 J4
Stiles Rd NWD/KWIPK L33 72 E3
The Stiles ORM L39 45 J6
Stillington Rd TOX L8 133 F5
Stiperstones Cl GTS/LS CH66 194 C3
Stirling Av CSBY/BLUN L23 69 F6
Stirling Cl WARR WA1 144 D2
Stirling Crs STHEL WA9 119 K1
Stirling Dr AIMK WN4 78 C5
Stirling Rd SPK/HALE L24 173 G2
Stirling St WAL/EG CH44 111 H5
Stirrup Cl WARRN/WOL WA2 124 C4
Stockbridge La HUY L36 116 C2
Stockbridge Pl EV L5 113 J1
Stockbridge St EV L5 113 J2
Stockdale Cl VAUX/LVPD L3 * 8 D1
Stockham Cl RUNC WA7 177 K5
Stockham La RUNC WA7 178 A6
Stockley Crs ORM L39 64 E1
Stockmoor Rd NG/CROX L11 98 D2
Stockpit Rd NWD/KWIPK L33 85 J1
Stockport Rd WARRS WA4 144 C6
Stocks Av STHEL WA9 104 C2
Stocks La WARRW/BUR WA5 140 E4
Stockswell Rd RAIN/WH L35 137 J5
Stockton Gv STHEL WA9 119 F1
Stockton La WARRS WA4 162 D2
Stockton Wood Rd
SPK/HALE L24 173 H2
Stockville Rd CALD/MH L18 135 F5
Stoddart Rd ANF/KKDL L4 97 J3
Stoke Cl PS/BROM CH62 184 B4
Stoke Gdns EP CH65 6 E7
Stoker Wy WLT/FAZ L9 82 D6
Stokesay CL/PREN CH43 130 A3
Stokesay Ct EP CH65 196 D6
Stokesley Av KKBY L32 84 B1
Stokes St GOL/RIS/CU WA3 125 G2
Stoke St BIRK CH41 * 2 B1
Stoke Wk EP CH65 6 E6
Stonebank Dr NSTN CH64 192 B3
Stonebarn Dr MGHL L31 62 A4
Stone Barn La RUNC WA7 187 J1
Stonebridge La AIN/FAZ L10 83 K5
NG/CROX L11 84 A6
Stoneby Dr WAL/NB CH45 95 G6
Stonechat Cl GOL/RIS/CU WA3 93 F3
NTHLY L27 136 B5
RUNC WA7 187 H2
Stonecroop CALD/MH L18 135 F4
Stonecrop Cl GOL/RIS/CU WA3 124 E3
RUNC WA7 187 J3
Stonecross Dr RAIN/WH L35 119 F6
Stone Cross La North
GOL/RIS/CU WA3 92 D4
Stone Cross La South
GOL/RIS/CU WA3 92 D5
Stonedale Crs NG/CROX L11 99 F1
Stonedale Pk NG/CROX L11 * 98 E1
Stonefield Rd DV/KA/FCH L14 115 K3
Stonegate Dr TOX L8 132 E5
Stonehaven Cl CHLDW L16 135 G1
Stonehaven Dr
WARRN/WOL WA2 124 C4
Stone Hay RAIN/WH L35 117 K4
Stonehey Dr WKBY CH48 146 D2
Stonehey Rd KKBY L32 84 D3
Stonehill Av ANF/KKDL L4 113 K1
BEB CH63 151 F5
Stonehills La RUNC WA7 11 J5
Stonehill St ANF/KKDL L4 113 K1
Stonehouse Ms CALD/MH L18 134 E6
Stonehouse Rd WAL/EG CH44 110 E2
Stonelea RUNC WA7 178 A3
Stoneleigh Cl STHP PR8 33 J5
Stoneleigh Gdns WARRS WA4 163 J2
Stoneleigh Gv RF/TRAN CH42 150 E3
Stone Pit Cl GOL/RIS/CU WA3 93 F2
Stoneridge Ct CL/PREN CH43 * 129 K1
Stone Sq BTL L20 82 B6
Stone St VAUX/LVPD L3 112 D3
Stoneville Rd CLB/OSW/ST L13 114 E3
Stoney Brow SKEL WN8 57 K3
Stoneycroft WD/CROXPK L12 115 F3
Stoneycroft Cl
CLB/OSW/ST L13 114 E2
Stoneycroft Crs
CLB/OSW/ST L13 114 E2
Stoney Hey Rd WAL/NB CH45 95 G6
Stoney Holt RUNC WA7 178 B5
Stoneyhurst Av AIN/FAZ L10 71 F6
Stoney La RAIN/WH L35 118 B3
Stonham Cl GR/UP/WCH CH49 129 F4
Stonyfield NTHTN L30 70 B4
Stonyhurst Cl RNFD/HAY WA11 88 E4
Stonyhurst Rd WLTN L25 154 E2
Stopford St TOX L8 132 E5
Stopgate La NWD/KWIPK L33 73 F3
WLT/FAZ L9 98 B2
Store St BTL L20 97 F4
Storeton Cl CL/PREN CH43 130 D6
Storeton La PEN/TH CH61 168 C1
Storeton Rd RF/TRAN CH42 150 C1
Stormont Rd ALL/GAR L19 153 J4
Storrington Av NG/CROX L11 98 E2
Storrington Heys NG/CROX L11 99 F2
Storrsdale Rd CALD/MH L18 153 J1
Stour Av RAIN/WH L35 118 E4
Stourcliffe Rd WAL/EG CH44 111 G4
Stour Ct EP CH65 6 C1
Stourport Cl
GR/UP/WCH CH49 * 128 D5
Stourton Rd KKBY L32 84 D3
STHP PR8 33 J5
Stourton St WAL/EG CH44 111 J5
Stourvale Rd HLWD L26 * 155 J4
Stowe Av AIN/FAZ L10 83 H1
Stowe Cl WLTN L25 154 E4
Stowell St EHL/KEN L7 9 J6
Stowford Cl NG/CROX L11 99 G3
Strada Wy VAUX/LVPD L3 9 J1
Stradbroke Cl GOL/RIS/CU WA3 93 H4
Strafford Dr BTL L20 5 J3
Straight Length
FROD/HEL WA6 200 B2
Straight Up La CHTN/BK PR9 24 A5
Straker Av EP CH65 195 J3
Strand Av AIMK WN4 79 G5
Strand Rd BTL L20 4 B5
HOY CH47 127 G2
Strand St CLVPS L1 8 C5
The Strand AIMK WN4 79 G5
CLVP L2 8 B4
Strange Rd AIMK WN4 78 C6
Stratford Cl STHP PR8 33 G3
Stratford Rd ALL/GAR L19 153 G3
NSTN CH64 191 J3
Strathallan Cl HES CH60 167 J3
Strathcona Rd WAL/NB CH45 111 H1
WAV L15 133 K2
Strathearn Rd HES CH60 180 E1
Strathlorne Cl RF/TRAN CH42 131 J6
Strathmore Av AIMK WN4 79 F4
Strathmore Dr CSBY/BLUN L23 69 F6
Strathmore Gv STHEL WA9 120 A1
Strathmore Rd NPK/KEN L6 114 A3
Stratton Cl RUNC WA7 188 A1
WAL/NB CH45 111 J1
WLTN L25 154 B1
Stratton Pk WDN WA8 138 E4
Stratton Rd KKBY L32 84 B2
WARRW/BUR WA5 141 J4
Strauss Cl TOX L8 133 G3
Strawberry Cl
GOL/RIS/CU WA3 124 E3
Strawberry Cross
CH/BCN CH1 * 202 E3
Strawberry Dr EP CH65 202 E3
Strawberry La CH/BCN CH1 202 A6
Strawberry Rd NG/CROX L11 98 C3
Streatham Av CALD/MH L18 134 A4
Street Hey La NSTN CH64 183 J5
Stretford Cl NWD/KWIPK L33 72 D4
Stretton Av GOL/RIS/CU WA3 * 92 E4
STHEL WA9 104 D2
WAL/EG CH44 111 G3
WGNW/BIL/O WN5 77 H4
Stretton Cl CL/PREN CH43 130 B6
PS/BROM CH62 184 B4
WD/CROXPK L12 100 A2
Stretton Dr CHTN/BK PR9 23 H5
Stretton Wy RAIN/WH L35 117 H6
Strickland Cl WARRS WA4 163 F4
Strickland St STHEL WA9 13 J2
Stringer Crs WARRS WA4 143 H5
Stringhey Rd WAL/EG CH44 111 J2
Stroma Av EP CH65 203 F3
Stroma Rd CALD/MH L18 153 J2
Stromness Cl
WARRN/WOL WA2 124 D4
Stroud Cl GR/UP/WCH CH49 128 D6
Stuart Av MOR/LEA CH46 109 K6
WLTN L25 155 F4
Stuart Cl MOR/LEA CH46 129 H1
Stuart Crs WGNW/BIL/O WN5 77 G4
Stuart Dr DV/KA/FCH L14 115 J4
WARRS WA4 162 E1
Stuart Gv BTL L20 97 F4
Stuart Rd ANF/KKDL L4 5 K6
CSBY/WL L22 81 F1
ECCL WA10 87 K5
MGHL L31 72 A6
RF/TRAN CH42 131 G6
RUNC WA7 178 A1
Stuart Rd North BTL L20 5 K4
Stubbs La CL/PREN CH43 130 B6
Stub La BRSC L40 46 A1
Studholme St BTL L20 96 E6
Studland Rd WLT/FAZ L9 98 C1
Studley Rd WAL/NB CH45 110 E1
Sturdee Rd CLB/OSW/ST L13 115 F6
Sturgess Cl ORM L39 45 K4
Sturgess St NEWLW WA12 105 K2
Suburban Rd NPK/KEN L6 114 A1
Sudbrook Cl
GOL/RIS/CU WA3 * 93 F3
Sudbury Cl WLTN L25 155 G1
Sudbury Rd CSBY/WL L22 80 C1
Sudbury Wy SPK/HALE L24 173 G1
Sudell Av MGHL L31 62 D5
Sudell La MGHL L31 62 B1
Sudley Gra AIG/SPK L17 153 F2
Sudworth Rd WAL/NB CH45 95 G6
Suez St NEWLW WA12 106 A2
WARR WA1 16 C5
Suffield Rd ANF/KKDL L4 97 F5
Suffolk Av EP CH65 195 J4
Suffolk Cl WARR WA1 144 C3
Suffolk Pl WDN WA8 157 H4
Suffolk Rd STHP PR8 34 C1
Suffolk St BTL L20 5 G2
CLVPS L1 9 F6
RUNC WA7 10 B3
Suffton Pk KKBY L32 84 B2
Sugar La PR/KW L34 100 D2
Sugar Stubbs La CHTN/BK PR9 25 G1
Sugnall St EHL/KEN L7 9 J6
Sulby Av CLB/OSW/ST L13 114 C2
WARRS WA4 142 E6
Sulby Cl STHP PR8 27 G4
Sulgrave Cl CHLDW L16 115 G6
Sullington Dr NTHLY L27 136 B3
Sullivan Av GR/UP/WCH CH49 129 G5
Sullivan's Wy STHEL WA9 103 K5
Sumley Cl RNFD/HAY WA11 89 G6
Summerfield PS/BROM CH62 171 F3
Summerfield Av ECCL WA10 102 B2
WARRW/BUR WA5 123 F5
Summerford Cl RF/TRAN CH42 131 H6
Summerhill Dr MGHL L31 71 J2
Summer La RUNC WA7 177 J4
WARRS WA4 189 G1
Summers Av BTL L20 5 J2
Summer Seat BTL L20 4 B5
VAUX/LVPD L3 112 E3
Summers Rd VAUX/LVPD L3 132 C4
Summer St SKEL WN8 56 B1
Summertrees Av
GR/UP/WCH CH49 128 E5
Summertrees Cl
GR/UP/WCH CH49 128 E5
Summertrees Rd GTS/LS CH66 202 C1
Summerville Gdns
WARRS WA4 162 E2
Summer Wy BTL L20 5 F1
Summerwood PEN/TH CH61 148 A4
Summerwood La ORM L39 44 A2
The Summit WAL/EG CH44 111 J2
Summit Wy WLTN L25 135 G6
Sumner Av ORM L39 51 H1
Sumner Cl EV L5 112 E2
RAIN/WH L35 119 F6
Sumner Gv NWD/KWIPK L33 72 E4
Sumner Rd CL/PREN CH43 130 C1
FMBY L37 49 F2
Sumner St RNFD/HAY WA11 89 K4
Sunbeam Rd CLB/OSW/ST L13 114 E4
Sunbeam St NEWLW WA12 106 C2
Sunbourne Rd AIG/SPK L17 152 C1
Sunbury Dr STHP PR8 33 H5
Sunbury Gdns WARRS WA4 162 D4
Sunbury Rd ANF/KKDL L4 97 K6
WAL/EG CH44 111 J4
Sunbury St ECCL WA10 * 102 E5
Suncroft Cl WARR WA1 144 D2
Suncroft Rd HES CH60 168 C6
Sundale Av RAIN/WH L35 118 B2
Sundew Cl BTL L20 82 C4
Sundridge St TOX L8 * 133 F5
Sunfield Cl GTS/LS CH66 195 G6
Sunfield Rd MOR/LEA CH46 109 K5
Sunflower Cl STHEL WA9 104 E6
Sunlight St NPK/KEN L6 114 A2
Sunloch Cl WLT/FAZ L9 83 G3
Sunningdale Av WDN WA8 157 G2
Sunningdale Cl HUY L36 116 C6
WARRW/BUR WA5 121 K1
Sunningdale Dr BEB CH63 183 J1
CSBY/BLUN L23 68 D3
PEN/TH CH61 148 D6
Sunningdale Gdns FMBY L37 48 E2
Sunningdale Rd WAL/NB CH45 95 F5
WAV L15 134 A1
Sunningdale Wy NSTN CH64 191 K5
Sunny Bank BEB CH63 150 C5
GR/UP/WCH CH49 129 G3
Sunnybank Av CL/PREN CH43 130 A5
Sunnybank Cl NEWLW WA12 106 C1
Sunny Bank Rd CHLDW L16 134 E2
Sunnydale RAIN/WH L35 119 F4
Sunnyfields ORM L39 46 A6
Sunnygate Rd ALL/GAR L19 * 153 H3
Sunnymede Dr MGHL L31 62 B4
Sunny Rd CHTN/BK PR9 23 J3
Sunnyside EP CH65 6 E2
ORM L39 53 G6
STHP PR8 27 G4
TOX L8 133 F4
WARRW/BUR WA5 141 F3
Sunnyside La RUNC WA7 178 D1
Sunnyside Rd AIMK WN4 78 E3
CSBY/WL L22 68 D6
Sunsdale Rd CALD/MH L18 * 134 B4
Sunset Cl NWD/KWIPK L33 73 F4
Superior Cl NTHLY L27 136 B4
Surby Cl CHLDW L16 135 F1
Surrey Av GR/UP/WCH CH49 129 F4
Surrey Dr WKBY CH48 146 D3
Surrey St BTL L20 5 G2
CLVPS L1 8 E7
RUNC WA7 10 D5
WAL/EG CH44 111 G4
WARRS WA4 143 G6
Surridge KNUT WA16 165 K6
Susan Dr WARRW/BUR WA5 140 E4
Susan Gv MOR/LEA CH46 128 E1
Susan St WDN WA8 158 D1
Sussex Cl BTL L20 5 G3
PEN/TH CH61 167 J1
Sussex Gv STHEL WA9 104 A3
Sussex Rd CHTN/BK PR9 15 H5
MGHL L31 62 C3
STHP PR8 28 B1
WKBY CH48 127 H6
Sussex St BTL L20 5 H3
CSBY/WL L22 * 80 D1
WDN WA8 19 J1
Sutch La BRSC L40 39 H5
Sutcliffe St NPK/KEN L6 113 K4
Sutherland Ct RUNC WA7 11 F4
Sutherland Dr PS/BROM CH62 184 A3

Sutherland Rd PR/KW L34 118 A1
Sutton Av NSTN CH64 191 K3
Sutton Cswy FROD/HEL WA6 187 H5
Sutton Cl PS/BROM CH62 184 B4
Sutton Hall Dr GTS/LS CH66 194 D3
Sutton Hall Gdns GTS/LS CH66 194 D3
Sutton Heath Rd STHEL WA9 119 G1
Sutton Moss Rd STHEL WA9 104 D5
Sutton Oak Dr STHEL WA9 104 A4
Sutton Park Dr STHEL WA9 104 A6
Sutton Rd FMBY L37 48 E4
WAL/NB CH45 95 H6
Sutton's La FMBY L37 50 A2
WDN WA8 18 E6
Sutton St CLB/OSW/ST L13 114 C2
RUNC WA7 11 G5
WARR WA1 17 F6
Sutton Wy EP CH65 6 A6
Sutton Wood Rd
SPK/HALE L24 173 H2
Swainson Rd AIN/FAZ L10 83 H4
Swale Av RAIN/WH L35 118 E4
Swaledale Av RAIN/WH L35 119 F4
Swaledale Cl PS/BROM CH62 184 B2
WARRW/BUR WA5 141 G2
Swalegate MGHL L31 62 A5
Swale Rd EP CH65 195 K2
Swallow Cl GOL/RIS/CU WA3 * 125 H3
NTHLY L27 136 C4
NWD/KWIPK L33 72 D2
WD/CROXPK L12 99 K2
Swallow Ct ECCL WA10 12 A5
Swallowfield Gdns
WARRS WA4 162 E6
Swallow Flds WLT/FAZ L9 98 D1
Swallowhurst Crs NG/CROX L11 98 E3
Swanage Cl WARRS WA4 162 D1
Swan Av STHEL WA9 104 E3
Swan Cl GTS/LS CH66 202 A1
Swan Crs WAV L15 134 C1
Swan Delph ORM L39 53 G3
Swan Gdns STHEL WA9 119 G1
Swan Hey MGHL L31 * 71 H2
Swan La ORM L39 62 C1
Swanpool La ORM L39 53 G3
Swan Rd NEWLW WA12 105 J1
Swanside Av DV/KA/FCH L14 115 J4
Swanside Rd DV/KA/FCH L14 115 J4
Swanston Av ANF/KKDL L4 97 J4
Swan St CLB/OSW/ST L13 114 D4
Swan Wk MGHL L31 71 H2
Sweden Gv CSBY/WL L22 * 80 E2
Sweet Briar Ct STHEL WA9 * 120 B4
Sweet Brier Ct STHEL WA9 120 B5
Sweetfield Gdns GTS/LS CH66 195 G2
Sweetfield Rd GTS/LS CH66 195 G2
Sweeting St CLVP L2 8 C4
Swift Cl WARRN/WOL WA2 124 A4
Swift Gv WD/CROXPK L12 99 K1
Swift's Cl NTHTN L30 70 A5
Swifts La NTHTN L30 70 B6
Swift St ECCL WA10 13 H2
Swinbrook Gn NG/CROX L11 98 D3
Swinburne Cl CHLDW L16 135 G1
Swinburne Rd ECCL WA10 12 A2
Swindale Av WARRN/WOL WA2 123 H4
Swindale Cl TOX L8 133 G2
Swinden Cl RUNC WA7 * 178 C3
Swinderby Dr KKBY L32 72 A6
Swindon Cl EV L5 97 F6
GR/UP/WCH CH49 128 D5
Swindon St EV L5 97 F6
Swinford Av WDN WA8 159 F1
Swisspine Gdns STHEL WA9 102 E6
Swiss Rd NPK/KEN L6 114 A4
Sword Wk NG/CROX L11 99 G2
Swynnerton Wy WDN WA8 139 G4
Sybil Rd ANF/KKDL L4 97 J6
Sycamore Av CSBY/BLUN L23 69 G3
GOL/RIS/CU WA3 92 B2
GR/UP/WCH CH49 128 E3
HLWD L26 155 H5
NEWLW WA12 106 C2
RNFD/HAY WA11 89 K6
WDN WA8 158 C1
Sycamore Cl ECCL WA10 102 D1
GR/UP/WCH CH49 128 E2
WLT/FAZ L9 98 A2
Sycamore Dr GTS/LS CH66 202 D2
LYMM WA13 145 J5
RUNC WA7 187 K3
SKEL WN8 56 A3
Sycamore Gdns ECCL WA10 88 B5
Sycamore Gv FMBY L37 48 C4
Sycamore La
WARRW/BUR WA5 141 J4
Sycamore Pk CALD/MH L18 154 A1
Sycamore Ri
GR/UP/WCH CH49 147 K1
Sycamore Rd CSBY/WL L22 81 F1
HUY L36 136 B1
RF/TRAN CH42 131 G5
RUNC WA7 177 F5
Sydenham Av AIG/SPK L17 133 H4
Sydney St RUNC WA7 176 A6
WLT/FAZ L9 82 D5
Syers Ct WARR WA1 143 H1
Sylvan Ct WLTN L25 154 D2
Sylvandale Gv PS/BROM CH62 171 F3
Sylvania Rd ANF/KKDL L4 97 G4
Sylvia Cl NG/CROX L11 84 A5
Sylvia Crs WARRN/WOL WA2 123 K6
Synge St WARRN/WOL WA2 143 F2
Syren St BTL L20 96 E5
Syston Av RNFD/HAY WA11 89 F5
Sytch Cft NSTN CH64 191 K1

T

Tabby Nook KIRK/FR/WA PR4 25 K4
Tabley Av WDN WA8 157 J1
Tabley Cl CL/PREN CH43 130 C6
Tabley Gdns STHEL WA9 119 F1
Tabley Rd WAV L15 133 J2
Tabley St CLVPS L1 8 E7
Tace Cl TOX L8 132 E2
Tadgers La FROD/HEL WA6 186 A6
Tadlow Cl FMBY L37 48 C4
Taggart Av CHLDW L16 134 E3
Tagus Cl TOX L8 133 G3
Tagus St TOX L8 133 G3
Tailor's La MGHL L31 71 H1
Talaton Cl CHTN/BK PR9 20 D6
Talbot Av BEB CH63 169 G4
NSTN CH64 192 A3
Talbot Cl ECCL WA10 12 E4
GOL/RIS/CU WA3 125 G4
NSTN CH64 192 A3
Talbot Ct CL/PREN CH43 130 D5
HUY L36 116 D6
Talbot Dr STHP PR8 14 E6
Talbot Gdns NSTN CH64 192 A3
Talbot Rd CL/PREN CH43 130 D5
GTS/LS CH66 195 J6
Talbot St AIMK WN4 * 79 J5
GOL/RIS/CU WA3 92 B3
STHP PR8 14 D7
Talbotville Rd CLB/OSW/ST L13 115 G6
Talgarth Wy WLTN L25 135 H2
Taliesin St EV L5 113 F2
Talisman Cl RUNC WA7 178 C6
Talisman Wy BTL L20 4 B2
Talland Cl HLWD L26 155 H2
Tallarn Rd KKBY L32 84 A1
Talman Gv AIMK WN4 79 J6
Talton Rd WAV L15 133 J2
Tamar Cl NPK/KEN L6 113 J3
Tamar Gv MOR/LEA CH46 128 E2
Tamarisk Gdns STHEL WA9 102 E6
Tamar Rd RNFD/HAY WA11 90 B5
Tamerton Cl WLTN L25 154 B1
The Tamneys SKEL WN8 56 B4
Tamworth St ECCL WA10 12 C4
TOX L8 132 D4
Tanar Cl PS/BROM CH62 170 D2
Tanat Dr CALD/MH L18 134 C5
Tancred Rd ANF/KKDL L4 97 J6
WAL/NB CH45 111 G2
Tanfields SKEL WN8 56 B4
Tan House La
WARRW/BUR WA5 122 A3
WDN WA8 19 H4
Tanhouse Rd CSBY/BLUN L23 69 J4
SKEL WN8 56 E5
Tankersley Gv
WARRW/BUR WA5 141 H4
Tanner's La GOL/RIS/CU WA3 92 C3
WARRN/WOL WA2 16 C3
Tannery La NSTN CH64 191 K1
WARRW/BUR WA5 140 D6
Tanning Ct WARR WA1 16 E5
Tansley Cl WKBY CH48 147 F1
Tanworth Gv MOR/LEA CH46 109 F6
Tapley Pl CLB/OSW/ST L13 114 D5
Taplow Cl WARRS WA4 162 D5
Taplow St NPK/KEN L6 113 K1
Tarbock Rd HUY L36 116 D6
SPK/HALE L24 173 J1
Tarbot Hey MOR/LEA CH46 128 D1
Target Rd HES CH60 167 F5
Tariff St EV L5 113 F2
Tarleswood SKEL WN8 56 B4
Tarleton Cl HLWD L26 155 H3
Tarleton Rd CHTN/BK PR9 23 J5
Tarleton St CLVPS L1 8 E4
Tarlscough La BRSC L40 31 H6
Tarlton Cl RAIN/WH L35 118 C2
Tarnbeck RUNC WA7 178 B6
Tarn Brow ORM L39 53 G2
Tarn Cl AIMK WN4 79 G4
Tarn Ct WARR WA1 144 E2
Tarn Gv RNFD/HAY WA11 88 E3
Tarn Rd FMBY L37 48 D2
Tarnway GOL/RIS/CU WA3 93 G4
Tarporley Cl CL/PREN CH43 130 C6
Tarporley Rd GTS/LS CH66 195 H5
Tarran Dr MOR/LEA CH46 109 H5
Tarran Rd MOR/LEA CH46 109 H5
Tarran Wy East
MOR/LEA CH46 109 H5
Tarran Wy North
MOR/LEA CH46 109 H5
Tarran Wy South
MOR/LEA CH46 109 H5
Tarran Wy West
MOR/LEA CH46 109 H4
Tarvin Cl CHTN/BK PR9 21 G6
EP CH65 6 E7
GOL/RIS/CU WA3 93 F4
RUNC WA7 187 F1
STHEL WA9 119 K3
Tarvin Rd FROD/HEL WA6 200 C6
PS/BROM CH62 184 C3
Tasker Ter RAIN/WH L35 118 E3
Tasman Cl WARRW/BUR WA5 141 K1
Tasman Gv STHEL WA9 103 G6
Tate Cl WDN WA8 * 157 J1
Tate St ANF/KKDL L4 97 H5
Tatlock Cl WGNW/BIL/O WN5 77 H4
Tatlock St EV L5 112 E3
Tattersall Rd LITH L21 81 H4
Tattersall Wy EHL/KEN L7 114 C5
Tatton Ct WARR WA1 * 144 C1
Tatton Dr AIMK WN4 78 E5
Tatton Rd RF/TRAN CH42 2 D7
WLT/FAZ L9 82 D5
Taunton Av STHEL WA9 120 B2
Taunton Dr AIN/FAZ L10 83 H1
Taunton Rd HUY L36 117 H5
WAL/NB CH45 110 E1
Taunton St WAV L15 133 K1
Taurus Pk WARRW/BUR WA5 122 D3
Taurus Rd DV/KA/FCH L14 116 A3
Tavener Cl BEB CH63 183 K2
Tavistock Dr STHP PR8 33 H3
Tavistock Rd WAL/NB CH45 110 E1
WARRW/BUR WA5 141 F5
Tavlin Av WARRW/BUR WA5 123 F6
Tavy Rd NPK/KEN L6 113 J3
Tawd Rd SKEL WN8 56 E5
Tawd St ANF/KKDL L4 97 G5
Tawny Ct RUNC WA7 177 H6
Tayleur Ter NEWLW WA12 * 106 D3
Taylor Av ORM L39 46 A6
Taylor Cl STHEL WA9 104 C5
Taylor Rd RNFD/HAY WA11 90 E5
Taylors Cl WLT/FAZ L9 97 H2
Taylor's La BTL L20 97 G2
WARRW/BUR WA5 159 H1
Taylors Rw RUNC WA7 11 J5
Taylor St BIRK CH41 3 G2
EV L5 113 F2
SKEL WN8 55 J4
STHEL WA9 104 C5
WARRS WA4 161 K2
WDN WA8 19 G1
Teakwood Cl NPK/KEN L6 113 K2
Teal Cl ORM L39 53 G3
RNFD/HAY WA11 88 E5
WARRN/WOL WA2 124 A4
Teal Gv GOL/RIS/CU WA3 125 H4
HLWD L26 155 H2
Teals Wy HES CH60 167 H5
Teasville Rd CALD/MH L18 135 F5
Tebay Cl MGHL L31 62 D5
Tebay Rd PS/BROM CH62 171 G5
Teck St EHL/KEN L7 113 J5
Tedburn Cl WLTN L25 135 K5
Tedbury Cl KKBY L32 84 D4
Tedbury Wk KKBY L32 84 D3
Tedder Av CHTN/BK PR9 23 J6
Tedder Sq WDN WA8 157 J3
Teddington Cl WARRS WA4 162 D6
Teehey Cl BEB CH63 150 C5
Teehey Gdns BEB CH63 150 C5
Teehey La BEB CH63 150 C5
Tees Cl ANF/KKDL L4 97 F4
Tees Ct EP CH65 195 K2
Teesdale Rd BEB CH63 170 A1
RNFD/HAY WA11 90 B4
Tees Pl ANF/KKDL L4 97 F4
Tees St ANF/KKDL L4 97 F4
BIRK CH41 111 F6
Teilo St TOX L8 133 F4
Telary Cl EV L5 112 E2
Telegraph Rd WKBY CH48 147 H5
Telford Cl CL/PREN CH43 130 E5
WDN WA8 138 C5
Telford Rd EP CH65 7 H7
Tempest Hey CLVP L2 8 C3
Temple Ct CLVP L2 8 D4
GOL/RIS/CU WA3 125 G1
Temple La CLVP L2 8 D3
Templemore Av CALD/MH L18 134 B6
Templemore Rd
CL/PREN CH43 130 D5
Temple Rd RF/TRAN CH42 150 B1
Temple St CLVP L2 * 8 D3
Templeton Crs WD/CROXPK L12 99 F4
Tenbury Cl WARRW/BUR WA5 122 A6
Tenbury Dr AIMK WN4 78 E5
Tenby Av LITH L21 81 H2
Tenby Cl WARRW/BUR WA5 123 F5
Tenby Dr MOR/LEA CH46 129 G2
RUNC WA7 177 G3
Tenby St EV L5 113 J1
Tennis St ECCL WA10 12 B2
Tennis St North ECCL WA10 12 C1
Tennyson Av RF/TRAN CH42 * 150 E2
Tennyson Dr ORM L39 45 H5
WARRN/WOL WA2 123 J5
Tennyson Rd EP CH65 6 A6
HUY L36 136 D1
WDN WA8 18 C1
Tennyson St BTL L20 4 C1
STHEL WA9 119 J5
Tensing Cl WARRW/BUR WA5 141 J1
Tensing Rd MGHL L31 62 B6
Tenterden St EV L5 * 113 F3
Tenth Av WLT/FAZ L9 83 G4
Terence Av WARR WA1 143 J2
Terence Rd CHLDW L16 134 E3
Terminus Rd HUY L36 116 B2
PS/BROM CH62 171 F2
Tern Cl NWD/KWIPK L33 72 D2
WDN WA8 139 G5
Ternhall Rd WLT/FAZ L9 98 D1
Ternhall Wy WLT/FAZ L9 98 D1
Tern Wy MOR/LEA CH46 109 F6
PR/KW L34 102 C6
Terrace Rd WDN WA8 158 B6
Terret Cft STBRV L28 100 B6
Tetbury St BIRK CH41 2 C6
Tetchill Cl GTS/LS CH66 202 B1
RUNC WA7 178 C5
Tetlow St ANF/KKDL L4 97 H5
Tetlow Wy ANF/KKDL L4 97 H5
Teversham SKEL WN8 56 B3
Tewit Hall Cl SPK/HALE L24 173 H2
Tewit Hall Rd SPK/HALE L24 173 H2
Tewkesbury SKEL WN8 * 56 A3
Tewkesbury Cl GTS/LS CH66 202 C4
WD/CROXPK L12 99 K1
WLTN L25 155 F1
Tewkesbury Rd
GOL/RIS/CU WA3 92 C3
Teynham Av PR/KW L34 100 D1
Teynham Crs NG/CROX L11 98 D3
Thackeray Cl TOX L8 * 132 E3
Thackeray Gdns NTHTN L30 82 A3
Thackeray Pl TOX L8 132 E3
Thackeray Sq TOX L8 132 E3
Thackeray St TOX L8 132 E3
Thackray Rd ECCL WA10 102 E5
Thamesdale EP CH65 6 B7
Thames Gdns EP CH65 195 K6
Thames Rd STHEL WA9 120 A1
Thames Side EP CH65 196 A6
Thames St TOX L8 133 G3
Thanet SKEL WN8 56 B3
Thatto Heath Rd ECCL WA10 103 F5
Thealby Cl SKEL WN8 56 A3
Thelwall La WARRS WA4 143 K6
Thelwall New Rd WARRS WA4 144 A6
Thelwall Rd GTS/LS CH66 195 H5
Thermal Rd PS/BROM CH62 171 F1
Thetford Rd WARRW/BUR WA5 141 F3
The Uplands RUNC WA7 177 J6
Thewlis St WARRW/BUR WA5 142 B4
Thickwood Moss La
RNFD/HAY WA11 75 G4
Thingwall Av DV/KA/FCH L14 115 H5
Thingwall Dr PEN/TH CH61 148 D5
Thingwall Hall Dr
DV/KA/FCH L14 115 H5
Thingwall La DV/KA/FCH L14 115 H4
Thingwall Rd PEN/TH CH61 148 C5
WAV L15 134 C1
Thingwall Rd East
PEN/TH CH61 148 D5
Third Av CL/PREN CH43 129 J3
CSBY/BLUN L23 * 68 E5
RUNC WA7 177 J6
WLT/FAZ L9 83 H4
Thirlemere Av AIMK WN4 79 H5
CL/PREN CH43 129 K3
FMBY L37 49 G3
LITH L21 82 A3
RNFD/HAY WA11 88 E3
SKEL WN8 57 K6
WARRN/WOL WA2 123 J4
Thirlmere Cl FROD/HEL WA6 201 G1
MGHL L31 62 C5
Thirlmere Dr LITH L21 82 A3
STHP PR8 33 H6
WAL/NB CH45 111 H2
Thirlmere Gn EV L5 113 J2
Thirlmere Ms HTWN L38 * 59 G3
Thirlmere Rd EP CH65 203 G1
EV L5 113 J2
GOL/RIS/CU WA3 92 D2
HTWN L38 59 G3
NSTN CH64 191 K3
Thirlmere Wk NWD/KWIPK L33 72 C5
Thirlmere Wy WDN WA8 157 G3
Thirlstane St AIG/SPK L17 133 G6
Thirsk SKEL WN8 56 A3
Thirsk Cl RUNC WA7 187 F1
Thistledown Cl AIG/SPK L17 133 F6
Thistleton Av BIRK CH41 130 C1
Thistleton Ms CHTN/BK PR9 15 H3
Thistlewood Rd EHL/KEN L7 114 C5
Thistley Hey Rd KKBY L32 84 E1
Thomas Cl ALL/GAR L19 153 K6
EP CH65 203 F1
Thomas Ct RUNC WA7 177 J6
Thomas Dr DV/KA/FCH L14 115 G5
RAIN/WH L35 117 J3
Thomas La DV/KA/FCH L14 115 H4
Thomasons Bridge La
WARRS WA4 161 H5
Thomas St BIRK CH41 3 G6
GOL/RIS/CU WA3 92 B3
RUNC WA7 11 F3
WDN WA8 18 C6
Thomaston St EV L5 113 G1
Thomas Winder Ct EV L5 * 113 F1
Thompson Av ORM L39 46 A6
Thompson St AIMK WN4 79 J5
BIRK CH41 131 H5
ECCL WA10 103 F4
GOL/RIS/CU WA3 125 G2
Thomson Rd LITH L21 81 H4
Thomson St NPK/KEN L6 113 K3
Thorburn Cl RF/TRAN CH42 151 G3
Thorburn Crs PS/BROM CH62 151 G3
Thorburn Rd PS/BROM CH62 151 G3
Thorburn St EHL/KEN L7 113 K6
Thorley Cl WAV L15 114 E6
Thornaby Gv STHEL WA9 119 F1
Thornbeck Av HTWN L38 59 F4
Thornbeck Ct WD/CROXPK L12 99 K2
Thornbridge Av BRSC L40 38 E6
LITH L21 82 A3
Thornbrook Cl WD/CROXPK L12 99 H6
Thornbury SKEL WN8 56 B3
Thornbury Av GOL/RIS/CU WA3 93 F4
Thornbury Rd ANF/KKDL L4 98 A6
Thornbush Cl GOL/RIS/CU WA3 93 F2
Thorncliffe Rd WAL/EG CH44 111 G4
Thorn Cl RUNC WA7 177 F6
WARRW/BUR WA5 141 G6
Thorncroft Dr PEN/TH CH61 168 B1
Thorndale Rd CSBY/WL L22 80 E1
Thorndyke Cl RAIN/WH L35 119 G6
Thorne Dr GTS/LS CH66 194 E5
Thornes Rd NPK/KEN L6 113 K4
Thorness Cl
GR/UP/WCH CH49 * 147 K1
Thorneycroft St BIRK CH41 130 D1
Thornfield Cl GOL/RIS/CU WA3 92 D3
Thornfield Hey BEB CH63 170 C3
Thornfield Rd CSBY/BLUN L23 69 H3
WLT/FAZ L9 82 C6
Thornham Av STHEL WA9 104 A5
Thornham Cl
GR/UP/WCH CH49 129 H2
Thornhead La WD/CROXPK L12 115 H1
Thornhill ORM L39 53 F4
Thornhill Rd AIMK WN4 78 B5
WAV L15 134 B2
Thornholme Crs NG/CROX L11 98 E4
Thornhurst KKBY L32 84 D4
Thornleigh Av PS/BROM CH62 184 C4
Thornleigh Dr GTS/LS CH66 195 H3
Thornley Rd LYMM WA13 145 H6
MOR/LEA CH46 128 C2
Thorn Rd ECCL WA10 102 E2
RUNC WA7 177 F6
WARR WA1 143 K1
Thorns Dr GR/UP/WCH CH49 147 K1
The Thorns MGHL L31 61 K5
Thornton WDN WA8 * 157 K3
Thornton Av BEB CH63 150 C3
BTL L20 82 A5
Thornton Cl AIMK WN4 78 E5
Thornton Common Rd
BEB CH63 169 H6
Thornton Crs HES CH60 181 G1
Thorntondale Dr
WARRW/BUR WA5 141 G2
Thornton Gv BEB CH63 150 B3
Thornton Rd BEB CH63 150 C3
BTL L20 5 F1
CHLDW L16 115 J6
CHTN/BK PR9 23 K6
EP CH65 7 H7
WAL/NB CH45 111 G1
WARRW/BUR WA5 141 J5
Thornton St BIRK CH41 130 D1
LITH L21 81 J5
Thorntree Cl AIG/SPK L17 133 F6
Thorntree Gn WARRS WA4 163 G6
Thornwood SKEL WN8 56 B3
Thornwood Cl NPK/KEN L6 113 K2
Thornwythe Gv GTS/LS CH66 195 H5
Thornycroft Rd WAV L15 133 J3
Thoroughgood Cl BRSC L40 46 D1
Thorpe SKEL WN8 56 B3
Thorpe Bank RF/TRAN CH42 150 E3
Thorstone Dr PEN/TH CH61 147 K4
Thorsway RF/TRAN CH42 150 E1
WKBY CH48 146 E3
Three Butt La WD/CROXPK L12 114 D1
Three Oaks Cl BRSC L40 47 H1
Three Pools CHTN/BK PR9 24 A2
Three Sisters Rd AIMK WN4 79 G3
Three Tuns La FMBY L37 49 F2
Threlfalls La CHTN/BK PR9 23 H3
Threlfall St TOX L8 133 F5
Thresher Av
GR/UP/WCH CH49 * 128 D5
The Threshers NTHTN L30 * 70 E5
Throne Rd NG/CROX L11 99 G2
Thurcroft Dr SKEL WN8 56 A3
Thurlby Cl AIMK WN4 79 J5
Thurlow GOL/RIS/CU WA3 93 F4
Thurne Wy WLTN L25 135 H3
Thurnham St NPK/KEN L6 114 A2
Thursby Cl KKBY L32 84 E3
STHP PR8 33 H6
Thursby Crs KKBY L32 84 E3
Thursby Rd PS/BROM CH62 171 G3
Thurstaston Rd HES CH60 167 J4
PEN/TH CH61 147 J5
Thurston SKEL WN8 56 A3
Thurston Cl WARRW/BUR WA5 142 A3
Thurston Rd ANF/KKDL L4 113 K1
Thynne St WARR WA1 16 B6
Tibbs Cross La WDN WA8 120 B6
Tichbourne Wy NPK/KEN L6 9 K1
Tickle Av STHEL WA9 104 B2
Tidal La WARRN/WOL WA2 143 J1
Tideswell Cl EHL/KEN L7 133 G1
Tide Wy WAL/NB CH45 94 E5
Tilbrook Dr STHEL WA9 120 B1
Tilbury Pl RUNC WA7 188 D1
Tilcroft SKEL WN8 56 A3
Tildsley Crs RUNC WA7 186 C1
Tilley St WARR WA1 17 F3
Tillotson Cl TOX L8 132 D4
Tilman Cl WARRW/BUR WA5 141 J1
Tilney St WLT/FAZ L9 82 D5
Tilstock Av PS/BROM CH62 151 G3
Tilstock Cl HLWD L26 155 K1
Tilstock Crs CL/PREN CH43 149 J2
Tilston Av WARRS WA4 143 K5
Tilston Cl WLT/FAZ L9 98 B2
Tilston Rd KKBY L32 84 B1
WAL/NB CH45 111 G1
WLT/FAZ L9 98 B1
Timberscombe Gdns
WARR WA1 144 D3
Time Pk RAIN/WH L35 118 B2
Timmis Cl WARRN/WOL WA2 124 C4
Timms Crs WDN WA8 18 C2
Timms Cl FMBY L37 41 F6
Timms La FMBY L37 41 F6
Timon Av BTL L20 5 J2
Timor Av STHEL WA9 103 G5
Timperley Av WARRS WA4 143 K5
Timperley St WDN WA8 * 18 E4
Timpron St EHL/KEN L7 133 H1
Timway Dr WD/CROXPK L12 99 J5
Tinas Wy GR/UP/WCH CH49 129 H4
Tinling Cl PR/KW L34 118 A1
Tinsley Av STHP PR8 28 B4
Tinsley's La STHP PR8 28 C6
Tinsley St ANF/KKDL L4 97 J6
WARRS WA4 143 J6
Tintagel SKEL WN8 55 K3
Tintagel Cl RUNC WA7 188 B1
Tintagel Rd NG/CROX L11 84 C6
Tintern Av AIMK WN4 79 J6
Tintern Cl WARRW/BUR WA5 * 122 E5
Tintern Dr FMBY L37 49 H3
MOR/LEA CH46 129 F1
Tiptree Cl WD/CROXPK L12 99 K1
Titchfield St EV L5 112 E3
Tithebarn Cl HES CH60 * 167 K6
Tithebarn Dr NSTN CH64 181 G5
Tithebarn Gv WAV L15 134 B2
Tithe Barn La KKBY L32 84 C2
Tithebarn La MGHL L31 71 K4
Tithebarn Rd AIMK WN4 90 B1
CSBY/BLUN L23 69 G4
PR/KW L34 100 D1
STHP PR8 15 K6
Tithebarn St CLVP L2 8 C3
SKEL WN8 * 57 K6

The Tithings RUNC WA7 ....177 H4
Tiverton Av SKEL WN8 ....56 A3
WAL/EG CH44 ....111 H3
Tiverton Cl HUY L36 ....117 H5
WDN WA8 ....138 B6
Tiverton Rd HLWD L26 ....155 H5
Tiverton Sq WARRW/BUR WA5 ..141 F5
Tiverton St WAV L15 ....133 K1
Tobermory Cl RNFD/HAY WA11....89 K6
Tobin Cl EV L5 ....112 E3
Tobin St WAL/EG CH44 ....111 K3
Tobruk Rd HUY L36 ....116 D3
Todd Rd STHEL WA9 ....13 J6
Todd's La CHTN/BK PR9 ....21 K5
Toft Cl WDN WA8 ....18 A2
Toft St EHL/KEN L7 ....114 A5
Toftwood Av RAIN/WH L35 ....119 G6
Tokenspire Pk
NWD/KWIPK L33 * 85 G4
Toll Bar Rd WARRN/WOL WA2 ....123 G4
Tollemache Rd BIRK CH41 ....130 B1
Tollemache St WAL/NB CH45 ....95 J5
Tollerton Rd WD/CROXPK L12 ....114 D1
Tollgate Rd BRSC L40 ....38 B6
Tolpuddle Rd WLTN L25 ....135 G6
Tolpuddle Wy ANF/KKDL L4 ....97 F5
Tolver St ECCL WA10 ....13 H4
Tomlinson Av
WARRN/WOL WA2 ....143 G1
Tom Mann Cl VAUX/LVPD L3 ....9 F2
Tonbridge Cl SPK/HALE L24 ....173 G1
Tonbridge Dr AIN/FAZ L10 ....71 G6
Tongbarn SKEL WN8 ....56 A3
Toothill Cl AIMK WN4 ....79 G4
Top Acre Rd SKEL WN8 ....56 E6
Topaz Cl ANF/KKDL L4 ....5 K7
Topcliffe Gv WD/CROXPK L12 ....100 A2
Top Delph ORM L39 ....46 A5
Topgate Cl HES CH60 ....168 B5
Topham Dr WLT/FAZ L9 ....82 E1
Topping Ct GOL/RIS/CU WA3 ....124 D3
Top Rd FROD/HEL WA6 ....201 G4
Topsham Cl WLTN L25 ....135 K5
Torcross Cl CHTN/BK PR9 ....20 D6
Torcross Wy HLWD L26 ....155 H3
WLTN L25 ....135 K5
Tordelow Cl NPK/KEN L6 ....113 J3
Toronto Cl HUY L36 ....116 D1
Toronto St WAL/EG CH44 ....112 A4
Torquay Dr WGNW/BIL/O WN5 ....77 H1
Torridon Gv GTS/LS CH66 ....195 J6
Torrington Dr HLWD L26 ....155 H5
PEN/TH CH61 ....148 E5
Torrington Gdns PEN/TH CH61 ..148 E4
Torrington Rd ALL/GAR L19 ....153 J4
WAL/EG CH44 ....111 G3
Torrisholme Rd WLT/FAZ L9 ....98 B2
Torr St EV L5 ....113 G1
Torus Rd CLB/OSW/ST L13 ....114 E3
Tor View Rd WAV L15 ....134 B3
Torwood CL/PREN CH43 ....130 A2
Tothale Turn NTHLY L27 ....136 C5
Totland Cl WARRW/BUR WA5 ....140 D2
Totnes Av HLWD L26 ....155 J2
Totnes Dr CHTN/BK PR9 ....20 D6
Totnes Rd NG/CROX L11 ....84 B6
Tourney Gn WARRW/BUR WA5 ..122 A5
Towcester St LITH L21 ....81 J5
Tower Buildings CHTN/BK PR9 *..15 G2
Tower End FMBY L37 ....40 C6
Tower Gdns VAUX/LVPD L3 ....8 B4
Tower Hl ORM L39 ....46 A6
RF/TRAN CH42 ....131 G6
Tower Hill Rd SKEL WN8 ....67 J2
Tower La LYMM WA13 ....165 G1
RUNC WA7 ....178 B6
Tower Nook SKEL WN8 ....67 J2
Tower Prom WAL/NB CH45 ....95 J4
Tower Quays BIRK CH41 * 3 F1
Tower Rd BIRK CH41 ....3 F1
RF/TRAN CH42 * 131 G6
Tower Rd North HES CH60 ....167 J3
Tower Rd South HES CH60 ....167 K4
Towers Av MGHL L31 ....62 A5
Towers Rd CHLDW L16 ....134 D3
The Towers RF/TRAN CH42 * 150 C1
Tower St VAUX/LVPD L3 ....132 C4
Tower Wy WLTN L25 ....135 H6
Tower Whf BIRK CH41 ....3 F1
Towneley Ct WDN WA8 ....18 C2
Townfield Av AIMK WN4 ....91 G1
Townfield Cl CL/PREN CH43 ....130 B6
Townfield Gdns BEB CH63 ....150 E4
Townfield La BEB CH63 ....150 E5
CL/PREN CH43 ....130 C6
FROD/HEL WA6 ....201 F2
Townfield Rd RUNC WA7 * 178 B3
WARRN/WOL WA2 * 123 F3
WKBY CH48 ....146 C1
Townfields AIMK WN4 ....79 F6
Townfield Vw RUNC WA7 ....178 B3
Town Green La ORM L39 ....53 G5
Town Hl WARR WA1 ....16 D4
Town La BEB CH63 ....150 D5
NSTN CH64 ....192 A3
SPK/HALE L24 ....174 E4
STHP PR8 ....28 B4
Town La (Kew) STHP PR8 ....27 K4
Town Meadow La
MOR/LEA CH46 ....109 G6
Town Rd RF/TRAN CH42 ....131 G6
Town Rw WD/CROXPK L12 ....99 F6
Townsend Av NG/CROX L11 ....98 C3
Townsend La NPK/KEN L6 ....98 A6
Townsend St BIRK CH41 ....110 E6
EV L5 ....112 D1
Townsend Vw LITH L21 ....81 J1
NG/CROX L11 ....98 C2
Townshend Av PEN/TH CH61 ....148 A6
Town Sq RUNC WA7 * 177 J6
Town Vw CL/PREN CH43 ....2 B6
Town Wk RUNC WA7 * 177 J6
Towson St EV L5 ....113 H1
Toxteth Gv TOX L8 ....133 F5
Toxteth St TOX L8 ....132 E4
Tracy Dr NEWLW WA12 ....106 E2
Trafalgar Av WAL/EG CH44 ....111 K2
Trafalgar Ct WDN WA8 ....158 B5
Trafalgar Dr BEB CH63 ....170 C1
Trafalgar Rd STHP PR8 ....27 F5
WAL/EG CH44 ....111 J2
Trafalgar St ECCL WA10 ....12 C3
Trafalgar Wy NPK/KEN L6 ....9 K1
Trafford Av WARRW/BUR WA5 ..142 B1
Trafford Crs RUNC WA7 ....187 F1
Tragan Dr WARRW/BUR WA5 ....140 E6
Tramway Rd AIG/SPK L17 ....133 H6
Trans Pennine Trail
CHLDW L16 ....135 G2
CLVPS L1 ....8 D5
MGHL L31 ....70 E3
TOX L8 ....133 G4
WARRW/BUR WA5 ....160 A2
WD/CROXPK L12 ....115 G3
WDN WA8 ....158 B6
WDN WA8 ....175 H2
WLT/FAZ L9 ....82 E6
Trap Hl FMBY L37 ....48 C4
Trapwood Cl ECCL WA10 ....102 D2
Travandon Cl NG/CROX L11 * 84 A5
Travers' Entry STHEL WA9 ....120 E1
Traverse St STHEL WA9 ....104 A2
Travis St WDN WA8 ....18 E3
Treborth St TOX L8 ....133 F4
Trecastle Rd NWD/KWIPK L33 ....73 F5
Tree Bank Cl RUNC WA7 ....176 D5
Treen Cl CHTN/BK PR9 ....20 E5
Treesdale Cl STHP PR8 ....27 G3
Tree Tops NSTN CH64 ....191 K4
Treetops Cl WARR WA1 ....143 J2
Treetops Dr BIRK CH41 ....110 D6
Treetop Vls CHTN/BK PR9 * 23 H1
Trefoil Cl GOL/RIS/CU WA3 ....124 E2
Treforris Rd WAL/NB CH45 ....95 F6
Trefula Pk WD/CROXPK L12 ....114 E1
Trelawney Cl WLTN L25 ....135 J3
Tremore Cl NG/CROX L11 ....99 G4
Trenance Cl RUNC WA7 ....188 A2
Trendeal Rd NG/CROX L11 ....84 C6
Trent Av DV/KA/FCH L14 ....115 K5
MGHL L31 ....62 D5
Trent Cl BRSC L40 ....39 F4
RAIN/WH L35 ....118 D4
STHEL WA9 ....120 A2
WD/CROXPK L12 ....99 H2
WDN WA8 ....139 G5
Trentdale EP CH65 ....196 A6
Trentham Av CALD/MH L18 ....134 A4
Trentham Cl WDN WA8 ....139 G5
Trentham Rd KKBY L32 ....84 B2
WAL/EG CH44 ....111 J4
Trentham St RUNC WA7 ....10 B3
Trent Rd AIMK WN4 ....79 K4
RAIN/WH L35 ....118 D4
WGNW/BIL/O WN5 ....77 F5
Trent St EV L5 ....112 E1
Trent Wy HES CH60 ....181 G1
LITH L21 ....81 H2
Tresham Dr WARRS WA4 ....163 F3
Tressel Dr STHEL WA9 ....119 J4
Tressell St WLT/FAZ L9 ....97 H2
Trevelyan St WLT/FAZ L9 ....97 H2
Treviot Cl NWD/KWIPK L33 ....72 C3
Trevor Dr CSBY/BLUN L23 ....69 G6
Trevor Rd BRSC L40 ....38 E5
STHP PR8 ....33 J5
WLT/FAZ L9 ....82 D5
The Triad BTL L20 ....4 E3
Trident Pk RUNC WA7 * 177 H6
Trimley Cl GR/UP/WCH CH49 ....129 F4
Tring Cl GR/UP/WCH CH49 ....129 H2
Trinity Ct GOL/RIS/CU WA3 ....125 H2
Trinity Gdns AIMK WN4 ....78 E5
STHP PR8 ....14 D7
Trinity Gv CSBY/BLUN L23 ....80 C1
Trinity La BIRK CH41 ....3 F3
Trinity Ms CHTN/BK PR9 ....15 H4
Trinity Pl BTL L20 ....5 G5
WDN WA8 ....18 E5
Trinity Rd BTL L20 ....4 E6
HOY CH47 ....127 G2
WAL/EG CH44 ....111 H2
Trinity St BIRK CH41 ....2 C3
STHEL WA9 ....104 A1
Trinity Wk VAUX/LVPD L3 ....9 H1
Trispen Cl HLWD L26 ....155 H3
Trispen Rd NG/CROX L11 ....99 H1
Triumph Wy SPK/HALE L24 ....154 C5
Triam Rd BTL L20 ....4 C3
Troon Cl BEB CH63 ....183 K2
RNFD/HAY WA11 ....89 K6
WD/CROXPK L12 ....115 J1
Trossach Cl WARRN/WOL WA2 ....124 A5
Trotwood Cl WLT/FAZ L9 ....83 G3
Troutbeck Av MGHL L31 ....62 C5
NEWLW WA12 ....105 J1
WARRW/BUR WA5 ....142 C2
Troutbeck Cl
GR/UP/WCH CH49 ....148 D1
RUNC WA7 ....187 K2
Troutbeck Gv RNFD/HAY WA11 ....88 E1
Troutbeck Rd AIMK WN4 ....79 H4
CALD/MH L18 ....134 E4
Trouville Rd ANF/KKDL L4 ....98 A6
Trowbridge St VAUX/LVPD L3 ....9 H4
Trueman Cl CL/PREN CH43 ....129 K1
Trueman St VAUX/LVPD L3 ....8 E2
Trumans La GTS/LS CH66 ....195 F2
Trundle Pie La ORM L39 ....44 A5
Truro Av CHTN/BK PR9 ....20 E6
NTHTN L30 ....70 C5
Truro Cl GTS/LS CH66 ....202 D3
RNFD/HAY WA11 ....89 G4
RUNC WA7 ....188 B1
WARR WA1 ....144 A1
Truro Rd WAV L15 ....134 B3
Truscott Rd BRSC L40 ....38 D5
Tudor Av BEB CH63 ....170 C2
WAL/EG CH44 ....112 A5
Tudor Cl EHL/KEN L7 ....9 K5
GTS/LS CH66 ....202 D3
RNFD/HAY WA11 ....75 F1
WARRS WA4 ....163 F1
Tudor Ct WARRS WA4 * 162 D2
Tudor Gra GR/UP/WCH CH49 ....128 E6
Tudor Rd CSBY/BLUN L23 ....68 E6
RF/TRAN CH42 ....131 H6
RUNC WA7 ....178 A2
STHP PR8 ....33 H3
WLTN L25 ....155 F4
Tudor St NPK/KEN L6 ....113 K4
Tudor Vw NWD/KWIPK L33 ....72 D4
Tudorville Rd BEB CH63 ....150 E6
Tudorway HES CH60 ....168 B5
Tue La WDN WA8 ....138 A3
Tuffins Cnr NTHLY L27 ....136 A4
Tulip Av BIRK CH41 ....130 C1
Tulip Rd RNFD/HAY WA11 ....90 E5
WAV L15 ....134 B2
Tulketh St STHP PR8 ....15 F5
Tullimore Rd CALD/MH L18 ....153 H2
Tullis St ECCL WA10 ....12 D7
Tulloch St NPK/KEN L6 ....113 K4
Tully Av NEWLW WA12 ....105 J2
Tumilty Av BTL L20 ....5 J2
Tunbridge Cl
WARRW/BUR WA5 ....141 H1
Tunnel Rd BIRK CH41 ....3 H6
EHL/KEN L7 ....133 G1
Tunnel Top North WARRS WA4 ..189 F3
Tunstall Cl GR/UP/WCH CH49 ....129 F4
Tunstall St EHL/KEN L7 ....133 H2
Tunstall's Wy STHEL WA9 ....120 B3
Tupelo Cl WD/CROXPK L12 ....99 K1
Tupman St TOX L8 ....132 E4
Turmar Av PEN/TH CH61 ....148 E5
Turnacre DV/KA/FCH L14 ....115 J4
FMBY L37 ....41 H5
Turnall Rd WDN WA8 ....157 G4
Turnberry SKEL WN8 ....55 K3
Turnberry Cl HUY L36 ....116 C6
LYMM WA13 ....145 H5
MOR/LEA CH46 ....109 F6
WD/CROXPK L12 ....115 K1
Turnberry Wy CHTN/BK PR9 ....21 G6
Turnbridge Rd MGHL L31 ....62 A4
Turner Av BTL L20 ....82 B5
Turner Cl WDN WA8 ....138 C6
Turner Gv NWD/KWIPK L33 ....72 D3
Turner St BIRK CH41 ....2 C7
Turney Rd WAL/EG CH44 ....111 G3
Turnill Dr AIMK WN4 ....91 G1
Turning La STHP PR8 ....35 J1
Turnpike Rd ORM L39 ....52 E4
Turnstone Av NEWLW WA12 ....106 C1
Turnstone Cl WD/CROXPK L12 ....99 J2
Turnstone Dr HLWD L26 ....155 H2
Turret Hall Dr GOL/RIS/CU WA3 ..93 F3
Turret Rd WAL/NB CH45 ....111 G1
Turriff Dr BEB CH63 ....183 K3
Turriff Rd DV/KA/FCH L14 ....116 A3
Turrocks Cl NSTN CH64 ....191 K4
Turrocks Cft NSTN CH64 ....191 K4
Turton Cl GOL/RIS/CU WA3 ....124 E2
Turton St EV L5 * 113 F1
GOL/RIS/CU WA3 ....92 B3
Tuscan Cl WDN WA8 ....139 G4
Tuson Dr WDN WA8 ....138 E5
Tutor Bank NEWLW WA12 ....106 D2
Tweed Cl NPK/KEN L6 ....114 A3
Tweedsmuir Cl
WARRN/WOL WA2 ....124 C3
Tweed St BIRK CH41 ....111 G6
Twenty Acre Rd
WARRW/BUR WA5 ....141 K1
Twickenham Dr HUY L36 ....116 C6
MOR/LEA CH46 ....110 A4
Twigden Cl AIN/FAZ L10 ....83 J3
Twig La HUY L36 ....116 C3
MGHL L31 ....62 B6
Twist Av GOL/RIS/CU WA3 ....92 D3
Twistfield Cl STHP PR8 ....27 G2
Two Acre Gv GTS/LS CH66 ....202 D2
Two Butt La RAIN/WH L35 ....118 C2
Twomey Cl EV L5 ....112 E3
Twyford Av LITH L21 ....81 J2
Twyford Cl MGHL L31 * 62 C6
WDN WA8 ....139 G5
Twyford La WDN WA8 ....139 J3
Twyford St NPK/KEN L6 ....113 K1
Tyberton Pl WLTN L25 ....155 F5
Tyburn Cl BEB CH63 ....170 B3
Tyburn Rd BEB CH63 ....170 B3
Tyndall Av CSBY/WL L22 ....81 G3
Tyne Cl ANF/KKDL L4 ....97 G5
STHEL WA9 ....119 F1
WARRN/WOL WA2 ....124 A5
Tynemouth Cl EV L5 ....113 J2
Tynemouth Rd RUNC WA7 ....188 B1
Tynesdale EP CH65 ....196 A6
Tyne St BIRK CH41 ....111 F6
Tynron Gv CL/PREN CH43 ....130 A4
Tynville Rd WLT/FAZ L9 ....83 F4
Tynwald Cl CLB/OSW/ST L13 ....114 D2
Tynwald Crs WDN WA8 ....138 E4
Tynwald Dr WARRS WA4 ....162 B4
Tynwald Hl CLB/OSW/ST L13 ....114 D3
Tynwald Pl CLB/OSW/ST L13 ....114 D3
Tynwald Rd WKBY CH48 ....146 B1
Tyrer Rd NEWLW WA12 ....106 C4
ORM L39 ....45 K4
Tyrer's Av MGHL L31 ....62 A2
Tyrers Cl FMBY L37 ....49 F3
Tyrer St BIRK CH41 ....111 F6
CLVPS L1 * 9 F4

U

Uldale Cl NG/CROX L11 ....98 E3
STHP PR8 ....33 H6
Uldale Wy NG/CROX L11 ....98 E3
Ullapool Cl GTS/LS CH66 ....194 C3
Ullet Rd AIG/SPK L17 ....133 J4
Ullswater Av CL/PREN CH43 ....129 K3
RNFD/HAY WA11 ....88 D3
WARRN/WOL WA2 ....123 J4
Ullswater Cl NWD/KWIPK L33 ....72 C5
Ullswater Gv RUNC WA7 ....187 G2
Ullswater Rd EP CH65 ....203 G1
GOL/RIS/CU WA3 ....92 D2
Ullswater St EV L5 ....113 J1
Ulster Rd CLB/OSW/ST L13 ....115 F4
Ultonia St ALL/GAR L19 ....172 B1
Ulverscroft CL/PREN CH43 ....130 C5
Ulverston Av
WARRN/WOL WA2 ....123 H4
Ulverston Cl MGHL L31 ....62 C5
RNFD/HAY WA11 ....89 K5
Ulverston Lawn NTHLY L27 ....136 C5
Umbria St ALL/GAR L19 ....172 B2
Underbridge La WARRS WA4 ....161 H5
Undercliffe Rd
CLB/OSW/ST L13 ....114 E3
Underhill Rd ECCL WA10 ....12 B7
Underley St EHL/KEN L7 ....133 H2
The Underway RUNC WA7 ....177 J5
Underwood Dr EP CH65 ....203 G1
Unicorn Rd NG/CROX L11 ....99 G1
Unicorn Wy BIRK CH41 ....3 H7
Union Bank La WDN WA8 ....119 K6
Union Ct CLVP L2 ....8 D4
Union St BIRK CH41 ....131 J6
CHTN/BK PR9 ....15 F3
ECCL WA10 ....13 G2
RUNC WA7 ....11 G5
VAUX/LVPD L3 ....8 B3
WAL/EG CH44 ....111 K3
Unit Rd STHP PR8 ....33 K4
Unity Gv PR/KW L34 ....85 F6
University Rd BTL L20 ....5 G5
Unsworth Av GOL/RIS/CU WA3 ....92 E2
Unsworth Ct
WARRN/WOL WA2 * 124 B6
Upavon Av GR/UP/WCH CH49 * 128 C6
Upchurch Cl TOX L8 ....132 E5
Upland Cl ECCL WA10 ....102 E5
Upland Dr AIMK WN4 ....79 J5
Upland Rd ECCL WA10 ....102 D5
GR/UP/WCH CH49 ....129 G3
Uplands Cl ECCL WA10 * 102 D5
Uplands Rd PS/BROM CH62 ....170 E4
Upper Aughton Rd STHP PR8 ....27 J3
Upper Baker St NPK/KEN L6 ....113 J4
Upper Beau St EV L5 ....113 G3
Upper Beckwith St BIRK CH41 ..130 E1
Upper Brassey St BIRK CH41 ....130 D1
Upper Bute St EV L5 ....113 G3
Upper Duke St CLVPS L1 ....9 G7
Upper Essex St TOX L8 ....132 E4
Upper Flaybrick Rd
CL/PREN CH43 ....130 B2
Upper Frederick St CLVPS L1 ....8 E7
Upper Hampton St TOX L8 ....132 E2
Upper Harrington St TOX L8 ....132 D4
Upper Hill St TOX L8 ....132 E3
Upper Hope Pl TOX L8 * 9 J6
Upper Huskisson St TOX L8 ....133 F2
Upper Mann St TOX L8 ....132 D4
Upper Mersey Rd WDN WA8 ....158 B6
Upper Mersey St EP CH65 ....6 E1
Upper Newington CLVPS L1 ....9 G5
Upper Park St TOX L8 ....132 E4
Upper Parliament St TOX L8 ....132 D2
Upper Pitt St CLVPS L1 ....9 F7
Upper Pownall St CLVPS L1 ....8 E7
Upper Raby Rd NSTN CH64 ....182 B5
Upper Rice La WAL/EG CH44 ....111 J2
Upper Stanhope St TOX L8 ....132 E2
Upper Warwick St TOX L8 ....132 E5
Upper William St
VAUX/LVPD L3 ....112 D3
Uppingham SKEL WN8 ....55 K4
Uppingham Av AIN/FAZ L10 ....83 H1
Uppingham Rd
CLB/OSW/ST L13 ....114 D2
WAL/EG CH44 ....111 F2
Upton Av STHP PR8 ....33 H3
Upton Barn MGHL L31 ....62 A5
Upton Bridle Pth WDN WA8 ....138 E5
Upton By-Pass
GR/UP/WCH CH49 ....129 F4
Upton Cl GOL/RIS/CU WA3 ....92 E3
GR/UP/WCH CH49 ....129 G4
SPK/HALE L24 * 173 K2
Upton Dr WARRW/BUR WA5 ....141 G4
Upton Gra WDN WA8 ....138 C6
Upton Gn SPK/HALE L24 * 173 K2
Upton La WDN WA8 ....138 E5
Upton Park Dr
GR/UP/WCH CH49 ....129 H3
Upton Rd CL/PREN CH43 ....129 K3
GTS/LS CH66 ....195 G5
Upwood Rd GOL/RIS/CU WA3 ....92 E4
Ure Ct EP CH65 ....195 K2
Urmson Rd WAL/NB CH45 ....111 H2
Urmston Av NEWLW WA12 ....91 G6
Ursula St BTL L20 ....97 F4
Utkinton Cl CL/PREN CH43 ....130 C6
Utting Av ANF/KKDL L4 ....97 K5
Utting Av East NG/CROX L11 ....98 C4
Uxbridge St EHL/KEN L7 * 113 K6

V

Vahler Ter RUNC WA7 ....11 H4
Vale Av WARRN/WOL WA2 ....142 E1
Vale Cl WLTN L25 ....154 C1
Vale Ct WARRS WA4 ....189 F4
Vale Crs STHP PR8 ....41 J1
Vale Cft SKEL WN8 ....67 J1
Vale Dr WAL/NB CH45 ....95 J6
Vale Gdns EP CH65 ....6 B7
FROD/HEL WA6 ....199 J5
Vale Gv KKBY L32 ....85 F2
Vale Ldg WLT/FAZ L9 * 97 J2
Valencia Gv PR/KW L34 ....102 C6
Valencia Rd WAV L15 ....134 B1
Valentia Rd HOY CH47 ....127 F3
Valentine Gv AIN/FAZ L10 ....83 H2
Valentine Rd NEWLW WA12 ....105 K2
Valentines Wy WLT/FAZ L9 ....83 F2
Vale Owen Rd
WARRN/WOL WA2 ....123 K6
Valerian Rd BIRK CH41 ....130 C2
Valerie Cl AIN/FAZ L10 ....84 A5
Vale Rd CSBY/BLUN L23 ....68 E5
EP CH65 ....6 B7
WLTN L25 ....154 C1
Valescourt Rd
WD/CROXPK L12 ....115 G2
Valiant Cl WARRN/WOL WA2 ....124 B5
WD/CROXPK L12 ....100 A3
Valiant Wy BIRK CH41 ....131 J5
Valkyrie Rd WAL/NB CH45 ....111 G2
Vallance Rd ANF/KKDL L4 ....98 A6
Valleybrook Gv BEB CH63 ....170 D3
Valley Cl AIN/FAZ L10 ....83 J2
CSBY/BLUN L23 ....69 J5
Valley Ct WARRN/WOL WA2 ....124 B6
Valley Dr GTS/LS CH66 ....195 G4
Valley Rd AIN/FAZ L10 ....83 K4
ANF/KKDL L4 ....113 J1
BIRK CH41 ....110 D5
KKBY L32 ....84 C2
PS/BROM CH62 ....171 F5
Valley Vw GTS/LS CH66 ....195 G4
NEWLW WA12 ....106 B4
Vanbrugh Crs ANF/KKDL L4 ....98 A6
Vanbrugh Rd ANF/KKDL L4 ....98 A5
Vancouver Rd NTHLY L27 ....136 B4
Vanderbilt Av WLT/FAZ L9 ....82 E3
Vanderbyl Av PS/BROM CH62 ....170 D3
Vandries St VAUX/LVPD L3 ....112 D3
Vandyke St TOX L8 ....133 H2
Vanguard Ct GOL/RIS/CU WA3 ..125 F3
Vanguard St EV L5 ....113 H1
Vanguard Wy BIRK CH41 ....131 J6
Vardon St BIRK CH41 ....2 D1
Varley Rd ALL/GAR L19 ....153 H2
STHEL WA9 ....104 A1
Varlian Cl BRSC L40 ....54 C2
Varthen St EV L5 ....113 J1
Vaudrey Dr WARR WA1 ....144 C2
Vaughan Cl FMBY L37 ....48 D1
Vaughan Rd STHP PR8 ....27 J3
WAL/NB CH45 ....95 J5
Vaughan St BIRK CH41 ....130 C1
Vaux Crs BTL L20 ....82 A6
Vauxhall Cl WARRW/BUR WA5 ....141 G5
Vauxhall Rd VAUX/LVPD L3 ....8 D1
Vaux Pl BTL L20 ....5 H1
Venables Cl BEB CH63 ....170 D4
Venables Dr BEB CH63 ....170 C3
Venice St EV L5 ....113 H1
Venmore St EV L5 ....113 H1
Venns Rd WARRN/WOL WA2 ....143 G2
Ventnor Cl WARRW/BUR WA5 ....140 E2
Ventnor Rd WAV L15 ....134 A1
Verbena Cl RUNC WA7 ....187 J3
Verdala Pk CALD/MH L18 * 154 A1
Verdi Av LITH L21 ....81 H5
Verdi St LITH L21 ....81 G6
Verdi Ter LITH L21 ....81 G6
Vere St TOX L8 * 132 D4
Vermont Av CSBY/BLUN L23 ....68 E5
Vermont Cl NWD/KWIPK L33 ....72 C3
WARRW/BUR WA5 ....141 K2
Vermont Rd CSBY/BLUN L23 ....68 E5
Vermont Wy BTL L20 ....4 E3
Verney Crs ALL/GAR L19 ....153 K3
Verney Crs South ALL/GAR L19 ..153 K3
Vernon Av GTS/LS CH66 ....184 D5
WAL/EG CH44 ....111 K5
Vernon Rd CHTN/BK PR9 ....23 J5
Vernon St CLVP L2 ....8 D2
STHEL WA9 ....104 A1
WARR WA1 ....16 E6
Verona St EV L5 ....113 H1
Veronica Wy GTS/LS CH66 ....195 G2
Verulam Cl TOX L8 ....133 F2
Verulam Rd CHTN/BK PR9 ....23 K2
Verwood Cl PEN/TH CH61 ....148 A4
Verwood Dr WD/CROXPK L12 ....100 A2
Veryan Cl HLWD L26 ....155 J2
Vescock St EV L5 ....113 F3
Vesta Rd ALL/GAR L19 ....172 C1
Vesuvius Pl EV L5 ....113 F1
Vetch Hey NTHLY L27 ....136 B4
Viaduct St NEWLW WA12 ....106 A2
Vicarage Cl CALD/MH L18 ....153 J1
FMBY L37 ....48 D1
ORM L39 ....54 B2
RF/TRAN CH42 ....150 A2
SPK/HALE L24 ....175 F4
Vicarage Dr RNFD/HAY WA11 ....89 K4
Vicarage Gdns BRSC L40 ....38 D5
Vicarage Gv WAL/EG CH44 ....111 J2
Vicarage Hl FROD/HEL WA6 ....199 K5
Vicarage La BRSC L40 ....54 D2
CHTN/BK PR9 ....21 J4
FROD/HEL WA6 ....199 K5
FROD/HEL WA6 ....201 F2
Vicarage Lawn WLTN L25 ....135 K4
Vicarage Pl PR/KW L34 ....117 J1
Vicarage Rd AIMK WN4 ....91 G1

FMBY L37 ....48 D1
RNFD/HAY WA11 ....89 K4
WDN WA8 ....18 D5
Vicarage Wk ORM L39 ....45 J6
Vicar Rd NPK/KEN L6 ....98 A6
Viceroy St EV L5 ....113 H1
Vickers Rd WDN WA8 ....176 B1
Victoria Av CSBY/BLUN L23 ....68 D5
DV/KA/FCH L14 ....115 H5
HES CH60 ....180 E1
RNFD/HAY WA11 ....88 D3
WARRS WA4 ....163 F1
WARRW/BUR WA5 ....140 E3
WAV L15 ....134 A1
WDN WA8 ....158 B1
Victoria Bridge Rd STHP PR8 ....15 G6
Victoria Cl AIG/SPK L17 ....133 K6
Victoria Ct STHP PR8 ....27 G3
WAV L15 ....134 B1
Victoria Dr RF/TRAN CH42 ....151 F2
WKBY CH48 ....146 B1
WLT/FAZ L9 ....82 C5
Victoria Flds RF/TRAN CH42 ....131 F5
Victoria Gdns CL/PREN CH43 ....130 E5
Victoria Gv WDN WA8 ....139 F6
Victoria La CL/PREN CH43 ....130 E5
Victoria Mt CL/PREN CH43 ....130 E5
Victoria Pde WAL/NB CH45 ....95 J4
Victoria Pk SKEL WN8 ....55 J4
Victoria Park Rd
RF/TRAN CH42 ....150 C1
Victoria Pl CLB/OSW/ST L13 ....114 E4
RAIN/WH L35 ....118 B4
WARRS WA4 ....162 B2
Victoria Rd AIG/SPK L17 ....153 F1
AIMK WN4 ....78 C5
BEB CH63 ....150 C5
CLB/OSW/ST L13 ....114 E4
CSBY/BLUN L23 ....68 E5
CSBY/WL L22 ....81 F3
EP CH65 ....6 C4
FMBY L37 ....40 B6
HTWN L38 ....60 A4
HUY L36 ....117 F5
NEWLW WA12 ....106 C1
NSTN CH64 ....192 B3
ORM L39 ....53 G2
RF/TRAN CH42 ....131 F5
RUNC WA7 ....10 E5
WAL/NB CH45 ....95 H5
WARRS WA4 ....162 C2
WARRW/BUR WA5 ....140 E5
WDN WA8 ....18 D5
WKBY CH48 ....146 B2
Victoria Sq ECCL WA10 ....13 G4
WDN WA8 ....18 D5
Victoria St BRSC L40 ....38 E4
CLVP L2 ....8 D4
ECCL WA10 ....13 G2
PS/BROM CH62 ....151 G6
RAIN/WH L35 ....118 E4
RNFD/HAY WA11 ....75 G2
STHP PR8 ....14 E3
WARR WA1 ....17 F4
WDN WA8 ....18 E5
Victoria Ter RAIN/WH L35 ....118 E4
WAV L15 ....134 B3
Victoria Wy FMBY L37 ....40 D6
STHP PR8 ....14 B5
Victor St WAV L15 ....133 J1
Victory Av CHTN/BK PR9 ....23 J6
Victory Cl NTHTN L30 ....82 B3
Vienna St EV L5 ....113 H1
Viennese Rd WLTN L25 * 135 J2
Viewpark Cl CHLDW L16 ....135 G2
View Rd RAIN/WH L35 ....118 E5
Viking Cl LITH L21 ....81 H4
STHP PR8 ....27 H3
Villagate La WARRS WA4 ....163 H6
Village Cl RUNC WA7 ....177 K5
SKEL WN8 ....55 K5
WAL/NB CH45 ....110 E1
WARRS WA4 ....144 D5
Village Ct AIG/SPK L17 ....152 D1
Village Green Ct
CL/PREN CH43 * 129 K1
Village Nook AIN/FAZ L10 * 83 H1
Village Rd BEB CH63 ....150 C5
CL/PREN CH43 ....130 D5
HES CH60 ....167 K6
WKBY CH48 ....146 D2
Village St NPK/KEN L6 ....113 H3
RUNC WA7 ....178 D3
The Village BEB CH63 ....151 F6
Village Vw WGNW/BIL/O WN5 ....77 H4
Village Wy HTWN L38 ....59 F3
SKEL WN8 ....55 K5
WAL/NB CH45 ....110 E2
Villa Gloria Cl ALL/GAR L19 ....153 H3
Villars St WARR WA1 ....17 G5
Villas Rd MGHL L31 ....63 F5
Villiers Crs ECCL WA10 ....87 G6
Villiers Rd PR/KW L34 ....85 G5
Vincent Cl WARRW/BUR WA5 ....141 J1
Vincent Ct CLVPS L1 ....9 F7
Vincent Rd LITH L21 ....81 K2
RAIN/WH L35 ....118 D3
Vincent St CLB/OSW/ST L13 ....114 D6
ECCL WA10 ....13 H4
Vine Crs WARRW/BUR WA5 ....141 F3
The Vineries WLTN L25 ....135 F6
Vine Rd GTS/LS CH66 ....202 D3
Vineside Rd WD/CROXPK L12 ....115 H2
Vine St EHL/KEN L7 ....133 F1
RUNC WA7 ....10 D5
WDN WA8 ....18 D5
Vine Ter RAIN/WH L35 * 157 F1
Vineyard St ALL/GAR L19 ....154 B6
Vining Rd RAIN/WH L35 ....118 B1
Vining St TOX L8 * 132 E3
Viola St BTL L20 ....96 E4
Violet Cl GOL/RIS/CU WA3 ....124 E4
Violet Rd BIRK CH41 ....130 C2
LITH L21 ....81 J5
Violet St AIMK WN4 ....91 G1
WDN WA8 ....18 C6
Virgil St ECCL WA10 ....12 C4
EV L5 ....113 F3
Virginia Av MGHL L31 ....62 A4
Virginia Gdns
WARRW/BUR WA5 ....141 J1
Virginia Gv MGHL L31 ....62 B4
Virginia Rd WAL/NB CH45 ....95 H4
Virginia St STHP PR8 ....15 G6
VAUX/LVPD L3 * 8 B2
Virgin's La CSBY/BLUN L23 ....69 G2
Viscount Rd WARRN/WOL WA2 ....124 A5
Vista Av NEWLW WA12 ....106 A1
Vista Rd NEWLW WA12 ....106 A1
RUNC WA7 ....176 D5
Vista Wy NEWLW WA12 ....106 A1
Vitesse Rd ALL/GAR L19 ....154 C5
Vittoria Cl BIRK CH41 ....2 D3
Vittoria Ct BIRK CH41 ....2 D2
Vittoria St BIRK CH41 ....2 C3
Vivian Av WAL/EG CH44 ....112 A5
Vivian Dr STHP PR8 ....27 H5
Voelas St TOX L8 ....133 F4
Vogan Av CSBY/BLUN L23 ....69 H6
Volunteer St ECCL WA10 ....13 F3
FROD/HEL WA6 ....187 F6
Vose Cl WARRW/BUR WA5 ....142 A3
Vronhill Cl TOX L8 ....133 F3
Vulcan Cl CL/PREN CH43 ....130 C1
NEWLW WA12 ....106 C4
WARRN/WOL WA2 ....124 B5
Vulcan St ALL/GAR L19 ....172 B1
BTL L20 ....4 B3
CHTN/BK PR9 ....15 G5
VAUX/LVPD L3 ....112 D3
Vyner Cl CL/PREN CH43 ....130 B3
Vyner Rd WAL/NB CH45 ....111 F2
Vyner Rd North CL/PREN CH43 ....130 A2
WLTN L25 ....135 H4
Vyner Rd South
CL/PREN CH43 ....130 A3
WLTN L25 ....135 H4
Vyrnwy St EV L5 ....97 H6

W

Waddicar La MGHL L31 ....71 K6
Waddington Cl
GOL/RIS/CU WA3 * 93 G3
WARRN/WOL WA2 ....124 B6
Wadebridge Rd NG/CROX L11 ....83 K5
Wadeson Rd ANF/KKDL L4 ....98 B3
Wadham Pk BTL L20 ....96 E4
Wadham Rd BTL L20 ....96 E4
Wagon La RNFD/HAY WA11 ....90 A5
Waine Gv RAIN/WH L35 ....118 C2
Waine St RNFD/HAY WA11 ....89 J5
STHEL WA9 ....104 B1
Wainwright Cl EHL/KEN L7 * 133 G1
Wainwright Gv ALL/GAR L19 ....153 K5
Wakefield Dr MOR/LEA CH46 ....109 K3
Wakefield Rd GTS/LS CH66 ....202 C2
NTHTN L30 ....70 E6
Wakefield St GOL/RIS/CU WA3 ....92 B4
VAUX/LVPD L3 ....9 G1
Walby Cl GR/UP/WCH CH49 ....149 F1
Walden Cl WARRS WA4 ....144 C6
Walden Rd DV/KA/FCH L14 ....115 G4
Waldgrave Pl WAV L15 ....115 F6
Waldgrave Rd WAV L15 ....114 E6
Walford Cl BEB CH63 ....170 B3
Walford Rd AIMK WN4 ....79 H6
Walker Av STHEL WA9 ....119 K4
Walker Cl FMBY L37 ....49 F3
Walker Dr BTL L20 ....81 K4
Walker Ms RF/TRAN CH42 ....131 G6
Walker Pl RF/TRAN CH42 ....131 G6
Walker Rd LITH L21 ....81 H4
Walker's Cft WAL/NB CH45 ....111 F2
Walkers La GTS/LS CH66 ....195 F3
STHEL WA9 ....119 J4
WARRW/BUR WA5 ....141 F6
Walker St HOY CH47 ....127 G2
NPK/KEN L6 ....113 J4
PS/BROM CH62 * 151 G5
RF/TRAN CH42 ....131 G6
WARRN/WOL WA2 ....16 B3
Walker Wy WLT/FAZ L9 ....82 C5
The Walk SPK/HALE L24 ....173 F3
STBRV L28 * 100 C6
STHP PR8 ....27 H2
Wallace Av HUY L36 ....117 F3
Wallace Dr HUY L36 ....117 F3
Wallace St WDN WA8 ....18 D3
WLT/FAZ L9 ....82 D5
Wallacre Rd WAL/EG CH44 ....110 E3
Wallasey Bridge Rd BIRK CH41 ....111 F6
Wallasey Rd WAL/EG CH44 ....111 G3
Wallasey Village WAL/EG CH44 ....110 E2
Wallcroft NSTN CH64 ....193 H2
Wallcroft St SKEL WN8 ....56 A5
Waller Cl ANF/KKDL L4 ....97 G6
Waller St BTL L20 ....81 H5
Wallgate Rd WLTN L25 ....135 G3
Wallgate Wy WLTN L25 ....135 G3
Wallingford Rd
GR/UP/WCH CH49 ....129 G4
Wallis St WARRS WA4 ....142 E6
Wallrake HES CH60 ....167 K6
Wallsend Ct WDN WA8 ....138 D6
Walmer Ct STHP PR8 ....27 G4
Walmer Rd CSBY/WL L22 ....81 F3
STHP PR8 ....27 H4
Walmesley Dr RNFD/HAY WA11 ....75 H4
Walmesley Rd ECCL WA10 ....87 H6
Walmsley St EV L5 ....112 E2
NEWLW WA12 ....106 D1
WAL/EG CH44 ....111 J2
WDN WA8 ....19 H3
Walney Rd WD/CROXPK L12 ....98 E5
Walnut Av WLT/FAZ L9 ....98 A2
Walnut Cl WARR WA1 ....144 D2
Walnut Gv GTS/LS CH66 ....202 D2
MGHL L31 ....71 K6
Walnut St STHP PR8 ....27 K3
Walpole Av RAIN/WH L35 ....118 B4
Walpole Gv WARRN/WOL WA2 ....123 J5
Walpole Rd RUNC WA7 ....186 E1
Walro Ms CHTN/BK PR9 ....23 J2
Walsh Cl EV L5 ....112 E3
NEWLW WA12 ....91 H6
Walsh Rd DV/KA/FCH L14 ....115 G5
Walsingham Ct WAL/EG CH44 ....111 K4
Walsingham Dr RUNC WA7 ....178 C3
Walsingham Rd CHLDW L16 ....115 J6
WAL/EG CH44 ....111 K4
WARRW/BUR WA5 ....141 G4
Walter Beilin Ct AIG/SPK L17 * 133 K4
Walter Gv STHEL WA9 ....104 D6
Walters Green Crs
GOL/RIS/CU WA3 ....92 B1
Walter St AIMK WN4 * 79 J5
VAUX/LVPD L3 ....112 D2
WARR WA1 ....143 H2
WDN WA8 ....19 J1
Waltham Ct RUNC WA7 ....178 D1
Waltham Rd NPK/KEN L6 ....114 A1
Waltho Av MGHL L31 ....62 C6
Walton Av WARRW/BUR WA5 ....141 F4
Walton Breck Rd ANF/KKDL L4 ....97 H6
Walton Hall Av ANF/KKDL L4 ....97 K3
NG/CROX L11 ....98 B2
Walton Heath Rd WARRS WA4 ....162 A2
Walton La ANF/KKDL L4 ....97 J4
Walton Lea Rd WARRS WA4 ....161 K4
Walton New Rd WARRS WA4 ....162 A3
Walton Pk WLT/FAZ L9 ....97 J1
Walton Park Gdns ANF/KKDL L4 ....97 J3
Walton Rd ANF/KKDL L4 ....97 G5
ECCL WA10 ....88 A5
GOL/RIS/CU WA3 ....125 G2
WARRS WA4 ....162 B3
Walton St BIRK CH41 * 3 F5
CHTN/BK PR9 ....15 G3
RUNC WA7 ....10 E5
Walton V WLT/FAZ L9 ....82 D5
Walton Village ANF/KKDL L4 ....97 H3
Wambo La WLTN L25 ....135 K4
Wandsworth Rd NG/CROX L11 ....98 D4
Wandsworth Wy WDN WA8 ....158 A6
Wango La AIN/FAZ L10 ....83 J2
Wanishar La ORM L39 ....43 J6
Wansfell Pl WARRN/WOL WA2 ....123 G4
Wantage Vw HUY L36 ....135 K1
Wapping VAUX/LVPD L3 ....8 D7
Wapping Quay VAUX/LVPD L3 ....132 B2
Wapshare Rd NG/CROX L11 ....98 C4
Warbler Cl HLWD L26 ....155 G1
Warbreck Av WLT/FAZ L9 ....82 D5
Warbreck Moor WLT/FAZ L9 ....82 E4
Warbreck Rd WLT/FAZ L9 ....82 D5
Warburton Hey RAIN/WH L35 ....118 D3
Warburton St WARRS WA4 ....162 C2
Ward Av FMBY L37 ....48 D3
Ward Cl WARRW/BUR WA5 ....122 B6
Warden St ANF/KKDL L4 ....97 G5
Wardgate Av WD/CROXPK L12 ....99 J2
Ward Gv RF/TRAN CH42 ....150 E3
Wardour St WARRW/BUR WA5 ....142 B3
Ward Rd CSBY/BLUN L23 ....68 B3
Ward St ECCL WA10 ....13 G3
PR/KW L34 ....101 K6
VAUX/LVPD L3 ....9 G3
Wareham Cl WARR WA1 ....144 B1
Wareing Rd WLT/FAZ L9 ....83 F5
Waresley Crs WLT/FAZ L9 ....98 C1
Wargrave Ms NEWLW WA12 ....106 C4
Wargrave Rd NEWLW WA12 ....106 C2
Warham Rd ANF/KKDL L4 ....98 A6
Waring Av RF/TRAN CH42 ....150 C1
STHEL WA9 ....105 F3
WARRS WA4 ....143 J4
Warkworth Cl WDN WA8 ....138 B6
Warmington Rd
DV/KA/FCH L14 ....115 G4
Warner Dr ANF/KKDL L4 ....98 A5
Warnerville Rd
CLB/OSW/ST L13 ....115 G6
Warnley Cl WDN WA8 ....138 C6
Warpers Moss Cl BRSC L40 ....39 F4
Warper's Moss La BRSC L40 ....39 G4
Warren Ct FROD/HEL WA6 ....201 G3
GTS/LS CH66 ....195 G6
STHP PR8 ....27 F2
Warren Cft RUNC WA7 ....178 B6
Warrender Dr BIRK CH41 ....130 C1
Warren Dr CL/PREN CH43 ....129 K3
GTS/LS CH66 ....195 H2
NEWLW WA12 ....107 F1
WAL/NB CH45 ....95 F5
WARRS WA4 ....162 B3
Warren Gn FMBY L37 ....48 D1
Warren Hey BEB CH63 ....170 C4
Warren House Rd CSBY/WL L22 ....80 C1
Warrenhouse Rd
NWD/KWIPK L33 ....73 F5
Warren La WARR WA1 ....144 C1
Warren Rd CHTN/BK PR9 ....23 J5
CSBY/BLUN L23 ....68 C5
HOY CH47 ....127 F2
WARRN/WOL WA2 ....123 K6
WARRS WA4 ....162 B4
The Warren GR/UP/WCH CH49 ....129 J4
Warren Wy HES CH60 ....167 H4
Warrington Av EP CH65 ....203 F1
Warrington New Rd STHEL WA9 ....13 K6
Warrington Old Rd STHEL WA9 ....13 J7
Warrington Rd AIMK WN4 ....91 G1
GOL/RIS/CU WA3 ....107 H2
GOL/RIS/CU WA3 ....124 E4
LYMM WA13 ....145 G5
NEWLW WA12 ....92 B5
RAIN/WH L35 ....118 A2
RAIN/WH L35 ....119 F4
RUNC WA7 ....177 K1
WARRS WA4 ....161 J5
WARRW/BUR WA5 ....140 E5
WDN WA8 ....19 G4
WDN WA8 ....139 J2
Warrington St BIRK CH41 ....131 H5
Warton Cl WARRW/BUR WA5 ....141 H6
Warton St BTL L20 ....81 H5
Warton Ter BTL L20 ....81 H5
Warwick Av AIMK WN4 ....91 J1
CSBY/BLUN L23 ....68 E6
NEWLW WA12 ....106 D3
WARRW/BUR WA5 ....140 E2
WARRW/BUR WA5 ....142 C2
Warwick Cl CL/PREN CH43 ....2 C6
HUY L36 ....117 G4
NSTN CH64 ....191 K4
STHP PR8 ....27 J4
Warwick Ct EP CH65 ....203 J1
Warwick Dr WAL/NB CH45 ....111 J1
WKBY CH48 ....146 D3
Warwick Rd BTL L20 ....5 H3
GR/UP/WCH CH49 ....129 G3
HUY L36 ....117 G4
Warwick St ECCL WA10 ....12 A6
STHP PR8 ....27 J3
TOX L8 ....132 D4
Wasdale Av MGHL L31 ....62 D5
RNFD/HAY WA11 ....88 E3
Wasdale Rd AIMK WN4 ....79 F1
WLT/FAZ L9 ....82 D6
Washbrook Av
CL/PREN CH43 * 129 K1
Washbrook Cl ECCL WA10 ....102 D1
Washbrook Wy ORM L39 ....53 J1
Washington Dr
NWD/KWIPK L33 ....72 C3
WARRW/BUR WA5 ....141 K2
Washington Pde BTL L20 ....4 E4
Wash La WARRS WA4 ....162 D1
Washway La ECCL WA10 ....88 D4
Wasley Cl WARRN/WOL WA2 ....124 B4
Wastdale Ct MOR/LEA CH46 ....109 G6
Wastdale Dr MOR/LEA CH46 ....109 G6
Wastdale Ms MOR/LEA CH46 ....109 G6
Wastle Bridge Rd HUY L36 ....116 E2
Watchyard La FMBY L37 ....49 G2
Waterbridge Ct WARRS WA4 ....162 C3
Waterdale Crs STHEL WA9 ....104 B6
Waterdale Pl STHEL WA9 ....104 B6
Waterfield Cl BEB CH63 ....150 C6
Waterfoot Av STHP PR8 ....33 H6
Waterford Dr NSTN CH64 ....192 B2
Waterford Rd CL/PREN CH43 ....130 B4
NTHLY L27 ....135 K3
Waterford Wy RUNC WA7 ....188 B1
Waterfront WARRS WA4 ....188 E1
Watergate La WLTN L25 ....154 E1
Watergate Wy WLTN L25 ....154 E1
Waterhouse Cl NPK/KEN L6 ....113 K2
Waterhouse St EV L5 * 113 H3
Waterland La STHEL WA9 ....104 D3
Water La CHTN/BK PR9 ....21 G6
RAIN/WH L35 ....137 G5
Waterloo Cl CSBY/WL L22 ....80 E3
EP CH65 ....6 E5
Waterloo Pl BIRK CH41 ....3 G6
Waterloo Rd CSBY/WL L22 ....81 F3
RUNC WA7 ....10 C4
STHP PR8 ....27 F6
VAUX/LVPD L3 ....112 D3
WAL/NB CH45 ....95 H4
WDN WA8 ....158 B6
Waterloo St ECCL WA10 ....13 F5
WAV L15 ....134 B2
Watermead Dr RUNC WA7 ....188 E2
Waterpark Cl CL/PREN CH43 ....149 J2
Waterpark Dr STBRV L28 ....99 K5
Waterpark Rd CL/PREN CH43 ....149 K2
Watersedge FROD/HEL WA6 ....187 G5
Watersedge Apartments
WAL/NB CH45 * 95 J4
Waterside NTHTN L30 ....70 B4
STHEL WA9 ....13 K3
WARRS WA4 ....162 C3
Waterside Ct STHEL WA9 ....13 K3
Waterside Dr FROD/HEL WA6 ....187 G5
Waterside Pk HUY L36 ....116 D6
Water St BIRK CH41 ....3 H4
CSBY/BLUN L23 ....69 J3
CSBY/WL L22 * 80 E3
ECCL WA10 ....13 F5
NEWLW WA12 ....106 C1
PS/BROM CH62 ....151 G5
RUNC WA7 ....10 E3
VAUX/LVPD L3 ....8 B4
WAL/EG CH44 ....111 K3
WDN WA8 ....158 B5
Water Tower Rd NSTN CH64 ....181 K5
Waterway Av NTHTN L30 ....70 E6
Waterways WARRW/BUR WA5 ....142 A3
Waterworks Dr NEWLW WA12 ....107 F1
Waterworks La GTS/LS CH66 ....184 B6
WARRN/WOL WA2 ....107 H6
Waterworks Rd ORM L39 ....46 A5
Waterworks St BTL L20 ....5 G4
Watery La FROD/HEL WA6 ....201 H4
STHEL WA9 ....104 C5
WARRN/WOL WA2 ....122 E1
Watford Rd ANF/KKDL L4 ....97 K6
Watkin Cl NTHTN L30 ....82 E2
Watkins Av NEWLW WA12 ....105 K2
Watkinson St CLVPS L1 ....132 C2
Watkinson Wy WDN WA8 ....19 G3
WDN WA8 ....138 E2
Watkin St WARRN/WOL WA2 ....16 D1
Watling Av LITH L21 ....81 H2
Watling Wy RAIN/WH L35 ....118 C2
Watmough St EV L5 ....113 G3
Watson Av AIMK WN4 ....79 H6
GOL/RIS/CU WA3 ....92 A2
Watson St BIRK CH41 ....2 E3
Watton Beck Cl MGHL L31 ....62 D5
Watton Cl WARRS WA4 ....144 B6
WD/CROXPK L12 ....100 A3
Watts Cl NWD/KWIPK L33 ....73 F5
Watts La BTL L20 ....82 B5
Wauchope St WAV L15 ....133 K1
Wavell Av CHTN/BK PR9 ....23 K6
WDN WA8 ....157 H3
Wavell Cl CHTN/BK PR9 ....23 K6
Wavell Rd HUY L36 ....116 E3
Waverley SKEL WN8 ....55 K4
Waverley Av WARRS WA4 ....162 C3
Waverley Dr HUY L36 ....117 F2
Waverley Gv RF/TRAN CH42 ....150 B1
Waverley Rd AIG/SPK L17 ....133 H5
CSBY/BLUN L23 ....68 D6
GOL/RIS/CU WA3 ....92 E2
HOY CH47 ....127 H2
Waverley St BTL L20 ....4 D4
STHP PR8 ....14 D4
Waverton Av CL/PREN CH43 ....149 H1
Waverton Rd GTS/LS CH66 ....195 H4
Wavertree Av
CLB/OSW/ST L13 ....114 C6
WDN WA8 ....18 C3
Wavertree Bvd EHL/KEN L7 ....114 B6
Wavertree Bvd South
EHL/KEN L7 ....114 C6
Wavertree Ct GTS/LS CH66 ....195 J2
Wavertree Gn WAV L15 ....134 B2
Wavertree Nook Rd WAV L15 ....115 G6
Wavertree Rd EHL/KEN L7 ....113 K6
Wavertree V WAV L15 ....133 J2
Wayfarers Ar STHP PR8 * 14 E4
Wayfarers Dr NEWLW WA12 ....106 E3
Wayford Cl FROD/HEL WA6 ....186 E6
Waylands Dr WLTN L25 ....154 E4
Wayside Cl LYMM WA13 ....164 E1
Wayville Cl CALD/MH L18 ....153 J1
Waywell Cl WARRN/WOL WA2 ....124 B4
Weald Dr GTS/LS CH66 ....194 D3
Weardale Rd WAV L15 ....133 K3
Wearhead Cl GOL/RIS/CU WA3 ....92 B4
Weasdale Cl STHEL WA9 ....104 B6
Weaste La WARRS WA4 ....163 J1
Weates Cl WDN WA8 ....139 K6
Weaver Av BRSC L40 ....39 F4
NWD/KWIPK L33 ....72 E3
RAIN/WH L35 ....118 D4
Weaver Crs FROD/HEL WA6 ....187 G6
Weaver Gv STHEL WA9 ....104 E2
Weaver La FROD/HEL WA6 ....186 E5
Weaver Rd EP CH65 ....196 B6
FROD/HEL WA6 ....187 G6
RUNC WA7 ....186 D1
Weaverside Av RUNC WA7 ....187 J3
Weavers La MGHL L31 ....71 J3
Weaver St WLT/FAZ L9 ....97 H2
Webb Cl EHL/KEN L7 ....114 A6
Webb Dr WARRW/BUR WA5 ....121 K1
Webber Rd NWD/KWIPK L33 ....85 G2
Webb St EHL/KEN L7 ....133 H2
STHEL WA9 ....104 B4
Webster Av BTL L20 ....5 J2
WAL/EG CH44 ....111 K2
Webster Dr KKBY L32 ....84 D1
Webster Rd WAV L15 ....133 J2
Websters La GTS/LS CH66 ....202 D1
Webster St LITH L21 ....81 J5
VAUX/LVPD L3 ....8 E2
Weddell Cl WARRW/BUR WA5 ....142 A2
Wedge Av RNFD/HAY WA11 ....89 K6
Wedgewood Gdns STHEL WA9 ....118 D1
Wedgewood St EHL/KEN L7 ....114 A5
Wedgwood Dr WDN WA8 ....139 G5
Wednesbury Dr
WARRW/BUR WA5 ....141 G3
Weedon Av NEWLW WA12 ....91 G6
Weightman Gv WLT/FAZ L9 ....82 D5
Weir La WARR WA1 ....144 D3
Weir St WARRS WA4 ....161 K2
Welbeck Av CALD/MH L18 ....134 A4
NEWLW WA12 ....106 D3
Welbeck Ct CSBY/WL L22 * 80 E2
Welbeck Rd AIMK WN4 ....79 G4
STHP PR8 ....27 G3
Welbeck Ter STHP PR8 ....27 G3
Welbourne Rd CHLDW L16 ....115 G6
Weld Blundell Av MGHL L31 ....61 K3
Weld Dr FMBY L37 ....48 D1
Weldon Dr ORM L39 ....53 K1
Weldon St ANF/KKDL L4 ....97 H3
Weld Pde STHP PR8 ....27 G3
Weld Rd CSBY/BLUN L23 ....68 D6
STHP PR8 ....27 F2
Welfield Pl TOX L8 ....133 F5
Welford Av CL/PREN CH43 ....149 J1
GOL/RIS/CU WA3 ....92 D4
Welland Cl HLWD L26 ....155 H6
Welland Rd AIMK WN4 ....79 K4
BEB CH63 * 150 C6
Wellbank Dr HLWD L26 ....155 K2
Wellbrae Cl GR/UP/WCH CH49 ....128 E4
Wellbrook Cl RUNC WA7 ....188 B2
SPK/HALE L24 * 173 J1
Wellbrooke Cl AIMK WN4 ....79 H6
Wellbrook Gn SPK/HALE L24 * 173 J2
Well Brow Rd ANF/KKDL L4 ....97 K3
Well Cl NSTN CH64 ....192 B5
Wellcroft Rd HUY L36 ....116 E3
Wellcross Rd SKEL WN8 ....67 K1
Weller St TOX L8 ....132 E4
Weller Wy TOX L8 ....133 F5
Wellesbourne Pl NG/CROX L11 ....98 E3
Wellesbourne Rd NG/CROX L11 ....98 E2
Wellesley Av EP CH65 ....6 E5
Wellesley Cl NEWLW WA12 ....91 G6
Wellesley Gv BEB CH63 ....151 F5
Wellesley Rd TOX L8 ....133 F5
WAL/EG CH44 ....111 H3
Wellesley Wk EP CH65 ....6 E5
Well Farm Cl WARR WA1 ....144 C1
Wellfield RNFD/HAY WA11 ....75 H5
RUNC WA7 ....188 D2

WDN WA8 139 F5
Wellfield Av KKBY L32 84 D2
Wellfield La BRSC L40 54 C3
Wellfield Rd WLT/FAZ L9 97 J1
Wellfield St WARRW/BUR WA5 142 B4
Wellgreen Rd WLTN L25 135 G2
Wellington Av WAV L15 133 J2
Wellington Cl AIN/FAZ L10 71 F6
EP CH65 6 E4
WARRN/WOL WA2 124 B5
Wellington Flds WAV L15 133 J3
Wellington Ga SPK/HALE L24 174 E3
Wellington Gv WAV L15 * 133 K1
Wellington Rd BEB CH63 151 F5
CL/PREN CH43 130 D5
EP CH65 6 C6
LITH L21 81 H4
TOX L8 132 E5
WAL/NB CH45 95 H4
WAV L15 133 K2
Wellington Rd North EP CH65 6 E5
Wellington St ALL/GAR L19 153 K6
CSBY/WL L22 80 E2
NEWLW WA12 106 A2
RUNC WA7 10 D3
STHP PR8 14 C6
WARR WA1 17 F5
WDN WA8 158 B5
Wellington Ter BIRK CH41 2 E7
ECCL WA10 13 G2
TOX L8 133 F4
Well La BEB CH63 150 C5
BTL L20 5 G4
GR/UP/WCH CH49 128 D6
HES CH60 181 F1
NSTN CH64 192 A4
ORM L39 43 G5
RF/TRAN CH42 150 D1
WARRW/BUR WA5 141 F6
WLTN L25 135 G2
Well Lane Gdns BTL L20 5 G4
Wells Av WGNW/BIL/O WN5 77 G4
Wells Cl GTS/LS CH66 202 C3
WARR WA1 144 A1
Wells St WAV L15 134 A2
Wellstead Cl WAV L15 134 B1
Wellstead Rd WAV L15 134 B1
Wellswood Rd GTS/LS CH66 195 H2
Welsby Cl WARRN/WOL WA2 124 B4
Welshampton Cl GTS/LS CH66 202 B1
Welshpool Cl
WARRW/BUR WA5 122 D4
Welsh Rd GTS/LS CH66 184 D6
Welton Av GR/UP/WCH CH49 129 G4
Welton Cl SPK/HALE L24 173 J2
Welton Gn SPK/HALE L24 173 J2
Welton Rd PS/BROM CH62 171 G2
Welwyn Av STHP PR8 33 K3
Welwyn Cl STHEL WA9 119 G1
WARRS WA4 144 B6
Wembley Gdns WLT/FAZ L9 82 C5
Wembley Rd CALD/MH L18 134 C4
CSBY/BLUN L23 * 69 G6
Wendell St TOX L8 133 H2
Wendover Av AIG/SPK L17 133 H6
Wendover Cl CL/PREN CH43 130 A5
Wendron Rd NG/CROX L11 * 84 C6
Wenger Rd WDN WA8 139 G4
Wenlock Cl WARR WA1 143 K1
Wenlock Dr HLWD L26 155 H4
Wenlock Gdns GTS/LS CH66 202 D1
Wenlock La GTS/LS CH66 202 D1
Wenlock Rd ANF/KKDL L4 97 K6
RUNC WA7 187 K3
Wenning Av MGHL L31 62 C5
Wennington Rd CHTN/BK PR9 23 H5
Wensley Av HLWD L26 155 H4
Wensleydale WLT/FAZ L9 82 D4
Wensleydale Av
PS/BROM CH62 184 B2
RAIN/WH L35 119 F4
Wensleydale Cl MGHL L31 61 K5
WARRW/BUR WA5 141 G1
Wensley Rd GOL/RIS/CU WA3 93 F4
WLT/FAZ L9 82 D4
Wentworth Av WAL/NB CH45 95 H6
WARR WA1 144 A2
Wentworth Cl CL/PREN CH43 130 A5
STHP PR8 33 J5
WDN WA8 139 F4
Wentworth Dr BEB CH63 183 J2
EV L5 113 H3
Wentworth Gv HUY L36 116 B5
Wentworth Rd AIMK WN4 78 E5
Wernbrook Cl CL/PREN CH43 130 A5
Wernbrook Rd ANF/KKDL L4 98 A6
Wervin Cl CL/PREN CH43 149 H1
Wervin Rd CL/PREN CH43 149 H1
KKBY L32 84 C2
Wesley Av RNFD/HAY WA11 90 D4
WAL/EG CH44 111 J2
Wesley Cl NSTN CH64 191 J2
Wesley Gv WAL/EG CH44 112 A4
Wesley St CSBY/WL L22 80 E3
STHP PR8 14 E6
Wessex Cl WARR WA1 144 C2
West Albert Rd AIG/SPK L17 133 G5
West Av GOL/RIS/CU WA3 92 C2
WARRN/WOL WA2 142 E1
WARRS WA4 162 B2
Westbank Av WAL/NB CH45 95 J6
West Bank Dock WDN WA8 158 A6
West Bank Dock Est WDN WA8 157 J6
West Bank Rd EHL/KEN L7 114 C5
Westbank Rd RF/TRAN CH42 131 F6
West Bank St WDN WA8 158 B6
Westbourne Av CSBY/BLUN L23 69 J3
Westbourne Gdns STHP PR8 27 F3
Westbourne Gv WKBY CH48 146 B1
Westbourne Rd CL/PREN CH43 2 B6
STHP PR8 26 E3
WAL/EG CH44 111 F3
WARRS WA4 162 A4
WKBY CH48 146 B1
Westbrook Av PR/KW L34 117 H1
WARRS WA4 162 C1
Westbrook Crs
WARRW/BUR WA5 122 C6
Westbrook Rd MOR/LEA CH46 128 D2
WLTN L25 135 K4
Westbrook Wy
WARRW/BUR WA5 122 B6
Westbury Cl AIG/SPK L17 152 D2
WARR WA1 143 K1
Westbury St BIRK CH41 131 H5
Westcliffe Rd STHP PR8 27 F2
WD/CROXPK L12 98 E6
West Cl CL/PREN CH43 130 A4
PR/KW L34 102 C6
Westcombe Rd ANF/KKDL L4 98 A6
Westcott Rd ANF/KKDL L4 113 K1
Westcott Wy CL/PREN CH43 130 A5
Westdale Rd RF/TRAN CH42 150 D1
WARR WA1 143 K2
WAV L15 134 A1
Westdale Vw WAV L15 134 A1
West Derby Rd
CLB/OSW/ST L13 114 C2
NPK/KEN L6 113 K3
West Derby St VAUX/LVPD L3 9 K3
West Derby Village
WD/CROXPK L12 99 F6
West Dr GR/UP/WCH CH49 129 H4
HES CH60 168 A6
NSTN CH64 191 J3
WARRW/BUR WA5 141 J5
West End Gv RNFD/HAY WA11 89 J5
West End Rd RNFD/HAY WA11 89 J5
Westenra Av EP CH65 195 J3
Western Av HUY L36 116 B4
PS/BROM CH62 171 F1
SPK/HALE L24 173 H2
Western Dr ALL/GAR L19 153 H4
Westerton Rd
WD/CROXPK L12 115 J1
Westfield Av AIMK WN4 79 F5
DV/KA/FCH L14 115 J5
Westfield Crs RUNC WA7 10 B7
Westfield Dr WD/CROXPK L12 99 J2
Westfield Ms RUNC WA7 10 B6
Westfield Rd RUNC WA7 10 A7
WAL/EG CH44 111 K6
WLT/FAZ L9 82 B5
Westfield St ECCL WA10 12 E6
Westfield Wk KKBY L32 84 A2
West Float BIRK CH41 * 111 H6
Westford Rd WARRS WA4 161 K2
Westgate SKEL WN8 55 K5
Westgate Rd PS/BROM CH62 170 D1
WAV L15 * 134 B4
West Gv HES CH60 167 K5
West Hall Ct KNUT WA16 165 K6
Westhaven Crs ORM L39 53 G5
Westhay Crs GOL/RIS/CU WA3 125 J2
Westhead Av GOL/RIS/CU WA3 93 F3
NWD/KWIPK L33 84 E1
Westhead Cl NWD/KWIPK L33 85 F2
Westhead Wk NWD/KWIPK L33 84 E1
West Heath Gv LYMM WA13 145 H5
Westhill STHP PR8 * 14 C7
Westhouse Cl BEB CH63 183 K2
West Hyde LYMM WA13 145 H6
West Kirby Rd WKBY CH48 128 D4
West Knowe CL/PREN CH43 * 130 C5
Westlands Cl NSTN CH64 182 A6
West La FMBY L37 41 F5
KNUT WA16 165 K5
RUNC WA7 177 H6
Westleigh Pl STHEL WA9 120 A2
West Mains SPK/HALE L24 174 B2
West Meade MGHL L31 61 K5
Westminster Av NTHTN L30 70 B5
Westminster Cl WARRS WA4 163 H1
WDN WA8 157 G3
Westminster Dr
PS/BROM CH62 184 A1
RNFD/HAY WA11 90 E4
STHP PR8 33 G4
Westminster Gv EP CH65 6 D3
PR/KW L34 117 G2
Westminster Pl WARR WA1 16 D4
Westminster Rd BTL L20 97 F4
EP CH65 6 D2
WAL/EG CH44 111 H3
Westmoreland Pl EV L5 113 F2
Westmoreland Rd STHP PR8 27 K2
WAL/NB CH45 95 J6
Westmorland Av NTHTN L30 69 K6
WDN WA8 18 E1
Westmorland Dr VAUX/LVPD L3 8 D1
Westmorland Pl EV L5 113 F2
Westmorland Rd HUY L36 116 E5
West Oakhill Pk
CLB/OSW/ST L13 114 E5
Westonby Ct AIMK WN4 79 J6
Weston Crs RUNC WA7 186 C1
Weston Gv HLWD L26 155 K5
MGHL L31 71 G3
Weston Point Dock RUNC WA7 175 K6
Weston Point Expy RUNC WA7 176 B4
Weston Rd RUNC WA7 176 C5
West Orchard La WLT/FAZ L9 83 G3
Westover Rd MGHL L31 62 A6
WARR WA1 143 J2
West Park Dr GTS/LS CH66 202 D3
West Park Rd ECCL WA10 12 B7
West Quay Rd
WARRN/WOL WA2 123 F4
West Rd CL/PREN CH43 130 A4
DV/KA/FCH L14 115 G5
EP CH65 196 B6
RUNC WA7 176 A6
WLT/FAZ L9 97 H2
Westry Cl MOR/LEA CH46 128 C1
West Side STHEL WA9 104 A3
West Side Av RNFD/HAY WA11 89 K5
West St ECCL WA10 103 F4
PR/KW L34 117 J1
STHP PR8 14 D5
WAL/NB CH45 * 111 H2
WARRN/WOL WA2 142 E2
West V NSTN CH64 191 K3
West Vw HUY L36 117 H5
RNFD/HAY WA11 * 75 G3
WARRN/WOL WA2 124 C6
West View Av HUY L36 117 H5
Westview Cl CL/PREN CH43 130 A5
West View Cl HUY L36 117 G5
Westward Ho WKBY CH48 146 E5
Westward Vw AIG/SPK L17 133 F6
CSBY/WL L22 80 C1
West Wy MOR/LEA CH46 109 J6
RUNC WA7 * 177 H5
Westway CL/PREN CH43 130 A5
GR/UP/WCH CH49 128 E5
HES CH60 180 E1
HTWN L38 59 F3
MGHL L31 62 A5
WAV L15 134 C1
Westwick Pl HUY L36 116 B4
Westwood RUNC WA7 178 B4
Westwood Cl STHP PR8 28 B4
Westwood Ct NSTN CH64 181 K5
Westwood Gv WAL/EG CH44 111 G3
Westwood Rd CALD/MH L18 153 K3
CL/PREN CH43 129 K3
Westy La WARRS WA4 143 H5
Wetherby Av WAL/NB CH45 110 E2
Wetherby Cl NEWLW WA12 91 H6
Wetherby Ct HUY L36 116 C2
Wetherby Wy GTS/LS CH66 194 E4
Wethersfield Rd
CL/PREN CH43 130 B5
Wetstone La WKBY CH48 146 D2
Wexford Av SPK/HALE L24 174 E3
Wexford Cl CL/PREN CH43 130 B5
Wexford Rd CL/PREN CH43 130 C5
Wexwood Gv RAIN/WH L35 118 A5
Weybourne Cl
GR/UP/WCH CH49 129 H2
Weybridge Cl WARRS WA4 162 D4
Weyman Av RAIN/WH L35 118 A4
Weymoor Cl BEB CH63 170 B3
Weymouth Av STHEL WA9 104 D4
Weymouth Cl CHLDW L16 135 G1
RUNC WA7 188 D1
Weymouth Rd
WARRW/BUR WA5 121 K1
Whaley La PEN/TH CH61 148 C5
Whalley Av ECCL WA10 88 B4
RNFD/HAY WA11 75 G3
Whalley Ct NTHTN L30 70 A5
Whalley Dr FMBY L37 49 G3
ORM L39 53 G6
Whalley Gv WDN WA8 139 J6
Whalley Rd RF/TRAN CH42 2 D7
Whalleys Rd SKEL WN8 56 D1
Whalley St TOX L8 * 132 E5
WARR WA1 17 G3
Wharf BRSC L40 36 D5
Wharfdale Cl
WARRW/BUR WA5 141 H2
Wharfedale RUNC WA7 188 A1
Wharfedale Av RF/TRAN CH42 150 A1
Wharfedale Dr PS/BROM CH62 184 C2
RAIN/WH L35 119 F4
Wharfedale Rd WAL/NB CH45 111 F1
Wharfe La EP CH65 195 K2
Wharford La RUNC WA7 178 D2
Wharf Rd NEWLW WA12 105 J3
Wharfside Ct WARRS WA4 162 D3
Wharf St PS/BROM CH62 151 G6
WARR WA1 17 H6
Wharmby Rd RNFD/HAY WA11 90 D5
Wharncliffe Rd
CLB/OSW/ST L13 114 E4
Wharton Cl GR/UP/WCH CH49 128 E3
Wharton St STHEL WA9 103 K4
Whatcroft Cl RUNC WA7 187 G1
Wheatacre SKEL WN8 56 A5
Wheat Cft WARRW/BUR WA5 * 141 K3
Wheatcroft Rd CALD/MH L18 153 K1
Wheatear Cl NTHLY L27 136 B5
Wheatfield Cl GTS/LS CH66 195 F6
MOR/LEA CH46 129 G2
NTHTN L30 70 E6
Wheatfield Rd WDN WA8 138 B4
Wheatfield Vw LITH L21 81 J1
Wheat Hill Rd NTHLY L27 136 B2
Wheatland Cl STHEL WA9 120 A3
Wheatland La WAL/EG CH44 111 K4
Wheatland Rd HES CH60 168 C6
Wheatlands RUNC WA7 177 H4
Wheatlands Cl NTHLY L27 136 A3
Wheat La BRSC L40 39 G6
Wheatley Av BTL L20 82 B6
NEWLW WA12 91 H6
Wheatsheaf Av STHEL WA9 120 B1
Wheeler Dr MGHL L31 72 A6
Whelan Gdns STHEL WA9 119 G1
Wheldrake Cl GTS/LS CH66 194 E4
Whernside WDN WA8 157 H1
Whetstone Hey GTS/LS CH66 195 G4
Whetstone La BIRK CH41 2 D5
RF/TRAN CH42 150 C1
Whickham Cl WDN WA8 138 E6
Whimbrel Av NEWLW WA12 106 C2
Whimbrel Cl RUNC WA7 187 J2
Whimbrel Pk HLWD L26 155 H2
Whinbury Ct STHEL WA9 120 A3
Whinchat Av NEWLW WA12 106 C1
Whinchat Cl GOL/RIS/CU WA3 93 F4
Whinchat Dr GOL/RIS/CU WA3 125 H4
Whinfell Gv RUNC WA7 187 H2
Whinfell Rd WD/CROXPK L12 115 G2
Whinfield Rd CSBY/BLUN L23 69 H3
WLT/FAZ L9 82 C5
Whinhowe Rd NG/CROX L11 99 F3
Whinmoor Cl CL/PREN CH43 130 A3
Whinmoor Rd AIN/FAZ L10 83 K4
WD/CROXPK L12 115 G2
Whinney Gv East MGHL L31 71 F3
Whinney Gv West MGHL L31 71 F3
Whiston La HUY L36 117 G3
Whitbarrow Rd LYMM WA13 145 H5
Whitburn Cl AIMK WN4 78 C5
Whitburn Rd NWD/KWIPK L33 73 F5
Whitby Av CHTN/BK PR9 21 F5
WAL/NB CH45 110 E2
WARRN/WOL WA2 123 K5
Whitby La CH/BCN CH1 202 E4
Whitby Rd EP CH65 6 C6
RUNC WA7 10 E7
Whitby St NPK/KEN L6 114 B1
Whitchurch Cl WARR WA1 143 K1
Whitchurch Wy RUNC WA7 187 G1
Whitcroft Rd NPK/KEN L6 114 B4
Whitebeam GTS/LS CH66 202 D2
Whitebeam Cl NWD/KWIPK L33 72 E3
RUNC WA7 178 B4
Whitebeam Dr WD/CROXPK L12 99 H2
Whitebeam Gdns STHEL WA9 118 E1
Whitebeam Wk
GR/UP/WCH CH49 147 J1
Whitechapel CLVPS L1 8 E4
Whitecroft Av GOL/RIS/CU WA3 93 F2
Whitecroft Rd GTS/LS CH66 202 C1
Whitecross Rd
WARRW/BUR WA5 142 B4
Whiteside Cl
GR/UP/WCH CH49 129 H5
Whitefield Av ANF/KKDL L4 97 G5
Whitefield Cl GR/UP/WCH CH49 129 J6
HTWN L38 59 F5
Whitefield Dr KKBY L32 84 A1
Whitefield La RAIN/WH L35 136 D3
Whitefield Rd ECCL WA10 12 A1
NPK/KEN L6 113 K3
WARRS WA4 162 A3
WLT/FAZ L9 82 D6
Whitefields CHNE CH2 198 C6
Whitefield Wy NPK/KEN L6 113 J3
Whitegate Cl PR/KW L34 100 D1
Whitegates Cl NSTN CH64 183 F6
Whitegates Crs NSTN CH64 193 F1
Whitehall Cl ANF/KKDL L4 97 F4
Whitehall Pl FROD/HEL WA6 200 E1
Whitehart Cl ANF/KKDL L4 97 K4
Whitehaven Cl STHP PR8 33 H6
Whitehedge Rd ALL/GAR L19 153 K4
Whitehey Rd SKEL WN8 56 A5
Whitehorn Dr STBRV L28 100 B6
Whitehouse Av FMBY L37 49 G2
White House Cl
RNFD/HAY WA11 90 A5
White House Dr WARR WA1 144 D2
Whitehouse Expy RUNC WA7 187 J2
White House La BRSC L40 30 B6
Whitehouse La FMBY L37 49 G2
HES CH60 168 D4
Whitehouse Rd
CLB/OSW/ST L13 115 F5
Whitehouse V RUNC WA7 * 188 E2
Whitelands Meadow
GR/UP/WCH CH49 129 F4
Whiteledge Rd SKEL WN8 56 D5
Whiteleggs La LYMM WA13 165 H2
Whiteley's La BRSC L40 54 C3
White Lodge Av HUY L36 116 D4
White Lodge Cl
PS/BROM CH62 184 B2
White Lodge Dr AIMK WN4 79 J5
Whitely Gv NWD/KWIPK L33 73 F3
White Meadow Dr
CSBY/BLUN L23 69 H3
Whitemere Ct EP CH65 * 6 D1
White Moss Rd SKEL WN8 55 J6
White Moss Rd South
SKEL WN8 56 A6
Whiterails Dr ORM L39 45 H5
Whiterails Ms ORM L39 45 G5
White Rock St NPK/KEN L6 113 K3
Whitesands Rd LYMM WA13 145 H5
Whiteside Av RNFD/HAY WA11 89 H6
Whiteside Cl EV L5 113 F2
Whiteside Rd RNFD/HAY WA11 90 A5
Whitestock SKEL WN8 56 A5
Whitestone Cl PR/KW L34 100 C3
White St CLVPS L1 9 F7
WARR WA1 16 B5
WARRS WA4 162 B2
WDN WA8 * 158 B6
Whitethorn Av
WARRW/BUR WA5 141 G4
Whitewell Dr
GR/UP/WCH CH49 129 G3
Whitewood Cl AIMK WN4 79 F3
Whitewood Pk WLT/FAZ L9 83 G5
Whitfield Av WARR WA1 143 J2
Whitfield Ct RF/TRAN CH42 131 G5
Whitfield Gv RNFD/HAY WA11 89 K5
Whitfield La HES CH60 168 A4
Whitfield St RF/TRAN CH42 131 G5
Whitford Rd RF/TRAN CH42 131 F5
Whitham Av CSBY/BLUN L23 81 G1
Whithorn St EHL/KEN L7 133 J1
Whitland Rd NPK/KEN L6 114 B4
Whitledge Gn AIMK WN4 79 F4
Whitledge Rd AIMK WN4 79 F4
Whitley Av WARRS WA4 143 K5
Whitley Cl RUNC WA7 176 C5
Whitley St VAUX/LVPD L3 112 D3
Whitlow Av GOL/RIS/CU WA3 92 A2
Whitman St WAV L15 133 K2
Whitmoor Cl RAIN/WH L35 119 G6
Whitney Pl WLTN L25 155 F1
Whitney Rd WLTN L25 135 K6
Whitstable Pk WDN WA8 138 D5
Whitstone Cl WLTN L25 154 B1
Whitstone Dr SKEL WN8 57 F6
Whittaker Av
WARRN/WOL WA2 123 K5
Whittaker Cl
CLB/OSW/ST L13 * 114 D6
Whittier St TOX L8 133 H2
Whittle Av RNFD/HAY WA11 89 K6
WARRW/BUR WA5 122 A6
Whittle Cl EV L5 113 G1
Whittle Dr ORM L39 45 J4
Whittle Hall La
WARRW/BUR WA5 141 G3
Whittle St ECCL WA10 103 F4
EV L5 113 G1
Whittlewood Cl
GOL/RIS/CU WA3 125 J2
Whittlewood Ct
NWD/KWIPK L33 72 E5
Whitwell Cl WARRW/BUR WA5 140 E2
Whitworth Cl GOL/RIS/CU WA3 125 G4
Wholesome La CHTN/BK PR9 30 B5
Wicket Cl NG/CROX L11 84 C6
Wickham Cl WAL/EG CH44 111 K5
Wicklow Cl GTS/LS CH66 194 D3
Wicks Crs FMBY L37 48 C1
Wicks Gdns FMBY L37 48 E2
Wicks Gn FMBY L37 48 C2
Wicks Green Cl FMBY L37 48 C1
Wicks La FMBY L37 48 C2
Wicksten Dr RUNC WA7 11 H5
Widdale Av RAIN/WH L35 * 119 F4
Widdale Cl WARRW/BUR WA5 141 G2
Widgeons Covert BEB CH63 182 A2
Widmore Rd WLTN L25 135 K5
Widnes Rd WDN WA8 18 E4
The Wiend BEB CH63 151 F6
RF/TRAN CH42 150 C2
Wigan Rd AIMK WN4 78 E2
AIMK WN4 79 G6
ORM L39 45 K6
SKEL WN8 56 B5
WGNW/BIL/O WN5 77 J2
Wiggins La BRSC L40 31 F2
Wight Cl EP CH65 203 G2
Wightman Av NEWLW WA12 91 H6
Wightman St NPK/KEN L6 113 K4
Wight Moss Wy STHP PR8 28 A4
Wigmore Cl GOL/RIS/CU WA3 125 J1
Wignall Cl KKBY L32 * 84 D4
Wignalls Meadow HTWN L38 59 F4
Wigston Cl STHP PR8 33 H5
Wilberforce Rd ANF/KKDL L4 97 K4
Wilbraham Pl EV L5 113 F2
Wilbraham St EV L5 113 F2
STHEL WA9 120 C4
Wilburn St ANF/KKDL L4 97 H4
Wilbur St STHEL WA9 104 C6
Wilcock Cl EV L5 113 F2
Wilcock Rd RNFD/HAY WA11 91 F3
Wilcote Cl WDN WA8 139 H5
Wilcove SKEL WN8 56 B4
Wild Arum Cl GOL/RIS/CU WA3 93 F3
Wildbrook Dr BIRK CH41 110 D5
Wildcherry Gdns STHEL WA9 102 D6
Wilderspool Cswy WARRS WA4 16 D7
Wilderspool Crs WARRS WA4 162 A2
Wilde St VAUX/LVPD L3 * 9 G3
Wilding Av RUNC WA7 11 G4
Wild Pl BTL L20 82 B4
Wildwood Gv WARR WA1 144 A2
Wilfer Cl EHL/KEN L7 133 H1
Wilfred Owen Dr
CL/PREN CH43 130 B2
Wilkes Av MOR/LEA CH46 110 B4
Wilkie St WAV L15 133 K2
Wilkinson Av WARR WA1 143 J3
Wilkinson Cl WDN WA8 158 B6
Wilkinson St BIRK CH41 2 C6
WARRN/WOL WA2 143 F2
Wilkinson Street Ms EP CH65 6 D2
Wilkinson St North EP CH65 6 D2
Wilkin St ANF/KKDL L4 * 97 G6
Willan St CL/PREN CH43 130 E5
Willard St BTL L20 82 A5
Willaston Dr HLWD L26 155 K5
Willaston Rd ANF/KKDL L4 97 K4
BEB CH63 182 E1
MOR/LEA CH46 109 H6
NSTN CH64 182 E5
Willedstan Av CSBY/BLUN L23 69 F6
William Brown St CLVPS L1 9 F3
William Harvey Cl NTHTN L30 70 C6
William Henry St BTL L20 4 D7
VAUX/LVPD L3 113 G4
William Jessop Wy
VAUX/LVPD L3 8 A2
William Morris Av BTL L20 82 B6
William Moult St EV L5 113 F2
William Penn Cl
WARRW/BUR WA5 * 141 F5
William Rd RNFD/HAY WA11 89 J6
William Roberts Av KKBY L32 84 B1
Williams Av BTL L20 5 K1
NEWLW WA12 91 H6
Williamson Ct WLTN L25 * 155 F2
Williamson Sq CLVPS L1 8 E4
Williamson St CLVPS L1 8 E4
Williams St PR/KW L34 117 K1
William St BIRK CH41 3 G4
ECCL WA10 * 13 G4
WAL/EG CH44 112 A5
WDN WA8 158 D1
William Wall Rd LITH L21 81 J1
Willingdon Rd CHLDW L16 115 J6
Willington Av PS/BROM CH62 184 B4
Willink Rd RNFD/HAY WA11 89 F4
Willis Cl RAIN/WH L35 117 K5
Willis La RAIN/WH L35 117 K5
Willis St WARR WA1 17 H2
Williton Rd CHLDW L16 135 F4
Willmer Rd ANF/KKDL L4 97 K6
RF/TRAN CH42 2 C7
Willoughby Cl
WARRW/BUR WA5 122 C6
Willoughby Dr ECCL WA10 102 D5
Willoughby Rd CSBY/WL L22 81 F2
DV/KA/FCH L14 115 J5
WAL/EG CH44 111 G3
Willow Av HUY L36 136 B1
KKBY L32 72 B6
NEWLW WA12 106 D1

RAIN/WH L35 117 K4
WDN WA8 158 C1
Willowbank Cl HUY L36 116 C2
Willow Bank Est
NEWLW WA12 107 F2
Willowbank Rd
PS/BROM CH62 151 G5
RF/TRAN CH42 131 G6
Willow Brook ORM L39 35 J3
Willowbrow Rd BEB CH63 182 E4
Willow Cl LYMM WA13 145 K5
RUNC WA7 176 E6
Willow Ct TOX L8 * 133 F5
Willow Crs BRSC L40 39 F3
WARR WA1 144 A1
WARRS WA4 * 160 D4
Willowcroft Rd
WAL/EG CH44 * 111 J5
Willowdale NEWLW WA12 106 E2
Willowdale Rd CALD/MH L18 134 A4
WLT/FAZ L9 97 J1
Willowdale Wy GTS/LS CH66 202 D3
Willow Dr SKEL WN8 56 A4
WARRS WA4 162 C2
Willow End BRSC L40 39 F5
Willowfield Gv AIMK WN4 91 F1
Willow Gn ORM L39 45 K6
WLTN L25 135 G5
Willow Gv AIMK WN4 79 K4
CHNE CH2 198 B6
CHTN/BK PR9 23 G6
FMBY L37 49 F1
GOL/RIS/CU WA3 92 B2
GTS/LS CH66 202 E2
MOR/LEA CH46 128 E2
RAIN/WH L35 118 A2
WAV L15 134 B1
Willowhey CHTN/BK PR9 23 H2
Willow Hey MGHL L31 71 H2
SKEL WN8 56 B4
Willow La BEB CH63 182 E4
Willow Lea CL/PREN CH43 130 C5
Willow Moss Cl MOR/LEA CH46 110 A5
Willow Pk GR/UP/WCH CH49 128 D5
Willow Rd ECCL WA10 102 E2
NEWLW WA12 106 E1
RNFD/HAY WA11 90 D4
WAV L15 133 K1
The Willows FROD/HEL WA6 201 F1
STHEL WA9 * 120 A3
STHP PR8 * 27 K3
WAL/NB CH45 94 E6
WARRW/BUR WA5 141 G4
Willow Tree Av STHEL WA9 120 B3
Willow Wk SKEL WN8 56 D1
Willow Wy CSBY/BLUN L23 69 F4
NG/CROX L11 84 C6
Wills Av MGHL L31 62 A5
Willsford Av KKBY L32 72 A6
Wilmcote Gv STHP PR8 33 H5
Wilmere La WDN WA8 139 F3
Wilmot Av WARRW/BUR WA5 141 G3
Wilmot Dr GOL/RIS/CU WA3 92 A4
Wilmslow Av GTS/LS CH66 195 H4
Wilmslow Crs WARRS WA4 144 C6
Wilmslow Dr GTS/LS CH66 195 H4
Wilne Rd WAL/NB CH45 * 111 G1
Wilsden Rd WDN WA8 157 G2
Wilsford Cl GOL/RIS/CU WA3 92 C2
Wilson Av WAL/EG CH44 112 A3
Wilson Cl ECCL WA10 12 D5
WARRS WA4 144 C6
WDN WA8 19 K1
Wilson Gv ALL/GAR L19 153 K5
Wilson La GOL/RIS/CU WA3 125 G2
Wilson Patten St WARR WA1 16 B6
Wilson Rd HUY L36 117 F5
RAIN/WH L35 117 K4
WAL/EG CH44 * 112 A3
Wilsons La LITH L21 81 J3
Wilson St TOX L8 133 F5
WARRW/BUR WA5 142 D2
Wilstan Av BEB CH63 150 C6
Wilton Gv CLB/OSW/ST L13 114 E5
Wilton La GOL/RIS/CU WA3 93 H6
Wilton Rd HUY L36 116 D5
RF/TRAN CH42 151 F2
Wiltons Dr PR/KW L34 100 C2
Wilton St AIMK WN4 78 E3
WAL/EG CH44 111 H3
Wiltshire Cl WARR WA1 144 C3
Wiltshire Gdns ECCL WA10 103 H3
Wimbledon St WAL/NB CH45 111 H2
WAV L15 133 K2
Wimborne Cl DV/KA/FCH L14 116 B1
Wimborne Pl DV/KA/FCH L14 116 B2
Wimborne Rd DV/KA/FCH L14 116 B2
Wimborne Wy PEN/TH CH61 148 A4
Wimbourne Av PEN/TH CH61 148 D6
Wimbrick Cl MOR/LEA CH46 129 G1
ORM L39 53 H1
Wimbrick Ct MOR/LEA CH46 * 129 G1
Wimbrick Crs ORM L39 53 H2
Wimbrick Hey MOR/LEA CH46 129 G1
Wimpole St EHL/KEN L7 113 K5
Winchester Av AIMK WN4 79 F6
AIN/FAZ L10 71 G6
CSBY/WL L22 80 D1
EP CH65 7 G7
WARRW/BUR WA5 141 K4
Winchester Cl WLTN L25 154 E4
Winchester Dr WAL/EG CH44 111 G2
Winchester Pl WDN WA8 157 H3
Winchester Rd NPK/KEN L6 114 A1
RNFD/HAY WA11 90 D2
Winchfield Rd WAV L15 134 A3
Windbourne Rd AIG/SPK L17 152 C1
Windermere Av
RNFD/HAY WA11 88 D3
WARRN/WOL WA2 123 J4
WDN WA8 139 G6
Windermere Cl NSTN CH64 192 A2
Windermere Crs STHP PR8 33 J6
Windermere Dr MGHL L31 62 C5
NWD/KWIPK L33 72 C5
RNFD/HAY WA11 66 B5
WD/CROXPK L12 99 G4
Windermere Rd
CL/PREN CH43 129 K4
EP CH65 203 G1
HTWN L38 59 G3
RNFD/HAY WA11 90 A5
Windermere St EV L5 113 J1
WDN WA8 139 G5
Windermere Ter TOX L8 * 133 G4
Windfield Cl NWD/KWIPK L33 73 F3
Windfield Gdns GTS/LS CH66 195 G2
Windfield Gn ALL/GAR L19 172 C2
Windfield Rd ALL/GAR L19 172 C1
Windle Ash MGHL L31 62 A5
Windle Av CSBY/BLUN L23 69 H5
Windlebrook Crs ECCL WA10 87 J5
Windle City ECCL WA10 88 C5
Windle Ct GOL/RIS/CU WA3 * 124 E3
NSTN CH64 181 K5
Windle Gv ECCL WA10 87 K5
Windle Hall Dr ECCL WA10 88 B4
Windlehurst Av ECCL WA10 88 B5
Windleshaw Rd ECCL WA10 12 B1
Windle St ECCL WA10 12 E2
Windle V ECCL WA10 12 C2
Windmill Av CSBY/BLUN L23 69 G4
ORM L39 45 G6
Windmill Cl NWD/KWIPK L33 * 72 D4
WARRS WA4 162 B5
Windmill Gdns STHEL WA9 104 B1
Windmill Hts SKEL WN8 57 J5
Windmill Hill Av RUNC WA7 178 C3
Windmill Hill Av East
RUNC WA7 178 C5
Windmill Hill Av North
RUNC WA7 178 B2
Windmill Hill Av South
RUNC WA7 178 C4
Windmill Hill Av West
RUNC WA7 178 B3
Windmill La WARRS WA4 162 B5
WARRS WA4 179 F6
WARRW/BUR WA5 141 F4
Windmill St RUNC WA7 11 G4
Window La ALL/GAR L19 172 B1
Windrows SKEL WN8 56 B4
Windscale Rd
WARRN/WOL WA2 124 C5
Windsor Av LITH L21 81 H3
NEWLW WA12 106 D3
Windsor Cl BRSC L40 38 E6
GR/UP/WCH CH49 128 E6
NTHTN L30 70 C4
PS/BROM CH62 151 F4
Windsor Ct BTL L20 82 B6
STHP PR8 27 F3
WARRS WA4 * 162 D2
Windsor Dr EP CH65 195 K6
RNFD/HAY WA11 91 F4
WARRS WA4 144 A6
Windsor Gv RUNC WA7 176 E5
Windsor Ms PS/BROM CH62 * 151 G4
Windsor Park Rd AIN/FAZ L10 71 H6
Windsor Rd AIMK WN4 91 G1
BTL L20 82 B6
CHTN/BK PR9 15 J5
CLB/OSW/ST L13 114 B1
ECCL WA10 12 A5
FMBY L37 48 E4
GOL/RIS/CU WA3 92 D3
HUY L36 116 B5
MGHL L31 71 F1
RAIN/WH L35 118 A3
SKEL WN8 57 J5
WDN WA8 139 F5
WGNW/BIL/O WN5 77 J4
Windsor St CL/PREN CH43 2 C6
TOX L8 132 E2
WAL/NB CH45 95 H4
WARRW/BUR WA5 142 B3
Windsor Vw TOX L8 133 G2
Windus St ECCL WA10 12 D5
Windways GTS/LS CH66 195 G2
Windy Arbor Cl RAIN/WH L35 117 K6
Windy Arbor Rd RAIN/WH L35 117 K6
Windy Bank PS/BROM CH62 151 G5
Windy Bank Av
GOL/RIS/CU WA3 93 F3
Windy Harbour Rd STHP PR8 34 A2
Wineva Gdns CSBY/BLUN L23 69 G6
Winfield Wy WDN WA8 19 F3
Winford St WAL/EG CH44 111 K4
Winfrith Cl BEB CH63 170 B3
Winfrith Dr BEB CH63 170 B3
Winfrith Rd WARRN/WOL WA2 124 C6
WLTN L25 135 K5
Wingate Av STHEL WA9 119 F1
Wingate Cl CL/PREN CH43 * 130 B5
Wingate Rd AIG/SPK L17 153 F1
NWD/KWIPK L33 72 E5
PS/BROM CH62 184 B2
Wingfield Cl SFTN L29 70 A1
Wingrave Wy NG/CROX L11 99 F4
Winhill WLTN L25 135 H5
Winifred La ORM L39 53 F4
Winifred Rd AIN/FAZ L10 84 A4
Winifred St EHL/KEN L7 113 K6
WARRN/WOL WA2 17 F1
Winkle St TOX L8 * 132 E4
Winmarleigh St WARR WA1 16 B5
Winmoss Dr NWD/KWIPK L33 72 E4
Winnington Rd HOY CH47 127 F5
Winnipeg Dr NTHLY L27 136 B4
The Winnows RUNC WA7 177 G4
Winsford Cl RNFD/HAY WA11 90 E4
Winsford Dr WARRW/BUR WA5 105 J6
Winsford Gv GTS/LS CH66 195 F6
Winsford Rd CLB/OSW/ST L13 114 D1
Winsham Cl KKBY L32 84 D3
Winsham Rd KKBY L32 84 D3
Winskill Rd NG/CROX L11 98 E4
Winslade Ct ANF/KKDL L4 97 K3
Winslade Rd ANF/KKDL L4 97 K4
Winslow Cl RUNC WA7 178 C5
Winslow St ANF/KKDL L4 97 H5
Winstanley Cl
WARRW/BUR WA5 141 K4
Winstanley Rd AIMK WN4 78 A2
CSBY/WL L22 81 F1
NSTN CH64 191 K4
PS/BROM CH62 151 G4
SKEL WN8 56 B5
WGNW/BIL/O WN5 77 K1
Winster Dr NTHLY L27 136 D6
The Winsters SKEL WN8 56 B4
Winston Av NEWLW WA12 106 B2
STHEL WA9 105 F3
Winston Crs STHP PR8 28 B5
Winston Dr CL/PREN CH43 129 K4
Winstone Rd DV/KA/FCH L14 116 A3
Winston Gv MOR/LEA CH46 129 F1
Winterburn Crs
WD/CROXPK L12 99 H6
Winter Gv STHEL WA9 105 F2
Winterhey Av WAL/EG CH44 111 H5
Winterlea Dr HLWD L26 155 K5
Winter St NPK/KEN L6 113 J4
Winthrop Pk CL/PREN CH43 130 B4
Winton Cl WAL/NB CH45 95 G5
Winton Gv RUNC WA7 * 178 C4
Winton Rd GOL/RIS/CU WA3 93 F6
Winwick La GOL/RIS/CU WA3 107 K3
Winwick Link Rd
WARRN/WOL WA2 123 H1
Winwick Park Av
WARRN/WOL WA2 123 G2
Winwick Rd NEWLW WA12 106 E3
WARRN/WOL WA2 16 D2
Winwick St WARR WA1 16 D4
Winwick Vw
WARRW/BUR WA5 105 H4
Wirral Cl BEB CH63 170 B2
Wirral Crs NSTN CH64 192 A4
Wirral Gdns BEB CH63 170 B2
Wirral Mt WAL/NB CH45 111 F2
WKBY CH48 146 E1
Wirral Vw ALL/GAR L19 153 G5
Wirral Vls WAL/NB CH45 110 E1
Wirral Wy CL/PREN CH43 129 K4
NSTN CH64 181 F4
NSTN CH64 192 B2
WKBY CH48 146 C1
Wisenholme Cl RUNC WA7 187 H3
Witham Cl NTHTN L30 70 D5
Witham Rd SKEL WN8 55 K4
Withburn Cl GR/UP/WCH CH49 129 F4
Withensfield WAL/NB CH45 111 H1
Withen's La WAL/NB CH45 111 H2
Withens Rd MGHL L31 62 B4
The Withens STBRV L28 100 B6
Withers Av WARRN/WOL WA2 143 G1
Wither's La KNUT WA16 164 D6
Withert Av BEB CH63 150 C3
Witherwin Av WARRS WA4 163 F4
Withington Rd SPK/HALE L24 174 A2
WAL/EG CH44 111 J4
Withins Fld HTWN L38 59 F4
Withins La HTWN L38 50 B6
Withins Rd RNFD/HAY WA11 90 D3
Within Wy SPK/HALE L24 175 F4
Withnell Cl CLB/OSW/ST L13 115 F5
Withnell Rd CLB/OSW/ST L13 115 F5
Withy Cl FROD/HEL WA6 201 F1
Withycombe Rd
WARRW/BUR WA5 141 F5
Witley Av MOR/LEA CH46 109 J6
Witley Cl MOR/LEA CH46 109 J6
Witney Cl GR/UP/WCH CH49 128 D6
Witney Gdns WARRS WA4 162 E5
Wittenham Cl
GR/UP/WCH CH49 * 129 G5
Wittering La HES CH60 167 H6
Wittom Rd CLB/OSW/ST L13 114 B1
Witton Wy RNFD/HAY WA11 75 H2
Witt Rd WDN WA8 18 C6
Wivern Pl RUNC WA7 11 G3
Woburn Av NEWLW WA12 106 D3
Woburn Cl CLB/OSW/ST L13 114 D3
RNFD/HAY WA11 90 E4
Woburn Dr WDN WA8 138 C4
Woburn Hl CLB/OSW/ST L13 114 D3
Woburn Pl RF/TRAN CH42 * 150 E1
Woburn Rd WAL/NB CH45 111 H1
WARRN/WOL WA2 123 G3
Wokefield Wy ECCL WA10 102 D1
Wokingham Gv HUY L36 136 B1
Wolfe Cl WARRS WA4 163 F3
Wolfenden Av BTL L20 82 B6
Wolferton Cl
GR/UP/WCH CH49 129 J2
Wolfe St TOX L8 132 D4
Wolfrick Dr BEB CH63 170 D4
Wolfson Sq AIMK WN4 78 E5
Wollaton Dr STHP PR8 28 C4
Wolmer St AIMK WN4 79 F5
Wolseley Rd ECCL WA10 12 E2
Wolsey Cl AIMK WN4 79 F4
Wolsey St BTL L20 96 E4
Wolstenholme Sq CLVPS L1 9 F6
Wolverham Rd EP CH65 196 B6
Wolverton SKEL WN8 56 B5
Wolverton Dr RUNC WA7 178 C4
Wolverton St NPK/KEN L6 114 A1
Woodacre Gv GTS/LS CH66 195 J1
Woodacre Rd GTS/LS CH66 195 H1
Woodale Cl WARRW/BUR WA5 141 F2
Woodall Dr RUNC WA7 11 F7
Wood Av BTL L20 5 K1
Woodbank Cl CHLDW L16 135 G1
Woodbank Pk CL/PREN CH43 130 B5
Woodbank Rd EP CH65 203 F1
WARRW/BUR WA5 141 H5
Woodberry Cl CL/PREN CH43 130 A5
NWD/KWIPK L33 72 E3
Woodbine St EV L5 97 F6
Woodbourne Rd
DV/KA/FCH L14 115 H3
Woodbridge Av HLWD L26 155 G1
Woodbrook Av WLT/FAZ L9 82 C5
Woodburn Bvd BEB CH63 150 D3
Woodburn Dr HES CH60 180 E1
Woodchurch Ct CL/PREN CH43 131 F6
Woodchurch La GTS/LS CH66 195 H4
RF/TRAN CH42 150 A1
Woodchurch Rd
CLB/OSW/ST L13 114 E3
GR/UP/WCH CH49 148 E2
RF/TRAN CH42 131 F6
Wood Cl BIRK CH41 2 E2
KKBY L32 84 C1
Woodclose GTS/LS CH66 184 D6
Woodcote Av EP CH65 203 F1
Woodcote Bank
RF/TRAN CH42 150 E4
Woodcote Cl NWD/KWIPK L33 73 F5
WARRN/WOL WA2 123 K6
The Woodcotes
PS/BROM CH62 184 A1
Woodcot La HES CH60 167 J4
Woodcroft SKEL WN8 56 B5
Woodcroft Dr PEN/TH CH61 167 K3
Woodcroft La BEB CH63 150 D3
Woodcroft Rd WAV L15 133 J2
Woodcroft Wy STHEL WA9 * 120 A3
Woodedge AIMK WN4 79 F6
Woodend PEN/TH CH61 167 K1
Woodend Av CSBY/BLUN L23 69 F3
MGHL L31 71 F2
SPK/HALE L24 155 F6
Wood End La NSTN CH64 193 F5
Woodend La SPK/HALE L24 173 H1
Woodend Rd EP CH65 195 J3
Woodene Cl KKBY L32 85 F4
Woodfall Cl NSTN CH64 192 B3
Woodfall Gv NSTN CH64 192 B3
Woodfall La NSTN CH64 192 A3
Woodfarm Hey STBRV L28 100 A5
Woodfield Av BEB CH63 150 D3
Woodfield Crs AIMK WN4 91 F1
Woodfield Rd BEB CH63 170 C2
ORM L39 53 G2
PEN/TH CH61 167 J1
WLT/FAZ L9 82 C6
Woodfield Rd North EP CH65 6 D4
Woodford Av GOL/RIS/CU WA3 92 E4
Woodford Cl RUNC WA7 186 E1
WARRS WA4 144 B6
Woodford Rd DV/KA/FCH L14 115 J3
ECCL WA10 87 K5
PS/BROM CH62 151 G3
Woodgate NTHLY L27 135 K3
Woodger St ALL/GAR L19 153 K6
Wood Gn CL/PREN CH43 * 129 K1
PR/KW L34 117 J1
Woodgreen Rd
CLB/OSW/ST L13 114 E3
Wood Gv CLB/OSW/ST L13 114 D5
Woodhall Av WAL/EG CH44 111 K3
Woodhall Cl WARRW/BUR WA5 141 H1
Woodhall Rd CLB/OSW/ST L13 114 E4
Woodham Gv NSTN CH64 192 A4
Woodhatch Rd RUNC WA7 187 K2
Woodhead Rd PS/BROM CH62 151 H5
Woodhead St PS/BROM CH62 151 G4
Woodhey Gv BEB CH63 150 E4
Woodhey Rd ALL/GAR L19 153 H3
BEB CH63 150 E4
Woodhouse Cl ANF/KKDL L4 97 G6
GOL/RIS/CU WA3 125 H4
Woodin Rd RF/TRAN CH42 151 F3
Woodkind Hey BEB CH63 170 C4
Woodland Av BRSC L40 36 D2
HOY CH47 108 B6
LYMM WA13 165 H1
NEWLW WA12 * 107 F2
WDN WA8 18 B1
Woodland Dr AIMK WN4 79 G4
GR/UP/WCH CH49 129 H6
LYMM WA13 165 G1
WAL/NB CH45 95 J6
Woodland Gv RF/TRAN CH42 150 E3
Woodland Rd ANF/KKDL L4 98 B5
EP CH65 203 F1
GR/UP/WCH CH49 129 H6
HLWD L26 155 H4
LITH L21 81 F4
MGHL L31 71 K5
RF/TRAN CH42 150 E3
WKBY CH48 147 F1
Woodlands Cl CHTN/BK PR9 15 K2
FMBY L37 48 D3
NSTN CH64 191 J1
ORM L39 54 A1
Woodlands Dr PEN/TH CH61 168 C1
WARRS WA4 144 C6
Woodlands Pk NEWLW WA12 * 91 H2
WD/CROXPK L12 114 E2
Woodlands Rd AIG/SPK L17 153 F1
FMBY L37 48 D3
HUY L36 116 B5
NSTN CH64 191 J1
PEN/TH CH61 148 A6
RNFD/HAY WA11 89 F4
WLT/FAZ L9 83 G5
The Woodlands BIRK CH41 2 D6
GR/UP/WCH CH49 129 G3
PR/KW L34 102 B6
STHP PR8 33 J4
Woodland Vw CSBY/BLUN L23 69 H2
Wood La FMBY L37 50 E4
GR/UP/WCH CH49 128 E4
HUY L36 117 H5
NSTN CH64 181 H5
NTHLY L27 136 C4
PR/KW L34 117 H1
RUNC WA7 187 J4
WAL/NB CH45 110 E1
WARRS WA4 162 D3
Wood Lea WD/CROXPK L12 99 J2
Woodlea Cl CHTN/BK PR9 21 G6
PS/BROM CH62 184 A2
Woodlee Rd WLTN L25 135 K5
Woodleigh Cl MGHL L31 61 K2
Woodley Fold
WARRW/BUR WA5 141 G5
Woodley Park Rd SKEL WN8 56 D1
Woodley Rd MGHL L31 71 F3
Woodmoss La STHP PR8 29 H5
Woodpecker Cl
GOL/RIS/CU WA3 125 H3
GR/UP/WCH CH49 128 E4
WD/CROXPK L12 99 K4
Woodpecker Dr HLWD L26 155 H1
Woodridge RUNC WA7 178 B4
Wood Rd HLWD L26 155 H4
Woodrock Rd WLTN L25 154 E1
Woodrow SKEL WN8 56 A5
Woodruff St TOX L8 132 E5
Woods Cl ORM L39 51 H1
Woodside Av AIMK WN4 79 F1
FROD/HEL WA6 201 G2
MOR/LEA CH46 128 E2
RNFD/HAY WA11 88 C3
STHP PR8 33 H6
Woodside Cl WD/CROXPK L12 99 F5
Woodside Ferry Ap BIRK CH41 3 J3
Woodside La LYMM WA13 165 J2
Woodside Rd PEN/TH CH61 148 B5
RNFD/HAY WA11 90 D4
WARRW/BUR WA5 141 G3
Woodside St EHL/KEN L7 113 K6
Woodside Wy NWD/KWIPK L33 72 E4
Wood's La AIMK WN4 79 H5
Woodsome Cl EP CH65 203 F2
Woodsome Dr EP CH65 203 F2
Woodsorrel Rd BIRK CH41 130 C2
WAV L15 134 C2
Wood Sorrel Wy
GOL/RIS/CU WA3 93 F3
Woodstock Av NEWLW WA12 106 D3
Woodstock Dr STHP PR8 34 B1
Woodstock Gdns WARRS WA4 162 E5
Woodstock Gv WDN WA8 157 J1
Woodstock Rd WAL/EG CH44 111 G4
Woodstock St EV L5 113 F2
Wood St ALL/GAR L19 153 K5
BIRK CH41 3 F2
CLVPS L1 9 F5
GOL/RIS/CU WA3 92 C3
HOY CH47 * 127 G2
LITH L21 81 J4
PR/KW L34 117 K1
PS/BROM CH62 151 G6
STHEL WA9 104 A1
WARR WA1 17 J3
WDN WA8 19 G2
Woodthorn Cl RUNC WA7 178 E1
Wood V STHEL WA9 119 G1
Woodvale Cl CL/PREN CH43 129 K1
WARRN/WOL WA2 124 A6
Woodvale Dr GOL/RIS/CU WA3 93 F2
Woodvale Rd GTS/LS CH66 195 G3
STHP PR8 41 K1
WD/CROXPK L12 99 K2
WLTN L25 154 E1
Woodview PR/KW L34 100 D2
Woodview Av WAL/EG CH44 111 K5
Woodview Crs WDN WA8 157 F3
Woodview Rd WDN WA8 157 F3
Wood View Rd WLTN L25 135 G4
Woodville Av CSBY/BLUN L23 68 E6
Woodville Pl WDN WA8 157 J2
Woodville Rd RF/TRAN CH42 131 F5
Woodville St ECCL WA10 13 J4
Woodville Ter NPK/KEN L6 113 K2
Woodward Rd NWD/KWIPK L33 73 H5
RF/TRAN CH42 151 F3
Woodway GR/UP/WCH CH49 128 E5
Woodyear Rd PS/BROM CH62 171 G6
Woolacombe Av STHEL WA9 120 A2
Woolacombe Cl WARRS WA4 143 G6
Woolacombe Rd CHLDW L16 135 F3
Wooler Cl MOR/LEA CH46 128 D1
Woolfall Cl HUY L36 116 B3
Woolfall Crs HUY L36 116 B3
Woolfall Heath Av HUY L36 116 D2
Woolfall Ter LITH L21 81 H5
Woolhope Rd WLT/FAZ L9 97 K3
Woolley Cl FROD/HEL WA6 187 G5
Woolmer Cl GOL/RIS/CU WA3 125 K1
Woolston Grange Av
WARR WA1 144 D1
WARRN/WOL WA2 124 E5
Woolston Rd RNFD/HAY WA11 90 C5
Woolton Bvd WLTN L25 154 E2
Woolton Cl AIMK WN4 78 E4
Woolton Ct GTS/LS CH66 195 H1
Woolton Hill Rd WLTN L25 135 F5
Woolton Mt WLTN L25 135 H6
Woolton Pk WLTN L25 135 H6
Woolton Park Cl WLTN L25 135 H6
Woolton Rd ALL/GAR L19 153 K5
WAV L15 134 B2
WLTN L25 135 G4
Woolton St WLTN L25 154 E1
Worcester Av
CLB/OSW/ST L13 * 98 B6
CSBY/WL L22 80 D1
GOL/RIS/CU WA3 * 92 C3
Worcester Cl ECCL WA10 12 E7
WARRW/BUR WA5 141 J4
Worcester Dr CLB/OSW/ST L13 98 B6
Worcester Dr North
CLB/OSW/ST L13 98 B6
Worcester Rd BTL L20 5 H2
CL/PREN CH43 130 A1
Worcester St EP CH65 6 E2
Worcester Wk EP CH65 6 E2
Wordsworth Av
RF/TRAN CH42 150 E2
STHEL WA9 119 J4
WARRS WA4 142 E6
WDN WA8 18 A3

Wordsworth Cl *ORM* L39 ....45 H5
Wordsworth St *BTL* L20 ....4 B1
TOX L8 ....133 H2
Wordsworth Wk *WKBY* CH48 ....146 C3
Wordsworth Wy *GTS/LS* CH66 ..202 C2
HUY L36 ....117 F6
Worrow Cl *NG/CROX* L11 ....99 F2
Worrow Rd *NG/CROX* L11 ....99 F2
Worsborough Av
WARRW/BUR WA5 ....141 J4
Worsley Av *WARRS* WA4 ....143 J5
Worsley Brow *STHEL* WA9 ....104 C5
Worsley Rd *WARRS* WA4 ....162 A2
Worsley St *GOL/RIS/CU* WA3 ....92 B3
RNFD/HAY WA11 ....89 J5
WARRW/BUR WA5 ....142 C2
Worthing Cl *STHP* PR8 ....27 G4
Worthing St *CSBY/WL* L22 ....80 D1
Worthington Cl *RUNC* WA7 ....177 K6
Worthington St *TOX* L8 ....132 C3
Wortley Rd *AIN/FAZ* L10 ....83 H3
Wotton Dr *AIMK* WN4 ....79 J6
Wray Av *STHEL* WA9 ....120 B3
Wrayburn Cl *EHL/KEN* L7 ....133 H1
Wrekin Cl *WLTN* L25 ....154 E3
Wrekin Dr *AIN/FAZ* L10 ....83 H1
Wrenbury Cl *CL/PREN* CH43 * 149 J1
Wrenbury St *EHL/KEN* L7 ....114 A5
Wren Cl *GOL/RIS/CU* WA3 ....125 H3
RUNC WA7 ....187 K1
Wrenfield Gv *AIG/SPK* L17 ....152 D1
Wren Gv *HLWD* L26 ....155 H2
Wrenshot La *KNUT* WA16 ....165 K6
Wrexham Cl *WARRW/BUR* WA5 ..122 E6
Wright Crs *WDN* WA8 ....176 D1
Wrights Gn *WARRS* WA4 * 163 F5
Wright's La *WARRW/BUR* WA5 ..121 J4
WDN WA8 ....159 G1
Wrights Ter *STHP* PR8 ....27 J4
WAV L15 ....134 B2
Wright St *AIMK* WN4 ....78 E3
CHTN/BK PR9 ....15 F4
EV L5 ....113 F2
WAL/EG CH44 ....111 K3
Wrigley Rd *RNFD/HAY* WA11 ....90 D5
Wrigleys Cl *FMBY* L37 ....41 F6
Wrigleys La *FMBY* L37 ....41 F6
Wroxham Cl *FROD/HEL* WA6 ....199 J5
GR/UP/WCH CH49 ....129 H4
Wroxham Dr
GR/UP/WCH CH49 ....129 H5
Wroxham Rd
WARRW/BUR WA5 ....141 F3
Wroxham Wy
GR/UP/WCH CH49 * 129 H4
Wryneck Cl *ECCL* WA10 ....102 D6
Wrynose Rd *PS/BROM* CH62 ....171 G5
Wulstan St *ANF/KKDL* L4 ....97 F6
Wyatt Gv *AIMK* WN4 ....79 J6
Wycherley Rd *RF/TRAN* CH42 ....131 G6
Wycherley St *PR/KW* L34 * 117 K1
Wychwood *GR/UP/WCH* CH49 ..129 G4
Wychwood Av *LYMM* WA13 ....145 H6
Wycliffe Rd *ANF/KKDL* L4 ....98 A6
GTS/LS CH66 ....195 J6
RNFD/HAY WA11 ....90 D4
Wycliffe St *RF/TRAN* CH42 * 150 E1
Wye Cl *RF/TRAN* CH42 ....131 J6
Wyedale *EP* CH65 ....196 A6
Wyedale Rd *RNFD/HAY* WA11 ....90 B5
Wye St *EV* L5 ....113 H1
Wyke Cop Rd *STHP* PR8 ....29 G4
Wykeham St *ANF/KKDL* L4 ....97 F6
Wykeham Wy *ANF/KKDL* L4 ....97 F6
Wyke La *CHTN/BK* PR9 ....24 A6
Wyken Gv *RNFD/HAY* WA11 ....89 F6
Wyke Rd *RAIN/WH* L35 ....118 A2
Wyke Wood La *CHTN/BK* PR9 ....24 D5
Wyllin Rd *NWD/KWIPK* L33 ....85 F1
Wylva Av *CSBY/BLUN* L23 ....69 H6
Wylva Rd *ANF/KKDL* L4 ....113 J1
Wyncroft Cl *EP* CH65 ....195 K6
WDN WA8 ....157 H4
Wyncroft Rd *WDN* WA8 ....157 H4
Wyncroft St *TOX* L8 ....133 F5
Wyndale Cl *CALD/MH* L18 ....134 C6
Wyndcote Rd *CALD/MH* L18 ....134 C4
Wyndham Av *DV/KA/FCH* L14 ....116 A5
Wyndham Crs *GTS/LS* CH66 ....202 C1
Wyndham Rd *WAL/NB* CH45 ....110 D2
Wyndham St *ANF/KKDL* L4 ....97 H3
Wynne Rd *ECCL* WA10 ....12 D2
Wynnstay Av *MGHL* L31 ....62 B4
Wynnstay St *TOX* L8 ....133 F3
Wynstay Rd *HOY* CH47 ....127 H1
Wynwood Pk *HUY* L36 ....116 C6
Wyre Rd *EV* L5 ....97 H6
Wyrescourt Rd
WD/CROXPK L12 ....115 H2
Wyresdale Av *ECCL* WA10 ....88 B4
STHP PR8 ....28 A3
Wyresdale Rd *WLT/FAZ* L9 ....82 E4
Wyrevale Gv *AIMK* WN4 ....79 H6
Wysall Cl *RNFD/HAY* WA11 ....89 G6
Wyswall Cl *HLWD* L26 ....155 H2
Wythburn Crs *RNFD/HAY* WA11 ..88 E3
Wythburn Gv *RUNC* WA7 ....187 H2
Wyvern Rd *MOR/LEA* CH46 ....129 F1

Y

Yanwath St *TOX* L8 ....133 G2
Yarcombe Cl *HLWD* L26 ....155 J2
Yardley Av *WARRW/BUR* WA5 ....142 C1
Yardley Dr *BEB* CH63 ....170 C4
Yardley Rd *NWD/KWIPK* L33 ....85 H2
Yarmouth Rd
WARRW/BUR WA5 ....141 F3
Yarrow Av *MGHL* L31 ....62 D5
Yates Cl *WARRW/BUR* WA5 ....141 K4
Yates' Ct *PR/KW* L34 ....117 K2
Yates St *TOX* L8 ....132 D4
Yeadon *SKEL* WN8 ....56 D4
Yeald Brow *LYMM* WA13 ....145 G6
Yellow House La *STHP* PR8 ....14 E7
Yelverton Cl *HLWD* L26 ....155 J2
Yelverton Rd *ANF/KKDL* L4 ....98 A6
RF/TRAN CH42 ....131 G6
Yeoman Cottages *HOY* CH47 ....127 H3
Yeoman Wy *GTS/LS* CH66 ....202 C2
Yeovil Cl *WARR* WA1 ....144 B1
Yew Bank Rd *CHLDW* L16 ....134 E2
Yewdale *SKEL* WN8 ....56 C4
Yewdale Av *RNFD/HAY* WA11 ....88 E2
Yewdale Dr *GTS/LS* CH66 ....202 D2
Yewdale Pk *CL/PREN* CH43 ....130 E5
Yewdale Rd *AIMK* WN4 ....79 F2
WLT/FAZ L9 ....97 K1
Yew Tree Av *NEWLW* WA12 ....106 A1
STHEL WA9 ....120 A1
Yew Tree Cl *LYMM* WA13 ....145 K5
WD/CROXPK L12 ....115 J1
Yewtree Cl *GR/UP/WCH* CH49 ....148 D1
NSTN CH64 ....192 A2
Yew Tree Ct
GOL/RIS/CU WA3 * 125 J2
Yew Tree Gn *MGHL* L31 ....72 A5
Yew Tree La *WARRS* WA4 ....163 H6
WD/CROXPK L12 ....115 J2
Yewtree La *WKBY* CH48 ....127 G6
Yewtree Rd *CALD/MH* L18 ....134 E6
Yew Tree Rd *BEB* CH63 ....170 A1
HUY L36 ....136 A1
MOR/LEA CH46 ....109 K5
ORM L39 ....45 K5
WLT/FAZ L9 ....97 H1
WLTN L25 ....155 F3
Yew Tree Wy *GOL/RIS/CU* WA3 ....92 C4
Yew Wy *MOR/LEA* CH46 ....109 K6
Yorkaster Rd *CALD/MH* L18 ....153 K2
York Av *AIG/SPK* L17 ....133 J3
CSBY/BLUN L23 ....68 E5
STHP PR8 ....27 H2
WAL/EG CH44 ....111 K4
WARRW/BUR WA5 ....141 F2
WKBY CH48 ....146 C3
York Cl *ECCL* WA10 ....12 E3
FMBY L37 ....41 F5
NTHTN L30 ....70 C4
York Ct *WARRS* WA4 * 162 D2
York Dr *WARRS* WA4 ....163 F1
York Gdns *STHP* PR8 ....27 H2
York Mnr *FMBY* L37 * 49 F2
York Pl *RUNC* WA7 ....10 E5
York Rd *AIMK* WN4 ....91 H1
CSBY/BLUN L23 ....69 F5
EP CH65 ....6 D5
FMBY L37 ....49 F2
HUY L36 ....117 G4
MGHL L31 ....71 G3
STHP PR8 ....27 G3
WAL/EG CH44 ....111 K5
WARRS WA4 ....163 F1
WDN WA8 ....157 H3
York Rd South *AIMK* WN4 ....91 H1
Yorkshire Gdns *ECCL* WA10 ....103 H3
York St *ALL/GAR* L19 ....172 B1
CLVPS L1 ....8 E6
CSBY/WL L22 ....80 E3
GOL/RIS/CU WA3 ....92 B2
PS/BROM CH62 ....151 J6
RUNC WA7 ....10 D5
WARRS WA4 ....17 F7
WLT/FAZ L9 ....97 H2
York Ter *CHTN/BK* PR9 ....15 H3
EV L5 ....113 G1
York Vls *EV* L5 * 97 H6
York Wy *ALL/GAR* L19 ....172 C2
Youatt Av *RAIN/WH* L35 ....118 A3
Youens Wy *DV/KA/FCH* L14 ....115 J3
Yoxall Dr *NWD/KWIPK* L33 ....72 D3
Yvonne Cl *AIMK* WN4 ....79 J4

Z

Zander Gv *WD/CROXPK* L12 ....100 A2
Zante Cl *EV* L5 ....113 G1
Zara Ct *RNFD/HAY* WA11 ....90 B4
Zenith Wk *WLTN* L25 ....135 H2
Zetland Rd *CALD/MH* L18 * 134 A4
WAL/NB CH45 ....95 F6
Zetland St *CHTN/BK* PR9 ....15 J5
Zig Zag Rd *WAL/NB* CH45 ....111 H1
WD/CROXPK L12 ....115 H2
Zircon Cl *LITH* L21 ....81 K3

Index - featured places

59 Rodney Street (NT)
CLVPS L1 ....9 H7
Abbey Farm Caravan Park
BRSC L40 ....46 C3
Abbey Lane Industrial Estate
BRSC L40 ....46 C2
Abbey Sefton Hospitals
CSBY/WL L22 ....81 F2
Abbeystead Medical Centre
WAV L15 ....134 C2
Abbotsfield Road Industrial
Park *STHEL* WA9 ....120 C2
Abbots Lea Special School
WLTN L25 ....135 F5
ABC Cinema
CALD/MH L18 ....134 C5
STHP PR8 ....14 E5
Abercromby Health Centre
TOX L8 ....133 F1
Abingdon Medical Centre
ANF/KKDL L4 ....98 A4
Acorn Business Centre
NWD/KWIPK L33 ....85 G2
Acorn Special School
CLB/OSW/ST L13 ....98 C5
Ainsdale CE Primary School
STHP PR8 ....33 K5
Ainsdale Clinic
STHP PR8 ....33 K6
Ainsdale High School
STHP PR8 ....33 J3
Ainsdale Sand Dunes
FMBY L37 ....40 E1
Aintree Hospitals NHS Trust
WLT/FAZ L9 ....83 G4
Aintree Industrial Estate
WLT/FAZ L9 ....82 E6
Aintree Osteopathic Clinic
WLT/FAZ L9 ....83 F4
Aintree Racecourse
WLT/FAZ L9 ....83 F2
Aintree Racecourse Retail &
Business Park *WLT/FAZ* L9 ....83 F2
AK Business Park
CHTN/BK PR9 ....28 D1
Alban Retail Park
WARRN/WOL WA2 ....123 G5
Albert Dock Village
VAUX/LVPD L3 ....8 B7
Albert Road Medical Centre
WDN WA8 ....19 F1
Alderman Bolton Community
School *WARRS* WA4 ....143 H6
Alder Root Golf Club
WARRW/BUR WA5 ....106 D6
Alexandra Industrial Estate
WDN WA8 ....18 B6
Alicia Hotel
AIG/SPK L17 ....133 H5
Allanson Street CP School
STHEL WA9 ....104 B3
Allerton Cemetery
WLTN L25 ....154 C4
Allerton Health Centre
WAV L15 ....134 B4
Allerton Park Golf Club
CALD/MH L18 ....154 A1
Allerton Remedial Clinic
AIG/SPK L17 ....133 K4
All Saints Catholic School
KKBY L32 ....84 D2
All Saints CE Primary School
RUNC WA7 ....10 D3
All Saints Junior School
NPK/KEN L6 ....114 A1
All Saints RC Infant School
ANF/KKDL L4 ....113 K1
All Saints RC Primary School
GOL/RIS/CU WA3 ....92 C3
All Saints Upton Primary
School *WDN* WA8 ....138 A6
Alsop High School
ANF/KKDL L4 ....97 J3
Alt Bridge Secondary
Support Centre *HUY* L36 ....117 F3
Alternative Medical Centre
ECCL WA10 ....13 F4
Andersons Industrial Estate
WDN WA8 ....18 D7
Anfield Cemetery
ANF/KKDL L4 ....97 J5
Anfield Comprehensive
School *ANF/KKDL* L4 ....97 K6
Anfield Crematorium
ANF/KKDL L4 ....97 J5
Anfield J & I School
ANF/KKDL L4 ....113 K1
Anfield Medical Centre
ANF/KKDL L4 ....97 K6
Appleton Thorn Trading
Estate *WARRS* WA4 ....163 J6
Archbishop Beck Catholic
Secondary School
WLT/FAZ L9 ....82 D5
Archbishop Blanch CE High
School *EHL/KEN* L7 ....113 J6
Argyle Health Centre
BIRK CH41 ....3 F5
Argyle Lawn Tennis Club
CHTN/BK PR9 ....23 G3
Arncot CP School
ANF/KKDL L4 ....97 H4
Arrowe Country Park
GR/UP/WCH CH49 ....148 C2
Arrowe Hill Primary School
GR/UP/WCH CH49 ....129 H6
Arrowe Park Hospital
GR/UP/WCH CH49 ....148 D2
Ashley Business Centre
PR/KW L34 ....117 K1
Ashley Retail Park
WDN WA8 ....19 F5
Ashley School
WDN WA8 ....157 J2
Ashton Grange Industrial
Estate *AIMK* WN4 ....79 G3
Ashton-in-Makerfield Golf
Club *AIMK* WN4 ....90 D1
Ashton Leisure Centre
AIMK WN4 ....79 F5
Ashton Medical Centre
AIMK WN4 ....79 F4
Ashton Town AFC
AIMK WN4 ....79 J5
Ashurst Health Centre
SKEL WN8 ....56 D1
Ashurst Primary School
RNFD/HAY WA11 ....89 G5
Ashville FC
WAL/NB CH45 ....110 D3
Ashworth Hospital
MGHL L31 ....62 E5
Asmall Primary School
ORM L39 ....45 H4
Astmoor Industrial Estate
RUNC WA7 ....177 J2
Astmoor Primary School
RUNC WA7 ....177 J3
Aston Primary School
RUNC WA7 ....188 B6
Atherton House School
CSBY/BLUN L23 ....68 E5
Atherton Infant School
EP CH65 ....195 J4
Atkinson Art Gallery
STHP PR8 ....14 E5
Atlanta Swimming
STHP PR8 ....27 H3
Auckland College
AIG/SPK L17 ....133 G6
Aughton Christ Church CE
Primary School *ORM* L39 ....53 G2
Austin Rawlinson Sports
Centre *SPK/HALE* L24 ....173 K2
Avalon School
WKBY CH48 ....146 D3
Balmoral Lodge Hotel
CHTN/BK PR9 ....15 H2
Bankfield School
WDN WA8 ....157 J2
Bank Quay Trading Estate
WARRW/BUR WA5 ....16 A7
Banks Health Centre
CHTN/BK PR9 ....21 J5
Banks Road Primary School
ALL/GAR L19 ....172 C1
Barlows Primary School
WLT/FAZ L9 ....83 G4
Barnston Primary School
HES CH60 ....168 C6
Barrow Hall CP School
WARRW/BUR WA5 ....141 F2
Baycliff Road Health Centre
WD/CROXPK L12 ....99 K6
BBC North & BBC Radio
Merseyside *CLVPS* L1 ....8 D5
Beach Road Primary School
LITH L21 ....81 H4
The Beacon CE Primary
School *EV* L5 ....113 G2
Beacon Country Park
SKEL WN8 ....57 G2
Beacon Park Public Golf
Centre *SKEL* WN8 ....57 G2
Beacon School
SKEL WN8 ....57 G5
Beamont Primary School
WARRN/WOL WA2 ....143 F2
The Beatles Story
VAUX/LVPD L3 ....8 B7
Beaufort Hotel
BRSC L40 ....46 B2
Beaufort Park CP School
TOX L8 ....132 E4
Beaufort Park School
TOX L8 ....132 E5
Bebington High School
Sports College
BEB CH63 ....150 D5
Bechers Business Centre
NTHTN L30 ....82 D1
Bedford Primary School
BTL L20 ....5 H6
Beechenhurst School
CALD/MH L18 ....134 E4
Beechwood CP School
HUY L36 ....116 C1
Beechwood Primary School
RUNC WA7 ....187 G2
Belair Industrial Estate
CSBY/BLUN L23 ....69 G6
Bellerive High School
TOX L8 ....133 G4
Belle Vale Health Centre
WLTN L25 ....135 J3
Belle Vale JMI School
WLTN L25 ....135 K4
Belle Vale Shopping Centre
WLTN L25 ....135 J3
Belle Vale Swimming Pool
WLTN L25 ....135 K3
The Belvedere School
TOX L8 ....133 G5
Bewsey Business Centre
WARRW/BUR WA5 ....16 A2
Bewsey Industrial Estate
WARRW/BUR WA5 ....16 A1
Bewsey Lodge Primary
School *WARRW/BUR* WA5 ....142 B2
BICC Athletic Club
RAIN/WH L35 ....118 B2
Bickerstaffe CE Primary
School *ORM* L39 ....64 E2
Bidston Avenue Primary
School *CL/PREN* CH43 ....130 B2
Bidston Golf Club
MOR/LEA CH46 ....110 C4
Bidston Industrial Estate
WAL/EG CH44 ....110 D4
Bigdale Medical Centre
NWD/KWIPK L33 ....73 F6
Bigham Road Medical Centre
NPK/KEN L6 ....114 A4
Billinge Chapel End Primary
School *WGNW/BIL/O* WN5 ....77 H5
Billinge Clinic
WGNW/BIL/O WN5 ....77 G5
Binns Road Industrial Estate
CLB/OSW/ST L13 ....114 C5
Birchwood CE Primary
School *GOL/RIS/CU* WA3 ....125 H3
Birchwood Community
High School
GOL/RIS/CU WA3 ....125 F4
Birchwood Golf Club
GOL/RIS/CU WA3 ....125 F1
Birchwood Medical Centre
GOL/RIS/CU WA3 ....125 G4
Birchwood One Business
Park *GOL/RIS/CU* WA3 ....125 G4
Birkdale Cemetery
STHP PR8 ....34 A2
Birkdale High School
STHP PR8 ....34 A2
Birkdale Primary School
STHP PR8 ....27 J4
Birkdale RC Cemetery
STHP PR8 ....34 A3
Birkdale Trading Estate
STHP PR8 ....27 G5
Birkenhead County Court
BIRK CH41 ....3 G5
Birkenhead High School
CL/PREN CH43 ....130 D4
Birkenhead High School
for Girls *CL/PREN* CH43 ....130 D4
Birkenhead Park Cricket Club
BIRK CH41 ....130 E3
Birkenhead Park RUFC
BIRK CH41 ....130 D2
Birkenhead Preparatory
School *CL/PREN* CH43 ....130 D4
Birkenhead Priory
BIRK CH41 ....3 J5
Birkenhead Priory & Museum
BIRK CH41 ....3 J5
Birkenhead School
CL/PREN CH43 ....130 C4
Birkenhead Sixth Form College
CL/PREN CH43 ....130 C2
Birleywood Health Centre
SKEL WN8 ....67 F1
Bishop David Sheppard CE
Primary School
CHTN/BK PR9 ....23 K6
Bishop Martin CE Primary
School *SKEL* WN8 ....57 F6
WLTN L25 ....154 D1
Blackbrook St Marys Catholic
Primary School
RNFD/HAY WA11 ....89 H5
Black Cat Industrial Estate
WDN WA8 ....18 B7
Black Horse Hill Infant School
WKBY CH48 ....127 J6
Black Horse Hill Junior School
WKBY CH48 ....127 J6
Blacklow Brow Primary
School *HUY* L36 ....116 D6
Blackmoor Park Infant
School *WD/CROXPK* L12 ....115 H1
Blackmoor Park Junior
School *WD/CROXPK* L12 ....115 H2
Black Moss School
SKEL WN8 ....55 K3
Bleak Hill Primary School
ECCL WA10 ....87 J5
Blessed Sacrament RC Infant
School *WLT/FAZ* L9 ....82 E5
Blessed Sacrament RC Junior
School *WLT/FAZ* L9 ....82 E5
Blowick Business Centre
CHTN/BK PR9 ....28 D1
Blueberry Park CP School
DV/KA/FCH L14 ....116 A1
The Blue Coat School
WAV L15 ....134 B3
Blue Planet Aquarium
EP CH65 ....203 H2
Blundells Hill Golf Club
RAIN/WH L35 ....118 D6
Boaler Street Industrial Estate
NPK/KEN L6 ....113 J4
Boat Museum
EP CH65 ....7 F1
Bold Business Centre
STHEL WA9 ....105 F6
Bold Hotel
CHTN/BK PR9 ....15 F3
Bold Industrial Estate
WDN WA8 ....139 H4
Bold Industrial Park
STHEL WA9 ....121 F1
Bold Street Medical Centre
WARR WA1 ....16 C6

Booker Avenue J & I School *CALD/MH* L18 ....153 J2
Bootle Cricket Club *BTL* L20 ....5 G7
Bootle Golf Club *NTHTN* L30 ....82 B2
Bootle High School *NTHTN* L30 ....70 D5
Bootle Leisure Centre *BTL* L20 ....4 E1
Bootle Stadium Sports Centre *BTL* L20 ....5 K3
Borough Cemetery *ECCL* WA10 ....88 A4
WDN WA8 ....139 F6
Borron Road Industrial Estate *NEWLW* WA12 ....106 C1
Botanic Estate *EHL/KEN* L7 ....114 B6
Botanic Gardens Museum *CHTN/BK* PR9 ....23 K3
Bousfield Health Centre *ANF/KKDL* L4 ....97 G6
Bowers Business Park *WDN* WA8 ....19 G5
The Bowler Hat Hotel *CL/PREN* CH43 ....130 D5
Bowling Alley *CLB/OSW/ST* L13 ....114 D6
NTHTN L30 ....70 D6
PS/BROM CH62 ....171 F2
WAL/NB CH45 ....95 H4
Bowring Comprehensive School *HUY* L36 ....116 B4
Bowring Park Golf Club *HUY* L36 ....116 B6
The Bowry Health Centre *STHEL* WA9 ....103 F5
Brackenwood Golf Club *BEB* CH63 ....169 K1
Brackenwood Infant School *BEB* CH63 ....150 E6
Brackenwood Junior School *BEB* CH63 ....150 D6
Bradshaw Primary School *WARRS* WA4 ....163 G1
Breckfield Community Comprehensive School *EV* L5 ....113 H2
Breckfield CP School *EV* L5 ....113 J1
Bridgehouse Clinic *BEB* CH63 ....150 C5
Bridge Industrial Estate *SPK/HALE* L24 ....154 E6
Bridgewater Community High School (Lower) *WARRS* WA4 ....162 C5
Bridgewater Upper School *WARRS* WA4 ....162 C4
Brindley Arts Centre *RUNC* WA7 ....10 E4
The British Lawnmower Museum *STHP* PR8 ....27 J2
Britonwood Trading Estate *NWD/KWIPK* L33 ....85 G4
Broadgreen Community Comprehensive School *CLB/OSW/ST* L13 ....115 F5
Broad Green JMI School *CLB/OSW/ST* L13 ....115 F5
Broad Oak Community Primary School *STHEL* WA9 ....104 E2
Broad Square Primary School *NG/CROX* L11 ....98 D5
Broadway Community High School *ECCL* WA10 ....102 E5
Bromborough Golf Club *BEB* CH63 ....183 J1
Bromborough Pool Primary School *PS/BROM* CH62 ....151 J6
Brook Acre Primary School *WARRN/WOL* WA2 ....124 A6
Brookdale Primary School *GR/UP/WCH* CH49 ....129 F6
Brookfield Comprehensive School *KKBY* L32 ....84 C3
Brookfield School *WDN* WA8 ....158 E1
Brookfields Primary School *SKEL* WN8 ....55 K3
Brook House Business Centre *WKBY* CH48 ....146 C1
Brookhurst Primary School *BEB* CH63 ....183 K1
Brook Lodge Primary School *RNFD/HAY* WA11 ....75 G1
Brooklyn Park & Country Club *CHTN/BK* PR9 ....24 E1
Brookside Primary School *DV/KA/FCH* L14 ....100 B6
GTS/LS CH66 ....195 H5
Brookvale Primary School *RUNC* WA7 ....188 A2
Brookvale Recreation Centre *RUNC* WA7 ....188 B1
Broomfield County Junior School *WARRS* WA4 ....162 D4
Broughton Hall C High School Technology College *WD/CROXPK* L12 ....115 J2
The Brow Primary School *RUNC* WA7 ....177 J4
Bruche Community Primary School *WARR* WA1 ....143 K2
Brunswick Business Park *VAUX/LVPD* L3 ....132 C5
Burscough Bridge Methodist Primary School *BRSC* L40 ....38 D4
Burscough Cricket Club *BRSC* L40 ....39 F5
Burscough Health Centre *BRSC* L40 ....38 E4
Burscough Industrial Estate *BRSC* L40 ....38 B4
Burscough Primary School *BRSC* L40 ....39 F4
Burscough Priory High School *BRSC* L40 ....38 D4
Burscough RC Primary School *BRSC* L40 ....46 E1
Burscough Sports Centre *BRSC* L40 ....38 E4
Burtonwood Industrial Centre *WARRW/BUR* WA5 ....105 K6
Burtonwood Primary School *WARRW/BUR* WA5 ....105 J6
Business Development Centre *STHEL* WA9 ....13 K3
Business Resource Centre *NWD/KWIPK* L33 ....85 H3
Byrchall High School *AIMK* WN4 ....91 G2
Byrne Avenue Recreation Centre *RF/TRAN* CH42 ....150 E2
Cabinet War Rooms *CLVP* L2 ....8 C3
Cables Retail Park *PR/KW* L34 ....117 K1
Calday Grange Grammar School *WKBY* CH48 ....146 E2
Calderstones Comprehensive School *CALD/MH* L18 ....134 D5
Caldy Golf Club *WKBY* CH48 ....147 F5
Camberley Medical Centre *WLTN* L25 ....155 F3
Cambridge Road Primary School *EP* CH65 ....6 E5
Cammell Laird's Sports Club *RF/TRAN* CH42 ....151 F2
Campanile Hotel *RUNC* WA7 ....10 D4
VAUX/LVPD L3 ....132 B2
Campion Catholic High School *EV* L5 ....113 G3
Canalside Industrial Estate *EP* CH65 ....7 G2
Canning Road Industrial Estate *CHTN/BK* PR9 ....28 D1
Cansfield High School *AIMK* WN4 ....79 F5
Capenhurst Grange Special School *GTS/LS* CH66 ....202 B1
Capenhurst Learning Centre *CH/BCN* CH1 ....202 A2
Capitol Trading Estate *NWD/KWIPK* L33 ....85 J1
Cardinal Heenan Catholic High *WD/CROXPK* L12 ....115 H2
Cardinal Newman RC High School *WARRS* WA4 ....143 J4
Carleton House Preparatory School *CALD/MH* L18 ....134 A6
Carlton Lawn Tennis Club *STHP* PR8 ....27 G5
Carmel College *ECCL* WA10 ....102 D4
Carr Lane Industrial Estate *HOY* CH47 ....127 H2
Carr Mill Infant School *RNFD/HAY* WA11 ....88 E3
Carr Mill Junior School *RNFD/HAY* WA11 ....89 F2
Castlefields Health Centre *RUNC* WA7 ....177 K3
Castleview Primary School *RUNC* WA7 ....177 G5
Castleway Primary School *MOR/LEA* CH46 ....110 A3
Catalyst Science Discovery Centre *WDN* WA8 ....158 B6
Cathcart Street Primary School *BIRK* CH41 ....2 D2
Causeway Medical Centre *WARRS* WA4 ....142 E6
Cavendish Medical Centre *BIRK* CH41 ....130 E2
Cavendish Special School *RUNC* WA7 ....186 E2
Cavern Club *CLVP* L2 ....8 D4
Cedar Cross Medical Centre *RAIN/WH* L35 ....117 K4
Centec Business Centre *NG/CROX* L11 ....84 A6
Central Clinic *ECCL* WA10 ....13 G3
Central Library *VAUX/LVPD* L3 ....9 F2
Chadwick Court Industrial Centre *VAUX/LVPD* L3 ....112 D4
Chaigley School *WARRS* WA4 ....144 D5
Chalon Way Industrial Estate *STHEL* WA9 ....13 H7
Chapelfield Clinic *WDN* WA8 ....157 G2
Chapel Street Clinic *WDN* WA8 ....18 D6
Cherryfield Primary School *KKBY* L32 ....84 D4
Cherry Tree Community School *LYMM* WA13 ....164 D1
Cheshire Oaks Retail Outlet *EP* CH65 ....203 J1
Chesnut Lodge School *WDN* WA8 ....157 K2
Chesterfield High School *CSBY/BLUN* L23 ....69 H5
Childer Thornton Primary School *GTS/LS* CH66 ....194 E1
Childwall CE Primary School *CHLDW* L16 ....134 E4
Childwall College:A specialist sports college *WAV* L15 ....134 D2
The Childwall Golf Club *NTHLY* L27 ....136 B2
Chinese Arch *CLVPS* L1 ....9 G7
Christ Church CE Primary School *BTL* L20 ....5 G3
EP CH65 ....203 F1
MOR/LEA CH46 ....129 F1
Christian Fellowship School *EHL/KEN* L7 ....133 G1
Christina Hartley Maternity Hospital *STHP* PR8 ....28 A2
Christ the King Catholic Primary School *WAV* L15 ....134 D1
Christ the King RC High School *STHP* PR8 ....27 J4
Christ the King RC Primary School *PS/BROM* CH62 ....171 G6
Chromolyte Industrial Estate *STHP* PR8 ....27 J2
Church Drive Primary School *PS/BROM* CH62 ....151 G5
Churchill Industrial Estate *WLT/FAZ* L9 ....83 F3
Church Road Medical Centre *BEB* CH63 ....170 C1
Church Square Shopping Centre *ECCL* WA10 ....13 G5
Church Street Industrial Estate *WARR* WA1 ....17 F5
Churchtown Medical Centre *CHTN/BK* PR9 ....23 J3
Churchtown Primary School *CHTN/BK* PR9 ....23 K3
Cineworld *ECCL* WA10 ....13 F5
RUNC WA7 ....177 J6
Cinnamon Brow CE Primary School *WARRN/WOL* WA2 ....124 B4
The Citadel *ECCL* WA10 ....13 G5
City of Liverpool Community College *VAUX/LVPD* L3 ....9 H5
Civic Hall *EP* CH65 ....6 C6
ORM L39 ....45 J6
Claremont Medical Centre *MGHL* L31 ....70 E1
Claremont Special School *WAL/NB* CH45 ....111 F1
Claremount School *MOR/LEA* CH46 ....110 A6
Clarence House School *FMBY* L37 ....40 E5
Clatterbridge Hospital *BEB* CH63 ....169 K4
Claughton Medical Centre *BIRK* CH41 ....130 D2
Clayton Square Shopping Centre *CLVPS* L1 ....9 F4
Cleveland Business Park *BIRK* CH41 ....2 C1
Clifford Holroyde Centre of Expertise *DV/KA/FCH* L14 ....115 H4
Clinic for the Handicapped *WARRN/WOL* WA2 ....16 C3
Clock Face Country Park *STHEL* WA9 ....120 D4
Clough Fold Primary School *SKEL* WN8 ....56 E3
Cobbs Brow Primary School *SKEL* WN8 ....56 C2
The Cobbs Infant School *WARRS* WA4 ....162 D3
Cockhedge Centre *WARR* WA1 ....16 E4
Cole Street Primary School *BIRK* CH41 ....2 B5
Collins Industrial Estate *STHEL* WA9 ....89 F6
Commercial Business Centre *RAIN/WH* L35 ....118 E4
Common Ground Sign Dance Theatre *CLVPS* L1 ....8 E5
Community Care for Health *WDN* WA8 ....18 D5
Concourse Shopping Centre *SKEL* WN8 ....56 D4
Conservation Centre *CLVPS* L1 ....8 E3
Constance Industrial Estate *WDN* WA8 ....158 B5
Copplehouse Medical Centre *AIN/FAZ* L10 ....83 K4
Corinthian Primary School *CLB/OSW/ST* L13 ....115 F3
Corner House Clinic *WKBY* CH48 ....146 C1
Cornerways Medical Centre *HUY* L36 ....116 C2
Corpus Christi Catholic Primary School *RNFD/HAY* WA11 ....75 G2
County Sessions House *VAUX/LVPD* L3 ....9 G2
Cowley Language College *ECCL* WA10 ....88 A5
Craighurst JMI School *WLTN* L25 ....135 H2
Craven Business Centre *BIRK* CH41 ....2 D4
Crawford Village Primary School *SKEL* WN8 ....67 G4
Croft Business Park *PS/BROM* CH62 ....171 G3
Cromdale Way Community Hall & Health Centre *WARRW/BUR* WA5 ....141 F3
Cronton CE Primary School *WDN* WA8 ....138 B3
Crosby Baths *CSBY/BLUN* L23 ....80 C1
Crosby High School *CSBY/BLUN* L23 ....69 F3
Cross Clinic *LYMM* WA13 ....145 K6
Crossens CC *CHTN/BK* PR9 ....24 B1
Crossens CE Primary School *CHTN/BK* PR9 ....21 F6
Cross Farm Primary School *NTHLY* L27 ....136 C5
Crowland Street Industrial Estate *CHTN/BK* PR9 ....28 C1
Crow Orchard Primary School *SKEL* WN8 ....56 B3
Croxteth Comprehensive School *NG/CROX* L11 ....84 B6
Croxteth Country Park *WD/CROXPK* L12 ....99 H3
Croxteth Family Health Centre *NG/CROX* L11 ....99 G1
Croxteth Hall *WD/CROXPK* L12 ....99 H4
Croxteth Primary School *NG/CROX* L11 ....99 H1
Croxteth Sports Centre *NG/CROX* L11 ....99 G1
Cunard Building *VAUX/LVPD* L3 ....8 B4
Daleacre Primary School *NTHTN* L30 ....69 K6
Dallam Community Primary School *WARRW/BUR* WA5 ....123 F6
Dalweb Industrial Park *CHTN/BK* PR9 ....25 G2
Daresbury Park Business Park *WARRS* WA4 ....178 E5
Daresbury Park Hotel *WARRS* WA4 ....179 F5
Daresbury Primary School *WARRS* WA4 ....179 G3
Davenhill Primary School *AIN/FAZ* L10 ....83 G1
Dawpool CE Primary School *PEN/TH* CH61 ....147 J5
Deacon Trading Estate *NEWLW* WA12 ....106 A3
De La Salle RC High School *NG/CROX* L11 ....99 F3
De La Salle School *ECCL* WA10 ....102 E1
The Dell Primary School *RF/TRAN* CH42 ....151 G2
Delph Side Primary School *SKEL* WN8 ....56 E5
Dental Hospital *VAUX/LVPD* L3 ....9 K3
Derby Lane Medical Centre *CLB/OSW/ST* L13 ....114 E4
Devaney Medical Centre *CL/PREN* CH43 ....2 A7
Devonshire Park Primary School *RF/TRAN* CH42 ....150 B1
Deyes High School *MGHL* L31 ....62 B6
Deysbrook Medical Centre *WD/CROXPK* L12 ....99 G6
Diamond Business Park *RNFD/HAY* WA11 ....75 J5
Dinas Lane Medical Centre *HUY* L36 ....116 C3
The District CE Primary School *NEWLW* WA12 ....106 A2
Ditton CE Primary School *WDN* WA8 ....157 F2
Ditton Medical Centre *WDN* WA8 ....157 H2
Dovecot Health Clinic *DV/KA/FCH* L14 ....115 K3
Dovecot JMI School *DV/KA/FCH* L14 ....116 A4
Dovedale County Infant School *CALD/MH* L18 ....134 B4
Dovedale Junior School *CALD/MH* L18 ....134 B4
Downall Green RC Primary School *AIMK* WN4 ....78 D3
Downholland Haskayne CE Primary School *ORM* L39 ....51 G2
Drug Dependency Clinic *CLVPS* L1 ....9 H5
WDN WA8 ....18 D6
Dunkirk Trading Estate *CH/BCN* CH1 ....202 B5
Dunnys Sports Club *WLT/FAZ* L9 ....97 J1
Eagle Sports Club *WARRW/BUR* WA5 ....141 H5
Earle Road Medical Centre *EHL/KEN* L7 ....133 H1
Eastcroft Park CP School *NWD/KWIPK* L33 ....72 E4
East Gillbrands Industrial Estate *SKEL* WN8 ....56 C6
Eastham Country Park *PS/BROM* CH62 ....171 J6
Eastham Lodge Golf Club *PS/BROM* CH62 ....184 D1
Eastside Industrial Estate *STHEL* WA9 ....104 A3
Eastway Primary School *MOR/LEA* CH46 ....109 J6
Eaton Road Medical Centre *WD/CROXPK* L12 ....115 G2
Eaves Primary School *STHEL* WA9 ....120 A1
Eccleston Lane Ends Primary School *PR/KW* L34 ....102 B6
Eccleston Medical Centre *ECCL* WA10 ....87 J6
Eccleston Mere Primary School *ECCL* WA10 ....102 C2
Eccleston Park Golf Club *STHEL* WA9 ....118 D1
Edge Hill Enterprise Training Centre *WLT/FAZ* L9 ....83 H5
Edge Hill Health Centre *EHL/KEN* L7 ....114 A6
Edge Hill University Sector College *ORM* L39 ....53 K2
Edge Lane Medical Centre *EHL/KEN* L7 ....113 K6
Edge Lane Retail Park *CLB/OSW/ST* L13 ....114 D5
Edwards Lane Industrial Estate *SPK/HALE* L24 ....155 F5
Egremont Medical Centre *WAL/EG* CH44 ....111 K3
Egremont Primary School *WAL/EG* CH44 ....111 K3
Elaine Norris Sports Centre *VAUX/LVPD* L3 ....112 E3
Elimu Academy *TOX* L8 ....133 G2
Elleray Park School *WAL/NB* CH45 ....95 G6
Ellergreen Medical Centre *NG/CROX* L11 ....98 D3
Ellesmere Port Business Centre *EP* CH65 ....6 C5
Ellesmere Port Catholic High School *EP* CH65 ....195 J6
Ellesmere Port Clinic *EP* CH65 ....6 C7
Ellesmere Port Golf Centre *GTS/LS* CH66 ....194 E1
Ellesmere Port Hospital *EP* CH65 ....202 E1
Ellesmere Port Stadium *EP* CH65 ....196 D6
Elmers Green Community Primary School *SKEL* WN8 ....57 F4
The Elms Special School *STBRV* L28 ....100 B5
Eltham Green Clinic *GR/UP/WCH* CH49 ....148 E1
Elton Primary School *CHNE* CH2 ....198 B5
Emmaus Primary School *WD/CROXPK* L12 ....99 K2
English Martyrs RC Primary School *LITH* L21 ....81 J3
RNFD/HAY WA11 ....90 C4
Epic Leisure Centre *EP* CH65 ....6 D7
Eric Moore Health Centre *WARRN/WOL* WA2 ....16 C3
Ernest Cookson Special School *WD/CROXPK* L12 ....115 F1
Erskine Street Industrial Estate *NPK/KEN* L6 ....9 K2
Estuary Business Park *SPK/HALE* L24 ....172 E1
Europa Pool *BIRK* CH41 ....2 E4
Evelyn Primary School *PR/KW* L34 ....102 A6
Evelyn Street Primary School *WARRW/BUR* WA5 ....142 B5
Everite Road Industrial Estate *WDN* WA8 ....157 G4
Everton FC (Goodison Park) *ANF/KKDL* L4 ....97 H5
Everton Park Sports Centre *EV* L5 ....113 G2
Everton Road Health Clinic *NPK/KEN* L6 ....113 H3
Everyman Theatre *VAUX/LVPD* L3 ....9 J5
Express by Holiday Inn *VAUX/LVPD* L3 ....8 B7
Express Industrial Estate *WDN* WA8 ....157 F4
Expressway Business Park *RF/TRAN* CH42 ....131 J6
Fairfield High School *WDN* WA8 ....139 G6
Fairfield Hospital *RNFD/HAY* WA11 ....88 B1
Fairfield J & I School *WDN* WA8 ....158 C1
Fairfield Medical Centre *NPK/KEN* L6 ....114 A4
Fairfield Primary School *WARR* WA1 ....17 G2
Fairfield RFC *RF/TRAN* CH42 ....150 E1
Fairlie CP School *SKEL* WN8 ....56 D2
Fairway Trading Estate *WDN* WA8 ....157 K4
Faith House Yoga & Natural Health Centre *WAL/NB* CH45 ....95 H5
Falcongate Industrial Estate *BIRK* CH41 ....111 H6
Family Health Centre *KKBY* L32 ....84 B1
Farnborough Road J & I School *STHP* PR8 ....34 B1
Farnworth CE Primary School *WDN* WA8 ....139 F5
Fazakerley High School *AIN/FAZ* L10 ....83 J4
Fazakerley Primary School *AIN/FAZ* L10 ....83 J4
Fazakerley Sports Centre *AIN/FAZ* L10 ....83 J3
Fearnhead Cross Medical Centre *WARRN/WOL* WA2 ....124 B5
Fender Primary School *GR/UP/WCH* CH49 ....129 K6
Fernhill Sports Centre *BTL* L20 ....82 A5
Ferries Industrial Estate *RF/TRAN* CH42 ....131 J6
Fingerprints of Elvis *VAUX/LVPD* L3 ....8 B6

Fir Grove Hotel *WARRS* WA4 143 K6
Fir Tree Drive South Medical Centre *WD/CROXPK* L12 99 K2
Fishwicks Industrial Estate *RNFD/HAY* WA11 90 E3
STHEL WA9 104 B5
Fleet Lane Industrial Estate *STHEL* WA9 104 C3
Fleming Industrial Estate *WARR* WA1 17 F4
Floral Pavilion Theatre *WAL/NB* CH45 95 J4
Florence Melly Comm Primary School *ANF/KKDL* L4 98 A4
Fordton Leisure Centre *WARRN/WOL* WA2 123 G4
Forefield Infant School *CSBY/BLUN* L23 69 H5
Forefield Junior School *CSBY/BLUN* L23 69 G5
Forest Hills Hotel & Leisure Complex *FROD/HEL* WA6 200 E3
The Forge Shopping Centre *WARRS* WA4 162 B2
Formby AFC *FMBY* L37 49 F2
Formby Business Park *FMBY* L37 49 J2
Formby CC *FMBY* L37 41 F6
Formby Golf Club *FMBY* L37 40 D6
Formby Hall Golf Club *FMBY* L37 41 J3
Formby High School *FMBY* L37 48 E1
Formby Junior Sports Club *FMBY* L37 41 G6
Formby Ladies Golf Club *FMBY* L37 40 D6
Formby Lawn Tennis Club *FMBY* L37 41 F6
The Fountains Abbey *ANF/KKDL* L4 97 G6
Four Acre Lane Shopping Centre *STHEL* WA9 119 K3
Foxfield School *MOR/LEA* CH46 128 E1
Freight Terminal Buildings (Euro-Rail) *LITH* L21 81 F5
Freshfield Primary School *FMBY* L37 49 G1
Freshlea Private Clinic *FMBY* L37 48 D4
Friary Primary School *EV* L5 113 G4
Frodsham CE Primary School *FROD/HEL* WA6 201 F2
Frodsham Golf Club *FROD/HEL* WA6 200 E4
Frodsham Science & Tech College *FROD/HEL* WA6 200 E1
Funland *STHP* PR8 14 D3
Fylde Road Industrial Estate *CHTN/BK* PR9 23 K1
Gallagher Industrial Estate *WAL/EG* CH44 111 H5
Garston CE Primary School *ALL/GAR* L19 154 A5
Garston Industrial Estate *ALL/GAR* L19 172 B1
Garston Leisure Centre *ALL/GAR* L19 153 K5
Garston Sports Centre *ALL/GAR* L19 153 K4
Garswood FC *AIMK* WN4 78 A4
Garswood Primary School *AIMK* WN4 78 B5
Garven Place Clinic *WARR* WA1 16 B5
Gateacre Comprehensive School *WLTN* L25 135 H4
Gateworth Industrial Estate *WARRW/BUR* WA5 142 A6
Gayton Primary School *HES* CH60 181 F1
Gemini Business Park *WARRW/BUR* WA5 122 E4
Gilbrook School *BIRK* CH41 3 H4
Gilded Hollins Primary School *LEIGH* WN7 93 K2
Gillmoss Industrial Estate *NG/CROX* L11 84 A5
Gillmoss Medical Centre *NG/CROX* L11 84 B6
Gilmour Infant School *ALL/GAR* L19 153 J4
Gilmour Junior School *ALL/GAR* L19 153 J4
Glenburn High School *SKEL* WN8 56 C5
Glenda Jackson Theatre *RF/TRAN* CH42 131 F6
Golborne Clinic *GOL/RIS/CU* WA3 92 C2
Golborne CP School *GOL/RIS/CU* WA3 92 B3
Golborne High School *GOL/RIS/CU* WA3 92 D2
Golden Square Shopping Centre *WARR* WA1 16 C5
Golden Triangle Industrial Estate *WDN* WA8 157 H5
Good Shepherd School *LITH* L21 81 K1
Gorse Covert Primary School *GOL/RIS/CU* WA3 125 K1
Gorsewood Primary School *RUNC* WA7 178 D6
Gorsthills Primary School *GTS/LS* CH66 195 F6
Grain Industrial Estate *TOX* L8 132 D5
Granada TV *VAUX/LVPD* L3 8 C6
The Grand National Experience *WLT/FAZ* L9 82 E2
The Grange Comprehensive School *RUNC* WA7 11 J7
The Grange Country Club *NSTN* CH64 182 A3
The Grange Infant School *RUNC* WA7 11 J6
The Grange Junior School *RUNC* WA7 11 J6
Grange Park Golf Club *ECCL* WA10 102 E4
Grange Primary School *NTHTN* L30 70 B4
The Grange Shopping Precinct *BIRK* CH41 2 E5
Grange Valley Primary School *RNFD/HAY* WA11 90 C6
Grappenhall Clinic *WARRS* WA4 163 G1
Grappenhall Cricket Club *WARRS* WA4 163 F2
Grappenhall Hall School *WARRS* WA4 163 G2
Grappenhall Heys Primary School *WARRS* WA4 163 F4
Grappenhall Sports Club *WARRS* WA4 162 E2
Greasby Health Centre *GR/UP/WCH* CH49 128 E6
Greasby Infant School *GR/UP/WCH* CH49 147 K1
Greasby Junior School *GR/UP/WCH* CH49 148 A2
Great Crosby RC Primary School *CSBY/BLUN* L23 69 G5
Great Homer Street Medical Centre *EV* L5 113 G2
Great Meols Primary School *HOY* CH47 108 C6
Great Sankey County High School *WARRW/BUR* WA5 141 F2
Great Sankey Primary School *WARRW/BUR* WA5 141 H4
Great Sutton Health Centre *GTS/LS* CH66 195 G5
Greenbank High School *STHP* PR8 27 F6
Greenbank Primary School *CALD/MH* L18 134 A4
Green Lane Medical Centre *CLB/OSW/ST* L13 114 C2
Green Lane Special School *WARR* WA1 144 A1
Greenleas School *WAL/NB* CH45 110 C1
Greenoaks Farm Industrial Estate *WDN* WA8 19 H3
Green Oaks Shopping Centre *WDN* WA8 19 F3
Green Park Primary School *MGHL* L31 61 K5
Greenways Special School *ALL/GAR* L19 153 G4
Gresford Medical Centre *DV/KA/FCH* L14 115 K4
Grove House Hotel *WAL/NB* CH45 94 E6
Grove Street Primary School *PS/BROM* CH62 151 F4
Guardian Medical Centre *WARRW/BUR* WA5 142 C3
Guardian Street Industrial Estate *WARRW/BUR* WA5 16 A3
Guinea Gap Baths & Recreation Centre *WAL/EG* CH44 112 A4
Gulliver's World Theme Park *WARRW/BUR* WA5 122 E6
Guys Industrial Estate *BRSC* L40 46 B1
Gwladys Street CP Schoolool *ANF/KKDL* L4 97 J4
Hale CE Primary School *SPK/HALE* L24 175 F4
Hale Road Industrial Estate *WDN* WA8 157 H6
Halewood CE Primary School *HLWD* L26 155 K2
Halewood Comprehensive School *HLWD* L26 155 H4
Halewood Health Centre *HLWD* L26 155 J4
Halewood St Marks Catholic Primary School *HLWD* L26 155 K3
Halewood Sports Centre *HLWD* L26 155 K4
Hall Green Clinic *SKEL* WN8 57 K6
Hall Street Medical Centre *ECCL* WA10 13 H5
Hallwood Park Primary School *RUNC* WA7 187 H1
Halsall St Cuthberts CE Primary School *ORM* L39 43 K2
Halsnead Community Primary School *RAIN/WH* L35 117 K5
Halton College *WDN* WA8 18 D5
Halton College of Further Education *WDN* WA8 18 C4
Halton General Hospital *RUNC* WA7 187 J1
Halton High School *RUNC* WA7 188 B2
Halton House School *RUNC* WA7 177 J4
Halton Lodge Primary School *RUNC* WA7 177 G5
Halton Magistrates Court *RUNC* WA7 177 J5
Hamblett School *ECCL* WA10 88 A5
Hanson Road Business Park *WLT/FAZ* L9 83 F6
The Hardshaw Shopping Centre *ECCL* WA10 13 H5
Harold Magnay Special School *WLTN* L25 135 G5
Hartley Trading Estate *WLT/FAZ* L9 82 E6
Haslemere Industrial Estate *AIMK* WN4 79 F1
Hatton Garden Industrial Estate *CLVP* L2 8 D2
Hatton Hill Primary School *LITH* L21 81 J1
Hawthorne Business Park *WARRW/BUR* WA5 142 C1
Haydock Cricket Club *RNFD/HAY* WA11 90 B5
Haydock High School *RNFD/HAY* WA11 90 B5
Haydock Lane Industrial Estate *RNFD/HAY* WA11 90 D3
Haydock Medical Centre *RNFD/HAY* WA11 90 C5
Haydock Park Golf Club *NEWLW* WA12 92 A6
Haydock Park Racecourse *NEWLW* WA12 91 H2
Hayfield School *GR/UP/WCH* CH49 129 H3
Hazel Business Park *RNFD/HAY* WA11 75 K5
The Heath Comprehensive School *RUNC* WA7 176 E6
Heath Road Medical Centre *RUNC* WA7 176 E5
Helsby Health Centre *FROD/HEL* WA6 199 J6
Helsby High School *FROD/HEL* WA6 200 A4
Hesketh Centre (Hospital) *CHTN/BK* PR9 15 H1
Hesketh Golf Club *CHTN/BK* PR9 23 G3
Heswall FC *HES* CH60 168 C6
Heswall Golf Club *HES* CH60 181 F2
Heswall Health Centre *HES* CH60 167 K4
Heswall Preparatory School *HES* CH60 167 J3
Heswall Primary School *PEN/TH* CH61 168 A4
Heygarth Primary School *PS/BROM* CH62 184 B2
Heygreen Comm Primary School *WAV* L15 133 K1
Higher Bebington Junior School *BEB* CH63 150 B5
Higher Side Community Comprehensive School *RAIN/WH* L35 118 B4
Highfield School *CL/PREN* CH43 130 B3
Highfield Special School *HLWD* L26 155 K4
High Legh CP School *KNUT* WA16 165 K6
Hilbre High School *WKBY* CH48 127 J6
Hillcrest Hotel *WDN* WA8 138 E4
Hillside Golf Club *STHP* PR8 27 F6
Hillside Health Centre *SKEL* WN8 56 E4
Hillside High School *BTL* L20 5 K5
Hillside Primary School *CL/PREN* CH43 130 A4
FROD/HEL WA6 200 A4
Hill Street Business Centre *TOX* L8 132 C3
Hillview Primary School *RUNC* WA7 187 H3
Hinderton School *EP* CH65 195 K6
Historic Warships *BIRK* CH41 111 K6
HM Customs & Excise National Museum *VAUX/LVPD* L3 8 A6
HM Prison Altcourse *WLT/FAZ* L9 83 G5
HM Prison Liverpool *WLT/FAZ* L9 82 C6
Holiday Inn *RNFD/HAY* WA11 91 G3
RUNC WA7 187 J3
WARR WA1 144 E2
Holland Business Park *BRSC* L40 55 J1
Holland Moor Primary School *SKEL* WN8 57 G6
Holly Lodge Girls College *WD/CROXPK* L12 114 E1
Holmeswood Methodist Primary School *KIRK/FR/WA* PR4 31 H1
Holy Angels RC Primary School *KKBY* L32 84 B1
Holy Cross Primary School *VAUX/LVPD* L3 8 E1
Holy Cross RC Primary School *BIRK* CH41 110 E6
ECCL WA10 13 J4
Holy Family Catholic Primary School *CHTN/BK* PR9 23 G6
Holy Family RC High School *CSBY/BLUN* L23 69 H3
Holy Family RC Primary School *WDN* WA8 138 C3
WLTN L25 155 G2
Holy Name RC Primary School *WLT/FAZ* L9 83 H4
Holy Rosary RC Junior School *AIN/FAZ* L10 71 G6
Holy Rosary RC Primary School *AIN/FAZ* L10 71 F6
Holy Spirit Catholic Primary School *STHEL* WA9 104 E2
The Holy Spirit RC Aided Primary School *RUNC* WA7 177 G5
Holy Spirit RC Primary School *NTHTN* L30 70 A6
Holy Trinity CE Primary School *CHTN/BK* PR9 15 G3
FMBY L37 48 E2
HOY CH47 127 H2
Holy Trinity RC Primary School *ALL/GAR* L19 154 A6
Homoeopathic Medical Centre *CLB/OSW/ST* L13 114 E4
Hood Manor Medical Centre *WARRW/BUR* WA5 141 K4
Hope School *HUY* L36 136 A2
Hope Street Natural Health Centre *CLVPS* L1 9 J7
Hope Valley CP School *EV* L5 97 H6
Hornspit Medical Centre *NG/CROX* L11 98 E5
Hotel Ibis *VAUX/LVPD* L3 8 D7
Houghwood Golf Club *WGNW/BIL/O* WN5 76 E2
Howard Johnson Hotel *PR/KW* L34 84 E5
Howley Quay Industrial Estate *WARR* WA1 17 H4
Hoylake Business Centre *HOY* CH47 127 H1
Hoylake Cottage Hospital *HOY* CH47 127 H1
Hoylake Golf Club *HOY* CH47 127 G3
Hoylake RFC *HOY* CH47 127 G2
Hudson Primary School *MGHL* L31 71 G2
Hugh Baird College of Technology *BTL* L20 5 F7
Hulmes Bridge Business Centre *ORM* L39 44 A1
Hunts Cross JMI School *WLTN* L25 155 F5
Hunts Cross Shopping Park *SPK/HALE* L24 154 D5
Hurlston Hall Country Caravan Park *BRSC* L40 45 G1
Hurlston Hall Golf Club *BRSC* L40 45 G1
Hurst School *ECCL* WA10 88 B5
Huyton & Prescot Golf Club *HUY* L36 117 G2
Huyton with Roby CE Primary School *HUY* L36 116 D4
Innkeeper's Lodge Hotel *ALL/GAR* L19 153 H3
CLB/OSW/ST L13 115 F3
GOL/RIS/CU WA3 93 F5
Interactive College *CLVP* L2 8 D3
Interchange Motorway Industrial Estate *HUY* L36 117 G6
International Business Centre *WARRW/BUR* WA5 122 C5
Irby Cricket Club *PEN/TH* CH61 148 A3
Irby Primary School *PEN/TH* CH61 148 B4
Irwin Road Health Centre *STHEL* WA9 104 B6
Isle of Man Ferry Terminal *VAUX/LVPD* L3 8 A3
Islington House Medical Centre *NPK/KEN* L6 9 K1
Job's Ferry *PS/BROM* CH62 171 J4
John Street Medical Centre *GOL/RIS/CU* WA3 92 B3
John Street Primary School *EP* CH65 6 D2
Jubilee Medical Centre *NG/CROX* L11 99 G3
Junction 1 Retail Park *WAL/EG* CH44 110 D4
Kensington CP J & I Schools *EHL/KEN* L7 113 K5
Kensington Industrial Estate *CHTN/BK* PR9 15 H6
Kensington Medical Centre *NPK/KEN* L6 113 J4
Kerfoot Business Park *WARRN/WOL* WA2 142 D1
Kew Medical Centre *STHP* PR8 28 B4
Kew Retail Park *STHP* PR8 28 D3
Kew Woods Primary School *STHP* PR8 28 B4
Kilgarth School *BIRK* CH41 130 E1
The King David High School *WAV* L15 134 D2
King David Primary School *WAV* L15 134 D2
King Edward Industrial Estate *VAUX/LVPD* L3 8 A1
Kingfisher Business Park *LITH* L21 81 J4
King George V College *STHP* PR8 28 B2
Kingsbury School *ORM* L39 45 H6
Kings Business Park *PR/KW* L34 117 G2
Kings Gap Court Hotel *HOY* CH47 127 F3
Kingsley Community School *TOX* L8 133 F2
Kings Meadow Primary School *STHP* PR8 33 J6
Kingsmead School *HOY* CH47 127 H1
Kingsway Industrial Park *VAUX/LVPD* L3 113 F3
Kingsway Primary School *WAL/EG* CH44 111 J5
Kingsway Surgery *CSBY/WL* L22 81 F1
Kingswood College *BRSC* L40 36 E3
Kirby-Liverpool Municipal Golf Club *AIN/FAZ* L10 84 A3
Kirkby CE Primary School *KKBY* L32 72 C6
Kirkby Sports Centre *KKBY* L32 84 B3
Kirkdale St Lawrence CE School *ANF/KKDL* L4 97 F5
Kirkfield Hotel *NEWLW* WA12 106 E1
Knotty Ash Primary School *DV/KA/FCH* L14 115 H3
Knowsley Business Park *PR/KW* L34 85 G6
Knowsley Central Primary Support Centre *HUY* L36 117 F3
Knowsley Community College *HUY* L36 116 C5
KKBY L32 84 C1
Knowsley Hey School *HUY* L36 117 F5
Knowsley Industrial Park *NWD/KWIPK* L33 85 F5
Knowsley Industrial Park *NWD/KWIPK* L33 85 H1
Knowsley Magistrates Court *HUY* L36 116 E5
Knowsley Medical Centre *PR/KW* L34 100 D2
Knowsley Northern Primary Support Centre *NWD/KWIPK* L33 72 E5
Knowsley Safari Park *PR/KW* L34 101 H4
Knowsley Village Primary School *PR/KW* L34 100 C3
Lady Lever Art Gallery *PS/BROM* CH62 151 G5
Ladymount RC Primary School *PEN/TH* CH61 167 K2
Lairdside Technology Park *BIRK* CH41 131 J5
Lakeside School *HUY* L36 136 A2
Lancaster House Medical Centre *ECCL* WA10 13 G3
Lance Lane Medical Centre *WAV* L15 134 B2
Lander Road Primary School *LITH* L21 81 K5
Landgate Industrial Estate *AIMK* WN4 79 F1
Landican Cemetery *GR/UP/WCH* CH49 148 E2
Landican Crematorium *GR/UP/WCH* CH49 148 E3
Langbank Medical Centre *NG/CROX* L11 98 D4
Langham Street Industrial Estate *ANF/KKDL* L4 97 H5
Larkfield Primary School *CHTN/BK* PR9 23 J2
Latchford CE Primary School *WARRS* WA4 16 E7
Latchford Medical Centre *WARRS* WA4 143 H6
Lathom County High School *SKEL* WN8 56 B2
Lathom Park CE Primary School *BRSC* L40 47 G3
Lathom Road Health Centre *HUY* L36 116 E4
Laurel Business Centre *EHL/KEN* L7 114 B5
Lea Green Business Park *STHEL* WA9 119 H3
Leamington Community School *NG/CROX* L11 98 B3
Leasowe Castle Hotel *MOR/LEA* CH46 109 J3
Leasowe Golf Club *MOR/LEA* CH46 109 K3
Leasowe Millennium Centre *MOR/LEA* CH46 110 A4
Leasowe Primary School *MOR/LEA* CH46 110 B3
Leasowe Recreation Centre *MOR/LEA* CH46 110 A4
Lee Park Golf Club *NTHLY* L27 136 A5
Legh Vale Primary School *RNFD/HAY* WA11 90 A5
Leisure Lakes *CHTN/BK* PR9 25 H5
Library & Rainford Gallery *ECCL* WA10 13 G4
Lifeboat House *HOY* CH47 127 F2

Linacre Primary School *BTL* L20 81 K6
Linaker Primary School *STHP* PR8 27 J2
Lincoln Road Health Centre *STHP* PR8 27 H6
Lingham Primary School *MOR/LEA* CH46 109 H6
Lingholme Health Centre *ECCL* WA10 13 F4
Lingley Mere Business Park *WARRW/BUR* WA5 141 F1
Lister Drive Infant School *CLB/OSW/ST* L13 114 C3
Lister Drive Junior School *CLB/OSW/ST* L13 114 C3
Litherland High School *LITH* L21 82 A1
Litherland Moss Primary School *LITH* L21 82 A2
Little Digmoor Primary School *SKEL* WN8 66 D1
Little Sutton CE Primary School *GTS/LS* CH66 194 D3
Little Theatre
CHTN/BK PR9 15 F4
CL/PREN CH43 2 C5
Liver Industrial Estate *WLT/FAZ* L9 98 A1
Liverpool Anglican Cathedral *CLVPS* L1 132 D2
Liverpool College *CALD/MH* L18 134 A5
Liverpool Community College *CLVPS* L1 9 G7
Liverpool Cricket Club *ALL/GAR* L19 153 G3
Liverpool Empire Theatre *CLVPS* L1 9 F3
Liverpool FC (Anfield) *ANF/KKDL* L4 97 J6
Liverpool FC Museum *ANF/KKDL* L4 97 J6
Liverpool Hope University College *CHLDW* L16 134 E3
Liverpool Hope University College *VAUX/LVPD* L3 9 J1
Liverpool John Lennon International Airport *SPK/HALE* L24 173 H3
Liverpool John Moores University *AIG/SPK* L17 153 G2
CLVPS L1 9 J5
EHL/KEN L7 114 B5
VAUX/LVPD L3 9 F1
VAUX/LVPD L3 9 H3
Liverpool Magistrates Court *CLVP* L2 8 D3
Liverpool Marriott Hotel
CLVPS L1 9 F3
SPK/HALE L24 172 E1
Liverpool Museum *VAUX/LVPD* L3 9 F2
Liverpool Playhouse Theatre *CLVPS* L1 9 F4
Liverpool St Helens RUFC *RNFD/HAY* WA11 87 H4
Liverpool University Botanic Gardens (Ness Gardens) *NSTN* CH64 192 B5
Liverpool Womens Hospital *TOX* L8 133 F1
Locking Stumps Primary School *GOL/RIS/CU* WA3 124 E2
Longbarn CP School *WARRN/WOL* WA2 124 D6
Long Lane CP School *WARRN/WOL* WA2 123 H6
Long Lane Medical Centre *WLT/FAZ* L9 98 D1
Longmoor Community Primary School *WLT/FAZ* L9 82 E5
Longton Lane Community Primary School *RAIN/WH* L35 118 D2
Longton Medical Centre *RAIN/WH* L35 118 D4
Longview J & I School *HUY* L36 116 E1
Lordsgate Township Primary School *BRSC* L40 38 E6
Lourdes Hospital *CALD/MH* L18 134 A5
Loushers Lane Special School
GOL/RIS/CU WA3 125 G4
WARRS WA4 162 C1
Lower Lee Special School *WLTN* L25 135 F5
Lowfield Industrial Estate *STHEL* WA9 119 H2
Lowton Business Park *GOL/RIS/CU* WA3 93 H3
Lowton High School *GOL/RIS/CU* WA3 93 J3
Lowton J & I School *GOL/RIS/CU* WA3 93 H4
Lowton St Marys CE Primary School *GOL/RIS/CU* WA3 93 H3
Lowton West Primary School *GOL/RIS/CU* WA3 92 D3
Lunts Heath Primary School *WDN* WA8 139 G4
Lydiate Primary School *MGHL* L31 62 A3
Lyme Community Primary School *NEWLW* WA12 105 K1
Lymm Golf Club *LYMM* WA13 145 J4
Lymm Hotel *LYMM* WA13 145 J6
Lymm RFC *LYMM* WA13 165 F2
The Lyndale School *PS/BROM* CH62 184 C2
Lyon Industrial Estate *STHEL* WA9 120 B3
Mab Lane Primary School *STBRV* L28 99 K6
Mackets Primary School *WLTN* L25 155 G2
Maghull Health Centre *MGHL* L31 62 B6
Maghull High School *MGHL* L31 71 F2
Manor Farm Medical Centre *HUY* L36 117 F6
Manor High School *CSBY/BLUN* L23 68 E3
The Manor House Primary School *FROD/HEL* WA6 187 F6
Manor Primary School *CL/PREN* CH43 129 K2
Mansfield Primary School *EP* CH65 195 J6
Marble Place Shopping Centre *STHP* PR8 14 E5
Margaret Beavan Special School *WD/CROXPK* L12 98 E6
The Margaret Thompson Medical Centre *SPK/HALE* L24 174 B1
Maricourt Catholic High School *MGHL* L31 71 H1
Marine FC *CSBY/BLUN* L23 68 E6
Market Hall
BIRK CH41 3 F5
EP CH65 6 D6
ORM L39 45 K6
SKEL WN8 56 D4
STHP PR8 14 E5
WARR WA1 16 D5
Marshside RSPB Reserve *WDN* WA8 20 A6
Martlew Day Hospital *STHEL* WA9 118 E2
Maryland Health Centre *CLVPS* L1 9 J6
Massey Hall School *WARRS* WA4 164 A1
Maternity & Child Welfare Clinic *STHEL* WA9 104 D2
Matthew Arnold Primary School *TOX* L8 133 F6
Mayflower Industrial Estate *FMBY* L37 49 G4
McKee School of Education *CALD/MH* L18 153 K1
Meadow Bank Special School *AIN/FAZ* L10 83 J3
Meadow Lane Industrial Park *EP* CH65 7 F3
Meadow Primary School *GTS/LS* CH66 202 C1
Meadowside School *GR/UP/WCH* CH49 148 D1
Melling Primary School *MGHL* L31 72 A5
Melrose Abbey *ANF/KKDL* L4 97 F4
Mendell Primary School *PS/BROM* CH62 171 G5
Meols Cop High School *STHP* PR8 28 C2
Meols Cop Retail Park *STHP* PR8 28 C3
Merchant Taylors Junior School for Girls *CSBY/BLUN* L23 68 E6
Merchant Taylors School for Boys *CSBY/BLUN* L23 81 F1
Merchant Taylors School for Girls *CSBY/BLUN* L23 68 E5
Mere Brow CE Primary School *KIRK/FR/WA* PR4 25 K3
Merefield Special School *STHP* PR8 33 H5
Mersey Ferries *VAUX/LVPD* L3 8 B5
Mersey Park Primary School *RF/TRAN* CH42 131 G6
Merseyside Maritime Museum *VAUX/LVPD* L3 8 A6
Mersey View *FROD/HEL* WA6 200 E2
Mersey View Special School *AIG/SPK* L17 153 F2
Merton Bank Primary School *STHEL* WA9 104 A1
Met Quarter *CLVP* L2 8 E4
Metropole Hotel *STHP* PR8 14 D6
Metropolitan Cathedral of Christ the King *VAUX/LVPD* L3 9 J4
Middlefield Primary School *SPK/HALE* L24 173 K2
Millbrook Business Centre *RNFD/HAY* WA11 75 K6
Millbrook Primary School *KKBY* L32 72 C6
Millfields Primary School *PS/BROM* CH62 184 B3
Mill Green Special School *NEWLW* WA12 106 E2
Millingford Industrial Estate *GOL/RIS/CU* WA3 92 C3
Mill Lane Industrial Estate *EP* CH65 196 E6
Millstead Special School *WAV* L15 134 B1
Mill Street Medical Centre *ECCL* WA10 13 F4
Miriam Health Centre *BIRK* CH41 130 C1
Model Village *STHP* PR8 14 C4
Monksdown Primary School *NG/CROX* L11 98 E4
Moore Primary School *WARRS* WA4 160 D6
Moore RUFC *WARRS* WA4 160 E5
Moorfield Primary School *WDN* WA8 139 J6
Moorfoot Road Industrial Estate *STHEL* WA9 104 D1
Moor Lane Business Centre *WDN* WA8 18 C6
Moorside Primary School *SKEL* WN8 57 G6
Moreton Medical Centre *MOR/LEA* CH46 129 F1
Mornington Business Centre *CLVPS* L1 9 H7
Mosscroft Primary School *HUY* L36 117 G4
Moss Industrial Estate *LEIGH* WN7 93 J2
Mosslands School *WAL/EG* CH44 110 E3
Moss Lane Sports Centre *LITH* L21 82 A2
Mossley Hill Hospital *CALD/MH* L18 133 K5
Mossock Hall Golf Club *ORM* L39 63 J3
Mosspits J & I School *WAV* L15 134 C3
Mother Teresa RC JMI School *EV* L5 113 F3
Mount Carmel Preparatory School *ORM* L39 53 H3
Mount Primary School *WAL/NB* CH45 95 G5
The Mount-St Marys Prep School *CSBY/BLUN* L23 68 C6
Much Woolton Catholic School *WLTN* L25 154 E1
Murdishaw Health Centre *RUNC* WA7 178 C6
Murrayfield Hospital *PEN/TH* CH61 149 G6
Museum of Liverpool Life *VAUX/LVPD* L3 8 B6
National Discovery Park *CLVPS* L1 8 D5
National Museums & Galleries Merseyside *CLVPS* L1 9 F3
National Wildflower Centre *CHLDW* L16 115 K6
Natural Health Clinic *PR/KW* L34 117 K1
Nature Reserve
BEB CH63 170 D6
FMBY L37 40 D2
FMBY L37 48 A5
Neptune Theatre *CLVPS* L1 8 E5
Neston CC *NSTN* CH64 191 H1
Neston High School *NSTN* CH64 182 A6
Neston Medical Centre *NSTN* CH64 191 K1
Neston Primary School *NSTN* CH64 191 K2
Neston Recreation Centre *NSTN* CH64 182 A6
Netherfield Family Health Clinic *EV* L5 113 G2
Netherley Health Centre *NTHLY* L27 136 B4
Netherley Sports Centre *NTHLY* L27 136 A4
Netherton Industrial Estate *NTHTN* L30 82 C3
Netherton Moss Primary School *NTHTN* L30 70 B6
Netherton Park Primary School *NTHTN* L30 82 C1
Newborough School *WLTN* L25 135 G6
New Brighton Primary School *WAL/NB* CH45 95 J5
New Brighton RUFC *MOR/LEA* CH46 109 K3
Newfield Special School *CSBY/BLUN* L23 69 J4
New Heys Comprehensive School *CALD/MH* L18 154 A2
New Hutte CP School *HLWD* L26 155 H5
New Lodge Industrial Estate *NWD/KWIPK* L33 85 G3
New Market Hall *RUNC* WA7 10 E3
New Mersey Retail Park *SPK/HALE* L24 154 C6
New Park Primary School *NPK/KEN* L6 113 K4
Newstead Abbey *TOX* L8 133 H2
Newton Bank Preparatory School *NEWLW* WA12 106 E1
Newton Community Hospital *NEWLW* WA12 106 B4
Newton Health Clinic *NEWLW* WA12 106 B1
Newton-le-Willows Cemetery *NEWLW* WA12 106 D3
Newton-le-Willows Community High School *NEWLW* WA12 91 J6
Newton-le-Willows Primary School *NEWLW* WA12 106 C2
Newton-le-Willows Sports Club *NEWLW* WA12 106 C1
New Way Business Centre *WAL/EG* CH44 111 K5
Nicol Mere School *AIMK* WN4 79 F4
Nine Tree Primary School *STBRV* L28 100 A4
Norman Pannell JMI School *NTHLY* L27 136 B4
Norris Green Family Health Clinic *NG/CROX* L11 98 C4
North Cheshire Trading Estate *CL/PREN* CH43 149 H3
North Clinic *CL/PREN* CH43 130 D2
Northcote Primary School *WLT/FAZ* L9 97 J2
Northern CC *CSBY/BLUN* L23 69 G3
North Meols Community Leisure Centre *CHTN/BK* PR9 21 K6
North Meols Lawn Tennis Club *CHTN/BK* PR9 23 J4
North Mersey Business Centre *NWD/KWIPK* L33 73 H5
North Mersey Community Hospital *WLT/FAZ* L9 83 G5
North Park Health Centre *BTL* L20 4 D1
Northway Primary School
MGHL L31 62 C4
WAV L15 115 F6
North Western Hall *CLVPS* L1 9 G3
North Wirral Coastal Park *MOR/LEA* CH46 109 H3
Norton Priory Museum and Gardens *RUNC* WA7 178 A2
Norton Priory Recreation Centre *RUNC* WA7 178 A3
Norwood Primary School *CHTN/BK* PR9 23 G6
Notre Dame Catholic High School *ANF/KKDL* L4 97 G6
Nugent House School *WGNW/BIL/O* WN5 77 G5
Nutgrove Methodist Primary School *STHEL* WA9 103 F6
Nye Bevan Swimming Pool *SKEL* WN8 56 D4
Oak Cottage Medical Centre *HUY* L36 116 E6
Oakdene Primary School *RAIN/WH* L35 118 E5
Oakfield Junior School *WDN* WA8 157 G3
Oak Remedial Clinic *WD/CROXPK* L12 99 J1
The Oaks Community Primary School *EP* CH65 196 C6
Oakwood Avenue Primary School *WARR* WA1 143 G2
Odeon Cinema
CLVPS L1 9 F3
NTHTN L30 70 D6
PS/BROM CH62 171 F3
Oil Refinery *EP* CH65 197 H6
Oil Terminal *RF/TRAN* CH42 131 K6
Old Boston Trading Estate *RNFD/HAY* WA11 91 F3
Oldershaw School *WAL/NB* CH45 111 G2
Old Foundry Estate *WDN* WA8 19 F6
Old Hall Farm Business Park *CHTN/BK* PR9 28 D2
Old Hall Primary School *WARRW/BUR* WA5 142 A1
Old Parkonians RFC *CL/PREN* CH43 130 D6
Old Rockferrians RFC *CL/PREN* CH43 149 J3
Old Swan Health Centre *CLB/OSW/ST* L13 114 E5
Ormskirk Business Park *ORM* L39 45 K5
Ormskirk CE Primary School *ORM* L39 45 K5
Ormskirk Cricket Club *ORM* L39 53 K1
Ormskirk & District General Hospital *ORM* L39 53 K1
Ormskirk Golf Club *BRSC* L40 46 E4
Ormskirk RUFC *ORM* L39 45 J5
Ormskirk School *BRSC* L40 46 B6
Orrell Primary School *BTL* L20 82 A6
Orrets Meadow School *MOR/LEA* CH46 129 G1
Our Lady Catholic High School *NPK/KEN* L6 113 J3
Our Lady Immaculate RCP School *EV* L5 113 G1
Our Lady Mother of the Saviour Catholic Primary *RUNC* WA7 187 K1
Our Lady of Compassion RC Primary School *FMBY* L37 49 G2
Our Lady of Good Help RC Primary School *WAV* L15 134 B1
Our Lady of Lourdes RC Primary School
MOR/LEA CH46 110 B3
STHP PR8 27 H6
Our Lady of Mount Carmel RC Primary School *TOX* L8 132 E4
Our Lady of Perpetual Succour RC Primary School *WDN* WA8 156 E3
Our Lady of Pity Primary School *GR/UP/WCH* CH49 148 A1
Our Lady of Reconciliation Primary School *VAUX/LVPD* L3 112 E3
Our Lady of the Assumption Primary School *WLTN* L25 135 J3
Our Lady of Walsingham RC Infant School *NTHTN* L30 82 B1
Our Lady of Walsingham RC Junior School *NTHTN* L30 82 B1
Our Lady Queen of Peace RC High School *SKEL* WN8 56 B1
Our Lady Queen of Peace RC Primary School *LITH* L21 81 H1
Our Lady RC Primary School *WARRS* WA4 143 H6
Our Lady & St Edwards RC Primary School *BIRK* CH41 130 E1
Our Lady & St Philomenas Primary School *WLT/FAZ* L9 98 D1
Our Lady & St Swithins Catholic Primary School *NG/CROX* L11 84 B6
Our Ladys Bishop Eton RC Primary School *CALD/MH* L18 134 D4
Our Ladys Catholic Infant School *EP* CH65 195 K6
Our Ladys RC Junior School *EP* CH65 195 K6
Our Ladys RC Primary School *PR/KW* L34 101 K6
Our Lady Star of the Sea RC Primary School *LITH* L21 81 H5
The Oval Sports Centre *BEB* CH63 151 F4
Overchurch J & I School *GR/UP/WCH* CH49 129 G3
Overdale Primary School *NWD/KWIPK* L33 72 E5
Oxton Cricket Club *CL/PREN* CH43 130 C5
Paddington House Hotel *WARR* WA1 143 K2
Padgate Business Centre *WARR* WA1 143 K1
Padgate CE Primary School *WARRN/WOL* WA2 124 C6
Padgate Community High School *WARRN/WOL* WA2 124 B5
Padgate Medical Centre *WARRN/WOL* WA2 124 C6
Paerr Hall *WARR* WA1 16 C6
Palacefields Primary School *RUNC* WA7 187 K1
Palace Theatre *WARR* WA1 16 D5
Palatine Industrial Estate *WARRS* WA4 143 F6
Palmerston Special School *WLTN* L25 135 F6
Paradise Street Bus Station *CLVP* L2 8 D5
Parish CE Primary School *ECCL* WA10 13 J3
Park Brow Primary School *KKBY* L32 85 F3
Parkdale Industrial Estate *WARR* WA1 17 G6
Parkfield Medical Centre *RF/TRAN* CH42 151 F3
Parkfield Special School *KKBY* L32 84 D3
Parkgate Primary School *NSTN* CH64 181 H6
Park High Lower School *BIRK* CH41 130 D2
Park High School Sports College *CL/PREN* CH43 2 A5
Park House Medical Centre *PR/KW* L34 117 K1
Park Industrial Estate *AIMK* WN4 78 D6
Parklands High School *SPK/HALE* L24 173 K2
Parklands Primary School *GTS/LS* CH66 195 G4
The Park Lane Hotel *AIG/SPK* L17 133 H6
Park Medical Centre *WKBY* CH48 146 B1
Park Pool *ORM* L39 45 J6
Park Primary School *WAL/EG* CH44 111 H4
The Park Primary School *RUNC* WA7 177 K4
Park Road Primary School *WARRW/BUR* WA5 141 F3
Park Road Sports Centre *TOX* L8 132 E4
Park View Primary School *HUY* L36 116 C3
Parliament Street North Waterfront Business Area *VAUX/LVPD* L3 132 B2
Parliament Street South Waterfront Business Area *CLVPS* L1 132 D2
Parr Industrial Estate *STHEL* WA9 104 C3
Parrs Corner Trading Estate *BTL* L20 5 F2
Parr Swimming Baths *STHEL* WA9 104 A2
Pasture Road Health Centre *MOR/LEA* CH46 109 J6

Patterdale Lodge Medical Centre *NEWLW* WA12 ....106 A2
Peatwood Medical Centre *KKBY* L32 ....84 E4
Peninsula Business Park *MOR/LEA* CH46 ....110 A5
Penketh Business Park *WARRW/BUR* WA5 ....141 J5
Penketh County High School *WARRW/BUR* WA5 ....141 G4
Penketh Health Clinic *WARRW/BUR* WA5 ....141 F5
Penketh Primary School *WARRW/BUR* WA5 ....140 E5
Penketh South Community Primary School *WARRW/BUR* WA5 ....141 G6
Penketh Swimming Baths *WARRW/BUR* WA5 ....141 F4
Penkford School *NEWLW* WA12 ....105 J3
Penlake Industrial Estate *STHEL* WA9 ....120 C1
Pennington Flash Country Park *LEIGH* WN7 ....93 K1
Penpoll Industrial Estate *BTL* L20 ....81 K5
Penpoll Trading Estate *BTL* L20 ....81 K5
Pensby Clinic *PEN/TH* CH61 ....168 A2
Pensby High School for Boys *PEN/TH* CH61 ....167 H2
Pensby High School for Girls *PEN/TH* CH61 ....167 H1
Pensby Infant School *PEN/TH* CH61 ....167 K2
Pensby Junior School *PEN/TH* CH61 ....167 K2
Pensby Park Primary School *PEN/TH* CH61 ....167 J1
Pensby Recreation Centre *PEN/TH* CH61 ....148 D6
Peterhouse School *CHTN/BK* PR9 ....23 K2
Peter Lloyd Leisure Centre *CLB/OSW/ST* L13 ....114 D2
Pewithall Primary School *RUNC* WA7 ....176 E6
Philharmonic Hall *CLVPS* L1 ....9 J6
Phoenix Medical Centre *ECCL* WA10 ....13 F4
Phoenix Primary School *EHL/KEN* L7 ....114 C5
Picture House Cinema *WLTN* L25 ....154 D1
Pinehurst Primary School *ANF/KKDL* L4 ....98 A6
Pinfold Primary School *BRSC* L40 ....36 D6
Pinners Brow Retail Park *WARRN/WOL* WA2 ....16 E3
Pius XII RC Primary School *GTS/LS* CH66 ....195 G3
Plantation Business Park *PS/BROM* CH62 ....171 H3
Plantation Primary School *HLWD* L26 ....155 J3
Platts Lane Industrial Estate *BRSC* L40 ....46 E1
Plaza Cinema *CSBY/WL* L22 ....80 E2
Pleasant Primary School *VAUX/LVPD* L3 ....9 H5
Pleasureland *STHP* PR8 ....14 A4
Plessington Catholic High School *BEB* CH63 ....151 F4
Pontville School *ORM* L39 ....53 H2
Poole Hall Industrial Estate *EP* CH65 ....185 J6
Pooltown Junior School *EP* CH65 ....195 J4
Port Arcades *EP* CH65 ....6 D5
Portland Primary School *BIRK* CH41 ....130 D1
Port of Liverpool *LITH* L21 ....81 F5
Port of Liverpool Building *VAUX/LVPD* L3 ....8 C5
Poulter Road Medical Centre *WLT/FAZ* L9 ....82 E4
Poulton Lancelyn Primary School *BEB* CH63 ....170 C3
Poulton Park Golf Club *WARRN/WOL* WA2 ....124 C3
Poulton Primary School *WAL/EG* CH44 ....111 G4
Premier Lodge *AIMK* WN4 ....91 G1
CLVPS L1 ....8 D3
GR/UP/WCH CH49 ....129 F5
HUY L36 ....116 B5
NTHTN L30 ....82 C1
RAIN/WH L35 ....119 G6
VAUX/LVPD L3 ....8 C7
WARR WA1 ....144 E3
WARRN/WOL WA2 ....123 G1
Prenton Golf Club *CL/PREN* CH43 ....150 A3
Prenton High School for Girls *RF/TRAN* CH42 ....150 C2
Prenton Infant & Junior Schools *CL/PREN* CH43 ....149 K2
Prenton Preparatory School *CL/PREN* CH43 ....130 E6
Prescot AFC *PR/KW* L34 ....101 K6
Prescot Leisure Centre *RAIN/WH* L35 ....118 A2
Prescot Medical Centre *PR/KW* L34 ....117 K1
Prescot Museum *PR/KW* L34 ....117 J1
Prescot Primary School *PR/KW* L34 ....118 B1
Prescot School *PR/KW* L34 ....101 J6
Presfield Special School *CHTN/BK* PR9 ....23 J2
Price Street Business Centre *BIRK* CH41 ....2 B1
Priestley Business Centre *WARRW/BUR* WA5 ....142 C4
Priestley Sixth Form College *WARRS* WA4 ....143 F6
Prince Edwin Adult Centre *EV* L5 ....113 G3
Princes Park Health Centre *TOX* L8 ....133 G3
Princess Drive Medical Centre *DV/KA/FCH* L14 ....116 A1
Princes Special School *TOX* L8 ....133 F2
The Priory CE Primary School *BIRK* CH41 ....2 C2
The Priory Medical Centre *NPK/KEN* L6 ....114 A2
Pump House Museum *BIRK* CH41 ....3 H3
Pyramid *WARR* WA1 ....16 C6
Pyramids Shopping Centre *BIRK* CH41 ....2 E5
Quality Hotel *GTS/LS* CH66 ....194 C3
SKEL WN8 ....67 H3
Quay Business Centre *WARRN/WOL* WA2 ....123 G4
Queen Elizabeth II Law Courts *CLVPS* L1 ....8 C5
Queenscourt Hospice *STHP* PR8 ....28 B3
Queens Dock Business Centre *VAUX/LVPD* L3 ....132 C2
Queens Drive Family Health Clinic *WLT/FAZ* L9 ....97 J2
Queens Park CE/URC Primary School *ECCL* WA10 ....12 B3
Queens Park Community Leisure Centre *ECCL* WA10 ....12 D4
Queensway Business Centre *WDN* WA8 ....158 A6
Racecourse Retail Park *WLT/FAZ* L9 ....83 F1
Radio City *CLVP* L2 ....8 D3
Radnor Medical Centre *NPK/KEN* L6 ....114 B2
Raeburn Primary School *PS/BROM* CH62 ....184 A1
RAF Burtonwood *WARRW/BUR* WA5 ....141 H2
Railway Centre *STHP* PR8 ....15 G6
Rainbow Medical Centre *STHEL* WA9 ....104 C6
Rainford CE Primary School *RNFD/HAY* WA11 ....75 G3
Rainford Health Centre *RNFD/HAY* WA11 ....75 H3
Rainford High School *RNFD/HAY* WA11 ....75 H1
Rainford Industrial Estate *RNFD/HAY* WA11 ....75 J5
Rainhill Clinic *RAIN/WH* L35 ....118 E4
Rainhill High School *RAIN/WH* L35 ....119 F5
Range High School *FMBY* L37 ....48 D5
Ravenhead Retail Park *STHEL* WA9 ....103 J4
Ravenscroft Primary School *NWD/KWIPK* L33 ....72 D4
Rawson Road Primary School *LITH* L21 ....81 G5
Record Business Park *WARRN/WOL* WA2 ....142 D1
Rectory CE Primary School *AIMK* WN4 ....78 C4
Redbridge High School *AIN/FAZ* L10 ....83 J3
Redgate Primary School *FMBY* L37 ....49 G3
Red Lion Shopping Centre *MGHL* L31 ....62 B6
Reginald Road Industrial Park *STHEL* WA9 ....120 D1
Renacres Hall Hospital *ORM* L39 ....35 K4
Rice Lane J & I Schools *WLT/FAZ* L9 ....82 D6
Richard Evans Community Primary School *RNFD/HAY* WA11 ....89 J5
Richard Evans Infant School *RNFD/HAY* WA11 ....89 K5
Ridgeway High School *CL/PREN* CH43 ....130 A5
Rimrose Business Park *BTL* L20 ....4 A1
BTL L20 ....4 B3
Rimrose Valley Country Park *CSBY/BLUN* L23 ....81 H1
Ringtail Industrial Estate *BRSC* L40 ....46 B1
Risley Moss Nature Park *GOL/RIS/CU* WA3 ....125 K3
Rivacre Business Centre *GTS/LS* CH66 ....195 H4
Rivacre Valley Country Park *GTS/LS* CH66 ....195 H1
Rivacre Valley CP School *GTS/LS* CH66 ....195 H2
Riverhill Hotel *CL/PREN* CH43 ....130 D6
Riverside Primary School *WAL/EG* CH44 ....112 A4
Riverside Retail Park *WARR* WA1 ....17 F6
Riverside Trading Estate *WARRW/BUR* WA5 ....160 A2
Rivington Primary School *ECCL* WA10 ....12 C1
R L Hughes Primary School *AIMK* WN4 ....79 F6
Roberts Primary School *BTL* L20 ....82 A4
Robins Lane Primary School *STHEL* WA9 ....104 A5
Robson Street Clinic *WARR* WA1 ....17 H3
Roby Medical Centre *HUY* L36 ....116 A5
Roby Mill CE Primary School *SKEL* WN8 ....57 K2
Roby Park Primary School *HUY* L36 ....116 B4
Rocket Trading Centre *DV/KA/FCH* L14 ....115 G6
Rock Ferry High School *RF/TRAN* CH42 ....150 E3
Rock Ferry Medical Centre *RF/TRAN* CH42 ....131 J6
Rock Ferry Primary School *RF/TRAN* CH42 ....150 E1
Rock Retail Park *BIRK* CH41 ....3 H7
Rodney Fertility Clinic *CLVPS* L1 ....9 H6
Roscoe Infant School *CLB/OSW/ST* L13 ....98 D6
Roseheath Primary School *HLWD* L26 ....155 J4
Rosehill Business Park *CHTN/BK* PR9 ....15 K6
Rossmore Primary School *GTS/LS* CH66 ....195 F2
Rother Drive Business Park *EP* CH65 ....195 K2
Rowan Park Special School *LITH* L21 ....82 A1
The Royal Birkdale Golf Club *STHP* PR8 ....26 E6
Royal Clifton Hotel *STHP* PR8 ....14 D4
Royal College of Nursing *CLVP* L2 ....8 C4
Royal Court Theatre *CLVPS* L1 ....9 F3
The Royal Hotel *CSBY/WL* L22 ....80 E3
Royal Liver Building *VAUX/LVPD* L3 ....8 B4
Royal Liverpool Childrens Hospital (Alder Hey) *WD/CROXPK* L12 ....115 G3
Royal Liverpool Golf Club *HOY* CH47 ....127 F3
Royal Liverpool University Hospital *EHL/KEN* L7 ....9 K3
Royal School for the Blind *WAV* L15 ....134 A2
Roy Castle International Centre for Lung Research *EHL/KEN* L7 ....9 K2
Rudston J & I School *CHLDW* L16 ....134 E1
Ruffwood Community School *NWD/KWIPK* L33 ....72 E6
Runcorn AFC *RUNC* WA7 ....11 G3
Runcorn County Court *RUNC* WA7 ....177 J5
Runcorn Golf Club *RUNC* WA7 ....176 D6
Runcorn Rowing Club *RUNC* WA7 ....187 G3
Runcorn Ski Slope *RUNC* WA7 ....178 A6
Runcorn Swimming Pool *RUNC* WA7 ....11 F3
Rutherford Medical Centre *CALD/MH* L18 ....134 C3
Sacred Heart RC High School *CSBY/BLUN* L23 ....69 F5
Sacred Heart RC Primary School *EHL/KEN* L7 ....113 J5
MOR/LEA CH46 ....109 K6
WARRW/BUR WA5 ....142 B4
St Aelreds RC Technology College *NEWLW* WA12 ....106 D1
St Agnes RC Primary School *HUY* L36 ....117 F6
St Aidans CE Primary School *WGNW/BIL/O* WN5 ....77 H4
St Aidans RC Primary School *HUY* L36 ....117 F4
St Albans RC Primary School *WAL/EG* CH44 ....111 G3
WARRW/BUR WA5 ....16 A2
St Alberts RC Primary School *STBRV* L28 ....100 A4
St Aloysius RC Primary School *HUY* L36 ....116 C3
St Ambrose Barlow RC High School *NTHTN* L30 ....70 D4
St Ambrose RC Primary School *SPK/HALE* L24 ....174 B3
St Andrews CE Primary School *BEB* CH63 ....150 E5
WARRN/WOL WA2 ....123 J4
St Andrews Maghull CE Primary School *MGHL* L31 ....62 B6
St Andrews RC Primary School *WLTN* L25 ....155 G4
St Annes CE Primary School *CLB/OSW/ST* L13 ....114 D4
St Annes RC Primary School *EHL/KEN* L7 ....133 G1
HUY L36 ....116 D6
ORM L39 ....53 H1
RF/TRAN CH42 ....150 E3
STHEL WA9 ....104 B6
St Anns CE Primary School *RAIN/WH* L35 ....118 E4
WARRN/WOL WA2 ....143 F1
St Anselms College *CL/PREN* CH43 ....130 D3
St Anselms Redcourt *CL/PREN* CH43 ....130 D4
St Anthony of Padua RC Primary School *CALD/MH* L18 ....134 A5
St Anthony's Shopping Centre *EV* L5 ....113 G2
St Augustine of Canterbury RC High School *RNFD/HAY* WA11 ....89 H6
St Augustines Catholic Primary School *WARRS* WA4 ....143 J5
St Augustines RC Primary School *RUNC* WA7 ....177 K3
St Austins RC Primary School *ALL/GAR* L19 ....153 J4
STHEL WA9 ....102 E6
St Barnabas CE Primary School *WARRW/BUR* WA5 ....142 C4
St Bartholomews RC Primary School *RAIN/WH* L35 ....119 G6
St Basil RC Primary School *RAIN/WH* L35 ....137 K6
St Bedes Catholic High School *ORM* L39 ....53 H1
St Bedes RC J & I School *WDN* WA8 ....18 D1
St Benedicts RC Primary School *WARRN/WOL* WA2 ....143 G2
St Benets RC Primary School *NTHTN* L30 ....70 C4
St Bernards RC Primary School *EP* CH65 ....196 C6
St Berteline CE Primary School *RUNC* WA7 ....178 B5
St Bridgets Catholic Primary School *WARRN/WOL* WA2 ....124 B4
St Bridgets CE Primary School *WKBY* CH48 ....146 C2
St Brigids RC Primary School *STBRV* L28 ....100 A6
St Catherines Centre for Girls *RNFD/HAY* WA11 ....89 H5
St Catherine's Hospital *RF/TRAN* CH42 ....131 G6
St Catherines RC Primary School *GOL/RIS/CU* WA3 ....93 F3
St Cecilias RC Infant School *CLB/OSW/ST* L13 ....114 C2
St Chads Catholic High School *RUNC* WA7 ....177 G6
St Charles RC Primary School *AIG/SPK* L17 ....152 D1
St Christophers RC Primary School *SPK/HALE* L24 ....173 J1
St Clares RC Primary School *WAV* L15 ....133 J2
St Clements RC Primary School *RUNC* WA7 ....10 D7
St Cleopas CE Primary School *TOX* L8 ....132 E5
St Columbas RC Primary School *HUY* L36 ....116 E2
St Cuthberts Catholic High School *STHEL* WA9 ....104 D4
St Cuthberts RC Primary School *CLB/OSW/ST* L13 ....114 D4
St Dominics RC J & I School *DV/KA/FCH* L14 ....116 B1
St Edmund Arrowsmith Catholic High School *AIMK* WN4 ....91 F1
St Edmund Arrowsmith RC Comprehensive School *RAIN/WH* L35 ....118 B2
St Edmund of Canterbury High School *DV/KA/FCH* L14 ....116 B1
St Edmunds & St Thomas Cath Primary School *CSBY/WL* L22 ....80 E2
St Edwards College (Secondary) *WD/CROXPK* L12 ....115 F2
St Edwards C Primary School *RUNC* WA7 ....11 G3
St Edwards Runnymede Junior School *WD/CROXPK* L12 ....115 F2
St Elizabeths Catholic Primary School *LITH* L21 ....81 K5
St Finbars Catholic Primary School *TOX* L8 ....133 F6
St Francis de Sales RC Infant School *ANF/KKDL* L4 ....5 K7
St Francis de Sales RC Junior School *ANF/KKDL* L4 ....97 G4
St Francis of Assisi RC Primary School *ALL/GAR* L19 ....153 K5
St Francis Xavier RC College *WLTN* L25 ....135 F5
St Gabriels CE Primary School *HUY* L36 ....117 G5
St George of England High School *BTL* L20 ....82 A5
St George's Hall *CLVPS* L1 ....9 F3
St Georges Medical Centre *WAL/NB* CH45 ....95 H6
St Georges Primary School *WAL/NB* CH45 ....110 E2
St Georges RC Primary School *MGHL* L31 ....71 G2
St Gerards RC School *EV* L5 ....113 F1
St Gregorys Catholic Primary School *MGHL* L31 ....62 A3
St Gregorys RC High School *WARRW/BUR* WA5 ....142 A4
St Gregorys RC JMI School *NTHLY* L27 ....136 B4
St Helens AFC *STHEL* WA9 ....104 D6
St Helens Bus Station *ECCL* WA10 ....13 H5
St Helens College *ECCL* WA10 ....13 F5
St Helens Crematorium *ECCL* WA10 ....87 K4
St Helens Cricket Club *ECCL* WA10 ....12 C2
St Helens Hospital *STHEL* WA9 ....104 A4
St Helens Museum & Art Gallery *ECCL* WA10 ....13 H4
St Helens Retail Park *STHEL* WA9 ....13 K6
St Helens RLFC (Knowsley Rd Stadium) *ECCL* WA10 ....102 E2
St Helens Theatre Royal *ECCL* WA10 ....13 H5
St Hildas CE High School *AIG/SPK* L17 ....133 J4
St Hughs JMI School *WAV* L15 ....133 J2
St James CE Primary School *BRSC* L40 ....54 E1
St James Primary School *RNFD/HAY* WA11 ....90 D5
St James RC Primary School *BTL* L20 ....4 C2
SKEL WN8 ....56 D1
St Joan of Arc RC Primary School *BTL* L20 ....4 A1
St John Almond RC Secondary School *ALL/GAR* L19 ....154 A5
St John Bosco RC Primary School *MGHL* L31 ....61 K5
St John Bosco RC Secondary School *NG/CROX* L11 ....99 F2
St John Fisher J & I School *WDN* WA8 ....19 K1
St John Fisher RC Primary School *PR/KW* L34 ....100 C1
St John's Beacon *CLVPS* L1 ....9 F4
St Johns Catholic J & I School *BEB* CH63 ....150 E4
St Johns CE Primary School *BRSC* L40 ....39 F4
CSBY/WL L22 ....80 E2
St Johns Primary School *ANF/KKDL* L4 ....97 G5
St Johns RC Primary School *SKEL* WN8 ....56 E4
St John's Shopping Centre & Market *CLVPS* L1 ....9 F4
St John Stone Catholic Primary School *STHP* PR8 ....41 K1
St John Vianney RC Primary School *STHEL* WA9 ....119 G1
St Josephs Catholic Primary School *WARRW/BUR* WA5 ....141 F4
St Josephs RC Infant School *KKBY* L32 ....84 D2
St Josephs RC Primary School *GR/UP/WCH* CH49 ....129 H4
HUY L36 ....117 F4
WAL/EG CH44 ....111 K5
St Julie RC Primary School *ECCL* WA10 ....102 C1
St Julies RC High School *WLTN* L25 ....154 D1
St Laurence Medical Centre *KKBY* L32 ....84 E2
St Laurence RC Primary School *KKBY* L32 ....84 E2
St Laurences RC Primary School *BIRK* CH41 ....2 E3
St Lawrence CE Primary School *ANF/KKDL* L4 ....97 G4
St Leos RC Primary School *RAIN/WH* L35 ....118 A5
St Lukes CE Primary School *FMBY* L37 ....48 D4
GOL/RIS/CU WA3 ....93 F4
St Lukes Halsall CE Primary School *CSBY/BLUN* L23 ....68 E4
St Lukes RC Primary School *FROD/HEL* WA6 ....201 F1
RAIN/WH L35 ....118 B3
SKEL WN8 ....67 G1
St Malachys RC Primary School *TOX* L8 ....132 D4
St Margaret Marys RC J & I School *DV/KA/FCH* L14 ....115 K4
St Margarets Anfield CE Primary School *NPK/KEN* L6 ....114 A2
St Margarets CE Controlled Infant School *WARRN/WOL* WA2 ....123 J5
St Margarets CE High School *AIG/SPK* L17 ....152 E2
St Margarets CE Primary School *TOX* L8 ....132 E2
WARRN/WOL WA2 ....123 J6
St Marie RC Primary School *NWD/KWIPK* L33 ....73 F6
St Marks Catholic Primary School *SKEL* WN8 ....57 G5

St Marks CE Primary School BRSC L40 36 B1
St Martins Catholic Primary School RUNC WA7 188 D1
St Mary & St Paul Primary School RAIN/WH L35 117 K3
St Marys Catholic College WAL/NB CH45 110 E1
St Marys Catholic Junior School NEWLW WA12 106 B1
St Marys Catholic School NEWLW WA12 106 C1
St Marys CE Primary School
BTL L20 4 D5
PS/BROM CH62 184 C2
RUNC WA7 177 K5
St Marys' Market ECCL WA10 13 H6
St Marys RC Primary School
BRSC L40 36 E2
CSBY/BLUN L23 69 F1
WGNW/BIL/O WN5 77 G5
St Marys West Derby Primary School WD/CROXPK L12 99 F6
St Mary & Thomas CE Primary School ECCL WA10 12 E4
St Matthews Catholic Primary School ANF/KKDL L4 98 B5
St Matthews CE Primary School STHEL WA9 102 E6
St Matthews RC Primary School SKEL WN8 57 F6
St Michael in the Hamlet Primary School AIG/SPK L17 133 G6
St Michael Jubilee Golf Club WDN WA8 157 K4
St Michaels Catholic Primary School NPK/KEN L6 113 K3
WDN WA8 157 H4
St Michaels CE Primary School ORM L39 53 F4
St Monicas RC Primary School
BTL L20 5 J1
WARRS WA4 162 C4
St Nicholas Catholic Primary School VAUX/LVPD L3 9 J5
St Nicholas CE Primary School CSBY/BLUN L23 68 C6
St Oswalds Catholic Junior School CLB/OSW/ST L13 114 E5
St Oswald's CE Primary School CL/PREN CH43 110 C6
NTHTN L30 70 C6
St Oswalds C Infant School CLB/OSW/ST L13 114 E4
St Oswalds RC J & I School AIMK WN4 79 G6
St Oswalds RC Primary School WARR WA1 143 H1
St Paschal Baylon RC Primary School CHLDW L16 135 G1
St Patricks Catholic Primary School TOX L8 132 E3
St Patricks RC Primary School CHTN/BK PR9 23 J3
St Paul of the Cross Catholic Primary School WARRW/BUR WA5 121 J1
St Pauls RC Primary School CL/PREN CH43 129 J2
St Pauls & St Timothys RC J & I School WD/CROXPK L12 99 G6
St Peter & Paul RC Primary School RNFD/HAY WA11 88 E4
WAL/NB CH45 95 G5
St Peter & St Paul RC High School WDN WA8 158 A1
St Peters Catholic Primary School WARR WA1 144 B2
St Peters CE Primary School
AIMK WN4 78 E3
FMBY L37 41 G6
HES CH60 167 K6
NEWLW WA12 106 D1
St Peters RC Primary School GR/UP/WCH CH49 129 K5
St Philips CE Primary School
LITH L21 81 K3
STHP PR8 15 H7
St Philips Church Community School WARRW/BUR WA5 122 B6
St Raymonds RC Primary School NTHTN L30 70 A5
St Richards Catholic Primary School SKEL WN8 55 J4
St Robert Bellarmine RC Primary School BTL L20 82 A4
St Saviours CE Aided Primary School CL/PREN CH43 130 D6
St Saviour's RC J & I School GTS/LS CH66 195 H6
St Sebastians Primary School EHL/KEN L7 114 B5
St Silas CE Primary School TOX L8 133 F4
Saints Peter & Paul Catholic School NWD/KWIPK L33 72 E4
St Stephens Catholic Primary School WARRN/WOL WA2 123 H4
St Stephens Primary School CHTN/BK PR9 21 K6
St Stephens School CHTN/BK PR9 21 J5
St Teresas Catholic Primary School ECCL WA10 12 B4
St Teresas CP School SKEL WN8 57 K4
St Teresas Junior School NG/CROX L11 98 D3
St Teresas of Lisieux Infant School NG/CROX L11 98 D3
St Teresas RC Infant School STHP PR8 27 H3
St Theresas Primary School STHEL WA9 120 A4
St Thomas Becket School HUY L36 117 G4
St Thomas CE Primary School
AIMK WN4 79 H6
GOL/RIS/CU WA3 92 C2
MGHL L31 62 B3
WARRS WA4 162 C2
St Thomas of Canterbury Catholic Primary School ECCL WA10 88 A5
St Thomas of Canterbury RC School CSBY/WL L22 81 F3
St Thomas the Martyr CE Primary School SKEL WN8 57 K6
St Vincent de Paul Catholic Primary School CLVPS L1 8 E7
St Vincents Catholic Primary School WARRW/BUR WA5 141 F6
St Vincents School WD/CROXPK L12 115 J1
St Weburgh CE Primary School WARRS WA4 162 A1
St Werburghs RC Primary School BIRK CH41 2 D7
St Wilfrids CE Aided Primary School WARRS WA4 163 G2
St Wilfrids RC High School LITH L21 81 K4
St William of York RC Primary School CSBY/BLUN L23 69 J4
St Winefrides Cath Primary School BTL L20 4 D5
St Winefrides RC Primary School NSTN CH64 192 A2
Sandfield Medical Centre ECCL WA10 12 E6
Sandfield Park Special School WD/CROXPK L12 115 F2
Sandhills Business Park EV L5 112 E1
Sandon Industrial Estate VAUX/LVPD L3 112 D1
Sandringham Medical Centre TOX L8 133 G5
Sandy Lane Health Centre SKEL WN8 55 K4
Sankey Bridge Industrial Estate WARRW/BUR WA5 141 K5
Sankey Medical Centre WARRW/BUR WA5 141 F2
Sankey Valley Country Park WARRW/BUR WA5 122 D6
Sankey Valley Industrial Estate NEWLW WA12 106 B3
NEWLW WA12 106 E4
Sankey Valley St James CE Primary School WARRW/BUR WA5 141 K3
Savio Catholic High School NTHTN L30 82 B2
Scarisbrick Hotel STHP PR8 14 D4
School of Good Shepherd ANF/KKDL L4 97 H4
Seabank Medical Centre WAL/NB CH45 95 H6
Seaforth Health Clinic LITH L21 81 H4
Sefton Business Park NTHTN L30 82 D3
Sefton CC AIG/SPK L17 133 H5
Sefton Lane Industrial Estate MGHL L31 70 D1
Sefton Park Medical Centre WAV L15 133 J3
Sefton Road Health Clinic LITH L21 81 J3
Senate Business Park NTHTN L30 82 C3
Shaw Hall Caravan Park BRSC L40 37 F5
Sherdley Business Park STHEL WA9 103 K5
Sherdley Park Golf Club STHEL WA9 103 J6
Sherdley Primary School STHEL WA9 120 A1
Shorefields Community Comprehensive School
AIG/SPK L17 133 G5
TOX L8 133 F6
Shoreside Primary School STHP PR8 33 H5
Shorrocks Hill Country Club FMBY L37 48 B4
Showcase Cinemas NG/CROX L11 98 E1
Silverdale Medical Centre HES CH60 167 K5
Simms Cross CP School WDN WA8 18 C4
Simonswood Industrial Park NWD/KWIPK L33 73 G3
Sir Alfred Jones Memorial Hospital ALL/GAR L19 153 K5
Sir Thomas Boteler High School WARRS WA4 143 H6
Skelmersdale & Ormskirk Colleges SKEL WN8 56 C4
Skelmersdale Park Primary School SKEL WN8 56 A4
Skelmersdale Sports Centre SKEL WN8 56 E6
Skelmersdale United FC SKEL WN8 55 J5
Skypark Industrial Estate SPK/HALE L24 173 G2
Slaidburn Industrial Estate CHTN/BK PR9 23 J1
Small Business Centre VAUX/LVPD L3 132 C4
Smithdown CP School EHL/KEN L7 133 G1
SMM Business Park WAL/EG CH44 111 J6
Somerville Primary School WAL/EG CH44 111 J4
Southbank Tennis Club STHP PR8 28 B3
Southdene Medical Centre KKBY L32 85 F3
Southern Primary Support Centre WLTN L25 155 G3
South Lancashire Industrial Estate AIMK WN4 79 G3
Southmead Primary School RAIN/WH L35 118 A5
Southport & Ainsdale Golf Club STHP PR8 33 J3
Southport & Birkdale CC STHP PR8 27 F4
Southport Business Centre CHTN/BK PR9 15 F4
Southport Business Park STHP PR8 27 H4
Southport College CHTN/BK PR9 15 G4
Southport Crematorium STHP PR8 28 E5
Southport FC STHP PR8 28 B2
Southport Flower Show Site STHP PR8 14 B5
Southport & Formby District General Hospital STHP PR8 28 B3
Southport & Formby Hospital CHTN/BK PR9 15 F4
Southport General Infirmary STHP PR8 28 A2
Southport Girls FC STHP PR8 28 C1
Southport Landing Area STHP PR8 26 E1
Southport Municipal Golf Club CHTN/BK PR9 22 E3
Southport New Synagogue STHP PR8 14 E6
Southport Old Links Golf Club CHTN/BK PR9 23 K4
Southport Pier STHP PR8 14 B1
Southport RFC STHP PR8 27 F6
Southport Sailing Club STHP PR8 14 D1
Southport Swimming Baths STHP PR8 14 B5
Southport Town Hall STHP PR8 14 E5
Southport Zoo & Conservation Trust STHP PR8 14 B4
South Sefton Business Centre BTL L20 4 D6
South Wirral High School PS/BROM CH62 184 A3
Speke Family Health Clinic SPK/HALE L24 173 K2
Speke Hall Industrial Estate SPK/HALE L24 173 G2
Sphynx Tennis Club STHP PR8 28 B3
The Sporting Edge Track ORM L39 54 A2
Springfield Special School KKBY L32 84 D4
Springwood Crematorium WLTN L25 154 C3
Springwood Primary School ALL/GAR L19 154 B3
SS Michael & All Angels RC Primary School GR/UP/WCH CH49 149 F1
The Stables Business Centre CLB/OSW/ST L13 98 C6
Stanley High School CHTN/BK PR9 23 H1
Stanley Medical Centre EV L5 113 F1
Stanley School PEN/TH CH61 148 D5
Stanney High School EP CH65 203 G1
Stanney Mill Industrial Estate CHNE CH2 203 K2
Stanney Mill Industrial Park EP CH65 196 E6
Stanney Ten Industrial Estate EP CH65 203 K1
Stanney Woods Country Park EP CH65 203 F2
Stanton Road Primary School BEB CH63 170 B2
Statham Primary School LYMM WA13 145 H5
Station Road Industrial Estate WARRS WA4 162 E1
Stockbridge Village Health Centre STBRV L28 100 A5
Stockton Heath Community Primary School WARRS WA4 162 B2
Stockton Heath Medical Centre WARRS WA4 162 B2
Stockton Wood Community Primary School SPK/HALE L24 173 H2
Stonebridge Business Park NG/CROX L11 83 K6
Stone Cross Business Park GOL/RIS/CU WA3 92 C4
Stopgate Medical Centre WLT/FAZ L9 98 B2
Storrsdale Medical Centre CALD/MH L18 134 C6
The Strand Medical Centre BTL L20 4 E2
Strand Shopping Centre BTL L20 4 E3
Streatham House School CSBY/BLUN L23 68 D5
Stutelea Hotel & Leisure Club CHTN/BK PR9 15 H1
Sudley House AIG/SPK L17 153 G1
Sudley Infant School AIG/SPK L17 153 F1
Sudley Junior School AIG/SPK L17 153 F2
Summerhill Primary School MGHL L31 71 H1
Sunnymede School STHP PR8 14 B7
Sutton Community Leisure Centre Track STHEL WA9 119 J1
Sutton Cricket Club STHEL WA9 120 A1
Sutton Green Primary School GTS/LS CH66 194 E4
Sutton Hall Golf Club RUNC WA7 187 K4
Sutton High School GTS/LS CH66 195 H4
Sutton High Sports College STHEL WA9 119 K1
Sutton Manor Community Primary School STHEL WA9 119 J5
Sutton Oak CE Primary School STHEL WA9 104 C5
Sycamore Lane Community Primary WARRW/BUR WA5 141 J4
Sylvester Primary School HUY L36 117 F6
Tanhouse Industrial Estate WDN WA8 19 H5
Tanning Court Industrial Estate WARR WA1 16 E6
Tate Gallery VAUX/LVPD L3 8 B7
Taylor Street Industrial Estate EV L5 113 F2
Thatto Heath Community Primary School STHEL WA9 103 G5
Theatre & Floral Hall STHP PR8 14 E2
Thelwall Infant School WARRS WA4 144 B6
Thelwall Junior School WARRS WA4 144 C6
Thelwall New Road Industrial Estate WARRS WA4 144 B5
Thelwall New Road Surgery WARRS WA4 144 A6
Thingwall Primary School PEN/TH CH61 148 D5
Thingwall Recreation Centre PEN/TH CH61 148 E5
Thomas Gray Infant School BTL L20 4 C2
Thomas Gray Junior School BTL L20 4 D1
Thornton Crematorium CSBY/BLUN L23 69 K2
Thornton Hall Hotel NSTN CH64 182 A2
Thornton Hough Primary School BEB CH63 169 H6
Thornton Primary School CSBY/BLUN L23 69 J3
Three Sisters Racing Circuit AIMK WN4 79 H2
Titanic Memorial VAUX/LVPD L3 8 A4
Tower College RAIN/WH L35 119 F6
Tower Dene Preparatory School CHTN/BK PR9 23 H3
Tower Hill Health Centre NWD/KWIPK L33 72 E4
Townfield Primary School CL/PREN CH43 130 B6
Town Green Primary School ORM L39 53 G5
Town Lane Infant School BEB CH63 150 D5
Toxteth Park Cemetery TOX L8 133 J3
Toxteth Sports Centre TOX L8 132 E3
Tranmere Rovers FC (Prenton Park) RF/TRAN CH42 150 B1
Tranmere Sports Centre RF/TRAN CH42 150 B1
Travel Inn
CLB/OSW/ST L13 114 E1
CLVP L2 8 D3
GOL/RIS/CU WA3 92 C4
NTHTN L30 70 E5
PS/BROM CH62 171 G4
RAIN/WH L35 136 E1
RUNC WA7 188 C3
STHEL WA9 119 H4
WARR WA1 16 D7
WLT/FAZ L9 82 E3
Travelodge
CLVP L2 8 E3
KNUT WA16 164 C5
PS/BROM CH62 184 C4
RNFD/HAY WA11 90 D3
VAUX/LVPD L3 132 C5
WARR WA1 16 C4
WDN WA8 19 G4
Tree Tops Country House Hotel FMBY L37 41 J2
Trentham Road Medical Centre KKBY L32 84 B1
Trident Industrial Estate GOL/RIS/CU WA3 125 G1
Trident Retail Park RUNC WA7 177 H6
Trinity Primary School SKEL WN8 56 A4
Triumph Trading Park SPK/HALE L24 154 D5
Twelve Quays Ferry Terminal BIRK CH41 112 B6
Twig Lane Clinic HUY L36 116 C3
UGC Cinema CLB/OSW/ST L13 114 D5
Unity Theatre CLVPS L1 9 H6
University Hospital Aintree WLT/FAZ L9 83 H5
University of Liverpool
EHL/KEN L7 9 K5
EHL/KEN L7 113 J6
VAUX/LVPD L3 9 J3
Upper Parliament Medical Centre EHL/KEN L7 133 G1
Upton CC GR/UP/WCH CH49 129 G4
Upton Hall FCJ School GR/UP/WCH CH49 129 G4
Upton Medical Centre WDN WA8 138 A6
Ursuline RC Primary School CSBY/BLUN L23 68 C6
Uveco Business Centre BIRK CH41 111 H6
Valewood Primary School CSBY/BLUN L23 68 E4
Valley Medical Centre
ANF/KKDL L4 97 G6
CHLDW L16 135 F2
Valley Road Business Park WAV L15 134 C1
VAT House & HM Customs & Excise VAUX/LVPD L3 132 B3
Vauxhall Business Centre VAUX/LVPD L3 112 E4
Vauxhall Health Centre EV L5 113 F3
Vernon Sangster Sports Centre ANF/KKDL L4 97 J6
Victoria Central Hospital WAL/EG CH44 111 H4
Victoria Park Arena WARRS WA4 17 J6
Victoria Road Primary School RUNC WA7 10 D6
Victoria Trading Estate RAIN/WH L35 118 E4
Village Medical Centre WLTN L25 154 D1
Villa Medical Centre CL/PREN CH43 149 K3
Virgin Cinemas CLB/OSW/ST L13 114 D6
Vittoria Medical Centre BIRK CH41 2 D2
VUE Cinema
BIRK CH41 3 F4
EP CH65 203 J2
Vulcan Industrial Estate NEWLW WA12 106 D4
Vyner Primary School CL/PREN CH43 110 D6
Wade Deacon County High School WDN WA8 158 B1
Wakefield Industrial Estate NTHTN L30 70 D6
Walker Art Gallery VAUX/LVPD L3 9 F2
Wallasey Golf Club WAL/NB CH45 94 D6
Wallasey RFC WAL/NB CH45 110 D2
Wallasey School MOR/LEA CH46 110 A4
Wallasey Town Hall WAL/EG CH44 112 A3
Walton Hall WARRS WA4 161 K5
Walton Hall Golf Club WARRS WA4 161 J4
Walton Hall Medical Centre ANF/KKDL L4 97 J4
Walton Hospital WLT/FAZ L9 97 H2
Walton Lea Crematorium WARRS WA4 161 K4
Walton Medical Centre ANF/KKDL L4 97 H3
Walton St Mary CE Primary School ANF/KKDL L4 97 H3
Walton Sports Centre WLT/FAZ L9 97 K3
Walton Village Medical Centre ANF/KKDL L4 97 J4
Wargrave House School NEWLW WA12 106 C4
Wargrave Primary School NEWLW WA12 106 C4
Warren Golf Club WAL/NB CH45 95 F6
Warrington Business Centre WARR WA1 16 D4
Warrington Business Park WARRN/WOL WA2 123 J6
Warrington Central Trading Estate WARRN/WOL WA2 16 B2
Warrington Collegiate Institute WARRN/WOL WA2 123 H6
Warrington Community Health Care WARRN/WOL WA2 123 F1

Warrington Golf Club *WARRS* WA4 ....162 B6
Warrington Hospital *WARRW/BUR* WA5 ....142 B3
Warrington Museum & Library *WARR* WA1 ....16 C6
Warrington New Town Cricket Club *WARRW/BUR* WA5 ....141 K4
Warrington Sports Club *WARRS* WA4 ....161 K4
Warrington Town AFC *WARRS* WA4 ....162 D1
Warrington Wolves RLFC (Halliwell Jones Stadium) *WARRN/WOL* WA2 ....16 C2
Waterfront Business Area *VAUX/LVPD* L3 ....132 B2
Watergate North Primary School *AIN/FAZ* L10 ....83 J3
Watergate Special School *WLTN* L25 ....154 E1
Waterloo FC *CSBY/BLUN* L23 ....68 C4
Waterloo Primary School *CSBY/WL* L22 ....81 F2
Wavertree Athletics Centre *WAV* L15 ....134 A2
Wavertree CE Primary School *WAV* L15 ....134 A2
Wavertree Cricket Club *WAV* L15 ....134 A1
Wavertree Health Clinic *WAV* L15 ....134 B3
Wavertree Retail Park *EHL/KEN* L7 ....114 A6
Wavertree Technology Park *EHL/KEN* L7 ....114 C6
Wavertree Town Hall *WAV* L15 ....134 B2
Wavertree Trading Estate *WAV* L15 ....133 K2
Weatherhead High School, Media Arts College *WAL/EG* CH44 ....111 F4
Weatherstone Business Centre *NSTN* CH64 ....192 D1
Weaver Industrial Estate *ALL/GAR* L19 ....172 B2
Weaver Park Industrial Estate *FROD/HEL* WA6 ....187 G5
Weaver Vale Primary School *FROD/HEL* WA6 ....187 F5
Welcome Lodge *WARRW/BUR* WA5 ....122 B4
Wellesbourne Primary School *NG/CROX* L11 ....98 D3
Wellington Employment Park *EV* L5 ....112 E1
Wellington Street Industrial Estate *WDN* WA8 ....18 C7
Well Lane Primary School *RF/TRAN* CH42 ....131 H6
Wesley House *ECCL* WA10 ....13 H4
West Bank Medical Centre *WDN* WA8 ....158 B6
West Bank Primary School *WDN* WA8 ....176 C1
Westbourne School *WAL/NB* CH45 ....111 J1
Westbrook Medical Centre *WARRW/BUR* WA5 ....122 C6
West Derby Cemetery *NG/CROX* L11 ....98 E1
West Derby Comprehensive School *CLB/OSW/ST* L13 ....114 E2
West Derby Golf Club *WD/CROXPK* L12 ....115 J1
West End Primary School *ORM* L39 ....45 J4
Westfield Primary School *RUNC* WA7 ....10 B6
West Gillbrands Industrial Estate *SKEL* WN8 ....56 A6
West Kirby Foot Health Clinic *WKBY* CH48 ....146 C1
West Kirby Girls Grammar School *WKBY* CH48 ....127 F5
West Kirby Health Centre & Swimming Pool *WKBY* CH48 ....146 B1
West Kirby Primary School *WKBY* CH48 ....127 F5
West Kirby Residential School *WKBY* CH48 ....126 E6
West Kirby Sailing Club *WKBY* CH48 ....146 C3
West Lancashire Golf Club *CSBY/BLUN* L23 ....68 B3
West Lancs Yacht Club *STHP* PR8 ....14 D1
Westminster Industrial Park *EP* CH65 ....195 J3
Westminster Medical Centre *ANF/KKDL* L4 ....97 G4
Westminster Retail Park *EP* CH65 ....7 F2
Westminster Road Swimming Pool *ANF/KKDL* L4 ....97 G6
Weston Point Primary School *RUNC* WA7 ....176 B6
Weston Primary School *RUNC* WA7 ....186 D1
West Park RFC *ECCL* WA10 ....102 D4
Westside Industrial Estate *STHEL* WA9 ....104 A3
Westvale Health Centre *KKBY* L32 ....84 B1
Westvale Primary School *KKBY* L32 ....84 A1
Wheathill Industrial Estate *NTHLY* L27 ....136 A3
Wheatland Business Park *WAL/EG* CH44 ....111 K5
Whetstone Lane Health Centre *BIRK* CH41 ....2 D6
Whiston Health Centre *RAIN/WH* L35 ....117 K4
Whiston Hospital *RAIN/WH* L35 ....118 B3
Whitby Heath Primary School *EP* CH65 ....196 A6
The Whitby High School *GTS/LS* CH66 ....202 E2
Whitefield CC *CHLDW* L16 ....115 K6
Whitefield JMI School *NPK/KEN* L6 ....113 J3
Whiteledge Centre *SKEL* WN8 ....56 D5
White Thorn Special School *WLT/FAZ* L9 ....83 F3
Widnes Community Midwifery & Ante-Natal *WDN* WA8 ....158 A1
Widnes Crematorium *WDN* WA8 ....138 E6
Widnes CC *WDN* WA8 ....139 G5
Widnes Golf Club *WDN* WA8 ....18 B1
Widnes Public Baths *WDN* WA8 ....18 D4
Widnes & Runcorn 6th Form College *WDN* WA8 ....138 D4
Widnes Vikings RLFC (The Auto Quest Stadium) *WDN* WA8 ....18 B4
Wildfowl & Wetlands Trust Martin Mere *CHTN/BK* PR9 ....31 G6
Willaston Primary School *NSTN* CH64 ....193 G1
William Beamont Community School *WARRN/WOL* WA2 ....123 H6
William Gladstone CE Primary School *LITH* L21 ....81 H4
William Stockton Primary School *EP* CH65 ....6 B4
Willowbank Holiday Home & Touring Park *STHP* PR8 ....41 H1
Willow Grove School *AIMK* WN4 ....79 K4
Willow Tree Primary School *STHEL* WA9 ....120 B3
Wilson Business Centre *HUY* L36 ....117 G6
Windlehurst Primary School *ECCL* WA10 ....88 B5
Windmill Farm *BRSC* L40 ....31 G3
Windmill Hill Primary School *RUNC* WA7 ....178 B3
Windmill Shopping Centre *WDN* WA8 ....19 F3
Windsor Primary School *TOX* L8 ....132 E3
Wingate Medical Centre *NWD/KWIPK* L33 ....73 F6
Winstanley Industrial Estate *WARRN/WOL* WA2 ....123 H6
Winwick CE Primary School *WARRN/WOL* WA2 ....123 H1
Winwick Parish Leisure Centre *WARRN/WOL* WA2 ....123 H1
Wirral Borough Magistrates Court *BIRK* CH41 ....3 J4
Wirral Business Centre *WAL/EG* CH44 ....111 J6
Wirral Business Park *GR/UP/WCH* CH49 ....129 G6
Wirral Country Park *NSTN* CH64 ....193 F2
PEN/TH CH61 ....166 D2
Wirral Grammar School for Boys *BEB* CH63 ....170 A1
Wirral Grammar School for Girls *BEB* CH63 ....170 A1
Wirral Hospital *BEB* CH63 ....169 K4
Wirral Hospital School *WAL/NB* CH45 ....110 C3
Wirral International Business Park *PS/BROM* CH62 ....171 H3
Wirral Ladies Golf Club *CL/PREN* CH43 ....130 B3
Wirral Metropolitan College *BIRK* CH41 ....3 F4
BIRK CH41 ....3 G1
PS/BROM CH62 ....171 J6
Wirral Museum *BIRK* CH41 ....3 H4
Wirral Stroke & Head Injury Clinic *CL/PREN* CH43 ....149 J2
Wirral Tennis & Sports Centre *BIRK* CH41 ....110 D5
Wirral Transport Museum *BIRK* CH41 ....3 H2
Wolverham Primary School *EP* CH65 ....7 F6
Woodchurch CE Primary School *GR/UP/WCH* CH49 ....148 E1
Woodchurch High School *GR/UP/WCH* CH49 ....130 A6
Woodchurch Leisure Centre *GR/UP/WCH* CH49 ....129 K6
Woodchurch Road Primary School *RF/TRAN* CH42 ....131 F5
Woodcote Hotel *GTS/LS* CH66 ....184 C6
Woodend Industrial Estate *SPK/HALE* L24 ....155 F6
Woodfall Infant School *NSTN* CH64 ....192 B3
Woodfall Junior School *NSTN* CH64 ....192 B3
Woodlands Industrial Estate *NEWLW* WA12 ....91 H5
Woodlands Infant School *GTS/LS* CH66 ....202 D1
Woodlands Junior School *GTS/LS* CH66 ....202 D2
Woodlands Primary School *BIRK* CH41 ....2 E7
FMBY L37 ....48 D2
Woodside Business Park *BIRK* CH41 ....3 J2
Woodside CP School *RUNC* WA7 ....177 H6
Woodside Ferry Landing Stage *BIRK* CH41 ....3 K2
Woodslee Primary School *PS/BROM* CH62 ....171 F3
Woodvale Airfield *FMBY* L37 ....41 F3
Woolston CE Primary School *WARR* WA1 ....144 B1
Woolston Community High School *WARR* WA1 ....144 A2
Woolston Community Primary School *WARR* WA1 ....144 B2
Woolton Golf Club *WLTN* L25 ....154 E3
Woolton House Medical Centre *WLTN* L25 ....154 D1
Woolton J & I School *WLTN* L25 ....135 J6
Woolton Swimming Pool *WLTN* L25 ....154 D1
World of Glass *ECCL* WA10 ....13 H6
Yew Tree Trading Estate *RNFD/HAY* WA11 ....90 C3

Acknowledgements

The Post Office is a registered trademark of Post Office Ltd. in the UK and other countries.

Schools address data provided by Education Direct.

Petrol station information supplied by Johnsons

One-way street data provided by © Tele Atlas N.V. Tele Atlas

The statement on the front cover of this atlas is sourced, selected and quoted from a reader comment and feedback form received in 2004

Garden centre information provided by

Garden Centre Association Britains best garden centres

Wyevale Garden Centres

Notes

Notes

Notes

Notes

Notes

AA Street by Street QUESTIONNAIRE

Dear Atlas User

Your comments, opinions and recommendations are very important to us. So please help us to improve our street atlases by taking a few minutes to complete this simple questionnaire.

You do not need a stamp (unless posted outside the UK). If you do not want to remove this page from your street atlas, then photocopy it or write your answers on a plain sheet of paper.

Send to: The Editor, AA Street by Street, FREEPOST SCE 4598, Basingstoke RG21 4GY

ABOUT THE ATLAS...

Which city/town/county did you buy?

____

Are there any features of the atlas or mapping that you find particularly useful?

____

____

____

Is there anything we could have done better?

____

____

____

Why did you choose an AA Street by Street atlas?

____

____

____

Did it meet your expectations?

Exceeded ☐ **Met all** ☐ **Met most** ☐ **Fell below** ☐

Please give your reasons

____

____

____

____

____

continued overleaf

Where did you buy it?

For what purpose? (please tick all applicable)

To use in your own local area ☐ **To use on business or at work** ☐

Visiting a strange place ☐ **In the car** ☐ **On foot** ☐

Other (please state)

LOCAL KNOWLEDGE...

Local knowledge is invaluable. Whilst every attempt has been made to make the information contained in this atlas as accurate as possible, should you notice any inaccuracies, please detail them below (if necessary, use a blank piece of paper) or e-mail us at ***streetbystreet@theAA.com***

ABOUT YOU...

Name (Mr/Mrs/Ms)

Address

Postcode

Daytime tel no

E-mail address

Which age group are you in?

Under 25 ☐ **25-34** ☐ **35-44** ☐ **45-54** ☐ **55-64** ☐ **65+** ☐

Are you an AA member? **YES** ☐ **NO** ☐

Do you have Internet access? **YES** ☐ **NO** ☐

Thank you for taking the time to complete this questionnaire. Please send it to us as soon as possible, and remember, you do not need a stamp (unless posted outside the UK).

We may want to contact you about other products and services provided by us, or our partners (by mail, telephone) but please tick the box if you DO NOT wish to hear about such products and services from us by mail or telephone. ☐

ML049z